The Adventures in Literature Program

ADVENTURES FOR READERS: BOOK ONE
Teacher's Manual
Test Booklet
Reading/Writing Workshop, Grade 7

ADVENTURES FOR READERS: BOOK TWO
Teacher's Manual
Test Booklet
Reading/Writing Workshop, Grade 8

ADVENTURES IN READING
Teacher's Manual
Test Booklet
Reading/Writing Workshop, Grade 9

ADVENTURES IN APPRECIATION
Teacher's Manual
Test Booklet
Reading/Writing Workshop, Grade 10

ADVENTURES IN AMERICAN LITERATURE
Teacher's Manual
Test Booklet
Lessons in Critical Reading and Writing:
Henry James's *Washington Square* and *Daisy Miller*

ADVENTURES IN ENGLISH LITERATURE
Teacher's Manual
Test Booklet
Lessons in Critical Reading and Writing:
Shakespeare's *Hamlet*

ADVENTURES IN MODERN LITERATURE
Teacher's Manual
Test Booklet

ADVENTURES IN WORLD LITERATURE
Teacher's Manual
Test Booklet
Lessons in Critical Reading and Writing:
Three Masters of Russian Fiction

FRANCIS X. CONNOLLY
Late of Fordham University, New York, New York
The Short Story, Biography, The Odyssey

JOYCE STRIBLING STEWARD
University of Wisconsin, formerly of LaFollette High School
Madison, Wisconsin
GENERAL TEACHING CONSULTANT
Poetry, Essays and Sketches, Teacher's Manual

VIRGINIA RUTLEDGE TAYLOR
Auburn High School, Auburn, Alabama
TEACHING CONSULTANT AND CONTRIBUTOR
Teacher's Manual

G. B. HARRISON
University of Michigan, Ann Arbor, Michigan
Shakespeare

A. R. GURNEY, JR.
Massachusetts Institute of Technology, Cambridge, Massachusetts
Drama

V. S. PRITCHETT
London
The Novel

ROBERT JAMESON
The Haverford School, Haverford, Pennsylvania
"Practice in Reading and Writing"

EVAN LODGE
Kent State University, Kent, Ohio
GENERAL CONSULTANT

THOMAS M. FOLDS
Dean of Education
Metropolitan Museum of Art, New York, New York
Fine Arts Program

ADVENTURES

in Reading

CLASSIC EDITION

Harcourt Brace Jovanovich, Publishers

ORLANDO NEW YORK CHICAGO ATLANTA DALLAS

FRANCIS X. CONNOLLY, late of Fordham University, edited *Man and His Measure* and *The Types of Literature;* is co-editor of *The Adventures in Literature* Series, Cardinal Newman Revised Edition; author of *A Rhetoric Case Book* and co-author of *The Sentence in Context.*

JOYCE STRIBLING STEWARD is an Associate Professor of English at the University of Wisconsin. She has taught at West High School and served as Chairman of the English Department at Robert M. LaFollette High School in Madison, Wisconsin. Mrs. Steward received a master's degree from Drake University, Iowa, and was a John Hay Fellow at Yale University in 1961–1962.

VIRGINIA RUTLEDGE TAYLOR teaches at Auburn High School, Alabama. Formerly Mrs. Taylor was a teacher of English at Itawamba Junior College and High School, Fulton, Mississippi, and Hulbert-West Memphis Schools, West Memphis, Arkansas.

G. B. HARRISON is Emeritus Professor of English at the University of Michigan. Editor of *Shakespeare: The Complete Works,* his other books include *The Elizabethan and Jacobean Journals, Introducing Shakespeare,* and *Shakespeare's Tragedies.*

A. R. GURNEY, JR. is an Associate Professor of English at the Massachusetts Institute of Technology. He is a graduate of the Yale School of Drama, and has produced and published several plays.

V. S. PRITCHETT is an English novelist, short story writer, and literary critic. He has worked also as a newspaper correspondent and has lectured on the novel at Princeton University. Among his works are *The Living Novel, Books in General, London Perceived,* and *New York Proclaimed.*

ROBERT JAMESON is Chairman of the English Department at The Haverford School, Haverford, Pennsylvania. Mr. Jameson received an A.B. from Harvard College, and has been a Visiting Associate Professor of English at Trinity College, Hartford, Connecticut. He is the Director of Reading for the College Board Advanced Placement Program, has written widely on educational subjects, and is the editor of *Essays Old and New.*

EVAN LODGE is an Associate Professor of English at Kent State University, Kent, Ohio, and a departmental consultant to high schools in the University area. Mr. Lodge served for many years as Supervisor and Directing Supervisor of English in the Cleveland Junior and Senior High Schools. He is the co-author of several literature and composition textbooks and a frequent contributor to various state and national professional journals.

THOMAS M. FOLDS is Dean of Education at the Metropolitan Museum of Art in New York. A graduate of Yale College and the Yale School of Fine Arts, Mr. Folds has been an instructor of English and Art Director at the Phillips Exeter Academy, New Hampshire, and a Professor of Art and Chairman of the Department of Art at Northwestern University.

Front cover photo by Susan McCartney.
Coin used as colophon courtesy of The American Numismatic Society.

Copyright © 1979, 1973, 1968 by Harcourt Brace Jovanovich, Inc.

PRINTED IN THE UNITED STATES OF AMERICA

ISBN 0–15–335120–9

CONTENTS

THE SHORT STORY

THEME AND IDEAS

TOTAL EFFECT

Part 2   *The Storyteller and the Story*   106

POETRY

PICTURES IN POETRY

POEMS OF JOY AND SORROW

THE SCOPE OF POETRY

Part 2   Five Poets: A Closer Look   220

ESSAYS AND SKETCHES

BIOGRAPHY AND PERSONAL RECOLLECTION

DRAMA

WILLIAM SHAKESPEARE

THE ODYSSEY: AN EPIC POEM

THE NOVEL

The Fine Arts Program

Adventures in Reading

THE SHORT STORY

A STORY TAKES PLACE in a world of the author's imagination—a world that may or may not be much different from our own. A story is not, like history, an attempt to tell what actually *did* happen; rather, it is an author's version of what we might *expect* to happen, given our knowledge of life and human nature and our awareness of the laws that operate in the author's story-world. J. R. R. Tolkien, a scholar and author of tales, has said that in a believable story

> What really happens is that the story-maker proves a successful "sub-creator." He makes a Secondary World which your mind can enter. Inside it, what he relates is "true": it accords with the laws of that world. You therefore believe it, while you are, as it were, inside. The moment disbelief arises, the spell is broken; the magic, or rather art, has failed. . . .
>
> Anyone inheriting the fantastic device of human language can say *the green sun.* . . . Many can then imagine or picture it. But that is not enough—. . .
>
> To make a Secondary World inside which the green sun will be credible, commanding Secondary Belief, will probably require labor and thought, and will certainly demand a special skill, a kind of elvish craft. Few attempt such difficult tasks. But when they are attempted and in any degree accomplished, then we have a rare achievement of Art: indeed narrative art, story-making in its primary and most potent mode.[1]

In a sense, when we read a story, we leave ourselves behind. We *stretch* ourselves—our knowledge and understanding—by entering the author's world and seeing imaginatively through other eyes.

[1] From *Tree and Leaf* by J. R. R. Tolkien. Reprinted by permission of Houghton-Mifflin Company.

PART 1 *Elements of the Short Story*

We may read a story simply for enjoyment. But when we try to talk about it, we find that we need to be aware of the various elements of which a story is composed. The stories in this book are organized to highlight the most important elements of storytelling.

When we consider the individual elements of a story, we are looking at the story from the storyteller's point of view. In writing their tales, authors will probably think about such basic questions as "Is the plot believable?" and "Are the characters real?" They want, in their stories, to succeed in creating a "Secondary World" in which all the conflicts, all the action, all the people are believable and real. This is also what we should decide for ourselves in discussing a story.

Among the most basic elements of any story are conflict and plot. *Plot* is the sequence in which the events of a story are arranged. Whatever happens in a story is part of the plot. A *conflict* is an opposition, a struggle, a clash or collision between two opposing forces that may be persons or may not. A conflict between two persons is usually easiest to recognize, but conflicts may take place between a person and an animal, a person and nature (or natural forces), and even within one's own mind. A straightforward conflict between two persons is set forth in the following passage from Saki's "The Interlopers" (page 14):

> The two enemies stood glaring at one another for a long silent moment. Each had a rifle in his hand. Each had hate in his heart and murder uppermost in his mind. The chance had come to give full play to the passions of a lifetime.

More subtle, but no less intense, is the conflict within Mathilde Loisel in De Maupassant's "The Necklace" (page 19):

> She grieved incessantly, feeling that she had been born for all the little niceties and luxuries of living. She grieved over the shabbiness of her apartment, the dinginess of the walls, the worn-out appearance of the chairs, the ugliness of the draperies. All these things . . . gnawed at her and made her furious. . . . She would dream of silent chambers, draped with Oriental tapestries and lighted by tall bronze floor lamps, and of two handsome butlers in knee breeches, who, drowsy from the heavy warmth cast by the central stove, dozed in large overstuffed armchairs.

Characterization, another of the important elements of the short story, is the means authors use to describe their characters and make them seem real. We may get our idea of characters from what they say, what they do, or what the author or other characters say about them. Sometimes an author tells us directly what to think, but much of the time we must decide for ourselves about a character. What impression, for example, do you get of Sam Carr in this paragraph from Morley Callaghan's "All the Years of Her Life" (page 57)?

> They were closing the drugstore, and Alfred Higgins, who had just taken off his white jacket, was putting on his coat and getting ready to go home. The little gray-haired man, Sam Carr, who owned the drugstore, was bending down behind the cash register, and when Alfred Higgins passed him, he looked up and said softly, "Just a moment, Alfred. One moment before you go."

Another element to consider when discussing a short story is its *theme.* The theme of a story is its central idea or meaning, the statement that its author makes or implies about life. Theme may be stated directly, but usually we must deduce theme from the story as a whole. Essentially, the theme of a story reflects the author's attitude, or point of view. Note, for example, the central idea expressed in this paragraph from O. Henry's story, "The Gift of the Magi" (page 77).

> The Magi, as you know, were wise men—wonderfully wise men—who brought gifts to the Babe in the manger. They invented the art of giving Christmas presents. Being wise, their gifts were no doubt wise ones, possibly bearing the privilege of exchange in case of duplication. And here I have lamely related to you the uneventful chronicle of two foolish children in a flat who most unwisely sacrificed for each other the greatest treasures of their house. But in a last word to the wise of these days let it be said that of all who gave gifts these two were the wisest. Of all who give and receive gifts, such as they are the wisest. Everywhere they are wisest. They are the Magi.

A story, of course, is (or should be) more than just a collection of isolated elements. In a good story, plot, conflict, characters, and theme are interwoven into a single whole, a *total effect* of impact and meaning. The last three stories in this unit—Stephen Crane's "A Gray Sleeve," James Thurber's "The Secret Life of Walter Mitty," and H. E. Bates' "The House with the Grapevine"—show how all these elements can be used by a storyteller for maximum effect.

The Lady or the Tiger?

FRANK R. STOCKTON

In the very olden time, there lived a semibarbaric king who was a man of exuberant fancy and of an authority so irresistible that, at his will, he turned his varied fancies into facts. He was greatly given to self-communing, and when he and himself agreed upon anything, the thing was done. When everything moved smoothly, his nature was bland and genial; but whenever there was a little hitch, he was blander and more genial still, for nothing pleased him so much as to make the crooked straight, and crush down uneven places.

Among his borrowed notions was that of the public arena, in which, by exhibitions of manly and beastly valor, the minds of his subjects were refined and cultured.

But even here the exuberant and barbaric fancy asserted itself. This vast amphitheater,[1] with its encircling galleries, its mysterious vault, and its unseen passages, was an agent of poetic justice, in which crime was punished, or virtue rewarded, by the decrees of an impartial and incorruptible chance.

[1] **amphitheater** (am′fə·thē´ə·tər): an open arena with rising tiers of seats.

When a subject was accused of a crime of sufficient importance to interest the king, public notice was given that on an appointed day the fate of the accused person would be decided in the king's arena.

When all the people had assembled in the galleries, and the king, surrounded by his court, sat high up on his throne of royal state on one side of the arena, he gave a signal, a door beneath him opened, and the accused subject stepped out into the amphitheater. Directly opposite him, on the other side of the enclosed space, were two doors, exactly alike and side by side. It was the duty and the privilege of the person on trial to walk directly to these doors and open one of them. He could open either door he pleased. He was subject to no guidance or influence but that of the aforementioned impartial and incorruptible chance. If he opened the one, there came out of it a hungry tiger, the fiercest and most cruel that could be procured, which immediately sprang upon him and tore him to pieces as a punishment for his guilt. The moment that the case of the criminal was thus decided, doleful iron bells were clanged, great wails went up from the hired mourners posted on the outer rim of the arena, and the vast audience, with bowed heads and downcast hearts, wended slowly their homeward way, mourning greatly that one so young and fair, or so old and respected, should have merited so dire a fate.

But if the accused person opened the other door, there came forth from it a lady, the most suitable to his years and station that His Majesty could select among his fair subjects; and to this lady he was immediately married, as a reward of his innocence. It mattered not that he might already possess a wife and family or that his affections might be engaged upon an object of his own selection. The king allowed no such arrangements to interfere with his great scheme of punishment and reward. The exercises, as in the other instance, took place immediately, and in the arena. Another door opened beneath the king, and a priest, followed by a band of choristers, and dancing maidens blowing joyous airs on golden horns, advanced to where the pair stood side by side, and the wedding was promptly and cheerily solemnized. Then the gay brass bells rang forth their merry peals, and the people shouted glad hurrahs, and the innocent man, preceded by children strewing flowers on his path, led his bride to his home.

This was the king's semibarbaric method of administering justice. Its perfect fairness is obvious. The criminal could not know out of which door would come the lady. He opened either he pleased, without having the slightest idea whether, in the next instant, he was to be devoured or married. On some occasions the tiger came out of one door, and on some, out of the other. The decisions were not only fair—they were positively decisive. The accused person was instantly punished if he found himself guilty, and if innocent, he was rewarded on the spot, whether he liked it or not. There was no escape from the judgments of the king's arena.

The institution was a very popular one. When the people gathered together on one of the great trial days, they never knew whether they were to witness a bloody slaughter or a hilarious wedding. This element of uncertainty lent an interest to the occasion which it could not otherwise have attained. Thus the masses were entertained and pleased, and the thinking part of the community could bring no charge of unfairness against this plan; for did not the accused person have the whole matter in his own hands?

This semibarbaric king had a daughter as blooming as his most rosy fancies, and with a soul as fervent and imperious as his own. As is usual in such cases, she was the apple of his eye, and was loved by him above all humanity. Among his courtiers was a young man of that fineness of blood and lowness of station common to the heroes of romance who love royal maidens. This royal maiden was well satisfied with

her lover, for he was handsome and brave to a degree unsurpassed in all this kingdom, and she loved him with an ardor that had enough of barbarism in it to make it exceedingly warm and strong. This love affair moved on happily for many months until, one day, the king happened to discover its existence. He did not hesitate nor waver in regard to his duty. The youth was immediately cast into prison, and a day was appointed for his trial in the king's arena. This, of course, was an especially important occasion, and His Majesty, as well as all the people, was greatly interested in the workings and development of this trial. Never before had such a case occurred—never before had a subject dared to love the daughter of a king. In after years such things became commonplace enough, but then they were, in no slight degree, novel and startling.

The tiger cages of the kingdom were searched for the most savage and relentless beasts, from which the fiercest monster might be selected for the arena, and the ranks of maiden youth and beauty throughout the land were carefully surveyed by competent judges, in order that the young man might have a fitting bride in case fate did not determine for him a different destiny. Of course, everybody knew that the deed with which the accused was charged had been done. He had loved the princess, and neither he, she, nor anyone else thought of denying the fact. But the king would not think of allowing any fact of this kind to interfere with the workings of the court of judgment, in which he took such great delight and satisfaction. No matter how the affair turned out, the youth would be disposed of, and the king would take pleasure in watching the course of events which would determine whether or not the young man had done wrong in allowing himself to love the princess.

The appointed day arrived. From far and near the people gathered and thronged the great galleries of the arena, while crowds, unable to gain admittance, massed themselves against its outside walls. The king and his court were in their places, opposite the twin doors—those fateful portals, so terrible in their similarity!

All was ready. The signal was given. A door beneath the royal party opened, and the lover of the princess walked into the arena. Tall, beautiful, fair, his appearance was greeted with a low hum of admiration and anxiety. Half the audience had not known so grand a youth had lived among them. No wonder the princess loved him! What a terrible thing for him to be there!

As the youth advanced into the arena, he turned, as the custom was, to bow to the king. But he did not think at all of that royal personage; his eyes were fixed upon the princess, who sat to the right of her father. Had it not been for the barbarism in her nature, it is probable that lady would not have been there. But her intense and fervid soul would not allow her to be absent on an occasion in which she was so terribly interested. From the moment that the decree had gone forth that her lover should decide his fate in the king's arena, she had thought of nothing, night or day, but this great event and the various subjects connected with it. Possessed of more power, influence, and force of character than anyone who had ever before been interested in such a case, she had done what no other person had done —she had possessed herself of the secret of the doors. She knew in which of the two rooms behind those doors stood the cage of the tiger, with its open front, and in which waited the lady. Through these thick doors, heavily curtained with skins on the inside, it was impossible that any noise or suggestion should come from within to the person who should approach to raise the latch of one of them. But gold, and the power of a woman's will, had brought the secret to the princess.

Not only did she know in which room stood the lady, ready to emerge, all blushing and radiant, should her door be opened, but she knew who the lady was. It was one of the fairest and loveliest of the damsels of the court who had been selected as the reward of the accused youth, should he be proved innocent of the crime of aspiring to one so far above him; and the princess hated her. Often had she seen, or imagined that she had seen, this fair creature throwing glances of admiration upon the person of her lover, and sometimes she thought these glances were perceived and even returned. Now and then she had seen them talking together. It was but for a moment or two, but much can be said in a brief space. It may have been on most unimportant topics, but how could she know that? The girl was lovely, but she had dared to raise her eyes to the loved one of the princess, and, with all the intensity of the savage blood transmitted to her through long lines of wholly barbaric ancestors, she hated the woman who blushed and trembled behind that silent door.

When her lover turned and looked at her, and his eye met hers as she sat there paler and whiter than anyone in the vast ocean of anxious faces about her, he saw, by that power of quick perception which is given to those whose souls are one, that she knew behind which door crouched the tiger, and behind which stood the lady. He had expected her to know it. He understood her nature, and his soul was assured that she would never rest until she had made plain to herself this thing, hidden to all other lookers-on, even to the king. The only hope for the youth in which there was any element of certainty was based upon the success of the prin-

cess in discovering this mystery, and the moment he looked upon her, he saw she had succeeded.

Then it was that his quick and anxious glance asked the question, "Which?" It was as plain to her as if he shouted it from where he stood. There was not an instant to be lost. The question was asked in a flash; it must be answered in another.

Her right arm lay on the cushioned parapet before her. She raised her hand, and made a slight, quick movement toward the right. No one but her lover saw her. Every eye but his was fixed on the man in the arena.

He turned, and with a firm and rapid step he walked across the empty space. Every heart stopped beating, every breath was held, every eye was fixed immovably upon that man. Without the slightest hesitation, he went to the door on the right and opened it.

Now, the point of the story is this: Did the tiger come out of that door, or did the lady?

The more we reflect upon this question, the harder it is to answer. It involves a study of the human heart which leads us through roundabout pathways of passion, out of which it is difficult to find our way. Think of it, fair reader, not as if the decision of the question depended upon yourself, but upon that hot-blooded, semibarbaric princess, her soul at a white heat beneath the combined fires of despair and jealousy. She had lost him, but who should have him?

How often, in her waking hours and in her dreams, had she started in wild horror and covered her face with her hands as she thought of her lover opening the door on the other side of which waited the cruel fangs of the tiger!

But how much oftener had she seen him at the other door! How in her grievous

reveries had she gnashed her teeth and torn her hair when she saw his start of rapturous delight as he opened the door of the lady! How her soul had burned in agony when she had seen him rush to meet that woman, with her flushing cheek and sparkling eye of triumph; when she had seen him lead her forth, his whole frame kindled with the joy of recovered life; when she had heard the glad shouts from the multitude, and the wild ringing of the happy bells; when she had seen the priest, with his joyous followers, advance to the couple, and make them man and wife before her very eyes; and when she had seen them walk away together upon their path of flowers, followed by the tremendous shouts of the hilarious multitude, in which her one despairing shriek was lost and drowned!

Would it not be better for him to die at once, and go to wait for her in the blessed regions of semibarbaric futurity?

And yet, that awful tiger, those shrieks, that blood!

Her decision had been indicated in an instant, but it had been made after days and nights of anguished deliberation. She had known she would be asked, she had decided what she would answer, and with-

out the slightest hesitation, she had moved her hand to the right.

The question of her decision is one not to be lightly considered, and it is not for me to presume to set up myself as the one person able to answer it. So I leave it with all of you: Which came out of the opened door—the lady or the tiger?

FOR STUDY AND DISCUSSION

1. The title of this story and the questions in its final paragraphs challenge you to guess who came out of the door. From what you know about the princess, which do you think she would point to: the lady or the tiger? Why? Draw up a list of reasons supporting your opinion and be prepared to challenge those who disagree.

2. If you had been the princess' lover, would you have opened the door she pointed to or the opposite one? Do you wish the author had not told you which door the hero chose to open? If this also had been left up to your imagination, would the story have had more impact or less? Why?

3. What was the king's way of determining innocence or guilt? Do you think his procedure was just? Why or why not? How does the king's "poetic justice" compare, in fairness of punishment, with the legal justice of a present-day court trial?

IRONY

Irony is a way of speaking in which we say the opposite of what we really mean. When we speak of a well-known gangster as "a leading citizen," we are being ironic. Writers often describe unpleasant characters or ideas ironically, pretending to accept them at face value in order to force us to realize how bad they are. In "The Lady or the Tiger?" Frank Stockton calls the king's system "poetic justice" with a perfectly straight face, as if he didn't know that it isn't just at all. He expects us to realize this for ourselves. In order to understand an author's irony, we must decide first on our own opinion of the facts. If the way things seem to us is very different from the way the author *speaks* (not thinks) of them, then the chances are that the author is being ironic. Explain why each of the following statements in "The Lady or the Tiger?" is ironic. If the irony is not clear, reread each statement in its context in the selection.

"[In] the public arena, . . . the minds of his subjects were *refined and cultured.*" (page 4)

"crime was punished, or virtue rewarded by the decrees of an *impartial and incorruptible* chance." (page 4)

"This was the king's semibarbaric method of administering justice. Its *perfect fairness* is obvious." (page 5)

Find other ironic statements in the story.

Why do you think authors use irony? Does their saying the opposite of what they really think help you to make your own judgment of the situation?

LANGUAGE AND VOCABULARY

This story contains many paired adjectives modifying a single noun. In the pairings listed below, find out exactly what each word means literally, then decide what the two together suggest—or *connote*—in the context of the sentence in which they appear. In the phrase "exhibitions of manly and beastly valor," for example, *manly* (literally, having the qualities of a man) and *beastly* (literally, like a beast) together suggest the degrading nature of the exhibitions in the arena, in which people act like beasts. What is connoted by each of the following pairs of words? How has the author strengthened the impression he wishes to give by using two adjectives rather than only one?

"*exuberant* and *barbaric* fancy . . ."

"a hungry tiger, the *fiercest* and *most cruel* . . ."

"a soul as *fervent* and *imperious* as his own."

"the most *savage* and *relentless* beasts . . ."

"her *intense* and *fervid* soul . . ."

"the lady, ready to emerge, all *blushing* and *radiant* . . ."

"that *hot-blooded, semibarbaric* princess . . ."

FOR COMPOSITION

1. As this story approaches its climax, the author gives the motives for its solution but not the actual solution. Which do you think the princess pointed to: the lady or the tiger? Write your version of the story's ending, telling what happened when the young man opened the door. You need not tell why you think the princess pointed to the lady or the tiger in your ending, but be ready to explain your view in class.

2. One of the most effective passages in this story is the author's explanation of the law of the arena. What makes it so effective is the clear, detailed account of the procedure followed on the day of a trial. Reread this account, beginning with paragraph 4. Then write your own account of the procedure followed on an occasion such as one of the following:

Trying out for a part in a play

Preparing for a picnic

Making a specific laboratory test

Electing a president

ABOUT THE AUTHOR

Frank R. Stockton (1834–1902) was born in Philadelphia and worked as an engraver, a newspaper reporter, and a magazine editor before turning to the writing of fiction. His novels and stories, which amount to twenty-three volumes, range from humorous tales to science fiction. "The Lady or the Tiger?"—his most famous story—was later made into an operetta. In this story Stockton anticipated O. Henry's use of the sudden, surprise ending.

Charles

SHIRLEY JACKSON

THE DAY my son Laurie started kindergarten, he renounced corduroy overalls with bibs and began wearing blue jeans with a belt; I watched him go off the first morning with the older girl next door, seeing clearly that an era of my life was ended, my sweet-voiced, nursery-school tot replaced by a long-trousered, swaggering character who forgot to stop at the corner and wave good-by to me.

He came home the same way, the front door slamming open, his cap on the floor, and the voice suddenly become raucous shouting, "Isn't anybody *here?*"

At lunch he spoke insolently to his father, spilled his baby sister's milk, and remarked that his teacher said we were not to take the name of the Lord in vain.

"How *was* school today?" I asked, elaborately casual.

"All right," he said.

"Did you learn anything?" his father asked.

Laurie regarded his father coldly. "I didn't learn nothing," he said.

"Anything," I said. "Didn't learn anything."

"The teacher spanked a boy, though," Laurie said, addressing his bread and butter. "For being fresh," he added, with his mouth full.

"What did he do?" I asked. "Who was it?"

Laurie thought. "It was Charles," he said. "He was fresh. The teacher spanked him and made him stand in a corner. He was awfully fresh."

"What did he do?" I asked again, but Laurie slid off his chair, took a cookie, and left, while his father was still saying, "See here, young man."

The next day Laurie remarked at lunch, as soon as he sat down, "Well, Charles was bad again today." He grinned enormously and said, "Today Charles hit the teacher."

"Good heavens," I said, mindful of the Lord's name, "I suppose he got spanked again?"

"He sure did," Laurie said. "Look up," he said to his father.

"What?" his father said, looking up.

"Look down," Laurie said. "Look at my thumb. Gee, you're dumb." He began to laugh insanely.

"Why did Charles hit the teacher?" I asked quickly.

"Because she tried to make him color with red crayons," Laurie said. "Charles wanted to color with green crayons so he hit the teacher and she spanked him and said nobody play with Charles but everybody did."

The third day—it was Wednesday of the first week—Charles bounced a seesaw onto the head of a little girl and made her bleed, and the teacher made him stay inside all during recess. Thursday Charles had to stand in a corner during story time because he kept pounding his feet on the floor. Friday Charles was deprived of blackboard privileges because he threw chalk.

On Saturday I remarked to my husband, "Do you think kindergarten is too unsettling for Laurie? All this toughness, and bad grammar, and this Charles boy sounds like such a bad influence."

"It'll be all right," my husband said reassuringly. "Bound to be people like Charles in the world. Might as well meet them now as later."

On Monday Laurie came home late, full of news. "Charles," he shouted as he came up the hill; I was waiting anxiously on the front steps. "Charles," Laurie yelled all the way up the hill, "Charles was bad again."

"Come right in," I said, as soon as he came close enough. "Lunch is waiting."

"You know what Charles did?" he demanded, following me through the door. "Charles yelled so in school they sent a boy in from first grade to tell the teacher she had to make Charles keep quiet, and so Charles had to stay after school. And so all the children stayed to watch him."

"What did he do?" I asked.

"He just sat there," Laurie said, climbing into his chair at the table. "Hi, Pop, y'old dust mop."

"Charles had to stay after school today," I told my husband. "Everyone stayed with him."

"What does this Charles look like?" my husband asked Laurie. "What's his other name?"

"He's bigger than me," Laurie said. "And he doesn't have any rubbers and he doesn't ever wear a jacket."

Monday night was the first Parent-Teachers meeting, and only the fact that the baby had a cold kept me from going; I wanted passionately to meet Charles's mother. On Tuesday Laurie remarked suddenly, "Our teacher had a friend come to see her in school today."

"Charles's mother?" my husband and I asked simultaneously.

"Naaah," Laurie said scornfully. "It was a man who came and made us do exercises; we had to touch our toes.

Look." He climbed down from his chair and squatted down and touched his toes. "Like this," he said. He got solemnly back into his chair and said, picking up his fork, "Charles didn't even *do* exercises."

"That's fine," I said heartily. "Didn't Charles want to do exercises?"

"Naaah," Laurie said. "Charles was so fresh to the teacher's friend he wasn't *let* do exercises."

"Fresh again?" I said.

"He kicked the teacher's friend," Laurie said. "The teacher's friend told Charles to touch his toes like I just did and Charles kicked him."

"What are they going to do about Charles, do you suppose?" Laurie's father asked him.

Laurie shrugged elaborately. "Throw him out of school, I guess," he said.

Wednesday and Thursday were routine; Charles yelled during story hour and hit a boy in the stomach and made him cry. On Friday Charles stayed after school again, and so did all the other children.

With the third week of kindergarten, Charles was an institution in our family; the baby was being a Charles when she cried all afternoon; Laurie did a Charles when he filled his wagon full of mud and pulled it through the kitchen; even my husband, when he caught his elbow in the telephone cord and pulled telephone, ash tray, and a bowl of flowers off the table, said, after the first minute, "Looks like Charles."

During the third and fourth weeks it looked like a reformation in Charles; Laurie reported grimly at lunch on Thursday of the third week, "Charles was so good today the teacher gave him an apple."

"What?" I said, and my husband added warily, "You mean Charles?"

"Charles," Laurie said. "He gave the

crayons around and he picked up the books afterward and the teacher said he was her helper."

"What happened?" I asked incredulously.

"He was her helper, that's all," Laurie said, and shrugged.

"Can this be true about Charles?" I asked my husband that night. "Can something like this happen?"

"Wait and see," my husband said cynically. "When you've got a Charles to deal with, this may mean he's only plotting."

He seemed to be wrong. For over a week Charles was the teacher's helper; each day he handed things out and he picked things up; no one had to stay after school.

"The P.T.A. meeting's next week again," I told my husband one evening. "I'm going to find Charles's mother there."

"Ask her what happened to Charles," my husband said. "I'd like to know."

"I'd like to know myself," I said.

On Friday of that week, things were back to normal. "You know what Charles did today?" Laurie demanded at the lunch table, in a voice slightly awed. "He told a little girl to say a word and she said it and the teacher washed her mouth out with soap and Charles laughed."

"What word?" his father asked unwisely, and Laurie said, "I'll have to whisper it to you, it's so bad." He got down off his chair and went around to his father. His father bent his head down, and Laurie whispered joyfully. His father's eyes widened.

"Did Charles tell the little girl to say *that?*" he asked respectfully.

"She said it *twice,*" Laurie said. "Charles told her to say it *twice.*"

"What happened to Charles?" my husband asked.

"Nothing," Laurie said. "He was passing out the crayons."

Monday morning Charles abandoned the little girl and said the evil word himself three or four times, getting his mouth washed out with soap each time. He also threw chalk.

My husband came to the door with me that evening as I set out for the P.T.A. meeting. "Invite her over for a cup of tea after the meeting," he said. "I want to get a look at her."

"If only she's there," I said prayerfully.

"She'll be there," my husband said. "I don't see how they could hold a P.T.A. meeting without Charles's mother."

At the meeting I sat restlessly, scanning each comfortable matronly face, trying to determine which one hid the secret of Charles. None of them looked to me haggard enough. No one stood up in the meeting and apologized for the way her son had been acting. No one mentioned Charles.

After the meeting I identified and sought out Laurie's kindergarten teacher. She had a plate with a cup of tea and a piece of chocolate cake; I had a plate with a cup of tea and a piece of marshmallow cake. We maneuvered up to one another cautiously and smiled.

"I've been so anxious to meet you," I said. "I'm Laurie's mother."

"We're all so interested in Laurie," she said.

"Well, he certainly likes kindergarten," I said. "He talks about it all the time."

"We had a little trouble adjusting, the first week or so," she said primly, "but now he's a fine little helper. With occasional lapses, of course."

"Laurie usually adjusts very quickly," I said. "I suppose this time it's Charles's influence."

"Charles?"

"Yes," I said, laughing, "you must

have your hands full in that kindergarten with Charles."

"Charles?" she said. "We don't have any Charles in the kindergarten."

FOR STUDY AND DISCUSSION

1. In a sense, "Charles" is about a child's conflict with his teacher. How does the child oppose the teacher? Why do you think he does so? How does the teacher handle his opposition? At the end of the story, who is winning? What makes you think so?

2. In part, "Charles" is about Laurie's parents' discovery of the true personality of their child. Did you suspect, before the teacher's final words, that there was no such person as Charles? If so, where in the story did you first suspect this? Which of Laurie's statements and actions might have given you a clue? Even if you didn't guess the truth, the author's hints carefully prepared you for (foreshadowed) the ending. What especially strong foreshadowing did the author give just before the teacher's final question?

3. Do you think that Laurie actually did all the things he said Charles did or that he was exaggerating in order to shock his parents? What in the story makes you think so?

4. Why did the author select Laurie's mother to tell his story? In answering this question, point out incidents and observations that only a parent would be likely to notice.

5. Is "Charles" a realistic report of actual classroom conditions? If you think it is, tell why. If you think it is not, does this lack of realism make the story seem less true to life? Explain.

THE EFFECT OF STYLE

In real life, Charles's actions in kindergarten would be cause for concern, and Charles would probably be referred to the school psychologist. Yet as Laurie tells about these actions, they are funny. Why can actions that are in reality quite serious seem funny when told about in fiction? At least part of the reason is that in reading a story we know that its incidents probably never really happened. But perhaps even more important is the author's *style,* or way of saying things. Choose two or three of Charles's worst actions, such as hitting the little girl with the seesaw or kicking the teacher's friend, and show how the author's choice and arrangement of words makes them seem amusing.

LANGUAGE AND VOCABULARY

1. Although the time span of "Charles" is about one month, the story does not seem to make huge jumps in time, but moves smoothly ahead from one incident to another. The reason for this smoothness of movement is the author's careful attention to *connectives*—connecting words that form bridges or transitions from one incident to the next. Notice how the author clearly marks the time of the first incident: "The day my son Laurie started kindergarten . . ." The connective words to the next incident are "The next day . . ." Find some other connective words that make clear the time sequence in the story.

2. How do the differences between Laurie's vocabulary and that of his parents help to make the characters seem real? Is there also a difference in syntax—that is, in the length and complexity of sentences? (How are most of Laurie's phrases connected into longer sentences?) Are length and complexity of sentences necessarily a sign of maturity? Why or why not?

FOR COMPOSITION

Laurie tells his parents about several interesting incidents involving "Charles." Choose one and tell the whole story, as you think it happened, including Charles's action and the reaction of his teacher.

ABOUT THE AUTHOR

Shirley Jackson (1919–1965) was a versatile American author. She wrote stories about children, including *Life Among the Savages,* and also a book for children, *The Witchcraft of Salem Village.* Many of her novels and short stories deal with strange characters set in the background of ordinary life. Her most famous story, "The Lottery," is a chilling illustration of the power of ignorant cruelty.

The Interlopers

SAKI (H. H. MUNRO)

In a forest of mixed growth somewhere on the eastern spurs of the Carpathians,[1] a man stood one winter night watching and listening, as though he waited for some beast of the woods to come within the range of his vision and, later, of his rifle. But the game for whose presence he kept so keen an outlook was none that figured in the sportsman's calendar as lawful and proper for the chase; Ulrich von Gradwitz patrolled the dark forest in quest of a human enemy.

The forest lands of Gradwitz were of wide extent and well stocked with game; the narrow strip of precipitous woodland that lay on its outskirt was not remarkable for the game it harbored or the shooting it afforded, but it was the most jealously guarded of all its owner's territorial possessions. A famous lawsuit, in the days of his grandfather, had wrested it from the illegal possession of a neighboring family of petty landowners; the dispossessed party had never acquiesced in the judgment of the Courts, and a long series of poaching affrays and similar scandals had embittered the relationships between the families for three generations. The neighbor feud had grown into a personal one since Ulrich had come to be head of his

family; if there was a man in the world whom he detested and wished ill to it was Georg Znaeym, the inheritor of the quarrel and the tireless game-snatcher and raider of the disputed border forest. The feud might, perhaps, have died down or been compromised if the personal ill-will of the two men had not stood in the way; as boys they had thirsted for one another's blood, as men each prayed that misfortune might fall on the other; and this wind-scourged winter night Ulrich had banded together his foresters to watch the dark forest, not in quest of four-footed quarry, but to keep a lookout for the prowling thieves whom he suspected of being afoot from across the land boundary. The roebuck, which usually kept in the sheltered hollows during a storm wind, were running like driven things tonight, and there was movement and unrest among the creatures that were wont to sleep through the dark hours. Assuredly there was a disturbing element in the forest, and Ulrich could guess the quarter from whence it came.

He strayed away by himself from the watchers whom he had placed in ambush on the crest of the hill and wandered far down the steep slopes amid the wild tangle of undergrowth, peering through the tree trunks and listening through the whistling and skirling of the wind and the restless beating of the branches for sight or sound of the marauders. If only on this wild night, in this dark, lone spot, he might come across Georg Znaeym, man to man, with none to witness—that was the wish that was uppermost in his thoughts. And as he stepped round the trunk of a huge beech he came face to face with the man he sought.

The two enemies stood glaring at one another for a long silent moment. Each had a rifle in his hand, each had hate in his heart and murder uppermost in his mind. The chance had come to give full play to the passions of a lifetime. But a man who has been brought up under the code of a restraining civilization cannot easily nerve himself to shoot down his neighbor in cold blood and without word spoken, except for an offense against his hearth and honor. And before the moment of hesitation had given way to action a deed of Nature's own violence overwhelmed them both. A fierce shriek of the storm had been answered by a splitting crash over their heads, and ere they could leap aside a mass of falling beech tree had thundered down on them. Ulrich von Gradwitz found himself stretched on the ground, one arm numb beneath him and the other held almost as helplessly in a tight tangle of forked branches, while both legs were pinned beneath the fallen mass. His heavy shooting boots had saved his feet from being crushed to pieces, but if his fractures were not as serious as they might have been, as least it was evident that he could not move from his present position till someone came to release him. The descending twigs had slashed the skin of his face, and he had to wink away some drops of blood from his eyelashes before he could take in a general view of the disaster. At his side, so near that under ordinary circumstances he could almost have touched him, lay Georg Znaeym, alive and struggling, but obviously as helplessly pinioned down as himself. All round them lay a thick-strewn wreckage of splintered branches and broken twigs.

Relief at being alive and exasperation at his captive plight brought a strange medley of pious thank-offerings and sharp curses to Ulrich's lips. Georg, who was nearly blinded with the blood which trickled across his eyes, stopped his struggling for a moment to listen and then gave a short, snarling laugh.

"So you're not killed, as you ought to be, but you're caught, anyway," he cried; "caught fast. Ho, what a jest, Ulrich von Gradwitz snared in his stolen forest. There's real justice for you!"

And he laughed again, mockingly and savagely.

"I'm caught in my own forest land," retorted Ulrich. "When my men come to release us you will wish, perhaps, that you were in a better plight than caught poaching on a neighbor's land, shame on you."

Georg was silent for a moment; then he answered quietly:

"Are you sure that your men will find much to release? I have men, too, in the forest tonight, close behind me, and *they* will be here first and do the releasing. When they drag me out from under these branches it won't need much clumsiness on their part to roll this mass of trunk right over on the top of you. Your men will find you dead under a fallen beech tree. For form's sake I shall send my condolences to your family."

"It is a useful hint," said Ulrich fiercely. "My men had orders to follow in ten minutes' time, seven of which must have gone by already, and when they get me out— I will remember the hint. Only as you will have met your death poaching on my lands I don't think I can decently send any message of condolence to your family."

"Good," snarled Georg, "good. We fight this quarrel out to the death, you and I and our foresters, with no cursed interlopers to come between us. Death and damnation to you, Ulrich von Gradwitz."

"The same to you, Georg Znaeym, forest-thief, game-snatcher."

Both men spoke with the bitterness of possible defeat before them, for each knew that it might be long before his men would seek him out or find him; it was a bare matter of chance which party would arrive first on the scene.

Both had now given up the useless struggle to free themselves from the mass of wood that held them down; Ulrich limited his endeavors to an effort to bring his one partially free arm near enough to his outer coat pocket to draw out his wine flask. Even when he had accomplished that operation, it was long before he could manage the unscrewing of the stopper or get any of the liquid down his throat. But what a heaven-sent draft it seemed! It was an open winter, and little snow had fallen as yet, hence the captives suffered less from the cold than might have been the case at that season of the year; nevertheless, the wine was warming and reviving to the wounded man, and he looked across with something like a throb of pity to where his enemy lay, just keeping the groans of pain and weariness from crossing his lips.

"Could you reach this flask if I threw it over to you?" asked Ulrich suddenly; "there is good wine in it, and one may as well be as comfortable as one can. Let us drink, even if tonight one of us dies."

"No, I can scarcely see anything; there is so much blood caked round my eyes," said Georg, "and in any case I don't drink wine with an enemy."

Ulrich was silent for a few minutes, and lay listening to the weary screeching of the wind. An idea was slowly forming and growing in his brain, an idea that gained strength every time that he looked across at the man who was fighting so grimly against pain and exhaustion. In the pain and languor that Ulrich himself was feeling the old fierce hatred seemed to be dying down.

"Neighbor," he said presently, "do as you please if your men come first. It was a fair compact. But as for me, I've changed my mind. If my men are the first to come you shall be the first to be helped, as though you were my guest. We have quarreled like devils all our lives over this stupid strip of forest, where the trees can't even stand upright in a breath of wind. Lying here tonight, thinking, I've come to think we've been rather fools; there are better things in life than getting the better of a boundary dispute. Neighbor, if you will help me to bury the old quarrel, I—I will ask you to be my friend."

Georg Znaeym was silent for so long that Ulrich thought, perhaps, he had fainted with the pain of his injuries. Then he spoke slowly and in jerks.

"How the whole region would stare and gabble if we rode into the market square together. No one living can remember seeing a Znaeym and a von Gradwitz talking to one another in friendship. And what peace there would be among the forester folk if we ended our feud tonight. And if we choose to make peace among our people there is none other to interfere, no interlopers from outside. . . . You would come and keep the Sylvester night [1] beneath my roof, and I would come and feast on some high day at your castle. . . . I would never fire a shot on your land, save when you invited me as a guest; and you should come and shoot with me down in the marshes where the wildfowl are. In all the countryside there are none that could hinder if we willed to make peace. I never thought to have wanted to do other than hate you all my life, but I think I have changed my mind about things too, this last half hour. And you offered me your wine-flask. . . . Ulrich von Gradwitz, I will be your friend."

For a space both men were silent, turning over in their minds the wonderful changes that this dramatic reconciliation would bring about. In the cold, gloomy forest, with the wind tearing in fitful gusts through the naked branches and whistling round the tree trunks, they lay and waited for the help that would now bring release and succor to both parties. And each prayed a private prayer that his men might be the first to arrive, so that he might be

[1] **Sylvester night:** New Year's Eve.

the first to show honorable attention to the enemy that had become a friend.

Presently, as the wind dropped for a moment, Ulrich broke silence.

"Let's shout for help," he said; "in this lull our voices may carry a little way."

"They won't carry far through the trees and undergrowth," said Georg, "but we can try. Together, then."

The two raised their voices in a prolonged hunting call.

"Together again," said Ulrich a few minutes later, after listening in vain for an answering halloo.

"I heard something that time, I think," said Ulrich.

"I heard nothing but the pestilential wind," said Georg hoarsely.

There was silence again for some minutes, and then Ulrich gave a joyful cry.

"I can see figures coming through the wood. They are following in the way I came down the hillside."

Both men raised their voices in as loud a shout as they could muster.

"They hear us! They've stopped. Now they see us. They're running down the hill toward us," cried Ulrich.

"How many of them are there?" asked Georg.

"I can't see distinctly," said Ulrich; "nine or ten."

"Then they are yours," said Georg; "I had only seven out with me."

"They are making all the speed they can, brave lads," said Ulrich gladly.

"Are they your men?" asked Georg. "Are they your men?" he repeated impatiently as Ulrich did not answer.

"No," said Ulrich with a laugh, the idiotic chattering laugh of a man unstrung with hideous fear.

"Who are they?" asked Georg quickly, straining his eyes to see what the other would gladly not have seen.

"Wolves."

1. Who are the interlopers? Why are they interlopers? How do you think their coming made the two men feel? At two previous places in the story Georg Znaeym spoke of interlopers. When he spoke of them, what was he sure of? Why is "The Interlopers" a better title for this story than "The Enemies," "Hate," or "The Fatal Feud"?

2. What details do the first paragraphs of "The Interlopers" give about the background of the feud? How are the place, the time, and the storm essential to the "deed of nature" that fells the two antagonists?

3. Do you think that, given the long-standing feud between their two families, the hatred of von Gradwitz and Znaeym for each other was a natural human feeling or that it was caused by their particular personalities? Have you ever encountered or read about similar feuds in this country?

4. Does this story convey a lesson or moral? If you think it does, state that lesson as exactly as you can. How could it be applied to situations in day-to-day life? If you think the story does not teach a lesson, tell why.

5. Like many good stories, "The Interlopers" tells of a change of heart. Hate turns to forgiveness. What are the motives—or reasons—for this change? Are these motives convincing? Why or why not? If von Gradwitz and Znaeym had been rescued and restored to health, would they have remained friends or gone back to hating each other? What in the story makes you think so?

LANGUAGE AND VOCABULARY

Often words reveal only one of their meanings when used in a particular sentence. Each of the words that follow has more meanings than you could guess from its use in this story. Find several meanings of each word, including the original or *etymological* meaning, and illustrate each meaning by using it in a sentence of your own.

precipitous	exasperation	acquiesce
reconciliation	pestilential	medley

FOR COMPOSITION

1. Reread the author's explanation in paragraph 2 of how the feud began and how it became personal. Which details make this paragraph convincing? Keeping this example in mind, write a short account of how an imaginary feud or a dispute began in your own town and how it grew. Let the class judge whose story is most convincing.

2. After Ulrich's offer of the wine flask, Georg Znaeym speculates on how their ending the feud would impress their neighbors. What good effects might follow from a similar action of your own? In a short composition, speculate on what might result from doing one of the following:

Saying hello to someone you have not been speaking to

Volunteering to do household chores

ABOUT THE AUTHOR

H. H. Munro (1870–1916) was born in India and educated in England. As a young man he spent a year in the Burma police force before illness forced him to return to England. He supported himself for a time by writing sketches of political figures and short stories distinguished for their wit and sardonic humor. (He adopted Saki as a pen name from the cupbearer in the *Rubáiyát* of Omar Khayyám.) Later, he became a foreign correspondent and spent several years in the Balkans, Russia, Poland, and France. When World War I broke out, he enlisted in the army. Although he became ill with malaria, he insisted on being at the front, where he was killed in action. Altogether, Saki wrote five books of short stories, many of which treated unconventional or unusual subjects and had strange and often grisly conclusions. "The Interlopers" is from his most famous book of stories, *Beasts and Superbeasts*.

The Necklace

GUY DE MAUPASSANT

SHE WAS one of those pretty and charming girls, born, as if by an accident of fate, into a family of clerks. With no dowry, no prospects, no way of any kind of being met, understood, loved, and married by a man both prosperous and famous, she was finally married to a minor clerk in the Ministry of Education.

She dressed plainly because she could not afford fine clothes, but was as unhappy as a woman who has come down in the world; for women have no family rank or social class. With them, beauty, grace, and charm take the place of birth and breeding. Their natural poise, their instinctive good taste, and their mental cleverness are the sole guiding principles which make daughters of the common people the equals of ladies in high society.

She grieved incessantly, feeling that she had been born for all the little niceties and luxuries of living. She grieved over the shabbiness of her apartment, the dinginess of the walls, the worn-out appearance of the chairs, the ugliness of the draperies. All these things, which another woman of her class would not even have noticed, gnawed at her and made her furious. The sight of the little Breton[1] girl who did her humble housework roused in her disconsolate regrets and wild daydreams. She

[1] **Breton** (bret′n): a native of Brittany, a province in northwestern France.

"The Necklace" by Guy de Maupassant, translated by Newbury LeB. Morse.

would dream of silent chambers, draped with Oriental tapestries and lighted by tall bronze floor lamps, and of two handsome butlers in knee breeches, who, drowsy from the heavy warmth cast by the central stove, dozed in large overstuffed armchairs.

She would dream of great reception halls hung with old silks, of fine furniture filled with priceless curios, and of small, stylish, scented sitting rooms just right for the four o'clock chat with intimate friends, with distinguished and sought-after men whose attention every woman envies and longs to attract.

When dining at the round table, covered for the third day with the same cloth, opposite her husband who would raise the cover of the soup tureen, declaring delightedly, "Ah! a good stew! There's nothing I like better . . ." she would dream of fashionable dinner parties, of gleaming silverware, of tapestries making the walls alive with characters out of history and strange birds in a fairyland forest; she would dream of delicious dishes served on wonderful china, of gallant compliments whispered and listened to with a sphinxlike smile as one eats the rosy flesh of a trout or nibbles at the wings of a grouse.

She had no evening clothes, no jewels, nothing. But those were the things she wanted; she felt that was the kind of life for her. She so much longed to please, be envied, be fascinating and sought after.

She had a well-to-do friend, a classmate of convent-school days whom she would no longer go to see, simply because she would feel so distressed on returning home. And she would weep for days on end from vexation, regret, despair, and anguish.

Then one evening, her husband came home proudly holding out a large envelope.

"Look," he said, "I've got something for you."

She excitedly tore open the envelope and pulled out a printed card bearing these words:

"The Minister of Education and Mme. Georges Ramponneau[1] beg M. and Mme. Loisel[2] to do them the honor of attending an evening reception at the ministerial mansion on Friday, January 18."

Instead of being delighted, as her husband had hoped, she scornfully tossed the invitation on the table, murmuring, "What good is that to me?"

"But, my dear, I thought you'd be thrilled to death. You never get a chance to go out, and this is a real affair, a wonderful one! I had an awful time getting a card. Everybody wants one; it's much sought after, and not many clerks have a chance at one. You'll see all the most important people there."

She gave him an irritated glance and burst out impatiently, "What do you think I have to go in?"

He hadn't given that a thought. He stammered, "Why, the dress you wear when we go to the theater. That looks quite nice, I think."

He stopped talking, dazed and distracted to see his wife burst out weeping. Two large tears slowly rolled from the corners of her eyes to the corners of her mouth; he gasped, "Why, what's the matter? What's the trouble?"

By sheer will power she overcame her outburst and answered in a calm voice while wiping the tears from her wet cheeks:

"Oh, nothing. Only I don't have an evening dress and therefore I can't go to that affair. Give the card to some friend at the office whose wife can dress better than I can."

He was stunned. He resumed, "Let's see, Mathilde.[3] How much would a suitable outfit cost—one you could wear for other affairs too—something very simple?"

She thought it over for several seconds, going over her allowance and thinking also of the amount she could ask for without bringing an immediate refusal and an exclamation of dismay from the thrifty clerk.

Finally, she answered hesitatingly, "I'm not sure exactly, but I think with four hundred francs[4] I could manage it."

He turned a bit pale, for he had set aside just that amount to buy a rifle so that, the following summer, he could join some friends who were getting up a group to shoot larks on the plain near Nanterre.[5]

However, he said, "All right. I'll give you four hundred francs. But try to get a nice dress."

As the day of the party approached, Mme. Loisel seemed sad, moody, and ill at ease. Her outfit was ready, however. Her husband said to her one evening, "What's the matter? You've been all out of sorts for three days."

And she answered, "It's embarrassing not to have a jewel or a gem—nothing to wear on my dress. I'll look like a pauper: I'd almost rather not go to that party."

He answered, "Why not wear some flowers? They're very fashionable this season. For ten francs you can get two or three gorgeous roses."

She wasn't at all convinced. "No.... There's nothing more humiliating than to look poor among a lot of rich women."

---

[1] **Mme. Georges Ramponneau** (mȧ·dȧm′ zhôrzh rȧm′pə·nō).

[2] **M. . . . Loisel** (mə·syûr′ . . . lwȧ·zĕl′).

[3] **Mathilde** (mȧ·tēld′).

[4] **four hundred francs:** at that time, about eighty dollars.

[5] **Nanterre** (nȧṅ·târ′): a town near Paris.

But her husband exclaimed, "My, but you're silly! Go see your friend Mme. Forestier [1] and ask her to lend you some jewelry. You and she know each other well enough for you to do that."

She gave a cry of joy, "Why, that's so! I hadn't thought of it."

The next day she paid her friend a visit and told her of her predicament.

Mme. Forestier went toward a large closet with mirrored doors, took out a large jewel box, brought it over, opened it, and said to Mme. Loisel: "Pick something out, my dear."

At first her eyes noted some bracelets, then a pearl necklace, then a Venetian cross, gold and gems, of marvelous workmanship. She tried on these adornments in front of the mirror, but hesitated, unable to decide which to part with and put back. She kept on asking, "Haven't you something else?"

"Oh, yes, keep on looking. I don't know just what you'd like."

All at once she found, in a black satin box, a superb diamond necklace; and her pulse beat faster with longing. Her hands trembled as she took it up. Clasping it around her throat, outside her high-necked dress, she stood in ecstasy looking at her reflection.

Then she asked, hesitatingly, pleading, "Could I borrow that, just that and nothing else?"

"Why, of course."

She threw her arms around her friend, kissed her warmly, and fled with her treasure.

The day of the party arrived. Mme. Loisel was a sensation. She was the prettiest one there, fashionable, gracious, smiling, and wild with joy. All the men turned to look at her, asked who she was, begged to be introduced. All the cabinet officials wanted to waltz with her. The minister took notice of her.

She danced madly, wildly, drunk with pleasure, giving no thought to anything in the triumph of her beauty, the pride of her success, in a kind of happy cloud composed of all the adulation, of all the admiring glances, of all the awakened longings, of a sense of complete victory that is so sweet to a woman's heart.

She left around four o'clock in the morning. Her husband, since midnight, had been dozing in a small empty sitting room with three other gentlemen whose wives were having too good a time.

He threw over her shoulders the wraps

---

[1] **Forestier** (fô·rə·styā′).

he had brought for going home, modest garments of everyday life whose shabbiness clashed with the stylishness of her evening clothes. She felt this and longed to escape, unseen by the other women who were draped in expensive furs.

Loisel held her back.

"Hold on! You'll catch cold outside. I'll call a cab."

But she wouldn't listen to him and went rapidly down the stairs. When they were on the street, they didn't find a carriage; and they set out to hunt for one, hailing drivers whom they saw going by at a distance.

They walked toward the Seine,[1] disconsolate and shivering. Finally on the docks they found one of those carriages that one sees in Paris only after nightfall, as if they were ashamed to show their drabness during daylight hours.

It dropped them at their door in the Rue des Martyrs, and they climbed wearily up to their apartment. For her, it was all over. For him, there was the thought that he would have to be at the ministry at ten o'clock.

Before the mirror, she let the wraps fall from her shoulders to see herself once again in all her glory. Suddenly she gave a cry. The necklace was gone.

Her husband, already half undressed, said, "What's the trouble?"

She turned toward him despairingly, "I . . . I . . . I don't have Mme. Forestier's necklace."

"What! You can't mean it! It's impossible!"

They hunted everywhere, through the folds of the dress, through the folds of the coat, in the pockets. They found nothing.

He asked, "Are you sure you had it when leaving the dance?"

"Yes, I felt it when I was in the hall of

the ministry."

"But if you had lost it on the street we'd have heard it drop. It must be in the cab."

"Yes, Quite likely. Did you get its number?"

"No. Didn't you notice it either?"

"No."

They looked at each other aghast. Finally Loisel got dressed again.

"I'll retrace our steps on foot," he said, "to see if I can find it."

And he went out. She remained in her evening clothes, without the strength to go to bed, slumped in a chair in the unheated room, her mind a blank.

Her husband came in about seven o'clock. He had had no luck.

He went to the police station, to the newspapers to post a reward, to the cab companies, everywhere the slightest hope drove him.

That evening Loisel returned, pale, his face lined; still he had learned nothing.

"We'll have to write your friend," he said, "to tell her you have broken the catch and are having it repaired. That will give us a little time to turn around."

She wrote to his dictation.

At the end of a week, they had given up all hope.

And Loisel, looking five years older, declared, "We must take steps to replace that piece of jewelry."

The next day they took the case to the jeweler whose name they found inside. He consulted his records. "I didn't sell that necklace, madame," he said. "I only supplied the case."

Then they went from one jeweler to another hunting for a similar necklace, going over their recollections, both sick with despair and anxiety.

They found, in a shop in Palais Royal,[2] a string of diamonds which seemed ex-

---

[1] **Seine** (sān): a river that runs through Paris.

[2] **Palais Royal** (pà·lā′ rwà·yàl′): a section of Paris with fashionable stores.

actly like the one they were seeking. It was priced at forty thousand francs. They could get it for thirty-six.

They asked the jeweler to hold it for them for three days. And they reached an agreement that he would take it back for thirty-four thousand if the lost one was found before the end of February.

Loisel had eighteen thousand francs he had inherited from his father. He would borrow the rest.

He went about raising the money, asking a thousand francs from one, four hundred from another, a hundred here, sixty there. He signed notes, made ruinous deals, did business with loan sharks, ran the whole gamut of moneylenders. He compromised the rest of his life, risked his signature without knowing if he'd be able to honor it, and then, terrified by the outlook for the future, by the blackness of despair about to close around him, by the prospect of all the privations of the body and tortures of the spirit, he went to claim the new necklace with the thirty-six thousand francs which he placed on the counter of the shopkeeper.

When Mme. Loisel took the necklace back, Mme. Forestier said to her frostily, "You should have brought it back sooner; I might have needed it."

She didn't open the case, an action her friend was afraid of. If she had noticed the substitution, what would she have thought? What would she have said? Would she have thought her a thief?

Mme. Loisel experienced the horrible life the needy live. She played her part, however, with sudden heroism. That frightful debt had to be paid. She would pay it. She dismissed her maid: they rented a garret under the eaves.

She learned to do the heavy housework, to perform the hateful duties of cooking. She washed dishes, wearing down her shell-pink nails scouring the grease from pots and pans; she scrubbed dirty linen, shirts, and cleaning rags which she hung on a line to dry; she took the garbage down to the street each morning and brought up water, stopping on each landing to get her breath. And, clad like a peasant woman, basket on arm, guarding sou [1] by sou her scanty allowance, she bargained with the fruit dealers, the grocer, the butcher, and was insulted by them.

Each month notes had to be paid, and others renewed to give more time.

Her husband labored evenings to balance a tradesman's accounts, and at night, often, he copied documents at five sous a page.

And this went on for ten years.

Finally, all was paid back, everything including the exorbitant rates of the loan sharks and accumulated compound interest.

Mme. Loisel appeared an old woman, now. She became heavy, rough, harsh, like one of the poor. Her hair untended, her skirts askew, her hands red, her voice shrill, she even slopped water on her floors and scrubbed them herself. But, sometimes, while her husband was at work, she would sit near the window and think of that long-ago evening when, at the dance, she had been so beautiful and admired.

What would have happened if she had not lost that necklace? Who knows? Who can say? How strange and unpredictable life is! How little there is between happiness and misery!

Then one Sunday when she had gone for a walk on the Champs Élysées [2] to relax a bit from the week's labors, she sud-

---

[1] **sou** (s$\overline{oo}$): a coin then worth about one cent.

[2] **Champs Élysées** (shäṅ zā·lē·zā′): the main avenue of Paris.

denly noticed a woman strolling with a child. It was Mme. Forestier, still young-looking, still beautiful, still charming

Mme. Loisel felt a rush of emotion. Should she speak to her? Of course. And now that everything was paid off, she would tell her the whole story. Why not?

She went toward her. "Hello, Jeanne."

The other, not recognizing her, showed astonishment at being spoken to so familiarly by this common person. She stammered, "But . . . madame . . . I don't recognize . . . You must be mistaken."

"No, I'm Mathilde Loisel."

Her friend gave a cry, "Oh, my poor Mathilde, how you've changed!"

"Yes, I've had a hard time since last seeing you. And plenty of misfortunes—and all on account of you!"

"Of me . . . How do you mean?"

"Do you remember that diamond necklace you loaned me to wear to the dance at the ministry?"

"Yes, but what about it?"

"Well, I lost it."

"You lost it! But you returned it."

"I brought you another just like it. And we've been paying for it for ten years now. You can imagine that wasn't easy for us who had nothing. Well, it's over now, and I am glad of it."

Mme. Forestier stopped short. "You mean to say you bought a diamond necklace to replace mine?"

"Yes. You never noticed, then? They were quite alike."

And she smiled with proud and simple joy.

Mme. Forestier, quite overcome, clasped her by the hands, "Oh, my poor Mathilde. But mine was only paste.[1] Why, at most it was worth only five hundred francs!"

---

[1] **paste:** a brilliant, glassy material used in imitation diamonds.

1. In the first seven paragraphs of this story, the author sketches Mme. Loisel's background. To what social class does she belong? Why does she envy those in a higher position? Why does she feel entitled to such a position? Do you agree that she is? Why or why not? Does Mme. Loisel value things because they are good in themselves or because they will impress others? What makes you think so? Do you think Mme. Loisel would have been contented even if she were wealthy?

2. The real action of the story begins when M. Loisel brings home the invitation to the reception. Why isn't Mme. Loisel delighted? What does her husband offer to let her do? From what you know of her, do you think she appreciates his offer? Why or why not?

3. When Mme. Loisel gets her dress, she complains that she needs a jewel. What are her reasons? Are they good ones? Do you agree with her husband's remark, "My, but you're silly"? Why or why not? Would you expect her to choose the most expensive-looking piece of jewelry in her friend's collection? Why?

4. The party is the high point of Mme. Loisel's happiness. Why is she so happy? How does her popularity affect her husband? Why does she become suddenly unhappy as she prepares to leave the party? What happens as a result of her hasty departure? How has Mme. Loisel's personality helped to cause her future misery?

5. What qualities of character does M. Loisel show by his actions after learning of the lost necklace? Do you admire him as a person? Why or why not?

6. The author offers no explanation of why the Loisels do not immediately confess to Mme. Forestier that they have lost the necklace. From what you know of them both, can you explain why?

7. Were you surprised by Mme. Loisel's "sudden heroism" in facing up to years of poverty? What do you think gave her the strength to endure such hardships? How does her meeting with Mme. Forestier show a change in her character? If, a few years before, looking as she did, Mme. Loisel had seen

Mme. Forestier, would she have spoken to her? Would she have told her the truth about the necklace? Does Mme. Forestier's revelation make you think that the Loisels have wasted their lives? Why or why not?

PLOT AND IRONY

As you saw in "The Lady or the Tiger?" *irony* involves a difference between the way things seem and how they really are. And in "The Necklace," De Maupassant is being ironic when he describes things, not as he or you or I might see them, but as they seem to Mme. Loisel.

Irony can be used not only in isolated statements but also in the plot or events of a story. A situation is ironic when the actual situation or state of affairs is quite different from what the characters—or the reader—suppose it to be. The irony is usually revealed by a sudden turn of events that is the opposite of what the characters—or reader—have been expecting. In "The Necklace," what ironic revelation occurs at the end of the story? What ironic surprise gives impact to the ending of "The Interlopers"? to the ending of "Charles"? to "The Lady or the Tiger?" Which door would it be ironic for the princess's lover to open? (Which door did he *expect* the princess to point to?)

LANGUAGE AND VOCABULARY

To gain a sense of a word's exact "weight" and meaning, we must study its use in a particular story, essay, or poem. Often, looking up a word in a dictionary is only the first step toward learning its meaning. After looking up each of the following words, show that you understand its exact meaning by using it in the same sense in a sentence of your own.

"Their natural *poise,* their *instinctive* good taste, and their mental cleverness are the sole guiding principles which make daughters of the common people the equals of ladies in high society."

"She grieved *incessantly* . . ."

"The sight of the little Breton girl who did her humble housework roused in her *disconsolate* regrets and wild daydreams."

"The next day she paid her friend a visit and told her of her *predicament.*"

"She danced madly, wildly, drunk with pleasure, . . . in a kind of happy cloud composed of all the *adulation,* of all the admiring glances . . ."

"terrified . . . by the prospect of all the *privations* of the body and tortures of the spirit, he went to claim the new necklace with the thirty-six thousand francs . . ."

FOR COMPOSITION

1. What is your attitude toward Mathilde and her dissatisfaction? Express your opinion in a short essay, explaining the reasons for your view.

2. Reread the five paragraphs beginning, "Mme. Loisel experienced the horrible life the needy live" (page 23). Notice how all the details in these paragraphs contribute to the impression of a life of poverty. In a similar manner, write a brief account depicting a life of leisure. You might begin like this: "All day long, Mme. Forestier had nothing to do but enjoy herself. . . ."

ABOUT THE AUTHOR

Guy de Maupassant (1850–1893) was born in Normandy of an old French family. As a young man he was introduced to the leading French writers, among them Gustave Flaubert, who taught him the craft of writing fiction. These lessons in brevity, precision, and scientifically accurate observation made De Maupassant the most successful short-story writer of his day. His experiences among the Norman peasants, as a soldier in the Franco-Prussian War, and as a Civil Service officer for the government were incorporated in a total of more than thirty volumes of short stories, novels, plays, and travel sketches. A close observer of human life, De Maupassant came to believe that people are victims of heredity and environment. His pessimistic attitude is evident in many of his most famous stories, such as "The Duel," "At Sea," "The White Wolf," and "La Mère Sauvage."

The Silver Mine

SELMA LAGERLÖF

Kɪɴɢ Gᴜsᴛᴀғ III [1] was traveling through Dalecarlia.[2] He was pressed for time, and all the way he wanted to drive like lightning. Although they drove with such speed that the horses were extended like stretched rubber bands and the coach cleared the turns on two wheels, the king poked his head out of the window and shouted to the postilion,[3] "Why don't you go ahead? Do you think you are driving over eggs?"

Since they had to drive over poor country roads at such a mad pace, it would have been almost a miracle had the harness and wagon held together! And they didn't, either; for at the foot of a steep hill the pole broke—and there the King sat! The courtiers sprang from the coach and scolded the driver, but this did not lessen the damage done. There was no possibility of continuing until the coach was mended.

When the courtiers looked around to try to find something with which the King

could amuse himself while he waited, they noticed a church spire looming high above the trees in a grove a short distance ahead. They intimated to the King that he might step into one of the coaches in which the attendants were riding and drive up to the church. It was a Sunday, and the King might attend services to pass the time until the royal coach was ready.

The King accepted the proposal and drove toward the church. He had been traveling for hours through dark forest regions; but here it looked more cheerful, with fairly large meadows and villages, and with the Dal River gliding on light and pretty, between thick rows of alder bushes.

But the King had ill luck to this extent: the bell ringer took up the recessional chant just as the King was stepping from the coach on the church knoll and the people were coming out from the service. But when they came walking past him, the King remained standing, with one foot in the wagon and the other on the footstep. He did not move from the spot—only stared at them. They were the finest lot of folk he had ever seen. All the men were above the average height, with intelligent and earnest faces, and the women were dignified and stately, with an air of Sabbath peace about them.

The whole of the preceding day the King had talked only of the desolate tracts he was passing through, and had said to his courtiers again and again, "Now I am certainly driving through the very poorest part of my kingdom!" But now, when he saw the people, garbed in the picturesque dress of this section of the country, he

[1] **Gustaf III** (gŏŏs′tāf): king of Sweden from 1771–1792.

[2] **Dalecarlia** (dal′ə·kär′li·ä): a region in west central Sweden.

[3] **postilion** (pōs·til′yən): a rider on one of the leading horses on a coach team.

forgot to think of their poverty; instead his heart warmed, and he remarked to himself, "The King of Sweden is not so badly off as his enemies think. So long as my subjects look like this, I shall probably be able to defend both my faith and my country."

He commanded the courtiers to make known to the people that the stranger who was standing among them was their King and that they should gather around him, so he could talk to them.

And then the King made a speech to the people. He spoke from the high steps outside the vestry, and the narrow step upon which he stood is there even today.

The King gave an account of the sad plight in which the kingdom was placed. He said that the Swedes were threatened with war by both Russians and Danes. Under ordinary circumstances it would not be such a serious matter; but now the army was filled with traitors, and he did not dare depend upon it. Therefore there was no other course for him to take than to go himself into the country settlements and ask his subjects if they would be loyal to their King and help him with men and money, so he could save the fatherland.

The peasants stood quietly while the King was speaking to them, and when he had finished they gave no sign either of approval or disapproval.

The King himself thought that he had spoken well. The tears had sprung to his eyes several times while he was speaking. But when the peasants stood there all the while, troubled and undecided, and could not make up their minds to answer him, the King frowned and looked displeased.

The peasants understood that it was becoming monotonous for the King to wait, and finally one of them stepped out from the crowd.

"Now, you must know, King Gustaf, that we were not expecting a royal visit in the parish today," said the peasant, "and therefore we are not prepared to answer you at once. I advise you to go into the vestry and speak with our pastor, while we discuss among ourselves this matter which you have laid before us."

The King apprehended that a more satisfactory response was not to be had immediately, so he felt that it would be best for him to follow the peasant's advice.

When he came into the vestry, he found no one there but a man who looked like a peasant. He was tall and rugged, with big hands toughened by labor, and he wore neither cassock nor collar but leather breeches and a long white homespun coat like all the other men.

He rose and bowed to the King when the latter entered.

"I thought I should find the parson in here," said the King.

The man grew somewhat red in the face. He thought it annoying to mention the fact that he was the parson of this parish, when he saw that the King had mistaken him for a peasant. "Yes," said he, "the parson is usually on hand in here."

The King dropped into a large armchair which stood in the vestry at that time and which stands there today, looking exactly like itself, with this difference: the congregation has had a gilded crown attached to the back of it.

"Have you a good parson in this parish?" asked the King, who wanted to appear interested in the welfare of the peasants.

When the King questioned him in this manner, the parson felt that he couldn't possibly tell who he was. "It's better to let him go on believing that I'm only a peasant," thought he, and replied that the parson was good enough. He preached a pure and clear gospel and tried to live as he taught.

The King thought that this was a good commendation, but he had a sharp ear and marked a certain doubt in the tone. "You sound as if you were not quite satisfied with the parson," said the king.

"He's a bit arbitrary," said the man, thinking that, if the King should find out later who he was, he would not think that the parson had been standing here and blowing his own horn; therefore he wished to come out with a little faultfinding also. "There are some, no doubt, who say the parson wants to be the only one to counsel and rule in this parish," he continued.

"Then, at all events, he has led and

managed in the best possible way," said the King. He didn't like it that the peasant complained of one who was placed above him. "To me it appears as though good habits and old-time simplicity were the rule here."

"The people are good enough," said the curate, "but then they live in poverty and isolation. Human beings here would certainly be no better than others if this world's temptations came closer to them."

"But there's no fear of anything of the sort happening," said the King, with a shrug.

He said nothing further but began thrumming on the table with his fingers. He thought he had exchanged a sufficient number of gracious words with this peasant and wondered when the others would be ready with their answer.

"These peasants are not very eager to help their King," thought he. "If I only had my coach, I would drive away from them and their palaver!" [1]

The pastor sat there troubled, debating with himself as to how he should decide an important matter which he must settle. He was beginning to feel happy because he had not told the King who he was. Now he felt that he could speak with him about matters which otherwise he could not have placed before him.

After a while the parson broke the silence and asked the King if it was an actual fact that enemies were upon them and that the kingdom was in danger.

The King thought this man ought to have sense enough not to trouble him further. He simply glared at him and said nothing.

"I ask because I was standing in here and could not hear very well," said the parson. "But if this is really the case, I want to say to you that the pastor of this congregation might perhaps be able to

---

[1] **palaver** (pə·lav′ər): discussion.

procure for the King as much money as he will need."

"I thought that you said just now that everyone here was poor," said the King, thinking that the man did not know what he was talking about.

"Yes, that's true," replied the rector, "and the parson has no more than any of the others. But if the King would condescend to listen to me for a moment, I will explain how the pastor happens to have the power to help him."

"You may speak," said the King. "You seem to find it easier to get the words past your lips than your friends and neighbors out there, who never will be ready with what they have to tell me."

"It is not so easy to reply to the King! I'm afraid that, in the end, it will be the parson who must undertake this on behalf of the others."

The King crossed his legs, folded his arms, and let his head sink down upon his breast. "You may begin now," he said, in the tone of one already asleep.

"Once upon a time there were five men from this parish who were out on a moose hunt," began the clergyman. "One of them was the parson of whom we are speaking. Two of the others were soldiers, named Olaf and Eric Svärd; the fourth man was the innkeeper in this settlement, and the fifth was a peasant named Israel Per Persson."

"Don't go to the trouble of mentioning so many names," muttered the King, letting his head droop to one side.

"Those men were good hunters," continued the parson, "who usually had luck with them, but that day they had wandered long and far without getting anything. Finally they gave up the hunt altogether and sat down on the ground to talk. They said there was not a spot in the whole forest fit for cultivation; all of it was only mountain and swampland. 'Our Lord has not done right by us in giving us such a poor land to live in,' said one. 'In other localities people can get riches for themselves in abundance, but here, with all our toil and drudgery we can scarcely get our daily bread.'"

The pastor paused a moment, as if uncertain that the King heard him, but the latter moved his little finger to show that he was awake.

"Just as the hunters were discussing this matter, the parson saw something that glittered at the base of the mountain where he had kicked away a moss tuft. 'This is a queer mountain,' he thought, as he kicked off another moss tuft. He picked up a sliver of stone that came with the moss and which shone exactly like the other. 'It can't be possible that this stuff is lead,' said he.

"Then the others sprang up and scraped away the turf with the butt ends of their rifles. When they did this, they saw plainly that a broad vein of ore followed the mountain.

"'What do you think this might be?' asked the parson.

"The men chipped off bits of stone and bit into them. 'It must be lead or zinc, at least,' said they.

"'And the whole mountain is full of it,' added the innkeeper."

When the parson had got thus far in his narrative, the King's head was seen to straighten up a little and one eye opened. "Do you know if any of these persons knew anything about ore and minerals?" he asked.

"They did not," replied the parson.

Then the King's head sank and both eyes closed.

"The clergyman and his companions were very happy," continued the speaker, without letting himself be disturbed by the King's indifference; "they fancied that now they had found that which would give them and their descendants wealth. 'I'll never have to do any more work,' said one. 'Now I can afford to do nothing at all the whole week through, and on Sundays I shall drive to church in a golden chariot!' They were otherwise sensible men, but the great find had gone to their heads, and they talked like children. Still they had enough presence of mind to put back the moss tufts and conceal the vein of ore. Then they carefully noted the place where it was and went home. Before they parted company, they agreed that the parson should travel to Falun and ask the mining expert what kind of ore this was. He was to return as soon as possible, and until then they promised one another on oath not to reveal to a soul where the ore was to be found."

The King's head was raised again a trifle, but he did not interrupt the speaker with a word. It appeared as though he was beginning to believe that the man actually had something of importance he wished to say to him, since he didn't allow himself to be disturbed by his indifference.

"Then the parson departed with a few samples of ore in his pocket. He was just as happy in the thought of becoming rich as were the others. He was thinking of rebuilding the parsonage, which at present was no better than a peasant's cottage, and then he would marry a dean's daughter whom he liked. He had thought that he might have to wait for her many years. He was poor and obscure and knew that it would be a long while before he should get any post that would enable him to marry.

"The parson drove over to Falun in two days, and there he had to wait another whole day because the mining expert was away. Finally he ran across him and showed him the bits of ore. The mining expert took them in his hand. He looked at them first, then at the parson.

The parson related how he had found them in a mountain at home in his parish and wondered if it might not be lead.

" 'No, it's not lead,' said the mining expert.

" 'Perhaps it is zinc, then?' asked the parson.

" 'Nor is it zinc,' said the mineralogist.

"The parson thought that all the hope within him sank. He had not been so depressed in many a long day.

" 'Have you many stones like this in your parish?' asked the mineralogist.

" 'We have a whole mountainful,' said the parson.

"Then the mineralogist came up closer, slapped the parson on the shoulder, and said, 'Let us see that you make such good use of this that it will prove a blessing both to yourselves and to the country, for this is silver.'

" 'Indeed?' said the parson, feeling his way. 'So it is silver.'

"The mineralogist began telling him how he should go to work to get legal rights to the mine and gave him many valuable suggestions; but the parson stood there dazed and did not listen to what the mineralogist was saying. He was thinking how wonderful it was that at home in his poor parish stood a whole mountain of silver ore, waiting for him."

The King raised his head so suddenly that the parson stopped short in his narrative. "It turned out, of course, that when he got home and began working the mine, he saw that the mineralogist had only been fooling him," said the King.

"Oh, no, the mineralogist had not fooled him," said the parson.

"You may continue," said the King as he settled himself more comfortably in the chair to listen.

"When the parson was at home again and was driving through the parish," continued the clergyman, "he thought that first of all he should inform his partners of the value of their find. And as he drove alongside the innkeeper Sten Stensson's place, he intended to drive up to the house to tell him they had found silver. But when he stopped outside the gate, he noticed that a broad path of evergreen was strewn all the way up to the doorstep.

" 'Who had died in this place?' asked the parson of a boy who stood leaning against the fence.

" 'The innkeeper himself,' answered the boy. Then he let the clergyman know that the innkeeper had drunk himself full every day for a week. 'Oh, so much brandy, so much brandy, has been drunk here!'

" 'How can that be?' asked the parson. 'The innkeeper used never to drink himself full.'

" 'Oh,' said the boy, 'he drank because he said he had found a mine. He was very rich. He should never have to do anything now but drink, he said. Last night he drove off, full as he was, and the wagon turned over and he was killed.'

"When the parson heard this, he drove homeward, distressed over what he had heard. He had come back so happy, rejoicing because he could tell the great news.

"When the parson had driven a few paces, he saw Israel Per Persson walking along. He looked about as usual, and the parson thought it was well that fortune had not gone to his head too. Him he would cheer at once with the good news that he was a rich man.

" 'Good day!' said Per Persson. 'Do you come from Falun now?'

" 'I do,' said the parson. 'And now I must tell you that it has turned out even better than we had imagined. The mineralogist said it was silver ore that we had found.'

"That instant Per Persson looked as though the ground had opened under him. 'What are you saying, what are you saying? Is it silver?'

" 'Yes,' answered the parson. 'We'll all be rich men now, all of us, and can live like gentlemen.'

" 'Oh, is it silver?' said Per Persson, looking more and more mournful.

" 'Why, of course it is silver,' replied the parson. 'You mustn't think that I want to deceive you. You mustn't be afraid to be happy.'

" 'Happy!' said Per Persson. 'Should I be happy? I believed it was only glitter that we had found, so I thought it would be better to take the certain for the uncertain; I have sold my share in the mine to Olaf Svärd for a hundred dollars.' He was desperate and, when the parson drove away from him, he stood on the highway and wept.

"When the clergyman got back to his home, he sent a servant to Olaf Svärd and his brother to tell them that it was silver they had found. He thought that he had had quite enough of driving around and spreading the good news.

"But in the evening, when the parson sat alone, his joy asserted itself again. He went out in the darkness and stood on a hillock upon which he contemplated building the new parsonage. It should be imposing, of course, as fine as a bishop's palace. He stood there long that night, nor did he content himself with rebuilding the parsonage! It occurred to him that, since there were such riches to be found in the parish, throngs of people would pour in and, finally, a whole city would be built around the mine. And then he would have to erect a new church in place of the old one. Toward this object a large portion of his wealth would probably go. And he was not content with this, either, but fancied that, when his church was ready, the King and many bishops would come to the dedication. Then the King would be pleased with the church; but he would remark that there was no place where a King might put up, and then he would have to erect a castle in the new city."

Just then one of the King's courtiers opened the door of the vestry and announced that the big royal coach was mended.

At the first moment the King was ready to withdraw, but on second thought he changed his mind. "You may tell your story to the end," he said to the parson. "But you can hurry it a bit. We know all about how the man thought and dreamed. We want to know about how he acted."

"But while the parson was still lost in his dreams," continued the clergyman, "word came to him that Israel Per Persson had made away with himself. He had not been able to bear the disappointment of having sold his share in the mine. He had thought, no doubt, that he could not endure to go about every day seeing

another enjoying the wealth that might have been his."

The King straightened up a little. He kept both eyes open. "Upon my word," he said, "if I had been that parson, I should have had enough of the mine!"

"The King is a rich man," said the parson. "He has quite enough, at all events. It is not the same thing with a poor curate who possesses nothing. The unhappy wretch thought instead, when he saw that God's blessing was not with his enterprise, 'I will dream no more of bringing glory and profit to myself with these riches, but I can't let the silver lie buried in the earth! I must take it out, for the benefit of the poor and needy. I will work the mine, to put the whole parish on its feet.'

"So one day the parson went out to see Olaf Svärd, to ask him and his brother as to what should be done immediately with the silver mountain. When he came in the vicinity of the barracks he met a cart surrounded by armed peasants, and in the cart sat a man with his hands tied behind him and a rope around his ankles.

"When the parson passed by, the cart stopped and he had time to regard the prisoner, whose head was tied up so it was not easy to see who he was. But the parson thought he recognized Olaf Svärd. He heard the prisoner beg those who guarded him to let him speak a few words with the parson.

"The parson drew nearer, and the prisoner turned toward him. 'You will soon be the only one who knows where the silver mine is,' said Olaf.

" 'What are you saying, Olaf?' asked the parson.

" 'Well, you see, parson, since we have learned that it was a silver mine we had found, my brother and I could no longer be as good friends as before. We were continually quarreling. Last night we got into a controversy over which one of us five it was who first discovered the mine. It ended in strife between us, and we came to blows. I have killed my brother and he has left me with a souvenir across the forehead to remember him by. I must hang now, and then you will be the only one who knows about the mine; therefore I wish to ask something of you.'

" 'Speak out!' said the parson. 'I'll do what I can for you.'

" 'You know that I am leaving several little children behind me,' began the soldier, but the parson interrupted him.

" 'As regards this, you can rest easy. That which comes to your share in the mine they shall have, exactly as if you yourself were living.'

" 'No,' said Olaf Svärd, 'it was another thing I wanted to ask of you. Don't let them have any portion of that which comes from the mine!'

"The parson staggered back a step. He stood there dumb and could not answer.

" 'If you do not promise me this, I cannot die in peace,' said the prisoner.

" 'Yes,' said the parson slowly and painfully. 'I promise you what you ask of me.'

"Thereupon the murderer was taken away, and the parson stood on the highway thinking how he should keep the promise he had given him. On the way home he thought of the wealth which he had been so happy over. What if it really were true that the people in this community could not stand riches? Already four were ruined who hitherto had been dignified and excellent men. He seemed to see the whole community before him, and he pictured to himself how this silver mine would destroy one after another. Was it befitting that he, who had been appointed to watch over these poor human beings' souls, should let loose upon them that which would be their destruction?"

All of a sudden the King sat bolt upright in his chair. "I declare!" said he, "you'll make me understand that a parson in this isolated settlement must be every inch a man."

"Nor was it enough with what had already happened," continued the parson, "for as soon as the news about the mine spread among the parishioners, they stopped working and went about in idleness, waiting for the time when great riches should pour in on them. All the ne'er-do-wells there were in this section streamed in, and drunkenness and fighting were what the parson heard talked of continually. A lot of people did nothing but tramp round in the forest searching for the mine, and the parson marked that as soon as he left the house people followed him stealthily to find out if he wasn't going to the silver mountain and to steal the secret from him.

"When matters were come to this pass, the parson called the peasants together to vote. To start with he reminded them of all the misfortunes which the discovery of the mountain had brought upon them, and he asked them if they were going to let themselves be ruined or if they would save themselves. Then he told them that they must not expect him, who was their spiritual adviser, to help on their destruction. Now he had declared not to reveal to anyone where the silver mine was, and never would he himself take riches from it. And then he asked the peasants how they would have it henceforth. If they wished to continue their search for the mine and wait upon riches, then he would go so far away that no word of their misery could reach him; but if they would give up thinking about the silver mine and be as heretofore, he would remain with them. 'Whichever way you may choose,' said the parson, 'remember this, that from me no one shall ever know anything about the silver mountain.' "

"Well," said the King, "how did they decide?"

"They did as their pastor wished," said the parson. "They understood that he meant well by them when he wanted to remain poor for their sakes. And they commissioned him to go to the forest and conceal the vein of ore with evergreen and stone, so that no one would be able to find it—neither they nor their posterity."

"And ever since the parson has been living here just as poor as the rest?"

"Yes," answered the curate, "he has lived here just as poor as the rest."

"He has married, of course, and built a new parsonage?" said the King.

"No, he couldn't afford to marry and he lives in the old cabin."

"It's a pretty story that you have told me," said the King. After a few seconds he resumed, "Was it of the silver mountain that you were thinking when you said that the parson here would be able to procure for me as much money as I need?"

"Yes," said the other.

"But I can't put the thumbscrews on him," said the King. "Or how would you advise that I get such a man to show me the mountain—a man who has renounced his sweetheart and the allurements of life?"

"Oh, that's a different matter," said the parson. "But if it's the fatherland that is in need of the fortune, he will probably give in."

"Will you answer for that?" asked the King.

"Yes, that I will answer for," said the clergyman.

"Doesn't he care, then, what becomes of his parishioners?"

"That can rest in God's hands."

The King rose from his chair and walked over to the window. He stood for a moment and looked upon the group of people outside. The longer he looked, the clearer his large eyes shone; and his figure seemed to grow. "You may greet the pastor of this congregation and say that for Sweden's King there is no sight more beautiful than to see a people such as this!"

Then the King turned from the window and looked at the clergyman. He began to smile. "Is is true that the pastor of this parish is so poor that he removes his black clothes as soon as the service is over and dresses himself like a peasant?" asked the King.

"Yes, so poor is he," said the curate,

and a crimson flush leaped into his rough-hewn face.

The King went back to the window. One could see that he was in his best mood. All that was noble and great within him had been quickened into life. "You must let that mine lie in peace," said the King. "Inasmuch as you have labored and starved a lifetime to make this people such as you would have it, you may keep it as it is."

"But if the kingdom is in danger?" said the parson.

"The kingdom is better served with men than with money," remarked the King. When he had said this, he bade the clergyman farewell and went out from the vestry.

Without stood the group of people, as quiet and taciturn as they were when he went in. As the King came down the steps, a peasant stepped up to him.

"Have you had a talk with our pastor?" said the peasant.

"Yes," said the King. "I have."

"Then of course you have our answer," said the peasant. "We asked you to go in and talk with our parson, that he might give you an answer from us."

"I have the answer," said the King.

FOR STUDY AND DISCUSSION

1. Which of the two stories is the main one —that of the King who stops on his travels, listens, and passes on or that of the parson's finding the silver mine? What is the function of the less important story? How does it add to the meaning of the main story?

2. Apparently the King learns a lesson from the parson's tale: "The kingdom is better served with men than with money." Do you think that the King will remember this lesson? Why or why not? Is the parson's tale actually more of a sermon—a persuasive speech on the evil that love of money works upon people—than it is a story? Did the parson tell it to teach the King a moral lesson, or to entertain him, or both? What in the story makes you think so? Can a story be both a story and a sermon?

3. What are the chief differences in personality between the King and the parson? Where are the differences first shown in the story? By the end of the story, do the two men seem more alike? What are they shown to have in common?

4. Contemporary critics of our "affluent society" often draw the same conclusions about the evil effects of money as the parson and the King do in "The Silver Mine." Do you think that the central idea of the story applies to the world today? Why or why not?

REVEALING CHARACTER

There are three ways in which an author can reveal character: by showing the character in question acting and speaking, by having other characters say what they think of that character, and by commenting on that character directly. In this story, how does the author characterize the King by each of these means? How does she characterize the parson? Which character is more fully revealed? Which of the three methods of characterization is used most effectively in this story?

LANGUAGE AND VOCABULARY

The words listed below help to characterize the King and the parson. Find out what they mean, then show how they help to suggest the character of each man. What other words could be used to replace these words and still keep the present meaning?

"it was becoming *monotonous* for the King to wait . . ."

"He's a bit *arbitrary* . . ." (the parson, about himself)

"if the King would *condescend* to listen to me for a moment . . ."

"without letting himself be *disturbed* by the King's *indifference* . . ."

"A man who has *renounced* his sweetheart and the *allurements* of life . . ." (the King, about the parson)

1. In the opening paragraphs Selma Lagerlöf shows the King's impatience by describing his rapid drive through Dalecarlia. Notice how her similes ("like lightning" . . . "like stretched rubber bands") contribute to the impression of impatience. In like manner, write a brief narrative showing the impatience of an automobile driver caught on a highway in the rush hour, or the anxiety of a student who is late for class or eager to reach the cafeteria at lunchtime. Try to use one or two similes in your account.

2. The parson's story (beginning with "Once upon a time . . .") is a tale that illustrates a moral point: the old saying that "Money is the root of all evil." What other old saying or proverb do you believe is true? Can you think of a story that would illustrate the truth of it? Write a brief tale of your own to illustrate such a saying. If you like, use one of the following:

    Liars Always Give Themselves Away
    A Stitch in Time Saves Nine
    Half a Loaf Is Better than None
    A Watched Pot Never Boils
    Judge People Not by What They Have,
      But by What They Are

ABOUT THE AUTHOR

Selma Lagerlöf (1858–1940) was born on her father's estate in Varmland, Sweden, where she lived for most of her life. A childhood attack of polio made it necessary for her to be tutored at home, where her grandmother supplemented the tutor's teaching with re-tellings of old Swedish folk legends. She later studied at the Royal Women's Academy for a time and taught at a girls' school. The source of Miss Lagerlöf's inspiration as a writer was always the land—its people and its legends—rather than the literature of her day. In 1909 she became the first woman to win the Nobel prize for literature; in 1914 she became the first woman member of the Swedish Academy of Arts and Letters. Her most famous books are *The Ring of the Lowenskolds,* about a peasant girl who lifts the curse from a noble family, and *The Wonderful Adventures of Nils.*

The Pacing Goose

JESSAMYN WEST

J ESS SAT in the kitchen at the long table by the west window where in winter he kept his grafting tools: the thin-bladed knife, the paper sweet with the smell of beeswax and the resin, the boxes of roots and scions.[1] Jess was a nurseryman and spring meant for him not only spirits' flowering—but the earth's. A week more of moderating weather and he'.d be out, still in gum boots, but touching an earth that had thawed, whose riches were once again fluid enough to be sucked upward, toward those burgeonings which by summer would have swelled into Early Harvests, Permains, and Sweet Bows.[2]

Spring's a various season, Jess thought, no two years the same: comes in with rains, mud deep enough to swallow horse and rider; comes in cold, snow falling so fast it weaves a web; comes in with a warm wind blowing about thy ears and bringing a smell of something flowering, not here, but southaways, across the Ohio, maybe, in Kentucky. Nothing here now but a smell of melting snow—which is no smell at all, but a kind of prickle in the

[1] **scions** (sī'ənz): plant shoots prepared for grafting.

[2] **Early . . . Bows:** varieties of apples.

nose, like a bygone sneeze. Comes in so various, winter put by and always so welcome.

"And us each spring so much the same."

"Thee speaking to me, Jess?"

"Nothing thee'd understand, Eliza."

Spring made Jess discontented with the human race—and with women, if anything, more than men. It looked as if spring put them all in the shade: the season so resourceful and they each year meeting it with nothing changed from last year, digging up roots from the same sassafras thicket, licking sulfur and molasses [1] from the big-bowled spoon.

Behind him the table was set for supper, plates neatly turned to cover the bone-handled knives and forks, spoon vase aglitter with steel well burnished by brick dust, dishes of jam with more light to them than the sun, which was dwindling away, peaked and overcast, outside his window.

"Spring opening up," he said, "and nobody in this house so much as putting down a line of poetry."

Eliza, who was lifting dried-peach pies from a hot oven, said nothing. She set the four of them in a neat row on the edge of her kitchen cabinet to cool, and slid her pans of cornbread into the oven. Then she turned to Jess, her cheeks red with heat, and her black eyes warm with what she had to say. "Thee'd maybe relish a nice little rhyme for thy supper, Jess Birdwell."

Jess sighed, then sniffed the pies, so rich with ripe peach flavor that the kitchen smelled like a summer orchard, nothing lacking but the sound of bees. "Now, Eliza," he said, "thee knows I wouldn't have thee anyways altered. Thee . . ."

"Thee," Eliza interrupted him, "is like

all men. Thee wants to have thy poetry and eat it too."

Jess wondered how what he'd felt about spring, a season with the Lord's thumbprint fresh on it, could've led to anything so unspringlike as an argument about a batch of dried-peach pies.

"Eliza," he said firmly, "I didn't mean thee. Though it's crossed my mind sometimes as strange that none of the boys have ever turned, this time of year, to rhyming."

"Josh writes poems," Eliza said.

"Thee ever read what Josh writes, Eliza?"

Eliza nodded.

Ah, well, Jess thought, no use at this late date to tell her what's the difference.

Eliza looked her husband over carefully. "Jess Birdwell," she said, "thee's full of humors. Thy blood needs thinning. I'll boil thee up a good cup of sassafras tea."

Jess turned away from the green and gold sunset and the patches of snow it was gilding and fairly faced the dried-peach pies and Eliza, who was dropping dumplings into a pot of beans.

[1] **sulfur and molasses:** an old-time "spring tonic."

"That's just it, Eliza," he said. "That's just the rub."

Eliza gave him no encouragement, but he went on anyway. "Earth alters, season to season, spring comes in never two times the same, only us pounding on steady as pump bolts and not freshened by so much as a grass blade."

"Jess, thee's got spring fever."

"I could reckon time and temperature, each spring, by the way thee starts honing[1] for geese. 'Jess, don't thee think we might have a few geese?' It's a tardy spring," Jess said. "Snow still on the ground and not a word yet from thee about geese."

Eliza pulled a chair out from the table and sat. "Jess, why's thee always been so set against geese?"

"I'm not set against geese. It's geese that's set against farming. They can mow down a half acre of sprouting corn while thee's trying to head them off—and in two minutes they'll level a row of pie plant it's taken two years to get started. No, Eliza, it's the geese that's against me."

"If thee had tight fences . . ." Eliza said.

"Eliza, I got tight fences, but the goose's never been hatched that'll admit fences exist. And an old gander'd just as soon go through a fence as hiss—and if he can't find a hole or crack in a fence he'll lift the latch."

"Jess," said Eliza flatly, "thee don't like geese."

"Well," said Jess, "I wouldn't go so far's to say I didn't like them, but I will say that if there's any meaner, dirtier animal, or one that glories in it more, I don't know it. And a thing I've never been able to understand about thee, Eliza, is what thee sees in the shifty-eyed birds."

"Geese," said Eliza, with a dreaminess unusual to her, "march along so lordly

[1] **honing:** yearning.

like . . . they're pretty as swans floating down a branch . . . in fall they stretch out their necks and honk to geese passing overhead as if they's wild. My father never had any trouble raising geese and I've heard him say many a time that there's no better food for a brisk morning than a fried goose egg."

Jess knew, with spring his topic, he'd ought to pass over Eliza's father and his fried goose egg but he couldn't help saying, "A fried goose egg always had a kind of bloated look to me, Eliza"—but then he went on fast. "The season's shaping up," he said. "I can see thee's all primed to say, 'Jess, let's get a setting of goose eggs.'"

Eliza went over to the bean kettle and began to lift out dumplings. "It's a forwarder season than thee thinks, Jess," she said. "I got a setting under a hen now."

Jess looked at his wife. He didn't know what had made him want spring's variety in a human being—nor Eliza's substituting doing for asking. And speaking of it just now, as he had, made opposition kind of ticklish.

"When'd thee set them?" he asked finally.

"Yesterday," said Eliza.

"Where'd thee get the eggs?"

"Overbys'," said Eliza. The Overbys were their neighbors to the south.

"Well, they got enough for a surety," Jess said, "to give a few away."

"The Overbys don't give anything away, as thee knows. I paid for them. With my own money," Eliza added.

"How many?" Jess asked.

"Eight," Eliza said.

Jess turned back to his window. The sun had set, leaving a sad green sky and desolate black and white earth. "Five acres of corn gone," he calculated.

"Thee said," Eliza reminded him, "that what thee wanted was a little variety in

me. 'Steady as a pump bolt,' were thy words."

"I know I did," Jess admitted glumly. "I talk too much."

"Draw up thy chair," Eliza said placidly, not contradicting him; "here's Enoch and the boys."

Next morning after breakfast Jess and Enoch left the kitchen together. The sun was the warmest the year had yet produced and the farm roofs were steaming; south branch, swollen by melting snow, was running so full the soft lap of its eddies could be heard in the barnyard; a rooster tossed his voice into the bright air, loud and clear as if aiming to be heard by every fowl in Jennings County.

"Enoch," said Jess to his hired man, "what's thy feeling about geese?"

Enoch was instantly equipped, for the most part, with feelings on every subject. Geese was a homelier topic than he'd choose himself to enlarge upon, not one that could be much embellished nor one on which Mr. Emerson,[1] so far's he could recall, had ever expressed an opinion. "In the fall of the year," he said, "long about November or December, there's nothing tastier on the table than roast goose."

"Goose on the table's not what I

<hr />

[1] **Mr. Emerson:** Ralph Waldo Emerson, American philosopher (1803–1882).

mean," Jess said. "I was speaking of goose on the hoof. Goose nipping off a stand of corn, Enoch, goose roistering round, honking and hissing so's thee can't hear thyself think, goose eying thee like a snake on stilts."

Enoch gazed at his employer for a few seconds. "Mr. Birdwell," he said, "I think that if they's an ornery bird, it's a goose. Ornery and undependable."

"I'm glad we's so like-minded about them," Jess said. "Otherwise, I'd not like to ask thee to do this little job." He pulled a long darning needle from beneath the lapel of his coat.

Enoch eyed it with some mistrust. "I can't say's I've been handy with a needle, Mr. Birdwell."

"Thee'll be handy enough for this," Jess said with hearty conviction. "To come to it, Enoch, Eliza's set eight goose eggs. Next year with any luck she'd have two dozen. And so on. More and more. Feeling the way thee does, Enoch, about geese, it's no more'n fair to give thee a chance to put a stop to this before it goes too far. One little puncture in each egg with this and the goose project's nipped in the bud and Eliza none the wiser."

"I'm mighty awkward with my hands," said Enoch, "doing fine work. Ticklish job like this I might drop an egg and break it."

"Enoch," said Jess, "thee's not developing a weakness for geese, is thee?"

"It ain't the geese," said Enoch frankly, "it's your wife. She's been mighty clever [1] to me and if she's got her heart set on geese, it'd go against the grain to disappoint her. Whyn't you do it, Mr. Birdwell?"

"Same reason," said Jess, "only more of them—and if Eliza ever asks if I tampered with that setting of eggs I figure on being able to say No." Jess held the needle nearer Enoch, who looked at it but still made no motion to take it.

"Likely no need to do a thing," Enoch said. "Two to one those eggs'll never hatch anyways. Overbys're such a fox-eared tribe they more'n likely sold her bad eggs to begin with."

"Thee's knowed about this," Jess asked, "all along?"

"Yes," Enoch said.

"Here's the needle," Jess said.

"You look at this," Enoch inquired, "not so much as a favor asked as a part of the day's work with orders from you?"

"Yes," Jess said, "that's about the way I look at it."

Enoch took the needle, held it somewhat gingerly, and with the sun glinting across its length walked slowly toward the chicken house.

It takes thirty days for a goose egg to hatch, and the time, with spring work to be done, went fast. The hen Eliza had picked was a good one and kept her mind strictly on her setting. Eliza kept her mind on the hen, and Jess and Enoch found their minds oftener than they liked on Eliza and her hoped-for geese.

At breakfast on the day the geese were due to break their shells Jess said, "If I's thee, Eliza, I wouldn't bank too much on them geese. I heard Enoch say a while back he wouldn't be surprised if not an

---

[1] **clever:** kind (a local use of the word).

egg hatched. Thought the eggs were likely no good."

Enoch was busy pouring coffee into a saucer, then busy cooling it, but Eliza waited until he was through. "Did thee say that, Enoch?"

Enoch looked at Jess. "Yes," he said, "I kind of recollect something of the sort."

"What made thee think so, Enoch?"

"Why," said Jess, for Enoch was busy with his coffee again, "it was the Overbys. Enoch's got a feeling they's kind of unreliable. Fox-eared, I think thee said, Enoch, didn't thee?"

Enoch's work took him outside almost at once and Jess himself said, "If thee'll just give me a little packet of food, Eliza, I won't trouble thee for anything at noon. I'm going to be over'n the south forty and it'll save time coming and going."

Eliza was surprised, for Jess'd usually come twice as far for a hot dinner at midday, but she made him fried ham sandwiches and put them and some cold apple turnovers in a bag.

"It's a pity thee has to miss thy dinner," she told him, but Jess only said, "Press of work, press of work," and hurriedly departed.

Jess came home that evening through the spring twilight, somewhat late, and found a number of things to do at the barn before he went up to the house. When he entered the kitchen nothing seemed amiss—lamps ruddy, table set, stove humming, and beside the stove a small box over which Eliza was bending. Jess stopped to look—and listen; from inside the box was coming a kind of birdlike peeping, soft and not unpleasant. Reluctantly he walked to Eliza's side. There, eating minced boiled egg, and between bites lifting its beak to Eliza, it seemed, and making those chirping sounds he'd heard, was a gray-gold gosling.

Eliza looked up pleasantly. "Enoch was right," she said. "The eggs were bad. Only one hatched. I plan to call it Samantha," she told Jess. "It's a name I've always been partial to."

"Samantha," said Jess without any enthusiasm whatever for either name or gosling. "How's thee know it's a she?"

"I don't," said Eliza, "but if it's a gander it's a name easily changed to Sam."

Enoch came in just then with a load of wood for the kitchen woodbox. "Enoch," asked Jess, "has thee seen Samantha—or Sam?"

Enoch mumbled but Jess understood him to say he had.

"It was my understanding, Enoch, that thy opinion was that all those eggs were bad."

"Well, Mr. Birdwell," said Enoch, "a man could make a mistake. He could count wrong."

"A man ought to be able to count to eight without going astray," said Jess.

Eliza was paying no attention to either of them; she was making little tweeting sounds herself, bending over the chirping gosling. "Does thee know," she asked Jess, "that this is the first pet I ever had in my life?"

"Thee's got Ebony," Jess said.

"I don't mean a caged pet," Eliza said, "but one to walk beside thee. I'm reconciled the others didn't hatch. With eight I'd've had to raise geese for the table. With one only I can make Samantha a pure pet."

A pure pet was what she made of her: Samantha ate what the family ate, with the exception of articles which Eliza thought might be indigestible and would risk on humans but not on her goose. Cake, pie, corn-on-the-cob, there was nothing too good for Samantha. From a big-footed, gold-downed gosling she swelled, almost at once, like a slack sail which gets a sudden breeze, into a full-rounded convexity.

"Emphasis on the vexity," Jess said when he thought of this. Samantha was everything he'd disliked in the general run of geese, with added traits peculiar to herself, which vexed him. Because she was fed at the doorstep, she was always underfoot. No shout, however loud, would move her before she's ready to move. If she's talked to too strong she'd flail you with her wings and pinch the calf of your leg until for some days it would look to be mortifying. She'd take food out of children's hands, and the pansies Jess had planted in a circle at the base of the Juneberry tree she sheared so close that

there was not a naked stem left to show for all his work. And when not being crossed in any way, Jess simply looking at her and meditating, trying to fathom Samantha's fascination for Eliza, the goose would suddenly extend her snake-like neck, and almost touching Jess, hiss with such a hint of icy disapprobation that Jess would involuntarily recoil.

But she was Eliza's pure pet, no two ways about that, and would lift her head for Eliza to scratch, and walk beside her with the lordly roll of the known elect.

"There was some goddess," Enoch remembered, "who always had a big bird with her." Jess supposed Enoch was thinking of Juno and her peacock, but the reference didn't convince him that a goose was a suitable companion for any goddess—let alone Eliza, and he couldn't honestly feel much regret when one evening toward the end of November Eliza told him Samantha was missing. "She'll turn up," Jess said. "That bird's too ornery to die young."

Eliza said nothing, but next evening she proved Jess was right. "Samantha's over at Overbys'," she said.

"Well, did thee fetch her home?" Jess asked.

"No," said Eliza with righteous indignation, "they wouldn't let me. They said they had forty geese—and forty's what they got now, and they don't think Samantha's there. They provoked me so, Jess, I told them they'd sold me seven bad eggs and now they try to take the eighth away from me."

Jess felt a little abashed at this, but he asked, "How can thee be so sure Samantha's there? She might've been carried off by a varmint."

Eliza was scornful. "Thee forgets I hand-raised Samantha from a gosling. I'd know her among four hundred—let alone forty."

"Whyn't thee buy her back then," Jess asked, "if that's the only way?"

"After what I said about their eggs," Eliza answered sadly, "the Overbys say they don't want any more dealings with me."

Eliza mourned so for the lost Samantha that first Enoch and then Jess went over to the Overbys' but no one there would admit the presence of a visiting goose—forty they had, and forty you could see by counting was what they had now. Short of force there didn't seem any way of getting Samantha home again.

When Eliza heard the Overbys were going to sell geese for Christmas eating she was frantic. "Jess," she said, "I just can't bear to think of Samantha, plucked naked and resting on a table waiting to be carved. She used to sing as sweet as any bird when she was little, and she'd walk by my side taking the air. She's the only goose I ever heard of," Eliza remembered mournfully, "who'd drink tea."

In Jess's opinion a goose'd eat anything at either end of the scale, but he didn't suppose this was a suitable time to mention it to Eliza. "Eliza," he said, "short of me and Enoch's going over there and using force on old man Overby—or sneaking over at night and breaking into their chicken pen, I don't know how in the world we're going to get Samantha back for thee."

"We could sue," said Eliza.

"Thee mean go to law?" Jess asked, astounded. Quakers stayed out of courts, believing in amicable settlements without recourse to law.

"Yes," said Eliza. "I'd do it for Samantha. I'd think it my duty. Going to law'd be a misery for us . . . but not so lasting a misery as being roasted would be for Samantha."

Jess couldn't deny this, but he said, "I'd have to think it over. I've never been to law yet in my life and suing for a gone goose don't seem to me a very likely place to start."

Next morning Eliza served a good but silent breakfast, not sitting herself to eat with the rest of her family.

"Thee feeling dauncy,[1] Eliza?" Jess asked.

"I just can't eat," she said, "for thinking of Samantha."

Labe and Mattie had tears in their eyes. Little Jess was mournfully bellowing. Enoch looked mighty glum. Jess felt ashamed to be swallowing victuals in the midst of so much sorrow. Eliza stood at the end of the stove where the gosling's box had rested for the first few weeks of its life, looking down, as if remembering how it had sung and lifted its beak to her.

Jess couldn't stand it. "Eliza," he said, "if thee wants to go through with it I'll go to Vernon and fee a lawyer for thee. Thee'll have to go to court, be on the witness stand—and even then I misdoubt thee'll ever get thy goose back. Does thee still want me to do it?"

Eliza came to the table and stood with her hand on Jess's shoulder. "Yes, Jess," she said, "I want thee to do it."

Jess went to Vernon, fee'd a lawyer, had a restraining order put on the Overbys so they couldn't sell or kill the goose Eliza said was Samantha, and awaited with misgivings the day of the trial. It came in mid-December.

Eliza, Jess. and Enoch rode to the trial through a fall of light, fresh snow. Brilliant sunlight, crisp air, glittering snow, and Rome's[2] spirited stepping made the occasion, in spite of its purpose, seem festive. Eliza made it seem festive. Jess, who did not forget its purpose, regarded her with some wonder. He couldn't say what it was about her—dress and bonnet appeared to be simply her First Day[3] best—but she had a holiday air.

He considered it his duty to warn her. "Eliza," he said, "thee understands thee's not going to Meeting?[4] They're not going to sit silent while thee tells them how much thee loves Samantha and how she sang when young and drank tea. Old man Overby'll have his say and he's got a lawyer hired for no other purpose than to trip thee up."

Eliza was unimpressed. "What's our lawyer fee'd for, Jess?" she asked.

Jess took another tack. "Eliza," he told her, "I don't figger thee's got a chance in a thousand to get Samantha back."

"This is a court of justice, isn't it?" Eliza asked.

"Yes," Jess said.

"Then there's no need for thee to fash[5] thyself, Jess Birdwell. I'll get Samantha back."

Not getting Samantha back wasn't what fashed Jess—he reckoned he could bear up under that mighty well. What fashed him was the whole shooting match . . . In some few cases, matters of life and death, going to court might be necessary, and he could imagine such. But a suit over a goose named Samantha wasn't one of them. And poor Eliza. Law to her was all Greek and turkey tracks . . . and here she was bound for court as chipper as if she was Chief Justice Taney[6] himself. Jess sighed and shook his head. Getting shut of Samantha would be no hardship for him, but he was downcast for Eliza's sake and the way she'd have to turn homeward empty-handed.

[3] **First Day:** Quaker name for Sunday.
[4] **Meeting:** Quaker church meeting.
[5] **fash:** worry.
[6] **Taney** (tā′nē): Roger B. Taney, a Chief Justice of the Supreme Court (1836–1864).

[1] **dauncy:** ill.
[2] **Rome:** Rome Beauty, the Birdwells' carriage horse.

In the courtroom, hard clear light reflected upward from the snow fell onto what Jess thought were hard faces: courthouse hangers-on; farmers whose slackening work made the diversion of a trial an inviting possibility; lovers of oddity who figured a tilt between a Quaker female, preacher to boot, and an old sinner like Milt Overby over the ownership of a goose ought to produce some enlivening quirks. They stared at Eliza, exchanged salutes with Milt Overby and inspected Samantha, who in her crate awaited the court's decision.

The two lawyers Jess considered to be on a par. Nothing fancy, either one ... old roadsters both, gone gray in service and with a knowledge of their business. The circuit judge was something else, unaccountably young, jug-eared and dressed more sprightly than a groom for his own wedding. A city whipper-snapper, born and trained north of the Mississinewa,[1] and now, in Jess's opinion, setting a squeamish foot in backwoods provinces, and irked to find himself trying so trifling a case. Didn't know a goose from a guinea hen, like as not, and would consider tossing a coin a more suitable manner of settling such a matter—just as near right in the end—and his valuable time saved.

Eliza, Jess saw, was of no such opinion. She, too, was scanning the young judge, and Jess, who knew her, saw from the look on her face that she was taken by him. A neat, thin, pious boy—far from home—he looked, no doubt to her; a young man who could do with better cooking and more regular eating.

The young man rapped the court to order. Spitting and shuffling slackened and in a high, precise voice he read, "Birdwell versus Overby. Charge, petty lar-

ceny. Appropriation and willful withholding of goose named Samantha." The name Samantha seemed to somewhat choke him, but he got it out.

"Ready for Birdwell," said Mr. Abel Samp, Eliza's lawyer.

"Ready for Overby," said the defendant's lawyer.

Eliza was the first witness on the stand. Jess sometimes forgot what a good-looking woman Eliza was, but the interest shown on lifted faces all about him refreshed his memory.

"Swear the plaintiff in," the judge said.

Eliza, in her sweet voice, spoke directly to the judge. "I don't swear," she said.

The judge explained that profanity was not asked for. "I understood," said Eliza, "that thee wasn't asking for profanity. No one would think that of thee. But we Quakers do not take oaths in court. We affirm."

"Permit Mrs. Birdwell to affirm," said the judge. Eliza affirmed.

Mr. Samp then proceeded to question Eliza as to Samantha's birth and habits.

"Judge," Eliza began.

"Address the judge," Mr. Samp said, "as Your Honor."

"We Quakers," Eliza told the judge, gently, "do not make use of such titles. What is thy name? I think thee'll go far in our state and thy name's one I'd like to know."

The judge appeared somewhat distraught, undecided as to whether to make the tone of the court brisk and legal (if possible) or to follow Eliza's lead of urbane sociability.

"Pomeroy," he said and made a slight bow in Eliza's direction.

Eliza returned the bow, deeper and with more grace. "Friend Pomeroy," she said, "it is indeed a pleasure to know thee."

Samantha's story as Eliza told it to

[1] **Mississinewa** (mis·is·sin′i·wä): a small river flowing into the Wabash River in Indiana.

Friend Pomeroy was surprisingly terse. Affecting, and losing nothing by Eliza's telling, but to the point.

"Mrs. Birdwell," said Samp, "how long have you had an acquaintanceship with geese and their habits?"

"Since I was a child," Eliza said. "My father was a great fancier of geese."

"And you think you could identify this goose Samantha, which you admit in looks was similar to the defendant's?"

"I could," Eliza said with much authority.

Mr. Samp, to Jess's surprise, left the matter there. "Take the witness," he said to Overby's lawyer—but the counsel for the defendant was in no hurry to cross-examine Eliza. Instead he put his client on the stand.

"Farewell, Samantha," Jess said to Enoch.

"You relieved?" Enoch asked.

"Putting Eliza first," Jess said, "as I do, no."

Milt Overby, whose natural truculence was somewhat stimulated by a nip he'd had to offset snappy weather, bellowed his way through his testimony. At one juncture he set the judge aright when he asked some elementary questions concerning the habits and configurations of geese. "Where in tarnation you from?" he snorted. "What they mean sending us judges down here who don't know Toulouse from Wyandotte,[1] or goose from gander?"

The young judge used voice and gavel to quiet the guffawing which filled the courtroom and the trial proceeded. A number of witnesses for both sides were brought to the stand and while it was shown that Overbys had maybe eaten a goose or two and neglected out of pure

fondness for the creatures to count them as among the departed, still nobody had been able to positively identify Samantha.

Mr. Overby's lawyer seemed somewhat loath to cross-examine Eliza, but he put her on the stand. She'd said she knew geese and her testimony had been direct and positive. "Mrs. Birdwell," he said, "how can you be so sure your goose was with my client's geese?"

Eliza's black eyes rested confidingly upon the judge. "Friend Pomeroy," she said, "I raised Samantha from a gosling."

Jess sighed. "Here it comes," he said, "how that goose could sing and drink tea."

Eliza continued, "And there's one thing about her that always set her apart from every other goose."

"Yes, Mrs. Birdwell," said Judge Pomeroy, who was inclined to forget, with Eliza on the stand, that he was in a courtroom.

"Samantha," said Eliza, with much earnestness, "from the day she was born had a gait unlike any other goose I ever saw and one that set her apart from all her Overby connections. I picked her out at once when I went over there, because of it. Thee couldn't've missed it, Friend Pomeroy."

"Yes, Mrs. Birdwell," said the judge with interest in his voice.

"Samantha," said Eliza, "was a born pacer. Thee knows what a pacer is?"

"Certainly," said Judge Pomeroy. "A pacer," he repeated with no surprise—and with obvious pleasure that Eliza'd hit upon so clear and differentiating an aspect of her goose and one that made identification possible.

A titter was mounting through the courtroom—Judge Pomeroy lifted his head. He had no desire to be further instructed as to the history, habits, and breeds of geese, and he liked to see a trial

[1] **Toulouse** (too·looz′) . . . **Wyandotte** (wī′ən·dot): breeds of fowl.

settled by some such little and too often overlooked subtlety. Judge Pomeroy brought down his gavel. "The court awards decision in favor of the plaintiff. Case dismissed." While the silence that followed on his words still prevailed Judge Pomeroy stepped briskly and with obvious pleasure out through the rear door.

Jess was also brisk about departure. No use lingering until friend Pomeroy had been more thoroughly informed as to gaits in general and geese in particular. Mid-afternoon's a quiet time in any season. In winter with snow on the ground, no leaves to rustle and bare limbs rigid as rock against a cloudless sky, the hush is deepest of all. Nothing broke that hush in the surrey,[1] except the squeak of leather and snow, the muffled footfalls of Rome Beauty. Jess and Eliza, on the front seat, rode without speaking. Enoch, in the back, seemed to meditate. Even Samantha in her crate at Enoch's feet was silent.

Maple Grove Nursery was in sight before Jess spoke. "Eliza," he said, "would thee mind telling me—did thee ever see a trotting goose?"

Enoch ceased to meditate and listened. He had been wondering about this himself.

"Certainly not," said Eliza. "Thee knows as well as I, Jess Birdwell, an ani-

mal can't trot without hind feet and fore-feet."

"So far, Eliza," Jess said, "we see eye to eye. Now maybe thee'd tell me—did thee ever see a goose that didn't pace?"

Eliza was truly amazed, it seemed. "Why, Jess," she said, "an ordinary goose just walks—but Samantha paces."

Jess was silent for a spell. "What'd thee say the difference is?"

"It's the swing, Jess Birdwell," said Eliza, "same as in a horse that nature's formed for a pacer . . . it's the natural bent, the way the spirit leads the beast to set his feet down. Samantha's a natural pacer."

That seemed as far as they'd likely get on the subject and Jess joined Enoch in meditation. In the barnyard, before she went up to the house, Eliza said, like an old hand at the business, "Attending court whettens the appetite. It's a little early but I thought if thee'd relish it"—and she looked at Jess and Enoch, never sparing a glance for Samantha, as if her menfolk's welfare was her sole concern—"I'd stir us up a bite to eat. Hot tea and fresh sweet-cakes, say. Might fry a little sausage and open some cherry preserves. If thee'd relish it," she repeated.

Jess wasn't taken in, but he'd relish it, and so would Enoch, and they both said so. They hustled with the unhitching so they could uncrate Samantha and note her progress with eyes newly instructed

[1] **surrey:** a light carriage.

as to what made a pacer. Jess dumped her in the snow, and Enoch tapped her with his hat. Samantha made for the back door.

"By sugar," said Jess, "Eliza's right. She paces." Samantha had the smooth roll of a racker [1]—there were no two ways about it. At heart she was a pacer, and what two legs could do in that line, Samantha accomplished.

"With four legs," Enoch said, "you could enter her in any county fair—rack on," he cried with enthusiasm. As they followed Samantha to the house, Enoch, for whom any event existed chiefly in its after aspects as a cud for rumination, asked, "How you feel in respect of court trials, now, Mr. Birdwell?"

"I'm still against them," Jess said, "though they's three things this trial's taught me I might never otherwise have learned. Two's about women."

Enoch revered all knowledge and he had a notion that information on this subject might have a more than transcendental [2] value. "What's the two things you learned about women, Mr. Birdwell?"

"Well, Enoch, I learned first, dependability's woman's greatest virtue. Steady as a pump bolt, day in, day out. When thee finds a woman like that, Enoch, don't try to change her. Not even in spring."

"No, sir," said Enoch, "I won't."

"Second, when it's a case of woman and the law—thee don't need to waste any worry on the woman."

"No, sir," said Enoch again.

When they reached the back steps, Enoch asked, "I understood you to say you'd learned three things, Mr. Birdwell. What's the third about?"

"Hired men," said Jess.

Enoch was taken aback, but he'd asked

[1] **racker:** a horse that paces or single-foots.
[2] **transcendental:** Pertaining to transcendentalism, the philosophy of Emerson, which Enoch admired.

for it. "Yes, Mr. Birdwell," he said.

"Never hire one," Jess told him, "till thee finds out first if he can count to eight. Save thyself a lot of trouble that way, Enoch."

"How's I to know the eighth'd turn out to be Samantha?" Enoch asked.

Samantha herself, who was waiting at the doorstep for an expected tidbit, reached out and, unhampered by either boots or work pants, nipped Enoch firmly through his thin Sunday best.

"Thee say something, Enoch?" Jess asked.

Enoch had but he didn't repeat it. Instead he said, "Pacer or no pacer, that's Samantha," and the two of them stepped out of the snow into the warm kitchen, scented with baking sweetcakes and frying sausage.

FOR STUDY AND DISCUSSION

1. Show how the humorous conflict between Jess and Eliza is a result of their different personalities. Why does Jess dislike geese? Why is Eliza fond of them? Are Eliza's reasons based on poetic sentiment and intuition? Are Jess's reasons based on convenience and common sense? Are Jess's and Eliza's attitudes toward geese consistent with their attitudes toward poetry and spring? Explain.

2. Despite their dispute over Samantha, Jess and Eliza continue to live in harmony. What evidence is there, in their speech and action, of mutual love and esteem? Where in the story does Jess show most clearly that his feeling for Eliza is stronger than his dislike of the goose?

3. Did Judge Pomeroy decide the case on the basis of the evidence or on the personality of the two persons involved? What makes you think so? In a lawsuit that becomes a question of who is telling the truth, should the personality of a witness count as part of the evidence? Do you think that in this case the judge was justified in deciding as he did? Why?

4. What is Enoch's part in the action of this story? How do his extensive reading and philosophic attitude cause him to act as he does?

SIMILE AND METAPHOR

Much of the interest in this story comes from its rich, colorful Quaker speech. Much of this speech is *figurative*—that is, it creates pictures in the imagination. The most frequent kinds of figurative language are *simile* and *metaphor*. Both compare two unlike things. A simile, however, makes the comparison by saying that one of the things is *like* the other, and usually uses the word *like* or *as* ("John is as brave as a tiger"). A metaphor, on the other hand, suggests that one of the things *is* the other ("John is a tiger"). Look at the expressions in italics in the following sentences. Which of them are similes? Which are metaphors? Which excite your interest? Why?

"a kind of prickle in the nose, *like a bygone sneeze.*"

"the kitchen smelled *like a summer orchard . . .*"

"a season with *the Lord's thumbprint fresh on it . . .*"

"only us pounding on steady *as pump bolts . . .*"

"a rooster *tossed his voice* into the bright air."

"goose eying thee *like a snake on stilts.*"

LANGUAGE AND VOCABULARY

In ordinary written prose, standard diction is generally preferred. In the realistic portrayal of character, however, dialect can be very useful—often even necessary. Look up the italicized words listed below. Which are dialect words? Which help to make the speaker seem real?

"Spring's a *various* season . . ."

"*Thee* speaking to me, Jess?"

"the sun . . . dwindling away, *peaked* and overcast . . ."

"thee's full of *humors.*"

"she'd . . . pinch the calf of your leg until . . . it would look to be *mortifying.*"

"She might've been carried off by a *varmint.*"

"Getting *shut* of Samantha would be no hardship . . ."

"Nothing fancy, either one . . . old *roadsters* both . . ."

"setting a *squeamish* foot in backwoods provinces . . ."

"Where in *tarnation* you from?"

"Attending court *whettens the* appetite."

FOR COMPOSITION

1. "Spring's a various season," thinks Jess, and goes on, in the second paragraph of the story, to tell why. What details does he use in his description to give a feeling of the variety of spring? What details might he have used to describe summer, winter, or fall? In a paragraph of your own, describe one of these other seasons, emphasizing its variety.

2. Eliza's victory at the trial is the result of her ability to describe "[the] one thing about her [Samantha] that always set her apart from [every other goose]." Imagine yourself in a situation similar to Eliza's and describe a pet, your car, or some other possession in such a way that it is clearly distinct from all other creatures or objects of the same kind.

ABOUT THE AUTHOR

Jessamyn West (1907–) was born in Indiana but grew up in California. She attended Whittier College, a Quaker school, and the University of California before marrying and going to study in England. When confined to bed with tuberculosis, she began to write. Her Quaker background provided the material for *The Friendly Persuasion,* a series of sketches about the life of a Quaker farm family in Indiana during the Civil War. This highly successful book was followed by *The Witch Diggers,* a novel about a poor farm; *Cress Delahanty,* a collection of stories about a teenage girl; and a book of short stories called *Love, Death, and the Ladies' Drill Team.* In all her works Miss West shows a real feeling for her characters, an original way with words and a down-to-earth sense of humor.

ELEMENTS OF ART

Drawings: Line and Tone

In real life we see objects as *tones* and *colors*. Tones, of course, may be dark or light, or they may be any shades or tints in between. When we make a drawing of an object, however, we usually begin it with *lines*. Such lines, of course, do not exist in nature. We use them simply as a convenience, as a direct way of communicating the basic idea of an object's shape. But lines can also be used to express feelings. Sharp, angular lines drawn boldly, for example, may indicate explosive action or sudden anger; whereas soft, wavy lines suggest gentleness and calm. Such linear effects are often found in cartoons and other types of drawings. You have probably expressed such feelings yourself from time to time in the lines of random scribbling, or "doodling."

Ever since prehistoric times, when artists drew with crude pieces of chalk on the walls of caves, people have used lines to describe their ideas and feelings about things they have seen or imagined. PLATE 1, an ink drawing on limestone made by an Egyptian artist more than 3,000 years ago, represents a pharaoh (king), accompanied by his hound, spearing a lion. The artist has used a diluted red ink to tint the pharaoh's flesh and portions of the two animals, but these tones of color are only added touches to what is basically a line drawing. Firm outlines enclose sharp, angular shapes, which converge swiftly toward the rearing body of the lion. Although the two animals are shown entirely in profile, the pharaoh is represented by a combination of profile and frontal views of various parts of his anatomy. Egyptian artists drew each detail as if seen separately and from its most characteristic angle.

PLATE 2 reproduces a watercolor brush drawing from the early sixteenth century, a picture of a young hare by the famous German artist Albrecht Dürer. The animal is shown as if seen from above and at an oblique angle instead of in profile, as the Egyptians would have represented it. Dürer has described the texture of the animal's fur in almost microscopic detail, with hundreds of tiny, delicate lines which curve and overlap one another in an extremely elaborate design. But of course this is not entirely a line drawing, for Dürer has also used broad areas of tone, mainly medium tones of browns and grays, to help give the figure an appearance of solidity.

One of the favorite drawing instruments of the eighteenth century was the quill pen, made from a wing or tail feather of a large bird such as a goose. A quill pen is so light and flexible that it responds instantly to the slightest pressure, allowing artists to move it quickly and gracefully across the surface of their paper. In PLATE 3 you can see what lively effects a skilled artist such as Tiepolo could achieve with this sensitive pen. In certain parts of the drawing, Tiepolo's line is very delicate and flowing, while in other parts it suddenly broadens into strong accents. To strengthen these accents, Tiepolo added dark tones with a brush, and to suggest lighter tones of shadow he diluted the brown ink, or *bistre,* with water.

The next drawing (PLATE 4), by the French artist Honore Daumier, dates from about a hundred years after Tiepolo. As you can see, Daumier's lines, especially in the figure of the clown, are free almost to the point of wildness, for, as they weave in and out, they suggest the frenzied rhythm of the drumbeat. Notice that all the lines, except the artist's signature ("h.d.") are drawn with a crayon, which makes a softer mark than a pen. On a slightly rough paper, crayon lines may vary from rich black to a sort of pebble-gray.

PLATE 5, a black crayon drawing by Georges Seurat, depends even more on the artist's use of the paper's grainy surface. Seurat has allowed tiny specks of white paper to show through most of his gray tones, especially the medium and lighter ones, so that they seem to sparkle with reflected light. But even the darkest shadows look rich and velvety. But notice also that Seurat's drawing contains no lines, no *outlines* around objects. His entire drawing is based on a very subtle use of tones.

In *Mid-Manhattan* (PLATE 6) Lyonel Feininger has made use of both line and tone. The tones are painted in watercolor washes. Hovering like shadows, they trace paths across the faces of low apartment houses in the foreground. Weaving in and out of these smudgy tones, thin crisp lines, drawn with charcoal, rise into the clear sky and outline the skeletons of skyscrapers. Tone and line seem almost completely independent of one another: each seems to go its own way.

Of course, drawings are made for various purposes. For instance, PLATES 1 and 3, and possibly PLATE 4, are sketches for paintings; whereas Dürer's drawing is a nature study. The drawings by Seurat and Feininger, however, are meant to be "finished" pictures.

PLATE 1. ARTIST UNKNOWN (Egyptian, between 1320–1085 B.C.): *King Spearing a Lion*.
Sketch in colored ink on limestone slab, from Valley of the Tombs of the Kings, 5 x 5½ inches.
(The Metropolitan Museum of Art, New York, The Carnavon Collection, Gift of Edward S.
Harkness, 1926)

PLATE 2. ALBRECHT DÜRER (German, 1471–1528): *The Hare*. 1502. Watercolor, $9\frac{5}{8}$ x $8\frac{5}{8}$ inches. (The Albertina, Vienna)

PLATE 3. GIOVANNI BATTISTA TIEPOLO (Venetian, 1696–1770): *Two Magicians and a Youth*. About 1735. Pen and wash drawing, $13\frac{5}{8}$ x $9\frac{15}{16}$ inches. (The Metropolitan Museum of Art, New York, Rogers Fund, 1937)

PLATE 4. HONORE DAUMIER (French, 1808–1879): *Clown*. About 1868. Charcoal and water-color, 14½ x 10¼ inches. (The Metropolitan Museum of Art, New York, Rogers Fund, 1937)

PLATE 5. GEORGES SEURAT (French, 1859–1891): *A Music Hall Artist*. About 1887. Pencil drawing, 12 x 9 inches. (Courtesy of the Fogg Art Museum, Harvard University, Cambridge, Mass., Bequest of Grenville L. Winthrop)

PLATE 6. ŁYONEL FEININGER (American, 1871–1956): *Mid-Manhattan*. 1952. Watercolor, charcoal, pen and ink on paper, 20¼ x 15⅝ inches. (The Metropolitan Museum of Art, New York, George A. Hearn Fund)

56

All the Years of Her Life

MORLEY CALLAGHAN

THEY WERE CLOSING the drugstore, and Alfred Higgins, who had just taken off his white jacket, was putting on his coat and getting ready to go home. The little gray-haired man, Sam Carr, who owned the drugstore, was bending down behind the cash register, and when Alfred Higgins passed him, he looked up and said softly, "Just a moment, Alfred. One moment before you go."

The soft, confident, quiet way in which Sam Carr spoke made Alfred start to button his coat nervously. He felt sure his face was white. Sam Carr usually said, "Good night," brusquely, without looking up. In the six months he had been working in the drugstore Alfred had never heard his employer speak softly like that. His heart began to beat so loud it was hard for him to get his breath. "What is it, Mr. Carr?" he asked.

"Maybe you'd be good enough to take a few things out of your pocket and leave them here before you go," Sam Carr said.

"What things? What are you talking about?"

"You've got a compact and a lipstick and at least two tubes of toothpaste in your pocket, Alfred."

"All the Years of Her Life" from *Now That April's Here* by Morley Callaghan, copyright, Canada, 1936 by The Macmillan Company of Canada Limited. Reprinted by permission of The Harold Matson Co., Inc.

"What do you mean? Do you think I'm crazy?" Alfred blustered. His face got red and he knew he looked fierce with indignation. But Sam Carr, standing by the door with his blue eyes shining bright behind his glasses and his lips moving underneath his gray mustache, only nodded his head a few times, and then Alfred grew very frightened and he didn't know what to say. Slowly he raised his hand and dipped it into his pocket, and with his eyes never meeting Sam Carr's eyes, he took out a blue compact and two tubes of toothpaste and a lipstick, and he laid them one by one on the counter.

"Petty thieving, eh, Alfred?" Sam Carr said. "And maybe you'd be good enough to tell me how long this has been going on."

"This is the first time I ever took anything."

"So now you think you'll tell me a lie, eh? What kind of a sap do I look like, huh? I don't know what goes on in my own store, eh? I tell you you've been doing this pretty steady," Sam Carr said as he went over and stood behind the cash register.

Ever since Alfred had left school he had been getting into trouble wherever he worked. He lived at home with his mother and his father, who was a printer. His two older brothers were married and his sister had got married last year, and it would have been all right for his parents now if Alfred had only been able to keep a job.

While Sam Carr smiled and stroked the side of his face very delicately with the tips of his fingers, Alfred began to feel that familiar terror growing in him that had been in him every time he had got into such trouble.

"I liked you," Sam Carr was saying. "I liked you and would have trusted you, and now look what I got to do." While Alfred watched with his alert, frightened blue eyes, Sam Carr drummed with his fingers on the counter. "I don't like to call a cop in point-blank," he was saying as he looked very worried. "You're a fool, and maybe I should call your father and tell him you're a fool. Maybe I should let them know I'm going to have you locked up."

"My father's not at home. He's a printer. He works nights," Alfred said.

"Who's at home?"

"My mother, I guess."

"Then we'll see what she says." Sam Carr went to the phone and dialed the number. Alfred was not so much ashamed, but there was that deep fright growing in him, and he blurted out arrogantly, like a strong, full-grown man, "Just a minute. You don't need to draw anybody else in. You don't need to tell her." He wanted to sound like a swaggering, big guy who could look after himself, yet the old, childish hope was in him, the longing that someone at home would come and help him. "Yeah, that's right, he's in trouble," Mr. Carr was saying. "Yeah, your boy works for me. You'd better come down in a hurry." And when he was finished Mr. Carr went over to the door and looked out at the street and watched the people passing in the late summer night. "I'll keep my eye out for a cop" was all he said.

Alfred knew how his mother would come rushing in; she would rush in with her eyes blazing, or maybe she would be crying, and she would push him away when he tried to talk to her and make him feel her dreadful contempt; yet he longed that she might come before Mr. Carr saw the cop on the beat passing the door.

While they waited—and it seemed a long time—they did not speak, and when at last they heard someone tapping on the closed door, Mr. Carr, turning the latch, said crisply, "Come in, Mrs. Higgins."

He looked hard-faced and stern.

Mrs. Higgins must have been going to bed when he telephoned, for her hair was tucked in loosely under her hat, and her hand at her throat held her light coat tightly across her chest so her dress would not show. She came in, large and plump, with a little smile on her friendly face. Most of the store lights had been turned out and at first she did not see Alfred, who was standing in the shadow at the end of the counter. Yet as soon as she saw him she did not look as Alfred thought she would look: she smiled, her blue eyes never wavered, and with a calmness and dignity that made them forget that her clothes seemed to have been thrown on her, she put out her hand to Mr. Carr and said politely, "I'm Mrs. Higgins. I'm Alfred's mother."

Mr. Carr was a bit embarrassed by her lack of terror and her simplicity, and he hardly knew what to say to her, so she asked, "Is Alfred in trouble?"

"He is. He's been taking things from the store. I caught him red-handed. Little things like compacts and toothpaste and lipsticks. Stuff he can sell easily," the proprietor said.

As she listened Mrs. Higgins looked at Alfred sometimes and nodded her head sadly, and when Sam Carr had finished

she said gravely, "Is it so, Alfred?"

"Yes."

"Why have you been doing it?"

"I been spending money, I guess."

"On what?"

"Going around with the guys, I guess," Alfred said.

Mrs. Higgins put out her hand and touched Sam Carr's arm with an understanding gentleness, and speaking as though afraid of disturbing him, she said, "If you would only listen to me before doing anything." Her simple earnestness made her shy; her humility made her falter and look away, but in a moment she was smiling gravely again, and she said with a kind of patient dignity, "What did you intend to do, Mr. Carr?"

"I was going to get a cop. That's what I ought to do."

"Yes, I suppose so. It's not for me to say, because he's my son. Yet I sometimes think a little good advice is the best thing for a boy when he's at a certain period in his life," she said.

Alfred couldn't understand his mother's quiet composure, for if they had been at home and someone had suggested that he was going to be arrested, he knew she would be in a rage and would cry out against him. Yet now she was standing there with that gentle, pleading smile on her face, saying, "I wonder if you don't think it would be better just to let him come home with me. He looks a big fellow, doesn't he? It takes some of them a long time to get any sense," and they both stared at Alfred, who shifted away with a bit of light shining for a moment on his thin face and the tiny pimples over his cheekbone.

But even while he was turning away uneasily Alfred was realizing that Mr. Carr had become aware that his mother was really a fine woman; he knew that Sam Carr was puzzled by his mother, as

if he had expected her to come in and plead with him tearfully, and instead he was being made to feel a bit ashamed by her vast tolerance. While there was only the sound of the mother's soft, assured voice in the store, Mr. Carr began to nod his head encouragingly at her. Without being alarmed, while being just large and still and simple and hopeful, she was becoming dominant there in the dimly lit store. "Of course, I don't want to be harsh," Mr. Carr was saying, "I'll tell you what I'll do. I'll just fire him and let it go at that. How's that?" and he got up and shook hands with Mrs. Higgins, bowing low to her in deep respect.

There was such warmth and gratitude in the way she said, "I'll never forget your kindness," that Mr. Carr began to feel warm and genial himself.

"Sorry we had to meet this way," he said. "But I'm glad I got in touch with you. Just wanted to do the right thing, that's all," he said.

"It's better to meet like this than never, isn't it?" she said. Suddenly they clasped hands as if they liked each other, as if they had known each other a long time. "Good night, sir," she said.

"Good night, Mrs. Higgins. I'm truly sorry," he said.

The mother and son walked along the street together, and the mother was taking a long, firm stride as she looked ahead with her stern face full of worry. Alfred was afraid to speak to her, he was afraid of the silence that was between them, so he only looked ahead too, for the excitement and relief was still pretty strong in him; but in a little while, going along like that in silence made him terribly aware of the strength and the sternness in her; he began to wonder what she was thinking of as she stared ahead so grimly; she seemed to have forgotten that he walked beside her; so when they were passing under the Sixth Avenue elevated [1] and the rumble of the train seemed to break the silence, he said in his old, blustering way, "Thank God it turned out like that. I certainly won't get in a jam like that again."

"Be quiet. Don't speak to me. You've disgraced me again and again," she said bitterly.

"That's the last time. That's all I'm saying."

"Have the decency to be quiet," she snapped. They kept on their way, looking straight ahead.

When they were at home and his mother took off her coat, Alfred saw that she was really only half-dressed, and she made him feel afraid again when she said, without even looking at him, "You're a bad lot. God forgive you. It's one thing after another and always has been. Why do you stand there stupidly? Go to bed, why don't you?" When he was going, she said, "I'm going to make myself a cup of tea. Mind, now, not a word about tonight to your father."

While Alfred was undressing in his bedroom, he heard his mother moving around the kitchen. She filled the kettle and put it on the stove. She moved a chair. And as he listened there was no shame in him, just wonder and a kind of admiration of her strength and repose. He could still see Sam Carr nodding his head encouragingly to her; he could hear her talking simply and earnestly, and as he sat on his bed he felt a pride in her strength. "She certainly was smooth," he thought. "Gee, I'd like to tell her she sounded swell."

And at last he got up and went along to the kitchen, and when he was at the door he saw his mother pouring herself a cup of tea. He watched and he didn't move. Her face, as she sat there, was a fright-

ened, broken face utterly unlike the face of the woman who had been so assured a little while ago in the drugstore. When she reached out and lifted the kettle to pour hot water in her cup, her hand trembled and the water splashed on the stove. Leaning back in the chair, she sighed and lifted the cup to her lips, and her lips were groping loosely as if they would never reach the cup. She swallowed the hot tea eagerly, and then she straightened up in relief, though her hand holding the cup still trembled. She looked very old.

It seemed to Alfred that this was the way it had been every time he had been in trouble before, that this trembling had really been in her as she hurried out half-dressed to the drugstore. He understood why she had sat alone in the kitchen the night his young sister had kept repeating doggedly that she was getting married. Now he felt all that his mother had been thinking of as they walked along the street together a little while ago. He watched his mother, and he never spoke, but at that moment his youth seemed to be over; he knew all the years of her life by the way her hand trembled as she raised the cup to her lips. It seemed to him that this was the first time he had ever looked upon his mother.

[1] **elevated:** a railway running above the street on elevated tracks.

FOR STUDY AND DISCUSSION

1. Who is the main character in this story? One way of answering this question is to ask yourself which character you can picture most clearly and which one aroused the greatest sympathy.

2. Point out incidents or statements in the story that underline the weaknesses in Alfred's character. What do you consider his chief weakness? How does it cause him to do what he does?

3. Put yourself in the place of Mrs. Higgins. Would you have defended Alfred in front of Mr. Carr, even though you knew he was guilty? Why or why not? Do you think that Mrs. Higgins was right in doing so or that she spoiled Alfred by coming to his defense? Should she have let him take his punishment?

4. One of the most effective ways of making characters real is to show them first as they appear to others, then as they are when they think they are alone. How does Morley Callaghan do this in "All the Years of Her Life"? In doing so, what does he show us about Mrs. Higgins?

5. At the end of the story, what does Alfred realize about his mother? about responsibility and growing up? Do you think this understanding will affect his future actions? If so, how? If not, why not?

LANGUAGE AND VOCABULARY

Callaghan's diction—his choice of words—is simple and informal, yet it succeeds in giving us a very good picture of the characters in his story. How do each of the following expressions help to give a specific picture or feeling of the character to whom it applies?

"with his eyes never meeting Sam Carr's eyes . . ." (Alfred)

"Alfred began to feel that familiar terror . . ." (Alfred)

"She came in, large and plump, with a little smile on her friendly face." (Mrs. Higgins)

"going along like that in silence made him terribly aware of the strength and the sternness in her . . ." (Alfred and Mrs. Higgins)

"her lips were groping loosely as if they would never reach the cup." (Mrs. Higgins)

FOR COMPOSITION

1. This story provides an excellent model of contrast in its presentation of Mrs. Higgins—as the confident woman who impresses Mr. Carr and as the disconsolate mother alone in the kitchen. Follow this model in developing one of the topics below. Devote one paragraph to what the character *seems* to be, and a second paragraph to his or her real feelings.

A shy girl (or boy) pretending to enjoy herself at a party, then confessing her self-consciousness later when alone

A parent pretending to be severe while scolding a child, but actually full of sympathy and tenderness

A high school speaker pretending to be confident, but actually quaking within

A football quarterback confidently predicting victory, but inwardly fearing defeat

2. In this story Alfred comes to realize his mother's inner self by seeing her first as she appears to others, and then as she is when she thinks she is alone. In a similar manner, write a brief narrative showing how you realized the inner character of some friend or member of your family

ABOUT THE AUTHOR

Morley Callaghan (1903–) was born in Toronto and studied at the University of Toronto, where he also boxed and played football. He began writing as a reporter on the *Toronto Star,* where he met Ernest Hemingway. Hemingway recognized Callaghan's talent and encouraged him to write short stories for experimental magazines such as *This Quarter, Transition,* and *The Exile.* Soon his work was appearing in prize short-story collections and in book form. Most of Callaghan's novels concern characters who have failed in life or who are the victims of unfortunate circumstances. His first two books of stories were *A Native Argosy* and *Now That April's Here.* He has also written several novels.

Luck

MARK TWAIN

IT WAS at a banquet in London in honor of one of the two or three conspicuously illustrious English military names of this generation. For reasons which will presently appear, I will withhold his real name and titles and call him Lieutenant-General Lord Arthur Scoresby, Y.C., K.C.B.,[1] etc., etc., etc. What a fascination there is in a renowned name! There sat the man, in actual flesh, whom I had heard of so many thousands of times since that day, thirty years before, when his name shot suddenly to the zenith from a Crimean battlefield, to remain forever celebrated. It was food and drink to me to look, and look, and look at that demigod; scanning, searching, noting: the quietness, the reserve, the noble gravity of his countenance; the simple honesty that expressed itself all over him; the sweet unconsciousness of his greatness—unconsciousness of the hundreds of admiring eyes fastened upon him, unconsciousness of the deep, loving, sincere worship welling out of the breasts of those people and flowing toward him.

The clergyman at my left was an old

[1] Y.C., K.C.B.: honorary titles.

"Luck" from *The Complete Short Stories of Mark Twain*, edited by Charles Neider. Reprinted by permission of Harper & Row, Publishers.

acquaintance of mine—clergyman now, but had spent the first half of his life in the camp and field and as an instructor in the military school at Woolwich. Just at the moment I have been talking about a veiled and singular light glimmered in his eyes and he leaned down and muttered confidentially to me—indicating the hero of the banquet with a gesture:

"Privately—he's an absolute fool."

This verdict was a great surprise to me. If its subject had been Napoleon, or Socrates, or Solomon, my astonishment could not have been greater. Two things I was well aware of: that the Reverend was a man of strict veracity and that his judgment of men was good. Therefore I knew, beyond doubt or question, that the world was mistaken about this hero: he *was* a fool. So I meant to find out, at a convenient moment, how the Reverend, all solitary and alone, had discovered the secret.

Some days later the opportunity came, and this is what the Reverend told me:

"About forty years ago I was an instructor in the military academy at Woolwich. I was present in one of the sections when young Scoresby underwent his preliminary examination. I was touched to the quick with pity, for the rest of the class answered up brightly and handsomely, while he—why, dear me, he didn't know *anything,* so to speak. He was evidently good, and sweet, and lovable, and guileless; and so it was exceedingly painful to see him stand there, as serene as a graven image, and deliver himself of answers which were veritably miraculous for stupidity and ignorance. All the compassion in me was aroused in his behalf. I said to myself, when he comes to be examined again he will be flung over, of course; so it will be simply a harmless act of charity to ease his fall as much as I can. I took him aside and found that he knew a little of Cæsar's history; and as he didn't know anything else, I went to work and drilled him like a galley-slave on a certain line of stock questions concerning Cæsar which I knew would be used. If you'll believe me, he went through with flying colors on examination day! He went through on that purely superficial "cram," and got compliments too, while others, who knew a thousand times more than he, got plucked. By some strangely lucky accident—an accident not likely to happen twice in a century—he was asked no question outside of the narrow limits of his drill.

It was stupefying. Well, all through his course I stood by him, with something of the sentiment which a mother feels for a crippled child; and he always saved himself—just by miracle, apparently.

Now, of course, the thing that would expose him and kill him at last was mathematics. I resolved to make his death as easy as I could; so I drilled him and crammed him, and crammed him and drilled him, just on the line of questions which the examiners would be most likely to use, and then launched him on his fate. Well, sir, try to conceive of the result: to my consternation, he took the first prize! And with it he got a perfect ovation in the way of compliments.

Sleep? There was no more sleep for me for a week. My conscience tortured me day and night. What I had done I had done purely through charity, and only to ease the poor youth's fall. I never had dreamed of any such preposterous results as the thing that had happened. I felt as guilty and miserable as Frankenstein. Here was

a wooden-head whom I had put in the way of glittering promotions and prodigious responsibilities, and but one thing could happen: he and his responsibilities would all go to ruin together at the first opportunity.

The Crimean War had just broken out. Of course there had to be a war, I said to myself. We couldn't have peace and give this donkey a chance to die before he is found out. I waited for the earthquake. It came. And it made me reel when it did come. He was actually gazetted to a captaincy in a marching regiment! Better men grow old and gray in the service before they climb to a sublimity like that. And who could ever have foreseen that they would go and put such a load of responsibility on such green and inadequate shoulders? I could just barely have stood it if they had made him a cornet; [1] but a captain—think of it! I thought my hair would turn white.

Consider what I did—I who so loved repose and inaction. I said to myself, I am responsible to the country for this, and I must go along with him and protect the country against him as far as I can. So I took my poor little capital that I had saved up through years of work and grinding economy, and went with a sigh and bought a cornetcy in his regiment, and away we went to the field.

And there—oh, dear, it was awful. Blunder?—why, he never did anything *but* blunder. But, you see, nobody was in the fellow's secret. Everybody had him focused wrong, and necessarily misinterpreted his performance every time. Consequently they took his idiotic blunders for inspirations of genius. They did, honestly! His mildest blunders were enough to make a man in his right mind cry; and they did make me cry—and rage

[1] **cornet:** the lowest-ranking commissioned officer of cavalry.

and rave, too, privately. And the thing that kept me always in a sweat of apprehension was the fact that every fresh blunder he made increased the luster of his reputation! I kept saying to myself, he'll get so high that when discovery does finally come it will be like the sun falling out of the sky.

He went right along up, from grade to grade, over the dead bodies of his superiors, until at last, in the hottest moment of the battle of —— down went our colonel, and my heart jumped into my mouth, for Scoresby was next in rank! Now for it, said I; we'll all land in Sheol [1] in ten minutes, sure.

The battle was awfully hot; the allies were steadily giving way all over the field. Our regiment occupied a position that was vital; a blunder now must be destruction. At this crucial moment, what does this immortal fool do but detach the regiment from its place and order a charge over a neighboring hill where there wasn't a suggestion of an enemy! "There you go!" I said to myself; "this *is* the end at last."

And away we did go, and were over the shoulder of the hill before the insane movement could be discovered and stopped. And what did we find? An entire and unsuspected Russian army in reserve! And what happened? We were eaten up? That is necessarily what would have happened in ninety-nine cases out of a hundred. But no; those Russians argued that no single regiment would come browsing around there at such a time. It must be the entire English army, and that the sly Russian game was detected and blocked; so they turned tail, and away they went, pell-mell, over the hill and down into the field, in wild confusion, and we after them; they themselves broke the solid Russian center in the field, and tore through, and in no time there was the

[1] **Sheol** (shē′ōl): Hell (in Hebrew).

most tremendous rout you ever saw, and the defeat of the allies was turned into a sweeping and splendid victory! Marshal Canrobert looked on, dizzy with astonishment, admiration, and delight; and sent right off for Scoresby, and hugged him, and decorated him on the field in presence of all the armies!

And what was Scoresby's blunder that time? Merely the mistaking his right hand for his left—that was all. An order had come to him to fall back and support our right; and, instead, he fell *forward* and went over the hill to the left. But the name he won that day as a marvelous military genius filled the world with his glory, and that glory will never fade while history books last.

He is just as good and sweet and lovable and unpretending as a man can be, but he doesn't know enough to come in when it rains. Now that is absolutely true. He is the supremest ass in the universe; and until half an hour ago nobody knew it but himself and me. He has been pursued, day by day and year by year, by a most phenomenal and astonishing luckiness. He has been a shining soldier in all our wars for a generation; he has littered his whole military life with blunders, and yet has never committed one that didn't make him a knight or a baronet or a lord or something. Look at his breast; why, he is just clothed in domestic and foreign decorations. Well, sir, every one of them is the record of some shouting stupidity or other; and, taken together, they are proof that the very best thing in all this world that can befall a man is to be born lucky. I say again, as I said at the banquet, Scoresby's an absolute fool."

FOR STUDY AND DISCUSSION

1. What does the word *luck* mean in this story? Do you believe in the existence of such luck? If you do, how large a part do you think

it plays in human affairs? Would a person be better off with brains and no luck or with luck and no brains? Defend your answer.

2. In your opinion, how does luck differ from fortune, fate, or providence? Could any of these words apply to Lord Scoresby's success? Why or why not?

3. Mark Twain is famous for his tall tales. Some of his "tallest" exaggerations, however, tend to call attention away from their underlying truth. Where does Twain exaggerate in this story? What factor or factors in this story do you think he meant to be taken seriously?

4. What is ironic about the events in this story? Is Twain's irony directed chiefly against Lord Scoresby, the educational system, or the world in general?

5. In a sense, the clergyman's story is offered as a proof of the idea that Lord Scoresby is "an absolute fool." Does the clergyman's story actually prove this? Why or why not?

THEME

The theme of a story is the central idea that underlies all its elements. In a good story, the theme is supported by the author's point of view, the plot, characters, setting, and even the language. What is the central idea of "Luck"? How is this theme reflected in the outcome of the plot? in the nature of the characters? in the author's attitude? Does the author succeed in convincing you that his central idea is true? Why or why not?

LANGUAGE AND VOCABULARY

Adverbs play an important part in indicating exact shades of thought and feeling. They are particularly important in this story because of the exaggerated nature of the incidents. How does each of the adverbs italicized below help to make the idea or the character clearer or more real?

"one of the two or three *conspicuously* illustrious English military names of this generation."

"*privately*—he's an absolute fool."

"By some *strangely* lucky accident . . ."

"Everybody . . . *necessarily* misinterpreted his performance every time."

FOR COMPOSITION

1. The clergyman's tale in "Luck" resembles the parson's tale in "The Silver Mine" in that it is a story within a story and also in that it is designed to prove a point. Using these stories as examples, write a first-person story that proves a point. If you like, write on one of the following:

John wants good grades more than anything in the world

Basketball is a rough game

It's not so hard to be a hero

2. Write a paragraph explaining why you think one of the following statements is true. Use incidents or details from the story.

Eliza Birdwell, in "The Pacing Goose," is an ideal wife

Mrs. Higgins, in "All the Years of Her Life," deserves our pity

ABOUT THE AUTHOR

Mark Twain (1835–1910), whose real name was Samuel Langhorne Clemens, was born and raised in Missouri towns along the Mississippi River. At the age of twelve he went to work as a printer. His later experiences as a steamboat pilot on the Mississippi, as a prospector and reporter in Nevada, and as a world traveler and lecturer provided him with plenty to write about. When he began to write, he took the pen name of Mark Twain—a cry he had often heard during his years on the river. ("Mark Twain" is the call for two fathoms, the minimum safe depth of water for a riverboat.) *Roughing It,* the story (with exaggerations) of his frontier adventures in Nevada, *Life on the Mississippi,* the story of his first years on the river, and *Innocents Abroad,* the rollicking tale of a shipload of tourists on a European tour, all came out of Twain's own experience. His masterpieces—*The Adventures of Tom Sawyer* and *The Adventures of Huckleberry Finn*—were based on his boyhood. Two of his best works not based on his own experience are *The Prince and the Pauper* and *A Connecticut Yankee in King Arthur's Court.* Mark Twain is known as a humorous writer, but he also wrote stories that bitterly ridiculed the foolishness of people.

The Split Cherry Tree

JESSE STUART

I DON'T MIND staying after school," I says to Professor Herbert, "but I'd rather you'd whip me with a switch and let me go home early. Pa will whip me anyway for getting home two hours late."

"You are too big to whip," says Professor Herbert, "and I have to punish you for climbing up in that cherry tree. You boys knew better than that! The other five boys have paid their dollar each. You have been the only one who has not helped pay for the tree. Can't you borrow a dollar?"

"I can't," I says. "I'll have to take the punishment. I wish it would be quicker punishment. I wouldn't mind."

Professor Herbert stood and looked at me. He was a big man. He wore a gray suit of clothes. The suit matched his gray hair.

"You don't know my father," I says to Professor Herbert. "He might be called a little old-fashioned. He makes us mind him until we're twenty-one years old. He believes: 'If you spare the rod you spoil the child.' I'll never be able to make him understand about the cherry tree. I'm the first of my people to go to high school."

"You must take the punishment," says

"The Split Cherry Tree" by Jesse Stuart from *Esquire Magazine,* © 1938 by Esquire, Inc. Reprinted by permission of *Esquire Magazine.*

Professor Herbert. "You must stay two hours after school today and two hours after school tomorrow. I am allowing you twenty-five cents an hour. That is good money for a high-school student. You can sweep the schoolhouse floor, wash the blackboards, and clean windows. I'll pay the dollar for you."

I couldn't ask Professor Herbert to loan me a dollar. He never offered to loan it to me. I had to stay and help the janitor and work out my fine at a quarter an hour.

I thought as I swept the floor, "What will Pa do to me? What lie can I tell him when I go home? Why did we ever climb that cherry tree and break it down for anyway? Why did we run crazy over the hills away from the crowd? Why did we do all of this? Six of us climbed up in a little cherry tree after one little lizard! Why did the tree split and fall with us? It should have been a stronger tree! Why did Eif Crabtree just happen to be below us plowing and catch us in his cherry tree? Why wasn't he a better man than to charge us six dollars for the tree?"

It was six o'clock when I left the schoolhouse. I had six miles to walk home. It would be after seven when I got home. I had all my work to do when I got home. It took Pa and me both to do the work. Seven cows to milk. Nineteen head of cattle to feed, four mules, twenty-five hogs, firewood and stovewood to cut, and water to draw from the well. He would be doing it when I got home. He would be mad and wondering what was keeping me!

I hurried home. I would run under the dark, leafless trees. I would walk fast uphill. I would run down the hill. The ground was freezing. I had to hurry. I had to run. I reached the long ridge that led to our cow pasture. I ran along this ridge. The wind dried the sweat on my face. I ran across the pasture to the house.

I threw down my books in the chip-yard. I ran to the barn to spread fodder on the ground for the cattle. I didn't take time to change my clean school clothes for my old work clothes. I ran out to the barn. I saw Pa spreading fodder on the ground for the cattle. That was my job. I ran up to the fence. I says, "Leave that for me, Pa. I'll do it. I'm just a little late."

"I see you are," says Pa. He turned and looked at me. His eyes danced fire. "What in th' world has kept you so? Why ain't you been here to help me with this work? Make a gentleman out'n one boy in th' family and this is what you get! Send you to high school and you get too onery fer th' buzzards to smell!"

I never said anything. I didn't want to tell why I was late from school. Pa stopped scattering the bundles of fodder. He looked at me. He says, "Why are you gettin' in here this time o' night? You tell me or I'll take a hickory withe to you right here on th' spot!"

I says, "I had to stay after school." I couldn't lie to Pa. He'd go to school and find out why I had to stay. If I lied to him it would be too bad for me.

"Why did you haf to stay atter school?" says Pa.

I says, "Our biology class went on a field trip today. Six of us boys broke down a cherry tree. We had to give a dollar apiece to pay for the tree. I didn't have the dollar. Professor Herbert is making me work out my dollar. He gives me twenty-five cents an hour. I had to stay in this afternoon. I'll have to stay in to-morrow afternoon!"

"Are you telling me th' truth?" says Pa.

"I'm telling you the truth," I says. "Go and see for yourself."

"That's jist what I'll do in th' mornin'," says Pa. "Jist whose cherry tree did you break down?"

"Eif Crabtree's cherry tree!"

"What was you doin' clear out in Eif Crabtree's place?" says Pa. "He lives four miles from th' county high school. Don't they teach you no books at that high school? Do they jist let you get out and gad over th' hillsides? If that's all they do I'll keep you at home, Dave. I've got work here fer you to do!"

"Pa," I says, "spring is just getting here. We take a subject in school where we have to have bugs, snakes, flowers, lizards, frogs, and plants. It is biology. It was a pretty day today. We went out to find a few of these. Six of us boys saw a lizard at the same time sunning on a cherry tree. We all went up the tree to get it. We broke the tree down. It split at the forks. Eif Crabtree was plowing down below us. He ran up the hill and got our names. The other boys gave their dollar apiece. I didn't have mine. Professor Herbert put mine in for me. I have to work it out at school."

"Poor man's son, huh," says Pa. "I'll attend to that myself in th' mornin'. I'll take keer o' 'im. He ain't from this county nohow. I'll go down there in th' mornin' and see 'im. Lettin' you leave your books and galavant all over th' hills. What kind of a school is it nohow! Didn't do that, my son, when I's a little shaver in school. All fared alike too."

"Pa, please don't go down there," I says, "just let me have fifty cents and pay the rest of my fine! I don't want you to go down there! I don't want you to start anything with Professor Herbert!"

"Ashamed of your old Pap are you, Dave," says Pa, "atter th' way I've worked to raise you! Tryin' to send you to school so you can make a better livin' than I've made.

"I'll straighten this thing out myself! I'll take keer o' Professor Herbert myself! He ain't got no right to keep you in and let the other boys off jist because they've got th' money! I'm a poor man. A bullet will go in a professor same as it will any man.

It will go in a rich man same as it will a poor man. Now you get into this work before I take one o' these withes and cut the shirt off'n your back!"

I thought once I'd run through the woods above the barn just as hard as I could go. I thought I'd leave high school and home forever! Pa could not catch me! I'd get away! I couldn't go back to school with him. He'd have a gun and maybe he'd shoot Professor Herbert. It was hard to tell what he would do. I could tell Pa that school had changed in the hills from the way it was when he was a boy, but he wouldn't understand. I could tell him we studied frogs, birds, snakes, lizards, flowers, insects. But Pa wouldn't understand. If I did run away from home it wouldn't matter to Pa. He would see Professor Herbert anyway. He would think that high school and Professor Herbert had run me away from home. There was no need to run away. I'd just have to stay, finish foddering the cattle, and go to school with Pa the next morning.

I would take a bundle of fodder, remove the hickory-withe band from around it, and scatter it on rocks, clumps of green briers, and brush, so the cattle wouldn't tramp it under their feet. I would lean it up against the oak trees and the rocks in the pasture just above our pigpen on the hill. The fodder was cold and frosty where it had set out in the stacks. I would carry bundles of the fodder from the stack until I had spread out a bundle for each steer. Pa went to the barn to feed the mules and throw corn in the pen to the hogs.

The moon shone bright in the cold March sky. I finished my work by moonlight. Professor Herbert really didn't know how much work I had to do at home. If he had known he would not have kept me after school. He would have loaned me a dollar to have paid my part on the cherry tree. He had never lived in the hills. He didn't know the way the hill boys had to work so that they could go to school. Now he was teaching in a county high school where all the boys who attended were from hill farms.

After I'd finished doing my work I went to the house and ate my supper. Pa and Mom had eaten. My supper was getting cold. I heard Pa and Mom talking in the front room. Pa was telling Mom about me staying in after school.

"I had to do all th' milkin' tonight, chop th' wood myself. It's too hard on me atter I've turned ground all day. I'm goin' to take a day off tomorrow and see if I can't remedy things a little. I'll go down to that high school tomorrow. I won't be a very good scholar fer Professor Herbert nohow. He won't keep me in atter school. I'll take a different kind of lesson down there and make 'im acquainted with it."

"Now, Luster," says Mom, "you jist stay away from there. Don't cause a lot o' trouble. You can be jailed fer a trick like that. You'll get th' Law atter you. You'll jist go down there and show off and plague your own boy Dave to death in front o' all th' scholars!"

"Plague or no plague," says Pa, "he don't take into consideration what all I haf to do here, does he? I'll show 'im it ain't right to keep one boy in and let the rest go scot free. My boy is good as th' rest, ain't he? A bullet will make a hole in a schoolteacher same as it will anybody else. He can't do me that way and get by with it. I'll plug 'im first. I aim to go down there bright and early in the mornin' and get all this straight! I aim to see about bug larnin' and this runnin' all over God's creation huntin' snakes, lizards, and frogs. Ransackin' th' country and goin' through cherry orchards and breakin' th' trees down atter lizards! Old Eif Crabtree ought to a-poured th' hot lead to 'em instead o' chargin' six dollars fer th' tree! He ought to a-got old Herbert th' first one!"

I ate my supper. I slipped upstairs and lit the lamp. I tried to forget the whole thing. I studied plane geometry. Then I studied my biology lesson. I could hardly study for thinking about Pa. "He'll go to school with me in the morning. He'll take a gun for Professor Herbert! What will Professor Herbert think of me! I'll tell him when Pa leaves that I couldn't help it. But Pa might shoot him. I hate to go with Pa. Maybe he'll cool off about it tonight and not go in the morning."

Pa got up at four o'clock. He built a fire in the stove. Then he built a fire in the fireplace. He got Mom up to get breakfast. Then he got me up to help feed and milk. By the time we had our work done at the barn, Mom had breakfast ready for us. We ate our breakfast. Daylight came and we could see the bare oak trees covered white with frost. The hills were white with frost. A cold wind was blowing. The sky was clear. The sun would soon come out and melt the frost. The afternoon would be warm with sunshine and the frozen ground with thaw. There would be mud on the hills again. Muddy water would then run down the little ditches on the hills.

"Now, Dave," says Pa, "let's get ready fer school. I aim to go with you this mornin' and look into bug larnin', frog larnin', lizard and snake larnin', and breakin' down cherry trees! I don't like no sicha foolish way o' larnin' myself!"

Pa hadn't forgot. I'd have to take him to school with me. He would take me to school with him. We were going early. I was glad we were going early. If Pa pulled a gun on Professor Herbert there wouldn't be so many of my classmates there to see him.

I knew that Pa wouldn't be at home in the high school. He wore overalls, big boots, a blue shirt and a sheepskin coat and a slouched black hat gone to seed at the top. He put his gun in its holster. We started trudging toward the high school across the hill.

It was early when we got to the county high school. Professor Herbert had just got there. I just thought as we walked up the steps into the schoolhouse, "Maybe Pa will find out Professor Herbert is a good man. He just doesn't know him. Just like I felt toward the Lambert boys across the hill. I didn't like them until I'd seen them and talked to them. After I went to school with them and talked to them, I liked them and we were friends. It's a lot in knowing the other fellow."

"You're th' Professor here, ain't you?" says Pa.

"Yes," says Professor Herbert, "and you are Dave's father."

"Yes," says Pa, pulling out his gun and laying it on the seat in Professor Herbert's office. Professor Herbert's eyes got big behind his black-rimmed glasses when he saw Pa's gun. Color came into his pale cheeks.

"Jist a few things about this school I want to know," says Pa. "I'm tryin' to make a scholar out'n Dave. He's the only one out'n eleven youngins I've sent to high school. Here he comes in late and leaves me all th' work to do! He said you's all out bug huntin' yesterday and broke a cherry tree down. He had to stay two hours atter school yesterday and work out money to pay on that cherry tree! Is that right?"

"Wwwwy," says Professor Herbert, "I guess it is."

He looked at Pa's gun.

"Well," says Pa, "this ain't no high school. It's a bug school, a lizard school, a snake school! It ain't no school nohow!"

"Why did you bring that gun?" says Professor Herbert to Pa.

"You see that little hole," says Pa as he picked up the long blue forty-four and put his finger on the end of the barrel, "a bullet can come out'n that hole that will kill a schoolteacher same as it will any other man. It will kill a rich man same as a poor man. It will kill a man. But atter I come in and saw you, I know'd I wouldn't need it. This maul o' mine could do you up in a few minutes."

Pa stood there, big, hard, brown-skinned, and mighty beside of Professor Herbert. I didn't know Pa was so much bigger and harder. I'd never seen Pa in a schoolhouse before. I'd seen Professor Herbert. He'd aways looked big before to me. He didn't look big standing beside of Pa.

"I was only doing my duty, Mr. Sexton," says Professor Herbert, "and following the course of study the state provided us with."

"Course o' study," says Pa, "what study, bug study? Varmint study? Takin' youngins to th' woods and their poor old Ma's and Pa's at home a-slavin' to keep 'em in school and give 'em a education! You know that's dangerous, too, puttin' a lot o' boys and girls out together like that!"

Students were coming into the schoolhouse now.

Professor Herbert says, "Close the door, Dave, so others won't hear."

I walked over and closed the door. I was shaking like a leaf in the wind. I thought Pa was going to hit Professor Herbert every minute. He was doing all the talking. His face was getting red. The red color was coming through the brown, weather-beaten skin on Pa's face.

"I was right with these students," says Professor Herbert. "I know what they got into and what they didn't. I didn't send one of the other teachers with them on

this field trip. I went myself. Yes, I took the boys and girls together. Why not?"

"It jist don't look good to me," says Pa, "a-takin' all this swarm of youngins out to pillage th' whole deestrict. Breakin' down cherry trees. Keepin' boys in atter school."

"What else could I have done with Dave, Mr. Sexton?" says Professor Herbert. "The boys didn't have any business all climbing that cherry tree after one lizard. One boy could have gone up in the tree and got it. The farmer charged us six dollars. It was a little steep, I think, but we had it to pay. Must I make five boys pay and let your boy off? He said he didn't have the dollar and couldn't get it. So I put it in for him. I'm letting him work it out. He's not working for me. He's working for the school!"

"I jist don't know what you could a-done with 'im," says Pa, "only a-larruped 'im with a withe! That's what he needed!"

"He's too big to whip," says Professor Herbert, pointing at me. "He's a man in size."

"He's not too big fer me to whip," says Pa. "They ain't too big until they're over twenty-one! It jist didn't look fair to me! Work one and let th' rest out because they got th' money. I don't see what bugs has got to do with a high school! It don't look good to me nohow!"

Pa picked up his gun and put it back in its holster. The red color left Professor Herbert's face. He talked more to Pa. Pa softened a little. It looked funny to see Pa in the high-school building. It was the first time he'd ever been there.

"We were not only hunting snakes, toads, flowers, butterflies, lizards," says Professor Herbert, "but, Mr. Sexton, I was hunting dry timothy grass to put in an incubator and raise some protozoa."

"I don't know what that is," says Pa.

"Th' incubator is th' new-fangled way o' cheatin' th' hens and raisin' chickens. I ain't so sure about th' breed o' chickens you mentioned."

"You've heard of germs, Mr. Sexton, haven't you?" says Professor Herbert.

"Jist call me Luster, if you don't mind," says Pa, very casual-like.

"All right, Luster, you've heard of germs, haven't you?"

"Yes," says Pa, "but I don't believe in germs. I'm sixty-five years old and I ain't seen one yet!"

"You can't see them with your naked eye," says Professor Herbert. "Just keep that gun in the holster and stay with me in the high school today. I have a few things I want to show you. That scum on your teeth has germs in it."

"What," says Pa, "you mean to tell me I've got germs on my teeth!"

"Yes," says Professor Herbert. "The same kind as we might be able to find in a living black snake if we dissect it!"

"I don't mean to dispute your word," says Pa, "but I don't believe it. I don't believe I have germs on my teeth!"

"Stay with me today and I'll show you. I want to take you through the school anyway! School has changed a lot in the hills since you went to school. I don't guess we had high schools in this county when you went to school!"

"No," says Pa, "jist readin', writin', and cipherin'. We didn't have all this bug larnin', frog larnin', and findin' germs on your teeth and in the middle o' black snakes! Th' world's changin'."

"It is," says Professor Herbert, "and we hope all for the better. Boys like your own there are going to help change it. He's your boy. He knows all of what I've told you. You stay with me today."

"I'll shore stay with you," says Pa. "I want to see th' germs off'n my teeth. I jist want to see a germ. I've never seen one

in my life. 'Seein' is believin',' Pap allus told me."

Pa walks out of the office with Professor Herbert. I just hoped Professor Herbert didn't have Pa arrested for pulling his gun. Pa's gun has always been a friend to him when he goes to settle disputes.

The bell rang. School took up. I saw the students when they marched in the schoolhouse look at Pa. They would grin and punch each other. Pa just stood and watched them pass in at the schoolhouse door. Two long lines marched in the house. The boys and girls were clean and well dressed. Pa stood over in the schoolyard under a leafless elm, in his sheepskin coat, his big boots laced in front with buckskin, and his heavy socks stuck above his boot tops. Pa's overalls legs were baggy and wrinkled between his coat and boot tops. His blue work shirt showed at the collar. His big black hat showed his gray-streaked black hair. His face was hard and weather-tanned to the color of a ripe fodder blade. His hands were big and gnarled like the roots of the elm tree he stood beside.

When I went to my first class I saw Pa and Professor Herbert going around over the schoolhouse. I was in my geometry class when Pa and Professor Herbert came in the room. We were explaining our propositions on the blackboard. Professor Herbert and Pa just quietly came in and sat down for awhile. I heard Fred Wurts whisper to Glenn Armstrong, "Who is that old man? Lord, he's a rough-looking scamp." Glenn whispered back, "I think he's Dave's Pap." The students in geometry looked at Pa. They must have wondered what he was doing in school. Before the class was over, Pa and Professor Herbert got up and went out. I saw them together down on the playground. Professor Herbert was explaining to Pa. I could see the prints of Pa's gun under his coat when he'd walk around.

At noon in the high school cafeteria Pa and Professor Herbert sat together at the little table where Professor Herbert always ate by himself. They ate together. The students watched the way Pa ate. He ate with his knife instead of his fork. A lot of the students felt sorry for me after they found out he was my father. They didn't have to feel sorry for me. I wasn't ashamed of Pa after I found out he wasn't going to shoot Professor Herbert. I was glad they had made friends. I wasn't ashamed of Pa. I wouldn't be as long as he behaved. He would find out about the high school as I had found out about the Lambert boys across the hill.

In the afternoon when we went to biology Pa was in the class. He was sitting on one of the high stools beside the microscope. We went ahead with our work just as if Pa wasn't in the class. I saw Pa take his knife and scrape tartar from one of his teeth. Professor Herbert put it on the lens and adjusted the microscope for Pa. He adjusted it and worked awhile. Then he says: "Now Luster, look! Put your eye right down to the light. Squint the other eye!"

Pa put his head down and did as Professor Herbert said. "I see 'im," says Pa. "Who'd a ever thought that? Right on a body's teeth! Right in a body's mouth. You're right certain they ain't no fake to this, Professor Herbert?"

"No, Luster," says Professor Herbert. "It's there. That's the germ. Germs live in a world we cannot see with the naked eye. We must use the microscope. There are millions of them in our bodies. Some are harmful. Others are helpful."

Pa holds his face down and looks through the microscope. We stop and watch Pa. He sits upon the tall stool. His knees are against the table. His legs are long. His coat slips up behind when he

bends over. The handle of his gun shows. Professor Herbert pulls his coat down quickly.

"Oh, yes," says Pa. He gets up and pulls his coat down. Pa's face gets a little red. He knows about his gun and he knows he doesn't have any use for it in high school.

"We have a big black snake over here we caught yesterday," says Professor Herbert. "We'll chloroform him and dissect him and show you he has germs in his body, too."

"Don't do it," says Pa. "I believe you. I jist don't want to see you kill the black snake. I never kill one. They are good mousers and a lot o' help to us on the farm. I like black snakes. I jist hate to see people kill 'em. I don't allow 'em killed on my place."

The students look at Pa. They seem to like him better after he said that. Pa with a gun in his pocket but a tender heart beneath his ribs for snakes, but not for man! Pa won't whip a mule at home. He won't whip his cattle.

"Man can defend hisself," says Pa, "but cattle and mules can't. We have the drop on 'em. Ain't nothin' to a man that'll beat a good pullin' mule. He ain't got th' right kind o' a heart!"

Professor Herbert took Pa through the laboratory. He showed him the different kinds of work we were doing. He showed him our equipment. They stood and talked while we worked. Then they walked out together. They talked louder when they got out in the hall.

When our biology class was over I walked out of the room. It was our last class for the day. I would have to take my broom and sweep two hours to finish paying for the split cherry tree. I just wondered if Pa would want me to stay. He was standing in the hallway watching the students march out. He looked lost among us. He looked like a leaf turned

brown on the tree among the treetop filled with growing leaves.

I got my broom and started to sweep. Professor Herbert walked up and says, "I'm going to let you do that some other time. You can go home with your father. He is waiting out there."

I laid my broom down, got my books, and went down the steps.

Pa says, "Ain't you got two hours o' sweepin' yet to do?"

I says, "Professor Herbert said I could do it some other time. He said for me to go home with you."

"No," says Pa. "You are goin' to do as he says. He's a good man. School has changed from my day and time. I'm a dead leaf, Dave. I'm behind. I don't belong here. If he'll let me I'll get a broom and we'll both sweep one hour. That pays your debt. I'll hep you pay it. I'll ast 'im and see if he won't let me hep you."

"I'm going to cancel the debt," says Professor Herbert. "I just wanted you to understand, Luster."

"I understand," says Pa, "and since I understand, he must pay his debt fer th' tree and I'm goin' to hep 'im."

"Don't do that," says Professor Herbert. "It's all on me."

"We don't do things like that," says Pa, "we're just and honest people. We don't want somethin' fer nothin'. Professor Herbert, you're wrong now and I'm right. You'll haf to listen to me. I've larned a lot from you. My boy must go on. Th' world has left me. It changed while I've raised my family and plowed th' hills. I'm a just and honest man. I don't skip debts. I ain't larned 'em to do that. I ain't got much larnin' myself but I do know right from wrong atter I see through a thing."

Professor Herbert went home. Pa and I stayed and swept one hour. It looked funny to see Pa use a broom. He never used one at home. Mom used the broom. Pa used the plow. Pa did hard work. Pa says, "I can't sweep. Durned if I can. Look at th' streaks o' dirt I leave on th' floor! Seems like no work a-tall fer me. Brooms is too light 'r somethin'. I'll jist do th' best I can, Dave. I've been wrong about th' school."

I says, "Did you know Professor Herbert can get a warrant out for you for bringing your pistol to school and showing it in his office! They can railroad you for that!"

"That's all made right," says Pa. "I've made that right. Professor Herbert ain't goin' to take it to court. He likes me. I like 'im. We jist had to get together. He had the remedies. He showed me. You must go on to school. I am as strong a man as ever come out'n th' hills fer my years and th' hard work I've done. But I'm behind, Dave. I'm a little man. Your hands will be softer than mine. Your clothes will be better. You'll allus look cleaner than your old Pap. Jist remember, Dave, to pay your debts and be honest. Jist be kind to animals and don't bother th'

snakes. That's all I got agin th' school. Puttin' black snakes to sleep and cuttin' 'em open."

It was late when we got home. Stars were in the sky. The moon was up. The ground was frozen. Pa took his time going home. I couldn't run like I did the night before. It was ten o'clock before we got the work finished, our suppers eaten. Pa sat before the fire and told Mom he was going to take her and show her a germ sometime. Mom hadn't seen one either. Pa told her about the high school and the fine man Professor Herbert was. He told Mom about the strange school across the hill and how different it was from the school in their day and time.

FOR STUDY AND DISCUSSION

1. There are a great many conflicts in this story. The students get in trouble with Farmer Crabtree, then with Professor Herbert. Dave is involved in difficulties with his father, and Pa confronts Professor Herbert. But there is a larger conflict, a conflict between two ways of life, that actually includes all of these. Where in the story is that conflict stated? How is it finally resolved?

2. Besides being a well-constructed story, "The Split Cherry Tree" is a study of human relations. What is Pa's attitude toward his children, particularly toward Dave? toward the high school with its new learning? What is Dave's attitude toward Pa? toward school? toward his fellow students? How does Professor Herbert show that he understands his pupils? that he understands Pa?

3. What are the advantages of telling this story from Dave's point of view? What is he able to tell us that Professor Herbert, or Pa, or an outsider could not? In telling a story, what are the advantages of a personal, first-person point of view? Are there any disadvantages? Discuss.

4. What is the significance of the title of this story? If you were asked to choose another

title, which of the following would you choose? Why?

> The Microscope and the Pistol
> New Ways and Old
> Pa and the Professor
> School Has Changed a Lot
> It's a Lot in Knowing the Other Person

5. Two themes—or central ideas—run through this story: the theme of change from old ways to new, and the theme of peace through understanding. What connection is there between these themes? How does the growth of mutual understanding affect the actions of Dave and Pa, of Dave and Professor Herbert, of Pa and Professor Herbert, and of Pa and Dave's classmates? Do you think that the idea of peace through understanding others' ways can be extended from individuals to groups—and even to nations? Why or why not?

LANGUAGE AND VOCABULARY

In this story there are three levels of writing: occasional passages of *formal* English, such as you would read in college textbooks or important speeches; many passages of *informal* English, such as you can hear in the speech of educated persons; and a good amount of *dialectal* English, such as you hear spoken by people of limited literary education or experience. Find examples of each kind of writing, and show how each kind contributes to the effectiveness of the story.

FOR COMPOSITION

1. Have you ever had an encounter such as Dave had with his teacher at the beginning of this story? If you haven't, can you imagine such an encounter? Without trying to reproduce the particular setting and speech patterns of "The Split Cherry Tree," write a narrative of an encounter with a teacher along the lines of Dave's with Professor Herbert.

2. In the paragraph that begins "Pa got up at four o'clock . . .", Jesse Stuart tells how the morning began in the Sexton house. In a paragraph of your own, tell about the morning routine in your house. Try to make your account as clear and orderly as Jesse Stuart's.

ABOUT THE AUTHOR

Jesse Stuart (1907–) was born in a one-room log cabin near Riverton, Kentucky. He studied at Plum Grove School and Greenup County High School between periods of work on farms for twenty-five cents a day, then worked his way through Lincoln Memorial University in Tennessee while editing the college paper and writing over five hundred poems. He made his first literary appearance by publishing a book of poems, *Man with a Bull Tongue Plough* (1934). The poet's eye, ear, and heart are evident in his autobiography, short stories, and novels. Some of Jesse Stuart's best short stories are contained in *Plowshare in Heaven: Tales Tall and True from the Kentucky Hills.*

which compelled even their angers and their ardors to chosen directions and chosen paces, their flight was as a flight of harnessed demons.

The captain's bay kept its pace at the head of the squadron with the lithe bounds of a thoroughbred, and this horse was proud as a chief at the roaring trample of his fellows behind him. The captain's glance was calmly upon the grove of maples whence the sharpshooters of the enemy had been picking at the blue line. He seemed to be reflecting. He stolidly rose and fell with the plunges of his horse in all the indifference of a deacon's figure seated plumply in church. And it occurred to many of the watching infantry to wonder why this officer could remain imperturbable and reflective when his squadron was thundering and swarming behind him like the rushing of a flood.

The column swung in a saber-curve toward a break in a fence, and dashed into a roadway. Once a little plank bridge was encountered, and the sound of the hoofs upon it was like the long roll of many drums. An old captain in the infantry turned to his first lieutenant and made a remark which was a compound of bitter disparagement of cavalry in general and soldierly admiration of this particular troop.

Suddenly the bugle sounded, and the column halted with a jolting upheaval amid sharp, brief cries. A moment later the men had tumbled from their horses and, carbines in hand, were running in a swarm toward the grove of maples. In the road one of every four of the troopers was standing with braced legs, and pulling and hauling at the bridles of four frenzied horses.

The captain was running awkwardly in his boots. He held his saber low, so that the point often threatened to catch in the turf. His yellow hair ruffled out from un-

der his faded cap. "Go in hard now!" he roared, in a voice of hoarse fury. His face was violently red.

The troopers threw themselves upon the grove like wolves upon a great animal. Along the whole front of woods there was the dry crackling of musketry, with bitter, swift flashes and smoke that writhed like stung phantoms. The troopers yelled shrilly and spanged bullets low into the foliage.

For a moment, when near the woods, the line almost halted. The men struggled and fought for a time like swimmers encountering a powerful current. Then with a supreme effort they went on again. They dashed madly at the grove, whose foliage, from the high light of the field, was as inscrutable as a wall.

Then suddenly each detail of the calm trees became apparent, and with a few more frantic leaps the men were in the cool gloom of the woods. There was a heavy odor as from burned paper. Wisps of gray smoke wound upward. The men halted; and, grimy, perspiring, and puffing, they searched the recesses of the woods with eager, fierce glances. Figures could be seen flitting afar off. A dozen carbines rattled at them in an angry volley.

During this pause the captain strode along the line, his face lit with a broad smile of contentment. "When he sends this crowd to do anything, I guess he'll find we do it pretty sharp," he said to the grinning lieutenant.

"Say, they didn't stand that rush a minute, did they?" said the subaltern. Both officers were profoundly dusty in their uniforms, and their faces were soiled like those of two urchins.

Out in the grass behind them were three tumbled and silent forms.

Presently the line moved forward again. The men went from tree to tree like hunters stalking game. Some at the left of the line fired occasionally, and those at the right gazed curiously in that direction. The men still breathed heavily from their scramble across the field.

Of a sudden a trooper halted and said: "Hello! there's a house!" Everyone paused. The men turned to look at their leader.

The captain stretched his neck and swung his head from side to side. "By George, it is a house!" he said.

Through the wealth of leaves there vaguely loomed the form of a large white house. These troopers, brown-faced from many days of campaigning, each feature of them telling of their placid confidence and courage, were stopped abruptly by the appearance of this house. There was some subtle suggestion—some tale of an unknown thing—which watched them from they knew not what part of it.

A rail fence girded a wide lawn of tangled grass. Seven pines stood along a driveway which led from two distant posts of a vanished gate. The blue-clothed troopers moved forward until they stood at the fence, peering over it.

The captain put one hand on the top rail and seemed to be about to climb the fence, when suddenly he hesitated and said in a low voice: "Watson, what do you think of it?"

The lieutenant stared at the house. "Derned if I know!" he replied.

The captain pondered. It happened that the whole company had turned a gaze of profound awe and doubt upon this edifice which confronted them. The men were very silent.

At last the captain swore and said: "We are certainly a pack of fools. Derned old deserted house halting a company of Union cavalry, and making us gape like babies!"

"Yes, but there's something—something—" insisted the subaltern in a half stammer.

"Well, if there's 'something—something' in there, I'll get it out," said the captain. "Send Sharpe clean around to the other side with about twelve men, so we will sure bag your 'something—something,' and I'll take a few of the boys and find out what's in the thing!"

He chose the nearest eight men for his "storming party," as the lieutenant called it. After he had waited some minutes for the others to get into position, he said "Come ahead" to his eight men, and climbed the fence.

The brighter light of the tangled lawn made him suddenly feel tremendously apparent, and he wondered if there could be some mystic thing in the house which was regarding this approach. His men trudged silently at his back. They stared at the windows and lost themselves in deep speculations as to the probability of there being, perhaps, eyes behind the blinds—malignant eyes, piercing eyes.

Suddenly a corporal in the party gave vent to a startled exclamation and half threw his carbine into position. The captain turned quickly, and the corporal said: "I saw an arm move the blinds. An arm with a gray sleeve!"

"Don't be a fool, Jones, now!" said the captain sharply.

"I swear t'—" began the corporal, but the captain silenced him.

When they arrived at the front of the house, the troopers paused, while the captain went softly up the front steps. He stood before the large front door and studied it. Some crickets chirped in the long grass, and the nearest pine could be heard in its endless sighs. One of the privates moved uneasily, and his foot crunched the gravel. Suddenly the captain swore angrily and kicked the door with a loud crash. It flew open.

II

The bright light of the day flashed into the old house when the captain angrily kicked open the door. He was aware of a wide hallway carpeted with matting and extending deep into the dwelling. There was also an old walnut hat rack and a little marble-topped table with a vase and two books upon it. Farther back was a great venerable fireplace containing dreary ashes.

But directly in front of the captain was a young girl. The flying open of the door had obviously been an utter astonishment to her, and she remained transfixed there in the middle of the floor, staring at the captain with wide eyes.

She was like a child caught at the time of a raid upon the cake. She wavered to and fro upon her feet, and held her hands behind her. There were two little points of terror in her eyes, as she gazed up at the young captain in dusty blue, with his reddish, bronze complexion, his yellow hair, his bright saber held threateningly.

These two remained motionless and silent, simply staring at each other for some moments.

The captain felt his rage fade out of him and leave his mind limp. He had been violently angry, because this house had made him feel hesitant, wary. He did not like to be wary. He liked to feel confident, sure. So he had kicked the door open, and had been prepared to march in like a soldier of wrath.

But now he began, for one thing, to wonder if his uniform was so dusty and old in appearance. Moreover, he had a feeling that his face was covered with a compound of dust, grime, and perspiration. He took a step forward and said, "I didn't mean to frighten you." But his voice was coarse from his battle-howling. It seemed to him to have hempen fibers in it.

The girl's breath came in little, quick gasps, and she looked at him as she would have looked at a serpent.

"I didn't mean to frighten you," he said again.

The girl, still with her hands behind her, began to back away.

"Is there anyone else in the house?" he went on, while slowly following her. "I don't wish to disturb you, but we had a fight with some rebel skirmishers in the woods, and I thought maybe some of them might have come in here. In fact, I was pretty sure of it. Are there any of them here?"

The girl looked at him and said, "No!" He wondered why extreme agitation made the eyes of some women so limpid and bright.

"Who is here besides yourself?"

By this time his pursuit had driven her to the end of the hall, and she remained there with her back to the wall and her hands still behind her. When she answered this question, she did not look at him, but down at the floor. She cleared her voice and then said, "There is no one here."

"No one?"

She lifted her eyes to him in that appeal that the human being must make even to falling trees, crashing boulders, the sea in a storm, and said, "No, no, there is no one here." He could plainly see her tremble.

Of a sudden he bethought him that she continually kept her hands behind her. As he recalled her air when first discovered, he remembered she appeared precisely as a child detected at one of the crimes of childhood. Moreover, she had always backed away from him. He thought now that she was concealing something which was an evidence of the presence of the enemy in the house.

"What are you holding behind you?" he said suddenly.

She gave a little quick moan, as if some grim hand had throttled her.

"What are you holding behind you?"

"Oh, nothing—please. I am not holding anything behind me; indeed I'm not."

"Very well. Hold your hands out in front of you, then."

"Oh, indeed, I'm not holding anything behind me. Indeed I'm not."

"Well," he began. Then he paused, and remained for a moment dubious. Finally, he laughed. "Well, I shall have my men search the house, anyhow. I'm sorry to trouble you, but I feel sure that there is someone here whom we want." He turned to the corporal, who, with the other men, was gaping quietly in at the door, and said: "Jones, go through the house."

As for himself, he remained planted in front of the girl, for she evidently did not dare to move and allow him to see what she held so carefully behind her back. So she was his prisoner.

The men rummaged around on the ground floor of the house. Sometimes the captain called to them. "Try that closet," "Is there any cellar?" But they found no one, and at last they went trooping toward the stairs which led to the second floor.

But at this movement on the part of the men the girl uttered a cry—a cry of such fright and appeal that the men paused. "Oh, don't go up there! Please don't go up there!—ple—ease! There is no one there! Indeed—indeed there is not! Oh, ple—ease!"

"Go on, Jones," said the captain calmly.

The obedient corporal made a preliminary step, and the girl bounded toward the stairs with another cry.

As she passed him, the captain caught

sight of that which she had concealed behind her back, and which she had forgotten in this supreme moment. It was a pistol.

She ran to the first step and, standing there, faced the men, one hand extended with perpendicular palm, and the other holding the pistol at her side. "Oh, please, don't go up there! Nobody is there—indeed, there is not! P-l-e-a-s-e!" Then suddenly she sank swiftly down upon the step and, huddling forlornly, began to weep in the agony and with the convulsive tremors of an infant. The pistol fell from her fingers and rattled down to the floor.

The astonished troopers looked at their astonished captain. There was a short silence.

Finally, the captain stooped and picked up the pistol. It was a heavy weapon of the army pattern. He ascertained that it was empty.

He leaned toward the shaking girl and said gently, "Will you tell me what you were going to do with this pistol?"

He had to repeat the question a number of times, but at last a muffled voice said, "Nothing."

"Nothing!" He insisted quietly upon a further answer. At the tender tones of the captain's voice, the phlegmatic corporal turned and winked gravely at the man next to him.

"Won't you tell me?"

The girl shook her head.

"Please tell me!"

The silent privates were moving their feet uneasily and wondering how long they were to wait.

The captain said: "Please, won't you tell me?"

Then this girl's voice began in stricken tones, half coherent, and amid violent sobbing: "It was grandpa's. He—he—he said he was going to shoot anybody who came in here—he didn't care if there were thousands of 'em. And—and I know he would, and I was afraid they'd kill him. And so —and—so I stole away his pistol—and I was going to hide it when you—you—you kicked open the door."

The men straightened up and looked at each other. The girl began to weep again.

The captain mopped his brow. He peered down at the girl. He mopped his brow again. Suddenly he said: "Ah, don't cry like that."

He moved restlessly and looked down at his boots. He mopped his brow again.

Then he gripped the corporal by the arm and dragged him some yards back from the others. "Jones," he said, in an intensely earnest voice, "will you tell me what in the devil I am going to do?"

The corporal's countenance became illuminated with satisfaction at being thus requested to advise his superior officer. He adopted an air of great thought, and finally said: "Well, of course, the feller with the gray sleeve must be upstairs, and we must get past the girl and up there somehow. Suppose I take her by the arm and lead her—"

"What!" interrupted the captain from between his clenched teeth. As he turned away from the corporal, he said fiercely over his shoulder: "You touch that girl and I'll split your skull!"

III

The corporal looked after his captain with an expression of mingled amazement, grief, and philosophy. He seemed to be saying to himself that there unfortunately were times, after all, when one could not rely upon the most reliable of men. When he returned to the group he found the captain bending over the girl and saying: "Why is it that you don't want us to search upstairs?"

The girl's head was buried in her crossed arms. Locks of her hair had escaped from their fastenings, and these fell upon her shoulder.

"Won't you tell me?"

The corporal here winked again at the man next to him.

"Because," the girl moaned—"because—there isn't anybody up there."

The captain at last said timidly: "Well, I'm afraid—I'm afraid we'll have to—"

The girl sprang to her feet again, and implored him with her hands. She looked deep into his eyes with her glance, which was at this time like that of the fawn when it says to the hunter, "Have mercy upon me!"

These two stood regarding each other. The captain's foot was on the bottom step, but he seemed to be shrinking. He wore an air of being deeply wretched and ashamed. There was a silence.

Suddenly the corporal said in a quick, low tone: "Look out, captain!"

All turned their eyes swiftly toward the head of the stairs. There had appeared there a youth in a gray uniform. He stood looking coolly down at them. No word was said by the troopers. The girl gave vent to a little wail of desolation, "Oh, Harry!"

He began slowly to descend the stairs. His right arm was in a white sling, and there were some fresh bloodstains upon the cloth. His face was rigid and deathly pale, but his eyes flashed like lights. The girl was again moaning in an utterly dreary fashion, as the youth came slowly down toward the silent men in blue.

Six steps from the bottom of the flight he halted and said, "I reckon it's me you're looking for."

The troopers had crowded forward a trifle and, posed in lithe, nervous attitudes, were watching him like cats. The captain remained unmoved. At the youth's question he merely nodded his head and said, "Yes."

The young man in gray looked down at the girl, and then, in the same even tone, which now, however, seemed to vibrate with suppressed fury, he said: "And is that any reason why you should insult my sister?"

At this sentence, the girl intervened, desperately, between the young man in gray and the officer in blue. "Oh, don't, Harry, don't! He was good to me! He was good to me, Harry—indeed he was!"

The youth came on in his quiet, erect fashion until the girl could have touched either of the men with her hand, for the captain still remained with his foot upon the first step. She continually repeated: "Oh, Harry! Oh, Harry!"

The youth in gray maneuvered to glare into the captain's face, first over one shoulder of the girl and then over the other. In a voice that rang like metal, he said: "You are armed and unwounded, while I have no weapons and am wounded; but—"

The captain had stepped back and sheathed his saber. The eyes of these two men were gleaming fire, but otherwise the captain's countenance was imperturbable. He said: "You are mistaken. You have no reason to—"

"You lie!"

All save the captain and the youth in gray started in an electric movement. These two words crackled in the air like shattered glass. There was a breathless silence.

The captain cleared his throat. His look at the youth contained a quality of singular and terrible ferocity, but he said in his stolid tone: "I don't suppose you mean what you say now."

Upon his arm he had felt the pressure of some unconscious little fingers. The girl was leaning against the wall as if she no longer knew how to keep her balance, but those fingers—he held his arm very still. She murmured: "Oh, Harry, don't! He was good to me—indeed he was!"

The corporal had come forward until he in a measure confronted the youth in gray, for he saw those fingers upon the captain's arm, and he knew that sometimes very strong men were not able to move hand nor foot under such conditions.

The youth had suddenly seemed to become weak. He breathed heavily and clung to the rail. He was glaring at the captain, and apparently summoning all his will power to combat his weakness. The corporal addressed him with profound straightforwardness: "Don't you be a derned fool!" The youth turned toward him so fiercely that the corporal threw up a knee and an elbow like a boy who expects to be cuffed.

The girl pleaded with the captain. "You won't hurt him, will you? He don't know what he's saying. He's wounded, you know. Please don't mind him!"

"I won't touch him," said the captain, with rather extraordinary earnestness; "don't you worry about him at all. I won't touch him!"

Then he looked at her, and the girl suddenly withdrew her fingers from his arm.

The corporal contemplated the top of the stairs, and remarked without surprise: "There's another of 'em coming!"

An old man was clambering down the stairs with much speed. He waved a cane wildly. "Get out of my house, you thieves! Get out! I won't have you cross my threshold! Get out!" He mumbled and wagged his head in an old man's fury. It was plainly his intention to assault them.

And so it occurred that a young girl became engaged in protecting a stalwart captain, fully armed, and with eight grim troopers at his back, from the attack of an old man with a walking stick!

A blush passed over the temples and brow of the captain, and he looked particularly savage and weary. Despite the girl's efforts, he suddenly faced the old man.

"Look here," he said distinctly, "we came in because we had been fighting in the woods yonder, and we concluded that some of the enemy were in this house, especially when we saw a gray sleeve at the window. But this young man is wounded, and I have nothing to say to him. I will even take it for granted that there are no others like him upstairs. We will go away, leaving your house just as we found it! And we are no more thieves and rascals than you are!"

The old man simply roared: "I haven't got a cow nor a pig nor a chicken on the place! Your soldiers have stolen everything they could carry away. They have torn down half my fences for firewood.

This afternoon some of your accursed bullets even broke my windowpanes!"

The girl had been faltering: "Grandpa! Oh, grandpa!"

The captain looked at the girl. She returned his glance from the shadow of the old man's shoulder. After studying her face a moment, he said: "Well, we will go now." He strode toward the door, and his men clanked docilely after him.

At this time there was the sound of harsh cries and rushing footsteps from without. The door flew open, and a whirlwind composed of bluecoated troopers came in with a swoop. It was headed by the lieutenant. "Oh, here you are!" he cried, catching his breath. "We thought—Oh, look at the girl!"

The captain said intensely: "Shut up, you fool!"

The men settled to a halt with a clash and a bang. There could be heard the dulled sound of many hoofs outside the house.

"Did you order up the horses?" inquired the captain.

"Yes. We thought—"

"Well, then, let's get out of here," interrupted the captain morosely.

The men began to filter out into the open air. The youth in gray had been hanging dismally to the railing of the stairway. He now was climbing slowly up to the second floor. The old man was addressing himself directly to the serene corporal.

"Not a chicken on the place!" he cried.

"Well, I didn't take your chickens, did I?"

"No, maybe you didn't but—"

The captain crossed the hall and stood before the girl in rather a culprit's fashion. "You are not angry at me, are you?" he asked timidly.

"No," she said. She hesitated a moment, and then suddenly held out her hand. "You were good to me—and I'm —much obliged."

The captain took her hand, and then he blushed, for he found himself unable to formulate a sentence that applied in any way to the situation.

She did not seem to heed that hand for a time.

He loosened his grasp presently, for he was ashamed to hold it so long without saying anything clever. At last, with an air of charging an entrenched brigade, he contrived to say: "I would rather do anything than frighten or trouble you."

His brow was warmly perspiring. He had a sense of being hideous in his dusty uniform and with his grimy face.

She said, "Oh, I'm so glad it was you instead of somebody who might have—might have hurt brother Harry and grandpa!"

He told her, "I wouldn't have hurt 'em for anything!"

There was a little silence.

"Well, good-by!" he said at last.

"Good-by!"

He walked toward the door past the old man, who was scolding at the vanishing figure of the corporal. The captain looked back. She had remained there watching him.

At the bugle's order, the troopers standing beside their horses swung briskly into the saddle. The lieutenant said to the first sergeant: "Williams, did they ever meet before?"

"Hanged if I know!"

"Well, say—"

The captain saw a curtain move at one of the windows. He cantered from his position at the head of the column and steered his horse between two flower beds.

"Well, good-by!"

The squadron trampled slowly past.

"Good-by!"

They shook hands.

He evidently had something enormously important to say to her, but it seemed that he could not manage it. He struggled heroically. The bay charger, with his great mystically solemn eyes, looked around the corner of his shoulder at the girl.

The captain studied a pine tree. The girl inspected the grass beneath the window. The captain said hoarsely: "I don't suppose—I don't suppose—I'll ever see you again!"

She looked at him affrightedly and shrank back from the window. He seemed to have woefully expected a reception of this kind for his question. He gave her instantly a glance of appeal.

She said: "Why, no, I don't suppose we will."

"Never?"

"Why, no, 'tain't possible. You—you are a—Yankee!"

"Oh, I know it, but—" Eventually he continued: "Well, some day, you know, when there's no more fighting, we might —" He observed that she had again withdrawn suddenly into the shadow, so he said: "Well, good-by!"

When he held her fingers she bowed her head, and he saw a pink blush steal over the curves of her cheek and neck.

"Am I never going to see you again?"

She made no reply.

"Never?" he repeated.

After a long time, he bent over to hear a faint reply: "Sometimes—when there are no troops in the neighborhood— grandpa don't mind if I—walk over as far as that old oak tree yonder—in the afternoons."

It appeared that the captain's grip was very strong, for she uttered an exclamation and looked at her fingers as if she expected to find them mere fragments. He rode away.

The bay horse leaped a flower bed. They were almost to the drive, when the girl uttered a panic-stricken cry.

The captain wheeled his horse violently, and upon his return journey went straight through a flower bed.

The girl had clasped her hands. She beseeched him wildly with her eyes. "Oh, please, don't believe it! I never walk to the old oak tree. Indeed I don't! I never— never—never walk there."

The bridle drooped on the bay charger's neck. The captain's figure seemed limp. With an expression of profound dejection and gloom he stared off at where the leaden sky met the dark green line of the woods. The long-impending rain began to fall with a mournful patter, drop and drop. There was a silence.

At last a low voice said, "Well—I might —sometimes I might—perhaps—but only once in a great while—I might walk to the old tree—in the afternoons."

FOR STUDY AND DISCUSSION

1. What qualities does the cavalry captain show in leading the charge across the field? Which actions show him to be courageous? forceful? proud? What change occurs in him and his troops when they come upon the house? Why do you think the house has such an effect on the troops?

2. How does Crane arouse your sympathy and admiration for the girl in the house? How do her appearance, her actions, and her pleas melt the sternness of the Yankee captain? Does the captain fall in love with the girl too quickly, or can you understand his feelings? Do you think you would have acted exactly as he did? Why or why not? If not, what would you have done differently?

3. Are the old grandfather and the wounded Confederate soldier believable characters? How are they unlike the Yankee soldiers, particularly the corporal, in their attitude toward war and honor? Would you call "A Gray Sleeve" a *romantic* story, true to the way we

would like people to be rather than the way they really are, or a *realistic* story, true to the actual behavior of men and women? Give reasons for your answer.

4. "A Gray Sleeve" may be compared to "The Lady or the Tiger?" in that both stories leave the reader uncertain about what will happen in the future. Do you think the girl will take a walk to the old tree? Why or why not?

TOTAL EFFECT

Looking at the story as a whole, what total effect or final impression do you think the author intended to create? Do you think his chief intention was to contrast the passions of war and private feelings? to show that love is stronger than hate or fear? to show the changeable nature of human feelings? Explain your choice. How is this intention shown in the actions of the characters? How is it shown in the author's comments on the events of the plot?

LANGUAGE AND VOCABULARY

The aim of a good storywriter is to make you sense the action as if you were actually present. In "A Gray Sleeve," Stephen Crane helps you to recreate the action in your imagination by choosing words that appeal to the ear and eye and other senses. In the following sentences, which words help you to see, hear, smell, taste, or feel the action? Pay attention to the sound of the words as well as to their meaning.

"On the springy turf the innumerable hoofs thundered in a swift storm of sound."

"Along the whole front of woods there was the dry crackling of musketry, with bitter, swift flashes and smoke that writhed like stung phantoms."

"One of the privates moved uneasily, and his foot crunched the gravel."

"She wavered to and fro upon her feet, and held her hands behind her."

"Moreover, he had a feeling that his face was covered with a compound of dust, grime, and perspiration."

"She gave a little quick moan, as if some grim hand had throttled her."

"The men began to filter out into the open air."

"His brow was warmly perspiring."

FOR COMPOSITION

In writing description, one of the most important things to keep in mind is point of view. Notice how the artillery captain's reaction to the cavalry helps to characterize this particular troop. Keeping in mind the importance of point of view, write a description following one of the suggestions given below.

Point of View	Action
A person standing on the roof of a high building	People and traffic in the street below
A supporter of football team A	The well-earned victory of team B

ABOUT THE AUTHOR

Stephen Crane (1871–1900) was descended from Methodist clergy on both sides of his family. After two years at college, he became a free-lance writer and reporter in New York. His fascination with the lives of the outcasts and the poor on the Bowery and in other New York slums led him to write *Maggie: A Girl of the Streets,* a bitterly realistic novel. War, his other overwhelming interest, led to his writing *The Red Badge of Courage,* a novel that imaginatively recreated the feelings of a young soldier in the War Between the States. This book made Crane famous overnight, and he began to get offers to cover wars and revolutions for newspaper syndicates. On his way to Cuba to report on an attempted invasion in 1896, Crane was shipwrecked off the Florida coast. He made use of this experience in his famous story "The Open Boat." Between assignments as a war correspondent, Crane wrote short stories—some with war settings, some set in the American West, and some based on the experiences of childhood. Despite his life-long love of sports and adventure, Crane was always physically frail. He died of tuberculosis at a health resort in Germany at the age of 29.

The Secret Life of Walter Mitty

JAMES THURBER

WE'RE GOING THROUGH!" The Commander's voice was like thin ice breaking. He wore his full-dress uniform, with the heavily braided white cap pulled down rakishly over one cold gray eye. "We can't make it, sir. It's spoiling for a hurricane, if you ask me." "I'm not asking you, Lieutenant Berg," said the Commander. "Throw on the power lights! Rev her up to 8,500! We're going through!" The pounding of the cylinders increased: ta - pocketa - pocketa - pocketa - *pocketa - pocketa*. The Commander stared at the ice forming on the pilot window. He walked over and twisted a row of complicated dials. "Switch on No. 8 auxiliary!" he shouted. "Switch on No. 8 auxiliary!" repeated Lieutenant Berg. "Full strength in No. 3 turret!" shouted the Commander. "Full strength in No. 3 turret!" The crew, bending to their various tasks in the huge, hurtling eight-engined Navy hydroplane, looked at each other and grinned. "The Old Man'll get us through," they said to one another. "The Old Man ain't afraid of Hell!" . . .

"Not so fast! You're driving too fast!" said Mrs. Mitty. "What are you driving so fast for?"

"The Secret Life of Walter Mitty" by James Thurber. Copyright © 1942 James Thurber. Copyright © 1970 Helen Thurber. From *My World—And Welcome To It* published by Harcourt Brace Jovanovich, Inc. Originally printed in *The New Yorker*. Reprinted by permission of Helen Thurber.

"Hmm?" said Walter Mitty. He looked at his wife, in the seat beside him, with shocked astonishment. She seemed grossly unfamiliar, like a strange woman who had yelled at him in a crowd. "You were up to fifty-five," she said. "You know I don't like to go more than forty. You were up to fifty-five." Walter Mitty drove on toward Waterbury in silence, the roaring of the SN202 through the worst storm in twenty years of Navy flying fading in the remote, intimate airways of his mind. "You're tensed up again," said Mrs. Mitty. "It's one of your days. I wish you'd let Dr. Renshaw look you over."

Walter Mitty stopped the car in front of the building where his wife went to have her hair done. "Remember to get those overshoes while I'm having my hair done," she said. "I don't need overshoes," said Mitty. She put her mirror back into her bag. "We've been all through that," she said, getting out of the car. "You're not a young man any longer." He raced the engine a little. "Why don't you wear your gloves? Have you lost your gloves?" Walter Mitty reached in a pocket and brought out the gloves. He put them on, but after she had turned and gone into the building and he had driven on to a red light, he took them off again. "Pick it up, brother!" snapped a cop as the light changed, and Mitty hastily pulled on his gloves and lurched ahead. He drove around the streets aimlessly for a time, and then he drove past the hospital on his way to the parking lot.

. . . "It's the millionaire banker, Wellington McMillan," said the pretty nurse. "Yes?" said Walter Mitty, removing his gloves slowly. "Who has the case?" "Dr. Ren haw and Dr. Benbow, but there are two specialists here, Dr. Remington from New York and Dr. Pritchard-Mitford from London. He flew over." A door opened down a long cool corridor and Dr.

Renshaw came out. He looked distraught and haggard. "Hello, Mitty," he said. "We're having the devil's own time with McMillan, the millionaire banker and close personal friend of Roosevelt. Obstreosis of the ductal tract. Tertiary. Wish you'd take a look at him." "Glad to," said Mitty.

In the operating room there were whispered introductions: "Dr. Remington, Dr. Mitty. Dr. Pritchard-Mitford, Dr. Mitty." "I've read your book on streptothricosis," said Pritchard-Mitford, shaking hands. "A brilliant performance, sir." "Thank you," said Walter Mitty. "Didn't know you were in the States, Mitty," grumbled Remington. "Coals to Newcastle,[1] bringing Mitford and me up here for a tertiary." "You are very kind," said Mitty. A huge, complicated machine, connected to the operating table, with many tubes and wires, began at this moment to go pocketa-pocketa-pocketa. "The new anaesthetizer is giving way!" shouted an intern. "There is no one in the East who knows how to fix it!" "Quiet, man!" said Mitty, in a low, cool voice. He sprang to the machine, which was now going pocketa-pocketa-queep-pocketa-queep. He began fingering delicately a row of glistening dials. "Give me a fountain pen!" he snapped. Someone handed him a fountain pen. He pulled a faulty piston out of the machine and inserted the pen in its place. "That will hold for ten minutes," he said. "Get on with the operation." A nurse hurried over and whispered to Renshaw, and Mitty saw the man turn pale. "Coreopsis has set in," said Renshaw nervously. "If you would take over, Mitty?" Mitty looked at him and at the craven figure of Benbow, who drank, and at the grave, uncertain faces of the two great specialists.

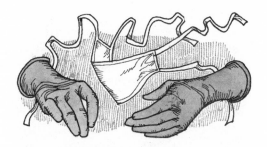

"If you wish," he said. They slipped a white gown on him; he adjusted a mask and drew on thin gloves; nurses handed him shining . . .

"Back it up, Mac! Look out for that Buick!" Walter Mitty jammed on the brakes. "Wrong lane, Mac," said the parking-lot attendant, looking at Mitty closely. "Gee. Yeh," muttered Mitty. He began cautiously to back out of the lane marked "Exit Only." "Leave her sit there," said the attendant. "I'll put her away." Mitty got out of the car. "Hey, better leave the key." "Oh," said Mitty, handing the man the ignition key. The attendant vaulted into the car, backed it up with insolent skill, and put it where it belonged.

They're so cocky, thought Walter Mitty, walking along Main Street; they think they know everything. Once he had tried to take his chains off, outside New Milford, and he had got them wound around the axles. A man had had to come out in a wrecking car and unwind them, a young, grinning garageman. Since then Mrs. Mitty always made him drive to a garage to have the chains taken off. The next time, he thought, I'll wear my right arm in a sling; they won't grin at me then. I'll have my right arm in a sling and they'll see I couldn't possibly take the chains off myself. He kicked at the slush on the sidewalk. "Overshoes," he said to himself, and he began looking for a shoe store.

When he came out into the street again, with the overshoes in a box under his arm,

[1] **Coals to Newcastle:** saying used to indicate unnecessary labor. Newcastle is a city in England that is famous for its production of coal.

Walter Mitty began to wonder what the other thing was his wife had told him to get. She had told him twice before they set out from their house for Waterbury. In a way he hated these weekly trips to town—he was always getting something wrong. Kleenex, he thought, Squibb's, razor blades? No. Toothpaste, toothbrush, bicarbonate, carborundum, initiative and referendum? He gave it up. But she would remember it. "Where's the what's-its-name?" she would ask. "Don't tell me you forgot the what's-its-name." A newsboy went by shouting something about the Waterbury trial.

. . . "Perhaps this will refresh your memory." The District Attorney suddenly thrust a heavy automatic at the quiet figure on the witness stand. "Have you ever seen this before?" Walter Mitty took the gun and examined it expertly. "This is my Webley-Vickers 50.80," he said calmly. An excited buzz ran around the courtroom. The Judge rapped for order. "You are a crack shot with any sort of firearms, I believe?" said the District Attorney, insinuatingly. "Objection!" shouted Mitty's attorney. "We have shown that the defendant could not have fired the shot. We have shown that he wore his right arm in a sling on the night of the fourteenth of July." Walter Mitty raised his hand briefly and the bickering attorneys were stilled. "With any known make of gun," he said evenly, "I could have killed Gregory Fitzhurst at three hundred feet *with my left hand.*" Pandemonium broke loose in the courtroom. A woman's scream rose above the bedlam and suddenly a lovely, dark-haired girl was in Walter Mitty's arms. The District Attorney struck at her savagely. Without rising from his chair, Mitty let the man have it on the point of the chin. "You miserable cur!" . . .

"Puppy biscuit," said Walter Mitty. He stopped walking and the buildings of Waterbury rose up out of the misty courtroom and surrounded him again. A woman who was passing laughed. "He said 'Puppy biscuit,'" she said to her companion. "That man said 'Puppy biscuit' to himself." Walter Mitty hurried on. He went into an A. & P., not the first one he came to but a smaller one farther up the street. "I want some biscuit for small, young dogs," he said to the clerk. "Any special brand, sir?" The greatest pistol shot in the world thought a moment. "It says 'Puppies Bark for It' on the box," said Walter Mitty.

His wife would be through at the hairdresser's in fifteen minutes, Mitty saw in looking at his watch, unless they had trouble drying it; sometimes they had trouble drying it. She didn't like to get to the hotel first; she would want him to be there waiting for her as usual. He found a big leather chair in the lobby, facing a window, and he put the overshoes and the puppy biscuit on the floor beside it. He picked up an old copy of *Liberty* and sank down into the chair. "Can Germany Conquer the World Through the Air?" Walter Mitty looked at the pictures of bombing planes and of ruined streets.

. . . "The cannonading has got the wind up in young Raleigh, sir," said the sergeant. Captain Mitty looked up at him through tousled hair. "Get him to bed," he said wearily, "with the others. I'll fly alone." "But you can't, sir," said the sergeant anxiously. "It takes two men to

handle that bomber and the Archies [1] are pounding hell out of the air. Von Richtman's circus [2] is between here and Saulier." "Somebody's got to get that ammunition dump," said Mitty. "I'm going over. Spot of brandy?" He poured a drink for the sergeant and one for himself. War thundered and whined around the dugout and battered at the door. There was a rending of wood and splinters flew through the room. "A bit of a near thing," said Captain Mitty carelessly. "The box barrage is closing in," said the sergeant. "We only live once, Sergeant," said Mitty, with his faint, fleeting smile. "Or do we?" He poured another brandy and tossed it off. "I never see a man could hold his brandy like you, sir," said the sergeant. "Begging your pardon, sir." Captain Mitty stood up and strapped on his huge Webley-Vickers automatic. "It's forty kilometers through hell, sir," said the sergeant. Mitty finished one last brandy. "After all," he said softly, "what isn't?" The pounding of the cannon increased; there was the rat-tat-tatting of machine guns, and from somewhere came the menacing pocketa-pocketa-pocketa of the new flame-throwers. Walter Mitty walked to the door of the dugout humming "Auprès de Ma Blonde." [3] He turned and waved to the sergeant. "Cheerio!" he said. . . .

Something struck his shoulder. "I've been looking all over this hotel for you," said Mrs. Mitty. "Why do you have to hide in this old chair? How did you expect me to find you?" "Things close in," said Walter Mitty vaguely. "What?" Mrs. Mitty said. "Did you get the what's-its-name? The puppy biscuit? What's in that box?" "Overshoes," said Mitty. "Couldn't

you have put them on in the store?" "I was thinking," said Walter Mitty. "Does it ever occur to you that I am sometimes thinking?" She looked at him. "I'm going to take your temperature when I get you home," she said.

They went out through the revolving doors that made a faintly derisive whistling sound when you pushed them. It was two blocks to the parking lot. At the drugstore on the corner she said, "Wait here for me. I forgot something. I won't be a minute." She was more than a minute. Walter Mitty lighted a cigarette. It began to rain, rain with sleet in it. He stood up against the wall of the drugstore, smoking. . . . He put his shoulders back and his heels together. "To hell with the handkerchief," said Walter Mitty scornfully. He took one last drag on his cigarette and snapped it away. Then, with that faint, fleeting smile playing about his lips, he faced the firing squad; erect and motionless, proud and disdainful, Walter Mitty the Undefeated, inscrutable to the last.

FOR STUDY AND DISCUSSION

1. Walter Mitty attempts to escape from real life through his daydreams. Why does he wish so strongly to escape? To what extent do you think Mrs. Mitty is a cause of his wishing to escape? Are Mrs. Mitty's remarks to her husband intentionally unkind, merely thoughtless, simply realistic, or all three? Explain.

2. Notice how Walter Mitty's fantasies are

---

[1] **Archies:** allied troops' name for the antiaircraft guns in World War I.

[2] **circus:** a squadron of planes flying in close formation.

[3] **"Auprès de Ma Blonde":** popular French song.

suggested by the actual events of a weekly shopping trip to town. While driving the car, he imagines himself to be a Navy flier; after his wife suggests a visit to the doctor, he pictures himself as a celebrated surgeon. Point out the connecting link between an actual event and the daydream it causes in two or three other places in the story.

3. The final incident of the story shows Walter Mitty dreaming of himself before a firing squad. How is this incident symbolic of his view of himself? Is this final daydream of Walter Mitty's an adequate summing-up of the total effect of the story? Why or why not?

4. This short story was the source of a full-length motion picture in which several of the incidents were greatly expanded. If you had been making that motion picture, which incidents would you have chosen to expand? Which incidents offer the best possibilities for further action? Why?

5. In your opinion, which of the statements listed below most closely approximates the theme or main idea of this story? Give reasons for your answer.

Walter Mitty has a decided inferiority complex.

All people lead secret dream lives.

There is both humor and sadness in the longings of average people who wish they could be heroes.

It is foolish to indulge in wishful thinking.

It is a terrible thing for people to lose control of their reason.

LANGUAGE AND VOCABULARY

One of the ways in which an author achieves the total, or overall, effect desired in a story is by using well-chosen words. The right word or words are those that exactly fit the situation they are meant to explain or describe. How does each of the italicized words below exactly fit the particular situation in the story? How does each word contribute to the total effect of the story?

"The *Old Man* ain't afraid of Hell!"

"She [his wife] seemed grossly *unfamiliar.*"

"The worst storm in twenty years of Navy flying fading in the *remote, intimate airways* of his mind."

" 'Coreopsis has set in,' said Renshaw *nervously.*"

"The attendant *vaulted* into the car, backed it up with *insolent skill,* and put it where it *belonged.*"

"and suddenly a *lovely, dark-haired* girl was in Walter Mitty's arms."

"*proud* and *disdainful,* Walter Mitty the Undefeated, *inscrutable* to the last."

FOR COMPOSITION

1. Reread question 4 in "For Study and Discussion"; then choose your favorite incident in the story and expand it. You might supply a more elaborate setting, more specific description, further action, additional dialogue. As you write, consider carefully the overall effect you wish to achieve.

2. Write a brief essay on the topic, "Humor in 'The Secret Life of Walter Mitty.'" Begin with a brief definition of humor, then give examples of situations and language in the story that make clear your definition.

ABOUT THE AUTHOR

James Thurber (1894–1961) achieved distinction in many fields—the essay, the short story, art, and drama. His early life—amusingly recalled in *My Life and Hard Times*—was spent in Columbus, Ohio, where he attended school and then the state university. After working on papers in Columbus, Paris, and New York, Thurber joined the staff of the *New Yorker* magazine as an editor and staff writer. Some of his experiences on the magazine are related in *The Years with Ross.* In all his work, Thurber was primarily a humorist. In both his writing and his drawing, he succeeded in exactly conveying both the humor and the meaning of a situation. As a result, many of his "pieces," as he called them, promise to become permanent American classics. In addition to the sophisticated essays and stories in *The Cream of Thurber* and *Thurber Country,* Thurber wrote several children's masterpieces, two of which are *The White Deer* and *The Thirteen Clocks.* Some of his best satire appears in *Fables for Our Time* and *Further Fables for Our Time.*

The House with the Grapevine

H. E. BATES

WHEN HE WAS a small boy he lived in a street that plunged down a long steep hill between lines of hard-baked bricks that were more like boxes than houses, and here and there a factory that was like a taller, darker box with the iron limb of a crane hanging like a gallows outside.

There were no trees in that street. But once, his father would tell him, and not so long ago, it had been a place of green fields, with oats and barley and meadows where there were now factory yards, and little spinneys of violets and a farmhouse with apple trees and a brook at the foot of the hill where sticklebacks swam among the cresses.

"And the farmhouse," his father would say, "had a grapevine. Like all the other old houses in the town. Nearly every one of them, in those days, had a grapevine."

"With grapes on?"

"Of course. Nice ones."

"Green ones? Like the ones we have at Christmas?"

No, his father would tell him, they were black ones. Or rather, dark plum-colored ones. Not big, of course, like those you bought in shops. "But about as big as your marbles," he would say.

"And whereabouts on the farmhouse did the grapevine grow?"

"On the south side. The other side from the road. It went all along that wall of the house. You couldn't see it from the road."

"Then how did you know it was there?"

"Because," his father would tell him, "I used to work there."

That was a very wonderful thing, he thought, the fact that his father had worked at a farmhouse.

"I never knew that," he said. "Did you work there all the time?"

"No," his father said. "Not all the time. Half-time."

That was a thing he did not quite understand: half-time. But his father could explain that.

"In those days," he said, "we went to school half-time. School in the mornings and then work in the afternoons."

That, too, he thought, was wonderful. "Wasn't it fun," he said, "only to have to go to school half the time and then work in the farmhouse for the rest of the time?"

"No," his father said, "I hated it."

That was something that was quite beyond him. He wished often that it would happen to him that he could go to school half the time and work among the apple trees and the grapevine for the rest of the time. That was the kind of life, he used to think, until his father said:

"I was eight. It was one winter when I worked there. There were no houses then between here and Evensford Hill in those days. I used to run all the way home in the dark, late at night, and my grandmother would be crying because she didn't know where I was."

"Which granny was that?"

"She's dead now," his father would tell him. "My mother died first. And then my grandmother. And after that——"

And gradually he knew that his father had been alone after that: though exactly how much alone and how often alone he did not know until long afterward. What he really cared about and what he really wanted to know about in those days was the farmhouse and the grapevine and how the grapes grew and what it was like before the brick boxes and the factories with the gallows-cranes came to smother and obliterate it all.

"Do you think the grapevine is still there?" he said.

"Well," his father said, "the house is still there. That's the only house left in the street. Of course the orchard isn't there. That was cut down when they built Packington's factory. But the old gates are there. And you can see it was a farm because it still has the stables there, and the pigeon cote in the top."

How marvelous it must have been, he thought, to have stables and a pigeon cote in the yard instead of only a water barrel and a slat fence where people beat their mats. What days they must have been—he simply couldn't believe his father hadn't liked them.

"Did you ever eat the grapes?"

"No."

"Weren't they good to eat?"

"Oh! yes. Only it was wintertime when I was there."

"But if you'd stayed till summertime would you have had some to eat?"

"There was never a boy," his father said, "who asked so many questions."

But every day, after that, when he went downhill to school, and again when he came back, he began to stop outside the gates that were now wedged between the gas-tarred wall of a house and the gaunt walls of a factory. He was aware of wanting to make a link with the past. All he could see of this link were the blocked-up holes of the dovecote in the stable, the stone walls of the house and once, when he peered through the keyhole of the gate,

a big dog kennel with a dirty dinner plate outside.

"When did the grapes ripen?" he said once.

"About September time."

Then he had a final, uneasy, haunting question:

"Weren't you very happy there?"

"No."

"Why not?"

"It isn't worth going into. It isn't worth bothering your head about."

"What did you have to do there? What work?"

"Oh! cleaning the hens out and cleaning the pigeons out. And sweeping the yard. And cleaning knives. And running errands. And looking for eggs—you know the sort of thing."

Yes: he knew the sort of thing. And again he could not think, for the life of him, why his father hadn't liked it.

"I just didn't," his father said. "I can't explain why. Perhaps some day there will be something that will make you unhappy and you won't know why it is. I hope not. But you can't always explain things. Things are funny that way sometimes."

Yes: things were funny, he thought. Grownup people were funny too.

He supposed he must have waited for three months or more, all through summer and into September, before he had courage enough to jump up and flick down the latch of the old house gate and then go, for the first time, into the yard on the other side.

He always remembered that day. It might have been chosen specially from all the days of the autumn because the air was so yellow with sunshine that the stone of the house seemed almost the color of a piece of plain Madeira cake,[1] and because even the small white clouds seemed warm.

[1] **Madeira** (mə·dir′ə) **cake:** a kind of poundcake.

To his surprise and joy there were also two or three apple trees, and a single pear, in the little garden beyond the stables. In the yard an old dog lay asleep by the kennel like a flabby bag of mangy brown leather with irregular black patches on its sides.

He was very terrified of dogs and he went across the yard in a wide circuit, on tiptoe, looking backward all the time over his shoulder.

And then all at once an old lady had him by the scruff of his collar. Her long hand pounced out from behind the corner of the house. With a cry she thrust into his eyes a long face like a parsnip that had a few suspended hairy roots hanging from the chin.

"Ah! you never see me, you never see me, did you?" she said. "You never see me."

It was impossible to speak; there was only a terrible thunder in all his veins.

"I know what you come for, I know what you come for. You come nickin' apples, didn't you, you come nickin' apples. Scrumpin'—nickin' other folkses things—scrumpin'—that's what you come for!"

He felt the horrible wiry hairs of her chin brush the back of his neck. He heard the dog stir on its chain and the sound came to him like the turn of a lock, imprisoning him there in the yard alone with her.

"That's what you come for, didn't you? I know. I catch 'em all the time. Every day. They're allus in here—but I git 'em. Like I got you——"

"I never——"

"Never what? If you didn't come for nickin' things what did you come for?"

There was a great cold stone in his throat. He swallowed several times but it wouldn't go down.

"Grapes," he managed to say at last.

"That's all I came for. Somebody said you had grapes to sell——"

"Grapes? Grapes? Somebody?—who's somebody? Who says so?"

"They said you had a grapevine—on the house. They said——"

"Grapes? They's never bin grapes here, not on this house, not since I lived here, and that's bin years a-new."

And suddenly she lifted him with her long skinny arm clean off the ground, screeching into his face:

"You know what they do to little snots like you?"

All his life was streaming out in terror through the soles of his feet and he couldn't answer.

"They git the policeman. Tek you to police station. Git you locked up there. Keep you in there so you can't nick things no more."

Her eyes were so near to him and so distended and bright that he could see swimming flecks of blood in them. Then she gave a great suck of her lips, drawing breath through her teeth, and said:

"Grapes? Somebody said they was grapes, did they? Where?"

"On the house."

"Come wi' me!" she screeched, "and I'll jist show you whether they is!"

With her long bony arm she lugged him across the yard and round the corner of the house. He was so small that she could twirl him at the end of her arm like a rope.

"Well—there y'are! There's your grapes—there y'are!"

That was the wall of the house, he knew quite well, that his father had described. It faced away from the road. That was the wall all right, but there were no grapes on it. It was empty; there was nothing there.

"You're a fibber, ain't you? You're a storyteller, ain't you?" she said. "You made it up, didn't you? You knew they wasn't no grapes there, didn't you? All the time. You tell lies."

He knew there had been grapes there. He knew because his father had told him so; but he couldn't say anything and she screeched:

"You know what they do to little monkeys what tell lies? You know what I've a good mind to do to you?" With craggy fingers she pointed to the windows of the stable. "Lock y'in there. Lock y'up in there while I git a policeman."

"No," he said. "No——"

"I locked one in there once. All day. That was a lesson to him. He never came back, nickin' folkses things. Nickin' things that never belonged to him. Shall I lock y'in there? Shall I?——"

"No!" he screamed.

Then he broke from her and he was running. The dog began lashing to and fro on the chain. The old woman gave a wild double stamping scurry with her feet as if she were chasing him. He was too small to reach the latch of the gate and the first time he leapt for it he missed it.

"You come in here once more and I'll lock y'up," she yelled, "and git the policeman and git you put in jail," and then he hit the latch and it was down and he was running in the street outside.

He never once spoke to his father about the grapes or the grapevine after that. He did not ask another single question about the house, the winter his father worked there, the way he had run home late at night to a weeping grandmother, or why he had been unhappy.

It was not because he did not believe in the grapevine; or that he believed his father had told a lie or had invented it or had made some mistake of memory about it over the years. He had great faith in his father. He knew that his father would not tell him a thing that was not right. He knew that his father would never let him be taken to the police station, that awful place. His father would protect him. He trusted his father. His father was a wonderful, kindly man.

"But," as his father said, "things are funny that way sometimes. You can't explain them. Perhaps some day there will be something that will make you unhappy and you won't be able to explain it to anyone—not even to somebody you love."

That was why, forever afterward, when he passed the gates of that house, he remembered the grapevine. That was why he too hated that house and, because of it, loved his father so much more.

FOR STUDY AND DISCUSSION

1. Why does the boy ask so many questions? What do the father's answers reveal about his own boyhood? How do the boy's questions help to create the total effect of the story? What does he especially want to find out? Why?

2. How was the boy's first impression of the house with the grapevine different from his father's impression? Although the boy did not find the grapevine, he refuses to believe that his father lied, or was mistaken, or had invented it. Why do you think he had such faith?

What did his faith show about his opinion of his father?

3. What did the house with the grapevine represent—or symbolize—for the father? How does it come to symbolize much the same thing for the son? Where in the story do you realize the exact nature of their feeling about the house?

4. This story is told from the point of view of an older man remembering his boyhood and his relations with his father. How is this point of view established in the story? (In considering your answer, pay special attention to the tenses of the verbs.)

5. The narrator speaks of his need to establish "a link with the past." What does he mean? Do you think that this is a common feeling in young children? What accounts for this feeling? Why would it lead children to ask endless questions?

6. In addition to telling a story, "The House with the Grapevine" tells a great deal about the father's life as an eight-year-old boy and about the changes that have taken place since that time in and about the countryside. What are some of these changes? What brought them about? Are they regrettable changes? Why or why not?

TOTAL EFFECT

The total effect of a story—its impact and meaning—depends on all its elements, especially conflict and plot, character, and theme. Which of these elements contributes most to the total effect of "The House with the Grapevine"? Which contributes most to "The Secret Life of Walter Mitty"? to "A Gray Sleeve"? In each story, how do the other elements also contribute? In which story do these elements combine most effectively to create the most powerful total effect?

LANGUAGE AND VOCABULARY

One way of making a story vivid is to use literary devices such as similes and metaphors. A striking simile in the first paragraph—"with the iron limb of a crane hanging like a gallows outside"—suggests the theme of this story.

Find three or four other similes or metaphors in the story and show how each gives a vivid impression of some character, action, or idea.

FOR COMPOSITION

1. "The House with the Grapevine" contains a vivid contrast between the farmhouse in its peaceful rural surroundings of the past and its grimy industrial setting of the present. Notice the details that the author uses to contrast the two. In a similar manner, write a brief description contrasting a single setting in two different times. If you like, write on one of the following:

An old farm before and after the coming of a new real-estate development

A small town before and after the new superhighway

The shores of the Hudson River (or any other river) in colonial or pioneer days and now

2. Have you ever had an unpleasant encounter like that of the boy with the old woman? Reread the author's version of this encounter in "The House with the Grapevine," noticing how he uses slang and specific details to give you a sense of the boy's feelings. Try to remember exactly what it was that made your own experience so frightening, and write the story of your encounter, using whatever words and details will give most impact in the telling.

ABOUT THE AUTHOR

Henry Ernest Bates (1905–1974) has long been regarded as one of England's outstanding short-story writers. Born in Rushden, a town in central England, he began his writing career as a reporter. His first original works were plays and novels, but after reading the short stories of Stephen Crane he became almost exclusively a writer of stories. Few modern anthologies of fiction do not contain one or more of Bates' stories. His books of stories, such as *The Purple Plain* and *The Jacaranda Tree,* are widely popular. Mr. Bates' study, *The Modern Short Story,* is one of the best such works written in recent years.

Description

How does an author go about writing a description? How should a reader go about reading one? Looking at some paragraphs from stories you have read may help you get some answers to these questions.

First of all, in writing a description, writers try to give clear pictures or impressions. They want readers to see with their own eyes, hear with their own ears, and experience with their own senses the scene, character, or object being described. Thus writers include concrete details in their descriptions, such as the chafing of sand between the toes or the salt taste of the sea. But a good description is more than a mass of details. In good descriptions, writers have organized their details so as to give exactly the impressions they intend. Sometimes they will begin by stating in the very first sentence the main impression that they wish to convey. What dominant impression do you get from this paragraph from "The Pacing Goose"?

Spring's a various season, Jess thought, no two years the same: comes in with rains, mud deep enough to swallow horse and rider; comes in cold, snow falling so fast it weaves a web; comes in with a warm wind blowing about thy ears and bringing a smell of something flowering, not here, but southaways, across the Ohio, maybe, in Kentucky. Nothing here now but a smell of melting snow—which is no smell at all, but a kind of prickle in the nose, like a bygone sneeze. Comes in so various, winter put by and always so welcome. (page 36)

1. What impression does this paragraph give you?

2. What phrase in the concluding sentence reinforces the paragraph's dominant impression?

3. What details does the author use to support the dominant impression? Which of these details give visual pictures? Which appeal to the other senses?

In writing a description, good writers try, through their dominant impressions, to give some sense of their own (or a character's) attitudes, or feelings. As you saw, what the paragraph you just read really showed was how Jess felt about the coming of spring. The author carefully prepared you, throughout the paragraph, to accept her final statement that spring is "always so welcome." Often, however, authors will not make such direct statements. Instead of making straightforward statements, they will try to suggest a single strong impression with a variety of vivid details. Without a general statement to make clear the meaning, they will have to take special care in selecting and ordering their details. Can you see the logic behind the order of the details in this paragraph from "A Gray Sleeve"?

At the edge of a grove of maples, across wide fields, there occasionally appeared little puffs of smoke of a dull hue in this gloom of sky which expressed an impending rain. The long wave of blue and steel in the field moved uneasily at the eternal barking of the faraway sharpshooters, and the men, leaning upon their rifles, stared at the grove of maples. Once a private turned to borrow some tobacco from a comrade in the rear rank, but, with his hand still stretched out, he continued to twist his head and glance at the distant trees. He was afraid the enemy would shoot him at a time when he was not looking. (page 82)

1. What would you say is the dominant impression of this paragraph? Can you state it in a single sentence?

2. What logic is behind the arrangement of details in this paragraph? If you were shooting this scene with a movie camera, which details would be distance shots? Which would be closeups?

3. How do the following phrases help to give a clear picture of the scene?

"At the edge of a grove of maples"

"in the field"

4. What do the following details contribute to the paragraph's dominant impression? What do they suggest about the men's attitude and feelings?

"of a dull hue"

"in this gloom of sky"

"moved uneasily"

"leaning upon their rifles"

5. Which senses does the writer arouse in this description? Which details help you to hear, smell, taste, or feel?

PRACTICING YOUR READING

In reading a description, you should always try to grasp the *dominant impression* given by the details used in the author's description. To practice this kind of reading, reread the following paragraphs in the short story unit, writing down a list of the details in each paragraph and a statement of the dominant impressions you receive.

With this in mind, reread the following paragraphs: page 58 ("Mrs. Higgins must . . .") and page 82 ("The yellow folds . . .").

WRITING A DESCRIPTION

In writing a description, you should try to:

1. Look hard at what you are describing to get a definite impression of what you want your reader to feel or see.

2. State or suggest this main impression in your very first sentence.

3. Reinforce or develop this impression with a logical arrangement of details.

Use these steps in writing the following paragraphs of description:

1. Write a paragraph describing some place you have recently seen. State your dominant impression of the place in a topic sentence, then support it with carefully selected details arranged in a logical order such as left to right, up to down, or near to far. Use transitional words or phrases (*on the left, beyond*) to indicate the direction of movement.

2. In a single paragraph, communicate your main impression of a person, place, or thing. Do not state this impression in your paragraph; *suggest* it with the details you select and the order you arrange them in.

SHARPENING YOUR WRITING

Modifiers are words that change (modify) another word by restricting it (making it more exact) in meaning. In "Spring's a various season," *various* is a modifier of *season*. It changes the statement from "spring is a season" to "spring is a particular kind of season." Without the modifier, the statement is rather stale and obvious; with it, it is fresh and interesting. Is this also the effect of the following modifiers?

"snow falling *so fast it weaves a web*"

"with a *warm* wind blowing about thy ears"

Many writers fail to make their modifiers exact enough. As a result, the modified statement is no more specific than the original one, and the extra word or words have added nothing. Go back over the paragraphs you have just written. If any of your modifiers seem weak or worthless, replace them with ones that are more exact and accurate.

ART AND LITERATURE

1. Describe one of the paintings on pages 51–56 to someone who has never seen it. State the dominant impression of the painting in a topic sentence; then support it with a logical, detailed description.

2. Describe one of the paintings on pages 51–56 as you might to a blind person, using only details that appeal to the senses of touch, hearing, taste, and smell. Try to suggest the painting's visual impression, using only non-visual details.

PART 2 *The Storyteller and the Story*

As you have seen in reading stories, every author uses the elements of storytelling—plot, conflict, characterization, theme—to create a total effect that is unique, that is unlike that of any other story. In addition to these elements, which are basic to most stories, is another very crucial element—that of the personality of the storyteller.

In this unit you will have an opportunity to read three outstanding stories by three outstanding American writers, each with his own attitudes and his own personal voice and style. Two of these writers lived in the nineteenth century; the other is contemporary with our time. All of them, however, could be called modern, for all are concerned with the inner problems, the personal conflicts and realizations that seem so important to us today.

The life of Edgar Allan Poe was almost as exciting and mysterious as his writings. Left an orphan at the age of two, he lived much of his life in a kind of wandering existence, without any real roots. The most famous of his stories are tales of horror, one of the most remarkable of which is "The Tell-Tale Heart" (page 108). The plot of this brief and chilling tale is simple, but the narrator's character and motivations are explored in depth through his own utterances. This story is an excellent example of Poe's theory that from the very first word a story should build up to a single overpowering effect. No word is wasted in "The Tell-Tale Heart."

Nathaniel Hawthorne, in many ways the opposite of Poe, lived a quiet life in cities and small towns, reading, writing, and walking through the streets and fields of New England. Like his life, his stories were introspective. Hawthorne searched within his characters and situations for essential meaning. The plot of "The Ambitious Guest" (page 114) unfolds slowly. This story is rich in character description, but its ending is constantly foreshadowed by extremely subtle means. The theme of the story, embodied in its characters and outcome, is a complex and many-sided thing.

John Steinbeck grew up on a ranch in California, where he learned to love animals and the land. All his writings show great sympathy with "ordinary" characters, with "ordinary" joys and disappointments. The theme of "The Gift" (page 130), though left unstated, has to do with faith and loss and the painfulness of growing up.

EDGAR ALLAN POE
(1809–1849)

In 1809 Edgar Allan Poe was born in Boston to a theatrical couple, but following the death of his mother two years later he became the ward of Mr. and Mrs. John Allan of Richmond, Virginia. The Allans gave the boy an extensive education in schools in Richmond and in England, where they lived for five years. He was especially brilliant in languages, and attended the University of Virginia with a good record. He fell deeply into debt, however, and when his foster father refused him more money, Poe, at the age of eighteen, enlisted in the army. After two years he entered West Point. But Poe soon became restless under military discipline and deliberately provoked a court-martial on charges of absence.

From the time of his leaving West Point, Poe's career was one of artistic success and personal sadness. His efforts as an editor on several magazines all failed. When his young wife died of tuberculosis at twenty-five, he was shattered by his loss. For the rest of his life he drifted in and out of literary circles, suffering from poverty almost constantly.

Despite the failures in his personal life, Poe succeeded as a poet, a short-story writer, and a critic. His hauntingly musical poetry suggests his longing for a pure life of the spirit. He was keenly aware that he stood apart from others. Melancholy and sadness are evident in nearly all of Poe's most famous poems, such as "The Bells," "The Raven," and "Annabel Lee."

Poe's short stories are even more widely known than his poetry. In fact, he has been called "the father of the modern short story"—not only because of the excellence of such stories as "The Fall of the House of Usher" and "The Cask of Amontillado," but also because of his original theories on how to write a story. Poe believed that a short story, like a poem, should create a single powerful impression and be short enough to be read in one sitting. The purpose of writing a story, he felt, was to create a mood. In his story the author should include no word or incident that does not support that pre-established mood. Pauses during reading, he believed, destroy the mood of a story and release the reader from the writer's control.

Poe's short stories are more varied than this theory might indicate. Some are poetic attempts to create an impression of sheer beauty; others are detective stories; still others are adventure stories. Although no one type of story is more typical of Poe than another, the type that best illustrates his theory of the short story are his tales of horror, such as "The Tell-Tale Heart".

The Tell-Tale Heart

TRUE!—nervous—very, very dreadfully nervous I had been and am; but why will you say that I am mad? The disease had sharpened my senses—not destroyed—not dulled them. Above all was the sense of hearing acute. I heard all things in the heaven and in the earth. I heard many things in hell. How, then, am I mad? Harken! and observe how healthily—how calmly I can tell you the whole story.

It is impossible to say how first the idea entered my brain; but once conceived, it haunted me day and night. Object there was none. Passion, there was none. I loved the old man. He had never wronged me. He had never given me insult. For his gold I had no desire. I think it was his eye! Yes, it was this! One of his eyes resembled that of a vulture—a pale blue eye, with a film over it. Whenever it fell upon me, my blood ran cold; and so by degrees—very gradually—I made up my mind to take the life of the old man and thus rid myself of the eye forever.

Now this is the point. You fancy me mad. Madmen know nothing. But you should have seen me. You should have seen how wisely I proceeded—with what caution—with what foresight—with what dissimulation I went to work! I was never kinder to the old man than during the whole week before I killed him. And every night, about midnight, I turned the latch of his door and opened it—oh, so gently! And then, when I had made an opening sufficient for my head, I put in a dark lantern, all closed, closed, so that no light shone out, and then I thrust in my head. Oh, you would have laughed to see how cunningly I thrust it in! I moved it slowly—very, very slowly, so that I might not disturb the old man's sleep. It took me an hour to place my whole head within the opening so far that I could see him as he lay upon his bed. Ha!—would a madman have been so wise as this? And then, when my head was well in the room, I undid the lantern cautiously—oh, so cautiously—cautiously (for the hinges creaked)—I undid it just so much that a single thin ray fell upon the vulture eye. And this I did for seven long nights—every night just at midnight—but I found the eye always closed; and so it was impossible to do the work; for it was not the old man who vexed me, but his Evil Eye. And every morning, when the day broke, I went boldly into the chamber and spoke courageously to him, calling him by name in a hearty tone, and inquiring how he had passed the night. So you see he would have been a very profound old man, indeed, to suspect that every night, just at twelve, I looked in upon him while he slept.

Upon the eighth night I was more than usually cautious in opening the door. A watch's minute hand moves more quickly than did mine. Never before that night had I felt the extent of my own powers—of my sagacity. I could scarcely contain my feelings of triumph. To think that there I was, opening the door, little by little, and he not even to dream of my secret deeds or thoughts. I fairly chuckled at the idea; and perhaps he heard me; for he moved on the bed suddenly, as if startled. Now you may think that I drew back—but no. His room was as black as pitch with the thick darkness (for the shutters were close-fastened, through fear of robbers), and so I knew that he could not see the opening of the door, and I kept pushing it on steadily, steadily.

I had my head in and was about to open the lantern, when my thumb slipped upon the tin fastening, and the old man sprang up in the bed, crying out—"Who's there?"

I kept quite still and said nothing. For a whole hour I did not move a muscle, and in the meantime I did not hear him lie down. He was still sitting up in the bed listening—just as I had done, night after night, harkening to the deathwatches[1] in the wall.

Presently I heard a slight groan, and I knew it was the groan of mortal terror. It was not a groan of pain or of grief—oh, no!—it was the low stifled sound that arises from the bottom of the soul when overcharged with awe. I knew the sound well. Many a night, just at midnight, when all the world slept, it has welled up from my own bosom, deepening, with its dreadful echo, the terrors that distracted me. I say I knew it well. I knew what the old man felt, and pitied him, although I chuckled at heart. I knew that he had been lying awake ever since the first slight noise, when he had turned in the bed. His fears had been ever since growing upon him. He had been trying to fancy them causeless, but could not. He had been saying to himself—"It is nothing but the wind in the chimney—it is only a mouse crossing the floor," or "It is merely a cricket which has made a single chirp." Yes, he had been trying to comfort himself with these suppositions; but he had found all in vain. All in vain; because Death, in approaching him, had stalked with his black shadow before him and enveloped the victim. And it was the mournful influence of the unperceived shadow that caused him to feel—although he neither saw nor heard—to feel the presence of my head within the room.

When I had waited a long time, very patiently, without hearing him lie down, I resolved to open a little—a very, very little crevice in the lantern. So I opened it—you cannot imagine how stealthily, stealthily—until, at length, a single dim ray, like the thread of the spider, shot from out the crevice and fell full upon the vulture eye.

It was open—wide, wide open—and I grew furious as I gazed upon it. I saw it with perfect distinctness—all a dull blue, with a hideous veil over it that chilled the very marrow in my bones; but I could see nothing else of the old man's face or person: for I had directed the ray as if by instinct, precisely upon the damned spot.

And now have I not told you that what you mistake for madness is but overacuteness of the senses?—now, I say, there came to my ears a low, dull, quick sound, such as a watch makes when enveloped in cotton. I knew that sound well, too. It was the beating of the old man's heart. It increased my fury, as the beating of a drum stimulates the soldier into courage.

But even yet I refrained and kept still. I scarcely breathed. I held the lantern motionless. I tried how steadily I could maintain the ray upon the eye. Meantime the hellish tattoo of the heart increased. It grew quicker and quicker and louder and louder every instant. The old man's terror must have been extreme! It grew louder, I say, louder every moment!—do you mark me well? I have told you that I am nervous: so I am. And now at the dead hour of the night, amid the dreadful silence of that old house, so strange a noise as this excited me to uncontrollable terror. Yet for some minutes longer I refrained and stood still. But the beating grew louder, louder! I thought the heart

[1] **deathwatches:** small insects which make a ticking sound believed by superstitious persons to be a forewarning of death.

must burst. And now a new anxiety seized me—the sound would be heard by a neighbor! The old man's hour had come! With a loud yell, I threw open the lantern and leaped into the room. He shrieked once —once only. In an instant I dragged him to the floor and pulled the heavy bed over him. I then smiled gaily, to find the deed so far done. But, for many minutes the heart beat on with a muffled sound. This, however, did not vex me; it would not be heard through the wall. At length it ceased. The old man was dead. I removed the bed and examined the corpse. Yes, he was stone, stone-dead. I placed my hand upon the heart and held it there many minutes. There was no pulsation. He was stone-dead. His eye would trouble me no more.

If still you think me mad, you will think so no longer when I describe the wise precautions I took for the concealment of the body. The night waned, and I worked hastily but in silence. First of all I dismembered the corpse. I cut off the head and the arms and the legs.

I then took up three planks from the flooring of the chamber, and deposited all between the scantlings.[1] I then replaced the boards so cleverly, so cunningly, that no human eye—not even his —could have detected anything wrong. There was nothing to wash out—no stain of any kind—no blood spot whatever. I had been too wary for that. A tub had caught all--ha! ha!

When I had made an end of these labors, it was four o'clock—still dark as midnight. As the bell sounded the hour, there came a knocking at the street door. I went down to open it with a light heart—for what had I now to fear? There entered three men, who introduced themselves, with perfect suavity, as officers of the police. A shriek had been heard by a neighbor during the

[1] **scantlings:** crosspieces.

night; suspicion of foul play had been aroused; information had been lodged at the police office, and they (the officers) had been deputed to search the premises.

I smiled—for what had I to fear? I bade the gentlemen welcome. The shriek, I said, was my own in a dream. The old man, I mentioned, was absent in the country. I took my visitors all over the house. I bade them search—search well. I led them, at length, to his chamber. I showed them his treasures, secure, undisturbed. In the enthusiasm of my confidence, I brought chairs into the room, and desired them here to rest from their fatigues, while I myself, in the wild audacity of my perfect triumph, placed my own seat upon the very spot beneath which reposed the corpse of the victim.

The officers were satisfied. My manner had convinced them. I was singularly at ease. They sat, and while I answered cheerily, they chatted familiar things. But, ere long, I felt myself getting pale and wished them gone. My head ached, and I fancied a ringing in my ears: but still they sat and still chatted. The ringing became more distinct; it continued and became more distinct. I talked more freely to get rid of the feeling, but it continued and gained definitiveness—until, at length, I found that the noise was not within my ears.

No doubt I now grew very pale; but I talked more fluently, and with a heightened voice. Yet the sound increased—and what could I do? It was a low, dull, quick sound—much such a sound as a watch makes when enveloped in cotton. I gasped for breath—and yet the officers heard it not. I talked more quickly—more vehemently; but the noise steadily increased. I arose and argued about trifles, in a high key and with violent gesticulations, but the noise steadily increased. Why would they not be gone? I paced the floor to and

fro with heavy strides, as if excited to fury by the observation of the men—but the noise steadily increased. Oh, God! What could I do? I foamed—I raved—I swore! I swung the chair upon which I had been sitting, and grated it upon the boards, but the noise arose over all and continually increased. It grew louder—louder—louder! And still the men chatted pleasantly and smiled. Was it possible they heard not? Almighty God!—no, no! They heard!—they suspected!—they knew!—they were making a mockery of my horror!—this I thought, and this I think. But anything was better than this agony! Anything was more tolerable than this derision! I could bear those hypocritical smiles no longer! I felt that I must scream or die!—and now—again!—hark! louder! louder! louder! louder!

"Villains!" I shrieked. "Dissemble no more! I admit the deed!—tear up the planks! here, here!—it is the beating of his hideous heart!"

FOR STUDY AND DISCUSSION

1. Do you think the narrator is just nervous, as he claims, or truly mad? What makes you think so? If you think he is mad, how do you explain the clear, logical way in which he tells the story?

2. Although this story is told in the first person, it succeeds in conveying to the reader just how the narrator's victim felt before the murder. How is this accomplished?

3. What single effect or predominant emotion do you think Poe aims to create in "The Tell-Tale Heart"? What means does he use to create it? Show how the single emotional effect is built up to the climax that occurs in the last two paragraphs.

4. A famous modern poet and critic, W. H. Auden, has said of Poe's stories, "They have one negative characteristic in common. There is no place in any of them for the human individual as he actually exists." In other words, Poe's characters, such as the narrator of "The

Tell-Tale Heart," do not seem real. Do you agree? Why or why not? If the narrator is not convincingly real, does that make the story less effective as a story? Why or why not?

LANGUAGE AND VOCABULARY

1. Effective writing consists not only of selecting the right word but also of selecting the right sequence of words or expressions to create an effect, a mood, or a feeling. In the first part of "The Tell-Tale Heart," Poe selects words that show the effect of the old man's eye on the narrator. He calls it ". . . the eye of a vulture—a pale blue eye, with a film over it." The effect of these words is to turn the speaker's blood cold. What other words or expressions add to this impression of the old man's eye? Which words or expressions in this sequence are especially effective in conveying the narrator's feeling about the eye?

2. Poe's readers were perhaps more familiar with words derived from Latin than present-day readers are. Poe took for granted that his readers would understand the basic meaning of such words as *dissimulation, sagacity, dismembered, suavity, audacity, gesticulations, derision*. Look up the original meaning of each of these words. For which of these words does the original meaning add most to your understanding of the story?

FOR COMPOSITION

Edgar Allan Poe believed that a short story should achieve a single, overpowering effect. "The Tell-Tale Heart" is one of the best examples of this belief. From the very first word of the story, every word, every detail, every mark of punctuation contributes to an overpowering impression that the narrator is mad. Reread the first few paragraphs of the story. Which words and details do the most to give this impression? Look closely at the description of the old man's eye. How does Poe suggest its eerie appearance in the narrator's mind? With these paragraphs fresh in your mind, write your own description of how a person might appear to someone who was overwrought, nervous, hysterical, or mad.

NATHANIEL HAWTHORNE

(1804–1864)

Nathaniel Hawthorne, one of America's finest writers, was born on the fourth of July in the year Lewis and Clark began their western expedition. Salem, his native town, was an active Massachusetts seaport peopled by merchants, ship-builders, sea captains, and sailors. His father, the master of a Yankee clipper, met his death on a voyage when Hawthorne was five.

From boyhood Hawthorne wanted to become a writer. Once he had learned to read, he began to lose himself in books. As he grew older, he became fascinated with the past of his native New England, especially with the history of his ances-tors. Stories of the Salem witchcraft trials both attracted and appalled him.

On graduating from Bowdoin College (in the same class with another famous writer, Henry Wadsworth Longfellow, and a future President, Franklin Pierce), he returned to his mother's house in Salem, where for twelve years he studied, wrote, and rewrote. He rarely came out of his "owl's nest," as he called his Salem home, except to take long walks in the evening, to swim in summer, and to take occasional walking tours through the New England countryside. Despite his hard work, fame came slowly. His tales and sketches appeared here and there in gift books and magazines, but were little noticed. Then in 1837 a friend secretly financed the pub-lication of *Twice-Told Tales,* a collection of Hawthorne's stories.

In 1842 Hawthorne married, and he lived for the next four years in a large old house in Concord, Massachusetts. During these years Hawthorne completed his second book of tales and sketches, *Mosses from an Old Manse.* By 1846, however, his growing family forced him to become a surveyor in the customs house in Salem. While holding this post, he wrote the novel *The Scarlet Letter,* his masterpiece.

In 1853 Hawthorne's college friend Franklin Pierce became President and ap-pointed Hawthorne a United States consul in England. When he returned home from Europe in 1860, Hawthorne was an ill man. He began several novels but lacked the strength to complete them. In May 1864 he died quietly in his sleep.

As a writer, Hawthorne cared chiefly for the truth of the human heart. Physical objects and traits of character were important only when they represented some inner reality. Most of the details in Hawthorne's stories have an extra symbolic significance. For example, in "The Ambitious Guest," which follows, the young traveler's yearning for a monument signifies his desire for fame. In all his works Hawthorne made his chief concern not the outer appearances of things but their essential or inner truth.

The Ambitious Guest

ONE September night a family had gathered round their hearth and piled it high with the driftwood of mountain streams, the dry cones of the pine, and the splintered ruins of great trees that had come crashing down the precipice. Up the chimney roared the fire and brightened the room with its broad blaze. The faces of the father and mother had a sober gladness; the children laughed; the eldest daughter was the image of happiness at seventeen; and the aged grandmother, who sat knitting in the warmest place, was the image of happiness grown old. They had found the "herb, heart's-ease," in the bleakest spot of all New England. This family was situated in the Notch of the White Hills,[1] where the wind was sharp throughout the year and pitilessly cold in the winter, giving their cottage all its fresh inclemency before it descended on the valley of the Saco. They dwelt in a cold spot and a dangerous one; for a mountain towered above their heads, so steep that the stones would often rumble down its sides and startle them at midnight.

The daughter had just uttered some simple jest that filled them all with mirth, when the wind came through the Notch and seemed to pause before their cottage —rattling the door, with a sound of wail-

[1] **White Hills:** the White Mountains, in northern New Hampshire.

ing and lamentation, before it passed into the valley. For a moment it saddened them, though there was nothing unusual in the tones. But the family were glad again when they perceived that the latch was lifted by some traveler, whose footsteps had been unheard amid the dreary blast which heralded his approach, and wailed as he was entering, and went moaning away from the door.

Though they dwelt in such a solitude, these people held daily converse with the world. The romantic pass of the Notch is a great artery, through which the life-blood of internal commerce is continually throbbing between Maine, on one side, and the Green Mountains and the shores of the St. Lawrence, on the other. The stagecoach always drew up before the door of the cottage. The wayfarer, with no companion but his staff, paused here to exchange a word, that the sense of loneliness might not utterly overcome him ere he could pass through the cleft of the mountain or reach the first house in the valley. And here the teamster, on his way to Portland market, would put up for the night; and, if a bachelor, might sit an hour beyond the usual bedtime and steal a kiss from the mountain maid at parting. It was one of those primitive taverns where the traveler pays only for food and lodging but meets with a homely kindness beyond all price. When the footsteps were heard, therefore, between the outer door and the inner one, the whole family rose up, grandmother, children, and all, as if about to welcome someone who belonged to them, and whose fate was linked with theirs.

The door was opened by a young man. His face at first wore the melancholy expression, almost despondency, of one who travels a wild and bleak road, at nightfall and alone, but soon brightened up when he saw the kindly warmth of his reception.

He felt his heart spring forward to meet them all, from the old woman, who wiped a chair with her apron, to the little child that held out its arms to him. One glance and smile placed the stranger on a footing of innocent familiarity with the eldest daughter.

"Ah, this fire is the right thing!" cried he; "especially when there is such a pleasant circle round it. I am quite benumbed; for the Notch is just like the pipe of a great pair of bellows; it has blown a terrible blast in my face all the way from Bartlett."

"Then you are going toward Vermont?" said the master of the house, as he helped to take a light knapsack off the young man's shoulders.

"Yes; to Burlington, and far enough beyond," replied he. "I meant to have been at Ethan Crawford's tonight, but a pedestrian lingers along such a road as this. It is no matter; for, when I saw this good fire, and all your cheerful faces, I felt as if you had kindled it on purpose for me and were waiting my arrival. So I shall sit down among you and make myself at home."

The frank-hearted stranger had just drawn his chair to the fire when something like a heavy footstep was heard without rushing down the steep side of the mountain, as with long and rapid strides, and taking such a leap in passing the cottage as to strike the opposite precipice. The family held their breath, because they knew the sound, and their guest held his by instinct.

"The old mountain has thrown a stone at us, for fear we should forget him," said the landlord, recovering himself. "He sometimes nods his head and threatens to come down; but we are old neighbors and agree together pretty well upon the whole. Besides, we have a sure place of refuge hard by if he should be coming in good earnest."

Let us now suppose the stranger to have finished his supper of bear's meat, and, by his natural felicity of manner, to have placed himself on a footing of kindness with the whole family, so that they talked as freely together as if he belonged to their mountain brood. He was of a proud, yet gentle spirit—haughty and reserved among the rich and great; but ever ready to stoop his head to the lowly cottage door and be like a brother or a son at the poor man's fireside. In the household of the Notch he found warmth and simplicity of feeling, the pervading intelligence of New England, and a poetry of native growth, which they had gathered when they little thought of it from the mountain peaks and chasms and at the very threshold of their romantic and dangerous abode. He had traveled far and alone; his whole life, indeed, had been a solitary path; for, with the lofty caution of his nature, he had kept himself apart from those who might otherwise have been his companions. The family, too, though so kind and hospitable, had that consciousness of unity among themselves, and separation from the world at large, which, in every domestic circle, should still keep a holy place where no stranger may intrude. But this evening a prophetic sympathy impelled the refined and educated youth to pour out his heart before the simple mountaineers and constrained them to answer him with the same free confidence. And thus it should have been. Is not the kindred of a common fate a closer tie than that of birth?

The secret of the young man's character was a high and abstracted ambition. He could have borne to live an undistinguished life but not to be forgotten in the grave. Yearning desire had been transformed to hope; and hope, long cherished, had become like certainty, that, obscurely as he journeyed now, a glory was to beam

confess that a gifted one had passed from his cradle to his tomb with none to recognize him.

"As yet," cried the stranger—his cheek glowing and his eye flashing with enthusiasm—"as yet, I have done nothing. Were I to vanish from the earth tomorrow, none would know so much of me as you: that a nameless youth came up at nightfall from the valley of the Saco, and opened his heart to you in the evening, and passed through the Notch by sunrise, and was seen no more. Not a soul would ask, 'Who was he? Whither did the wanderer go?' But I cannot die till I have achieved my destiny. Then, let Death come! I shall have built my monument!"

There was a continual flow of natural emotion, gushing forth amid abstracted reverie, which enabled the family to understand this young man's sentiments, though so foreign from their own. With quick sensibility of the ludicrous, he blushed at the ardor into which he had been betrayed.

"You laugh at me," said he, taking the eldest daughter's hand, and laughing himself. "You think my ambition as nonsensical as if I were to freeze myself to death on the top of Mount Washington, only that people might spy at me from the country round about. And, truly, that would be a noble pedestal for a man's statue!"

"It is better to sit here by this fire," answered the girl, blushing, "and be comfortable and contented, though nobody thinks about us."

"I suppose," said her father, after a fit of musing, "there is something natural in what the young man says, and if my mind had been turned that way, I might have felt just the same. It is strange, wife, how his talk has set my head running on things that are pretty certain never to come to pass."

on all his pathway—though not, perhaps, while he was treading it. But when posterity should gaze back into the gloom of what was now the present, they would trace the brightness of his footsteps, brightening as meaner glories faded, and

"Perhaps they may," observed the wife. "Is the man thinking what he will do when he is a widower?"

"No, no!" cried he, repelling the idea with reproachful kindness. "When I think of your death, Esther, I think of mine, too. But I was wishing we had a good farm in Bartlett, or Bethlehem, or Littleton, or some other township round the White Mountains; but not where they could tumble on our heads. I should want to stand well with my neighbors and be called Squire, and sent to General Court for a term or two; for a plain, honest man may do as much good there as a lawyer. And when I should be grown quite an old man, and you an old woman, so as not to be long apart, I might die happy enough in my bed, and leave you all crying around me. A slate gravestone would suit me as well as a marble one—with just my name and age, and a verse of a hymn, and something to let people know that I lived an honest man and died a Christian."

"There now!" exclaimed the stranger; "it is our nature to desire a monument, be it slate, or marble, or a pillar of granite, or a glorious memory in the universal heart of man."

"We're in a strange way, tonight," said the wife, with tears in her eyes. "They say it's a sign of something, when folks' minds go a-wandering so. Hark to the children!"

They listened accordingly. The younger children had been put to bed in another room but with an open door between, so that they could be heard talking busily among themselves. One and all seemed to have caught the infection from the fireside circle, and were outvying each other in wild wishes and childish projects of what they would do when they came to be men and women. At length a little boy, instead of addressing his brothers and sisters, called out to his mother.

"I'll tell you what I wish, mother," cried he. "I want you and father and grandma'm, and all of us, and the stranger too, to start right away, and go and take a drink out of the basin of the Flume!"

Nobody could help laughing at the child's notion of leaving a warm bed and dragging them from a cheerful fire to visit the basin of the Flume, a brook which tumbles over the precipice deep within the Notch. The boy had hardly spoken when a wagon rattled along the road and stopped a moment before the door. It appeared to contain two or three men, who were cheering their hearts with the rough chorus of a song, which resounded in broken notes between the cliffs, while the singers hesitated whether to continue their journey or put up here for the night.

"Father," said the girl, "they are calling you by name."

But the good man doubted whether they had really called him and was unwilling to show himself too solicitous of gain by inviting people to patronize his house. He therefore did not hurry to the door; and the lash being soon applied, the travelers plunged into the Notch, still singing and laughing, though their music and mirth came back drearily from the heart of the mountain.

"There, mother!" cried the boy again. "They'd have given us a ride to the Flume."

Again they laughed at the child's pertinacious fancy for a night ramble. But it happened that a light cloud passed over the daughter's spirit; she looked gravely into the fire and drew a breath that was almost a sigh. It forced its way in spite of a little struggle to repress it. Then starting and blushing, she looked quickly round the circle as if they had caught a glimpse into her bosom. The stranger asked what she had been thinking of.

"Nothing," answered she, with a downcast smile. "Only I felt lonesome just then."

"Oh, I have always had a gift of feeling what is in other people's hearts," said he, half seriously. "Shall I tell the secrets of yours? For I know what to think when a young girl shivers by a warm hearth and complains of lonesomeness at her mother's side. Shall I put these feelings into words?"

"They would not be a girl's feelings any longer if they could be put into words," replied the mountain nymph, laughing, but avoiding his eye.

All this was said apart. Perhaps a germ of love was springing in their hearts, so pure that it might blossom in paradise, since it could not be matured on earth; for women worship such gentle dignity as his; and the proud, contemplative, yet kindly soul is oftenest captivated by simplicity like hers. But while they spoke softly and he was watching the happy sadness, the lightsome shadows, the shy yearnings of a maiden's nature, the wind through the Notch took a deeper and drearier sound. It seemed, as the fanciful stranger said, like the choral strain of the spirits of the blast, who in old Indian times had their dwelling among these mountains and made their heights and recesses a sacred region. There was a wail along the road, as if a funeral were passing. To chase away the gloom, the family threw pine branches on their fire till the dry leaves crackled and the flame arose, discovering once again a scene of peace and humble happiness. The light hovered about them fondly and caressed them all. There were the little faces of the children, peeping from their bed apart, and here the father's frame of strength, the mother's subdued and careful mien, the high-browed youth, the budding girl, and the good old grandam, still knitting in the warmest place. The aged woman looked

up from her task, and, with fingers ever busy, was the next to speak.

"Old folks have their notions," said she, "as well as young ones. You've been wishing and planning and letting your heads run on one thing and another, till you've set my mind a-wandering too. Now what should an old woman wish for, when she can go but a step or two before she comes to her grave? Children, it will haunt me night and day till I tell you."

"What is it, mother?" cried the husband and wife at once.

Then the old woman, with an air of mystery which drew the circle closer round the fire, informed them that she had provided her grave-clothes some years before—a nice linen shroud, a cap with a muslin ruff, and everything of a finer sort than she had worn since her wedding day. But this evening an old superstition had strangely recurred to her. It used to be said, in her younger days, that if anything were amiss with a corpse, if only the ruff were not smooth, or the cap did not set right, the corpse in the coffin and beneath the clods would strive to put up its cold hands and arrange it. The bare thought made her nervous.

"Don't talk so, grandmother!" said the girl, shuddering.

"Now," continued the old woman, with singular earnestness, yet smiling strangely at her own folly, "I want one of you, my

children—when your mother is dressed
and in the coffin—I want one of you to
hold a looking-glass over my face. Who
knows but I may take a glimpse at myself
and see whether all's right?"

"Old and young, we dream of graves
and monuments," murmured the stranger
youth. "I wonder how mariners feel when
the ship is sinking, and they, unknown
and undistinguished, are to be buried together in the ocean—that wide and nameless sepulcher?"

For a moment, the old woman's ghastly
conception so engrossed the minds of
her hearers that a sound abroad in the
night, riding like the roar of a blast, had
grown broad, deep, and terrible, before
the fated group were conscious of it. The
house and all within it trembled; the foundations of the earth seemed to be shaken,
as if this awful sound were the peal of the
last trump.[1] Young and old exchanged
one wild glance and remained an instant,

[1] **the last trump:** the trumpet whose sound is
supposed to announce the end of the world.

pale, affrighted, without utterance or
power to move. Then the same shriek
burst simultaneously from all their lips.

"The slide! The slide!"

The simplest words must intimate but
not portray the unutterable horror of the
catastrophe. The victims rushed from
their cottage and sought refuge in what
they deemed a safer spot—where, in contemplation of such an emergency, a sort
of barrier had been reared. Alas! they had
quitted their security and fled right into
the pathway of destruction. Down came
the whole side of the mountain in a cataract of ruin. Just before it reached the

house, the stream broke into two branches —shivered not a window there, but overwhelmed the whole vicinity, blocked up the road, and annihilated everything in its dreadful course. Long ere the thunder of the great slide had ceased to roar among the mountains, the mortal agony had been endured, and the victims were at peace. Their bodies were never found.

The next morning, the light smoke was seen stealing from the cottage chimney up the mountainside. Within, the fire was yet smoldering on the hearth, and the chairs in a circle round it, as if the inhabitants had but gone forth to view the devastation of the slide and would shortly return to thank heaven for their miraculous escape. All had left separate tokens, by which those who had known the family were made to shed a tear for each. Who has not heard their name? The story has been told far and wide and will forever be a legend of these mountains. Poets have sung their fate.

There were circumstances which led some to suppose that a stranger had been received into the cottage on this awful night and had shared the catastrophe of all its inmates. Others denied that there were sufficient grounds for such a conjecture. Woe for the high-souled youth, with his dream of earthly immortality! His name and person utterly unknown; his history, his way of life, his plans, a mystery never to be solved; his death and his existence equally a doubt! Whose was the agony of that death moment?

FOR STUDY AND DISCUSSION

1. In the first paragraphs of the story, Hawthorne carefully develops his setting. What impression of the family's life does he convey? How is this shown in their attitude toward the stranger? In what sense have they found the "herb, heart's-ease"?

2. As the daughter utters a "simple jest,"

the wind passes "with a sound of wailing and lamentation." How does this occurrence prepare you for the ending of the story? What other "signs" throughout the story foreshadow the ending?

3. Early in the story, Hawthorne refers to the *romantic* pass and later to the family's *romantic* and dangerous abode. What is the meaning of *romantic* on these occasions? Is there any connection between a place being romantic and being dangerous? What is your idea of a romantic—as opposed to a realistic—story?

4. In several previous stories, you have already encountered irony of fate and circumstance. In this story, Hawthorne uses irony in referring to both the ambitious guest and to his contented hosts. In view of the fate in store for all these characters, what is ironic about the attitude of each? How does irony add to the pathos or tragic emotion of the story?

LANGUAGE AND VOCABULARY

Look up the italicized words in the phrases below and tell what each expression means in the context of the story. What expression with about the same meaning could be substituted for each one of these?

the guest's natural "*felicity* of manner . . ."

the close tie between "*kindred* of a common fate . . ."

the stranger's "quick *sensibility* of the *ludicrous* . . ."

"the child's *pertinacious* fancy . . ."

the guest's "*contemplative,* yet kindly soul . . ."

"the unutterable horror of the *catastrophe* . . ."

FOR COMPOSITION

Hawthorne characterizes his setting as "the bleakest spot of all New England." Study his description, paying special attention to the details he chooses to give this impression, then write a description of your own about the bleakest spot you have ever seen. If you like, include people in your scene.

ELEMENTS OF ART

Paintings in Watercolor

Watercolor paints can be used in many different ways. When artists apply them with fine, pointed brushes, they can render the most delicate details, as we saw in Dürer's watercolor drawing of a young hare (page 52). With larger brushes, however, they can apply the paints more boldly, in broad "washes" of color. If they thin the washes out with water, the whiteness of the paper will show through, making the colors appear luminous. Certain types of watercolor washes look wet even after they have dried, which often gives them a special beauty of their own.

One of the masters of watercolor was a nineteenth-century American painter named Winslow Homer. From long experience he had learned to control wet, running washes of color with incredible skill. For example, look how he has represented the sky in his picture called *Palm Tree, Nassau* (PLATE 1). Within an almost continuous wash, he gradually changed the tone of this gray sky from a cool, light gray at the top to a warmer and darker gray down near the horizon. He did this to create an effect of movement across the sky. But he also needed a darker background in the lower part of the sky to set off the white silhouette of the lighthouse. This tiny white shape is very important to the picture's whole design, for it helps to counterbalance the off-center position of the great palm tree. To balance the towering height of the tree, Homer has grouped all his brightest colors near the bottom of the picture.

John Singer Sargent's painting called *Simplon Pass: The Lesson* (PLATE 2) shows quite a different watercolor style. Sargent seems to have been less interested in the fluidity of his color washes than in the crisp edges he could create with them. Look, for instance, how sharply he has silhouetted the blue shadow which runs along the sleeve of the girl at the right. Sargent began this watercolor with the very lightest tints, such as the yellow in the background behind the face of the girl at the left. Then, either while these tints were still damp, or after some of them had dried—depending on the effects he wanted—Sargent added other layers of color, saving the darkest of all until last.

PLATE 3 shows an exciting night scene which the great English artist J. M. W. Turner viewed from his hotel roof in Venice: the sudden flashing of rockets through the sky illuminating the huge domed silhouette of Santa Maria della Salute in the distance. Turner's composition is almost as explosive as the fireworks themselves. The dome of the church, for instance, leans slightly to the right, as if pulling away from the curving path of the rocket. Yet these dynamic forms are anchored at the same time by the quiet horizontal shape of the gondola below.

The kind of paint Turner used here is known as *gouache*—watercolor mixed with an opaque white pigment to give it more "body" and to make it less transparent. Notice that Turner has painted his picture on a brownish paper, which he has allowed to show through in certain places as part of the overall color scheme. For his lightest accents, Turner used strokes of white chalk.

The watercolors in PLATES 4 and 5 were painted by two twentieth-century American artists, John Marin and Edward Hopper. In PLATE 4 you can see how dramatically Marin expressed the hustle and bustle of modern city life. He painted the figures of people and cars with quick strokes of his brush, barely suggesting them, as if their shapes had been shattered by the white sunlight. The light reaches a terrific climax toward the top of the skyscraper, where the building seems almost to burst from the paper, leaving patches of blue sky behind it.

Hopper's watercolor (PLATE 5) also captures impressions of outdoor light. But Hopper painted slowly and deliberately, rather than on impulse. Although there is nothing fussy about the way he has laid down his broad washes of color, he seems to have planned his composition well in advance. As you can see, the design is weighted heavily on the left by the dark tones of the old barn. But it is balanced by the diagonal blue shadows which seem to move toward the right. Hopper has concentrated the warmest and richest colors along the bottom of the picture, contrasting them with the cooler blue of the shadows.

Our last picture, PLATE 6, is a masterly demonstration of the "wet" watercolor technique. Emil Nolde painted this dramatic seascape with extraordinary skill, manipulating virtual puddles of floating pigment until they settled into the exact formations he wanted. If you examine Nolde's picture carefully, you will see how much he has varied the edges of his shapes. Ranging them from crisp to blurry, he has suggested the surging motion of waves and the thick, massive forms of dark storm clouds.

PLATE 1. WINSLOW HOMER (American, 1836–1910): *Palm Tree, Nassau.* 1898. Watercolor, 23⅜ x 15 inches. (The Metropolitan Museum of Art, New York, Lazarus Fund, 1910)

PLATE 2. JOHN SINGER SARGENT (American, 1856–1925): *Simplon Pass: The Lesson.* 1911. Watercolor, 15 x 18$\frac{1}{4}$ inches. (Courtesy, Museum of Fine Arts, Boston, Hayden Collection)

PLATE 3. JOSEPH MALLORD WILLIAM TURNER (English, 1775–1851): *Santa Maria della Salute, Venice: Night Scene with Rockets*. About 1835. Watercolor (gouache) and chalk on brown paper. $9\frac{1}{2}$ x 12 inches. (The British Museum, London)

PLATE 4. JOHN MARIN (American, 1870–1953): *Municipal Building—New York*. 1912. Watercolor, 18½ x 15¾ inches. (Philadelphia Museum of Art, A. E. Gallatin Collection)

126

PLATE 5. EDWARD HOPPER (American, 1882–1967): *House on Pamet River*. 1934. Water-color, 19¾ x 24⅞ inches. (Collection of the Whitney Museum of American Art, New York)

PLATE 6. EMIL NOLDE (German, 1867–1956): *Auf Hoher See.* 1939. Watercolor, $6\frac{9}{16}$ x 9 inches. (Sprengel Collection, Hanover, Germany)

JOHN STEINBECK

(1902–1968)

When John Steinbeck was born in Salinas, California, in 1902, Salinas was a small town of ranches and farms, populated by pioneers from the central states, fishers from the coast, Mexicans, Indians, and other groups borne by the great river of history to the farthest shore of the frontier. It was the right place for a novelist to be born—full of stories about the Spanish conquest, the Mexican revolution, and the gold-rush days of robbery and violence. The fertile San Fernando Valley, locked in between great mountains, was alternately the scene of droughts and flash floods. Both prosperity and poverty put people to the test. Steinbeck soaked up this background in his youth and later put it to good use in his stories.

Steinbeck grew up in a fairly well-to-do middleclass family. During summer vacation, he worked on farms and, during the school year, he held odd jobs in town. In high school he was particularly interested in science and worked for a year after graduation as an assistant chemist in a laboratory. He then entered Stanford University and for five years attended courses of his own choosing. Every so often he would take time off to work on a ranch or a road crew, in a factory or a laboratory, or on his own as a painter or carpenter. Five years after entering college, he left Stanford without a degree. He had made up his mind to become a writer.

In 1936, in the middle of the Depression, Steinbeck wrote a series of newspaper articles on the farm workers who were streaming into California from the barren Dust Bowl of the Central Plains. He became so interested in their plight that the next year he went to Oklahoma, joined a group of farmers bound for California, and lived with them in worker's camps. In a fury of pity for their hopeless lives, he wrote a vigorous novel of social protest known as *The Grapes of Wrath*.

The Grapes of Wrath captured the American imagination, and Steinbeck was acclaimed for his deep sympathy and uncompromising truthfulness. These same qualities are present in nearly all his writing, especially in his stories and short novels. His most famous short novel is *The Pearl*, a haunting parable of the viciousness aroused in people by money. His most gripping short stories are those in *The Long Valley*, many of which, like "The Gift," which you will read here, are about ranch life and growing up. Here you will see how Steinbeck writes to create great realism, a realism that includes understanding and sympathy for people as they are, without attempting to pass judgment on them or to point out what they should be.

During his long career John Steinbeck received many literary awards, including, in 1962, the Nobel Prize for literature.

The Gift

At daybreak Billy Buck emerged from the bunkhouse and stood for a moment on the porch looking up at the sky. He was a broad, bandy-legged little man with a walrus mustache, with square hands, puffed and muscled on the palms. His eyes were a contemplative, watery gray and the hair which protruded from under his Stetson hat was spiky and weathered. Billy was still stuffing his shirt into his blue jeans as he stood on the porch. He unbuckled his belt and tightened it again. The belt showed, by the worn shiny places opposite each hole, the gradual increase of Billy's middle over a period of years. When he had seen to the weather, Billy cleared each nostril by holding its mate closed with his forefinger and blowing fiercely. Then he walked down to the barn, rubbing his hands together. He curried and brushed two saddle horses in the stalls, talking quietly to them all the time; and he had hardly finished when the iron triangle started ringing at the ranch house. Billy stuck the brush and currycomb together and laid them on the rail, and went up to breakfast. His action had been so deliberate and yet so wasteless of time that he came to the house while Mrs. Tiflin was still ringing the triangle. She nodded her gray head to him and withdrew into the kitchen. Billy Buck sat down on the steps, because he was a cowhand and it wouldn't be fitting that he should go first into the dining room.

He heard Mr. Tiflin in the house, stamping his feet into his boots.

The high jangling note of the triangle put the boy Jody in motion. He was only a little boy, ten years old, with hair like dusty yellow grass and with shy polite gray eyes, and with a mouth that worked when he thought. The triangle picked him up out of sleep. It didn't occur to him to disobey the harsh note. He never had: no one he knew ever had. He brushed the tangled hair out of his eyes and skinned his nightgown off. In a moment he was dressed—blue chambray shirt and overalls. It was late in the summer, so of course there were no shoes to bother with. In the kitchen he waited until his mother got from in front of the sink and went back to the stove. Then he washed himself and brushed back his wet hair with his fingers. His mother turned sharply on him as he left the sink. Jody looked shyly away.

"I've got to cut your hair before long," his mother said. "Breakfast's on the table. Go on in, so Billy can come."

Jody sat at the long table which was covered with white oilcloth washed through to the fabric in some places. The fried eggs lay in rows on their platter. Jody took three eggs on his plate and followed with three thick slices of crisp bacon. He carefully scraped a spot of blood from one of the egg yolks.

Billy Buck clumped in. "That won't hurt you," Billy explained. "That's only a sign the rooster leaves."

Jody's tall stern father came in then and Jody knew from the noise on the floor that he was wearing boots, but he looked under the table anyway, to make sure. His father turned off the oil lamp over the table, for plenty of morning light now came through the windows.

Jody did not ask where his father and Billy Buck were riding that day, but he wished he might go along. His father was a disciplinarian. Jody obeyed him in everything without questions of any kind. Now Carl Tiflin sat down and reached for the egg platter.

"Got the cows ready to go, Billy?" he asked.

"In the lower corral," Billy said. "I could just as well take them in alone."

"Sure you could. But a man needs company. Besides your throat gets pretty dry." Carl Tiflin was jovial this morning.

Jody's mother put her head in the door. "What time do you think to be back, Carl?"

"I can't tell. I've got to see some men in Salinas. Might be gone till dark."

The eggs and coffee and big biscuits disappeared rapidly. Jody followed the two men out of the house. He watched them mount their horses and drive six old milk cows out of the corral and start over the hill toward Salinas. They were going to sell the old cows to the butcher.

When they had disappeared over the crown of the ridge Jody walked up the hill in back of the house. The dogs trotted around the house corner hunching their shoulders and grinning horribly with pleasure. Jody patted their heads— Doubletree Mutt with the big thick tail and yellow eyes, and Smasher, the shepherd, who had killed a coyote and lost an ear in doing it. Smasher's one good ear stood up higher than a collie's ear should. Billy Buck said that always happened. After the frenzied greeting the dogs lowered their noses to the ground in a businesslike way and went ahead, looking back now and then to make sure that the boy was coming. They walked up through the chicken yard and saw the quail eating with the chickens. Smasher chased the chickens a little to keep in practice in case there should ever be sheep to herd. Jody continued on through the large vegetable patch where the green corn was higher than his head. The cow-pumpkins were green and small yet. He went on to the sagebrush line where the cold spring ran out of its pipe and fell into a round wooden tub. He leaned over and drank close to the green mossy wood where the water tasted best. Then he turned and looked back on the ranch, on the low, white-washed house girded with red geraniums, and on the long bunkhouse by the cypress tree where Billy Buck lived alone. Jody could see the great black kettle under the cypress tree. That was where the pigs were scalded. The sun was coming over the ridge now, glaring on the whitewash of the houses and barns, making the wet grass blaze softly. Behind him, in the tall sagebrush, the birds were scampering on the ground, making a great noise among the dry leaves; the squirrels piped shrilly on the side-hills. Jody looked along at the farm buildings. He felt an uncertainty in the air, a feeling of change and of loss and of the gain of new and unfamiliar things. Over the hillside two big black buzzards sailed low to the ground and their shadows slipped smoothly and quickly ahead of them. Some animal had died in the vicinity. Jody knew it. It might be a cow or it might be the remains of a rabbit. The buzzards overlooked nothing. Jody hated them as all decent things hate them, but they could not be hurt because they made away with carrion.

After a while the boy sauntered downhill again. The dogs had long ago given him up and gone into the brush to do things in their own way. Back through the vegetable garden he went, and he paused for a moment to smash a green muskmelon with his heel, but he was not happy about it. It was a bad thing to do, he knew perfectly well. He kicked dirt over the ruined melon to conceal it.

Back at the house his mother bent over

his rough hands, inspecting his fingers and nails. It did little good to start him clean to school for too many things could happen on the way. She sighed over the black cracks on his fingers, and then gave him his books and his lunch and started him on the mile walk to school. She noticed that his mouth was working a good deal this morning.

Jody started his journey. He filled his pockets with little pieces of white quartz that lay in the road, and every so often he took a shot at a bird or at some rabbit that had stayed sunning itself in the road too long. At the crossroads over the bridge he met two friends and the three of them walked to school together, making ridiculous strides and being rather silly. School had just opened two weeks before. There was still a spirit of revolt among the pupils.

It was four o'clock in the afternoon when Jody topped the hill and looked down on the ranch again. He looked for the saddle horses, but the corral was empty. His father was not back yet. He went slowly, then, toward the afternoon chores. At the ranch house, he found his mother sitting on the porch, mending socks.

"There's two doughnuts in the kitchen for you," she said. Jody slid to the kitchen and returned with half of one of the doughnuts already eaten and his mouth full. His mother asked him what he had learned in school that day, but she didn't listen to his doughnut-muffled answer. She interrupted, "Jody, tonight see you fill the wood-box clear full. Last night you crossed the sticks and it wasn't only about half full. Lay the sticks flat tonight. And Jody, some of the hens are hiding eggs, or else the dogs are eating them. Look about in the grass and see if you can find any nests."

Jody, still eating, went out and did his chores. He saw the quail come down to eat with the chickens when he threw out the grain. For some reason his father was proud to have them come. He never allowed any shooting near the house for fear the quail might go away.

When the wood-box was full, Jody took his twenty-two rifle up to the cold spring at the brush line. He drank again and then aimed the gun at all manner of things, at rocks, at birds on the wing, at the big black pig kettle under the cypress tree, but he didn't shoot for he had no cartridges and wouldn't have until he was twelve. If his father had seen him aim the rifle in the direction of the house he would have put the cartridges off another year. Jody remembered this and did not point the rifle down the hill again. Two years was enough to wait for cartridges. Nearly all of his father's presents were given with reservations which hampered their value somewhat. It was good discipline.

The supper waited until dark for his father to return. When at last he came in with Billy Buck, Jody could smell the delicious brandy on their breaths. Inwardly he rejoiced, for his father sometimes talked to him when he smelled of brandy, sometimes even told things he had done in the wild days when he was a boy.

After supper, Jody sat by the fireplace and his shy polite eyes sought the room corners, and he waited for his father to tell what it was he contained, for Jody knew he had news of some sort. But he was disappointed. His father pointed a stern finger at him.

"You'd better go to bed, Jody. I'm going to need you in the morning."

That wasn't so bad. Jody liked to do the things he had to do as long as they weren't routine things. He looked at the floor and his mouth worked out a question before he spoke it. "What are we going to do in the morning, kill a pig?" he asked softly.

"Never you mind. You better get to bed."

When the door was closed behind him, Jody heard his father and Billy Buck chuckling and he knew it was a joke of some kind. And later, when he lay in bed, trying to make words out of the murmurs in the other room, he heard his father protest, "But, Ruth, I didn't give much for him."

Jody heard the hoot-owls hunting mice down by the barn, and he heard a fruit tree limb tap-tapping against the house. A cow was lowing when he went to sleep.

When the triangle sounded in the morning, Jody dressed more quickly even than usual. In the kitchen, while he washed his face and combed back his hair, his mother addressed him irritably. "Don't you go out until you get a good breakfast in you."

He went into the dining room and sat at the long white table. He took a steaming hotcake from the platter, arranged two fried eggs on it, covered them with another hotcake and squashed the whole thing with his fork.

His father and Billy Buck came in. Jody knew from the sound on the floor that both of them were wearing flat-heeled shoes, but he peered under the table to make sure. His father turned off the oil lamp, for the day had arrived, and he looked stern and disciplinary, but Billy Buck didn't look at Jody at all. He avoided the shy questioning eyes of the boy and soaked a whole piece of toast in his coffee.

Carl Tiflin said crossly, "You come with us after breakfast!"

Jody had trouble with his food then, for he felt a kind of doom in the air. After Billy had tilted his saucer and drained the coffee which had slopped into it, and had wiped his hands on his jeans, the two men stood up from the table and went out into the morning light together, and Jody respectfully followed a little behind them. He tried to keep his mind from running ahead, tried to keep it absolutely motionless.

His mother called, "Carl! Don't you let it keep him from school."

They marched past the cypress, where a singletree [1] hung from a limb to butcher the pigs on, and past the black iron kettle, so it was not a pig killing. The sun shone over the hill and threw long, dark shadows of the trees and buildings. They crossed a stubble-field to shortcut to the barn. Jody's father unhooked the door and they went in. They had been walking toward the sun on the way down. The barn was black as night in contrast and warm from the hay and from the beasts. Jody's father moved over toward the one box stall. "Come here!" he ordered. Jody could begin to see things now. He looked into the box stall and then stepped back quickly.

A red pony colt was looking at him out of the stall. Its tense ears were forward and a light of disobedience was in its eyes. Its coat was rough and thick as an airedale's fur, and its mane was long and tangled. Jody's throat collapsed in on itself and cut his breath short.

"He needs a good currying," his father said, "and if I ever hear of you not feeding him or leaving his stall dirty, I'll sell him off in a minute."

Jody couldn't bear to look at the pony's eyes any more. He gazed down at his hands for a moment, and he asked very shyly, "Mine?" No one answered him. He put his hand out toward the pony. Its gray nose came close, sniffing loudly, and then the lips drew back and the strong teeth closed on Jody's fingers. The pony

---

[1] **singletree:** a crossbar to which horses can be harnessed for pulling.

shook its head up and down and seemed to laugh with amusement. Jody regarded his bruised fingers. "Well," he said with pride—"Well, I guess he can bite all right." The two men laughed, somewhat in relief. Carl Tiflin went out of the barn and walked up a side-hill to be by himself, for he was embarrassed, but Billy Buck stayed. It was easier to talk to Billy Buck. Jody asked again—"Mine?"

Billy became professional in tone. "Sure! That is, if you look out for him and break him right. I'll show you how. He's just a colt. You can't ride him for some time."

Jody put out his bruised hand again, and this time the red pony let his nose be rubbed. "I ought to have a carrot," Jody said. "Where'd we get him, Billy?"

"Bought him at a sheriff's auction," Billy explained. "A show went broke in Salinas and had debts. The sheriff was selling off their stuff."

The pony stretched out his nose and shook the forelock from his wild eyes. Jody stroked the nose a little. He said softly, "There isn't a—saddle?"

Billy Buck laughed. "I'd forgot. Come along."

In the harness room he lifted down a little saddle of red morocco leather. "It's just a show saddle," Billy Buck said disparagingly. "It isn't practical for the brush, but it was cheap at the sale."

Jody couldn't trust himself to look at the saddle either, and he couldn't speak at all. He brushed the shining red leather with his fingertips, and after a long time he said, "It'll look pretty on him though." He thought of the grandest and prettiest things he knew. "If he hasn't a name already, I think I'll call him Gabilan Mountains," he said.

Billy Buck knew how he felt. "It's a pretty long name. Why don't you just call him Gabilan? That means hawk. That would be a fine name for him." Billy felt glad. "If you will collect tail hair, I might be able to make a hair rope for you sometime. You could use it for a hackamore."[1]

Jody wanted to go back to the box stall. "Could I lead him to school, do you think—to show the kids?"

But Billy shook his head. "He's not even halter-broke yet. We had a time getting him here. Had to almost drag him. You better be starting for school though."

"I'll bring the kids to see him here this afternoon," Jody said.

Six boys came over the hill half an hour early that afternoon, running hard, their heads down, their forearms working, their

[1] **hackamore:** a halter, used to lead horses.

breath whistling. They swept by the house and cut across the stubble-field to the barn. And then they stood self-consciously before the pony, and then they looked at Jody with eyes in which there was a new admiration and a new respect. Before today Jody had been a boy, dressed in overalls and a blue shirt—quieter than most, even suspected of being a little cowardly. And now he was different. Out of a thousand centuries they drew the ancient admiration of the footman for the horseman. They knew instinctively that a man on a horse is spiritually as well as physically bigger than a man on foot. They knew that Jody had been miraculously lifted out of equality with them, and had been placed over them. Gabilan put his head out of the stall and sniffed them.

"Why'n't you ride him?" the boys cried. "Why'n't you braid his tail with ribbons like in the fair?" "When you going to ride him?"

Jody's courage was up. He too felt the superiority of the horseman. "He's not old enough. Nobody can ride him for a long time. I'm going to train him on the long halter. Billy Buck is going to show me how."

"Well, can't we even lead him around a little?"

"He isn't even halter-broke," Jody said. He wanted to be completely alone when he took the pony out the first time. "Come and see the saddle."

They were speechless at the red morocco saddle, completely shocked out of comment. "It isn't much use in the brush," Jody explained. "It'll look pretty on him though. Maybe I'll ride bareback when I go into the brush."

"How you going to rope a cow without a saddle horn?"

"Maybe I'll get another saddle for every day. My father might want me to help him with the stock." He let them feel the red

saddle, and showed them the brass chain throat-latch on the bridle and the big brass buttons at each temple where the headstall and brow band [1] crossed. The whole thing was too wonderful. They had to go away after a little while, and each boy, in his mind, searched among his possessions for a bribe worthy of offering in return for a ride on the red pony when the time should come.

Jody was glad when they had gone. He took brush and currycomb from the wall, took down the barrier of the box stall and stepped cautiously in. The pony's eyes glittered, and he edged around into kicking position. But Jody touched him on the shoulder and rubbed his high arched neck as he had always seen Billy Buck do, and he crooned, "So-o-o Boy," in a deep voice. The pony gradually relaxed his tenseness. Jody curried and brushed until a pile of dead hair lay in the stall and until the pony's coat had taken on a deep red shine. Each time he finished he thought it might have been done better. He braided the mane into a dozen little pigtails, and he braided the forelock, and then he undid them and brushed the hair out straight again.

Jody did not hear his mother enter the barn. She was angry when she came, but when she looked in at the pony and at Jody working over him, she felt a curious

[1] **headstall and brow band:** parts of a bridle.

pride rise up in her. "Have you forgot the wood-box?" she asked gently. "It's not far off from dark and there's not a stick of wood in the house, and the chickens aren't fed."

Jody quickly put up his tools. "I forgot, ma'am."

"Well, after this do your chores first. Then you won't forget. I expect you'll forget lots of things now if I don't keep an eye on you."

"Can I have carrots from the garden for him, ma'am?"

She had to think about that. "Oh—I guess so, if you only take the big tough ones."

"Carrots keep the coat good," he said, and again she felt the curious rush of pride.

Jody never waited for the triangle to get him out of bed after the coming of the pony. It became his habit to creep out of bed even before his mother was awake, to slip into his clothes and to go quietly down to the barn to see Gabilan. In the gray quiet mornings when the land and the brush and the houses and the trees were silver-gray and black like a photograph negative, he stole toward the barn, past the sleeping stones and the sleeping cypress tree. The turkeys, roosting in the tree out of coyotes' reach, clicked drowsily. The fields glowed with a gray frost-like light and in the dew the tracks of rabbits and of field mice stood out sharply. The good dogs came stiffly out of their little houses, hackles up and deep growls in their throats. Then they caught Jody's scent, and their stiff tails rose up and waved a greeting—Doubletree Mutt with the big thick tail, and Smasher, the incipient shepherd—then went lazily back to their warm beds.

It was a strange time and a mysterious journey, to Jody—an extension of a dream. When he first had the pony he liked to torture himself during the trip by thinking Gabilan would not be in his stall, and worse, would never have been there. And he had other delicious little self-induced pains. He thought how the rats had gnawed ragged holes in the red saddle, and how the mice had nibbled Gabilan's tail until it was stringy and thin. He usually ran the last little way to the barn. He unlatched the rusty hasp of the barn door and stepped in, and no matter how quietly he opened the door, Gabilan was always looking at him over the barrier of the box stall and Gabilan whinnied softly and stamped his front foot, and his eyes had big sparks of red fire in them like oakwood embers.

Sometimes, if the work horses were to be used that day, Jody found Billy Buck in the barn harnessing and currying. Billy stood with him and looked long at Gabilan and he told Jody a great many things about horses. He explained that they were terribly afraid for their feet, so that one must make a practice of lifting the legs and patting the hooves and ankles to remove their terror. He told Jody how horses love conversation. He must talk to the pony all the time, and tell him the reasons for everything. Billy wasn't sure a horse could understand everything that was said to him, but it was impossible to say how much was understood. A horse never kicked up a fuss if someone he liked explained things to him. Billy could give examples, too. He had known, for instance, a horse nearly dead beat with fatigue to perk up when told it was only a little farther to his destination. And he had known a horse paralyzed with fright to come out of it when his rider told him what it was that was frightening him. While he talked in the mornings, Billy Buck cut twenty or thirty straws into neat three-inch lengths and stuck them into his hatband. Then during the whole day,

if he wanted to pick his teeth or merely to chew on something, he had only to reach up for one of them.

Jody listened carefully, for he knew and the whole country knew that Billy Buck was a fine hand with horses. Billy's own horse was a stringy cayuse [1] with a hammer head, but he nearly always won the first prizes at the stock trials. Billy could rope a steer, take a double half-hitch about the horn with his riata,[2] and dismount, and his horse would play the steer as an angler plays a fish, keeping a tight rope until the steer was down or beaten.

Every morning, after Jody had curried and brushed the pony, he let down the barrier of the stall, and Gabilan thrust past him and raced down the barn and into the corral. Around and around he galloped, and sometimes he jumped forward and landed on stiff legs. He stood quivering, stiff ears forward, eyes rolling so that the whites showed, pretending to be frightened. At last he walked snorting to the water-trough and buried his nose in the water up to the nostrils. Jody was proud then, for he knew that was the way

to judge a horse. Poor horses only touched their lips to the water, but a fine spirited beast put his whole nose and mouth under, and only left room to breathe.

Then Jody stood and watched the pony, and he saw things he had never noticed about any other horse, the sleek, sliding flank muscles and the cords of the buttocks, which flexed like a closing fist, and the shine the sun put on the red coat. Having seen horses all his life, Jody had never looked at them very closely before. But now he noticed the moving ears which gave expression and even inflection of expression to the face. The pony talked with his ears. You could tell exactly how he felt about everything by the way his ears pointed. Sometimes they were stiff and upright and sometimes lax and sagging. They went back when he was angry or fearful, and forward when he was anxious and curious and pleased; and their exact position indicated which emotion he had.

Billy Buck kept his word. In the early fall the training began. First there was the halter-breaking, and that was the hardest because it was the first thing. Jody held a carrot and coaxed and promised and pulled on the rope. The pony set his feet

---

[1] **cayuse:** a tough little range horse.
[2] **riata:** lariat, lasso.

like a burro when he felt the strain. But before long he learned. Jody walked all over the ranch leading him. Gradually he took to dropping the rope until the pony followed him unled wherever he went.

And then came the training on the long halter. That was slower work. Jody stood in the middle of a circle, holding the long halter. He clucked with his tongue and the pony started to walk in a big circle, held in by the long rope. He clucked again to make the pony trot, and again to make him gallop. Around and around Gabilan went thundering and enjoying it immensely. Then he called, "Whoa," and the pony stopped. It was not long until Gabilan was perfect at it. But in many ways he was a bad pony. He bit Jody in the pants and stomped on Jody's feet. Now and then his ears went back and he aimed a tremendous kick at the boy. Every time he did one of these bad things, Gabilan settled back and seemed to laugh to himself.

Billy Buck worked at the hair rope in the evenings before the fireplace. Jody collected tail hair in a bag, and he sat and watched Billy slowly constructing the rope, twisting a few hairs to make a string and rolling two strings together for a cord, and then braiding a number of cords to make the rope. Billy rolled the finished rope on the floor under his foot to make it round and hard.

The long-halter work rapidly approached perfection. Jody's father, watching the pony stop and start and trot and gallop, was a little bothered by it.

"He's getting to be almost a trick pony," he complained. "I don't like trick horses. It takes all the—dignity out of a horse to make him do tricks. Why, a trick horse is kind of like an actor—no dignity, no character of his own." And his father said, "I guess you better be getting him used to the saddle pretty soon."

Jody rushed for the harness-room. For some time he had been riding the saddle on a sawhorse. He changed the stirrup length over and over, and could never get it just right. Sometimes, mounted on the sawhorse in the harness-room, with collars and hames and tugs [1] hung all about him, Jody rode out beyond the room. He carried his rifle across the pommel. He saw the fields go flying by, and he heard the beat of the galloping hoofs.

It was a ticklish job, saddling the pony the first time. Gabilan hunched and reared and threw the saddle off before the cinch could be tightened. It had to be replaced again and again until at last the pony let it stay. And the cinching was difficult, too. Day by day Jody tightened the girth a little more until at last the pony didn't mind the saddle at all.

Then there was the bridle. Billy explained how to use a stick of licorice for a bit until Gabilan was used to having something in his mouth. Billy explained, "Of course we could force-break him to everything, but he wouldn't be as good a horse if we did. He'd always be a little bit afraid, and he wouldn't mind because he wanted to."

The first time the pony wore the bridle he whipped his head about and worked his tongue against the bit until the blood oozed from the corners of his mouth. He tried to rub the headstall [2] off on the manger. His ears pivoted about and his eyes turned red with fear and with general rambunctiousness. Jody rejoiced, for he knew that only a mean-souled horse does not resent training.

And Jody trembled when he thought of the time when he would first sit in the saddle. The pony would probably throw

[1] **hames and tugs:** parts of a harness.
[2] **headstall:** the part of a bridle that fits over the horse's head.

him off. There was no disgrace in that. The disgrace would come if he did not get right up and mount again. Sometimes he dreamed that he lay in the dirt and cried and couldn't make himself mount again. The shame of the dream lasted until the middle of the day.

Gabilan was growing fast. Already he had lost the long-leggedness of the colt; his mane was getting longer and blacker. Under the constant currying and brushing his coat lay as smooth and gleaming as orange-red lacquer. Jody oiled the hoofs and kept them carefully trimmed so they would not crack.

The hair rope was nearly finished. Jody's father gave him an old pair of spurs and bent in the side bars and cut down the strap and took up the chainlets until they fitted. And then one day Carl Tiflin said:

"The pony's growing faster than I thought. I guess you can ride him by Thanksgiving. Think you can stick on?"

"I don't know," Jody said shyly. Thanksgiving was only three weeks off. He hoped it wouldn't rain, for rain would spot the red saddle.

Gabilan knew and liked Jody by now. He nickered when Jody came across the stubble-field, and in the pasture he came running when his master whistled for him. There was always a carrot for him every time.

Billy Buck gave him riding instructions over and over. "Now when you get up there, just grab tight with your knees and keep your hands away from the saddle, and if you get throwed, don't let that stop you. No matter how good a man is, there's always some horse can pitch him. You just climb up again before he gets to feeling smart about it. Pretty soon, he won't throw you no more, and pretty soon he *can't* throw you no more. That's the way to do it."

"I hope it don't rain before," Jody said.

"Why not? Don't want to get throwed in the mud?"

That was partly it, and also he was afraid that in the flurry of bucking Gabilan might slip and fall on him and break his leg or his hip. He had seen that happen to men before, had seen how they writhed on the ground like squashed bugs, and he was afraid of it.

He practiced on the sawhorse how he would hold the reins in his left hand and a hat in his right hand. If he kept his hands thus busy, he couldn't grab the horn if he felt himself going off. He didn't like to think of what would happen if he did grab the horn. Perhaps his father and Billy Buck would never speak to him again, they would be so ashamed. The news would get about and his mother would be ashamed too. And in the school yard—it was too awful to contemplate.

He began putting his weight in a stirrup when Gabilan was saddled, but he didn't throw his leg over the pony's back. That was forbidden until Thanksgiving.

Every afternoon he put the red saddle on the pony and cinched it tight. The pony was learning already to fill his stomach out unnaturally large while the cinching was going on, and then to let it down when the straps were fixed. Sometimes Jody led him up to the brush line and let him drink from the round green tub, and sometimes he led him up through the stubble-field to the hilltop from which it was possible to see the white town of Salinas and the geometric fields of the great valley, and the oak trees clipped by the sheep. Now and then they broke through the brush and came to little cleared circles so hedged in that the world was gone and only the sky and the circle of brush were left from the old life. Gabilan liked these trips and showed it by keeping his head very high and by quivering his nostrils with interest. When the two came back from an expedition, they smelled of the sweet sage they had forced through.

Time dragged on toward Thanksgiving, but winter came fast. The clouds swept down and hung all day over the land and brushed the hilltops, and the winds blew shrilly at night. All day the dry oak leaves drifted down from the trees until they covered the ground, and yet the trees were unchanged.

Jody had wished it might not rain before Thanksgiving, but it did. The brown earth turned dark and the trees glistened. The cut ends of the stubble turned black with mildew; the haystacks grayed from exposure to the damp, and on the roofs the moss, which had been all summer as gray as lizards, turned a brilliant yellow-green. During the week of rain, Jody kept the pony in the box stall out of the dampness, except for a little time after school when he took him out for exercise and to drink at the water-trough in the upper corral. Not once did Gabilan get wet.

The wet weather continued until little new grass appeared. Jody walked to school dressed in a slicker and short rubber boots. At length one morning the sun came out brightly. Jody, at his work in the box stall, said to Billy Buck, "Maybe I'll leave Gabilan in the corral when I go to school today."

"Be good for him to be out in the sun," Billy assured him. "No animal likes to be cooped up too long. Your father and me are going back on the hill to clean the leaves out of the spring." Billy nodded and picked his teeth with one of his little straws.

"If the rain comes, though—" Jody suggested.

"Not likely to rain today. She's rained herself out." Billy pulled up his sleeves and snapped his arm bands. "If it comes on to rain—why a little rain don't hurt a horse."

"Well, if it does come on to rain, you put him in, will you, Billy? I'm scared he might get cold so I couldn't ride him when the time comes."

"Oh sure! I'll watch out for him if we get back in time. But it won't rain today."

And so Jody, when he went to school, left Gabilan standing out in the corral.

Billy Buck wasn't wrong about many things. He couldn't be. But he was wrong about the weather that day, for a little after noon the clouds pushed over the hills and the rain began to pour down. Jody heard it start on the schoolhouse roof. He considered holding up one finger for permission to go to the outhouse and, once outside, running for home to put the pony in. Punishment would be prompt both at school and at home. He gave it up and took ease from Billy's assurance that rain couldn't hurt a horse. When school was finally out, he hurried home through the dark rain. The banks at the sides of the road spouted little jets of muddy water. The rain slanted and swirled under a cold and gusty wind. Jody dog-trotted home, slopping through the gravelly mud of the road.

From the top of the ridge he could see Gabilan standing miserably in the corral. The red coat was almost black, and streaked with water. He stood head down with his rump to the rain and wind. Jody arrived running and threw open the barn door and led the wet pony in by his forelock. Then he found a gunny sack and rubbed the soaked hair and rubbed the legs and ankles. Gabilan stood patiently, but he trembled in gusts like the wind.

When he had dried the pony as well as he could, Jody went up to the house and brought hot water down to the barn and soaked the grain in it. Gabilan was not very hungry. He nibbled at the hot mash, but he was not very much interested in it, and he still shivered now and then. A little steam rose from his damp back.

It was almost dark when Billy Buck and Carl Tiflin came home. "When the rain started we put up at Ben Herche's place, and the rain never let up all afternoon," Carl Tiflin explained. Jody looked reproachfully at Billy Buck and Billy felt guilty.

"You said it wouldn't rain," Jody accused him.

Billy looked away. "It's hard to tell, this time of year," he said, but his excuse was lame. He had no right to be fallible, and he knew it.

"The pony got wet, got soaked through."

"Did you dry him off?"

"I rubbed him with a sack and I gave him hot grain."

Billy nodded in agreement.

"Do you think he'll take cold, Billy?"

"A little rain never hurt anything," Billy assured him.

Jody's father joined the conversation then and lectured the boy a little. "A horse," he said, "isn't any lap-dog kind of thing." Carl Tiflin hated weakness and sickness, and he held a violent contempt for helplessness.

Jody's mother put a platter of steaks on the table and boiled potatoes and boiled squash, which clouded the room with their steam. They sat down to eat. Carl Tiflin still grumbled about weakness put into animals and men by too much coddling.

Billy Buck felt bad about his mistake. "Did you blanket him?" he asked.

"No. I couldn't find any blanket. I laid some sacks over his back."

"We'll go down and cover him up after we eat, then." Billy felt better about it then. When Jody's father had gone in to the fire and his mother was washing dishes, Billy found and lighted a lantern. He and Jody walked through the mud to

the barn. The barn was dark and warm and sweet. The horses still munched their evening hay. "You hold the lantern!" Billy ordered. And he felt the pony's legs and tested the heat of the flanks. He put his cheek against the pony's gray muzzle and then he rolled up the eyelids to look at the eyeballs and he lifted the lips to see the gums, and he put his fingers inside the ears. "He don't seem so chipper," Billy said. "I'll give him a rub-down."

Then Billy found a sack and rubbed the pony's legs violently and he rubbed the chest and the withers. Gabilan was strangely spiritless. He submitted patiently to the rubbing. At last Billy brought an old cotton comforter from the saddle-room, and threw it over the pony's back and tied it at neck and chest with string.

"Now he'll be all right in the morning," Billy said.

Jody's mother looked up when he got back to the house. "You're late up from bed," she said. She held his chin in her hard hand and brushed the tangled hair out of his eyes and she said, "Don't worry about the pony. He'll be all right. Billy's as good as any horse doctor in the country."

Jody hadn't known she could see his worry. He pulled gently away from her and knelt down in front of the fireplace until it burned his stomach. He scorched himself through and then went in to bed, but it was a hard thing to go to sleep. He awakened after what seemed a long time. The room was dark but there was a grayness in the window like that which precedes the dawn. He got up and found his overalls and searched for the legs, and then the clock in the other room struck two. He laid his clothes down and got back into bed. It was broad daylight when he awakened again. For the first time he had slept through the ringing of the triangle. He leaped up, flung on his clothes and went out of the door still buttoning his shirt. His mother looked after him for a moment and then went quietly back to her work. Her eyes were brooding and kind. Now and then her mouth smiled a little but without changing her eyes at all.

Jody ran on toward the barn. Halfway there he heard the sound he dreaded, the hollow rasping cough of a horse. He broke into a sprint then. In the barn he found Billy Buck with the pony. Billy was rubbing its legs with his strong thick hands. He looked up and smiled gaily. "He just took a little cold," Billy said. "We'll have him out of it in a couple of days."

Jody looked at the pony's face. The eyes were half closed and the lids thick and dry. In the eye corners a crust of hard mucus stuck. Gabilan's ears hung loosely sideways and his head was low. Jody put out his hand, but the pony did not move close to it. He coughed again and his whole body constricted with the effort. A little stream of thin fluid ran from his nostrils.

Jody looked back at Billy Buck. "He's awful sick, Billy."

"Just a little cold, like I said," Billy insisted. "You go get some breakfast and then go back to school. I'll take care of him."

"But you might have to do something else. You might leave him."

"No, I won't. I won't leave him at all. Tomorrow's Saturday. Then you can stay with him all day." Billy had failed again, and he felt badly about it. He had to cure the pony now.

Jody walked up to the house and took his place listlessly at the table. The eggs and bacon were cold and greasy, but he didn't notice it. He ate his usual amount. He didn't even ask to stay home from school. His mother pushed his hair back when she took his plate. "Billy'll take care of the pony," she assured him.

He moped through the whole day at school. He couldn't answer any questions nor read any words. He couldn't even tell anyone the pony was sick, for that might make him sicker. And when school was finally out he started home in dread. He walked slowly and let the other boys leave him. He wished he might continue walking and never arrive at the ranch.

Billy was in the barn, as he had promised, and the pony was worse. His eyes were almost closed now, and his breath whistled shrilly past an obstruction in his nose. A film covered that part of the eyes that was visible at all. It was doubtful whether the pony could see any more. Now and then he snorted, to clear his nose, and by the action seemed to plug it tighter. Jody looked dispiritedly at the pony's coat. The hair lay rough and unkempt and seemed to have lost all of its old luster. Billy stood quietly beside the stall. Jody hated to ask, but he had to know.

"Billy, is he—is he going to get well?"

Billy put his fingers between the bars under the pony's jaw and felt about. "Feel here," he said and he guided Jody's fingers to a large lump under the jaw. "When that gets bigger, I'll open it up and then he'll get better."

Jody looked quickly away, for he had heard about that lump. "What is it the matter with him?"

Billy didn't want to answer, but he had to. He couldn't be wrong three times. "Strangles,"[1] he said shortly, "but don't you worry about that. I'll pull him out of it. I've seen them get well when they were worse than Gabilan is. I'm going to steam him now. You can help."

"Yes," Jody said miserably. He followed Billy into the grain room and watched him make the steaming bag ready. It was a long canvas nose bag with straps to go over a horse's ears. Billy filled it one-third full of bran and then he added a couple of handfuls of dried hops. On top of the dry substance he poured a little carbolic acid and a little turpentine. "I'll be mixing it all up while you run to the house for a kettle of boiling water," Billy said.

When Jody came back with the steaming kettle, Billy buckled the straps over Gabilan's head and fitted the bag tightly around his nose. Then through a little hole in the side of the bag he poured the boiling water on the mixture. The pony started away as a cloud of strong steam rose up, but then the soothing fumes crept through his nose and into his lungs, and the sharp steam began to clear out the nasal passages. He breathed loudly. His legs trembled in an ague, and his eyes closed against the biting cloud. Billy poured in more water and kept the steam rising for fifteen minutes. At last he set down the kettle and took the bag from Gabilan's nose. The pony looked better.

[1] **Strangles:** distemper; an infectious disease affecting horses.

He breathed freely, and his eyes were open wider than they had been.

"See how good it makes him feel," Billy said. "Now we'll wrap him up in the blanket again. Maybe he'll be nearly well by morning."

"I'll stay with him tonight," Jody suggested.

"No. Don't you do it. I'll bring my blankets down here and put them in the hay. You can stay tomorrow and steam him if he needs it."

The evening was falling when they went to the house for their supper. Jody didn't even realize that someone else had fed the chickens and filled the wood-box. He walked up past the house to the dark brush line and took a drink of water from the tub. The spring water was so cold that it stung his mouth and drove a shiver through him. The sky above the hills was still light. He saw a hawk flying so high that it caught the sun on its breast and shone like a spark. Two blackbirds were driving him down the sky, glittering as they attacked their enemy. In the west, the clouds were moving in to rain again.

Jody's father didn't speak at all while the family ate supper, but after Billy Buck had taken his blankets and gone to sleep in the barn, Carl Tiflin built a high fire in the fireplace and told stories. He told about the wild man who ran naked through the country and had a tail and ears like a horse, and he told about the rabbit-cats of Moro Cojo that hopped into the trees for birds. He revived the famous Maxwell brothers who found a vein of gold and hid the traces of it so carefully that they could never find it again.

Jody sat with his chin in his hands; his mouth worked nervously, and his father gradually became aware that he wasn't listening very carefully. "Isn't that funny?" he asked.

Jody laughed politely and said, "Yes,

sir." His father was angry and hurt, then. He didn't tell any more stories. After a while, Jody took a lantern and went down to the barn. Billy Buck was asleep in the hay, and, except that his breath rasped a little in his lungs, the pony seemed to be much better. Jody stayed a little while, running his fingers over the red rough coat, and then he took up the lantern and went back to the house. When he was in bed, his mother came into the room.

"Have you enough covers on? It's getting winter."

"Yes, ma'am."

"Well, get some rest tonight." She hesitated to go out, stood uncertainly. "The pony will be all right," she said.

Jody was tired. He went to sleep quickly and didn't awaken until dawn. The triangle sounded, and Billy Buck came up from the barn before Jody could get out of the house.

"How is he?" Jody demanded.

Billy always wolfed his breakfast. "Pretty good. I'm going to open that lump this morning. Then he'll be better maybe."

After breakfast, Billy got out his best knife, one with a needle point. He whetted the shining blade a long time on a little carborundum[1] stone. He tried the point and the blade again and again on his calloused thumb-ball, and at last he tried it on his upper lip.

On the way to the barn, Jody noticed how the young grass was up and how the stubble was melting day by day into the new green crop of volunteer. It was a cold sunny morning.

As soon as he saw the pony, Jody knew he was worse. His eyes were closed and sealed shut with dried mucus. His head hung so low that his nose almost touched the straw of his bed. There was a little

groan in each breath, a deep-seated, patient groan.

Billy lifted the weak head and made a quick slash with the knife. Jody saw the yellow pus run out. He held up the head while Billy swabbed out the wound with weak carbolic acid salve.

"Now he'll feel better," Billy assured him. "That yellow poison is what makes him sick."

Jody looked unbelieving at Billy Buck. "He's awful sick."

Billy thought a long time what to say. He nearly tossed off a careless assurance, but he saved himself in time. "Yes, he's pretty sick," he said at last. "I've seen worse ones get well. If he doesn't get pneumonia, we'll pull him through. You stay with him. If he gets worse, you can come and get me."

For a long time after Billy went away, Jody stood beside the pony, stroking him behind the ears. The pony didn't flip his head the way he had done when he was well. The groaning in his breathing was becoming more hollow.

Doubletree Mutt looked into the barn, his big tail waving provocatively, and Jody was so incensed at his health that he found a hard black clod on the floor and deliberately threw it. Doubletree Mutt went yelping away to nurse a bruised paw.

In the middle of the morning, Billy Buck came back and made another steam bag. Jody watched to see whether the

---

[1] **carborundum:** an abrasive for sharpening knives.

pony improved this time as he had before. His breathing eased a little, but he did not raise his head.

The Saturday dragged on. Late in the afternoon Jody went to the house and brought his bedding down and made up a place to sleep in the hay. He didn't ask permission. He knew from the way his mother looked at him that she would let him do almost anything. That night he left a lantern burning on a wire over the box stall. Billy had told him to rub the pony's legs every little while.

At nine o'clock the wind sprang up and howled around the barn. And in spite of his worry, Jody grew sleepy. He got into his blankets and went to sleep, but the breathy groans of the pony sounded in his dreams. And in his sleep he heard a crashing noise which went on and on until it awakened him. The wind was rushing through the barn. He sprang up and looked down the lane of stalls. The barn door had blown open, and the pony was gone.

He caught the lantern and ran outside into the gale, and he saw Gabilan weakly shambling away into the darkness, head down, legs working slowly and mechanically. When Jody ran up and caught him by the forelock, he allowed himself to be led back and put into his stall. His groans were louder, and a fierce whistling came from his nose. Jody didn't sleep any more then. The hissing of the pony's breath grew louder and sharper.

He was glad when Billy Buck came in at dawn. Billy looked for a time at the pony as though he had never seen him before. He felt the ears and flanks. "Jody," he said, "I've got to do something you won't want to see. You run up to the house for a while."

Jody grabbed him fiercely by the forearm. "You're not going to shoot him?"

Billy patted his hand. "No. I'm going to open a little hole in his windpipe so he can breathe. His nose is filled up. When he gets well, we'll put a little brass button in the hole for him to breath through."

Jody couldn't have gone away if he had wanted to. It was awful to see the red hide cut, but infinitely more terrible to know it was being cut and not to see it. "I'll stay right here," he said bitterly. "You sure you got to?"

"Yes. I'm sure. If you stay, you can hold his head. If it doesn't make you sick, that is."

The fine knife came out again and was whetted again just as carefully as it had been the first time. Jody held the pony's head up and the throat taut, while Billy felt up and down for the right place. Jody sobbed once as the bright knife point disappeared into the throat. The pony plunged weakly away and then stood still, trembling violently. The blood ran thickly out and up the knife and across Billy's hand and into his shirtsleeve. The sure square hand sawed out a round hole in the flesh, and the breath came bursting out of the hole, throwing a fine spray of blood. With the rush of oxygen, the pony took a sudden strength. He lashed out with his hind feet and tried to rear, but Jody held his head down while Billy mopped the new wound with carbolic salve. It was a good job. The blood stopped flowing and the air puffed out the hole and sucked it in regularly with a little bubbling noise.

The rain brought in by the night wind began to fall on the barn roof. Then the triangle rang for breakfast. "You go up and eat while I wait," Billy said. "We've got to keep this hole from plugging up."

Jody walked slowly out of the barn. He was too dispirited to tell Billy how the barn door had blown open and let the pony out. He emerged into the wet gray morning and sloshed up to the house, taking a perverse pleasure in splashing through all the puddles. His mother fed him and put dry clothes on. She didn't question him. She seemed to know he couldn't answer questions. But when he was ready to go back to the barn she brought him a pan of steaming meal. "Give him this," she said.

But Jody did not take the pan. He said, "He won't eat anything," and ran out of the house. At the barn, Billy showed him how to fix a ball of cotton on a stick, with which to swab out the breathing hole when it became clogged with mucus.

Jody's father walked into the barn and stood with them in front of the stall. At length he turned to the boy. "Hadn't you better come with me? I'm going to drive over the hill." Jody shook his head. "You better come on, out of this," his father insisted.

Billy turned on him angrily. "Let him alone. It's his pony, isn't it?"

Carl Tiflin walked away without saying another word. His feelings were badly hurt.

All morning Jody kept the wound open and the air passing in and out freely. At noon the pony lay wearily down on his side and stretched his nose out.

Billy came back. "If you're going to stay with him tonight, you better take a little nap," he said. Jody went absently out of the barn. The sky had cleared to a hard thin blue. Everywhere the birds were busy with worms that had come to the damp surface of the ground.

Jody walked to the brush line and sat on the edge of the mossy tub. He looked down at the house and at the old bunkhouse and at the dark cypress tree. The place was familiar, but curiously changed. It wasn't itself any more, but a frame for things that were happening. A cold wind blew out of the east now, signifying that the rain was over for a little while. At his feet Jody could see the little arms of new weeds spreading out over the ground. In the mud about the spring were thousands of quail tracks.

Doubletree Mutt came sideways and embarrassed up through the vegetable patch, and Jody, remembering how he had thrown the clod, put his arm about the dog's neck and kissed him on his wide black nose. Doubletree Mutt sat still, as though he knew some solemn thing was happening. His big tail slapped the ground gravely. Jody pulled a swollen tick out of Mutt's neck and popped it dead between his thumb-nails. It was a nasty thing. He washed his hands in the cold spring water.

Except for the steady swish of the wind, the farm was very quiet. Jody knew his mother wouldn't mind if he didn't go in to eat his lunch. After a little while he went slowly back to the barn. Mutt crept into his own little house and whined softly to himself for a long time.

Billy Buck stood up from the box and surrendered the cotton swab. The pony still lay on his side and the wound in his throat bellowsed in and out. When Jody saw how dry and dead the hair looked, he knew at last that there was no hope for the pony. He had seen the dead hair before on dogs and on cows, and it was a sure sign. He sat heavily on the box and let down the barrier of the box stall. For a long time he kept his eyes on the moving wound, and at last he dozed, and the afternoon passed quickly. Just before dark his mother brought a deep dish of stew and left it for him and went away. Jody ate a little of it, and, when it was dark, he set the lantern on the floor by the pony's head so he could watch the wound and keep it open. And he dozed again until the night chill awakened him. The wind was blowing fiercely, bringing the north cold with it. Jody brought a blanket from his bed in the hay and wrapped himself in it. Gabilan's breathing was quiet at last; the hole in his throat moved gently. The owls flew through the hayloft, shrieking and looking for mice. Jody put his hands down on his head and slept. In his sleep he was aware that the wind had increased. He heard it slamming about the barn.

It was daylight when he awakened. The barn door had swung open. The pony was gone. He sprang up and ran out into the morning light.

The pony's tracks were plain enough, dragging through the frostlike dew on the young grass, tired tracks with little lines between them where the hoofs had dragged. They headed for the brush line halfway up the ridge. Jody broke into a run and followed them. The sun shone on the sharp white quartz that stuck through the ground here and there. As he followed the plain trail, a shadow cut across in front of him. He looked up and saw a high circle of black buzzards, and the slowly revolving circle dropped lower and lower. The solemn birds soon disappeared over the ridge. Jody ran faster then, forced on by panic and rage. The trail entered the brush at last and followed a winding route among the tall sage bushes.

At the top of the ridge Jody was winded. He paused, puffing noisily. The blood pounded in his ears. Then he saw what he was looking for. Below, in one of the little clearings in the brush, lay the red pony. In the distance, Jody could see the legs moving slowly and convulsively. And in a circle around him stood the buzzards, waiting for the moment of death they know so well.

Jody leaped forward and plunged down the hill. The wet ground muffled his steps and the brush hid him. When he arrived, it was all over. The first buzzard sat on the pony's head and its beak had just risen dripping with dark eye fluid. Jody plunged into the circle like a cat. The black brotherhood arose in a cloud, but the big one on the pony's head was too late. As it hopped along to take off, Jody caught its wing tip and pulled it down. It was nearly as big as he was. The free wing crashed into his face with the force of a club, but he hung on. The claws fastened on his leg and the wing elbows battered his head on either side. Jody groped blindly with his free hand. His fingers found the neck of the struggling bird. The red eyes looked into his face, calm and fearless and fierce; the naked head turned from side to side. Then the beak opened and vomited a stream of putrefied fluid. Jody brought up his knee and fell on the great bird. He held the neck to the ground with one hand while his other found a piece of sharp white quartz. The first blow broke the beak sideways and black blood spurted from the twisted, leathery mouth corners. He struck again and missed. The red fearless eyes still looked at him, impersonal and unafraid and detached. He struck again and again, until the buzzard lay dead, until its head was a red pulp. He was still beating the dead bird when Billy Buck pulled him off and held him tightly to calm his shaking.

Carl Tiflin wiped the blood from the boy's face with a red bandana. Jody was limp and quiet now. His father moved the buzzard with his toe. "Jody," he explained, "the buzzard didn't kill the pony. Don't you know that?"

"I know it," Jody said wearily.

It was Billy Buck who was angry. He had lifted Jody in his arms, and had turned to carry him home. But he turned back on Carl Tiflin. " 'Course he knows it," Billy said furiously, "Good Lord! man, can't you see how he'd feel about it?"

1. What impression do you have of Jody? How is he different from his father? How does he feel toward his father? How does his father feel toward him? Why is Carl Tiflin so strict with his son? Why do you think he gives him the red pony?

2. What effect does Jody's owning the red pony have on his schoolmates? on Jody himself? How do you know that he appreciates the gift?

3. What are some of the things that Billy Buck taught Jody? Was his advice to Jody always good? What is Jody's attitude toward Billy at the beginning of the story? Does his attitude change because of what happens in the story? What makes you think so?

4. How does Jody's love for his pony make him more attentive to the pony's appearance and actions? Does his love for the pony also make him more aware of other life around him? What makes you think so?

5. How does the author describe the animal life on and around the farm? What details in the story suggest the cruelty of life and the "law of the wild"? How do these details help to *foreshadow* (prepare for) the ending of the story?

6. Gabilan's sickness and death are the central incidents of the story. How do Jody, Billy, and Carl react to these events? What does each character's reaction reveal about his personality?

7. "The Gift" is the first part of a longer story, "The Red Pony," that tells of Jody's growing up. What do his experiences in this story teach him? Would you expect him, in the next part of the story, to squash melons thoughtlessly or throw stones? Why or why not?

SYMBOLISM

Many authors use objects and words as *symbols*—that is, to suggest a larger meaning than we usually associate with a particular object or word. The buzzards described in "The Gift" are literally birds of prey. Symbolically, however, they represent death, the common end of all living things. The fierceness of Jody's fight with the buzzard suggests how deeply he feels the death of Gabilan. It is this symbolic connection—what the buzzard represents to Jody—that his father fails to understand.

Reread Steinbeck's description of the buzzards, both at the beginning and at the end of the story. Which details most powerfully suggest their larger meaning? What realistic action of the largest buzzard sets off Jody's fury? What is symbolized by this action?

What other symbols can you find in the story? What are their larger meanings?

FOR COMPOSITION

1. In one section of this story, Billy Buck teaches Jody how to break the red pony and how to ride him. Reread this section and notice particularly each stage of the pony's training. Then, in a similar fashion, write a composition telling your classmates how to train a dog or another animal, or how to swim or fish. Make sure to indicate clearly each step in the process you choose to explain.

2. Reread Steinbeck's description of Jody's journey up the hill behind the ranch, in the paragraph beginning, "When they had disappeared . . ." Notice the details Steinbeck uses to give a vivid picture of the dogs, the chicken yard, the vegetable patch, the cold spring, and the distant ranch yard. What connecting words and phrases does he use to lead the reader's attention from one place to the next? Write your own description of a walk through places you know well, using vivid details and appropriate connecting words to lead from one place to another.

3. Most young people of Jody's age have not had firsthand contact with life on a ranch, where they can come to know both the beauty and cruelty of nature. What do you think are the advantages of country life compared with life in a city? What are the disadvantages? Would you prefer to live in the country or in a city? Why? Express your personal opinion in a short composition, including one paragraph on the advantages of country life, another on the disadvantages, and a third explaining your own preference.

Narration

Narration is storytelling, and a paragraph of narration, like a story, is a series of events or actions. In a good paragraph, as in a good story, the order of incidents is clear and logical: one action leads to another in a way that seems right and natural. The most natural order for such a series of events is *chronological*—that is, in the same order as they would naturally occur in time.

A good story begins—and a good paragraph may begin—in a way that arouses your curiosity and anticipation. Once your interest is aroused, you are more alert to all the details of the actions and readier to draw your own conclusions. Reading narration demands a special alertness and readiness to draw conclusions. The author very often simply tells what happened, leaving it up to you to form your own opinion of the character or characters involved and what their actions show about them. What opinion do you get from the following paragraph from "The Gift"?

> The high jangling note of the triangle put the boy Jody in motion. He was only a little boy, ten years old, with hair like dusty yellow grass and with shy polite gray eyes, and with a mouth that worked when he thought. The triangle picked him up out of sleep. It didn't occur to him to disobey the harsh note. He never had: no one he knew ever had. He brushed the tangled hair out of his eyes and skinned his nightgown off. In a moment he was dressed—blue chambray shirt and overalls. It was late in the summer, so of course there were no shoes to bother with. In the kitchen he waited until his mother got from in front of the sink and went back to the stove. Then he washed himself and brushed back his wet hair with his fingers. His mother turned sharply on him as he left the sink. Jody looked shyly away. (page 130)

1. Are the events in this paragraph told in chronological order? List them in the order they occur.
2. Does the very first sentence or two arouse your curiosity about Jody and what will happen to him?
3. Which do you think is more important in this paragraph—Jody's actions or what we learn about him from these actions?

In narration, as in all writing, a good writer —and a good reader—gives special attention to the way a paragraph begins and ends. A truly good beginning should not only intrigue the reader, arouse curiosity and anticipation, but should give some hint of what the paragraph will be about. The end of a paragraph, ideally, should be a kind of climax of the paragraph's main action or impression. Of course, not all paragraphs have equally forceful endings. The paragraph from "The Gift" which you have just read ends quietly, but this ending supports the impression created throughout the paragraph and gives you a clear sense of what Jody is like. The following paragraph, from "The Tell-Tale Heart," has an even more definite beginning and end. In reading it, what do you come to realize? What is the real answer to the narrator's opening question?

> I smiled—for what had I to fear? I bade the gentlemen welcome. The shriek, I said, was my own in a dream. The old man, I mentioned, was absent in the country. I took my visitors all over the house. I bade them search—search well. I led them, at length, to his chamber. I showed them his treasures, secure, undisturbed. In the enthusiasm of my confidence, I brought chairs into the room, and desired them here to rest from their fatigue, while I

myself, in the wild audacity of my perfect triumph, placed my own seat upon the very spot beneath which reposed the corpse of the victim. (page 110)

1. What question does the narrator raise in the opening sentence of this paragraph? Does this sentence provoke interest? Why?

2. Do the events take place in chronological order? List them in the order in which they occur. Is there a definite progression, a sense of movement in space as well as in time? Explain.

3. About halfway through the paragraph, the narrator reinforces the progression in time by using a phrase that indicates *transition:* "I led them, *at length,* to his chamber." Look back at the paragraph from "The Gift" and find two or three words and phrases that indicate time or space transitions.

4. What is the climax of the paragraph from "The Tell-Tale Heart"? How does it finally make clear the answer to the opening question?

PRACTICING YOUR READING

In reading narration, you should always try to follow the *sequence of events* that leads to the climax of each episode. To practice this kind of reading, reread the following paragraphs in the "Storyteller and the Story" unit, writing down the events in sequence as they take place in each:

p. 109—"But even yet . . ."
p. 110—"No doubt I now . . ."
p. 114—"The daughter had just . . ."
p. 119—"The simplest words . . ."
p. 131—"When they had disappeared . . ."

WRITING NARRATION

In writing a narrative, you should:

1. Decide on what you want the climax, the end result of your story, to be.

2. Plan a logical—and chronological—series of events that will lead up to your climax.

3. Try to interest your readers with the very first event of your story. Make them curious and eager to read on.

Write the following "narratives," keeping the above steps in mind:

1. Carefully plan and write an account of some event or incident you saw or were involved in. Tell your story in a single paragraph with a definite beginning and ending. Make sure your sequence of events leads logically to the climax of the episode.

2. Tell about an exciting incident you saw, or read, or heard about. Work out a logical, believable sequence of events and actions, and write a "short story" several paragraphs long.

SHARPENING YOUR WRITING

As you know, vivid *modifiers* that say exactly what you mean are very important in good writing. Try substituting other words with similar meanings for the modifiers in the following phrases and sentences. How does this change the meaning?

"The *high jangling* note of the triangle"
"hair *like dusty yellow grass*"
"*shy polite gray* eyes"
"turned *sharply* on him"
"Jody looked *shyly* away."

Choice of *verbs,* words expressing action, is especially important in narration. Look back over your own writing for weak verbs and modifiers. In each case, try to think of a word that will say *exactly* what you mean.

ART AND LITERATURE

1. Often a story—a sequence of events or incidents—will be suggested to a writer by a particular atmosphere or *setting*. Look at the watercolor paintings on pages 123–28. Which of them most strongly suggests a story that might have taken place in such a setting? List the sequence of events that might have taken place in the story you imagine.

2. Write the story behind the painting you have chosen, using the list of actions and events that you drew up for the preceding question. Try to give your story an interesting beginning, a logical sequence, and an exciting end.

POETRY

W HAT IS POETRY?
        Like many simple questions, this one is difficult to answer. So
many people have defined poetry in so many different ways that the
only certainty is that no one can agree on a single definition. One way,
however, to begin thinking about this question is to look at what
poets themselves have said about poetry.

On the printed page of a book, the first thing you notice about
poetry is that it is arranged in lines, with much more white space
around it than is the case with prose. You also see that the first word
of each line usually begins with a capital letter. And you notice that
the last words of certain lines often rhyme with each other. Even
when there is no rhyme, it is often easy to pick out within the lines
of a poem certain vowels and consonants that are repeated. Sometimes, too, words and phrases are repeated. Echoing forwards and
backwards throughout the poem, such repetitions help to establish
pattern and unity. In spite of its use of all kinds of repetition, we
notice that in poetry every word counts. A good poem seems to say
more in fewer words than is the case with prose—and often what is
said is expressed more beautifully, more impressively, and more
effectively than can be done in prose. All this, perhaps, is what the
English poet Samuel Taylor Coleridge was referring to when he defined poetry as "the best words in the best order."

The choice and handling of words are indeed most important in
poetry. But in addition to the *form* of a poem, there is another essential element to consider: that is, the *content* of a poem. The content
of poetry has its roots in the experiences of life. Just as all of us respond to the events of life, so does poetry. A sensitive and imaginative poet can make us more fully aware than we might otherwise be
of the quality of an experience or a relationship—of the world in
general. As the American poet Archibald MacLeish has pointed out,
"the deepest meanings of human life are revealed in poems."

In reacting to the world around us, a poet may simply express delight in being part of the physical universe. The poet Robert Frost is one of many who express delight in the world. In his definition of poetry, however, he goes one step further by saying that a poem "begins in delight and ends in wisdom." Poetry, he feels, starts with a moment of joy experienced by the poet and ends with a moment of insight.

As we have said, poetry can be defined in many ways. But the emphasis on *form* in Coleridge's definition of poetry and the emphasis on *content* in MacLeish's and Frost's definitions point out for us two of the major considerations in poetry. Let's try out both of these ideas in reading the following poem.

Summer Evening

WALTER DE LA MARE

The sandy cat by the farmer's chair
Mews at his knee for dainty fare;
Old Rover is in his moss-greened house
Mumbles a bone, and barks at a mouse.
In the dewy fields the cattle lie
Chewing the cud 'neath a fading sky.
Dobbin at manger pulls his hay:
Gone is another summer's day.

Examine the *form* of this poem. Do certain lines rhyme with each other? Are certain vowels and consonants repeated? Are you aware of a specific rhythm? Can you convey the idea of this poem more effectively, and in fewer words, in prose?

And what about *content?* What "delight" is found in the beginning of this poem? What "meaning of human life," what "wisdom," is found in the ending?

In the poems in the following pages, you will not only have many opportunities to test the definitions of poetry offered here, but you will have equal opportunity to formulate a definition of your own.

This unit is divided into two parts. Part 1, called "An Introduction to Poetry," is in turn divided into five separate sections, the first four of which spotlight a particular aspect of poetry.

"Summer Evening" by Walter de la Mare. Reprinted by permission of the Literary Trustees of Walter de la Mare and The Society of Authors as their representatives.

In the first of these sections, "Stories in Poetry," we shall study examples of narrative verse. These include poems such as "The Wife of Usher's Well," a folk ballad which has come down to us from medieval times. "Allen-a-Dale," by Sir Walter Scott, the famous nineteenth-century English poet and novelist, and "The Sailing of the Sword" by William Morris, another nineteenth-century English poet, are both examples of poetry that was inspired by old folk ballads such as "The Wife of Usher's Well." Moving up closer to our own day, we shall study "The Ballad of William Sycamore," a story in poetry by the American poet Stephen Vincent Benét.

In the second section, called "Music in Poetry," we shall discover how various poets have created exciting musical effects in their verse through the effective use of poetic elements such as rhythm, rhyme, alliteration, and assonance. In Alfred, Lord Tennyson's "Bugle Song," for example, the poet helps us hear the echo of the bugle sounding in the distant hills. In Housman's "Reveille" we shall see how the poet uses rhythm for effect. And in "maggie and milly and molly and may," by the twentieth-century American poet E. E. Cummings, we shall see how a modern writer uses both sound and meaning to create a very original kind of music.

In "Pictures in Poetry," the third section of Part 1, we shall see how different poets have used their special powers of description to make us see in our mind's eye everything from a playful cat, a sleepy fawn, and a whirling sea, to the silvery world of Walter de la Mare and the rushing night clouds of Amy Lowell.

We shall encounter both joyous and sad or reflective verse in the section entitled "Poems of Joy and Sorrow." William Wordsworth's "My Heart Leaps Up" and Shelley's "Dirge" are good examples of the range of feeling expressed in this section.

In "The Scope of Poetry," the last of the five sections of Part 1, we shall sample the great range of human concern which can be expressed in poetry and which, in fact, has been expressed by poets throughout the ages, from the song of a psalmist of Biblical times, to the reflections of a seventeenth-century poet as he views a cluster of daffodils, to those of a contemporary American as he gazes at a well-known national monument. We shall also see how two quite different poets—one a man of the nineteenth-century, the other a woman of our own century—have expressed humor in verse.

In Part 2 (page 220) of this unit on poetry, we shall make use of what we have learned in Part 1 of various elements in poetry, as we take a close look at the poetry of five well-known poets—old and new, English and American.

The Wife of Usher's Well

There lived a wife at Usher's Well,
  And a wealthy wife was she;
She had three stout and stalwart sons,
  And sent them o'er the sea.

They hadna been a week from her,   5
  A week but barely one,
When word came to the carline° wife
  That her three sons were gone.

They hadna been a week from her,
  A week but barely three,   10
When word came to the carline wife
  That her sons she'd never see.

"I wish the wind may never cease,
  Nor fashes° in the flood,
Till my three sons come home to me,   15
  In earthly flesh and blood."

It fell about the Martinmas,°
  When nights are long and murk,
The carline wife's three sons came home,
  And their hats were o' the birk.°   20

It neither grew in syke° nor ditch,
  Nor yet in any sheugh;°
But at the gates o' Paradise,
  That birk grew fair enough.

"Blow up the fire, my maidens,   25
  Bring water from the well;
For a' my house shall feast this night,
  Since my three sons are well."

And she has made to them a bed,
  She's made it large and wide,   30
And she's ta'en her mantle her about,
  Sat down at the bedside.

Up then crew the red, red cock
  And up and crew the gray;
The eldest to the youngest said,   35
  " 'Tis time we were away."

The cock he hadna crawed but once,
  And clapp'd his wings at a',
When the youngest to the eldest said,
  "Brother, we must awa'.   40

"The cock doth craw, the day doth daw,
  The channerin'° worm doth chide;
Gin° we be missed out o' our place,
  A sair° pain we maun bide.°

"Fare ye well, my mother dear!   45
  Farewell to barn and byre!°
And fare ye well, the bonny lass
  That kindles my mother's fire!"

7. **carline** (kär'lin): old. 14. **fashes**: troubles.
17. **Martinmas**: the Feast of St. Martin (November 11). 20. **birk**: birch. 21. **syke**: a trench.
22. **sheugh** (shükh): gully.

42. **channerin'**: devouring. 43. **Gin**: If. 44. **sair**: sore. **Maun bide**: must endure. According to ancient belief, spirits had to return to the world of the dead at the first sign of dawn or be punished. 46. **byre**: stable.

1. A ballad is a short story told in verse. What happens in the ballad of "The Wife of Usher's Well"? Is the story exciting simply as a plot?

2. What was the old mother's wish? How was it fulfilled? What is ironic about this fulfillment?

3. Lines 20–24 describe the appearance of the three sons. How do you know that they are ghosts? Does their mother realize this? Which of her actions suggest that she expects them to stay?

4. Why must the sons leave when the cock crows? To what things in life does the youngest son say goodbye? Which of them does he seem saddest to leave?

5. Because the ballad often tells a fairly long story in a few stanzas, much of what happens is left to the reader's imagination. In the last stanza of "The Wife of Usher's Well," the youngest son says farewell forever to his mother, his home, and a pretty girl. How does he feel at that moment? The author of the ballad does not say. We must imagine this for ourselves. The stanza suggests or implies more than it states directly. Why is this economical way of telling the story so effective? Would the son's farewell be as dramatic if the last stanza had explained in great detail just how sad he felt? Why or why not?

THE FOLK BALLAD

Folk, or traditional, ballads are old poems whose authors are now unknown. They were composed by the *folk,* or common people, and were passed on by word of mouth for generations before being written down. In the process, of course, they were shaped and altered by each storyteller, and over the years appeared in many different versions. Most folk ballads tell stories of adventure and daring, disappointed love, sudden disaster, and ghostly mysteries. Which of these elements are present in "The Wife of Usher's Well"?

Most folk ballads are divided into four-line stanzas with a definite pattern of rhythm and rhyme. "The Wife of Usher's Well" is a good example of this pattern. In this ballad, how many strong beats or accents occur in the first and third lines of each stanza? in the second and fourth lines? Which of the lines in each stanza rhyme?

Allen-a-Dale

SIR WALTER SCOTT

Allen-a-Dale has no faggot for burning,
Allen-a-Dale has no furrow for turning,
Allen-a-Dale has no fleece for the spinning,
Yet Allen-a-Dale has red gold for the winning.
Come, read me my riddle! come, harken my tale!   5
And tell me the craft of bold Allen-a-Dale.

The Baron of Ravensworth prances in pride,
And he views his domains upon Arkindale side,
The mere for his net, and the land for his game,
The chase for the wild, and the park for the tame: 10
Yet the fish of the lake, and the deer of the vale,
Are less free to Lord Dacre than Allen-a-Dale!

Allen-a-Dale was ne'er belted a knight,°
Though his spur be as sharp, and his blade be as bright;
Allen-a-Dale is no baron or lord,   15
Yet twenty tall yeomen will draw at his word;
And the best of our nobles his bonnet will vail,
Who at Rere-Cross on Stanmore meets Allen-a-Dale.

Allen-a-Dale to his wooing is come;
The mother, she asked of his household and home: 20
"Though the castle of Richmond stand fair on the hill,
My hall," quoth bold Allen, "shows gallanter still;
'Tis the blue vault of heaven, with its crescent so pale,
And with all its bright spangles!" said Allen-a-Dale.

The father was steel, and the mother was stone;   25
They lifted the latch, and they bade him be gone;
But loud, on the morrow, their wail and their cry!
He had laughed on the lass with his bonny black eye,
And she fled to the forest to hear a love-tale,
And the youth it was told by was Allen-a-Dale!   30

13. **belted a knight:** In the ceremony of being knighted, a young man was given a sword and a belt.

FOR STUDY AND DISCUSSION

1. Tell the story of the poem in your own words. What details does each stanza contribute to the story? At what point in the poem does the story actually begin?

2. What is the answer to the riddle with which the poem begins? What is Allen's "craft"? Why is his gold "red"? What do you learn about Allen from stanzas 2 and 3 and from his answer to the girl's parents in stanza 4? Why do you think the girl's parents object to him as a possible husband?

3. The girl goes with Allen despite her parents' objections. Do you think she admires the same things about him that her parents object to?

4. Explain the meaning of the following lines:

"Yet the fish of the lake, and the deer of the vale,
  Are less free to Lord Dacre than Allen-a-Dale!"   (lines 11–12)

"My hall," quoth bold Allen, "shows gallanter still;
'Tis the blue vault of heaven, . . ."

(lines 22–23)

5. Poetry is often particularly effective because the poet has described things so specifically and vividly that we can picture the action. For instance, Scott says,

"The father was steel, and the mother was stone;
  They lifted the latch, and they bade him be gone;"

Compare Scott's lines to: "The parents were cold and unyielding and made him leave." What words and details in Scott's description help you to picture what happened?

THE LITERARY BALLAD

The literary ballad, which first became popular in the early nineteenth century, is a poem which imitates the old folk ballads in both style and subject matter. Like the folk ballad, the literary ballad is usually full of romance, adventure, and danger, and the poet makes a point of using all the traditional musical devices such as rhyme and rhythm to add to the excitement of the poem. "Allen-a-Dale" by Sir Walter Scott is a good example of the literary ballad. What other literary ballads can you find in this unit?

ALLITERATION

One of the musical devices most commonly found in both folk and literary ballads is *alliteration,* the repetition of consonant sounds at the beginning of words. In "Allen-a-Dale" there are three good examples of alliteration in line 16: "Yet *twenty tall yeomen will* draw at his *word*." Point out other examples of alliteration in the poem.

LANGUAGE AND VOCABULARY

Scott has used several words in this poem which dictionaries mark *archaic* or *obsolete.* (If necessary, look up the meaning of *archaic* and *obsolete.* In your dictionary, how are these terms abbreviated?) Look up *mere, vail, quoth.* What is the meaning of each? Why are they marked archaic or obsolete? Other words such as *vale* (valley) may be marked *poetic.* Why are archaic words appropriate in poems such as "Allen-a-Dale"?

ABOUT THE POET

Sir Walter Scott (1771–1832) came to love the stories and songs of his native Scotland when he went to his grandfather's country home to recover from infantile paralysis. Although Scott was educated to be a lawyer, he spent most of his life writing. At first he wrote long narrative poems such as *Marmion* and *The Lady of the Lake,* but it was through his novels that he achieved his greatest success and fame. Many of his novels are noted for their pictures of exciting periods in Scottish history. Two of his most popular novels are *Ivanhoe* and *The Talisman,* both filled with romance and vigorous action.

The Sailing of the Sword

WILLIAM MORRIS

Across the empty garden beds
   When the Sword went out to sea,
I scarcely saw my sisters' heads
   Bowed each beside a tree.
I could not see the castle leads,°   5
   When the Sword went out to sea.

Alicia wore a scarlet gown,
   When the Sword went out to sea,
But Ursula's was russet brown:
   For the mist we could not see   10
The scarlet roofs of the good town,
   When the Sword went out to sea.

Green holly in Alicia's hand,
   When the Sword went out to sea,
With sere° oak leaves did Ursula stand;
   O! yet alas for me!   16
I did but bear a peel'd white wand,
   When the Sword went out to sea.

O, russet brown and scarlet bright,
   When the Sword went out to sea,   20
My sisters wore; I wore but white:
   Red, brown, and white, are three;
Three damozels;° each had a knight,
   When the Sword went out to sea.

Sir Robert shouted loud, and said: 25
   When the Sword went out to sea,
"Alicia, while I see thy head,
   What shall I bring for thee?"
"O, my sweet lord, a ruby red":
   The Sword went out to sea.   30

5. **leads** (ledz): lead sheets on the roof of the castle. 15. **sere** (sir): dried up, withered. 23. **damozels:** young ladies, girls.

Sir Miles said, while the sails hung down:
When the Sword went out to sea,
"O, Ursula! while I see the town,
    What shall I bring for thee?"
"Dear knight, bring back a falcon brown":
The Sword went out to sea.   36

But my Roland, no word he said
When the Sword went out to sea,
But only turn'd away his head;
    A quick shriek came from me: 40
"Come back, dear lord, to your white
    maid."
The Sword went out to sea.

The hot sun bit the garden beds
When the Sword came back from sea;
Beneath an apple tree our heads   45
    Stretched out toward the sea;
Gray gleam'd the thirsty castle leads,
When the Sword came back from sea.

Lord Robert brought a ruby red,
When the Sword came back from sea;
He kissed Alicia on the head: 51
    "I am come back to thee;
'Tis time, sweet love, that we were wed,
Now the Sword is back from sea!"

Sir Miles he bore a falcon brown,   55
When the Sword came back from sea;
His arms went round tall Ursula's gown:
    "What joy, O love, but thee?
Let us be wed in the good town,
    Now the Sword is back from sea!"   60

My heart grew sick, no more afraid,
When the Sword came back from sea;
Upon the deck a tall white maid
    Sat on Lord Roland's knee;
His chin was press'd upon her head,   65
When the Sword came back from sea!

FOR STUDY AND DISCUSSION

1. The story of this ballad is told in two scenes—the sailing of the *Sword* and its return. What happens in each scene? What clues in the first scene suggest the final outcome of the story?

2. Describe the setting of the two scenes. What is the weather in the first scene? What is the time of year? How are these different from the weather and time of year of the second scene? How does the setting of each scene match the action described? How does it match the mood of the sisters?

3. How does the color of the sisters' gowns affect your first impression of them? With which sister does the author make you most sympathetic? What do you learn about the first two sisters from the gifts they ask for? (Notice how the author unifies the poem by

echoing the colors of the sisters' gowns in the gifts they request.) For what gift does the third sister ask? How does the order of their asking concentrate attention on the third sister and create suspense?

REFRAIN

A refrain is a phrase, a line, or a group of lines that is repeated throughout a poem. In "The Sailing of the Sword" the refrain underlines the basic action of the two scenes: the *Sword's* sailing and its return. Does this constant emphasis through repetition increase or lesson the force of the poem? Does repetition add suspense and foreboding to the mood of the poem? Explain.

A refrain also has a musical effect. Note how the repetition of a phrase or an entire line not only rounds off each stanza but adds extra rhythm to the movement of sounds within a poem.

FOR COMPOSITION

Some writers of fiction always try to conclude their stories with a happy ending. Can you think of such an ending for "The Sailing of the Sword"? Rewrite the last stanza of the poem, keeping only the refrain, so as to bring the third sister and Roland together again. Read your version in class as part of the whole poem. Do you think the happy endings written by you and your classmates are as convincing as the original ending of the poem?

ABOUT THE POET

William Morris (1834–1896) was one of the most versatile men of his time. He was known as a painter, architect, interior decorator, and designer of furniture, as well as an essayist and poet. His interest in art is evident in the color and design of his poetry.

Something of Morris's philosophy of life is suggested in one of his letters. When he was in college and trying to decide on a career, he wrote to his mother, "You see I do not hope to be great at all in anything, but perhaps I may reasonably hope to be happy in my work."

Eldorado

EDGAR ALLAN POE

Eldorado was the legendary "city of gold" that for centuries was sought in vain by Spanish explorers and soldiers of fortune. It has often been used by poets to represent an unattainable ideal.

Gaily bedight,°
A gallant knight,
In sunshine and in shadow,
Had journeyed long,
Singing a song,   5
In search of Eldorado.

But he grew old—
This knight so bold—
And o'er his heart a shadow
Fell as he found   10
No spot of ground
That looked like Eldorado.

And, as his strength
Failed him at length,
He met a pilgrim shadow—   15
"Shadow," said he,
"Where can it be—
This land of Eldorado?"

"Over the mountains
Of the moon,   20
Down the valley of the shadow,
Ride, boldly ride,"
The shade replied—
"If you seek for Eldorado!"

1. **bedight:** decked out, dressed.

FOR STUDY AND DISCUSSION

1. The knight begins his journey eagerly. What change occurs in him? What phrase in stanza 2 best describes this change? Do you think the change is caused mostly by the

knight's growing old or by his failure to find Eldorado? What makes you think so?

2. How is the journey described by the "pilgrim shadow" different from the kind of journey the knight apparently expected when he began his search? Do you think he will ever find Eldorado? Why?

3. In this poem Eldorado seems to stand for—to *symbolize*—any goal that we want very much to reach. If we consider that the knight's journey represents someone's efforts to reach such a goal, what lesson is there in the advice given him by the pilgrim shadow?

4. Poe, who believed that poetry should be concerned more with beauty than with meaning, was very skillful at creating especially musical combinations of words. Read the poem aloud, giving special attention to its strong and regular rhyme. What is the rhyme scheme of the poem? What word is used as a refrain? What effect does its repetition have on the mood of the poem?

ASSONANCE

As you know, alliteration is the repetition of the sounds of consonants in a poem. *Assonance* is the repetition of vowel sounds. One good example of assonance is in lines 16–18 of "Eldorado":

> "Shadow," said he,
> "Where can it be—
> This land of Eldorado?"

What other examples of assonance can you find in this poem? Which is most prominent—assonance or alliteration? Where are the strongest examples of alliteration in the poem?

FOR COMPOSITION

Suppose you were writing a poem about how an adventurer finds Eldorado. How would you describe this ideal city? What details of its appearance would you use to suggest to the reader as dazzling a picture as possible? List three or four details that you might use to suggest the city's splendor. Which detail would you tell first—or reserve for last—for greatest impact on your reader's imagination? Explain the reasons for your choice.

ABOUT THE POET

Edgar Allan Poe (1809–1849) is best known as a writer of stories of mystery and horror. An erratic genius who died at an early age, his life was largely one of pain and disappointment. Despite these personal difficulties, however, his writings and his literary criticism exerted a profound influence over later writers of stories and poetry. For more on the life of Poe, see page 107.

Incident of the French Camp

ROBERT BROWNING

This poem is based upon an actual incident which occurred during Napoleon's Austrian campaign in 1809. Marshal Lannes, one of Napoleon's most trusted commanders, stormed the fortified city of Ratisbon in a battle which was crucial for the French.

You know, we French stormed Ratisbon.
  A mile or so away,
On a little mound, Napoleon
  Stood on our storming-day;
With neck out-thrust, you fancy how,   5
  Legs wide, arms locked behind,
As if to balance the prone brow
  Oppressive with its mind.

Just as perhaps he mused "My plans
  That soar, to earth may fall,   10
Let once my army leader Lannes
  Waver at yonder wall"—
Out 'twixt the battery smokes there flew
  A rider, bound on bound
Full galloping; nor bridle drew   15
  Until he reached the mound.

Then off there flung in smiling joy,
  And held himself erect
By just his horse's mane, a boy:
  You hardly could suspect—   20

(So tight he kept his lips compressed,
   Scarce any blood came through)
You looked twice ere you saw his breast
   Was all but shot in two.

"Well," cried he, "Emperor, by God's
     grace   25
   We've got you Ratisbon!
The Marshal's in the market-place,
   And you'll be there anon°
To see your flag-bird flap his vans°
   Where I, to heart's desire,   30
Perched him!" The chief's eye flashed;
     his plans
   Soared up again like fire.

The chief's eye flashed; but presently
   Softened itself, as sheathes
A film the mother-eagle's eye   35
   When her bruised eaglet breathes;
"You're wounded!" "Nay," the soldier's
     pride
   Touched to the quick, he said:
"I'm killed, Sire!" And, his chief beside,
   Smiling, the boy fell dead.   40

28. **anon:** right away. 29. **vans:** wings. The emblem on Napoleon's banner was an eagle.

FOR STUDY AND DISCUSSION

1. Show that this narrative poem contains the three basic elements of a short story: characters, setting, and plot.

2. According to lines 27–31, what part did the boy play in the battle? Some historians say that a man, not a boy, performed the act of bravery. Why is Browning's choice of a boy more effective in arousing the reader's sympathy?

3. Look again at the description of the boy's ride (lines 14–24). In which line do we realize that the rider is a boy? Why would an observer see him at first as simply "a rider"? Does the information that he is a boy come at the best dramatic moment? Are the other details in the description presented as they might meet the eye of a bystander? Are they arranged in order for the greatest dramatic impact? If not, how would you change the order?

4. What special qualities does the narrator see in Napoleon that might inspire devotion such as that of the wounded boy?

THE SPEAKER IN THE POEM

In many poems, especially those by Robert Browning, the speaker has an identity entirely different from that of the poet. In reading such poems it is important not to confuse the speaker with the poet. What is your impression of the person who tells the story in "Incident of the French Camp"? Does he seem to be a veteran of many battles? What about his attitude toward the battle might make you think so? Would you guess that he is telling about the event just after it happened or years later? Why? What is his attitude toward the boy? Does he seem to admire him or think him foolish?

SIMILE

To describe Napoleon's reaction to the boy's injury, the poet uses a *simile* (lines 34–36). A simile is a figure of speech that compares one thing to another, using the words *like* or *as* to suggest the similarity the poet sees between two things. In "Incident of the French Camp," Napoleon's eye softens *as* a mother eagle's eye is sheathed by a membranous film. What is Napoleon compared to in this simile? What does this comparison suggest about his reaction to the boy's wound? Can you find another effective simile in this poem?

LANGUAGE AND VOCABULARY

What is the meaning of the word *oppressive* in line 8? What is another common meaning of this word? Look up the root of the word *oppress* in a dictionary. What is the meaning of the Latin word from which it came? Does this original meaning of the word give you a more vivid sense of what it means to be *oppressed*? How is the *oppression* of a dictator, for instance, different from that of Napoleon's mind? How are the two similar?

FOR COMPOSITION

Suppose you wanted to describe to someone what it was like on an *oppressively* hot day in the middle of summer. One way to make your description vivid would be to use a simile. You might start thinking about it this way: what else is as heavy and stifling as a hot, humid day? When you have thought of something similar, express the similarity in a simile. (Be sure to use either *like* or *as* in your simile.) After you have described a summer day, try to describe a winter day by using simile.

ABOUT THE POET

Robert Browning (1812–1889), one of England's greatest poets, is noted for the dramatic situations and vivid characters in his poems. Fascinated by history, he frequently drew upon the past of other countries, especially Italy and France, for his subjects. His elopement with the English poet Elizabeth Barrett, one of the world's famous love stories, has been told by numerous biographers and dramatized by Rudolf Besier in the play *The Barretts of Wimpole Street*.

A Dutch Picture

HENRY WADSWORTH LONGFELLOW

Simon Danz has come home again,
   From cruising about with his buccaneers;
He has singed the beard of the King of Spain,
And carried away the Dean of Jaen°
   And sold him in Algiers.°   5

In his house by the Maese,° with its roof of tiles,
   And weathercocks flying aloft in air,
There are silver tankards of antique styles,
Plunder of convent and castle, and piles
   Of carpets rich and rare.   10

---

4. **Dean of Jaen** (hä·än′): a high-ranking Spanish church official.   5. **Algiers:** a North African city and center of the slave trade.   6. **the Maese** (māz): the Meuse (myooz) River.

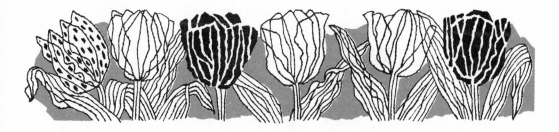

In his tulip garden there by the town,
   Overlooking the sluggish stream,
With his Moorish cap and dressing gown,
The old sea captain, hale and brown,
   Walks in a waking dream.   15

A smile in his gray mustachio lurks
   Whenever he thinks of the King of Spain;
And the listed° tulips look like Turks,
And the silent gardener as he works
   Is changed to the Dean of Jaen.   20

The windmills on the outermost
   Verge° of the landscape in the haze,
To him are towers on the Spanish coast,
With whiskered sentinels at their post,
   Though this is the river Maese.   25

But when the winter rains begin,
   He sits and smokes by the blazing brands,°
And old seafaring men come in,
Goat-bearded, gray, and with double chin,
   And rings upon their hands.   30

They sit there in the shadow and shine
   Of the flickering fire of the winter night;
Figures in color and design
Like those by Rembrandt° of the Rhine,
   Half darkness and half light.   35

And they talk of ventures lost or won,
   And their talk is ever and ever the same,
While they drink the red wine of Tarragon,°
From the cellars of some Spanish Don,°
   Or convent set on flame.   40

18. **listed** (lis′tid): set in a straight line.   22. **Verge** (vûrj): edge.   27. **brands:** logs.   34. **Rembrandt** (rem′brant): a great Dutch painter of the seventeenth century.   38. **Tarragon :** a province in northeastern Spain.   39. **Don:** the title of a Spanish nobleman.

Restless at times with heavy strides
    He paces his parlor to and fro;
He is like a ship that at anchor rides,
And swings with the rising and falling tides,
    And tugs at her anchor tow.   45

Voices mysterious far and near,
    Sound of the wind and sound of the sea,
Are calling and whispering in his ear,
"Simon Danz! Why stayest thou here?
    Come forth and follow me!"   50

So he thinks he shall take to the sea again
    For one more cruise with his buccaneers,
To singe the beard of the King of Spain,
And capture another Dean of Jaen
    And sell him in Algiers.   55

FOR STUDY AND DISCUSSION

1. Which objects in Simon's surroundings might make him dream of Algiers? How does he spend winter evenings? Why do you think he dwells with such pleasure on his memories?

2. How does Longfellow in the last few stanzas of the poem emphasize Simon's fascination with the sea? In which lines do assonance and alliteration create a musical, wave-like sound? In which lines does the rhythm suggest a rolling or an ebbing motion?

METAPHOR

Like a simile, a metaphor compares two things that are basically unsimilar. A simile, as you know, is introduced by the word *like* or *as*. A metaphor omits these connecting words. A simile says that one thing is *like* another ("My love is like a rose"), whereas a metaphor says that one thing *is* another ("My love is a rose").

There is a good example of metaphor in lines 21–23 of "A Dutch Picture," where "windmills . . . are towers on the Spanish coast." In Simon's mind, the windmills are towers, and through this comparison they have, for the moment, a grandeur that we do not usually think of them as having. How would you rephrase this metaphor as a simile? As a simile? As you read, look for other similes and metaphors.

FOR COMPOSITION

In "A Dutch Picture" Longfellow explores the memories of an old Dutch sea captain. Perhaps an actual portrait painting inspired the writing of this poem. Select one of the portraits reproduced in this book and study it closely. Is the person's expression alert, thoughtful, vague, or dreamy? Can you imagine what the person is thinking of? how the person feels? Write a brief paragraph describing the person in the portrait.

ABOUT THE POET

Old sea captains must have been plentiful in the little town of Portland, Maine, where Henry Wadsworth Longfellow (1807–1882) was born, but he himself followed a far different calling. After graduating from Bowdoin College at the age of eighteen, Longfellow spent several years in Europe, traveling and studying, before returning to Bowdoin to teach modern languages. Upon publication of his long poems based on American legends—"The Song of Hiawatha," "Evangeline," and "The Courtship of Miles Standish"—Longfellow became his country's best-known poet. Apart from his own poetry, his numerous and excellent translations of European literature did much to make the best of other cultures available to Americans.

The Ballad of William Sycamore

STEPHEN VINCENT BENÉT

My father, he was a mountaineer,
His fist was a knotty hammer;
He was quick on his feet as a running deer,
And he spoke with a Yankee stammer.

My mother, she was merry and brave, 5
And so she came to her labor,
With a tall green fir for her doctor grave
And a stream for her comforting neighbor.

And some are wrapped in the linen fine,
And some like a godling's scion;° 10
But I was cradled on twigs of pine
In the skin of a mountain lion.

And some remember a white, starched lap
And a ewer° with silver handles;
But I remember a coonskin cap 15
And the smell of bayberry candles.

The cabin logs, with the bark still rough,
And my mother who laughed at trifles,
And the tall, lank visitors, brown as snuff,
With their long, straight squirrel rifles. 20

I can hear them dance, like a foggy song,
Through the deepest one of my slumbers,
The fiddle squeaking the boots along
And my father calling the numbers.

The quick feet shaking the puncheon
floor,° 25
The fiddle squeaking and squealing,
Till the dried herbs rattled above the door
And the dust went up to the ceiling.

There are children lucky from dawn till
dusk,
But never a child so lucky! 30
For I cut my teeth on "Money Musk"°
In the Bloody Ground of Kentucky!

When I grew tall as the Indian corn,
My father had little to lend me, 34
But he gave me his great old powderhorn
And his woodsman's skill to befriend me.

With a leather shirt to cover my back,
And a redskin nose to unravel
Each forest sign, I carried my pack
As far as a scout could travel. 40

Till I lost my boyhood and found my wife,
A girl like a Salem clipper!
A woman straight as a hunting knife
With eyes as bright as the Dipper!

We cleared our camp where the buffalo
feed, 45
Unheard-of streams were our flagons;°
And I sowed my sons like appleseed
On the trail of the Western wagons.

They were right, tight boys, never sulky or
slow,
A fruitful, a goodly muster. 50
The eldest died at the Alamo.°
The youngest fell with Custer.°

The letter that told it burned my hand.
Yet we smiled and said, "So be it!"
But I could not live when they fenced the
land, 55
For it broke my heart to see it.

10. scion (sī'ən): a descendant, child. 14. ewer
(yōō'ər): a pitcher. 25. puncheon floor: a floor
of heavy timbers.

31. "Money Musk": a mountain tune. 46. flag-
ons: drinking vessels. 51. the Alamo: a fort in
Texas whose defenders were massacred by Mexi-
can troops (1836). 52. Custer: Colonel George A.
Custer, whose entire army was massacred by the
Sioux (1876).

I saddled a red, unbroken colt
And rode him into the day there;
And he threw me down like a thunderbolt
And rolled on me as I lay there.　　　60

The hunter's whistle hummed in my ear
As the city men tried to move me,
And I died in my boots like a pioneer
With the whole wide sky above me.

Now I lie in the heart of the fat, black soil,
Like the seed of a prairie-thistle;　　66
It has washed my bones with honey and
　　oil
And picked them clean as a whistle.

And my youth returns, like the rains of
　　spring,
And my sons, like the wild geese flying; 70
And I lie and hear the meadowlark sing
And have much content in my dying.

Go play with the towns you have built of
　　blocks,
The towns where you would have bound
　　me!
I sleep in my earth like a tired fox,　　75
And my buffalo have found me.

FOR STUDY AND DISCUSSION

1. Judging from the first two stanzas, what were the special characteristics of William's parents? Did William's sons possess the same characteristics?

2. What memories did William Sycamore have of his childhood? Where did he grow up? What in his surroundings and home life made him think of himself as lucky?

3. After reading this ballad, what do you remember best about William Sycamore—his

disappointments and losses or his spirited way of meeting them? What great disappointment finally broke his spirit? Did it remain broken or did he regain his hope and confidence? What made him content to die?

4. To whom is the last stanza of the poem addressed? Why would a pioneer like William Sycamore think of towns as "built of blocks"? Do you agree with his opinion of towns and cities? Why or why not?

5. Look again at the description of the ballad stanza following "The Wife of Usher's Well." In what ways is the stanza pattern of "The Ballad of William Sycamore" like that of a folk ballad such as "The Wife of Usher's Well"? What rhyme scheme does Benét use in his poem? How does it differ from that of "The Wife of Usher's Well"?

6. Find three or four striking similes and metaphors in the poem. Which do you consider the most striking figure of speech? Why?

FOR COMPOSITION

As you know, a literary ballad is written by a poet who wants to tell a story in the exciting manner of the old folk ballads. Do you know an exciting story worth the telling? Try to put it in the form of a ballad, with four-line stanzas whose second and fourth lines rhyme. Make your lines short and exciting, and don't stop to tell *why* anyone does anything. Just tell what happened.

ABOUT THE POET

Stephen Vincent Benét (1898–1943) published his first book of poems at seventeen, and throughout his lifetime never supported himself with any occupation other than writing. He was made famous by *John Brown's Body,* his long epic about the War Between the States, a collection of prose, ballads, and other verse that was an immediate best seller and won the Pulitzer prize. Benét's most famous short story, *The Devil and Daniel Webster,* is also set in American history and underlines Benét's passionate hatred of cruelty and inhumanity. Among his most striking writings are a series of nightmare fantasies on the dangers of the machine age.

Bugle Song

ALFRED, LORD TENNYSON

The splendor falls on castle walls
  And snowy summits old in story;
The long light shakes across the lakes,
  And the wild cataract leaps in glory.
Blow, bugle, blow, set the wild echoes flying,   5
Blow, bugle; answer, echoes, dying, dying, dying.

O, hark, O, hear! how thin and clear,
  And thinner, clearer, farther going!
O, sweet and far from cliff and scar
  The horns of Elfland faintly blowing!   10
Blow, let us hear the purple glens replying,
Blow, bugle; answer, echoes, dying, dying, dying.

O love, they die in yon rich sky,
  They faint on hill or field or river;
Our echoes roll from soul to soul,   15
  And grow forever and forever.
Blow, bugle, blow, set the wild echoes flying,
And answer, echoes, answer, dying, dying, dying.

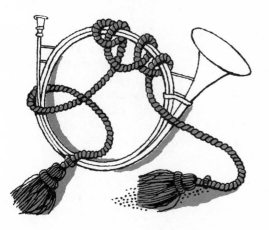

FOR STUDY AND DISCUSSION

1. Notice that, except for the last two lines, the first stanza of this poem presents a picture and the second adds sound effects. What does the speaker see in the first stanza of the poem? Which words in stanza 2 link its sound effects to the setting described in stanza 1?

2. What happens to the bugle's sound in the second stanza? Do you think the "horns of Elfland" are other, faraway horns or the bugle's own echoes? How are the last two lines of this stanza different from the last two lines of the first stanza? Which lines make the bugle and its echoes seem farther away?

3. To whom is the speaker speaking in the last stanza? In lines 13–14, to what does "they" refer? What does the speaker say "our echoes" will do that "they" did not. To whom besides the speaker do "our echoes" belong?

THE MUSIC OF THE POEM

Most of the music in "Bugle Song" comes from repetition—of words, sounds, phrases, and even whole lines. The last two lines of each stanza use repetition of words and sounds to suggest the bugle and its echo. Read the lines aloud. How does the sound suggest what is happening in the lines?

As you know, the repetition of the sounds of consonants is called *alliteration*. The words "Blow, bugle, blow" are a striking example of this. Find two or three other examples of alliteration that contribute to the music of the poem.

Rhyme is another kind of repetition. Which lines in each stanza rhyme? Notice that two lines in each stanza have *internal rhyme*—a rhyme within the line itself.

The splendor *falls* on castle *walls*.

Find some other examples of internal rhyme.

Since "Bugle Song" is so musical, much of its effect depends on how well it is read. As with all poems, it is important to read the punctuation and to pause only where punctuation occurs. Try reading the poem aloud once more, being careful to follow the punctuation.

ABOUT THE POET

Alfred, Lord Tennyson (1809–1892) wrote an epic poem at the age of twelve, a blank verse drama at fourteen, and he published a book containing several of his best poems before he was twenty-four. Although hard-pressed for money after being swindled out of his inheritance, he refused to take a job that would interfere with his writing of poetry. His faith in himself proved justified since he became one of England's most popular poets and was later named poet laureate. Among his most popular poems are those on the legends of King Arthur called *The Idylls of the King*. For more on the life of Alfred, Lord Tennyson, see page 245.

Hunting Song

SIR WALTER SCOTT

Waken, lords and ladies gay,
On the mountain dawns the day,
All the jolly chase is here,
With hawk, and horse, and hunting-spear!
Hounds are in their couples° yelling,   5
Hawks are whistling, horns are knelling,
Merrily, merrily, mingle they,
"Waken, lords and ladies gay."

Waken, lords and ladies gay,
The mist has left the mountain gray,   10
Springlets in the dawn are steaming,
Diamonds on the brake° are gleaming:
And foresters have busy been
To track the buck in thicket green;
Now we come to chant our lay,°   15
"Waken, lords and ladies gay."

Waken, lords and ladies gay,
To the greenwood haste away;
We can show you where he lies,
Fleet of foot, and tall of size: 20
We can show the marks he made,
When 'gainst the oak his antlers frayed;
You shall see him brought to bay,
"Waken, lords and ladies gay."

Louder, louder chant the lay,   25
Waken, lords and ladies gay!
Tell them youth, and mirth, and glee,
Run a course as well as we;
Time, stern huntsman! who can balk,°
Staunch as hound, and fleet as hawk?   30
Think of this, and rise with day,
Gentle lords and ladies gay.

5. **couples:** leashes.   12. **brake:** clumps of bushes, thickets of shrubs.   15. **lay:** song, ballad.   29. **balk:** hinder, stop.

1. To what are the lords and ladies being awakened in the first three stanzas? Which details are most effective in giving you a picture of the woods, the quarry, and the preparations for the hunt?

2. In the fourth stanza the hunters become the hunted. What does this stanza contribute to the general significance of the poem?

3. Explain the following lines:

"Diamonds on the brake are gleaming . . ."
(line 12)

"Tell them youth, and mirth, and glee,
Run a course as well as we . . ." (lines 27–28)

What figure of speech does the poet use in these last two lines?

RHYME AND RHYTHM

Read the poem aloud and notice how rapidly it moves. To achieve this rapid movement, the poet has used several kinds of repetition, including both rhyme and rhythm.

What is the rhyme scheme of "Hunting Song"? Two consecutive lines that rhyme with each other are called a *couplet*. How does Scott use couplets that end in –*ay* to link the various stanzas? Do these rhymes slow or speed the movement of the poem?

As you know, a repeated line, such as "Waken, lords and ladies gay," is called a refrain. How many times is the refrain repeated in this poem? Does it become more or less stirring through repetition?

Rhythm is the rise and fall of stressed and unstressed syllables in a poem. What is the poet's rhythm pattern in "Hunting Song"? Do most of the lines begin with a stressed or an unstressed syllable? Is this a strong or a weak beginning? Do most of the lines end with a stressed or an unstressed syllable? How does the poet's rhythm pattern speed up the movement of the poem?

ABOUT THE POET

Sir Walter Scott (1771–1832) was England's most popular writer of historical novels. For background on the life of Scott, see page 157.

Reveille

A. E. HOUSMAN

Wake: the silver dusk returning
  Up the beach of darkness brims,
And the ship of sunrise burning
  Strands° upon the eastern rims.

Wake: the vaulted shadow shatters,   5
  Trampled to the floor it spanned,
And the tent of night in tatters
  Straws the sky-pavilioned land.

Up, lad, up, 'tis late for lying:
  Hear the drums of morning play;   10
Hark, the empty highways crying
  "Who'll beyond the hills away?"

Towns and countries woo together,
  Forelands beacon, belfries call;
Never lad that trod on leather   15
  Lived to feast his heart with all.

Up, lad: thews° that lie and cumber°
  Sunlit pallets° never thrive;
Morns abed and daylight slumber
  Were not meant for man alive.   20

Clay lies still, but blood's a rover;
  Breath's a ware° that will not keep.
Up, lad: when the journey's over
  There'll be time enough to sleep.

4. **strands:** runs aground. 17. **thews:** muscles. **cumber:** encumber, weigh down on. 18. **pallet:** a cot or mattress, usually of straw. 22. **ware:** product.

"Reveille" from "A Shropshire Lad"—Authorised Edition—from *The Collected Poems of A. E. Housman.* Copyright 1939, 1940, © 1965 by Holt, Rinehart and Winston. Copyright © 1967, 1968 by Robert E. Symons. Reprinted by permission of Holt, Rinehart and Winston, Publishers, The Society of Authors as the literary representative of the Estate of A. E. Housman, and Jonathan Cape Ltd., publishers of A. E. Housman's *Collected Poems.*

FOR STUDY AND DISCUSSION

1. Check the dictionary for the meaning and pronunciation of *reveille*. How does the title suggest the poem's purpose and meaning?

2. The first two stanzas present a dramatic picture of the dawn. What is the "beach of darkness"? What is the "ship of sunrise"? On what is it stranded? In stanza 2, what happens to night with the approach of morning? Which words and phrases make the picture of this event vivid and exciting?

3. In stanzas 3 and 4, what calls to the lad to get up? Which lines best suggest the adventure that lies "beyond the hills"? Restate in your own words the meaning of lines 15–16.

4. What does the poet mean by "Clay lies still, but blood's a rover"? To what does *clay* refer? To what does *blood* refer? In what sense is breath "a ware that will not keep"?

5. In "Hunting Song" Scott says that in life, we are, in a sense, being hunted by time. In lines 23–24, what is Housman's comment on life? How are the two statements similar? Which statement do you think most forcefully expresses the poet's thought? Why?

RHYTHM

Housman begins each line of "Reveille" with a heavy beat—a stressed syllable much like a bugle call. What is the rhythm pattern of the first two lines? Is this pattern repeated throughout the poem? How is the rhythm pattern of "Reveille" different from that of "Bugle Song"? In which poem does the rhythm convey a greater sense of urgency? How is the rhythm of each poem affected by its punctuation? by its rhyme?

LANGUAGE AND VOCABULARY

If none of the following words had been explained by footnotes, could you have guessed their meaning from how they are used in the poem?

strands (line 4)	pallets (line 18)
thews (line 17)	ware (line 22)
cumber (line 17)	

Look up the complete definitions of these words in a dictionary. Try substituting a more familiar word with the same meaning for each word where it appears in the poem. Now read the poem aloud. Can you see why the poet used the more unusual word? What is there about the sound or rhythm or the meaning of Housman's words that makes them a better choice? If any of your substitutions seem better to you than the original word, see if the rest of the class agrees.

ABOUT THE POET

During his lifetime A. E. Housman (1859–1936) was considered something of a mystery. Gay and lively as a boy, with many friends, during his college years he suddenly became shy and melancholy. His poems are the poems of doomed youth—of beauty that must fade and young men who must die. Anyone familiar with his work can understand why he described the writing of poetry as a fever that he could endure only for short periods of time. His collections of poetry include *A Shropshire Lad* and *Last Poems*. Housman, a renowned classical scholar, was professor of Latin at Cambridge University, England, for many years.

The Lorelei

HEINRICH HEINE

Translated by Louis Untermeyer

I cannot tell why this imagined
Sorrow has fallen on me;
The ghost of an unburied legend
   That will not let me be.

The air is cool, and twilight   5
   Flows down the quiet Rhine;
A mountain alone in the high light
   Catches the faltering shine.

One rosy peak half gleaming
   Reveals, enthroned in air,   10
A goddess, lost in dreaming,
   Who combs her golden hair.

With a golden comb she is combing
   Her hair as she sings a song;
Heard and reheard in the gloaming   15
   It hurries the night along.

The boatman has heard what has bound him
   In throes of a strange, wild love.
He is blind to the reefs that surround him,
   Who sees but the vision above.   20

And lo, the wild waters are springing—
   The boat and the boatman are gone. . . .
Then silence. And this with her singing,
   The Lorelei has done.

FOR STUDY AND DISCUSSION

1. At what time of day does the boatman encounter the Lorelei? What kind of mood might you expect him to be in at this time of day? Do you think such a mood would make him more likely to fall under the Lorelei's spell? Why or why not?

2. How does the maiden make the boatman unaware of his danger? To which two of his senses does she appeal?

3. What hint of approaching disaster is given in stanza 5? Were you, despite this hint, surprised by the suddenness of the disaster? Did your surprise help you to understand what happened to the boatman?

4. The poem begins with a reference to an "imagined sorrow." Whom has the sorrow "fallen on"? Why do you think the poet describes the river, the mountain, and the maiden so much more fully than the actual disaster? Can an argument be made that the poem is not so much about the boatman's disaster as about the poet's sorrow? Why or why not?

5. If you have read about Odysseus' encounter with the sirens, who also lured passing ships to disaster, compare the two stories. Whose appeal is more alluring—the sirens' or the Lorelei's? Why was Odysseus able to avoid the boatman's fate?

THE USE OF SOUND

In translating this poem, the translator—who is himself a poet—was careful to preserve its musical quality. He has done this by repeating the sounds of certain vowels and consonants throughout the poem. The repetition of consonant sounds, as you know, is called *alliteration,* and the repetition of vowel sounds is called *assonance.* Which consonant sounds are repeated most often in "The Lorelei"? Which vowel sounds?

Did you notice, in looking for alliteration, that most of the consonant sounds in the poem are "soft" sounds? Consonants such as *l, s, m,* and *n* are not spoken with the explosive force of such "hard" sounds as *b, p, d,* and *g.*

Why are soft sounds more appropriate to this poem?

At what point in the poem would hard sounds be appropriate to the action of the poem? In which consecutive lines did the translator use *b, p, d,* and *g* all together to give a feeling of sudden violence? In the last two lines of the poem, what kinds of sounds does the translator use to suggest the closing of the waters over the wreck?

ABOUT THE POET

Heinrich Heine (1797–1856), a truly Romantic poet, fell in love with his cousin Amalie at seventeen and with her sister Therese at twenty-three. While at law school he was exiled from the town for challenging another student to a duel. Later he was forced to live outside Germany because of official outrage at his satiric writing. All of his poetry iş musical and full of intense feeling.

London Town

JOHN MASEFIELD

Oh London Town's a fine town, and London sights are rare,°
And London ale is right ale, and brisk's the London air,
And busily goes the world there, but crafty grows the mind,
And London Town of all towns I'm glad to leave behind.

Then hey for croft and hop-yard,° and hill, and field, and pond, 5
With Bredon Hill before me and Malvern Hill beyond.
The hawthorn white i' the hedgerow, and all the spring's attire
In the comely° land of Teme and Lugg, and Clent, and Clee, and Wyre.°

Oh London girls are brave° girls, in silk and cloth o' gold,
And London shops are rare shops where gallant things are sold, 10
And bonnily° clinks the gold there, but drowsily blinks the eye,
And London Town of all towns I'm glad to hurry by.

---

1. **rare:** excellent, fine. 5. **croft and hop-yard:** a small farm; a courtyard of hops, an herb used in brewing. 8. **comely:** attractive. **Teme . . . Wyre:** place names of the Severn Valley in western England. 9. **brave:** finely dressed, splendid. 11. **bonnily:** merrily, attractively.

Then, hey for covert° and woodland, and ash and elm and oak,
Tewkesbury inns, and Malvern roofs, and Worcester chimney smoke,
The apple trees in the orchard, the cattle in the byre,°   15
And all the land from Ludlow town to Bredon church's spire.

Oh London tunes are new tunes, and London books are wise,
And London plays are rare plays, and fine to country eyes,
But wretchedly fare the most there, and happily fare the few,
And London Town of all towns I'm glad to hurry through.   20

So hey for the road, the west road, by mill and forge and fold,
Scent of the fern and song of the lark by brook, and field, and wold,°
To the comely folk at the hearthstone and the talk beside the fire,
In the hearty land, where I was bred, my land of heart's desire.

13. **covert:** a thicket, a shady place.   15. **byre:** stable.   22. **wold:** wood.

FOR STUDY AND DISCUSSION

1. The structure of this poem emphasizes the contrast between the English countryside and London Town. Which stanzas deal with the city? which with the country? In what ways is the country different from the city?

2. What good things does the speaker admit can be found in London? In the last part of lines 3, 11, and 19, what bad effects does he suggest that city life has on people?

3. In stanzas 2, 4, and 6, how does the speaker give a sense of open spaces and fresh country air? Do the pauses called for by punctuation make the lines more or less open? How do the place names mentioned by the speaker suggest an actual journey?

4. As you know, a refrain is a phrase or sentence that is repeated a number of times in a poem. In "London Town" one refrain is used in speaking of the city and another in speaking of the country. What phrase is repeated, with the variation of a word or two, in stanzas 1, 3, and 5? What phrase is repeated in stanzas 2, 4, and 6? How do these refrains contribute to the contrast between city and country in the poem?

FOR COMPOSITION

1. Poets often write about real places where they once were or would very much like to be. A. E. Housman, who wrote the poem "Rev-eille," wrote many poems about the towns and countryside that Masefield speaks of in "London Town." Is there a place that you have seen or read about to which you long to go? In a short composition describe such a place, telling why it appeals to you. Or, if you like, try to express your feelings about the place in a short poem.

2. Which do you prefer, the city or the country? Why? Give the reasons for your preference in a short composition, with one paragraph on what you like about one, either city or country, and another paragraph on what you dislike about the other.

ABOUT THE POET

John Masefield (1874–1967) tramped the English countryside as a boy and went to sea at the age of fourteen. Three years later, tired of this life, he disembarked in New York City and proceeded to support himself by odd jobs that included working in a bakery, a livery stable, and a saloon. This varied experience of life made him want to read and write poetry, and for a few years he read eagerly all the great English poets. At the end of that time he returned to England and a few years later published *Salt Water Ballads,* his first and finest book of poems. His poetry became popular immediately and eventually earned him the title of poet laureate.

An Old Song

SOLOMON BLOOMGARDEN

Translated by Marie Syrkin

In the blossom-land Japan
Somewhere thus an old song ran.
Said a warrior to a smith,
"Hammer me a sword forthwith.
Make the blade   5
Light as wind on water laid.
Make it long
As the wheat at harvest song.
Supple, swift
As a snake, without rift,   10
Full of lightnings, thousand-eyed!
Smooth as silken cloth and thin
As the web that spiders spin.
And merciless as pain, and cold."

"On the hilt what shall be told?"   15

"On the sword's hilt, my good man,"
Said the warrior of Japan,
"Trace for me
A running lake, a flock of sheep,   19
And one who sings her child to sleep."

"An Old Song" by Solomon Bloomgarden, translated by Marie
Syrkin. Reprinted by permission of Marie Syrkin.

FOR STUDY AND DISCUSSION

1. What contrast is there between what the
warrior wants in the blade of his sword and
what he wants traced on the sword's hilt? Do
you think the scene on the hilt represents
something he dreams of having or something
he is fighting to protect? What comment does
the poem make on the reasons we go to war?

2. With the exception of the first two lines,
this poem consists of a dialogue. Who are the
speakers?

3. The warrior describes the blade of his
sword in a series of similes. How many similes
does he use in his description? Japanese poetry
is noted for its vivid pictures of nature. Which
of the warrior's similes do you find most
striking?

4. In translating this poem from Yiddish,
the language in which Solomon Bloomgarden
wrote it, the translator has tried to preserve
the light, musical character of the original
source, an old Japanese song. Where has she
used rhyme to emphasize key words?

ABOUT THE POET

Solomon Bloomgarden (1870–1927) grew
up in Lithuania. At the age of twenty he came
to America, where he worked for ten years
before falling ill with tuberculosis. Forced to
enter a sanitarium for a rest cure, he began to
devote all his time to writing. He is known
not only for his poems but for his essays and
translations, notably his translation of the
Old Testament into Yiddish.

maggie and milly and molly and may

E. E. CUMMINGS

maggie and milly and molly and may
went down to the beach(to play one day)

and maggie discovered a shell that sang
so sweetly she couldn't remember her troubles,and

milly befriended a stranded star   5
whose rays five languid fingers were;

and molly was chased by a horrible thing
which raced sideways while blowing bubbles:and

may came home with a smooth round stone
as small as a world and as large as alone.   10

For whatever we lose(like a you or a me)
it's always ourselves we find in the sea

FOR STUDY AND DISCUSSION

1. Each of the girls described by the poet looks at the world of the seashore differently. Judging from their reactions, which girl is the kindest? which is the most excitable? which is inclined to daydream? How would you describe the fourth girl's reaction? With which girl (or girls) did you feel most sympathy? Why?

2. How does the poet's statement in the last two lines of the poem apply to the girls' experiences? How did each of them, in a sense, find herself in the sea? Explain in your own words the meaning of the poem's last two lines.

CONNOTATIVE WORDS

In a poem, the music of the words and rhythms helps to arouse specific sensations in the reader, as do the words' meanings. Words that arouse feelings through the ideas they suggest or that imply a meaning additional to the literal meaning are said to have *connotations*. What connotations are aroused by "a shell that sang"? by "a horrible thing/ which raced sideways"? Which words in these lines are most successful in suggesting—or *connoting*—additional meanings? How do the sounds of these words add to their connotations?

ABOUT THE POET

E. E. Cummings (1894–1962) enlisted in the French Ambulance Corps and then in the American Infantry in World War I. After the war he divided his time between New York and Paris, writing and painting. Unlike many poets, he earned his living entirely through the sale and reading of his poems. A deep believer in the value of love, Cummings resorted to all sorts of experiments and "tricks" of language and punctuation to communicate to his readers the beauty of what he saw around him.

PICTURES IN POETRY

Night Clouds

AMY LOWELL

The white mares of the moon rush along the sky
Beating their golden hoofs upon the glass Heavens;
The white mares of the moon are all standing on their hind legs
Pawing at the green porcelain doors of the remote Heavens.
Fly, mares!   5
Strain your utmost,
Scatter the milky dust of stars,
Or the tiger sun will leap upon you and destroy you
With one lick of his vermilion tongue.

FOR STUDY AND DISCUSSION

1. This poem begins with a *metaphor* (see page 164). To the poet, what do the night clouds seem to be? What characteristic of the appearance of clouds at night might have suggested this metaphor to the poet?

2. Which actions of the "white mares of the moon" are especially violent? Which create an impression of swiftness? How might night clouds "scatter the milky dust of stars"?

3. What does the poet urge the mares to do? Why? What does the poem's last metaphor (lines 8–9) suggest about the sun?

IMAGERY

Poetry, like all forms of art, attempts to share an experience. Some poets are particularly gifted at making us aware, through the very language of their poems, of what they have seen, heard, touched, or tasted. Words and phrases that communicate such sense impressions are called *imagery,* and a single picture or impression is called an *image.*

Imagery appeals to the imagination. A good poet uses words in a fresh or unusual way to reveal some new relationship or meaning. To do this, the poet often uses figures of speech such as similes (page 162) and metaphors (page 164).

In "Night Clouds" Amy Lowell describes the night sky in images that suggest a fairy tale. The moonlit clouds are "white mares of the moon" and the morning sun is a leaping tiger with a bright red-orange tongue. What other images are there in the poem? What do they represent in nature? Which words create striking color images? Which image suggests a startling sound?

ABOUT THE POET

Amy Lowell (1874–1925) was born and raised in Massachusetts. She acquired most of her education by studying in her father's library. When she became interested in writing poetry, she displayed the same self-reliance and determination, shutting herself up in her room with books and paper. Within a few years she became an accomplished poet. Later she became the leader of a group of poets called the Imagists. She worked tirelessly in their behalf and published their poems.

"Night Clouds" from *What's O'Clock* by Amy Lowell. Reprinted by permission of Houghton Mifflin Company.

Silver

WALTER DE LA MARE

Slowly, silently, now the moon
Walks the night in her silver shoon;°
This way, and that, she peers, and sees
Silver fruit upon silver trees;
One by one the casements catch   5
Her beams beneath the silvery thatch;
Couched in his kennel, like a log,
With paws of silver sleeps the dog;
From their shadowy cote° the white breasts peep
Of doves in a silver-feathered sleep;   10
A harvest mouse goes scampering by,
With silver claws and a silver eye;
And moveless fish in the water gleam,
By silver reeds in a silver stream.

2. **shoon:** shoes.   9. **cote:** coop.

FOR STUDY AND DISCUSSION

1. Which word links the various images in this poem into one dominant impression? What is that impression? What objects and animals are silvered by the moonlight? In what way does the word *silver* function as a refrain in the poem?

2. Which words in the poem suggest motion? How is the pace of this movement different from that in "Night Clouds"? What is the rhyme scheme of "Silver"?

3. Find several examples of alliteration in this poem. Which consonant sounds are repeated most frequently?

4. *Consonance* is the repetition of several identical consonant sounds, either in a single word or in words which follow each other. The very first line of "Silver" begins with consonance: *"Slowly, silently . . ."* These same liquid sounds, *s* and *l*, are repeated frequently throughout the poem. Why do you think these soft, musical sounds are appropriate to the mood of this poem?

PERSONIFICATION

Personification is a figure of speech that gives human qualities or characteristics to an animal, object, or idea. Where in this poem does the poet personify the moon by speaking of it as if it were a person? Which words in the poem suggest that the moon is human?

Did any of the metaphors in "Night Clouds" involve personification? How do you know?

ABOUT THE POET

Walter de la Mare (1873–1956) was born in England and educated in London. He became a clerk in a London office at the age of seventeen. Stifled by the dullness of this life, he took refuge in writing poems based on dreams and fantasy. Within a few years, his very distinctive poems won him a government pension that enabled him to devote all his time to writing. Most of his poems suggest an eerie sense of the supernatural. One of his best known collections of verse is *The Veil.*

Travel

ROBERT LOUIS STEVENSON

I should like to rise and go
Where the golden.apples grow;
Where below another sky
Parrot islands anchored lie,
And, watched by cockatoos and goats, 5
Lonely Crusoes building boats;
Where in sunshine reaching out
Eastern cities, miles about,
Are with mosque and minaret
Among sandy gardens set, 10
And the rich goods from near and far
Hang for sale in the bazaar;
Where the Great Wall round China goes,
And on one side the desert blows,
And with bell and voice and drum, 15
Cities on the other hum;
Where are forests, hot as fire,
Wide as England, tall as a spire,
Full of apes and coconuts
And the Negro hunters' huts; 20
Where the knotty crocodile
Lies and blinks in the Nile,
And the red flamingo flies

Hunting fish before his eyes;
Where in jungles, near and far, 25
Man-devouring tigers are,
Lying close and giving ear
Lest the hunt be drawing near,
Or a comer-by be seen
Swinging in a palanquin;° 30
Where among the desert sands
Some deserted city stands,
All its children, sweep° and prince,
Grown to manhood ages since,
Not a foot in street or house, 35
Not a stir of child or mouse,
And when kindly falls the night,
In all the town no spark of light.
There I'll come when I'm a man
With a camel caravan; 40
Light a fire in the gloom
Of some dusty dining room;
See the pictures on the walls,
Heroes, fights, and festivals;
And in a corner find the toys 45
Of the old Egyptian boys.

30. **palanquin** (pal'ən·kēn'): an enclosed chair or litter carried on projecting poles; used in India and China. 33. **sweep**: a chimney sweeper. Small children often cleaned chimneys in Stevenson's time.

FOR STUDY AND DISCUSSION

1. Of the places suggested in the poem, how many can you identify? Does the poet seem to be writing about specific places or trying to give a general impression of exotic foreign scenes? Which lines in the poem make you think so?

2. How old, would you guess, is the speaker in the poem? Where do you think he has gotten his information about the places he dreams of visiting?

3. Most of the images in this poem are visual—they make the reader *see*. Which pictures do you find most striking? Why? Which images appeal to other senses?

ABOUT THE POET

Robert Louis Stevenson (1850–1894) is better known for his stories and novels than for his poetry, but one of his books of poems, *A Child's Garden of Verses*, has always been extremely popular. Much of his best work was written for children; he delighted in seeing the world as if through a child's eyes. In addition to stories, essays, and travel sketches, Stevenson wrote a number of exciting novels, including *Kidnapped, Treasure Island,* and *The Master of Ballantrae.* Two exceptional long stories are "Markheim" and "The Strange Case of Dr. Jekyll and Mr. Hyde." Stevenson is unexcelled as a writer of adventure stories.

Oread

H. D.

This little poem is spoken by an oread—a nymph of the mountains. In Greek mythology, the nymphs were immortal maidens who inhabited the mountains, the forests, and the sea.

> Whirl up, sea—
> Whirl your pointed pines.
> Splash your great pines
> On our rocks.
> Hurl your green over us—   5
> Cover us with your pools of fir.

ALLUSION

In line 6 of "Travel" ("Lonely Crusoes building boats"), Stevenson uses a literary *allusion*—a reference to a work of literature with which he expects his readers to be familiar. What do you need to know about *Robinson Crusoe* to understand Stevenson's allusion in line 6?

Ancient myths and legends, especially, are often alluded to by writers. The "golden apples" in line 2 of "Travel," for instance, might be an allusion to the golden apples in Greek mythology, which grew in an enchanted garden.

Allusions do much to enrich our understanding of a writer's meaning. But they need not always refer to other works of literature. Allusions can be made to almost anything real or fictitious outside the literary work you are reading. The test of an effective allusion, whether a literary allusion or not, is its appropriateness and its relevance to the author's point.

Where is there an allusion in "Oread"? (What part of the poem needed a preliminary explanation?) How does this allusion enrich the meaning of this brief and simple poem? What other poems that you have read have made allusions to history, mythology, or legend?

FOR STUDY AND DISCUSSION

1. This entire poem is actually a single metaphor—a description of one thing as something else. To what is the oread speaking? What else, in her mind, does it seem to be?

2. What are the "pointed pines" of the sea? What other likenesses does the oread see between the forests and the sea?

3. What does the oread urge the sea to do? What action words does the poet use to suggest the speaker's mood? How do the poem's short lines and irregular rhythms emphasize this mood?

ABOUT THE POET

Hilda Doolittle (1886–1961), who wrote under the pen name of H. D., grew up in Philadelphia. After beginning to write poetry, she, like Amy Lowell (see page 176), became a member of the Imagists, a group of poets who believed that a poem should consist of a single, powerful image. Her own poetry—simple and direct—was extremely successful in achieving the Imagist ideal. In addition to her poetry, H. D. is known for her translations of Greek and Latin poems. Most of her life was spent in Europe, in self-imposed exile, including about thirty years in Switzerland.

The Fawn

EDNA ST. VINCENT MILLAY

There it was I saw what I shall never forget
And never retrieve.
Monstrous and beautiful to human eyes, hard to believe,
He lay, yet there he lay,
Asleep on the moss, his head on his polished cleft small ebony hooves,   5
The child of the doe, the dappled child of the deer.

Surely his mother had never said, "Lie here
Till I return," so spotty and plain to see
On the green moss lay he.
His eyes had opened; he considered me.   10

I would have given more than I care to say
To thrifty ears, might I have had him for my friend
One moment only of that forest day:

Might I have had the acceptance, not the love
Of those clear eyes;   15
Might I have been for him the bough above
Or the root beneath his forest bed,
A part of the forest, seen without surprise.

Was it alarm, or was it the wind of my fear lest he depart
That jerked him to his jointy knees   20
And sent him crashing off, leaping and stumbling
On his new legs, between the stems of the white trees?

FOR STUDY AND DISCUSSION

1. What about the fawn caused the poet's wonder? Why did he seem "monstrous" as well as beautiful? (What meaning of the word is the poet using here?) Which pictures in the poem help you to share the poet's wonder?

2. What kind of relationship with the fawn did the poet wish for? What is the difference between "acceptance" and "love," as these words are used in line 14? Why was the poet disappointed when the fawn became frightened and ran away?

3. Point out three or four striking images in the poem. Which pictures are so clear and sharply defined that they seem almost like photographs?

ABOUT THE POET

Edna St. Vincent Millay (1892–1950) wrote a prize poem at the age of nineteen, acted with the Provincetown Players, in Greenwich Village, and finally married and retired to the Berkshire Hills. For more information on Edna St. Vincent Millay, see page 241.

Poem

WILLIAM CARLOS WILLIAMS

As the cat
climbed over
the top of

the jamcloset
first the right   5
forefoot

carefully
then the hind
stepped down

into the pit of   10
the empty
flower pot

FOR STUDY AND DISCUSSION

1. What is unusual about the form of this poem? How does it suggest the movement of the cat? Which words in particular make you feel that you are watching the cat?

2. In writing this poem in free verse, the poet omitted all punctuation. Try reading the poem aloud. Do you notice the lack of punctuation, or do the line and stanza breaks provide the necessary pauses? If you had written the poem, would you have ended it with a period? Why or why not?

FREE VERSE

Free verse is poetry that does not have a fixed pattern of rhyme, rhythm, or line length. By deliberately not restricting themselves to a set rhyme scheme or a certain number of syllables to a line, poets are able to fit their sounds and rhythms more closely to the meaning of their poems. The free verse of William Carlos Williams is remarkable for its use of everyday language and natural speech rhythms.

FOR COMPOSITION

Observe a simple action of some animal as carefully as Williams must have observed a cat. Then, in a short composition, describe the action in exact detail. If you like, indicate pauses and hesitations by writing your composition in free verse.

ABOUT THE POET

William Carlos Williams (1883–1963) was born in New Jersey. Perhaps because of his varied ancestry, which included large mixtures of British, French, Spanish, and Jewish blood, he always felt a keen sympathy for all kinds and nationalities of people. For most of his life, in addition to writing stories, poems, and essays, he was a practicing pediatrician. A close and careful observer of the life around him, Williams shows in all his writing a deep responsiveness to the inner qualities of things. For example, a board fence painted a certain color and weathered by the elements is to him a splendid subject for a poem.

A Narrow Fellow in the Grass

EMILY DICKINSON

A narrow fellow in the grass
Occasionally rides;
You may have met him—did you not?
His notice sudden is.

The grass divides as with a comb,   5
A spotted shaft is seen;
And then it closes at your feet
And opens further on.

He likes a boggy acre,
A floor too cool for corn.   10
Yet when a boy, and barefoot,
I more than once, at noon,

Have passed, I thought, a whiplash
Unbraiding in the sun—
When, stooping to secure it,   15
It wrinkled, and was gone.

Several of nature's people
I know, and they know me;
I feel for them a transport°
Of cordiality;   20

But never met this fellow,
Attended or alone,
Without a tighter breathing,
And zero at the bone.

19. **transport:** strong feeling.

FOR STUDY AND DISCUSSION

1. Which images in the poem are particularly effective in helping you to share the speaker's experience? Which details of the snake's appearance make him seem real?

2. In stanza 2, three different figures of speech—simile, metaphor, and personification—all contribute to a single picture. Identify each of these. Which do you consider the most striking image? Why?

IMAGERY

Much of the impact of imagery comes from words that are both exact and unexpected. Emily Dickinson's poems are full of words that surprise the reader with highly accurate pictures. What more ordinary word might the poet have used in place of each of the following? How does the word she used present a more vivid picture?

"rides"—line 2   "wrinkled"—line 16
"notice"—line 4   "tighter"—line 23
"unbraiding"—line 14   "zero"—line 24

FOR COMPOSITION

Recall some event that gave you a sudden feeling of terror—a "zero at the bone." Describe what happened in such exact and vivid pictures that your classmates will share your reaction to the incident as fully as you felt it at the time.

ABOUT THE POET

Emily Dickinson (1830–1886) lived practically all of her life in Amherst, Massachusetts. A sensitive young girl, she became increasingly disillusioned with the world around her and kept more and more to herself as the years went on. During the last part of her life, she rarely left her father's house and garden. She wrote her poems, expressions of her deepest thoughts and feelings, on scraps of paper, including the backs of envelopes and old grocery bills. Her poetry is remarkable for its striking pictures and original phrasings. In her poetry, even the most familiar things seem to take on new significance and meaning.

Desert Places

ROBERT FROST

Snow falling and night falling fast, oh, fast
In a field I looked into going past,
And the ground almost covered smooth in snow,
But a few weeds and stubble showing last.

The woods around it have it—it is theirs.   5
All animals are smothered in their lairs.
I am too absent-spirited to count;
The loneliness includes me unawares.

And lonely as it is, that loneliness
Will be more lonely ere it will be less—   10
A blanker whiteness of benighted° snow
With no expression, nothing to express.

They cannot scare me with their empty spaces
Between stars—on stars where no human race is.
I have it in me so much nearer home   15
To scare myself with my own desert places.

11. **benighted:** overtaken by the night or darkness.

FOR STUDY AND DISCUSSION

1. What scene is described in stanza 1? Which details suggest blankness or emptiness? What time of day is it? How long has it been snowing? How do lines 5 and 6 heighten the mood of the scene? Which single word would you say best describes this mood?

2. Frost first mentions his own state of mind in line 7. What does he mean by "absent-spirited"? How does "the loneliness" include him "unawares"? Who is unaware of his being included—Frost or "the loneliness," or both?

3. In stanza 3, the poet looks into the future. What change does he foresee in the scene? in his own mood?

4. The last stanza of the poem is entirely about the poet. Who is the "they" in line 13? Why can't they frighten him?

SYMBOLS

A *symbol* suggests or stands for a broad, abstract idea or meaning. In time, certain objects become associated with certain meanings, such as a flag with patriotism, scales with justice, a rose with love or beauty. What, for example, does the color red suggest or symbolize to you? What do you think the "desert places" symbolize in this poem?

ABOUT THE POET

Robert Frost (1874–1963) was born in San Francisco but spent most of his life in New England. He worked at a variety of odd jobs, teaching, and farming for many years before gaining recognition as a poet. Since then he has won four Pulitzer prizes for his poetry.

My Heart Leaps Up

WILLIAM WORDSWORTH

My heart leaps up when I behold
A rainbow in the sky.
So was it when my life began;
So is it now I am a man,
So be it when I shall grow old,   5
   Or let me die!
The child is father of the man;
And I could wish my days to be
Bound each to each by natural piety.°

9. **natural piety:** reverent regard for nature.

FOR STUDY AND DISCUSSION

1. In these nine lines William Wordsworth, a poet who has been called "the high priest of nature," expresses much of his personal philosophy. What is it that he wants to keep throughout his lifetime? Why might a child rather than an adult be more likely to have this quality? What does the phrase "natural piety" suggest about Wordsworth's attitude toward nature? Is he serious about it? Does he seem to feel a kind of awe? Why might someone call him "the high priest of nature"?

2. Explain how the heart can "leap up" at the sight of beauty. Is the poet speaking literally or figuratively? What is this figure of speech called? What others like it are there in the poem?

3. A statement such as line 7, "The child is father of the man," is called a *paradox*, because it at first seems self-contradictory and therefore untrue, but on further thought it can be seen to contain an element of truth. In what sense is a child the "father" of the man he eventually becomes? What does Wordsworth feel an adult should have learned from childhood?

LYRIC POETRY

Originally, in the ancient world, lyrics were sung to the accompaniment of a lyre, a harplike instrument. Today, the word "lyric" is used to describe a short poem in which the poet expresses a personal thought or feeling. Love poems and meditative poems are among the most common lyrics.

Lyric poets attempt to make their readers share their thoughts or feelings. In his lyric "My Heart Leaps Up," Wordsworth uses both sound and imagery to convey his feelings. Where does he use word repetition for greater force and emphasis? Where does he use a short line for emphasis? Which figure of speech most strikingly suggests the speaker's feelings?

ABOUT THE POET

William Wordsworth (1770–1850) grew up in the English countryside and lived close to nature all his life. Most of his finest poems are brief lyrics praising nature and meditating on its meaning in our lives. Intensely sensitive to the beauty of his natural surroundings, he hated all that was false or artificial.

Music

RALPH WALDO EMERSON

Let me go where're I will
I hear a sky-born music still:
It sounds from all things old,
It sounds from all things young,
From all that's fair, from all that's foul, 5
Peals out a cheerful song.

It is not only in the rose,
It is not only in the bird,
Not only where the rainbow glows,
Nor in the song of woman heard, 10
But in the darkest, meanest things
There always, always something sings.

'Tis not in the high stars alone,
Nor in the cup of budding flowers,
Nor in the redbreast's mellow tone, 15
Nor in the bow that smiles in showers,
But in the mud and scum of things
There always, always something sings.

FOR STUDY AND DISCUSSION

1. What is the mood of Emerson's poem? Judging from this poem, would you call him an optimist or a pessimist? Which lines sum up his way of looking at things? What is his attitude toward things that are usually considered disagreeable?

2. Only a few of the objects the poet mentions can actually sing or create sound. Why, then, do you think he speaks of "music"? What figure of speech is he using here? In what sense is the music "sky-born"?

3. Although the poet says there is beauty in the ugliest of things, he gives no examples of such beauty. In view of this, why is his argument as convincing as it is? How does he prepare you, in the first stanza of the poem, to see beauty in all kinds of things?

MUSIC AND LYRIC POETRY

Ever since their beginnings as songs, lyrics have been extremely musical. In writing lyrics, poets have found all sorts of musical devices (such as rhythm, rhyme, assonance, and alliteration) effective in helping them to communicate their thoughts and feelings.

Read Emerson's poem aloud. How does the music of the poem suggest the music the poet hears around him? Which musical devices do most to create the music of the poem?

FOR COMPOSITION

In a paragraph or two, compare "Music" with "My Heart Leaps Up." How are the two poems alike? How are they different? Which poet is concerned more with the world around him? Which is concerned more with his own feelings? Which poem did you prefer? Why?

ABOUT THE POET

Ralph Waldo Emerson (1803–1882) is remembered as a lecturer and writer of thoughtful essays, but he was also a poet. His philosophy of Transcendentalism, a belief that there are truths in the world which "transcend," or "go beyond," what is provable by everyday logic, was an important influence on American ideas. In his writings, Emerson offered his own strong New England belief in the virtues of honesty, endurance, and self-reliance as fundamental American ideals.

Psalm 96

THE KING JAMES BIBLE

O sing unto the Lord a new song:
Sing unto the Lord, all the earth.
Sing unto the Lord, bless His name;
Show forth His salvation from day to day.
Declare His glory among the heathen,   5
His wonders among all people.
For the Lord is great, and greatly to be praised:
He is to be feared above all gods.
For all the gods of the nations are idols:
But the Lord made the heavens.   10
Honor and majesty are before Him:
Strength and beauty are in His sanctuary.
Give unto the Lord, O ye kindreds of the people,
Give unto the Lord glory and strength.
Give unto the Lord the glory due unto His name: 15
Bring an offering, and come into His courts.
O worship the Lord in the beauty of holiness:
Fear before Him, all the earth.
Say among the heathen that the Lord reigneth:
The world also shall be established that it shall not be moved: 20
He shall judge the people righteously.
Let the heavens rejoice, and let the earth be glad;
Let the sea roar, and the fullness thereof.
Let the field be joyful, and all that is therein:
Then shall all the trees of the wood rejoice   25
Before the Lord: for He cometh,
For He cometh to judge the earth:
He shall judge the world with righteousness,
And the people with His truth.

FOR STUDY AND DISCUSSION

1. What reasons does the poet give for singing praises to the Lord? According to the poet, in what ways can people praise the Lord?

2. What message is to be given to the heathen? How will the Lord judge the people? What reaction to this message does the speaker foresee throughout the world?

3. The ancient Hebrew poets were fond of using images from nature. How does the poet use nature imagery in Psalm 96 to build a joyful climax? How might the heavens "rejoice" and the earth "be glad"?

THE PSALMS

The Psalms are one of the earliest forms of free verse. Although they do not have a regular pattern of rhyme or rhythm, they make strong use of rhythm and nearly every other poetic technique.

One of the devices most frequently used in the poetry of the Psalms is that of *parallelism*—a repetition of rhythm or wording. In rhythmic parallelism, the rhythm of one verse or line corresponds with that of another, so that lines seem to balance or echo each other. Notice examples of parallelism in lines 7, 11–12, 22, and 28–29. What are some others?

What other poetic devices has the poet used to emphasize the meaning of the poem? Where has assonance been used? alliteration?

THE KING JAMES BIBLE

In the vigor, simplicity, and dignity of its language, the King James translation of the Bible (1611)—named after James I, who authorized its preparation—has never been equaled by later translations. Probably the language of no other single book has so profoundly influenced the style of later literature written in English. From the time of its publication to modern times, writers have echoed Biblical phrasing and parallelisms.

Abraham Lincoln Walks at Midnight
in Springfield, Illinois

VACHEL LINDSAY

It is portentous, and a thing of state
That here at midnight, in our little town,
A mourning figure walks, and will not rest,
Near the old courthouse pacing up and down,

Or by his homestead, or in shadowed yards   5
He lingers where his children used to play,
Or through the market, on the well-worn stones,
He stalks until the dawn stars burn away.

A bronzed, lank man! His suit of ancient black,
A famous high top hat and plain worn shawl   10
Make him the quaint great figure that men love,
The prairie lawyer, master of us all.

He cannot sleep upon his hillside now.
He is among us—as in times before!
And we who toss and lie awake for long   15
Breathe deep, and start, to see him pass the door.

His head is bowed. He thinks on men and kings.
Yea, when the sick world cries, how can he sleep?
Too many peasants fight, they know not why,
Too many homesteads in black terror weep.   20

The sins of all the warlords burn his heart.
He sees the dreadnoughts° scouring every main.°
He carries on his shawl-wrapped shoulders now
The bitterness, the folly, and the pain.

He cannot rest until a spirit dawn   25
Shall come—the shining hope of Europe free:
The league of sober folk, the workers' earth,
Bringing long peace to cornland, alp, and sea.

It breaks his heart that kings must murder still,
That all his hours of travail here for men   30
Seem yet in vain. And who will bring white peace
That he may sleep upon his hill again?

22. **dreadnoughts** (dred′nôts′): battleships used by the British in World War I.   **main:** sea.

FOR STUDY AND DISCUSSION

1. This poem is based on a legend that the ghosts of great leaders are restless when their nations are in trouble. It was written in 1914, when World War I began. What references to the war are there in the poem? From what you know about Lincoln, why would he be especially likely to feel "The bitterness, the folly, and the pain" of this worldwide violence?

2. How is Lincoln pictured in the poem? Which details of his appearance are familiar to you from other descriptions? Is it Lincoln's appearance or his behavior that gives him his strange and haunting dignity?

3. While President, what "hours of travail" did Lincoln undergo? If he could return to see our world today, do you think he would find all those hours "yet in vain"? Why or why not?

ABOUT THE POET

Vachel Lindsay (1879–1931) was a poet, an artist, a missionary, and a vagabond. As a young man he went on walking tours throughout the country, reading his poems aloud and trading poetry and drawings for bed and board. Later in life, he made grand tours over the same ground, reciting his poems to jazz rhythms. Lindsay's poetry reveals his love of beauty and hatred of cruelty.

Dirge

PERCY BYSSHE SHELLEY

Rough wind, that moanest loud
  Grief too sad for song;
Wild wind, when sullen cloud
  Knells all the night long;
Sad storm, whose tears are vain,   5
Bare woods, whose branches strain,
Deep caves and dreary main—
  Wail, for the world's wrong!

FOR STUDY AND DISCUSSION

1. Look up the word *dirge* in a dictionary. How well does the title fit this poem?
2. How many of the poet's words suggest sadness and pain? How does the weather contribute to the mood of the poem?

ABOUT THE POET

Percy Bysshe Shelley (1792–1822) lived a life as romantic as his poetry. Always a rebel, he eloped at the age of nineteen and spent much of his life in Europe and in Greece before drowning in a storm at sea.

Uphill

CHRISTINA ROSSETTI

Does the road wind uphill all the way?
  Yes, to the very end.
Will the day's journey take the whole long day?
  From morn to night, my friend.

But is there for the night a resting place?   5
  A roof for when the slow dark hours begin.
May not the darkness hide it from my face?
  You cannot miss that inn.

Shall I meet other wayfarers at night?
  Those who have gone before.   10
Then must I knock, or call when just in sight?
  They will not keep you standing at that door.

Shall I find comfort, travel-sore and weak?
  Of labor you shall find the sum.
Will there be beds for me and all who seek?   15
  Yea, beds for all who come.

1. In form and language, "Uphill" at first seems simple. You probably did not read far before suspecting that the poem is about more than a simple journey. Where did you first become aware of the real subject of the poem? What "journey" is the poet speaking of? What is its destination? What other symbols are there in the poem?

2. This poem is a series of questions and answers. How has the poet arranged the questions and answers to make clear who is speaking? How do the rhymes and line lengths help to distinguish the two speakers?

3. Anyone might ask the questions in this poem. Who do you think answers them?

TONE AND MOOD

Just as tone of voice often indicates a speaker's attitude, so also is an author's attitude toward subject matter revealed by *tone*. What is the tone of the questioner in "Uphill"? Does it differ from that of the second speaker? Are the answers offered frightening or reassuring? How would you read the last line?

What mood does the author's tone produce? Which words do most to create this mood?

ABOUT THE POET

Christina Rossetti (1830–1894) was concerned all her life with religious questions. She knew sorrow at first-hand, having forced herself to refuse two marriages for religious reasons. Her poetry is notable for its honesty and sincerity of purpose, and her pure and subdued lyrics rank among the best English poems of their kind.

Gulls

ROBERT HAYDEN

In sun-whetted
    morning,
the dropped gull
    splayed
on sand,   5
    wind
picking at
    its feathers.

Over the headlong
    toppling   10
rush and leashed-back
    mica'd
fall of the sea,
    gulls
scouting and   15
    crying.

FOR STUDY AND DISCUSSION

1. What has happened to the gull in the first stanza? What might have caused it to drop from the sky? What picture of the gull's condition do you get from lines 4–8?

2. In line 12, what does the word "mica'd" suggest about the color and texture of the sea?

3. How is the sea affected by what has happened? What is the reaction of the other gulls?

ABOUT THE POET

Robert Hayden (1913–) was born in Detroit and went to the University of Michigan. He has won several awards and fellowships for his poetry and now teaches at Fisk University in Nashville, Tennessee. Although he often writes free verse, his lines are always carefully controlled and disciplined.

The Summit Temple

LI PO

Tonight I stay at the Summit Temple.
Here I could pluck the stars with my hand.
I dare not speak aloud in the silence,
For fear of disturbing the dwellers of heaven.

—Translated by Shigeyoshi Obata

FOR STUDY AND DISCUSSION

1. What mood is captured in this poem? How does the poet feel when he says he "could pluck the stars"? Why does he not dare to speak aloud?

2. Who do you think are "the dwellers of heaven"? Why might they be disturbed by someone's speaking aloud?

3. Do you think the poet will ever return from the Summit Temple? Do you think he would be changed if he did return? Explain.

FOR COMPOSITION

The poet does not describe the Summit Temple, except that it seems close to the heavens and full of silence. Do you think the Temple is beautiful? Why? In a short composition (or free-verse poem), describe the appearance of the Summit Temple as you imagine it to be. If you like, base your description on a picture you have seen of an oriental temple.

ABOUT THE POET

Li Po (701?–762) grew up in the mountains of western China in the T'ang Dynasty, the Golden Age of Chinese poetry. A bright child, he had read nearly all the Chinese classics by the time he was ten and preferred writing poetry to any other career. Except for a few years as court poet to the Emperor Hsuan Tsung, Li Po lived all his life among his friends at home. The popular legend of his death is that he drowned one night while trying to embrace the beautiful reflection of the moon in the water.

i thank You God

E. E. CUMMINGS

i thank You God for most-this amazing
day:for the leaping greenly spirits of trees
and a blue true dream of sky;and for everything
which is natural which is infinite which is yes

(i who have died am alive again today,   5
and this is the sun's birthday;this is the birth
day of life and of love and wings:and of the gay
great happening illimitably earth)

how should tasting touching hearing seeing
breathing any—lifted from the no   10
of all nothing—human merely being
doubt unimaginable You?

(now the ears of my ears awake and
now the eyes of my eyes are opened)

FOR STUDY AND DISCUSSION

1. To whom is the poet speaking in this poem? For what is he thankful? What is the season of the year? Why, in this season, might natural things give a feeling of "infinite" and of "yes"? What season is suggested by the "no" out of which all these things have come?

2. In stanza 2, which is placed in parentheses, the poet turns aside from giving thanks for a moment to explain more fully why he is thankful. Why is this day "the sun's birthday"? In what sense is the sun "born"? What season gives birth to "wings"? What is the "gay great happening"?

3. In your own words, explain what the poet says in stanza 3. What added meaning does he gain by arranging the words as he does?

4. In what respect is this poem like Psalm 96? Which lines best express the poet's affirmative point of view?

EXPERIMENTS IN POETRY

As you have seen in both "i thank You God" and "maggie and milly and molly and may," E. E. Cummings likes to experiment with poetry. He does this in order to give fresh expression to emotions people have experienced since time began.

The form of "i thank You God" is an old one. It is a *sonnet,* a fourteen-line lyric poem, with a traditional rhyme scheme. Which lines rhyme (more or less) in each stanza? Does each stanza contain a complete thought?

Within the traditional sonnet form, Cummings experiments with both language and punctuation. What is unusual about the punctuation in the poem? Where has punctuation been omitted to permit a more rapid flow of thought? In which lines do you notice the absence of punctuation most? How does the omission of space after punctuation in other lines affect your reading of the poem?

Paintings in Tempera and Fresco

In our age of mass production, most painters buy their materials ready-made. But during the Middle Ages and the Renaissance, painters prepared many of their pigments in their own workshops. They made them out of colored materials and pieces of earth, which they ground into fine powder and mixed with water to form a paste. They knew how bright or dull certain colors would appear after drying, and they knew fairly well what their paintings would look like after ten, twenty, or even a hundred years. Because artists in those days knew their materials so well, many of their paintings are still in excellent condition.

Look, for instance, at the clear, beautiful colors in the fifteenth-century manuscript illumination reproduced here (PLATE 1). The ultramarine blue used for both the sea and the sky was made from a semi-precious stone called *lapis lazuli*. Before applying each mixture of pigment and water, the artist added a gummy substance to make the paint adhere firmly. Manuscript illuminators often used the white of an egg, but painters who worked on canvas or wooden panels used the yolk. *Egg tempera,* as this kind of paint is called, dries so fast that each new stroke of color can be added almost instantly without blurring or mixing. In a period such as the early Renaissance, when precision of detail was so highly admired, egg tempera was the perfect medium.

Panel paintings were often much larger than manuscript illuminations but could be just as precise in detail (PLATES 2 and 3). The surface of the panel was prepared with many layers of a fine white plaster called *gesso,* rubbed down to a smooth finish. The first colors were often laid on in flat tones and then shaded from light to dark with many tiny strokes of a pointed brush. You can see this kind of shading in the path at the lower left of PLATE 2 and in the highlights of the young man's hair in PLATE 3. If you look closely at the flesh tones in PLATE 3, you can see that they have been underpainted in green. This cool color was used to set off the warmer pink and ivory colors, and to give them a vibrancy they would otherwise lack.

In Renaissance art, two or more events of a story were often illustrated within the same picture. PLATE 1 shows Jonah being tossed to the whale by his shipmates; yet he appears again in the distance, being spewed up by the whale onto the far shore. PLATE 2 shows John the Baptist both in the foreground and again in the distant wilderness. In this picture the artist wanted to make each part of the story equally important, so he made both figures the same size. Notice, though, that the landscape in between helps to give some illusion of space and distance.

When Italian artists of the fifteenth and sixteenth centuries painted pictures on the stone walls of churches and palaces, they used another kind of water paint called *fresco*. In pure fresco painting, the wall was first coated with plaster and allowed to dry. When the artist was ready to begin each day's work, the assistants would spread a fresh layer of plaster over the part of the wall which the artist expected to finish by sundown. The artist would then paint on the plaster while it was still moist, using a mixture of only pigment and water. No egg, glue, or any other adhesive was needed, because the paint dried with the plaster, so that it finally looked as if it were actually part of the wall itself.

PLATES 4 and 5 show sections of large fresco paintings by two famous Italian Renaissance artists, Piero della Francesca and Michelangelo. The figure of Adam by Michelangelo is only one of several hundred huge figures which cover the ceiling of the Sistine Chapel in Rome. Before Michelangelo began painting each part of this gigantic fresco, he first made many detailed drawings on paper. This was essential, for in fresco painting last minute changes are not easy to make. The artist must know well in advance how the finished picture will look.

Since the Renaissance, oil painting has become more popular than either tempera or fresco. But some artists still prefer the older techniques. The American painter Ben Shahn, for example, has worked mainly in tempera, using its quick-drying quality to good advantage in rendering minute details. Look at the delicate grating of the stairway and the tiny rocks in the foreground of his picture called *The Red Stairway* (PLATE 6). But notice that Shahn has painted the sky and the walls of the building with a much looser brushstroke, making us conscious of the paint's thickness and texture. In this respect, his use of tempera is different from that of Renaissance artists. Yet some of Shahn's colors—especially his pearly grays and gray-blues—are similar to beautiful passages in certain paintings of ꞁ fifteenth century.

PLATE 1. ARTIST UNKNOWN (French, 15th century): *Jonah Thrown to the Whale*. Page from the prayer book of René of Lorraine. Illuminated manuscript, $8\frac{3}{16}$ x $5\frac{1}{2}$ inches. (Bibliotheque Nationale, Paris)

2. GIOVANNI DI PAOLO (Sienese, 1403–1482): *St. John in the Wilderness*. About Tempera on wood panel, 27 x 14¼ inches. (Courtesy of The Art Institute of Chicago)

PLATE 3. SEBASTIANO MAINARDI (Florentine, about 1460–1513): *Portrait of a Young Man*. About 1480–90. Tempera on wood panel, $16\frac{3}{4}$ x $12\frac{7}{8}$ inches. (Staatliche Museum, Berlin)

ᴀᴛᴇ 4. PIERO DELLA FRANCESCA (Florentine, about 1416–1492): *Grooms and Horses*,
᷂le of the *Queen of Sheba* panel from the series *The Story of the Finding of the True Cross*.
᷂59. Fresco. Entire wall is 11 x 24 feet. (Church of San Francesco, Arrezzo, Italy)

PLATE 5. MICHELANGELO (Florentine, 1475–1564): *Adam*. 1511. Detail from the *Creation of Adam*, on the ceiling of the Sistine Chapel in the Vatican. Fresco. Entire ceiling is 130 feet 6 inches by 43 feet 6 inches; highest point above the floor is 59 feet. (Vatican, Rome)

PLATE 6. BEN SHAHN (American, 1898–): *The Red Stairway*. 1944. Tempera on masonite, 16 x 23⅝ inches. (City Art Museum of Saint Louis)

THE SCOPE OF POETRY

Psalm 23

THE KING JAMES BIBLE

Psalm 23 was composed by David, a young shepherd boy in Biblical times, who grew up to become king of his people. David, a gifted singer and harpist, wrote many of the Psalms, of which this is probably the best known and loved.

> The Lord is my shepherd; I shall not want.
> He maketh me to lie down in green pastures:
> He leadeth me beside the still waters.
> He restoreth my soul:
> He leadeth me in the paths of righteousness for His name's sake.   5
> Yea, though I walk through the valley of the shadow of death,
> I will fear no evil: for Thou art with me;
> Thy rod and Thy staff they comfort me.
> Thou preparest a table before me in the presence of mine enemies:
> Thou anointest my head with oil; my cup runneth over.   10
> Surely goodness and mercy shall follow me all the days of my life:
> And I will dwell in the house of the Lord forever.

FOR STUDY AND DISCUSSION

1. This is probably the best known of the Old Testament Psalms. Which line of the poem functions as a kind of topic sentence—a sentence that states the main idea of the poem? In what ways is the poet's Lord like a shepherd? What qualities do you associate with a shepherd? gentleness? kindness? leadership? Why is it natural that a poet living in Old Testament times might think of the Lord as a shepherd?

2. Who is the *Thou* that the poet begins to speak to halfway through the poem? How does this shift to direct address heighten the dramatic tension of the poem?

3. Which lines describe the Lord as guide and guardian? as provider and host? What is the speaker's feeling toward the Lord? How does his attitude toward the Lord compare with that of the speaker in Psalm 96?

4. This poem is full of images. Which are most striking? Which suggest symbolic meanings? What is suggested by "green pastures"? by "the still waters"? by "the valley of the shadow of death"? by "the house of the Lord"?

5. What examples of parallelism (see page 187) are there in this poem? In which lines does the poet most effectively use balance and repetition to emphasize his meaning?

The Goat Paths

JAMES STEPHENS

The crooked paths go every way
  Upon the hill—they wind about
  Through the heather, in and out
Of a quiet sunniness.

And the goats, day after day,   5
  Stray in sunny quietness;
Cropping here, and cropping there—
  As they pause, and turn, and pass—
Now a bit of heather spray,
  Now a mouthful of the grass.   10

In the deeper sunniness;
  In the place where nothing stirs;
Quietly in quietness;
  In the quiet of the furze°
They stand awhile; they dream; they lie;
They stare upon the roving sky.   16

If you approach they run away!
  They will stare, and stamp, and bound,
  With a sudden angry sound,
To the sunny quietude;   20
  To crouch again where nothing stirs,
  In the quiet of the furze:
To crouch them down again and brood,
In the sunny solitude.

Were I but as free as they,   25
  I would stray away and brood;
I would beat a hidden way,
Through the quiet heather spray,
  To a sunny solitude.

And should you come I'd run away!   30
  I would make an angry sound,
  I would stare, and stamp, and bound

14. **furze:** a spiny shrub with yellow flowers.

To the deeper quietude;
  To the place where nothing stirs
  In the quiet of the furze.   35

In that airy quietness
  I would dream as long as they:
Through the quiet sunniness
  I would stray away and brood,
All among the heather spray,   40
  In a sunny solitude.

I would think until I found
  Something I can never find;
Something lying on the ground,
  In the bottom of my mind.   45

FOR STUDY AND DISCUSSION

1. What words are repeated—sometimes in slightly different forms—over and over again in the poem? What mood is created by this repetition?

2. Why does the poet envy the goats' way of life? What do the crooked goat paths mean to the poet? Where do the paths lead? What would the poet like to do? What do you think keeps him from doing it? Is the "you" he would hide from a particular person, or people in general? What makes you think so?

3. The last stanza of the poem is striking because of its paradox: a statement which at first seems absurd or contrary to common sense but which really is not. Restate the idea of this stanza in your own words. Why is the poet's way of saying it more memorable?

ABOUT THE POET

James Stephens (1882–1950) lacked a formal education, but through his own reading he made himself an authority on art and folk music, as well as a successful novelist and poet. His first success was a book of fairy stories, *The Crock of Gold*. All of his writing is full of fantasy and deep imagination. A small man who looked much like a leprechaun, Stephens could hold a group spellbound for hours with Irish stories, legends, and poetry.

Heart of the Woods

WESLEY CURTRIGHT

Deep in the woods we'll go,
Hand in hand
Let the woods close about us,
Let the world outside be lost—
And let us find that Secret City   5
Lost so long ago—
In the Heart of the Woods.

MOOD AND LANGUAGE

The mood of "Goat Paths" is created chiefly through the repetition of words, phrases, even whole lines and sounds. One of the sounds repeated most frequently is the *s* sound. Find two or three places in the poem where this sound is used most often. What does it contribute to the mood?

The poet uses comparatively few rhymes. Which rhymed words are repeated? how many times? Do the repeated rhymes tend to speed up or slow down your reading of the poem?

The wandering or straying movement of the goats is emphasized by repeating patterns of words or lines. Look, for example, at stanza 2. How do repeated words and rhythms suggest the movement of the goats? How do the rhymes help to suggest a back-and-forth motion? Find words and lines that are repeated in other stanzas to give a sense of the goats' aimless wandering.

FOR STUDY AND DISCUSSION

1. In "Heart of the Woods," to whom is the poet speaking? What in the poem makes you think so? Does the poet seem to think mostly about finding the Secret City or simply about escaping from the outside world?

2. The "Secret City" and "Heart of the Woods," especially since they are capitalized, suggest a special meaning, but they may mean different things to different readers. What do you think they symbolize in the poem? Is the Secret City a real place that the poet remembers, or does it exist only in his imagination? What makes you think so?

3. What musical devices does the poet use in this free-verse poem? What word is repeated for emphasis? Which consonant sounds in the middle of the poem suggest a soft flowing quality?

FOR COMPOSITION

1. Many writers have described places where they could meditate and get to know themselves. Thoreau, an American writer, described a place in the woods where he had a "withdrawing room." Where do you go to think and be alone? In a paragraph or two, describe your own retreat and tell why you find it a good place to go.

2. Is there a place that suggests to you a certain mood? Describe this place in a short composition, using words that suggest its mood.

ABOUT THE POET

Wesley Curtright (1910–) was born in Georgia, and went to school in New York City and to college in California. Before going to live on a farm in Michigan, he spent several years in the Civil Service of New York State.

Curfew

HENRY WADSWORTH LONGFELLOW

I

Solemnly, mournfully,
 Dealing its dole,
The curfew bell
 Is beginning to toll.

Cover the embers,   5
 And put out the light;
Toil comes with the morning,
 And rest with the night.

Dark grow the windows,
 And quenched is the fire;   10
Sound fades into silence—
 All footsteps retire.

No voice in the chambers,
 No sound in the hall!
Sleep and oblivion   15
 Reign over all!

II

The book is completed,
 And closed, like the day;
And the hand that has written it
 Lays it away.   20

Dim grow its fancies;
 Forgotten they lie;
Like coals in the ashes,
 They darken and die.

Song sinks into silence,   25
 The story is told,
The windows are darkened,
 The hearthstone is cold.

Darker and darker
 The black shadows fall;   30
Sleep and oblivion
 Reign over all.

FOR STUDY AND DISCUSSION

1. The very first words of "Curfew" create a mood. What is the dominant feeling of the poem? Which words and pictures contribute to this feeling?

2. This poem is about the ending of a day. What else does the poet suggest is ending? In line 15, what is suggested by the word *oblivion?* How does the association of sleep with oblivion add an additional finality to this night's curfew? Of what does the curfew seem to be announcing the ending?

3. The poet first mentions "the book" in stanza 5. Do you think this book is about some specialized subject or about all of human life? Who do you think has written it? Who "lays it away"? Which images in the last half of the poem suggest most vividly how the book's contents are forgotten? What is the "all" that is reigned over by oblivion?

SOUND, REPETITION, AND MEANING

Longfellow uses many devices of repetition to create the mood of this poem. What words and patterns of phrasing are repeated? Which two lines are used as a refrain?

In addition to regular rhymes, Longfellow uses long vowel sounds to slow the movement of the poem. Notice the number of long *o* (as in *toll*), long *i* (as in *light*), and long *a* (as in *day*) sounds in the poem. How many of these occur in the rhymes?

How many other musical devices does Longfellow use in this poem?

ABOUT THE POET

Henry Wadsworth Longfellow (1807–1882), the first American to be accepted as a first-rate poet by European readers, was a masterful creator of atmosphere and mood. For more on Longfellow's life, see page 164.

To Sleep

WILLIAM WORDSWORTH

A flock of sheep that leisurely pass by,
One after one; the sound of rain, and bees
Murmuring; the fall of rivers, winds and seas,
Smooth fields, white sheets of water, and pure sky:
I have thought of all by turns, and yet do lie   5
Sleepless! and soon the small birds' melodies
Must hear, first uttered from my orchard trees;
And the first cuckoo's melancholy cry.
Even thus last night, and two nights more, I lay,
And could not win thee, Sleep! by any stealth: 10
So do not let me wear tonight away:
Without Thee what is all the morning's wealth?
Come, blessed barrier between day and day,
Dear mother of fresh thoughts and joyous health!

FOR STUDY AND DISCUSSION

1. In his last few lines, the poet expresses the main thought of the poem. Restate this thought in your own words. What is "the morning's wealth"? Why is it of no value without sleep?

2. How many nights has the poet had trouble sleeping? At about what time of night do you think he is writing the poem? What in the poem makes you think so?

3. In the first four lines, Wordsworth lists the things he has thought of in order to fall asleep. In what ways do the pictures and sounds suggest sleep and relaxation? How do the images in these lines reveal Wordsworth's sympathy with nature? Which make the strongest impression on your senses?

4. How is .Wordsworth's attitude toward sleep different from that of Longfellow, as expressed in "Curfew"?

SOUND AND MEANING

In "To Sleep," Wordsworth uses *l* sounds to give the lines a liquid flow. Why are they appropriate in a poem about sleep? What other soft consonant sound is used in the poem to make the lines flow smoothly and evenly?

ABOUT THE POET

William Wordsworth (1770–1850), one of England's greatest poets, believed that nature has a healing influence on people. For details about his life, see page 184.

Time, You Old Gypsy Man

RALPH HODGSON

Time, you old gypsy man,
    Will you not stay,
Put up your caravan
    Just for one day?

All things I'll give you   5
Will you be my guest,
Bells for your jennet°
Of silver the best,
Goldsmiths shall beat you
A great golden ring,   10
Peacocks shall bow to you,
Little boys sing,
Oh, and sweet girls will
Festoon you with may.°
Time, you old gypsy,   15
Why hasten away?

Last week in Babylon,
Last night in Rome,
Morning, and in the crush
Under Paul's° dome;   20
Under Paul's dial
You tighten your rein—
Only a moment,
And off once again;
Off to some city   25
Now blind in the womb,
Off to another
Ere that's in the tomb.

Time, you old gypsy man,
    Will you not stay,   30
Put up your caravan
    Just for one day?

FOR STUDY AND DISCUSSION

1. Gypsies are not often seen today, but you have probably heard about them in legends or stories. What characteristics do you associate with gypsies? How do you picture an old gypsy man?

2. What cities has Time, the old gypsy, recently visited? How important were these cities in their time of greatest power? What city is Time visiting at the time the poem was written? What does the third stanza (lines 17–28) suggest about the permanence of power and rule?

3. What does the poet ask Time to do? Do you think he expects Time to agree? Why or why not? Are the gifts the poet offers the sort of thing that would appeal to a gypsy? How do you think Time will answer the poet's question? What in the poem makes you think so?

ABOUT THE POET

Ralph Hodgson (1871–1962) was a lover of animals and of the past, who believed deeply in personal privacy. As a young man he was co-founder of a printing house called The Sign of the Flying Flame, where his first books of poetry were printed. He gained a considerable reputation for the short, powerful lines and rich pictures in poems such as "The Bull" and "Eve." Then suddenly, at the age of forty-six, he stopped publishing his poetry, except for a few volumes which appeared after a lapse of over fourteen years.

7. **jennet:** a donkey.   14. **may:** hawthorn blossoms. The hawthorn bears white, pink, or red blossoms in May.   20. **Paul's:** St. Paul's Cathedral in London.

To Daffodils

ROBERT HERRICK

Fair daffodils, we weep to see
  You haste away so soon;
As yet the early rising sun
  Has not attained his noon.
    Stay, stay,   5
Until the hasting day
    Has run
But to the evensong;°
And, having prayed together, we
  Will go with you along.   10

We have short time to stay, as you
  We have as short a spring;
As quick a growth to meet decay
  As you, or anything.
    We die,   15
As your hours do, and dry
    Away,
Like to the summer's rain;
Or as the pearls of morning's dew,
  Ne'er to be found again.   20

8. **evensong:** evening prayer service.

FOR STUDY AND DISCUSSION

1. What does the poet want the daffodils to do? Why? Who are the "we" that he speaks of in the poem? In what ways are "we" like the daffodils?

2. Which of the following statements most nearly captures the poem's central thought or theme?

  The beauty of flowers such as daffodils makes us appreciate nature.

  Youth and life itself pass all too quickly and are over all too soon.

  The loveliness of flowers and rain will not last all day.

Which lines of the poem best express this theme? Which images most vividly communicate the poet's meaning? To which do you respond more strongly—the prose statement of the theme or the poet's images? Why?

3. In what way are the attitudes expressed in "To Daffodils" and "Time, You Old Gypsy Man" similar? Which poem best communicates the poet's feeling? Which is the most musical? Which has the most striking imagery?

ABOUT THE POET

Robert Herrick (1591–1674), who lived the early part of his life in London, at the age of thirty-eight left the city to become a minister in a small and remote English village. At first, he found country life dull. Soon, however, he began to notice the birds and flowers and all the other life around him and, becoming fascinated with nature, he wrote an enormous number of short and simple poems that sparkle like tiny jewels among the finest examples of English lyric poetry.

In a London Square

ARTHUR HUGH CLOUGH

Put forth thy leaf, thou lofty plane,°
  East wind and frost are safely gone;
With zephyr° mild and balmy rain
  The summer comes serenely on;
Earth, air, and sun and skies combine   5
  To promise all that's kind and fair:
But thou, O human heart of mine,
  Be still, contain thyself, and bear.

December days were brief and chill,
  The winds of March were wild and drear,
And, nearing and receding still,   11
  Spring never would, we thought, be here.
The leaves that burst, the suns that shine,
  Had, not the less, their certain date:
And thou, O human heart of mine,   15
  Be still, refrain thyself, and wait.

1. **plane:** a plane tree, one of the trees that buds earliest in spring. 3. **zephyr** (zef′ər): the west wind.

FOR STUDY AND DISCUSSION

1. In this poem, as in others you have read, a scene in nature calls forth the poet's inner feelings. Judging from the title of the poem, where is the poet standing? What does he see? Is his own mood similar or opposite to the mood of the season? What in the poem makes you think so?

2. Which images in the poem suggest the poet's mood? What comfort does he gain from witnessing the change in the weather? What is the meaning of lines 13–14? How are these lines a promise of better things? What do they suggest may happen in the poet's own life?

3. Which of these statements best summarizes the meaning of the poem?

  We must all learn patience, for good and troubled times come and go as do the seasons.

  The human heart can bear anything.

  Spring and summer bring happiness, while winter brings only waiting.

Summer Evening

WALTER DE LA MARE

The sandy cat by the farmer's chair
Mews at his knee for dainty fare;
Old Rover in his moss-greened house
Mumbles a bone, and barks at a mouse.
In the dewy fields the cattle lie   5
Chewing the cud 'neath a fading sky.
Dobbin at manger pulls his hay:
Gone is another summer's day.

FOR STUDY AND DISCUSSION

1. In this poem Walter de la Mare uses details as exactly as a photographer. How many "photographs" does he create with words? Which pictures are clearest and most striking? What details make them so?

2. What general impression or mood is created by the pictures in the poem? How does the last line contribute to this mood? Why do you think "Summer Evening" is a good title for this poem?

FOR COMPOSITION

What happens on a summer evening at your home? Can you describe it in a series of images? Write a short poem entitled "Summer Evening," using as many visual images and musical devices as you can.

ABOUT THE POETS

Arthur Hugh Clough (1819–1861), whose name is pronounced *Cluff*, led a quiet life, spending many years as a student and teacher at Oxford. After leaving Oxford when he was nearly forty, he lived most of the rest of his life in London.

Walter de la Mare (1873–1956) was a master at creating atmosphere, whether of fantasy or everyday life. For more on his life, see the biographical sketch on page 177.

Washington Monument by Night

CARL SANDBURG

1

The stone goes straight.
A lean swimmer dives into night sky,
Into half-moon mist.

2

Two trees are coal black.
This is a great white ghost between.   5
It is cool to look at.
Strong men, strong women, come here.

3

Eight years is a long time
To be fighting all the time.

4

The republic is a dream.   10
Nothing happens unless first a dream.

5

The wind bit hard at Valley Forge one
    Christmas.
Soldiers tied rags on their feet.
Red footprints wrote on the snow . . .
. . . and stone shoots into stars here   15
. . . into half-moon mist tonight.

6

Tongues wrangled dark at a man.
He buttoned his overcoat and stood alone.
In a snowstorm, red hollyberries, thoughts,
    he stood alone.   20

7

Women said: He is lonely
. . . fighting . . . fighting . . . eight years . . .

8

The name of an iron man goes over the
    world.
It takes a long time to forget an iron man.

9

. . .   .
. . .   .

FOR STUDY AND DISCUSSION

1. Have you ever seen a picture of the Washington Monument? Can you imagine how it would look at night? What aspect of the monument's appearance is suggested by the images in stanza 1? by the images in stanza 2? Which images in these stanzas convey a sense of George Washington's idealism? of his dreams?

2. In what sense is the monument Washington's "ghost"? How do the statements in stanzas 3 and 4 apply to the life of Washington? What was Washington's dream?

3. What do you know about Washington's hardships and frustrations at Valley Forge? What hardships are described in stanza 5? What does stanza 6 suggest about the way Washington responded to those who thought him foolish and advised him to surrender?

4. As he is pictured in this poem, what kind of man was Washington? How does the Washington Monument, especially as it appears at night, suggest his outstanding qualities?

5. Which images do you find most striking in this free-verse poem? What figure of speech is used in each?

6. What does the unfinished last stanza suggest about the poet's thoughts on George Washington?

ABOUT THE POET

Carl Sandburg (1878–1967), son of Swedish immigrants, is known for his first-hand acquaintance with all parts of the United States and for his deep sympathies with all who work and suffer. For a biography of Sandburg, see page 221.

Fable

RALPH WALDO EMERSON

The mountain and the squirrel
Had a quarrel;
And the former called the latter "Little Prig."
Bun° replied,
"You are doubtless very big;   5
But all sorts of things and weather
Must be taken in together,
To make up a year
And a sphere.
And I think it no disgrace   10
To occupy my place.
If I'm not so large as you,
You are not so small as I,
And not half so spry.
I'll not deny you make   15
A very pretty squirrel track;
Talents differ; all is well and wisely put;
If I cannot carry forests on my back,
Neither can you crack a nut."

4. **Bun:** a regional name for a squirrel.

FOR STUDY AND DISCUSSION

1. A *fable* is a brief story or poem that illustrates a moral—a lesson concerning proper conduct—and often uses animals or objects to represent human characteristics. Which lines state the moral of this fable? What is the "sphere" referred to in line 9? How does Emerson use rhyme and rhythm to set off and emphasize the key ideas of the poem?

2. What talents does the squirrel feel make up for its small size? Do you think it overestimates its own importance in the scheme of things? A prig is someone who feels superior to others. Do you agree with the mountain that the squirrel is a "Little Prig"? Why or why not?

3. When writing is moralistic, the moral is usually easier to swallow if it is made amusing. What words and turns of thought make this poem amusing?

4. How are the ideas expressed by Emerson in "Fable" like those in "Music" (page 185)? From these poems, would you say Emerson was an optimist or a pessimist? State in a sentence, in your own words, what seems to be his attitude toward life.

FOR COMPOSITION

Can you make up a fable of your own or remember one from your reading? Try your hand at writing a free-verse version of a fable, using animal characters to illustrate some moral truth.

ABOUT THE POET

Ralph Waldo Emerson (1803–1882) is famous as an American essayist and thinker, as well as a poet. For more information on his life and writings, see page 185.

At Woodward's Gardens

ROBERT FROST

A boy, presuming on his intellect,
Once showed two little monkeys in a cage
A burning-glass they could not understand
And never could be made to understand.
Words are no good: to say it was a lens   5
For gathering solar rays would not have helped.
But let him show them how the weapon worked.
He made the sun a pinpoint on the nose
Of first one, then the other, till it brought
A look of puzzled dimness to their eyes   10
That blinking could not seem to blink away.
They stood arms laced together at the bars,
And exchanged troubled glances over life.
One put a thoughtful hand up to his nose
As if reminded—or as if perhaps   15
Within a million years of an idea.
He got his purple little knuckles stung.
The already known had once more been confirmed
By psychological experiment,
And that were all the finding to announce   20
Had the boy not presumed too close and long.
There was a sudden flash of arm, a snatch,
And the glass was the monkeys', not the boy's.
Precipitately° they retired back-cage
And instituted an investigation   25
On their part, though without the needed insight.
They bit the glass and listened for the flavor.
They broke the handle and the binding off it.
Then none the wiser, frankly gave it up,
And having hid it in their bedding straw   30
Against the day of prisoners' ennui,°
Came dryly forward to the bars again
To answer for themselves: Who said it mattered
What monkeys did or didn't understand?
They might not understand a burning-glass.   35
They might not understand the sun itself.
It's knowing what to do with things that counts.

24. **Precipitately:** hurriedly.   31. **ennui** (än′wē): boredom.

"At Woodward's Gardens" from *The Poetry of Robert Frost* edited by Edward Connery Lathem. Copyright 1936 by Robert Frost. Copyright © 1964 by Lesley Frost Ballantine. Copyright © 1969 by Holt, Rinehart and Winston. Reprinted by permission of Holt, Rinehart and Winston, Publishers.

1. This poem, like Emerson's, is a fable. What happens in the story it tells? What is the moral of the tale?

2. Who does Frost think really knew more —the boy or the monkeys? Why? Do you agree? What comment does this poem make on our use of scientific knowledge to develop bigger and better weapons?

3. What does Frost mean when he says the boy is "presuming on his intellect"? How would you describe this attitude in everyday language? Why is Frost's rather elegant phrase a better reflection of the boy's state of mind?

4. Which lines in this poem give the clearest pictures of what is happening? Which words in these lines have a humorous effect? Why are they amusing?

5. What is the tone of this poem? What words might you use to describe the author's tone?

ABOUT THE POET

Among the things for which Robert Frost (1875–1963) is famous are his wit and common sense. For more on his life, see page 183.

The Shift of Gears

MELVIN TOLSON

The mechanic probes
The belly of the car,
And smears the jaw
With the zigzag scar,
And puckers his brow 5
As he wrenches a bar.

The driver curses,
And strikes a match,
And rams his hat,

And mops his thatch.   10
"What's wrong?" he taunts,
With lording dispatch.

The mechanic speaks
In the language of peers:
"A car or a man   15
Can outwear the years,
If horse sense handles
The shift of gears."

FOR STUDY AND DISCUSSION

1. In this poem two people are involved in a very common occurrence. Who are the two people? What is each of them doing? What do you learn of their moods or personalities from the way they act and speak?

2. What is the rhyme scheme of the poem? How do the strong rhyming words help give force to the lines?

3. What does the mechanic mean by his final statement? Could his statements be applied to more than the driver's broken car?

ABOUT THE POET

Melvin Tolson (1900–1966) was born in Missouri, but lived most of his life in the Southwest—in Texas and in Oklahoma. In addition to teaching literature and writing poetry, he served as director of the Dust Bowl Theater in Oklahoma and as Mayor of Langston, Oklahoma. Melvin Tolson won a number of awards for his poetry. In his work he reveals a deep concern for basic human problems, such as social injustice and misunderstanding.

Father William

LEWIS CARROLL

"You are old, Father William," the young man said,
    "And your hair has become very white;
And yet you incessantly stand on your head—
    Do you think, at your age, it is right?"

"In my youth," Father William replied to his son,   5
    "I feared it might injure the brain;
But now that I'm perfectly sure I have none,
    Why, I do it again and again."

"You are old," said the youth, "as I mentioned before,
    And have grown most uncommonly fat;   10
Yet you turned a back-somersault in at the door—
    Pray, what is the reason of that?"

"In my youth," said the sage, as he shook his gray locks,
    "I kept all my limbs very supple
By the use of this ointment—one shilling the box—   15
    Allow me to sell you a couple?"

"You are old," said the youth, "and your jaws are too weak
    For anything tougher than suet;°
Yet you finished the goose, with the bones and the beak—
    Pray, how did you manage to do it?"   20

"In my youth," said his father, "I took to the law,
    And argued each case with my wife;
And the muscular strength which it gave to my jaw
    Has lasted the rest of my life."

"You are old," said the youth, "one would hardly suppose   25
    That your eye was as steady as ever;
Yet you balanced an eel on the end of your nose—
    What made you so awfully clever?"

"I have answered three questions, and that is enough,"
    Said his father. "Don't give yourself airs!   30
Do you think I can listen all day to such stuff?
    Be off, or I'll kick you downstairs!"

18. **suet:** animal fat used in cooking.

1. Like most of Lewis Carroll's "nonsense" poems, "Father William" has a ring of truth. What is the young man's attitude toward Father William? Is his tone friendly or sneering? Which lines make you think so?

2. What is Father William's attitude toward the young man? Does he take his questions seriously? How does each of his answers turn the tables on his questioner?

3. Who is younger in spirit—Father William or his son? How is this shown in what they say and do? Which one do you like better? Why? Which one has more common sense? What makes you think so?

4. While Father William's tricks and answers are unexpected, his final method of disposing of his questioner is fairly common. Do you think he has run out of answers, or is he just tired of the game? How does his rebuke make his son seem like a small child?

IRONY

When something a character does or says brings about an entirely unexpected result, perhaps the opposite of what is intended, the outcome of the effort is *ironic*. "Father William," like most of Lewis Carroll's poetry, is a series of unexpected, ironic twists. What is ironic or "upside down" in a young person's saying to an old one, "Act your age"? What is ironic about an old man's having more of a spirit of fun than his son? What is especially ironic about Father William's final answer to his son's questions?

Lewis Carroll was often asked what he meant by some of his "nonsense." How does "Father William" provide an answer to this kind of question?

ABOUT THE POET

Lewis Carroll (1832–1898) was the pen name of Charles Lutwidge Dodgson, a well-known and highly respected professor of mathematics. Professor Dodgson lived a quiet life while his other self, writer Lewis Carroll, explored vast underground regions of fantasy and imagination. His double life did create some problems. When Queen Victoria, who had been delighted by *Alice's Adventures in Wonderland,* requested a copy of the author's next book, she received, some months later, Professor Dodgson's *Elementary Treatise on Determinants.*

Inventors, Keep Away from My Door

PHYLLIS MC GINLEY

Ah, where's the patented device
   That I can learn to master?
My icebox yields me melted ice,
   My oven, but disaster.
From stranded cars it is my fate   5
   To view the rural scenery;
For I'm the poor unfortunate
   Undone by all machinery.

Other people's robots keep a willing head up.
   All their cheerful keyholes welcome in the key.   10
Other people's toasters do not burn their bread up.
   But nothing ever works for me.

The gadgets come, the gadgets go,
    Ambitious for the attic.
Tune up my stubborn radio—   15
    It screams with rage and static.
The vacuum sweeper roundabout
    With slippery strength encoils me.
Locks treacherously lock me out.
    The simple corkscrew foils me.   20

Other people's mousetraps sometimes bring a mouse down.
    Other people's furnaces sing in cozy glee.
Mine huffs and it puffs till it brings the quaking house down.
    Nothing ever runs for me.

The humblest tools in my abode   25
    Know half a hundred ruses°
To leak or sputter or explode,
    Catch fire or short their fuses.
In all things made of steel or wire,
    Inanimate, unholy,   30
There lurks some dark, ancestral ire°
    Directed at me, solely;
There lurks some black, malicious spite
    Amid the wheels and prisms,
And what shall save me from the might   35
    Of wrathful mechanisms?

Other people's watches do not send them late for
    Amorous appointment or literary tea.
Other people's telephones bring the word they wait for.
    But *nothing* ever works for me.   40

26. **ruses:** ingenious, cunning tricks. 31. **ire:** anger.

INVENTORS, KEEP AWAY FROM MY DOOR   215

1. What line is used as a refrain to sum up the speaker's feelings about modern inventions? About which "patented devices" does she seem most bitter? Which devices does she personify? What does she feel their attitude is toward her?

2. Which words and phrases most vividly suggest the treachery of the machines? What figures of speech does the poet use in these lines? Is she laughing at the inventions, at herself, or at both? What in the poem makes you think so?

3. Read the poem aloud. How do its rhythm and rhyme contribute to the humor? Which lines suggest, through repetition, the mechanical movements of the inventions? Which lines and phrases in the poem are most amusing?

4. What idea is expressed in lines 13–14? More seriously than Miss McGinley, an earlier American, Henry David Thoreau, argued that we clutter up our lives with "things." In his book *Walden* he speaks of "furniture" and "trumpery" and says, "The more you have of such things the poorer you are." What do you think Thoreau meant by this? Do you agree? Why or why not?

FOR COMPOSITION

Did you ever feel that some mechanical thing was actually defying you? Write a humorous account of a losing battle you have had —or might have had—with a gadget or machine. Use images and sounds to suggest your frustration.

ABOUT THE POET

Phyllis McGinley (1905–1978) grew up in Colorado and Utah, but spent most of her life writing and teaching in New York. She is known as a writer of children's books and poetry, especially as a writer of light verse. In her verse, however amusing, there is always a touch of truth. She received a Pulitzer prize in 1961. She also wrote the filmscript for the movie *The Emperor's Nightingale,* based on a Hans Christian Andersen fairy tale.

The Last of the Books

ALFRED NOYES

Is it too strange to think
    That, when all life at last from earth is gone,
And round the sun's pale blink
    Our desolate planet wheels its ice and stone,
Housed among storm-proof walls there yet may abide,   5
    Defying long the venoms of decay,
A still dark throng of books, dumb books of song
    And tenderest fancies born of youth and May?

A quiet remembering host,
    Outliving the poor dust that gave them birth,   10
Unvisited by even a wandering ghost,
    But treasuring still the music of our earth,

In little fading hieroglyphs they shall bear
   Through death and night, the legend of our spring,
And how the lilac scented the bright air   15
   When hearts throbbed warm, and lips could kiss and sing.

And, ere that record fail,
   Strange voyagers from a mightier planet come
On wingèd ships that through the void can sail
   And gently alight upon our ancient home;   20
Strange voices echo, and strange flares explore,
   Strange hands, with curious weapons, burst these bars,
Lift the brown volumes to the light once more,
   And bear their stranger secrets through the stars.

FOR STUDY AND DISCUSSION

1. What fate does the poet foretell for our planet? In lines 3–4, what has happened to the earth? What has happened to the sun? What scientific basis is there for believing that this is what might actually happen? How does Noyes's version of the end of the world compare with that imagined by other writers?

2. How have we discovered what we know today of past civilizations? What past discoveries are suggested by the word *hieroglyphs* (line 13)? What other objects besides books can help to preserve a record of human history? Why are books so important in doing this?

3. About what kind of books does the poet seem to be speaking? Which images suggest what is told in them? From the strangers' treatment of the books, do you think they properly appreciate their importance? What do you think they will do with them?

4. How is the situation in this poem similar to that in Longfellow's "Curfew" (page 204)? How do the poets' conclusions differ?

FOR COMPOSITION

1. What do you know about our present storehouses of relics from other times? Look up information in several sources on such remarkable archives or libraries as the British Museum in London, the Vatican Library in Rome, and the Library of Congress in Washington, D.C. Report on the outstanding features of one of these famous libraries or museums.

2. Has Noyes's poem about the future made you wonder about the great civilizations of the past? After checking several different sources, write a short report on the remarkable features of one of the following:

The Ancient Cities of Nineveh, Troy, and
   Pompeii
The Golden Age of China
The Indian Civilizations of America:
   Mayans, Aztecs, Incas
Stonehenge

ABOUT THE POET

Alfred Noyes (1880–1958) never had to undergo the difficulties and financial struggle that have been the lot of most young poets. An athlete at Oxford, he published his first book of poems at twenty-two and soon became highly popular. Fond of heroic subjects, he wrote an epic poem on Sir Francis Drake and a poetic drama on Robin Hood, but his most popular writings are his exciting ballads, such as *The Highwayman*. Not at all a "literary" man, Noyes's work for the British government during World War I earned him public recognition as a Commander of the Order of the British Empire.

Reading and Writing about Poetry

Reading poetry generally requires more concentration and greater care than reading prose. An individual sentence of poetry may be as complex in its structure as a whole paragraph of prose. Also, poetry is written to be read aloud, with all the variations of voice and tone—pace, pitch, volume, rhythm—that can give hints of meaning. No one can tell you everything about how to read a poem, but the following suggestions may help you develop your own methods of doing so:

1. Read the entire poem through several times. Read more slowly than you would read prose. Read in sentences rather than lines. At least once, read aloud.

2. Check the meaning of any unfamiliar words. You may need to consult a dictionary and study certain words carefully in the context of the sentences in which they appear. Remember that many words have more than one meaning, and that poets tend to be unusually aware of a word's derivations and root meaning.

3. If the meaning of a sentence is unclear, study its structure (syntax) and its punctuation; look for key words, and words that indicate transitions. As a check, you might try to rephrase a sentence in your own words. (If you do, make sure that your paraphrase makes sense in the context of the poem.)

4. In studying the poem as a whole, ask yourself these questions:

Does the poem make a statement and support that statement with details? Is there more than one general statement? If so, how are they related?

Who is the speaker in the poem? What does the character of the speaker have to do with the poem's meaning?

Are there repetitions of words or phrases or ideas? Are there parallel structures? comparisons and contrasts? If so, what purpose do they serve?

Is there more than one level of meaning in the poem? If so, which lines are primarily concerned with each?

Try applying these procedures to the following poem by Walter de la Mare, and see if they don't help you better understand the total meaning of the poem:

An Epitaph

Here lies a most beautiful lady,
Light of step and heart was she;
I think she was the most beautiful lady
That ever was in the West Country.
But beauty vanishes; beauty passes;   5
However rare—rare it be;
And when I crumble, who will remember
This lady of the West Country?

What is an *epitaph?* What does the title suggest about the purpose of the poem?

Line 1 of "An Epitaph" makes a general statement; lines 2–4 develop or expand that statement with description and personal comment.

Line 5 makes a second statement, commented on in line 6 and linked up with the first four lines by the question asked in lines 7–8.

Thus the total, literal structure of the poem is this: The speaker (one who evidently thought highly of the lady) makes two statements: "Here lies a lady . . ." and "Beauty vanishes . . ." Each statement is enlarged on ("Light of step . . ."; "rare . . .") and commented on ("I think . . ." and "when I crumble . . .").

In this simple poem, the speaker is actually developing two kinds of ideas, two levels of meaning: a statement about the death of a lady and a personal commentary on that lady. The poem is both an epitaph and a love poem. Note that lines 1–2 and 5–6 might be called factual, or philosophical; whereas lines 3–4 and 7–8 are personal, sad, and exaggerated to express the speaker's feelings.

In the following poem, William Wordsworth develops an idea similar to that in "An Epitaph." Read the poem carefully for total meaning, following the steps suggested above.

Lucy

She dwelt among the untrodden ways
  Beside the springs of Dove,
A maid whom there were none to praise
  And very few to love:

A violet by a mossy stone   5
  Half hidden from the eye!
—Fair as a star, when only one
  Is shining in the sky.

She lived unknown, and few could know
  When Lucy ceased to be;   10
But she is in her grave, and, oh,
  The difference to me!

1. *Sentences.* How many sentences are there in the poem? Where are the important breaks in punctuation? What is the subject of stanza 2? How does the punctuation in lines 7 and 11 affect your reading of the poem?

2. *Words.* The language of the poem is simple, but you may need to check the meaning of *ways* and *untrodden.* (The Dove is a river in the north of England.) How does the phrase "untrodden ways" relate to other lines and pictures in the poem?

3. *Imaginative language.* Familiar words such as *violet* and *star* are used as *images* in this poem to give us a striking picture of how Lucy appears in the poet's imagination. What does the image of the violet tell us about Lucy? What does the image of the star suggest about the poet's feelings?

4. *Structure of the poem.* The poem makes three specific statements: lines 1–4 ("She dwelt..."), lines 9–10 ("She lived..."), and lines 11–12 ("she is in her grave..."). What is the relation of stanza 2 (lines 5–8) to the rest of the poem?

Which lines in the poem are statements of fact? Which are expressions of personal feeling? What do we learn about the speaker from his expressions of feeling?

WRITING ABOUT POETRY

Read (or reread) the following poem by Robert Herrick, using the procedures suggested above to get at its total meaning:

To Daffodils

Fair daffodils, we weep to see
  You haste away so soon;
As yet the early rising sun
  Has not attained his noon.
    Stay, stay,   5
Until the hasting day
    Has run
But to the evensong;
And, having prayed together, we
  Will go with you along.   10

We have short time to stay, as you
  We have as short a spring;
As quick a growth to meet decay
  As you, or anything.
    We die,   15
As your hours do, and dry
    Away,
Like to the summer's rain;
Or as the pearls of morning's dew,
  Ne'er to be found again.   20

Read the poem carefully, in sentences, as you search for the whole meaning. Look for clues in the sentence syntax (structure) and punctuation, and the way the statements and details are arranged. (Be sure to check unfamiliar words for their meaning in the context of the poem.)

When you have finished your examination, write an analysis of the poem. Base your analysis on your own step-by-step observations. In your final paragraph, discuss the poem's total meaning. Do you think it says more than one thing?

ART AND LITERATURE

Write a short poem about one of the paintings on pages 195–200, describing either the painting itself or your personal reaction to it.

PART 2 *Five Poets: A Closer Look*

In Part 1 of this unit on poetry we learned how, over the years, various poets have used the elements of their craft—rhythm, rhyme, imagery, and figures of speech such as metaphor and simile—to achieve, all in their own ways, a variety of poetic effects as they expressed themselves on a variety of subjects. Now, in Part 2 of this unit, we shall use our new understanding of the poet's craft as we take a close look at the work of five well-known poets. And, since an understanding of writers' lives does a great deal to aid our understanding of their work, we shall take a closer look at the lives of these poets as well as at the background of the times in which they wrote their poems.

The first of these five poets is Carl Sandburg, the well-known, twentieth-century American who is as well known for his monumental biography of Abraham Lincoln as for his poetry. From Sandburg we shall turn to Rudyard Kipling, an Englishman who lived in many parts of the world—India, South Africa, and the United States— and whose poetry and stories made him the spokesman of his country and his age.

Turning back to the eighteenth century, we shall then come to "Bobby" Burns, whom Scotland claims as her national poet and whose verse has for two hundred years delighted Scots and non-Scots alike.

Edna St. Vincent Millay, the fourth poet at whom we shall have a close look, we have already encountered in Part 1 (page 180). This twentieth-century American, who wrote stories and verse plays as well as poetry, is remembered chiefly for her intense and imaginative lyric poems.

We shall turn finally to Alfred, Lord Tennyson, the Poet Laureate of Victorian England and one of the most famous of all English poets. Tennyson, like Robert Burns, was greatly admired by his countrymen; no Victorian parlor table was considered complete without its volume of Tennyson's poems.

The poems chosen to represent these five poets are, of course, only a few of the many each has written. The "close look" you are about to take at these poets is meant to encourage you to read further, not only in the works of these very same poets, but in the works of other poets as well.

CARL SANDBURG
(1878–1967)

Perhaps you have seen Carl Sandburg on television, or even on the stage —a tall man with bright, piercing eyes and long white hair—reading his own poetry or singing American folk songs and now and then accompanying himself on a guitar. He has been called the poet of the people because of his wide acquaintance and sympathy with all kinds of people. His personal hero was Abraham Lincoln, also a man of the people. Sandburg's monumental biography of Lincoln conveys a sense of Lincoln's true greatness.

Carl Sandburg was born in Galesburg, a small town in Illinois. His parents were poor, hardworking Swedish immigrants, and Carl had to quit school at the age of thirteen to work full-time and help support his family. He worked at almost everything—sweeping an office, handling a paper route, carrying cans of milk, washing pop bottles, managing a concessions stand, sweeping out a barber shop. At nineteen, life began to seem cramped in Galesburg, and he decided to go on the road. Riding the rails from town to town, he got to know America and Americans through all sorts of jobs. He worked his way through Illinois, Missouri, Kansas, Colorado, Nebraska, and home again. By the time he reached Galesburg he had a new understanding of education. After volunteering for service in the Spanish-American War and encountering only seasickness and mosquitoes, he returned to Galesburg and worked as a firefighter to put himself through college. After college, he worked at political jobs and as a reporter to support himself while writing poetry.

Sandburg's first success came with the publication of *Chicago Poems,* which appeared in 1916 when he was thirty-seven years old. His poetry was immediately praised for its realistic portrayal of American cities, with their proud and relentless industry, and of the Western expanse, with its small towns and farms. Sandburg went on to write a great many more books of poems, and eventually won the Pulitzer prize for both poetry and history. After a full life, he retired to a farm at Flat Rock, North Carolina.

Carl Sandburg is first of all a poet of everyday life and common things. He believed that a real poet can make poetry out of anything. In fact, he said: "When men lose their poetic feeling for ordinary life and cannot write poetry of ordinary things, their exalted poetry is likely to lose its strength of exaltation, in the way men cease to build beautiful churches when they have lost happiness in building shops." Sandburg's poems are full of pictures that make his readers aware, in a new way, of the most ordinary things. He once said of himself, "From the age of six I had a mania for drawing the forms of things. By the time I was fifty I had published an infinity of designs."

The form of Sandburg's poetry is very free. He saw no reason to cramp his imagination with regular rhyme and rhythm, and he was critical of the strictness of formal poetry. Above all, he did not want to write "formal poetry perfect only in form," with little impact or meaning. To him, such verse seemed "all dressed up and having nowhere to go." In place of regular form, Sandburg valued pictures and life in words and richness of thought and meaning. This, for him, is what makes poetry alive, like "a living fish aswim in bright waters," and not "a dead mackerel in the moonshine."

A Fence

Now the stone house on the lake front is finished and the workmen are
    beginning the fence.
The palings are made of iron bars with steel points that can stab the life out
    of any man who falls on them.
As a fence, it is a masterpiece, and will shut off the rabble and all vagabonds
    and hungry men and all wandering children looking for a place to play.
Passing through the bars and over the steel points will go nothing except
    Death and the Rain and Tomorrow

Lost

Desolate and lone
All night long on the lake
Where fog trails and mist creeps,
The whistle of a boat
Calls and cries unendingly,   5
Like some lost child
In tears and trouble
Hunting the harbor's breast
And the harbor's eyes.

Fire-Logs

Nancy Hanks dreams by the fire;
Dreams, and the logs sputter,
And the yellow tongues climb.
Red lines lick their way in flickers.
Oh, sputter, logs.
　　　Oh, dream, Nancy.   5
Time now for a beautiful child.
Time now for a tall man to come.

Wind Song

Long ago I learned how to sleep,
In an old apple orchard where the wind swept by counting its money and
　　　throwing it away,
In a wind-gaunt orchard where the limbs forked out and listened or never
　　　listened at all,
In a passel° of trees where the branches trapped the wind into whistling,
　　　"Who, who are you?"
I slept with my head in an elbow on a summer afternoon and there I took a
　　　sleep lesson.   5
There I went away saying: I know why they sleep, I know how they trap
　　　the tricky winds.
Long ago I learned how to listen to the singing wind and how to forget
　　　and how to hear the deep whine,
Slapping and lapsing under the day blue and the night stars:
　　　　　　　Who, who are you?

　　　　　　　Who can ever forget   10
　　　　　　　listening to the wind go by
　　　　　　　counting its money
　　　　　　　and throwing it away?

---

4. **passel** (pas″l): a dialect word for *parcel*. Sandburg uses it here in the sense of "a bunch."

Sand Scribblings

The wind stops, the wind begins.
The wind says stop, begin.

A sea shovel scrapes the sand floor.
The shovel changes, the floor changes.

The sandpipers, maybe they know.   5
Maybe a three-pointed foot can tell.
Maybe the fog moon they fly to, guesses.

The sandpipers cheep "Here" and get away.
Five of them fly and keep together flying.

Night hair of some sea woman   10
Curls on the sand when the sea leaves
The salt tide without a good-by.

Boxes on the beach are empty.
Shake 'em and the nails loosen.
They have been somewhere.   15

Boxes and Bags

The bigger the box the more it holds.
Empty boxes hold the same as empty heads.
Enough small empty boxes thrown into a big empty box fill it full.
A half-empty box says, "Put more in."
A big enough box could hold the world.   5
Elephants need big boxes to hold a dozen elephant handkerchiefs.
Fleas fold little handkerchiefs and fix them nice and neat in flea handkerchief-
      boxes.
Bags lean against each other and boxes stand independent.
Boxes are square with corners unless round with circles.
Box can be piled on box till the whole works come tumbling.   10
Pile box on box and the bottom box says, "If you will kindly take notice
      you will see it all rests on me."
Pile box on box and the top one says, "Who falls farthest if or when we fall?
      I ask you."
Box people go looking for boxes and bag people go looking for bags.

See the Trees

See the trees lean to the wind's way of learning.
See the dirt of the hills shape to the water's way of learning.
See the lift of it all go the way the biggest wind and the strongest water
    want it.

FOR STUDY AND DISCUSSION

A FENCE

1. This poem is a series of statements, each contributing to the total effect. What do the first two statements tell you about the house? about the fence? What is the purpose of the fence? Are the poet's sympathies with the people who are having the fence built or with those it is meant to keep out? What in the poem makes you think so?

2. Who or what can defy the fence and those who built it? Is this true of all fences, no matter who builds them? What general conclusions about fences and people who build fences around themselves can you draw from Sandburg's poem?

3. Notice how the poet uses familiar words in such a way that they appeal vividly to your senses. Which words suggest the strength of the fence? Which suggest its sharpness? Which words make clear the property owners' apparent opinion of the rest of the world?

LOST

1. This poem is a striking simile. What scene does the poet describe? Of what do the boat's "calls and cries" remind him? What human emotion does the boat seem to feel?

2. How does the poet describe the harbor?

What figure of speech does he use? How has he prepared for this figure of speech in his description of the boat? What does he suggest that the boat's search for the harbor is similar to?

3. In this poem Carl Sandburg uses words and images to create a mood. Which words create a feeling of loneliness? Which other words intensify this feeling?

FIRE-LOGS

1. Who was Nancy Hanks? Who is the "tall man to come"? Which of Sandburg's favorite subjects serves as the basis for this ·poem?

2. Which images in this poem make the fire seem vivid and real?

WIND SONG

1. Where did the poet learn how to sleep and listen to the wind? When "trapped" in the branches, what did the wind whistle?

2. Do you think that the wind's question is an unusual one, one that most people would have to think about before answering? How would you answer if the wind asked you this question?

• 3. What is the wind's "money"? What does the wind do with things it scoops up off the ground? What do the wind's actions suggest about the permanence of our world and of people?

4. As you know, Carl Sandburg wrote free verse—verse without regular patterns of rhythm and rhyme. Every so often someone argues that this kind of poetry is not poetry at all, but merely prose which has been broken up into short lines. Use "Wind Song" to prove to such doubters that Sandburg's free verse is highly poetic. How many poetic devices, such as assonance and alliteration, can you discover in these lines? How do they help to make the lines "alive"?

SAND SCRIBBLINGS

1. What elements of nature leave their marks, or "scribblings," on the sand? What is the "sea shovel" made of? How do you know?

2. Are the scribblings clear or mysterious? Why does the poet think the sandpipers might know what they mean? What special resources of experience and instinct do the sandpipers have that the poet does not?

3. What is the "night hair of some sea woman" that the ebbing tide adds to the scribblings? How have the boxes, which once held humanity's possessions, been treated by the wind and sea? What has happened to them? Does the poet have any idea where they have been? What does the last stanza add to the meaning of the poem?

BOXES AND BAGS

1. Which lines in this poem resemble proverbs or folk sayings? Restate in your own words the meaning of each. Which do you think best suggests a general truth?

2. How does Sandburg's use of "boxes" in all his sayings make them more amusing? What is especially amusing about lines 6 and 7? What kind of people might be described as "elephants"? What kind might be thought of as "fleas"?

3. In line 2 Sandburg compares empty boxes to empty heads. How does this prepare you to hear the boxes speaking? How many boxes speak in the poem? How does Sandburg's manner of phrasing make the boxes seem like real people?

SEE THE TREES

1. What forces of nature does Sandburg say determine the shape of the trees and the land? Which words suggest the strength of these forces?

2. What does Sandburg mean by "the wind's way of learning"? Who is learning, the trees or the wind? What is being learned?

3. In this poem Sandburg personifies the trees, the wind, and the water. Can what is learned be applied to human life as well? How are human beings also shaped by pressures in their environment? What are some of the forces that shape people?

SUMMING UP

1. Judging from the poems you have just read, list a few general statements about Carl Sandburg's poetry. For instance, does he choose ordinary or unusual subjects? Does he use ordinary or unusual figures of speech? Does he often personify inanimate things? Explain your answer.

2. Which of Carl Sandburg's comments on life most impressed you with their wisdom?

3. What is your opinion of Sandburg's use of free verse? Do the rhythms in any of his poems remind you of the parallel rhythms of the Psalms? How well do his verse rhythms suit the subjects of his poems?

FOR COMPOSITION

1. Reread "A Fence" and write a short description of the family you picture living in the stone house surrounded by the fence.

2. Try, in a short free-verse poem, to communicate a feeling such as the one Sandburg describes in "Lost." Try to find a single, effective simile that expresses your emotion.

3. Choose a single line from "Boxes and Bags" and use it as the basis for a short composition.

4. Another poet, Alexander Pope, once wrote, "Just as the twig is bent the tree's inclined." How is this idea similar to that expressed in "See the Trees"? Write a short account of a personal experience that illustrates or disproves this idea.

RUDYARD KIPLING

(1865–1936)

Joseph Rudyard Kipling was a striking exception to the belief that writers, and poets in particular, usually starve. While still in his early twenties, he began to publish at an incredible rate in newspapers and magazines and soon found himself one of the hugest and youngest successes of any writer who ever lived. His short stories, novels, and poems were enormously popular, especially in England, the United States, and India, and he was one of the first writers to be published in paperback books.

Kipling was born in Bombay, the "Gateway of India." As a young boy he spoke Hindustani as well as he did English, and was brought up on Indian tales and legends told by his nurse in local dialect. He even went to both Christian and Hindu religious services, depending on which servant had charge of him that day. When he was five-and-a-half, he was sent to England for his education, but he returned to India before he was seventeen. An intelligent and inquisitive young man, he observed closely everything around him—the customs and the people, the plants and the animals, the usual and the unusual. This India that he learned to know so well was to furnish the characters, plots, and setting for many of his stories and poems.

At the age of twenty-three, Kipling returned to England from India with a suitcase full of stories and poems which launched his early success as a writer. A few years after his success in England, Kipling married an American and lived for four years in Vermont, traveling widely in America and giving lectures. He was also, for a time, a correspondent in South Africa during the Boer War, in which British troops suffered a humiliating defeat at the hands of the local Dutch settlers. Finally, he and his wife settled in a country home in Sussex, on the English Channel in southern England, where he spent the rest of his life writing and exploring the history of the region.

Kipling is thought of not only as representing the period in which he lived but as helping to shape it. In this period, the latter part of the nineteenth century, England achieved its greatest height as a colonial empire, accepting responsibilities in India and elsewhere throughout the world. Kipling's poems and stories did much to make the English aware of their overseas colonies and the responsibilities that their country had undertaken. Kipling seemed to understand more fully than any other writer of his period not only the tradition of the English, with their set standards of conduct and ideals, but also the feelings of the common British soldier and native Indians.

Kipling wrote over two hundred fifty short stories and over a thousand pages of poetry. All of this writing is full of the action and interest that the author had a habit of arousing with his very first line, a skill that was probably, at least in part, a result of his newspaper training. Also like a good newspaper writer, he was never afraid to look hard at life and to write exactly what he saw. What he saw was an often cruel world, which we must face with ideals and courage. Nowhere does Kipling state these beliefs more clearly than in his poetry.

Kipling's poetry is easy to identify once you have read a few of his poems. In force and rhythm, in excitement and realistic detail, they are like no one else's. The lines are strong and spontaneous and packed with sound, with a ringing and vigorous music all their own.

If

If you can keep your head when all about you
    Are losing theirs and blaming it on you,
If you can trust yourself when all men doubt you,
    But make allowance for their doubting too;
If you can wait and not be tired by waiting,   5
    Or being lied about, don't deal in lies,
Or being hated don't give way to hating,
    And yet don't look too good, nor talk too wise:

If you can dream—and not make dreams your master;
    If you can think—and not make thoughts your aim,   10
If you can meet with Triumph and Disaster
    And treat those two impostors just the same;
If you can bear to hear the truth you've spoken
    Twisted by knaves to make a trap for fools,
Or watch the things you gave your life to, broken,   15
    And stoop and build 'em up with worn-out tools:

If you can make one heap of all your winnings;
    And risk it on one turn of pitch-and-toss,
And lose, and start again at your beginnings
    And never breathe a word about your loss;   20
If you can force your heart and nerve and sinew
    To serve your turn long after they are gone
And so hold on when there is nothing in you
    Except the Will which says to them: "Hold on!"

If you can talk with crowds and keep your virtue,   25
    Or walk with Kings—nor lose the common touch,
If neither foes nor loving friends can hurt you,
    If all men count with you, but none too much;
If you can fill the unforgiving minute
    With sixty seconds' worth of distance run,   30
Yours is the Earth and everything that's in it,
    And—which is more—you'll be a Man, my son!

The Ballad of East and West

Oh East is East, and West is West, and never the twain shall meet,
Till Earth and Sky stand presently at God's great Judgment Seat,
But there is neither East nor West, Border, nor Breed, nor Birth,
When two strong men stand face to face, though they come from the ends
    of the earth!

Kamal° is out with twenty men to raise the Border side,   5
And he has lifted the Colonel's mare that is the Colonel's pride.
He has lifted her out of the stable door between the dawn and the day,
And turned the calkins° upon her feet, and ridden her far away.
Then up and spoke the Colonel's son that led a troop of the Guides:°
"Is there never a man of all my men can say where Kamal hides?"   10
Then up and spoke Mohammed Khan, the son of the Ressaldar:°
"If ye know the track of the morning mist, ye know where his pickets are.
"At dusk he harries the Abazai°—at dawn he is into Bonair,°
"But he must go by Fort Bukloh to his own place to fare.
"So if ye gallop to Fort Bukloh as fast as a bird can fly,   15
"By the favor of God ye may cut him off ere he win to the Tongue of Jagai.

5. **Kamal** (kä·mäl′): the leader of the Afghans.   8. **calkins** (kô′kənz): the turned-down edges
of a horseshoe.   9. **the Guides**: native troops who served with the English as guides and
interpreters.   11. **Ressaldar** (rəs·ôl′dər): a native Indian commander of a troop of native
cavalry.   13. **Abazai** (ə·bäsē′), **Bonair** (bun·âr′): settlements on the frontier of the Punjab
district in northwest India.

"But if he be past the Tongue of Jagai, right swiftly turn ye then,
"For the length and the breadth of that grisly plain is sown with Kamal's men.
"There is rock to the left, and rock to the right, and low lean thorn between,
"And ye may hear a breech-bolt° snick where never a man is seen."   20
The Colonel's son has taken horse, and a raw rough dun was he,
With the mouth of a bell and the heart of Hell and the head of a gallows tree.
The Colonel's son to the Fort has won, they bid him stay to eat—
Who rides at the tail of a Border thief, he sits not long at his meat.
He's up and away from Fort Bukloh as fast as he can fly,   25
Till he was aware of his father's mare in the gut of the Tongue of Jagai,
Till he was aware of his father's mare with Kamal upon her back,
And when he could spy the white of her eye, he made the pistol crack.
He has fired once, he has fired twice, but the whistling ball went wide.
"Ye shoot like a soldier," Kamal said. "Show now if ye can ride!"   30
It's up and over the Tongue of Jagai, as blown dust devils go,
The dun he fled like a stag of ten, but the mare like a barren doe.
The dun he leaned against the bit and slugged his head above,
But the red mare played with the snaffle bars,° as a maiden plays with a
     glove.
There was rock to the left and rock to the right, and low lean thorn be-
     tween,   35
And thrice he heard a breech-bolt snick tho' never a man was seen.
They have ridden the low moon out of the sky, their hoofs drum up the dawn,
The dun he went like a wounded bull, but the mare like a new-roused fawn.
The dun he fell at a watercourse—in a woeful heap fell he,
And Kamal has turned the red mare back, and pulled the rider free.   40
He has knocked the pistol out of his hand—small room was there to strive,
"'Twas only by favor of mine," quoth he, "ye rode so long alive:
"There was not a rock for twenty mile, there was not a clump of tree,
"But covered a man of my own men with his rifle cocked on his knee.
"If I had raised my bridle hand, as I have held it low,   45
"The little jackals that flee so fast were feasting all in a row.
"If I had bowed my head on my breast, as I have held it high,
"The kite° that whistles above us now were gorged till she could not fly."
Lightly answered the Colonel's son: "Do good to bird and beast,
"But count who come for the broken meats before thou makest a feast.   50
"If there should follow a thousand swords to carry my bones away,
"Belike the price of a jackal's meal were more than a thief could pay.
"They will feed their horse on the standing crop, their men on the garnered
     grain.
"The thatch of the byres° will serve their fires when all the cattle are slain.
"But if thou thinkest the price be fair—thy brethren wait to sup,   55

---

20. **breech-bolt:** the part of a gun drawn back to cock it for firing.   34. **snaffle bars:** the part
of a bit that is placed in the horse's mouth.   48. **kite:** buzzard.   54. **byre:** cow barn.

"The hound is kin to the jackal spawn—howl, dog, and call them up!
"And if thou thinkest the price be high, in steer and gear and stack,
"Give me my father's mare again, and I'll fight my own way back!"
Kamal has gripped him by the hand and set him upon his feet.
"No talk shall be of dogs," said he, "when wolf and gray wolf meet.   60
"May I eat dirt if thou hast hurt of me in deed or breath;
"What dam° of lances brought thee forth to jest at the dawn with Death?"
Lightly answered the Colonel's son: "I hold by the blood of my clan:
"Take up the mare for my father's gift—by God, she has carried a man!"
The red mare ran to the Colonel's son, and nuzzled against his breast;   65
"We be two strong men," said Kamal then, "but she loveth the younger best.
"So she shall go with a lifter's dower, my turquoise-studded rein,
"My 'broidered saddle and saddlecloth, and silver stirrups twain."
The Colonel's son a pistol drew, and held it muzzle-end,
"Ye have taken the one from a foe," said he. "Will ye take the mate from a
        friend?"   70
"A gift for a gift," said Kamal straight; "a limb for the risk of a limb.
"Thy father has sent his son to me, I'll send my son to him!"
With that he whistled his only son, that dropped from a mountain crest—

62. **dam:** mother.

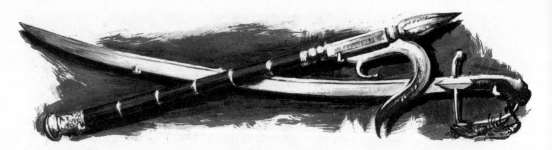

He trod the ling° like a buck in spring, and he looked like a lance in rest.

"Now here is thy master," Kamal said, "who leads a troop of the Guides,

"And thou must ride at his left side as shield on shoulder rides.   76

"Till Death or I cut loose the tie, at camp and board and bed,

"Thy life is his—thy fate it is to guard him with thy head.

"So, thou must eat the White Queen's° meat, and all her foes are thine,

"And thou must harry thy father's hold for the peace of the Border-line.   80

"And thou must make a trooper tough and hack thy way to power—

"Belike they will raise thee to Ressaldar when I am hanged in Peshawur!"°

They have looked each other between the eyes, and there they found no fault.

They have taken the Oath of the Brother-in-Blood on leavened bread and salt:

They have taken the Oath of the Brother-in-Blood on fire and fresh-cut sod,   85

On the hilt and the haft of the Khyber knife,° and the Wondrous Names of God.°

The Colonel's son he rides the mare and Kamal's boy the dun,

And two have come back to Fort Bukloh where there went forth but one.

And when they drew to the Quarter-Guard,° full twenty swords flew clear—

There was not a man but carried his feud with the blood of the mountaineer.   90

"Ha' done! ha' done!" said the Colonel's son. "Put up the steel at your sides!

"Last night ye had struck at a Border thief—tonight 'tis a man of the Guides!"

Oh, East is East, and West is West, and never the twain shall meet,

Till Earth and Sky stand presently at God's great Judgment Seat;

But there is neither East nor West, Border, nor Breed, nor Birth,   95

When two strong men stand face to face, though they come from the ends
of the earth!

74. **ling:** heather. 79. **the White Queen:** Queen Victoria. 82. **Peshawur** (pə·shä′wər): the seat of the British government in the northwest frontier province of India. 86. **Khyber knife** (kī′bər): a kind of knife used in the Khyber Pass, a narrow road between India and Afghanistan. **Wondrous Names of God:** the one hundred Mohammedan names given to God. 89. **Quarter-Guard:** sentry post.

Recessional

A recessional is the hymn which is sung as the choir and clergy are leaving the church at the end of a service. Kipling's "Recessional" was written in 1897, the year of England's celebration of the sixtieth anniversary—the Diamond Jubilee—of the reign of Queen Victoria. In that year, England was at the height of its dominion as a world power.

God of our fathers, known of old,
    Lord of our far-flung battle line,
Beneath whose awful Hand we hold
    Dominion over palm and pine—
Lord God of Hosts, be with us yet,   5
Lest we forget—lest we forget!

The tumult and the shouting dies;
    The captains and the kings depart:
Still stands Thine ancient sacrifice,
    An humble and a contrite heart.   10
Lord God of Hosts, be with us yet,
Lest we forget—lest we forget!

Far-called, our navies melt away;
    On dune and headland sinks the fire:
Lo, all our pomp of yesterday   15
    Is one with Nineveh and Tyre!°
Judge of the Nations, spare us yet,
Lest we forget—lest we forget!

If, drunk with sight of power, we loose
    Wild tongues that have not Thee in awe,
Such boasting as the Gentiles° use,   21
    Or lesser breeds without the Law°—
Lord God of Hosts, be with us yet,
Lest we forget—lest we forget!

16. **Nineveh and Tyre** (nin'ə·və and tīr): great cities which were centers of ancient civilizations until they neglected God's commandments and decayed. 21. **Gentiles** (jen'tīlz): Kipling is using the word in the Biblical sense of "outsider"—those not belonging to the "chosen people." 22. **the Law:** the Hebrew Law of the Old Testament. Kipling is thinking of the English, who in his day ruled much of the world, as a "chosen people," like the Israelites of ancient times.

For heathen heart that puts her trust   25
    In reeking tube and iron shard,°
All valiant dust that builds on dust,
    And guarding, calls not Thee to guard,
For frantic boast and foolish word—
Thy Mercy on Thy People, Lord!   30

26. **shard:** a hard or brittle fragment—here, a bullet from the "reeking tube" of guns.

Cities and Thrones and Powers

Cities and Thrones and Powers
    Stand in Time's eye,
Almost as long as flowers,
    Which daily die:
But, as new buds put forth   5
    To glad° new men,
Out of the spent and unconsidered Earth
    The Cities rise again.

This season's Daffodil,
    She never hears   10
What change, what chance, what chill,
    Cut down last year's;
But with bold countenance,
    And knowledge small,
Esteems her seven days' continuance   15
    To be perpetual.

So Time that is o'er-kind
    To all that be,
Ordains us e'en as blind,
    As bold as she: 20
That in our very death,
    And burial sure,
Shadow to shadow, well persuaded, saith,
    "See how our works endure!"

6. **glad:** to make glad, to gladden.

IF

1. Look closely at lines 9–12. What does Kipling mean by "not make dreams your master"? by "not make thoughts your aim"? In what way are triumph and disaster "impostors"? How would one treat them "just the same"?

2. Which of the qualities cited by Kipling do you admire most? Are there any you think are not good qualities? Can you think of any other qualities that might be added to Kipling's list? Are the qualities in your final list ones that are prominent in our world leaders and famous figures of today?

3. Which quality named in "If" do you think is most important in a person? What character in history or literature is an outstanding example of this quality? How would you describe this quality in your own words? What words or images make Kipling's description especially vivid?

BALLAD OF EAST AND WEST

1. A ballad is a poem that tells a story. What happens in the story of Kamal and the Colonel's son? How does this story illustrate the statement in the first and last stanzas of the poem? Considering both the story and the refrain, state in your own words the theme of the poem.

2. What does Kamal mean when he says, "No talk shall be of dogs when wolf and gray wolf meet" (line 60)? What does he admire about the Colonel's son? Which of the qualities described in "If" are evident in the Colonel's son? Does Kamal also show these qualities? does Kamal's son?

3. What final gift does Kamal send back with the Colonel's son? How does he hope this will benefit his own son? What is the purpose of the oaths sworn by the sons of Kamal and the Colonel? Which of the things they swear on make the oath seem a solemn ritual? Which of these objects suggest or symbolize some wider meaning?

RECESSIONAL

1. In what things does Kipling say his nation should not put its trust? Why should it reject these sources of power? On what would Kipling have his compatriots rely?

2. What examples does Kipling give to prove that success in war and conquest will not keep a nation great? Why, as an empire expands, might its power tend to "melt away"? How might a nation's puffing up with a sense of its own importance hasten this process?

3. What lines does Kipling use as a refrain (see page 159)? How does the refrain grow in effect and meaning each time it is repeated in the poem? Where does Kipling vary this refrain? What new ideas are introduced in these variations?

CITIES AND THRONES AND POWERS

1. This poem may remind you of several others you have read, especially "Daffodils" by Robert Herrick. In Kipling's poem, why is the daffodil bold? What does it not understand? How are each of us as "blind" and "bold" about our own place in time?

2. Who are the "shadows" in lines 23–24? What are they "well persuaded" of? Why is it a kindness to us that Time does not let us, like the daffodils, realize that our accomplishments will not endure?

3. In this poem do you think Kipling is warning England as he does in "Recessional"? If so, what is the warning?

SUMMING UP

1. If you were writing a poem such as "If" today, what qualities would you include? Why? Do today's heroes have the qualities that Kipling most admires? Are the virtues that he recommends still as important as they were?

2. Read Kipling's "Just So Stories," *The Jungle Book, Captains Courageous,* or *Kim.* Report on your reading to the class and be ready to discuss relationships between the ideas in Kipling's poetry and his prose.

ROBERT BURNS

(1759–1796)

Robert Burns, Scotland's chief poet, has caught popular imagination as few other writers ever have. His personal story, both romantic and tragic, has given rise to a vast number of stories and legends, most of them exaggerated and untrue. Even without such exaggerations, however, the life of Robert Burns was dramatic, difficult, and full of struggle.

Burns was born at Ayr, a Scottish farm community. His parents were peasants, and the whole family's energies were absorbed in the exhausting attempt to coax a living out of the thin soil. Burns' formal education was meager, consisting only of a few years with a local schoolmaster, but his father encouraged his eagerness to borrow books and to read widely in English and Scottish literature. Early in his life, an old nurse taught him Scotland's traditional songs and stories, and as he grew up he loved to hear the people sing. He himself had difficulty carrying a tune, but he listened eagerly to others and learned all the old songs. Later, while whistling and walking behind a plow on his family's farm, he composed many of his poems to the tune of old Scottish songs. In all his poetry a melody seems to lie just beneath the words, and many of his poems which were written to no special tune have since had tunes written for them.

Unlike most Scottish peasants, Robert Burns never willingly accepted as his lot the hard life of a poor farmer. His means of escape was poetry. As a boy and young man he practiced writing and earned money by writing letters to girls for young men who could not write themselves. As his ability with words grew, he began to put his feelings into poetry. When the father of his sweetheart, Jean Armour, refused to let them marry, he made up his mind to leave Scotland and published a book of poems to raise money for his transportation. His poetry aroused such interest, however, that Burns changed his mind and went instead to Edinburgh, the literary capital of Scotland, where he was flattered and applauded in the finest social circles. Within a short time, however, he grew sick of the poses of society, and society grew equally tired of him. He went home, married Jean, and wrote his best poetry. At the age of thirty-seven, at the height of his genius as a poet, he died of tuberculosis.

The poems of Robert Burns are a remarkable mixture of Scottish music and Scottish common sense. No one else has ever used the Scottish dialect and idiom so simply and forcefully and with such feeling for its inner music. The themes of Burns's poems are few. Many of them speak of personal love; others glorify the virtues of home and country life. Burns wrote often in a spirit of independence and freedom and, speaking out for the cause of the French Revolution, championed the cause of the common folk. A man who was close to nature, Burns often uses nature imagery in his poetry. The Scottish countryside—its flowers, trees, birds, hills, and streams—all come alive in his lines. But most of all, his poetry is full of honest feeling.

Bannockburn

In 1314, at the Battle of Bannockburn, Robert the Bruce led the badly outnumbered Scots to victory over the English—a triumph that was the turning point in the Scottish struggle for independence. Burns's poem is a rallying cry that Robert the Bruce might have made to his men just before the crucial battle.

Scots, wha hae° wi' Wallace bled,
Scots, wham Bruce has aften led;
Welcome to your gory bed,
    Or to victory!

Now's the day, and now's the hour;   5
See the front o' battle lour;°
See approach proud Edward's power—
    Chains and slavery!

Wha will be a traitor knave?
Wha can fill a coward's grave?   10
Wha sae base as be a slave?
    Let him turn and flee!

Wha for Scotland's king and law
Freedom's sword will strongly draw,
Freeman stand, or Freeman fa',   15
    Let him follow me!

By oppression's woes and pains!
By your sons in servile chains!
We will drain our dearest veins,
    But they shall be free!   20

Lay the proud usurpers low!
Tyrants fall in every foe!
Liberty's in every blow!—
    Let us do or die!°

1. **wha hae:** who have. 6. **lour:** threaten, scowl.

24. **die:** Scottish pronunciation is dē.

Sweet Afton

Mary Campbell, one of Burns's first sweethearts, died of typhoid fever while they were engaged. This memorable poem recalls their days together on the shores of the river Afton.

Flow gently, sweet Afton! among thy green braes,°
Flow gently, I'll sing thee a song in thy praise;
My Mary's asleep by thy murmuring stream,
Flow gently, sweet Afton, disturb not her dream.

Thou stock dove whose echo resounds through the glen,   5
Ye wild whistling blackbirds in yon thorny den,
Thou green crested lapwing, thy screaming forbear,
I charge you, disturb not my slumbering Fair.

How lofty, sweet Afton, thy neighboring hills,
Far marked with the courses of clear, winding rills;   10
There daily I wander as noon rises high,
My flocks and my Mary's sweet cot in my eye.

How pleasant thy banks and green valleys below,
Where, wild in the woodlands, the primroses blow;°
There oft, as mild ev'ning weeps over the lea,   15
The sweet-scented birk° shades my Mary and me.

Thy crystal stream, Afton, how lovely it glides,
And winds by the cot where my Mary resides;
How wanton thy waters her snowy feet lave,°
As, gathering sweet flowerets, she stems thy clear wave.   20

Flow gently, sweet Afton, among thy green braes,
Flow gently, sweet river, the theme of my lays;°
My Mary's asleep by thy murmuring stream,
Flow gently, sweet Afton, disturb not her dream.

1. **braes** (brāz): hillsides.   14. **blow:** bloom, blossom.   16. **birk:** birch.   19. **lave:** wash, bathe.   22. **lays:** songs.

Of A' the Airts

Of a' the airts° the wind can blaw,
  I dearly like the west,
For there the bonnie° lassie lives,
  The lassie I lo'e best:
There's wild woods grow, and rivers row,
  And mony a hill between;   6
But day and night my fancy's flight
  Is ever wi' my Jean.

I see her in the dewy flowers,
  I see her sweet and fair: 10
I hear her in the tunefu' birds,
  I hear her charm the air:
There's not a bonnie flower that springs,
  By fountain, shaw,° or green;
There's not a bonnie bird that sings, 15
  But minds me o' my Jean.

    1. **airts:** directions. 3. **bonnie:** pretty. 14. **shaw:**
woods, a thicket of trees or bushes.

John Anderson My Jo

John Anderson my jo,° John,
  When we were first acquent,°
Your locks were like the raven,
  Your bonnie brow was brent;°
But now your brow is beld,° John,   5
  Your locks are like the snow;
But blessings on your frosty pow,°
  John Anderson, my jo.

John Anderson my jo, John,
  We clamb the hill thegither;   10
And mony a canty° day, John,
  We've had wi' ane anither:
Now we maun° totter down, John,
  And hand in hand we'll go,
And sleep thegither at the foot, 15
  John Anderson, my jo.

    1. **jo:** joy, sweetheart. 2. **acquent:** acquainted.
4. **brent:** unwrinkled. 5. **beld:** bald. 7. **pow:**
head. 11. **canty:** happy. 13. **maun:** must.

A Man's a Man for A' That

Is there, for honest poverty,
  That hings his head, an' a' that?
The coward slave, we pass him by,
  We dare be poor for a' that!
    For a' that, an' a' that,   5
      Our toils obscure, an' a' that;
    The rank is but the guinea's stamp;°
    The man's the gowd° for a' that.

What tho' on hamely fare we dine,
  Wear hodden-gray,° an' a' that;   10
Gie fools their silks, and knaves their
      wine,
  A man's a man for a' that.
    For a' that, an' a' that,
      Their tinsel show, an' a' that;
    The honest man, though e'er sae
      poor,   15
    Is king o' men for a' that.

Ye see yon birkie,° ca'd a lord,
  Wha struts, an' stares, an' a' that;
Tho' hundreds worship at his word,
  He's but a coof° for a' that.   20
    For a' that, an' a' that,
      His riband, star,° an' a' that,
    The man o' independent mind,
      He looks and laughs at a' that.

A prince can mak' a belted knight,   25
  A marquis, duke, an' a' that;
But an honest man's aboon° his might,
  Guid faith he mauna fa'° that!
    For a' that, an' a' that,
      Their dignities, an' a' that,   30
    The pith o' sense, an' pride o' worth,
    Are higher rank than a' that.

Then let us pray that come it may,
  As come it will for a' that,
That sense and worth, o'er a' the earth,
  May bear the gree,° an' a' that.   36
    For a' that, an' a' that,
      It's coming yet, for a' that,
    That man to man, the warld o'er,
      Shall brothers be for a' that.   40

36. **bear the gree:** take the prize.

FOR STUDY AND DISCUSSION

BANNOCKBURN

1. Which words and phrases make this poem a stirring challenge to the fight for liberty? Which words make the alternatives of freedom and slavery vividly real? Which words suggest what may happen to those who choose to fight for freedom?

2. Read the poem aloud as an oration intended to rouse an army just before battle. Before you begin, notice the punctuation of the poem. Why do you think the exclamation marks increase toward the end of the poem? In what tone of voice would Robert the Bruce utter the questions in stanza 3?

3. How many lines rhyme within each stanza? How does this add to the emotion of the poem? How do the rhymes in the last line of each stanza function as a kind of refrain?

SWEET AFTON

1. What mood is created in the first stanza? Which words do the most to create this mood? The second stanza interrupts the mood with sounds of life and excitement. How does the poet react to this interruption? Why does he ask the Afton to "flow gently"? How might it disturb "her dream"?

2. Line 3 contains a good example of *onomatopoeia*—a literary device in which the sound of a word echoes its meaning. How is this true of the word *murmuring?* Where else can you find onomatopoeia in the poem?

3. Burns said that he wrote this poem as a compliment to "the small river Afton," which "has some charming, wild, romantic scenery

---

7. **guinea's stamp:** mold for stamping out gold coins. 8. **gowd:** gold. 10. **hodden-gray:** coarse cloth. 17. **birkie:** fellow. 20. **coof:** fool. 22. **riband, star:** insignia of titles and honors. 27. **aboon:** above. 28. **mauna fa':** cannot make.

on its banks." Which lines picture this scenery? Which lines link the scenery with Mary? Do you think Burns was writing about his love for Mary or about the river Afton? What in the poem makes you think so?

4. Read the poem aloud, paying special attention to the smooth, gliding effect of the words. Which words suggest the river's slow and dreamy motion? What sounds in the first and last stanzas make these lines seem to flow?

OF A' THE AIRTS

1. This poem is a tribute to Jean Armour, written soon after Burns was married. Which lines and words convince you of the genuineness of his feeling? Is Burns's mood in this poem lonely or happy? What in the poem makes you think so?

2. Read the poem aloud to fully appreciate its music. What is the rhyme scheme? How does it compare to that of a folk ballad such as "The Wife of Usher's Well"? Where in this poem does Burns add an "extra" rhyme?

3. As you know, a *ballad stanza* contains four lines—alternating lines with four accents or heavy beats (lines 1 and 3 of the stanza) and lines with three accents (lines 2 and 4). What is the metrical pattern in "Of A' the Airts"? What variation is it of the ballad stanza? Does the varying length of the lines add to the music of the poem?

JOHN ANDERSON MY JO

1. Who is the speaker in this poem? How old is she? How has her sweetheart changed? Does she still love him? How do you know?

2. What does the speaker recall about their days with one another? What symbolic meaning is suggested by the phrases "clamb the hill" and "totter down"? What is the symbolic meaning of line 15?

3. Read the poem aloud, paying special attention to the words in Scottish dialect. Which words rhyme? Which are examples of alliteration? How does repetition of words and phrases contribute to the music of the poem?

A MAN'S A MAN FOR A' THAT

1. In your own words, state the theme or central meaning of the poem. Burns lived in the time of both the American and French Revolutions and openly applauded the French Revolution's creed of "Liberty, Equality, Fraternity." How does "A Man's a Man for A' That" express the ideals of this rising republic?

2. For greater compression, a poet often leaves out words that would be included in prose. For instance, in prose, the first two lines of this poem might be written, "Is there any man who just because he's poor, hangs his head, and all that kind of thing?" Why does Burns call such a person a "coward slave"? How is this attitude like that expressed in "Bannockburn"? Go through the poem carefully and list the qualities that Burns thinks make a real person. How do these qualities compare with those proposed in "If"?

3. Which lines show how strongly Burns feels about pomp and social poses? What is his attitude toward titles and rank? What does he feel it is that "stamps" rank on a person? What quality in a person is "the gowd" that is more important than official rank?

4. What Scottish phrase is used as a refrain in the poem? How does its repetition make the poem more stirring especially when read aloud? What wider meaning do the words and "a' that" take on as they are used again and again in the poem?

SUMMING UP

1. Which of Burns's poems do you think best illustrate each of the following characteristics?
His gift for creating music in Scottish dialect
His sensitivity to the beauty of nature
His belief in simple honesty and friendship
His belief in personal pride and courage
His sincerity and deep feeling

2. Which one of Burns's poems did you like best? Why? Study it closely for word music, pictures, and striking phrasing, and be ready to defend your choice.

EDNA
ST. VINCENT
MILLAY
(1892–1950)

Edna St. Vincent Millay, a lovely, slender woman with red hair, green eyes, and an innocent smile, combined in her poetry two very different worlds—the Maine coast where she spent her childhood, and the sophisticated, exciting world of Greenwich Village, New York, where she lived with other young actors and writers in the early part of the twentieth century. Someone meeting Vincent Millay (as she liked to be called) for the first time was usually struck at once either by her intense seriousness or her bubbling humor. Her large eyes could shine for hours as she listened to someone who had caught her interest, or they could light up with mischievous gaiety as she kept up a running stream of nonsense.

Edna St. Vincent Millay was born in 1892 in Rockland, Maine. As a young girl, she began to write and recite poetry, and her first poems were printed in *St. Nicholas Magazine* when she was still in school. Her first book of poetry, *Renascence,* was published the year of her graduation from Vassar College, and she went, with this small book as an introduction, to New York City to seek her fortune. For several years she lived in New York, acting with a small theater group and writing plays, stories, and poems. She won the Pulitzer prize for poetry in 1923. Shortly afterward she married and, after traveling a while, finally settled down on a farm in western Massachusetts. Here she died in 1950.

Although Vincent Millay wrote stories, verse plays, and an opera libretto, her best work is her lyric poems. Like most writers of lyrics, she had her own highly personal gift of seeing and feeling—an intense imagination, and vivid, personal emotions. Her poems are full of wonder and delight in the world around her and a deep conviction that beauty is everywhere, just waiting to be seen. Yet over all is the shadow of its own death, the inevitable fact that no beauty can endure.

Edna St. Vincent Millay did not believe in hiding or hoarding. For that, life was too short. She gave freely of herself in her poetry and never tried to conceal her innermost heart.

Travel

The railroad track is miles away,
    And the day is loud with voices speaking,
Yet there isn't a train goes by all day
    But I hear its whistle shrieking.

All night there isn't a train goes by,   5
    Though the night is still for sleep and dreaming,
But I see its cinders red on the sky,
    And hear its engine steaming.

My heart is warm with the friends I make,
    And better friends I'll not be knowing;   10
Yet there isn't a train I wouldn't take,
    No matter where it's going.

Winter Night

Pile high the hickory and the light
Log chestnut struck by the blight.
Welcome-in the winter night.

The day has gone in hewing and felling,
Sawing and drawing wood to the dwelling
For the night of talk and storytelling.   6

These are the hours that give the edge
To the blunted ax and the bent wedge,
Straighten the saw and lighten the sledge.

Here are question and reply,   10
And the fire reflected in the thinking eye.
So peace, and let the bobcat cry.

The Courage
That My Mother Had

The courage that my mother had
Went with her, and is with her still:
Rock from New England quarried;
Now granite in a granite hill.

The golden brooch my mother wore   5
She left behind for me to wear;
I have no thing I treasure more:
Yet, it is something I could spare.

Oh, if instead she'd left to me
The thing she took into the grave!—   10
That courage like a rock, which she
Has no more need of, and I have.

God's World

O world, I cannot hold thee close enough!
　Thy winds, thy wide gray skies!
　Thy mists that roll and rise!
Thy woods, this autumn day, that ache and sag
And all but cry with color! That gaunt crag　　　　　　　5
To crush! To lift the lean of that black bluff!
World, world, I cannot get thee close enough!

Long have I known a glory in it all,
　But never knew I this;
　Here such a passion is　　　　　　　　　　　　　10
As stretcheth me apart. Lord, I do fear
Thou'st made the world too beautiful this year.
My soul is all but out of me—let fall
No burning leaf; prithee,° let no bird call.

14. **prithee:** a shortened form of "I pray thee."

Autumn Chant

Now the autumn shudders
　In the rose's root.
Far and wide the ladders
　Lean among the fruit.

Now the autumn clambers　　　5
　Up the trellised frame,
And the rose remembers
　The dust from which it came.

Brighter than the blossom
　On the rose's bough　　　　10
Sits the wizened, orange,
　Bitter berry now;

Beauty never slumbers;
　All is in her name;
But the rose remembers　　　　15
　The dust from which it came.

FOR STUDY AND DISCUSSION

TRAVEL

1. What does the speaker hear and see all day and night? What about her surroundings makes this surprising? Do you think she is happy or unhappy with her present life?

2. Sometimes people travel to escape; sometimes they travel to get from one place to another. Why does the speaker want to travel? How would you describe the emotion she expresses in the poem?

3. Compare this poem with Robert Louis Stevenson's poem "Travel" (page 178). Which speaker seems to have the strongest desire to travel? What in the poems make you think so?

WINTER NIGHT

1. Would you say that a particular part of the country is used as the setting for this poem? What kind of work was done during the day? Why is the evening welcome?

2. What is the effect of the night of talk and

storytelling on the weary workers? How does it affect them physically? How does it affect them mentally? Explain how these quiet hours of fireside talk on a winter night can have the effect the poet describes in stanza 3.

3. What is the rhyme scheme of this poem? The poem begins with an image of piling logs on the fire. In the same way, the poet piles rhymes on each other within each stanza. How does this repeated rhyming reinforce the slow, deliberate rhythm of the poem? How does the rhythm match the mood of the winter night?

THE COURAGE THAT MY MOTHER HAD

1. This poem is based on a comparison of courage and New England granite. Why is this comparison a good one?

2. What did the poet inherit from her mother? Why, although she treasures it, can she spare it? Do you think that, in general, personal qualities such as courage are a more necessary "inheritance" than valuable material objects? Why or why not?

3. Read the poem aloud, noticing how the poet suggests pauses of differing lengths by using different punctuation marks. Which punctuation mark calls for the longest pause? which for the shortest? Why? Notice especially the exclamation point in the last stanza. How does it emphasize the poet's feelings?

GOD'S WORLD

1. What details of the autumn day impress the poet with their beauty? Which verbs suggest the strength of her feeling for this beauty? Which words suggest that this feeling is painful as well as wonderful?

2. What desire causes the poet's outcry in line 7: "World, world, I cannot get thee close enough!" Why might such a desire be felt more deeply in autumn than in summer or in spring when the world's beauty is younger?

3. Stanza 1 is addressed to the world. To whom does the poet speak in stanza 2? How does this change to direct address, as in Psalm 23 (page 201), intensify the ending of this poem?

4. What musical devices does the poet use in this poem? Which are most effective in making you share her feelings?

AUTUMN CHANT

1. What is the meaning of the lines the poet repeats: "And the rose remembers/ The dust from which it came." What ideas do you associate with a *rose?* with *dust?* What do these words symbolize (see page 183)? What do these two lines suggest about the change in seasons and living things? Together with sadness at beauty's departure, does the poem seem to promise its return? What in the last stanza might make you think so?

2. Each stanza of the poem contains an image of a beginning and of an ending. For instance, stanza 1 includes both "the rose's root" and the harvest ladders among the ripe fruit. What images of beginning and ending can you find in the other three stanzas? How do these repeated images contribute to the theme or central meaning of the poem?

3. How does this description of autumn compare with that in "God's World"? Which is more emotional? In which is the poet more resigned to the changes of fall? Which poem suggests a deeper sadness at these changes?

SUMMING UP

1. Some critics find Edna St. Vincent Millay's poetry overdramatic and excessive in feeling. What is your response to her poetry? Would you say her poetry is an expression of youth?

2. Go back over Millay's poems and notice her skill at creating music with words. Does she use a variety of stanzas? of rhymes? of rhythm patterns? In which poems does she most obviously choose her words for their music as well as for their meaning?

FOR COMPOSITION

A writer uses vivid images to communicate emotion to a reader. Try expressing one of your own feelings in either prose or poetry. Ask yourself what pictures will best suggest your feeling to others and help them to share it.

Here are some possible titles, suggested by Millay poems.

"Stay, Stay!"
"Spring's Gift"
"Time to Work, Time to Wonder"

ALFRED, LORD TENNYSON

(1809–1892)

Alfred Tennyson, a tall, dark, handsome man, was poet laureate of England for over forty years, and was finally made Lord Tennyson in honor of his achievements as a poet. Since the period during which he was poet laureate overlapped with much of the reign of Queen Victoria, he has often been called "the voice of the Victorian Age." No other poet of his time so well expressed the hopes, faith, doubts, and joys of the people of that day—their patriotism, their questions about science and religion, their ideals and high goals for the perfection of life and society. His belief in England's progress, his admiration for her mighty navy and powerful machines, was balanced by a personal sympathy for human suffering and loss.

At the age of five, Tennyson said, "I hear a voice that's speaking in the wind," and not long afterward he began to write poetry. As you might expect from this beginning, Tennyson's idea of a poet was a lofty one. He considered the poet as a kind of prophet, one who speaks truth to the world. The surroundings of Tennyson's childhood home were ideal for the making of a poet, with woods, hills, bluffs, dunes, and marshes all nearby to see and walk upon. Alfred gained quite a reputation among the villagers for the long and aimless walks he took in the countryside. It was secretly whispered that he must be mad.

Their surroundings and their father's library had somewhat the same effect on several of the Tennyson children. While still in college, Alfred and his brother Charles published a book of poems called *Poems by Two Brothers,* and many critics of the time could not decide which brother had the greater talent as a poet. Then suddenly, in his early twenties, Alfred came face to face with personal grief and unhappiness. His father died and then his best friend, Arthur Hallam, a brilliant young man of whom all his friends expected great things. Alfred Tennyson, shocked into a deep sadness, withdrew from life and lived in seclusion at his family's country home. For ten years he published no poetry. He did, after a while, fall in love with Emily Sellwood, a girl who lived nearby, but her father refused to let them marry until Alfred proved that he could support a family. They became engaged, but it was thirteen years before they married.

In contrast to his early life of hardship and frustration, Tennyson's later life was filled with fame and honors. He and Emily went to live on the Isle of Wight, off the southern coast of England. When tourists and autograph-seekers overran the island, they began spending summers on the mainland, in southwestern England. All his life Tennyson avoided publicity and the public glare. While still a young man, he wrote, "I require quiet, and myself to myself, more than any man when I write." And he was always writing.

Tennyson was a remarkable lyricist—a singer in words who could work musical variations on all sorts of patterns of rhythm and rhyme. He is unsurpassed in his use of musical devices to create atmosphere and mood in his poetry. An excellent observer of nature, Tennyson filled his poems with pictures of natural beauty. Although one of his favorite themes was progress, his finest poems are probably those whose setting is in the past. In works such as *Idylls of the King*, about the legend of King Arthur and his Round Table, Tennyson brings the past before our eyes in poetry of haunting beauty. Whether he writes about the legends of King Arthur and his knights, about an eagle on a crag, a flower rooted in a wall, a flowing river, or a hero's temptations in ancient times, everything he writes of comes to life with vivid freshness in the poetry of Alfred Tennyson.

The Poet's Song

The rain had fallen, the poet arose,
   He passed by the town and out of the street;
A light wind blew from the gates of the sun,
   And waves of shadow went over the wheat;
And he sat him down in a lonely place,
   And chanted a melody loud and sweet,   5
That made the wild swan pause in her cloud,
   And the lark drop down at his feet.

The swallow stopped as he hunted the fly,
   The snake slipped under a spray,°
The wild hawk stood with the down on his beak,   10
   And stared, with his foot on the prey;
And the nightingale thought, "I have sung many songs,
   But never a one so gay,
For he sings of what the world will be
   When the years have died away."   15

10. **spray:** a small flowering branch.

The Eagle

He clasps the crag with crooked hands,
Close to the sun in lonely lands,
Ringed with the azure° world, he stands.

The wrinkled sea beneath him crawls;
He watches from his mountain walls,   5
And like a thunderbolt he falls.

3. **azure** (azh'ər): sky blue.

Flower in the Crannied Wall

Flower in the crannied° wall,
I pluck you out of the crannies,
I hold you here, root and all, in my hand,
Little flower—but *if* I could understand
What you are, root and all, and all in all,
I should know what God and man is.   6

1. **crannied:** containing crannies—small holes or crevices in a wall.

A Farewell

Flow down, cold rivulet, to the sea,
   Thy tribute wave deliver;
No more by thee my steps shall be,
   Forever and forever.

Flow, softly flow, by lawn and lea,°   5
   A rivulet, then a river:
Nowhere by thee my steps shall be,
   Forever and forever.

But here will sigh thine alder tree,
   And here thine aspen shiver;   10
And here by thee will hum the bee,
   Forever and forever.

A thousand suns will stream on thee,
   A thousand moons will quiver;
But not by thee my steps shall be,   15
   Forever and forever.

5. **lea:** meadow.

The Lotus-Eaters

After the Trojan War, one of the adventures of Odysseus and his men as they made their long voyage home to the island of Ithaca was a visit to the land of the lotus-eaters. Here Odysseus speaks to his men as they first sight the shore.

"Courage!" he said, and pointed toward the land,
"This mounting wave will roll us shoreward soon."
In the afternoon they came unto a land
In which it seemed always afternoon.
All round the coast the languid air did swoon,   5
Breathing like one that hath a weary dream.
Full-faced above the valley stood the moon;
And, like a downward smoke, the slender stream
Along the cliff to fall and pause and fall did seem.

A land of streams! some, like a downward smoke,   10
Slow-dropping veils of thinnest lawn,° did go;
And some through wavering lights and shadows broke,
Rolling a slumbrous sheet of foam below.
They saw the gleaming river seaward flow
From the inner land; far off, three mountaintops,   15
Three silent pinnacles of aged snow,
Stood sunset-flushed; and, dewed with showery drops,
Up-clomb the shadowy pine above the woven copse.°

The charmèd sunset lingered low adown
In the red west; through mountain clefts the dale   20
Was seen far inland, and the yellow down°
Bordered with palm, and many a winding vale
And meadow, set with slender galingale;°
A land where all things always seemed the same!
And round about the keel with faces pale,   25
Dark faces pale against that rosy flame,
The mild-eyed melancholy Lotus-eaters came.

Branches they bore of that enchanted stem,
Laden with flower and fruit, whereof they gave
To each, but whoso did receive of them   30
And taste, to him the gushing of the wave
Far, far away did seem to mourn and rave
On alien shores; and if his fellow spake,
His voice was thin, as voices from the grave;
And deep asleep he seemed, yet all awake,   35
And music in his ears his beating heart did make.

11. **lawn:** a thin, sheer fabric. 18. **copse:** a thicket of bushes or small trees. 21. **down:** rolling, upland countryside. 23. **galingale** (gal'in·gāl): a tall, grasslike herb of southern England.

They sat them down upon the yellow sand,
Between the sun and moon upon the shore;
And sweet it was to dream of fatherland,
Of child, and wife, and slave; but evermore   40
Most weary seemed the sea, weary the oar,
Weary the wandering fields of barren foam.
Then someone said, "We will return no more";
And all at once they sang, "Our island home
Is far beyond the wave; we will no longer roam."   45

FOR STUDY AND DISCUSSION

THE POET'S SONG

1. What does this poem reveal about Tennyson's idea of the function of the poet? What special powers must the poet possess to sing of "what the world will be"? Which images in the first stanza suggest the nature of the poet's song?

2. In lines 7–8 the swan and the lark pause to listen to the poet. What is even more surprising about the reactions of the creatures in lines 9–12? When they pause, what are the swallow and the hawk in the act of doing? Why is it significant that they pause? What is so compelling about the poet's song?

3. The Victorian period was a time of great optimism and hope that people eventually could create a perfect civilization and social order.

What suggestions are there of such a hope in "The Poet's Song"?

THE EAGLE

1. In the first stanza, would you say that the poet observes the eagle at close range or from far off? Which words make his picture particularly vivid?

2. Why does the sea seem "wrinkled"? Which words and phrases in the poem suggest the eagle's power? Which remind you that he is a bird of prey?

3. Tennyson is a master at creating musical effects with words. What is the rhyme scheme of this poem? How do the rhymes build up within each stanza to the climax of the eagle's "fall"? What vowel and consonant sounds build up, through repetition, a similar tension in the poem?

FLOWER IN THE CRANNIED WALL

1. What simple experience is described in this poem? What broad conclusion does the poet draw from that experience?

2. During the Victorian period, when Tennyson wrote, people expected to learn all the secrets of the universe through science. Do you agree with Tennyson's suggestion that a small flower might contain within itself all the secrets of the universe? Why or why not? What is added to the mystery of the flower by the fact that it was found growing in a tiny cranny in a wall?

3. Reread lines 4 and 5. Do you think the poet expects ever to understand "all in all"? What in these lines makes you think so?

A FAREWELL

1. To what is the poet saying "farewell"? Describe the setting of the poem. Which lines or phrases suggest that nature will go on the same, despite the poet's departure?

2. Which lines contain the most striking pictures in the poem? In what way might trees "sigh" and "shiver"? How would suns "stream" on water? How would moons "quiver"? Which images are most effective in helping you share the poet's feeling?

3. What musical devices does Tennyson use in "A Farewell"? How does the sound of the poem help create its mood?

THE LOTUS-EATERS

1. Odysseus speaks at the beginning of the poem to men who are tired, worn out from hard rowing through the sea. What natural features of the land of the lotus-eaters would make it seem particularly attractive to tired and weary people? What is the overall impression of the scene they see? What do phrases such as "slow-dropping veils" and "like a downward smoke" suggest about the atmosphere of the scene?

2. Which lines present a picture of the lotus-eaters as they crowd around the keel of the ship? Which details in this description make them seem exotic and strange? Which words suggest the effects of their eating of the lotus? When they give the mariners lotus-blossoms, how does eating the "enchanted stem" affect

the men? Which lines suggest the growing remoteness of the world and its responsibilities?

3. Two of Tennyson's outstanding skills as a poet are particularly evident in "The Lotus-Eaters"—his ability to create a mood with pictures and with musical words or lines. What images create the "slow motion" effect in the first stanza? What words and lines add to the mood of quiet and laziness? How do the liquid *s* and *l* sounds in stanza 2 affect this mood? How does repetition of both words and sounds create an overwhelming feeling of tiredness in lines 40–42: ". . . but evermore / Most weary seemed the sea, weary the oar, / Weary the wandering fields of barren foam."

SUMMING UP

1. Tennyson is a master at creating pictures and music with words. Which of these—his pictures or his music—do you find most striking and effective? Find lines in his poems that are especially striking examples of his skill.

2. After studying this sample of Tennyson's poetry, you may want to read other poems by him. Some good choices would be "Break, Break, Break," "The Lady of Shalott," "Morte d'Arthur," "Ulysses," and "Crossing the Bar." Or you might want to try some of the longer poems, based on the King Arthur legends, in *Idylls of the King*. Applying what you've just learned, explain how, in these other poems, Tennyson uses sound and pictures to create an atmosphere or mood.

FOR COMPOSITION

1. Do you ever get in a mood when you would like to spend some time in a land of dreams like the land of the lotus-eaters? Write a composition expressing your feelings at such a time; or take another approach and write about how it feels to come back to reality after such a period of escape.

2. Which of the poets you have studied in this unit—Sandburg, Kipling, Burns, Millay, or Tennyson—did you like best as a person and as a poet? In a short composition, describe your impression of his (or her) personality and qualities as a poet. Or, compare him or her to another poet in this group.

Reading and Writing about Poetry

In "Reading and Writing about Poetry" (pages 218–19), you were asked to make careful analyses of three poems, based on a list of suggested procedures for reading the poems and understanding their structure and language. In the exercises that follow, you will be asked to write in a more general way about a number of poems. Here you will be able to make use of everything you have learned in studying the poems in this book and in your previous work on pages 218–19. As in all work with poetry, each of these exercises calls for careful reading and careful writing.

PARAPHRASING A POEM

Paraphrasing (rephrasing a passage in different words) can be a useful way of getting at the meaning of a poem. Restating a poem, or part of it, in your own words often helps you to realize exactly what it means.

Read the first and last stanzas of "A Farewell," by Tennyson, quoted below:

Flow down, cold rivulet, to the sea,
  Thy tribute wave deliver;
No more by thee my steps shall be,
  Forever and forever.

A thousand suns will stream on thee,   5
  A thousand moons will quiver;
But not by thee my steps shall be,
  Forever and forever.

As an example, a possible paraphrase of the first stanza would be: "Flow down to the sea, cold little brook; give it your contribution. I'll never walk alongside you again, ever."

Now try it yourself. Study the last stanza carefully, and then rewrite it in your own words. Be sure to "translate" any figurative language into literal English and not to omit any part of the idea the poet is stating.

After completing your paraphrase, compare it to the original. Which is clearer in meaning? more forceful? more moving?

COMPARISON AND CONTRAST

One way of getting a better sense of exactly what a poem is saying is to compare and contrast it with another poem that has somewhat the same subject, theme, or meaning. You may have read already one of the following two poems; the other you probably have not. What differences can you see in them, in the attitude toward autumn of the two poets?

Autumn Chant

Now the autumn shudders
  In the rose's root.
Far and wide the ladders
  Lean among the fruit.

Now the autumn clambers   5
  Up the trellised frame,
And the rose remembers
  The dust from which it came.

Brighter than the blossom
  On the rose's bough   10
Sits the wizened orange,
  Bitter berry now;

Beauty never slumbers;
  All is in her name;
But the rose remembers   15
  The dust from which it came.

                Edna St. Vincent Millay

Indian Summer

These are the days when birds come back,
A very few, a bird or two,
To take a backward look.

These are the days when skies put on
The old, old sophistries of June—   5
A blue and gold mistake.

Oh, fraud that cannot cheat the bee,
Almost thy plausibility
Induces my belief,

Till ranks of seeds their witness bear,   10
And softly through the altered air
Hurries a timid leaf!

Oh, sacrament of summer days,
Oh, last communion in the haze,
Permit a child to join,   15

Thy sacred emblems to partake,
Thy consecrated bread to break,
Taste thy immortal wine!

               Emily Dickinson

Read and reread these poems carefully, using the procedures you have learned. Paraphrase any lines or stanzas that seem difficult or obscure. When you feel you understand the poems, compare them in an essay. Include your answers to the following questions:

1. Which poem suggests greater sadness about the approach of autumn?

2. Which poet seems to have a clearer view of what goes on in nature?

3. Which poem most fully succeeds in conveying a sense of the passing seasons?

4. Which poem do you find most thought provoking?

5. Which poem do you find most difficult?

6. In which poem did the use of language appeal to you most? Why?

7. Which poem do you prefer? Why?

WHAT IS POETRY?

Below are a number of statements by critics and poets about the nature of poetry. Use one (or more) of them as the main idea in an essay about the poetry you have read, referring to two or three of the poems in this book as examples. You may, of course, either agree or disagree with any of these ideas.

1. "Poetry is the art of uniting pleasure with truth, by calling imagination to the help of reason."

2. "Poetry is the spontaneous overflow of powerful feelings."

3. "A poem is the very image of life expressed in its eternal truth."

4. "Poetry is nothing less than the most perfect speech of man, that in which he comes nearest to being able to utter the truth."

5. "A poem begins in delight and ends in wisdom."

COMPARING POETRY

Compare the following versions of a stanza from Robert Burns' "Bannockburn." (Be sure to read aloud in comparing them.) Which version is better poetry? In what way or ways has "revision" damaged Burns' poem?

Now's the day, and now's the hour;
See the front o' battle lour;
See approach proud Edward's power—
   Chains and slavery!

Now's the day, and now's the fatal hour;
See the front o' dismal battle lour;
See approach proud Edward's mighty power—
   Chains and wretched slavery!

Are the added modifiers exact or vague? Do they add to the meaning of the lines? Which version has a more forceful rhythm?

ART AND LITERATURE

1. Study Rogier van der Weyden's "Portrait of a Lady" on page 267. Imagine yourself to be a poet, who, greatly impressed by this painting, wishes to express an impression of the lady in a poem. In a brief essay, explain which details in the painting you would emphasize, and why. What significance or meaning would you try to express in your poem?

2. Study the paintings on pages 267–72 and think back over the poems you have read in this book. Then write an essay in support of or in disagreement with this statement: "What really matters in art and poetry is the power, not the beauty, of a painting or a poem. The crucial thing is how forcefully the work expresses the artist's (or poet's) point of view." Support your argument with references to details in paintings and lines in poems.

ESSAYS AND SKETCHES

IT WAS Michel de Montaigne, the sixteenth-century French writer who coined the word *essai* and who wrote the first real essay. He thought of this literary form as an attempt in prose (the French *J'essai* means "I try") to set forth his ideas in a limited and personal manner on any number of topics. Although the essay has taken many forms since Montaigne's day, Montaigne's basic definition still holds true. Today an essay can be loosely defined as almost any piece of prose writing which deals with its subject briefly and from a personal point of view. In this sense, newspaper editorials, book and film reviews, letters, and so on, are essays, or, to be more exact, *familiar* essays, since their style is informal and expresses the writer's personality.

Style—a point of view and how it is expressed—is the most unique feature of the familiar essay. Style is determined by a writer's personality and attitude toward a subject. Two authors—or three or four or more—can write about the same subject with very different results. The style of each writer is the special ingredient that distinguishes one work from another.

In the following pages, we shall study the style of six prominent authors who represent a span of three centuries. We shall see, for example, how one writer's style is characterized by "balanced sentences" and a strict and logical presentation of ideas, how another writer uses words effectively to create a contrast between his subject and his tone, how another employs exaggeration, how yet another, by careful choice of details, can suggest a specific mood or picture, thus communicating his own very personal way of seeing things.

From style stems the greatest pleasure of essay reading, for it introduces us not only to the writing of distinguished writers, but also to the people themselves.

Essays

FROM *Delight*

J. B. PRIESTLEY

(1894–   )

Like poets, most writers of essays try to convey their personal feelings about things they have seen or experienced. John Boynton Priestley, who opens his collection *Delight* with the remark, "I have always been a grumbler," is just such a writer. Ever since he was a boy in Yorkshire, England, says Priestley, he has been convinced that he was sent to the wrong planet. He describes himself as "grumbling" through boyhood, through the first World War, through Cambridge University, and finally "all over the world."

In his essays called *Delight,* Priestley says, he decided to make up for his life of grumbling by writing of the things which have given him special pleasure. In sharing his private delights with us, he hopes to arouse our own sense of wonder and of humor over things that we might otherwise overlook.

In its original meaning, the word *essay* meant "attempt." Even today, an essay is essentially an attempt to say something that the writer hopes will prove memorable and lasting. Authors try to communicate directly to the reader the wisdom or humor of their ideas and observations. Many of the early essayists were moralists—writers whose first concern was to preach or instruct—and their writings were intended as sensible advice or guides to proper conduct. Priestley writes on less serious subjects and in a less serious tone than these early writers, but, like them, he bases his essays on a single idea, which he enlarges or explains. He opens each of his small, paragraph-like essays with a general statement about a specific pleasure. This statement, sometimes only a fragment of a sentence, he uses as a kind of topic sentence, which he then develops with vivid examples or details in the rest of the paragraph.

In all of these little essays, the author's style of writing communicates a sense of vitality and exuberance as well as pleasure. Priestley shows a warmth and spontaneity of feeling and a quick good humor that show him to be a remarkably good-natured grumbler.

READING IN BED
ABOUT FOUL WEATHER

There is a peculiar delight, which I can still experience though I knew it best as a boy, in cozily reading about foul weather when equally foul weather is beating hard against the windows, when one is securely poised between the wind and rain and sleet outside and the wind and rain and sleet that leap from the page into the mind. The old romancers must have been aware of this odd little bonus of pleasure for the reader, and probably that is why so many of their narratives, to give them a friendly start, began with solitary horsemen, cloaked to the eyebrows, riding through the night on urgent business for the Duke, sustained by nothing more than an occasional and dubious ragout [1] or pasty [2] and a gulp or two of sour wine (always fetched by surly innkeepers or their scowling slatterns [3]), on side roads deep in mire, with wind, rain, thunder and lightning, sleet, hail, snow, all turned on

---

[1] **ragout** (ra·gōō′): a French stew.
[2] **pasty:** an English meat dish.
[3] **slattern:** an untidy woman, here a servant in an inn.

at the full. With the windows rattling away and hailstones drumming at the paper in the fireplace, snug in bed except for one cold elbow, I have traveled thousands and thousands of mucky miles with these fellows, braving the foulest nights, together crying "Bah!"

BRAGGING

It is true, as my family have pointed out more than once (families overdo this kind of thing), that now and again I delight in bragging. But I do it, as of course I do everything, from the best of motives. When I am with people who think I am a fine fellow and have done some good work in my time, I am (or at least I imagine I am) modest, almost ready to blush, candid about my faults, humbly aware of how little I have done to merit such praise, etc., etc., etc. But there are some persons who do not appear to understand that I exist just as they and their friends exist, that what I do seems as important to me as what they do seems to them, that I have a world of my own just as they and their kind have a world of their own. They are people composed of blank stares, ignorance, incredulity, and insensitiveness. In a ruder society, they could be taken

out into the castle yard and banged over the head with spiked maces. In our society, this is not possible. So I assert myself, I become aggressive, I begin to brag. But I am not doing this merely for myself. I am proclaiming the existence of a whole world of wonder and glory. I am taking my stand for Literature and Drama and the author's way of life. I am glaring and shouting on behalf of Sophocles and Shakespeare, Cervantes and Molière.[1] Mightier than the sword, Major Fawcett![2] Yes, and let me tell *you* something——

LONG TROUSERS

There was a time when merely wearing long trousers brought me delight. In those days, when I must have been about fifteen, I had only one suit—my best—with long trousers. My other suits had knee breeches, buttoning tightly just below the knee and worn with thick long

[1] **Sophocles . . . Molière:** four of the world's greatest writers.

[2] **Mightier . . . Fawcett:** Priestley argues his point by quoting Lord Bulwer-Lytton's famous declaration, "The pen is mightier than the sword." "Major Fawcett" is an imaginary officer whom Priestley charges with denying the importance of anything outside his military world.

stockings, turned down at the top. There was really nothing wrong with my appearance when I wore these knee breeches and long stockings, for after years of football I had muscular, well-shaped legs; but whenever I wore them I felt I was still imprisoned, a shamefaced giant, in the stale miniature world of childhood. Condemned—and I use this term because there were strict rules at home about which suits could be worn—to wear these knee breeches, I felt that no glimpse of my real self could catch the town's eye: I might almost have been sent to school in a pram.[1] Conversely, I felt that as soon as I put on the long trousers, then appearance and reality were gloriously one; I joined the world of men; and even without doing anything more than wear these trousers—and leaving the other wretched things at home—I could feel my whole nature expanding magnificently. On the occasional days when I was allowed to wear the adult trousers to go to school, I almost floated there. Never did eighteen inches of cloth do more for the human spirit. On those mornings now when I seem to stare sullenly at the wreck of a shining world, why do I not remind myself that although I grow old and fat and peevish *at least I am wearing my long trousers?*

NO SCHOOL REPORT

We fathers of families have one secret little source of delight that is closed to other men. As we read the school reports upon our children, we realize with a sense of relief that can rise to delight that—thank Heaven—nobody is reporting in this fashion upon us. What a nightmare it would be if our personalities were put through this mincing machine! I can imagine my own report: *"Height and weight at beginning of term—5 feet, 9 inches: 13 stone,[2] 10 lbs. At end of term—5 feet, 8 inches: 14 stone, 2 lbs.* Note: Through greed and lack of exercise, J. B. is putting on weight and is sagging. He must get out more and eat and drink less. *Conduct*—Not satisfactory. J. B. is increasingly irritable, inconsiderate, and uncooperative. He is inclined to blame others for faults in himself. He complains of lack of sleep but persists in remaining awake to finish rubbishy detective stories. He smokes far too much and on several occasions has been discovered smoking in bed. There is no real harm in him, but, at the present time, he tends to be self-indulgent, lazy, vain, and touchy. He should be encouraged to spend some weeks this summer with the Sea Scouts or at a Harvest Camp. *Eng. Lang. & Lit.:* Fair, but inclined to be careless. *French:* A disappointing term. *History:* Has not made the progress here that we expected of him. Should read more. *Mathematics:* Very poor. *Art:* Has made some attempts both at oils and water color but shows little aptitude. Has been slack in his Appreciation and did not attend Miss Mulberry's excellent talks on the Italian Primitives. *Music:* Fair, but will not practice. *Natural History:* Still professes an interest but finds it impossible to remember names of birds, butterflies, flowers. Has not joined in the Rambles[3] this term. *Chemistry:* Clearly has no interest in this subject. *Physics:* Poor, though occasionally shows interest. Fails to comprehend basic laws. *Physical Culture:* Sergeant Beefer reports

[1] **pram:** a baby carriage.

"No School Report" from *Delight* by J. B. Priestley, copyright 1949 by J. B. Priestley. Reprinted by permission of The Harold Matson Co., Inc.

[2] **stone:** an English unit of weight equal to fourteen pounds. Thirteen stone would be 182 pounds.
[3] **Rambles:** walks through the woods and countryside.

that J. B. has been frequently absent and is obviously far from keen. A bad term. *General Report:* J. B. is not the bright and helpful member of our little community that he once promised to be. He lacks self-discipline and does not try to cultivate a cheery outlook. There are times when he still exerts himself—e.g., he made a useful contribution to the end-of-term production of *A Comedy of Errors*—but he tends to be lazy and egoistical. His housemaster has had a talk with him, but I suggest that stronger parental guidance would be helpful and is, indeed, necessary." And then I would be asked to see my father and would find him staring and frowning at this report, and then he would stare and frown at me and would begin asking me, in his deep and rather frightening voice, what on earth was the matter with me. But it can't happen, not this side of the grave. I am knee-deep in the soggy world of graying hair and rotting teeth, of monstrous taxes and overdrafts,[1] of vanishing friends and fading sight; but at least, I can tell myself delightedly, nobody is writing a school report on me.

[1] **overdrafts:** overdrawings from a bank account.

WALK IN A PINE WOOD

Near the house, high on a hill, were woods of pine and fir; and, slipping away from the others, I followed a path that led me into one of these woods, through a tunnel of green gloom and smoky blue dusk. It was very quiet, very remote, in there. My feet sank into the pile of the pine needles. The last bright tatters of sunlight vanished. Some bird went whirring and left behind a deeper silence. I breathed a different air, ancient and aromatic. I had not gone a hundred paces before I had walked out of our English South Country and was deep in the Northern forest itself, with a thickness of time, centuries and centuries of it, pressing against me. Little doors at the back of my mind were softly opened. It was not the mere quickening of fancy that brought me delight then, but an atavistic [2] stirring and heightening of the imagination, as if all my distant ancestors, who were certainly

[2] **atavistic** (at'ə·vis'tik): returning to a more primitive type of being, characteristic of one's earliest ancestors.

of the North, were whispering and pointing in this sudden dusk. Any turn now might bring me to the magical smithy, the cave of the dragon; a horn might blow and shatter the present time like so much painted glass; the world of legend, hung about these trees like the spiders' webs, was closing round me. No doubt my precious ego, challenged at every step, felt a touch of fear; but my true self, recognizing this enlargement of life, finding its place for a moment or two in that procession which is the real life of Man, drew deeper breaths, lived in its own world during these moments, and was delighted.

COOKING PICNICS

Like most men and unlike nearly all women, those atavistic creatures, I detest picnics. One reason is that I am usually very hungry out in the open and I dislike the kind of food provided by picnics. Thus, there are few things to eat better than a properly dressed salad in a fine big salad bowl, but there are few things less appetizing than an undressed salad out of a paper bag or cardboard box. Then, except for thick slices of ham between thin slices of bread, I have a growing distaste for the whole sandwich family, especially paste, egg or cheese sandwiches. Again, anything with jam in it or on it is a curse on a summer's day. Finally, there is a peculiarly hard, green, sour little apple that must be grown specially for picnic boxes. Nevertheless, I have delighted in my time—and am not yet past it—in one kind of picnic, namely, the cooking picnic. This is for great souls. The instrumental basis of it is the frying pan. Sausages will do, though steak of course is better. Fried potatoes are essen-

From "Cooking Picnics" from *Delight* by J. B. Priestley, copyright 1949 by J. B. Priestley. Reprinted by permission of The Harold Matson Company, Inc.

tial, and persons whose stomachs shrink from a greasy chip [1] rather underdone should stay at home and nibble health foods. Coffee, which stands up to wood smoke better than tea, is the beverage. The cooking picnic is, I will admit, a smoky job, at least in this damp climate of ours. I have superintended cooking picnics—and I am a natural superintendent on all these occasions—with inflamed and streaming eyes and every sinus wrecked, spluttering and coughing and choking, damning and blasting, glaring at would-be helpful children until they ran away and howled. I have stoked and fried and stewed and dished out portions until there was nothing left for me but a few bits of greasy muck and a half a cup of coffee grounds. And even my pipe has tasted all wrong in the inferno of wood smoke. Yet I would not have missed a moment of it for a five-pound [2] lunch in a private room on somebody else's expense sheet. Somewhere among the damp obstinate sticks, the dwindling sausages, the vanishing fat, the potatoes that would not brown and the water that would not boil, the billowing smoke on the hillside, the monstrous appetites of the company, there has been delight like a crumb of gold.

[1] **chip:** slice of potato.
[2] **five-pound:** about $15.00.

FOR STUDY AND DISCUSSION

READING IN BED ABOUT FOUL WEATHER

1. Have you ever been delighted by being snug indoors and not having to go out into a stormy night? How did the stories that Priestley remembers reading in bed add to his pleasure on such occasions? Why is the word *peculiar* a good one to describe this feeling?

2. Why do the riders in the stories say "Bah"? Why does Priestley?

3. Have you read adventure stories such as Priestley describes? Is his description of the

solitary horsemen and their ride in the spirit of the "old romancers"? Which details in his description are especially effective in conveying this spirit?

BRAGGING

1. We usually consider bragging offensive. How does Priestley justify his bragging? What kind of person provokes his bragging? Why? When he brags, he says, he is "proclaiming the existence of a whole world of wonder and glory." What is this world of glory? How does mentioning the names of great writers add dignity and importance to Priestley's cause?

2. Is it true that it is easy to be modest when one is praised but hard to remain quiet when one is ignored? Have you known people who ignore others and seem to care only for a little "world of their own"?

LONG TROUSERS

1. The essence of Priestley's delight in long trousers is expressed in the sentence beginning "Conversely I felt that as soon as I put on the long trousers . . ." What does the author mean by "appearance and reality were gloriously one"? How can clothing help one's "whole nature" expand?

2. How does Priestley imply that his view of the adult world and its accessories has changed since he was fifteen? How has it changed? What facts of middle age have caused this world to lose some of its glamor?

NO SCHOOL REPORT

1. Which items on Priestley's imaginary school report are most amusing? Which tell you most about Priestley? In which items has he best captured the tone of a teacher? Judging from this essay, what would you say Priestley thinks of school reports?

2. Priestley states the source of his delight in the first two sentences of "No School Report," and then restates it in the last sentence. What is added to the main idea in this final sentence? How has this new element of the main idea been prepared for by Priestley's

description of himself in his imaginary school report?

WALK IN A PINE WOOD

1. Which details make the pine wood most vividly real? What about the wood suggests to Priestley a magic world of legendary times?

2. This essay attempts to convey a feeling which at some time you may have shared. Feeling his "precious ego" challenged, Priestley recognizes an "enlargement of life, . . . in that procession which is the real life of Man." Can you explain this feeling? As Priestley becomes absorbed in this feeling, what happens to his sense of time?

COOKING PICNICS

1. What does Priestley dislike about picnics served from paper bags or cardboard boxes?

2. Why does Priestley think that "cooking picnics" are for "great souls"? What about them would dismay a lesser person? Priestley paints a rather dismal picture of cooking picnics. Why do you think he delights in them?

THE WRITER'S STYLE

One of the major factors in a writer's style—a personal way of saying things—is the choice of details. A good writer selects details that suggest to the reader's imagination the mood or picture that the writer wishes the reader to sense or to see.

In "Walk in a Pine Wood" Priestley writes, "My feet sank into the pile of the pine needles." What does this detail tell you about the woods? How does it help to suggest a sense of the past, "ancient and aromatic"? How does the next detail, the "last bright tatters of sunlight," help you to see the woods in a particular setting? Which other details in Priestley's essays are especially striking? Why?

FOR COMPOSITION

Pay tribute to one of your special delights by writing a short essay on it. Make a special effort to use specific details in your paragraph.

The Genuine Mexican Plug

MARK TWAIN

(1835–1910)

As is typical of essayists, the writings of Mark Twain (the pen name of Samuel Langhorne Clemens) are based on his personal experience. Having been a printer, a river pilot, a prospector, a reporter, a lecturer, and a world traveler, he had a great many first-hand impressions to write about.

Perhaps more than any other writer, Mark Twain captured in his stories and sketches the sprawling humor of the American frontier. As a boy on the Mississippi River and a young reporter in the western territories, he gained a feeling for the rugged frontier spirit and its tall tales.

In all his writing, Twain was first of all a storyteller whose chief interest was to make his readers laugh. He would not hesitate to exaggerate a detail or an incident in order to develop the humor of a story, but his exaggerations were always based on close observation of human nature. His incidents might never have actually happened, but no one could say that they never could happen.

"The Genuine Mexican Plug" appears in *Roughing It,* Twain's account of his adventures in the Far West. As in most informal essays, much of our interest in this sketch lies in the author's style—his way of expressing himself. Twain left the stamp of his personal style on a wide variety of writing, from newspaper columns and humorous sketches

"The Genuine Mexican Plug" from *Roughing It, Vol. 1,* by Mark Twain. Reprinted by permission of Harper & Row, Publishers.

to classics, such as *Tom Sawyer* and *Huckleberry Finn*. But it is in the essay, perhaps more than in any other form of writing, that writers speak in their own voices and express their own thoughts and opinions in their own characteristic choice of words. In "The Genuine Mexican Plug," the voice of the author overshadows the story he is telling. It is not the story as much as the author's way of telling it that keeps us reading.

I RESOLVED to have a horse to ride. I had never seen such wild, free, magnificent horsemanship outside of a circus as these picturesquely clad Mexicans, Californians, and Mexicanized Americans displayed in Carson [1] streets every day. How they rode! Leaning just gently forward out of the perpendicular, easy and nonchalant, with broad slouch-hat brim blown square up in front, and long riata [2] swinging above the head, they swept through the town like the wind! The next minute they were only a sailing puff of dust on the far desert. If they trotted, they sat up gallantly and gracefully, and seemed part of the horse; did not go jiggering up and down after the silly Miss-Nancy fashion of the riding schools. I had quickly learned to tell a horse from a cow and was full of anxiety to learn more. I was resolved to buy a horse.

While the thought was rankling in my mind, the auctioneer came scurrying through the plaza on a black beast that had as many humps and corners on him as a dromedary,[3] and was necessarily uncomely; but he was "going, going, at twenty-two!—horse, saddle and bridle at twenty-two dollars, gentlemen!" and I could hardly resist.

A man whom I did not know (he turned out to be the auctioneer's brother) noticed

[1] **Carson:** Carson City, Nevada.
[2] **riata:** Mexican name for a lasso or lariat.
[3] **dromedary:** a camel with one hump.

the wistful look in my eye, and observed that that was a very remarkable horse to be going at such a price; and added that the saddle alone was worth the money. It was a Spanish saddle, with ponderous *tapidaros*,[1] and furnished with the ungainly sole-leather covering with the unspellable name. I said I had half a notion to bid. Then this keen-eyed person appeared to me to be "taking my measure"; but I dismissed the suspicion when he spoke, for his manner was full of guileless candor and truthfulness. Said he:

"I know that horse—know him well. You are a stranger, I take it, and so you might think he was an American horse, maybe, but I assure you he is not. He is nothing of the kind; but—excuse my speaking in a low voice, other people being near—he is, without the shadow of a doubt, a Genuine Mexican Plug!"

I did not know what a Genuine Mexican Plug was, but there was something about this man's way of saying it that made me swear inwardly that I would own a Genuine Mexican Plug, or die.

"Has he any other—er—advantages?" I inquired, suppressing what eagerness I could.

He hooked his forefinger in the pocket of my army shirt, led me to one side, and breathed in my ear impressively these words:

"He can outbuck anything in America!"

"Going, going, going—at *twent-ty*-four dollars and a half, gen—" "Twenty-seven!" I shouted, in a frenzy.

"And sold!" said the auctioneer and passed over the Genuine Mexican Plug to me.

I could scarcely contain my exultation. I paid the money and put the animal in a neighboring livery stable to dine and rest himself.

[1] *tapidaros:* stirrup flaps or coverings.

In the afternoon I brought the creature into the plaza, and certain citizens held him by the head, and others by the tail, while I mounted him. As soon as they let go, he placed all his feet in a bunch together, lowered his back, and then suddenly arched it upward, and shot me straight into the air a matter of three or four feet! I came as straight down again, lit in the saddle, went instantly up again, came down almost on the high pommel, shot up again, and came down on the horse's neck—all in the space of three or four seconds. Then he rose and stood almost straight up on his hind feet, and I, clasping his lean neck desperately, slid back into the saddle, and held on. He came down, and immediately hoisted his heels into the air, delivering a vicious kick at the sky, and stood on his fore feet. And then down he came once more, and began the original exercise of shooting me straight up again.

The third time I went up I heard a stranger say: "Oh, *don't* he buck, though!"

While I was up, somebody struck the horse a sounding thwack with a leathern strap, and when I arrived again the Genuine Mexican Plug was not there. A Californian youth chased him up and caught him and asked if he might have a ride. I granted him that luxury. He mounted the Genuine, got lifted into the air once, but sent his spurs home as he descended, and the horse darted away like a telegram. He soared over three fences like a bird and disappeared down the road toward the Washoe Valley.

I sat down on a stone with a sigh, and by a natural impulse one of my hands sought my forehead and the other the base of my stomach. I believe I never appreciated, till then, the poverty of the human machinery—for I still needed a hand or two to place elsewhere. Pen cannot describe how I was jolted up. Imagination cannot conceive how disjointed I was— how internally, externally, and universally I was unsettled, mixed up, and ruptured. There was a sympathetic crowd around me, though.

One elderly-looking comforter said:

"Stranger, you've been taken in. Everybody in this camp knows that horse. Any child, any Injun, could have told you that he'd buck; he is the very worst devil to buck on the continent of America. You hear *me*. I'm Curry. *Old* Curry. Old *Abe* Curry. And moreover, he is a simon-pure, out-and-out, genuine, d—d Mexican plug, and an uncommon mean one at that, too. Why, you turnip, if you had laid low and kept dark, there's chances to buy an *American* horse for mighty little more than you paid for that bloody old foreign relic."

I gave no sign; but I made up my mind that if the auctioneer's brother's funeral took place while I was in the territory I would postpone all other recreations and attend it.

After a gallop of sixteen miles, the Californian youth and the Genuine Mexican Plug came tearing into town again, shedding foam-flakes like the spume-spray that drives before a typhoon, and, with one final skip over a wheelbarrow and a Chinaman, cast anchor in front of the "ranch."

Such panting and blowing! Such spreading and contracting of the red equine [1] nostrils, and glaring of the wild equine eye! But was the imperial beast subjugated? Indeed, he was not. His lordship the Speaker of the House thought he was and mounted him to go down to the Capitol; but the first dash the creature made was over a pile of telegraph poles half as high as a church; and his time to the Capitol—one mile and three-quarters —remains unbeaten to this day. But then he took an advantage—he left out the mile and only did the three-quarters. That is to say, he made a straight cut across lots, preferring fences and ditches to a crooked road; and when the Speaker got to the Capitol, he said he had been in the air so much he felt as if he had made the trip on a comet.

In the evening the Speaker came home afoot for exercise and got the Genuine towed back behind a quartz-wagon. The next day I loaned the animal to the Clerk of the House to go down to the Dana silver mine, six miles, and *he* walked back for exercise and got the horse towed. Everybody I loaned him to always walked back; they never could get enough exercise any other way. Still, I continued to loan him to anybody who was willing to borrow him, my idea being to get him crippled, and throw him on the borrower's hands, or killed, and make the borrower pay for him. But somehow nothing ever happened to him. He took chances that

[1] **equine** (ē′kwīn): pertaining to or like a horse.

no other horse ever took and survived, but he always came out safe. It was his daily habit to try experiments that had always before been considered impossible, but he always got through. Sometimes he miscalculated a little and did not get his rider through intact, but *he* always got through himself. Of course I had tried to sell him; but that was a stretch of simplicity which met with little sympathy. The auctioneer stormed up and down the streets on him for four days, dispersing the populace, interrupting business, and destroying children, and never got a bid— at least never any but the eighteen-dollar one he hired a notoriously substanceless bummer to make. The people only smiled pleasantly and restrained their desire to buy, if they had any. Then the auctioneer brought in his bill, and I withdrew the horse from the market. We tried to trade him off at private vendue [1] next, offering him at a sacrifice for secondhand tombstones, old iron, temperance tracts [2]—any kind of property. But holders were stiff, and we retired from the market again. I never tried to ride the horse any more. Walking was good enough exercise for a man like me that had nothing the matter

with him except ruptures, internal injuries, and such things. Finally I tried to *give* him away. But it was a failure. Parties said earthquakes were handy enough on the Pacific coast—they did not wish to own one. As a last resort I offered him to the Governor for the use of the "Brigade." His face lit up eagerly at first but toned down again, and he said the thing would be too palpable.

Just then the livery-stable man brought in his bill for six weeks' keeping—stall room for the horse, fifteen dollars; hay for the horse, two hundred and fifty! The Genuine Mexican Plug had eaten a ton of the article, and the man said he would have eaten a hundred if he had let him.

I will remark here, in all seriousness, that the regular price of hay during that year and a part of the next was really two hundred and fifty dollars a ton. During a part of the previous year, it had sold at five hundred a ton, in gold, and during the winter before that, there was such scarcity of the article that in several instances small quantities had brought eight hundred dollars a ton in coin! The consequence might be guessed without my telling it: people turned their stock loose to starve, and before the spring arrived Carson and Eagle Valleys were almost literally carpeted with their carcasses!

[1] **vendue** (ven·do͞o′): an auction or public sale.
[2] **temperance tracts:** pamphlets warning against the consumption of liquor.

Any old settler there will verify these statements.

I managed to pay the livery bill, and that same day I gave the Genuine Mexican Plug to a passing Arkansas emigrant whom fortune delivered into my hand. If this ever meets his eye, he will doubtless remember the donation.

Now whoever has had the luck to ride a real Mexican plug will recognize the animal depicted in this chapter and hardly consider him exaggerated—but the uninitiated will feel justified in regarding his portrait as a fancy sketch, perhaps.

FOR STUDY AND DISCUSSION

1. What about the horsemen in Carson City makes Twain yearn to own a horse? What statement in the very first paragraph suggests his ignorance of horses?

2. What observations about human nature does Twain make throughout his story of the Genuine Mexican Plug? Who does the man who advised him to buy the horse turn out to be? Why was Twain so easily deceived? Do you think people are often fooled for this same reason?

3. Which details of Twain's attempt to ride the Plug did you find the most humorous? Why? Do you think this scene would be as funny in a movie version as it is in Twain's account of it? Is the humor of the scene more in the events themselves or in the way Twain describes them? Which words and phrases make Twain's description of how he was "jolted up" particularly funny?

4. By the end of Twain's essay, you probably feel as though you know the Genuine Mexican Plug rather well. What human habits and characteristics does Twain say he has? What is the "personality" of the Plug?

5. In the last three paragraphs, Twain neatly protects himself against the charge of exaggeration. What methods does he use in these paragraphs to make his experience seem real?

THE WRITER'S STYLE

Much of Mark Twain's humor stems from his style of writing, and from his choice and arrangement of words in his sentences and paragraphs. He often creates laughter by using a striking, and exaggerated, comparison. For instance, he describes the western way of riding as not at all like the "jiggering up and down after the silly Miss-Nancy fashion of the riding schools." Or he describes the Plug as having "as many humps and corners on him as a dromedary" or as "tearing into town . . . shedding foam-flakes like the spume-spray that drives before a typhoon." Such exaggerated statements are the very heart of Mark Twain's humor.

Another favorite device of Twain's is the indirect statement. There is a similar kind of exaggeration in the roundabout manner and avoidance of direct statement in sentences such as these:

"I never appreciated, till then, the poverty of the human machinery—for I still needed a hand or two to place elsewhere."

"I made up my mind that if the auctioneer's brother's funeral took place while I was in the territory I would postpone all other recreations and attend it."

Can you see why these statements are much more humorous than what Twain might have said ("I had a great many bumps and bruises" and "I was furious at the fellow who had cheated me")? In your own writing, remember that exaggeration can be a very important source of humor.

FOR COMPOSITION

Write a sketch in which you attempt to be humorous by exaggerating your predicament in some ironic event in which you were directly involved. You might try a title like one of these:

The Tables Turned
The Practical Joke That Boomeranged
The Story That Turned Out to Be True
The Laugh Was on Me

ELEMENTS OF ART

Oil Painting

No one really knows when oil painting was invented. But there is evidence that by the end of the fourteenth century Flemish artists were mixing their color pigments with linseed oil instead of the water medium used for tempera and fresco. One advantage of oil was that it dried slowly, allowing artists time to blend their colors after they had spread them on a picture's surface. They could now paint tones ranging so gradually from light to dark that no brushstrokes were visible.

One of the masters of this new style was Rogier van der Weyden, whose *Portrait of a Lady* is shown here as PLATE 1. When Italian artists in the early fifteenth century first saw portraits of this type, they were astonished at the softness of the flesh tones and the exquisite textures of the clothing—quite different from the hard, sculptural modeling of forms in their own tempera paintings, such as Mainardi's *Portrait of a Young Man* (page 197).

Such Flemish pictures were usually painted on wooden panels prepared with a smooth surface of white plaster, like the kind used for tempera. The color pigments were diluted with oil and then applied in thin glazes, somewhat like the washes used in watercolor painting. When each color glaze had dried, another was applied, and then another, until the picture had a rich enamel-like finish. After many such glazes, the darker colors became deep and velvety. In lighter areas, however, the whiteness of the plaster showed through the thin color glazes in a soft and luminous glow. You can see this effect in the lighter flesh tones of Van der Weyden's portrait.

During the next two hundred years, more and more artists chose to paint on stretched canvas rather than on wood panels. To create more realistic effects of brilliant light and deep shadow, they invented new ways of applying the paint. Look closely, for example, at Jan Vermeer's painting *Mistress and Maid* (PLATE 2). Instead of applying the thinnest glazes in the highlights so that the white ground would show through (as it does in Van der Weyden's portrait), Vermeer built up these light tones with the thickest layers of pigment. Thick layers of pigment like this are almost pastelike, what the Italians call *impasto*. Because of their opaqueness, they tend to reflect light, whereas the much thinner layers of dark paint in the shadows tend to absorb it.

Now compare Vermeer's picture with another oil painting on canvas of almost two hundred years later: Géricault's *Mounted Officer of the Imperial Guard* (PLATE 3). Like Vermeer, Géricault applied his paints rather thickly in the lighter tones, but the effect of his brushstrokes—the way he applied his colors to the canvas—is considerably different. The entire picture seems to have been painted more rapidly and spontaneously, an effect which helps to dramatize the action Géricault was trying to represent in this battle scene.

Oil paints, as you have seen by now, can be used in many different ways to produce a wide variety of effects. PLATES 4, 5, and 6 show how differently three artists of our century have used them.

Charles Sheeler, in his picture called *Upper Deck* (PLATE 4), applied his paint in thin, but fairly opaque, layers. The colors are laid on so smoothly and uniformly that we are hardly aware of the actual process of painting. Such a smooth, impersonal technique seems particularly appropriate for the subject Sheeler has represented here.

The French artist Henri Matisse, on the other hand, calls our attention to the highly individual way he has put down each stroke of paint on the canvas—as if it were his own handwriting. You can see this in PLATE 5, a still life of the 1920's. Note especially the way Matisse has painted the reddish brown curtain with highlights of gleaming yellow-gold laid on in a thick impasto. The lemons and flowers in the center carry our attention to the left, where the whole composition seems to explode in a joyous, exuberant burst of color.

Some modern painters apply their oil paints to the canvas in thick slabs with a *palette knife,* a flat-bladed instrument similar to a kitchen spatula. Nicolas de Staël used this technique in his *Landscape Study* (PLATE 6). Here, the surface of the paint is smooth and lustrous, like an enamel with an extremely high gloss. At first glance, you may think de Staël's picture is completely abstract, but as you study it carefully, you can see that its design is a geometric simplification of a view of a seashore. Slabs of different colors represent houses, boats, the beach, and open spaces beyond, such as the sea and sky.

PLATE 1. ROGIER VAN DER WEYDEN (Flemish, 1399/1400–1464): *Portrait of a Lady*. About 1455. Oil on wood, 14½ x 10¾ inches. (National Gallery of Art, Washington, D.C., Andrew Mellon Collection)

PLATE 2. JAN VERMEER (Dutch, 1632–1675): *Mistress and Maid*. About 1670. Oil on canvas, 35¼ x 30¾ inches. (Copyright The Frick Collection, New York)

PLATE 3. THÉODORE GÉRICAULT (French, 1791–1824): *Mounted Officer of the Imperial Guard*. 1812. Oil on paper, mounted on canvas, 20½ x 15 inches. (The Louvre, Paris)

PLATE 4. CHARLES SHEELER (American, 1883–1965): *Upper Deck*. 1931. Oil on canvas, 48 x 36 inches. (Courtesy of the Fogg Art Museum, Harvard University, Cambridge, Mass.)

PLATE 5. HENRI MATISSE (French, 1869–1954): *Fruits and Flowers of Nice*. 1925. Oil on canvas, 32 x 39½ inches. (Ittleson Collection, New York)

PLATE 6. NICHOLAS DE STAEL (French, 1914–1955): *Landscape Study*. 1952. Oil on composition board. $12\frac{7}{8}$ x $18\frac{1}{2}$ inches. (Reproduced by courtesy of the Trustees. The Tate Gallery, London)

FROM *Diedrich Knickerbocker's History of New York*

WASHINGTON IRVING

(1783–1859)

In the early 1800's most Europeans looked on Americans as crude country folk of little or no culture. Americans, in common opinion, might be quite capable of doing simple tasks, such as cutting down forests and plowing a straight line, but they were as likely to be able to write well and entertainingly as mice were likely to fly. The writer who forced Europeans to change their minds was Washington Irving.

Especially in creating the atmosphere of a place and time, Irving proved himself the equal of any European writer. In his introduction to his most popular book of essays and tales, *The Sketch-Book,* he wrote of himself as a painter who sketches in words. In this same introduction he wrote of himself:

> I was always fond of visiting new scenes and observing strange characters and manners. Even when a mere child I began my travels and made many tours of discovery into foreign parts and unknown regions of my native city, to the frequent alarm of my parents and the emolument[1] of the town crier. As I grew into boyhood, I extended the range of my observations. My holiday afternoons were spent in rambles about the surrounding country. I made myself familiar with all its places famous in history or fable. I knew every spot where a murder or robbery had been committed or a ghost seen. I visited the neighboring villages and added greatly to my stock of knowledge by noting their habits and customs and conversing with their sages and great men.

Since Irving traveled a good deal and lived abroad for many years, he was able to enjoy to the full his fondness for visiting new scenes, and wherever he went he kept a record of his impressions, filling his notebooks with descriptions and ideas for essays and tales. During the course of his lifetime, Irving sketched in words not only New York and the Hudson Valley (his boyhood home) but also England, the Netherlands (the land of his ancestors), Spain, and America's western frontier.

The following selection, which might be called a descriptive essay or sketch, appears in *Diedrich Knickerbocker's History of New York,* Irving's first book, in which he showed all the best qualities of a writer of essays—wit, charm, a graceful style, and a liking for speaking directly to the reader. Here Irving takes a look at the Dutch settlers of New Amsterdam and, in picturesque detail, tells us something of their customs and daily life.

I WILL NOT grieve my readers' patience by describing minutely the increase and improvement of New Amsterdam.[2] Their own imaginations will doubtless present to them the good burghers,[3] like so many painstaking and persevering beavers, slowly and surely pursuing their labors—they will behold the prosperous transfor-

---

[1] **emolument** (i·mol′yə·mənt): payment for services; reward. It was the custom to tip the town crier when he brought home a lost child.

[2] **New Amsterdam:** the Dutch settlement established on Manhattan Island in 1625. The city was renamed New York in 1664 after the English took over New Netherlands, the Dutch colony in which New Amsterdam was situated.

[3] **burghers** (bûr′gərz): citizens.

turns and labyrinths, which distinguish certain streets of New York at this very day.

The houses of the higher class were generally constructed of wood, excepting the gable end, which was of small black and yellow Dutch bricks, and always faced on the street, as our ancestors, like their descendants, were very much given to outward show, and were noted for putting the best leg foremost. The house was always furnished with abundance of large doors and small windows on every floor, the date of its erection was curiously designated by iron figures on the front, and on the top of the roof was perched a fierce little weathercock, to let the family into the important secret, which way the wind blew. These, like the weathercocks on the tops of our steeples, pointed so many different ways that every man could have a wind to his mind; the most staunch and loyal citizens, however, always went according to the weathercock on the top of the governor's house, which was certainly the most correct, as he had a trusty servant employed every morning to climb up and set it to the right quarter.

In those good days of simplicity and sunshine, a passion for cleanliness was the leading principle in domestic economy and the universal test of an able housewife—a character which formed the utmost ambition of our unenlightened grandmothers. The front door was never opened except on marriages, funerals, New Year's Days, the festival of St. Nicholas, or some such great occasion. It was ornamented with a gorgeous brass knocker, curiously wrought, sometimes in the device of a dog, and sometimes of a lion's head, and was daily burnished with such religious zeal that it was ofttimes worn out by the very precautions taken for its preservation. The whole house was constantly in a state of inundation, under

mation from the rude log hut to the stately Dutch mansion, with brick front, glazed windows, and tiled roof; from the tangled thicket to the luxuriant cabbage garden; and from the skulking Indian to the ponderous burgomaster.[1] In a word, they will picture to themselves the steady, silent, and undeviating march of prosperity, incident to a city destitute of pride or ambition, cherished by a fat government, and whose citizens do nothing in a hurry.

The sage council not being able to determine upon any plan for the building of their city—the cows, in a laudable fit of patriotism, took it under their peculiar charge, and as they went to and from pasture, established paths through the bushes, on each side of which the good folks built their houses; which is one cause of the rambling and picturesque

[1] **burgomaster:** mayor.

the discipline of mops and brooms and scrubbing brushes; and the good housewives of those days were a kind of amphibious animal, delighting exceedingly to be dabbling in water—insomuch that a historian of the day gravely tells us that many of his townswomen grew to have webbed fingers like unto a duck; and some of them, he had little doubt, could the matter be examined into, would be found to have the tails of mermaids—but this I look upon to be a mere sport of fancy, or what is worse, a wilful misrepresentation.

The grand parlor was the sanctum sanctorum,[1] where the passion for cleaning was indulged without control. In this sacred apartment no one was permitted to enter, excepting the mistress and her confidential maid, who visited it once a week for the purpose of giving it a thorough cleaning and putting things to rights—always taking the precaution of leaving their shoes at the door and entering devoutly on their stocking feet. After scrubbing the floor, sprinkling it with fine white sand, which was curiously stroked into angles, and curves, and rhomboids,[2] with a broom—after washing the windows, rubbing and polishing the furniture, and putting a new bunch of evergreens in the fireplace—the window shutters were again closed to keep out the flies, and the room carefully locked up until the revolution of time brought round the weekly cleaning day.

As to the family, they always entered in at the gate and most generally lived in the kitchen. To have seen a numerous household assembled round the fire, one would have imagined that he was transported back to those happy days of primeval simplicity, which float before our imagina-

tions like golden visions. The fireplaces were of a truly patriarchal[3] magnitude, where the whole family, old and young, master and servant, black and white, nay, even the very cat and dog, enjoyed a community of privilege and had each a right to a corner. Here the old burgher would sit in perfect silence, puffing his pipe, looking in the fire with half shut eyes, and thinking of nothing for hours together; the *goede vrouw*[4] on the opposite side would employ herself diligently in spinning yarn or knitting stockings. The young folks would crowd around the hearth, listening with breathless attention to some old crone of a servant, who was the oracle of the family, and who, perched like a raven in a corner of the chimney, would croak forth for a long winter afternoon a string of incredible stories about New England witches—grisly ghosts, horses without heads—and hairbreadth escapes and bloody encounters among the Indians.

[1] **sanctum sanctorum:** the holy of holies, the most holy place.
[2] **rhomboids** (rom′boidz): rectangles with oblique angles.

[3] **patriarchal** (pā′trē·är′kəl): here, large enough to accommodate a large family. A patriarch is the oldest man of a clan or family, usually an old man.
[4] *goede vrouw* (gœdə vrō): literally, "good lady," meaning the lady of the house.

In those happy days a well-regulated family always rose with the dawn, dined at eleven, and went to bed at sunset. Dinner was invariably a private meal, and the fat old burghers showed incontestable signs of disapprobation and uneasiness at being surprised by a visit from a neighbor on such occasions. But though our worthy ancestors were thus singularly averse to giving dinners, yet they kept up the social bands of intimacy by occasional banquetings, called tea parties.

These fashionable parties were generally confined to the higher classes, or noblesse,[1] that is to say, such as kept their own cows and drove their own wagons. The company commonly assembled at three o'clock and went away about six, unless it was in winter time, when the fashionable hours were a little earlier that the ladies might get home before dark. The tea table was crowned with a huge earthen dish, well stored with slices of fat pork, fried brown, cut up into morsels, and swimming in gravy. The company being seated round the genial board, and each furnished with a fork,

evinced their dexterity in launching at the fattest pieces in this mighty dish—in much the same manner as sailors harpoon porpoises at sea or our Indians spear salmon in the lakes. Sometimes the table was graced with immense apple pies or saucers full of preserved peaches and pears; but it was always sure to boast an enormous dish of balls of sweetened dough, fried in hog's fat, and called doughnuts, or *olykoeks*—a delicious kind of cake, at present scarce known in this city, except in genuine Dutch families.

The tea was served out of a majestic delft [2] teapot, ornamented with paintings of fat little Dutch shepherds and shepherdesses tending pigs—with boats sailing in the air, and houses built in the clouds, and sundry other ingenious Dutch fantasies. The beaux [3] distinguished themselves by their adroitness in replenishing this pot from a huge copper teakettle, which would have made the pygmy macaronies of these degenerate days sweat merely to look at it. To sweeten the beverage, a lump of sugar was laid beside each cup—and the company alternately nibbled and sipped with great decorum, until an improvement was introduced by a shrewd and economic old lady, which was to suspend a large lump directly over the tea table, by a string from the ceiling, so that it could be swung from mouth to mouth—an ingenious expedient, which is still kept up by some families in Albany; but which prevails without exception in Communipaw, Bergen, Flatbush, and all our uncontaminated Dutch villages.

At these primitive tea parties the utmost propriety and dignity of deportment prevailed. No flirting nor coqueting—no gambling of old ladies nor hoyden [4] chattering and romping of young ones—no

---

[1] **noblesse** (nō·bles'): nobility.

[2] **delft:** a glazed pottery made in Holland.
[3] **beaux** (bōz): young men.
[4] **hoyden** (hoid'n): rude, noisy behavior.

self-satisfied struttings of wealthy gentlemen with their brains in their pockets—nor amusing conceits and monkey divertissements[1] of smart young gentlemen with no brains at all. On the contrary, the young ladies seated themselves demurely in their rush-bottomed chairs, and knit their own woolen stockings; nor ever opened their lips excepting to say *yah Mynheer,* or *yah ya Vrouw,*[2] to any question that was asked them; behaving, in all things, like decent, well-educated damsels. As to the gentlemen, each of them tranquilly smoked his pipe and seemed lost in contemplation of the blue and white tiles with which the fireplaces were decorated; wherein sundry passages of Scripture were piously portrayed—Tobit and his dog figured to great advantage, Haman swung conspicuously on his gibbet, and Jonah appeared most manfully bouncing out of the whale, like Harlequin[3] through a barrel of fire.

The parties broke up without noise and without confusion. They were carried home by their own carriages, that is to say, by the vehicles nature had provided them, excepting such of the wealthy as could afford to keep a wagon. The gentlemen gallantly attended their fair ones to their respective abodes and took leave of them with a hearty smack at the door: which, as it was an established piece of etiquette, done in perfect simplicity and honesty of heart, occasioned no scandal at that time nor should it at the present—if our great-grandfathers approved of the custom, it would argue a great want of reverence in their descendants to say a word against it.

[1] **conceits . . . divertissements:** witty ideas and amusements.

[2] *yah Mynheer* (yà mīn·hâr′): yes, Sir. *yah ya Vrouw* (yà yà vrō): yes, yes, Ma'am (Dutch).

[3] **Tobit . . . Haman . . . Jonah:** Biblical characters. **Harlequin:** an amusing character in comedies and in pantomimes; a goblin.

FOR STUDY AND DISCUSSION

1. In your own words, describe the appearance of the houses and the streets of New Amsterdam. How does Irving say the pattern of the streets in New York developed? Is this a reasonable explanation?

2. What does Irving suggest about human nature in his description of the houses and their weathercocks? Is the direction of the wind actually an "important secret"? Why might everyone want "a wind to his mind"? Why would "loyal citizens" agree with the weathercock on top of the governor's house?

3. What passion dominated the life of the Dutch housewife? What was the ironic result of her careful polishing of the brass knocker? What was ironic about her thorough cleaning of the parlor?

4. According to Irving, what did the people do at their tea parties? Would you want to go to one? Why or why not? Do you believe the story of the old lady and her large lump of sugar? Is it consistent with other customs at these tea parties? What are the chief characteristics of the people as Irving describes them?

5. Do you think people were really as quietly behaved at these parties as Irving says? Why or why not? Is this an idea that most younger generations have about the behavior of their parents and their grandparents?

Even though this essay is not a formal piece of writing, it is arranged in carefully organized paragraphs, each of which is concerned with a particular aspect of life in New Amsterdam. Since the author is describing and not explaining or persuading, he does not always state the subject of a paragraph in a topic sentence. Nevertheless, you should be able to name the contribution each paragraph makes to the whole description. In your own words describe the role played by each paragraph, starting as suggested below and continuing throughout the sketch:

the city then and now

the cowpath streets

the houses of the Dutch settlers

Your own essays and compositions should also consist of paragraphs arranged in a logical order in order to convey to the reader, point by point, your line of thought. Before beginning to write, know what you want your reader to see in each paragraph.

FOR COMPOSITION

1. In the first paragraph of this selection, Irving compares New Amsterdam to the Indian village that once stood on Manhattan Island. What further comparisons can be made? What other changes have taken place in New York City? Use Irving's paragraph as a basis for a short composition, adding a phrase of your own to each of his comparisons to bring the description up to date. For instance, when Irving speaks of the "transformation from the rude log hut to the stately Dutch mansion," you might complete his description by adding "to the Empire State Building."

2. A photographer following Irving throughout this essay would take several pictures of the houses and the streets, move the camera inside to catch the women at work, the family at its fireside, and a tea party with an assortment of guests. Imagine yourself a writer-photographer following in Irving's footsteps. How would your camera move from one still shot to another? Divide up the essay as you would for camera shots, making each shot a separate paragraph.

The Adventures of a Shilling

JOSEPH ADDISON

(1672–1719)

In the early eighteenth century, one of the favorite pastimes of Londoners was conversation. Most educated people had opinions on a great many topics and were eager to express them to acquaintances and friends. Writers, wits, philosophers, and people of leisure would gather daily at Will's, the Turk's Head, the Grecian, or one of the other London coffee houses to exchange opinions and the latest news. Such conversations, over steaming cups of tea and coffee, were usually leisurely, relaxed, and entertaining.

These same qualities could be found in the *Tatler,* one of the first English newspapers. The *Tatler* was founded in 1709 by Richard Steele, a former army captain and pamphlet writer with a flair for creating lively characters. Steele didn't tell in the paper who the "Tatler" was, but his friend Joseph Addison, then a member of Parliament, recognized a remark he had made to Steele when it appeared in print. Before long Addison was writing for the *Tatler* too. When Steele stopped publishing the *Tatler,* Addison, with Steele's help, started the *Spectator,* perhaps the most famous of English newspapers. The gossip and essays in both of these papers were eagerly read in the coffee houses.

Today Joseph Addison is recognized as one of the greatest English writers of the *informal* or *familiar* essay. In this kind of essay, as in conversation, the author has no intention of exploring any particular topic thoroughly.

Rather the mind and imagination are allowed to wander at will. The only requirement of the familiar essay is that the topic be interesting and the ideas well expressed.

Like Addison, many other essayists have been amused observers of human nature, and have poked fun at ridiculous habits and attitudes. Few, however, have succeeded as well as Addison. Even when he mocks or satirizes someone, Addison rarely gives offense. He is tolerant of all kinds of human behavior and would rather smile than condemn. Others might write a sermon on the foolishness of people's attitudes toward money, but Addison would rather tell his readers a story about the adventures of a shilling.

Per varios casus, per tot discrimina rerum,
Tendimus—

Virgil, *Aeneid* I, 209

"Through various hazards, and events, we move."

I WAS LAST NIGHT visited by a friend of mine, who has an inexhaustible fund of discourse, and never fails to entertain his company with a variety of thoughts and hints that are altogether new and uncommon. Whether it were in complaisance[1] to my way of living or his real opinion, he advanced the following paradox: that it required much greater talents to fill up and become a retired life than a life of business. Upon this occasion he rallied[2] very agreeably the busy men of the age, who only value themselves for being in motion and passing through a series of trifling and insignificant actions. In the heat of his discourse, seeing a piece of money lying on my table, "I defy," says he, "any of these active persons to produce half the adventures that this twelve-penny piece[3] has been engaged in were it possible for him to give us an account of his life."

My friend's talk made so odd an impression upon my mind that soon after I was abed I fell insensibly into an unaccountable reverie that had neither moral nor design in it, and cannot be so properly called a dream as a delirium.

Methought the shilling that lay upon the table reared itself upon its edge and, turning the face toward me, opened its mouth and, in a soft silver sound, gave me the following account of his life and adventures:

"I was born," says he, "on the side of a mountain, near a little village of Peru, and made a voyage to England in an ingot under the convoy of Sir Francis Drake.[4] I was, soon after my arrival, taken out of my Indian habit,[5] refined, naturalized, and put into the British mode with the face of Queen Elizabeth on one side and the arms of the country on the other. Being thus equipped, I found in me a wonderful inclination to ramble and visit all the parts of the new world into which I was brought. The people very much favored my natural disposition and shifted me so fast from hand to hand that, before I was five years old, I had traveled into almost every corner of the nation. But in the beginning of my sixth year, to my unspeakable grief, I fell into the hands of a miserable old fellow, who clapped me into an iron chest where I found five hundred more of my own quality who lay under the same confinement. The only relief we had was to be taken out and counted over in the fresh air every morning and evening. After an imprisonment of several years, we heard

---

[1] **complaisance** (kəm·plā′zəns): a desire to please others.

[2] **rallied:** scolded in a teasing manner.

[3] **twelve-penny piece:** a shilling. The British shilling is now worth about fourteen cents in American money.

[4] **Sir Francis Drake** (1540?–1596): an English sea captain and explorer in the New World.

[5] **habit:** dress, clothing.

somebody knocking at our chest and breaking it open with a hammer. This we found was the old man's heir, who, as his father lay dying, was so good as to come to our release. He separated us that very day. What was the fate of my companions I know not: as for myself, I was sent to the apothecary's shop for a pint of sack.[1] The apothecary gave me to an herb-woman, the herb-woman to a butcher, the butcher to a brewer, and the brewer to his wife, who made a present of me to a nonconformist preacher. After this manner I made my way merrily through the world; for, as I told you before, we shillings love nothing so much as traveling. I sometimes fetched in a shoulder of mutton, sometimes a play-book, and often had the satisfaction to treat a templer[2] at a twelve-penny ordinary[3] or carry him with three friends to Westminster Hall.

"In the midst of this pleasant progress, which I made from place to place, I was arrested by a superstitious old woman, who shut me up in a greasy purse in pursuance of a foolish saying, 'that while she kept a Queen Elizabeth's shilling about her, she would never be without money.' I continued here a close prisoner for many months until, at last, I was exchanged for eight-and-forty farthings.[4]

"I thus rambled from pocket to pocket until the beginning of the civil wars when, to my shame be it spoken, I was employed in raising soldiers against the king: for, being of a very tempting breadth, a sergeant made use of me to inveigle country fellows and lift them into the service of the Parliament.

"As soon as he had made one man sure,

his way was to oblige him to take a shilling of a more homely figure and then practice the same trick upon another. Thus I continued doing great mischief to the crown.

"After many adventures which it would be tedious to relate, I was sent to a young spendthrift, in company with the will of his deceased father. The young fellow, who I found was very extravagant, gave great demonstrations of joy at the receiving of the will: but opening it, he found himself disinherited and cut off from the possession of a fair estate by virtue of my being made a present to him. This put him into such a passion that, after having taken me in his hand and cursed me, he squirred me away from him as far as he could fling me. I chanced to light in an unfrequented place under a dead wall where I lay undiscovered and useless during the usurpation of Oliver Cromwell.[5]

"About a year after the King's return, a poor cavalier that was walking there about dinnertime fortunately cast his eye upon me and, to the great joy of us both, carried me to a cook's shop where he dined upon me and drank the King's health. When I came again into the world, I found that I had been happier in my retirement than I thought, having probably by that means escaped wearing a monstrous pair of breeches.[6]

"Being now of great credit and antiquity, I was rather looked upon as a medal than an ordinary coin; for which reason a gamester laid hold of me and converted me to a counter,[7] having got together some dozens of us for that use. We led a melancholy life in his possession, being busy at those hours wherein current coin is at

---

[1] **sack:** a dry, white wine.

[2] **templer:** a law student.

[3] **ordinary:** a cheap meal at an inn.

[4] **farthing:** formerly a British coin worth about a fourth of a penny; now extinct.

[5] **Oliver Cromwell:** the leader of the Puritan forces in the English civil wars (1643–1651) and Lord Protector of the Puritan Commonwealth.

[6] **monstrous . . . breeches:** the coins issued by the Commonwealth had markings that resembled a large W or pair of breeches.

[7] **counter:** a coin used in gambling games.

rest and partaking the fate of our master, being in a few moments valued at a crown, a pound, or a sixpence, according to the situation in which the fortune of the cards placed us. I had at length the good luck to see my master break, by which means I was again sent abroad under my primitive denomination of a shilling.

"I shall pass over many other accidents of less moment and hasten to that fatal catastrophe when I fell into the hands of an artist, who conveyed me under ground and, with an unmerciful pair of shears, cut off my titles, clipped my brims, retrenched my shape, rubbed me to my inmost ring; and, in short, so spoiled and pillaged me that he did not leave me worth a groat. You may think what confusion I was in to see myself thus curtailed and disfigured. I should have been ashamed to have shown my head had not all my old acquaintance been reduced to the same shameful figure, excepting some few that were punched through the belly. In the midst of this general calamity, when everybody thought our misfortune irretrievable and our case desperate, we were thrown into the furnace together and, as it often happens with cities rising out of a fire, appeared with greater beauty and luster than we could ever boast of before. What has happened to me since this change of sex which you now see, I shall take

some other opportunity to relate. In the meantime, I shall only repeat two adventures as being very extraordinary, and neither of them having ever happened to me above once in my life. The first was my being in a poet's pocket who was so taken with the brightness and novelty of my appearance that it gave occasion to the finest burlesque poem in the British language, entitled, from me, *The Splendid Shilling*. The second adventure, which I must not omit, happened to me in the year 1703 when I was given away in charity to a blind man; but indeed this was by mistake, the person who gave me having thrown me heedlessly into the hat among a pennyworth of farthings."

FOR STUDY AND DISCUSSION

1. What tragedies or mishaps occurred in the course of the shilling's travels? For how many of these was the shilling at least partly responsible?

2. Look again at the shilling's account of its experiences with the miser, the superstitious old woman, and the gamester. Does the shilling's account make clear the author's attitude toward each kind of person? What is his attitude toward each?

3. Addison's readers would have been familiar with the events of the bloody civil wars that were fought in England toward the middle of the seventeenth century. The Puritans won the war and ruled England for nearly ten years

before the death of their leader, Oliver Cromwell. After the strictness of Puritan rule, the restoration of the King in 1660 was a cause for celebration in most of England. The shilling does not say directly which side of the controversy it favors, but the way it speaks of both makes its preference clear. Reread the references to the civil wars, the King, and Oliver Cromwell. With which side do the author's sympathies seem to lie?

4. What is the "paradox" proposed by Addison's friend in paragraph 1? Do you agree with it? Why or why not? Do the shilling's adventures tend to prove or disprove the paradox? Are the shilling's actions "trifling and insignificant"? Do they seem so to the shilling? What kind of life, busy or retired, does the shilling find more enjoyable?

5. Which two of the shilling's adventures did you find most amusing? Which was more amusing—the events themselves or the author's way of telling about them?

THE WRITER'S STYLE

In this essay Joseph Addison expresses the idea that people often act foolishly, especially in connection with money. Yet he never says this directly. Instead, he *shows* us a succession of people acting foolishly. In other words, he tells a story.

Addison's chief purpose in "The Adventures of a Shilling" is to mock, or poke fun at—to satirize—human foolishness. By showing us people acting foolishly in an imaginary story, he makes his point in a far more convincing and entertaining manner than if he had simply stated that people are foolish.

In your own writing, keep in mind that the most effective and entertaining way of conveying an idea is often to bring that idea to life in a story.

FOR COMPOSITION

What events similar to those described by Addison might occur today to an American quarter? Satirizing foolish attitudes toward money, write your own story about the possible adventures of a modern quarter.

The Decline of Sport

A Preposterous Parable

E. B. WHITE

(1899–)

One reviewer of *The Second Tree from the Corner,* the essay collection by Elwyn Brooks White in which "The Decline of Sport" appears, stated flatly that, in his opinion, E. B. White is "the finest essayist in the United States." Many readers would agree with this judgment.

As can be said of any good writer, and especially writers of essays, no one else writes quite like E. B. White. In "The Decline of Sport," his way of beginning with a preposterous assumption and proceeding by simple, logical steps to an even more preposterous conclusion is a unique experience in reading. In this strange world of exaggeration, everything that happens is fantastic and improbable, yet at the same time all too possible and true.

In most of his writing, E. B. White shows us human nature in a mirror—not an ordinary mirror, but one from the fun house, which shows us ourselves at peculiar angles, not at all as we like to think we are. This exaggeration of the odd contradictions in human nature shows us, in a humorous fashion, the way we look to others from time to time. As E. B.

White himself once wrote: "Humor plays close to the big, hot fire which is truth, and the reader often feels the heat."

E. B. White's approach to style is one of the chief secrets of his success as a writer of essays. He is the first to admit, however, that this secret is difficult to define. Most writing, he says, is laborious and slow and intensely personal. You can tell, with writers who have found their style, how they are different from other people. As White puts it: "Style not only reveals the spirit of the man, it reveals his identity, as surely as would his fingerprints." The only real approach to style is to set down your own thoughts honestly. In White's own words, "The approach to style is by way of plainness, simplicity, orderliness, sincerity." These qualities—plainness, simplicity, orderliness, and sincerity—are the distinguishing marks of E. B. White's own writing.

Ⅰɴ ᴛʜᴇ ᴛʜɪʀᴅ decade of the supersonic age, sport gripped the nation in an ever-tightening grip. The horse tracks, the ball parks, the fight rings, the gridirons, all drew crowds in steadily increasing numbers. Every time a game was played, an attendance record was broken. Usually some other sort of record was broken, too—such as the record for the number of consecutive doubles hit by left-handed batters in a Series game, or some such thing as that. Records fell like ripe apples on a windy day. Customs and manners changed, and the five-day business week was reduced to four days, then to three, to give everyone a better chance to memorize the scores.

Not only did sport proliferate but the demands it made on the spectator became greater. Nobody was content to take in one event at a time, and thanks to the magic of radio and television nobody had to. A Yale alumnus, class of 1962, returning to the Bowl with 197,000 others to see the Yale-Cornell football game would take along his pocket radio and pick up the Yankee Stadium, so that while his eye might be following a fumble on the Cornell twenty-two-yard line, his ear would be following a man going down to second in the top of the fifth, seventy miles away. High in the blue sky above the Bowl, skywriters would be at work writing the scores of other major and minor sporting contests, weaving an interminable record of victory and defeat, and using the new high-visibility pink news-smoke perfected by Pepsi-Cola engineers. And in the frames of the giant video sets, just behind the goal posts, this same alumnus could watch Dejected win the Futurity [1] before a record-breaking crowd of 349,872 at Belmont, each of whom was tuned to the Yale Bowl and following the World Series game in the video and searching the sky for further news of events either under way or just completed. The effect of this vast cyclorama [2] of sport was to divide the spectator's attention, oversubtilize [3] his appreciation, and deaden his passion. As the fourth supersonic decade was ushered in, the picture changed and sport began to wane.

A good many factors contributed to the decline of sport. Substitutions in football had increased to such an extent that there were very few fans in the United States capable of holding the players in mind during play. Each play that was called saw two entirely new elevens lined up, and the players whose names and faces you had familiarized yourself with in the first period were seldom seen or heard of again. The spectacle became as diffuse as

[1] **the Futurity:** the Futurity Stakes, a yearly racing event at Belmont Park.

[2] **cyclorama** (sī′klə·ram′ə): a pictured representation of a scene on a circular wall, often used as a backdrop for a stage set; a circular panorama or view.

[3] **oversubtilize:** overrefine, spread too thin.

Kent 4 — Dummer 3

the main concourse in Grand Central [1] at the commuting hour.

Express motor highways leading to the parks and stadia had become so wide, so unobstructed, so devoid of all life except automobiles and trees that sport fans had got into the habit of traveling enormous distances to attend events. The normal driving speed had been stepped up to ninety-five miles an hour, and the distance between cars had been decreased to fifteen feet. This put an extraordinary strain on the sport lover's nervous system, and he arrived home from a Saturday game, after a road trip of three hundred and fifty miles, glassy-eyed, dazed, and spent. He hadn't really had any relaxation and he had failed to see Czlika (who had gone in for Trusky) take the pass from Bkeeo (who had gone in for Bjallo) in the third period, because at that moment a youngster named Lavagetto had been put in to pinch-hit for Art Gurlack in the bottom of the ninth with the tying run on second, and the skywriter who was attempting to write "Princeton 0—Lafayette 43" had banked the wrong way, muffed the "3," and distracted everyone's atten-

tion from the fact that Lavagetto had been whiffed.[2]

Cheering, of course, lost its stimulating effect on players, because cheers were no longer associated necessarily with the immediate scene but might as easily apply to something that was happening somewhere else. This was enough to infuriate even the steadiest performer. A football star, hearing the stands break into a roar before the ball was snapped, would realize that their minds were not on him, and would become dispirited and grumpy. Two or three of the big coaches worried so about this that they considered equipping all players with tiny ear sets, so that they, too, could keep abreast of other sporting events while playing, but the idea was abandoned as impractical, and the coaches put it aside in tickler files,[3] to bring up again later.

I think the event that marked the turning point in sport and started it downhill was the Midwest's classic Dust Bowl game of 1975, when Eastern Reserve's great right end, Ed Pistachio, was shot by a spectator. This man, the one who did the shooting, was seated well down in the

[1] **Grand Central:** a large and usually crowded railroad station in New York City.

[2] **whiffed:** struck out.
[3] **tickler files:** memorandum files.

stands near the forty-yard line on a bleak October afternoon and was so saturated with sport and with the disappointments of sport that he had clearly become deranged. With a minute and fifteen seconds to play and the score tied, the Eastern Reserve quarterback had whipped a long pass over Army's heads into Pistachio's waiting arms. There was no other player anywhere near him, and all Pistachio had to do was catch the ball and run it across the line. He dropped it. At exactly this moment, the spectator—a man named Homer T. Parkinson, of 35 Edgemere Drive, Toledo, O.—suffered at least three other major disappointments in the realm of sport. His horse, Hiccough, on which he had a five-hundred-dollar bet, fell while getting away from the starting gate at Pimlico and broke its leg (clearly visible in the video); his favorite shortstop, Lucky Frimstitch, struck out and let three men die on base in the final game of the Series (to which Parkinson was tuned); and the Governor Dummer [1] soccer team, on which Parkinson's youngest son played goalie, lost to Kent, 4–3, as recorded in

[1] **Governor Dummer:** Governor Dummer Academy, a New England preparatory school, as is the Kent School.

the sky overhead. Before anyone could stop him, he drew a gun and drilled Pistachio, before 954,000 persons, the largest crowd that had ever attended a football game and the *second*-largest crowd that had ever assembled for any sporting event in any month except July.

This tragedy, by itself, wouldn't have caused sport to decline, I suppose, but it set in motion a chain of other tragedies, the cumulative effect of which was terrific. Almost as soon as the shot was fired, the news flash was picked up by one of the skywriters directly above the field. He glanced down to see whether he could spot the trouble below, and in doing so failed to see another skywriter approaching. The two planes collided and fell, wings locked, leaving a confusing trail of smoke, which some observers tried to interpret as a late sports score. The planes struck in the middle of the nearby eastbound coast-to-coast Sunlight Parkway, and a motorist driving a convertible coupé stopped so short, to avoid hitting them, that he was bumped from behind. The pileup of cars that ensued involved 1,482 vehicles, a record for eastbound parkways. A total of more than three thousand persons lost their lives in the highway accident, including the two pilots, and when panic broke out in the stadium, it cost another 872 in dead and injured. News of the disaster spread quickly to other sports arenas and started other panics among the crowds trying to get to the exits, where they could buy a paper and study a list of the dead. All in all, the afternoon of sport cost 20,003 lives, a record. And nobody had much to show for it except one small Midwestern boy who hung around the smoking wrecks of the planes, captured some aero news-smoke in a milk bottle, and took it home as a souvenir.

From that day on, sport waned. Through long, noncompetitive Saturday afternoons, the stadia slumbered. Even the parkways fell into disuse as motorists rediscovered the charms of old, twisty roads that led through main streets and past barnyards, with their mild congestions and pleasant smells.

FOR STUDY AND DISCUSSION

1. Judging from this essay, what does E. B. White think of America's craze for competitive sports? What does he find ridiculous about it? Do you think his attitude is sensible or too extreme? Why? Do you think White would feel the same about individual sports such as swimming or sailing as he does about mass spectator sports? Why or why not?

2. Do you think any of the events that White describes have ever actually occurred? Have events very much like them, though not as exaggerated, actually happened? Which incidents in the story seem most likely to be real?

3. What were the causes of Homer T. Parkinson's derangement? How did he react? How did the crowd react? Compare the crowd's reaction to the reactions of crowds you have seen at baseball or football games? Is White's account an accurate, though exaggerated, reflection of mob behavior?

4. This essay is subtitled "A Preposterous Parable." A parable is a short tale that teaches

a lesson by telling a story about familiar, everyday things. It is similar to a fable, except that its "point" or lesson is not stated in so many words. Why does E. B. White call this essay a *preposterous* parable? What lesson does it teach?

THE WRITER'S STYLE

Good writers try in the very first sentence to interest their readers, even to startle them, so that they will be sure to continue reading. In this essay, E. B. White's opening sentence is a short and forceful declaration: "In the third decade of the supersonic age, sport *gripped* the nation in an ever-tightening *grip*." The tone of the sentence seems to suggest that something ominous has happened. But what is so ominous? This strange contrast of subject and tone, or manner of speaking, intrigues us and makes us want to read on.

The beginning of "The Decline of Sport" also prepares us for the development of the rest of the essay. As we read on, the grip of sport on the nation becomes more and more sinister and at the same time more and more preposterous. We can appreciate the essay fully because the author has pointed us in the right direction with his very first sentence.

Even the ending of the essay is made more effective by White's beginning. Compare the last sentence or two of the essay with the first sentence. The force of the opening sentence gives way to the slow words and relaxed feeling of "long, noncompetitive Saturday afternoons" and "the charms of old, twisty roads." Like any good beginning and ending, the opening and closing sentences of "The Decline of Sport" provide an effective frame for the ideas the author developed in the body of his essay.

FOR COMPOSITION

1. The craze for competitive sports is a subject which sparks many discussions. Write a short paper for or against the stress placed on competitive sports.

2. Choose a fad that grips many of your friends and write about its rise and fall, using striking opening and closing sentences.

Of Studies

FRANCIS BACON
(1561–1626)

Sir Francis Bacon, unlike the other writers in this section, wrote only *formal essays*. In these essays he attempted to set down his thoughts on important subjects, such as friendship, truth, learning, honor, youth, and age. Each essay is a kind of summing-up of his own understanding of that subject, including all that he had seen and learned. His concern was to communicate wisdom, not to provide pleasant reading. As a result, his writing is much less personal than that of most essayists today.

Before Bacon's time, most serious writing was in Latin, which scholars and the learned felt was a more enduring language than the "common tongue" spoken by the people. Bacon's essays and his many other writings convinced his readers that the most profound and weighty thoughts could be expressed in English with no loss of dignity or meaning. In their careful balance and structure, Bacon's sentences are like those of the classic Latin writers; he also occasionally uses a Latin phrase. These Latin influences are always appropriate, however, to the seriousness of his subjects and the extremely careful organization of his ideas.

Bacon lived in a time—the English Renaissance—when new ideas were bursting like flares on the consciousness of all. Bacon himself was the source of many of these ideas. Despite a life spent in public service, he found time not only to write essays and treatises but to introduce to the general public many of the ideas of modern science. An ambitious man, Bacon declared in one of his writings: "I have taken all knowledge to be my province." Nowhere is this more clearly revealed than in his essays. In each he offers the judgment of a man who has thought deeply and seen much.

Bacon expressed his ideas clearly, forcefully, and in a few, well-chosen words. Where another writer might take a paragraph to develop and elaborate an idea, Bacon states his meaning in a phrase and then goes on to the next idea. Of course, this style requires extremely careful reading as well as writing.

Essentially, Bacon's essays are practical guidebooks, packed with information and ideas. His intention was to teach what he had learned of life, especially to the young who wanted to get ahead. His essays help us to understand the world and the proper use of things. You at times may have wondered, for example, about the use of studies. In his fifty-seven essays, Sir Francis Bacon has provided an answer to this and to many other questions.

Studies serve for delight, for ornament, and for ability. Their chief use for delight is in privateness and retiring; for ornament, is in discourse; and for ability, is in the judgment and disposition of business; for expert men [1] can execute, and perhaps judge of particulars, one by one; but the general counsels, and the plots and marshaling of affairs come best from those that are learned. To spend too much time in studies is sloth; to use them too much for ornament is affectation; to make judgment wholly by their rules is the humor [2] of a scholar. They perfect nature, and are perfected by experience; for natural abilities are like natural plants, that need pruning by study; and studies themselves do give forth directions too much at large, except they be bounded in by experience.

Crafty [3] men contemn [4] studies, simple [5]

---

[1] **expert men:** experienced men of practical affairs.
[2] **humor:** temperament, disposition.
[3] **Crafty:** skilled in crafts.
[4] **contemn:** despise.
[5] **simple:** unlettered.

Two sixteenth-century scholars converse on a hill overlooking Oxford University.

men admire [1] them, and wise men use them; for they teach not their own use; but that is a wisdom without them and above them, won by observation. Read not to contradict and confute, nor to believe and take for granted, nor to find talk and discourse, but to weigh and consider. Some books are to be tasted, others to be swallowed, and some few to be chewed and digested; that is, some books are to be read only in parts; others to be read but not curiously; and some few to be read wholly, and with diligence and attention. Some books also may be read by deputy, and extracts made of them by others; but that would be only in the less important arguments and the meaner sort of books; else distilled books are, like common distilled waters, flashy [2] things.

Reading maketh a full man; conference a ready man; and writing an exact man. And, therefore, if a man write little, he had need have a great memory; if he confer little, he had need have a present wit; and if he read little, he had need have much cunning, to seem to know that he doth not. Histories make men wise; poets, witty; the mathematics, subtle; natural philosophy, deep; moral, grave; logic and rhetoric, able to contend: *Abeunt studia in mores!* [3]

Nay, there is no stand [4] or impediment in the wit but may be wrought out by fit studies; like as diseases of the body may have appropriate exercises. Bowling is good for the stone and reins, [5] shooting for the lungs and breast, gentle walking

[1] **admire:** wonder at.
[2] **flashy:** tasteless.

[3] *Abeunt . . . mores:* studies are turned into habits (Latin).
[4] **stand:** obstacle.
[5] **stone and reins:** old name for a kidney ailment.

for the stomach, riding for the head, and the like. So if a man's wit be wandering, let him study the mathematics; for in demonstrations, if his wit be called away never so little, he must begin again. If his wit be not apt to distinguish or find differences, let him study the schoolmen; for they are *cymini sectores!*[1] If he be not apt to beat over matters, and to call up one thing to prove and illustrate another, let him study the lawyers' cases. So every defect of the mind may have a special receipt.[2]

[1] *cymini sectores:* hair-splitters (Latin). The "schoolmen" (medieval scholars) were known for their closely reasoned arguments.
[2] **receipt:** prescription, remedy.

Sir Francis Bacon, as shown in a detail from the title page of one of his works.

FOR STUDY AND DISCUSSION

1. According to Bacon, what are the three uses of studies? For what kind of decisions are they especially useful? Why is this true?

2. What are the three ways in which studies can be misused? Which kind of misuse do you think does most harm? Do you agree that in order to truly understand the knowledge gained from books, it is necessary also to have direct experience of life? Why or why not?

3. What opinion do crafty, simple, and wise people have of studies? What is a wise person's aim in reading?

4. What does a person gain from reading? from writing? from conversation? What does a person need who does little of any of these? Why?

THE WRITER'S STYLE

In building an argument or persuading a reader to agree with you, it is important to organize your ideas logically. A good writer adds one part of an argument to another as carefully as an architect constructs the various parts of a house. In modern writing, each major idea introduced in an argument is usually set off in a separate paragraph. Bacon, however, wrote his essays as single paragraph units. Look back at the essay above and con-sider the paragraph divisions made in printing it here. Do the paragraph divisions seem logical to you? Does each division indicate another major idea in the total structure of the essay? In what way does the paragraphing help you as a reader?

Bacon's sentences are as carefully put together as are his ideas. He often uses *balanced sentences,* a good way of setting forth parallel ideas or examples or of contrasting opposite sides of a single idea. Notice the balance in the following sentences:

"Crafty men contemn studies, simple men admire them, and wise men use them . . .

"Reading maketh a full man; conference a ready man; and writing an exact man."

"They perfect nature, and are perfected by experience . . ."

Do such sentences give a sense of authority to the essay? Find other examples of balanced sentences in "Of Studies."

FOR COMPOSITION

After class discussion of Bacon's ideas on studies, write an essay summing up your position on this subject. Explain why you agree or disagree with Bacon.

Exposition

Exposition is the statement or explanation of facts, ideas, or personal opinions. More than any other kind of writing, exposition involves the direct expression of ideas and reasons. Because of this, it must be especially logical in its organization. The structure of an expository paragraph or essay must be clear, for it is easier for readers to lose their way in exposition than when reading narration, where they are following a story; or in description, where the writer is appealing to the senses. What is the logic behind the following paragraph from "The Decline of Sport"? What is the writer trying to explain?

In the third decade of the supersonic age, sport gripped the nation in an ever-tightening grip. The horse tracks, the ball parks, the fight rings, the gridirons, all drew crowds in steadily increasing numbers. Every time a game was played, an attendance record was broken. Usually some other sort of record was broken, too—such as the record for the number of consecutive doubles hit by left-handed batters in a Series game, or some such thing as that. Records fell like ripe apples on a windy day. Customs and manners changed, and the five-day business week was reduced to four days, then to three, to give everyone a better chance to memorize the scores.

(page 283)

1. What generalization is made in the first sentence of this paragraph? Does the paragraph have a concluding, or "clincher," sentence?
2. Which details in the paragraph support the statement in the opening sentence?
3. Is the order of details logical? What does the order of presentation suggest to you about the author's attitude toward sports?
4. What "clue words" help to make clear the movement of the author's thought?

A paragraph of exposition may be intended primarily to give information, to develop an idea, or to express the writer's personal opinion. There are many different ways of doing each of these. One way is to state the topic of a paragraph in an opening sentence, and then support it with facts, examples, or illustrations; another is to build up to it gradually. Which way is used by J. B. Priestley in his essay on bragging?

It is true, as my family have pointed out more than once (families overdo this kind of thing), that now and again I delight in bragging. But I do it, as of course I do everything, from the best of motives. When I am with people who think I am a fine fellow and have done some good work in my time, I am (or at least I imagine I am) modest, almost ready to blush, candid about my faults, humbly aware of how little I have done to merit such praise, etc., etc., etc. But there are some persons who do not appear to understand that I exist just as they and their friends exist, that what I do seems as important to me as what they do seems to them, that I have a world of my own just as they and their kind have a world of their own. They are people composed of blank stares, ignorance, incredulity, and insensitiveness. In a ruder society, they could be taken out into the castle yard and banged over the head with spiked maces. In our society, this is not possible. So I assert myself, I become aggressive, I begin to brag. But I am not doing this merely for myself. I am proclaiming the existence of a whole world of wonder and glory. I am taking my stand for Literature and Drama and the author's way of life. I am glaring and shouting on behalf of Sophocles and Shakespeare, Cervantes and Molière. Mightier than the sword, Major Fawcett! Yes, and let me tell *you* something—— (page 255)

1. What point is Priestley making in this little essay? Is his real topic stated or implied?

2. How does he support his main idea with facts? with examples? with narration? with description?

3. What devices does the author use in this essay to help you follow his thought?

4. How is the last sentence (incomplete) a kind of "clincher" for the main idea of the essay as a whole?

PRACTICE IN READING EXPOSITION

In reading exposition, you should try to understand the writer's main idea and decide whether it is convincing. With this in mind, reread the following paragraphs and write down the main idea (and your opinion) of each:

page 262—"Stranger, you've been taken in . . ."

page 274—"In those good days . . ."

page 276—"At these primitive tea parties . . ."

page 284—"Express motor highways . . ."

page 287—"Studies serve for delight . . ."

WRITING EXPOSITION

In writing exposition, you should try to do the following:

1. Keep your main idea firmly in mind.

2. Think of facts, examples, reasons, or arguments that will support or develop your main idea.

3. Arrange them in a logical order that will best express your point.

4. Write clearly and persuasively, making all shifts and turnings of your thought clear with "clue words" or transitions.

Keep these steps in mind while doing the following writing:

1. Reread the following paragraph from "The Decline of Sport," noticing the author's selection and organization of details. How does he support the main idea expressed in his topic sentence?

Not only did sport proliferate but the demands it made on the spectator became greater. Nobody was content to take in one event at a time, and thanks to the magic of radio and television nobody had to. A Yale alumnus, class of 1962, returning to the Bowl with 197,000 others to see the Yale-Cornell football game would take along his pocket radio and pick up the Yankee Stadium, so that while his eye might be following a fumble on the Cornell twenty-two-yard line, his ear would be following a man going down to second in the top of the fifth, seventy miles away. High in the blue sky above the Bowl, skywriters would be at work writing the scores of other major and minor sporting contests, weaving an interminable record of victory and defeat, and using the new high-visibility pink news-smoke perfected by Pepsi-Cola engineers. And in the frames of the giant video sets, just behind the goal posts, this same alumnus could watch Dejected win the Futurity before a record-breaking crowd of 349,872 at Belmont, each of whom was tuned to the Yale Bowl and following the World Series game in the video and searching the sky for further news of events either under way or just completed. The effect of this vast cyclorama of sport was to divide the spectator's attention, oversubtilize his appreciation, and deaden his passion. As the fourth supersonic decade was ushered in, the picture changed and sport began to wane.
(page 283)

Now write a paragraph of your own in which you develop a topic sentence with examples, as E. B. White did in this paragraph from "The Decline of Sport." You may use one of these beginnings or make up one of your own:

Getting good marks (or doing anything else) is getting harder every year.

What a time I had learning to ski (or surf or water-ski or . . .).

In the city (country, town) there's always plenty going on.

Arrange your examples in a logical order and use transitional words and phrases to make clear how each fits into the design of your paragraph.

2. Another way to develop a point is with narration—by telling a little story that illustrates and reinforces your opinion. Think of

an incident that illustrates one of your own opinions and tell about it in a paragraph or two.

SHARPENING YOUR WRITING

In exposition it is especially important to express your meaning clearly. Sometimes the first attempt is not enough, and further explanations are required to communicate clearly and completely what you mean. Even as talented and thoughtful a writer as Francis Bacon often found it necessary to retrace his steps at times and restate an idea from a different angle, as in these two examples:

Some books are to be tasted, others to be swallowed, and some few to be chewed and digested; that is, some books are to be read only in parts; others to be read but not curiously; and some few to be read wholly, and with diligence and attention.

Reading maketh a full man; conference a ready man; and writing an exact man. And, therefore, if a man write little, he had need have a great memory; if he confer little, he had need have a present wit; and if he read little, he had need have much cunning, to seem to know that he doth not. (page 288)

Often in your own writing expressing an idea another way will suddenly make it come clear. Look back over your paragraphs of exposition. Does anything seem unclear? Perhaps using different wording will make things clearer. The logic of your paragraphs should be strong and solid, without any gaps in reasoning.

SENTENCE SKILLS

As you know, good writers vary the length of their sentences to avoid monotony. They will also vary the beginnings of their sentences. Look closely at the following paragraph from "Long Trousers." How does Priestley vary the length of his sentences and their beginnings?

There was a time when merely wearing long trousers brought me delight. In those days, when I must have been about fifteen, I had only one suit—my best—with long trousers. My other suits had knee breeches, buttoning tightly just below the knee and worn with thick long stockings, turned down at the top. There was really nothing wrong with my appearance when I wore these knee breeches and long stockings, for after years of football I had muscular, well-shaped legs; but whenever I wore them I felt I was still imprisoned, a shamefaced giant, in the stale miniature world of childhood. Condemned—and I use this term because there were strict rules at home about which suits could be worn—to wear these knee breeches, I felt that no glimpse of my real self could catch the town's eye: I might almost have been sent to school in a pram. Conversely, I felt that as soon as I put on the long trousers, then appearance and reality were gloriously one; I joined the world of men; and even without doing anything more than wear these trousers—and leaving the other wretched things at home—I could feel my whole nature expanding magnificently. On the occasional days when I was allowed to wear the adult trousers to school, I almost floated there. Never did eighteen inches of cloth do more for the human spirit. On those mornings now when I seem to stare sullenly at the wreck of a shining world, why do I not remind myself that although I grow old and fat and peevish *at least I am wearing my long trousers?*

(pages 255–56)

Which is the longest sentence in this paragraph? Which is the shortest? Which expresses most forcefully the paragraph's main idea? Which sentences begin with the subject? with a modifier? with a prepositional phrase?

ART AND LITERATURE

Write a short expository essay explaining which of the paintings on pages 307–12 seems to you to have the greatest significance.

BIOGRAPHY
AND PERSONAL
RECOLLECTION

I N OTHER PARTS of this book, you can read the works of famous
writers of different eras and different lands. In this unit, you will
have a chance to read about the lives of a number of these writers.
Reading biography is one of the easiest and most pleasurable ways
of expanding the limits of one's own life. By reading about the lives
of other people we can share all kinds of experiences, many of which
we will never have a chance to sample for ourselves.

In the following pages, you can visit sixteenth-century Stratford-
on-Avon and sample the boyhood world of William Shakespeare, one
of the greatest of all writers and the author of the play *Romeo and
Juliet* (page 434). And jumping forward three centuries, you can
sample nineteenth-century London where Charles Dickens, the English novelist who wrote *Great Expectations* (page 560), grew up. On
this side of the Atlantic Ocean, you can meet Mark Twain, an American contemporary of Dickens who became one of this country's best
known writers. In "The Genuine Mexican Plug" (page 260), we shall
sample one of Twain's adventures in the old West.

Also in this unit, two modern American writers, James Thurber
and John Steinbeck, reminisce about episodes in their own lives.
James Thurber, author of "The Secret Life of Walter Mitty" (page
74), recalls an eventful day in his youth, and John Steinbeck, author
of "The Gift" (page 130), recounts some of his travel experiences.
The selections in this unit of the book should help you consider each
of these writers—both the individuals and their work—in deeper than
usual dimension.

The Young Shakespeare

MARCHETTE CHUTE

THE SON of the High Bailiff, young William Shakespeare, was four years old and had a two-year-old brother named Gilbert to keep him company. The center of his life must have been at first the house on Henley Street, with its sturdy oak framework and slanting roof; and he must have known the premises thoroughly from the pointed gables of the attic to his father's shop with its leathers and its tools on the ground floor.

The house was on the edge of town, just south of the gravel pits that marked the northern limits of the borough, but it was only a short walk down Henley Street to the intersection where the real business of town began. Here was the pump where the Stratford housewives washed their clothes and hung them, rather improperly, on the Market Cross to dry. It was here that John Shakespeare had his stall on market days; and a square wooden structure on pillars not only supported the clock with its gilded dial but had a ledge encircling it from which a small boy could comfortably dangle his legs and watch the shoppers below.

East of Market Cross was Bridge Street, the thoroughfare that led towards Oxford and London, and most of the im-

portant shops in Stratford were concentrated along its length. Here were the smithies and the taverns, the shoemakers and the bake shops, and also Stratford's four excellent inns. An inn like the Swan could boast of leaded panes and velvet cushions, and its walls were engagingly decorated with pictures of ancient worthies like Tobias [1] dressed in Elizabethan doublet and trunk hose.

Beyond Bridge Street a causeway led to the great stone bridge that Sir Hugh Clopton had built over the river Avon. In those days the Avon was "a river in summer and a little sea in winter" and the parapet of the bridge was low enough so that even the smallest of small boys could see over its edge. Along the river bank between the town and the bridge was Butt Close, where the townsmen were supposed to practice their archery, and beyond that was Bank Croft, where the ducks and cattle and sheep of Stratford had their communal pasture. The practice of archery was not only supposed to distract the citizens' minds from "unlawful" games like bowling and cards but also to fit them for soldiering when the Queen needed them, although the development of gunpowder had made archers obsolete and England's own armament industry had reached such proportions that English mariners complained the enemy was destroying them with guns of English manufacture.

Each of the prosperous inhabitants of Stratford had his own barn and his own garden, and the garden that adjoined the guild buildings was noted for its apples and plums. The town was green and leafy in summer, for there were over a thousand elms in its small confines and forty ash— that wood which "being cut down green it burneth green and bright." Around

From *Shakespeare of London* by Marchette Chute, copyright 1949 by E. P. Dutton & Co., Inc. Reprinted by permission of the publishers.

[1] **Tobias:** a character in the Old Testament of the Bible.

Stratford was farm land, the parallel strips that were still being tilled on the communal system that had served the people well in medieval times. But as a boy grew more adventurous there lay for his delight along the horizon what was now called the Woodland but had been known in ancient times as the Forest of Arden.

As a Stratford boy grew older he found less time for roaming, for school was a serious business in his community. There had always been a free school in Stratford, financed before the Reformation by the Guild of the Holy Cross and since then by borough revenues. The Stratford charter stipulated that the town was to have a "free grammar school for the training and education of children" to be "continued forever," and the boys in Stratford were expected to enter it for a free education as soon as they knew how to read and write.

By the end of the century [1] there was a man in Stratford who taught the children reading and writing while his wife taught needlework, and unless there was a similar arrangement when William Shakespeare was a small boy he probably learned his letters from the parish clerk. The Stratford grammar school was not supposed to handle elementary work of this kind, although it was apparently sometimes forced to assume what it called the "tedious trouble" of teaching the young to read. It was a trouble to the young also, and one weak-minded English uncle of the previous decade spent twenty times as much on sugar plums as on hornbooks before his nephew succeeded in learning his letters.

The hornbook was a slab of wood on which a page full of letters had been fastened and which was covered over with a thin, transparent sheet of horn to protect it from grubby small fingers. Countless generations of children had learned to read clutching the handle of a hornbook and William Shakespeare could hardly have been an exception. From that he probably graduated to *The ABC and Little Catechism,* which gave the youth of England their letters and their religious instruction simultaneously and sold in England at the rate of ten thousand copies in eight months.

Shakespeare learned to form his letters in the way all the little boys in rural districts formed them. The new Italian hand, which corresponds roughly to the modern way of writing, had made great headway in court and city circles, but the medieval way of writing, the one called the secretary hand, was still being used in the country. Some of Shakespeare's fellow dramatists, like George Peele, used the new Italian way of writing; some of them, like Thomas Kyd and George Chapman, used both fashions interchangeably, and at least one of them, Ben Jonson, [2] worked out an efficient compromise between the two. The few signatures which are all that remain of Shakespeare's writing are done in the old-fashioned secretary hand he was taught in Stratford, and it is probable that he did not bother to change it after he came to London.

As soon as he could read and write and knew his Catechism, young William Shakespeare was ready to enter Stratford grammar school. He was the son of one of the most prominent men in Stratford, but he received the same education that was democratically open to every boy in town and there was no charge for the instruction.

The curriculum of Stratford grammar school, like that of every other grammar

---

[1] This refers to the end of the sixteenth century. Shakespeare was born in 1564.

[2] **Ben Jonson:** next to Shakespeare, the most important dramatist of the Elizabethan period.

school in England, was serious, thorough, and dull. There was no attempt whatever to fit the boys for the ordinary life they were going to find when they graduated, for all school theory in England was based on the medieval system. The purpose of schools in the Middle Ages was to turn out learned clerks for church positions, and therefore what the little boys of Renaissance England learned was Latin, more Latin, and still more Latin. About a decade after Shakespeare entered the classroom, a London teacher urged that English should also be taught in the schools, but no one paid any attention to so radical a suggestion.

The chief difference between the education given Shakespeare and that given Geoffrey Chaucer[1] two centuries earlier was that Chaucer's comparatively simple instruction book, called the Donat, had been replaced by an authorized Latin grammar written by William Lily. Lily was the first headmaster of the school at St. Paul's Cathedral, and his book must have made him more cordially hated by harassed seven-year-olds than any man before or since. The whole of the English educational system united to pound Lily's Latin grammar into the heads of the young, and if a schoolboy was wise he resigned himself to having to memorize the whole book.

Not one boy in a hundred had any real use for Latin in his subsequent career, and it is sad to think how the young Quineys and Walkers[2] and Shakespeares worked over their construing in the schoolroom, in what one London teacher compassionately called "an unnatural stillness," while the whole of the sunlit world waited for them outside. One of their number was eventually to become an actor and no doubt the strict training in memory-work did him a certain amount of good, but it is hard to see how their work in the schoolroom really benefited most of them.

In the average grammar school the boys worked at their grammar about four years, although an earlier educationalist had urged a little more consideration of the boy's own point of view. "By the time he cometh to the sweet and pleasant reading of old authors, the sparks of fervent desire for learning is extinct with its burden of grammar." Another reformer agreed that it was "cold and uncomfortable" for both teacher and pupil when grammar was taught without an allied course of reading, but he added gloomily that it was "the common way." It was much easier to teach rules than to give boys a real love of Latin literature, and the average teacher took the easier way.

Here and there an imaginative teacher who loved his work triumphed over Lily and kindled a love of Latin writers in the hearts of the young. William Camden, the great London teacher, lit such a fire in the heart of one of his students that Ben Jonson worshiped both Camden and the classics all his life. Somewhere at Cambridge Christopher Marlowe[3] evidently found a teacher who did the same, but there is no indication that any schoolmaster set off a similar spark in young William Shakespeare. Like Geoffrey Chaucer before him, Shakespeare preferred to approach his Latin authors through a translation whenever he could.

Like Chaucer, Shakespeare's one real love among the schoolroom worthies was

---

[1] **Geoffrey Chaucer:** The first great English poet (1340?–1400), author of *The Canterbury Tales*.

[2] **Quineys and Walkers:** These were names of families who lived in Stratford during Shakespeare's lifetime. The sons of these families, Richard Quiney and Henry Walker, were contemporaries and friends of Shakespeare.

[3] **Christopher Marlowe:** an English dramatist (1564–1593), who, like Jonson, was a friend and contemporary of Shakespeare. He is the author of a number of magnificent tragic dramas.

Above, Shakespeare's birthplace in Stratford-on-Avon, seen from the garden at the rear of the house. Left, student production of a Shakespearean play, given in front of Shakespeare's old school. Below, a desk from Shakespeare's school which is thought to have been used by Shakespeare himself. This desk can be seen today in the house where Shakespeare was born.

Ovid,[1] but it was never difficult to arouse a schoolboy's interest in Ovid. The chief difficulty, rather, was to distract his mind from that amorous and delightful story-teller. Nearly all the mythology that Shakespeare knew came from Ovid's *Metamorphoses*, as did that of most of his fellow writers, but it is evident that Shakespeare was much more familiar with the first book or two than he was with the rest of it and even in the case of Ovid he was not above working with a translation.

Apart from learning to read Latin and write Latin, an English schoolboy was also expected to recite Latin, and here again was an aspect of the curriculum that might conceivably be of some use to a future actor. There was considerable emphasis on good public speaking and a controlled, intelligent use of the voice, and many schoolmasters let their boys act out Latin plays by Plautus and Terence to give them experience in handling the spoken word.

Richard Mulcaster, who was head for many years of the excellent school conducted by the Merchant Tailors in London, always kept the spoken word in the forefront of his mind when he taught Latin. When he expounded the mysteries of punctuation to his classes he did it as a singing teacher might, with the emphasis on "tunable uttering." A parenthesis meant the use of a lower and quicker voice, a comma was a place to catch the breath a little, and a period was a place where the breath could be caught completely. This sort of training would have been of great use to William Shakespeare when he started work as a professional actor and had to learn to translate the words written on a cue sheet into the sound of a living voice, and if he did not learn it from some imaginative teacher in the schoolroom, it was one of the many things he had to pick up for himself after he reached London.

Apart from teaching him Latin, Stratford grammar school taught Shakespeare nothing at all. It did not teach him mathematics or any of the natural sciences. It did not teach him history, unless a few pieces of information about ancient events strayed in through Latin quotations. It did not teach him geography, for the first (and most inadequate) textbook on geography did not appear until the end of the century, and maps and atlases were rare even in university circles. It did not teach him modern languages, for when a second language was taught at a grammar school it was invariably Greek.

What Shakespeare learned about any of these subjects he learned for himself later, in London. London was the one great storehouse in England of living, contemporary knowledge, and in that great city an alert and intelligent man could find out almost anything he wanted to know. It was in London, for instance, that Shakespeare learned French; and French was taught by Frenchmen who worked in competition with each other and used oral, conversational methods that were designed to get colloquial French into the student's head as quickly as possible.

When French was finally accepted into the grammar school curriculum it was subjected to the heavy emphasis on rules and grammar with which the Latin tongue was already burdened, and Shakespeare was probably very fortunate that no one tried to teach him English by the same system. All the rules, the ritual, and the reverent embalming were focused on Latin, and as a result the writers of the late sixteenth century had a lighthearted sense of freedom where their native tongue was concerned because it had never been laid out in the schoolroom and expounded. Much

[1] **Ovid:** a Roman poet.

respect was given to the Latin language, but all the affection, the excited experimentation, and the warm sense of personal ownership went into the English. If a writer needed an effective word, he could not go to a dictionary for it. There were no English dictionaries, although Richard Mulcaster remarked it would be a praiseworthy deed to compile one. The writer could either reach back into his memory, a practice that forced every writer to be also an alert listener, or else he could invent a new word entirely.

There was still some doubt among thoughtful men whether it was quite respectful to the language to use it in so lighthearted a fashion. George Puttenham [1] apologized for using such "strange and unaccustomed" new words as *idiom, method, impression, numerous, penetrate, savage,* and *obscure.* Gabriel Harvey [2] was scolded for using such abnormalities as *theory* and *jovial* and *negotiation;* and Ben Jonson, who could never forget his classical education, was horrified by a fellow playwright who used such outlandish words as *damp, clumsy, strenuous,* and *puffy.*

This use of new words could degenerate into complete confusion in the hands of incompetent writers, but it gave Shakespeare exactly the freedom he needed. He felt at complete liberty to pick up effective new words and combinations of words wherever he could find them, and a play like *Hamlet* is so full of them that it would have made a schoolmaster turn pale if he had had any responsibility for teaching his charges the English language. Fortunately he had no such responsibility, and young William Shakespeare

was free to discover the great reaches of the English language as a freeborn and independent citizen.

Every weekday, summer and winter, from the time when he was about seven years old, young Shakespeare went to school. He walked down Henley Street, turned at the Market Cross, and went the two long blocks to the guild buildings. During most of Shakespeare's boyhood the schoolroom was upstairs over the Council room, except for a short period when it had to be repaired, and the same bell that called William to school every morning called his father about once a month to the Council meeting in one of the rooms downstairs.

No single schoolmaster can be assigned the honor of having given William Shakespeare his schooling, since there happened to be a succession of teachers in Stratford during Shakespeare's boyhood. When he entered school the master was Walter Roche, who left because he was given a rectory. Roche's successor was Simon Hunt, who left in 1575 to become a Jesuit. [3] The teacher for the next four years was Thomas Jenkins, and when Jenkins left his post Shakespeare was fifteen and certainly no longer in school. All these men were university graduates, each of them holding a degree from Oxford, for the pay in Stratford was excellent and the twenty pounds a year that went to the schoolmaster was almost twice what he would have received in a large town like Warwick. All three men were presumably competent and well trained, since there must have been many candidates for the post. It is to be hoped that at least one of them had a spark of Mulcaster's imagination, but they may have been merely the routine pedagogues that the educational system of the time encouraged.

[1] **George Puttenham:** a contemporary of Shakespeare, reputed to be the author of a treatise of English literary criticism.

[2] **Gabriel Harvey:** another contemporary of Shakespeare, a writer of satiric poetry.

[3] **Jesuit** (jezh'o͞o·it): a religious order of the Roman Catholic Church.

Water pageants were a popular form of court entertainment in Elizabethan days. In the woodcut above, Queen Elizabeth I, seated on her throne in the upper left, witnesses a pageant including a floating castle and a group of sea nymphs.

The illustration at the left pictures a typical English inn built around a rectangular courtyard. The Elizabethan acting companies that toured the provinces often played in such courtyards. The spectators stood in the yard or sat in the galleries above.

When a boy had completed the curriculum of the grammar school in Stratford, he would have his head well stocked with the principles of Latin grammar and also with a miscellaneous collection of quotations from Latin authors, designed to illustrate the different parts of speech and supply him with a little moral education besides. He had probably been taught to keep a commonplace book, in which he was encouraged to write down any quotations that pleased him in his reading from ancient authors. He had learned how to make a pen neatly, cutting off the goose feathers with his penknife and softening the nib with his tongue. He had learned to sit upright when he was writing so that the humors of the brain would not fall down into his forehead and affect his eyesight, and he had learned how to endure the discipline of long hours of labor.

The school hours for the average English boy were long, usually extending from seven in the morning to five at night, with two hours off in the middle of the day to go home for dinner. The only difference made by the coming of summer was that the school hours were generally longer because there were more hours of daylight. Since curfew was at eight in the summertime, a well-brought-up little Stratfordian had comparatively few hours to play. For the rest, each small scholar was supposed to supply his own books and satchel and pens and ink, with candles extra in the winter; and, as William Lily opened his grammar by pointing out sternly, he was also supposed to come to school with his face washed and his hair combed, and on no account was he to loiter by the way.

It has been suggested that on one hot evening in July, when William Shakespeare was eleven years old, he was taken to the castle at Kenilworth to see part of the show with which the Earl of Leicester was entertaining Queen Elizabeth. On Monday evening the water devices included a dolphin and a mermaid, and the event is therefore said to be the origin of the lovely lines in *A Midsummer Night's Dream* in which Oberon [1] describes the mermaid singing on the dolphin's back. But the Kenilworth water show was grotesque rather than beautiful, since the mermaid was eighteen feet long and the dolphin twenty-four. Both had actors perched on their backs and were propelled by elaborate mechanical equipment, and except for the fact they both appeared in the same show they had no connection with each other. It is very unlikely, in any case, that Shakespeare would have been allowed to leave school in July and make so long a trip. Fifteen miles in those days was a journey of real magnitude; and since no one in Stratford could have known how charmingly suitable it would have been for England's great future dramatist to meet England's great queen, it must remain exceedingly unlikely that he ever made the trip to Kenilworth at all.

In Stratford itself, young William Shakespeare would have had many opportunities to see public entertainments. Stratford was famous for its fairs, and the people of Warwickshire came from miles around to shop at the special booths and stalls that were set up in Market Street in May and again in September. Wherever there were people in England there were entertainers, and no fair would have been complete without its acrobats and performing animals, any more than without its pies.

Stratford also had its share of regular stage productions. The first of the touring companies of actors came to Stratford the year that Shakespeare's father

[1] **Oberon** (ō'bə·ron): the king of the fairies in Shakespeare's play *A Midsummer Night's Dream*.

was High Bailiff and they were welcomed by him in his official capacity. After that, one of the large companies stopped there every year or so, showing plays at Stratford in their regular yearly tour through the provinces.

The acting companies were rigidly licensed under an Act of Parliament, for nothing could have been more sinister to the Elizabethan mind than any group of men traveling around the country without proper credentials. To escape being listed as vagabonds, each acting company operated under someone's patronage, the smaller groups under local dignitaries or incorporated towns and the larger ones under prominent court officials like the Earl of Leicester or the Earl of Warwick.

When a company of actors arrived in Stratford they first presented themselves before the High Bailiff and showed their credentials so that they could be licensed for playing in town. The first show was put on at the guildhall before the Bailiff and other members of the Council. Admission to the first show was evidently free to the public, since the Council was paying the bill, and there was always an enthusiastic attendance. In Bristol, for instance, when Shakespeare was twelve years old, part of the iron bar on the guildhall door had to be repaired because of "the press of people at the play."

Since William Shakespeare was the son of one of the most prominent of the Council members he probably always had a good place to see and hear. Perhaps, like a small boy named Willis of about his own age in Gloucester, he stood between his father's legs while John Shakespeare sat on one of the benches. The main room of the guildhall made an excellent theater, being long and narrow, with the players acting on a platform at the south end of the hall and using the smaller room, at right angles to it, to change their costumes and wait for their cues.

There must have been a great deal of activity in this improvised tiring room,[1] for the touring companies were small and each actor was expected to play several characters. A company of six players thought nothing of putting on a play like *Horestes,* which called for a cast of twenty-five, and long practice had made them adept at leaping in and out of their costumes and assuming new parts. In the play of *Cambises,* for instance, two actors handled fourteen roles between them, and in *The Repentance of Mary Magdalene* four men wrestled with fourteen parts that included Carnal Concupiscence, Infidelity, Knowledge of Sin, Mary Magdalen, and Christ Jesus.[2] The chief character here was Infidelity, who carried the comedy role known as the Vice; and since vice was always punished in the end while the better and nobler abstractions triumphed, the audience had the comfortable feeling of seeing a play that was "not only godly, learned, and fruitful, but also well furnished with pleasant mirth and pastime."

From the point of view of a small boy the whole thing was evidently pure enchantment. The little boy in Gloucester could still remember, seventy years later, every detail of the show he had seen while he stood between his father's legs. He especially remembered the scene in which the wicked hero was transformed into a swine (being a typical small boy he took a deep interest in the way this was handled with a mask and wires) and the splendid climax in which an actor dressed in blue, portraying End-of-the-World, makes the lovely ladies like Pride and

[1] **tiring room:** a small room, offstage, used as a dressing room.

[2] These characters were found in many early plays. Because such plays aimed at teaching a moral lesson to the audience, they were called *morality plays.*

An illustration from a sixteenth-century edition of *Everyman,* the most famous of the English morality plays.

Luxury vanish from the stage and the hero is carried off howling by devils. The plots of these morality plays lent themselves to a great deal of violent physical action and to the low comedy that English audiences had been trained to expect ever since the old miracle plays [1] were acted in carts in the town streets.

No reasonable man could object to an entertainment that was full of moral lessons and did not disturb those settled principles that the schools and the parents worked so hard to inculcate. If the plays that went on tour did not deal with moral abstractions, they dealt with equally impeccable and improving stories. The subject might be Biblical, like *The Comedy of the Most Virtuous and Godly Susanna,* or it might be classical and introduce characters like Menelaus and Clytemnestra [2] to English country audiences. The most careful of Stratford parents would have been willing to let his son see plays like

these, and even if the boys acted the plots out afterwards in the elm-shaded gardens of Stratford, they could do very little injury to their moral natures.

The effect of these traveling actors on the small boys of Stratford can be measured by the effect of a similar group of English players on another small boy who was Dauphin [3] of France. Louis managed to remain cool and dignified until a moment arrived in the plot when one of the characters had his head cut off. This made a profound impression on the small Dauphin, and for two weeks thereafter his favorite game was playing actor, costuming himself in whatever was handy, taking long strides, and announcing to his mother that he was the whole of the acting company. If the small boys of Stratford played actor for weeks after the players left, they had an advantage over the Dauphin since there were more of them to share the parts, but it is not likely they were any less excited or less impressed than the boy at Fontainebleau. [4]

The actors were made increasingly welcome at Stratford, and soon they were coming at the rate of two companies a year. When Shakespeare was twelve, the companies of both the Earl of Warwick and the Earl of Worcester paid a visit to Stratford. When he was thirteen the Earl of Worcester's men played a return engagement and the town was also honored by a visit from some of the most brilliant actors in England, those under the patronage of the Earl of Leicester. [5]

---

[1] **miracle plays:** dramatizations of the lives of the saints, forerunners of the morality plays described above.

[2] **Menelaus** (men′ə·lā′əs) **and Clytemnestra** (klī′təm·nes′trə): names of two famous characters of ancient Greek legends.

[3] **Dauphin** (dō·faṅ′): a title used from 1349 to 1830 to designate the eldest son of the king of France.

[4] **Fontainebleau** (fôṅ·ten·blō′): a palace which was formerly the home of the kings of France.

[5] **Earl of Leicester** (les′tər): The head of the Earl of Leicester's company was actor James Burbage, whose son Richard became the most famous actor of his day. As a member of Shakespeare's acting company, Richard Burbage played the leading roles in Shakespeare's plays *Hamlet, Othello,* and *King Lear.*

1. Comparatively little is known about the early life of William Shakespeare, but by painstaking research through old records, Marchette Chute has managed to show us what life must have been like when Shakespeare was a boy in Stratford. Do you think she has presented a vivid picture of Shakespeare's early days? Why or why not?

2. What kind of town was Stratford in Shakespeare's boyhood? What facilities were available for recreation? for business? for education?

3. Describe Shakespeare's education at Stratford. In what ways did it differ from your own early education? What was the medieval theory of education that still survived in Shakespeare's time? Do you think the curriculum of the Stratford grammar school was too demanding? Why or why not? How did the teaching method of the Stratford schoolmasters differ from the methods of teachers like William Camden and Richard Mulcaster?

4. In Shakespeare's time, English was used more freely and informally than Latin or French. What was the reason for this? How did Shakespeare benefit from this free and experimental use of English? Miss Chute says that Richard Mulcaster wished someone would compile an English dictionary. What, do you think, are the advantages of having a dictionary of a language?

5. Of Shakespeare's training at school, Miss Chute writes: ". . . it is hard to see how their [the students'] work in the classroom really benefited most of them." Yet Shakespeare learned to write imperishable poetry and other schoolmates surely made their marks on life. Does this lead you to think that someone like Shakespeare would have written great plays no matter what his education was like? Explain your answer.

6. Miss Chute describes in detail the kind of dramatic entertainment that was popular when Shakespeare was a boy. Why do you think she has included all of these details in this biography? Does knowing something about this feature of Elizabethan life help you to understand Shakespeare or his work? Why or why not?

In describing Shakespeare's early life, Marchette Chute uses some terminology that would be easily understood by an Elizabethan or by the English of today. To most Americans, however, many of these terms are unfamiliar. Look up the meaning of each of the terms listed below. To what customs or attitudes do they refer? By what names would Americans today describe these things?

guildhall	secretary hand
parish clerk	humors of the brain
worthies	tiring room
commonplace book	doublet and trunk hose
High Bailiff	

FOR COMPOSITION

Drama was very popular in Elizabethan England, but, as you must have noticed from Miss Chute's account, the plays which enchanted Shakespeare as a boy were very different from the plays we enjoy today. From outside reading and from a review of Miss Chute's description on pages 302–03, write a brief report on the type of drama that was popular when Shakespeare was a boy. Show how these forms of drama differ from the plays and movies of today.

ABOUT THE AUTHOR

Marchette Chute (1909–) was born in Wayzata, Minnesota, and studied at the University of Minnesota. Her early literary works were poems for children called *Rhymes About Ourselves* (1932) and a study of the Bible called *The Search for God* (1941). Her special interest in literary biography began with the publication of *Geoffrey Chaucer of England* (1946). Since that time she has written *Shakespeare of London, Ben Jonson of Westminster,* and *Two Gentlemen: The Lives of George Herbert and Robert Herrick.* Miss Chute's writing is both scholarly and readable. Her vivid style enables her to make the past come alive, and her characters speak and act as if they were our contemporaries. Miss Chute has received numerous awards for both poetry and biography.

Color in Paintings

Color has three main attributes. One is *hue*—the color itself. When we speak of a red barn and a blue sky, we are talking about different hues. How many hues are there? We all know of the "primaries"—red, yellow, and blue—and the "secondaries"—purple, green, and orange. Most color charts represent about eighteen others as well—such "in-between" hues as yellow-orange, yellow-green, and violet-blue. But there is actually an infinite number of other hues in between these that the human eye cannot distinguish.

Another attribute of color is its strength, or degree of *saturation*. Each hue is a "pure" color—a color at full saturation. However, most colors we see are not at full strength. At certain times of day, for instance, the blue of the sky may change to a gray blue, or it may even change completely to gray. At such a moment, its saturation would be zero: all its color (blue) would have disappeared. You can dull any color simply by mixing gray with it. If you mix orange with a medium gray, for instance, you will get a golden brown. If you mix yellow with a very light gray, you will get beige.

Every color, whether pure or mixed, has *tone*. Tone refers to the degree of a color's darkness or lightness. When we speak of a dark red barn, we refer not only to its hue (red), but also to its tonal value (dark). Some hues are naturally darker in tonal value than others. Purple-blue is darker than red, for example, whereas red is darker than orange.

In painting a picture, artists take all of these attributes into account. Even though they may want to reproduce colors they see in everyday life, they must change them so that their pictures will have balance and unity. A painting is not simply a mirror of the real world: it is a creation in its own right, with its own special kind of logic.

Now let us see how six different artists have used color. First, look at Milton Avery's painting called *The Fencers* (PLATE 1). You can see at once that its color scheme is rather limited. The picture is dominated by large areas of gray greenish-blue and a kind of salmon pink. But the range of tones is extremely wide—from white to almost black. Most areas, though, are fairly light, with little saturation. The salmon-pink ground, for example, is a mixture of orange-red and lots of very light gray. Avery used the darker tones as accents. Notice that he has repeated the dark gray of the left fencer first in the mat at lower right, and then again on the helmet of the other fencer, thus tying the picture together in a triangle of dark tones.

In Claude Monet's *La Grenouillère* (PLATE 2), we find more hues and many more shades of hues. However, the range of tones from dark to light is much more limited. The only colors that are close to full strength are the yellow reflections in the water and the orange stripes on the boats. Yet despite the grayed look of most of the colors and the narrow range of tones, Monet has made his picture appear lively and interesting. By grouping his darker colors mainly around the edges of the picture, he has emphasized the sparkling light on the surface of the water.

Painters often use effects of light and shadow as dynamic elements of composition. In Edgar Degas's picture *The Rehearsal* (PLATE 3), for instance, we sense the movement of light across a room as it pours in through the windows from outside. Degas has combined this right-to-left movement of light with a pointing accent of color (the red-orange on one of the dancer's legs) to help counterbalance the extreme off-center grouping of the figures. And notice that Degas has painted fairly strong colors into the shadows along the wall between the windows—different colors in each section to harmonize with the different colors of the figures in front.

Sometimes a painter will use color mainly to express mood. For example, in an early painting called *The Old Guitarist* (PLATE 4), Pablo Picasso used many tones of gray-blue to suggest the sadness and despair of a lonely, impoverished old man. In a later painting called *Dog and Cock* (PLATE 5), Picasso created an entirely different kind of mood with brighter colors and a much wider range of tones. The way he has set off sharp patterns of white against darker tones gives this picture an extremely vibrant, lively quality.

At first glance the abstract painting by Josef Albers in PLATE 6 seems extremely simple. But appearances are often deceptive. The title of this painting is *White Front,* yet the "white" is actually a light gray. The darker yellow seems denser and heavier than the bright yellow in the background, yet the two small rectangles of heavy yellow appear to be floating in space. The more you study this picture, the more surprises you will discover.

PLATE 1. MILTON AVERY (American, 1893–1965): *The Fencers*. 1944. Oil on canvas, 49 x 32 inches. (The Santa Barbara Museum of Art, California)

PLATE 2. CLAUDE MONET (French, 1840–1926): *La Grenouillère*. About 1866–67. Oil on canvas, 29$\frac{3}{8}$ x 39$\frac{1}{4}$ inches. (The Metropolitan Museum of Art, New York. Bequest of Mrs H. O

308

PLATE 3. EDGAR DEGAS (French, 1834–1917): *The Rehearsal*. About 1879. Oil on canvas, 18¾ x 23¾ inches. (Copyright The Frick Collection, New York)

PLATE 4. PABLO PICASSO (French, 1881–1973): *The Old Guitarist*. 1903. Oil on wood, 47¾ x 32¼ inches. (Courtesy of The Art Institute of Chicago)

PLATE 5. PABLO PICASSO (French, 1881–1973): *Dog and Cock*. 1921. Oil on canvas, 60⅞ x 30⅛ inches. (Yale University Art Gallery, New Haven, Conn., Gift of Stephen Carlton Clark)

PLATE 6. JOSEF ALBERS (American, 1888–1976): *White Front.* 1958. Oil on masonite, 23½ x 27 inches. (Collection of the University of Michigan Museum of Art, Ann Arbor)

Charles Dickens: The Boy of the London Streets

RUPERT SARGENT HOLLAND

T HE LITTLE FELLOW who worked all day long in the tumble-down old house by the river Thames pasting oil-paper covers on boxes of blacking [1] fell ill one afternoon. One of the workmen, a big man named Bob Fagin, made him lie down on a pile of straw in the corner and placed blacking bottles filled with hot water beside him to keep him warm. There he lay until it was time for the men to stop work, and then his friend Fagin, looking down upon the small boy of twelve, asked if he felt able to go home. The boy got up looking so big-eyed, white-cheeked, and thin that the man put his arm about his shoulder.

"Never mind, Bob; I think I'm all right now," said the boy. "Don't you wait for me; go on home."

"You ain't fit to go alone, Charley. I'm comin' along with you."

" 'Deed I am, Bob. I'm feelin' as spry as a cricket." The little fellow threw back his shoulders and headed for the stairs.

[1] **blacking:** shoe polish.

"Charles Dickens: The Boy of the London Streets" by Rupert Sargent Holland from *St. Nicholas Magazine*, copyright 1909 by The Century Company. Reprinted by permission of the publishers, Appleton-Century-Crofts, Inc.

Fagin, however, insisted on keeping him company; and so the two, the shabbily dressed undersized youth and the big strapping man, came out into the murky London twilight and took their way over the Blackfriars Bridge.

"Been spendin' your money at the pastry shops, Charley, again? That's what was the matter with you, I take it."

The boy shook his head. "No, Bob. I'm trying to save. When I get my week's money, I put it away in a bureau drawer, wrapped in six little paper packages, with a day of the week on each one. Then I know just how much I've got to live on, and Sundays don't count. Sometimes I do get hungry, though; so hungry! Then I look in at the windows and play at being rich."

They crossed the bridge, the boy's big eyes seeming to take note of everything, the man, duller-witted, listening to his chatter. Several times the boy tried to say good night, but Fagin would not be shaken off. "I'm goin' to see you to your door, Charley lad," he said each time.

At last they came into a little street near the Southwark Bridge. The boy stopped by the steps of a house. "Here 't 's, Bob. Good night. It was good of you to take the trouble for me."

"Good night, Charley."

The boy ran up the steps, and, as he noticed that Fagin still stopped, he pulled the doorbell. Then the man went on down the street. When the door opened, the boy asked if Mr. Fagin lived there, and being told that he did not, said he must have made a mistake in the house. Turning about, he saw that his friend had disappeared around a corner. With a little smile of triumph, he made off in the other direction.

The door of the Marshalsea Prison stood open like a great black mouth. The boy, tired with his long tramp, was glad to reach it and to run in. Climbing several long flights of stairs, he entered a room on the top story where he found his family, his father, a tall pompous-looking man dressed in black, his mother, an amiable but extremely fragile woman, and a small brother and sister seated at a table eating supper. The room was very sparsely furnished; the only bright spot in it was a small fire in a rusty grate, flanked by two bricks to prevent burning too much fuel.

There was a vacant place at the table for Charles, and he sat down upon a stool and ate as ravenously as though he had not tasted food for months. Meanwhile the tall man at the head of the table talked solemnly to his wife at the other end, using strange long words which none of the children could understand.

Supper over, Mr. and Mrs. Dickens (for that was their name) and the two younger children sat before the tiny fire, and Mr. Dickens talked of how he might raise enough money to pay his debts, leave the prison, and start fresh in some new business. Charles had heard these same plans from his father's lips a thousand times before, and so he took from the cupboard an old book which he had bought at a little secondhand shop a few days before, a small tattered copy of *Don Quixote*,[1] and read it by the light of a tallow candle in the corner.

The lines soon blurred before the boy's tired eyes, his head nodded, and he was fast asleep. He was awakened by his father's deep voice. "Time to be leaving, Charles, my son. You have not forgotten that my pecuniary situation prevents my choosing the hour at which I shall close the door of my house. Fortunately it is a predicament which I trust will soon be obviated to our mutual satisfaction."

---

[1] *Don Quixote* (dôn kē·hō′tä): a novel by the Spanish writer Cervantes, considered one of the finest literary works of the world.

The small fellow stood up, shook hands solemnly with his father, kissed his mother, and took his way out of the great prison. Open doors on various landings gave him pictures of many peculiar households; sometimes he would stop as though to consider some unusually puzzling face or figure.

Into the night again he went, and wound through a dismal labyrinth of the dark and narrow streets of old London. Sometimes a rough voice or an evil face would frighten him, and he would take to his heels and run as fast as he could. When he passed the house where he had asked for Mr. Fagin, he chuckled to himself; he would not have had his friend know for worlds that his family's home was the Marshalsea Prison.

Even that room in the prison, however, was more cheerful than the small back attic chamber where the boy fell asleep for the second time that night. He slept on a bed made up on the floor, but his slumber was no less deep on that account.

The noise of workmen in a timber yard under his window woke Charles when it seemed much too dark to be morning. It was, however, and he was quickly dressed and making his breakfast from the penny cottage loaf of bread, a section of cream cheese, and a small bottle of milk, which were all he could afford to buy from the man who rented him the room. Then he took the roll of paper marked with the name of the day from the drawer of his bureau and counted out the pennies into his pocket. They were not many; he had to live on seven shillings [1] a week, and he tucked them away very carefully in a pocket lest he lose them and have to do without his lunch.

He was not yet due at the blacking factory, but he hurried away from his room and joined the crowd of early morning people already on their way to work. He went down the embankment along the Thames until he came to a place where a bench was set in a corner of a wall. This was his favorite lounging place; London Bridge was just beyond, the river lay in front of him, and he was far enough away from people to be secure from interruption. As he sat there watching the bridge and the Thames, a small girl came to join him. She was no bigger than he, perhaps a year or two older, but her face was already shrewd enough for that of a grown-up woman. She was the maid-of-all-work at a house in the neighborhood, and she had fallen into the habit of stopping to talk for a few moments with the boy on her way to work in the morning. She liked to listen to his stories. This was his hour for inventing them. He could spin wonderful tales about London Bridge, the Tower, and the wharves along the river. Sometimes he made up stories about the people who passed in front of them, and

[1] **shilling:** a British coin; the shilling was worth about 25¢ at the time.

they were such astonishing stories that the girl remembered them all day as she worked in the house. He seemed to believe them himself; his eyes would grow far away and dreamy and his words would run on and on until a neighboring clock brought him suddenly back to his own position.

"You do know a heap o' things, don't you?" said the little girl, lost in admiration. "I'd rather have a shillin', though, than all the fairy tales in the world."

"I wouldn't," said Charles stoutly. "I'd rather read books than do anything else."

"You've got to eat, though," objected his companion; "and books won't make you food. 'T ain't common sense." She relented in an instant. "It's fun, though Charley Dickens. Good-by till tomorrow."

Charles went on down to the old blacking factory by Hungerford Stairs, a ramshackle building almost hanging over the river, damp and overrun with rats. His place was in a recess of the counting room on the first floor, and as he covered the bottles with the oil-paper tops and tied them on with a string, he could look from time to time through a window at the slow coal barges swinging down the river.

There were very few boys about the place. At lunch time he would wander off by himself and, selecting his meal from a careful survey of several pastry cooks' windows, invest his money for the day in fancy cakes or a tart. He missed the company of friends his own age. Even Fanny, his oldest sister, he only saw on Sundays, when she came back to the Marshalsea from the place where she worked to spend the day with her family. It was only grown-up people that he saw most of the time, and they were too busy with their own affairs to take much interest in the small shabby boy who looked

just like any one of a thousand other children of the streets. In all the men at the factory it was only the big clumsy fellow named Fagin who would stop to chat with the lad. So it was that Charles was forced to make friends with whomever he could, people of any age or condition; and was driven to spend much of his spare time roaming about the streets, lounging by the river, reading stray books by a candle in the prison or in the little attic where he slept. It was not a boyhood that seemed to promise much.

In time the boy left the factory and tried being a lawyer's clerk, then a reporter, and at last wrote a book of his own. The book was *Pickwick Papers,* and it was so original that people clamored for more. Then the young man took note of all the strange types of people among whom he had lived as a boy, and those days of poverty and drudgery were turned to wonderful account because he could write of such people and such scenes as he remembered them. The little maid-of-all-work became the "Marchioness" in the *Old Curiosity Shop,* Bob Fagin loaned his name to *Oliver Twist,* and in *David Copperfield* we read the story of the small boy who had to fight his way through London alone. Those days of his boyhood had given him a deep insight into human nature, into the humor and pathos of other people's lives; and it was that rare insight that enabled him to become in time one of the greatest of all English writers, Charles Dickens, the beloved novelist of the Anglo-Saxon people.

1. At the beginning of this selection, Bob Fagin walks young Charley home. What does this account tell you about Dickens's poverty? What does it tell you about Fagin's attitude toward his young friend? about Dickens's feeling of shame?

2. How does the author of this selection show you that Charles Dickens loved to read? How does he show that the boy liked to observe things? Contrast Dickens's attitude toward books with that of the servant girl.

3. In the last paragraph, the author tells us something of Dickens's future. Does he suggest that Dickens's sufferings during childhood were the main reasons for his later success as a novelist? What personal qualities do you think also helped to account for his success?

4. The author of this biographical sketch tells us that Charles Dickens used real people as models for characters in his novels. Do you think that good novelists like Dickens reproduce characters exactly as they are in real life? Do you think imagination also plays a part in the creation of characters? What details in this account indicate that Dickens had a rich imagination even as a boy?

5. Dickens's parents had been sent to Marshalsea Prison, where debtors were confined. Do you think it is right to confine people to prison for nonpayment of debts? Why or why not? Investigate the subject of debtors' prisons, particularly Marshalsea, and be prepared to discuss the effect of confining families to the prison.

LANGUAGE AND VOCABULARY

Define each italicized word in the phrases and sentences below. What does each word suggest about the London that Charles Dickens knew as a child?

"into the *murky* London twilight . . ."

"The room was very *sparsely* furnished . . ."

"through a *dismal labyrinth* of the dark and narrow streets . . ."

"a *ramshackle* building almost hanging over the river . . ."

FOR COMPOSITION

1. Note the organization of the account you have just read:

   a. first, it presents a series of scenes to illustrate an average day in Dickens's life;

   b. then, it briefly summarizes Dickens's boyhood;

   c. finally, it gives a quick glimpse into Dickens's future.

Which paragraphs in the selection cover these three categories? Using a similar organization, write a short biographical essay about a prominent person. Use the research facilities of your library to gather facts needed to fill in items *b* and *c*. Then after checking all of your biographical facts, let your own imagination help you to fill in the various details for item *a*.

2. As he took us through a typical day with young Charles Dickens, the author carefully described the sights that Charley saw. As a result, he has given us a good picture of the London that Dickens knew so well. Write an essay about a typical day in your own life. Present a series of scenes which illustrate where you go during the day and whom and what you see. Take special care to give your reader a clear description of your daily surroundings.

ABOUT THE AUTHOR

Rupert Sargent Holland (1878–1952), born in Louisville, Kentucky, knew from the time he was ten that he wished to become a writer. At Harvard University he was an editor and writer for no less than three campus publications. Eventually he became a lawyer and settled in Philadelphia. Throughout his life, however, he maintained his literary interests. He wrote more than fifty books of history and fiction, many of them appearing in the celebrated *St. Nicholas Magazine*. The subjects of his stories ranged from the adventures of Boy Scouts and knights of old to the daring deeds of pirates. His *Historic Boyhoods* (1909) and *Historic Girlhoods* (1910) contain biographical sketches like "Charles Dickens: The Boy of the London Streets."

Mark Twain

STEPHEN LEACOCK

LIFE ON THE MISSISSIPPI, 1857–1861

WHEN THE youthful Sam Clemens turned his back on printing to follow his fortune on the river and in the West, he may be said, in a modern overworked phrase, to have "found himself." Put very simply, he turned into Mark Twain.

It was the West, the river and the prairie, the Nevada desert and the Rocky Mountains and the sunlit shores of the Pacific, and with it the new civilization of the West, raw but virile, that nurtured the genius that never could have blossomed in a New York boarding house or a Philadelphia printing room. The West made Mark Twain. All that he wrote has its basis there. It supplies the point of view, the "eye of innocence," with which he was able later on to look upon Europe. His western life began on the Mississippi River. It resumed the play of childhood, broken ten years before.

Readers of the book that was published later as *Life on the Mississippi* do not need to be reminded of the romance, the interest, and the humors of Mark Twain's pilot days. He has told the story so well that no one can follow him. The fascination of the river steamers, the pomp and luxury with which they seemed to glitter

in an age of ox wagons, mules, frame houses, and log churches, make the position of the pilot, seated sky-high in the pilothouse, almost one of majesty. Mark Twain, as a young man, had no higher ambition than to go on the river as a pilot. No doubt, in the dull hours of trying to set "10,000 ems [1] of type a day," he often dreamed himself just such a sky-high pilot, the envy of mankind. In vain he had often sought an opening. And now by chance fate threw it in his way when he was stranded in New Orleans looking vainly toward South America. Chance threw him into the company of one Mr. Horace Bixby, a famous pilot of his day. and afterwards his lifelong friend. He agreed with the young man to "teach him the Mississippi River from New Orleans to St. Louis" for the sum of five hundred dollars chargeable against his future wages.

Mark Twain records how he "entered

[1] **em:** a unit of measurement in printing. A pica em is approximately one sixth of an inch.

This drawing of a pilot house is from the original edition of *Life on the Mississippi*.

on the small enterprise of 'learning' twelve or thirteen hundred miles of the Mississippi River" with easy confidence, and records how he felt disillusioned, appalled, and hopeless to find that he must know the river not only by day but in total darkness, not only upwards but downwards, not only at high water but at any water; must learn to follow all the shifts of sand bars and snags, and that, too, at a day when the Mississippi bore neither buoys nor lights to indicate its tortuous channels. "If my ears hear aright," he reflected, in the course of his early instruction, "I have not only to get the names of all the towns and islands and bends, but I must get up a warm personal acquaintance with every old snag and one-limbed cottonwood and obscure woodpile that ornaments the banks of this river for twelve hundred miles!"

What is more, he did it. Within eighteen months he got his license; before the job ended (with the War Between the States) he was second to few on the river. His knowledge of the great river and his abiding feeling for it became part of his life and the inspiration, as in the pages of *Huckleberry Finn,* of the finest of his work.

From his Mississippi days Samuel Clemens also carried away his pen name of Mark Twain.

The origin of the *nom de plume* [1] runs thus: "Mark Twain" is the pilot's designation for two fathoms of water. Now it happened that there was in Sam Clemens's pilot days an ancient and experienced pilot, a Captain Sellers, who sometimes contributed to the New Orleans papers little bits of wisdom and forecast about the river, as crude in form as they were valuable in fact. These contributions to the press were signed "Mark Twain."

[1] *nom de plume:* French expression for pen name.

A steamboat on the Mississippi River.

Clemens, still something of a journalist at heart, wrote a little burlesque of his senior's prophecies which called forth a laugh that echoed up the Mississippi—and incidentally broke old Sellers's heart with its ridicule. Young Clemens learned forever a lesson in the cruelty of "fun," and seldom sinned again. But later on, when Sellers was dead and beyond injury, he annexed the pen name for himself.

Mark Twain's pilot days were ended by the outbreak of the War Between the States and the blockade of the river. He succeeded in getting north from New Orleans to his own state on the last boat that got up the river (January 1861). The part he took at the opening of the war was unheroic if not inglorious. He enlisted, as a Confederate, in some sort of irregular band which professed to be cavalry. Their aim was to "liberate the soil of Missouri" —from what, it was not clearly understood.

But Mark Twain dropped out of the conflict almost at once and saw nothing of warfare. He himself has narrated the episode with that characteristic mixture of fact and exaggeration which baffles foreign readers in all his "western" books, in his sketch called *A Campaign That Failed.*

But the truth is that his heart was not in the war on either side. His common sense showed him that the war, in spite of the urgent denials of President Lincoln and the rest, had something to do with slavery. He could not fight to maintain *that*. But he was equally far from being a "Yankee." His brief sojourn as a youth at New York and Philadelphia was that of a stranger in a strange land. Of New England and its traditions of liberty, piety, intolerance, and "culture" he as yet knew nothing at all; nor ever sympathized with it later. His heart was neither in the North nor the South, but in the new West.

Thither he decided to go. His older brother, Orion Clemens, had contrived to secure an appointment as secretary of the new territory of Nevada. Sam Clemens offered to go along with his brother as "private secretary to the secretary," an office which he himself describes as a "unique sinecure," there being "nothing to do and no salary." Indeed, it was Sam Clemens's savings as a pilot which financed the journey to the West, his brother Orion being invited by the United States, as was Mr. Pickwick [1] by the Pickwick Club, to travel at his own expense.

These, of course, were the days of the rise of the American West, from a vast untraversed wilderness to an El Dorado [2] of gold and silver. The gold discoveries in California had started the "forty-niners" on the trail. In the decade following, a flock of prospectors found their way into the mountains and disclosed the fabulous wealth of silver-bearing lodes of the district of the Carson Valley, a part of the Mormon territory of Utah. It was the organization of this district as the territory of Nevada which gave to the two Clemens brothers the opportunity of taking part in the western movement. To get to Nevada they must go overland by the stage. There was as yet no railway across the continent, nor was there till some years after the War Between the States. To reach California one might make the stormy voyage around Cape Horn; or choose the dangerous Isthmus route, by Panama or Nicaragua; or the stage route over the prairies and mountains. For Nevada the stage route—only seventeen hundred miles!—was the obvious choice.

Behold, then, the Clemens brothers mounting the coach at St. Jo,[3] Missouri, climbing up on the mail sacks to bid farewell to warfare in the East and seek peace among the savages.

ROUGHING IT IN THE WEST, 1861–1866

Orion Clemens, secretary for the territory of Nevada, and his brother Sam, ex-pilot and retired Confederate soldier, set out from St. Jo for Carson City, Nevada, on the 26th of July 1861. Before them was seventeen hundred miles of prairie, mountain, and desert, and nineteen days of glorious transit.

Mark Twain, in his book called *Roughing It,* has recalled in his own way his experience of the journey. There is no doubt of the exhilaration, the excitement, the thrill of it. But his account of it, like all his western books, is a standing perplexity to many of his British admirers. Where do

[1] **Mr. Pickwick:** a character in *The Pickwick Papers* by Charles Dickens.

[2] **El Dorado:** Spanish for "the gilded," a name used to refer to any place of great richness.

[3] **St. Jo:** a familiar name for the city of St. Joseph.

the facts end and the lies began? How much is statistical fact and how much is sheer exuberant exaggeration? For instance, is there, asks the reader, such an animal as the "Jackass Rabbit"? Is it true that such an animal sits and "thinks about its sins," and then moves off so fast that "long after he is out of sight you can hear him whizz"? Many British readers have felt that this is open to doubt.

Or take the account of the Mormon settlement at Salt Lake. Is it really true that Brigham Young[1] looked round to find one of his children and then gave up and said, "I thought I would have known the little cub again, but I don't"? Seems a little hard to believe, doesn't it? Or again, is the water in the Humbolt county so full of alkali that it is like lye? or the water in Lake Tahoe so clear that one can see through eighty feet of it? or is there a "washoe" wind which upsets stage-coaches and which blows so hard in Carson City as to account for the prevalence of so many baldheaded people, and which is described as a "soaring dust drift about the size of the United States"?

In this wonderland of marvel and adventure the American reader easily finds his way. He knows by instinct that Mark Twain did *not* hear the same story told about Horace Greeley[2] four hundred and eighty-four times; and he knows, on the other hand, that the claims staked out on the Ophir mine *were* worth four thousand dollars a foot; and that Mark and his friends *were* caught at night in a snowstorm and *did* actually give themselves up for lost and huddle to sleep in the snow, waking to find a hotel forty-five feet away. But he does not believe the story, told in

another connection, of the group of congressmen snowbound on a western train, driven at last to cannibalism and making their choice of successive victims with the proper forms of legislative procedure. One is reminded of poor John Bright's[3] perplexity over hearing Mark Twain's contemporary, Artemus Ward,[4] lecture in London. "Many of the young man's statements," he said, "appear overdrawn and open to question." Mark Twain himself has humorously explained this western method of his narration. "I speak," he says in the *Innocents Abroad,* "of the north shore of Lake Tahoe, where one can count the scales on a trout at a depth of a hundred and eighty feet. I have tried to get this statement off at par here [he is writing from Europe], but with no success; so I have been obliged to negotiate it at fifty percent discount. At this rate I find some takers; perhaps the reader will receive it on the same terms, ninety feet instead of a hundred and eighty." What is one to make of this? It seems to be giving the reader "what the traffic will bear."

But though overdrawn in the single statement, Mark Twain's western writings give in their entirety a wonderful and fascinating picture of the new land of hope. It has all passed away so long ago and the country changed so completely that perhaps the fascination is all the greater. "Where once the silent prairie saw the Indian and the scout, the Swede sets rows of cabbage out,"—so has a later songster chronicled the passing of frontier west.

Mark Twain's western life lasted, in all, some five and a half years. From his sinecure duties as secretary he turned to mining, caught for a time the fever of the

---

[1] **Brigham Young** (1801–1877): leader of the Mormon community.

[2] **Horace Greeley** (1811–1872): American journalist and political leader who founded the New York *Tribune*.

[3] **John Bright** (1811–1889): English orator and political figure.

[4] **Artemus Ward** (1834–1867): pseudonym of Charles Farrar Browne, an American humorist.

day, and once only missed a fortune by quitting his washing out of pay dirt a few bucketsful too soon. By a natural and easy transition he turned to journalism. These were the palmy days of the little local paper, favored by isolation, springing up as easily as mushrooms and cultivated by hand. Such papers were the natural ground for local jests and squibs, and the practical jokes and hoaxes which passed for fun with the people of eighty years ago.

Sam Clemens, working as a surface miner, began contributing a little to a paper called the *Territorial Enterprise,* published by Joe Goodman at Virginia City. The editor—who was also the proprietor—was struck by the quality of the sketches, and sent to the writer a proposal to join in the editorship at a salary of twenty-five dollars a week. Clemens dropped the pick and shovel, walked a hundred and thirty miles to take over the job, and with that stepped into a new life.

At the time when Sam Clemens abandoned mining and betook himself definitely to journalism (August 1862), he was twenty-six years old. He was a robust-looking young man with a mop of sandy hair turning to auburn and a blue eye filled with life and intelligence. In his infancy he had been a puny child, but the outdoor life of farm and bush and river had done its work and had presently endowed him with that deep-seated energy and vital power which is the birthright of the frontiersman.

As a young and rising pilot he had liked to make himself in point of dress a mirror of fashion. As a miner he did the exact opposite, outdoing his fellows in the careless roughness of his dress and the lazy slouch of his walk. He possessed, and accentuated by use, a slow and drawling speech. In short, he tried to make himself a "character," and succeeded to the full measure of his wish. A large part of his popularity and his local reputation in his Nevada days sprang from the attraction of this easy and careless manner and appearance. Second nature though it became, there was beneath it an eager and a restless mind, filled in his mining days with the fever of the search for gold, dreaming of fortune. At times even his robust health broke under the strain of the intensity of his pursuit of fortune.

But the outside world saw nothing of this. By nature easy and optimistic, on the surface at least, he enjoyed at this time all the careless exuberance of the morning of life, while his easy disposition and his peculiar cast of thought and drollery of speech endeared him to those about him. Many of the friends he made at this time he made for life, such as Horace Bixby, his pilot master, Joe Goodman and Steve Gillis of the *Enterprise.*

By disposition Mark Twain was peaceful rather than belligerent. He lived in a rough world among rough men, with untamed Indians, desperadoes, and outlaws as part of the environment of a western life. Under such circumstances no one could venture to be timorous, but Mark was at least not looking for a fight. He himself has described his feelings on finding himself in close contact with Slade, the most notorious "bad man" and "dead shot" of the West—afterwards to be hanged by the Vigilantes of Montana. Slade was at that time in charge of one of the eating places of the Overland Company. "He was about to take some coffee," says the author of *Roughing It,* "when he saw that my cup was empty. He politely offered to fill it, but although I wanted it, I politely declined. I was afraid he had not killed anybody that morning and might be needing diversion."

Never was man more happily cast in his lot than young Sam Clemens when he

The press room of the *Territorial Enterprise*.

joined the *Territorial Enterprise*. If he had become a reporter on the staff of an ordinary paper, he would have sickened rapidly at the drudgery of the task, the circumscribed round of duty, the necessity of carrying out the commands and ideas of other men. In fact, he did so sicken of it when later he held such a position as a reporter in San Francisco, and even as an editor and part-proprietor in Buffalo. But the *Enterprise* was an entirely different matter. The public of the roaring mining settlements cared nothing about foreign dispatches and world politics. Even the sound of the great war tearing the soil of the continent came faintly across the intervening two thousand miles. What the readers wanted was local stuff—news of robberies, scraps, lucky finds—and above all, such was the mood of the time and place, local "fun" about "local" characters,

personal touches, practical jokes, lies, and interchange of sarcastic "cracks" between rival papers. For all this stuff "Mark Twain" and his fellows were given a free hand. They wrote what they felt like writing; they were not so much "reporters" as "minstrels." Looking back now on the surviving fragments of what Mark Twain wrote then, we can see emerging in it the outline of a clear and beautiful style, we can see already a striking power of phrase to convey the sights and sounds of nature. But we could hardly see all this except in the light of what happened after. In and of themselves Mark Twain's western sketches are of no account. Here, for example, is the "Petrified Man," which set the camp in a roar because they appreciated it as the "crack" at the local coroner who was supposed to hold an inquest over a body turned to rock centuries ago. But the story got somehow into the eastern papers as a fact, and that to the western mind was funnier still. The people in the West at that time seemed to have been moved to Homeric laughter [1] every time they told a huge lie and got someone to believe it. Here again is "My Bloody Massacre," as entirely imaginary as the "Petrified Man," but meant as a slap against a California mining company. The terrific joke lay in the fact that the "massacre" was committed—in the story—at a place where it couldn't have happened. The eastern papers, not knowing the locality, copied the story as an item of crime, at which the West slapped Mark on the back and roared again.

Into such life and such work the character of Sam Clemens fitted as into a mold. His skits and "take-offs" and "write-ups" became the delight of the territory. When he presently went to Carson City to "write up" the legislature, he became about as important as the legislature itself and far more popular.

This may well have been the happiest time of Mark Twain's life. He and his fellow minstrels led a roaring life, painting the town red, drinking imported champagne at the French restaurant, playing cards all night and practical jokes all day. Into their midst one day blew the young man Charles F. Browne (Artemus Ward), for whom the world still has a smile and a tear. He was of the same stamp and kind as Clemens, but his feet were already higher on the ladder of success. He was "lecturing" in his own droll way, about anything or nothing, making money, touching Heaven and raising Hell. He "caught on" instantly to Mark Twain, not as a local "cut-up," but as a real genius—

urged him to strike out, to come East, to conquer the world.

There is something in the life of a new and roaring settlement—a mining town, a boom town—cut off from the rest of the world, which intensifies local interest, local character, and local personality. All men seem giants. All character is exceptional. All jokes become a roar. All lives appear intense. All episodes become Homeric and historic. Read, if one will, the history of early San Francisco or talk with the surviving old-timers of the Manitoba boom.

Such was the setting supplied for Mark Twain by the environment of Virginia City. "Mark Twain" he was now by deliberate designation. The name was first signed to an *Enterprise* article of February 2, 1863. Henceforth he was Mark for the West.

The merry journalistic life at Virginia City was ended in a duel, the outcome of some particularly insulting jokes. How serious or how comic the duel was, heaven only knows. The account given in *Roughing It* is at least, like all else in that great work, partly true. But the new Territory in a moral moment had passed a law against dueling, and Mark Twain had to "skip out." He skipped to San Francisco. There he got a real place as a real reporter on the *Call,* a job which soon put the iron into his soul. It was no part of his nature to work at a routine task in a routine way. The management of the *Call* soon found him listless and careless in his work and "let him go." But he stayed on in San Francisco for a while—according to his own account, a poor outcast mendicant on the fringe of want. But this is only a legend, the western lie reasserting itself. In reality he never lacked the means of support; he wrote daily "letters" for his old paper, the *Enterprise,* and did some "pieces" for the *Californian Maga-*

[1] **Homeric** (hō·mer′ik) **laughter:** uproarious and irrepressible laughter. Something that is "Homeric" is so large in size that it is suggestive of the epic tales told by the ancient Greek writer Homer.

zine, and did very well. More than that, he was thrown in with Bret Harte [1] and the group of young men whose genius was ripening under the favoring isolation of the Pacific coast.

But again his journalism got him into trouble. His letters to the Virginia City *Enterprise* denouncing municipal corruption in San Francisco hurt the feelings of the city police. They decided to make it hot for him, on which Mark Twain again skipped out, this time to the hills. Here he found refuge at the mining camp of Jim Gillis, the "truthful James" of Bret Harte, a brother of the Steve Gillis of Nevada. Here and in the nearby Calaveras County Mark Twain spent the rainy winter of 1864–65, scratching round for surface gold and listening to the endless yarns of the miners of Angel's Camp (see Bret Harte for *Abner Dean of Angel's*). Here was a solemn jackass who used to repeat to the point of weariness a solemn story about a frog—a jumping frog into which someone put shot to shut it out in what the Germans would call a frog-jump-money-bet-competition, and the English an "open frog jump." Mark Twain wrote up the story and sent it to New York for Artemus Ward's funny book. It missed the book, drifted into a newspaper, and became the famous "Jumping Frog"— vastly admired by those who haven't read it. But long before the "Jumping Frog" had found its way into print, its author had thrown down pick and shovel (missing a snug little fortune by one bucketful of dirt) and drifted back to San Francisco.

Here then was Mark Twain at the age of thirty, the period of his western life drawing to a close, his career of success about to begin. His biographers have greatly exaggerated the amount of his achievement at this period. His western success as a journalist and a wit was purely local. A few of his "pieces" had drifted into the eastern papers, but the world at large had never heard of him.

Indeed, nothing that he had written was of any real value. The "Jumping Frog" he himself declared to be "a villainous backwoods sketch," and he was just about right. We are told that when it appeared in the New York press it set all America in a roar. This is nonsense. Even the America of 1865 did not roar so easily as that. The legend rests on the phrase of a California correspondent in New York who sent home items to a home paper, and is merely the kind of legend that grows up round the life story of a great man. The truth is that Mark Twain was practically unknown, and deserved to be.

But now things changed. A San Francisco newspaper offered the young man a job as a special correspondent to go forth and "write up" the Sandwich Islands, in those days (1865) an unknown paradise, lost in the Pacific. Mark Twain undertook the task and carried it out with wonderful success; saw, traversed, explored, and described the islands as no one else could have done; and sent also to his paper, by a piece of journalistic good luck, the first news of a disaster at sea— a "scoop" of the first magnitude. His Sandwich Islands letters attracted great attention in California. They well deserved it. Apart from any incidental humor, they reveal that power of vivid description, that marvelous facility in conveying the sights and sounds in nature, which henceforth constitutes one of the distinctive charms of Mark Twain's work. He returned to San Francisco in a blaze of glory.

The blaze was rapidly turned to a conflagration. His friends persuaded him to

[1] **Bret Harte** (1836–1902): American journalist and writer of short stories about the gold rush period in the Far West.

give a lecture on his Sandwich Islands trip. This was new. Until now Mark had spoken a few times "for fun" and made a burlesque speech or two on Carson City politics. But to attempt to talk for *money* —for a dollar a seat in a big public place—to be "funny" on a platform at a set hour, was as new and exciting as it was terrifying. His friends shoved him to it and took the biggest theater in town. Mark advertised that the "doors open at seven o'clock. The trouble begins at eight o'clock," and in due course found him-self thrust out before the lights, a huge manuscript in his hand, to receive a welcoming roar of applause that must be repaid in services. An hour or so later, when he ended his talk that had been carried along in billows of laughter, he left the platform with his head among the clouds, and on it a golden crown (October 2, 1866).

This was the beginning of his success as a lecturer, unrivaled except by that of his senior contemporary, Charles Dickens. The lecture on the Sandwich Islands was carried around the state of California and repeated in theaters, in halls, and on improvised platforms in mining camps, amid a continuous roar of laughter.

Mark Twain was now "started" in earnest. He dreamed of wider fields—of a trip around the world. Alexander the Great wanted to conquer the world, Mark Twain wanted to write it up. He determined to follow the rising star of his success, to reverse the advice of Horace Greeley to his contemporaries and to "go East." He made a rough-and-ready arrangement with the *Alta* newspaper for sending them letters from somewhere or anywhere, then set off on the steamship *America* on December 15, 1866, to reach the East by the Isthmus route, and landed in New York on January 11, 1867. The Innocent was abroad.

INNOCENTS ABROAD AND AT HOME, 1867–1870

When Mark Twain landed in New York in January of 1867, he had in his mind an idea of traveling round the world and writing letters about it. But he was still a little vague as to how to begin. He started writing "letters" from New York to the *Alta* of San Francisco, made a trip to the Mississippi to see his mother at St. Louis, visited his native town of Hannibal, made arrangements about publishing a book of sketches, and then opportunity came to him, just as it should, at the opportune moment.

He learned that the luxurious paddle-wheel steamer *Quaker City* would leave New York on an excursion trip across the Atlantic to the Mediterranean and the Holy Land. The ship would be "provided with every necessary comfort, including library and musical instruments"; it would carry "an experienced physician"; it would proceed—but it is unnecessary to give further details. All the world knows of the *Quaker City* and its cargo of Innocents Abroad.

Mark Twain leaped at the chance. He proposed to the proprietors of the *Alta* that he should go on the excursion. They accepted the offer, forwarded his passage money, and promised him twenty dollars a letter for his correspondence.

To the elation caused by this prospect there was added just before he sailed the satisfaction of another laurel in his new crown of success. His friend, "Governor Frank Fuller"—governor once of Utah and hence "Governor" forever—was in New York. He insisted that Mark should lecture; prophesied fame and a fortune, took the Cooper Institute and advertised "a serio-humorous lecture concerning Kanakadom," by "Mark Twain" (there was no Mr. Clemens anymore). At the last moment it began to seem clear,

The *Quaker City* as shown in an illustration from the first edition of *Innocents Abroad*.

to the lecturer's horror, that nobody was coming. Mark Twain as yet was not worth fifty cents. A great flood of free tickets was sent to all the school teachers within range. The lecture was given in a hall crowded to capacity, to an audience suffocated with laughter. Financially the lecture was a failure: it cost $500; the receipts were $300. The generous "Governor" made good the deficit. "It's all right, Mark," he said; "the fortune didn't come, but the fame has arrived."

And on June 8, 1867, in the glow of a new notoriety, Mark Twain sailed as one of the "lions" of the *Quaker City*.

The sea voyage, as judged by our pampered standards of today, was dingy and drab enough. The paddle-wheel steamer, luxurious in 1867, would seem cramped and dim today; the speed a crawl.

The excursionists "did" the Continent, from Paris to the Crimea, with Asia to the Holy Land and Africa to the pyramids. They got their money's worth. Without Mark Twain they would have been only a set of spectacled American tourists, thumbing their guidebooks, and trying to admire Giotto [1] and remember when Vermicelli lived. Mark Twain waved over them the magic wand of inspired genius, and turned them into the merry group of Innocents Abroad, whose pilgrimage is part of history. The letters which he sent home to the *Alta* in California and to the *Tribune* in New York reached the public this time—east, west, and everywhere— and deserved to. When the boat returned to America (November 19, 1867), Mark Twain stepped off the *Quaker City* a celebrity. He had gone away a lamb—or at best a western mustang—he came back a lion.

Success greeted him on his return like a tidal wave. All of a sudden, it seemed, the American nation knew him and acclaimed him. His success was not as sudden, as sweeping, and as phenomenal as that of Dickens after the *Pickwick Papers*.

[1] **Giotto** (jôt′tō): an Italian painter of the late thirteenth and early fourteenth centuries.

But it was second only to it. And it had in it the same ingredient of personal affection. The public took Mark to its heart, as England had taken young "Boz";[1] and with an added feeling of national pride unknown and unnecessary in the case of Dickens. Here was, at last, an *American* author. The Longfellows and the Hawthornes and the Fenimore Coopers had written English literature in America. Here at last was a man who wrote American literature, and wrote it in and on Europe. The publication of the *Innocents Abroad* was the first step in the Americanization of Europe now reaching its climax.

No wonder success came in a flood. A lecture bureau offered him a contract for eighteen nights at a hundred dollars a night. A western senator wanted him as literary secretary. The New York *Tribune* put him on their staff. All of the papers—the *Tribune,* the *Herald,* the San Francisco *Alta,* the Chicago press, the magazines, wanted letters and articles. And meanwhile his first book, *The Celebrated Jumping Frog of Calaveras County and Other Sketches,* which had appeared (May 1, 1867) just before the *Quaker City* left, was on the market and selling.

Bigger things were to come.

[1] **"Boz":** a pen name used by Charles Dickens.

FOR STUDY AND DISCUSSION

1. Leacock states the principal theme of the first section of this biography in his first two paragraphs. His story is about how Sam Clemens found himself in the West, or, in other words, about how "the West made Mark Twain." Make a list of Mark Twain's "western" experiences. What did Twain experience in the West that he could not have experienced in the East or the South? What effect did the West have on Twain?

2. Mark Twain's use of exaggeration is said to be the most important feature of his humor.
In what ways might his years in the West have nurtured Twain's talent for exaggeration? Point out several of his exaggerations referred to in this essay. Where has Twain used exaggeration in his story "Luck," on page 62 of this book? Why are exaggerations funny? Are all exaggerations funny? Why or why not?

3. According to Leacock, what aspect of Mark Twain's writings perplexed British readers? Were American readers perplexed by these things? In your opinion, what might account for this difference between British and American readers?

4. In most good biographies of writers, an attempt is made to show a connection between the writer's experiences and literary works. Leacock mentions ten examples of Mark Twain's writings. Would you say that the connection between Twain's writing and his experiences is clearly made? Why or why not?

FOR COMPOSITION

Starting on page 322 with the paragraph that begins "Sam Clemens, working as a surface miner," Leacock devotes five paragraphs to a description of Mark Twain at the age of twenty-six. Notice that the author describes not only Twain's appearance but also his character and that he uses an anecdote to illustrate one aspect of his disposition. Using these five paragraphs as models, write a short essay in which you describe someone you know personally or some historical character with whose life you are familiar.

ABOUT THE AUTHOR

Stephen Butler Leacock (1869–1944) was born in England but went to Canada with his parents in 1876. Originally a student of languages, he eventually became Chairman of the Department of Economics and Political Science at McGill University in Montreal. He had written several books on economics and political science when, just before he was forty years old, he turned to comic writing. Today his fame rests on his witty essays and humorous short stories.

The Day the Dam Broke

JAMES THURBER

MY MEMORIES of what my family and I went through during the 1913 flood in Ohio I would gladly forget. And yet neither the hardships we endured nor the turmoil and confusion we experienced can alter my feeling toward my native state and city. I am having a fine time now and wish Columbus were here, but if anyone ever wished a city was in hell it was during that frightful and perilous afternoon in 1913 when the dam broke or, to be more exact, when everybody in town *thought* that the dam broke. We were both ennobled and demoralized by the experience. Grandfather especially rose to magnificent heights which can never lose their splendor for me, even though his reactions to the flood were based upon a profound misconception; namely, that Nathan Bedford Forrest's [1] cavalry was the menace we were called upon to face. The only possible means of escape for us was to flee the house, a step which grandfather sternly forbade, brandishing his old army saber in his hand. "Let 'em come!" he roared. Meanwhile hundreds of people were

[1] **Nathan Bedford Forrest** (1821–1877): a cavalry general in the Confederate Army during the War Between the States.

streaming by our house in wild panic, screaming "Go east! Go east!" We had to stun grandfather with the ironing board. Impeded as we were by the inert form of the old gentleman—he was taller than six feet and weighed almost a hundred and seventy pounds—we were passed, in the first half-mile, by practically everybody else in the city. Had grandfather not come to, at the corner of Parson Avenue and Town Street, we would unquestionably have been overtaken and engulfed by the roaring waters—that is, if there had *been* any roaring waters.

Later, when the panic had died down and people had gone rather sheepishly back to their homes and their offices, minimizing the distances they had run and offering various reasons for running, city engineers pointed out that even if the dam had broken, the water level would not have risen more than two additional inches in the West Side. The West Side was, at the time of the dam scare, under thirty feet of water—as, indeed, were all Ohio river towns during the great spring floods of forty years ago. The East Side (where we lived and where all the running occurred) had never been in any danger at all. Only a rise of some ninety-five feet could have caused the flood waters to flow over High Street—the thoroughfare that divided the east side of town from the west—and engulf the East Side.

The fact that we were all as safe as kittens under a stove did not, however, assuage in the least the fine despair and the grotesque desperation which seized upon the residents of the East Side when the cry spread like a grass fire that the dam had given way. Some of the most dignified, staid, cynical, and clear-thinking men in town abandoned their wives, stenographers, homes, and offices and ran east. There are few alarms in the world more terrifying than "The dam has broken!" There are few persons capable of stopping to reason when that clarion cry strikes upon their ears, even persons who live in towns no nearer than five hundred miles to a dam.

The Columbus, Ohio, broken-dam rumor began, as I recall it, about noon of March 12, 1913. High Street, the main canyon of trade, was loud with the placid hum of business and the buzzing of placid businessmen arguing, computing, wheedling, offering, refusing, compromising. Darius Conningway, one of the foremost corporation lawyers in the Middle West, was telling the Public Utilities Commission in the language of Julius Caesar that they might as well try to move the Northern Star as to move him. Other men were making their little boasts and their little gestures. Suddenly somebody began to run. It may be that he had simply remembered, all of a moment, an engagement to meet his wife, for which he was now frightfully late. Whatever it was, he ran east on Broad Street (probably toward the Maramor Restaurant, a favorite place for a man to meet his wife).

Somebody else began to run, perhaps a newsboy in high spirits. Another man, a portly gentleman of affairs, broke into a trot. Within ten minutes, everybody on High Street, from the Union Depot to the Courthouse was running. A loud mumble gradually crystallized into the dread word "dam."

"The dam has broke!" The fear was put into words by a little old lady in an electric,[1] or by a traffic cop, or by a small boy; nobody knows who, nor does it now really matter. Two thousand people were abruptly in full flight. "Go east!" was the cry that arose—east away from the river, east to safety. "Go east! Go east! Go east!"

---

[1] **an electric:** a battery-powered automobile.

Black streams of people flowed eastward down all the streets leading in that direction; these streams, whose headwaters were in the dry-goods stores, office buildings, harness shops, movie theaters, were fed by trickles of housewives, children, cripples, servants, dogs, and cats, slipping out of the houses past which the main streams flowed, shouting and screaming. People ran out leaving fires burning and food cooking and doors wide open. I remember, however, that my mother turned out all the fires and that she took with her a dozen eggs and two loaves of bread. It was her plan to make Memorial Hall, just two blocks away, and take refuge somewhere in the top of it, in one of the dusty rooms where war veterans met and where old battle flags and stage scenery were stored. But the seething throngs, shouting "Go east!" drew her along and the rest of us with her.

When grandfather regained full consciousness, at Parsons Avenue, he turned upon the retreating mob like a vengeful prophet and exhorted the men to form ranks and stand off the rebel dogs, but at length he, too, got the idea that the dam had broken and, roaring "Go east!" in his powerful voice, he caught up in his one arm a small child and in the other a slight, clerkish man of perhaps forty-two, and we slowly began to gain on those ahead of us.

A scattering of firemen, policemen, and army officers in dress uniforms—there had been a review at Fort Hayes, in the northern part of town—added color to the surging billows of people. "Go east!" cried a little child in a piping voice, as she ran past a porch on which drowsed a lieutenant-colonel of infantry. Used to quick decisions, trained to immediate obedience, the officer bounded off the porch and, running at full tilt, soon passed the child, bawling "Go east!" The two of

them emptied rapidly the houses of the little street they were on.

"What is it? What is it?" demanded a fat, waddling man who intercepted the colonel. The officer dropped behind and asked the little child what it was. "The dam has broke!" gasped the girl. "The dam has broke!" roared the colonel.

"Go east! Go east! Go east!" He was soon leading, with the exhausted child in his arms, a fleeing company of three hundred persons who had gathered around him from living rooms, shops, garages, back yards, and basements.

Nobody has ever been able to compute with any exactness how many people took part in the great rout of 1913, for the panic, which extended from the Winslow Bottling Works in the South End to Clintonville, six miles north, ended as abruptly as it began and the bobtail and ragtag and velvet-gowned groups of refugees melted away and slunk home, leaving the streets peaceful and deserted. The shouting, weeping, tangled evacuation of the city lasted not more than two hours in all. Some few people got as far east as Reynoldsburg, twelve miles away; fifty or more reached the Country Club, eight miles away; most of the others gave up,

exhausted, or climbed trees in Franklin Park, four miles out. Order was restored and fear dispelled finally by means of militiamen riding about in motor lorries [1] bawling through megaphones: "The dam has *not* broken!" At first this tended only to add to the confusion and increase the panic, for many stampeders thought the soldiers were bellowing "The dam has *now* broken!" thus setting an official seal of authentication on the calamity.

All the time, the sun shone quietly and there was nowhere any sign of oncoming waters. A visitor in an airplane, looking down on the straggling, agitated masses of people below, would have been hard put to it to divine a reason for the phenomenon. It must have inspired, in such an observer, a peculiar kind of terror, like the sight of the *Marie Celeste,* [2] abandoned at sea, its galley fires peacefully burning, its tranquil decks bright in the sunlight.

An aunt of mine, Aunt Edith Taylor, was in a movie theater on High Street

[1] **lorries:** trucks.
[2] **Marie Celeste:** a vessel en route from New York to Genoa which vanished in the Atlantic and was found abandoned weeks later with crew missing.

when, over and above the sound of the piano in the pit (a W. S. Hart [1] picture was being shown), there rose the steadily increasing tromp of running feet. Persistent shouts rose above the tromping. An elderly man, sitting near my aunt, mumbled something, got out of his seat, and went up the aisle at a dogtrot. This started everybody. In an instant the audience was jamming the aisles. "Fire!" shouted a woman who always expected to be burned up in a theater; but now the shouts outside were louder and coherent.

"The dam has broke!" cried somebody. "Go east!" screamed a small woman in front of my aunt. And east they went, pushing and shoving and clawing, knocking women and children down, emerging finally into the street, torn and sprawling.

Inside the theater, Bill Hart was calmly calling some desperado's bluff and the brave girl at the piano played "Row! Row! Row!" loudly and then "In My Harem."

Outside, men were streaming across the statehouse yard, others were climbing trees, a woman managed to get up onto the "These Are My Jewels" statue, whose bronze figures of Sherman, Stanton, Grant, and Sheridan [2] watched with cold unconcern the going-to-pieces of the capital city.

"I ran south to State Street, east on State to Third, south on Third to Town, and out east on Town," my Aunt Edith has written me. "A tall spare woman with grim eyes and a determined chin ran past me down the middle of the street. I was still uncertain as to what was the matter, in spite of all the shouting. I drew alongside the woman with some effort, for although she was in her late fifties, she had a beautiful easy running form and seemed to be in excellent condition. 'What is it?' I puffed. She gave me a quick glance, and then looked ahead again, stepping up her pace a trifle. 'Don't ask me, ask God!' she said.

"When I reached Grant Avenue, I was so spent that Dr. H. R. Mallory—you remember Dr. Mallory, the man with the white beard who looks like Robert Browning?—well, Dr. Mallory, whom I had drawn away from at the corner of Fifth and Town, passed me. 'It's got us!' he shouted, and I felt sure that whatever it was *did* have us, for you know what conviction Dr. Mallory's statements always carried. I didn't know at the time what he meant, but I found out later.

"There was a boy behind him on roller skates, and Dr. Mallory mistook the swishing of the skates for the sound of rushing water. He eventually reached the Columbus School for Girls, at the corner of Parsons Avenue and Town Street, where he collapsed, expecting the cold frothing waters of the Scioto to sweep him into oblivion. The boy on the skates swirled past him, and Dr. Mallory realized for the first time what he had been running from. Looking back up the street, he could see no signs of water, but nevertheless, after resting a few minutes, he jogged on east again. He caught up with me at Ohio Avenue, where we rested together. I should say that seven hundred people passed us.

"A funny thing was that all of them were on foot. Nobody seemed to have had the courage to stop and start his car; but as I remember it, all cars had to be cranked in those days, which is probably the reason."

The next day, the city went about its business as if nothing had happened, but

---

[1] **W. S. Hart** (1872–1946): popular actor in silent movies, especially Westerns.

[2] **Sherman . . . Sheridan:** Stanton was U. S. Secretary of War 1862–1867; Sherman, Grant, and Sheridan were all generals of the Union forces in the War Between the States.

there was no joking. It was two years or more before you dared treat the breaking of the dam lightly. And even now, many years after, there are a few persons, like Dr. Mallory, who will shut up like a clam if you mention the Afternoon of the Great Run.

FOR STUDY AND DISCUSSION

1. Which sentences in the first paragraph clearly convey the humorous intention of this essay? How is that intention carried out in the essay by the use of amusing exaggerations?

2. Each of the main characters mentioned in this memoir did some memorable thing during the panic. What action or actions were taken by the following:

grandfather
mother
a lieutenant-colonel of infantry
Aunt Edith Taylor
Dr. Mallory

3. What attitude toward the panic does Thurber take? What do you think such an attitude reveals about the character of Thurber?

LANGUAGE AND VOCABULARY

1. Although written in an informal style, this essay uses many words that are not usually found in ordinary conversation. You miss some of Thurber's humor if you do not know exactly the meaning of each word the author uses. Define each italicized word in the sentences below. How does Thurber's use of these words appeal to your sense of the ridiculous?

"*Impeded* as we were by the *inert* form of the old gentleman . . . we were passed . . . by practically everybody else in the city."

"The fact that we were all . . . safe . . . did not, however, *assuage* in the least the *fine despair* and the *grotesque desperation* which seized upon the residents of the East Side"

"many stampeders thought the soldiers were bellowing 'The dam has now broken!' thus setting an official seal of *authentication* on the *calamity*."

2. Note the vivid pictures of movement that James Thurber suggests in this essay. Thurber accomplishes this through the use of picturesque verbs. Some of these picturesque verbs are italicized in the phrases below. What vivid picture of movement does each word suggest? What verbs might a less imaginative person have used in each case?

"grandfather, . . . *brandishing* his old army saber . . ."

"the officer *bounded* off the porch . . ."

"groups of refugees . . . *slunk* home . . ."

"The boy on the skates *swirled* past him . . ."

"he *jogged* on east again."

FOR COMPOSITION

1. Almost every family can remember a day when everything went wrong. In a humorous vein, write a personal recollection of such a day. As Thurber did in "The Day the Dam Broke," characterize various personalities by describing just what they did on that occasion. You might use one of the following as the title of your essay.

The Day Mother Lost Her Temper

On Some Days It Doesn't Pay to Get Up

How Our Family Reacts to an Emergency

2. Note how Thurber's essay develops the main idea stated in the sentence, "We were both ennobled and demoralized by the experience." In like manner, write an essay developing the idea stated in one of the following topic sentences:

Life in the Space Age is both inspiring and frightening.

An after-school job can build you up and tear you down.

Family dinners bring out the best and the worst in almost all of us.

ABOUT THE AUTHOR

You have already encountered the writing of James Thurber in "The Secret Life of Walter Mitty," in the Short Story unit of this book (page 94). In "The Day the Dam Broke," the same author looks back at a humorous incident in his own life. For biographical details about James Thurber, see page 98.

Travels with Charley

JOHN STEINBECK

Travels with Charley is the account by an American Nobel prize winner of his long and eventful trip throughout the length and breadth of the United States. In the selections which follow, John Steinbeck writes of his reasons for making the trip, of his visit to Yellowstone National Park, to the redwood forests of the Northwest, and to the Mojave Desert.

My PLAN was clear, concise, and reasonable, I think. For many years I have traveled in many parts of the world. In America I live in New York or dip into Chicago or San Francisco. But New York is no more America than Paris is France or London is England. Thus I discovered that I did not know my own country. I, an American writer, writing about America, was working from memory, and the memory is at best a faulty, warpy reservoir. I had not heard the speech of America, smelled the grass and trees and sewage, seen its hills and water, its color and quality of light. I knew the changes only from books and newspapers. But more than this, I had not felt the country for twenty-five years. In short, I was writing of something I did not know about, and it seems to me that in a so-called

writer this is criminal. My memories were distorted by twenty-five intervening years.

Once I traveled about in an old bakery wagon, a double-doored rattler with a mattress on its floor. I stopped where people stopped or gathered, I listened and looked and felt, and in the process had a picture of my country the accuracy of which was impaired only by my own shortcomings.

So it was that I determined to look again, to try to rediscover this monster land. Otherwise, in writing, I could not tell the small diagnostic truths which are the foundations of the larger truth. One sharp difficulty presented itself. In the intervening twenty-five years my name had become reasonably well known. And it has been my experience that when people have heard of you, favorably or not, they change; they become, through shyness or the other qualities that publicity inspires, something they are not under ordinary circumstances. This being so, my trip demanded that I leave my name and my identity at home. I had to be peripatetic eyes and ears, a kind of moving gelatin plate. I could not sign hotel registers, meet people I knew, interview others, or even ask searching questions. Furthermore, two or more people disturb the ecologic complex of an area. I had to go alone and I had to be self-contained, a kind of casual turtle carrying his house on his back.

With all this in mind I wrote to the head office of a great corporation which manufactures trucks. I specified my purpose and my needs. I wanted a three-quarter-ton pickup truck, capable of going anywhere under possibly rigorous conditions, and on this truck I wanted a little house built like the cabin of a small boat. A trailer is difficult to maneuver on mountain roads, is impossible and often illegal to park, and is subject to many restrictions. In due time, specifications came through, for a tough, fast, comfortable vehicle, mounting a camper top—a little house with double bed, a four-burner stove, a heater, refrigerator and lights operating on butane, a chemical toilet, closet space, storage space, windows screened against insects—exactly what I wanted. It was delivered in the summer to my little fishing place at Sag Harbor near the end of Long Island. Although I didn't want to start before Labor Day, when the nation settles back to normal living, I did want to get used to my turtle shell, to equip it and learn it. It arrived in August, a beautiful thing, powerful and yet lithe. It was almost as easy to handle as a passenger car. And because my planned trip had aroused some satiric remarks among my friends, I named it Rocinante, which you will remember was the name of Don Quixote's [1] horse.

Since I made no secret of my project, a number of controversies arose among my friends and advisers. (A projected journey spawns advisers in schools.) I was told that since my photograph was as widely distributed as my publisher could make it, I would find it impossible to move about without being recognized. Let me say in advance that in over ten thousand miles, in thirty-four states, I was not recognized even once. I believe that people identify things only in context. Even those people who might have known me against a background I am supposed to have, in no case identified me in Rocinante.

I was advised that the name Rocinante painted on the side of my truck in sixteenth-century Spanish script would cause curiosity and inquiry in some places.

I do not know how many people recognized the name, but surely no one ever asked about it.

Next, I was told that a stranger's purpose in moving about the country might cause inquiry or even suspicion. For this reason I racked a shotgun, two rifles, and a couple of fishing rods in my truck, for it is my experience that if a man is going hunting or fishing, his purpose is understood and even applauded. Actually, my hunting days are over. I no longer kill or catch anything I cannot get into a frying pan; I am too old for sport killing. This stage setting turned out to be unnecessary.

It was said that my New York license plates would arouse interest and perhaps questions, since they were the only outward identifying marks I had. And so they did—perhaps twenty or thirty times in the whole trip. But such contacts followed an invariable pattern, somewhat as follows:

Local man: "New York, huh?"

Me: "Yep."

Local man: "I was there in nineteen thirty-eight—or was it thirty-nine? Alice, was it thirty-eight or thirty-nine we went to New York?"

Alice: "It was thirty-six. I remember because it was the year Alfred died."

Local man: "Anyway, I hated it. Wouldn't live there if you paid me."

There was some genuine worry about my traveling alone, open to attack, robbery, assault. It is well known that our roads are dangerous. And here I admit I had senseless qualms. It is some years since I have been alone, nameless, friendless, without any of the safety one gets from family, friends, and accomplices. There is no reality in the danger. It's just a very lonely, helpless feeling at first—a kind of desolate feeling. For this reason I took one companion on my journey—an old French gentleman poodle known as

---

[1] **Don Quixote** (dôn kē·hō′tā): the hero of a great Spanish novel which ridicules tales of chivalry. Rocinante (rō′thē·nän′tā) was the broken-down nag which carried Don Quixote to all his adventures.

Charley. Actually his name is Charles le Chien. He was born in Bercy on the outskirts of Paris and trained in France, and while he knows a little poodle-English, he responds quickly only to commands in French. Otherwise he has to translate, and that slows him down. He is a very big poodle, of a color called *bleu*, and he is blue when he is clean. Charley is a born diplomat. He prefers negotiation to fighting, and properly so, since he is very bad at fighting. Only once in his ten years has he been in trouble—when he met a dog who refused to negotiate. Charley lost a piece of his right ear that time. But he is a good watch dog—has a roar like a lion, designed to conceal from night-wandering strangers the fact that he couldn't bite his way out of a *cornet de papier*.[1] He is a good friend and traveling companion, and would rather travel about than anything he can imagine. If he occurs at length in this account, it is because he contributed much to the trip. A dog, particularly an exotic like Charley, is a bond between strangers. Many conversations en route began with "What degree of a dog is that?"

The techniques of opening conversation are universal. I knew long ago and rediscovered that the best way to attract attention, help, and conversation is to be lost. A man who seeing his mother starving to death on a path kicks her in the stomach to clear the way, will cheerfully devote several hours of his time giving wrong directions to a total stranger who claims to be lost.

I must confess to a laxness in the matter of national parks. I haven't visited many of them. Perhaps this is because they enclose the unique, the spectacular, the astounding—the greatest waterfall, the deepest canyon, the highest cliff, the most stupendous works of man or nature. And I would rather see a good Brady photograph than Mount Rushmore. For it is my opinion that we enclose and celebrate the freaks of our nation and of our civilization. Yellowstone National Park is no more representative of America than is Disneyland.

This being my natural attitude, I don't know what made me turn sharply south and cross a state line to take a look at Yellowstone. Perhaps it was a fear of my neighbors. I could hear them say, "You mean you were that near to Yellowstone and didn't go? You must be crazy." Again it might have been the American tendency in travel. One goes, not so much to see but to tell afterward. Whatever my purpose in going to Yellowstone, I'm glad I went because I discovered something about Charley I might never have known.

A pleasant-looking National Park man checked me in and then he said, "How about that dog? They aren't permitted in except on leash."

"Why?" I asked.

"Because of the bears."

"Sir," I said, "this is a unique dog. He does not live by tooth or fang. He respects the right of cats to be cats although he doesn't admire them. He turns his steps rather than disturb an earnest caterpillar. His greatest fear is that someone will point out a rabbit and suggest that he chase it. This is a dog of peace and tranquility. I suggest that the greatest danger to your bears will be pique at being ignored by Charley."

The young man laughed. "I wasn't so much worried about the bears," he said. "But our bears have developed an intolerance for dogs. One of them might demonstrate his prejudice with a clip on the chin, and then—no dog."

"I'll lock him in the back, sir. I promise

---

[1] *cornet de papier* (kôr·ne′ də pȧ·pyȧ′): the French name for "paper bag."

you Charley will cause no ripple in the bear world, and as an old bear-looker, neither will I."

"I just have to warn you," he said. "I have no doubt your dog has the best of intentions. On the other hand, our bears have the worst. Don't leave food about. Not only do they steal but they are critical of anyone who tries to reform them. In a word, don't believe their sweet faces or you might get clobbered. And don't let the dog wander. Bears don't argue."

We went on our way into the wonderland of nature gone nuts, and you will have to believe what happened. The only way I can prove it would be to get a bear.

Less than a mile from the entrance I saw a bear beside the road, and it ambled out as though to flag me down. Instantly a change came over Charley. He shrieked with rage. His lips flared, showing wicked teeth that have some trouble with a dog biscuit. He screeched insults at the bear, which hearing, the bear reared up and seemed to me to overtop Rocinante. Frantically I rolled the windows shut and, swinging quickly to the left, grazed the animal, then scuttled on while Charley raved and ranted beside me, describing in detail what he would do to that bear if he could get at him. I was never so astonished in my life. To the best of my knowledge Charley had never seen a bear, and in his whole history had showed great tolerance for every living thing. Besides all this, Charley is a coward, so deepseated a coward that he has developed a technique for concealing it. And yet he showed every evidence of wanting to get out and murder a bear that outweighed him a thousand to one. I don't understand it.

A little farther along two bears showed up, and the effect was doubled. Charley became a maniac. He leaped all over me, he cursed and growled, snarled and

John Steinbeck and his dog Charley.

screamed. I didn't know he had the ability to snarl. Where did he learn it? Bears were in good supply, and the road became a nightmare. For the first time in his life Charley resisted reason, even resisted a cuff on the ear. He became a primitive killer lusting for the blood of his enemy, and up to this moment he had had no enemies. In a bearless stretch, I opened the cab, took Charley by the collar, and locked him in the house. But that did no good. When we passed other bears he leaped on the table and scratched at the windows trying to get out at them. I could hear canned goods crashing as he struggled in his mania. Bears simply brought out the Hyde in my Jekyll-headed dog. What could have caused it? Was it a prebreed memory of a time when the wolf was in him? I know him well. Once in a while he tries a bluff, but it is a palpable

"... a well-favored bear can bat a dog like a tennis ball."

lie. I swear that this was no lie. I am certain that if he were released he would have charged every bear we passed and found victory or death.

It was too nerve-wracking, a shocking spectacle, like seeing an old, calm friend go insane. No amount of natural wonders, of rigid cliffs and belching waters, of smoking springs could even engage my attention while that pandemonium went on. After about the fifth encounter I gave up, turned Rocinante about, and retraced my way. If I had stopped the night and bears had gathered to my cooking, I dare not think what would have happened.

At the gate the park guard checked me out. "You didn't stay long. Where's the dog?"

"Locked up back there. And I owe you an apology. That dog has the heart and soul of a bear-killer and I didn't know it. Heretofore he has been a little tender-hearted toward an underdone steak."

"Yeah!" he said. "That happens sometimes. That's why I warned you. A bear

dog would know his chances, but I've seen a Pomeranian go up like a puff of smoke. You know, a well-favored bear can bat a dog like a tennis ball."

I moved fast, back the way I had come, and I was reluctant to camp for fear there might be some unofficial nongovernment bears about. That night I spent in a pretty auto court near Livingston. I had my dinner in a restaurant, and when I had settled in with a drink and a comfortable chair and my bathed bare feet on a carpet with red roses, I inspected Charley. He was dazed. His eyes held a faraway look and he was totally exhausted, emotionally no doubt. He couldn't eat his dinner, he refused the evening walk, and once we were in he collapsed on the floor and went to sleep. In the night I heard him whining and yapping, and when I turned on the light his feet were making running gestures and his body jerked and his eyes were wide open, but it was only a night bear. I awakened him and gave him some water. This time he went to sleep and didn't stir all night. In the morning he was still tired. I wonder why we think the thoughts and emotions of animals are simple.

I stayed two days close to the bodies of the giants,[1] and there were no trippers, no chattering troupes with cameras. There's a cathedral hush here. Perhaps the thick soft bark absorbs sound and creates a silence. The trees rise straight up to zenith; there is no horizon. The dawn comes early and remains dawn until the sun is high. Then the green fernlike foliage so far up strains the sunlight to a green gold and distributes it in shafts or rather in stripes of light and shade. After the sun passes zenith it is afternoon and quickly evening with a whispering dusk as long as was the morning.

Thus time and the ordinary divisions of the day are changed. To me dawn and dusk are quiet times, and here in the redwoods nearly the whole of daylight is a quiet time. Birds move in the dim light or flash like sparks through the stripes of sun, but they make little sound. Underfoot is a mattress of needles deposited for over two thousand years. No sound of footsteps can be heard on this thick blanket. To me there's a remote and cloistered feeling here. One holds back speech for fear of disturbing something—what? From my earliest childhood I've felt that something was going on in the groves, something of which I was not a part. And if I had forgotten the feeling, I soon got it back.

At night, the darkness is black—only straight up a patch of gray and an occasional star. And there's a breathing in the black, for these huge things that control the day and inhabit the night are living

"There's a cathedral hush here. . . . The trees rise straight up to zenith; there is no horizon."

---

[1] **the giants:** the giant redwood trees of southern Oregon.

things and have presence, and perhaps feeling, and, somewhere in deep-down perception, perhaps communication. I have had lifelong association with these things. (Odd that the word "trees" does not apply.) I can accept them and their power and their age because I was early exposed to them. On the other hand, people lacking such experience begin to have a feeling of uneasiness here, of danger, of being shut in, enclosed and overwhelmed. It is not only the size of these redwoods but their strangeness that frightens them. And why not? For these are the last remaining members of a race that flourished over four continents as far back in geologic time as the upper Jurassic period.[1] Fossils of these ancients have been found dating from the Cretaceous era, while in the Eocene and Miocene they were spread o er England and Europe and America. And then the glaciers moved down and wiped the Titans out beyond recovery. And only these few are left—a stunning memory of what the world was like once long ago. Can it be that we do not love to be reminded that we are very young and callow in a world that was old when we came into it? And could there be a strong resistance to the certainty that a living world will continue its stately way when we no longer inhabit it?

It would be pleasant to be able to say of my travels with Charley, "I went out to find the truth about my country and I found it." And then it would be such a simple matter to set down my findings and lean back comfortably with a fine sense of having discovered truths and taught them to my readers. I wish it were that easy. But what I carried in my head and deeper in my perceptions was a barrel of

---

[1] **upper Jurassic period:** about 150 million years ago. The other periods mentioned are more recent.

worms. I discovered long ago in collecting and classifying marine animals that what I found was closely intermeshed with how I felt at the moment. External reality has a way of being not so external after all.

This monster of a land, this mightiest of nations, this spawn of the future, turns out to be the macrocosm of microcosm me. If an Englishman or a Frenchman or an Italian should travel my route, see what I saw, hear what I heard, their stored pictures would be not only different from mine but equally different from one another. If other Americans reading this account should feel it true, that agreement would only mean that we are alike in our Americanness.

From start to finish I found no strangers. If I had, I might be able to report them more objectively. But these are my people and this my country. If I found matters to criticize and to deplore, they were tendencies equally present in myself. If I were to prepare one immaculately inspected generality it would be this: For all of our enormous geographic range, for all of our sectionalism, for all of our interwoven breeds drawn from every part of the ethnic world, we are a nation, a new breed. Americans are much more American than they are Northerners, Southerners, Westerners, or Easterners. And descendants of English, Irish, Italian, Jewish, German, Polish are essentially American. This is not patriotic whoop-de-do; it is carefully observed fact. California Chinese, Boston Irish, Wisconsin German, and Alabama Negroes have more in common than they have apart. And this is the more remarkable because it has happened so quickly. It is a fact that Americans from all sections and of all racial extractions are more alike than the Welsh are like the English, the Lancashireman like the Cockney, or for that matter the Lowland Scot like the

Highlander. It is astonishing that this has happened in less than two hundred years and most of it in the last fifty. The American identity is an exact and provable thing.

Starting on my return journey, I realized by now that I could not see everything. My impressionable gelatin plate was getting muddled. I determined to inspect two more sections and then call it a day—Texas and a sampling of the Deep South.

This journey had been like a full dinner of many courses, set before a starving man. At first he tries to eat all of everything, but as the meal progresses he finds he must forgo some things to keep his appetite and his taste buds functioning.

I bucketed Rocinante out of California by the shortest possible route—one I knew well from the old days of the 1930's. From Salinas to Los Banos, through Fresno and Bakersfield, then over the pass and into the Mojave[1] Desert, a burned and burning desert even this late in the year, its hills like piles of black cinders in the distance, and the rutted floor sucked dry by the hungry sun. It's easy enough now, on the high-speed road in a dependable and comfortable car, with stopping places for shade and every service station vaunting its refrigeration. But I can remember when we came to it with prayer, listening for trouble in our laboring old motors, drawing a plume of steam from our boiling radiators. Then the broken-down wreck by the side of the road was in real trouble unless someone stopped to offer help. And I have never crossed it without sharing something with those early families foot-dragging through this terrestrial hell, leaving the white skeletons of horses and cattle which still mark the way.

The Mojave is a big desert and a frightening one. It's as though nature tested a man for endurance and constancy to prove whether he was good enough to get to California. The shimmering dry heat made visions of water on the flat plain. And even when you drive at high speed, the hills that mark the boundaries recede before you. Charley, always a dog for water, panted asthmatically, jarring his whole body with the effort, and a good eight inches of his tongue hung out flat as a leaf and dripping. I pulled off the road into a small gulley to give him water from my thirty-gallon tank. But before I let him drink I poured water all over him and on my hair and shoulders and shirt. The air is so dry that evaporation makes you feel suddenly cold.

I sat well inside the shade of Rocinante, looking out at the sun-pounded plain, dotted here and there with clumps of sagebrush.

About fifty yards away two coyotes stood watching me, their tawny coats blending with sand and sun. I knew that with any quick or suspicious movement of mine they could drift into invisibility. With the most casual slowness I reached down my new rifle from its sling over my bed—the .222 with its bitter little high-speed, long-range stings. Very slowly I brought the rifle up. Perhaps in the shade of my house I was half hidden by the blinding light outside. The little rifle has a beautiful telescope sight with a wide field. The coyotes had not moved.

I got both of them in the field of my telescope, and the glass brought them very close. Their tongues lolled out so that they seemed to smile mockingly. They were favored animals, not starved, but well furred, the golden hair tempered with black guard hairs. Their little lemon-yellow eyes were plainly visible in the glass. I moved the cross hairs to the breast of the right-hand animal, and pushed the safety. My elbows on the table steadied the gun. The cross hairs lay unmoving on the brisket. And then the coyote sat down like a dog and its right rear paw came up to scratch the right shoulder.

My finger was reluctant to touch the trigger. I must be getting very old and my ancient conditioning worn thin. Coyotes are vermin. They steal chickens. They thin the ranks of quail and all other game birds. They must be killed. They are the enemy. My first shot would drop the sitting beast, and the other would whirl to fade away. I might very well put him down with a running shot because I am a good rifleman.

And I did not fire. My training said, "Shoot!" and my age replied, "There isn't a chicken within thirty miles, and if there are any they aren't my chickens. And this waterless place is not quail country. No, these boys are keeping their figures with kangaroo rats and jack rabbits, and that's vermin eat vermin. Why should I interfere?"

"Kill them," my training said. "Everyone kills them. It's a public service." My finger moved to the trigger. The cross was steady on the breast just below the panting tongue. I could imagine the splash and jar of angry steel, the leap and struggle until the torn heart failed, and then, not too long later, the shadow of a buzzard, and another. By that time I would be long gone—out of the desert and across the Colorado River. And beside the sagebrush there would be a naked, eyeless skull, a few picked bones, a spot of black dried blood and a few rags of golden fur.

I guess I'm too old and too lazy to be a good citizen. The second coyote stood sidewise to my rifle. I moved the cross hairs to his shoulder and held steady. There was no question of missing with that rifle at that range. I owned both animals. Their lives were mine. I put the safety on and laid the rifle on the table. Without the telescope they were not so intimately close. The hot blast of light tousled the air to shimmering.

Then I remembered something I heard long ago that I hope is true. It was unwritten law in China, so my informant told me, that when one man saved another's life he became responsible for that life to the end of its existence. For, having interfered with a course of events, the savior could not escape his responsibility. And that has always made good sense to me.

Now I had a token responsibility for two live and healthy coyotes. In the delicate world of relationships, we are tied together for all time. I opened two cans of dog food and left them as a votive.[1]

I have driven through the Southwest many times, and even more often have flown over it—a great and mysterious wasteland, a sun-punished place. It is a mystery, something concealed and waiting. It seems deserted, free of parasitic man, but this is not entirely so. Follow the double line of wheel tracks through sand and rock and you will find a habitation somewhere huddled in a protected place, with a few trees pointing their roots at under-earth water, a patch of starveling corn and squash, and strips of jerky[2] hanging on a string. There is a breed of desert men, not hiding exactly but gone to sanctuary from the sins of confusion.

At night in this waterless air the stars come down just out of reach of your fingers. In such a place lived the hermits of the early church piercing to infinity with unlittered minds. The great concepts of oneness and of majestic order seem always to be born in the desert. The quiet counting of the stars, and observation of their movements, came first from desert places. I have known desert men who chose their places with quiet and slow

---

[1] **votive:** an action done to fulfill a vow or obligation.
[2] **jerky:** an Americanization of the Spanish word *charqui,* meaning cured meat.

"... these boys are keeping their figures with kangaroo rats and jack rabbits ..."

passion, rejecting the nervousness of a watered world. These men have not changed with the exploding times except to die and be replaced by others like them.

And always there are mysteries in the desert, stories told and retold of secret places in the desert mountains where surviving clans from an older era wait to re-emerge. Usually these groups guard treasures hidden from the waves of conquest, the golden artifacts of an archaic Montezuma,[1] or a mine so rich that its discovery would change the world. If a stranger discovers their existence, he is killed or so absorbed that he is never seen again. These stories have an inevitable pattern untroubled by the question, If none return, how is it known what is there? Oh, it's there all right, but if you find it you will never be found.

And there is another monolithic tale which never changes. Two prospectors in partnership discover a mine of preternatural richness—of gold or diamonds or rubies. They load themselves with samples, as much as they can carry, and they mark the place in their minds by land-

marks all around. Then, on the way out to the other world, one dies of thirst and exhaustion, but the other crawls on, discarding most of the treasure he has grown too weak to carry. He comes at last to a settlement, or perhaps is found by other prospecting men. They examine his samples with great excitement. Sometimes in the story the survivor dies after leaving directions with his rescuers, or again he is nursed back to strength. Then a well-equipped party sets out to find the treasure, and it can never be found again. That is the invariable end of the story—it is never found again. I have heard this story many times, and it never changes. There is nourishment in the desert for myth, but myth must somewhere have its roots in reality.

And there are true secrets in the desert. In the war of sun and dryness against living things, life has its secrets of survival. Life, no matter on what level, must be moist or it will disappear. I find most interesting the conspiracy of life in the desert to circumvent the death rays of the all-conquering sun. The beaten earth appears defeated and dead, but it only appears so. A vast and inventive organiza-

[1] **Montezuma** (mon′tə·zoo′mə): the last Aztec emperor of Mexico.

tion of living matter survives by seeming to have lost. The gray and dusty sage wears oily armor to protect its inward small moisture. Some plants engorge themselves with water in the rare rainfall and store it for future use. Animal life wears a hard, dry skin or an outer skeleton to defy the desiccation. And every living thing has developed techniques for finding or creating shade. Small reptiles and rodents burrow or slide below the surface or cling to the shaded side of an outcropping. Movement is slow to preserve energy, and it is a rare animal which can or will defy the sun for long. A rattlesnake will die in an hour of full sun. Some insects of bolder inventiveness have devised personal refrigeration systems. Those animals which must drink moisture get it at second hand—a rabbit from a leaf, a coyote from the blood of a rabbit.

One may look in vain for living creatures in the daytime, but when the sun goes and the night gives consent, a world of creatures awakens and takes up its intricate pattern. Then the hunted come out and the hunters, and hunters of the hunters. The night awakes to buzzing and to cries and barks.

When, very late in the history of our planet, the incredible accident of life occurred, a balance of chemical factors, combined with temperature, in quantities and in kinds so delicate as to be unlikely, all came together in the retort of time and a new thing emerged, soft and helpless and unprotected in the savage world of unlife. Then processes of change and variation took place in the organisms, so that one kind became different from all others. But one ingredient, perhaps the most important of all, is planted in every life form—the factor of survival. No living thing is without it, nor could life exist without this magic formula. Of course, each form developed its own machinery for survival, and some failed and disappeared while others peopled the earth. The first life might easily have been snuffed out and the accident may never have happened again—but, once it existed, its first quality, its duty, preoccupation, direction, and end, shared by every living thing, is to go on living. And so it does and so it will until some other accident cancels it. And the desert, the dry and sun-lashed desert, is a good school in which to observe the cleverness and the infinite variety of techniques of survival under pitiless opposition. Life could not change the sun or water the desert, so it changed itself.

The desert, being an unwanted place, might well be the last stand of life against unlife. For in the rich and moist and wanted areas of the world, life pyramids against itself and in its confusion has finally allied itself with the enemy nonlife. And what the scorching, searing, freezing, poisoning weapons of nonlife have failed to do may be accomplished to the end of its destruction and extinction by the tactics of survival gone sour. If the most versatile of living forms, the human, now fights for survival as it always has, it can eliminate not only itself but all other life. And if that should transpire, unwanted places like the desert might be the harsh mother of repopulation. For the inhabitants of the desert are well trained and well armed against desolation. Even our own misguided species might re-emerge from the desert. The lone man and his sun-toughened wife who cling to the shade in an unfruitful and uncoveted place might, with their brothers in arms—the coyote, the jack rabbit, the horned toad, the rattlesnake, together with a host of armored insects—these trained and tested fragments of life might well be the last hope of life against nonlife. The desert has mothered magic things before this.

1. Explain why Steinbeck decided he must rediscover the United States. Why did he wish to leave his name and identity at home? Why was it appropriate that Steinbeck name his truck Rocinante? What purpose did Charley serve on the trip?

2. Steinbeck's account of Charley's behavior in Yellowstone National Park resembles a short story in its structure. Notice that this account has a theme, expressed at the conclusion of the "story" by the sentence "I wonder why we think the thoughts and emotions of animals are simple." Show how this account also resembles a short story in that it has believable characters involved in some sort of conflict. Do you think Steinbeck exaggerated Charley's "personality"? Explain your answer.

3. How did Steinbeck react to the giant redwood forest in southern Oregon? Show how his account of the redwoods combines a knowledge of scientific facts with a description of personal feelings. How are Steinbeck's observations about the trees affected by his scientific knowledge of them?

4. As he begins to tell about his return journey, Steinbeck sums up his impressions of his trip thus far. His chief impression is that "the American identity is an exact and provable thing." Discuss this statement. What does it mean to be "American"? What characteristics distinguish Americans from people of other nations? Do all nations have "an exact and provable" identity? Explain.

5. Steinbeck's descriptive narrative of his trip through the Mojave Desert relates the incident of the two coyotes. Did this story interest you? Why or why not? How did it help you understand John Steinbeck's attitude toward life?

6. What are the "mysteries" of the desert? What are the "true secrets" in the desert? How does Steinbeck's account of these secrets reveal his interest in science?

LANGUAGE AND VOCABULARY

1. As indicated in questions 3 and 6 above, Steinbeck brought considerable scientific knowledge to his rediscovery of America. You might also have noticed that he sometimes used his fund of literary knowledge in describing the trip. Look up the terms listed below and tell how an understanding of them is necessary for a full appreciation of Steinbeck's description of the redwood forest. Which terms are scientific? Which term refers to literature?

geologic time	Eocene era
upper Jurassic period	Miocene era
Cretaceous era	Titans

2. Study the italicized words in the passage below. Look up each word you do not know and then explain the relationship of each italicized word to one of the other words in the same passage.

"A projected journey *spawns* advisers in schools."

"there were no *trippers,* no chattering troupes with cameras."

"There's a cathedral hush here.... To me there's a remote and *cloistered* feeling here."

"This monster of a land, this mightiest of nations,... turns out to be the *macrocosm* of microcosm me."

FOR COMPOSITION

1. Steinbeck's descriptions of the redwood forest and the desert are distinctive because they not only give the particular flavor of each place, but they also reveal Steinbeck's own feelings for each spot. Write a brief essay describing a place that has made a great impression on you, perhaps a mountain, the seashore, or a city. In your essay, indicate to your reader why this particular place means something special to you.

2. Steinbeck's adventures with his dog Charley may remind you of experiences you yourself have had with animals. Write an account of some incident that involved you and an animal. Try to describe, as Steinbeck did, the personality of the animal.

ABOUT THE AUTHOR

John Steinbeck (1902–1968) is one of America's best known contemporary writers. For biographical details, see page 129.

Description, Narration, and Exposition

In most writing, including biography, authors will probably use a combination of description, narration, and exposition. They will use narration in biography because they are telling a life story, description because the story contains people and places that greatly influenced the person whose story is being told, and exposition to explain and give reasons and perhaps to express opinions. As you read, learn to recognize the kind of writing being used. Which kind of writing is used in each of the following examples? Why does the author use this particular kind of writing? Which kind, for example, is this paragraph from "The Young Shakespeare"?

The curriculum of Stratford grammar school, like that of every other grammar school in England, was serious, thorough, and dull. There was no attempt whatever to fit the boys for the ordinary life they were going to find when they graduated, for all school theory in England was based on the medieval system. The purpose of schools in the Middle Ages was to turn out learned clerks for church positions, and therefore what the little boys of Renaissance England learned was Latin, more Latin, and still more Latin. About a decade after Shakespeare entered the classroom, a London teacher urged that English should also be taught in the schools, but no one paid any attention to so radical a suggestion. (pages 295–96)

1. In this example of expository writing, a reader should look for the *main idea*. What is the main idea of this paragraph?

2. The topic sentence of this paragraph says that the curriculum of Shakespeare's school was *serious, thorough,* and *dull*. What evidence of each of these is given?

In reading each of the following paragraphs, from "Travels with Charley" and "Mark Twain," identify the kind of writing—description, narration, or exposition—and then determine the sequence of events or the main idea or impression. After reading each paragraph, write down on a separate sheet of paper

1. the kind of writing in the paragraph
2. the paragraph's main events (narration), dominant impression (description), or main idea (exposition).

Thus time and the ordinary divisions of the day are changed. To me dawn and dusk are quiet times, and here in the redwoods nearly the whole of daylight is a quiet time. Birds move in the dim light or flash like sparks through the stripes of sun, but they make little sound. Underfoot is a mattress of needles deposited for over two thousand years. No sound of footsteps can be heard on this thick blanket. To me there's a remote and cloistered feeling here. One holds back speech for fear of disturbing something—what? From my earliest childhood I've felt that something was going on in the groves, something of which I was not a part. And if I had forgotten the feeling, I soon got it back. (page 339)

But now things changed. A San Francisco newspaper offered the young man a job as a special correspondent to go forth and "write up" the Sandwich Islands, in those days (1865) an unknown paradise, lost in the Pacific. Mark Twain undertook the task and carried it out with wonderful success; saw, traversed, explored, and described the islands as no one else could have done; and sent also to his paper, by a piece of journalistic good luck, the first news of a disaster at sea—a "scoop" of the first magnitude. His Sandwich Islands letters attracted great attention in California. They well deserved it. Apart from any incidental humor, they reveal that power of vivid description, that marvelous facility in conveying the sights and sounds in nature, which henceforth constitutes one of the distinctive charms of Mark Twain's work. He returned to San Francisco in a blaze of glory. (page 325)

Success greeted him on his return like a tidal wave. All of a sudden, it seemed, the American nation knew him and acclaimed him. His success was not as sudden, as sweeping, and as phenomenal as that of Dickens after the *Pickwick Papers,* but it was second only to it. And it had in it the same ingredient of personal affection. The public took Mark to its heart, as England had taken young "Boz"; and with an added feeling of national pride unknown and unnecessary in the case of Dickens. Here was, at last, an *American* author. The Longfellows and the Hawthornes and the Fenimore Coopers had written English literature in America. Here at last was a man who wrote American literature, and wrote it in and on Europe. The publication of the *Innocents Abroad* was the first step in the Americanization of Europe now reaching its climax.
(pages 327–28)

The desert, being an unwanted place, might well be the last stand of life against unlife. For in the rich and moist and wanted areas of the world, life pyramids against itself and in its confusion has finally allied itself with the enemy nonlife. And what the scorching, searing, freezing, poisoning weapons of nonlife have failed to do may be accomplished to the end of its destruction and extinction by the tactics of survival gone sour. If the most versatile of living forms, the human, now fights for survival as it always has, it can eliminate not only itself but all other life. And if that should transpire, unwanted places like the desert might be the harsh mother of repopulation. For the inhabitants of the desert are well trained and well armed against desolation. Even our own misguided species might re-emerge from the desert. The lone man and his sun-toughened wife who cling to the shade in an unfruitful and uncoveted place might, with their brothers in arms—the coyote, the jack rabbit, the horned toad, the rattlesnake, together with a host of armored insects— these trained and tested fragments of life might well be the last hope of life against nonlife. The desert has mothered magic things before this. (page 344)

YOUR OWN WRITING

Write a paragraph of descriptive exposition about some person in public life, explaining your opinion of this person and including details in support of your opinion.

READING BIOGRAPHY

The following passage from the selection about Dickens by Rupert Holland contains narration, description, and exposition. Watch for each as you read.

He was not yet due at the blacking factory, but he hurried away from his room and joined the crowd of early morning people already on their way to work. He went down the embankment along the Thames until he came to a place where a bench was set in a corner of a wall. This was his favorite lounging place: London Bridge was just beyond, the river lay in front of him, and he was far enough away from people to be secure from interruption. As he sat there watching the bridge and the Thames, a small girl came to join him. She was no bigger than he, perhaps a year or two older, but her face was already shrewd enough for that of a grown-up woman. She was the maid-of-all-work at a house in the neighborhood, and she had fallen into the habit of stopping to talk for a few moments with the boy on her way to work in the morning. She liked to listen to his stories. This was his hour for inventing them. He could spin wonderful tales about London Bridge, the Tower, and the wharves along the river. Sometimes he made up stories about the people who passed in front of them, and they were such astonishing stories that the girl remembered them all day as she worked in the house. He seemed to believe them himself; his eyes would grow far away and dreamy and his words would run on and on until a neighboring clock brought him suddenly back to his own position.

"You do know a heap o'things, don't you?" said the little girl, lost in admiration. "I'd rather have a shillin', though, than all the fairy tales in the world."

"I wouldn't," said Charles stoutly. "I'd rather read books than do anything else."

"You've got to eat, though," objected his companion; "and books won't make you food. 'T ain't common sense." She relented in an instant. "It's fun, though, Charley Dickens. Good-by till tomorrow."

Charles went on down to the old blacking factory by Hungerford Stairs, a ramshackle building almost hanging over the river, damp and overrun with rats. His place was in a recess of the counting room on the first floor, and as he covered the bottles with the oil-paper tops and tied them on with a string, he could look from time to time through a window at the slow coal barges swinging down the river.

There were very few boys about the place. At lunch time he would wander off by himself and, selecting his meal from a careful survey of several pastry cooks' windows, invest his money for the day in fancy cakes or a tart. He missed the company of friends his own age. Even Fanny, his oldest sister, he only saw on Sundays, when she came back to the Marshalsea from the place where she worked to spend the day with her family. It was only grown-up people that he saw most of the time, and they were too busy with their own affairs to take much interest in the small shabby boy who looked just like any one of the thousand other children of the streets. In all the men at the factory it was only the big clumsy fellow named Fagin who would stop to chat with the lad. So it was that Charles was forced to make friends with whomever he could, people of any age or condition; and was driven to spend much of his spare time roaming about the streets, lounging by the river, reading stray

books by a candle in the prison or in the little attic where he slept. It was not a boyhood that seemed to promise much.

In time the boy left the factory and tried being a lawyer's clerk, then a reporter, and at last wrote a book of his own. The book was *Pickwick Papers,* and it was so original that people clamored for more. Then the young man took note of all the strange types of people among whom he had lived as a boy, and those days of poverty and drudgery were turned to wonderful account because he could write of such people and such scenes as he remembered them. The little maid-of-all-work became the "Marchioness" in the *Old Curiosity Shop,* Bob Fagin loaned his name to *Oliver Twist,* and in *David Copperfield* we read the story of the small boy who had to fight his way through London alone. Those days of his boyhood had given him a deep insight into human nature, into the humor and pathos of other people's lives; and it was that rare insight that enabled him to become in time one of the greatest of all English writers, Charles Dickens, the beloved novelist of the Anglo-Saxon people. (pages 315–16)

List the main events that make up the narrative portions of this passage, the main ideas of the paragraphs of exposition, and the descriptive details that support these main ideas and help make the narrative alive and vivid.

SENTENCE SKILLS

As you know, variety in sentences is important in good writing. Look again at the paragraphs from "Mark Twain" (pages 346–47) and *Travels with Charley* (page 346), and notice the variety of sentence lengths and beginnings. Then revise your own writing for greater variety where needed.

ART AND LITERATURE

Choose one of the portraits on pages 379–84 that you find especially interesting, and tell, as in a biographical sketch, what you find most interesting about that person.

DRAMA

The drama is as old as civilization. The urge to play, to pretend, to re-enact seems to be an instinctive characteristic of the human race. Imagine a caveman returning from the hunt with a sabre-tooth tigerskin slung over his shoulder. As his tribe surrounds the campfire, imagine the hunter stepping into the center of the circle to retell the tale of the kill. See him move around the circle, brandishing his spear, stalking, crouching, pantomiming each phrase of the hunt until, as his story reaches its climax, he drives his spear quivering into the ground in front of him. Here is primitive drama in all its elements. And don't you imagine that the hunter, seeing his audience enthralled, would add a detail here, exaggerate an incident there, complicating and extending his story in order to squeeze out the last drop of excitement from the onlookers? You might almost say that the first playwright was one of these cave dwellers. Perhaps year after year, he would be asked to tell again the great story of the tiger hunt, and others would counter with their own dramatic stories.

From the beginning of language on, some people have wanted to tell stories while others have wanted to listen to them. There seems to be some special thrill in hearing, in a group, an exciting story well told—which, in drama, means well acted out. We tend to sympathize and identify with the hero, and at the same time, in the comfortable anonymity of the group, we know that we are not actually in danger. The tiger can't really kill us, but we like to pretend that it can. This odd, double feeling of being half involved in, half detached from, the story is an experience which the drama can give us more completely than any other form of literature. It is designed to do so.

A play, or a drama, is a story which is supposed to be performed in front of an audience. All three ingredients—story, performance, and audience—are essential elements. There must be a story, or no one will bother to sit quietly for any length of time; the story must be performed by actors, or puppets, or moving pictures of actors, otherwise we are simply in the realm of fiction, not drama; and finally, we, as readers or playgoers, must have the sense of being part of an audience, part of a group experiencing the play together and simultaneously, or else one of the great aspects and effects of drama is lost.

These three elements of the drama lead to a number of possibilities. The story normally has suspense which keeps us eagerly alert and interested until the end; because it was written to be performed, the good play normally has vital, clearly conceived characters, since actors must have roles which they can grasp and project; and finally, the play must speak to its audience, appealing to certain common denominators, so that a contagious, electric sense of sharing the experience will pulse through the theater. Costume, scenery, gestures, even the location of a character on the stage can all contribute to the telling of the story. A play may seem, in its printed form, to be merely a number of people saying a number of words. To see it staged, to see these people come alive and move on the stage, to hear their pauses as well as their words, is to experience drama. No abstract definitions or cozy readings of plays will really do the trick. Anybody who has been to a good play or movie has felt at least a small part of what the drama is all about.

One final word is necessary about the problems of reading plays rather than attending them as a part of an audience. Certainly there are some advantages in being able to pause over a speech, ponder a stage direction, and reflect at our own pace about the play we hold in our hands. Yet we must always remember that drama is intended to be performed. The playwright has worked long and hard over how the work will look and sound to an assembled multitude sitting in a theater for a certain designated period of time. To read the dialogue of a play, alone, at home, is to approach the work from a distorted, narrow position. Even Shakespeare's plays, which seem to stand up so well in the library under the close scrutiny of scholars of literature, show new and different dimensions and perspectives when they are seen on the stage.

Yet because we can't always go to plays, because we have to read them at home in books, we should still try to stage them as much as possible in our own minds. Our imaginations must create the theater for us, cast the characters, design their costumes and the scenery. The more this visual side, this theatricality, comes alive for us, the more we will appreciate the play.

The Boor

A Jest in One Act

ANTON CHEKHOV
(1860–1904)

In real life, people do not always act logically: they are often torn between what they want to do and what they think they should do. Neither do people in real life always speak logically: they often jump from topic to topic, sometimes making no connection between them. Sometimes, too, the reactions people have are difficult to explain. In serious moments, some people laugh; in funny situations, others may cry or become angry.

Anton Chekhov, who was trained as a doctor of medicine but who is generally considered as Russia's finest playwright, knew a great deal about human nature. Few writers have shown so detailed an acquaintance with the workings of the human mind. Rather than present his characters from a romantic or idealized point of view, he showed them as human beings—often foolish, often unexplainable, but always psychologically true to life. This is just what we find in Chekhov's one-act play, *The Boor*. Here the dramatist reveals his characters in a variety of differing moods, not all of them logical or explainable. The heroine "smiles through her tears," the hero continually contradicts himself, and neither the hero nor the heroine behaves as, ideally, we might expect a hero or a heroine to behave. Nevertheless, the reactions of Chekhov's characters are entirely believable. The play is an amusing one and a good introduction to comedy. In subtitling the play "a jest," Chekhov asks us to laugh with him at the foolishness of human beings and their poses.

Born the grandson of a serf in a tiny provincial town, Chekhov spent much of his youth working in his father's shop, where he waited on all kinds of people. Judging from his later knowledge of human nature, he missed nothing that went on. Although he struggled to work his way through medical school, he hardly ever practiced medicine: he discovered while he was still in school that he could make more money writing jokes and humorous stories for newspapers and magazines. Despite illness and financial pressures, it was not long before the success of his stories made Chekhov the chief breadwinner of his family. His talent grew steadily, and, before he was thirty, he was recognized as one of Russia's most promising young writers. He is remembered today both as a dramatist and as a short-story writer. His plays have had an enormous influence on the drama of our century. Aside from his plays, his short stories alone, with their exactness of detail and subtlety of mood, would have assured his worldwide reputation.

Though an early work, *The Boor* reveals the realistic approach to his characters that is so characteristic of all of Chekhov's writing. For this reason, there is probably no better introduction than *The Boor* to the work of this master dramatist.

Characters

YELENA IVANOVNA POPOVA,[1] *a little widow with dimpled cheeks, a land-owner*

GRIGORY STEPANOVICH SMIRNOV,[2] *a middle-aged gentleman farmer*

LUKA,[3] *Mme. Popova's footman, an old man*

The drawing room in Mme. Popova's manor house. Mme. Popova, in deep mourning, her eyes fixed on a photograph. Luka is on stage.

LUKA. It isn't right, madam. You're just killing yourself. The maid and the cook have gone berrying, every living thing rejoices, even the cat knows how to enjoy life and wanders through the courtyard catching birds, but you stay in the house as if it were a convent and take no pleasure at all. Yes, really! It's a whole year now, I figure, that you haven't left the house!

MME. POPOVA. And I never will leave it . . . What for? My life is over. He lies in his grave, and I have buried myself within these four walls. We are both dead.

LUKA. There you go again! I oughtn't to listen to you, really. Nikolay Mihailovich is dead; well, there is nothing to do about it, it's the will of God; may the kingdom of Heaven be his. You have grieved over it, and that's enough; there's a limit to everything. One can't cry and wear mourning forever. The time came when my old woman, too, died. Well? I grieved over it, I cried for a month, and that was enough for her, but to go on wailing all my life, why, the old woman isn't worth it. *(Sighs)* You've forgotten all your

neighbors. You don't go out and you won't receive anyone. We live, excuse me, like spiders—we never see the light of day. The mice have eaten the livery.[4] And it isn't as if there were no nice people around—the county is full of gentlemen. A regiment is quartered at Ryblov and every officer is a good-looker; you can't take your eyes off them. And every Friday there's a ball at the camp, and 'most every day the military band is playing. Eh, my dear lady, you're young and pretty, just peaches and cream, and you could lead a life of pleasure. Beauty doesn't last forever, you know. In ten years' time you'll find yourself wanting to strut like a peahen and dazzle the officers, but it will be too late.

MME. POPOVA *(resolutely)*. I beg you never to mention this to me again! You know that since Nikolay Mihailovich died, life has been worth nothing to me. You think that I am alive, but it only seems so to you! I vowed to myself that never to the day of my death would I take off my mourning or see the light. Do you hear me? Let his shade[5] see how I love him! Yes, I know, it is no secret to you that he was often unjust to me, cruel, and . . . even unfaithful, but I shall be true to the end and prove to him how I can love. There, in the other world, he will find me just the same as I was before he died . . .

LUKA. Instead of talking like that, you ought to go and take a walk in the garden or have Toby or Giant put in the shafts and drive out to pay calls on the neighbors.

MME. POPOVA. Oh! *(Weeps)*

LUKA. Madam! Dear madam! What's wrong? Bless you!

MME. POPOVA. He was so fond of Toby! When he drove out to the Korchagins and

[1] **Yelena Ivanovna Popova** (yel′ən·ə ē′vàn·ōv′nə pop′ōv′ə).
[2] **Grigory Stepanovich Smirnov** (grig′ôr·ē step·an′·ə·vich smûr′nov).
[3] **Luka** (lōō′kə).

[4] **livery:** servants' uniforms.
[5] **shade:** ghost, spirit.

the Vlasovs it was always with Toby. What a wonderful driver he was! How graceful he was when he pulled at the reins with all his might! Do you remember? Toby, Toby! Tell them to give him an extra measure of oats today.

LUKA. Very well, madam. (*The door-bell rings sharply.*)

MME. POPOVA (*startled*). Who is it? Say that I am at home to no one.

LUKA. Very good, madam. (*Exits.*)

MME. POPOVA (*looking at the photograph*). You shall see, Nicolas, how I can love and forgive. My love will die only with me, when my poor heart stops beating. (*Laughs through her tears*) And aren't you ashamed? I am a good, faithful little wife; I've locked myself in and shall remain true to you to the grave, and you ... aren't you ashamed, you naughty boy? You were unfaithful to me, you made scenes, you left me alone for weeks ... (LUKA *enters.*)

LUKA (*disturbed*). Madam, someone is asking for you, wants to see you ...

MME. POPOVA. But you told him, didn't you, that since my husband's death I receive no one?

LUKA. Yes, I did, but he wouldn't listen to me; he says it's a very urgent matter.

MME. POPOVA. I do not receive anyone!

LUKA. I told him, but ... he's a perfect devil ... he curses and barges right in ... he's in the dining room now.

MME. POPOVA (*annoyed*). Very well, ask him in ... What rude people! (*Exit* LUKA.) How irritating! What do they want of me? Why do they have to intrude on my solitude? (*Sighs*) No, I see I shall really have to enter a convent. (*Pensively*) Yes, a convent ... (*Enter* SMIRNOV *and* LUKA.)

SMIRNOV (*to* LUKA). Blockhead, you talk too much. You jackass! (*Seeing* MME. POPOVA, *with dignity*) Madam, I have the honor to introduce myself: Land-owner Grigory Stepanovich Smirnov, lieutenant of the artillery, retired. I am compelled to disturb you in connection with a very weighty matter.

MME. POPOVA (*without offering her hand*). What do you wish?

SMIRNOV. At his death your late husband, with whom I had the honor of being acquainted, was in my debt to the amount of 1200 rubles,[1] for which I hold two notes. As I have to pay interest on a loan to the Land Bank tomorrow, I must request you, madam, to pay me the money today.

MME. POPOVA. Twelve hundred.... And for what did my husband owe you the money?

SMIRNOV. He used to buy oats from me.

MME. POPOVA (*sighing, to* LUKA). So don't forget, Luka, to tell them to give Toby an extra measure of oats. (*Exit* LUKA. *To* SMIRNOV) If Nikolay Mihailovich owed you money, I shall pay you, of course; but you must excuse me, I haven't any ready cash today. The day after tomorrow my steward[2] will be back from town and I will see that he pays you what is owing to you, but just now I cannot comply with your request. Besides, today is exactly seven months since my husband's death and I am in no mood to occupy myself with money matters.

SMIRNOV. And I am in the mood to be carried out feet foremost if I don't pay the interest tomorrow. They'll seize my estate!

MME. POPOVA. The day after tomorrow you will receive your money.

SMIRNOV. I need the money today, not the day after tomorrow.

MME. POPOVA. I am sorry, but I cannot pay you today.

---

[1] **1,200 rubles:** approximately $600.00. At the time this play was written, the ruble was worth about fifty cents in present-day American money.

[2] **steward:** the manager of an estate.

SMIRNOV. And I can't wait till the day after tomorrow.

MME. POPOVA. But what can I do if I don't have the money now!

SMIRNOV. So you can't pay me?

MME. POPOVA. No, I can't.

SMIRNOV. H'm . . . So that's your last word?

MME. POPOVA. My last word.

SMIRNOV. Your last word? Positively?

MME. POPOVA. Positively.

SMIRNOV. Many thanks. I'll make a note of it. (Shrugs his shoulders) And they want me to keep cool! I meet the tax commissioner on the road, and he asks me: "Why are you always in a bad humor, Grigory Stepanovich?" But in heaven's name, how can I help being in a bad humor? I'm in desperate need of money. I left home yesterday morning at dawn and called on all my debtors and not one of them paid up! I wore myself out, slept the devil knows where, in some inn next to a barrel of vodka . . . Finally I come here, fifty miles from home, hoping to get something, and I'm confronted with a "mood." How can I help getting in a temper?

MME. POPOVA. I thought I made it clear to you that you will get your money as soon as my steward returns from town.

SMIRNOV. I didn't come to your steward, but to you! What the devil—pardon the expression—do I care for your steward!

MME. POPOVA. Excuse me, sir, I am not accustomed to such language or to such a tone. I won't listen to you any more. (Exits rapidly.)

SMIRNOV. That's a nice thing! Not in the mood . . . husband died seven months ago! What about me? Do I have to pay the interest or don't I? I'm asking you: do I have to pay the interest or don't I? Well, your husband died, you're not in the mood, and all that . . . and your steward, devil take him, has gone off somewhere, but what do you want me to do? Am I to escape my creditors in a balloon, eh? Or take a running start and dash my head against a wall? I call on Gruzdev, he's not at home, Yaroshevich is hiding, I had an awful row with Kuritzyn and nearly threw him out of the window; Mazutov has an upset stomach, and this one isn't in the mood! Not one scoundrel will pay up! And it's all because I've spoiled them, because I'm a milksop, a softy, a weak sister. I'm too gentle with them altogether! But wait! You'll find out what I'm like! I won't let you make a fool of me, devil take it! I'll stay right here till she pays up! Ugh! I'm in a perfect rage today, in a rage! Every one of my nerves is trembling with fury, I can hardly breathe. Ouf! Good Lord, I even feel sick! (Shouts) You there! (Enter LUKA.)

LUKA. What do you wish?

SMIRNOV: Give me some kvass [1] or a drink of water! (Exit LUKA.) No, but the logic of it! A fellow is in desperate need of cash, is on the point of hanging himself, but she won't pay up, because, you see, she isn't in the mood to occupy herself with money matters! Real petticoat logic! That's why I've never liked to talk to women, and I don't now. I'd rather sit on a powder keg than talk to a woman. Brr! I'm getting gooseflesh—that skirt made me so furious! I just have to see one of these poetic creatures from a distance and my very calves begin to twitch with rage. It's enough to make me yell for help. (Enter LUKA.)

LUKA (handing SMIRNOV a glass of water). Madam is ill and will see no one.

SMIRNOV. Get out! (Exit LUKA.) Ill and will see no one! All right, don't see me. I'll sit here until you pay up. If you're sick for a week, I'll stay a week; if you're sick a year, I'll stay a year. I'll get my own

[1] **kvass:** a Russian drink resembling beer.

back, my good woman. You won't get round me with your widow's weeds [1] and your dimples . . . We know those dimples! *(Shouts through the window)* Semyon, take out the horses! We're not leaving so soon! I'm staying on! Tell them at the stables to give the horses oats. You block-head, you've let the left outrider's leg get caught in the reins again! *(Mimicking the coachman)* "It don't matter" . . . I'll show you "don't matter." *(Walks away from the window)* It's horrible . . . the heat is terrific, nobody has paid up, I slept badly, and here's this skirt in mourning, with her moods! I have a headache. Shall I have some vodka? Yes, I think I will. *(Shouts)* You there! *(Enter LUKA.)*

LUKA. What do you wish?

SMIRNOV. Give me a glass of vodka. *(Exit LUKA.)* Ouf! *(Sits down and looks himself over)* I cut a fine figure, I must say! All dusty, boots dirty, unwashed, un-combed, straw on my vest. The little lady must have taken me for a highwayman. *(Yawns)* It's a bit uncivil to barge into a drawing room in such shape, but never mind . . . I'm no caller, just a creditor, and there are no rules as to what the creditor should wear. *(Enter LUKA.)*

LUKA *(handing SMIRNOV the vodka)*. You allow yourself too many liberties, sir . . .

[1] **widow's weeds:** mourning dress.

SMIRNOV *(crossly)*. What?

LUKA. I . . . nothing . . . I just meant . . .

SMIRNOV. To whom do you think you're talking? Shut up!

LUKA *(aside)*. There's a demon in the house . . . The Evil Spirit must have brought him . . . *(Exit LUKA.)*

SMIRNOV. Oh, what a rage I'm in! I'm mad enough to grind the whole world to powder. I feel sick. *(Shouts)* You there! *(Enter MME. POPOVA.)*

MME. POPOVA *(with downcast eyes)*. Sir, in my solitude I've long since grown unaccustomed to the human voice, and I cannot bear shouting. I beg you not to disturb my peace!

SMIRNOV. Pay me my money and I'll drive off.

MME. POPOVA. I told you in plain language, I have no ready cash now. Wait till the day after tomorrow.

SMIRNOV. And I had the honor of telling you in plain language that I need the money today, not the day after tomorrow. If you don't pay me today, I'll have to hang myself tomorrow.

MME. POPOVA. But what shall I do if I have no money? How odd!

SMIRNOV. So you won't pay me now, eh?

MME. POPOVA. I can't.

SMIRNOV. In that case I stay and I'll sit here till I get the money. *(Sits down)* You'll pay me the day after tomorrow?

Excellent. I'll sit here till the day after tomorrow. *(Jumps up)* I ask you: Do I have to pay the interest tomorrow or don't I? Or do you think I'm joking?

MME. POPOVA. Sir, I beg you not to shout. This is no stable.

SMIRNOV. Never mind the stable, I'm asking you: Do I have to pay the interest tomorrow or not?

MME. POPOVA. You don't know how to behave in the presence of ladies!

SMIRNOV. No, madam, I do know how to behave in the presence of ladies!

MME. POPOVA. No, you do not! You are a rude, ill-bred man! Decent people don't talk to women that way!

SMIRNOV. Admirable! How would you like me to talk to you? In French, eh? *(Rages, and lisps)* Madame, je vous prie,[1] I am delighted that you do not pay me my money . . . Ah, pardonnez-moi[2] if I have discommoded you! It's such delightful weather today! And how your mourning becomes you! *(Scrapes his foot)*

MME. POPOVA. That's rude and silly.

SMIRNOV *(mimicking her)*. Rude and silly! I don't know how to behave in the presence of ladies! Madam, I've seen more ladies than you've seen sparrows! I've fought three duels on account of women, I've jilted twelve women and been jilted by nine! Yes, madam! Time was when I played the fool, sentimentalized, used honeyed words, went out of my way to please, bowed and scraped . . . I used to love, pine, sigh at the moon, feel blue, melt, freeze . . . I loved passionately, madly, all sorts of ways, devil take me; I chattered like a magpie about the emancipation of women, I wasted half my fortune on affairs of the heart, but now, please excuse me! Now you won't bamboozle me! Enough! Dark eyes, burning eyes, ruby lips, dimpled cheeks, the moon, whispers, timid breathing . . . I wouldn't give a brass farthing[3] for all this now, madam. Present company excepted, all women, young or old, put on airs, pose, gossip, are liars to the marrow of their bones, are malicious, vain, petty, cruel, revoltingly unreasonable, and as for this *(Taps his forehead)*, pardon my frankness, a sparrow can give ten points to any philosopher in skirts! You look at one of these poetic creatures: She's all muslin and fluff, an airy demigoddess, a million transports, but look into her soul and what do you see but a common crocodile! *(Grips the back of his chair so that it cracks and breaks)* But what is most revolting, this crocodile for some reason imagines that the tender feelings are her special province, her privilege, her monopoly! Why, devil take it, hang me by my feet on that nail, but can a woman love anything except a lap dog? When she's in love all she can do is whimper and turn on the waterworks! While a man suffers and makes sacrifices, her love finds expression only in swishing her train and trying to get a firmer grip on your nose. You, madam, have the misfortune of being a woman, so you know the nature of women down to the ground. Tell me honestly, then, did you ever see a woman who was sincere, faithful, and constant? You never did! Only old women and frights are faithful and constant. You'll sooner come across a horned cat or a white woodcock than a constant woman!

MME. POPOVA. Allow me to ask, then, who, in your opinion, is faithful and constant in love? Not man?

SMIRNOV. Yes, madam, man!

MME. POPOVA. Man! *(With bitter laughter)* Man is faithful and constant in love! That's news! *(Hotly)* What earthly right do you have to say that? Men faithful

---

[1] *je vous prie* (zhə vōō prē): I beg of you (French).
[2] *pardonnez-moi* (par·dôn′ā·mwa′): pardon me (French).

[3] **brass farthing**: a worthless coin.

and constant! If such is the case, let me tell you that of all the men I have ever known my late husband was the best. I loved him passionately, with my whole soul, as only a young, deep-natured women can love. I gave him my youth, my happiness, my life, my fortune; I lived and breathed by him; I worshiped him like a heathen, and . . . and what happened? This best of men deceived me shamelessly at every step! After his death I found a whole drawerful of love letters in his desk, and while he was alive—I can't bear to recall it!—he would leave me alone for weeks on end; he made love to other women before my very eyes, and he was unfaithful to me; he squandered my money and mocked my feelings. And in spite of it all, I loved him and was faithful to him. More than that, he died, and I am still faithful to him, still constant. I have buried myself forever within these four walls, and I will not take off my mourning till I go to my grave.

SMIRNOV (laughing scornfully). Mourning! I wonder who you take me for! As if I didn't know why you are masquerading in black like this and why you've buried yourself within four walls! Of course I do! It's so mysterious, so poetic! Some cadet or some puny versifier will ride past the house, glance at the windows, and say to himself: "Here lives the mysterious Tamara who, for love of her husband, has buried herself within four walls." We know those tricks!

MME. POPOVA (flaring up). What! How dare you say this to me!

SMIRNOV. You've buried yourself alive, but you haven't forgotten to powder your nose.

MME. POPOVA. How dare you talk to me like that!

SMIRNOV. Please don't scream, I'm not your steward! Allow me to call a spade a spade. I'm no woman and I'm used to talking straight from the shoulder! So please don't shout!

MME. POPOVA. I'm not shouting, you are shouting! Please leave me alone!

SMIRNOV. Pay me my money, and I'll go.

MME. POPOVA. I won't give you any money.

SMIRNOV. No, madam, you will!

MME. POPOVA. Just to spite you, I won't give you a penny. Only leave me alone!

SMIRNOV. I haven't the pleasure of being either your husband or your fiancé, so kindly, no scenes. (Sits down) I don't like them.

MME. POPOVA (choking with rage). You've sat down?

SMIRNOV. I've sat down.

MME. POPOVA. I ask you to leave.

SMIRNOV. Give me my money . . . (Aside) Oh, what a rage I'm in, what a rage!

MME. POPOVA. Such impudence! I don't want to talk to you. Please get out. (Pause) Are you going? No?

SMIRNOV. No.

MME. POPOVA. No?

SMIRNOV. No!

MME. POPOVA. Very well, then. (Enter LUKA.)

MME. POPOVA. Luka, show this gentleman out!

LUKA (approaching SMIRNOV). Sir, be good enough to leave when you are asked to. Don't be——

SMIRNOV (jumping to his feet). Shut up! Who do you think you're talking to! I'll make hash of you!

LUKA (clutching at his heart). Mercy on us! Holy saints! (Drops into an armchair) Oh, I'm sick, I'm sick! I can't get my breath!

MME. POPOVA. But where is Dasha? Dasha? (Shouts) Dasha! Pelageya! Dasha! (Rings)

LUKA. Oh, they've all gone berrying .... There's no one here ... I'm sick, water!

MME. POPOVA (to SMIRNOV). Please, get out!

SMIRNOV. Can't you be a little more civil?

MME. POPOVA (clenching her fists and stamping her feet). You're a boor! A brute, a bully, a monster!

SMIRNOV. What! What did you say?

MME. POPOVA. I said that you were a brute, a monster.

SMIRNOV (advancing upon her). Excuse me, but what right have you to insult me?

MME. POPOVA. Yes, I insulted you. What of it? Do you think I'm afraid of you?

SMIRNOV. And you think, just because you're a poetic creature, you can insult people with impunity, eh? I challenge you!

LUKA. Mercy on us! Holy saints! Water!

SMIRNOV. We'll shoot it out!

MME. POPOVA. Just because you have big fists and bellow like a bull, you think I'm afraid of you, eh? Bully!

SMIRNOV. I challenge you! I won't allow anybody to insult me, and it makes no difference to me that you're a woman, a member of the weaker sex.

MME. POPOVA (trying to outshout him). Brute, brute, brute!

SMIRNOV. It's high time to abandon the prejudice that men alone must pay for insults. Equal rights are equal rights, devil take it! I challenge you!

MME. POPOVA. You want to shoot it out? Well and good.

SMIRNOV. This very minute.

MME. POPOVA. This very minute. I have my husband's pistols. I'll bring them directly. (Walks rapidly away and turns back) What pleasure it will give me to put a bullet into your brazen head! Devil take you! (Exits.)

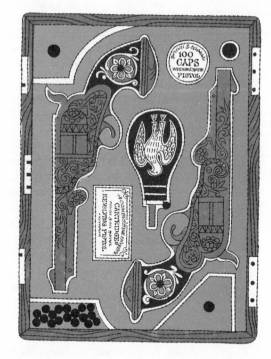

SMIRNOV. I'll bring her down like a duck. I'm no boy, no sentimental puppy. There's no weaker sex as far as I'm concerned.

LUKA (to SMIRNOV). Master, kind sir! (Going down on his knees) Have pity on an old man, do me a favor—go away from here! You've frightened me to death, and now you want to fight a duel!

SMIRNOV (not listening to him). A duel! That's equal rights, that's emancipation! That's equality of the sexes for you! I'll bring her down as a matter of principle. But what a woman! (Mimics her) "Devil take you ... I'll put a bullet into your brazen head." What a woman! She flushed and her eyes shone! She accepted the challenge! Word of honor, it's the first time in my life that I've seen one of the stripe.

LUKA. Kind master, please go away, and I will pray for you always.

SMIRNOV. That's a woman! That's the kind I understand! A real woman! Not a sour-faced, spineless crybaby, but a creature all fire and gunpowder, a cannon ball! It's a pity I have to kill her!

LUKA (crying). Sir, kind sir, please go away!

SMIRNOV. I positively like her! Positively! Even though she has dimples in her cheeks, I like her! I am even ready to forgive her the debt . . . And I'm not angry any more. A remarkable woman! (Enter MME. POPOVA with the pistols.)

MME. POPOVA. Here are the pistols. But before we fight, please show me how to shoot. I never held a pistol in my hands before.

LUKA. Lord, have mercy on us! I'll go and look for the gardener and the coachman. Why has this calamity befallen us? (Exits.)

SMIRNOV (examining the pistols). You see, there are several makes of pistols. There are Mortimers, specially made for duelling, they are fired with the percussion cap. What you have here are Smith and Wesson triple-action, central-fire revolvers with extractors. Excellent pistols! Worth ninety rubles a pair at least. You hold the revolver like this . . . (Aside) The eyes, the eyes! A woman to set you on fire!

MME. POPOVA. Like this?

SMIRNOV. Yes, like this. Then you cock the trigger . . . and you take aim like this . . . throw your head back a little! Stretch your arm out properly . . . Like this . . . Then you press this gadget with this finger, and that's all there is to it. . . . The main thing is: Keep cool and take aim slowly. . . . And try not to jerk your arm.

MME. POPOVA. Very well. It's inconvenient to shoot indoors; let's go into the garden.

SMIRNOV. All right. Only I warn you, I'll fire into the air.

MME. POPOVA. That's all that was wanting. Why?

SMIRNOV. Because . . . because . . . It's my business why.

MME. POPOVA. You're scared, eh? Ah, ah, ah! No, sir, don't try to get out of it! Be so good as to follow me. I shan't rest until I've drilled a hole in your forehead . . . this forehead that I hate so! Scared?

SMIRNOV. Yes, I am scared.

MME. POPOVA. You're lying! Why do you refuse to fight?

SMIRNOV. Because . . . because I . . . like you.

MME. POPOVA (laughing bitterly). He likes me! He dares to say that he likes me! (Shows him the door) You may go.

SMIRNOV (silently puts down the revolver, takes his cap and walks to the door; there he stops and for half a minute the pair look at each other without a word; then he says, hesitatingly approaching MME. POPOVA). Listen . . . Are you still angry? I'm in a devil of a temper myself, but you see . . . how shall I put it? . . . the thing is . . . you see . . . it's this way . . . in fact . . . (Shouts) Well, am I to blame if I like you? (Clutches the back of his chair; it cracks and breaks) The devil! What fragile furniture you have! I like you. You understand. I've almost fallen in love.

MME. POPOVA. Go away from me. I hate you.

SMIRNOV. God, what a woman! Never in my life have I seen anything like her! I'm lost. I'm done for. I'm trapped like a mouse.

MME. POPOVA. Go away or I'll shoot.

SMIRNOV. Shoot! You can't understand what happiness it would be to die before those enchanting eyes . . . to die of a revolver shot fired by this little velvet hand! I've lost my mind. Think a moment and decide right now, because if I leave this house, we'll never see each other again. Decide. I'm a landed gentleman, a decent fellow, with an income of ten thousand a year; I can put a bullet through a penny thrown into the air; I have a good stable. Will you be my wife?

MME. POPOVA (*indignant, brandishing the revolver*). We'll shoot it out! Come along! Get your pistol.

SMIRNOV. I've lost my mind. I don't understand anything. (*Shouts*) You there! Some water!

MME. POPOVA (*shouts*). Come! Let's shoot it out!

SMIRNOV. I've lost my mind. I've fallen in love like a boy, like a fool. (*Seizes her by the hand; she cries out with pain.*) I love you. (*Goes down on his knees*) I love you as I've never loved before. I jilted twelve women and was jilted by nine. But I didn't love one of them as I do you. I've gotten sentimental. I'm melting. I'm weak as water. Here I am on my knees like a fool, and I offer you my hand. It's a shame, a disgrace! For five years I've not been in love. I took a vow. And suddenly I'm bowled over, swept off my feet. I offer you my hand—yes or no? You won't? Then don't! (*Rises and walks rapidly to the door*)

MME. POPOVA. Wait a minute.

SMIRNOV (*stops*). Well?

MME. POPOVA. Never mind. Go . . . But no, wait a minute . . . No, go, go! I detest you! Or no . . . don't go! Oh, if you knew how furious I am, how furious! (*Throws the revolver on the table*) My fingers are cramped from holding this vile thing. (*Tears her handkerchief in a fit of temper*) What are you standing there for? Get out!

SMIRNOV. Good-by.

MME. POPOVA. Yes, yes, go! (*Shouts*) Where are you going? Wait a minute . . . But no, go away . . . Oh, how furious I am! Don't come near me, don't come near me!

SMIRNOV (*approaching her*). I'm disgusted with myself! Falling in love like a

mooncalf, going down on my knees. It gives me gooseflesh. (*Rudely*) I love you. What on earth made me fall in love with you? Tomorrow I have to pay the interest. And we've started mowing. And here are you! . . . (*Puts his arm around her waist*) I shall never forgive myself for this.

MME. POPOVA. Get away from me! Hands off! I hate you! Let's shoot it out!

[*A prolonged kiss. Enter* LUKA *with an axe, the gardener with a rake, the coachman with a pitchfork, and hired men with sticks.*]

LUKA (*catching sight of the pair kissing*). Mercy on us! Holy saints! (*Pauses*)

MME. POPOVA (*dropping her eyes*). Luka, tell them at the stables that Toby isn't to have any oats at all today.

FOR STUDY AND DISCUSSION

1. At the beginning of a play, the playwright usually introduces the characters by providing facts about their personalities and background. What facts does Chekhov provide in the first four speeches of *The Boor?* Why has Mme. Popova shut herself up in her house? Is she suffering from real grief, or is she trying to prove something? What in her speeches makes you think so?

2. Smirnov announces himself as a "lieutenant of the artillery, retired." How is his rough-and-ready military background reflected in his personality and behavior?

3. Why does Mme. Popova say she can't pay Smirnov? Are her excuses believable? Why does Smirnov insist on immediate payment? Do you think his case is as urgent as he says it is? What makes you think so?

4. What does Smirnov vow to do when Mme. Popova refuses to pay him? Which seems to make him angrier, not getting his money or encountering a woman "with a 'mood' "?

5. What are Smirnov's and Mme. Popova's different views of the attitudes of men and

women toward each other? What personal experiences have given them such different views? In what way were their experiences similar?

6. When Mme. Popova tells Smirnov why she is still in mourning, what does Smirnov suggest is the real reason for her mourning? Who do you think is nearer the truth? Why?

7. What hints, besides her dimples, does Chekhov give us that Mme. Popova is not really suited to everlasting mourning? What indication does he give that Smirnov really likes ladies despite his complaints about them?

8. How does Mme. Popova "insult" Smirnov? Why does he challenge her to a duel? How does she react to his challenge? Why is her reaction "in character"—that is, would you expect her to react this way from what you have seen of her so far in the play?

9. Where did you first feel that Mme. Popova likes Smirnov? Where does Smirnov first show his liking for her? Is his sudden admiration for her believable? Why or why not?

10. Reread the part of the play where Smirnov explains the pistols to Mme. Popova and demonstrates how they work. What is amusing about this situation? How is Smirnov's preoccupation with the pistols, despite his real feelings, typical of the actions of both characters throughout the play?

11. Comedy often pokes fun at the poses of human beings—at the differences between how people behave toward others and how they really feel. *The Boor* is in this tradition. Where in the play do the characters hide behind make-believe poses instead of admitting what they really feel? Are they more honest with themselves at the end of the play than they were at the beginning?

THE CRAFT OF THE DRAMATIST

1. So that the audience can respond to the plot and characters, early in the play dramatists must make the audience aware of essential background facts: they must identify their characters and describe the situation in which they find themselves. Chekhov provides his background facts—the *exposition,* as it is called—in the first four speeches of *The Boor.* How essential are these speeches to the unfolding action of the play? How does Chekhov enable his exposition to develop naturally out of the dialogue?

2. What is the function of Luka in the play? of the servants who appear at the end of the play? How would the play be different without these characters? What would be lost if Chekhov had not written these characters into his play?

3. Who is Toby? What does he stand for in the play? Why did Mme. Popova order that he be given extra oats? Why does she order, at the end of the play, that he be given no oats at all?

4. Toward the end of *The Boor,* Chekhov calls for his two main characters to stop "for half a minute . . . [and] look at each other without a word" (page 359). What is the reason for this long pause? What function does it serve in the play?

5. Like most good dramatists, Chekhov makes effective use of props and costumes to underscore the meaning of his dialogue and action on stage. How do the following things emphasize important aspects of the play?

Mme. Popova's black clothes
The photograph of Mme. Popova's husband
Smirnov's dusty clothes and dirty boots
The glasses of water and vodka brought by Luka
The chair that breaks
The dueling pistols
The axe, rake, pitchfork, and sticks brought by the servants at the end of the play

6. Did you find the play funny? What makes it funny? Are there any really witty lines, or does Chekhov get his humor out of character and situation? What did you feel was the most amusing scene?

FOR COMPOSITION

From the information given in the play, write a character sketch of Mme. Popova's husband, describing what he looked like and how he treated her. In a final paragraph, tell why, given the kind of man he was, you think Mme. Popova was or was not foolish to mourn so deeply over him.

Abe Lincoln in Illinois

═══════════

ROBERT E. SHERWOOD

(1896–1955)

We all know a good deal about Abraham Lincoln. In writing this play, Robert Sherwood realized that his audience would already know who Lincoln was, what he did, and what he strove for. Sherwood's task as a playwright was to show the man behind the President, to take the audience beyond Lincoln as a public official and enable them to share a great man's human fears. In doing this, Sherwood had to deal with ideas and feelings as well as with historical fact, but he worked hard to discover all he could about Lincoln so that his own interpretation of him would be as close as possible to the truth.

In this play, then, is an opportunity to study biography as well as drama. As you read the play, keep on the lookout for ideas of Lincoln that are new to you—personal glimpses that help you to see the man behind the many legends about him. Also watch for the techniques of playwriting that Sherwood uses to present his portrait of Lincoln on the stage.

Like Carl Sandburg, Robert Sherwood won Pulitzer prizes in two different fields. Sherwood's prizes were for history and drama. His most powerful plays are based on the characters of people who are forced to move from detachment to involvement in life's affairs. *Abe Lincoln in Illinois*, *Idiot's Delight*, and *There Shall Be No Night* all deal with this theme, and all won the Pulitzer prize.

Since *Abe Lincoln in Illinois* is an attempt to present on the stage a number of different sides of Lincoln's personality, every scene contributes something toward that end, and in each you should learn something new about Abe Lincoln. Perhaps the best way to look at this play is to consider every word and incident a beam of light thrown upon Lincoln the man. Look, for example, at the three scenes of Act I: first, we see Lincoln, as a student, attempting to understand the world around him; next, we see him among men and with a pretty girl; and finally, we learn more of what is going on inside him. Through all these scenes, we come to realize that Abe is hardly the simple, uncomplicated backwoodsman we might once have thought he was.

Characters

ABE LINCOLN

MENTOR GRAHAM, *a school teacher*

ANN RUTLEDGE, *Lincoln's sweetheart, daughter of New Salem tavern owner*

BEN MATTLING, *Revolutionary War veteran*

JUDGE BOWLING GREEN and NANCY GREEN, *New Salem lawyer and his wife, old friends to Lincoln*

NINIAN EDWARDS and ELIZABETH EDWARDS, *prominent Springfield citizen and his wife, later, Lincoln's brother- and sister-in-law*

JOSHUA SPEED, *Springfield merchant, Lincoln's closest friend*

TRUM COGDAL, *elderly New Salem conservative*

JACK ARMSTRONG, BAB, FEARGUS, JASP, *New Salem rowdies*

SETH, AGGIE, and JIMMY GALE, *frontiersman, an early acquaintance of Lincoln, his wife and child*

GOBEY, *freed slave, servant to the Gales*

WILLIAM (BILLY) HERNDON, *Lincoln's law clerk and, later, partner*

MARY TODD, *sister to Elizabeth Edwards, later Lincoln's wife*

STEPHEN A. DOUGLAS, *Lincoln's political opponent*

WILLIE, TAD, and ROBERT LINCOLN, *Lincoln's sons*

CRIMMIN, *Eastern politician*

BARRICK, *Episcopal minister from Boston*

STURVESON, *wealthy manufacturer from Philadelphia*

JED and PHIL, *helpers at Lincoln's campaign headquarters*

KAVANAGH and MAJOR, *officers assigned to guard Lincoln*

ACT I

SCENE I

MENTOR GRAHAM'S *cabin near New Salem, Illinois. In the late 1830's, late at night. There is one rude table, piled with books and papers. Over it hangs an oil lamp, the only source of light.*

At one side of table sits MENTOR GRAHAM, *a middle-aged, patient school teacher. Across from him is* ABE LINCOLN, *a young man, gaunt, tired but intent, dressed in the ragged clothes of a backwoodsman.* MENTOR *is leaning on table.* ABE'S *chair is tilted back, so that his face is out of the light.* MENTOR *turns a page in a grammar book.*

MENTOR. The Moods. (MENTOR *closes book and looks at* ABE.) Every one of us has many moods. You yourself have more than your share of them, Abe. They express the various aspects of your character. So it is with the English language—and you must try to consider this language as if it were a living person, who may be awkward and stumbling, or pompous and pretentious, or simple and direct. Name me the five moods.

ABE. The Indicative, Imperative, Potential, Subjunctive and Infinitive.

MENTOR. And what do they signify?

ABE. The Indicative mood is the easy one. It just indicates a thing—like "He loves," "He is loved"—or, when you put it in the form of a question, "Does he love?" or "Is he loved?" The Imperative mood is used for commanding, like "Get out!"

MENTOR. Is that the best example you can think of?

ABE. Well, you can put it in the Bible way—like "Give us this day our daily bread and forgive us our trespasses."

MENTOR. Yes—here—— (*Reaches for newspaper in the mess on the table*) I want you to read this—it's a speech delivered by Mr. Webster [1] before the United States Senate. A fine document, and a perfect usage of the Imperative mood in its hortatory [2] sense. Here it is—read this down here.

ABE (*moves into light*). "'While the Union lasts,' the Senator continued in the deep rich tones of the historic church bells of his native Boston, 'we have high prospects spread out before us, for us and our children. Beyond that I seek not to penetrate the veil. God grant that in my day, at least, the curtain may not rise.'"

MENTOR. Don't read it off as if it were an inventory of Denton Offut's groceries. Imagine that you're making the speech before the Senate with the fate of your country at stake. Put your own life into it!

ABE (*reads*). "When my eyes shall be turned to behold for the last time the sun in heaven, may I not see him shining on the broken and dishonored fragments of a once glorious Union; on States dissevered, discordant, belligerent; on a land rent with civil feuds, or drenched, it may be, in fraternal blood! Let their last feeble

---

[1] **Daniel Webster:** American lawyer and statesman, famed for his powerful speeches.

[2] **hortatory** (hôr′tə·tôr′e′): intended to excite or rouse to action.

glance rather behold the glorious ensign of the republic, now known and honored throughout the earth, not a single star of it obscured, bearing for its motto no such miserable——"

MENTOR. "Interrogatory."

ABE. "—interrogatory as 'What is all this worth?' Nor those other words of delusion and folly, 'Liberty first and Union afterwards'; but everywhere, spread all over in characters of living light, that other sentiment, dear to every true American heart—Liberty and Union . . ."

MENTOR. Emphasize the *"and."*

ABE. "Liberty *and* Union, now and forever, one and inseparable!" *(He puts paper back on table.)* He must have had 'em up on their feet cheering with *that,* all right.

MENTOR. Some cheered, and some spat, depending on which section they came from.

ABE. What was he talking about?

MENTOR. It was in the debate over the right of any state to secede from the Union. Calhoun had pleaded South Carolina's cause—pleaded it ably. He said that just as we have liberty as individuals—so have we liberty as states—to go as we please. Which means, if we don't like the Union, as expressed by the will of its majority, then we can leave it, and set up a new nation or many nations—so that this continent might be as divided as Europe. But Webster answered him, all right. He proved that without union we'd have precious little liberty left. Now—go on with the Potential mood.

ABE. That signifies possibility—usually of an unpleasant nature. Like, "If I ever get out of debt, I will probably get right back in again."

MENTOR *(smiles).* Why did you select that example, Abe?

ABE. Well—it just happens to be the thought that's always heaviest on my mind.

MENTOR. Is the store [1] in trouble again?

ABE *(calmly).* Yes. Berry's drunk all the whiskey we ought to have sold, and we're going to have to shut up any day now. I guess I'm my father's own son, all right. Give me a steady job, and I'll fail at it.

MENTOR. You haven't been a failure here, Abe. There isn't a man-jack in this community that isn't fond of you and anxious to help you get ahead.

ABE *(with some bitterness).* I know—just like you, Mentor, sitting up late nights to give me learning, out of the goodness of your heart. And now Josh Speed and Judge Green and some of the others I owe money to want to get me the job of postmaster, thinking maybe I can handle that, since there's only one mail comes in a week. I've got my friends, all right—the best friends. But they can't change my luck, or maybe it's just my nature.

MENTOR. What you want to do is get

[1] **the store:** a grocery store in New Salem in which Lincoln was a partner.

out of New Salem. This poor little forgotten town will never give anyone an opportunity.

ABE. Yes—I've thought about moving, think about it all the time. My family have always been movers, shifting about, never knowing what they were looking for, and whatever it was, never finding it. My old father ambled from Virginia to one place after another in Kentucky, where I was born, and then into Indiana and then here in Illinois. About all I can remember of when I was a boy was hitching up, and then unhitching, and then hitching up again. (*He changes the subject.*) As a matter of fact, Seth Gale and me have been talking a lot about moving—out to Kansas or Nebraska Territory. But—wherever I go it'll be the same story—more friends, more debts.

MENTOR. Well, Abe, just bear in mind that there are always two professions open to people who fail at everything else; there's schoolteaching and there's politics.

ABE. Then I'll choose schoolteaching. You go into politics, and you may get elected.

MENTOR. Yes—there's always that possibility.

ABE. And if you get elected, you've got to go to the city. I don't want none of that.

MENTOR. What did I say about two negatives?

ABE. I meant, "any of that."

MENTOR. What's your objection to cities, Abe? Have you ever seen one?

ABE. Sure. I've been down river twice to New Orleans. And, do you know, every minute of the time I was there I was scared?

MENTOR. Scared of what, Abe?

ABE. Well—it sounds kind of foolish—I was scared of people.

MENTOR. What on earth do you mean?

ABE (*serious*). I was scared they'd kill me.

MENTOR (*also serious*). Why? Why should they want to kill you?

ABE. I don't know.

MENTOR (*after a moment*). You think a lot about death, don't you?

ABE. I've had to, because it has seemed to be so close in the forest where I grew up. When I was no higher than this table, we buried my mother. The milk sick [1] got her, poor creature. I helped Paw make the coffin—whittled the pegs for it with my jackknife. We buried her in a timber clearing beside my grandmother, old Betsy Sparrow. I used to go there often and look at the place—used to watch the deer running over her grave with their little feet. I never could kill a deer after that. One time I catched it from Paw because when he was taking aim I knocked his gun up. And I always compare the looks of those deer with the looks of men—like

[1] **milk sick:** poisoning from cow's milk.

the men in New Orleans—that you could see had murder in their hearts.

MENTOR. You're a hopeless mess of inconsistency, Abe Lincoln.

ABE. How do you mean, Mentor?

MENTOR. I've never seen anyone who is so friendly and at the same time so misanthropic.

ABE. What's that?

MENTOR. A misanthrope is one who distrusts men and avoids their society.

ABE. Well—maybe that's how I am. Oh—I like people well enough—when you consider 'em one by one. But they seem to look different when they're put into crowds, or mobs, or armies. *(He stands up.)* I came here to listen to you, and then I do all the talking.

MENTOR. Go right on, Abe. I'll correct you when you say things like "catched it."

ABE *(grins)*. I know. Whenever I get talking about Paw, I sort of fall back into his language. *(Stands up)* But—you've got your own school to teach tomorrow. I'll get along.

MENTOR. Wait a minute. . . . *(He is fishing about among the papers. He takes out a copy of an English magazine.)* There's just one more thing I want to show you. It's a poem. Here it is. *(He finds place in magazine.)* You read it, Abe. *(He hands ABE magazine.)*

ABE *(reads)*. "On Death," written at the age of nineteen by the late John Keats.[1]

"Can death be sleep, when life is but a
    dream,
And scenes of bliss pass as a phantom by?
The transient *(He hesitates on that word.)*
    pleasures as a vision seem,
And yet we think the greatest pain's to die.
(He moves closer to the light.)
How strange it is that man on earth should
    roam,
And lead a life of woe, but not forsake

His rugged path—nor dare he view alone
His future doom—which is but to awake."

(He looks at MENTOR.*)* That sure is good, Mentor. It's fine! *(He is reading it again, to himself, when the lights fade.)*

SCENE 2

Rutledge Tavern, New Salem. Noon, July 4th.

It is a large room, with log walls but with curtains on the windows and pictures on the walls to give it an air of dressiness. The pictures include likenesses of all the Presidents from Washington to Jackson. The sun is shining brightly. The furniture of the room consists of two tables, two benches, and various chairs and stools. BEN MATTLING *is seated on a bench at the end of the room. He is an ancient, paunchy, watery-eyed veteran of the Revolution, and he wears a cocked hat and the tattered but absurd semblance of a Colonial uniform.* JUDGE BOWLING GREEN *and* NINIAN EDWARDS *come in, followed by* JOSHUA SPEED. BOWLING *is elderly, fat, gentle.* NINIAN *is young, tall, handsome, prosperous.* JOSH *is quiet, mild, solid, thoughtful, well-dressed.*

BOWLING *(coming to table)*. This is the Rutledge Tavern, Mr. Edwards. It's not precisely a gilded palace of refreshment. *(*JOSH *goes to door.* NINIAN *comes down to table.)*

NINIAN. Make no apologies, Judge Green.

JOSH *(calls)*. Miss Rutledge.

ANN *(apprearing in doorway)*. Yes, Mr. Speed?

JOSH. Have you seen Abe Lincoln?

ANN. No. He's probably down at the foot races.[2]

---

[1] **John Keats:** English poet (1795–1821).

[2] **foot races:** New Salem is celebrating the Fourth of July.

JOSH (*turns to* BOWLING). I'll find Abe and bring him here.

NINIAN. Remember, Josh, we've got to be back in Springfield before sundown. (JOSH *goes.*)

BOWLING. Ah, good day, Uncle Ben. Have a seat, Mr. Edwards. (*They sit at table.*)

BEN. Good day to you, Bowling.

ANN (*coming in*). Hello, Judge Green.

BOWLING. Good morning, Ann. We'd be grateful for a bottle of your father's best whiskey.

ANN. Yes, Judge. (*She starts.*)

BEN (*stopping her*). And git me another mug of that Barbados rum.

ANN. I'm sorry, Mr. Mattling, but I've given you one already and you know my father said you weren't to have any more till you paid for . . .

BEN. Yes, wench—I know what your father said. But if a veteran of the Revolutionary War is to be denied so much as credit, then this country has forgot its gratitude to them that made it.

BOWLING. Bring him the rum, Ann. I'll be happy to pay for it.

[TRUM COGDAL *comes in.*]

TRUM. Ann, bring me a pot of Sebago tea.

ANN. Yes, Mr. Cogdal. (*She goes out.* TRUM *sits.*)

BEN. I have to say thank you, Judge.

BOWLING. Don't say a word, Ben.

TRUM. Well, Mr. Edwards—what's your impression of our great and enterprising metropolis?

NINIAN. Distinctly favorable, Mr. Cogdal. I could not fail to be impressed by the beauty of your location, here on this hilltop . . . (ANN *comes in with tray.*) . . . in the midst of the prairie land.

TRUM. Well, we're on the highroad to the west—and when we get the ragtag and bobtail cleaned out of here, we'll grow. Yes, sir—we'll grow.

NINIAN. I'm sure of it. (ANN *has been taking things off tray.*)

BOWLING. Thank you, Ann.

ANN. Has the mud wagon come in yet?

TRUM. No. I been waiting for it. (ANN *starts to go.*)

BOWLING. Not by any chance expecting a letter, are you, Ann?

ANN. Oh, no—who'd be writing to me, I'd like to know?

BOWLING. Well—you never can tell what might happen on the Fourth of July. (*He lifts his glass.* NINIAN *lifts his.*) But I beg to wish you all happiness, my dear. And let me tell you that Mr. Edwards here is a married man, so you can keep those lively eyes to yourself.

ANN. Oh, Judge Green—you're just joking me. (*She goes out.*)

NINIAN. A mighty pretty girl.

TRUM. Comes of good stock, too.

NINIAN. With the scarcity of females in these parts, it's a wonder someone hasn't snapped her up.

BOWLING. Someone has. The poor girl promised herself to a man named McNeil —it turned out his real name's McNamar. Made some money out here and then left town, saying he'd return soon. She's still waiting for him. (*Looks back at* NINIAN) But your time is short, Mr. Edwards, so if you'll tell us just what it is you want in New Salem, we'll do our utmost to . . .

NINIAN. I'm sure you gentlemen know what I want.

TRUM. Naturally, you want votes. Well—you've got mine. Anything to frustrate that tyrant, Andy Jackson. (*He shakes his fist at picture of Jackson on back wall.*)

NINIAN. I assure you that I yield to none in my admiration for the character of our venerable President, but when he goes to the extent of ruining our banking structure, destroying faith in our currency, and even driving sovereign states to the point of secession, then, gentlemen, it is time to call a halt.

BOWLING. We got two more years of him—if the old man lives that long. You can't make headway against his popularity.

NINIAN. But we can start now to drive out his minions here in the government of the State of Illinois. We have a great battle cry, "End the reign of Andrew Jackson."

[JACK ARMSTRONG *and three others of the Clary's Grove boys have come in during this speech. The others are named* BAB, FEARGUS *and* JASP. *They are a tough lot.*]

JACK (*going to door*). Miss Rutledge.

ANN (*appearing in doorway*). What do you want, Jack Armstrong?

JACK. Your humble pardon, Miss Rutledge, and we will trouble you for a keg of liquor.

BAB (*down to bench by window*). And we'll be glad to have it quick because we're powerful dry.

ANN. You get out of here—you get out of here right now—you low *scum!*

JACK. I believe I said a keg of liquor. Did you hear me say it, boys?

FEARGUS (*by bench right of* BEN). That's how it sounded to me, Jack.

JASP (*back of* BOWLING). Come along with it, Annie——

ANN. If my father were here, he'd take a gun to you, just as he would to a pack of prairie wolves.

JACK. If your paw was here he'd be scareder than you. 'Cause he knows we're the wildcats of Clary's Grove, worse'n any old wolves, and we're a-howlin' and a-spittin' for drink. So get the whiskey, Miss Annie, and save your poor old paw a lot of expenses for damages to his property. (ANN *goes.*)

TRUM (*in undertone to* NINIAN). That's the ragtag and bobtail I was .

JACK. And what are you mumblin' about, old measely-weasely Trum Cogdal—with your cup of tea on the Fourth of July

BAB. He's a cottonmouthed traitor and I think we'd better whip him for it.

FEARGUS. Squeeze that 'ar tea outen him, Jack.

JASP (*crosses past* BEN; *shouting*). Come on you, Annie, with that liquor!

JACK. And you, too, old fat-pot Judge Bowling Green that sends honest men to prison—and who's the stranger? Looks kind of elegant for New Salem.

BOWLING. This is Mr. Ninian Edwards of Springfield, Jack—and for the Lord's sake shut up, and sit down, and behave yourselves.

JACK. Ninian Edwards, eh! The governor's son, I presume. Well—well!

NINIAN. You've placed me.

JACK. No wonder you've got a New Orleans suit of clothes and a gold fob and a silverheaded cane. (*Picks up cane*) I reckon you can buy the best of everything with that steamin' old pirate land-grabber for a paw. I guess them fancy pockets of yourn are pretty well stuffed with the money your paw stole from us taxpayers—eh, Mr. Edwards?

BAB. Let's take it offen him, Jack.

FEARGUS (*moves down a step*). Let's give him a lickin', Jack.

JACK (*still to* NINIAN). What you come here for anyway? Lookin' for a fight? Because if that's what you're a-cravin', I'm your man (ANN *enters.*)—wrasslin', clawin', bitin' and tearin'.

ANN (*coming in*). Jack Armstrong, here's your liquor! Drink it and go away.

JASP. He told you to bring a keg!

[ANN *carries four mugs.* BAB *crosses to* ANN.]

JACK (*contemplating the glasses*). One little noggin apiece? Why—that ain't enough to fill a hollow tooth! Get the keg, Annie.

FEARGUS. Perhaps she can't tote it. I'll get it, Jack. (*Goes to kitchen.*)

ANN. Wait a minute! (*Follows him to door. Desperate. Turns*) Aren't there any of you men can do anything to protect decent people from these ruffians?

NINIAN. I'll be glad to do whatever I . . . (*He starts to rise.*)

BOWLING (*restraining him*). I'd be rather careful, Mr. Edwards.

JACK (*sitting on table*). That's right, Mr. Edwards. You be careful. Listen to the old squire. He's got a round pot but a level head. He's seen the Clary's Grove boys in action, and he can tell you you might get that silverheaded cane rammed down your gullet. Hey, Bab—you tell him what we did to Hank Spears and Gus Hocheimer. Just tell him!

BAB. Jack nailed the two of 'em up in a barr'l and sent 'em rollin' down Salem hill and it jumped the bank and fotched up in the river and when we opened up the barr'l they wasn't inclined to move much. (*Crosses down to bench*)

JACK (*rising and crossing to* BOWLING). Of course, it'd take a bigger barr'l to hold you and your friends here, Squire, but I'd do it for you and I'd do it for any rapscallions and sons of thieves that come here a-preachin' treachery (FEARGUS *returns* *with keg, sets it on fireplace bench, and stands beside it.*) and disunion and pisenin'[1] the name of Old Hickory,[2] the people's friend.

BEN. Kill him, boys! You're the only *real* Americans we got left!

NINIAN (*rising*). If you gentlemen will step outside, I'll be glad to accommodate you with the fight you seem to be spoiling for. (BAB *stands at door right of* NINIAN.)

TRUM. You're committing suicide, Mr. Edwards.

JACK. Oh, no—he ain't. We ain't killers—we're just bone-crushers. After a few months, you'll be as good as new, which ain't saying much. You bring that keg, Feargus.

[*They are about to go when* ABE *appears in door. He now is slightly more respectably dressed, wearing a battered claw-hammer coat*[3] *and pants that have been "foxed"*[4] *with buckskin. He carries the mail. Behind him is* JOSH SPEED.]

ABE. Hello, Jack.

JACK. Hello, Abe.

ABE. The mud wagon's in! Hello, Jack—boys. Hello, Miss Ann. Got a letter for you.

ANN. Thank you, Abe.

[*There is a marked shyness in his attitude toward* ANN. *She snatches letter away and runs out with it.*]

BEN. Abe, there's goin' to be a fight!

NINIAN (*to* JACK). All right—come on, if you're coming.

JACK. All right, boys. (*General ad lib*[5])

ABE. Fight? Who—and why?

[1] **pisenin'** (pī′sə·nin) (dialect): poisoning.
[2] **Old Hickory:** nickname for President Jackson, given him because of his toughness.
[3] **claw-hammer coat:** a swallow-tailed dress coat.
[4] **"foxed":** reinforced.
[5] *ad lib:* speeches not given in the script.

JACK. This is the son of Ninian Edwards, Abe. Come from Springfield lookin' for a little hoist, and I'm aimin' to oblige. (ABE *looks* NINIAN *over.*)

BOWLING. Put a stop to it, Abe. It'd be next door to murder.

JACK. You shut your trap, Pot Green! Murder's too good for any goose-livered enemy of Andy Jackson. Come on, boys!

ABE. Wait a minute, boys. Jack, have you forgotten what day it is?

JACK. No, I ain't! But I reckon the Fourth of July is as good a day as any to whip a politician!

ABE (*amiably*). Well, if you've just got to fight, Jack, you shouldn't give preference to strangers. Being postmaster of this thriving town, I can rate as a politician myself, so you'd better try a fall with me—— (*He turns to* NINIAN.) And as for you, sir, I haven't the pleasure of your acquaintance; but my name's Lincoln, and I'd like to shake hands with a brave man.

NINIAN (*shaking hands with* ABE). I'm greatly pleased to know you, Mr. Lincoln.

ABE. You should be. Because I came just in time to save you quite some embarrassment, not to mention injury. Got a couple of letters for you, Bowling. Here's your Cincinnati *Journal,* Trum.

JACK. Look here, Abe—you're steppin' into something that ain't none of your business. This is a private matter of patriotic honor . . .

ABE. Everything in this town is my business, Jack. It's the only kind of business I've got. And besides—I saw Hannah down by the grove and she says to tell you to come on to the picnic and that means *now* or she'll give the cake away to the Straders children and you and the boys'll go hungry. So get moving.

FEARGUS. Are you goin' to let Abe talk you out of it?

ABE. Sure he is. (*He turns to* TRUM.) Say, Trum—if you ain't using that *Jour-nal* for a while, would you let me have a read?

TRUM. By all means, Abe. Here you are. (*He tosses paper to* ABE.)

ABE. Thanks. (*He turns again to* JACK.) Better hurry, Jack—or you'll get a beatin' from Hannah.

[*Starts to take wrapper off, goes over to chair.* JACK *looks at* ABE *a moment, then laughs.*]

JACK (*to* NINIAN). All right! Abe Lincoln's saved your hide. I'll consent to callin' off the fight just because he's a friend of mine.

ABE. And also because I'm the only one around here you can't lick.

JACK. But I just want to tell you, Mr. Ninian Edwards, Junior, that the next time you come round here a-spreadin' pisen and——

ABE. Go on, Jack, Hannah's waiting.

JACK (*over to* ABE). I'm going, Abe. But I warn you—you'd better stop this foolishness of reading, reading, reading morning, noon, and night, or you'll be getting soft, and you won't be the same fighting man you are now. And it would break my heart to see you licked by anybody—including me. (*He laughs, slaps* ABE *on back, and turns to go.*) Glad to have met you, Mr. Edwards.

[*He makes a feinting pass at* NINIAN *as he goes out door, followed by* BAB *and* JASP. FEARGUS *picks up keg and starts after them.*]

NINIAN (*to* JACK). It's been a pleasure. (*Returns to seat right of table*)

ABE. Where'd you get that keg, Feargus?

FEARGUS (*at door, nervously*). Jack told me to take it outen Mis' Rutledge's kitchen, and I——

ABE. Well, put it down—If you see Seth Gale, tell him I've got a letter for him.

FEARGUS. I'll tell him, Abe. *(He puts down keg and goes out.)*

JOSH *(laughs and comes up to table).* Congratulations, Ninian. I shouldn't have enjoyed taking you home to Mrs. Edwards after those boys had done with you. *(Picks up drink from table)*

NINIAN *(grinning).* I was aware of the certain consequences, Josh. *(Turns to* ABE*)* I'm deeply in your debt, Mr. Lincoln.

ABE. Never mind any thanks, Mr. Edwards. Jack Armstrong talks big but he means well.

NINIAN. Won't you join us in a drink?

ABE. No, thank you. *(He's reading paper.* BOWLING *fills glasses.)*

JOSH. Put that paper down, Abe. We want to talk to you.

ABE. Me? What about? *(He looks curiously at* JOSH, BOWLING *and* NINIAN.)

JOSH. I brought Mr. Edwards here for the sole purpose of meeting you—and with his permission, I shall tell you why.

NINIAN. Go right ahead, Josh. *(All are looking intently at* ABE.)

JOSH. Abe—how would you like to run for the State Assembly?

ABE *(looks at group).* When?

JOSH. Now—for the election in the fall.

ABE. Why?

NINIAN. Mr. Lincoln, I've known you for only a few minutes, but that's long enough to make me agree with Josh Speed that you're precisely the type of man we want. The whole Whig organization [1] will support your candidacy.

ABE. Is this your idea, Josh?

JOSH *(smiling).* Oh, no, Abe—you're the people's choice.

TRUM. What do you think of it, Bowling?

BOWLING *(heartily).* I think it's as fine

---

[1] **Whig organization:** a political party formed about 1834 to oppose the Democrats.

a notion as I ever heard. Why, Abe—I can hear you making speeches right and left, taking your stand on all the issues—secession, Texas, the National Bank crisis, abolitionism—it'll be more fun than we ever had in our lives!

ABE *(rises).* Isn't anybody going to ask what *I* think?

JOSH *(laughs).* All right, Abe—*I'll* ask you.

ABE *(after a moment's pause).* It's a comical notion, all right—and I don't know if I can give you an answer to it, off-hand. But my first hasty impression is that I don't think much of it.

BOWLING. Don't overlook the fact that, if elected, your salary would be three whole dollars a day.

ABE. That's fine money. No doubt of that. And I see what you have in mind, Bowling. I owe you a considerable sum of money; and if I stayed in the legislature for, say, twenty years, I'd be able to pay off . . . $2.50 a day—— *(Figuring on fingers)*

BOWLING. I'm not thinking about the debts, Abe.

ABE. I know you ain't, Bowling. But I've got to. And so should you, Mr. Edwards. The Whig Party is the party of sound money and God save the National Bank, ain't it?

NINIAN. Why, yes—among other things . . .

ABE. Well, then—how would it look if you put forward a candidate who has demonstrated no earning power but who has run up the impressive total of fifteen hundred dollars of debts?

BOWLING *(to* NINIAN*).* I can tell you something about those debts. Abe started a grocery store in partnership with an unfortunate young man named Berry. Their stock included whiskey, and Berry started tapping the keg until he had consumed all the liquid assets. *(Chuckles)* So the store went bankrupt—and Abe voluntarily assumed all the obligations. Fifteen hundred dollars' worth! That may help to explain to you, Mr. Edwards, why we think pretty highly of him around here.

NINIAN. It's a sentiment with which I concur most heartily.

ABE. I thank you one and all for your kind tributes, but don't overdo them, or I'll begin to think that three dollars a day ain't enough!

JOSH (*rises and takes a step toward* ABE). What's the one thing that you want most, Abe? You want to learn. This will give you your chance to get at a good library, to associate with the finest lawyers in the State.

ABE. I've got a copy of Blackstone [1] already. Found it in an old junk barrel. And how can I tell that the finest lawyers would welcome association with *me?*

NINIAN. You needn't worry about that. I saw how you dealt with those ruffians. You quite obviously know how to handle men.

ABE. I can handle the Clary's Grove boys because I can outwrassle them—but I can't go around Sangamon County throwing *all* the voters.

BOWLING (*laughing*). I'll take a chance on that, Abe. (JOSH *goes up to fireplace bench—sits.*)

ABE (*crossing and sitting on table. To* NINIAN). Besides—how do you know that my political views would agree with yours? How do you know I wouldn't say the wrong thing?

NINIAN. What *are* your political leanings, Mr. Lincoln?

ABE. They're all toward staying out. What sort of leanings do you want?

NINIAN. We need good conservative men to counteract all the radical fire-

---

[1] **William Blackstone:** a noted English jurist (1723–1780), whose works are studied by all students of law.

brands that have swept over this country in the wake of Andrew Jackson. We've got to get this country back to first principles!

ABE. Well—I'm conservative, all right. If I got into the legislature you'd never catch me starting any movements for reform or progress. I'm pretty certain I wouldn't even have the nerve to open my mouth.

JOSH. I told you, Ninian—he's just the type of candidate you're looking for. (*They both laugh and* NINIAN *rises.*)

NINIAN (*crossing to* ABE). As postmaster, Mr. Lincoln, you're in an excellent position to establish contacts. While delivering letters, you can also deliver speeches and campaign literature with which our headquarters will keep you supplied. The fact is—(*Crosses to* ABE) we want to spike the rumor that ours is the party of the more privileged classes. That is why we seek men of the *plain* people for candidates——

ABE. Would you supply me with a suit of store clothes? A candidate mustn't look *too* plain.

NINIAN (*glances at* BOWLING. *Smiling*). I think then that could be arranged, eh, Judge?

BOWLING. I think so.

NINIAN. So—think it over, Mr. Lincoln, and realize that this is opportunity unlimited in scope. Just consider what it means to be starting up the ladder in a nation which is now expanding southward, across the vast area of Texas; and westward, to the Empire of the Californias on the Pacific Ocean. We're becoming a continent, Mr. Lincoln—and all that we need is men! (*He looks at his watch.* BOWLING, TRUM *and* JOSH *rise. Turns to* BOWLING *and* TRUM *and back.*) And now, gentlemen, if you will excuse me—I must put in an appearance at the torchlight procession in Springfield this evening, so I shall have to be moving on. Good-by, Mr. Lincoln. This meeting has been a happy one for me.

ABE. *(shaking hands)*. Good-by, Mr. Edwards. Good luck in the campaign.

NINIAN. And the same to you. *(Turns and goes out quickly.* TRUM *starts to go.)*

ABE *(crossing up to door. Stops* TRUM*)*. Oh, Trum—here's your Cincinnati *Journal.*

TRUM. Go ahead and finish it, Abe. I won't be looking at it yet awhile.

ABE. Thanks, Trum. I'll leave it at your house. (TRUM *and* NINIAN *have gone.)*

BOWLING *(as he is going out)*. I'll see you later, Abe. Tell Ann I'll be back to pay the bill.

ABE. I'll tell her, Bowling. (BOWLING *has gone.* JOSH *is looking at* ABE *who, after a moment, turns to him.* ABE, *crossing to* JOSH.*)* I'm surprised at you, Josh. I thought you were my friend.

JOSH. I know, Abe. But Ninian Edwards asked me is there anybody in that godforsaken town of New Salem that stands a chance of getting votes, and the only one I could think of was you. I can see you're embarrassed by this—and you're annoyed. But—whether you like it or not—you've got to grow; and here's your chance to get a little scrap of importance.

ABE. Am I the kind that wants importance?

JOSH. You'll deny it, Abe—but you've got a funny kind of vanity—which is the same as saying you've got some pride— and it's badly in need of nourishment. So, if you'll agree to this—I don't think you'll be sorry for it or feel that I've betrayed you. (SETH GALE *comes in.)*

SETH. Hey, Abe—Feargus said you've got a letter for me.

ABE *(turns)*. Yes.

SETH. Hello, Mr. Speed.

JOSH. How are you, Mr. Gale?

ABE *(giving* SETH *letter)*. Here you are, Seth.

[*He hands him letter.* SETH *takes it, sits down, and starts to read.*]

JOSH *(crossing to door and out)*. I've got to get home to Springfield, Abe, but I'll be down again in a week or so.

ABE *(goes to chair, sits)*. I'll be here, Josh.

BEN *(angrily)*. Are you going to do it, Abe? Are you goin' to let them make you into a *candidate?*

ABE. I ain't had time to think about it yet.

BEN. Well—I tell you to stop thinkin' before it's too late. Don't let 'em get you. Don't let 'em put you in a store suit that's the uniform of degradation in this miserable country. You're an honest man, Abe Lincoln. You're a good-for-nothin', debt-ridden loafer—but you're an honest man. And you have no place in that den of thieves that's called gov'ment. They'll corrupt you as they've corrupted the whole United States. Look at Washington, look at Jefferson, and John Adams—— *(He points grandly to the pictures.)* where are they today? Dead! And everything they stood for and fought for and *won*—that's dead too. (ANN *comes in, clears table and goes out.)* Why— we'd be better off if we was all held in the bonds of slavery. *They* get fed—*they* get looked after when they're old and sick. (ABE *turns and looks at* ANN. *She does not see him.)* But *you* don't care—you ain't listenin' to me, neither . . . *(He starts slowly toward door.)*

ABE. Of course I'm listening, Ben.

BEN *(crossing up into doorway).* No, you ain't. *I* know. You're goin' to the Assembly and join the wolves who're feedin' off the carcass of Liberty. *(He has gone.)*

ABE. You needn't worry. I'm not going. (ANN *picks up glasses. She seems extremely subdued.* ABE *looks at her, curiously.)* Bowling Green said to tell you he'd be back later to pay you what he owes.

ANN *(curtly).* That's all right. (ANN *puts glasses and bottles on tray and picks it up.* ABE *jumps to his feet.)*

ABE. Can I help you with that, Ann?

ANN *(irritably).* No—leave it alone! I can carry it!

ABE. Excuse me, Ann . . .

ANN *(stopping).* Well?

ABE. Would you come back after you're finished with that? I—I'd like to talk to you.

[SETH *has finished the letter. Its contents seem to have depressed him.]*

ANN. All right. I'll talk to you—if you want. *(She goes out.* SETH *comes to table.)*

SETH. Abe . . . Abe—that letter was from my folks back in Maryland. It means

—I guess I've got to give up the dream we had of moving out into Nebraska Territory, for the time being, at any rate.

ABE. What's happened, Seth?

SETH *(despondently).* Well—for one thing the old man's took sick, and he's pretty feeble.

ABE. I'm sorry to hear that, Seth.

SETH. So am I. They've sent for me to come back and work the farm. Measly little thirty-six acres—sandy soil. I tell you, Abe, it's a bitter disappointment to me when I had my heart all set on going out into the West. And the worst of it is— I'm letting you down on it, too.

ABE. *(with a glance toward kitchen).* Don't think about that, Seth. Maybe I won't be able to move for awhile, myself. And when your father gets to feeling better, you'll come back . . .

SETH. He won't get to feeling better. Not at his age. I'll be stuck there, just like he was. I'll be pushed in and cramped all the rest of my life, till the malaria gets me, too . . . Well—there's no use crying about it. If I've got to go back East, I've got to go. I'll tell you good-by, Abe, before I leave.

[*He goes out.* ANN *comes back from kitchen.* ABE *looks at her, she at him.*]

ANN. Well—what is it, Abe?

ABE. I just thought—you might like to talk to me.

ANN *(sharply).* What about?

ABE. The letter you got from New York State.

ANN. What do you know about that letter?

ABE. I'm the postmaster. I know more than I ought to about people's private affairs. I couldn't help seeing that that was the handwriting of Mr. McNamar—or McNeil. And I couldn't help seeing, from the look on your face that the bad news you've been afraid of has come.

[ANN *looks at him with surprise. He is a lot more observant than she had thought. Her attitude of hostility softens. She sits down on bench.*]

ANN. Whatever the letter said, it's no concern of yours, Abe.

ABE. I know that, Ann. But—it appears to me that you've been crying—and it makes me sad to think that something could have hurt you. The thing is—I think quite a lot of you—always have—ever since I first came here and met you. I wouldn't mention it, only when you're distressed about something it's a comfort sometimes even to find a pair of ears to pour your troubles into—and the Lord knows my ears are big enough to hold a lot.

[ANN *rewards him with a tender smile. Into her sharp little mind has darted the thought that perhaps he can be of help, not much help, but some.*]

ANN. You're a Christian gentleman, Abe Lincoln.

ABE. No, I ain't. I'm a plain, common sucker with a shirttail so short I can't sit on it.

ANN (*laughs*). Well—sit down anyway, Abe—here, by me. (ABE *crosses and sits near her.*) You can always say something to make a person laugh, can't you?

ABE. Well—I don't even have to *say* anything. A person just has to look at me.

ANN. You're right about that letter, Abe. It's the first I've heard from him in months—and now he says he's delayed by family troubles and doesn't know when he'll be able to get to New Salem again. By which he probably means—never.

ABE. I wouldn't say that, Ann.

ANN. I would. (*She looks at him.*) I reckon you think I'm a silly fool for ever having promised myself to Mr. McNeil.

ABE. I think no such thing. I liked him

myself, and still do, and whatever reasons he had for changing his name I'm sure were honorable. He's a smart man, and a handsome one—and I—I wouldn't blame any girl for—loving him.

ANN. I guess I don't love him, Abe. I guess I couldn't love anybody that was as—as faithless as that.

ABE (*trying to appear unconcerned*). Well, then, there's nothing to fret about. Now—poor Seth Gale—he got some *really* bad news. His father's sick, and he has to give up his dream which was to go and settle out West.

ANN (*looks at him*). I don't believe you know much about females, Abe.

ABE. Probably I don't—although I certainly spend enough time thinking about 'em.

ANN. You're a big man, and you can lick anybody, and you can't understand the feelings of somebody who is weak. But—I'm a female, and I can't help thinking what they'll be saying about me—all the old gossips, all over town. They'll make it out that he deserted me; I'm a rejected woman. They'll give me their sympathy to my face, but they'll snigger at me behind my back.

ABE. Yes—that's just about what they would do. But—would you let *them* disturb you?

ANN. I told you—it's just weakness—it's just vanity. It's something you couldn't understand, Abe.

[*She has crossed to window and is staring out.* ABE *twists in his chair to look at her.*]

ABE. Maybe I can understand it, Ann. I've got a kind of vanity myself. Josh Speed said so, and he's right. . . . It's—it's nothing but vanity that's kept me from declaring my inclinations toward you. (*She turns, amazed, and looks at him.*) You see, I don't like to be sniggered at, either. I know what I am—and I know what I look like—and I know that I've got nothing to offer any girl that I'd be in love with.

ANN. Are you saying that you're in love with me, Abe?

ABE. (*rises. With deep earnestness*). Yes—I am saying that. (*He stands facing her. She looks intently into his eyes.*) I've been loving you—a long time—with all my heart. You see, Ann, you're a particularly fine girl. You've got sense, and you've got bravery—those are two things that I admire particularly. And you're powerful good to look at, too. So it's only natural I should have a great regard for you. But—I don't mean to worry you about it, Ann. I only mentioned it because—if you would do me the honor of keeping company with me for a while, it might shut the old gossips' mouths. They'd figure you'd chucked McNeil for—for someone else. Even me.

[ANN *goes to him, puts her hand on his hand, which is clutching a lapel.*]

ANN. I thought I knew you pretty well, Abe. But I didn't.

ABE. Why do you say that? Do you consider I was too forward in speaking out as I did?

ANN (*gravely*). No, Abe . . . I've always thought a lot of you—the way I thought you were. But—the idea of love between you and me—I can't say how I feel about that, because now you're like some other person that I'm meeting for the first time.

ABE (*quietly*). I'm not expecting you to feel anything for me. I'd never dream of expecting such a thing.

ANN. I know that, Abe. You'd be willing to give everything you have and never expect anything in return. Maybe you're different in that way from any man I ever heard of. And I can tell you this much—

now and truthfully, Abe—if I ever do love you, I'll be happy about it—and lucky, to be loving a good, decent man. . . . If you just give me time, Abe—to think about it. . . .

ABE (*unable to believe his eyes and ears*). You mean—if you took time—you might get in your heart something like the feeling I have for you?

ANN (*with a great tenderness*). I don't know, Abe. But I do know that you're a man who could fill anyone's heart—yes, fill it and warm it and make it glad to be living.

[*He stares at her so hard that she again looks away from him. He takes her hand between both of his and works it around in his terrific grasp. It is some time before he finds words.*]

ABE. Ann—I've always tried hard to believe what the orators tell us—that this is a land of equal opportunity for all. But I've never been able to believe it, any more than I could believe God made all men in His own image. But—if I could win you, Ann—I'd be willing to disbelieve everything I've ever seen with my own eyes, and have faith in everything that I've ever dreamed of. (*Both are silent for a moment.*) But—I'm not asking you to say anything now. And I won't ask you until the day comes when I know I've got a right to.

[*He lets go of her hand, picks up the newspaper, rises, and walks quickly toward door.*]

ANN. Abe! Where are you going?

ABE. I'm going to find Bowling Green and tell him a good joke. (*He grins. He is standing in the doorway.*)

ANN (*worried*). A *joke?* What about?

ABE. I'm going to tell him that I'm a candidate for the assembly of the State of Illinois. (*He goes. The light fades.*)

Portrait Painting

When artists paint portraits, they usually try for more than simply a physical likeness. They try to tell us something about a person's character or type of life—what it is that makes that person interesting.

One way an artist can do this is by representing the subjects of portraits in their usual surroundings. For example, the nineteenth-century French painter Edgar Degas portrayed one of his friends, another painter named James Tissot, by posing the man in his own studio (PLATE 1). To make Tissot seem to be part of the room around him, Degas placed his figure in the background. The paintings we see are all by Tissot, except for a small sixteenth-century portrait of a German prince on the wall just above his left shoulder. Degas placed this compact little picture in the very center of his composition to exaggerate, by contrast, Tissot's casual pose and the slimness of his figure.

Not all portraits are so informal, however. For example, Sir Anthony van Dyck's seventeenth-century picture of Philip, Lord Wharton (PLATE 2) was intended not as an intimate likeness of a friend, but as a stately portrait of a young nobleman. Since lords and ladies of this period loved to play at being shepherds, Van Dyck has shown this young English lord holding a shepherd's staff, and he has painted every fold and wrinkle of his costume in exquisite detail. Notice that the main areas of light tones—the patch of sky, the orange drapery, and the highlights along the sleeve of the jacket—all lead directly to the face. Yet the features of this haughty, reserved aristocrat are almost expressionless. Nor does the setting tell us very much about him. The green drapery adds to his elegant appearance, but it bears no relation to the rest of the scene, which is set outdoors. The landscape itself represents no particular place, but serves merely as a picturesque backdrop.

On the page opposite Van Dyck's picture is a very different kind of portrait, a self-portrait by the great Dutch painter Rembrandt van

Rijn (PLATE 3). At first this picture may appear simpler than either of the two we have just seen, for it represents principally the figure itself—no drapery, landscape, or other objects in the background. But in the way it is painted, it is infinitely more complex. Although Rembrandt has used only a few colors, he has broken each one down into so many subtle changes of *tone* that the figure appears to emerge gradually from the shadows around it. Compare the sharp contrast between the dark hat and the light forehead with softer modulations in other areas. Just to the right, for instance, the lower part of the hat almost dissolves into shadow. Rembrandt's self-portrait, one of many he painted throughout his career, is a profound study of his own personality.

PLATE 4 reproduces an earlier portrait than any we have seen so far. It is another picture of a man shown in his usual surroundings: a merchant in his London shop, painted in the sixteenth century by a German artist named Hans Holbein the Younger. Here the figure has emerged from shadow but has been carefully lighted as if he were on display, like the many objects in the room around him. Holbein has defined clearly the outside contours of every form in the picture. Even the tiny lettering on the various papers seems to be in sharp focus. But notice that Holbein has grouped the most elaborate details around the edges of the picture. He has painted the upper part of the figure's jacket, his hat, his hair, and most of his face in broad, flat areas of color, calling attention to his eyes and the way he is looking at us.

Now look at a much simpler composition: Vincent van Gogh's straightforward likeness of Armand Roulin (PLATE 5). Here, as in Rembrandt's self-portrait, there are no objects to identify the figure. There seems to be nothing distinctive about Roulin; he is shown merely as a pleasant young man wearing everyday clothes. Yet there is something extremely compelling about his facial expression, a look which seems not the least bit artificial. Van Gogh has brought out this candid expression by using clear, strong light colors for the coat and the background. In fact, this is the first portrait we have looked at that is predominantly *light* in tone. Dark colors are used here mainly as accents.

Amedeo Modigliani's *Gypsy Woman with Baby* (PLATE 6) suggests feelings of tenderness and protectiveness. The young mother's long, thin face and neck emphasize the fuller, more rounded curves of her arms and shoulders, which enclose the sleeping child. Notice also the soft, feathery texture of Modigliani's brushstrokes. What we see here is more of a "picture" than a "portrait"—more of an idealized image than an exact likeness.

PLATE 1. EDGAR DEGAS (French, 1834–1917): *Portrait of the Painter James Tissot*. About 1868. Oil on canvas, $59\frac{1}{3}$ x $44\frac{1}{4}$ inches. (The Metropolitan Museum of Art, New York, Rogers Fund, 1939)

PLATE 2. SIR ANTHONY VAN DYCK (Flemish, 1599–1641): *Philip, Lord Wharton.* 1632.
Oil on canvas, $52\frac{1}{2}$ x $41\frac{7}{8}$ inches. (National Gallery of Art, Washington, D.C., Andrew Mellon
Collection)

PLATE 3. REMBRANDT VAN RIJN (Dutch, 1606–1669): *Self-Portrait*. 1661. Oil on canvas, 35$\frac{13}{16}$ x 30$\frac{5}{16}$ inches. (Rijksmuseum, Amsterdam)

PLATE 4. HANS HOLBEIN, THE YOUNGER (German, 1497–1543): *George Gisze*. 1532.
Oil on wood panel, $37\frac{3}{4}$ x $34\frac{3}{4}$ inches. (Staatliche Museum, Berlin)

PLATE 5. VINCENT VAN GOGH (Dutch, 1853–1890): *Armand Roulin*. 1888. Oil on canvas, 24¾ x 22½ inches. (Folkwang Museum, Essen, Germany)

PLATE 6. AMEDEO MODIGLIANI (French, 1884–1920): *Gypsy Woman with Baby.* 1919. Oil on canvas, $45\frac{5}{8}$ x $28\frac{3}{4}$ inches. (National Gallery of Art, Washington, D.C., Chester Dale Collection)

SCENE 3

BOWLING GREEN'S *house near New Salem.*

It is a small room, but the walls are lined with books and family pictures. In center is a table with a lamp on it. Another light—a candle in a glass globe—is on a bookcase at back, toward right. There are comfortable chairs at either side of table, and a sofa at left. At back, toward left, is the front door. A rifle is leaning against wall by door. There is another door in right wall. Toward right at the back is a ladder fixed against wall leading up through an opening to the attic.

It is late in the evening, a year or so after Scene 2. A storm is raging outside.

BOWLING *is reading aloud from a sort of pamphlet. His comfortable wife,* NANCY, *is listening and sewing.*

BOWLING (*reads*). "And how much more interesting did the spectacle become when, starting into full life and animation, as a simultaneous call for 'Pickwick' burst from his followers, that illustrious man slowly mounted into the Windsor chair, on which he had been previously seated, and addressed the club he himself had founded." [1] (BOWLING *chuckles.* NANCY *laughs.*)

NANCY. He sounds precisely like *you*, Bowling. (*There is a knock at door. Nervous*) That's not Abe's knock. Who can it be?

BOWLING (*rising*). We don't know yet, my dear.

NANCY. It's a strange hour for anyone to be calling. (BOWLING *unbolts and opens door. It is* JOSH SPEED.)

BOWLING. Why—Josh Speed!

JOSH. Good evening, Bowling.

BOWLING. We haven't seen you in a coon's age.

NANCY. Good evening, Mr. Speed.

[1] Bowling is reading from Charles Dickens's *Pickwick Papers.*

JOSH. Good evening, Mrs. Green. And I beg you to forgive me for this untimely intrusion.

NANCY. We're delighted to see you, Mr. Speed. Take your wrap off.

JOSH. (*hangs up hat and coat*). Thank you. I've just come down from Springfield. I heard Abe Lincoln was in town and I was told I might find him here.

BOWLING. He's been sleeping here, up in the attic.

NANCY. But he's out now at the Rutledge Farm, tending poor little Ann.

JOSH. Miss Rutledge? What's the matter with her?

NANCY. She's been taken with the brain sickness. It's the most shocking thing. People have been dying from it right and left.

BOWLING. But Ann's young. She'll pull through, all right. Sit down, Josh.

JOSH (*crossing to sofa*). Thank you.

[*He sits.* BOWLING *goes to bookcase, fills and lights pipe.*]

NANCY. I suppose you know that Abe came rushing down from Vandalia the moment he heard she was taken. He's deeply in love with her.

BOWLING. Now, Nancy—don't exaggerate. (JOSH *is listening to all this intently.*)

JOSH. So Abe is in love. I wondered what has been the matter with him lately.

NANCY. Why, it's written all over his poor, homely face.

JOSH. The last time I saw him he seemed pretty moody. But when I asked him what was wrong, he said it was his liver.

BOWLING (*laughing*). That sounds more likely. Has he been getting on well in the assembly?

JOSH. No, he has just been sitting there—drawing his three dollars a day—and taking no apparent interest in the proceedings. Do you fancy that Miss Rutledge cares anything for him?

NANCY. Indeed she does! She broke her promise to that Mr. McNeil because of her feelings for Abe.

JOSH. Has he any notion of marrying her?

NANCY. It's the only notion of his life right now. And the sooner they are married, the better for both of them.

BOWLING. Better for her, perhaps—but worse for him.

NANCY. And why? The Rutledges are fine people, superior in every way to those riffraff Hankses and Lincolns that are Abe's family.

BOWLING. I think you feel as I do, Josh—Abe has his own way to go, and sweet and pretty as Ann undoubtedly is, she'd only be a hindrance to him.

JOSH. I guess it wouldn't matter much if she could give him a little of the happiness he's never had.

NANCY. That's just it! I think as much of Abe as you do, Bowling. But we can't deny that he's a poor man, and he's failed in trade, and he's been in the legislature for a year without accomplishing a blessed thing.

BOWLING. He could go to Springfield and set up a law practice and make a good thing of it. Ninian Edwards would help him to get started. And he'd soon forget little Ann. He has just happened to fasten on her his own romantic ideal of what's beautiful and unattainable. Let him ever attain her, and she'd break his heart.

NANCY (comes back to table. Sits). Do you agree with Bowling on that, Mr. Speed?

JOSH. I can't say, Mrs. Green. I've abandoned the attempt to predict anything about Abe Lincoln.

[There is a knock on the door.]

BOWLING. That's Abe now. (BOWLING gets up and opens it. ABE comes in, bareheaded, wet by the storm. He now wears a fairly respectable dark suit of clothes. He looks considerably older and grimmer.) Why, hello, Abe! We've been sitting up waiting for you. Come on in. (BOWLING shuts and bolts door behind him and crosses up by stove.)

NANCY. We were reading "The Posthumous Papers of the Pickwick Club" when Mr. Speed came in.

ABE. Hello, Josh. Glad to see you.

JOSH. Hello, Abe. (Then ABE turns to NANCY.)

ABE. Nancy . . .

NANCY. Yes, Abe?

ABE. She's dead.

BOWLING. Ann? She's dead?

ABE. Yes. Tonight the fever suddenly got worse. They couldn't seem to do anything for it. (NANCY goes to ABE and takes his hand.)

NANCY. Oh, Abe—I'm so sorry. She was such a dear little girl. Everyone who knew her will join in mourning for her.

ABE. I know they will. But it won't do any good. She's dead.

BOWLING. Sit down, Abe, and rest yourself.

ABE. No—I'm not fit company for anybody. I'd better be going. (He goes to door and unbolts it. NANCY turns sharply.)

JOSH (stopping him). No you don't, Abe. You'll stay right here.

BOWLING. You better do what Josh tells you.

NANCY (crosses to chair center). Come here, Abe. Please sit down. (ABE looks from one to the other, then obediently goes to a chair and sits.) Your bed is ready for you upstairs when you want it.

ABE (dully). You're the best friends I've got in the world, and it seems a pretty poor way to reward you for all that you've given me, to come here now and inflict you with a corpse.

BOWLING. This is your home, Abe. This is where you're loved.

ABE. I know that. And I love you, Bowling and Nancy. But I loved her more than everything else that I've ever known.

NANCY. I know you did, Abe. I know it.

ABE. (*He has stood up.*) I'm making a poor exhibition of myself—and I'm sorry —but—I can't stand it. I can't live with myself any longer. I've got to die and be with her again, or I'll go crazy! (*He goes to door and opens it and stands looking out.*) I can't bear to think of her out there alone!

[NANCY *looks at* BOWLING *with frantic appeal. He goes to* ABE, *who is standing in doorway, looking out.*]

BOWLING (*going to* ABE. *With great tenderness*). Abe . . . I want you to go upstairs and see if you can't get some sleep. . . . Please, Abe—as a special favor to Nancy and me.

ABE (*after a moment*). All right, Bowling. (*He turns and goes to ladder.*)

NANCY (*takes candle from bookcase*). Here's a light for you, dear Abe. (*She hands him the candle.*)

ABE. Thank you, Nancy. . . . Good night. (*He goes up ladder into the attic. They all look up after him.*)

NANCY (*tearful*). Poor lonely soul. (BOWLING *cautions her to be quiet.*)

JOSH (*putting on his coat*). Keep him here with you, Mrs. Green. Don't let him out of your sight.

BOWLING. We won't, Josh.

JOSH. Good night. (*Goes and closes door.*)

BOWLING. Good night, Josh.

[*He bolts door, then comes down to table and picks up lamp.* NANCY *looks up once more, then goes out.* BOWLING *blows out lamp and follows her out. He closes door behind him, so that the only light on stage is the beam from the attic.*]

FOR STUDY AND DISCUSSION

1. In Act I we meet a number of minor characters who have important influences on Abe. Make sure that you know who they all are and what influence they have on Lincoln. Consider particularly the following characters and write a sentence or two giving a thumbnail sketch of each character and his or her relationship to Lincoln.

Mentor Graham	Joshua Speed
Ben Mattling	Seth Gale
Judge Bowling Green	Nancy Green
Ninian Edwards	

2. Describe Abe's life before he came to New Salem. You can learn about this from a number of remarks made by others and by Abe himself.

3. Why did Abe's store fail? Was its failure his fault in any way? How does the failure reveal something about his character? What does the store episode show about his feeling of responsibility?

4. What qualities of Abe's character are shown in his encounter with Jack Armstrong and the Clary's Grove boys?

5. What qualities in Abe do we see for the first time in the way he acts toward Ann?

6. Josh Speed tells Abe, in urging him to run for the legislature, "Whether you like it or not—you've got to grow; and here's your chance to get a little scrap of importance." What does he mean? What does Abe think of this kind of "importance"? In what way does Josh think Abe has to "grow"?

7. In Scene 3, Nancy Green argues with her husband and Josh Speed about whether it will be good for Abe to marry Ann. Which one do you think is right? Why?

8. Does Abe's reaction to the death of Ann increase or lessen your admiration for him as a person? Why?

9. What is Ben Mattling's opinion of Abe and politics? From what you have seen of Abe, do you think he agrees with either part of this opinion? Does he seem reluctant to run for the Illinois State Assembly because of doubts about the Assembly or because of doubts about himself? From his behavior in the Assembly, do his doubts appear to be right? Explain your answer.

10. Make a list of the qualities and characteristics of Lincoln that you learned about for the first time in Act I of this play.

THE CRAFT OF THE DRAMATIST

1. The playwright obviously had no way of knowing exactly what went on in a typical lesson in Mentor Graham's cabin. Therefore, in this opening scene he was free to imagine a conversation that would reveal as much as possible about Lincoln's character. What do you learn about Abe from each of the following:

Abe's and Mentor's discussion of the five "moods" in English grammar (Why does this turn out to be more revealing than a discussion of spelling or punctuation might have been?)

Abe's reading of Daniel Webster's speech

Abe's reaction to Keats's poem on death

2. How, in the dialogue between the Bowling Greens and Josh Speed in Scene 3, does the playwright prepare the audience for Ann's death? How does the lightheartedness of the Greens at the beginning of the scene make Abe's grief more dramatic and moving?

ACT II

SCENE 4

Law office of Stuart and Lincoln on the second floor of the Courthouse in Springfield, Illinois, in the 1840's.

A sunny summer's afternoon, some five years after the preceding scene. The room is small with two windows and one door, upstage, which leads to hall and staircase. At back is a table and chair, at left an old desk, littered with papers. At right is a ramshackle bed, with a buffalo robe thrown over it. Below the windows are some rough shelves, sagging with law books. There is an old wood stove. On wall above desk is hung an American flag with twenty-six stars. Between the windows is an election poster, for Harrison and Tyler, with a list of electors, the last of whom is Ab'm Lincoln, of Sangamon.

BILLY HERNDON *is working at the table. He is young, slight, serious-minded, smoldering. He looks up as* ABE *comes in.* ABE *wears a battered plug hat, a light alpaca coat, and carries an ancient threadbare carpetbag. He is evidently not in a talkative mood. His boots are caked with mud. He leaves office door open, and lettered on it we see the number 4, and the firm's name—Stuart & Lincoln, Attorneys & Counselors at Law.* ABE *goes directly down to desk.*

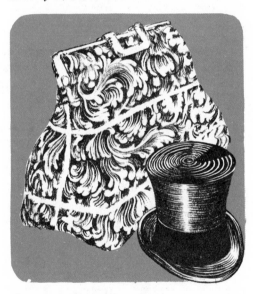

BILLY. How de do, Mr. Lincoln. Glad to see you back.

ABE (*sits*). Good day, Billy. (*He sets down carpetbag, takes off his hat, removes from it various papers, puts hat on the rack and tosses the papers on desk.*)

BILLY. How was it on the circuit,[1] Mr. Lincoln?

ABE. About as usual.

[1] **circuit:** When Lincoln was a young lawyer, judges journeyed about, holding court at appointed times on an established route or circuit. Lawyers concerned with a case had to follow the judges.

BILLY. Have you been keeping in good health?

ABE. Not particularly. But Doc Henry dosed me enough to keep me going. (*He starts looking at letters and papers that have accumulated during his absence. He takes little interest in them, pigeonholing some letters unopened.*)

BILLY. Did you have occasion to make any political speeches?

ABE. Oh—they got me up on the stump a couple of times. Ran into Stephen Douglas [1]—he was out campaigning, of course—and we had some argument in public.

BILLY (*greatly interested. Rises and crosses to* ABE.) That's good! What issues did you and Mr. Douglas discuss?

ABE. Now—don't get excited, Billy. We weren't taking it serious. There was no blood shed. . . . What's the news here?

BILLY. Judge Stuart wrote that he arrived safely in Washington and the campaign [2] there is getting almost as hot as the weather. Mrs. Frain stopped in to say she couldn't possibly pay your fee for awhile.

ABE. I should hope not. I ought to be paying her, seeing as I defended her poor husband and he hanged.

[BOWLING GREEN *comes in, followed by* JOSH SPEED.]

BILLY. Mr. Lincoln, I'd like to . . .

BOWLING. Are we interrupting the majesty of the law?

ABE. Bowling! (*Rises and crosses to* BOWLING. *Shakes hand*) How are you, Bowling?

BOWLING. Tolerably well, Abe—and glad to see you.

ABE. Glad to see you.—This is Billy

[1] **Stephen Douglas:** a young man campaigning for the state legislature.

[2] **the campaign:** Van Buren's term as President was ending, and the Democrats had nominated him for another term.

Herndon—Squire Green, of New Salem. Hello, Josh.

JOSH. Hello, Abe.

BILLY. I'm proud to know you, sir. Mr. Lincoln speaks of you constantly.

BOWLING. Thank you, Mr. Herndon. Are you a lawyer, too?

BILLY (*seriously*). I hope to be, sir. I'm serving here as a clerk in Judge Stuart's absence.

BOWLING. So now you're teaching others, Abe?

ABE. Just providing a bad example.

BOWLING. I can believe it. Look at the mess on that desk. Shameful!

ABE. Give me another year of law practice and I'll need a warehouse for the overflow. . . . But—sit yourself down, Bowling, and tell me what brings you to Springfield?

BOWLING (*sits above table*). I've been up to Lake Michigan fishing—came in today on the steam-cars.—Scared me out of a year's growth—but how are you doing, Abe? Josh says you're still broke, but you're a great social success.

ABE. True—on both counts. I'm greatly in demand at all the more elegant functions. You remember Ninian Edwards?

BOWLING. Of course.

ABE. Well, sir, I'm a guest at his mansion regularly. He's got a house so big you could race horses in the parlor. And his wife is one of the Todd family from Kentucky. Very high-grade people. They spell their name with two D's— which is pretty impressive when you consider that one was enough for God.

JOSH. Tell Bowling whom you met over in Rochester.

ABE. The President of the United States!

BOWLING. You don't tell me so!

ABE. Do you see that hand? (*He holds out his right hand, palm upward.*)

BOWLING. Yes—I see it.

ABE. It has shaken the hand of Martin Van Buren!

BOWLING. Was the President properly respectful to you, Abe?

ABE (*crossing up to door, then down to table*). Indeed he was! He said to me, "We've been hearing great things of you in Washington." I found out later he'd said the same thing to every other cross-roads politician he'd met. (*He laughs.*) But Billy Herndon here is pretty disgusted with me for associating with the wrong kind of people. Billy's a firebrand—a real, radical Abolitionist,[1] and he can't stand anybody who keeps his mouth shut and abides by the Constitution. If he had his way, the whole Union would be set on fire and we'd all be burned to a crisp. Eh, Billy?

BILLY (*grimly*). Yes, Mr. Lincoln. And if you'll permit me to say so, I think you'd be of more use to your fellowmen if you allowed some of the same incendiary impulses to come out in you.

ABE. You see, Bowling? He wants me to get down into the blood-soaked arena and grapple with all the lions of injustice and oppression.

BOWLING. Mr. Herndon—my profound compliments.

BILLY (*rising*). Thank you, sir. (*To* ABE, *taking his hat*) I have the writ prepared in the Wilcox case. I'll take it down to the Clerk of Court to be attested.

ABE. All right, Billy.

BILLY (*goes to door and turns*). Squire Green, Mr. Lincoln regards you and Mr. Speed as the best friends he has on earth, and I should like to beg you, in his presence, to drag him out of this stagnant pool in which he's rapidly drowning himself. Good day, sir—good day, Mr. Speed. (*Goes out quickly*)

JOSH. Good day, Billy.

[1] **Abolitionist:** one in favor of abolishing slavery in the United States.

BOWLING. That's a bright young man, Abe. Seems to have a good grasp of things.

ABE (*looking after* BILLY). He's going downstairs to the Clerk's office, but he took his hat. Which means that before he comes back to work, he'll have paid a little visit to the Chenery House saloon.

BOWLING. Does the boy drink?

ABE. Yes. He's got great fires in him, but he's putting 'em out fast. . . . Now—tell me about New Salem. (*He sits down on* BILLY's *table.*)

BOWLING. Practically nothing of it left.

ABE. How's that blessed wife of yours?

BOWLING. Nancy's busier than ever, and more than ever concerned about your innermost thoughts and yearnings. In fact she instructed me expressly to ask what on earth is the matter with you?

ABE (*laughs*). You can tell her there's nothing the matter. I've been able to pay off my debts to the extent of some seven cents on the dollar, and I'm sound of skin and skeleton.

BOWLING. But why don't we hear more from you and of you?

ABE. Josh can tell you—I've been busy.

BOWLING. What at?

ABE. I'm a candidate.

JOSH (*points to poster*). Haven't you noticed his name? It's here—at the bottom of the list of electors on the Whig ticket.

ABE. Yes, sir—if old Tippecanoe[2] wins next fall, I'll be a member of the Electoral College.[3]

BOWLING. The Electoral College. Is that the best you can do?

ABE. Yes—in the limited time at my disposal. I had a letter from Seth Gale—

[2] **old Tippecanoe:** a nickname for William Henry Harrison, the Whig candidate for President.

[3] **Electoral College:** pledged electors who cast their ballots for the candidate elected by the voters of their state.

you remember him—used to live in New Salem and was always aimin' to move West. He's settled down in Maryland now—and has a wife and son. He says that back East they're powerful worried about the annexation of Texas.

BOWLING. They have reason to be. It would probably mean extending slavery through all the territories from Kansas and Nebraska right out to Oregon and California. That would give the South absolute rule of the country—and God help the rest of us in the free states.

JOSH. It's an ugly situation, all right. It's got the seeds in it of nothing more nor less than civil war.

ABE (crossing to bed and stretching out on it). Well, if so, it'll be the Abolitionists' own fault. They know where this trouble might lead, and yet they go right on agitating. They ought to be locked up for disturbing the peace, all of them.

BOWLING. I thought you were opposed to slavery, Abe. Have you changed your mind about it?

ABE. No. I am opposed to slavery. But I'm even more opposed to going to war. And, on top of that, I know what you're getting at, both of you. (He speaks to them with the utmost good nature.) You're following Billy Herndon's lead—troubling your kind hearts with concerns about me and when am I going to amount to something? Is that it?

BOWLING. Oh, no, Abe. Far be it from me to interfere in your life.

JOSH. Or me, either. If we happen to feel that, so far, you've been a big disappointment to us, we'll surely keep it to ourselves.

ABE (laughs. He has slid down from table and ambled over to window.) I'm afraid you'll have to do what I've had to do—which is, learn to accept me for what I am. I'm no fighting man. I found that out when I went through the Black

Hawk War,[1] and was terrified that I might have to fire a shot at an Indian. Fortunately, the Indians felt the same way, so I never saw one of them. Now, I know plenty of men who like to fight; they're willing to kill, and not scared of being killed. All right. Let them attend to the battles that have to be fought.

BOWLING. Peaceable men have sometimes been of service to their country.

ABE. They may have been peaceable when they started, but they didn't remain so long after they'd become mixed in the great brawl of politics. Suppose I ran for Congress and got elected. (Sits up.) I'd be right in the thick of that ugly situation you were speaking of. One day I might have to cast my vote on the terrible issue of war or peace. It might be war with Mexico over Texas; or war with England over Oregon; or even war with our own people across the Ohio River. What attitude would I take in deciding which way to vote? "The liberal attitude," of course. And what is the liberal attitude? To go to war for a tract of land or a moral principle? Or to avoid war at all costs? No, sir. The place for me is in the Electoral College, where all I have to do is vote for the President whom everybody else elected four months previous.

BOWLING. Well, Abe—you were always an artful dodger—and maybe you'll be able to go on to the end of your days (NINIAN EDWARDS comes in. He is a little stouter and more prosperous.) avoiding the clutch of your own conscience.

ABE. Hello, Ninian.

JOSH. Hello, Ninian.

NINIAN. Hello. I saw Billy Herndon at the Chenery House and he said you were in. (He sees BOWLING.) Why—it's my good friend Squire Green. How de do,

[1] the Black Hawk War (1830–1832): led by Chief Black Hawk, concerning land which the United States government had taken over.

and welcome to Springfield.

BOWLING. Thank you, Mr. Edwards. *(They shake hands.)*

NINIAN *(he turns to* ABE*).* I just called in, Abe, to tell you you must dine with us. And, Squire, Mrs. Edwards would be honored to receive you, if your engagements will permit—and you, too, Josh.

JOSH. Delighted.

NINIAN. We're proudly exhibiting my sister-in-law, Miss Mary Todd, who has just come from Kentucky to grace our home. She's a very gay young lady—speaks French like a native, recites poetry at the drop of a hat, and knows the names and habits of all the flowers. I've asked Steve Douglas and some of the other eligibles to meet her, so you boys had better get in early.

BOWLING. My compliments to Mrs. Edwards, but my own poor wife awaits me impatiently.

NINIAN. I appreciate your motives, Squire, and applaud them. You'll be along presently, Abe?

ABE. I wouldn't be surprised.

NINIAN. Good. You'll meet a delightful young lady. And I'd better warn you, she's going to survey the whole field of matrimonial prospects and select the one who promises the most. So you'd better be on your guard, Abe, unless you're prepared to lose your standing as a free man.

ABE. I thank you for the warning, Ninian.

NINIAN. Good day to you, Squire. See you later, Josh. *(He goes out.)*

ABE. There, Bowling—you see how things are with me. Hardly a day goes by but what I'm invited to meet some eager young female who has all the graces including an ability to speak the language of diplomacy.[1]

BOWLING. I'm sorry, Abe, that I shan't be able to hear you carrying on a flirtation in French. *(He gets his hat.)*

ABE. I'm not pretending with you, Bowling—or you, Josh. I couldn't fool you any better than I can fool myself. I know what you're thinking about me, and I think so too. Only I'm not so merciful in considering my own shortcomings or so ready to forgive them as you are. *(Rises)* But—you talk about civil war—there seems to be one going on inside me all the time. Both sides are right and both sides are wrong and equal in strength. I'd like to be able to rise superior to the struggle—but—it says in the Bible that a house divided against itself cannot stand, so I reckon there's not much hope. One of these days I'll just split asunder, and part company with myself—and it'll be a good riddance from both points of view. However—come on. *(He takes his hat from desk.* BOWLING *rises and so does* SPEED. ABE *rises and goes to door.)* You've got to get back to Nancy, and Josh and I have got to make a good impression upon Miss Mary Todd, of Kentucky. *(He is waving them to door as lights fade out.)*

SCENE 5

Parlor of the Edwards house in Springfield. An evening in November, some six months after preceding scene. There is a fireplace at left, a heavily curtained bay window at back, and a door at left leading into front hall. At right by fireplace are a small couch and an easy chair. Another couch at left, and a table and chairs at back. There are family portraits on the walls. It is all moderately elegant. NINIAN *is standing before the fire, in conversation with* ELIZABETH, *his wife. She is highbred, ladylike—excessively so. She is at the moment in a state of some agitation.*

---

[1] **language of diplomacy:** French, used by diplomats of all nations, served as an international language.

ELIZABETH (*sitting on couch*). I can not believe it! It is an outrageous reflection on my sister's good sense.

NINIAN (*standing by fire*). I'm not so sure of that. Mary has known Abe for several months, and she has had plenty of chance to observe him closely.

ELIZABETH. She has been entertained by him, as we all have. But she has been far more attentive to Mr. Webb and Stephen Douglas and many others who are distinctly eligible.

NINIAN. Isn't it remotely possible that she sees more in Abe than you do?

ELIZABETH. Nonsense! Mr. Lincoln's chief virtue is that he hides no part of his simple soul from anyone. He's a most amiable creature, to be sure; but as the husband of a highbred, high-spirited young lady . . .

NINIAN. Quite so, Elizabeth. Mary *is* high-spirited! And she's abnormally ambitious. That is just why she set her cap for him. (ELIZABETH *looks at him sharply, then laughs.*)

ELIZABETH. You're making fun of me, Ninian. You're deliberately provoking me into becoming excited about nothing.

NINIAN (*crosses to* ELIZABETH). No, Elizabeth—I am merely trying to prepare you for a rude shock. You think Abe Lincoln would be overjoyed to capture an elegant, cultivated girl, daughter of the President of the Bank of Kentucky, descendant of a long line of English gentlemen. Well, you are mistaken.

[MARY TODD *comes in. She is twenty-two —short, pretty, remarkably sharp. She stops short in the doorway, and her suspecting eyes dart from* ELIZABETH *to* NINIAN. *He has sat on couch.*]

MARY. What were you two talking about?

NINIAN (*rises and turns to* MARY). I was telling your sister about the new song the boys are singing:

"What is the great commotion, motion,
  Our country through?
It is the ball a-rolling on
For Tippecanoe and Tyler, too—for
    Tippecanoe . . ."

MARY (*with a rather grim smile*). I compliment you for thinking quickly, Ninian. But you were talking about *me*. (*She looks at* ELIZABETH, *who quails a little before her sister's determination.*) Weren't you?

ELIZABETH (*crossing over to* MARY). Yes, Mary, we were.

MARY. And quite seriously, I gather.

NINIAN. I'm afraid that our dear Elizabeth has become unduly alarmed.

ELIZABETH (*snapping at him*). Let me say what I have to say! (*She goes up to right of* MARY.) Mary—you must tell me the truth. Are you—have you ever given one moment's serious thought to the possibility of marriage with Abraham Lincoln? (ELIZABETH *turns away.*) I promise you, Mary, that to me such a notion is too far beyond the bounds of credibility to be . . .

MARY. But Ninian has raised the horrid subject, hasn't he? He has brought the evil scandal out into the open, and we must face it, fearlessly. Let us do so at once, by all means. I shall answer you, Elizabeth. I have given more than one moment's thought to the possibility you mentioned—and I have decided that I shall be Mrs. Lincoln. (MARY *goes to couch and sits.*) I have examined, carefully, the qualifications of all the young gentlemen, and some of the old ones, in this neighborhood. Those of Mr. Lincoln seem to me superior to all others, and he is my choice.

ELIZABETH. Do you expect me to congratulate you upon this amazing selection?

MARY. No! I ask for no congratulations, nor condolences, either.

ELIZABETH. Then I shall offer none. (*Goes to chair and sits with her back to* NINIAN *and* MARY.)

NINIAN. Forgive me for prying, Mary, but have you as yet communicated your decision to the gentleman himself?

MARY (*with a slight smile at* NINIAN). Not yet. But he is coming to call this evening, and he will ask humbly for my hand in marriage; and, after I have displayed the proper amount of surprise and confusion, I shall murmur, timidly, "Yes!"

ELIZABETH (*half turns toward them. Pitiful*) You make a brave jest of it, Mary. But as for me, I am deeply and painfully shocked. I don't know what to say to you. But I urge you, I beg you, as your elder sister, responsible to our father and our dead mother for your welfare . . .

MARY (*with a certain tenderness*). I can assure you, Elizabeth—it is useless to beg or command. I have made up my mind.

NINIAN. I admire your courage, Mary, but I should like . . .

ELIZABETH. I think, Ninian, that this is a matter for discussion solely between my sister and myself. (NINIAN *starts to rise.* MARY *stops him.*)

MARY. No! I want to hear what Ninian has to say. (*To* NINIAN) What is it?

NINIAN. I only wondered if I might ask you another question.

MARY (*calmly*). You may.

NINIAN. Understand, my dear—I'm not quarreling with you. My affection for Abe is eternal, but I'm curious to know what it is about him that makes you choose him for a husband?

MARY (*betraying her first sign of uncertainty*). I should like to give you a plain, simple answer, Ninian. But I cannot.

ELIZABETH (*rising and crossing to* MARY). Of course you cannot! You're rushing blindly into this. You have no conception of what it will mean to your future.

MARY. You're wrong about that, Elizabeth. This is not the result of wild, tempestuous infatuation. I have not been swept off my feet. Mr. Lincoln is a Westerner, but that is his only point of resemblance to Young Lochinvar.[1] I simply feel that of all the men I've ever known, he is the one whose life and destiny I want most to share.

ELIZABETH. Haven't you sense enough to know you could never be happy with him? His breeding—his background—his manner—his whole point of view . . . ?

MARY (*gravely*). I could not be content with a "happy marriage" in the accepted sense of the word. I have no craving for comfort and security.

---

[1] **Young Lochinvar** (lok'in·vär): the hero of a ballad by Sir Walter Scott. According to the story, Lochinvar "came out of the West," swept a young girl onto his horse, and carried her off to be his bride.

ELIZABETH (*turns*). And have you a craving for the kind of life you would lead? A miserable cabin, without a servant, without a stitch of clothing that is fit for exhibition in decent society?

MARY (*raising her voice*). I have not yet tried poverty, so I can not say how I should take to it. But I might well prefer it to anything I have previously known—so long as there is forever before me the chance for high adventure—so long as I can know that I am always going forward, with my husband, along a road that leads across the horizon. (*This last is said with a sort of mad intensity.*)

ELIZABETH. And how far do you think you will go with anyone like Abe Lincoln, who is lazy and shiftless and prefers to stop constantly along the way to tell jokes?

MARY (*rises—furious. Crosses to* ELIZABETH.) He will not stop, if I am strong enough to make him go on. And I am strong. I know what you expect of me. You want me to do precisely as you have done and marry a man like Ninian; and I know many that are just like him. But with all due respect to my dear brother-in-law, I don't want that, and I won't have it. Never! You live in a house with a fence around it, presumably to prevent the common herd from gaining access to your sacred precincts but really to prevent you yourselves from escaping from your own narrow lives. In Abraham Lincoln I see a man who has split rails for other men's fences, but who has never built one around himself.

ELIZABETH (*turns away*). What are you saying, Mary? You are talking with a degree of irresponsibility that is not far from sheer madness.

MARY (*scornfully. Follows her*). I imagine it does seem like insanity to you. You married a man who was settled and established in the world, with a comfortable inheritance, and no problems to face. And you've never made a move to change your condition or improve it. You consider it couldn't be improved. To you, all this represents perfection. But it doesn't to me. I want the chance to shape a new life, for myself, and for my husband. Is that irresponsibility?

MAID (*entering at doorway*). Mr. Lincoln, ma'am.

ELIZABETH. He's here.

MARY. I shall see him. (*Crosses over to window*)

MAID. Will you step in, Mr. Lincoln?

ABE (*comes in wearing a new suit, his hair nearly neat*). Good evening, Mrs. Edwards. Good evening, Miss Todd.

ELIZABETH. Good evening.

MARY. Good evening, Mr. Lincoln.

NINIAN (*rises*). Glad to see you, Abe.

[*He goes to* ABE. ABE *sees that there is electricity in the atmosphere of this parlor. He tries hard to be affably casual.* MARY *has sat on couch.*]

ABE. Ninian, good evening. I'm afraid I'm a little late in arriving, but I ran into an old friend of mine, wife of Jack Armstrong, the champion rowdy of New Salem. I believe you have some recollection of him, Ninian?

NINIAN (*sits on couch. Smiling*) I most certainly have. What's he been up to now?

ABE. Oh, he's all right, but—Hannah, his wife, is in fearful trouble because her son Duff is up for murder and she wants me to defend him. I went over to the jail to interview the boy and he looks pretty tolerably guilty to me. But I used to give him lessons in the game of marbles while his mother foxed my pants for me. (*He turns to* ELIZABETH.) That means she sewed buckskin around the legs of my pants so I wouldn't tear 'em to shreds going through underbrush when I was surveying. Well—in view of old times, I felt I had to take the case and do what I can to obstruct the orderly processes of justice.

NINIAN *(laughs, with some relief)*. And the boy will be acquitted. I tell you, Abe, this country would be law-abiding peaceful if it weren't for you lawyers. But *(Rises)* if you will excuse Elizabeth and me, we must hear the children's prayers and see them safely abed.

ABE. Why, I'd be glad to hear their prayers, too.

NINIAN. Oh, no! You'd only keep them up till all hours with your stories. Come along, Elizabeth.

[ELIZABETH *doesn't want to go but doesn't know what to do to prevent it.*]

ABE. Kiss them good night for me. (ELIZABETH *rises.*)

NINIAN. We'd better not tell them you're in the house, or they'll be furious.

ELIZABETH *(making one last attempt, crosses to* MARY*)*. Mary! Won't you come with us and say good night to the children?

NINIAN *(takes* ELIZABETH *by shoulders)*. No, my dear. Leave Mary here—to keep Abe entertained. *(He guides* ELIZABETH *out, following her.)*

MARY *(with a little laugh)*. I don't blame Ninian for keeping you away from those children. They all adore you.

ABE. Well, I always seemed to get along well with children. Probably it's because they never want to take me seriously.

MARY. You understand them—that's the important thing. But, do sit down, Mr. Lincoln.

ABE. Thank you, I will.

[*He crosses to chair by fire and sits opposite* MARY. *His back is to the audience.* MARY *looks at him with melting eyes. The lights fade.*]

SCENE 6

Again the law office. It is afternoon of New Year's Day, a few weeks after the preceding scene.

ABE *is sitting, slumped in his chair, staring at his desk. He has his hat on, and a muffler is hanging about his neck, untied.* JOSH SPEED *is half-sitting on table at left. He is reading a long letter with most serious attention. At length he finishes it, refolds it very carefully, stares at floor.*

ABE. Have you finished it, Josh?

JOSH. Yes.

ABE. Well—do you think it's all right?

JOSH. No, Abe, I don't. (ABE *turns and looks at him.*) I think the sending of this letter would be a most grave mistake— and that is putting it mildly and charitably.

ABE. Have I stated the case too crudely?

[ABE *is evidently in a serious state of distress, although he is making a tremendous effort to disguise it by speaking in what he intends to be a coldly impersonal tone. He is struggling mightily to hold himself back from the brink of nervous collapse.*]

JOSH. No—I have no quarrel with your choice of words. None whatever. If anything, the phraseology is too correct. But your method of doing it, Abe! It's brutal, it's heartless, it's so unworthy of you that I'm at a loss to understand how you ever thought you could do it this way.

ABE. I've done the same thing before with a woman to whom I seemed to have become attached. She approved of my action.

JOSH. This is a different woman. (*He walks over to window, then turns again toward* ABE.) You cannot seem to accept the fact that women are human beings, too, as variable as we are. You act on the assumption that they're all the same one and that one is a completely unearthly being of your own conception. This letter isn't written to Mary Todd, it's written to yourself. Every line of it is intended to provide salve for your own conscience.

ABE (*coldly*). Do I understand that you will not deliver it for me?

JOSH. No, Abe, I shall not.

ABE (*angrily*). Then someone else will!

JOSH. Yes. You could give it to the minister to hand to the bride when he arrives for the ceremony. But—I hope, Abe, you won't send it till you're feeling a little calmer in your mind. . . .

ABE. How can I ever be calm in my mind until this thing is settled and out of the way, once and for all? Have you got eyes in your head, Josh? Can't you see that I'm desperate?

JOSH. I can see that plainly, Abe. I think your situation is more desperate even than you imagine, and I believe you should have the benefit of some really intelligent medical advice.

ABE. The trouble with me isn't anything that a doctor can cure.

JOSH. There's a good man named Dr. Drake, who makes a specialty of treating people who get into a state of mind like yours, Abe. . . .

ABE (*utterly miserable*). So that's how you've figured it! I've done what I've threatened to do many times before: I've gone crazy. Well—you know me better than most men, Josh, and perhaps you're not far off right. I just feel that I've got to the end of my rope, and I must let go, and drop—and where I'll land I don't know, and whether I'll survive the fall—I don't know that either. . . . But—this I do know: I've got to get out of this thing—I can't go through with it—I've got to have my release!

[JOSH *has turned to window. Suddenly he turns back toward* ABE.]

JOSH. Ninian Edwards is coming up. Why not show this letter to him and ask for his opinion. . . .

ABE (*interrupting, with desperation*). No, no! Don't say a word about this to him! Put that letter in your pocket. I can't bear to discuss this business with him now. (JOSH *puts letter in his pocket, sits on bed. He looks out.*)

JOSH. Hello, Ninian.

NINIAN. Hello, Josh! Happy New Year! (NINIAN *comes in. He wears a handsome fur-trimmed great-coat, and carries two silverheaded canes.*) And Happy New Year, Abe—in fact, the happiest of your whole life! (*Lays canes on table*)

ABE. Thank you, Ninian. And Happy New Year to you.

NINIAN (*opening his coat*). That didn't sound much as if you meant it. (*He goes*

to stove to warm his hands.) However, you can be forgiven today, Abe. I suppose you're inclined to be just a wee bit nervous. *(He chuckles and winks at* JOSH.*)* It's cold in here! Don't you ever light this stove?

ABE. The fire's all laid. Go ahead and light it, if you want.

NINIAN *(striking match).* You certainly are in one of your less amiable moods today. *(He lights stove.)*

JOSH. Abe's been feeling a little under the weather.

NINIAN *(at stove).* So it seems. He looked to me as if he'd been to a funeral.

ABE. That's where I have been.

NINIAN *(disbelieving, turns and crosses to table).* What? A funeral on your wedding day?

JOSH. They buried Abe's oldest friend, Bowling Green, this morning.

NINIAN *(shocked, sits beside table).* Oh—I'm mighty sorry to hear that, Abe. And—I hope you'll forgive me for—not having known about it.

ABE. Of course, Ninian.

NINIAN. But I'm glad you were there, Abe, at the funeral. It must have been a great comfort to his family.

ABE. I wasn't any comfort to anyone. They asked me to deliver an oration, a eulogy of the deceased—and I tried—and I couldn't say a thing. Why do they expect you to strew a lot of flowery phrases over anything so horrible as a dead body? Do they think that Bowling Green's soul needs quotations to give it peace? All that mattered to me was that he was a good, just man—and I loved him—and he's dead.

NINIAN. Why didn't you say that, Abe?

ABE. I told you—they wanted an oration.

NINIAN. Well, Abe—I think Bowling himself would be the first to ask you to put your sadness aside in the prospect of your own happiness, and Mary's—and I'm only sorry that our old friend didn't live to see you two fine people married. *(He is making a gallant attempt to assume a more cheery nuptial tone.)* I've made all the arrangements with the Reverend Dresser, and Elizabeth is preparing a bang-up dinner—so you can be sure the whole affair will be carried off handsomely *and* painlessly.... *(*BILLY HERNDON *comes in. He is already more than a little drunk and sullen but abnormally articulate.)* Ah, Billy—Happy New Year!

BILLY. The same to you, Mr. Edwards. *(He goes up by stove and takes his coat off and warms his hands.)*

NINIAN. I brought you a wedding present, Abe. Thought you'd like to make a brave show when you first walk out with your bride. *(He picks up one of the canes and hands it proudly to* ABE, *who takes it and inspects it gravely.)* It came from the same place in Louisville where I bought mine.

ABE. It's very fine, Ninian. And I thank you. (*He turns and puts it on desk.*)

NINIAN. Well—I'll frankly confess that in getting it for you, I was influenced somewhat by consideration for Mary and her desire for keeping up appearances. And in that connection—I know you'll forgive me, Josh, and you, too, Billy, if I say something of a somewhat personal nature?

BILLY (*turns. Truculent*) If you want me to leave you, I shall be glad to . . .

NINIAN. No—please, Billy—I merely want to speak a word or two as another of Abe's friends; it's my last chance before the ceremony. Of course, the fact that the bride is my sister-in-law gives me a little added responsibility in wishing to promote the success of this marriage. (*He turns to* ABE.) And a success it will be . . . if only, Abe, you will bear in mind one thing: you must keep a tight rein on her ambition. My wife tells me that even as a child she had delusions of grandeur— she predicted to one and all that the man she would marry would be President of the United States. (*He turns to* JOSH.) You know how it is—every boy in the country plans some day to be President, and every little girl plans to marry him. (*Again to* ABE) But Mary is one who hasn't entirely lost those youthful delusions. So I urge you to beware. Don't let her talk you into any gallant crusades or wild goose chases. Let her learn to be satisfied with the estate to which God hath brought her. With which I shall conclude my pre-nuptial sermon. (*He buttons his coat.*) I shall see you all at the house at five o'clock, and I want you to make sure that Abe is looking his prettiest. (*He goes out.*)

BILLY. Mr. Lincoln, I beg leave to drink to your health and happiness . . . and to that of the lady who will become your wife. (ABE *makes no response.* BILLY *drinks it down, then puts cup back on table. Huskily*) You don't want to accept my toast because you think it wasn't sincere. And, I'll admit, I've made it plain that I've regretted the step you've taken. I thought that in this marriage you were lowering yourself—you were trading your honor for some exalted family connections. . . . I wish to apologize for so thinking. . . .

ABE. No apologies required, Billy.

BILLY. I doubt that Miss Todd and I will ever get along well together. But I'm now convinced that our aims are the same —particularly since I've heard warnings delivered by her brother-in-law. (*A note of scorn colors his allusion to* NINIAN.) If she really is ambitious for you—if she will never stop driving you, goading you— then I say, God bless her and give her strength! (BILLY *pours himself another drink, nearly emptying the large bottle.* ABE *turns and looks at him.*)

ABE. Have you had all of that bottle today?

BILLY. This bottle? Yes—I have.

JOSH. And why not? It's New Year's Day!

BILLY. Thank you, Mr. Speed. Thank you for the defense. (*Crossing to* ABE.) To the President of the United States and Mrs. Lincoln! (*He drinks.*)

ABE (*grimly*). I think we can do without any more toasts, Billy.

BILLY. Very well! That's the last one— until after the wedding. And then, no doubt, the Edwards will serve us with the costliest champagne. And, in case you're apprehensive, I shall be on my best behavior in that distinguished gathering!

ABE. There is not going to be a wedding. (ABE *rises.*) I have a letter I want you to deliver to Miss Todd.

BILLY. What letter? What is it?

ABE. Give it to him, Josh. (JOSH *takes letter out of his pocket and puts it in the stove and crosses down by windows.* ABE *jumps up.*) You have no right to do that!

JOSH. I know I haven't! But it's done. (ABE *is staring at* JOSH.) And don't look at me as if you were planning to break my neck. Of course you could do it, Abe— but you won't. (JOSH *turns to* BILLY.) In that letter Mr. Lincoln asked Miss Todd for her release. He told her that he had made a mistake in his previous protestations of affection for her, and so he couldn't go through with a marriage which could only lead to endless pain and misery for them both.

ABE (*deeply distressed*). If that isn't the truth, what is? (*He leans on desk.*)

JOSH. I'm not disputing the truth of it. I'm only asking you to tell her so to her face, in the manner of a man.

ABE. It would be a more cruel way. It would hurt her more deeply. For I couldn't help blurting it *all* out—all the terrible things I didn't say in that letter. (*He is speaking with passion.*) I'd have to tell her that I have hatred for her infernal ambition—that I don't want to be ridden and driven, upward and onward through life, with her whip lashing me and her spurs digging into me! If her poor soul craves importance in life, then let her marry Stephen Douglas. He's ambitious, too. I want only to be left alone! (*Sits at end of table*)

JOSH. Very well, then—tell her all that! It will be more gracious to admit that you're afraid of her, instead of letting her down flat with the statement that your ardor, such as it was, has cooled.

[BILLY *has been seething with a desire to get into this conversation. Now, with a momentary silence, he plunges.*]

BILLY. May I say something?

ABE. I doubt that you're in much of a condition to contribute . . .

JOSH. What is it, Billy?

BILLY. It's just this. Mr. Lincoln, you're not abandoning Miss Mary Todd. No! You're only using her as a living sacrifice, offering her up in the hope that you will thus gain forgiveness of the gods for your failure to do your own great duty!

ABE. Yes! My own great duty. Everyone feels called upon to remind me of it, but no one can tell me what it is.

BILLY. I can tell you! I can tell you what is the duty of every man who calls himself an American! It is to perpetuate those truths which were once held to be self-evident: that all men are created equal —that they are endowed with certain inalienable rights—that among these are the right to life, liberty, and the pursuit of happiness.

ABE. And are those rights denied to *me?*

BILLY. Could you ever enjoy them while your mind is full of the awful knowledge that two millions of your fellow beings in this country are slaves? Can you take any satisfaction from looking at that flag above your desk when you know that ten of its stars represent states which are willing to destroy the Union rather than yield their property rights in the flesh and blood of those slaves? And what of all the states of the future? All the territories of the West—clear out to the Pacific Ocean? Will they be the homes of freemen? Are you answering that question to your own satisfaction? That's your flag, Mr. Lincoln, and you're proud of it. But what are you doing to save it from being ripped into shreds? (ABE *jumps to his feet and towers over* BILLY.)

ABE. I'm minding my own business— that's what I'm doing! And there'd be no threat to the Union if others would do the same. And as to slavery, I'm sick and tired of this righteous talk about it. When you know more about law, you'll know that those property rights you mentioned are guaranteed by the Constitution. And if the Union can't stand the Constitution, then let it fall! (*Crosses to above desk chair*)

BILLY (*turns to face* ABE). This is a matter of the rights of living men to freedom—and those came before the Constitution! When the law denies those rights, then the law is wrong, and it must be changed, if not by moral protest, then by force! There's no course of action that isn't justified in the defense of freedom! And don't dare to tell me that anyone in the world knows that better than you do, Mr. Lincoln. You, who honor the memory of Elijah Lovejoy and every other man who ever died for that very ideal!

ABE (*turning away from him*). Yes—I honor them—and envy them—because they could believe that their ideals are *worth* dying for. (*He turns to* JOSH *and speaks with infinite weariness.*) All right, Josh, I'll go up now and talk to Mary—and then I'm going away. . . . (*Going*)

JOSH. Where, Abe?

ABE. I don't know. (*He goes out.* BILLY *rushes to door and shouts after him.*)

BILLY. You're quitting, Mr. Lincoln. As surely as there's a God in Heaven, He knows that you're running away from your obligations to Him, and to your fellowmen, and your own immortal soul!

JOSH (*who is by other window*). Leave him alone, Billy. He's a sick man.

BILLY. What can we do for him, Mr. Speed? What can we do?

JOSH. *I* don't know, Billy. (*He goes to window and looks out.* BILLY *sits at table.*) He'll be in such a state of emotional upheaval he'll want to go away by himself for a long time. Just as he did after the death of poor little Ann Rutledge. He'll go out and wander on the prairies, aimlessly, trying to grope his way back into the wilderness from which he came. There's nothing we can do for him, Billy. He'll have to do it for himself.

BILLY (*fervently*). May God be with him!

SCENE 7

On the prairie near New Salem. It is a clear, cool, moonlit evening, nearly two years after the preceding scene. In the foreground is a campfire. Around it are packing cases, blanket rolls and one ancient trunk. In the background is a covered wagon, standing at an angle, so that the opening at the back of it is visible to the audience.

SETH GALE *is standing by the fire, holding his eight-year-old son,* JIMMY, *in his arms. The boy is wrapped up in a blanket.*

JIMMY. I don't want to be near the fire, Paw. I'm burning up. Won't you take the blanket offen me, Paw?

SETH. No, son. You're better off if you keep yourself covered.

JIMMY. I want some water, Paw. Can't I have some water?

SETH. Yes! Keep quiet, Jimmy! Gobey's getting the water for you now. (*He looks off, sees someone coming.*) Hello, Jack. I was afraid you'd got lost.

JACK (*coming in*). I couldn't get lost anywheres around New Salem. How's the boy?

SETH (*with a cautionary look at* JACK). He's—he's a little bit thirsty. Did you find Abe?

JACK. Yes—it took me some time because he'd wandered off—went out to the old cemetery across the river to visit Ann Rutledge's grave.

SETH. Is he coming here?

JACK. He said he'd better go get Doc Chandler who lives on the Winchester Road. He'll be along in a while. (*He*

comes up to JIMMY.) How you feeling, Jimmy?

JIMMY. I'm thirsty. (AGGIE *appears, sees* JACK.)

AGGIE. Oh, I'm glad you're back, Mr. Armstrong.

JACK. There'll be a doctor here soon, Mrs. Gale.

AGGIE. Thank God for that! Bring him into the wagon, Seth. I got a nice soft bed all ready for him.

SETH. You hear that, Jimmy? Your ma's fixed a place where you can rest comfortable. (AGGIE *retreats into wagon.*)

JIMMY. When'll Gobey come back? I'm thirsty. When'll he bring the water?

SETH. Right away, son. You can trust Gobey to get your water. (*He hands* JIMMY *into the wagon.*)

JACK. He's worse, ain't he?

SETH (*in a despairing tone*). Yes. The fever's been raging something fierce since you left. It'll sure be a relief when Abe gets here. He can always do something to put confidence in you.

JACK. How long since you've seen Abe, Seth?

SETH. Haven't laid eyes on him since I left here—seven—eight years ago. We've corresponded some.

JACK (*sits behind fire to right*). Well, you may be surprised when you see him. He's changed plenty since he went to Springfield. He climbed up pretty high in the world, but he appears to have slipped down lately. He ain't much like his old comical self.

SETH. Well, I guess we all got to change. (*Hearing* GOBEY *return, he rises and goes to the left.*) Aggie! (GOBEY *has come in carrying bucket of water.* AGGIE *appears at wagon flap.*) Here's Gobey with the water.

GOBEY. Yes, Miss Aggie. Here you are. (*Hands up pail to her*)

AGGIE. Thanks, Gobey. (*Goes back into wagon*)

GOBEY. How's Jimmy now, Mr. Seth?

SETH. About the same.

GOBEY (*shakes head*). I'll get some more water for the cooking. (*Picks up kettle, goes off.*)

JACK. How long you been on the road, Seth?

SETH. More than three months. Had a terrible time in the Pennsylvania mountains. Fearful rains and every stream flooded. I can tell you there was more than one occasion when I wanted to turn back and give up the whole idea. (*He looks.*) Say! Is that Abe coming now?

JACK (*rises and looks off*). Yep. That's him.

SETH. Lord, look at him! Store clothes and a plug hat! Hello, Abe!

ABE (*goes to fire*). Hello, Seth. (*They shake hands.*) I'm awful glad to see you again, Seth.

SETH. And me too, Abe.

ABE. It did my heart good when I heard you were on your way West. Where's your boy?

SETH. He's in there—in the wagon.

AGGIE (*appearing on the wagon*). Is that the doctor?

SETH. No, Aggie. This is the man I was telling you about I wanted so much to see. This is Mr. Abe Lincoln—my wife, Mrs. Gale.

ABE (*goes to her*). Pleased to meet you, Mrs. Gale.

AGGIE. Pleased to meet you, Mr. Lincoln.

ABE. Doc Chandler wasn't home. They said he was expected over at the Boger farm at midnight. I'll go there then and fetch him.

SETH. It'll be a friendly act, Abe.

AGGIE. We'll be in your debt, Mr. Lincoln.

ABE. In the meantime, Mrs. Gale, I'd like to do whatever I can . . .

SETH. There's nothing to do, Abe. The boy's got the swamp fever, and we're just trying to keep him quiet.

AGGIE (*desperately*). There's just one thing I would wish.—Is there any kind of a preacher around this godforsaken place?

SETH (*worried*). Preacher?

ABE. Do you know of any, Jack?

JACK. No. There ain't a preacher within twenty miles of New Salem now.

AGGIE. Well—I only thought if there was, we might get him here to say a prayer for Jimmy. (*She goes back into wagon. SETH looks after her with great alarm.*)

SETH. She wants a preacher. That looks as if she'd given up, don't it?

JACK. It'd probably just comfort her.

ABE. Is your boy very sick, Seth?

SETH. Yes—he is.

JACK. Why don't you speak a prayer, Abe? You could always think of something to say.

ABE. I'm afraid I'm not much of a hand at praying. I couldn't think of a blessed thing that would be of any real help.

SETH. Never mind. It's just a—a religious idea of Aggie's. Sit down, Abe.

ABE. So you've got your dream at last, Seth. You're doing what you and I used to talk about—you're moving.

SETH. Yes, Abe. We got crowded out of Maryland. The city grew up right over our farm. So—we're headed for a place where there's more room. I wrote you, Abe—about four months back—to tell you we were starting out, and I'd like to meet up with you here. I thought it was just possible you might consider joining in this trip.

ABE. It took a long time for your letter to catch up with me, Seth. I've just been drifting—down around Indiana and Kentucky where I used to live. Do you aim to settle in Nebraska?

SETH. No, we're not going to stop there. We're going to Oregon.

ABE. Oregon?

JACK. Sure. That's where they're all heading for now.

SETH. We're making first for a place called Westport Landing—that's in Kansas right on the frontier—where they outfit the wagon trains for the far West. You join up there with a lot of others who are like-minded, so you've got company when you're crossing the plains and the mountains.

ABE. It's staggering to think of the distance you're going. And you'll be taking the frontier along with you.

SETH. It may seem like a foolhardy thing to do, but we heard too many tales of the black earth out there, and the balance of rainfall and sunshine.

JACK. Why don't you go with them, Abe? That country out West is getting settled fast. Why, last week alone, I counted more than two hundred wagons went past here—people from all over— Pennsylvania, Connecticut, Vermont— all full of jubilation at the notion of getting land. By gosh, I'm going too, soon as I can get me a wagon. They'll need men like me to fight the Indians for 'em and they'll need men with brains, like you, Abe, to tell 'em how to keep the peace.

ABE. It's a temptation to go, I can't deny that.

JACK. Then what's stopping you from doing it? You said yourself you've just been drifting.

ABE. Maybe that's it, maybe I've been drifting too long. Do you think it will be free in Oregon?

SETH. Of course it will! It's got to—

ABE. Oh, no, it hasn't, Seth. Not with the politicians in Washington selling out the whole West piece by piece to the slave traders.

SETH (vehemently). That territory has got to be free! If this country ain't strong enough to protect its citizens from slavery, then we'll cut loose from it and join with Canada. Or, better yet, we'll make a new country out there in the far West.

ABE. A new country?

SETH. Why not?

ABE. I was just thinking—old Mentor Graham once said to me that some day the United States might be divided up into many hostile countries, like Europe.

SETH. Well—let it be! Understand—I love this country and I'd fight for it. And I guess George Washington and the rest of them loved England and fought for it when they were young—but they didn't hesitate to cut loose when the government failed to play fair and square with 'em.

JACK. By gum, if Andy Jackson was back in the White House, he'd run out them traitors with a horsewhip!

ABE. (grimly). It'd be a bad day for us Americans, Seth, if we lost you, and your wife, and your son.

SETH. My son!—Oh, I've been talking big but it's empty talk. If he dies there won't be enough spirit left in us to push on any further. What's the use of working

for a future when you know there won't be anybody growing up to enjoy it? Excuse me, Abe, but I'm feeling pretty scared.

ABE (suddenly rises). You mustn't be scared, Seth. I know I'm a poor one to be telling you that—because I've been scared all my life. And seeing you now, and thinking of the big thing you've set out to do—well, it's made me feel pretty small. It's made me feel that I've got to do something, too, to keep you and your kind in the United States of America. You mustn't give up, Seth. Don't let anything beat you—don't ever give up.

AGGIE (comes out of wagon and runs to SETH). Seth!

SETH. What is it, Aggie?

AGGIE. He's worse, Seth. He's moaning in his sleep, and he's gasping for breath. (Breaks down)

SETH (takes her in his arms). Never mind, honey, never mind. When the doctor gets here, he'll fix him up in no time. It's all right, honey. He'll get well.

ABE. If you wish me to, Mrs. Gale, I'll try to speak a prayer.

JACK (crosses to ABE). That's the way to talk, Abe.

SETH. We'd be grateful for anything you might say, Abe.

ABE (takes off his hat and starts speaking). Oh God, the Father of all living, I ask You to look with gentle mercy upon this little boy who is here, lying sick in this covered wagon. His people are traveling far to seek a new home in the wilderness, to do Your work, God, to make this earth a good place for Your children to live in. They can see clearly where they're going, and they're not afraid to face all the perils that lie along the way. I humbly beg You not to take their child from them. Grant him the freedom of life. Do not condemn him to the imprisonment of death. Do not deny him his birthright.

Let him know the sight of great plains and high mountains, of green valleys and wide rivers. For this little boy is an American, and these things belong to him, and he to them. Spare him, that he too may strive for the ideal for which his fathers have labored, so faithfully and for so long. Spare him and give him his father's strength—give us all strength, oh God, to do the work that is before us. Amen.

SETH and AGGIE *(murmuring)*. Amen! (ABE *puts his hat on.*)

ABE. It must be getting near midnight. I'll go after the doctor. *(He goes out.)*

SETH. Thank you, Abe.

AGGIE. Thank you—thank you, Mr. Lincoln. *(The lights fade quickly.)*

SCENE 8

Again the parlor of the Edwards house a few days after preceding scene. MARY *is seated, reading a book. Night. After a moment the* MAID *enters.*

MAID. Miss Mary, Mr. Lincoln is here.

MARY. Mr.—Lincoln! *(She sits still a moment in an effort to control her emotions, then sharply closes book, rises and goes to one side.)*

MAID. Will you see him, Miss Mary?

MARY. Yes—in one moment. (MAID *goes off.* MARY *turns, thinking, drops her book on sofa, then turns and moves right; at fireplace she stops and turns to face* ABE *as he enters.)* I'm glad to see you again, Mr. Lincoln.

ABE. Thank you, Mary. You may well wonder why I have thrust myself on your mercy in this manner.

MARY. I'm sure you're always welcome in Ninian's house.

ABE. After my behavior at our last meeting here, I have not been welcome company for myself.

MARY. You've been through a severe illness, Abe. Joshua Speed has kept us informed of it. We've been greatly concerned.

ABE. It is most kind of you.

MARY. But you're restored to health now—you'll return to your work, and no doubt you'll be running for the assembly again—or perhaps you have larger plans—?

ABE. I have no plans, Mary. *(He seems to brace himself.)* But I wish to tell you that I am sorry for the things that I said on that unhappy occasion which was to have been our wedding day.

MARY. You need say nothing about that, Abe. Whatever happened then, it was my own fault.

ABE *(tortured by these coals of fire)*. Your fault? It was my miserable cowardice——

MARY. I was blinded by my own self-confidence! I—I loved you. *(For a moment her firm voice falters, but she immediately masters that tendency toward weakness.)* And I believed I could make you love me. I believed we might achieve a real communion of spirit, and the fire of my determination would burn in you. You would become a man and a leader of men! But you didn't wish that. *(She turns away.)* I knew you had strength, but I did not know you would use it, all of it, to resist your own magnificent destiny.

ABE. It is true, Mary, you once had faith in me which I was far from deserving. But the time has come, at last, when I wish to strive to deserve it. (MARY *looks at him, sharply.)* When I behaved in that shameful manner toward you, I did so because I thought that our ways were separate and could never be otherwise. I've come to the conclusion that I was wrong. I believe that our destinies are together, for better or for worse, and I again presume to ask you to be my wife. I fully realize, Mary, that taking me back now would involve humiliation for you.

MARY. I am not afraid of humiliation, if I know it will be wiped out by ultimate triumph. But there can be no triumph unless you yourself are sure. What was it brought you to the change of heart and mind?

ABE. On the prairie I met an old friend of mine who was moving West, with his wife and child, in a covered wagon. He asked me to go with him, and I was strongly tempted to do so. But then I knew that was not my direction. The way I must go is the way you have always wanted me to go.

MARY. And you will promise that never again will you falter, or turn to run away?

ABE. I promise, Mary—if you will have me—I shall devote myself for the rest of my days to trying—to do what is right—as God gives me power to see what is right.

MARY. Then I will be your wife. I shall fight by your side—till death do us part. (*These words are spoken with an almost triumphant exaltation. She moves to him.*) Abe! I love you—oh, I love you. Whatever becomes of the two of us, I'll die loving you.

[*She is sobbing wildly on his shoulder. Awkwardly he lifts his hands and takes hold of her in a loose embrace. He is staring down at the carpet over her shoulder.*]

FOR STUDY AND DISCUSSION

1. What is your impression of Billy Herndon? What faults does he have? what virtues? How is he similar to Abe? How is he different?

2. What does Abe say in Scene 4 that shows his understanding of both sides of the controversy that is threatening to divide the nation? Why is he against the fanatics on both sides?

3. What is your impression of Mary Todd? In answering, consider what she says, what she does, and what others say about her. Many historians have given us a picture of Mary Todd that is quite unpleasant. Does she have any saving virtues? Judging from the play, how great an influence did she have on Lincoln's life and career?

4. Compare Mary Todd with Ann Rutledge. In what ways are they different? How is Lincoln's attitude toward Mary different from his attitude toward Ann?

5. In Scene 5, Mary says, "In Abraham Lincoln I see a man who has split rails for other men's fences, but who has never built one around himself!" What does she mean? From what you have seen of Lincoln in the play, do you agree? Why or why not? In your own words tell what this statement suggests about the personality of Lincoln.

6. In Act I we saw Lincoln's reaction to the death of Ann. What is his reaction to the death of Bowling Green? What causes him to leave his law office and his waiting bride to go out on the prairies and "grope his way back into the wilderness from which he came"? Does he succeed in finding his way to some sort of inner peace? How does he react to the threatened death of the son of his friend Seth? How is the way he meets this crisis different from his shyness at the funeral of Bowling Green? What new maturity does this difference show in Lincoln?

7. Why does Abe run away from his marriage to Mary? How is his unwillingness to marry like his unwillingness to seek public office? How does his encounter with Seth Gale and his family on the prairie change Lincoln's mind about accepting responsibility? What is he reminded of by seeing Seth and his sick son?

8. What kind of man does Abe say, near the end of Scene 6, that he admires and envies? What does this suggest about the kind of person that he may eventually become?

9. In a way, the contradictions in Abe are like the contradictions in the nation, and the two sides of his sympathies are like the two opposing factions that are threatening to split the Union. How does Abe's struggle to reconcile the two opposing impulses in his own nature make him particularly well suited to

become President of a troubled nation? At what moment in the play does he succeed in reconciling the two sides of his nature? What in his prayer for Seth's son suggests that he is also dedicating himself to the future of the nation?

10. What new sides of Lincoln's character were brought out in the five scenes of Act II?

THE CRAFT OF THE DRAMATIST

1. One of the basic skills of a dramatist is to use characters for purposes of contrast. By showing us a character who acts differently from the main character, the dramatist enables us to see more clearly the nature of each. What do we learn about Abe Lincoln from the way in which each of the following characters contrasts with him?

Billy Herndon   Josh Speed
Ninian Edwards   Mary Todd

2. Sherwood himself said of Scene 7 that it was "the most completely fictitious, and the one which presented the greatest difficulty in the writing." Why did he have to include this scene? How is it a turning point in the play?

ACT III

SCENE 9

Parlor of the Lincoln home in Springfield. Afternoon of a day in the spring of 1860.

ABE *is sitting on couch with his seven-year-old son,* TAD. *Beside them is another son,* WILLIE, *aged nine. The eldest son,* ROBERT, *a young Harvard student of seventeen, is sitting by the window, importantly smoking a pipe and listening to the story* ABE *has been telling the children.* JOSHUA SPEED *is sitting at left of stage.*

ABE. You must remember, Tad, the roads weren't much good then—mostly nothing more than trails, and it was hard to find my way in the darkness. . . .

WILLIE. Were you scared?

ABE. Yes—I was scared.

WILLIE. Of Indians?

ABE. No, there weren't any of them left around here. I was afraid I'd get lost, and the boy would die, and it would be all my fault. But finally I found the doctor. He was very tired, and wanted to go to bed, and he grumbled a lot, but I made him come along with me then and there.

WILLIE. Was the boy dead?

ABE. No. The doctor gave him a lot of medicine.

TAD. Did it taste bad, Pa?

ABE. I presume it did. But it worked. I never saw those nice people again, but I've heard from them every so often. That little boy was your age, Willie, but now he's a grown man with a son as big as Tad. He lives on a great big farm, in a valley with a river that runs right down from the tops of the snow mountains. . . . (MARY *comes in.*)

MARY. Robert! You are smoking in my parlor!

ROBERT (*wearily—rising*). Yes, Mother.

MARY. I have told you that I shall not tolerate tobacco smoke in my parlor or, indeed, in any part of my house, and I mean to . . .

ABE. Come, come, Mary—you must be respectful to a Harvard man. Take it out to the woodshed, Bob.

ROBERT (*starts up*). Yes, Father.

MARY. And this will not happen again!

ROBERT. No, Mother. (*He goes out.*)

ABE. I was telling the boys a story about some pioneers I knew once.

MARY. It's time for you children to make ready for your supper. (*The* CHILDREN *promptly get up to go.*)

WILLIE. But what happened after that, Pa?

ABE. Nothing. Everybody lived happily ever after. Now run along. (WILLIE *and* TAD *run out.* MARY *is shaking the smoke out of the curtains.*)

JOSH. Half-past four, Abe. Those men will be here any minute.

ABE (*rising*). Good Lord!

MARY. What men?

ABE. Some men from the East. One of them's a political leader named Crimmin—and there's a Mr. Sturveson—he's a manufacturer—and . . .

MARY (*impressed*). Henry D. Sturveson?

ABE. That's the one—and also the Reverend Dr. Barrick from Boston.

MARY (*sharply*). What are they coming here for?

ABE. I don't precisely know—but I suspect that it's to see if I'm fit to be a candidate for President of the United States. (MARY *is, for the moment, speechless.*) I suppose they want to find out if we still live in a log cabin and keep pigs under the bed. . . .

MARY (*in a fury*). And you didn't *tell* me!

Abraham Lincoln at the age of fifty-one.

ABE. I'm sorry, Mary—the matter just slipped my . . .

MARY (*crossing to* ABE). You forgot to tell me that we're having the most important guests who ever crossed the threshold of my house!

ABE. They're not guests. They're only here on business.

MARY (*bitterly*). Yes! Rather important business, it seems to me. They want to see us as we *are*—crude, sloppy, vulgar Western barbarians, living in a house that reeks of foul tobacco smoke.

ABE. We can explain about having a son at Harvard.

MARY. If I'd only *known!* If you had only given me a little time to prepare for them. Why didn't you put on your best suit? And those filthy old boots!

ABE. Why, Mary, I clean forgot.

MARY. I declare, Abraham Lincoln, I believe you would have treated me with much more consideration if I had been your slave, instead of your wife! You have never, for one moment, stopped to think that perhaps I have some interests, some concerns, in the life we lead together.

ABE. I'll try to clean up my boots a little, Mary.

[*He goes out, glad to escape from this painful scene.* MARY *looks after him. Her lip is quivering. She wants to avoid tears.*]

MARY (*sits on side of sofa. Bitterly*). You've seen it all, Joshua Speed. Every bit of it—courtship, if you could call it that, change of heart, change back again, and marriage, eighteen years of it. And you probably think just as all the others do—that I'm a bitter, nagging woman, and I've tried to kill his spirit and drag him down to my level. . . .

JOSH (*quietly*). No, Mary. I think no such thing. Remember—I know Abe, too.

MARY. There never could have been another man such as he is! I've read about many that have gone up in the world, and all of them seemed to have to fight to assert themselves every inch of the way against the opposition of their enemies and the lack of understanding in their own friends. But he's never had any of that. He's never had an enemy, and every one of his friends has always been completely confident in him. Even before I met him I was told that he had a glorious future, and after I'd known him a day I was sure of it myself. But he didn't believe it—or, if he did, secretly, he was so afraid of the prospect that he did all in his power to avoid it. He had some poem in his mind, about a life of woe, along a rugged path, that leads to some future doom, and it has been an obsession with him. All these years I've tried and tried to stir him out of it, but all my efforts have been like so many puny waves, dashing against the Rock of Ages. And now opportunity, the greatest opportunity, is coming here, to him, right into his own house. And what can I do about it He *must* take it! He *must* see that this is what he was meant for! But I can't persuade him of it! I'm tired—I'm tired to death! (*The tears now come.*) I thought I could help to shape him as I knew he should be, and I've succeeded in nothing—but in breaking myself. . . . (*She sobs bitterly.* JOSH *rises, goes close to her.*)

JOSH (*tenderly. Sits beside her*). I know, Mary. But there's no reason in heaven and earth for you to reproach yourself. Whatever becomes of Abe Lincoln is in the hands of a God who controls the destinies of all of us, including lunatics and saints. (ABE *comes back.*)

ABE. I think they look all right now, Mary. (*He looks at* MARY, *who is now trying hard to control her emotion. He looks at* JOSH.)

MARY (*rises*). You can receive the gentlemen in here. I'll try to prepare some refreshment for them in the dining room.

[*She goes out.* ABE *looks after her, miserably, and sits down. A few moments of silence. At length* ABE *speaks, in an offhand manner.*]

ABE. I presume these men are pretty influential.

JOSH. They'll have quite a say in the delegations of three states that may swing the nomination away from Seward.[1]

ABE. Suppose, by some miracle or fluke, they did nominate me; do you think I'd stand a chance of winning the election?

JOSH. An excellent chance, in my opinion. There'll be four candidates in the field, bumping each other, and opening up the track for a dark horse.

ABE. But the dark horse might run in the wrong direction.

JOSH. Yes—you can always do that. Abe. I know *I* wouldn't care to bet two cents on you.

ABE (*grinning*). It seems funny to be comparing it to a horse race, with an old spavined hack[2] like me. But I've had some mighty energetic jockeys—Mentor Graham, Bowling Green, Bill Herndon, you, and Mary—most of all, Mary.

JOSH (*looking at* ABE). They don't count now, Abe. You threw 'em all, long ago. When you finally found yourself running against poor little Douglas you got the bit between your teeth and went like greased lightning. You'd do the same thing to him again, if you could only decide to get started, which you probably won't. . . .

ABE. I expect that's them now.

JOSH. I'll go see if I can help Mary.

[1] **Seward:** William Henry Seward, a prominent senator and antislavery leader. He later became Lincoln's Secretary of State.

[2] **spavined** (spav'ind) **hack:** a lame, worn-out horse.

(He starts for the door but turns and looks at ABE, *and speaks quietly.)* I'd just like to remind you, Abe—there are pretty nearly thirty million people in this country; most of 'em are common people like you. They're in serious trouble and they need somebody who understands 'em as you do. So—when these gentlemen come in—try to be a little bit polite to them. (ABE *grins.* JOSH *looks off.*) However—you won't listen to any advice from me.

[JOSH *goes. The door is opened by a* MAID, *and* STURVESON, BARRICK, *and* CRIMMIN *come in.* STURVESON *is elderly, wealthy, and bland.* DR. BARRICK *is a soft Episcopalian dignitary.* CRIMMIN *is a shrewd, humorous fixer.*]

ABE. Come right in, gentlemen. Glad to see you again, Mr. Crimmin. *(They shake hands.)*

CRIMMIN. How de do, Mr. Lincoln. This is Dr. Barrick of Boston and Mr. Sturveson of Philadelphia.

BARRICK. Mr. Lincoln.

STURVESON. I'm honored, Mr. Lincoln.

ABE. Thank you, sir. Pray sit down, gentlemen.

STURVESON. Thank you. *(They sit.)*

CRIMMIN. Will Mrs. Lincoln seriously object if I light a seegar?

ABE. Go right ahead, Mr. Crimmin. I regret that Mrs. Lincoln is not here to receive you, but she will join us presently.

BARRICK *(with great benignity).* I am particularly anxious to meet Mrs. Lincoln for I believe, with Mr. Longfellow, that "as unto the bow the cord is, so unto the man is woman."

STURVESON *(very graciously).* And we are here dealing with a bow that is stout indeed. (ABE *bows slightly in acknowledgment of the compliment.*) And one with a reputation for shooting straight. So you'll forgive us, Mr. Lincoln, for coming directly to the point.

ABE. Yes, sir. I understand that you wish to inspect the prairie politician in his native lair, and here I am.

STURVESON. It is no secret that we are desperately in need of a candidate—one who is sound, conservative, safe—and clever enough to skate over the thin ice of the forthcoming campaign. Your friends—and there's an increasingly large number of them throughout the country—believe that you are the man.

ABE. Well, Mr. Sturveson—I can tell you that when first I was considered for political office—that was in New Salem, twenty-five years ago—I assured my sponsors of my conservatism. I have subsequently proved it by never progressing anywhere.

BARRICK. Then you agree that you are the man we want?

ABE. I'm afraid I cannot go quite that far in self-esteem, Dr. Barrick, especially when you have available a statesman and gentleman as eminent as Mr. Seward who, I believe, is both ready and willing.

STURVESON. That's as may be. But please understand that this is not an inquisition. *(Both laugh.)* We merely wish to know you better, to gain a clearer idea of your theories on economics—religion—and national affairs in general. (CRIMMIN *nods, wisely.*) To begin with, in one of your memorable debates with Senator Douglas, your opponent indulged in some of his usual demagoguery about industrial conditions in the North, and you replied shrewdly that whereas the slaves in the South . . .

ABE. Yes, I remember the occasion. I replied that I was thankful that laborers in free states have the right to strike. But that wasn't shrewdness, Mr. Sturveson. It was just the truth.

STURVESON. It has gained for you substantial support from the laboring classes, which is all to the good. It has also caused a certain amount of alarm among businessmen, like myself.

ABE. I cannot enlarge on the subject. It seems obvious to me that this nation was founded on the supposition that men have the right to protest, violently if need be, against authority that is unjust or oppressive. The Boston Tea Party was a kind of strike. So was the Revolution itself. So was Nicholas Biddle's[1] attempt to organize the banks against the Jackson administration.

STURVESON. Which is all perfectly true —but—the days of anarchy are over. We face an unprecedented era of industrial expansion—mass production of every conceivable kind of goods—railroads and telegraph lines across the continent— all promoted and developed by private enterprise. In this great work we must have a free hand, and a firm one, Mr. Lincoln. To put it bluntly, would you, if elected, place the interests of labor above those of capital?

ABE. I cannot answer that, bluntly, or any other way; because I cannot tell what I should do, if elected.

STURVESON. But you must have inclinations toward one side or the other. . . .

ABE. All I can say is, if it came to a conflict between those two forces, I should attempt to consider them as equals.

STURVESON. But you must have inclinations toward one side or the other. . . .

ABE. I think you know, Mr. Sturveson, that I am opposed to slavery.

BARRICK. And we of New England applaud your sentiments! We deplore the inhumanity of our Southern friends in . . .

ABE (to BARRICK). There are more forms of slavery than that which is inflicted upon the Negroes in the South. I am opposed

to all of them. (*He turns again to* STURVESON.) I believe in our democratic system —the just and generous system which opens the way to all—gives hope to all, and consequent energy and progress and improvement of condition to all, including employer and employee alike.

BARRICK. We support your purpose, Mr. Lincoln, in steadfastly proclaiming the rights of men to resist unjust authority. But I am most anxious to know whether you admit One Authority to whom devotion is unquestioned?

ABE. I presume you refer to the Almighty?

BARRICK. I do.

ABE. I think there has never been any doubt of my submission to His will.

BARRICK. I'm afraid there is a great deal of doubt as to your devotion to His church.

ABE. I realize that, Doctor. They say I'm an atheist, because I've always refused to become a church member.

BARRICK. What have been the grounds of your refusal?

ABE. I have found no churches suitable for my own form of worship. I could not give assent without mental reservations to the long, complicated statements of Christian doctrine which characterize their articles of belief and confessions of faith. But I can promise you, Dr. Barrick—I shall gladly join any church at any time if its sole qualification for membership is obedience to the Savior's own statement of Law and Gospel: "Thou shalt love the Lord thy God with all thy heart and with all thy soul and with all thy mind, and thou shalt love thy neighbor as thyself." . . . But—I beg you gentlemen to excuse me for a moment. I believe Mrs. Lincoln is preparing a slight collation,[2] and I must see if I can help with it. . . .

---

[1] **Nicholas Biddle:** a director of the Bank of the United States, attacked by President Jackson as favoring the interests of the rich over the good of the people.

[2] **collation** (kə·lā′shən): a light meal.

CRIMMIN. Certainly, Mr. Lincoln. (ABE *goes, closing door behind him.* CRIMMIN *looks at door, then turns to others.*) Well?

BARRICK. The man is unquestionably an infidel. An idealist—in his curious primitive way——

STURVESON. And a radical!

CRIMMIN. A radical? Forgive me, gentlemen, if I enjoy a quiet laugh at that.

STURVESON. Go ahead and enjoy yourself, Crimmin—but I did not like the way he evaded my direct question. I tell you, he's as unscrupulous a demagogue as Douglas. He's a rabble-rouser!

CRIMMIN. Of course he is! As a dealer in humbug he puts Barnum[1] himself to shame.

STURVESON. Quite possibly, but he isn't *safe!*

CRIMMIN. Not safe, eh? And what do you mean by that?

STURVESON. Just what I say. A man who devotes himself so wholeheartedly to currying favor with the mob develops the mob mentality. He becomes a preacher of discontent, of mass unrest. . . .

CRIMMIN. And what about Seward? If we put him up, he'll start right in demanding liberation of the slaves—and then there *will* be discontent and unrest! I ask you to believe me when I tell you that this Lincoln *is* safe—in economics and theology and everything else. After all, what is the essential qualification that we demand of the candidate of our party? It is simply this: that he be able to get himself elected! And there is the man who can do that.

STURVESON (*smiling*). I should like to believe you!

BARRICK. So say we all of us!

CRIMMIN. Then just keep faith in the eternal stupidity of the voters, which is what he will appeal to. (*He points off*

[1] **Barnum:** Phineas T. Barnum, the famous circus manager and showman.

stage.) In that uncouth rail-splitter you may observe one of the smoothest, slickest politicians that ever hoodwinked a yokel mob! You complain that he evaded your questions. Of course he did and did it perfectly! Ask him about the labor problem, and he replies, "I believe in democracy." Ask his views on religion, and he says, "Love thy neighbor as thyself." Now—you know you couldn't argue with that, either of you. I tell you, gentlemen, he's a vote-getter if I ever saw one. His very name is right—Abraham Lincoln! Honest Old Abe! He'll play the game with us now, and he'll go right on playing it when we get him into the White House. He'll do just what we tell him. . . .

BARRICK (*cautioning him*). Careful, Mr. Crimmin . . . (ABE *returns.*)

ABE. If you gentlemen will step into the dining room, Mrs. Lincoln would be pleased to serve you with a cup of tea.

BARRICK (*has risen*). Thank you. (*He goes.*)

STURVESON. That is most gracious.

ABE. Or perhaps something stronger for those who prefer it. (STURVESON *and* DR. BARRICK *go.* CRIMMIN *is looking for a place to throw his cigar.*) Bring your seegar with you, Mr. Crimmin.

CRIMMIN. Thank you—thank you!

[*He smiles at* ABE, *gives him a slap on arm, and goes out,* ABE *following. The lights fade.*]

SCENE 10

Lincoln campaign headquarters in the Illinois State House. The evening of Election Day, November 6th, 1860. It is a large room with two tall windows opening out to a wide balcony. There are doors upper right and upper left. At left is a table littered with newspapers and clippings. There are many chairs about and a liberal supply of spittoons. At the back,

*between the windows, is a huge chart of
the thirty-three states, with their electoral
votes, and a space opposite each side for
the posting of bulletins. A short ladder
gives access to Alabama and Arkansas
at the top of the list. On wall at left is an
American flag. At right is a map of the
United States, on which each state is
marked with a red, white, or blue flag.*

ABE *is at left, reading newspaper clippings. He wears his hat and has spectacles on.* MRS. LINCOLN *is sitting at right,
her eyes darting nervously from* ABE, *to
chart, to map. She wears her bonnet,
tippet* [1] *and muff.* ROBERT LINCOLN *is
standing near her, studying map.* JOSH
SPEED *and* NINIAN EDWARDS *are sitting
in center, smoking cigars, and watching
chart. The door at right is open, and
through it the clatter of telegraph instruments can be heard. The window at left
is partly open, and we can hear band
music from the square below, and frequent cheers from the assembled mob,
who are watching the election returns
flashed from a magic lantern on the State
House balcony. Every now and then a
telegraph operator named* JED *comes in
from right and tacks a new bulletin up on
chart. Another man named* PHIL *is out on
the balcony taking bulletins from* JED.

ROBERT. Mr. Speed, what do those little
flags mean, stuck into the map?

JOSH (*without looking up*). Red means
the state is sure for us. (JED *enters.*) White
means doubtful. Blue means hopeless.
(ABE *tosses clipping he has been reading
on table and picks up another.* JED *comes
in and goes up to pin bulletins opposite
Illinois, Maryland and New York.*)

NINIAN (*rising to look*). Lincoln and
Douglas neck and neck in Illinois.

JOSH. Maryland is going all for Brecken-

1860 Lincoln campaign tintype with ribbon.

ridge and Bell. Abe—you're nowhere in
Maryland.

MARY (*with intense anxiety*). What of
New York?

JED. Say, Phil—when you're not getting bulletins, keep that window closed.
We can't hear ourselves think.

PHIL. All right. Only have to open 'er
again. (*He closes window.*)

MARY. What does it say about New
York? (JED *goes.*)

NINIAN. Douglas a hundred and seventeen thousand—Lincoln a hundred and
six thousand.

MARY (*desperately, to* ABE). He's winning from you in New York, Abe.

JOSH. Not yet, Mary. These returns so
far are mostly from the City, where Douglas is bound to run the strongest.

ABE (*interested in clipping*). I see the

New York *Herald* says I've got the soul of a Uriah Heep[1] encased in the body of a baboon. *(He puts clipping aside and starts to read another.)*

NINIAN *(who has resumed his seat).* You'd better change that flag on Illinois from red to white, Bob. It looks doubtful to me. (ROBERT, *glad of something to do, changes flag.)*

MARY. What does it look like in Pennsylvania, Ninian?

NINIAN. There's nothing to worry about there, Mary. It's safe for Abe. In fact, you needn't worry at all.

MARY. Yes—you've been saying that over and over all evening: There's no need to worry. But how can we help worrying when every new bulletin shows Douglas ahead?

JOSH. Nearly all of them show Abe gaining.

NINIAN. Just give them time to count all the votes in New York and you'll be on your way to the White House.

MARY. Oh—why don't they hurry with it! Why don't those returns come in?

ABE *(preoccupied).* They'll come in—soon enough.

BILLY *(enters. He has been doing a lot of drinking, but has hold of himself. Goes to chair).* That mob down there is sickening. They cheer every bulletin that's flashed on the wall, whether the news is good or bad. And they cheer every picture of every candidate, including George Washington, with the same fine ignorant enthusiasm.

JOSH. That's logical. They can't tell 'em apart.

BILLY *(to ABE).* There are a lot of journalists down there. They want to know what will be your first official action after you're elected.

NINIAN. What do you want us to tell them, Abe?

ABE *(still reading).* Tell 'em I'm thinking of growing a beard.

JOSH. A beard?

NINIAN. Whatever put that idea into your mind?

ABE *(picking up another clipping).* I had a letter the other day from some little girl. She said I ought to have whiskers to give more dignity. And I'll need it—if elected.

[JED *enters with more bulletins—Connecticut and Missouri. They all huddle together.*]

MARY. What do they say now? Is there anything new from New York?

NINIAN *(has gone to study map and board).* Connecticut—Abe far in the lead. That's eleven safe electoral votes, anyway. (JED *has gone to window, knocked on it, and* PHIL *opens it—loud cheers are heard.)* Missouri—Douglas thirty-five thousand—Bell thirty-three—Breckinridge sixteen—Lincoln eight[2] ——

MARY. What are they cheering for?

BILLY. They don't know. (MARY *closes window and sounds die down.)*

ABE *(with another clipping).* The Chicago *Times* says, "Lincoln breaks down. Lincoln's heart fails him! His legs fail him! His tongue fails him! He fails all over! The people refuse to support him! They laugh at him! Douglas is champion of the people. Douglas skins the living dog." *(He tosses clipping aside.)*

MARY *(her voice trembling).* I can't stand it any longer!

ABE *(rising quickly).* Yes, my dear—I think you'd better go home. I'll join you presently.

---

[1] **Uriah** (yoō·rī′ə) **Heep:** a slippery, hand-rubbing character in Dickens' novel *David Copperfield.*

[2] **Douglas . . . eight:** In this election, Lincoln was the candidate of the Republican Party. A split in the Democratic Party had produced three Democratic candidates: Douglas, Breckinridge, and Bell.

MARY (*hysterically*). No. I won't go home! You only want to get rid of me. That's what you've wanted ever since the day we were married—and before that. Anything to get me out of your sight, because you hate me! And it's the same with all of you—all of his friends—you hate me—you wish I'd never come into his life!

JOSH. No, Mary——

[ABE *has stood up, quickly, at the first storm signal. He himself is in a fearful state of nervous tension—in no mood to treat* MARY *with patient indulgence. He looks sharply at* NINIAN *and at others.*]

ABE. Will you please step out for a moment?

NINIAN. Certainly, Abe.

[*He and others go into telegraph office.* JOSH *gestures to* ROBERT *to go with them.* ROBERT *casts a black look at* MARY *and goes. . . .* ABE *turns on* MARY *with strange savagery.*]

ABE. Confound you! Confound you for taking every opportunity you can to make a public fool of me—and yourself! It's bad enough, Lord knows, when you act like that in the privacy of our own home. But here—in front of people! You're not to do that again. Do you hear me? You're never to do that again!

[MARY *is so aghast at this outburst that her hysterical temper vanishes, giving way to blank terror.*]

MARY (*in a faint, strained voice*). Abe! You cursed at me. Do you realize what you did? You cursed at me.

[ABE *has the impulse to curse at her again, but with considerable effort he controls it.*]

ABE (*in a strained voice*). I lost my temper, Mary. And I'm sorry for it. But I still think you should go home rather than stay here and endure the strain of this—this death watch.[1]

MARY (*stares at him, uncomprehendingly, then*). This is the night I dreamed about when I was a child, when I was an excited young girl, and all the gay young gentlemen of Springfield were courting me and I fell in love with the least likely of them all. This is the night when I'm waiting to hear that my husband has become President of the United States. And even if he does—it's ruined for me. It's too late.

[ABE *turns and looks at her.* MARY *opens door and goes out.* ABE *looks after her, anguished, then goes quickly to door and calls.*]

ABE. Bob! (*Steps back from door.* ROBERT *enters.*) Go home with your mother.

ROBERT. Do I have to?

ABE. Yes! Hurry! Keep right with her till I get home. (ROBERT *goes out and* ABE *turns up to window at back.*)

PHIL (*comes to window and opens it*). Do you think you're going to make it, Mr. Lincoln?

ABE. Oh—there's nothing to worry about.

[*As window opens there is the murmur of the crowd and they begin to sing "Old Abe Lincoln Came Out of the Wilderness" through once.* PHIL *stands at window during song, at end of which there is a big cheer, and he closes window.* NINIAN, BILLY, JOSH *and* JED *enter, the latter to post bulletins.* ABE *turns from window.* JED *exits again after having distributed bulletins.*]

NINIAN. It looks like seventy-four electoral votes sure for you. Twenty-seven

---

[1] **death watch:** a vigil at the bedside of a person who is dying.

more probable. New York's will give you the election. (BILLY *is at board.*)

JOSH (*has been looking at* ABE). Abe, could I get you a cup of coffee?

ABE. No, thanks, Josh.

NINIAN. Getting nervous, Abe?

ABE. No. I'm just thinking what a blow it would be to Mrs. Lincoln if I should lose.

NINIAN. And what about me? I have ten thousand dollars bet on you.

BILLY (*scornfully*). I'm afraid that the loss to the nation would be somewhat more serious than that.

JOSH. How would you feel, Abe?

ABE. I guess I'd feel the greatest sense of relief of my life. (JED *comes in with a news dispatch.*)

JED. Here's a news dispatch. (*He hands it over and goes.*)

NINIAN (*reads*). "Shortly after nine o'clock this evening, Mr. August Belmont stated that Stephen A. Douglas has piled up a majority of fifty thousand votes in New York City and carried the State."

BILLY. Mr. Belmont be hanged!

[CRIMMIN *has come in, smoking cigar, looking contented.*]

CRIMMIN. Good evening, Mr. Lincoln. Good evening, gentlemen—and how are you all feeling *now?*

NINIAN. Look at this, Crimmin. (*He hands dispatch to* CRIMMIN.)

CRIMMIN (*smiles*). Well—August Belmont—he's going to fight to the last ditch, which is just what he's lying in now. I've been in Chicago and the outlook there is cloudless. In fact, Mr. Lincoln, I came down tonight to protect you from the office-seekers. (JED *comes in with more bulletins to put on chart.*) They're lining up downstairs already. On the way in I counted four Ministers to Great Britain and eleven Secretaries of State. (JED *goes to window.*)

BILLY (*at chart*). New York! (JED *leaves.*) Douglas a hundred and eighty-three thousand—Lincoln a hundred and eighty-*one* thousand! (PHIL *opens window.*)

JOSH. Look out, Abe. You're catching up! (*Window closed*)

CRIMMIN. The next bulletin from New York will show you winning. Mark my words, Mr. Lincoln, this election is all wrapped up tightly in a neat bundle, ready for delivery on your doorstep tonight. We've fought the good fight, and we've won!

ABE. Yes—we've fought the good fight—in the dirtiest campaign in the history of corrupt politics. And if I have won, then I must cheerfully pay my political debts. All those who helped to nominate and elect me must be paid off. I have been gambled all around, bought and sold a hundred times. And now I must fill all the dishonest pledges made in my name.

NINIAN. We realize all that, Abe—but the fact remains you're even beating the coalition in Rhode Island.

ABE. I've got to step out for a moment. (*He goes out.*)

NINIAN (*cheerfully*). Poor Abe.

CRIMMIN. You gentlemen have all been close friends of our candidate for a long time so perhaps you could answer a question that's been puzzling me considerably. Can I possibly be correct in supposing that he doesn't want to win?

JOSH. The answer is—yes.

CRIMMIN. Well—I can only say that, for me, this is all a refreshingly new experience.

BILLY (*belligerently, crosses to* CRIMMIN). Would you want to become President of the United States at this time? Haven't you been reading the newspapers lately?

CRIMMIN. Why, yes—I try to follow the events of the day. (*Sits at table*)

BILLY. Don't you realize that they've raised ten thousand volunteers in South Carolina? They're arming them. The governor has issued a proclamation saying that if Mr. Lincoln is elected the state will secede tomorrow, and every other state south of the Mason-Dixon line [1] will go with it. Can you see what that means? It means war. Civil war. And he'll have the whole terrible responsibility for it—a man who has never wanted anything in his life but to be let alone, in peace.

NINIAN. Calm down, Billy. Go get yourself another drink.

JED (*rushes in with news dispatch which he gives to* NINIAN). Mr. Edwards—here it is.

[*He then goes to window and attracts* PHIL'S *attention.* PHIL *opens window and hands him a megaphone, as* JED *steps outside.*]

NINIAN (*reads*). "At 10:30 tonight the New York *Herald* conceded that Mr. Lincoln has carried the State by a majority of at least twenty-five thousand and has won the election." He's won! He's won! Hurrah! (*Throws dispatch in the air*)

JED (*outside window—through megaphone as crowd is stilled for the announcement*). Lincoln is elected! Honest Old Abe is our next President.

[*There is a terrifying cheer outside, the band plays "Illinois." Abe returns, and the characters on stage move toward* ABE *in congratulations, embracing and slapping each other on the back.*]

BILLY. God be praised! God be praised! (*Shakes* ABE'S *hand*)

CRIMMIN. I knew it! I never had a doubt of it!

NINIAN. You've carried New York,

[1] **Mason-Dixon line:** the boundary between Pennsylvania and Maryland.

THE RESULT.
END OF THE GREAT NATIONAL CONTEST

ABRAHAM LINCOLN,
OF ILLINOIS,
ELECTED PRESIDENT,
AND
HANNIBAL HAMLIN,
OF MAINE,
VICE PRESIDENT,
OF THE
UNITED STATES.

News of Lincoln's election on front page of the New York *Herald*, November 7, 1860.

Abe! You've won!

BILLY. The New York *Herald* has admitted it!

NINIAN. Congratulations, Abe—congratulations!

BILLY. You're President, Mr. Lincoln —you're President of the United States!

CRIMMIN. And my congratulations, Mr. President. This is a mighty achievement for all of us.

JED (*has closed window when cheers are at height, left megaphone outside, and come down to* ABE). And me, too, Mr. President. (*Shakes* ABE'S *hand and goes out*)

ABE (*solemnly*). Thank you—thank you all very much.

JOSH (*comes to table to shake hands with* ABE). I congratulate you, Abe.

ABE. Thanks, Josh.

NINIAN. Listen to them, Abe. Listen to that crazy, howling mob down there.

CRIMMIN. It's all for you, Mr. Lincoln.

NINIAN (*above table*). Abe—come on —get out there and let them see you!

ABE. No. I don't want to go out there. (*He waves hand in refusal.* BILLY *closes window and sound dies down.*) I guess I'll be going on home to tell Mary.

[*He is about to start for door when* KAVANAGH *enters, followed by two others who stand either side of door. By this time all sound off-stage has stopped. Move crowd to left side of stage.*]

CRIMMIN. This is Captain Kavanagh, Mr. Lincoln.

KAVANAGH (*salutes*). I've been detailed to accompany you, Mr. Lincoln, in the event of your election.

ABE. I'm grateful, Captain. But I don't need you.

KAVANAGH. I'm afraid you must have us, Mr. Lincoln. I don't like to be alarming, but I guess you know as well as I do what threats have been made.

ABE (*wearily*). Well—good night, Josh, Ninian—Mr. Crimmin—Billy. Thanks for your good wishes. (*He starts for door as they bid him good night.* KAVANAGH *steps down before him.*)

KAVANAGH. With your permission, sir, I'll go first.

[*He turns on his heel in an about-face and marches off.* ABE *follows him off and the other two officers close in behind him as lights dim down and out.*]

SCENE 11

When the music stops as the lights come up on the scene, a shrill train whistle is heard.

The yards of the railroad station at Springfield, February 11th, 1861.

At right, at an angle toward audience, is the back of a railroad car. From behind this, off to upper left runs a platform.

Flags and buntings are draped above.

Along platform, on both sides of it, are soldiers, with rifles and bayonets fixed, and packs on their backs, standing at ease. Off to left is a large crowd, whose excited murmur can be heard.

In foreground is KAVANAGH. MILITIA MAJOR *enters down ramp.*

MAJOR. You men form up along this ramp. (*A* BRAKEMAN *with a lantern is inspecting the wheels of the car.* KAVANAGH *is pacing up and down, chewing a dead cigar. He looks at his watch.* MAJOR, *to* KAVANAGH, *with a trace of scorn*) You seem nervous, Captain Kavanagh.

KAVANAGH. Well—I am nervous. For three months I've been guarding the life of a man who doesn't care what happens to him. I heard today that they're betting two to one in Richmond that he won't be alive to take the oath of office on March 4th.

MAJOR. I'd like to take some of that money. The State Militia is competent to protect the person of our Commander-in-Chief.

KAVANAGH. I hope the U. S. Army is competent to help. But those Southerners are mighty good shots. And I strongly suggest that your men be commanded to keep watch through every window of every car, especially whenever the train stops—at a town, or a tank, or anywhere. And if any alarm is sounded, at any point along the line . . .

MAJOR (*a trifle haughty*). There's need to command my men to show courage in an emergency.

KAVANAGH. No slur was intended, Major—but we must be prepared in advance for everything.

[*A brass band strikes up the campaign song, "Old Abe Lincoln Came Out of the Wilderness." The crowd starts to*

Despite cold, rainy weather, hundreds of friends and neighbors gathered at the station to bid President-Elect Lincoln farewell as he left Springfield for Washington, D.C. (February, 1861).

sing it, more and more voices taking it up. A CONDUCTOR *comes out of car and looks at his watch. There is a commotion as* NINIAN *and* ELIZABETH EDWARDS *and* JOSH, BILLY, *and* CRIMMIN *come in and are stopped by the soldiers. The* MAJOR *goes forward, bristling with importance.*]

MAJOR *(going up ramp).* Stand back, there! Keep the crowd back there, you men!

NINIAN. I'm Mr. Lincoln's brother-in-law.

MAJOR. What's your name?

KAVANAGH. I know him, Major. That's Mr. and Mrs. Edwards, and Mr. Speed and Mr. Herndon with them. I know them all. You can let them through.

MAJOR. Very well. You can pass. *(They come down.* MAJOR *goes off.* KAVANAGH *tips his hat.)*

CRIMMIN. How is the President feeling today? Happy?

NINIAN. Just as gloomy as ever.

BILLY *(emotionally).* He came down to the office, and when I asked him what I should do about the sign, "Lincoln and Herndon," he said, "Let it hang there. Let our clients understand that this election makes no difference to the firm. If I live, I'll be back some time, and then we'll go right on practicing just as if nothing had happened."

ELIZABETH. He's always saying that— "if I live." . . . *(A tremendous cheer starts and swells off-stage at left.* MAJOR *comes on, briskly.)*

NINIAN. Here's Abe!

MAJOR *(to* KAVANAGH*).* The President has arrived! *(To his men)* Attention! Right shoulder—arms! (MAJOR *strides down platform and takes his position by car.)*

KAVANAGH (*to* NINIAN *and the others*). Would you mind stepping back there? We want to keep this space clear for the President's party. (*They move. The cheering is now very loud.*)

MAJOR. Present—arms!

[*The* SOLDIERS *come to the "present." MAJOR salutes. Preceded by OGLEBY and DONNER, who are looking sharply to right and left, ABE comes in along platform. He will be fifty-two years old tomorrow. He wears a beard. Over his shoulder is his plaid shawl. In his right hand, he carries his carpetbag, his hand is leading TAD. Behind him are MARY, ROBERT and WILLIE, and the MAID. All, except MARY, are also carrying bags. She carries a bunch of flowers. When they come to car, ABE hands his bag up to the CONDUCTOR, then lifts TAD up. MARY, ROBERT, WILLIE, and the MAID get on board, while ABE steps over to talk to NINIAN and the others. During this, there is considerable commotion as crowd tries to surge forward. MAJOR rushes forward.*]

MAJOR. Keep 'em back! Keep 'em back, men!

[*The* SOLDIERS *have broken their file on platform and are in line, facing crowd. KAVANAGH, OGLEBY, and DONNER are close to ABE. Each of them has his hand in his pocket and is keeping a sharp lookout.*]

KAVANAGH (*at step of car, upper end*). Better get on board, Mr. Lincoln.

[*As* ABE *climbs up on car's back platform there is a great increase in the cheering when crowd sees him. They shout "Speech—Speech"—"Give us a speech, Abe," "Speech, Mr. President," "Hurray for Old Abe," etc.* ABE *turns to crowd, takes off his hat and waves a*

halfhearted gesture. Cheering dies down.]

NINIAN. Say something, Abe. (*For a moment* ABE *stands still, looking off.*)

ABE. My dear friends—I have to say good-by to you. I am going now to Washington, with my new whiskers—of which I hope you approve.

[*The crowd roars with laughter at that. More shouts of "Good Old Abe!" In its exuberant enthusiasm, crowd surges forward at and around SOLDIERS who shout, "Get back there," and "Stand back, you."*]

MAJOR. Keep 'em back, men.

ABE. It's all right, Major—let them come on. They're all old friends of mine.

MAJOR. All right, men. Fall back.

[SOLDIERS *fall back, forming ring about end of car, and crowd pushes its way in.* MAJOR *goes to end of car. Silence falls.*]

ABE. No one, not in my situation, can appreciate my feelings of sadness at this parting. To this place, and the kindness of you people, I owe everything. I have lived here for a quarter of a century, and passed from a young to an old man. Here my children have been born, and one is buried. I now leave, not knowing when or whether ever I may return. I am called upon to assume the Presidency at a time when eleven of our sovereign states have announced their intention to secede from the Union, when threats of war increase in fierceness from day to day. It is a grave duty which I now face. In preparing for it I have tried to inquire what great principle or idea it is that has kept this Union so long together. And I now believe that it was not the mere matter of separation of the colonies from the motherland, but that sentiment in the Declaration of Independence which gave liberty to the people of this country and hope to all the world. This sentiment was the fulfillment of an ancient dream, which men have held through all time, that they might one day shake off their chains and find freedom in the brotherhood of life. We gained democracy, and now there is a question whether it is fit to survive. Perhaps we have come to the dreadful day of awakening, and the dream is ended. If so, I am afraid it must be ended forever. I cannot believe that ever again will men have the opportunity we have had. Perhaps we should admit that and concede that our ideals of liberty and equality are decadent and doomed. I have heard of an Eastern monarch who once charged his wise men to invent him a sentence which would be true and appropriate in all times and situations. They presented him with the words, "And this, too, shall pass away." That is a comforting thought in times of affliction —"and this, too, shall pass away." And yet (*Suddenly speaks with quiet but urgent authority*) let us believe that it is not true! Let us live to prove that we can cultivate the natural world that is about us and the intellectual and moral world that is within us, so that we may secure an individual, social, and political prosperity whose course shall be forward, and which, while the earth endures, shall not pass away. I commend you to the care of the Almighty, as I hope that in your prayers you will remember me. Good-by, my friends and neighbors.

[*He leans over rail of car platform to say good-by to* NINIAN, ELIZABETH, JOSH, BILLY, CRIMMIN, *etc., shaking hands. The crowd begins to sing "John Brown's Body." The cheering swells.* CONDUCTOR *looks at his watch and speaks to* MAJOR, *who gets on board. Crowd shouts, "Good-by, Abe," "Good luck," "We trust you, Mr. Lincoln," etc., and*

we hear the refrain "Glory, Glory, Hallelujah." The crowd starts to sing, increasing the number of voices with each word.* KAVANAGH *tries to speak to* ABE *but cannot be heard. He touches* ABE'S *arm;* ABE *turns to him quickly.*]

KAVANAGH. Time to pull out, Mr. Lincoln, better get inside.

[*The song increases in volume and the crowd surges toward the car.* ABE *gives one last wistful wave to the crowd as he enters the car. The* SOLDIERS *clamber on board the platform and on the last note of the song the lights are down and out. The curtain falls.*]

FOR STUDY AND DISCUSSION

1. What is Lincoln like as a father and as a husband? What seems to be his attitude toward Mary? toward his sons? Do you think he has cause to be angry with Mary on election night? From Mary's point of view, how might he be exasperating as a husband?

2. How does Lincoln show himself, in Scene 9, to be an able and quick-thinking politician? How does he handle the crisis of Bob's pipe in the living room? What does he invite Crimmin to do with his cigar? Do you think he has forgotten that Mary objects to smoking? Do you think Mary will object to Crimmin's cigar? Why or why not?

3. Why do the politicians finally decide that Lincoln is the one for them? What surprises are they in for? What obstacles and problems will Abe have to overcome as President? Why is he better suited than any other person to solve them?

4. Reread Lincoln's farewell speech. How does it summarize all that has passed? How does it predict what is to come?

5. Some years after Lincoln's death, Mary Todd Lincoln was pronounced insane. Can you see the seeds of her insanity in Act III? What effect has her ambition on Abe's career? on his attitude toward other people?

6. In Lincoln's farewell speech there is a phrase, "Not knowing when or whether ever I may return," about which the playwright

has declared, "That strange and beautiful construction is comparable to 'The world will little note nor long remember . . .' in the Gettysburg Address." Find other phrases in this speech or elsewhere in the play that seem to be examples of Lincoln's "poetry."

THE CRAFT OF THE DRAMATIST

1. Despite the fact that we already know what the result of the election will be, the playwright manages to make Scene 10 tense and exciting. How does he do this? Throughout the scene how does he focus attention on the outcome in New York? How does he emphasize Abe's calm detachment in contrast to the other characters in the scene?

2. The threat of Lincoln's impending death looms over the entire play, but nowhere is it more overwhelming than in the final scene. How are we reminded in this scene of the threats on Lincoln's life? of his feelings about death?

THE PLAY AS A WHOLE

1. In addition to having a hero, most plays have a villain—someone or something we can root *against*. Is there any such villain in this play, any force or influence that we hope Abe will either avoid or conquer? In order to reach real greatness, what reluctance within himself must Abe first overcome?

2. This play is the story of a man's maturing. How does Abe change from the young man we first see with Mentor Graham to the man who says farewell as President? In which scenes do we see the greatest evidence of new growth?

3. Which scene in this play contains the *climax*—the point at which tension is greatest, the decisive turning point in the play? What makes this scene the high point of tension in the play?

4. Throughout the play, there are many references to Abe's fear of death. What attitude toward death is expressed in the poem by John Keats in Scene 1? Does this attitude eventually become Abe's own? Does he seem concerned, in his farewell speech, about his own life or death? Express in your own words

Lincoln's final attitude toward the importance of his own life and his ideals.

5. Do you think this play is better suited to the stage or to the movies? Which scenes would be more effective if presented through a camera able to move from place to place, showing just what it wished? Which are more exciting with live actors confronting each other on the stage? If you had your choice between the two, how would you present the play?

6. If you were making a movie of *Abe Lincoln in Illinois,* which scene would offer the most opportunity for various changes of location? What shots would you add of off-stage happenings that could not be included in a stage play? Go through the scene you think would benefit most by being shot as a movie, and indicate where you would add to the tension by reminding the audience of something else that was happening at the same time.

FOR COMPOSITION

1. From what you learned about him in the play, write a character sketch of Abe Lincoln. Try to give a clear picture of his appearance and the way he acts toward people. In your final paragraph, tell which episode in the play showed you the most about Lincoln, and explain what it showed you.

2. Write a sketch of the character in this play, other than Abraham Lincoln, that you found most interesting. In the last paragraph of your character sketch, explain how the life of this character and his (or her) personality affected Lincoln's.

3. Considering the example in this play of Abe Lincoln, what would you say are the qualities of a good politician? Write a short description of your idea of a good politician, including several examples, from Abe's actions in the play, of how to be considerate of other people's feelings.

4. Reread Abe's prayer for Seth's son in Scene 7 and his farewell speech in the last scene. How well do you think his hopes for his nation have been fulfilled? In a short composition, tell why you think America today has fallen short of, or gone beyond, Lincoln's dreams.

Reading and Writing about Drama

What is a play? What are the ingredients of drama? One way to approach these questions is to read some plays yourself. Another way is to see if what critics and authors have written on the subject can help you gain some insight or understanding. The following paragraph, by an author who has written plays himself, attempts to suggest some of the elements of a stage performance by glancing at the broader meanings we associate with the words *drama* and *play:*

> We tend to use the words "play" and "drama" interchangeably, though perhaps "drama" suggests something more serious. Both words, though, have broader meanings that extend beyond what happens on a stage. We see children at play, and play at games ourselves, and in both cases the word implies a temporary pretense or make-believe. A child playing fireman with a truck or a batter trying to connect with a ball both have to convince themselves that what they are doing is highly important and very "real." When this kind of serious pretending becomes a story presented on a stage, we call it a *play,* admitting that it is not real. The word *drama,* too, often steps out of the theater. We have all been in situations in our lives which can be called *dramatic*—moments full of drama, charged with suspense or feeling. In plays and drama, art imitates life, and life imitates art, and people seem to have an instinctive urge to involve themselves in both. (A. R. Gurney)

1. Describe a situation in real life in which you "made believe" as in a play.
2. Describe a situation in real life that you would call *dramatic*. What elements of this situation made it dramatic?
3. Explain in a paragraph or two how both *make-believe* and *dramatic* action are important in a good play. To support your explanation, show how both of these elements exist in *The Boor* or in *Abe Lincoln in Illinois*.

A less general topic than the nature of drama is the nature of a particular kind of play. *The Boor,* for example, is usually described as a kind of comedy called *farce*. What is farce? Here is one view:

> Farce-comedy is, in its plausibility, about halfway between burlesque and polite comedy. It is funny and frequently absurd, but not altogether impossible. It depends for its hilarious fun, not on the characters, but on the situation—that is, on the fast-moving action which sweeps the characters along in spite of themselves to a happy ending. It is to this type of comedy that *The Boor* belongs. In it the author presents the lighter side of Russian country life in such a way that he seems to be inviting his audience to cast off all restraint and laugh uproariously with him at the ridiculous situation in which these stupidly naive people find themselves. Not only does he invite the audience to participate, but he insists on wholehearted and enthusiastic participation of those who would present the play. (Jean Carter, *The Play Book.*)

1. What do you think are the best examples in *The Boor* of the following elements of farce:
   "the fast-moving action which sweeps the characters along in spite of themselves"
   "the ridiculous situation in which these stupidly naive people find themselves"
2. Explain in your own words the nature of farce-comedy as defined in the quote above, using specific examples from *The Boor* to make clear exactly what you mean.

Reading about the *kind* of play that we have read or seen can help us appreciate its structure and other qualities. It is also useful to read about the characteristics of a particular play and discuss what the playwright means. One writer wrote the following about *The Boor:*

"In this play, Chekhov asks us to laugh at the foolishness of poses assumed by men and women with regard to love by showing how easily the walls they construct for themselves come tumbling down when another opportunity for love comes along. The playwright suggests that love and life go together, that widowhood and confinement are unnatural. We are asked to feel that Madame Popova's fruitless moral combat with her dead husband is not only foolish but precarious. We are glad to see her succumb to a new love, and we can see why it happened so quickly." (A. R. Gurney)

1. List examples of the foolish poses of Smirnov and Mme. Popova with regard to love.

2. In a few paragraphs, explain how Chekhov's handling of the characters and action makes us glad to see Mme. Popova "succumb to a new love" and able to see why it happened so quickly.

Few characters in drama are so central to a play as Lincoln is in *Abe Lincoln in Illinois.* The whole play, in a sense, hangs on his shoulders, as is suggested by the writer of the following:

"Since *Abe Lincoln in Illinois* is an attempt to present on the stage a number of different facets of Lincoln's personality, . . . every detail in each scene must have been selected for its particular relevance. Perhaps the best way to look at this play is to consider every word and incident a beam of light thrown upon this mysterious man, so that by the end of the play he will have been more fully illuminated. Abe Lincoln is shown, in this play, to be a complicated man, both by what he says and does himself and by what others say about him. Yet for all his complexities and personal doubts, we meet no one who dislikes him, and we ourselves, as an audience, cannot help but like him too." (A. R. Gurney)

1. Choose two or three scenes in the play and point out at least one important thing we learn in each about the personality of Lincoln.

2. Write a few paragraphs discussing how "Abe Lincoln is shown, in this play, to be a complicated man."

Another critic had this to say about the character of Lincoln:

"Lincoln is affecting precisely because he is so unpretentious, because he is so much like other men in his waverings, and because he shrinks from every course of action that might lead to bloodshed even when his antislavery sentiments would dictate another course of action." (John Gassner)

1. Make a list of places in the play that show Lincoln's unpretentiousness, his wavering, and his tendency to shrink from bloodshed and violence.

2. Using these character-revealing moments as supporting illustrations, write an essay on Robert Sherwood's interpretation of the character of Lincoln.

ART AND LITERATURE

Which of the paintings on pages 451–56 seems to you the most dramatic and exciting? In a short essay explain what is dramatic about the situation shown, by comparing it with another, less dramatic painting.

WILLIAM SHAKESPEARE

WE KNOW FEW FACTS about Shakespeare's childhood and early manhood. Church records show that he was born in April 1564 in Stratford-on-Avon, a small English town in Warwickshire. He married at the age of eighteen and was the father of three children before he was twenty-one. Although there are few certain facts about Shakespeare's life in Stratford-on-Avon, a good many local legends have risen. One such story tells that, as a young man, Shakespeare got into trouble for poaching deer.

Although we do not know just what caused Shakespeare to go to London, it is clear that by the time he wrote *Romeo and Juliet* he had been in London for several years, acting in and writing plays. In 1594 he became a shareholder in a company of actors called the Chamberlain's Men, for whom he wrote *Romeo and Juliet,* probably in the same year. Within another few years, Shakespeare was prosperous enough to buy a large house in Stratford-on-Avon. He had also become widely recognized as a great English dramatist. A few of his plays had been printed, with or without his company's permission, and they sold well.

When King James came to the English throne in 1603, one of his first acts was to make the Chamberlain's Men the "King's Men." As a result, Shakespeare's plays were performed even more frequently at court. At about this time, Shakespeare retired from the stage. From 1610 on, he spent most of his time in Stratford-on-Avon, where he died on April 23, 1616.

Shakespeare is the most famous of all writers in the English language. He wrote sonnets, narrative poems, songs, and thirty-seven plays—tragedies, comedies, histories, farces. His works—above all his plays—still give delight to readers and playgoers of every age and kind, for he had the deepest understanding of men and of women. Most works seem tired after a third reading. Shakespeare's plays are always fresh. Each time we read them we find something new. Moreover, he had such supreme skill in words that we can find a quotation in Shakespeare to express almost every mood and every situation. His infinite variety never grows stale.

Songs and Speeches
from the Plays

When Icicles Hang by the Wall

One of Shakespeare's early plays, *Love's Labor's Lost,* concludes with two songs—one describing winter and one describing spring. This is the song of winter.

When icicles hang by the wall,
   And Dick the shepherd blows° his nail,
And Tom bears logs into the hall,
   And milk comes frozen home in pail,
When blood is nipped and ways° be foul
Then nightly sings the staring owl—   6
      "Tu-whit,
Tu-who!"—a merry note,
While greasy Joan doth keel° the pot.

When all aloud the wind doth blow,   10
   And coughing drowns the parson's saw,°
And birds sit brooding in the snow,
   And Marian's nose looks red and raw,
When roasted crabs° hiss in the bowl,
Then nightly sings the staring owl—   15
      "Tu-whit,
Tu-who!"—a merry note,
While greasy Joan doth keel the pot.

2. **blows:** blows on. 5. **ways:** roads. 9. **keel:** stir. 11. **saw:** moral saying. 14. **crabs:** crabapples.

Full Fathom Five

In Shakespeare's last great play, *The Tempest,* Prospero, the lord of an enchanted island, has his helper Ariel sing this song to persuade the young prince Ferdinand that his father has been drowned in a shipwreck.

Full fathom° five thy father lies,
   Of his bones are coral made,
Those are pearls that were his eyes.
   Nothing of him that doth fade
But doth suffer a sea change   5
Into something rich and strange.
Sea nymphs° hourly ring his knell°:
                    Ding-dong!
Hark! now I hear them—ding-dong, bell!

1. **fathom:** a measurement of depth equal to six feet. 7. **nymphs:** beautiful young maidens. **knell:** the tolling of a bell to announce a death.

Who Is Silvia?

Silvia is one of the heroines of another of Shakespeare's early plays, *The Two Gentlemen of Verona.* In the play, one of Silvia's suitors has this song sung under her window.

Who is Silvia? What is she,
   That all our swains° commend her?
Holy, fair, and wise is she;
   The Heaven such grace did lend her,
That she might admirèd be.   5

Is she kind as she is fair?
   For beauty lives with kindness.
Love° doth to her eyes repair°
   To help him of his blindness,
And, being helped, inhabits there.   10

Then to Silvia let us sing,
   That Silvia is excelling;
She excels each mortal thing
   Upon the dull earth dwelling.
To her let us garlands bring.   15

2. **swains:** young men in love. 8. **Love:** Cupid, the little blind god of love. **repair:** retreat.

1. How, in his description of winter, does Shakespeare create a feeling of biting cold? Which lines of "When Icicles Hang by the Wall" best suggest the bitter cold?

2. Why, on a winter's night, with the day's work done, does the owl's call seem merry? How do the last three lines of each stanza of "When Icicles Hang by the Wall" give a feeling of snugness and warmth?

3. In "Who Is Silvia?" what does the singer admire in Silvia? List her good qualities. Which quality does the singer most admire? It is traditional for a serenading lover to exaggerate the good qualities of his beloved. Where do you think this singer exaggerates?

4. Where do the rhythmical stresses fall in the lines of "Who Is Silvia?"? What is the rhyme scheme of this song? How do the rhythm and rhyme help to tie the lines together and round off each stanza?

5. Do you think "Full Fathom Five" should succeed in persuading the prince that his father has been drowned? If so, point out lines that are especially convincing. If you think the song is not convincing, tell why.

6. What is the rhyme scheme of "Full Fathom Five"? How do the rhymes help to create a feeling of finality like the tolling of a knell?

How Sweet the Moonlight

Lorenzo and Jessica, two young lovers in *The Merchant of Venice,* are outdoors on a beautiful moonlit night. Lorenzo, who has called for music to be played, turns to Jessica and speaks.

> How sweet the moonlight sleeps upon this bank!
> Here will we sit and let the sounds of music
> Creep in our ears. Soft stillness and the night
> Become the touches of sweet harmony.
> Sit, Jessica. Look how the floor of heaven   5
> Is thick inlaid with patines° of bright gold.

6. **patines:** metal disks.

There's not the smallest orb° which thou behold'st
But in his motion like an angel sings,°
Still quiring° to the young-eyed cherubins.
Such harmony is in immortal souls,   10
But whilst this muddy vesture of decay°
Doth grossly close it in, we cannot hear it.
Come, ho! and wake Diana° with a hymn!
With sweetest touches pierce your mistress' ear,
And draw her home with music.   15

7. **orb:** sphere, star.   8. **in his motion . . . sings:** In Shakespeare's time it was believed that each planet in its course around the earth made a sweet, unearthly sound—the "music of the spheres."   9. **quiring:** choiring, singing.   11. **muddy vesture of decay:** our earthly bodies.   13. **Diana:** goddess of the moon. Lorenzo is calling to the musicians to welcome Portia home.

The Seven Ages of Man

In one of Shakespeare's most popular romantic comedies, *As You Like It*, a banished Duke takes refuge in the Forest of Arden. Among his faithful followers is Jaques, a disillusioned gentleman who loves to talk about the follies of the world. In the following speech, Jaques sums up human life as a series of scenes in a universal comedy.

All the world's a stage,
And all the men and women merely players.
They have their exits and their entrances,
And one man in his time plays many parts,
His acts being seven ages. At first the infant,   5
Mewling and puking in the nurse's arms.
Then the whining schoolboy, with his satchel
And shining morning face, creeping like snail
Unwillingly to school. And then the lover,
Sighing like furnace, with a woeful ballad   10
Made to his mistress' eyebrow. Then a soldier,

Full of strange oaths and bearded like the pard,°
Jealous in honor, sudden and quick in quarrel,
Seeking the bubble reputation
Even in the cannon's mouth. And then the justice,   15
In fair round belly with good capon° lined,
With eyes severe and beard of formal cut,
Full of wise saws° and modern instances,°
And so he plays his part. The sixth age shifts
Into the lean and slippered Pantaloon°   20
With spectacles on nose and pouch on side,
His youthful hose, well saved, a world too wide
For his shrunk shank, and his big manly voice,
Turning again toward childish treble, pipes
And whistles in his sound. Last scene of all,   25
That ends this strange eventful history,
Is second childishness and mere oblivion,
Sans° teeth, sans eyes, sans taste, sans everything.

12. **pard:** leopard. 16. **capon:** chicken. 18. **saws:** moral sayings. **modern instances:** obvious examples. 20. **Pantaloon:** a foolish old figure, usually a man. Pantaloon was a stock character in Italian comedies. 28. **sans:** without (French).

FOR STUDY AND DISCUSSION

1. At what are Lorenzo and Jessica looking during most of Lorenzo's speech? What do they see? What are "the floor of heaven" and the "patines of bright gold"?

2. In "How Sweet the Moonlight," two of Shakespeare's verbs, *creep* in line 3 and *draw* in line 15, not only create a vivid picture but also contribute to the overall effect of the speech. Point out other words in the speech that suggest, by their sound or meaning, the harmony of music and the hush of night.

3. In "The Seven Ages of Man," which age do you think is captured most vividly in Jaques' description? Which details most effectively help you to *see* the person he describes?

4. According to Jaques, what are the characteristics of a lover? a soldier? a judge? How is a soldier "jealous in honor"? What is "the bubble reputation" that he seeks? Why would a judge be likely to be "Full of wise saws and modern instances"?

5. Much of the effect of Jaques' description comes from the use of adjectives. Find several adjectives that help to give an unexpected and yet accurate picture of an age.

Shakespeare's Theater

In Shakespeare's time, the theater was small and open to the sky. The stage was a large platform. At the back, on each side of the platform, were two large doors. In the center of the platform was a recess or inner stage, which was usually concealed by a curtain. When desired, this curtain could be drawn aside allowing the recess to serve (in *Romeo and Juliet,* for example) as Friar Laurence's cell or Juliet's tomb. Above the recess was a balcony flanked by windows. From this balcony Juliet spoke to Romeo, and Romeo descended after their wedding night. There was no front curtain to hide the stage completely and separate the actors from their audience. All the characters appearing in a scene had to make their entrances and exits in full view of the audience.

None of the elaborate equipment of our modern theater was available in Shakespeare's day. He had no scenery to rely on, no electricity or artificial lighting, and none of the subtle effects of mood that contemporary lighting experts can create. Shakespeare's plays were always performed during daylight hours. The greater simplicity of the sixteenth-century theater had its advantages, however. With no scenery to be changed, the action of the play could flow more quickly. One scene could be ended and another begun simply by having one group of actors leave the stage and another group come on. Thus Shakespeare could have as many scenes as he wished, unrestricted by the need for expensive sets. Also because there were no sets, to create atmosphere in this theater, playwrights and actors had to rely on their own words and actions. When Romeo and Juliet, for instance, met in the garden, the whole feeling of a moonlit night had to be evoked by words alone.

The Globe Theater

In a modern Broadway production, an appropriate actor is selected for each part in a new play. Shakespeare's actors, on the other hand, were a permanent company of players, who together filled all the parts and shared in the profits of their plays. Usually there were about fifteen full members in the company, a few stagehands, and two or three boys who were learning the art of acting and who played the young women's parts. In such a small company, the actors soon became thoroughly familiar with each other's style of playing, thus permitting effective group playing.

Shakespeare's audiences were varied. The poor spectators stood in the yard around the platform stage; the rich paid extra and sat in one of the galleries. His widely varied audience made it essential for Shakespeare to satisfy many different tastes and to include in a single play the most vigorous action, the most boisterous humor, and the highest-soaring poetry he could produce.

Above, a model of the Globe Theater, where many of Shakespeare's plays were given. Far left, Laurence Olivier and Jean Simmons in a scene from Shakespeare's *Henry V*. Left, Terence Scammell and Maria Tucci in Shakespeare's *Romeo and Juliet*.

Shakespeare as Playwright

In Shakespeare's plays, the poetry does much more than set the scene. The rhythms of the verse add emphasis to the spoken words and force the audience to feel as the speaker feels. Shakespeare's audiences enjoyed powerful language and expected to hear it in the theater. They were alert to every effect of sound and rhythm, to elaborate plays on words, and to every suggestion of symbolic meaning.

Magnificent as it is, there is, however, much more than poetry to appreciate in Shakespeare's plays. First of all, there is *plot*. In Shakespeare's best plays, the plot is so devised that the spectators, gripped by the opening words and action, are led compellingly from scene to scene with hardly a slackening of dramatic tension, until at the end of the play they are left with a sense of conclusion and with all their questions answered. Although Shakespeare did not invent the story of *Romeo and Juliet,* which was well known and popular, he did most skillfully devise the plot. From the opening quarrel between the followers of Montague and Capulet, we are led naturally from event to event until the final, inevitable tragedy. We never feel that any of the events is an unnatural result of what has gone before.

In this play, as in all good plays, plot depends on *character,* since in a play, as in life, events are caused by people's actions. In a good play, the characters act according to their individual natures, and we understand from our knowledge of human nature why different characters act as they do. In a good play, we can believe that the characters are real. In *Romeo and Juliet,* Shakespeare has created remarkably human characters; at no time in the play do we feel that they could have behaved otherwise. Old Capulet's anger at Juliet's defiance in Act IV, for instance,

Portrait of Shakespeare in *The First Folio.*

is entirely natural. Though he is very fond of his only daughter, he does not like to be crossed.

Not the least of Shakespeare's skills is what we can call his *stage sense*—that is, his knack for making each scene interesting and exciting and true-to-life. For example, note as you read *Romeo and Juliet* that there is very little action in the scene where the Nurse tells Juliet about Romeo's arrangements for their wedding. Nevertheless, the scene is both exciting and funny, for the Nurse is at first too tired and grumpy either to sympathize with Juliet's natural impatience or to tell her news. In life, we feel as we watch this scene unfold, it would have happened just this way.

There is much to look for in a play by Shakespeare. It takes care and practice to appreciate fully the richness of Shakespeare's art, but once you have trained yourself to respond to what Shakespeare offers, you will understand why he is considered the greatest of all writers in the English language. Such an appreciation, once achieved, is lasting.

Romeo and Juliet

Romeo and Juliet is the story of a family feud and how it ended. In the ancient city of Verona, bitter feuding between the two leading families of Montague and Capulet is forever breaking out into street fights and murder. The only son of Lord Montague is Romeo; the only daughter and only child of Lord Capulet is Juliet. Shakespeare's play is the tragedy of their ill luck.

The Characters

THE MONTAGUES

LORD MONTAGUE
LADY MONTAGUE
ROMEO, *son of Montague*
BENVOLIO, *nephew of Montague and friend of Romeo*
BALTHASAR, *servant of Romeo*

THE CAPULETS

LORD CAPULET
LADY CAPULET
JULIET, *daughter of Capulet*
TYBALT, *nephew of Lady Capulet*
NURSE *of Juliet*
SERVANT *of Lord Capulet*

PRINCE ESCALUS, *ruler of Verona*
MERCUTIO, *friend of Romeo*
FRIAR LAURENCE, *a Franciscan priest*
FRIAR JOHN, *another Franciscan priest*
COUNT PARIS, *a young nobleman*
APOTHECARY
PAGE *of Paris*
CHIEF WATCHMAN

KINSMEN of both houses, DANCERS, GUARDS, OFFICERS, WATCHMEN, and SERVANTS

THE TIME: The fourteenth century
THE PLACE: Verona, Italy

Prologue

[*From the back of the stage the* CHORUS *enters to introduce and explain the theme of the play*.]

CHORUS. Two households, both alike in dignity,
    In fair Verona, where we lay our scene,
    From ancient grudge break to new mutiny,°
    Where civil blood makes civil hands unclean.
    From forth the fatal loins of these two foes   5
    A pair of star-crossed° lovers take their life,
    Whose misadventured piteous overthrows
    Do with their death bury their parents' strife.
    The fearful passage of their death-marked love,
    And the continuance of their parents' rage,   10
    Which, but their children's end, naught could remove,
    Is now the two hours' traffic° of our stage;
    The which if you with patient ears attend,
    What here shall miss, our toil shall strive to mend.°

                               [*Exit*.]

ACT I

SCENE I

[*The two doors at the side of the stage represent the feuding houses of* MONTAGUE AND CAPULET. *From one door* SERVANTS *of* MONTAGUE *come out, and from the other door* SERVANTS *of* CAPULET. *They meet, insult each other, and begin to fight. Then from the* MONTAGUE *door* BENVOLIO, *a young gentleman of the family, emerges. He draws his sword and tries to stop the brawl*.]

BENVOLIO. Part, fools! [*Beating down their weapons*.]
    Put up your swords. You know not what you do.

[*From the* CAPULET *door comes young* TYBALT, *with sword drawn.* TYBALT *is hot-tempered and a quick striker*.]

TYBALT. What, art thou drawn among these heartless hinds?°
    Turn thee, Benvolio, look upon thy death.
BENVOLIO. I do but keep the peace. Put up thy sword,   5
    Or manage it to part these men with me.
TYBALT. What, drawn, and talk of peace! I hate the word
    As I hate Hell, all Montagues, and thee.
    Have at thee, coward!

    3. **mutiny:** riot. 6. **star-crossed:** doomed by unlucky stars. 12. **traffic:** business. 14. **mend:** make clearer.
    3. **heartless hinds:** cowardly servants.

[BENVOLIO *and* TYBALT *join in the fight. Aroused by the shouts,* CITIZENS *come out through both doors and take sides. The* OFFICERS *of the city try to restore order.*]

FIRST OFFICER. Clubs, bills, and partisans!° Strike! Beat them down!   10
  Down with the Capulets! Down with the Montagues!

[*Old* CAPULET *comes out, with his wife hanging onto his sleeve to pull him back.*]

CAPULET. What noise is this? Give me my long sword, ho!
LADY CAPULET. A crutch, a crutch! Why call you for a sword?
CAPULET. My sword, I say! Old Montague is come,
  And flourishes his blade in spite of° me.   15

      [*Old* MONTAGUE *likewise enters with his wife.*]

MONTAGUE. Thou villain Capulet!—Hold me not, let me go.
LADY MONTAGUE. Thou shalt not stir one foot to seek a foe.

[PRINCE ESCALUS *enters with his* BODYGUARD. *At first no one heeds him in the din.*]

PRINCE. Rebellious subjects, enemies to peace,
  Profaners of this neighbor-stainèd steel°—
  Will they not hear? What ho!

      [*At last the rioters are abashed and silenced by his anger.*]

                              You men, you beasts,   20
  That quench the fire of your pernicious rage
  With purple fountains issuing from your veins,
  On pain of torture, from those bloody hands
  Throw your mistempered° weapons to the ground,
  And hear the sentence of your movèd prince.   25
  Three civil brawls, bred of an airy° word,
  By thee, old Capulet and Montague,
  Have thrice disturbed the quiet of our streets,
  And made Verona's ancient citizens
  Cast by their grave beseeming ornaments°   30
  To wield old partisans, in hands as old,
  Cankered° with peace, to part your cankered hate.
  If ever you disturb our streets again,
  Your lives shall pay the forfeit of the peace.
  Once more, on pain of death, all men depart.   35
      [*Exeunt* all but* MONTAGUE, LADY MONTAGUE, *and* BENVOLIO.]

---

10. **bills and partisans:** different kinds of spears.   15. **in spite of:** to spite.   19. **Profaners . . . steel:** who profanely stain your swords in the blood of your neighbors.   24. **mistempered:** angry. 26. **airy:** light.   30. **ornaments:** peaceful garments.   32. **Cankered:** rusted, corroded.   ***Exeunt:** plural form of "Exit."

MONTAGUE. Who set this ancient quarrel new abroach?°
    Speak, Nephew, were you by when it began?
BENVOLIO. Here were the servants of your adversary°
    And yours close fighting ere° I did approach.
    I drew to part them. In the instant came   40
    The fiery Tybalt, with his sword prepared,
    Which as he breathed defiance to my ears,
    He swung about his head and cut the winds,
    Who, nothing hurt withal,° hissed him in scorn.
    While we were interchanging thrusts and blows,   45
    Came more and more, and fought on part and part
    Till the Prince came, who parted either part.
LADY MONTAGUE. Oh, where is Romeo? Saw you him today?
    Right glad I am he was not at this fray.

[ROMEO, *says* BENVOLIO, *is suffering from moody melancholy, shutting himself
away from daylight and from his friends. No one knows why. As* BENVOLIO
speaks of him, ROMEO *approaches.*]

BENVOLIO. See where he comes. So please you, step aside.   50
    I'll know his grievance, or be much denied.
MONTAGUE. I would thou wert so happy° by thy stay
    To hear true shrift.° Come, madam, let's away.
                                    [*Exeunt* MONTAGUE *and* LADY.]
BENVOLIO. Good morrow,° Cousin.
ROMEO.   Is the day so young?
BENVOLIO. But new struck nine.
ROMEO.   Aye me, sad hours seem long!   55
    Was that my father that went hence so fast?
BENVOLIO. It was. What sadness lengthens Romeo's hours?
ROMEO. Not having that which, having, makes them short.
BENVOLIO. In love?
ROMEO. Out——   60
BENVOLIO. Of love?
ROMEO. Out of her favor where I am in love.
BENVOLIO. Tell me in sadness,° who is that you love?
ROMEO. What, shall I groan and tell thee?
BENVOLIO.   Groan! Why, no,
    But sadly tell me who.   65
ROMEO. Bid a sick man in sadness make his will.
    Ah, word ill urged to one that is so ill!
    In sadness, Cousin, I do love a woman.
BENVOLIO. I aimed so near when I supposed you loved.

---

    36. **abroach:** afoot, astir. 38. **adversary:** enemy. 39. **ere** (âr): before. 44. **withal:** by this.
52. **happy:** fortunate. 53. **shrift:** confession. 54. **Good morrow:** good morning. "Cousin" is a
name used for any relative. 63. **sadness:** seriousness.

ROMEO. A right good mark-man! And she's fair love.   70
BENVOLIO. A right fair mark, fair Coz, is soonest hit.
ROMEO. Well, in that hit you miss. She'll not be hit
    With Cupid's arrow.
    She hath forsworn to° love, and in that vow
    Do I live dead, that live to tell it now.   75
BENVOLIO. Be ruled by me, forget to think of her.
ROMEO. Oh, teach me how I should forget to think.
BENVOLIO. By giving liberty unto thine eyes.
    Examine other beauties.
ROMEO.   'Tis the way
    To call hers exquisite, in question more.°   80
    These happy masks° that kiss fair ladies' brows,
    Being black, put us in mind they hide the fair.
    He that is stricken blind cannot forget
    The precious treasure of his eyesight lost.
    Show me a mistress that is passing° fair,   85
    What doth her beauty serve but as a note
    Where I may read who passed° that passing fair?
    Farewell. Thou canst not teach me to forget.
BENVOLIO. I'll pay that doctrine,° or else die in debt.

[They go off together.]

74. **forsworn to:** sworn not to.   80. **in question more:** by comparing her beauty more with others.
81. **masks:** masks were worn by ladies of fashion.   85. **passing:** very.   87. **passed:** surpassed.
89. **pay that doctrine:** pay you for teaching me how to forget.

SCENE II

[*Old* CAPULET *enters with* COUNT PARIS, *a young nobleman related to the* PRINCE. *A* SERVANT *follows.*]

CAPULET. But Montague is bound° as well as I,
    In penalty alike, and 'tis not hard, I think,
    For men so old as we to keep the peace.
PARIS. Of honorable reckoning° are you both,
    And pity 'tis you lived at odds so long.   5
    But now, my lord, what say you to my suit?
CAPULET. But saying o'er what I have said before.
    My child is yet a stranger in the world—
    She hath not seen the change of fourteen years.
    Let two more summers wither in their pride   10
    Ere we may think her ripe to be a bride.
PARIS. Younger than she are happy mothers made.
CAPULET. And too soon marred are those so early made.
    The earth hath swallowed all my hopes but she,
    She is the hopeful lady of my earth.°   15
    But woo her, gentle Paris, get her heart.
    My will to her consent is but a part;
    An° she agree, within her scope° of choice
    Lies my consent and fair according° voice.
    This night I hold an old accustomed feast,   20
    Whereto I have invited many a guest
    Such as I love, and you among the store,
    One more, most welcome, makes my number more.

    [*To the* SERVANT, *giving him a list of the invited guests.*]

    Go, sirrah,° trudge about
    Through fair Verona. Find those persons out   25
    Whose names are written there, and to them say
    My house and welcome on their pleasure stay.

                    [*Exeunt* CAPULET *and* PARIS.]
SERVANT. [*Who cannot read*]. Find them out whose names are written here!
    I am sent to find those persons whose names are here writ, and can never
    find what names the writing person hath here writ. I must to the learned.
    In good time.°   31

[*Enter* BENVOLIO *and* ROMEO, *still talking of Romeo's love. The* SERVANT *goes up to them.*]

ROMEO. Godden,° good fellow.
SERVANT. God gi' godden. I pray, sir, can you read?

---

    1. **bound:** pledged to keep the peace.   4. **reckoning:** reputation.   15. **earth:** body, "flesh and blood."   18. **An:** if.   **scope:** range.   19. **according:** agreeing.   24. **sirrah:** a name used in addressing servants.   31. **In good time:** What luck! Just in time!   32. **Godden:** good afternoon.

ROMEO. Aye, mine own fortune in my misery.

SERVANT. Perhaps you have learned it without book, but I pray, can you read anything you see?   36

ROMEO. Aye, if I know the letters and the language.

SERVANT. Ye say honestly. Rest you merry!°

ROMEO. Stay, fellow, I can read. [*He reads out the names.*]
    A fair assembly. Whither should they come?   40

SERVANT. Up.

ROMEO. Whither?

SERVANT. To supper, to our house.

ROMEO. Whose house?

SERVANT. My master's.   45

ROMEO. Indeed I should have asked you that before.

SERVANT. Now I'll tell you without asking. My master is the great rich Capulet, and if you be not of the House of Montagues, I pray come and crush° a cup of wine. Rest you merry!

                                                  [*Exit.*]

BENVOLIO. At this same ancient feast of Capulet's   50
    Sups the fair Rosaline whom thou so lovest,
    With all the admirèd beauties of Verona.
    Go thither, and with unattainted° eye
    Compare her face with some that I shall show,
    And I will make thee think thy swan a crow.   55

ROMEO. One fairer than my love! The all-seeing sun
    Ne'er saw her match since first the world begun.

BENVOLIO. Tut, you saw her fair, none else being by,
    Herself poised° with herself in either eye.
    But in that crystal scales let there be weighed   60
    Your lady's love against some other maid
    That I will show you shining at this feast,
    And she shall scant° show well that now seems best.

ROMEO. I'll go along, no such sight to be shown,
    But to rejoice in splendor of mine own.   65
                                                  [*Exeunt.*]

38. **Rest you merry:** God keep you merry. 48. **crush:** drink. 53. **unattainted:** unprejudiced.
59. **poised:** balanced. 63. **scant:** scarcely, hardly.

SCENE III

[At home in CAPULET'S *house,* LADY CAPULET *enters with* JULIET'S *old* NURSE.]

LADY CAPULET. Nurse, where's my daughter? Call her forth to me.
NURSE. Where's this girl? What, Juliet!

[Enter JULIET.]

JULIET. How now! Who calls?
NURSE. Your mother.
JULIET. Madam, I am here. What is your will?   5
LADY CAPULET. This is the matter. Nurse, give leave° awhile,
    We must talk in secret.—Nurse, come back again,
    I have remembered me, thou'st° hear our counsel.
    Thou know'st my daughter's of a pretty age.
NURSE. Faith, I can tell her age unto an hour.   10
LADY CAPULET. She's not fourteen.
NURSE. Come Lammas° Eve at night shall she be fourteen.
    Susan and she—God rest all Christian souls!—
    Were of an age. Well, Susan is with God.
    She was too good for me.—But, as I said,   15
    On Lammas Eve at night shall she be fourteen.
    That shall she, marry, I remember it well.
    'Tis since the earthquake now eleven years.
    For then she could stand high-lone°—nay, by the rood,°
    She could have run and waddled all about,   20
    For even the day before, she broke° her brow,
    And then my husband—God be with his soul!
    A'° was a merry man—took up the child.
    "Yea," quoth he, "dost thou fall upon thy face?"
LADY CAPULET. Enough of this. I pray thee hold thy peace.   25
NURSE. Peace, I have done. God mark° thee to His grace!
LADY CAPULET. Tell me, daughter Juliet,
    How stands your disposition to be married?
JULIET. It is an honor that I dream not of.
LADY CAPULET. Well, think of marriage now. Younger than you   30
    Here in Verona, ladies of esteem,
    Are made already mothers. By my count,
    I was your mother much upon these years°
    That you are now a maid. Thus then in brief—
    The valiant Paris seeks you for his love.   35

---

    6. **give leave:** leave us alone. 8. **thou'st:** you shall. 12. **Lammas:** a church festival celebrated
August 1. 19. **high-lone:** all alone, by herself. **rood:** cross, crucifix. 21. **broke:** cut, broke the skin.
23. **A'** (ä): he. 26. **mark:** select, choose. 33. **much upon these years:** at much the same age.

NURSE. A man, young lady! Lady, such a man
    As all the world——Why, he's a man of wax.°
LADY CAPULET. Speak briefly. Can you like of Paris' love?
JULIET. I'll look to like, if looking liking move.°
    But no more deep will I endart mine eye   40
    Than your consent° gives strength to make it fly.

                  [Enter a SERVANT.]

SERVANT. Madam, the guests are come, supper served up, you called, my young
    lady asked for, the nurse cursed in the pantry, and everything in extremity.°
    I must hence to wait. I beseech you, follow straight.°

                                       [Exeunt.]

SCENE IV

[ROMEO *and* BENVOLIO, *with their friend* MERCUTIO *and others, all wearing masks
and carrying torches, are on their way to* CAPULET'S *house.* ROMEO *is depressed
and reluctant.* MERCUTIO, *who is a great talker, tries to cheer him.*]

MERCUTIO. Nay, gentle Romeo, we must have you dance.
ROMEO. Not I, believe me. You have dancing shoes
    With nimble soles. I have a soul of lead
    So stakes me to the ground I cannot move.
MERCUTIO. You are a lover. Borrow Cupid's wings,   5
    And soar with them above a common bound.°
ROMEO. I am too sore enpiercèd° with his shaft°
    To soar with his light feathers, and so bound,
    I cannot bound a pitch° above dull woe.
    Under love's heavy burden do I sink.—   10
    I dreamed a dream tonight.°
MERCUTIO.   And so did I.
ROMEO. Well, what was yours?
MERCUTIO.   That dreamers often lie.
ROMEO. In bed asleep, while they do dream things true.
MERCUTIO. Oh then, I see Queen Mab° hath been with you.
    She is the fairies' midwife, and she comes
    In shape no bigger than an agate stone°   15
    On the forefinger of an alderman,
    Drawn with a team of little atomies°

37. **man of wax:** perfect, like a wax model. 39. **move:** arouse. 41. **consent:** approval. 43. **extremity:** confusion. 44. **straight:** right away, at once.
   6. **bound:** leap. 7. **enpiercèd:** pierced, wounded. **shaft:** arrow. 9. **bound a pitch:** leap in flight.
11. **tonight:** last night. 14. **Queen Mab:** the Queen of the Fairies. 16. **agate** (ag′it) **stone:** large
seal ring. 18. **atomies:** atoms, tiny things.

Athwart men's noses as they lie asleep—
Her wagon spokes made of long spinners'° legs;   20
The cover, of the wings of grasshoppers;
Her traces,° of the smallest spider's web;
Her collars, of the moonshine's watery beams;
Her whip, of cricket's bone; the lash, of film;°
Her wagoner,° a small gray-coated gnat   25
Not half so big as a round little worm
Pricked from the lazy finger of a maid.°
Her chariot is an empty hazelnut,
Made by the joiner° squirrel or old grub,
Time out o' mind the fairies' coachmakers.   30
And in this state° she gallops night by night
Through lovers' brains, and then they dream of love;
O'er courtiers' knees, that dream on curtseys straight;
O'er lawyers' fingers, who straight dream on fees;
O'er ladies' lips, who straight on kisses dream,   35
Which oft the angry Mab with blisters plagues
Because their breaths with sweetmeats° tainted are.
Sometime she gallops o'er a courtier's nose,
And then dreams he of smelling out a suit.°
And sometime comes she with a tithe pig's° tail   40
Tickling a parson's nose as a' lies asleep,
Then dreams he of another benefice.°
Sometime she driveth o'er a soldier's neck,
And then dreams he of cutting foreign throats,
Of breaches, ambuscadoes, Spanish blades,   45
Of healths five fathom deep; and then anon
Drums in his ear, at which he starts and wakes,
And being thus frighted swears a prayer or two,
And sleeps again.
ROMEO.   Peace, peace, Mercutio, peace!
Thou talk'st of nothing.
MERCUTIO.   True, I talk of dreams,   50
Which are the children of an idle brain,
Begot of nothing but vain fantasy,
Which is as thin of substance as the air
And more inconstant than the wind, who woos
Even now the frozen bosom of the North,   55
And, being angered, puffs away from thence,
Turning his face to the dew-dropping South.

20. **spinners:** spiders. 22. **traces:** harness. 24. **film:** spider's thread. 25. **wagoner:** coachman. 26–27. **worm . . . maid:** In Shakespeare's time, it was a popular superstition that lazy maids grew worms in their fingers. 29. **joiner:** carpenter. 31. **state:** grand style. 37. **sweetmeats:** sweets; candy, cakes. 39. **suit:** a petition for special favor. 40. **tithe** (tīth) **pig:** the parson was often paid in goods, such as a pig, instead of money. 42. **benefice:** church appointment, source of income.

BENVOLIO. This wind you talk of blows us from ourselves.
    Supper is done, and we shall come too late.
ROMEO. I fear, too early. For my mind misgives°   60
    Some consequence, yet hanging in the stars,
    Shall bitterly begin his fearful date°
    With this night's revels, and expire the term°
    Of a despisèd life closed in my breast
    By some vile forfeit of untimely death.   65
    But He that hath the steerage of my course
    Direct my sail! On, lusty gentlemen.
BENVOLIO. Strike, drum.

                                  [Exeunt.]

SCENE V

[In CAPULET'S *house. As the* MASKED GUESTS, *ladies with their gentlemen escorts, enter the great chamber,* CAPULET *comes forward to greet them.* JULIET *and others of his family are present.* ROMEO, BENVOLIO, MERCUTIO *and their party, masked and unrecognized, mingle with the guests in their enemy's house.]*

CAPULET. Welcome, gentlemen! Ladies that have their toes
    Unplagued with corns will have a bout with you.
    Ah ha, my mistresses! Which of you all
    Will now deny to dance? She that makes dainty,°
    She, I'll swear, hath corns—am I come near ye° now?   5
    Welcome, gentlemen! I have seen the day
    That I have worn a visor,° and could tell
    A whispering tale in a fair lady's ear
    Such as would please. 'Tis gone, 'tis gone, 'tis gone.
    You are welcome, gentlemen! Come, musicians, play   10
    A hall, a hall!° Give room! And foot it, girls.

                  [Music plays, and they dance.]

    More light, you knaves, and turn the tables up,
    And quench the fire, the room is grown too hot.

       *[*ROMEO *sees* JULIET *and instantly falls in love with her.]*

ROMEO. *[To a* SERVANT] What lady's that which doth enrich the hand
    Of yonder knight?   15
SERVANT. I know not sir.

---

60. **misgives:** fears. 62. **date:** time, period. 63. **expire the term (of):** bring to an end.
  4. **makes dainty:** pretends to be shy. 5. **come near ye:** touching a tender spot. 7. **visor:** mask.
11. **a hall:** clear the hall for dancing!

ROMEO. Oh, she doth teach the torches to burn bright!
　　It seems she hangs upon the cheek of night
　　Like a rich jewel in an Ethiop's ear—
　　Beauty too rich for use, for earth too dear!°　　　　　　20
　　So shows a snowy dove trooping with crows
　　As yonder lady o'er her fellows shows.
　　The measure° done, I'll watch her place of stand,
　　And, touching hers, make blessèd my rude hand.
　　Did my heart love till now? Forswear it, sight!　　　　25
　　For I ne'er saw true beauty till this night.
TYBALT. This, by his voice, should be a Montague.
　　Fetch me my rapier, boy. What dares the slave
　　Come hither, covered with an antic face,
　　To fleer° and scorn at our solemnity?°　　　　　　　　30
　　Now, by the stock and honor of my kin,
　　To strike him dead I hold it not a sin.
CAPULET. [*Noticing* TYBALT's *anger*] Why, how now, kinsman! Wherefore storm
　　you so?

20. **dear:** precious.　23. **measure:** dance.　30. **fleer:** sneer.　**solemnity:** celebration.

TYBALT. Uncle, this is a Montague, our foe,
    A villain, that is hither come in spite   35
    To scorn at our solemnity this night.
CAPULET. Young Romeo, is it?
TYBALT.   'Tis he, that villain Romeo.
CAPULET. Content thee, gentle Coz, let him alone,
    He bears him like a portly° gentleman.
    And, to say truth, Verona brags of him   40
    To be a virtuous and well-governed youth.
    I would not for the wealth of all this town
    Here in my house do him disparagement.°
    Therefore be patient, take no note of him.
    It is my will, the which if thou respect,   45
    Show a fair presence and put off these frowns,
    An ill-beseeming semblance° for a feast.
TYBALT. It fits when such a villain is a guest.
    I'll not endure him.
CAPULET. *(Losing his temper)* He shall be endured.
    What, goodman boy,° I say he shall. Go to,   50
    Am I the master here, or you? Go to.
    You'll not endure him!
TYBALT. Why, Uncle, 'tis a shame.
CAPULET.   Go to, go to,
    You are a saucy boy. Is't so, indeed?
    Be quiet, or—More light, more light! For shame!   55
    I'll make you quiet. What, cheerly, my hearts!°
TYBALT. Patience perforce° with willful choler° meeting
    Makes my flesh tremble in their different greeting.
    I will withdraw. But this intrusion shall,
    Now seeming sweet, convert to bitterest gall.   60

[TYBALT *strides out in a rage.* ROMEO *goes up to* JULIET *and takes her by the hand.*]

ROMEO. If I profane with my unworthiest hand
    This holy shrine, the gentle fine° is this,
    My lips, two blushing pilgrims, ready stand
    To smooth that rough touch with a tender kiss.
JULIET. Good pilgrim,° you do wrong your hand too much,   65
    Which mannerly devotion shows in this;

---

39. **portly:** dignified. 43. **disparagement** (dis·par′ij·mənt): disrespect, insult. 47. **semblance:** appearance. 50. **goodman boy:** a contemptuous term. *Goodman* indicates a rank under that of gentleman: *boy,* youngster, is an insulting term. 56. **hearts:** friends. 57. **perforce:** forced (on me). **choler** (kol′ər): anger. 62. **fine:** punishment. 65. **Good pilgrim:** Juliet goes along with Romeo's suggestion that he is a pilgrim and she, a saint.

For saints have hands that pilgrims' hands do touch,
And palm to palm is holy palmers'° kiss.
ROMEO. Have not saints lips, and holy palmers too?
JULIET. Aye, pilgrim, lips that they must use in prayer.   70
ROMEO. Oh then, dear saint, let lips do what hands do.
    They pray. Grant thou, lest faith turn to despair.
JULIET. Saints do not move, though grant for prayers' sake.
ROMEO. Then move not while my prayer's effect I take.
    Thus from my lips by thine my sin is purged.   75

[Kissing her.]

JULIET. Then have my lips the sin that they have took.
ROMEO. Sin from my lips? Oh, trespass sweetly urged!
    Give me my sin again.
JULIET.   You kiss by the book.°
NURSE. Madam, your mother craves a word with you.
ROMEO. What is her mother?
NURSE.   Marry, bachelor,   80
    Her mother is the lady of the house,
    And a good lady, and a wise and virtuous.
    I nursed her daughter, that you talked withal.°
    I tell you, he that can lay hold of her
    Shall have the chinks.°
ROMEO.   Is she a Capulet?   85
    Oh, dear account! My life is my foe's debt.°
BENVOLIO. Away, be gone. The sport is at the best.
ROMEO. Aye, so I fear. The more is my unrest.
CAPULET. Nay, gentlemen, prepare not to be gone,
    We have a trifling foolish banquet toward.   90
    Is it e'en so? Why then, I thank you all,.
    I thank you, honest gentlemen. Good night.
    More torches here! Come on, then, let's to bed.
    Ah, sirrah, by my fay,° it waxes° late.
    I'll to my rest.   95

[Exeunt all but JULIET *and* NURSE. JULIET *too has fallen in love, but at first she
    hides her feelings.]*

JULIET. Come hither, Nurse. What is yond gentleman?
NURSE. The son and heir of old Tiberio.
JULIET. What's he that now is going out of door?
NURSE. Marry, that, I think, be young Petruchio.

---

    68. **palmer:** a pilgrim who carried a palm leaf to show that he had been to the Holy Land.   78. **by
the book:** as if you had learned how out of a book.   83. **withal:** with.   85. **chinks:** "dough" (inheritance).   86. **is my foe's debt:** belongs to my enemy.   94. **fay:** faith. **waxes:** grows.

JULIET. What's he that follows there, that would not dance?   100
NURSE. I know not.
JULIET. Go ask his name. [*To herself.*] If he be marrièd,
      My grave is like to be my wedding bed.
NURSE. His name is Romeo, and a Montague,
      The only son of your great enemy.   105
JULIET. My only love sprung from my only hate!
      Too early seen unknown, and known too late!
NURSE. [*Suspicious of* JULIET'S *sudden interest in a stranger*] What's this? What's this?
JULIET.   A rhyme I learned even now
      Of one I danced withal. [*Someone calls,* "Juliet."]
NURSE.   Anon, anon!
      Come, let's away, the strangers all are gone.   110

[*Exeunt.*]

FOR STUDY AND DISCUSSION

1. In the Prologue, what does the Chorus tell us about the play? How does the Chorus help to prepare us for the story which follows?

2. What does the quarrel at the opening of Scene i show about the feud between the Montagues and the Capulets? How long has the feud been going on? Is feeling between the two families bitter? Explain.

3. What is the Prince's attitude toward the feud? What penalty does he set for the next man who breaks the peace? Which character in this opening scene might you expect to cause further trouble?

4. At the beginning of Scene ii, what does Paris urge Capulet to do? To what does Capulet agree?

5. What is Juliet's feeling about marriage before she meets Romeo? What does she mean when she says, "I'll look to like, if looking liking move" (Scene iii, line 39)? Does she keep this promise? How are the results different from what Lady Capulet expected?

6. Mercutio's long speech about Queen Mab is a famous passage. Which lines did you find especially amusing? Besides being remarkable poetry, the speech serves to tell us much about Mercutio's attitude toward life. What word (or words) best describe his attitude? Is Mercutio a likable person, one his friends would be likely to admire?

7. What is Romeo's reaction when he first sees Juliet? Are his feelings toward her the same as those he had toward Rosaline? Do you think he is sincere? Was he sincere in his feelings for Rosaline? Explain your answer.

8. Why is Tybalt so furious at seeing Romeo at Capulet's party? Is his anger justified, at least in part? After being rebuked by Capulet, what does Tybalt swear to do?

9. How does Romeo react to the information that Juliet is a Capulet? How does Juliet react when she learns that Romeo is a Montague? Would an obstacle such as a family feud be likely to lessen or increase their attraction to each other? Why?

ACT II FOLLOWS ON PAGE 457

The Artist's Point of View

Ordinarily, we use the phrase "point of view" to mean a personal opinion. But if we think of its literal meaning—a *single vantage point* from which something is observed—we will understand what is meant by an artist's point of view in composing a picture. When artists draw a house, for example, they could look straight ahead at the front door, or down from an airplane, or even up from below; and they could observe it either from close up or from a considerable distance. Wherever they place themselves in relation to the house determines the visual point of view for the picture.

Some pictures, however, show figures and objects as if seen from more than one vantage point. For example, in PLATE 1, a view of Venice by an unknown fifteenth-century artist, we seem to be looking down upon the scene from high above; yet we see boats, swans, and some buildings as if they were more or less on our eye level. And notice the disproportionate sizes of certain figures—especially the swans, which appear almost as large as the boats. What we see here is really a combination of picture and map, in which figures and objects are represented by general *symbols* rather than by realistic likenesses.

Compare this fifteenth-century view of Venice with Jan Vermeer's seventeenth-century picture of the Dutch town of Delft (PLATE 2). Vermeer shows us a scene very much as he must have observed it from a single fixed point across the river, fairly high off the shoreline. His picture has the sort of vividness we usually associate with color photographs; yet Vermeer has arranged many details in a way no photographer could have. After first calling our attention to the silhouettes of the buildings (by placing them low in the picture, at our eye level), he leads us gently back and forth from one side of the composition to the other, so that we gradually move upward through a marvelous expanse of sky—until we finally come to a wide dark cloud at the top, which completes the picture by balancing the long strip of shadows below.

449

In Vincent van Gogh's *Thatched Roofs—Auvers* (PLATE 3) the artist's point of view, and ours too, is much closer to the subject. Here we seem to be so close, in fact, that the ground the two men are standing on at the lower left appears to be out in front of the picture. Notice that both figures are framed in a doorway so as to anchor this corner of the composition, which otherwise would appear to slide diagonally down toward the right. Van Gogh seems to have brought us up close even to the very paint itself by making every brushstroke stand out in thick sculptural relief, giving the whole picture a roughly textured surface.

Now look at a picture showing a view from only a few feet away: a nineteenth-century painting by the Frenchman Edgar Degas, called *At the Milliner's* (PLATE 4). Here we seem to have suddenly swooped down upon a small part of a room, shutting out everything except the immediate area around one seated figure. The space in the picture seems very crowded indeed, but notice that Degas has left just enough elbow room at the right to call attention to the figure's movements. By showing us such a close-up view, he has forced us to examine certain details which we might otherwise have overlooked, such as the highlights on the chair and details of the woman's hand and face.

Degas continually experimented with different points of view. In another painting, for instance, he shows us the left side of a stage from a point about ten or fifteen feet above the footlights (PLATE 5). Degas was intensely interested in the strange effects of theatrical lighting, such as the way a dancer's face suddenly goes into shadow when the head tilts back away from the glaring lights below. In this picture the main figure has an entire stage to herself. But notice how she seems to take command of this empty space with her various gestures—pointing her head back to the figures in the wings, extending one arm toward the rear of the stage, and reaching out toward the audience with the other.

Perhaps artists have never expressed their visual "points of view" more forcefully than in our own century. We see the world around us today from many vantage points, which are constantly changing. For example, when the American artist Charles Sheeler decided to use the Golden Gate Bridge in San Francisco as a theme for one of his paintings, he tried to express the visual impact of a sudden upward view of one of its giant pylons (PLATE 6). Parts of the bridge seem to be transparent as they overlap other parts, like a double exposure in a photograph. Or are they merely shadows? All we can really be certain about is the dizzying effect of looking up at something that seems to thrust into infinite space.

PLATE 1. ARTIST UNKNOWN (English, about 1400): *View of Venice,* page from *The Book of Marco Polo.* Illuminated manuscript, 9 x 8 inches. (Bodleian Library, Oxford)

PLATE 2. JAN VERMEER (Dutch, 1632–1675): *View of Delft.* 1658. Oil on canvas, $38\frac{3}{4}$ x $46\frac{1}{4}$ inches. (Royal Picture Gallery Mauritshuis, The Hague)

452

PLATE 3. VINCENT VAN GOGH (Dutch, 1853–1890): *Thatched Roofs—Auvers*. 1890. Oil on canvas, $25\frac{5}{8}$ x $31\frac{7}{8}$ inches. (Kunsthaus, Zurich)

PLATE 4. EDGAR DEGAS (French, 1834–1917): *At the Milliner's*. About 1882. Pastel draw ing, 26⅜ x 26⅜ inches. (Collection, The Museum of Modern Art, New York, Gift of Mrs. David M. Levy)

PLATE 5. EDGAR DEGAS (French, 1834–1917): *Dancer on the Stage*. About 1876. Pastel drawing, $23\frac{5}{8}$ x $17\frac{5}{8}$ inches. (Jeu de Paume, The Louvre, Paris)

PLATE 6. CHARLES SHEELER (American, 1883–1965): *Golden Gate.* 1955. Oil on canvas, 25 x 34 inches. (The Metropolitan Museum of Art, New York, George A. Hearn Fund, 1955)

ACT II

SCENE I

[*Later the same night.* ROMEO *enters alone. He is lingering beneath* JULIET'S *bedroom window.*]

ROMEO. Can I go forward when my heart is here?
 Turn back, dull earth,° and find thy center° out.

[*He hears* BENVOLIO'S *and* MERCUTIO'S *voices, and hides behind a pillar.*]

BENVOLIO. Romeo! My cousin Romeo!
MERCUTIO.   He is wise,
 And, on my life, hath stol'n him home to bed.
BENVOLIO. He ran this way, and leaped this orchard wall.   5
 Call, good Mercutio.
MERCUTIO. Romeo!
 I conjure thee by Rosaline's bright eyes,
 By her high forehead and her scarlet lip,
 That in thy likeness thou appear to us!   10

[*As there is no answer,* BENVOLIO *and* MERCUTIO *go on their way.* ROMEO, *who has overheard* MERCUTIO'S *joking, comes from his hiding place and looks up at* JULIET'S *window.*]

ROMEO. He jests° at scars that never felt a wound.

[JULIET *appears above at the window, as yet unaware of* ROMEO.]

 But, soft! What light through yonder window breaks?
 It is the east, and Juliet is the sun!
 Arise, fair sun, and kill the envious moon,
 Who is already sick and pale with grief   15
 That thou her maid art far more fair than she.
 Be not her maid, since she is envious.
 Her vestal livery° is but sick and green,
 And none but fools do wear it. Cast it off.
 It is my lady, oh, it is my love!   20
 Oh, that she knew she were!
 She speaks, yet she says nothing. What of that?
 Her eye discourses,° I will answer it.
 I am too bold, 'tis not to me she speaks.
 Two of the fairest stars in all the heaven,   25
 Having some business, do entreat her eyes

---

2. **earth:** body. **center:** the center of the earth, to which all things are attracted. The center of Romeo's world is Juliet. 11. **jests:** laughs, jokes. 18. **vestal livery:** maiden's dress. 23. **discourses:** speaks.

To twinkle in their spheres° till they return.
What if her eyes were there, they in her head?
The brightness of her cheek would shame those stars
As daylight doth a lamp; her eyes in heaven   30
Would through the airy region stream so bright
That birds would sing and think it were not night.
See how she leans her cheek upon her hand!
Oh, that I were a glove upon that hand,
That I might touch that cheek!

JULIET.   Aye me!
ROMEO. [*Softly, to himself*]   She speaks.   35
Oh, speak again, bright angel! For thou art
As glorious to this night, being o'er my head,
As is a wingèd messenger of Heaven
Unto the white-upturnèd wondering eyes
Of mortals that fall back to gaze on him   40
When he bestrides the lazy-pacing clouds
And sails upon the bosom of the air.

JULIET. O Romeo, Romeo, wherefore° art thou Romeo?
Deny thy father and refuse thy name,
Or, if thou wilt not, be but sworn my love   45
And I'll no longer be a Capulet.

ROMEO. [*To himself*] Shall I hear more, or shall I speak at this?
JULIET. 'Tis but thy name that is my enemy.
Thou art thyself, though not° a Montague.
What's Montague? It is nor hand, nor foot,   50
Nor arm, nor face, nor any other part
Belonging to a man. Oh, be some other name!
What's in a name? That which we call a rose
By any other name would smell as sweet.
So Romeo would, were he not Romeo called,   55
Retain that dear perfection which he owes°
Without that title. Romeo, doff thy name,
And for thy name, which is no part of thee,
Take all myself.

ROMEO. [*Going nearer and answering her*] I take thee at thy word.
Call me but love, and I'll be new baptized.   60
Henceforth I never will be Romeo.

JULIET. [*Frightened*] What man art thou that, thus bescreened in night,
So stumblest on my counsel?°

ROMEO.   By a name
I know not how to tell thee who I am.
My name, dear saint, is hateful to myself   65

27. **twinkle in their spheres** (sfirz): take their place in the sky. 43. **wherefore:** why; that is, why
are you an enemy of the Capulets? 49. **though not:** even if you were not. 56. **owes:** owns.
63. **counsel:** innermost thoughts.

Because it is an enemy to thee.
Had I it written, I would tear the word.
JULIET. My ears have yet not drunk a hundred words
Of thy tongue's uttering, yet I know the sound.
Art thou not Romeo, and a Montague?   70
ROMEO. Neither, fair saint, if either thee dislike.
JULIET. How camest thou hither, tell me, and wherefore?
The orchard walls are high and hard to climb,
And the place death, considering who thou art,
If any of my kinsmen find thee here.   75
ROMEO. With love's light wings did I o'erperch° these walls,
For stony limits cannot hold love out.
And what love can do, that dares love attempt,
Therefore thy kinsmen are no let° to me.
JULIET. If they do see thee, they will murder thee.   80
ROMEO. Alack, there lies more peril in thine eye
Than twenty of their swords. Look thou but sweet,
And I am proof° against their enmity.
JULIET. I would not for the world they saw thee here.
ROMEO. I have night's cloak to hide me from their eyes,   85
And but° thou love me, let them find me here.
My life were better ended by their hate
Than death prorogùed,° wanting of° thy love.
JULIET. By whose direction found'st thou out this place?
ROMEO. By love, that first did prompt me to inquire.   90
He lent me counsel, and I lent him eyes.
I am no pilot, yet wert thou as far
As that vast shore washed with the farthest sea,
I would adventure for such merchandise.
JULIET. Thou know'st the mask of night is on my face,   95
Else would a maiden blush bepaint my cheek
For that which thou hast heard me speak tonight.
Fain° would I dwell on form,° fain, fain deny
What I have spoke. But farewell compliment!°
Dost thou love me? I know thou wilt say "Aye,"   100
And I will take thy word. Yet if thou swear'st,
Thou mayst prove false. At lovers' perjuries°
They say Jove° laughs. O gentle Romeo,
If thou dost love, pronounce it faithfully.
Or if thou think'st I am too quickly won,   105
I'll frown and be perverse and say thee nay,
So° thou wilt woo; but else, not for the world.

76. **o'erperch:** climb over. 79. **let:** hindrance, obstacle. 83. **proof:** armored, safe. 86. **And but:** unless. 88. **prorogùed** (prō·rōg′d): postponed. **wanting of:** lacking. 98. **Fain:** gladly. **dwell on form:** behave in the customary way. 99. **compliment:** polite manners. 102. **perjuries:** broken promises. 103. **Jove** (jōv): in classical mythology, the chief of the gods. 107. **So:** so long as.

In truth, fair Montague, I am too fond,°
And therefore thou mayst think my 'havior light.
But trust me, gentleman, I'll prove more true   110
Than those that have more cunning to be strange.°
I should have been more strange, I must confess,
But that thou overheard'st, ere I was ware,°
My true love's passion. Therefore pardon me,
And not impute this yielding to light love,   115
Which the dark night hath so discovered.°

ROMEO. Lady, by yonder blessed moon I swear,
    That tips with silver all these fruit-tree tops——
JULIET. Oh, swear not by the moon, th' inconstant moon,
    That monthly changes in her circled orb,°   120
    Lest that thy love prove likewise variable.
ROMEO. What shall I swear by?
JULIET.   Do not swear at all.
    Or, if thou wilt, swear by thy gracious self,
    Which is the god of my idolatry,
    And I'll believe thee.
ROMEO.   If my heart's dear love——   125
JULIET. Well, do not swear. Although I joy in thee,
    I have no joy of this contract tonight.
    It is too rash, too unadvised, too sudden,
    Too like the lightning, which doth cease to be
    Ere one can say "It lightens." Sweet, good night!   130
    This bud of love, by summer's ripening breath,
    May prove a beauteous flower when next we meet.
    Good night, good night! As sweet repose and rest
    Come to thy heart as that within my breast!
ROMEO. Oh, wilt thou leave me so unsatisfied?   135
JULIET. What satisfaction canst thou have tonight?
ROMEO. The exchange of thy love's faithful vow for mine.
JULIET. I gave thee mine before thou didst request it,
    And yet I would it were to give again.
ROMEO. Wouldst thou withdraw it? For what purpose, love?   140
JULIET. But to be frank,° and give it thee again.
    And yet I wish but for the thing I have.
    My bounty° is as boundless as the sea,
    My love as deep; the more I give to thee,
    The more I have, for both are infinite.   145
    I hear some noise within. Dear love, adieu!

[*The* NURSE *calls from within.*]

108. **fond:** foolish.   111. **strange:** cold, distant.   113. **ware:** aware.   116. **discovered:** revealed.
120. **orb:** orbit.   141. **frank:** generous.   143. **bounty:** generosity.

Anon,° good Nurse! Sweet Montague, be true.
Stay but a little, I will come again.

[*Exit.*]

ROMEO. Oh, blessed, blessed night! I am afeard,
    Being in night, all this is but a dream,   150
    Too flattering-sweet to be substantial.°

      [JULIET *comes back to the window.*]

JULIET. Three words, dear Romeo, and good night indeed.
    If that thy bent° of love be honorable,
    Thy purpose marriage, send me word tomorrow
    By one that I'll procure to come to thee,   155
    Where and what time thou wilt perform the rite,
    And all my fortunes at thy foot I'll lay,
    And follow thee my lord throughout the world.
NURSE. [*From within*] Madam!
JULIET. I come, anon.—But if thou mean'st not well, I do beseech thee—— 160
NURSE. [*Within*] Madam!
JULIET.   By and by,° I come—
    To cease thy suit, and leave me to my grief.
    Tomorrow will I send.
ROMEO.   So thrive my soul——
JULIET. A thousand times good night!

[*Exit.*]

---

   147. **Anon:** in a minute. 151. **substantial:** real. 153. **bent:** intention. 161. **By and by:** right
away.

ROMEO. A thousand times the worse, to want thy light.   165
      Love goes toward love as schoolboys from their books,
      But love from love toward school with heavy looks.

          [JULIET *returns to the window*.]

JULIET. Hist! Romeo, hist!
ROMEO.   My dear?
JULIET.   At what o'clock tomorrow
      Shall I send to thee?
ROMEO.   At the hour of nine.
JULIET. I will not fail. 'Tis twenty years till then.   170
      I have forgot why I did call thee back.
ROMEO. Let me stand here till thou remember it.
JULIET. I shall forget, to have thee still stand there,
      Remembering how I love thy company.
ROMEO. And I'll still stay, to have thee still forget,   175
      Forgetting any other home but this.
JULIET. 'Tis almost morning. I would have thee gone,
      And yet no farther than a wanton's° bird,
      Who lets it hop a little from her hand,
      Like a poor prisoner in his twisted gyves,°   180
      And with a silk thread plucks it back again,
      So loving-jealous of his liberty.
ROMEO. I would I were thy bird.
JULIET.   Sweet, so would I.
      Yet I should kill thee with much cherishing.
      Good night, good night! Parting is such sweet sorrow   185
      That I shall say good night till it be morrow.
                                      [*Exit*.]

ROMEO. Sleep dwell upon thine eyes, peace in thy breast!
      Would I were sleep and peace, so sweet to rest!
      Hence will I to my ghostly° father's cell,
      His help to crave and my dear hap° to tell.   190
                                      [*Exit*.]

SCENE II

[*Very early in the morning. From the back of the stage,* FRIAR LAURENCE *enters, carrying a basket*.]

FRIAR LAURENCE. The gray-eyed morn smiles on the frowning night,
      Checkering the eastern clouds with streaks of light,
      And fleckèd darkness like a drunkard reels
      From forth day's path and Titan's° fiery wheels.

    178. **wanton:** spoiled child. 180. **gyves** (jīvz): fetters. 189. **ghostly:** spiritual. 190. **dear hap:** good fortune.
    4. **Titan:** the sun.

Now, ere the sun advance his burning eye,   5
The day to cheer and night's dank dew to dry,
I must upfill° this osier cage° of ours
With baleful° weeds and precious-juicèd flowers.
Oh, mickle° is the powerful grace° that lies
In herbs, plants, stones, and their true qualities.   10
For naught so vile that on the earth doth live,
But to the earth some special good doth give;
Nor aught so good but, strained from that fair use,
Revolts from true birth, stumbling on abuse.°
Within the infant rind of this small flower   15
Poison hath residence and medicine power.
In man as well as herbs, grace and rude will°;
And where the worser is predominant,°
Full soon the canker° death eats up that plant.

[*Enter* ROMEO.]

ROMEO. Good morrow, Father.
FRIAR LAURENCE.   Benedicite!   20
What early tongue so sweet saluteth me?
Young son, it argues a distempered° head
So soon to bid good morrow to thy bed.
Therefore thy earliness doth me assure
Thou art uproused by some distemperature.°   25
Or if not so, then here I hit it right,
Our Romeo hath not been in bed tonight.
ROMEO. That last is true. The sweeter rest was mine.
FRIAR LAURENCE. God pardon sin! Wast thou with Rosaline?
ROMEO. With Rosaline, my ghostly father? No.   30
I have forgot that name and that name's woe.
FRIAR LAURENCE. That's my good son. But where hast thou been, then?
ROMEO. I'll tell thee ere thou ask it me again.
I have been feasting with mine enemy,
Where on a sudden one hath wounded me   35
That's by me wounded. Both our remedies
Within thy help and holy physic° lies.
I bear no hatred, blessed man, for, lo,
My intercession° likewise steads° my foe.
FRIAR LAURENCE. Be plain, good son, and homely° in thy drift.°   40
Riddling° confession finds but riddling shrift.°
ROMEO. Then plainly know my heart's dear love is set
On the fair daughter of rich Capulet.

7. **upfill:** fill up. **osier cage:** wicker basket. 8. **baleful:** poisonous. 9. **mickle:** great. **grace:** goodness. 14. **abuse:** misuse. 17. **will:** natural desire, for evil. 18. **predominant:** stronger. 19. **canker:** worm. 22. **distempered:** disturbed. 25. **distemperature:** sickness. 37. **physic:** curing, remedy. 39. **intercession:** prayer, plea.. **steads:** benefits. 40. **homely:** simple, plain. **drift:** speech. 41. **Riddling:** speaking in riddles. **shrift:** absolution, forgiveness.

As mine on hers, so hers is set on mine,
And all combined° save what thou must combine   45
By holy marriage. When, and where, and how,
We met, we wooed and made exchange of vow,
I'll tell thee as we pass; but this I pray,
That thou consent to marry us today.

FRIAR LAURENCE. Holy Saint Francis, what a change is here!   50
Is Rosaline, that thou didst love so dear,
So soon forsaken? Young men's love then lies
Not truly in their hearts, but in their eyes.

ROMEO. Thou chid'st° me oft for loving Rosaline.

FRIAR LAURENCE. For doting, not for loving, pupil mine.   55

ROMEO. And bad'st me bury love.

FRIAR LAURENCE.   Not in a grave
To lay one in, another out to have.

ROMEO. I pray thee, chide not. She whom I love now
Doth grace for grace and love for love allow.
The other did not so.

FRIAR LAURENCE.   Oh, she knew well   60
Thy love did read by rote° and could not spell.
But come, young waverer, come, go with me,
In one respect I'll thy assistant be;
For this alliance may so happy prove,
To turn your households' rancor° to pure love.   65

ROMEO. Oh, let us hence. I stand on sudden haste.°

FRIAR LAURENCE. Wisely and slow. They stumble that run fast.

[*Exeunt.*]

---

45. **combined:** united.   54. **chid'st:** scolded.   61. **by rote:** by heart.   65. **rancor:** hatred.   66. **haste:** impatience.

SCENE III

[Enter BENVOLIO *and* MERCUTIO.]

MERCUTIO. Where the devil should this Romeo be?
    Came he not home tonight?
BENVOLIO. Not to his father's, I spoke with his man.
MERCUTIO. Ah, that same pale hardhearted wench, that Rosaline,
    Torments him so that he will sure run mad.   5
BENVOLIO. Tybalt, the kinsman of old Capulet,
    Hath sent a letter to his father's house.
MERCUTIO. A challenge, on my life.
BENVOLIO. Romeo will answer it.
MERCUTIO. Any man that can write may answer a letter.   10
BENVOLIO. Nay, he will answer the letter's master, how he dares, being dared.
MERCUTIO. Alas, poor Romeo, he is already dead! Stabbed with a white wench's
    black eye, shot through the ear with a love song, the very pin° of his heart
    cleft with the blind bowboy's butt shaft.° And is he a man to encounter
    Tybalt?   15

*[*ROMEO *enters, quite changed, no longer dull and melancholy but full of zest. As
he exchanges jokes with* BENVOLIO *and* MERCUTIO, *the* NURSE *approaches
with* PETER, *her man.* MERCUTIO *and* BENVOLIO *leave, and* ROMEO *is at last
able to give the* NURSE *his message for* JULIET.]

ROMEO. Bid her devise
    Some means to come to shrift° this afternoon,
    And there she shall at Friar Laurence' cell
    Be shrived and married. Here is for thy pains.
NURSE. No, truly, sir, not a penny.   20
ROMEO. Go to, I say you shall.
NURSE. This afternoon, sir? Well, she shall be there.
ROMEO. And stay, good Nurse, behind the abbey wall.
    Within this hour my man shall be with thee,
    And bring thee cords made like a tackled stair,°   25
    Which to the high topgallant° of my joy
    Must be my convoy in the secret night.
    Farewell. Be trusty, and I'll quit thy pains.°
    Farewell, commend me to thy mistress.
NURSE. Now God in Heaven bless thee! Hark you, sir.   30
ROMEO. What say'st thou, my dear nurse?
NURSE. Is your man secret?° Did you ne'er hear say
    Two may keep counsel, putting one away?°
ROMEO. I warrant thee, my man's as true as steel.

---

13. **pin:** center of a target, bulls-eye.   14. **blind . . . shaft:** Cupid's arrow.   17. **shrift:** confession.
25. **tackled stair:** rope ladder.   26. **topgallant:** topmast.   28. **quit thy pains:** reward your trouble.
32. **secret:** to be trusted.   33. **Two . . . away:** Two can keep a secret—if only one of them knows it.

NURSE. Well, sir, my mistress is the sweetest lady—Lord, Lord, when 'twas   35
    a little prating thing—Oh, there is a nobleman in town, one Paris, but she,
    good soul, had as lieve° see a toad, a very toad, as see him. I anger her
    sometimes, and tell her that Paris is the properer° man. But I'll warrant
    you, when I say so, she looks as pale as any clout° in the versal° world.

ROMEO. Commend me to thy lady.   40

NURSE. Aye, a thousand times. [*Exit* ROMEO.] Peter!

PETER. Anon?

NURSE. Peter, take my fan, and go before, and apace.°

SCENE IV

[JULIET *enters, impatiently waiting for the return of her* NURSE. *It is now noon.*]

JULIET. The clock struck nine when I did send the nurse.
    In half an hour she promised to return.
    Perchance she cannot meet him. That's not so.
    Oh, she is lame! Love's heralds should be thoughts,
    Which ten times faster glide than the sun's beams,   5
    Driving back shadows over lowering° hills.
    Therefore do nimble-pinioned° doves draw love,
    And therefore hath the wind-swift Cupid wings.
    Now is the sun upon the highmost hill
    Of this day's journey, and from nine till twelve   10
    Is three long hours; yet she is not come.
    Had she affections and warm youthful blood,
    She would be as swift in motion as a ball,
    My words would bandy° her to my sweet love,
    And his to me.   15

[*Enter* NURSE.]

    Oh, God, she comes! honey Nurse, what news?
    Hast thou met with him?
    Now, good sweet Nurse—Oh, Lord, why look'st thou sad?
    Though news be sad, yet tell them merrily;
    If good, thou shamest the music of sweet news   20
    By playing it to me with so sour a face.

NURSE. I am aweary, give me leave° a while.
    Fie, how my bones ache! What a jaunce° have I had!

JULIET. I would thou hadst my bones and I thy news.
    Nay, come, I pray thee, speak, good, good Nurse, speak.   25

---

   37. **lieve:** soon.   38. **properer:** handsomer.   39. **clout:** dishcloth.   **versal:** universal.   43. **apace:**
quickly.
   6. **lowering:** frowning.   7. **nimble-pinioned:** quick-winged.   14. **bandy:** bat, hit (like a tennis ball).
22. **give me leave:** let me alone.   23. **jaunce:** run back and forth.

NURSE. Jesu, what haste? Can you not stay a while?
　　Do you not see that I am out of breath?
JULIET. How art thou out of breath when thou hast breath
　　To say to me that thou art out of breath?
　　The excuse that thou dost make in this delay　　　　　　30
　　Is longer than the tale thou dost excuse.
　　Is thy news good, or bad? Answer to that.
　　Say either, and I'll stay the circumstance.°
　　Let me be satisfied, is 't good or bad?
NURSE. Well, you have made a simple choice. You know not how to choose　35
　　a man. Romeo! No, not he, though his face be better than any man's, yet
　　his leg excels all men's; and for a hand, and a foot, and a body, though they
　　be not to be talked on, yet they are past compare. He is not the flower of
　　courtesy,° but, I'll warrant him, as gentle as a lamb. Go thy ways, wench,
　　serve God. What, have you dined at home?　　　　　　40
JULIET. No, no. But all this did I know before.
　　What says he of our marriage? What of that?
NURSE. Lord, how my head aches! What a head have I!
　　It beats as it would fall in twenty pieces.
　　My back o' t' other side—ah, my back, my back!　　　　　45
　　Beshrew° your heart for sending me about
　　To catch my death with jauncing up and down!
JULIET. I' faith, I am sorry that thou art not well.
　　Sweet, sweet, sweet Nurse, tell me, what says my love?
NURSE. Your love says, like an honest gentleman, and a courteous, and a　50
　　kind, and a handsome, and, I warrant, a virtuous—Where is your mother?
JULIET. Where is my mother! Why, she is within,
　　Where should she be? How oddly thou repliest!
　　"Your love says, like an honest gentleman,
　　Where is your mother?"
NURSE.　　　　　　　　　　　Oh, God's Lady dear!°　　　　55
　　Are you so hot°? Marry, come up, I trow.°
　　Is this the poultice° for my aching bones?
　　Henceforward do your messages yourself.
JULIET. Here's such a coil!° Come, what says Romeo?
NURSE. Have you got leave to go to shrift today?　　　　　60
JULIET. I have.
NURSE. Then hie° you hence to Friar Laurence' cell,
　　There stays a husband to make you a wife.
　　Now comes the wanton blood up in your cheeks,
　　They'll be in scarlet straight at any news.　　　　　　65
　　Hie you to church, I must another way,

33. **stay the circumstance:** wait for details.　39. **flower of courtesy:** perfect gentleman.　46. **be-shrew:** a plague on.　55. **God's Lady dear:** God's dear Mother (the Virgin Mary).　56. **hot:** impatient. **Marry...trow:** Come, come, you're too impatient, I say.　57. **poultice:** remedy.　59. **coil:** fuss. 62. **hie:** hurry.

To fetch a ladder by the which your love
Must climb a bird's nest soon when it is dark.
Go, I'll to dinner, hie you to the cell.
JULIET. Hie to high fortune! Honest Nurse, farewell.   70

[*Exeunt.*]

SCENE V

[FRIAR LAURENCE'S *cell. Through the curtains at the back of the stage, which represents* FRIAR LAURENCE'S *cell, the* FRIAR *and* ROMEO *enter. They are waiting for* JULIET.]

FRIAR LAURENCE. So smile the Heavens upon this holy act
That afterhours with sorrow chide us not!
ROMEO. Amen, amen! But come what sorrow can,
It cannot countervail° the exchange of joy
That one short minute gives me in her sight.   5
Do thou but close our hands with holy words,
Then love-devouring death do what he dare,
It is enough I may but call her mine.
FRIAR LAURENCE. These violent delights have violent ends.
Therefore, love moderately, long love doth so,   10
Too swift arrives as tardy as too slow.

4. **countervail:** counterbalance, outweigh.

[Enter JULIET.]

Here comes the lady. Oh, so light a foot
Will ne'er wear out the everlasting flint.°
JULIET. Good even° to my ghostly confessor.
FRIAR LAURENCE. Romeo shall thank thee, daughter, for us both.　　　　15
JULIET. As much° to him, else is his thanks too much.
ROMEO. Ah, Juliet, if the measure of thy joy
　　　Be heaped like mine, and that thy skill be more
　　　To blazon° it, then sweeten with thy breath
　　　This neighbor air, and let rich music's tongue　　　　20
　　　Unfold the imagined happiness that both
　　　Receive in either by this dear encounter.
JULIET. They are but beggars that can count their worth,
　　　But my true love is grown to such excess,
　　　I cannot sum up sum of half my wealth.　　　　25
FRIAR LAURENCE. Come, come with me, and we will make short work,
　　　For, by your leaves, you shall not stay alone
　　　Till Holy Church incorporate two in one.

[They go in together to their wedding.]

---

13. **flint:** hard stone.　14. **Good even:** good evening.　16. **As much:** the very same greeting.
19. **blazon** (blā′zən): describe.

FOR STUDY AND DISCUSSION

1. Why does Juliet wish that Romeo had some other name? If he can't give up his name, what does she say she will do? From what you have seen of Juliet so far in the play, do you think she would?

2. How does Romeo happen to be in the Capulets' garden? After he overhears Juliet, what is she afraid he will think of her? From what you know of Romeo, do you think he would?

3. How does Juliet ask Romeo to prove his love for her? What is the first thing she speaks of each time she comes back to the window?

4. The balcony scene is famous for its poetry. How does the poetry in this scene help you to share the feelings of Romeo and Juliet? Which lines are especially good at enabling you to share the speaker's feeling?

5. What is Friar Laurence's first reaction when he hears that Romeo has a new love? Why does he finally agree to marry Romeo and Juliet? What does he hope their marriage will accomplish?

6. What plans does Romeo make for his secret marriage to Juliet? If you were Romeo, would you trust the Nurse? Does it ever occur to him not to trust her? What does this show about Romeo?

7. What makes Scene iv so amusing? Why do you think the Nurse drives Juliet to the end of her patience before telling her of Romeo's plans? What does this scene reveal about the seriousness of Juliet's love?

8. As they wait for Juliet to arrive for her wedding, does Friar Laurence share Romeo's joy? What is the Friar's attitude now toward the marriage? Of what is he fearful?

9. Just before they are married, what does Romeo ask Juliet to do? What is her answer? Of the two, who speaks with more common sense and practicality? Is this difference between Romeo and Juliet also evident in the balcony scene (Scene i)? Which lines best illustrate this difference?

ACT III

SCENE I

[*Enter* MERCUTIO, BENVOLIO, PAGE, *and* SERVANTS.]

BENVOLIO. I pray thee, good Mercutio, let's retire.
    The day is hot, the Capulets abroad,
    And if we meet, we shall not 'scape a brawl;
    For now these hot days is the mad blood stirring.

[*Enter* TYBALT *and other* CAPULETS, *looking for trouble.*]

BENVOLIO. By my head, here come the Capulets. 5
MERCUTIO. By my heel, I care not.
TYBALT. Follow me close, for I will speak to them.
    Gentlemen, good-den—a word with one of you.
MERCUTIO. And but one word with one of us? Couple it with something—make it
    a word and a blow. 10
TYBALT. You shall find me apt enough to that, sir, an you will give me occasion.
MERCUTIO. Could you not take some occasion without giving?
TYBALT. Mercutio, thou consort'st° with Romeo——
MERCUTIO. Consort! What, dost thou make us minstrels?° An thou make minstrels
    of us, look to hear nothing but discords. Here's my fiddlestick,° here's 15
    that shall make you dance. 'Zounds,° consort!
BENVOLIO. We talk here in the public haunt of men.
    Either withdraw unto some private place,
    And reason coldly of your grievances,
    Or else depart. Here all eyes gaze on us. 20
MERCUTIO. Men's eyes were made to look, and let them gaze.
    I will not budge for no man's pleasure, I.

[*Enter* ROMEO. *Now that* JULIET *is his wife, he is full of friendly thoughts for the*
CAPULETS, *who have become his kinsmen by marriage.*]

TYBALT. Well, peace be with you, sir. Here comes my man.°
MERCUTIO. But I'll be hanged, sir, if he wear your livery.°
    Marry, go before to field,° he'll be your follower. 25
    Your worship in that sense may call him man.
TYBALT. Romeo, the hate I bear thee can afford
    No better term than this—thou art a villain.
ROMEO. Tybalt, the reason that I have to love thee
    Doth much excuse the appertaining rage° 30

---

13. **consort'st:** are friendly with.   14. **minstrels:** Mercutio puns on another meaning of consort: a party of musicians.   15. **fiddlestick:** weapon.   16. **'Zounds:** by Christ's wounds.   23. **my man:** the man I am looking for.   24. **livery:** servant's uniform. Mercutio pretends that Tybalt has used "man" in the sense of "servant" or "follower" (line 25).   25. **field:** dueling place.   30. **appertaining rage:** the anger with which I would otherwise respond.

To such a greeting. Villain am I none,
Therefore farewell. I see thou know'st me not.°
TYBALT. Boy, this shall not excuse the injuries
That thou hast done me, therefore turn and draw.
ROMEO. I do protest I never injured thee,   35
But love thee better than thou canst devise°
Till thou shalt know the reason of my love.
And so, good Capulet—which name I tender°
As dearly as mine own—be satisfied.
MERCUTIO. [*Who supposes that* ROMEO'S *weakness is due to cowardice*] Oh,
calm, dishonorable, vile submission!   40
Alla stoccata° carries it away. [*He draws his sword.*]
Tybalt, you ratcatcher, will you walk?
TYBALT. What wouldst thou have with me?
MERCUTIO. Good King of Cats,° nothing but one of your nine lives, that I mean to
make bold withal, and, as you shall use me hereafter, dry-beat° the rest   45
of the eight. Will you pluck your sword out of his pilcher° by the ears?
Make haste, lest mine be about your ears ere it be out.
TYBALT. [*Also drawing*] I am for you.
ROMEO. Gentle Mercutio, put thy rapier up.
MERCUTIO. Come, sir, your passado.°   50

[*As they begin to fight,* ROMEO *appeals to* BENVOLIO *to help him stop the quarrel.*]

ROMEO. Draw, Benvolio, beat down their weapons.
Gentlemen, for shame, forbear this outrage!
Tybalt, Mercutio, the Prince expressly hath
Forbid this bandying° in Verona streets.
Hold, Tybalt, good Mercutio!

[ROMEO *comes between them. Seeing his chance,* TYBALT *stabs* MERCUTIO, *whose
vision is blocked by* ROMEO. TYBALT *and the other* CAPULETS *run away.*]

MERCUTIO.   I am hurt.   55
A plague o'both your houses! I am sped.°
Is he gone, and hath nothing?
BENVOLIO.   What, art thou hurt?
MERCUTIO. Aye, aye, a scratch, a scratch—marry, 'tis enough.
Where is my page? Go, villain,° fetch a surgeon.

[*Exit* PAGE.]

ROMEO. Courage, man, the hurt cannot be much.   60
MERCUTIO. No, 'tis not so deep as a well nor so wide as a church door, but 'tis
enough, 'twill serve. Ask for me tomorrow and you shall find me a grave

32. **know'st me not:** know not that I am now married to your cousin.   36. **devise:** guess, imagine.
38. **tender:** regard, care for.   41. **Alla stoccata:** a thrust in fencing. Mercutio supposes that Romeo
is afraid of Tybalt's skill as a fencer.   44. **King of Cats:** In the folk tale of Reynard the Fox, Tibert
(Tybalt) is Prince of Cats.   45. **dry-beat:** bruise.   46. **pilcher:** scabbard.   50. **passado:** lunge.
54. **bandying:** quarreling.   56. **sped:** done for.   59. **villain:** term used in addressing a servant.

man.° I am peppered,° I warrant, for this world. A plague o' both your
houses! 'Zounds, a dog, a rat, a mouse, a cat, to scratch a man to death!
A braggart, a rogue, a villain, that fights by the book of arithmetic!° Why 65
the devil came you between us! I was hurt under your arm.

ROMEO. I thought all for the best.

MERCUTIO. Help me into some house, Benvolio,
Or I shall faint. A plague o' both your houses!
They have made worms' meat of me. I have it, 70
And soundly too—your houses!

[BENVOLIO *supports* MERCUTIO *through the nearest door.*]

ROMEO. This gentleman, the Prince's near ally,
My very friend, hath got his mortal hurt
In my behalf, my reputation stained
With Tybalt's slander—Tybalt, that an hour 75
Hath been my kinsman. O sweet Juliet,
Thy beauty hath made me effeminate,°
And in my temper softened valor's steel!

[BENVOLIO *returns.*]

BENVOLIO. O Romeo, Romeo, brave Mercutio's dead!
That gallant spirit hath aspired° the clouds, 80
Which too untimely here did scorn the earth.

ROMEO. This day's black fate on more days doth depend,°
This but begins the woe others must end.

[TYBALT *comes back.*]

BENVOLIO. Here comes the furious Tybalt back again.

ROMEO. Alive, in triumph! And Mercutio slain! 85
Away to Heaven, respective lenity,°
And fire-eyed fury be my conduct° now!
Now, Tybalt, take the "villain" back again
That late thou gavest me; for Mercutio's soul
Is but a little way above our heads, 90
Staying for thine to keep him company.
Either thou, or I, or both, must go with him.

TYBALT. Thou, wretched boy, that didst consort him here,
Shalt with him hence.

ROMEO.   This shall determine that.

[ROMEO, *roused to fury, quickly overcomes* TYBALT, *who falls dead.*]

BENVOLIO. Romeo, away, be gone! 95

62–63. **grave man:** another pun by Mercutio, who is now dying. 63. **peppered:** shot, wounded.
65. **book of arithmetic:** textbook on fencing. 77. **effeminate:** womanly. 80. **aspired:** soared to.
82. **on more . . . depend:** will be followed by more fatal days. 86. **respective lenity:** considerate
mercy (which Romeo has shown to Juliet's kin). 87. **conduct:** guide.

The citizens are up, and Tybalt slain.
Stand not amazed. The Prince will doom thee death
If thou art taken. Hence, be gone, away!
ROMEO. Oh, I am fortune's fool!
BENVOLIO.   Why dost thou stay?

[*Exit* ROMEO. *Citizens come running out both doors.*]

FIRST CITIZEN. Which way ran he that killed Mercutio?   100
Tybalt, that murderer, which way ran he?
BENVOLIO. There lies that Tybalt.
FIRST CITIZEN.   Up, sir, go with me.
I charge thee in the Prince's name, obey.

[*The* PRINCE *and his guard come out.* MONTAGUE *and* CAPULET *with their wives
and followers join the crowd.*]

ROMEO AND JULIET   473

PRINCE. Where are the vile beginners of this fray?

BENVOLIO. O noble Prince, I can discover° all   105
    The unlucky manage° of this fatal brawl.
    There lies the man, slain by young Romeo,
    That slew thy kinsman, brave Mercutio.

LADY CAPULET. Tybalt, my cousin! Oh, my brother's child!
    O Prince! O Cousin! Husband! Oh, the blood is spilt   110
    Of my dear kinsman! Prince, as thou art true,
    For blood of ours shed blood of Montague.
    O Cousin, Cousin!

PRINCE. Benvolio, who began this bloody fray?

BENVOLIO. Tybalt, here slain, whom Romeo's hand did slay—   115
    Romeo that spoke him fair, bade him bethink
    How nice° the quarrel was, and urged withal
    Your high displeasure.
    This is the truth, or let Benvolio die.

LADY CAPULET. He is a kinsman to the Montague,   120
    Affection makes him false, he speaks not true.
    Some twenty of them fought in this black strife,
    And all those twenty could but kill one life.
    I beg for justice, which thou, Prince, must give.
    Romeo slew Tybalt, Romeo must not live.   125

PRINCE. Romeo slew him, he slew Mercutio.
    Who now the price of his dear blood doth owe?

MONTAGUE. [*Pleading for his son*] Not Romeo, Prince, he was Mercutio's
    friend.
    His fault concludes but what the law should end,
    The life of Tybalt.   130

PRINCE. [*His anger roused*] And for that offense
    Immediately we do exile him hence.
    I have an interest° in your hate's proceeding,
    My blood° for your rude brawls doth lie a-bleeding.
    But I'll amerce° you with so strong a fine   135
    That you shall all repent the loss of mine.°
    I will be deaf to pleading and excuses,
    Nor tears nor prayers shall purchase out° abuses.
    Therefore use none. Let Romeo hence in haste,
    Else, when he's found, that hour is his last.   140
    Bear hence this body, and attend our will.°
    Mercy but murders, pardoning those that kill.

                        [*Exeunt, carrying the body of* TYBALT.]

---

105. **discover:** reveal. 106. **manage:** circumstances. 117. **nice:** trifling, trivial. 133. **interest:**
concern. Mercutio was the Prince's kin. 134. **My blood:** the blood of my kin. 135. **amerce:** punish.
136. **mine:** my kin's blood. 138. **purchase out:** pay for. 141. **attend our will:** come to receive my
judgment.

SCENE II

[Later the same day JULIET, *as yet ignorant of the death of her cousin* TYBALT, *is waiting impatiently for night and the coming of* ROMEO.]

JULIET. Gallop apace, you fiery-footed steeds,
    Toward Phoebus'° lodging. Come, civil night,
    Thou sober-suited matron, all in black,
    Come, night, come, Romeo, come, thou day in night,
    For thou wilt lie upon the wings of night   5
    Whiter than new snow on a raven's back.
    Come, gentle night, come, loving, black-browed night,
    Give me my Romeo; and when he shall die,
    Take him and cut him out in little stars,
    And he will make the face of heaven so fine   10
    That all the world will be in love with night,
    And pay no worship to the garish° sun.

    [Enter the NURSE, *carrying the ladder of cords and weeping.]*

    Now, Nurse, what news!
    What hast thou there? The cords
    That Romeo bid thee fetch?   15
NURSE. Aye, aye, the cords. *[Throws them down.]*
JULIET. Aye me! What news? Why dost thou wring thy hands?
NURSE. Ah, welladay! He's dead, he's dead, he's dead.
    We are undone, lady, we are undone.
    Alack the day! He's gone, he's killed, he's dead.   20
JULIET. Can Heaven be so envious?
NURSE.   Romeo can,
    Though Heaven cannot. O Romeo, Romeo!
    Who ever would have thought it? Romeo!
JULIET. What devil art thou that dost torment me thus?
    This torture should be roared in dismal Hell.   25
    Hath Romeo slain himself?
NURSE. I saw the wound, I saw it with mine eyes—
    God save the mark!—here on his manly breast.
    A piteous corse,° a bloody piteous corse,
    Pale, pale as ashes, all bedaubed in blood,   30
    All in gore blood, I swounded° at the sight.
JULIET. Oh, break, my heart! Poor bankrupt, break at once!
    To prison, eyes, ne'er look on liberty!
    Vile earth to earth resign, end motion here,
    And thou and Romeo press one heavy bier!   35
NURSE. O Tybalt, Tybalt, the best friend I had!
    O courteous Tybalt! Honest gentleman!

---

    2. **Phoebus** (fē′bəs): the sun god, who according to legend was drawn daily across the sky in his chariot. 12. **garish:** gaudy. 29. **corse:** corpse. 31. **swounded:** swooned, fainted.

That ever I should live to see thee dead!

JULIET. What storm is this that blows so contrary?
　　Is Romeo slaughtered, and is Tybalt dead?　　　　40
　　My dear-loved cousin, and my dearer lord?
　　Then, dreadful trumpet,° sound the general doom!
　　For who is living if those two are gone?

NURSE. Tybalt is gone, and Romeo banishèd—
　　Romeo that killed him, he is banishèd.　　　　　45

JULIET. Oh, God! Did Romeo's hand shed Tybalt's blood?

NURSE. It did, it did. Alas the day, it did!

JULIET. Oh, serpent heart, hid with a flowering face!
　　Oh, that deceit should dwell
　　In such a gorgeous palace!

NURSE. 　　　　　　　　　　There's no trust,　　　　50
　　No faith, no honesty in men—all perjured,
　　All forsworn, all naught, all dissemblers.°
　　Ah, where's my man? Give me some aqua vitae.°
　　These griefs, these woes, these sorrows, make me old.
　　Shame come to Romeo!

JULIET. 　　　　　　　　　　Blistered be thy tongue　　55
　　For such a wish! He was not born to shame.
　　Upon his brow shame is ashamed to sit,
　　For 'tis a throne where honor may be crowned
　　Sole monarch on the universal earth.
　　Oh, what a beast was I to chide at him!　　　　　60

NURSE. Will you speak well of him that killed your cousin?

JULIET. Shall I speak ill of him that is my husband?
　　Ah, poor my lord, what tongue shall smooth thy name
　　When I, thy three-hours wife, have mangled it?
　　But wherefore, villain, didst thou kill my cousin?　65
　　That villain cousin would have killed my husband.
　　My husband lives, that Tybalt would have slain,
　　And Tybalt's dead, that would have slain my husband.
　　All this is comfort, wherefore weep I, then?
　　Some word there was, worser than Tybalt's death,　70
　　That murdered me. I would forget it fain,°
　　But, oh, it pressed to my memory
　　Like damnèd guilty deeds to sinners' minds.
　　"Tybalt is dead, and Romeo banishèd."
　　That "banishèd," that one word "banishèd,"　　　75
　　Hath slain ten thousand Tybalts. Tybalt's death
　　Was woe enough if it had ended there.
　　"Romeo is banishèd." To speak that word
　　Is father, mother, Tybalt, Romeo, Juliet,

---

42. **dreadful trumpet:** the trumpet which is supposed to announce the end of the world.　52. **dissemblers:** pretenders, hypocrites.　53. **aqua vitae** (vī′tē): spirits.　71. **fain:** gladly, willingly.

All slain, all dead. "Romeo is banishèd."   80
There is no end, no limit, measure, bound,
In that word's death; no words can that woe sound.
Where is my father, and my mother, Nurse?
NURSE. Weeping and wailing over Tybalt's corse.
Will you go to them? I will bring you thither.   85
JULIET. Wash they his wounds with tears. Mine shall be spent,
When theirs are dry, for Romeo's banishment.
NURSE. [*Suddenly sobered by a note of desperation in* JULIET] Hie to your cham-
ber. I'll find Romeo
To comfort you. I wot° well where he is.
Hark ye, your Romeo will be here at night.   90
I'll to him—he is hid at Laurence' cell.
JULIET. Oh, find him! Give this ring to my true knight,
And bid him come to take his last farewell.

[*Exeunt.*]

SCENE III

[*The curtains at the back of the stage open on* FRIAR LAURENCE'S *cell. Enter*
FRIAR LAURENCE.]

FRIAR LAURENCE. Romeo, come forth, come forth, thou fearful° man.
Affliction is enamored of thy parts,°
And thou art wedded to calamity.

[*Enter* ROMEO *in great distress.*]

ROMEO. Father, what news? What is the Prince's doom?°
What sorrow craves acquaintance at my hand   5
That I yet know not?
FRIAR LAURENCE.   Too familiar
Is my dear son with such sour company.
I bring thee tidings of the Prince's doom.

89. **wot:** know.
1. **fearful:** full of fear.   2. **Affliction . . . parts:** misfortune has fallen in love with your good qualities (and so follows wherever you go).   4. **doom:** sentence.

ROMEO. What less than Doomsday is the Prince's doom?

FRIAR LAURENCE. A gentler judgment vanished° from his lips,   10
    Not body's death, but body's banishment.

ROMEO. Ha, banishment! Be merciful, say "death,"
    For exile hath more terror in his look,
    Much more, than death. Do not say "banishment."

FRIAR LAURENCE. Hence from Verona art thou banishèd.   15
    Be patient, for the world is broad and wide.

ROMEO. [Almost hysterical with grief] There is no world without° Verona·walls,
    But Purgatory, torture, Hell itself.
    Hence banishèd is banished from the world,
    And world's exile is death. Then "banishèd"   20
    Is death mistermed. Calling death "banishèd,"
    Thou cut'st my head off with a golden ax,
    And smilest upon the stroke that murders me.

FRIAR LAURENCE. Oh, deadly sin! Oh, rude unthankfulness!
    Thy fault our law calls death, but the kind Prince,   25
    Taking thy part, hath rushed° aside the law,
    And turned that black word "death" to "banishment."
    This is dear° mercy, and thou seest it not.

ROMEO. 'Tis torture, and not mercy. Heaven is here,
    Where Juliet lives, and every cat and dog   30
    And little mouse, every unworthy thing,
    Live here in Heaven and may look on her,
    But Romeo may not. More validity,
    More honorable state, more courtship, lives
    In carrion flies than Romeo. They may seize   35
    On the white wonder of dear Juliet's hand,
    And steal immortal blessing from her lips.
    But Romeo may not, he is banishèd.
    This may flies do, but I from this must fly.
    They are free men, but I am banishèd.   40
    And say'st thou yet that exile is not death?

FRIAR LAURENCE. Thou fond° madman, hear me but speak a word.

ROMEO. Oh, thou wilt speak again of banishment.

FRIAR LAURENCE. I'll give thee armor to keep off that word,
    Adversity's sweet milk, philosophy,   45
    To comfort thee, though thou art banishèd.

ROMEO. Yet "banishèd"? Hang up philosophy!
    Unless philosophy can make a Juliet,
    Displant° a town, reverse a Prince's doom,
    It helps not, it prevails not. Talk no more.   50
    Thou canst not speak of that thou dost not feel.

---

10. **vanished:** escaped from.   17. **without:** outside.   26. **rushed:** brushed.   28. **dear:** precious.
42. **fond:** foolish.   49. **displant:** uproot.

Wert thou as young as I, Juliet thy love,
An hour but married, Tybalt murderèd,
Doting like me, and like me banishèd,
Then mightst thou speak, then mightst thou tear thy hair   55
And fall upon the ground, as I do now,
Taking the measure of an unmade grave.

[*As he throws himself on the ground, someone knocks at the door.*]

FRIAR LAURENCE. Arise, one knocks. Good Romeo, hide thyself.
ROMEO. Not I, unless the breath of heartsick groans
    Mistlike enfold me from the search of eyes. [*Knocking.*]   60
FRIAR LAURENCE. Hark how they knock! Who's there? Romeo, arise,
    Thou wilt be taken.—Stay awhile!—Stand up, [*Knocking.*]
    Run to my study.—By and by!—God's will,
    What simpleness is this!—I come, I come! [*Knocking.*]
    Who knocks so hard? Whence come you? What's your will?   65

[*The voice of the* NURSE *is heard from outside.*]

NURSE. Let me come in, and you shall know my errand.
    I come from Lady Juliet.
FRIAR LAURENCE.   Welcome, then.

[*Enter* NURSE.]

NURSE. O holy Friar, oh, tell me, holy Friar,
    Where is my lady's lord, where's Romeo?
FRIAR LAURENCE. There on the ground, with his own tears made drunk.   70
NURSE. Oh, he is even in my mistress' case,
    Just in her case! Even so lies she,
    Blubbering and weeping, weeping and blubbering.
    Stand up, stand up, stand, an you be a man.
    For Juliet's sake, for her sake, rise and stand.   75
    Why should you fall into so deep an O?°
ROMEO. Nurse!
NURSE. Ah sir, ah sir! Well, death's the end of all.
ROMEO. [*Eagerly*] Spakest thou of Juliet? How is it with her?
    Doth she not think me an old° murderer,   80
    Now I have stained the childhood of our joy
    With blood removed but little from her own?
    Where is she? And how doth she? And what says
    My concealed lady° to our canceled love?
NURSE. Oh, she says nothing, sir, but weeps and weeps,   85
    And now falls on her bed, and then starts up
    And Tybalt calls, and then on Romeo cries,
    And then down falls again.

76. **O:** cry of grief. 80. **old:** common. 84. **concealed lady:** secret bride.

ROMEO.   As if that name,
          Shot from the deadly level° of a gun,
          Did murder her, as that name's cursèd hand   90
          Murdered her kinsman. Oh, tell me, Friar, tell me,
          In what vile part of this anatomy°
          Doth my name lodge? Tell me, that I may sack°
          The hateful mansion. [*Drawing his dagger.*]
FRIAR LAURENCE.   Hold thy desperate hand.
          Art thou a man? Thy form cries out thou art.   95
          Thy tears are womanish, thy wild acts denote
          The unreasonable fury of a beast.
          What, rouse thee, man! Thy Juliet is alive,
          For whose dear sake thou wast but lately dead.
          There art thou happy. Tybalt would kill thee,   100
          But thou slew'st Tybalt. There art thou happy too.
          The law, that threatened death, becomes thy friend
          And turns it to exile. There art thou happy.
          A pack of blessings lights upon thy back,
          Happiness courts thee in her best array;   105
          But, like a misbehaved and sullen wench,
          Thou pout'st upon thy fortune and thy love.
          Take heed, take heed, for such die miserable.
          Go, get thee to thy love, as was decreed,
          Ascend her chamber—hence and comfort her.   110
          But look thou stay not till the watch be set,°
          For then thou canst not pass to Mantua,
          Where thou shalt live till we can find a time
          To blaze° your marriage, reconcile your friends,
          Beg pardon of the Prince, and call thee back   115
          With twenty hundred thousand times more joy
          Than thou went'st forth in lamentation.
          Go before, Nurse. Commend me to thy lady,
          And bid her hasten all the house to bed,
          Which heavy sorrow makes them apt unto.   120
          Romeo is coming.
NURSE. Oh Lord, I could have stayed here all the night
          To hear good counsel. Oh, what learning is!
          My lord, I'll tell my lady you will come.
ROMEO. Do so, and bid my sweet prepare to chide.   125
NURSE. Here, sir, a ring she bid me give you, sir.
          Hie you, make haste, for it grows very late.

                                                                        [*Exit.*]

89. **level:** aim.   92. **anatomy:** body.   93. **sack:** destroy.   111. **watch be set:** watchmen go on duty
at the gates.   114. **blaze:** make public.

ROMEO. How well my comfort is revived by this!

FRIAR LAURENCE. Go hence, good night, and here stands all your state°

    Either be gone before the watch be set,   130

    Or by the break of day disguised from hence.

    Sojourn° in Mantua. I'll find out your man,

    And he shall signify from time to time

    Every good hap° to you that chances here.

    Give me thy hand, 'tis late. Farewell, good night.   135

ROMEO. But that a joy past joy calls out on me,

    It were a grief so brief to part with thee.

    Farewell.

[ROMEO *goes forth eagerly.*]

SCENE IV

[*In* CAPULET'S *house.* CAPULET *enters with* LADY CAPULET *and* PARIS, *who is hoping for a favorable answer from* JULIET.]

CAPULET. Things have fall'n out, sir, so unluckily,

    That we have had no time to move° our daughter.

    Look you, she loved her kinsman Tybalt dearly,

    And so did I. Well, we were born to die.

    'Tis very late, she'll not come down tonight.   5

    I promise you, but for your company

    I would have been abed an hour ago.

PARIS. These times of woe afford no time to woo.

    Madam, good night. Commend me to your daughter.

LADY CAPULET. I will, and know her mind early tomorrow;   10

    Tonight she's mewed up to her heaviness.°

CAPULET. [*Suddenly struck by what seems to be a good plan*] Sir Paris, I will

      make a desperate tender°

    Of my child's love. I think she will be ruled

    In all respects by me—nay, more, I doubt it not.

    Wife, go you to her ere you go to bed,   15

    Acquaint her here of my son° Paris' love,

    And bid her, mark you me, on Wednesday next—

    But, soft! what day is this?

PARIS.   Monday, my lord.

CAPULET. Monday! Ha, ha! Well, Wednesday is too soon.

    O' Thursday let it be. O' Thursday, tell her,   20

---

129. **here . . . state:** on this depends all your good fortune.   132. **Sojourn:** remain.   134. **hap:** happening.

2. **move:** make your proposal to.   11. **mewed . . . heaviness:** shut up in seclusion with her sorrow. 12. **desperate tender:** bold offer.   16. **son:** future son-in-law.

She shall be married to this noble Earl.
Will you be ready? Do you like this haste?
We'll keep no great ado, a friend or two;
For, hark you, Tybalt being slain so late,°
It may be thought we held him carelessly,°   25
Being our kinsman, if we revel much.
Therefore we'll have some half a dozen friends,
And there an end. But what say you to Thursday?
PARIS. My lord, I would that Thursday were tomorrow.
CAPULET. Well, get you gone. O' Thursday be it, then.   30
Go you to Juliet ere you go to bed,
Prepare her, wife, against° this wedding day.
Farewell, my lord. Light to my chamber, ho!
Afore me,° it is so very very late
That we may call it early by and by.   35
Good night.

[*Exeunt.*]

SCENE V

[ROMEO *and* JULIET *appear above, at her window.*]

JULIET. Wilt thou be gone? It is not yet near day.
It was the nightingale, and not the lark,°
That pierced the fearful hollow of thine ear.
Nightly she sings on yond pomegranate tree.
Believe me, love, it was the nightingale.   5
ROMEO. It was the lark, the herald of the morn,
No nightingale. Look, love, what envious streaks
Do lace° the severing° clouds in yonder east.
Night's candles are burnt out, and jocund° day
Stands tiptoe on the misty mountaintops.   10
I must be gone and live, or stay and die.
JULIET. Yond light is not daylight, I know it, I.
It is some meteor that the sun exhales,
To be to thee this night a torchbearer
And light thee on thy way to Mantua.   15
Therefore stay yet—thou need'st not to be gone.
ROMEO. Let me be ta'en, let me be put to death,
I am content, so thou wilt have it so.
Come, death, and welcome! Juliet wills it so.
How is't, my soul? Let's talk. It is not day.   20

---

24. **late:** lately, recently. 25. **held him carelessly:** did not care about him. 32. **against:** in readiness for. 34. **Afore me:** an oath meaning "before God."
2. **nightingale ... lark:** The nightingale sings at night; the lark sings in the early morning. 8. **lace:** stripe. **severing:** parting. 9. **jocund:** joyful.

JULIET. [*Wildly*] It is, it is. Hie hence, be gone, away!
  It is the lark that sings so out of tune.
  Oh, now be gone, more light and light it grows.
ROMEO. More light and light. More dark and dark our woes!

[*The warning voice of the* NURSE *is heard.*]

NURSE. Madam!   25
JULIET. Nurse?
NURSE. Your lady mother is coming to your chamber.
  The day is broke, be wary, look about.
JULIET. Then, window, let day in, and let life out.
ROMEO. Farewell, farewell! One kiss, and I'll descend.   30

[*He climbs down by the ladder of cords to the stage below.*]

JULIET. [*Looking down from the window*] Art thou gone so? Love, lord, ay,
    husband, friend!
  I must hear from thee every day in the hour,
  For in a minute there are many days.
  Oh, by this count I shall be much in years
  Ere I again behold my Romeo!   35
ROMEO. Farewell!
  I will omit no opportunity
  That may convey my greetings, love, to thee.
JULIET. Oh, think'st thou we shall ever meet again?

ROMEO. I doubt it not, and all these woes shall serve   40
    For sweet discourses in our time to come.
JULIET. Oh God! I have an ill-divining° soul.
    Methinks I see thee, now thou art below,
    As one dead in the bottom of a tomb.
    Either my eyesight fails or thou look'st pale.   45
ROMEO. And trust me, love, in my eye so do you.
    Dry sorrow drinks° our blood. Adieu, adieu!

                                        [*He turns and goes out.*]

        [*From inside the voice of* LADY CAPULET *is heard.*]

LADY CAPULET. Ho, daughter! Are you up?
JULIET. Who is't that calls? It is my lady mother!
    Is she not down so late, or up so early?   50
    What unaccustomed cause procures her hither?

                    [*Enter* LADY CAPULET.]

LADY CAPULET. Why, how now, Juliet!
JULIET.   Madam, I am not well.
LADY CAPULET. Evermore weeping for your cousin's death?
    What, wilt thou wash him from his grave with tears?
    And if thou couldst, thou couldst not make him live,   55
    Therefore have done. Some grief shows much of love,
    But much of grief shows still some want of wit.
JULIET. Yet let me weep for such a feeling° loss.
LADY CAPULET. So shall you feel the loss, but not the friend
    Which you weep for.
JULIET.   Feeling so the loss,   60
    I cannot choose but ever weep the friend.
LADY CAPULET. Well, girl, thou weep'st not so much for his death
    As that the villain lives which slaughtered him.
JULIET. What villain, madam?
LADY CAPULET.   That same villain, Romeo.
JULIET. [*To herself*] Villain and he be many miles asunder.   65
    God pardon him! I do, with all my heart,
    And yet no man like° he doth grieve my heart.
LADY CAPULET. That is because the traitor murderer lives.
JULIET. Aye, madam, from the reach of these my hands.
    Would none but I might venge my cousin's death!   70
LADY CAPULET. We will have vengeance for it, fear thou not.
    But now I'll tell thee joyful tidings, girl.
JULIET. And joy comes well in such a needy time.
    What are they, I beseech your ladyship?

    42. **ill-divining:** fearful.   47. **drinks:** drains.   58. **feeling:** deeply felt.   67. **like:** as much as.

LADY CAPULET. Well, well, thou hast a careful father, child, 75
 One who, to put thee from thy heaviness,
 Hath sorted° out a sudden day of joy,
 That thou expect'st not, nor I looked not for.
JULIET. Madam, in happy time,° what day is that?
LADY CAPULET. Marry, my child, early next Thursday morn, 80
 The gallant, young, and noble gentleman,
 The County Paris, at Saint Peter's Church,
 Shall happily make thee there a joyful bride.
JULIET. [*Wildly*] Now, by Saint Peter's Church, and Peter too,
 He shall not make me there a joyful bride. 85
 I wonder at this haste, that I must wed
 Ere he that should be husband comes to woo.
 I pray you tell my lord and father, madam,
 I will not marry yet. And when I do, I swear
 It shall be Romeo, whom you know I hate, 90
 Rather than Paris. These are news indeed!
LADY CAPULET. Here comes your father, tell him so yourself
 And see how he will take it at your hands.

[CAPULET, *very cheerful, enters with the* NURSE *and sees* JULIET *weeping*.]

CAPULET. When the sun sets, the air doth drizzle dew,
 But for the sunset of my brother's son 95
 It rains downright.
 How now! A conduit,° girl? What, still in tears?
 Evermore showering? How now, wife!
 Have you delivered to her our decree?
LADY CAPULET. Aye, sir, but she will none, she gives you thanks. 100
 I would the fool were married to her grave!
CAPULET. Soft! Take me with you, take me with you,° wife.
 How! Will she none? Doth she not give us thanks?
 Is she not proud? Doth she not count her blest,
 Unworthy as she is, that we have wrought 105
 So worthy a gentleman to be her bridegroom?
JULIET. Not proud you have, but thankful that you have.
 Proud can I never be of what I hate,
 But thankful even for hate that is meant love.
CAPULET. [*Losing his temper*] How, how! How, how! Chop-logic!° What is
 this? 110
 "Proud," and "I thank you," and "I thank you not,"
 And yet "not proud." Mistress minion,° you,
 Thank me no thankings, nor proud me no prouds,

---

77. **sorted:** chosen. 79. **in happy time:** indeed. 97. **conduit:** fountain. 102. **take me with you:** what do you mean? 110. **Chop-logic:** hair-splitting. 112. **Mistress minion:** saucy miss.

But fettle° your fine joints 'gainst Thursday next,
To go with Paris to Saint Peter's Church,   115
Or I will drag thee on a hurdle° thither.
Out, you green-sickness carrion!° Out, you baggage!
You tallow-face!

[*He becomes so violent that even his wife is shocked.*]

LADY CAPULET.   Fie, fie! What, are you mad?
JULIET. Good Father, I beseech you on my knees,
Hear me with patience but to speak a word.   120
CAPULET. Hang thee, young baggage! Disobedient wretch!
I tell thee what. Get thee to church o' Thursday
Or never after look me in the face.
Speak not, reply not, do not answer me.
My fingers itch. Wife, we scarce thought us blest   125
That God had lent us but this only child,
But now I see this one is one too much,
And that we have a curse in having her.
Out on her, hilding!°
NURSE.   God in Heaven bless her!
You are to blame, my lord, to rate° her so.   130
CAPULET. [*Turning on the* NURSE] And why, my lady wisdom? Hold your tongue,
Good prudence. Smatter° with your gossips, go.
NURSE. I speak no treason.
CAPULET.   Oh, God ye godden.
NURSE. May not one speak?
CAPULET.   Peace, you mumbling fool!
Utter your gravity° o'er a gossip's bowl,   135
For here we need it not.
LADY CAPULET.   You are too hot.
CAPULET. [*Turning his anger back to* JULIET] God's bread! It makes me mad.
Day, night, hour, tide, time, work, play,
Alone, in company, still° my care hath been
To have her matched. And having now provided   140
A gentleman of noble parentage,
Of fair demesnes,° youthful, and nobly trained,
Stuffed, as they say, with honorable parts,°
Proportioned as one's thought would wish a man—
And then to have a wretched puling fool,   145
A whining mammet,° in her fortune's tender,°

---

114. **fettle:** get ready. 116. **hurdle:** a frame used to carry condemned criminals to execution.
117. **green-sickness carrion:** anemic lump of flesh. 129. **hilding:** worthless girl. 130. **rate:** scold.
132. **smatter:** chatter. 135. **gravity:** wise words. 139. **still:** always. 142. **demesnes** (di·mānz′):
estates, wealth. 143. **parts:** qualities. 146. **mammet:** doll. **in her fortune's tender:** when good
fortune is offered to her.

To answer "I'll not wed, I cannot love,
I am too young, I pray you, pardon me."
But an you will not wed, I'll pardon you.
Graze where you will, you shall not house with me.   150
Look to 't, think on 't, I do not use to° jest.
Thursday is near. Lay hand on heart, advise.°
An you be mine, I'll give you to my friend.
An you be not, hang, beg, starve, die in the streets,
For, by my soul, I'll ne'er acknowledge thee,   155
Nor what is mine shall never do thee good—
Trust to 't, bethink you, I'll not be forsworn.°

                                          [*He stamps out.*]

JULIET. Is there no pity sitting in the clouds
    That sees into the bottom of my grief?
    O sweet my mother, cast me not away!   160
    Delay this marriage for a month, a week;
    Or, if you do not, make the bridal bed
    In that dim monument where Tybalt lies.

LADY CAPULET. Talk not to me, for I'll not speak a word.
    Do as thou wilt, for I have done with thee.   165
                                          [*Exit.*]

JULIET. Oh, God!—O Nurse, how shall this be prevented?
    My husband is on earth, my faith in Heaven.
    How shall that faith return again to earth
    Unless that husband send it me from Heaven
    By leaving earth? Comfort me, counsel me.   170
    What say'st thou? Hast thou not a word of joy?
    Some comfort, Nurse.

NURSE.   Faith, here it is.
    Romeo is banished, and all the world to nothing°
    That he dares ne'er come back to challenge° you;
    Or if he do, it needs must be by stealth.   175
    Then, since the case so stands as now it doth,
    I think it best you married with the County.
    Oh, he's a lovely gentleman!
    Romeo's a dishclout to him.°
    Beshrew my very heart,   180
    I think you are happy in this second match,
    For it excels your first. Or if it did not,
    Your first is dead, or 'twere as good he were
    As living here and you no use of him.

JULIET. Speakest thou from thy heart?   185

---

151. **use to:** usually.   152. **advise:** be careful.   157. **be forsworn:** break my vow.   173. **all . . .
nothing:** the odds are overwhelming.   174. **challenge:** claim.   179. **to him:** compared to him.

NURSE. And from my soul too, else beshrew them both.

JULIET. Amen!

NURSE. What?

JULIET. Well, thou hast comforted me marvelous much.
Go in, and tell my lady I am gone, 190
Having displeased my father, to Laurence' cell,
To make confession and to be absolved.

NURSE. Marry, I will, and this is wisely done.

[*Exit.*]

JULIET. Go, counselor. Thou and my bosom° henceforth shall be twain.
I'll to the Friar, to know his remedy. 195
If all else fail, myself have power to die.

[*Exit.*]

194. **bosom:** secrets, inner thoughts.

FOR STUDY AND DISCUSSION

1. Why is Tybalt angry at Romeo? Why does Romeo ignore Tybalt's insult? Why does Mercutio take up the fight? How is Romeo the cause of Mercutio's death?

2. Why, after killing Tybalt, does Romeo call himself "fortune's fool"?

3. Do you consider the Prince's penalty mild, severe, or entirely just? Of what fact is the Prince unaware? Does he seem to be influenced by the fact that Mercutio is his own kin?

4. When Juliet first hears about the duel from her Nurse, what is her reaction? Later in the scene, what "second thoughts" does she have? Which do you think is more admirable: her first impulse or her later change of heart? Why? What do Juliet's reactions in this scene show about her?

5. Why is Romeo in the depths of despair when he learns of the Prince's judgment? What causes his sudden change in spirits? Where else in the play has Romeo undergone such a sudden change in spirits?

6. Which is the stronger character, Juliet or Romeo? How is this shown in their reactions to Romeo's banishment?

7. How does Capulet seem to feel toward Paris? Why might he assume that Juliet shares his feelings? Is the suddenness of his decision that they shall marry typical of Capulet?

8. How does Lady Capulet expect Juliet to react to the news of her coming wedding? How do Lord and Lady Capulet react to Juliet's refusal? What does Capulet threaten if Juliet remains stubborn? Is the violence of his reaction surprising? Why or why not?

9. What does the Nurse advise Juliet to do? Does Juliet agree? What do you think of the Nurse's advice? of Juliet's reaction to it?

ACT IV

SCENE I

[*The curtains at the back open on* FRIAR LAURENCE'S *cell. He enters with* PARIS, *who has come to arrange for his wedding to* JULIET. *The* FRIAR *is much worried at this unexpected news.*]

FRIAR LAURENCE. On Thursday, sir? The time is very short.
PARIS. My father° Capulet will have it so,
    And I am nothing slow to slack his haste.
FRIAR LAURENCE. You say you do not know the lady's mind.
    Uneven is the course, I like it not.   5
PARIS. Immoderately she weeps for Tybalt's death,
    And therefore have I little talked of love,
    For Venus smiles not in a house of tears.
    Now, sir, her father counts it dangerous
    That she doth give her sorrow so much sway,   10
    And in his wisdom hastes our marriage,
    To stop the inundation° of her tears,
    Which, too much minded° by herself alone,
    May be put from her by society.°
    Now do you know the reason of this haste.   15
FRIAR LAURENCE. [*To himself*] I would I knew not why it should be slowed.
    Look, sir, here comes the lady toward my cell.

[*Enter* JULIET.]

PARIS. Happily met, my lady and my wife!
JULIET. That may be, sir, when I may be a wife.
PARIS. That may be must be, love, on Thursday next.   20
JULIET. What must be shall be.
FRIAR LAURENCE.   That's a certain text.
PARIS. Come you to make confession to this Father?
JULIET. To answer that, I should confess to you.
PARIS. Do not deny to him that you love me.
JULIET. I will confess to you that I love him.   25
PARIS. So will ye, I am sure, that you love me.
JULIET. If I do so, it will be of more price
    Being spoke behind your back than to your face.
    Are you at leisure, holy Father, now,
    Or shall I come to you at evening mass?   30
FRIAR LAURENCE. My leisure serves me, pensive° daughter, now.
    My lord, we must entreat the time alone.
PARIS. God shield° I should disturb devotion!

2. **father:** future father-in-law. 12. **inundation:** flood. 13. **minded:** brooded over. 14. **society:** the company of others. 31. **pensive:** thoughtful, solemn. 33. **shield:** forbid.

Juliet, on Thursday early will I rouse ye.
Till then, adieu, and keep this holy kiss.   35

                                                                          [*Exit.*]

JULIET. Oh, shut the door, and when thou hast done so,
    Come weep with me—past hope, past cure, past help!
FRIAR LAURENCE. Ah, Juliet, I already know thy grief,
    It strains me past the compass° of my wits.
    I hear thou must, and nothing may prorogue° it,   40
    On Thursday next be married to this County.
JULIET. Tell me not, Friar, that thou hear'st of this,
    Unless thou tell me how I may prevent it.
    If in thy wisdom thou canst give no help,
    Do thou but call my resolution wise,   45

                    [*She draws out a dagger.*]

    And with this knife I'll help it presently.
    God joined my heart and Romeo's, thou our hands,
    Therefore, out of thy long-experienced time,
    Give me some present counsel; or, behold,
    'Twixt my extremes° and me this bloody knife   50
    Shall play the umpire.
FRIAR LAURENCE. Hold, daughter. I do spy a kind of hope.
    If, rather than to marry County Paris,
    Thou hast the strength of will to slay thyself,
    Then is it likely thou wilt undertake   55
    A thing like death to chide away this shame,
    And, if thou darest, I'll give thee remedy.
JULIET. Oh, bid me leap, rather than marry Paris,
    From off the battlements of yonder tower;
    Or bid me go into a new-made grave,   60
    And hide me with a dead man in his shroud—
    Things that to hear them told have made me tremble—
    And I will do it without fear or doubt,
    To live an unstained wife to my sweet love.
FRIAR LAURENCE. Hold, then, go home, be merry, give consent   65
    To marry Paris. Wednesday is tomorrow.
    Tomorrow night look that thou lie alone,
    Let not thy nurse lie with thee in thy chamber.

                    [*He produces a small bottle.*]

    Take thou this vial, being then in bed,
    And this distillèd liquor drink thou off,   70
    When presently through all thy veins shall run
    A cold and drowsy humor;° for no pulse

---

39. **compass:** reach.   40. **prorogue:** postpone.   50. **extremes:** misfortunes.   72. **humor:** moisture.

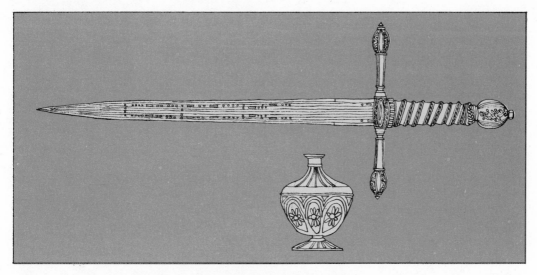

Shall keep his native progress, but surcease.°
No warmth, no breath, shall testify thou livest.
And in this borrowed likeness of shrunk death   75
Thou shalt continue two and forty hours,
And then awake as from a pleasant sleep.
Now, when the bridegroom in the morning comes
To rouse thee from thy bed, there art thou dead.
Then, as the manner of our country is,   80
In thy best robes uncovered on the bier
Thou shalt be borne to that same ancient vault
Where all the kindred of the Capulets lie.
In the meantime, against thou shalt awake,
Shall Romeo by my letters know our drift,°   85
And hither shall he come, and he and I
Will watch thy waking, and that very night
Shall Romeo bear thee hence to Mantua.
And this shall free thee from this present shame,
If no inconstant toy° nor womanish fear   90
Abate thy valor in the acting it.

                [JULIET *takes the bottle.*]

JULIET. Give me, give me! Oh, tell not me of fear!
FRIAR LAURENCE. Hold, get you gone, be strong and prosperous
    In this resolve. I'll send a friar with speed
    To Mantua, with my letters to thy lord.   95
JULIET. Love give me strength! And strength shall help afford.
    Farewell, dear Father!

                           [*Exeunt.*]

73. **surcease:** cease. 85. **drift:** purpose, intention. 90. **inconstant toy:** fickle fancy, foolish whim.

SCENE II

[*In* CAPULET'S *house. Hasty preparations are being made for the wedding. Enter* CAPULET, LADY CAPULET, *the* NURSE, *and* TWO SERVANTS.]

CAPULET. So many guests invite as here are writ.

[*Exit* FIRST SERVANT.]

    Sirrah, go hire me twenty cunning cooks.

SECOND SERVANT. You shall have none ill, sir, for I'll try if they can lick their
    fingers.

CAPULET. How canst thou try them so?   5

SECOND SERVANT. Marry, sir, 'tis an ill cook that cannot lick his own fingers.
    Therefore he that cannot lick his fingers goes not with me.

CAPULET. Go, be gone.

[*Exit* SECOND SERVANT.]

    We shall be much unfurnished° for this time.

    What, is my daughter gone to Friar Laurence?   10

NURSE. Aye, forsooth.

CAPULET. Well he may chance to do some good on her.

    A peevish self-willed harlotry° it is.

[JULIET *approaches*.]

NURSE. See where she comes from shrift° with merry look.

CAPULET. [*Who has recovered from his recent rage*] How now, my headstrong!

    Where have you been gadding?   15

JULIET. [*Lowering her eyes*] Where I have learned me to repent the sin

    Of disobedient opposition

    To you and your behests,° and am enjoined°

    By holy Laurence to fall prostrate° here,

    To beg your pardon.

[*She kneels*.]

    Pardon, I beseech you!   20

    Henceforward I am ever ruled by you.

CAPULET. Send for the County, go tell him of this.

    I'll have this knot knit up tomorrow morning.

JULIET. I met the youthful lord at Laurence' cell,

    And gave him what becomèd° love I might,   25

    Not stepping o'er the bounds of modesty.

CAPULET. Why, I am glad on 't, this is well. Stand up.

    This is as 't should be. Let me see the County.

    Aye, marry, go, I say, and fetch him hither.

    Now, afore God, this reverend holy Friar,   30

    All our whole city is much bound° to him.

---

9. **unfurnished:** unprepared. 13. **harlotry:** hussy. 14. **shrift:** confession. 18. **behests:** commands. **enjoined:** ordered, bidden. 19. **prostrate:** on my knees. 25. **becomèd:** suitable, proper. 31. **bound:** in debt.

JULIET. Nurse, will you go with me into my closet,°
    To help me sort° such needful ornaments
    As you think fit to furnish me tomorrow?
LADY CAPULET. No, not till Thursday, there is time enough.   35
CAPULET. Go, Nurse, go with her. We'll to church tomorrow.

                  [*Exeunt* JULIET *and* NURSE.]

LADY CAPULET. We shall be short in our provision.
    'Tis now near night.
CAPULET.   Tush, I will stir about,
    And all things shall be well, I warrant thee, wife.
    Go thou to Juliet, help to deck up her.   40
    I'll not to bed tonight, let me alone,
    I'll play the housewife for this once. What ho!
    They are all forth. Well, I will walk myself
    To County Paris, to prepare him up
    Against tomorrow. My heart is wondrous light   45
    Since this same wayward girl is so reclaimed.

                        [*Exeunt.*]

SCENE III

[*In* JULIET'S *bedroom,* JULIET *and the* NURSE *are busy selecting clothes for the wedding.*]

JULIET. Aye, those attires are best. But, gentle Nurse,
    I pray thee leave me to myself tonight.

             [*Enter* LADY CAPULET.]

LADY CAPULET. What, are you busy, ho? Need you my help?
JULIET. No, madam, we have culled° such necessaries
    As are behooveful° for our state° tomorrow.   5
    So please you, let me now be left alone,
    And let the nurse this night sit up with you,
    For I am sure you have your hands full all
    In this so sudden business.
LADY CAPULET.   Goodnight.
    Get thee to bed and rest, for thou hast need.   10

        [*Exeunt* LADY CAPULET *and* NURSE, *leaving* JULIET *alone.*]

JULIET. Farewell! God knows when we shall meet again.
    I have a faint cold fear thrills through my veins
    That almost freezes up the heat of life.
    I'll call them back again to comfort me.
    Nurse!—What should she do here?   15

---

32. **closet:** small private room. 33. **sort:** select.
4. **culled:** selected. 5. **behooveful:** suitable. **state:** condition, situation (as bride).

My dismal scene I needs must act alone.
Come, vial.
What if this mixture do not work at all?
Shall I be married then tomorrow morning?
No, no, this shall forbid it. Lie thou there.   20

[She lays the dagger beside her on the bed.]

What if it be a poison which the Friar
Subtly hath ministered° to have me dead,
Lest in this marriage he should be dishonored
Because he married me before to Romeo?
I fear it is. And yet methinks it should not,   25
For he hath still been tried° a holy man.
How if, when I am laid into the tomb,
I wake before the time that Romeo
Come to redeem me? There's a fearful point.
Shall I not then be stifled in the vault,   30
To whose foul mouth no healthsome air breathes in,
And there die strangled ere my Romeo comes?
Or if I live, is it not very like,
The horrible conceit° of death and night,
Together with the terror of the place,   35
As in a vault, an ancient receptacle,
Where for this many hundred years the bones
Of all my buried ancestors are packed;
Where bloody Tybalt, yet but green in earth,°
Lies festering in his shroud; where, as they say,   40
At some hours in the night spirits resort—
Alack, alack, is it not like that I
So early waking, what with loathsome smells
And shrieks like mandrakes'° torn out of the earth,
That living mortals hearing them run mad?   45
Oh, if I wake, shall I not be distraught,
Environèd with all these hideous fears,
And madly play with my forefathers' joints,
And pluck the mangled Tybalt from his shroud,
And in this rage, with some great kinsman's bone,   50
As with a club, dash out my desperate brains?

[She imagines that she sees a horrible vision.]

Oh, look! Methinks I see my cousin's ghost
Seeking out Romeo, that did spit his body

---

22. **ministered:** provided.   26. **tried:** found to be.   34. **conceit:** idea.   39. **green in earth:** newly buried.   44. **mandrakes':** forked roots, which, according to superstition, screamed when dug up.

Upon a rapier's point. Stay, Tybalt, stay!
Romeo, I come! This do I drink to thee. 55

[*She takes up the bottle and drinks. Then she closes the curtains of the bed, and falls down on the bed within.*]

SCENE IV

[*On the stage below, the excitement is growing.* LADY CAPULET *and the* NURSE *enter*]

LADY CAPULET. Hold, take these keys, and fetch more spices, Nurse.
NURSE. They call for dates and quinces in the pastry.°

       [*Enter* CAPULET, *who proceeds to get in everyone's way.*]

CAPULET. Come, stir, stir, stir! The second cock hath crowed,
    The curfew bell hath rung, 'tis three o'clock.
    Look to the baked meats, good Angelica. 5
    Spare not for cost.
NURSE.   Go, you cotquean,° go,
    Get you to bed. Faith, you'll be sick tomorrow
    For this night's watching.
CAPULET. No, not a whit. What! I have watched ere now
    All night for lesser cause, and ne'er been sick. 10
LADY CAPULET. Aye, you have been a mousehunt° in your time,
    But I will watch you from such watching now.
                  [*Exeunt* LADY CAPULET *and* NURSE.]
CAPULET. A jealoushood,° a jealoushood!

    [*Enter three or four servants, with spits, and logs, and baskets.*]

                Now, fellow, What's there?
FIRST SERVANT. Things for the cook, sir, but I know not what.
CAPULET. Make haste, make haste. 15

[*The music of the bridegroom's party is heard.* CAPULET *sends the* NURSE *to rouse* JULIET *and bid her come down.*]

---

2. **pastry:** the room where baking was done. 6. **cotquean** (kot′kwēn): a man who meddles in women's affairs. 11. **mousehunt:** one who follows the girls, a "wolf". 13. **jealoushood:** jealousy.

SCENE V

[*The* NURSE *enters* JULIET'S *bedroom. The curtains are still closed around the bed.*]

NURSE. Mistress! What, mistress! Juliet! Fast, I warrant her, she.
    Why, lamb! Why, lady! Fie, you slugabed!
    Why, love, I say! Madam! Sweetheart! Why, bride!
    What, not a word? How sound is she asleep!
    I needs must wake her. Madam, madam, madam! 5

[*She draws apart the curtains on the bed.*]

    What, dressed! And in your clothes! And down again!
    I must needs wake you. Lady, lady, lady!
    Alas, alas! Help, help! My lady's dead!
    Oh, welladay that ever I was born!
    Some aqua vitae, ho! My lord! My lady! 10

[*Enter* LADY CAPULET.]

LADY CAPULET. What noise is here?
NURSE.   Oh, lamentable day!
LADY CAPULET. What is the matter?
NURSE.   Look, look! Oh, heavy day!
LADY CAPULET. Oh me, oh me! My child, my only life,
    Revive, look up, or I will die with thee.
    Help! help! Call help. 15

[*Enter* CAPULET.]

CAPULET. For shame, bring Juliet forth, her lord is come.
NURSE. She's dead, deceased, she's dead, alack the day!
LADY CAPULET. Alack the day, she's dead, she's dead, she's dead!
CAPULET. Ha! Let me see her. Out, alas! She's cold.
    Her blood is settled and her joints are stiff. 20
    Life and these lips have long been separated.
    Death lies on her like an untimely frost
    Upon the sweetest flower of all the field.
NURSE. Oh, lamentable day!
LADY CAPULET.   Oh, woeful time!
CAPULET. Death, that hath ta'en her hence to make me wail, 25
    Ties up my tongue and will not let me speak.

[*Enter* FRIAR LAURENCE *and* PARIS, *with* MUSICIANS.]

FRIAR LAURENCE. Come, is the bride ready to go to church?
CAPULET. Ready to go, but never to return.

Death is my son-in-law, Death is my heir,
My daughter he hath wedded. I will die, 30
And leave him all—life, living, all is Death's.
PARIS. Have I thought long to see this morning's face
And doth it give me such a sight as this?
LADY CAPULET. Accurst, unhappy, wretched, hateful day!
Most miserable hour that e'er time saw 35
In lasting labor of his pilgrimage!
But one, poor one, one poor and loving child,
But one thing to rejoice and solace° in,
And cruel death hath catched it from my sight!
NURSE. Oh, woe! Oh, woeful, woeful, woeful day! 40
Most lamentable day, most woeful day,
That ever, ever, I did yet behold!
Oh, day, oh, day, oh, day! Oh, hateful day!
Never was seen so black a day as this.
Oh, woeful day, oh, woeful day! 45
PARIS. Beguiled, divorced, wronged, spited, slain!
Most detestable death, by thee beguiled,
By cruel cruel thee quite overthrown!
Oh, love! Oh, life! Not life, but love in death!
CAPULET. Despised, distressed, hated, martyred, killed! 50
Dead art thou! Alack, my child is dead,
And with my child my joys are burièd!
FRIAR LAURENCE. Peace ho, for shame! Confusion's cure lives not
In these confusions. Heaven and yourself
Had part in this fair maid, now Heaven hath all, 55
And all the better is it for the maid.
Your part in her you could not keep from death,
But Heaven keeps his part in eternal life.
CAPULET. All things that we ordainèd° festival
Turn from their office to black funeral. 60
Our instruments to melancholy bells,
Our wedding cheer to a sad burial feast,
Our solemn hymns to sullen dirges change,
Our bridal flowers serve for a buried corse,
And all things change them to the contrary. 65
FRIAR LAURENCE. Sir, go you in, and, madam, go with him.
And go, Sir Paris, everyone prepare
To follow this fair corse unto her grave.
The Heavens do lour° upon you for some ill;°
Move them no more by crossing their high will. 70
[Exeunt.]

38. solace: take comfort. 59. ordained: intended for. 69. lour: frown, scowl. ill: misdeed.

1. Why has Paris come to Friar Laurence's cell? Why do you think the Friar doesn't tell him or the Capulets that Juliet is already married to Romeo? From what you know of the Friar, do you think he is wary for his own sake or for the sake of Romeo and Juliet?

2. How does Paris greet Juliet? How does she reply? What do her replies show about her attitude toward Paris? Is he aware of her attitude? How do you know?

3. When Paris has gone, what does Juliet threaten to do? What plan does the Friar propose as a way out of her difficulty? What is the time limit on the plan? How is Romeo to be informed of his part in the plan?

4. When Juliet returns home, why does she pretend to accept her father's wishes? In his joy at her seeming change of heart, what change does Capulet make in the wedding plans? How will this change affect the timing of the Friar's plan? Why doesn't Juliet think of this?

5. What doubts does Juliet have before drinking the Friar's potion? How does she reassure herself? What is her great fear? What finally causes her to drink the potion? How does she show herself to be a courageous person?

6. What is ironic about the cheerful bustle of the wedding preparations?

7. As Juliet drinks the potion, are things working out as the Friar intended? According to his plan, what is the next step? What could still go wrong?

ACT V

SCENE I

[At Mantua, ROMEO *is waiting for news from Verona.]*

ROMEO. If I may trust the flattering truth of sleep,°
    My dreams presage° some joyful news at hand.
    My bosom's lord° sits lightly in his throne,
    And all this day an unaccustomed spirit
    Lifts me above the ground with cheerful thoughts.   5
    I dreamed my lady came and found me dead
    And breathed such life with kisses in my lips
    That I revived and was an emperor.

        [Enter BALTHASAR, ROMEO'S SERVANT *in riding clothes.]*

    News from Verona! How now, Balthasar!
    Dost thou not bring me letters from the Friar?   10
    How doth my lady? Is my father well?
    How fares my Juliet? That I ask again;
    For nothing can be ill if she be well.
BALTHASAR. Then she is well, and nothing can be ill.
    Her body sleeps in Capels' monument,   15

---

1. **flattering . . . sleep:** happy dreams that seemed true.   2. **presage:** foretell.   3. **bosom's lord:** heart.

And her immortal part with angels lives.
I saw her laid low in her kindred's vault,
And presently took post° to tell it you.
Oh, pardon me for bringing these ill news,
Since you did leave it for my office,° sir.   20

ROMEO. Is it e'en so? Then I defy you, stars!
Thou know'st my lodging. Get me ink and paper,
And hire post° horses. I will hence tonight.

BALTHASAR. I do beseech you, sir, have patience.
Your looks are pale and wild, and do import°   25
Some misadventure.°

ROMEO.   Tush, thou art deceived.
Leave me, and do the thing I bid thee do.
Hast thou no letters to me from the Friar?

BALTHASAR. No, my good lord.

ROMEO.   No matter. Get thee gone,
And hire those horses. I'll be with thee straight.   30

[*Exit* BALTHASAR.]

Well, Juliet, I will lie with thee tonight.
Let's see for means.—O mischief, thou art swift
To enter in the thoughts of desperate men!
I do remember an apothecary,
And hereabouts he dwells, which late I noted   35
In tattered weeds,° with overwhelming° brows,
Culling of simples.° Meager were his looks,
Sharp misery had worn him to the bones.
And in his needy shop a tortoise hung,
An alligator stuffed and other skins   40
Of ill-shaped fishes; and about his shelves
A beggarly account° of empty boxes,
Green earthen pots, bladders, and musty seeds,
Remnants of packthread and old cakes of roses,°
Were thinly scattered, to make up a show.   45
Noting this penury, to myself I said,
"An if a man did need a poison now,
Whose sale is present death in Mantua,
Here lives a caitiff° wretch would sell it him."
Oh, this same thought did but forerun my need,   50
And this same needy man must sell it me.
As I remember, this should be the house.
Being holiday, the beggar's shop is shut.
What ho! Apothecary!

---

18. **took post:** rode fast.   20. **office:** duty.   23. **post:** fast.   25. **import:** suggest, imply.   26. **misadventure:** misfortune.   36. **weeds:** clothes.   **overwhelming:** overhanging.   37. **simples:** herbs.   42. **account:** collection.   44. **roses:** rose leaves.   49. **caitiff** (kā′tif): miserable.

[*The* APOTHECARY *opens the door of his shop.*]

APOTHECARY. Who calls so loud?

ROMEO. Come hither, man. I see that thou art poor. 55
Hold, there is forty ducats. Let me have
A dram of poison, such soon-speeding gear°
As will disperse itself through all the veins,
That the life-weary taker may fall dead.

APOTHECARY. Such mortal drugs I have, but Mantua's law 60
Is death to any he that utters° them.

ROMEO. Art thou so bare and full of wretchedness,
And fear'st to die? Famine is in thy cheeks,
Need and oppression starveth in thy eyes,
Contempt and beggary hangs upon thy back, 65
The world is not thy friend, nor the world's law.
The world affords no law to make thee rich,
Then be not poor, but break it, and take this.

APOTHECARY. My poverty, but not my will, consents.

ROMEO. I pay thy poverty and not thy will. 70

[*The* APOTHECARY *goes back into the shop and returns with a small packet.*]

APOTHECARY. Put this in any liquid thing you will,
And drink if off, and if you had the strength
Of twenty men, it would dispatch you straight.

ROMEO. There is thy gold, worse poison to men's souls,
Doing more murder in this loathsome world 75
Than these poor compounds that thou mayst not sell.
I sell thee poison, thou hast sold me none.
Farewell. Buy food, and get thyself in flesh.

57. **gear:** stuff. 61. **utters:** sells.

Come, cordial° and not poison, go with me
To Juliet's grave, for there must I use thee.   80

[Exeunt.]

SCENE II

[Outside FRIAR LAURENCE'S cell. FRIAR JOHN enters in great haste.]

FRIAR JOHN. Holy Franciscan friar! Brother, ho!

[Enter FRIAR LAURENCE.]

FRIAR LAURENCE. This same should be the voice of Friar John.
    Welcome from Mantua. What says Romeo?
    Or if his mind be writ, give me his letter.
FRIAR JOHN. Going to find a barefoot brother out,   5
    One of our order, to associate° me
    Here in this city visiting the sick,
    And finding him, the searchers of the town,
    Suspecting that we both were in a house
    Where the infectious pestilence° did reign,   10
    Sealed up the doors and would not let us forth,
    So that my speed to Mantua there was stayed.
FRIAR LAURENCE. Who bare my letter, then, to Romeo?
FRIAR JOHN. I could not send it—here it is again—
    Nor get a messenger to bring it thee,   15
    So fearful were they of infection.
FRIAR LAURENCE. Unhappy fortune! By my brotherhood.
    The letter was not nice,° but full of charge°
    Of dear import,° and the neglecting it
    May do much danger. Friar John, go hence.   20
    Get me an iron crow° and bring it straight
    Unto my cell.
FRIAR JOHN. Brother, I'll go and bring it thee.

[Exit.]

FRIAR LAURENCE. Now must I to the monument alone.
    Within this three hours will fair Juliet wake.   25
    She will beshrew° me much that Romeo
    Hath had no notice of these accidents.
    But I will write again to Mantua,
    And keep her at my cell till Romeo come.
    Poor living corse, closed in a dead man's tomb.   30

[Exit.]

---

79. **cordial:** restorative medicine.
   6. **associate:** accompany. 10. **pestilence:** plague. When a case of the plague was discovered, all persons living in the house were locked in to prevent the infection from spreading. 18. **nice:** trivial. **charge:** instructions. 19. **dear import:** great importance. 21. **crow:** crowbar. 26. **beshrew:** blame.

SCENE III

[The curtains at the back of the stage are drawn aside, showing the doorway of the CAPULETS' *family tomb.* PARIS *enters with his* PAGE, *who carries flowers and a torch.]*

PARIS. Give me thy torch, boy. Hence, and stand aloof.
  Yet put it out, for I would not be seen.
  Under yond yew trees lay thee all along,°
  Holding thine ear close to the hollow ground.
  So shall no foot upon the churchyard tread,   5
  Being loose, unfirm, with digging up of graves,
  But thou shalt hear it. Whistle then to me,
  As signal that thou hear'st something approach.
  Give me those flowers. Do as I bid thee, go.
PAGE. *[To himself]* I am almost afraid to stand alone   10
  Here in the churchyard, yet I will adventure.

[He withdraws to one side of the stage.]

PARIS. Sweet flower, with flowers thy bridal bed I strew—
  Oh, woe! Thy canopy is dust and stones—
  The obsequies° that I for thee will keep
  Nightly shall be to strew thy grave and weep.   15

[The PAGE *whistles.]*

  The boy gives warning something doth approach.
  What cursèd foot wanders this way tonight?
  What, with a torch! Muffle° me, night, awhile.

[He hides as ROMEO *and* BALTHASAR *enter, carrying a torch, a mattock, and a crowbar.]*

ROMEO. Give me that mattock and the wrenching iron.
  Hold, take this letter. Early in the morning   20
  See thou deliver it to my lord and father.
  Give me the light. Upon thy life, I charge thee,
  Whate'er thou hear'st or seest, stand all aloof,
  And do not interrupt me in my course.
  Why I descend into this bed of death   25
  Is partly to behold my lady's face,
  But chiefly to take thence from her dear finger
  A precious ring, a ring that I must use
  In dear employment.° Therefore hence, be gone.
  But if thou, jealous,° dost return to pry   30
  In what I farther shall intend to do,
  By Heaven, I will tear thee joint by joint

---

3. **all along:** at full length. 14. **obsequies** (ob'sə·kwēz): funeral ceremonies. 18. **Muffle:** conceal.
29. **In dear employment:** for an important purpose. 30. **jealous:** curious.

And strew this hungry churchyard with thy limbs.
BALTHASAR. I will be gone, sir, and not trouble you.
ROMEO. So shalt thou show me friendship. Take thou that.   35
    Live, and be prosperous, and farewell, good fellow.
BALTHASAR. [*To himself*] For all this same, I'll hide me hereabout.
    His looks I fear, and his intents I doubt. [*He hides.*]
ROMEO. Thou detestable maw,° thou womb of death,
    Gorged with the dearest morsel of the earth,   40
    Thus I enforce thy rotten jaws to open,
    And in despite° I'll cram thee with more food.

      [*With the mattock, he pries open the door of the tomb.*]

PARIS. This is that banished haughty Montague
    That murdered my love's cousin, with which grief
    It is supposèd the fair creature died,   45
    And here is come to do some villainous shame
    To the dead bodies. I will apprehend° him.

      [*He comes forward and confronts* ROMEO.]

    Stop thy unhallowed toil, vile Montague!
    Can vengeance be pursued further than death?
    Condemnèd villain, I do apprehend thee.   50
    Obey, and go with me, for thou must die.
ROMEO. I must indeed, and therefore came I hither.
    Good gentle youth, tempt not a desperate man.
    Fly hence and leave me. Think upon these gone,
    Let them affright thee. I beseech thee, youth,   55
    Put not another sin upon my head,
    By urging me to fury. Oh, be gone!
    By Heaven I love thee better than myself,
    For I come hither armed against myself.
    Stay not, be gone. Live, and hereafter say   60
    A madman's mercy bid thee run away.

39. **maw:** stomach.   42. **despite:** scorn, defiance.   47. **apprehend:** arrest.

PARIS. I do defy thy conjurations°
 And apprehend thee for a felon here.
ROMEO. Wilt thou provoke me? Then have at thee, boy!

[*They draw their swords and fight.*]

PAGE. Oh, Lord, they fight! I will go call the watch.   65

[*He runs out.*]

PARIS. Oh, I am slain! If thou be merciful,
 Open the tomb, lay me with Juliet.

[PARIS *falls and dies.*]

ROMEO. In faith, I will. Let me peruse this face.
 Mercutio's kinsman, noble County Paris!
 What said my man, when my betossèd° soul   70
 Did not attend° him as we rode? I think
 He told me Paris should have married Juliet.
 Said he not so? Or did I dream it so?
 Or am I mad, hearing him talk of Juliet,
 To think it was so? Oh, give me thy hand,   75
 One writ with me in sour misfortune's book!
 I'll bury thee in a triumphant grave—
 A grave? Oh, no, a lantern,° slaughtered youth;
 For here lies Juliet, and her beauty makes
 This vault a feasting presence° full of light.   80
 Death, lie thou there, by a dead man interred.

[*He drags* PARIS'S *body inside the tomb.*]

 How oft when men are at the point of death
 Have they been merry! Which their keepers call
 A lightning° before death. Oh, how may I
 Call this a lightning?

[*He sees* JULIET *lying on a bier.*]

                    O my love! My wife!   85
 Death, that hath sucked the honey of thy breath,
 Hath had no power yet upon thy beauty.
 Thou art not conquered; beauty's ensign° yet
 Is crimson in thy lips and in thy cheeks,
 And death's pale flag is not advancèd there.   90
 Tybalt, liest thou there in thy bloody sheet?
 Oh, what more favor can I do to thee
 Than with that hand that cut thy youth in twain

---

62. **conjurations:** spells. 70. **betossèd:** upset, agitated. 71. **attend:** listen to. 78. **lantern:** lofty tomb.
80. **a feasting presence:** like a hall brightly lit for a feast. 84. **lightning:** brightening. 88. **ensign:** flag.

To sunder° his that was thine enemy?
Forgive me, Cousin! Ah, dear Juliet,   95
Why art thou yet so fair?
Here, here will I remain
With worms that are thy chambermaids. Oh, here
Will I set up my everlasting rest,
And shake the yoke of inauspicious° stars   100
From this world-wearied flesh. Eyes, look your last!
Arms, take your last embrace! And lips, O you
The doors of breath, seal with a righteous kiss
A dateless° bargain to engrossing° death!
Come, bitter conduct,° come, unsavory guide!   105
Thou desperate pilot, now at once run on
The dashing rocks thy seasick weary bark.°
Here's to my love!

[*He drinks the poison.*]

     O true apothecary!
Thy drugs are quick. Thus with a kiss I die.

[*He falls dead beside* JULIET. *Through one of the doors* FRIAR LAURENCE *enters,
carrying a lantern, a crowbar, and a spade.*]

FRIAR LAURENCE. Saint Francis be my speed!° How oft tonight   110
    Have my old feet stumbled at graves! Who's there?
BALTHASAR. Here's one a friend, and one that knows you well.
FRIAR LAURENCE. Bliss be upon you! Tell me, good my friend,
    What torch is yond that vainly lends his light
    To grubs and eyeless skulls? As I discern,   115
    It burneth in the Capel's monument.
BALTHASAR. It doth so, holy sir, and there's my master,
    One that you love.
FRIAR LAURENCE.   Who is it?
BALTHASAR.   Romeo.
FRIAR LAURENCE. How long hath he been there?
BALTHASAR.   Full half an hour.
FRIAR LAURENCE. Go with me to the vault.
BALTHASAR.   I dare not, sir.   120
    My master knows not but I am gone hence,
    And fearfully did menace me with death
    If I did stay to look on his intents.
FRIAR LAURENCE. Stay, then, I'll go alone. Fear comes upon me—
    Oh, much I fear some ill unlucky thing.   125
BALTHASAR. As I did sleep under this yew tree here,

---

94. **sunder:** cut off. 100. **inauspicious:** unlucky. 104. **dateless:** unending. **engrossing:** all-encompassing. 105. **conduct:** guide. 107. **bark:** ship. 110. **speed:** help.

I dreamed my master and another fought,
And that my master slew him.

FRIAR LAURENCE.   Romeo!

[*He approaches the open door of the tomb.*]

Alack, alack, what blood is this which stains
The stony entrance of this sepulcher?   130
What mean these masterless and gory swords
To lie discolored by this place of peace?

[*He enters the tomb.*]

Romeo! Oh, pale! Who else? What, Paris too?
And steeped in blood? Ah, what an unkind hour
Is guilty of this lamentable chance!   135
The lady stirs.

[JULIET *opens her eyes.*]

JULIET. O comfortable° Friar! Where is my lord?
I do remember well where I should be,
And there I am. Where is my Romeo?

[*Noise within.*]

FRIAR LAURENCE. I hear some noise. Lady, come from that nest   140
Of death, contagion, and unnatural sleep.
A greater power than we can contradict
Hath thwarted our intents. Come, come away.
Thy husband in thy bosom there lies dead,
And Paris too. Come, I'll dispose of thee   145
Among a sisterhood of holy nuns.
Stay not to question, for the watch is coming.
Come, go, good Juliet, I dare no longer stay.

JULIET. Go, get thee hence, for I will not away.

[FRIAR LAURENCE *hurries away.* JULIET, *now fully awake, sees* ROMEO *lying dead
by her side.*]

What's here? A cup, closed in my true love's hand?   150
Poison, I see, hath been his timeless° end.
O churl! Drunk all, and left no friendly drop
To help me after? I will kiss thy lips—
Haply° some poison yet doth hang on them
To make me die with a restorative.°   155

[*She kisses him.*]

Thy lips are warm.

[*The voice of a watchman is heard off-stage.*]

137. **comfortable:** comforting.   151. **timeless:** untimely.   154. **haply:** perhaps.   155. **restorative:**
a drug that restores to life.

FIRST WATCHMAN. Lead, boy. Which way?

JULIET. Yea, noise? Then I'll be brief. O happy dagger!

[*Snatching* ROMEO'S *dagger.*]

This is thy sheath. [*Stabs herself.*] There rust, and let me die.

[JULIET *falls dead on* ROMEO'S *body. The* WATCH *enters, led by* PARIS'S PAGE.]

PAGE. This is the place—there, where the torch doth burn.   160

FIRST WATCHMAN. The ground is bloody. Search about the churchyard.
　　Go, some of you, whoe'er you find attach.°
　　Pitiful sight! Here lies the County slain,
　　And Juliet bleeding, warm, and newly dead,
　　Who here hath lain this two days burièd.   165
　　Go tell the Prince. Run to the Capulets,
　　Raise up the Montagues. Some others search.
　　We see the ground whereon these woes do lie,
　　But the true ground° of all these piteous woes
　　We cannot without circumstance° descry.°   170

[*Reenter some of the* WATCH, *with* BALTHASAR.]

SECOND WATCHMAN. Here's Romeo's man. We found him in the churchyard.

FIRST WATCHMAN. Hold him in safety till the Prince come hither.

[*Reenter* FRIAR LAURENCE, *and another* WATCHMAN.]

THIRD WATCHMAN. Here is a friar that trembles, sighs, and weeps.
　　We took this mattock and this spade from him
　　As he was coming from this churchyard's side.   175

FIRST WATCHMAN. A great suspicion. Stay the friar too.

[*Enter the* PRINCE *and* ATTENDANTS.]

PRINCE. What misadventure is so early up
　　That calls our person from our morning rest?

[*Enter* CAPULET, LADY CAPULET, *and others.*]

CAPULET. What should it be that they so shriek abroad?

LADY CAPULET. The people in the street cry Romeo,   180
　　Some Juliet, and some Paris, and all run
　　With open outcry toward our monument.

PRINCE. What fear is this which startles in our ears?

FIRST WATCHMAN. Sovereign, here lies the County Paris slain,
　　And Romeo dead, and Juliet, dead before,   185
　　Warm and new-killed.

PRINCE. Search, seek, and know how this foul murder comes.

FIRST WATCHMAN. Here is a friar, and slaughtered Romeo's man,

162. **attach:** arrest.　169. **ground:** cause.　170. **circumstance:** knowledge of the facts.　**descry:** understand.

With instruments upon them fit to open
These dead men's tombs.   190
CAPULET. Oh, heavens! O wife, look how our daughter bleeds!
This dagger hath mista'en, for, lo, his house°
Is empty on the back of Montague,
And it mis-sheathèd in my daughter's bosom!
LADY CAPULET. Oh me! This sight of death is as a bell°   195
That warns° my old age to a sepulcher.

[*Enter* MONTAGUE *and others*.]

PRINCE. Come, Montague, for thou art early up,
To see thy son and heir more early down.
MONTAGUE. Alas, my liege, my wife is dead tonight,
Grief of my son's exile hath stopped her breath.   200
What further woe conspires against mine age?
PRINCE. Look, and thou shalt see.
MONTAGUE. O thou untaught! What manners is in this,
To press before thy father to a grave?
PRINCE. Seal up the mouth of outrage° for a while   205
Till we can clear these ambiguities
And know their spring,° their head, their true descent.

[*The door of the tomb is closed*.]

Bring forth the parties of suspicion.°
FRIAR LAURENCE. I am the greatest, able to do least,
Yet most suspected, as the time and place   210
Doth make against me, of this direful murder.
And here I stand, both to impeach° and purge°
Myself condemnèd and myself excused.
PRINCE. Then say at once what thou dost know in this.
FRIAR LAURENCE. I will be brief, for my short date of breath°   215
Is not so long as is a tedious tale.
Romeo, there dead, was husband to that Juliet,
And she, there dead, that Romeo's faithful wife.
I married them, and their stol'n marriage day
Was Tybalt's doomsday, whose untimely death   220
Banished the new-made bridegroom from this city,
For whom, and not for Tybalt, Juliet pined.
You, to remove that siege of grief from her,
Betrothed and would have married her perforce
To County Paris. Then comes she to me,   225
And with wild looks bid me devise some mean
To rid her from this second marriage,

192. **house:** sheath. 195. **bell:** church bells tolled for the dead. 196. **warns:** tells me that soon
I too must die. 205. **mouth of outrage:** the tomb where terrible deeds were done. 207. **spring:** source.
208. **parties of suspicion:** suspected persons. 212. **impeach:** accuse. **purge:** clear (of guilt). 215. **my
short . . . breath:** the little life left me.

Or in my cell there would she kill herself.
Then gave I her, so tutored by my art,
A sleeping potion, which so took effect   230
As I intended, for it wrought on her
The form of death. Meantime I writ to Romeo
That he should hither come as this° dire night,
To help to take her from her borrowed° grave,
Being the time the potion's force should cease.   235
But he which bore my letter, Friar John,
Was stayed by accident, and yesternight
Returned my letter back. Then all alone
At the prefixèd hour of her waking
Came I to take her from her kindred's vault,   240
Meaning to keep her closely° at my cell
Till I conveniently could send to Romeo.
But when I came, some minute ere the time
Of her awaking, here untimely lay
The noble Paris and true Romeo dead.   245
She wakes, and I entreated her come forth,
And bear this work of Heaven with patience.
But then a noise did scare me from the tomb,
And she too desperate would not go with me,
But, as it seems, did violence on herself.   250
All this I know, and to the marriage
Her nurse is privy.° And if aught in this
Miscarried by my fault, let my old life
Be sacrificed some hour before his time
Unto the rigor of severest law.   255
PRINCE. We still° have known thee for a holy man.
    Where's Romeo's man? What can he say in this?
BALTHASAR. I brought my master news of Juliet's death,
    And then in post° he came from Mantua
    To this same place, to this same monument.   260
    This letter he early bid me give his father,
    And threatened me with death, going in the vault,
    If I departed not and left him there.
PRINCE. Give me the letter, I will look on it.
    Where is the County's page, that raised the watch?   265
    Sirrah, what made° your master in this place?
PAGE. He came with flowers to strew his lady's grave,
    And bid me stand aloof, and so I did.
    Anon comes one with light to ope the tomb,
    And by and by my master drew on him,   270
    And then I ran away to call the watch.

---

233. **as this:** this same. 234. **borrowed:** temporary. 241. **closely:** secretly. 252. **is privy:** shares the secret. 256. **still:** always. 259. **post:** haste. 266. **made:** did.

PRINCE. This letter doth make good the Friar's words,
    Their course of love, the tidings of her death.
    And here he writes that he did buy a poison
    Of a poor 'pothecary, and therewithal   275
    Came to this vault to die and lie with Juliet.
    Where be these enemies? Capulet! Montague!
    See what a scourge° is laid upon your hate
    That Heaven finds means to kill your joys with love!
    And I, for winking° at your discords too,   280
    Have lost a brace° of kinsmen. All are punished.
CAPULET. O Brother Montague, give me thy hand.
    This is my daughter's jointure,° for no more
    Can I demand.
MONTAGUE.   But I can give thee more.
    For I will raise her statue in pure gold,   285
    That whiles Verona by that name is known
    There shall no figure at such rate° be set
    As that of true and faithful Juliet.
CAPULET. As rich shall Romeo's by his lady's lie,
    Poor sacrifices of our enmity!   290
PRINCE. A glooming peace this morning with it brings,
    The sun for sorrow will not show his head.
    Go hence, to have more talk of these sad things.
    Some shall be pardoned and some punishèd.
    For never was a story of more woe   295
    Than this of Juliet and her Romeo.

[All walk off sorrowfully.]

278. **scourge:** punishment. 280. **winking:** shutting my eyes. 281. **brace:** pair. 283. **jointure:** wedding gift. 287. **rate:** value.

FOR STUDY AND DISCUSSION

1. What is Romeo's mood before he receives the news of Juliet? How does he react to the news? Is this reaction similar to some of his earlier reactions? Explain.

2. What argument does Romeo use to persuade the Apothecary to sell him poison? Is his argument convincing?

3. Why wasn't Friar John able to deliver Friar Laurence's message to Romeo? Why couldn't he get anyone else to deliver it? How does this affect the Friar's plan?

4. Why does Paris come to the tomb? Why is he so angry when he sees Romeo? What does Romeo's reply to Paris reveal about Romeo's mood? What effect does Paris's last request have on Romeo?

5. How is Romeo affected by the sight of Juliet in the tomb? How does Romeo swear his love for the last time?

6. When Juliet awakens, what does Friar Laurence want her to do? Why won't she? Why do you think the Friar doesn't force her to come away with him?

7. Why does Juliet kill herself so quickly? Is her determination and the suddenness of her decision typical of her? Where else in the play does she deeply commit herself by making a quick decision?

8. Are the final explanations after Juliet's death necessary to bring the play to an end? Is the play primarily about Romeo and Juliet or about the feud between their families? What in the play makes you think so?

9. What is represented, or symbolized, by the golden statues that Montague and Capulet promise to erect? Why is it ironic that the parents wish to erect a monument to their children's love? How would they have reacted to their love earlier in the play?

THE PLAY AS A WHOLE

1. Reread the opening speech of the Chorus. Is it an accurate summary of the play? Does it leave out any important elements of the plot? Which words in this speech take on new meaning after you have read the play? In what sense do you think the "dignity" of the two houses is responsible for the catastrophe? Do you agree with lines 10–11 that nothing but the lovers' death could end the feud? Why or why not?

2. One of the excellent things about Shakespeare's plays is that each scene is written to achieve one principal result. The purpose of the first scene, for example, could be to show the violence of the feud between the Montagues and the Capulets. What would you say is the purpose of the second scene? (What is the main incident in this scene?) Make an outline of the purpose or main action of each scene in the play. Does your outline contain all the main events of the play?

3. Many of the events in *Romeo and Juliet* are "accidents"—that is, they do not necessarily happen because of what has occurred earlier. Consider, for example, Romeo's meeting the servant with invitations to Capulet's feast. Is this "accident" believable, or is it an obvious device on the part of the author? Point out three other "accidents" and show why they are or are not believable.

4. What is Juliet like when she first appears in the play? How does she change when she meets Romeo? Where else in the play does she show new and different sides of her character? By the end of the play, what kind of person has she shown herself to be?

5. At the beginning of the play, Romeo does not know Juliet. Summarize briefly the events that lead them to meet and fall in love. In order to marry, Romeo and Juliet had to overcome many obstacles. At what points in the play might lesser persons have found the obstacles too great and given up? What qualities in Romeo and Juliet enabled them to persevere?

6. What is your final impression of Friar Laurence? Did he mean well in everything he did? Was it at all his fault that his plans went wrong? Several times in the play the Friar cautions Romeo against being impatient. Do you think he could have profited from following his own advice? Support your answer with specific examples from the play.

FOR COMPOSITION

1. Romeo and Tybalt are about the same age but very different as individuals. In a short composition, explain how each differs from the other in temperament.

2. Friar Laurence and the Nurse are both colorful and important supporting characters in this play. In a short composition analyze the differences between these two characters. How would you describe the way in which each speaks and acts? How does each react to the incidents of the play? In your final paragraph, state which character you like better, and why.

3. Lord Capulet is another extremely well-drawn character. What kind of person is he? In a short composition, point out Capulet's dominant traits and characteristics, giving examples from the text of the play. Be sure to explain, for example, why Capulet stops Tybalt from challenging Romeo at the party in Act I, Scene v; why he decides suddenly in Act III, Scene iv, that Juliet shall marry Paris without delay; and why he reacts as he does, in Scene v, when Juliet refuses.

4. Reread Romeo's description of the Apothecary's shop. Using the details given in Act V, Scene i, and adding some of your own, write a descriptive paragraph about the Apothecary's shop. Try to convey your impression upon stepping into the shop.

Reading and Writing about Shakespeare

One way of gaining a better understanding of Shakespeare's plays is to read what has been written about them. Look, for example, at the following comments on *Romeo and Juliet*. Read each one carefully, then write a paragraph or two supporting or contradicting the writer's argument with quotations and evidence from the play.

This is a tragedy of youth, as youth sees it, and age is not let play a very distinguished part. Friar Laurence is sympathetic, but he is compact of maxims, of pedagogic kindness; he is just such a picture of an old man as a young man draws, all unavailing wisdom. (Harley Granville-Barker, *Prefaces to Shakespeare*.)

Is Friar Laurence "compact [full] of maxims" and "pedagogic kindness"? (Check the exact meanings of these words.) Is his wisdom "unavailing"?

The Nurse, whatever her age, is a triumphant and complete achievement. She stands foursquare, and lives and breathes in her own right from the moment she appears. You may, indeed, take any sentence the Nurse speaks throughout the play, and only she could speak it. (Granville-Barker, *Prefaces to Shakespeare*.)

What does "She stands foursquare" suggest about the Nurse's character? Do you agree with the last sentence?

Juliet begins as a demure girl who is prepared to listen respectfully to the advice of her mother. When she has fallen in love, she becomes suddenly a woman of great courage and resource, who will face even death and fantastic horror to regain her husband. (G. B. Harrison, *Shakespeare: The Complete Works*.)

When we first see Juliet, is she demure? Where does she later show other qualities?

In reading each of the following quotations, ask yourself the kind of questions suggested in the previous examples.

Romeo's hearing of Juliet's death is best taken with a terrible quiet . . . giving a new depth to contrast with his earlier abandon. His description of the Apothecary is very important, and should be done slowly. New worlds are swimming into his ken. Tragic experience now for the first time opens his eyes to suffering and impoverished humanity. (G. Wilson Knight, *Shakespearian Production*.)

In *Romeo and Juliet* the beauty and ardor of young love is seen by Shakespeare as the irradiating glory of sunlight and starlight in a dark world. The dominating image is *light* . . . the sun, moon, stars, fire, lightning, the flash of gunpowder, and the reflected light of beauty and of love; while by contrast we have night, darkness, clouds, rain, mist, and smoke. Each of the lovers thinks of the other as light. (Caroline Spurgeon, "The Imagery of Romeo and Juliet.")

ART AND LITERATURE

You have seen how Shakespeare used light and darkness in the imagery of *Romeo and Juliet*. Painters as well as poets are concerned with this fundamental opposition. Select a painting from pages 451–56 which shows a striking use of light and darkness, and discuss this use in a short essay.

THE ODYSSEY

An Epic Poem

THE *Iliad* and the *Odyssey,* the two great epic poems by the Greek poet Homer, have long been known and admired throughout the western world. An *epic* is a long narrative poem about the exploits of a national or legendary hero. The ancient Greeks recited Homer's epics in public every four years before a great convocation in Athens at the festival of Athene, the goddess of wisdom and patroness of the city. In time, the study of Homer's epics became the basis of Greek education. From Homer, Greek youths learned how to tell a story, to portray character, to give a speech, and to express the Greek ideals of thought and action. It was also from Homer's suggestions that the great Greek philosophers started their inquiries on the nature of God and human life.

Later, Roman poets and writers, notably Virgil, modeled their epics on Homer's works, and for centuries European school children read Homer. Great poets, among them Dryden and Pope, translated and paraphrased him. To this day Homer is read the world over. Who was this poet whose work has delighted so many successive generations? What quality in Homer's work has enabled it to survive?

We know few firmly established facts about Homer, the man, except that he lived and wrote. He most probably lived between 850 and 800 B.C. Although seven cities claimed him as a native son, we cannot be sure where he was born. We do know that during his lifetime he was greatly honored as the first poet to combine isolated tales about various heroic exploits into a single, coherent whole, thus creating the epic. A persistent tradition tells us that Homer became blind and that, after his death, his grave was venerated as a sacred shrine.

We know a great deal more about Homer's poetry than we do about the poet. First of all, we know that the Trojan war, the background of Homer's epics, was a definite event, and not, as was long supposed, an imaginary happening. About 1200 B.C., some four hundred years before the composition of the *Iliad* (the tale of Ilios, or Troy) and the *Odyssey* (the tale of Odysseus), 100,000 Greeks, under the leadership of Agamemnon, King of Mycenae, sailed from Greece to Asia Minor in about twelve hundred ships to besiege, conquer, and then destroy the ancient city of Troy. The reason for this massive invasion was revenge. Paris, son of Priam, the King of Troy, had carried off Helen, the beautiful wife of Agamemnon's brother. Agamemnon and his brother, Menelaus, persuaded the princes of other Greek tribes and cities to join them in an expedition to recapture Helen and redeem their honor.

The siege of Troy lasted for ten years. During that time, there took place all the usual happenings of a great war. Heroes emerged: Achilles, Odysseus, and Ajax among the Greeks; Hector and Aeneas among the Trojans. Both sides performed acts of valor and cowardice, of candor and guile, of wisdom and stupidity. In hand-to-hand combat, the heroes and villains showed their strength and weakness, and both nations discovered the extent of their courage and patriotism. The experience was never to be forgotten.

Shortly after the fall of Troy, poets began to sing or chant their heroes' praise. In time, the numerous versions of the deeds of their heroes prompted the ever-agile Greek mind to ask not only what happened, but why it happened. Homer's answer to the question *why* is a great part of his achievement as a poet.

THE ILIAD

Let us begin with the *Iliad,* since it not only precedes the *Odyssey* in time but serves as its prelude.

Homer's account of the Trojan war in the *Iliad* answered the question *why* by reducing a mass of conflicting legends to an artistic whole. How did he do this? First, he began his story at a time when the events of the war approached their crisis. The *Iliad* deals with just fifty-one days in the tenth and last year of the war, the very moment, so to speak, when the war reached its climax in the final overthrow of Troy. Second, Homer concentrated on one main hero, Achilles, the supreme warrior among the Greeks, and on one main antagonist, Hector, the noblest of the Trojans. Finally, Homer presented his story as a straightforward sequence of events. The *Iliad* begins with Achilles' angry fight with Agamemnon over a captive slave girl. When Agamemnon refuses to yield, Achilles refuses to fight the war. With Achilles absent from the field, the Trojans take heart and begin to beat back the Greeks. It is only when Hector kills Patroclus, Achilles' best friend, that Achilles, enraged, returns to combat and slays Hector. Though Achilles himself is struck down by a Trojan arrow, his victory demoralizes the Trojans and, soon after the fall of Hector, Troy itself finally falls.

By emphasizing one important hero, concentrating on one continuous action, and selecting an underlying theme for the *Iliad,* Homer told his audience *why* the events happened the way they did. The action of the whole poem can be traced to a single cause, the wrath of Achilles. Though Achilles is noble, courageous in battle, a superb orator, and a passionately loyal friend, his intense anger causes him to sulk in his tent and thereby encourage the Trojans to renew the fight. After the death of Patroclus, Achilles' anger flares again. Furious, he returns to battle and kills Hector at the price of his own life. Thus all the principal events of the *Iliad* derive from its very first line: "Sing, Muse, the wrath of Achilles . . ."

THE ODYSSEY

Homer's *Iliad* tells of the great Greek victory at Troy; his *Odyssey* tells of the return home of the Greek heroes. In this epic also Homer concentrates on one main hero, Odysseus (often called Ulysses), who won fame during the Trojan war for his shrewdness and fortitude. It was Odysseus who conceived the bold plan to leave a huge wooden horse, filled with Greek warriors, outside the gates of Troy. When the Trojans took the horse inside, the Greeks crept out and opened the city gates to their own army. Thus Odysseus was directly responsible for the fall of Troy. The gods who had sympathized with the Trojans were angry and vowed that Odysseus would have a long and difficult journey home. Thus Odysseus was tested anew during his homeward journey: to rejoin his wife Penelope and his son Telemachus in his native Ithaca, Odysseus had to survive storms, temptations, the anger of the god Poseidon, and the stratagems of his enemies at home. The *Iliad* shows a hero great even in death, the *Odyssey* a hero great in victory and success.

Of the two epics, the *Odyssey* is the more popular. One of its recent translators calls it "the best story ever written" and few disagree with him. The *Odyssey* is not only the story of a national hero but also the universal story of every human being. We all, like Odysseus, spend many years trying to reach our own personal land of peace and joy. Like him, we must achieve that land by testing ourselves against all the temptations and obstacles in life. Small wonder that our journey through life is often called our "odyssey."

The theme of the *Odyssey,* like that of the *Iliad,* also answers the question *why.* Odysseus wins his way home because of his heroic strength, courage, and wisdom. But, as you will see, his journey is by no means an easy one. It is ten long years before he finally reaches his native land, and even then he is forced to put his enemies to the sword before he can live in peace in his own home.

While the structure or plot reveals the themes of the *Odyssey,* the characterization and the incidental description combine to give us a vivid picture of ancient Greek life. In addition, Odysseus, wise and courageous, Penelope, a patient and faithful wife, and Telemachus, a brave and trusting son, offer us lifelike symbols of the virtues most admired by the Greeks. Humbler characters such as Eumæus the swineherd, and Eurycleia, Penelope's nurse and servant, also contribute to a full and rounded view of the Greek way of life. Nor should we forget that the gods, particularly Zeus, Athene, and Poseidon, are truly characters in this epic poem. They are personifications of human traits raised to their highest power but never free of human defects. They do not so much rule the universe as they administer the rules of fate. They take sides, as Athene does for Odysseus, and as Poseidon does against him. They walk the earth in various disguises and participate in human action.

HOMER'S MYTHS

Besides simply enjoying the story, in reading the *Odyssey* we should remember that the dangers that Odysseus and his men encounter are mythical exaggerations of the perils and trials of the everyday world. Myths are highly imaginative tales that attempt to explain the mysteries of human life. You have encountered myths in fairy tales, for instance, where evil is caused by a wicked witch and good by a fairy godmother, or in American Indian lore, where the mists surrounding a waterfall are explained as the tears of a maiden mourning for her lost warrior. Homer's myths are essentially the same as these. The chief difference is simply this: Homer uses myth to illustrate the character of his epic hero. Thus the myth of the lotus-eaters is used to underline Odysseus' ability to overcome the temptation of idleness. The myth of the Sirens shows how Odysseus uses reason, strength of will, and clever planning to triumph over the pleasures of the senses. In Homer, myth is employed not just to entertain but to convey a meaningful truth. Myth, in short, is a way of expressing the truth the poet has seen and felt.

The Odyssey

HOMER

[Odysseus [1] is in the banquet hall of Alcinous,[2] king of Phæacia,[3] who helps him on his way after all his comrades have been killed and his last vessel destroyed. Odysseus tells the story of his adventures thus far.]

I am
Odysseus, great Laertes'° son,
For cunning plans of every kind
Known among men; and even to heaven
Has spread my fame. My native land   5
Is Ithaca,° a sun-bright island
Low of shore which lies far out
To sea and toward the west. Rugged
It is, this land of mine, yet breeds
A sturdy youth, and I can find   10
No land more sweet to me than this,
My native land.
              But come,
For I will tell the many sorrows
Zeus° sent upon me as I traveled
Homeward from Troy.   15

THE LAND OF THE LOTUS-EATERS

Great Zeus, who guides the clouds, sent forth
Against our ships a wild north wind,
A raging tempest, and enshrouded
In dark clouds land and sea. Deep night

Came rolling from on high. Our ships   20
Drove headlong, while their sails were riven
Asunder by that gale; but these
We stored beneath the decks, still toiling
In dread of death, and striving ever,
Rowed on and reached the land   25
Where dwell the Lotus-eaters, men
Whose food is flowers. And we all
Here went ashore and drew us water,
And by the sides of their swift ships
My men prepared their meal. And now
When we at last had had our fill   31
Of meat and drink, I sent forth men
To learn what manner of mankind
That live by bread might dwell here. Two
I chose to go and sent with them   35
A third, a herald. And these quickly
Went forth into that land and mingled
Among the Lotus-eaters. Never
Did these men, eaters of the lotus,
Plan evil to my men, and yet   40
They gave them of the lotus flower
And bade them eat of it, and lo,
Whatever man of them but tasted
That blossom strange and honey-sweet,
Naught cared he then to hasten back   45
With tidings to the ships, or ever
Turn homeward any more, but longed
To dwell there with the Lotus-eaters,
And pluck and eat the lotus blossoms
And think no more of home.
              But these   50
I brought back to the ships by force,
Though they lamented, and I dragged them
Aboard the hollow ships and bound them
Beneath the benches. Then I bade
The rest, my true companions, hasten   55
Aboard the ships, lest one of them
Taste of the lotus, too, and lose
All memory of home. So straightway
They came aboard and sat them down
In order on the thwarts° and smote   60
The foaming sea with oars.

THE CYCLOPS

So thence
We sailed upon our way sad-hearted.
And now we came unto the land
Where dwell the Cyclopes°—arrogant
And lawless beings, who, with trust   65
In the undying gods, plow not
Nor plant with hands a single plant.
Yet crops spring up for them unsown
On fields untended—wheat and barley
And vines that bear full-clustered grapes
To make them wine. The rain of Zeus   71
Still brings increase in all. These men
Have neither meeting place for council
Nor settled laws. They live apart
On lofty mountain ridges, dwelling   75
In hollow caverns. Each makes laws
For wife and child, and gives no heed
To any save himself.

                 There lies,
Facing the Cyclopes' land, an island,
Sheltering the haven's outer side,   80
Not near, nor yet far out. Thither we
   sailed
Seeking the land. Surely it was
Some god that gave us guidance thither
Through the dense night, for we could see
Nothing before our eyes: the mist   85
Shut close about the ships; no moon
Showed forth in heaven, for clouds en-
   closed it.
So no man with his eyes beheld
That isle or saw the long seas rolling
Against the land till we had beached   90
Our well-benched ships.

                Now we looked
And saw not far away the mainland
Where dwelt the Cyclopes. And we saw
Smoke rise, and heard the speech of men
And bleat of sheep and goats. Then came
The setting of the sun and darkness;   96
And there we slept beside the breakers.
But when the earliest dawn appeared

Rose-fingered, then I called together
My men and spoke to all:

              "Rest here,   100
Dear comrades, while with my own ship
And my own men I go to learn
What men these are—if wild and cruel
And ignorant of right, or kind
To every stranger and with hearts   105
That fear the gods."

            Now when we reached
That land that lay hard by, we saw
Upon its utmost point a cave
Close to the sea: high-roofed it was,
With laurel overhung, and many   110
The flocks of sheep and goats that there
Found shelter in the night. Around it
A courtyard lay, high-walled with stones
Set deep in earth, with lofty pines
And high-leaved oaks.

            Within this lair   115
A man was wont° to sleep, a monster
Who grazed his sheep far off, alone,
Nor ever mingled with his kind,
But lonely dwelt—lawless and evil.
And marvelously was he shapen—   120
This monstrous being, not like mortals
That live by bread, but like a peak

---

64. **Cyclopes** (sī·klō′pēz): plural form of Cyclops (sī′klops).

116. **wont** (wunt): accustomed or used.

That rising rough with woods stands
   forth
Apart from other hills.
               And I
Now bade my trusty men to bide   125
Close by the ship and guard the ship,
But twelve I chose, the best of all,
And we set forth.
            I bore with me
A goatskin filled with dark sweet wine,
Sweet and unmixed, a drink for gods. 130
Who drank that red wine, honey-sweet,
He took one cup, no more, and served it
Mingled with water twenty times
The measure of the wine, and yet
Up from the mixing bowl there rose   135
Rare scent and sweetness, till no man
Could find it easy to refrain
From drinking of that wine. I filled
A great skin with this, and I bore it
As I set forth, and bore besides   140
Food in a leathern sack. For now
My fearless heart foresaw a meeting
With a strange man of monstrous might—
A savage, scornful of the gods
And of man's law.
          Straightway we reached   145
His cave and entered, but we found not
The man within. For far away
He herded, while they grazed at pasture,
His goodly flock. So on we passed   149
Far into that great cave and marveled
At all we saw within. Here stood
Crates heaped with cheese and here were
   pens
Crowded with lambs and kids.
                My men
Besought me eagerly to carry
The cheeses thence, and come again 155
And loose the kids and lambs and drive
   them
In haste to our swift ship, then sail
Away o'er the salt sea. But this
I would not grant, though better far
Had I but done so! For I hoped   160
To look upon this man—he might

Give gifts of friendship. But, alas,
When he appeared, he was to bring
My poor men little joy!
            So there
We kindled fire and of that cheese   165
We made an offering, and ate
Ourselves thereof, and sat and waited
Until at last he entered, driving
His flock before him.
             He bore in
Dry wood to cook his meal, a load   170
Of wondrous weight, and down he flung
   it
Within the cave, with such a crash
We cowered back with fear and crouched
In the cave's corner. Then he drove
Into that spacious cave the sheep   175
That he must milk, and left the others—
The rams and goats—without, to roam
The high-walled court.
           Then in its place
He set the massive rock that closed
The doorway of the cave: he raised it 180
Lightly aloft, a weight so vast
That never two and twenty wagons,
Four-wheeled and firmly built, might stir
   it
From where it lay on earth—so great
That towering crag was that he set   185
To close his door.
          Now sat he down
And milked his sheep and bleating goats

That he might sup thereon. And now,
When he had labored busily
And finished every task, he stayed   190
And kindled up the fire and saw us
And asked us:

        "Strangers, who are you,
And whence do you come sailing hither
Over the sea's wet ways? What errand
Can bring you hither? Or perchance   195
You wander purposeless, like robbers
Who rove the seas and venture life
To bring to strangers in far lands
An evil fortune."

        So he spoke,
And at his words our hearts within us   200
Were crushed and broken, for we feared
The man's deep voice and monstrous
   body.
Yet I spoke up and answered, saying:
"We are Achæans° come from Troy;
We wander blown by every wind   205
Over the sea's great gulf, still striving
To reach our homes, yet ever go
On alien ways, by paths we never
Have willed to travel—so it pleases
Zeus to decree. Now we come   210
Hither before your knees to pray you
Give welcome to your guests and grant us
Such gifts as guests should have. Respect,
O mighty one, the gods, for we
Are suppliants,° and Zeus avenges   215
The suppliant and stranger: he
Is god of strangers, watching over
Each worthy wanderer."

        So I spoke,
And pitiless of heart, he answered:
"Stranger, you either are a fool   220
Or come from a far land, to bid me
Fear or beware the gods! We Cyclopes
Fear not your ægis-wielding° Zeus
Nor any god above. For we
Are mightier far than they. I would not
Show mercy to your men or you   226

To shun the wrath of Zeus, nay, never
Unless my own heart bade. But come,
Tell me, where left you your good ship
When you came hither? Was it near   230
Or at the land's far end? Nay, tell me,
For I would know."

        So asked he, striving
To trap the truth from me, but caught
  not
My tried mind unaware. So thus
With crafty words I spoke:

        "The god   235
Who shakes the earth, Poseidon,° broke
My ship asunder, for he drove her
Upon the cliffs that line your land
And dashed her on the rocks. A tempest
Had blown us in from sea, and I   240
And these my comrades here but barely
Escaped sheer death."

        So I replied.
He, cruel-hearted, made no answer,
But springing up, reached forth his hands
And seized my comrades. Two at once
He snatched up in his grasp and dashed
  them   246
To earth like helpless puppies. Forth
The brains flowed, moistening the ground.
Then limb from limb he tore their bodies
And made his meal, devouring them   250
Savagely as a lion bred
Among the mountains. Naught of them
He left uneaten—flesh or entrails
Or marrowy bones. And we cried out
In lamentation and uplifted   255
Our hands to Zeus, to see a deed
So horrible. Numb terror laid
Hold on our hearts.

        And now the Cyclops,
When he had filled that monstrous belly
With flesh of men, and followed this   260
With draughts of unmixed milk, lay
  stretched
Full length upon the cavern floor
Among his flock.

---

204. **Achæans** (ə·kē′ənz): Greeks. 215. **suppliants** (sup′lē·ənts): those who beg or ask a favor.
223. **ægis-wielding** (ē′jis·wēld′ing): shield-bearing.

236. **Poseidon** (pō·sī′dən): god of the sea, whom the Romans called Neptune.

The Odyssey *in Art*

An adventurer, explorer, and warrior perhaps even more renowned for his clever ideas than his prowess with spear and sword, Odysseus is the center of Homer's only story about one hero. Odysseus inherited his love of travel from his father Laertes, who had gone with the Argonauts under Jason in quest of the Golden Fleece. King of Ithaca, Odysseus reluctantly left his wife and home and sailed with twelve ships to fight at Troy. After the city's fall, he traveled for ten long years until, without any of his companions remaining, he finally returned home. Although Odysseus is thought to have lived thirty-two centuries ago, his adventures have inspired artists up to the present day.

During the sack of Troy, Odysseus was a valiant hero, but when he was awarded the armor of the dead Achilles, he generously gave it to the latter's son. PLATE 1 shows this touching scene painted on the inside of a drinking cup. The shield held by Odysseus is of the "dumbbell" shape which had been used in Crete about the time these heroes were supposed to have lived.

Led by Odysseus, the Greeks built a wooden horse which they used to hide their soldiers inside the Trojan walls. PLATE 2 reproduces a fifteenth-century interpretation of this scene. But here the horse is of metal and is shown in a charming medieval city, where knights in armor are substituted for Greek and Trojan warriors.

After the fall of Troy, Odysseus's ships began their perilous voyage homeward without map, compass, or proper rudder. They could depend only on the strong arms of the oarsmen and the shifting winds in their sails. Blown off course, the ships came to the land of the Cyclopes, one-eyed cannibals. The cartoonlike figures on the water jar in PLATE 3 represent Odysseus and his companions blinding the giant Polyphemos after Polyphemos had trapped them in his cave.

Although we have many vases from classical times, very little painting of large proportions has survived to this day, especially when compared to what remains of classical sculpture and architecture. One of the exceptions is shown in PLATE 4. which reproduces one of the eight wall paintings in the famous *Odyssey* landscape series. Since each scene in this series is separated by painted pilasters, when we look at these paintings we feel that we are looking out of a window at an actual event. PLATE 4 shows the Greek fleet in a beautiful harbor where it had sought refuge from storms. Giant cannibals of the island splinter Odysseus's boats and crush his companions with huge rocks. Only Odysseus's ship will escape. You can see his men frantically rowing to the right, with the huge steering oar in place at the stern. They are headed for Circe's lovely island, perhaps the one with rolling, misty hills in the right background. Warm sun lights the rocks and ships; the brown silhouettes of the Laestrygonians are caught in vigorous action against the calm Mediterranean. The sketchy brushwork used to indicate oars and broken timber almost convinces us that this painting must have been painted in our own time rather than two thousand years ago.

As we have seen, the *Odyssey* was a source of inspiration not only to the classical world but to painters of the medieval and Renaissance periods as well. In PLATE 5 you see a fifteenth-century interpretation of the story of Circe. Odysseus's scouting party is shown timorously approaching the enchantress, who is beautifully arrayed in a Renaissance costume. They have good reason to look frightened, for near them are two men already turned to swine by her magic. Odysseus, in the stern of his ship, gestures toward Circe as he prepares to go to the rescue. The artist has not hesitated to put the Greeks in fifteenth-century armor nor to change Circe's Mycenaean palace into a fortified castle.

In PLATE 6, the Greek legend is again set in modern dress, this time in the sixteenth century. The artist shows Penelope at her loom while her son Telemachus rushes in to her perhaps to give news of his father. The dapper young men in Renaissance garb must be the impatient suitors, while in the doorway we see Odysseus in his disguise as a beggar. Here too, just as was done seventeen centuries before (PLATE 4), the artist has used the device of the window to tell of events in the *Odyssey*. You can see Odysseus's ship, far more elaborately portrayed than in classical times, as well as the Sirens and Circe's island. For the first time in these paintings of the *Odyssey* we see a conscious, almost self-conscious, use of perspective. Note the lines of the floor, loom, and walls. In this painting Pintoricchio has tried to tell many things at once: through the window, past events; with the loom, how Penelope kept away the suitors; and with the bow and quiver on the wall, how Odysseus will slay the suitors at the end of the story.

PLATE 1. DOURIS (Greek, 5th century B.C.): *Odysseus Gives Achilles's Son His Father's Arms*. About 490 B.C. Attic red-figured clay kylix, 5 x $13\frac{5}{16}$ inches. (Kunsthistorisches Museum, Vienna)

PLATE 2. ARTIST UNKNOWN (French, late 15th century): *The Trojan Horse*. Miniature on vellum from Raoul Lefèvres's *Recueil*, $8\frac{9}{16}$ x 12 inches. (Bibliothèque Nationale, Paris)

PLATE 3. ARTIST UNKNOWN (Greek, 6th century B.C.): *The Blinding of Polyphemos*. About 530 B.C. Caeretan clay hydria. $16\frac{5}{16}$ x $39\frac{3}{8}$ inches. (Villa Guilia Museum, Rome)

PLATE 4. ARTIST UNKNOWN (Graeco-Roman, late 1st century B.C.): *The Laestrygonians Hurling Rocks at the Fleet of Odysseus.* Fresco, wall from a house on the Esquiline Hill, 59 x 61 inches. (Vatican Library, Rome)

PLATE 5. JEAN MIELOT (French or Flemish, 15th century) *Ulysses and His Companions at Circe's Palace*, 1461. Miniature from Christine de Pisan's *Epître d'Othéa*, $6\frac{3}{16}$ x 5 inches. (Copyright Bibliothèque Royale, Brussels)

PLATE 6. BERNARDINO PINTORICCHIO (Umbrian, about 1454–1513): *The Return of Odysseus.* About 1509. Fresco transferred to canvas, from the Pandolfo Petrucci Palace, Siena, 49 x 57½ inches. (Reproduced by courtesy of the Trustees, The National Gallery, London)

And now I formed
This plan within my daring heart—
To venture nearer and to draw   265
My keen sword from my thigh and thrust
    it
Deep in his breast, straight to the spot
Where lay his liver, feeling first
To seek the place; and yet a thought
Withheld me, for we all, each man,   270
Must then have met sheer death; for never
Could our strength stir from that high
    door
The massive stone he set there. So
Lamenting there we sat and waited
The sacred dawn.

        And when the dawn   275
Came, rosy-fingered, then once more
He kindled fire and milked his flock
Of wondrous sheep, in order due,
Setting her young by each; and now
When he had labored busily   280
And finished every task, he seized
Once more upon two men and made
His morning meal. And after this,
His breakfast done, he drove away
His goodly flock, moving with ease   285
The mighty door-stone thence, then set it
In place as lightly as a man
Would set the lid upon a quiver.
And now I pondered how I best
Might find revenge, if but Athene°   290
Would hear my prayer. And this plan
    seemed
Best to my mind at last:

        There lay
Close by the pens, a mighty staff
Cut by the Cyclops. Olive wood
It was, still green, for he had cut it   295
To use when it had dried: it seemed,
As we stood gazing, the great mast
Of some broad ship of twenty oars,
Laden with cargo, a black ship
That sails the great gulf of the sea,   300
So long and thick it seemed. So there

I took my stand by it and cut
A fathom's length away, and this
I gave my men and bade them shape it.
They made it smooth, while I stood by
And brought it to a point and charred it
In glowing fire; and then I took it   307
And hid it in the dung that lay
In heaps about the cave.

        I bade then
My company cast lots to see   310
Which men of them would dare to join me
And lift that stake and bore it deep
Into his eye when gentle slumber
Should come upon him. And the lot
Fell on the four I should have chosen,
And I myself became the fifth   316
To share the venture.

        And now came
The Cyclops home at evening, herding
His well-fleeced flocks. Straightway he
    drove
Into that cavern, one and all,   320
His goodly flocks, nor left he any
In the wide court without.° He felt,
Perhaps, some sense of coming evil;
Perhaps some god had warned him. Next
He set in place the massive door-stone,
Lifting it lightly, then once again   326
He seized on two of my companions
And made his evening meal.

        And now
I stood before him, and thus spoke,
The while I held forth in my hands   330
An ivy bowl, filled with dark wine:
"Here, Cyclops, take this wine, and drink
After your feast of human flesh,
And learn how good a drink we kept
Hidden within our ship. I brought it   335
An offering to you, in hope
You might have pity on my sorrows
And help me home. But you, alas,
In rage exceed all patience! Madman!
How shall there ever come hereafter   340
Another stranger here to seek you

290. **Athene** (ə·thē′nə): Athena, the Greek goddess of wisdom.

322. **without:** outside.

From any land on earth, if you
Thus scorn all human laws!"
                              So said I.
He took the wine and drank it. Vastly
That sweet drink pleased him. And again
He begged of me:
                    "In goodness give me   346
Yet more, I pray. And tell me now
Your name, and quickly! I will give you
A gift to make your heart rejoice."
So thrice I bore that glowing wine   350
And gave it him, and thrice in folly
He drained it off. Then when the wine
Had stolen round his wits, I spoke
And said in honeyed words:
                              "O Cyclops,
You ask my far-famed name, and this   355
I now will tell you. Give me therefore
The stranger's gift, as you have promised.
My name is Noman."
                    So I spoke,
And he with cruel heart replied:
"Noman, of all his company,   360
I shall eat last; and all the others
I'll eat before him. This shall be
My gift to you—my guest.
                          So spoke he,
Then down he sank and on his back
Lay flat, his thick neck bent aside,   365
And from his throat there poured forth
  wine
And fragments of men's flesh.
                          And now
Deep under heaped-up coals I thrust
That stake till it grew hot, and stirred
The courage of my men with speech   370
Lest one of them should shrink with fear
And fail my need.
                  And now that stake
Of olive wood, green as it was,
Was ready to burst forth in flame,
All glowing with fierce heat. I drew it   375
Forth from the fire, while round about me
My men stood ready. Then—for surely
Some god had breathed into our hearts
High courage—they laid hold upon   379

That sharpened olive stake and thrust it
Deep in his eye, the while above them
I leaned upon its top and turned it
As one who with an auger bores
A great ship timber. Those below him
Twist it by thongs on either side,   385
And still it ever turns unceasing.
So holding that huge stake of wood
Deep in his eye, we kept it turning.
Round that hot brand, forth poured the
  blood;
And round it all his brows and lashes   390
Were singed off by the blast that came
Out of that burning eye. Its roots
Seethed in the fire. As when a smith
Dips a great ax or adz° in water
To temper it, and loud it hisses—   395
For so steel gets its strength—even so
His eye hissed round that olive stake.
And loud his cry and terrible
Till the rocks echoed and we fled
Away in fear. Then from his eye   400
He wrenched away that stake, thick clot-
  ted
With his own blood and raging hurled it
Out of his hands. Then loud he shouted
To all the Cyclopes who dwelt round him
In caves upon the windy heights.   405
They heard his shout and straggling gath-
  ered,
One here, one there, from every side,
And standing all about his cave
They asked what grieved him.
                          "What can ail you,
O Polyphemus,° that so loudly   410
You cry out in the heavenly night
And keep us sleepless? Is some man,
Some mortal, driving off your flocks
Against your will; or is some man
Now slaying you by force or cunning?"
And thus in answer from his cave   416

---

394. **adz:** a tool like an ax, but with a curved
blade set across the end of the handle. 410. **Polyphemus** (pol′i-fē′məs): the name of the Cyclops who
has imprisoned Odysseus.

Spoke mighty Polyphemus:

               "Friends,
Noman is slaying me by cunning,
Nor uses force at all!"

         And they
With winged words thus replied:

           "Since no man   420
Now does you violence, while you
Are there alone, this illness sent
By mighty Zeus, no man may shun
In any way. But pray you now   424
To your great father, Lord Poseidon."
So said they and then went their way.
And in my heart I laughed to think
How with that name and my shrewd plan
I had deceived them.

          But the Cyclops,
Groaning in agony and anguish,   430
Went groping with his hands, and lifted
The great rock from the door and there
He sat athwart° the doorway, stretching
His hands, to catch, if it might be,
Any who sought to pass the door   435
Among the sheep; for in his heart
He hoped that I might prove so foolish
As thus to venture. But I still
Sat planning how to bring this peril
To a good end and win us all—   440
My men and me—escape. Full many
The plan and trick I fashioned, striving
For life itself, for great the peril
And close at hand. And at the last
This, as I deemed, was of them all   445
The wisest plan.

        There in the cave
Were well-grown rams of thickest wool,
Fair beasts and great, and dark of fleece.
These silently I bound together   449
With twisted willow withes,° whereon
The Cyclops slept, that savage monster
Who knew no law nor right. I bound them
By threes together and the midmost
Bore under him a man; the others,

One on each side, were to conceal   455
And save my comrades: so there went
A man to each three sheep. And I,
Myself, now seized upon a ram,
The best of all that flock, and grasped
His back from underneath, and lay   460
Beneath his shaggy belly; there
Twisting my fingers deep within
That wondrous fleece, I hung, face up-
  ward,
With steadfast heart. And so, lamenting,
We waited sacred dawn.

           And now,   465
When earliest dawn came rosy-fingered,
Then forth the rams went to the pasture,
But all the unmilked ewes went bleating
About their pens with swollen udders.
Their lord, though torn by cruel pain,   470
Yet, ere each ram passed, made him stand
And felt along his back. He guessed not
In his dull mind that there beneath
Those fleecy breasts were bound my men.
Now to the door, last of them all,   475
The great ram slowly came, weighed
  down
With heavy fleece and with the burden
Of me and my shrewd plans. Upon him
The mighty Polyphemus then
Laid searching hands, and said:

             "Dear ram,   480
Why do you cross the cave so slowly,
Last of the flock? Till now, you never
Lagged thus, but ever first of all
Sped forth with mighty strides to crop

---

433. **athwart** (ə·thwôrt'): across. 450. **withes**
(wĭᴛʜz): slender twigs or branches, especially those
used as bands or ropes.

The soft bloom of the grass, and ever 485
Were first to reach the running waters,
And first, when evening came, to long
To turn back home. And yet you now
Come last of all. Surely you sorrow
Over your lord's lost eye! A villain   490
Has quenched its sight—he and his crew
Of wretched fellows, mastering
My wits with wine, this fellow Noman!
Not yet, I say, has he escaped   494
The death that waits him. Would but you
Could know my thought and had the
   power
To speak in words and let me know
Where he is skulking from my wrath!
For I should smite him down and dash
His brains about the cave—here, there, 500
Aye, on the ground! By such a deed
My heart might find some ease from all
The evils that this worthless Noman
Has brought upon me."

                              So he spoke,
And sent the ram forth through the door-
   way.   505
And now, when we were safe outside
That cavern and its yard, I loosed
My grip upon the great ram's fleece
And then unbound my men in turn,
Setting them free. And then in haste   510
We drove that flock before us—sheep
Most rich in fat, most long of stride—
And yet we often turned our heads
To glance behind us ere we came
Safe to our ship. Welcome indeed   515
We were to our dear comrades, snatched
From death itself; and yet they wept,
Lamenting those we lost. But this
I would not suffer, but forbade,
With lifted brows, all lamentation,   520
And bade them quickly bear aboard
Into the ship those many sheep
So fine of fleece, and sail away
Across the salt sea waves. And they   524
Went then aboard and took their seats
Each in his place, and smote with oars
The whitening sea.

                              And now, when yet
A shout might reach the land, I called
To Cyclops, taunting him:
                              "O Cyclops,
You were not, then, to find that man   530
A helpless weakling—him whose men
You ate there in your hollow cave
With might and cruel strength. For surely
These evil deeds of yours are doomed
To overtake you. O mad fool   535
Who felt no shame, but must devour
Your guests in your own home! May Zeus
And all the other gods send vengeance
Upon you for such deeds!"
                              So spoke I,
And he in heart grew angrier yet   540
And tearing off a hill's great summit,
He hurled it. And it fell beyond
Our dark-bowed ship: the sea surged high
As that great rock crashed down. A wave
Came rolling back, a mighty billow   545
Out of the deep, and swept our ship
In toward the land. Swiftly I grasped
A great pole in my hands and thrust
The ship from shore and bade my men,
Nodding my brows, fall to and pull   550
Their best upon the oars and flee
Out of that danger; and they all
Bent to their oars.
                              But when we now
Were twice as far from shore as we
Had been before, once more I called   555
Unto the Cyclops, but my men
With pleading words came all about me
And begged me stay:
                              "Why, like a madman,
Will you enrage this savage monster
Who made but now so great a cast   560
He drove our ship, then far at sea,
Back to the land. We thought that we
Were lost indeed there. Had he heard
A man of us but stir or speak,   564
He would have shattered all our heads
And our ship's timbers, too, so rugged
A rock he would have cast, so strongly
He sends it on its way!"

So spoke they.
But did not move my lordly spirit,
And once again with angry heart   570
I called back, saying:
     "If, O Cyclops,
A mortal man shall ever ask you
How it befell your eye was blinded
So hideously, then answer thus:
It was Odysseus blinded you,   575
Taker of Troy, Laërtes' son,
Who dwells in Ithaca."
     So spoke I,
And with a groan he spoke and answered:
"Alas, for now are come upon me
The ancient oracles. A prophet   580
Once dwelt here, a great man and good,
And he foretold me everything
That time should bring to pass—that I
Should lose my sight here at the hand
Of one Odysseus. But I ever   585
Watched for the coming of a man
Tall, handsome, armed with wondrous
   strength;
And now this little worthless fellow
Has robbed me of my eye by craft,
First mastering me with wine. Yet now
Come hither, O Odysseus, come!   591
For I would give my guest his gifts
And would implore the far-famed god
Who shakes the shores to give you help
Upon your way. I am his son: 595
He owns himself my father. He,

And he alone, can make me whole
If so he will, but this no other
Can do, no other of the gods
On high or mortal men who perish."   600
So spoke he and I answered thus:
"Would I could be as sure that I
Could strip you bare of soul and being,
And send you to Death's house, as I
Am sure of this:—that none shall ever
Restore your eye, not even he   606
Who makes earth tremble!"
     So I spoke,
And he with hands upraised in prayer
To starry heaven, thus besought
The lord Poseïdon:
     "Hear me now,   610
Thou dark-haired god who mak'st earth
   tremble!
If I be verily thy son
And thou wilt own thyself my father,
Grant that Odysseus, he who took
The towers of Troy, come never home.
Yet, should it be his fate to see   616
His friends once more and come at last
To his good house and native land,
Late may he come, in evil fortune,
With loss of all his men, and borne   620
Within a stranger's ship, and meet
In his own home affliction.'
     So
He spoke in prayer, and to his words
The dark-haired god gave ear.

1. Odysseus' adventures are interesting for their own sake, but, in addition, almost all of them illustrate some facet of Odysseus' character. What specific characteristics of Odysseus are revealed in the episode in the land of the lotus-eaters?

2. When the three men sent by Odysseus had eaten of the lotus blossoms, they lost all desire to return home. Do you think Odysseus was justified in forcing them to board the ship and sail away with the others? Why or why not?

3. Do you think that the land of the lotus-eaters symbolizes what we today would call *escapism*—that is, withdrawal from reality into a dream world? If you do, point out lines that support your view. If you do not, give reasons for your opinion.

4. Odysseus' men urge him to go back to the ship before the Cyclops returns and finds them in his cave. Was this good advice? Why does Odysseus insist on waiting for the Cyclops? What does his desire to see the Cyclops show about his character? Do you think this trait is admirable? Why or why not?

5. Why does Odysseus call the Cyclopes arrogant and lawless, even though they "trust in the undying gods"? How is the Cyclopes' attitude toward strangers different from that of the Greeks, who were accustomed to being received with courtesy and hospitality? What actions of the Cyclops toward Odysseus and his men are most cruel and inhuman?

6. Odysseus' craftiness is clearly displayed in this episode. Where does he show himself to be exceptionally resourceful and clever? Point out three or four specific actions that show his ability to outwit his opponent.

7. After gouging out Polyphemus' eye, Odysseus gloats over his cleverness. Later, after escaping from the cave, Odysseus shouts defiance to the Cyclops despite the pleas of his companions. What are the consequences to Odysseus of telling the Cyclops his name? Do you think his final outcries are bold and heroic or foolish and boastful? Why?

8. How does the Cyclops' final speech (lines 610–22) sum up his character in contrast to that of Odysseus? What is the chief difference between the two? What lines in this speech suggest that Odysseus will have to face other trials? How does this foreshadowing add to the suspense of the poem?

9. The story of the Cyclops, like other episodes in the *Iliad* and the *Odyssey*, is legendary—that is, it is a story handed down by tradition and accepted as true but impossible to prove. Suppose the events in this episode never actually happened. In what sense can they still be "true"? Have you ever met or read about people who are in some way like the Cyclops? What is his attitude toward others? What kind of person does he represent or symbolize?

[The Cyclops' curse is heard by Poseidon, who sends fierce winds to blow Odysseus' ships far from home. The next time they land, all the ships but one are destroyed, and their crews devoured, by the Læstrygonians,[1] a race of savage giants. Odysseus' own ship proceeds to the island of Aeaea,[2] where his crew is cast under a spell by the goddess Circe.[3] A year later, the goddess agrees to let them continue their journey, and Odysseus sails his ship to the Land of the Dead, where he asks the ghost of a famous prophet, Teiresias,[4] what he must do in order to reach his native land. The prophet foretells great pain and hardship, but Odysseus nevertheless vows to go on. Before setting out, he returns briefly to Circe's island, where the goddess gives him a further warning.]

CIRCE'S WARNINGS

Then mighty Circe
Spoke thus, and said:
      "Now all these things   625
Are past and ended. Listen well
To what I have to tell. May heaven
Help you to heed it. You will first
Come to the Sirens, to those women

---

[1] **Læstrygonians** (lēs·tri·gō′nē·ənz). [2] **Aeaea** (ē′ē·ə).
[3] **Circe** (sûr′sē). [4] **Teiresias** (Tâ·rē′sē·əs).

Who weave a magic spell that masters
All men who hear their song. For he   631
Who turns him from his way in folly
To hear the Sirens' song—no more
Shall he behold his wife and children
Coming to greet him, glad of heart   635
That he is home again. They sit,
These Sirens, in a grassy meadow,
And here they sing their clear, sweet song
And weave their spell. And all about them
Lie heaps of gleaming bones; and bodies
Shriveled, with shreds of skin.
                              Row swiftly   641
And drive your ship till safely past.
But first mold honeyed wax and stop
Your comrades' ears, that none of them
May hear that song. Yet if you long   645
With your own ears to hear it, bid them
First bind you hand and foot and lash you
Upright in your swift ship, your back
Against the mast, with ropes cast round
  you.
So you may listen with delight   650
And hear the Sirens' song. Yet first
Command your men that if you beg them
To set you free, they then must bind you
In faster lashings.
                    When your men
Have urged your ship past these—what
  road   655
You next must take, I shall not tell you.
Take counsel with your heart, and choose.
I will make both ways plain. On one
Great rocks o'erhang the sea: against
  them
Roll in and break the mighty waves   660
Of dark-eyed Amphitrite.° Thence
No ship of man escapes, if once
She turn her thither. There together
Forevermore the planks of ships
And bodies of slain men go tossing   665
At will of rolling waves, and swept
By tempests of dread fire.

                              There rise
Beside the other way two crags,
And one of these soars high to heaven
With pointed peak. About the summit
A cloud hangs ever, dark and sullen,   671
Nor ever passes thence. Nor ever
Does the clear light of heaven touch
That peak, in summer or in harvest.
No mortal man might climb it—nay,   675
Nor find him foothold, though he had
A score of hands and feet, that rock
Rises so smooth, like polished stone
On every side. Midmost the front
Of this great crag, and deep in shadow   680
There lies a cave. Westward it looks
And toward the land of Death. And
  thither,
You must, illustrious Odysseus,
Steer with your ship.
                      Within this cave
Dwells Scylla,° ever uttering   685
Her dreadful yelping cry, her voice
Shrill as a new-born whelp's. There dwells
  she,
A monstrous shape of evil. No one
Can see that sight unshaken, nay,
Not though a god should face her.
  Twelve   690
Her hanging feet are, and six necks
She stretches forth, on each a head
Hideous to see, and in each head
Teeth in three rows, close-set and bris-
  tling,
Filled with black death. And there she
  sits,   695
Sunk to her middle in that cave,
And stretches forth from that dread gulf
Her fearful heads, and fishes, groping
About the crag for sharks or dolphins
Or whatso greater beast her fortune   700
May make her prey—for many such
The deep-voiced sea-nymph Amphi-
  trite

661. **Amphitrite** (am'fə·trī'tē): wife of Poseidon
and goddess of the sea.

685. **Scylla** (sil'ə).

Has in her pastures. Not one seaman
Can boast his ship has passed her by
Without some hurt. From each dark ship
She ever snatches, with each head,   706
One man away to death.

                  And now,
Odysseus, you shall see, close by,
The second crag. Lower it lies
Yet near the other: one could shoot   710
A shaft° across to it. Upon it
There stands a fig tree, great and tall
And all in leaf. And under this
The dread Charybdis° swallows in
The dark sea-water. Thrice each day   715
She sends it up and thrice again
She sucks it down, and terrible
That sight to see. I pray that you
May not be there when she is sucking
The water in, for no one then   720
Could save you from that evil—nay,
Not he that shakes the earth. So turn
Your ship to Scylla's crag and drive her
Swiftly upon her way. Far better
Lose six men from your ship than all   725
Should die together."

                So she spoke,
And answering her I said:

                  "Nay, goddess,
Tell but this, and truly: may not
I find me out some way to shun
This dire Charybdis and yet fight   730
That other from my ship when she
Would make my men her prey?"

                 So spoke I,
And thus at once the goddess answered,
"Rash you are ever, with a heart
Set upon war and deeds of danger.   735
Can you not yield, when this must be,
To the immortal gods! This monster
Is not a mortal, but a thing
Of living evil none may slay,
Dread, fierce, unconquerable: no man   740
May fight against. Courage here
Avails you nothing. This alone

Is best—to flee from her! What though
You linger by her rock and arm you,
I fear lest then she once again   745
Stretch forth those fearful heads and
  snatch
As many more. Nay, rather drive
Full speed upon your way.

             And now you reach
The island of Thrinacia.° Here
Are pastured all the Sungod's cattle   750
And his fat flocks. For seven herds
Of cattle graze here, seven flocks
Of goodly sheep, and there are fifty
In every flock. They bear no young
Nor do they ever die. If these   755
You leave unharmed and fix your hearts
Upon the homeward way, you yet
May come, though suffering sore perils,
To Ithaca. But if you harm them,
Then naught can I foresee but ruin   760
For you and ship and men. Nay, though
Yourself, you yet escape, then late,
In evil plight you shall come home,
With loss of all your men."

               So said she,
And straightway came the dawn, rose-
  fingered,   765
And thence the goddess passed away
Up through the island. Then I turned
Back to the ship, and bade my men
Embark and loose the cables.

THE SONG OF THE SIRENS

                 Quickly
They went aboard and took their seats,
Each man in his own place, and smote
The whitened sea with oars. And now   772
There came, behind our dark-prowed
  ship,
A favoring wind to fill our sail,
A welcome comrade, sent by Circe,   775
That fair-tressed goddess of dread
  power,

---

711. **shaft:** arrow.   714. **Charybdis** (kə·rib′dis).

749. **Thrinacia** (thrin·ā′shə).

Who speaks with mortals. So we trimmed
Our good ship's tackle right, and then
Sat at our ease, while wind and helmsman
Held her course true.
                    And now I said, 780
Sad-hearted, to my men:
                    "Unfitting
It is, friends, that but one or two
Should hear the sacred prophecies
Of that dread goddess, Circe. These
I now shall tell you, for then either   785
We die foreknowing what shall fall,
Or we escape and shun the death
And doom that wait us.
                    This she first
Bids us:—to shun the wondrous Sirens,
With their sweet voices and their mead-
    ows   790
Abloom with flowers. For she bade
That I alone should hear their song.
So bind me fast in bonds—aye, lash me
Upright against the mast, that thence
I may not stir, and cast strong ropes   795
About me, too. If I entreat you
And bid you set me free, then bind me
Yet tighter than before."
                    And so
I told them all she said. And ever
Our good ship sailed on swiftly, nearing
The Sirens' island, for the wind   801
Blew fair and drove her on. And now
The wind ceased suddenly; there came
A calm without a breath: some god
Laid all the sea to sleep. So now   805
My men rose, furled the sail, and stowed
    it
Within the hollow ship, and sitting
In order on the thwarts, they smote
With polished oars the whitening sea.
But I, with my keen blade, now cut   810
A great round lump of wax, and kneaded
The fragments with my hands, till swiftly
The wax was softened. With this, I
    stopped
The ears of all my crew, in turn;
Then fast they bound me, hand and foot

Upright in my swift ship, my back   816
Against the mast, with ropes cast round
    me.
Then once again they sat and smote
The foaming sea with oars.
                    And now
When we were but so far away   820
As a man's cry may reach, and lightly
Went driving on, our ship's swift flight,
As close to land she sped, escaped not
The Sirens' sight, and they upraised
At once their clear, sweet song:
                    "Come hither,
O famed Odysseus, mighty glory   826
Of the Achæans. Turn your ship
But hither to the shore and hearken
The song we sing, for no man ever
Has steered his black ship hence till he
Has heard the honey-sweet delight   831
Of music from our lips; then forth
He went upon his way with joy
And fuller wisdom. For we know
All that the Argives° and the Trojans° 835
Endured on Troy's wide plains; we know
All that befalls mankind on earth,
The nourisher of all."
                    So sang they,
Uttering their sweet song. My heart
Yearned to hear further, and I bade   840
My men to loose me, and I frowned
My bidding with my brows, but they
Bent busier to their oars, and two,
Eurylochus° and Perimedes,°
Arose and bound me ever faster   845
With double lashings. But at last,
When we had passed them and no more
Might hear the song those Sirens sang
And their sweet voices, then my men
Took quickly from their ears the wax 850
Wherewith I stopped them, and they
    loosed
The bonds that bound me.

835. **Argives** (är'jīvz): as used by Homer, almost
any Greeks; **Trojans** (trō'jənz): people of Troy.
884. **Eurylochus** (yoŏ·ril'ə·kus): **Perimedes** (per'ə-
mē'dēz).

SCYLLA AND CHARYBDIS

And we now
Had left that isle behind, but soon
I saw the smoke of flying spray,
And huge seas rolling, and I heard   855
The boom of breakers. From the hands
Of my affrighted men the oars
Fell and trailed idle, roaring through
The running sea beside us. Quickly
The ship lost way and stopped, for now
My men no longer toiled, with hands   861
Upon the tapered oars. Now swiftly
I passed through all the ship and paused
By each in passing, cheering him
With gentle words:

"We are not, friends,
Untried in danger. This new peril   866
That lies before us is no greater
Then when the Cyclops caught and held us
Fast in his hollow cave. Yet thence
We found escape—all through my valor
And wit and shrewdness; and I think 871
That we shall live to tell the tale
Of this day too. But rouse you now.
Do as I bid you. Take your seats
Upon the thwarts and drive your oars
Deep in the sea whose billows roll   876
So steep against us. We shall see
If Zeus will grant us to escape
Out of this place of death. And you,
Helmsman, I charge you, fix my words
Fast in your heart, for you alone   881
Hold in your hand the helm that guides
Our hollow ship. Steer boldly forth
Out of these smoking seas and head her

Straight for yon crag, and take good heed
Lest she swing wide and sweep us all 886
Into sore peril!

So I spoke,
And they obeyed my order quickly,
And yet I did not speak of Scylla,
That monster none may face, in fear   890
Lest they from terror drop their oars
And hide within the hold.

Slight heed
I gave to Circe's hard command
I should not arm me. I put on
My glorious armor and I grasped   895
Two spears in hand and took my station
On the decked prow, for there I thought
I first should see appear this Scylla
That dwelt within the rock, to bring
My men destruction.

And yet nowhere 900
Could I behold her, and my eyes
Wearied with wandering up and down
That shadowy wall of stone.

So onward
Into that strait we sailed lamenting—
On one side Scylla, on the other   905
Dreadful Charybdis. Terribly
She swallowed down the salt seawater
Then vomited it forth till all
Was tossed and whirling like a caldron
Above a raging fire; and spray   910
Flew high and fell upon the tops
Of the tall crags. But when once more
She sucked the salt sea down, we saw
The whirl's wild depths laid bare; the waters
Roared loud about the rocks; far down

We saw the bottom of the deep   916
Blackened with sand.
                          Pale terror then
Laid hold on us: we saw the monster
And feared death near.
                          And on that instant
Scylla reached forth and snatched my
    men   920
Out of my hollow ship—six men,
My best in strength and courage. Lo,
Even as I looked along the ship
To seek them, there I saw, above me,
Their hands and feet as up she swung
    them   925
Aloft in air. And loud they cried,
Calling, for the last time, my name,
In agony of heart. And even
As one who fishes from a rock
That juts far out to sea, casts down   930
His bait to lure small fish and tosses
Into the deep a bit of horn
From kine° of his own field—aye, even
As he, if then he takes a fish,
Flings it aloft out of the sea   935
All quivering, even so she swung them
All quivering up to her high crag.
There she devoured them, one and all,
Before her doorway, while they shrieked
And still stretched out their hands to me
In dying agony. That sight   941
Was saddest of all sights my eyes
Have ever seen, while through sore trials
I wandered the sea's ways.
                          So now
We had escaped the Clashing Rocks, 945
And Scylla and the dread Charybdis.

933. **kine:** cattle.

FOR STUDY AND DISCUSSION

1. What do the Sirens promise Odysseus in
their song? Which of the things they promise
would be most tempting to Odysseus? Why?

2. Faced with a choice between Scylla and
Charybdis, Odysseus does as Circe advises
and chooses Scylla. From what happens when
the ship passes between the two, do you think
Odysseus made the right choice? Do you think
he was justified in choosing Scylla, knowing
that this would mean the sacrifice of six of
his men? Why or why not? Why is Scylla the
lesser of two evils?

3. What information about the dangers
they must face did Odysseus withhold from
his crew? Why did he do this? Do you think
he had a right or a responsibility as a leader
to do so? Why or why not?

4. Although Circe warns him of all that will
happen, Odysseus is unable to ignore the
Sirens' song or to save his six men from Scylla.
Is Odysseus less of a hero because of these
failures? Why or why not?

5. Reread Circe's description of the dangers
that Odysseus must face. From what she says
about them, what in real life do you think each
of these dangers represents? Do these dangers illustrate examples of—and lessons in—
human conduct?

═══════════════════

[Remembering Circe's warning not to harm
the Sungod's cattle, Odysseus tries to persuade his men to bypass Thrinacia. The men,
however, insist on landing. After adverse
winds force them to remain on the island,
their supplies give out and, ignoring the goddess' warning, one day, while Odysseus is
sleeping, his men slaughter some of the cattle.
Vengeance is not long in coming, Almost as
soon as they put to sea, the ship is swept up
in a raging storm and all but Odysseus are
drowned. Clinging to a raft, he is washed
ashore on the island of Phæacia. After hearing the story of Odysseus' wanderings, the
king of Phæacia offers him a boat and crew
to take him home to Ithaca. Thus Odysseus
returns to his own land after an absence of
twenty years.

The goddess Athene appears to Odysseus
on the beach to warn him of the state of affairs
in Ithaca. During his absence, young men
from nearby lands, considering Odysseus dead,
have come to woo his beautiful wife Penelope.[1]
Penelope herself does not believe that Odys-

[1] **Penelope** (pə·nel′ə·pē).

seus is dead and keeps putting off the wooers. The wooers, however, refuse to leave and remain at Odysseus' house, eating and drinking at his expense. Penelope is helpless to make them leave, because Odysseus' most loyal followers went with him long ago to Troy. The wooers, realizing Penelope's helplessness, are even plotting to murder her son Telemachus [1] before he is old enough to inherit his father's lands. Telemachus, who also is hoping for Odysseus' return, has gone to Lacedæmon [2] (Sparta) to ask for news of him.

After bringing Odysseus up to date, Athene leaves for Sparta to bring back Telemachus. Odysseus, disguised as a beggar, takes shelter meanwhile in the hut of his faithful old servant, the swineherd Eumæus.[3]]

THE MEETING OF ODYSSEUS AND TELEMACHUS

And now Athene went her way
To Lacedæmon, for she sought
Noble Odysseus' son, to bid him
Return to his own home. And there   950
She found him, and drew near to him,
And said:

      "It is no longer wise,
Telemachus, to wander here
So far from home, leaving your house
And all the wealth there in the power   955
Of the proud wooers. Now I warn you,
And heed my words: Their leaders lie
Already watching at the straits
And plan to slay you ere you come
To your own land. So steer your ship   960
Outside the islands, and sail swiftly
By day and night. The god who watches
And keeps you safe will send a wind
To help you on your way.

      And when
You reach the utmost point of land   965
That juts to sea from Ithaca,

Send then your ship and all your men
On to the city. You yourself
Shall seek the farm where dwells the swineherd
Who keeps your herds of swine, whose heart   970
Is ever faithful."

      At her words
Telemachus aroused his comrades
And bade them make his good ship ready
And loose the cables. And Athene
Sent a fair wind across the sea.   975
Odysseus and the goodly swineherd
Together in the hut at dawn
Prepared their breakfast, kindling fire,
When they had sent the men away
To drive the swine afield. And now   980
Telemachus drew near. The dogs,
Though wont to bark, now wagged their tails
Nor barked at all; and great Odysseus
Saw how they wagged their tails, and heard   984
The sound of footsteps, and spoke quickly
With winged words to Eumæus:

      "Surely,
Eumæus, there comes hither now
A friend or one you know!"

      And scarcely
Had he thus said, when his dear son
Stood in the doorway. Then the swineherd   990
Sprang up, surprised, and from his hands
Let fall the bowl with which he labored
Mingling the glowing wine. He hastened
To greet his master and he kissed him.
So in now stepped Telemachus   995
Over the sill of stone. His father
Rose from his seat to give him place,
But this he would not have, and stayed him,
And said:

      "Nay, stranger, sit. For we,
Here on this farm of ours, with ease   1000
Shall find a seat, and this man here
Will soon provide one."

---

[1] **Telemachus** (tə·lem′ə·kəs).   [2] **Lacedæmon** (las·ə-dē′mən).   [3] **Eumæus** (yoo·mē′əs).

So he spoke.
Back to his seat then turned Odysseus,
And the good swineherd heaped fresh
  bushes
And spread a fleecy skin upon them   1005
And here now sat Telemachus,
Odysseus' own dear son.
                        And now,
When food and drink had stayed their
  hunger,
He said to the good swineherd:
                        "Whence,
Good father, comes this stranger?"
                        Then,   1010
Swineherd Eumæus, thus you° answered:
"From Crete, he told me, but through
  many
A city of mankind he passed
In wandering hither. He has come   1014
To my own house, and to your charge
I give him now. Do with him, then
Whate'er you will. He is, he says,
Your suppliant."
                Then thus replied
Prudent Telemachus:
                        "Eumæus,
Your words pierce to my heart. How can I
Receive a guest at home? But go   1021
Quickly, my good old friend—go tell
Prudent Penelope that I
Am safe here, come from Pylos."°
                                So
Then spoke Telemachus, and sent   1025
The swineherd on his way. And yet
He did not go his way unseen
By great Athene, for she came,
In form a woman, fair and tall,   1029
And skilled in dainty crafts, and stood
Close by the door. Odysseus saw her;
His son beheld her not, though standing
Before his face, nor knew her presence,

For not to all men do the gods
Appear in open sight. Odysseus   1035
Saw, and the dogs saw too; they barked
  not,
But whimpering slunk off in fear
Across the farmland. With her brows
She signed° to him. Odysseus saw
And understood, and forth he came   1040
By the great courtyard wall and there
He stood before her. Then to him
Thus spoke Athene:
                        "Shrewd Odysseus,
Laërtes' son, now you shall tell   1044
Your son your secret; now no longer
Need you keep silence. And you twain°
Shall plan together death and doom
For the proud wooers."
                        Upon his body
She put a fresh new cloak and tunic,
And mightier she made him seem   1050
And fairer, and the deeper hue
Of youth came back.
                        And now Odysseus
Entered the lodge, and his son marveled
Beholding him, and turned his eyes
Away in awe, lest this might be   1055
A god before him, and he spoke
In winged words:
                        "You are changed, O stranger,
From what you seemed but now. Your
  garments
Are not the same; your very flesh
Is altered. Surely you are one   1060
Of the immortal gods that have
Wide heaven for home. Show, now,
Compassion on us!"
                        Then replied
Noble, long-tried Odysseus:
                        "Nay,
I am no god! Why liken me   1065
To those that die not? I am he
Whom you so long have wept," His son,
Who could not yet believe that this
Could be his father, answered him

1011. **Eumæus, thus you:** this direct form of
address is used by Homer to show an especially
warm feeling toward the old servant. 1024. **Pylos**
(pī′lôs): a seaport southwest of Sparta.

1039. **signed:** signaled. 1046. **twain:** two.

And said:

       "No, you are not Odysseus;   1070
My own dear father! Some strange god
Enchants my eyes, to make me weep
In greater grief hereafter. Never
Could any mortal man so change."
Then Odysseus answered and said:

               "Telemachus,
It is unworthy of you thus   1076
To stare and marvel beyond measure
At your own father, when at last
He stands before you! No Odysseus
But I will ever come! For I   1080
It is, I that you see before you,
Who have borne perils and have wandered
In many lands, and now at last
Come, after twenty years, again
To my own native land."

             So said he, 1085
And sat him down. Then round his neck
His son cast both his arms and sobbed
And poured forth tears. Upon them both
Came longing and wild weeping. Loud
Rose their lament, and never ceased—
Like the shrill cry of birds, of sea-hawks
Or crook-clawed cormorants, whose
   young   1092
The country-folk bear off, ere yet
Their wings are fit for flight: even so
All piteously beneath their brows   1095
Their tears then fell.

           At last thus spoke
Noble Odysseus: "Hither now
I come at counsel of Athene,
That you and I may plan the slaying
Of all our enemies. Go you   1100
Tomorrow morning home; there join
The haughty wooers. And the swineherd
Shall bring me in, an aged beggar.
Then, if they treat me with foul insult
In my own home, still let your breast 1105
Endure it all. Nay, though they drag me
About the hall, and hurl their missiles,
Look on in patience: speak smooth words
And bid them cease, but they will heed
  not,

For on them comes their fated day.   1110
And this I say now: mark it well:
If you are truly mine, the son
Of my own ancient blood, let no one
Learn that Odysseus is returned—
No, not Laertes, not the swineherd 1115
Nor any of the house, nay, not
Penelope herself! We two
Alone will find what loyalty
Still dwells here in my house, what hearts
Are faithful yet!"

            And now at evening, 1120
Back came the swineherd to Odys-
  seus
And his brave son, and there they made
Their supper ready. But Athene
Had first drawn near and touched Odys-
  seus
With her gold wand, and once again 1125
She made him agèd to behold
And meanly clad, lest the good swineherd
Should look upon his face and know him,
And go to wise Penelope
And tell his tidings.   1130
Now when the earliest dawn appeared
Rose-fingered, then Telemachus,
Dear son of great Odysseus, bound
Upon his feet his sandals fair
And took his mighty spear that fitted 1135
His hand so readily. And now,
Ere he set forth to town, thus said he
To the good swineherd:

            "Now, old friend,
I go to town so that my mother
May see me, for she will not cease, 1140
I know, her piteous tears and weeping
Till she herself has seen me. This
I leave for you to do, to guide
This stranger to the town, that there
The man may beg his bread. Who chooses
May give him then a crust to eat, 1146
A drink too from his cup. I have not
A home for every guest; too many
The troubles that come pressing on me
To vex my heart. So, if this stranger 1150
Should take this ill, the worse for him!

I love, myself, plain speaking."
                    Then
Thus answered wise Odysseus:
                         "Nay,
Good friend, I have no wish to stay here.
In town a beggar fares far better   1155
Than on the farm, for there a man
Can beg him food, and whoso will
May give him freely. I am now
Too old to live here on a farm
And labor at each task my master   1160
May lay upon me. Go your way,
And, as for me, this man shall guide me
As you have bidden, after I
Have warmed me well beside the fire
And the sun gains in strength, for poorly
I now am clad; the frosts of morning 1166
Might do me hurt: the town, they tell me,
Lies far away."
              So spoke Odysseus,
And now Telemachus went forth
Across the farmland. Fast he walked 1170
With hurrying feet, still planning evil
Against the wooers.
                   And at last
He reached the stately house and set
The spear he carried in its place
By a great pillar. Then he entered   1175
O'er the stone threshold. First of all
To see him was old Eurycleia,°
His nurse, as he was spreading fleeces
Upon the carven chairs. And swiftly
She came with flowing tears to meet him;
And kissed him on the face and shoul-
    ders.   1181
And now there came forth from her room
Penelope, like Artemis,°
Or golden Aphrodite.° Weeping,
She cast her arms about her son   1185
And kissed his face and his fair eyes.
And said, in winged words:

1177. **Eurycleia** (yo͞o′ri·klē′yə). 1183. **Artemis**
(är′tə·mis): goddess of the moon and hunting;
the Romans called her Diana. 1184. **Aphrodite**
(af′rə·dī′tē): goddess of love and beauty; the Romans called her Venus.

                              "Now at last
You come, Telemachus, more welcome
Than the sun's light. I thought my eyes
Should never see you more, when you
Went off so secretly to Pylos   1191
Aboard your ship, to seek for tidings
Of your dear father. Tell me now.
What saw you on your way?"
                             Then thus
Telemachus replied:
                     "Nay, mother,   1195
Start not my tears nor stir my heart
Within my bosom, for I barely
Escaped the stroke of death."

FOR STUDY AND DISCUSSION

1. Why doesn't Odysseus tell Telemachus
who he is when they first meet? What might he
want to find out about Telemachus? What
kind of person does Telemachus, through his
actions, show himself to be? Which actions
reveal his character most clearly?

2. What qualities of character are evident
in the actions of the old swineherd Eumæus?
In what sense could he be considered more
"noble" than the suitors of noble birth who
have come to woo Penelope?

3. Many scenes in the *Odyssey* contain the
germ of a subsequent scene or scenes. What
future action do you anticipate after Odysseus' meeting with his son? What does Odysseus promise Telemachus they will do?

4. How do Odysseus and Telemachus plan
to get rid of the suitors? As part of this plan,
what does Odysseus caution Telemachus to
be sure not to do? Why do you think Odysseus
considers this part of the plan so vital?

5. In this scene, as elsewhere in the *Odyssey,* the goddess Athene takes part in the
action of the story. What part does she play
in this scene? What distinctly human traits
are given her by Homer? How does she use
godlike powers?

6. The last half of the *Odyssey* contains
many details of everyday life in Homer's time.
Point out some of these details in the scene
in Eumæus' hut. How do these details help
to make the events of the scene seem real?

[Guided by the swineherd, Odysseus approaches his home. He is still disguised as a beggar.]

Now a dog
Lay near, and heard, and straightway lifted
His head and ears. For this was Argos,
Steadfast Odysseus' dog—a dog   1201
He reared long since, but never used,
For ere he used him, he went thence
To sacred Ilium.° Young men,   1204
In days now gone, would take the dog
To chase wild goats and deer and hares,
But now, his master far away,
He lay despised upon the dung
Left by the cattle and the mules
Heaped high before the doors. There 1210
Argos, this dog, now lay, all foul
With vermin. Yet when he beheld,
Weak though he was, Odysseus near him,
He wagged his tail and dropped both ears,
Though he had now no strength to move
Nearer his master.

1204. **Ilium** (il′ē·əm): Troy.

And Odysseus   1216
Saw him, but drew not near. He wiped
A tear away before Eumæus
Might see he wept; then thus he spoke
And said:
        "Now this is strange, Eumæus.   1220
Why should a dog like this lie here
Upon a dunghill? For this dog
Is finely formed: I cannot say
Whether his speed can match his beauty,
Or if he be but of those dogs   1225
That masters keep for show at table."
Then, good Eumæus, you replied:
"Aye, he who owned this dog has perished
In a far land. Were this dog now
What he was once, in grace of form   1230
And feats of hunting—on the day
His master went to Ilium
And left him here—you would be seized
With sudden wonder did you see
His swiftness and his strength. No beast
That he once started from his lair   1236
In the dense forest depths escaped him;
Keenly he followed scent. But now
His evil days have come. His master
Has perished far away; the women   1240

Care not and let him lie untended.
For slaves, when masters pass from
   power,
Give no more heed to toil. When once
Ill fortune brings a man to bondage
Far-thundering Zeus then takes from him
Full half his worth."
                    So spoke Eumæus,   1246
Then entered that fair house and passed
Straight down the hall and through the
   midst
Of those proud wooers. Then on Argos
Death's dark end came, when he had seen
Odysseus, gone for twenty years.

[Odysseus enters the hall and passes among
the suitors to beg. Failing to recognize the
master of the house in his beggar's rags, they
taunt and jeer at him. Odysseus, however,
bides his time, planning their murder. When
Penelope hears that the "stranger" has news
of her long-absent husband, she sends for him
and says:]

                    "This first, O stranger,   1251
I fain° would know: what man are you?
And of what land? Who are your kin
And what your city?"
                    Then in answer
Spoke shrewd Odysseus:
                    "No man, lady,   1255
Of all the mortal men that dwell
Upon unmeasured earth, can blame you.
Your fame is spread as wide as heaven.
Even a king whom all men praise,
Who rules, in fear of God, a folk   1260
Many and great, upholding justice,
Can win no greater fame. For ever
Beneath his kindly rule, the earth
On its dark soil bears wheat and barley,
The trees bend low with fruit, the flocks
Breed sturdy lambs, the sea yields fish,
And all his people prosper. Ask me   1267
Of what things else you will, since I
Am in your house, but do not ask

My race or native land, or fill   1270
My soul with still more suffering
By waking memory. For many
A sorrow I have known. And yet,
Here in another's house, I would not
Sit weeping and lamenting. Sorrow   1275
Grows only worse through endless weep-
   ing.
Nay, one of these maids here or you
Might blame me, saying that my eyes
Swim thus in tears because the wine
Lies deep about my wits."
                    Then answered   1280
Prudent Penelope and said:
                    "Alas,
O stranger, but now all wherein
I once excelled, in form or face,
The gods laid waste that day the Argives
Embarked for Ilium; for with them   1285
My husband went away, Odysseus!
Would he might come again to watch
Over my life here: better far
Would be my fame, and fairer. Now
I can but suffer. Such the evil   1290
Some power from on high has sent
For my affliction. So I give
But little heed to wanderers
Or suppliants or heralds serving
The people's need, but ever long   1295
After Odysseus, wasting ever
My heart away.
                    These men would hasten
My marriage day, so I must spin
A skein° of trickery. And first
Some power whispered to my heart   1300
That I should build me in my hall
A great loom, and should weave me here
A robe, a garment rich and wide.
So then I said to all:
                    'Young men   1304
Who come to woo me—this I pray you:
Though great Odysseus now lie dead,
Forbear to urge this marriage. Wait
But till this robe I weave is finished—

1252. **fain:** gladly.

1299. **skein** (skān): a dense coil of yarn or thread.

I would not have its threads all wasted!
This is a shroud° for lord Laertes°   1310
When the dread doom of death shall take
    him
And leave long sorrow. I must do this
Lest some Achæan woman blame me
In my own land, if he should lie
Without a shroud, who once was lord
Of wealth so great.'
                        So then I spoke, 1316
And their proud hearts agreed. And so
Each day I wove at my great web,
But every night I bade them bring
Torches to light me, and unraveled   1320
All I had wrought by day. And thus
Three years I did, unseen, and ever
Deceived the wooers. But at length,
When the fourth year came round, my
    maids,   1324
Ungrateful, like base dogs, betrayed me.
The wooers came and caught me. Harshly
They railed against° me. So, compelled,
And through no will of mine, I brought
That weaving to its end. And now
I can no longer put off marriage   1330
Or shape me a new plan."
                        Indeed
Odysseus' heart was filled with pity
At his wife's weeping. Yet he kept
His eyes beneath his eyelids steady
As horn or iron, and with craft   1335
He hid his tears from sight.
                        But now,
When she with many a tear had taken
Her fill of sorrow, once again
She spoke and answered:
                        "Now I mean
To try you, stranger. I would know   1340
If you in truth received my husband
As guest in your own hall."
                        Answered

The wise Odysseus:
                "Noble lady,
This is a hard thing to tell rightly
After so long a time, for now   1345
Full twenty years have gone their way
Since he set forth and left my land.
Yet I will tell you how my heart
Still sees his picture. Great Odysseus
Then wore a cloak of purple wool   1350
In double fold. Upon it shone
A brooch of gold: two clasps it had.
And thus its front was carved: a dog
Held with its paws a dappled fawn
Struggling, and gripped it in its jaws; 1355
And all who saw it marveled how,
Though wrought of lifeless gold, that dog
Held the fawn gripped, and strangled it,
While, striving to escape, the fawn
Still struggled with its feet. I marked 1360
His tunic, too, that shone as bright
Upon his body as the skin
That gleams upon a sun-dried onion,
So smooth it was, and shining like
The sun itself. And many a woman   1365
Gazed at him wondering. And this
I say besides; mark well: I know not
If he was wont to wear this clothing

1310. **shroud:** garment for a corpse; **lord Laertes:**
Odysseus' father is now a very old man. The word
lord is used to indicate respect for his former greatness. 1327. **railed against:** scolded.

At home, or if some comrade gave it
When he embarked in his swift ship, 1370
Or if some host had given it him,
For he was loved by many, few
So loved as he. And I myself
Gave him a sword of bronze, a cloak
With double fold, of fairest purple, 1375
And a fringed tunic, and so sent him,
With love and honor, on his way
In his good ship."

        So he spoke,
And once again he waked in her
The need of weeping, for she knew 1380
So well each token that Odysseus
Told her so clearly. But at length
She answered:

        "From this moment, stranger,
You who have been a sight for pity,
Shall be beloved and honored. I 1385
It was, with my own hand, who gave him
Those garments you have told of. First
In my own room, I folded them
And fixed upon them the bright brooch,
That precious jewel. Yet I never 1390
Shall greet him now, returning hither
To his own land."

        And thus Odysseus
Answered her, saying:

        "Honored wife
Of great Odysseus, mar no more
Your lovely flesh, nor waste away 1395
Your heart with weeping for your hus-
  band.
And yet I blame you not. No woman
But weeps to lose her lord, the man
She loved, whose children she has borne—
Aye, even though he were far other 1400
Than was Odysseus who, men say,
Is like the gods. But cease your weeping
And heed my words, for I will speak
Truth only and will hold back naught
Of all I lately heard: Odysseus. 1405
They say, is near at hand and safe,
I say that he is safe. Already
He is at hand: no longer now

Will he delay and linger far
From friends and native land. Nay, more,
I add my oath. Be witness, now, 1411
Zeus, highest of the gods and best,
And let this hearth of good Odysseus,
Where I now stand, be witness too
That now, this very year, Odysseus 1415
Shall come here, aye, as this moon passes
And the new moon begins."

FOR STUDY AND DISCUSSION

1. Odysseus' encounter with his dog Argos is one of the most moving episodes in the *Odyssey*. Which details in Homer's description of Argos are especially effective in arousing your sympathy for him? What truths about people and life in general are suggested by the story of Argos?

2. What does Penelope want to learn from the "stranger"? What does Odysseus want to learn from Penelope? Which of them is more successful? Why?

3. What in the story Odysseus tells Penelope is not true? Why does he lie to her? Do you think, under the circumstances, that his lying is justified? Why or why not?

4. To what does Penelope refer when she speaks of a "skein of trickery" (line 1299)? What does this scheme reveal about her?

5. Note how Odysseus describes himself to his wife, especially in lines 1372–73. What hints do we have that Odysseus is enjoying the humor of this particular situation?

ODYSSEUS' TRIUMPH

[Odysseus returns to the hall where the suitors are feasting and once again is mocked and insulted. The suitors summon Penelope to the hall and demand that she choose one of them at once. Penelope replies that she will marry whoever can string Odysseus' bow and shoot an arrow through a row of twelve axes, as Odysseus used to do. All the suitors try to match this feat, but cannot even bend the bow to string it. Last of all, Odysseus, still disguised, steps forward and takes the bow.]

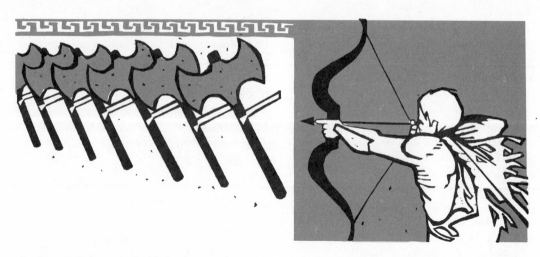

And now Odysseús held the bow
And turned it, side to side, and tried it
In every part, lest worms, the while 1420
Its lord was far away, had eaten
Into the horn. And one who watched
Would say, quick glancing at his neighbor.
"This fellow must be used to bows,
A clever rascal. He may have 1425
A bow like this laid by at home
Or studies how to make one. Look:
See how the idle beggar turns it
This way and that with ready hands,
Well tried in mischief!"

                    And another 1430
Of the proud youths would say:

                              "May he
Meet ever such good luck as now
Will be his lot, when he shall fail
To bend the bow!"

                    So spoke the wooers. 1434
But wise Odysseus, who had handled
That mighty bow, testing each part,
At once as easily as a man,
A singer, skillful with the lyre,
Stretches a string in place and fits it
To its new peg, and at each end 1440
Makes fast the twisted gut—even so
With ready ease Odysseus bent
And strung that mighty bow.

                              He took it
In his right hand and tried the bowstring,

And at his touch it rang out loud, 1445
Clear as a swallow's cry.

                    Then fell
A deadly dread on all the wooers,
And every face turned pale. Zeus sent
His sign from heaven in loud thunder,
And great Odysseus, who so long 1450
Had suffered and endured, rejoiced
To hear this signal from the son
Of artful Cronus.°

                    Now he took
A swift shaft in his hand: it lay
Before him, drawn, upon the table; 1455
For in the hollow quiver yet
The rest lay waiting—as the Achæns
Ere long should learn.

                    And now he laid
The arrow in the rest,° and seated 1459
There on the bench, he drew the string
And the notched arrow. Straight he aimed,
And loosed the shaft.

                    And not one axe
Of all it missed. Through every one
From the first axe, that bronze-tipped ar-
    row
Went speeding to the very last 1465
And out beyond. Then thus Odysseus
Spoke to Telemachus:

1453. **Cronus** (krō′nəs): a Titan who was father
of Zeus and ruler of the world. 1459. **rest:** that
part of a bow where the arrow rests.

"This stranger,
Telemachus, who as your guest
Sits in your hall, has not, you see,
Brought shame on you. I have not missed
The mark nor made a mighty labor   1471
Of stringing the great bow. My strength
Is even as of old, nor fails me now
As these in insult deemed.
                    At last
The time is come, the destined hour 1475
To bid these wooers sup with us,
Through yet it is full day! And we
Have sport for them besides—the dance
And twanging of the lyre, to crown
This coming feast!"
                    So spoke Odysseus, 1480
And gave, with bended brows, the signal.
And, on the instant, his dear son
Telemachus girt by his side
His keen-edged sword and took his stand
Beside his father's seat, all armed   1485
In glittering bronze.

[With the help of Telemachus, Odysseus
kills the suitors in a bloody and merciless fight.
The old nurse, Eurycleia, who has kept silent
even though she recognized Odysseus before
the battle, now rushes to Penelope to tell her
that the suitors are dead, slain by Odysseus,
her husband. Penelope cannot believe such
good news and answers:]

                    "Dear nurse,
The gods have made you mad; for they
Can turn to folly even him
Who is the wisest, and can set
The fool upon the way to wisdom.   1490
And they have turned your wits astray.
Your mind, till now, was ever steady.
Why do you mock me, now my spirit
Is heavy with its grief, to tell me
Such tales as this, awaking me   1495
From the sweet sleep that held me fast
And sealed my eyes?"
                    Then replied
Her dear nurse Eurycleia:

                    "Nay,
Dear child, I do not mock you. Here
In very truth, Odysseus now   1500
Is with us, he himself. For he
Was the poor stranger every man
Insulted in the hall. Long since,
Telemachus knew well that he   1504
Was here among us, but with foresight
He hid his knowledge, that his father
Might all the better take his vengeance
For all the cruel wrongs these men
Have wrought in arrogance."
                    So said she.
Gladly her mistress heard and sprang
Up from her bed and cast her arms   1511
Round the old woman. In winged words
She said:
                    "Now, prithee, tell me truly,
My own dear nurse. If he indeed
Is come again, as you are saying,   1515
To his own home, how could he then
So quickly lay his hands in vengeance
Upon the shameless wooers—he
Being but one, while they are many,
Thronging the house!"
                    And thus replied   1520
Her dear nurse Eurycleia:
                    "Nay,
I saw not, and I heard no tidings,
Nay, not a sound, save for the groans
Of those he slew. For we in fear
Sat shrinking in the farthest corner   1525
Of our own sheltered room, fast barring
Its close-set doors, until at last
I heard your son Telemachus
Call from the hall, for so his father
Had bid him call. I found Odysseus   1530
Amidst the bodies of the slain,
For all about him they were lying
Upon the trodden floor, aye, many,
Each close upon the other. Glad   1534
Your heart too would have been, had you
But seen him then! Now all the bodies
Are gathered in a heap together
Hard by the courtyard gate, while kindling
A mighty fire, he now is cleansing

The noble hall with brimstone.° Hither
I come to call you, for he bade me. 1541
Follow me now that you may both
Enjoy your happiness together
With loving hearts, for you have both
Borne many a sorrow."

        Then replied 1545
Prudent Penelope:
        "Dear nurse,
Now be not over-quick to boast
And laugh with joy. You know indeed
How welcome he would be to all
In his own house, and most to me 1550
And to the son I bore him. Yet
This tale you tell cannot be true:
Alas, it is some god came hither
And slew those haughty wooers, angered
At the rash insults of their pride 1555
And all their evil deeds. They honored
No man upon the earth, no man
Or good or evil who dared come
Among them here. So for their crimes
They met this end. But far away 1560
Odysseus now has lost forever
All hope of his returning hither—
Nay, he himself is lost!"

        Then answered
Her dear nurse Eurycleia:
        "Child,
What words are these that now have
   passed 1565
The portal of your teeth! To say
That your own husband, he who now
Stands here upon his hearth, will never
Come home again! Your heart is ever
Slow to believe. Yet I can tell you 1570
Another sign, a sign yet surer,
The scar of the deep wound the boar
Once gave with his bright tusk. I spied it
That day I washed his feet, and longed
To tell you what I saw. But he 1575
Laid hand upon my mouth and so
With his wise foresight, stopped my
   speech."

1540. **brimstone:** sulfur, burned as a cleansing
agent.

Then wise Penelope replied:
"Dear nurse, wise as you are, 'tis hard
To guard against the secret purpose 1580
Of the eternal gods. And yet
Let us go down and seek my son
And see these wooers who lie slain
And him that slew them"

        So she spoke,
And down she passed then from her room,
And sorely was her heart divided 1586
Whether to stand far off and question
Her own dear lord or stand beside him
And kiss his face and clasp his hand.
But when she entered and passed over
The threshold of carved stone, she went
And sat her down, facing Odysseus, 1592
In firelight, by the farther wall.
And he still sat with downcast eyes
By the tall pillar and awaited 1595
In wonder if his stately wife
Would speak to him when she should turn
Her eyes and see him. A long time
She sat in silence, and amazement
Was in her heart; then for a time 1600
She gazed upon him face to face,
And then again she knew him not,
For he still wore upon his body
A beggar's raiment.

        And her son,
Telemachus, now spoke, and said, 1605
Reproaching her:
        "Mother of mine,
Unmotherly, why is your heart
So hard? Why do you ever keep
Far from my father? Why not sit
Close by his side, and question him, 1610
And ask him all his story? Nay,
There is no other woman living
Would stand aside thus, hardening
A stubborn heart against her husband
Who after many a peril past, 1615
Comes, in the twentieth year, once more
To his own land. Your heart is ever
Harder than stone!"

        Then thus replied
Prudent Penelope:

"My son,
My spirit is amazed within me.   1620
I have no power to speak or question
Or look upon his face. And yet,
If this can be Odysseus' self,
And he has now come home, we two
May know each other far more surely
Than any other may, for we   1626
Have secret tokens known to us,
Hidden from all besides."
                    So said she,
And great Odysseus smiled and quickly
Thus to Telemachus he spoke   1630
In winged words:
                    "Go, Telemachus,
And leave your mother in the hall
To test me. She shall learn ere long
More surely what I am. But now,
Because I am unclean to see,   1635
And wear base garments on my body,
She holds me in dishonor, saying
That I am not her lord."

1. What is the suitors' reaction when the "old beggar" takes the bow? Is Homer's description of them as "proud youths" a good one? How is this description borne out by their actions?

2. Odysseus' shooting of an arrow through the holes in a row of twelve battle-axes is a remarkable, almost incredible feat, yet centuries of readers have found this deed believable and entirely convincing. How do the character of Odysseus and his previous actions make such a feat seem possible for him?

3. When the nurse Eurycleia tells Penelope that Odysseus has slain the suitors, Penelope doesn't believe it. Who does she think was responsible for slaying the suitors? Why? How does the nurse know it was Odysseus?

4. When Penelope enters the hall, she is uncertain whether to go to Odysseus or to speak to him from a distance. Why does she feel uncertain? Do you think she is sensible or foolish to hesitate? Why?

PENELOPE TESTS ODYSSEUS

[Odysseus leaves the hall long enough to bathe and dress himself in kingly garments. Athene herself restores his former handsome appearance.]

                    So he came
Forth from the bath, and seemed in presence
Like the immortal gods. And thus   1640
He came once more back to the seat
Whence he had risen, and there sat
Facing his wife. He spoke to her
And said:
                    "O most perplexing woman,
Surely the dwellers on Olympus   1645
Have given you a harder heart
Than other tender women."
                    Answered
The wise Penelope:
                    "O man
Perplexing to my soul—nay, I
Am not held off by pride, nor scorn you,
But I am lost in wonder. Well   1651
I know what you were once when, sailing
Away in your oared ship, you left
Your home in Ithaca. But come
Now, Eurycleia, and make ready   1655
His firm-built bed. Make it outside
The room he built him himself. Aye, move
His firm-built bedstead forth and strew
Upon it bedding—fleeces, covers,
And bright-hued rugs."
                    All this she said   1660
To try her husband. But Odysseus
Was angered at her words, and thus
He spoke to his true wife:
                    "What, woman!
What words are these you now have said
To pierce my heart! Who can have set
My bed in a new place? That task   1666
Would be a hard one, aye, too hard
Even for the cleverest, unless
A god should come and easily
Remove it at his will and set it   1670
In a new place. No mortal man

Of living men, in his full strength,
Could ever move it easily
Out of its present place. For in it,
Wrought in its very frame, is hidden 1675
A secret token, and no other
Wrought this, but I alone.
                              There grew
Within our yard an olive tree,
Long-leaved and thriving, strong of
  growth,
Thick as a pillar. Round its trunk   1680
I shaped my room and built it thus
Till all was finished, walling it
With massive stone, and well I fashioned
The roof to cover it and hung
And fitted its joined doors. And then,
From that long-leaved tall olive tree 1686
I cut the crown away and squared,
Using my ax, the stem remaining
Above the roots; then with the adz
I smoothed it and made true the line, 1690
And thus I made my bedpost. Next
I bored it all with a keen auger
And, so beginning, ever worked
On to the end, and it stood finished.
I decked it all with gold and silver   1695
And ivory, and across it stretched
Long strips of oxhide bright and red.
This is the token that I mean.

Now, wife, I do not know if still
That bed is standing there, or whether
Someone has cut that olive stem   1701
And moved it elsewhere.”
                              So he spoke,
And at his words her knees grew weak
And all her soul within, for well
She knew this token that Odysseus   1705
Had told so plainly. And she wept,
And straight to him she ran, and cast
Her arms about her husband’s neck
And kissed his face and said:
                              “Odysseus,
Pray be not angry with me. You   1710
Have ever been, through every fortune,
Wisest of men. The gods have sent
Sore grief upon us, for they grudged us
That we should side by side together
Share the delight of youth and cross 1715
The threshold of old age. Yet be not,
I pray you, wroth° with me or blame me,
Because I did not, when I saw you,
Run thus to greet you! For my heart
Within my breast was shuddering ever
Lest some strange man should come and
  cheat me   1721
With lying words. For many a man
Will plot base deeds for gain. Lo, now
You quite convince this heart of mine,
Stubborn what though it be!”
                       So spoke she, 1725
And stronger still there came upon him
A yearning need of tears, and there,
Holding his wise and faithful wife,
He wept with joy. And she beside him,
Like men that see the land with gladness—
Seamen whose sturdy ship Poseidon 1731
Has smitten on the deep and shattered
With storm and mighty seas, and few
Are they who from the foaming waters
Escape to swim to shore: their skin   1735
Is crusted with the brine, but happy
They step to land once more, delivered
Out of their danger—with such gladness
She gazed upon her husband.
   1717. **wroth** (rôth): angry.

1. Penelope's deception of the suitors and her testing of Odysseus show a cleverness much like her husband's. What other qualities do she and Odysseus have in common? Where are they revealed in her thoughts, words, and actions? Penelope is one of the most admired characters in all literature. Why do you think this is so?

2. Odysseus' long description of his tree-bed could be considered a digression from the main story. Do you think it is? Why or why not? What purpose does it serve in the story?

3. What moment do you consider the main climax of the last part of the *Odyssey?* What makes that particular moment more powerful than any other?

LANGUAGE AND VOCABULARY

1. In the opening lines of this translation of the *Odyssey*, Odysseus describes himself as well known for his "*cunning* plans." In other translations of this work, this adjective has been translated as *sagacious, strategic, wily, guileful,* and even *deceitful.* Check the meaning of each of these words in a dictionary. Which word best fits Odysseus? Why? Which of these words has a favorable meaning? Which unfavorable? If you were translating the *Odyssey,* which word would you use to describe Odysseus? Why?

2. The concluding lines of the Scylla-Charybdis episode contain a Homeric simile. As you know, a simile is a comparison of two unlike actions or objects that are usually linked by *like* or *as.* An Homeric simile is an extended comparison of two actions or objects that develops mounting excitement and usually ends in a climax. In this passage (lines 928–37), Scylla seizing Odysseus' men is compared to a fisherman landing a fish. Notice how the simile is extended by describing the actions of a fisherman and the parallel actions of the monster. How does Homer's choice of details make the action rise in excitement? How does this extended simile make the action more vivid and gripping?

3. To describe the reunion of Odysseus and Telemachus, Homer uses another extended simile. To what does he compare their lament? What details in the simile suggest the emotions of Odysseus and Telemachus at this moment? Look also at the two similes Homer uses to describe Odysseus' bending of the bow. Which is most strikingly effective? Why?

4. Like the extended simile, the *epithet* is a favorite device of the ancient epic poets. In the *Odyssey* Homer speaks repeatedly of "*rosy-fingered* dawn," "*hollow* ships," the "*wine-dark*" sea," and so on. What epithet is most often applied to Penelope? Does this epithet accurately describe the most essential feature of her character? Why or why not? What epithets are applied to Odysseus? Which of them do you think best fits his character?

FOR COMPOSITION

1. You may be surprised to learn that Greek boys (and some girls) learned how to write by imitating passages from the *Odyssey*. It is easy to see why Homer was such a good model: he had a simple and exciting way of telling a story, of explaining a situation, of describing a battle or a storm, of arousing sympathy. Look again at some part of the *Odyssey* and write a composition on one of the following topics:

In up-to-date, informal English tell the story of Odysseus' outwitting of Polyphemus.

In your own language, explain the perils of passing between Scylla and Charybdis and tell why that passage can symbolize one's journey through life.

Describe Odysseus' return to Ithaca from his own point of view. Relate his reactions upon seeing Telemachus, Eumæus, and Penelope.

Retell Penelope's story in such a way that you arouse admiration for her character and pity for her suffering.

2. Write a brief composition on one of the following topics suggested by the *Odyssey:*

The status of women in Greek life and their status today

The code of the hero

The hero's attitude toward the gods

The hero's relations with others

The Greek respect for civilization

Odysseus as a representative of Greek ideals

Reading and Writing about the Odyssey

Much has been written about the *Iliad* and the *Odyssey,* Homer's two great epic poems. Reading comments on these poems by scholars and critics familiar with them and the time in which they were written can deepen both our enjoyment and understanding. One noted scholar writes this about Homer's style:

Even if we allow for many differences between the *Iliad* and the *Odyssey,* the resemblances are more numerous and striking. In both there is the same generous understanding of humanity, the same pleasure in the good things of life, in wealth and courtesy and hospitality, in skill at shooting or ship-building, in the numerous details of pastoral life, in cows, sheep and pigs, finally in all the natural sights of the Greek world, in the sea-birds diving or perching on rafters, in the rise and fall of the wind, in the return of evening and morning, in the sun and the sea and the sky. If Homer was blind . . . he remembered well what he once saw. Few poets have the gift of conveying visible things so clearly as he can. (C. M. Bowra, *Ancient Greek Literature.*)

What incidents or comments in the *Odyssey* show Homer's "generous understanding of humanity"? his "pleasure in the good things of life"? Which passages best illustrate Homer's gift for "conveying visible things"?

In the following quotation, another writer answers one of the *Odyssey's* central questions: what kind of hero is Odysseus and why is he able to overcome all obstacles?

Odysseus is a good example of a man who indulges in his share of folly but who wins through successfully by faith in the gods and the employment of as much self control

and intelligence as he can command. (Ennis Rees, *The Iliad of Homer.*)

Where does Odysseus indulge in folly? Which is more important to his winning through: his faith in the gods or his intelligence and self control? What does the last part of the author's statement suggest about Odysseus' stature as a hero?

WRITING ABOUT THE ODYSSEY

In a short essay, agree or disagree with one of these statements from the Introduction to the *Odyssey* (pages 515–16).

The *Odyssey* is not only the story of a national hero but also the universal story of every human being. Each of us, like Odysseus, spends many years trying to reach his own personal land of peace and joy. Like him, we must achieve that land by testing ourselves against all the temptations and obstacles in life. Small wonder that our journey through life is often called our "odyssey."

Homer uses myth to illustrate the character of his epic hero. Thus the myth of the lotus-eaters is used to underline Odysseus' ability to overcome the temptation of idleness. The myth of the Sirens shows how Odysseus uses reason, strength of will, and clever planning to triumph over the lure of the pleasures of the senses. [Homer uses] myth . . . to convey a meaningful truth.

ART AND LITERATURE

After studying the art (pages 523–28) and literature in this unit, write an essay giving your impression of Greek art, culture, and ideals.

THE NOVEL

To MANY people one of the great pleasures in life is to curl up with a good novel. Novels are so familiar to us that we might easily assume that they have been in existence for as long as, for example, the drama, which dates back for centuries. However, the novel is one of the most recent forms of literature. It came into being only about three hundred years ago. Essentially, a novel is a long story which often has many characters and more than one plot or story line. It is usually written in prose.

For centuries before the development of the novel, stories were frequently written in verse. During the Middle Ages, many of these stories were known as *romances*. They were largely about kings, queens, heroes, knights in armor, and magicians—all people whose lives were quite unlike the lives of ordinary folk who have to work for their living. The problems faced by farmers, servants, or shopkeepers, and the events of their everyday lives were not regarded as suitable subject matter for literature.

Gradually, however, people came to see that literature could also be interesting and meaningful when it dealt with problems within their own experience. Beginning with the Renaissance, in the fifteenth and sixteenth centuries, and afterwards as well, many social, economic, and scientific developments took place which changed peoples' attitudes toward life and literature.

The world's horizons were widened with the exciting geographical discoveries of such places as India and the Americas. The wealth which poured into Europe through trade with these and other far-off places brought power and prestige to an important new group, the merchants. As the merchants acquired wealth, they moved into the cities. There, books, produced in large quantities at relatively low prices by the newly invented printing press, were gradually made available to them. Practical and hard-headed, these people were more interested in reading about real people and real things than about the make-believe world of the romances.

To meet the demands of their readers, the new storytellers began to write in plain everyday prose about the adventures of ordinary people. They soon saw that the adventures of a servant could be just as exciting as those of a noble master and that the person who sold stockings could be as interesting as the great lord who wore them. The heroes of this new type of literature were often former servants, some honest, some dishonest, who wandered from place to place seeking their fortunes. The amusing stories of these rogues' adventures were called *picaresque,* from *picaro,* the Spanish word for "rascal."

Some people felt that even these characters were too far removed from their own experience. In the eighteenth-century novel *Robinson Crusoe,* the English author Daniel Defoe vividly recreated the experiences of an ordinary trader who was shipwrecked on a desert island. Defoe describes how Crusoe struggled to obtain food and shelter, how he was frightened at night, how he prayed for rescue, and even what he dreamed about. Later in the eighteenth century, the English author Henry Fielding wrote *Joseph Andrews,* a novel in which he described the adventures of a young servant as he traveled about meeting different types of people. These novels, in which the hero travels about and has exciting experiences, are known as *adventure* or *journey* novels. Many famous novels in English and American literature, including *Oliver Twist, David Copperfield, Tom Sawyer,* and *Huckleberry Finn* are adventure novels.

Another type of novel, the *plot* novel, also was developed in eighteenth-century England. An early example of this type of novel is Samuel Richardson's *Pamela; or Virtue Rewarded,* about a servant who is pursued by her rich young master. The plot novel, unlike the adventure novel, is usually set in one place. The reader encounters many people in the adventure novel but becomes only slightly acquainted with them. In the plot novel we meet perhaps only a few people but get to know them well. The adventure novel is usually a collection of adventures and incidents which could go on forever. In the plot novel, the reader's attention must be caught and kept with an interesting and compelling story. Plot novels relate stories about love between men and women, fathers and sons, mothers and daughters, and between friends. These works help us to understand how other people—ordinary human beings, often like ourselves—feel and think and how they react to others and to their surroundings. Since its beginnings, the novel has generally pictured real life. It has reflected the people, customs, and problems of each of the periods through which it has passed.

ELEMENTS OF THE NOVEL

A novel is made up of various elements. The manner in which the novelist approaches the story is very important. To give the novel meaning, the writer begins by introducing one or more *themes,* or overall attitudes toward life, which are developed throughout the work. For example, the theme of *Pamela* is that a good or virtuous person will be rewarded if he or she remains good without faltering. Richardson carries this idea even further, indicating that if good prevails it will not only defeat the bad but actually reform it. Since the novel is a long work, there is time and space to explore and develop important ideas and problems such as these.

The *plot* of a novel is the pattern or system of events and actions that make up the story. It may consist both of the difficulties that combine to prevent the hero or heroine from achieving their goals, as well as the events through which he or she eventually obtains them. As the plot develops and becomes more involved, the novel finally reaches its *climax,* or point of highest interest, when the fate of the hero or heroine is decided. The climax leads to the *dénouement,* when the novelist resolves the complications of the plot. *Dénouement* is a French word meaning "untying" or "solution."

An interesting theme and a compelling plot alone are not enough to make a good novel. Effective *characterization,* the creation of interesting characters, is also essential. It is the presence of people in a book that makes it come alive. However, these should not be just any people, not just any sailor, or farmer, or millionaire, or orphan. The novelist has to give these people character, a special quality which distinguishes them one from the other and makes them so full of life that they become very real to the reader. Some characters are so lifelike in manner that the reader may be either strongly drawn to them or strongly repelled by them. These characters develop and grow as their circumstances or their relationships with others change.

Some novelists, on the other hand, choose to portray their characters with less depth, allowing them to fall into certain expected attitudes or categories. For example, an author may show just the typical outward actions of a lonely old man who seems to hate children and continually chases them away from his front porch, without revealing why the character does this and how he became that way. Another novelist may concentrate on the background, the motives, the emotions of the old man, examining his mind and his feelings and showing how they account for his behavior.

Another important aspect of the novel is its *setting* or actual physical background. The conditions and atmosphere of the time and place in which the action occurs often have a direct bearing on the plot and characterization. Frequently the settings are so well described that readers can see and understand a world that is far removed from their own experiences. *Tom Sawyer,* for example, gives a very vivid picture of life along the Mississippi River in the mid-nineteenth century and *Johnny Tremain* recreates the atmosphere of colonial New England during the Revolutionary period.

POINT OF VIEW AND STYLE

There are many ways of writing a novel. For example, novelists can either look at their characters from the outside or they can write about them from the inside, giving first importance to their inner thoughts and feelings. Early novels were often written in a series of letters which were sent back and forth between the characters. Another technique is that of the *omniscient* or all-knowing author, who stands outside the story, carefully controlling the characters and determining beforehand how each one thinks, feels, and acts. Some authors tell their story through the point of view of a character in the novel. In this method, the actions and responses of the other characters are interpreted by the point of view of the character through whose eyes they are seen. Occasionally novelists pretend to be a character in the story and tell it in the first person. In such novels, it is important to remember that it is the character and not the author who is speaking.

The presence of the author in a novel is felt chiefly through *style,* the author's characteristic mode of expression. Some authors write in an elaborate, involved style, using difficult words and complicated grammatical constructions. Other novelists use everyday speech, writing in simple, brief sentences. Other variations in style include humorous versus serious writing and a warm personal approach versus a removed, objective attitude. The factor of style, as well as all the other elements of the novel, combine to produce in the reader the sense of sustained involvement, immediacy, and identification which the novel at its best can evoke perhaps better than any other literary form.

GREAT EXPECTATIONS

Great Expectations by Charles Dickens is one of the most famous English novels. The story, which is told in the first person by its young hero Pip, traces his emotional and moral growth as he develops from a confused, self-centered boy into a responsible and mature adult. In describing Pip's development, Dickens drew on the memories of his own youthful experiences. (Look back, for example, at "Charles Dickens: Boy of the London Streets," by Rupert Sargent Holland, pages 313–16.)

When Dickens was twelve years old, his father was imprisoned for debts and the boy had to support himself. Left on his own, he met various types of people, including prison inmates, rough laborers, and common servants, some of whom later appeared as characters in his many novels. At eighteen, Dickens fell in love with a young girl, who heartlessly turned him down. He later married Catherine Hogarth, the daughter of an editor and music critic.

After working as a lawyer's clerk and reporter, Dickens took up writing and published his first story in 1833. With the appearance of his novel *The Pickwick Papers* in serial form, in 1836–37, he became well known in England. He was also admired in the United States, which he visited in 1842.

Great Expectations, which was written in 1860–61, was first printed in weekly installments in a magazine which Dickens edited. It appeared in book form in 1861. In this work, Dickens created some of his most memorable characters. Its blend of humor, excitement, and suspense has made *Great Expectations* one of Dickens' most popular and enduring novels.

V. S. PRITCHETT

Great Expectations

A NOVEL BY

CHARLES DICKENS

CHAPTER 1

*In this chapter we meet Pip,
who meets a convict
in a graveyard.*

My FATHER'S FAMILY name being Pirrip, and my Christian name Philip, my infant tongue could make of both names nothing more explicit than Pip. So I called myself Pip, and came to be called Pip.

I gave Pirrip as my father's family name, on the authority of his tombstone and my sister—Mrs. Joe Gargery, who married the blacksmith. I never saw my father or my mother, and never saw a picture of either of them.

Ours was the marsh country, down by the river, within twenty miles of the sea. My first vivid impression of things seems to me to have been gained on a memorable raw afternoon toward evening. At such a time I found out for certain that this bleak place was the churchyard; and that Philip Pirrip, late of this parish, and Georgiana,

Great Expectations by Charles Dickens, as abridged by Blanche Jennings Thompson, copyright 1950 by Harcourt Brace Jovanovich, Inc. Reprinted by permission of the publishers.

wife of the above, were dead and buried. I knew that the dark flat wilderness beyond was the marshes; and that the low leaden line beyond was the river; and that the distant savage lair from which the wind was rushing was the sea; and that the small bundle of shivers growing afraid of it all and beginning to cry was Pip.

"Hold your noise!" cried a terrible voice, as a man started up from among the graves. "Keep still, you little devil, or I'll cut your throat!"

A fearful man, all in coarse gray, with a great iron on his leg. A man with no hat, and with broken shoes, and with an old rag tied round his head. A man who had been soaked in water, and smothered in mud, and lamed by stones, and cut by flints, and stung by nettles, and torn by briars; who limped and shivered, and glared and growled; and whose teeth chattered in his head as he seized me by the chin.

"Oh! Don't cut my throat, sir," I pleaded in terror. "Pray don't do it, sir."

"Tell us your name!" said the man. "Quick!"

"Pip, sir."

"Once more," said the man, staring at me. "Give it mouth!"

"Pip. Pip, sir."

"Show us where you live," said the man. Pint out the place!"

I pointed to where our village lay, a mile or more from the church.

The man, after looking at me for a moment, turned me upside down and emptied my pockets. There was nothing in them but a piece of bread. He ate the bread ravenously.

"You young dog," said the man, licking his lips. "What fat cheeks you ha' got. Darn me if I couldn't eat 'em, and if I han't half a mind to't!"

I held tighter to the tombstone on which he had put me; partly, to keep myself upon it; partly, to keep myself from crying.

"Now lookee here!" said the man. "Where's your mother?"

"There, sir!" said I.

He started, made a short run, and stopped and looked over his shoulder.

"There, sir!" I timidly explained. "Also Georgiana. That's my mother."

"Oh!" said he, coming back. "And is that your father alonger your mother?"

"Yes, sir," said I; "him too."

"Ha!" he muttered. "Who d'ye live with—supposin' you're kindly let to live, which I han't made up my mind about?"

"My sister, sir—Mrs. Joe Gargery—wife of Joe Gargery, the blacksmith, sir."

"Blacksmith, eh?" said he. And looked down at his leg.

After darkly looking at his leg and at me several times, he came closer, took me by both arms, and tilted me back as far as he could hold me.

"Now lookee here," he said, "the question being whether you're to be let to live. You know what a file is?"

"Yes, sir."

"And you know what wittles ¹ is?"

"Yes, sir."

After each question he tilted me over a little more, so as to give me a greater sense of helplessness and danger.

"You get me a file." He tilted me again. "And you get me wittles." He tilted me again. "You bring 'em both to me." He tilted me again. "Or I'll have your heart and liver out."

I was dreadfully frightened, and so giddy that I clung to him with both hands and said, "If you would kindly please to let me keep upright, sir, perhaps I shouldn't be sick, and perhaps I could attend more."

He gave me a most tremendous dip and roll. Then he held me by the arms in an upright position and went on in these fearful terms:

"You bring me, tomorrow morning early, that file and them wittles to that old Battery ¹ over yonder. You do it, and you never dare to say a word or dare to make a sign concerning your having seen such a person as me, or any person sumever, and you shall be let to live. You fail, or you go from my words in any partickler, no matter how small it is, and your heart and your liver shall be tore out, roasted, and ate. Now, I ain't alone, as you may think I am. There's a young man hid with me. That young man hears the words I speak. That young man has a secret way of getting at a boy, and at his heart, and at his liver. It is in wain for a boy to attempt to hide himself from that young man. A boy may lock his door, may be warm in bed, may tuck himself up, may draw the clothes over his head, may think himself comfortable and safe, but that young man will creep his way to him and tear him open. I am a-keeping that young man from harming of you at the present moment, with great difficulty. I find it wery hard to hold that young man off of

---

¹ **wittles:** victuals (vit'lz), food. Throughout the novel several characters pronounce *v* like *w*.

² **Battery** (bat'ər·ē): a bank of earth on which large guns are mounted.

your inside. Now, what do you say?"

I said that I would get him the file, and I would get him what broken bits of food I could, and I would come to him at the Battery early in the morning.

"Say, Lord strike you dead if you don't!" said the man.

I said so, and he took me down.

"Now," he pursued, "you remember what you've undertook, and you remember that young man, and you get home."

He hugged his shuddering body in both his arms and limped toward the low church wall. He got over it, like a man whose legs were numbed and stiff, and then turned round to look for me. I looked all around for the horrible young man, and could see no signs of him. But now I was frightened again, and ran home without stopping.

CHAPTER 2

*We now meet Mrs. Joe Gargery,
Pip's sister, and Joe Gargery
the blacksmith, his brother-in-law.*

My SISTER, Mrs. Joe Gargery, was more than twenty years older than I, and had established a great reputation with herself and the neighbors because she had brought me up "by hand." Knowing her to have a hard and heavy hand, and to be much in the habit of laying it upon her husband as well as upon me, I supposed that Joe Gargery and I were both brought up by hand.

She was not a good-looking woman, my sister; and I had a general impression that she must have made Joe Gargery marry her by hand. Joe was a fair man, with curls of flaxen hair on each side of his smooth face, and with eyes of a very undecided blue. He was a mild, good-natured, sweet-tempered, easygoing, foolish, dear fellow —a sort of Hercules in strength, and also in weakness. My sister, Mrs. Joe, with black hair and eyes, was tall and bony, and almost always wore a coarse apron, fastened over her figure behind with two loops.

Joe's forge adjoined our house, which was a wooden house, as many of the dwellings in our country were. When I ran home from the churchyard, the forge was shut up, and Joe was sitting alone in the kitchen. Joe and I being fellow sufferers, Joe imparted a confidence to me the moment I raised the latch of the door and peeped in at him.

"Mrs. Joe has been out a dozen times looking for you, Pip. And she's out now making it a baker's dozen."

"Is she?"

"Yes, Pip," said Joe, "and what's worse, she's got Tickler with her."

At this dismal intelligence, I twisted the only button on my waistcoat round and round, and looked in great depression at the fire. Tickler was a wax-ended piece of cane, worn smooth by collision with my tickled frame.

"She sot down," said Joe, "and she got up, and she made a grab at Tickler, and she Ram-paged [1] out. That's what she did," said Joe, "she Ram-paged out, Pip."

"Has she been gone long, Joe?" I always treated him as a larger child, and as no more than my equal.

"Well," said Joe, "she's been on the Ram-page, this last spell, about five minutes, Pip. She's a-coming! Get behind the door, old chap."

I took the advice. My sister, Mrs. Joe, throwing the door wide open, and finding an obstruction behind it, immediately divined the cause, and applied Tickler.

[1] **Ram-paged:** Joe is giving added emphasis to the word *rampage,* to storm about wildly.

She concluded by throwing me at Joe, who passed me on into the chimney and quietly fenced me up there with his great leg.

"Where have you been, you young monkey?" said Mrs. Joe, stamping her foot. "Tell me directly what you've been doing to wear me away with fret and fright and worrit, or I'd have you out of that corner if you was fifty Pips, and he was five hundred Gargerys."

"I have only been to the churchyard," said I, from my stool, crying and rubbing myself.

"Churchyard!" repeated my sister. "If it warn't for me you'd have been to the churchyard long ago, and stayed there. Who brought you up by hand?"

"You did," said I.

"And why did I do it, I should like to know?" exclaimed my sister.

I whimpered, "I don't know."

"*I* don't!" said my sister. "I'd never do it again! I know that. It's bad enough to be a blacksmith's wife, and him a Gargery, without being your mother."

My thoughts strayed from that question as I looked disconsolately at the fire. For, the fugitive out on the marshes with the ironed leg, the mysterious young man, the file, the food, and the dreadful pledge I was under to commit a larceny on those sheltering premises, rose before me in the avenging coals.

My sister had a way of cutting our bread-and-butter for us that never varied. First, with her left hand she jammed the loaf hard against her bib. Then she took some butter (not too much) and spread it on the loaf, then sawed a very thick round off the loaf and hewed it into two halves, of which Joe got one, and I the other. Though I was hungry, I dared not eat my slice. I felt that I must have something in reserve for my dreadful acquaintance and his ally, the still more dreadful young

man. I resolved to put my hunk of bread-and-butter down the leg of my trousers.

Joe was about to take a bite when his eye fell on me, and he saw that my bread-and-butter was gone.

The wonder and consternation with which Joe stopped and stared at me were too evident to escape my sister's observation.

"What's the matter now?" said she.

"I say, you know!" muttered Joe, shaking his head at me in a very serious remonstrance. "Pip, old chap! You'll do yourself a mischief. It'll stick somewhere. You can't have chawed it, Pip."

"What's the matter *now*?" repeated my sister, more sharply than before.

"If you can cough any trifle on it up, Pip, I'd recommend you to do it," said Joe, all aghast. "Manners is manners, but still your 'elth's your 'elth."

By this time, my sister was quite desperate, so she pounced on Joe, and, taking him by the two whiskers, knocked his head for a little while against the wall behind him while I sat in the corner looking guiltily on.

"Now, perhaps you'll mention what's the matter," said my sister, out of breath, "you staring great stuck pig."

Joe looked at her in a helpless way; then took a helpless bite and looked at me again.

"Been bolting his food, has he?" cried my sister.

"You know, old chap," said Joe, "I bolted, myself, when I was your age, but I never see your bolting equal yet, Pip."

My sister made a dive at me, and fished me up by the hair, saying nothing more than the awful words, "You come along and be dosed."

Some medical beast had revived tar water [1] in those days as a fine medicine,

---

[1] **tar water:** a solution of tar and water regarded as a cure-all and also used as a tonic.

and Mrs. Joe always kept a supply of it in the cupboard. The urgency of my case demanded a pint of this mixture, which was poured down my throat while Mrs. Joe held my head under her arm.

Conscience is a dreadful thing. The guilty knowledge that I was going to rob Mrs. Joe—I never thought I was going to rob Joe, for I never thought of any of the housekeeping property as his—united to the necessity of always keeping one hand on my bread-and-butter as I sat, or when I was ordered about the kitchen on any small errand, almost drove me out of my mind.

It was Christmas Eve, and I had to stir the pudding for next day with a copper stick. I tried it with the load upon my leg (and that made me think afresh of the man with the load on *his* leg), and found the tendency of exercise to bring the bread-and-butter out at my ankle quite unmanageable. Happily I slipped away and deposited that part of my conscience in my garret bedroom.

"Hark!" said I, when I had done my stirring, and was taking a final warm in the chimney corner before being sent up to bed. "Was that great guns, Joe?"

"Ah!" said Joe. "There's another conwict off."

"What does that mean, Joe?" said I.

"There was a conwict off last night," said Joe, "after sunset-gun. And they fired warning of him. And now it appears they're firing warning of another."

"*Who's* firing?" said I.

"Drat that boy," interposed my sister, frowning at me over her work; "what a questioner he is. Ask no questions, and you'll be told no lies."

"Mrs. Joe," said I, "I should like to know—if you wouldn't much mind—where the firing comes from?"

"Lord bless the boy!" exclaimed my sister, as if she didn't quite mean that but

rather the contrary. "From the Hulks!"

"And please what's Hulks?" said I.

"That's the way with this boy!" exclaimed my sister, pointing me out with her needle and thread, and shaking her head at me. "Answer him one question, and he'll ask you a dozen directly. Hulks are prison ships, right 'cross th' meshes." We always used that name for marshes in our country.

"I wonder who's put into prison ships, and why they're put there?" said I, in a general way, and with quiet desperation.

It was too much for Mrs. Joe, who immediately rose. "I tell you what, young fellow," said she; "I didn't bring you up by hand to badger people's lives out. People are put in the Hulks because they murder, and because they rob, and forge, and do all sorts of bad; and they always begin by asking questions. Now, you get along to bed!"

I was never allowed a candle to light me to bed, and, as I went upstairs in the dark, I was in mortal terror of the young man who wanted my heart and liver; I was in mortal terror of the man with the iron leg; I was in mortal terror of myself, from whom an awful promise had been extracted.

As soon as the great black velvet pall outside my little window was shot with gray, I got up and went downstairs, every board upon the way, and every crack in every board, calling after me, "Stop thief!" and "Get up, Mrs. Joe!" I had no time to spare. I stole some bread, some rind of cheese, and about half a jar of mincemeat (which I tied up in my pocket handkerchief with my last night's slice), some brandy from a stone bottle, diluting the stone bottle from a jug in the kitchen cupboard, a meat bone with very little on it, and a beautiful round compact pork pie.

There was a door in the kitchen com-

municating with the forge; I unlocked and unbolted that door and got a file from among Joe's tools. Then I put the fastenings as I had found them, opened the door at which I had entered when I ran home last night, shut it, and ran for the misty marshes.

CHAPTER 3

A second convict appears.

IT WAS a rimy morning and very damp. On every rail and gate, wet lay clammy, and the marsh mist was thick. However fast I went, I couldn't warm my feet, to which the damp cold seemed riveted as the iron was riveted to the leg of the man I was running to meet. I knew my way to the Battery, for I had been down there with Joe, and Joe had told me that, when I was apprenticed to him, we would have such larks there! I had just crossed a ditch which I knew to be very near the Battery, and had just scrambled up the mound beyond, when I saw the man sitting before me. His back was toward me, and he had his arms folded and was nodding forward, heavy with sleep, so I went forward softly and touched him on the shoulder. He instantly jumped up, and it was not the

same man, but another man!

And yet this man was dressed in coarse gray, too, and had a great iron on his leg, and was lame, and hoarse, and cold, and everything that the other man was except that he had not the same face, and had a flat, broad-brimmed, low-crowned felt hat on. He swore an oath at me and then he ran into the mist, stumbling twice as he went.

"It's the young man!" I thought, feeling my heart shoot as I identified him. I dare say I should have felt a pain in my liver, too, if I had known where it was.

I was soon at the Battery, and there was the right man—hugging himself and limping to and fro, as if he had never all night left off hugging and limping—waiting for me. He was awfully cold, to be sure. His eyes looked awfully hungry, too. He did not turn me upside down this time, but left me right side upward while I opened the bundle and emptied my pockets.

"What's in the bottle, boy?" said he.

"Brandy," said I.

He was already handing mincemeat down his throat in the most curious manner—more like a man who was putting it away somewhere in a violent hurry, than a man who was eating it—but he left off to take some of the liquor. He shivered all the while so violently that it was quite as much as he could do to keep the neck of the bottle between his teeth without biting it off.

"I think you have got the ague,"[1] said I.

"I'm much of your opinion, boy," said he.

"It's bad about here," I told him. "You've been lying out on the meshes."

"I'll eat my breakfast afore they're the death of me," said he. "I'd do that if I was going to be strung up to that there gallows over there, directly arterward. I'll

---

[1] **ague** (ā′gyōō): chills.

beat the shivers so far, *I'll* bet you."

He was gobbling mincemeat, meat bone, bread, cheese, and pork pie, all at once; staring distrustfully while he did so at the mist all around us, and often stopping to listen. Some real or fancied sound, some clink upon the river or breathing of beast upon the marsh, now gave him a start, and he said, suddenly:

"You're not a deceiving imp? You brought no one with you?"

"No, sir! No!"

"Well," said he, "I believe you. You'd be but a fierce young hound indeed, if at your time of life you could help to hunt a wretched warmint, hunted as near death as this poor wretched warmint is!"

Something clicked in his throat as if he had works in him like a clock, and was going to strike. And he smeared his ragged rough sleeve over his eyes.

Pitying his desolation, and watching him as he gradually settled down upon the pie, I made bold to say, "I am glad you enjoy it."

"Thankee, my boy. I do."

"I am afraid you won't leave any of it for him," said I, timidly. "There's no more to be got where that came from."

"Leave any for him? Who's him?" said my friend, stopping in his crunching of piecrust.

"The young man. That you spoke of. That was hid with you."

"Oh, ah!" he returned, with something like a gruff laugh. "Him? Yes, yes! *He* don't want no wittles."

"I thought he looked as if he did," said I.

The man stopped eating and regarded me with the keenest scrutiny and the greatest surprise.

"Looked? When?"

"Just now."

"Where?"

"Yonder," said I, pointing; "over there, where I found him nodding asleep, and thought it was you."

He held me by the collar and stared at me so that I began to think his first idea about cutting my throat had revived.

"Dressed like you, you know, only with a hat," I explained, trembling; "and —and—" I was very anxious to put this delicately—"and with—the same reason for wanting to borrow a file. Didn't you hear the cannon last night?"

"When a man's alone on these flats, with a light head and a light stomach, perishing of cold and want, he hears nothin' all night but guns firing and voices calling. But this man—did you notice anything in him?"

"He had a badly bruised face," said I.

"Not here?" exclaimed the man, striking his left cheek.

"Yes, there!"

"Where is he?" He crammed what little food was left into the breast of his gray jacket. "Show me the way he went. I'll pull him down, like a bloodhound. Curse this iron on my sore leg! Give us hold of the file, boy."

He was down on the rank wet grass, filing at his iron like a madman, and not minding me or minding his own leg, which had an old chafe upon it and was bloody, but which he handled as roughly as if it had no more feeling in it than the file.

I was very much afraid of him again, now that he had worked himself into this fierce hurry, and I was likewise very much afraid of keeping away from home any longer. I told him I must go, but he took no notice, so I thought the best thing I could do was to slip off. The last I saw of him, his head was bent over his knee and he was working hard at his fetter, muttering impatient imprecations at it and his leg. The last I heard of him, I stopped in the mist to listen, and the file was still going.

CHAPTER 4

*We meet the Christmas
dinner guests:
Mr. Wopsle, the parish clerk;
Mr. and Mrs. Hubble,
a wheelwright and his wife;
and Mr. Pumblechook, Joe's uncle,
a corn merchant.*

I FULLY expected to find a constable in the kitchen, waiting to take me up. But not only was there no constable there, but no discovery had yet been made of the robbery. Mrs. Joe was prodigiously busy in getting the house ready for the festivities of the day.

"And where the deuce ha' *you* been?" was Mrs. Joe's Christmas salutation, when I and my conscience showed ourselves.

I said I had been down to hear the carols. "Ah, well!" observed Mrs. Joe. "You might ha' done worse." Joe secretly crossed his two forefingers and exhibited them to me as our token that Mrs. Joe was in a cross temper.

We were to have a superb dinner, consisting of a leg of pickled pork and greens, and a pair of roast stuffed fowls. A handsome mince pie had been made yesterday morning (which accounted for the mincemeat not being missed), and the pudding was already on the boil. My sister, having so much to do, was going to church vicariously; that is to say, Joe and I were going. In his working clothes, Joe was a well-knit, characteristic-looking blacksmith; in his holiday clothes, he was more like a scarecrow in good circumstances than anything else. Nothing that he wore then fitted him or seemed to belong to him. As to me, when I was taken to have a new suit of clothes, the tailor had orders to make them like a kind of reformatory, and on no account to let me have the free use of my limbs. Joe and I going to church, therefore, must have been a moving spectacle for compassionate minds. Yet what I suffered outside was nothing to what I underwent within. The terrors that had assailed me whenever Mrs. Joe had gone near the pantry were only to be equalled by the remorse with which my mind dwelt on what my hands had done.

Mr. Wopsle, the clerk at church, was to dine with us; and Mr. Hubble, the wheelwright, and Mrs. Hubble; and Uncle Pumblechook, who was a well-to-do corn-chandler in the nearest town, and drove his own chaise-cart.[1] The dinner hour was half-past one. When Joe and I got home, we found the table laid, and Mrs. Joe dressed, and the dinner dressing, and the front door unlocked (it never was at any other time) for the company to enter by, and everything most splendid. And still, not a word of the robbery.

The time came, without bringing with it any relief to my feelings, and the company came. Mr. Wopsle, united to a Roman nose and a large, shining, bald forehead, had a deep voice which he was uncommonly proud of. He punished the *amens* tremendously; and when he gave out the psalm, he looked all round the congregation first, as much as to say, "You have heard our friend overhead; oblige me with your opinion of this style!"

I opened the door to the company, first to Mr. Wopsle, next to Mr. and Mrs. Hubble, and last of all to Uncle Pumblechook. (*I* was not allowed to call him "uncle," under the severest penalties.)

"Mrs. Joe," said Uncle Pumblechook— a large, hard-breathing, middle-aged, slow man, with a mouth like a fish, dull staring

[1] **chaise-cart** (shāz-kärt): a two-wheeled one-horse carriage with a folding top.

eyes, and sandy hair standing upright on his head, so that he looked as if he had just been all but choked, and had that moment come to—"I have brought you as the compliments of the season—I have brought you, mum, a bottle of sherry wine—and I have brought you, mum, a bottle of port wine," Every Christmas Day he presented himself, as a profound novelty, with exactly the same words, and carrying the two bottles like dumbbells.

We dined on these occasions in the kitchen, and adjourned, for the nuts and oranges and apples, to the parlor. Among this good company I should have felt myself, even if I hadn't robbed the pantry, in a false position. I should not have minded that if they would only have left me alone. But they wouldn't leave me alone. They seemed to think the opportunity lost if they failed to point the conversation at me, every now and then, and stick the point into me.

It began the moment we sat down to dinner. Mr. Wopsle said grace with theatrical declamation and ended with the very proper aspiration that we might be truly grateful. Upon which my sister fixed me with her eye and said in a low reproachful voice. "Do you hear that? Be grateful."

"Especially," said Mr. Pumblechook, "be grateful, boy, to them which brought you up by hand."

Joe always aided and comforted me when he could, in some way of his own, and he always did so at dinnertime by giving me gravy, if there were any. There being plenty of gravy today, Joe spooned into my plate, at this point, about half a pint.

"He was a world of trouble to you, ma'am," said Mrs. Hubble, commiserating my sister.

"Trouble?" echoed my sister. "Trouble?" And then entered on a fearful catalogue of all the illnesses I had been guilty of, and all the acts of sleeplessness I had committed, and all the high places I had tumbled from, and all the low places I had tumbled into, and all the injuries I had done myself, and all the times she had wished me in my grave, and I had contumaciously [1] refused to go there. Everybody looked at me with indignation and abhorrence.

"Have a little brandy, uncle," said my sister.

O Heavens, it had come at last! He would find it was weak, he would say it was weak, and I was lost! I held tight to the leg of the table with both hands and awaited my fate.

My sister went for the stone bottle, came back with the stone bottle, and poured his brandy out: no one else taking any. The wretched man trifled with his glass—took it up, looked at it through the light, put it down—prolonged my misery. All this time Mrs. Joe and Joe were briskly clearing the table for the pie and pudding.

I couldn't keep my eyes off him. I saw the miserable creature finger his glass playfully, take it up, smile, throw his head back, and drink the brandy off. Instantly, the company was seized with unspeakable consternation, owing to his springing to his feet, turning round several times in an appalling, spasmodic whooping-cough dance, and rushing out at the door; he then became visible through the window, making the most hideous faces and apparently out of his mind.

I held on tight, while Mrs. Joe and Joe ran to him. I didn't know how I had done it, but I had no doubt I had murdered him somehow. In my dreadful situation, it was a relief when he was brought back, and,

---

[1] **contumaciously:** stubbornly, disobediently.

surveying the company all round as if *they* had disagreed with him, sank down into his chair with the one significant gasp, "Tar!"

I had filled up the bottle from the tar-water jug!

"Tar!" cried my sister, in amazement. "Why, how ever could tar come there?"

But Uncle Pumblechook, who was omnipotent in that kitchen, wouldn't hear the word, wouldn't hear of the subject, imperiously waved it all away with his hand, and asked for hot gin-and-water. My sister, who had begun to be alarmingly meditative, had to employ herself actively in getting the gin, the hot water, the sugar, and the lemon peel, and mixing them. For the time at least, I was saved. I still held on to the leg of the table, but clutched it now with the fervor of gratitude.

By degrees, I became calm enough to release my grasp and partake of pudding. Mr. Pumblechook partook of pudding. All partook of pudding. I began to think I should get over the day, when my sister said to Joe, "Clean plates—cold."

I clutched the leg of the table again immediately. I foresaw what was coming, and I felt that this time I really was gone.

"You must taste," said my sister, addressing the guests with her best grace, "you must taste, to finish with, a pie; a savory pork pie."

My sister went out to get it. I heard her steps proceed to the pantry. I saw Mr. Pumblechook balance his knife. I heard Joe say, "You shall have some, Pip." I felt that I could bear no more, and that I must run away. I released the leg of the table and ran for my life.

But I ran no farther than the house door, for there I ran head foremost into a party of soldiers with their muskets, one of whom held out a pair of handcuffs to me, saying: "Here you are, look sharp, come on!"

CHAPTER 5

The sergeant finds the two convicts.

THE APPARITION of a file of soldiers ringing down the butt ends of their loaded muskets on our doorstep caused the dinner party to rise from table in confusion, and caused Mrs. Joe, re-entering the kitchen empty-handed, to stop short and stare in her wondering lament of "Gracious goodness gracious me, what's gone—with the—pie!"

The sergeant and I were in the kitchen when Mrs. Joe stood staring. It was the sergeant who had spoken to me, and he was now looking round at the company, with his handcuffs invitingly extended toward them in his right hand, and his left on my shoulder.

"Excuse me, ladies and gentlemen," said the sergeant, "but I want the blacksmith. You see, blacksmith," said the sergeant, who had by this time picked out Joe with his eye, "we have had an accident with these, and I find the lock of one of 'em goes wrong. As they are wanted for immediate service, will you throw your eye over them?"

Joe threw his eye over them and pronounced that the job would necessitate the lighting of his forge fire, and would take nearer two hours than one. "Will it? Then will you set about it at once, blacksmith?" said the offhand sergeant, "as it's on His Majesty's service." With that he called to his men, who came trooping into the kitchen one after another and piled their arms in a corner.

I was in an agony of apprehension. But, beginning to perceive that the handcuffs were not for me, and that the military had so far got the better of the pie as to put it in the background, I collected a little more of my scattered wits.

"How far might you call yourselves from the marshes, hereabouts? Not above a mile, I reckon?"

"Just a mile," said Mrs. Joe.

"That'll do. We begin to close in upon 'em about dusk. That'll do."

"Convicts, sergeant?" asked Mr. Wopsle, in a matter-of-course way.

"Aye!" returned the sergeant. "Two. They're pretty well known to be out on the marshes still, and they won't try to get clear of 'em before dusk. Anybody here seen anything of any such game?"

Everybody, myself excepted, said no, with confidence. Nobody thought of me.

"Well," said the sergeant, "they'll find themselves trapped in a circle. Now, blacksmith! If you're ready, His Majesty the King is."

Joe had got his coat and waistcoat and cravat [1] off, and his leather apron on, and passed into the forge. One of the soldiers opened its wooden windows, another lighted the fire, another turned to at the bellows, the rest stood round the blaze, which was soon roaring. Then Joe began to hammer and clink, hammer and clink, and we all looked on.

At last Joe's job was done, and the ringing and roaring stopped. As Joe got on his coat, he mustered courage to propose that some of us should go down with the soldiers and see what came of the hunt. Mr. Wopsle said he would go, if Joe would. Joe said he was agreeable and would take me.

The sergeant took a polite leave of the ladies, and his men resumed their muskets and fell in. Mr. Wopsle, Joe, and I received strict charge to keep in the rear and to speak no word after we reached the marshes. When we were all out in the raw air and were steadily moving toward our business, I treasonably whispered to Joe, "I hope, Joe, we shan't find them." And Joe whispered to me, "I'd give a shilling if they had cut and run, Pip."

We were joined by no stragglers from the village, for the weather was cold and threatening, the way dreary, the footing bad, darkness coming on, and the people had good fires indoors, and were keeping the day.[2] We struck out on the open marshes, through the gate at the side of the churchyard. A bitter sleet came rattling against us here on the east wind, and Joe took me on his back.

Now that we were out upon the dismal wilderness where they little thought I had been within eight or nine hours, and had seen both men hiding, I considered for the first time, with great dread, if we should come upon them, would my particular convict suppose that it was I who had brought the soldiers there? He had asked me if I was a deceiving imp, and he said I should be a fierce young hound if I joined the hunt against him. Would he believe that I was both imp and hound in treacherous earnest, and had betrayed him?

It was of no use asking myself this question now. There I was, on Joe's back, and there was Joe beneath me, charging at the ditches like a' hunter. The soldiers were in front of us, extending into a pretty wide line with an interval between man and man.

With my heart thumping like a blacksmith at Joe's broad shoulder, I looked all about for any sign of the convicts. I could see none, I could hear none. The soldiers were moving on in the direction of the old Battery, and we were moving on a little way behind them, when, all of a sudden, we all stopped. For there had reached us, on the wings of the wind and rain, a long

---

[1] **cravat** (krə·vat'): necktie.

[2] **keeping the day:** observing Christmas Day.

shout. It was repeated. The sergeant, a decisive man, ordered that the sound should not be answered, but that the course should be changed, and that his men should make toward it "at the double."

It was a run indeed now. Down banks and up banks, and over gates, and splashing into dikes, and breaking among coarse rushes, no man cared where he went. As we came nearer to the shouting, it became more and more apparent that it was made by more than one voice. After a while, we could hear one voice calling "Murder!" and another voice, "Convicts! Runaways! Guard! This way for the runaway convicts!" Then both voices would seem to be stifled in a struggle, and then would break out again. And when it had come to this, the soldiers ran like deer, and Joe too.

The sergeant ran in first, and two of his men ran in close upon him. Their pieces [1] were cocked and leveled when we all ran in.

"Here are both men!" panted the sergeant, struggling at the bottom of a ditch. "Surrender, you two! and confound you for two wild beasts! Come asunder!"

Water was splashing, and mud was flying, and oaths were being sworn, and blows were being struck, when some more men went down into the ditch to help the sergeant, and dragged out, separately, my convict and the other one. Both were bleeding and panting and execrating and struggling; but of course I knew them both directly.

"Mind," said my convict, wiping blood from his face with his ragged sleeves, and shaking torn hair from his fingers, "*I* took him! *I* give him up to you! Mind that!"

"It's not much to be particular about," said the sergeant. "It'll do you small good,

¹ **pieces:** muskets.

my man, being in the same plight yourself. Handcuffs there!"

"I don't expect it to do me any good. I don't want it to do me more good than it does now," said my convict, with a greedy laugh. "I took him. He knows it. That's enough for me."

The other convict, in addition to the old bruised left side of his face, seemed to be bruised and torn all over. He could not so much as get his breath to speak, until they were both separately handcuffed, but leaned upon a soldier to keep himself from falling.

"Take notice, guard—he tried to murder me," were his first words.

"Tried to murder him?" said my convict disdainfully. "Try, and not do it? I took him, and giv' him up; that's what I done. I not only prevented him getting off the marshes, but I dragged him here. He's a gentleman if you please, this villain. Now the Hulks has got its gentleman again, through me. Murder him? When I could do worse and drag him back!"

The other one still gasped, "He tried—he tried—to—murder me. Bear—bear witness."

"Lookee here!" said my convict to the sergeant. "Singlehanded I got clear of the prison ship; I made a dash and I done it. I could ha' got clear of these death-cold flats likewise—look at my leg: you won't find much iron on it—if I hadn't made discovery that *he* was here. Let *him* go free? Let *him* profit by means as I found out? Let *him* make a tool of me afresh and again? Once more? No, no, no. If I had died at the bottom there," and he made an emphatic swing at the ditch with his manacled hands, "I'd have held to him with that grip, that you should have been safe to find him in my hold."

The other fugitive, who was evidently in extreme horror of his companion, repeated, "He tried to murder me. I should have been a dead man if you had not come up."

"He lies!" said my convict, with fierce energy. "He's a liar born, and he'll die a liar. Look at his face; ain't it written there? Let him turn those eyes of his on me. I defy him to do it."

The other looked at the soldiers, and looked about at the marshes and at the sky, but certainly did not look at the speaker.

"Do you see him?" pursued my convict. "Do you see what a villain he is? Do you see those groveling and wandering eyes? That's how he looked when we were tried together. He never looked at me."

The other, turning his eyes restlessly about him far and near, did at last turn them for a moment on the speaker, with the words, "You are not much to look at," and with a half-taunting glance at the bound hands. At that point, my convict became so frantically exasperated that he would have rushed upon him but for the interposition of the soldiers. "Didn't I tell you," said the other convict then, "that he would murder me, if he could?" And anyone could see that he shook with fear, and that there broke out upon his lips curious white flakes, like thin snow.

"Enough of this parley," said the sergeant. "Light those torches."

As one of the soldiers, who carried a basket, went down on his knee to open it, my convict looked round him for the first time and saw me. I had alighted from Joe's back on the brink of the ditch when we came up, and had not moved since. I looked at him eagerly when he looked at me, and slightly moved my hands and shook my head. I had been waiting for him to see me, that I might try to assure him of my innocence. He gave me a look that I did not understand, and it all passed in a moment. But if he had looked at me for an hour or for a day, I could not have

remembered his face ever afterwards, as having been more attentive.

The soldier with the basket soon lighted three or four torches. Before we departed from that spot, four soldiers, standing in a ring, fired twice into the air. Presently we saw other torches kindled at some distance behind us, and others on the marshes on the opposite bank of the river. "All right," said the sergeant. "March."

We had not gone far when three cannon were fired ahead of us with a sound that seemed to burst something inside my ear. "You are expected on board," said the sergeant to my convict. "They know you are coming. Don't straggle, my man. Close up here."

The two were kept apart, and each walked surrounded by a separate guard. I had hold of Joe's hand now, and Joe carried one of the torches. Mr. Wopsle had been for going back, but Joe was resolved to see it out, so we went on with the party. The two prisoners limped along in the midst of the muskets. We could not go fast, because of their lameness; and they were so spent, that two or three times we had to halt while they rested.

After an hour or so, we came to a rough wooden hut and a landing place. Then we went into the hut, where there was a smell of tobacco and whitewash, and a bright fire, and a lamp.

My convict never looked at me, except that once. While we stood in the hut, he turned to the sergeant and remarked:

"I wish to say something respecting this escape. It may prevent some persons laying under suspicion alonger me."

"You can say what you like," returned the sergeant, standing coolly looking at him with his arms folded, "but you have no call to say it here. You'll have opportunity enough to say about it, and hear about it, before it's done with, you know."

"I know, but this is another matter. A

man can't starve; at least *I* can't. I took some wittles, up at the village over yonder."

"You mean stole," said the sergeant.

"And I'll tell you where from. From the blacksmith's."

"Halloa!" said the sergeant, staring at Joe.

"Halloa, Pip!" said Joe, staring at me.

"It was some broken wittles—that's what it was—and a dram of liquor, and a pie."

"Have you happened to miss such an article as a pie, blacksmith?" asked the sergeant confidentially.

"My wife did, at the very moment when you came in. Don't you know, Pip?"

"So," said my convict, turning his eyes on Joe in a moody manner, and without the least glance at me; "so you're the blacksmith, are you? Then I'm sorry to say, I've eat your pie."

"God knows you're welcome to it—so far as it was ever mine," returned Joe, with a saving remembrance of Mrs. Joe. "We don't know what you have done, but we wouldn't have you starved to death for it, poor miserable fellow creature. Would us, Pip?"

The something that I had noticed before clicked in the man's throat again, and he turned his back. The boat had returned, and his guard were ready, so we followed him to the landing place, and saw him put into the boat, which was rowed by a crew of convicts like himself. No one seemed surprised to see him, or interested in seeing him, or glad to see him, or sorry to see him, or spoke a word except that somebody in the boat growled as if to dogs, "Give way, you!" which was the signal for the dip of the oars. By the light of the torches, we saw the black Hulk lying out a little way from the mud of the shore, like a wicked Noah's ark. Cribbed and barred and moored by massive rusty chains, the prison ship seemed in my young eyes to be ironed like the prisoners. We saw the boat go alongside, and we saw him taken up the side and disappear. Then, the ends of the torches were flung hissing into the water, and went out, as if it were all over with him.

I do not recall that I felt any tenderness of conscience in reference to Mrs. Joe, when the fear of being found out was lifted off me. But I loved Joe—perhaps for no better reason in those days than because the dear fellow let me love him —and it was much on my mind that I ought to tell Joe the whole truth. Yet I did not, and for the reason that I mistrusted that if I did, he would think me worse than I was. The fear of losing Joe's confidence tied up my tongue. In a word, I was too cowardly to do what I knew to be right, as I had been too cowardly to avoid doing what I knew to be wrong.

CHAPTER 6

*We meet Mr. Wopsle's
great-aunt and Biddy,
her granddaughter.*

WHEN I was old enough, I was to be apprenticed to Joe, and until I could assume that dignity I was not to be what Mrs. Joe called "Pompeyed," or (as I render it) pampered. Therefore, I was not only odd boy about the forge, but if any neighbor happened to want an extra boy to frighten birds, or pick up stones, or do any such job, I was favored with the employment. A money box was kept on the kitchen mantel shelf, into which it was publicly made known that all my earnings were dropped, but I had no hope of any personal participation in the treasure.

Mr. Wopsle's great-aunt kept an evening school in the village. She was a ridiculous old woman who used to go to sleep from six to seven every evening, in the society of youth who paid twopence [1] per week each for the improving opportunity of seeing her do it. She rented a small cottage, and Mr. Wopsle had the room upstairs, where we students used to overhear him reading aloud in a most dignified and terrific manner, and occasionally bumping on the ceiling. There was a fiction that Mr. Wopsle "examined" the scholars once a quarter. What he did on those occasions was to turn up his cuffs, stick up his hair, and give us Mark Antony's oration over the body of Caesar.

Mr. Wopsle's great-aunt, besides keeping this educational institution, kept—in the same room—a little general shop. She had no idea what stock she had, or what the price of anything in it was; but there was a little greasy memorandum book kept in a drawer, which served as a catalogue of prices, and by this oracle Biddy arranged all the shop transactions. Biddy was Mr. Wopsle's great-aunt's granddaughter. She was an orphan like myself; like me, too, had been brought up by hand. Her hair always wanted brushing, her hands always wanted washing, and her shoes always wanted mending and pulling up at heel.

More by the help of Biddy than of Mr. Wopsle's great-aunt, I struggled through the alphabet as if it had been a bramblebush, getting considerably worried and scratched by every letter. After that, I fell among those thieves, the nine figures, who seemed every evening to do something new to disguise themselves and baffle recognition. But at last I began, in a groping way, to read, write, and cipher,[2] on the very smallest scale.

One night, I was sitting in the chimney corner with my slate, expending great efforts on the production of a letter to Joe. I think it must have been a full year after our hunt upon the marshes, for it was a long time after, and it was winter and a hard frost. With an alphabet on the hearth at my feet for reference, I contrived in an hour or two to print and smear this epistle:

mI deEr JO i opE U r krWitE wELl i opE i sHAl soN B haBell 4 2 teeDge U JO aN theN wE sHOrl b sO gLOdd aN wEn i M preNgtD 2 u JO woT larX aN blEvE ME inF xn PiP.

There was no necessity for my communicating with Joe by letter, inasmuch as he sat beside me and we were alone. But I delivered this written communication (slate and all) with my own hand, and Joe received it as a miracle of erudition.

"I say, Pip, old chap!" cried Joe, opening his blue eyes wide. "What a scholar

---

[1] **twopence** (tup'əns): about four cents in American money in Dickens' time.

[2] **cipher:** calculate with numbers.

you are! Ain't you?"

"I should like to be," said I, glancing at the slate as he held it, with a misgiving that the writing was rather hilly.

"Why, here's a J," said Joe, "and a O equal to anythink! Here's a J and a O, Pip, and a J-O, Joe."

I had never heard Joe read aloud to any greater extent than this monosyllable, and I had observed at church last Sunday, when I accidentally held our prayer book upside down, that it seemed to suit his convenience quite as well as if it had been all right. Wishing to embrace the present occasion of finding out whether, in teaching Joe, I should have to begin quite at the beginning, I said, "Ah! But read the rest, Joe."

"The rest, eh, Pip?" said Joe, looking at it with a slowly searching eye. "One, two, three. Why, here's three J's, and three O's, and three J-O, Joe's, in it, Pip!"

I leaned over Joe, and, with the aid of my forefinger, read him the whole letter.

"Astonishing!" said Joe, when I had finished. "You *are* a scholar."

"How do you spell Gargery, Joe?" I asked.

"I don't spell it at all," said Joe.

"But supposing you did?"

"It *can't* be supposed," said Joe. "Tho' I'm oncommon fond of reading, too."

"Are you, Joe?"

"Oncommon. Give me," said Joe, "a good book, or a good newspaper, and sit me down afore a good fire, and I ask no better. Lord!" he continued, after rubbing his knees a little, "when you *do* come to a J and a O, and says you, 'Here, at last, is a J-O, Joe,' how interesting reading is!"

I derived from this last, that Joe's education, like steam, was yet in its infancy. Pursuing the subject, I inquired:

"Didn't you ever go to school, Joe, when you were as little as me?"

"No, Pip."

"Why didn't you ever go to school, Joe, when you were as little as me?"

"Well, Pip," said Joe, taking up the poker, and settling himself to his usual occupation, when he was thoughtful, of slowly raking the fire between the lower bars, "I'll tell you. My father, Pip, he were given to drink, and when he were overtook with drink, he hammered away at my mother most onmerciful. My mother and me we ran away from my father several times; and then my mother she'd go out to work, and she'd say, 'Joe,' she'd say, 'now, please God, you shall have some schooling, child,' and she'd put me to school. But my father were that good in his heart that he couldn't a-bear to be without us. So, he took us home and hammered us. Which, you see, Pip," said Joe, "were a drawback on my learning."

"Certainly, poor Joe!"

"Though mind you, Pip," said Joe, "rendering unto all their doo, and maintaining equal justice betwixt man and man, my father were that good in his heart, don't you see?"

I didn't see; but I didn't say so.

"'Consequence, my father didn't make objections to my going to work; so I went to work at my present calling, and I worked tolerable hard, I assure *you*, Pip. In time I were able to keep him, and I kep him till he went off in a purple leptic fit.[1] My mother, she were in poor 'elth, and quite broke. She waren't long of following, poor soul, and her share of peace come round at last."

Joe's blue eyes turned a little watery. "It were but lonesome then," said Joe, "living here alone, and I got acquainted with your sister. Now, Pip," Joe looked firmly at me, as if he knew I was not going

[1] **purple leptic fit:** Joe probably means an *apoplectic* (ap'ə·plek'tik) *fit Apoplexy* is a sudden paralysis or loss of consciousness, sometimes called a *stroke.*

to agree with him, "your sister is a fine figure of a woman."

I could not help looking at the fire, in an obvious state of doubt.

"Whatever family opinions, or whatever the world's opinions, on that subject may be, Pip, your sister is," Joe tapped the top bar with the poker after every word following, "a—fine—figure—of—a—woman!"

I could think of nothing better to say than "I am glad you think so, Joe."

"So am I," returned Joe. "When I offered to your sister to keep company, and to be asked in church, at such times as she was willing and ready to come to the forge, I said to her, 'And bring the poor little child. God bless the poor little child,' I said to your sister, 'there's room for *him* at the forge!'"

I broke out crying and hugged Joe round the neck, who dropped the poker to hug me, and to say, "Ever the best of friends; ain't us, Pip? Don't cry, old chap!"

When this little interruption was over, Joe resumed:

"Well, you see, Pip, and here we are! Now, when you take me in hand in my learning, Pip (and I tell you beforehand I am awful dull, most awful dull), Mrs. Joe mustn't see too much of what we're up to. It must be done, as I may say, on the sly. I'll tell you why, Pip.

"Your sister is given to government," said Joe. "Which I meantersay the government of you and myself."

"Oh!"

"And she ain't overpartial to having scholars on the premises," Joe continued, "and in partickler would not be over-partial to my being a scholar, for fear as I might rise. Like a sort of rebel, don't you see?"

Young as I was, I believe that I dated a new admiration of Joe from that night.

We were equals afterward, as we had been before; but afterward, at quiet times when I sat looking at Joe and thinking about him. I had a new sensation of feeling conscious that I was looking up to Joe in my heart.

"However," said Joe, rising to replenish the fire, "here's the Dutch clock a-working himself up to being equal to strike eight of 'em, and she's not home yet!"

Mrs. Joe made occasional trips with Uncle Pumblechook on market days to assist him in buying such household stuffs and goods as required a woman's judgment, Uncle Pumblechook being a bachelor. This was market day, and Mrs. Joe was out on one of these expeditions.

Joe made the fire and swept the hearth, and then we went to the door to listen for the chaise-cart. It was a dry, cold night.

"Here comes the mare," said Joe, "ringing like a peal of bells!"

Mrs. Joe was soon landed, and Uncle Pumblechook was soon down too, and we were soon all in the kitchen, carrying so much cold air with us that it seemed to drive all the heat out of the fire.

"Now," said Mrs. Joe, unwrapping herself with haste and excitement, and throwing her bonnet back on her shoulders, where it hung by the strings, "if this boy ain't grateful this night, he never will be!"

I looked as grateful as any boy possibly could who was wholly uninformed why he ought to assume that expression.

"It's only to be hoped," said my sister, "that he won't be Pompeyed. But I have my fears."

"She ain't in that line, mum," said Mr. Pumblechook. "She knows better."

She? I looked at Joe, making the motion with my lips and eyebrows. "She?" Joe looked at me, making the motion with *his* lips and eyebrows. "She?" My sister catching him in the act, he drew the back of his hand across his nose with his usual conciliatory air on such occasions, and looked at her.

"Well?" said my sister, in her snappish way. "What are you staring at? Is the house afire?"

"Which some individual," Joe politely hinted, "mentioned she."

"And she is a she, I suppose?" said my sister. "Unless you call Miss Havisham a he. And I doubt if even you'll go so far as that."

"Miss Havisham uptown?" said Joe.

"Is there any Miss Havisham downtown?" returned my sister. "She wants this boy to go and play there. And of course he's going. And he had better play there," said my sister, shaking her head at me as an encouragement to be extremely light and sportive, "or I'll work him."

I had heard of Miss Havisham uptown—everybody for miles round had heard of Miss Havisham uptown—as an immensely rich and grim lady who lived in a large and dismal house barricaded against robbers, and who led a life of seclusion.

"Well, to be sure!" said Joe, astounded. "I wonder how she comes to know Pip!"

"Noodle!" cried my sister. "Who said she knew him?"

"Which some individual," Joe again politely hinted, "mentioned that she wanted him to go and play there."

"And couldn't she ask Uncle Pumblechook if he knew of a boy to go and play there? Isn't it just barely possible that Uncle Pumblechook may be a tenant of hers, and that he may sometimes go there to pay his rent? And couldn't she then ask Uncle Pumblechook if he knew of a boy to go and play there? And couldn't Uncle Pumblechook—being always considerate and thoughtful for us, though you may not think it, Joseph, then mention this boy that I have forever been a willing slave to?"

"Good again!" cried Uncle Pumblechook. "Well put! Good indeed! Now, Joseph, you know the case."

"No, Joseph," said my sister, in a reproachful manner, "you do not yet—though you may not think it—know the case. Uncle Pumblechook, being sensible that this boy's fortune may be made by his going to Miss Havisham's, has offered to take him into town tonight in his own chaise-cart and to keep him tonight and to take him with his own hands to Miss Havisham's tomorrow morning. And Lor-a-mussy [1] me!" cried my sister, casting off her bonnet in sudden desperation, "here I stand talking to mere mooncalfs, with Uncle Pumblechook waiting, and the mare catching cold at the door, and the boy grimed with crock and dirt from the hair of his head to the sole of his foot!"

With that she pounced on me, like an eagle on a lamb, and my face was squeezed into wooden bowls in sinks, and my head was put under taps of water butts, and I was soaped, and kneaded, and toweled, and thumped, and harrowed, and rasped, until I really was quite beside myself.

When my ablutions were completed, I was put into clean linen of the stiffest character, and was trussed up in my tightest and fearfulest suit. I was then delivered over to Mr. Pumblechook, who formally received me as if he were the sheriff, and who let off upon me the speech that I knew he had been dying to make all along: "Boy, be forever grateful to all friends, but especially unto them which brought you up by hand!"

"Good-by, Joe!"

[1] **Lor-a-mussy:** Lord have mercy (on).

"God bless you, Pip, old chap!"

I had never parted from him before, and what with my feelings and what with soap-suds, I could at first see no stars from the chaise-cart. But they twinkled out one by one, without throwing any light on the questions why on earth I was going to play at Miss Havisham's, and what on earth I was expected to play at.

CHAPTER 7

*We are introduced to Miss
Havisham and her ward Estella.*

MR. PUMBLECHOOK'S premises in the High Street of the market town were of a peppercorny character, as the prem-ises of a corn chandler and seedsman should be. It was in the early morning after my arrival that I entertained this speculation. On the previous night, I had been sent straight to bed in an attic with a sloping roof, which was so low in the corner where the bedstead was that I calculated the tiles as being within a foot of my eyebrows.

Mr. Pumblechook and I breakfasted at eight o'clock in the parlor behind the shop while his shopman took his mug of tea and hunch of bread-and-butter on a sack of peas in the front premises. I considered Mr. Pumblechook wretched company. Besides giving me as much crumb as possible in combination with as little butter, and putting a great quantity of warm water in my milk, his conversation consisted of nothing but arithmetic. On my politely bidding him good morning, he said pompously, "Seven times nine, boy?" And how should *I* be able to answer, dodged in that way, in a strange place, on an empty stomach! I was hungry, but be-fore I had swallowed a morsel, he began a running sum that lasted all through the breakfast. "Seven?" "And four?" "And eight?" "And six?" "And two?" "And ten?" And so on.

I was very glad when ten o'clock came and we started for Miss Havisham's. Within a quarter of an hour we came to Miss Havisham's house, which was of old brick, and dismal, and had a great many iron bars to it. Some of the windows had been walled up; of those that remained, all the lower were rustily barred. There was a courtyard in front, and that was barred; so we had to wait, after ringing the bell, until someone should come to open it. While we waited at the gate, I saw that at the side of the house there was a large brew-ery. No brewing was going on in it, and none seemed to have gone on for a long time.

A window was raised, and a clear voice demanded, "What name?" To which my conductor replied, "Pumblechook." The voice returned, "Quite right," and the window was shut again, and a young lady came across the courtyard, with keys in her hand.

"This," said Mr. Pumblechook, "is Pip."

"This is Pip, is it?" returned the young lady, who was very pretty, and seemed very proud. "Come in, Pip."

Mr. Pumblechook was coming in also, when she stopped him with the gate.

"Oh!" she said. "Did you wish to see Miss Havisham?"

"If Miss Havisham wished to see me," returned Mr. Pumblechook, discomfited.

"Ah!" said the girl. "But you see she don't."

She said it so finally, that Mr. Pumble-chook could not protest. But he eyed me severely—as if *I* had done anything to him!—and departed with the words re-proachfully delivered: "Boy! Let your

behavior here be a credit unto them which brought you up by hand!"

My young conductress locked the gate, and we went across the courtyard. It was paved and clean, but grass was growing in every crevice. The brewery beyond stood open, and all was empty and disused. The cold wind seemed to blow colder there than outside the gate; and it made a shrill noise in howling in and out at the open sides of the brewery, like the noise of the wind in the rigging of a ship at sea.

"What is the name of this house, miss?"

"Its name was Satis; which is Greek, or Latin, or Hebrew, or all three—or all one to me—for enough."

"Enough House!" said I. "That's a curious name, miss."

"Yes," she replied, "but it meant more than it said. It meant, when it was given, that whoever had this house, could want nothing else. They must have been easily satisfied in those days, I should think. But don't loiter, boy."

Though she called me "boy" so often, and with a carelessness that was far from complimentary, she was of about my own age. She seemed much older than I, of course, being a girl, and beautiful and self-possessed; and she was a scornful of me as if she had been one-and-twenty, and a queen.

We went into the house by a side door —the great front entrance had two chains across it outside—and the first thing I noticed was that the passages were all dark, and that she had left a candle burning there. She took it up, and we went through more passages and up a staircase, and still it was all dark, and only the candle lighted us.

At last we came to the door of a room, and she said, "Go in."

I answered, more in shyness than politeness, "After you, miss."

To this she returned, "Don't be ridiculous, boy; I am not going in." And scornfully walked away, and—what was worse —took the candle with her.

This was very uncomfortable, and I was half afraid. However, the only thing to be done being to knock at the door, I knocked, and was told from within to enter. I entered, therefore, and found myself in a pretty large room, well lighted with wax candles. No glimpse of daylight was to be seen in it. It was a dressing room, as I supposed from the furniture. But prominent in it was a draped table with a gilded looking glass, and that I made out at first sight to be a fine lady's dressing table.

In an armchair, with an elbow resting on the table and her head leaning on that hand, sat the strangest lady I have ever seen, or shall ever see.

She was dressed in rich materials— satins, and lace, and silks—all of white. Her shoes were white. And she had a long white veil dependent from her hair, and she had bridal flowers in her hair, but her hair was white. Some bright jewels sparkled on her neck and on her hands, and some other jewels lay sparkling on the table. Dresses and half-packed trunks were scattered about. She had not quite finished dressing, for she had but one shoe on—the other was on the table near her hand—her veil was but half arranged, her watch and chain were not put on, and some lace for her bosom lay with those trinkets, and with her handkerchief, and gloves, and some flowers, and a prayer book, all confusedly heaped about the looking glass.

But I saw that everything within my view which ought to be white had lost its luster, and was faded and yellow. I saw that the bride within the bridal dress had withered like the dress, and like the flowers, and had no brightness left but the brightness of her sunken eyes. I saw that the dress had been put upon the rounded figure of a young woman, and that the figure upon which it now hung loose had shrunk to skin and bone.

"Who is it?" said the lady at the table.

"Pip, ma'am."

"Pip?"

"Mr. Pumblechook's boy, ma'am. Come—to play."

"Come nearer; let me look at you. Come closer."

It was when I stood before her, avoiding her eyes, that I took note of the surrounding objects in detail, and saw that her watch had stopped at twenty minutes to nine, and that a clock in the room had stopped at twenty minutes to nine.

"Look at me," said Miss Havisham. "You are not afraid of a woman who has never seen the sun since you were born?"

I regret to state that I was not afraid of telling the enormous lie comprehended in the answer, "No."

"Do you know what I touch here?"

she said, laying her hands, one upon the other, on her left side.

"Yes, ma'am."

"What do I touch?"

"Your heart."

"Broken!"

She uttered the word with an eager look, and with strong emphasis, and with a weird smile that had a kind of boast in it.

"I am tired," said Miss Havisham. "I sometimes have sick fancies, and I have a sick fancy that I want to see some play. There, there!" with an impatient movement of the fingers of her right hand, "play, play, play!"

I stood looking at Miss Havisham in what I suppose she took for a stubborn manner, inasmuch as she said, when we had taken a good look at each other:

"Are you sullen and obstinate?"

"No ma'am, I am very sorry for you, and very sorry I can't play just now. If you complain of me, I shall get into trouble with my sister, so I would do it if I could; but it's so new here, and so strange, and so fine—and melancholy—" I stopped, fearing I might say too much, or had already said it, and we took another look at each other.

Before she spoke again, she turned her eyes from me, and looked at the dress she wore, and at the dressing table, and finally at herself in the looking glass.

"So new to him," she muttered, "so old to me; so strange to him, so familiar to me; so melancholy to both of us! Call Estella."

As she was still looking at the reflection of herself, I thought she was still talking to herself, and kept quiet.

"Call Estella," she repeated, flashing a look at me. "You can do that. Call Estella. At the door."

To stand in the dark in a mysterious passage of an unknown house, bawling

Estella to a scornful young lady neither visible nor responsive, and feeling it a dreadful liberty so to roar out her name, was almost as bad as playing to order. But, she answered at last, and her light came along the dark passage like a star.

Miss Havisham beckoned her to come close, and took up a jewel from the table, and tried its effect against her pretty brown hair. "Your own, one day, my dear, and you will use it well. Let me see you play cards with this boy."

"With this boy! Why, he is a common laboring boy!"

I thought I overheard Miss Havisham answer—only it seemed so unlikely— "Well? You can break his heart."

"What do you play, boy?" asked Estella of me, with the greatest disdain.

"Nothing but beggar my neighbor, miss."

"Beggar him," said Miss Havisham to Estella. So we sat down to cards.

It was then I began to understand that everything in the room had stopped, like the watch and the clock, a long time ago. I noticed that Miss Havisham put down the jewel exactly on the spot from which she had taken it up. As Estella dealt the cards, I glanced at the dressing table again, and saw that the shoe upon it, once white, now yellow, had never been worn. I glanced down at the foot from which the shoe was absent, and saw that the silk stocking on it, once white, now yellow, had been trodden ragged.

Miss Havisham sat, corpselike, as we played at cards.

"He calls the knaves jacks, this boy!" said Estella with disdain, before our first game was out. "And what coarse hands he has! And what thick boots!"

I had never thought of being ashamed of my hands before; but her contempt for me was so strong that it became infectious, and I caught it.

She won the game, and I dealt. I misdealt, as was only natural when I knew she was lying in wait for me to do wrong; and she denounced me for a stupid, clumsy, laboring boy.

"You say nothing of her," remarked Miss Havisham to me, as she looked on. "She says many hard things of you, yet you say nothing of her. What do you think of her?"

"I don't like to say," I stammered.

"Tell me in my ear," said Miss Havisham, bending down.

"I think she is very proud," I replied, in a whisper.

"Anything else?"

"I think she is very pretty."

"Anything else?"

"I think she is very insulting." (She was looking at me then with a look of supreme aversion.)

"Anything else?"

"I think I should like to go home."

"And never see her again, though she is so pretty?"

"I am not sure that I shouldn't like to see her again, but I should like to go home now."

"You shall go soon," said Miss Havisham aloud. "Play the game out."

I played the game to an end with Estella, and she beggared me. She threw the cards down on the table when she had won them all, as if she despised them for having been won of me.

"When shall I have you here again?" said Miss Havisham. "Let me think. Come again after six days. You hear?"

"Yes, ma'am."

"Estella, take him down. Let him have something to eat, and let him roam and look about him while he eats. Go, Pip."

I followed the candle down, as I had followed the candle up, and she stood it in the place where we had found it.

"You are to wait here, you boy," said

Estella. She disappeared and closed the door.

I took the opportunity of being alone to look at my coarse hands and my common boots. They had never troubled me before, but they troubled me now. I determined to ask Joe why he had ever taught me to call those picture cards jacks, which ought to be called knaves. I wished Joe had been rather more genteelly brought up, and then I should have been so too.

She came back, with some bread and meat and a little mug of beer. She put the mug down on the stones of the yard, and gave me the bread and meat without looking at me, as insolently as if I were a dog in disgrace. I was so humiliated, hurt, spurned, offended, angry, sorry, that tears started to my eyes. The moment they sprang there, the girl looked at me with a quick delight in having been the cause of them. This gave me power to keep them back and to look at her; so she gave a contemptuous toss—but with a sense, I thought, of having made too sure that I was so wounded—and left me.

But, when she was gone, I got behind one of the gates in the brewery lane, and leaned my sleeve against the wall there, and leaned my forehead on it, and cried. As I cried, I kicked the wall, and took a hard twist at my hair, so bitter were my feelings.

I got rid of my injured feelings for the time, by kicking them into the brewery wall, and twisting them out of my hair, and then I smoothed my face with my sleeve, and came from behind the gate. The bread and meat were acceptable, and the beer was warming and tingling.

Even with those aids, I might not have come to myself as soon as I did, but that I saw Estella approaching with the keys to let me out. She gave me a triumphant glance in passing me, as if she rejoiced that my hands were so coarse and my boots were so thick, and she opened the gate and stood holding it. I was passing out without looking at her, when she touched me with a taunting hand.

"Why don't you cry?"

"Because I don't want to."

"You do," said she. "You have been crying till you are half blind, and you are near crying again now."

She laughed contemptuously, pushed me out, and locked the gate upon me. I went straight to Mr. Pumblechook's, and was immensely relieved to find him not at home. So, leaving word with the shopman on what day I was wanted at Miss Havisham's again, I set off on the four-mile walk to our forge, pondering, as I went along, on all I had seen, and that I was a common laboring boy; that my hands were coarse; that my boots were thick; that I was much more ignorant than I had considered myself last night; and generally that I was in a low-lived, bad way.

CHAPTER 8

Pip tells some tall tales.

WHEN I reached home, my sister was very curious to know all about Miss Havisham's, and asked a number of questions. And I soon found myself getting heavily bumped from behind in the nape of the neck and the small of the back, and having my face ignominiously shoved against the kitchen wall, because I did not answer those questions at sufficient length.

I felt convinced that if I described Miss Havisham's as my eyes had seen it, I should not be understood. Not only that, but I felt convinced that Miss Havisham too would not be understood; and although she was perfectly incomprehensible to me, I entertained an impression that there would be something coarse and treacherous in my dragging her as she really was (to say nothing of Miss Estella) before the contemplation of Mrs. Joe. Consequently, I said as little as I could, and had my face shoved against the kitchen wall.

The worst of it was that bullying old Pumblechook, preyed upon by a devouring curiosity to be informed of all I had seen and heard, came gaping over in his chaise-cart at teatime, to have the details divulged to him.

"Well, boy," Uncle Pumblechook began, as soon as he was seated in the chair of honor by the fire. "How did you get on uptown?"

I answered, "Pretty well, sir," and my sister shook her fist at me.

"Pretty well?" Mr. Pumblechook repeated. "Pretty well is no answer. Tell us what you mean by pretty well, boy?"

My sister with an exclamation of impatience was going to fly at me—I had no shadow of defense, for Joe was busy in the forge—when Mr. Pumblechook interposed with "No! Don't lose your temper. Leave this lad to me, ma'am; leave this lad to me." Mr. Pumblechook then turned me toward him, as if he were going to cut my hair, and said: "Boy! What like is Miss Havisham?" Mr. Pumblechook began, folding his arms tight on his chest.

"Very tall and dark," I told him.

"Is she, uncle?" asked my sister.

Mr. Pumblechook winked assent, from which I at once inferred that he had never seen Miss Havisham, for she was nothing of the kind.

"Good!" said Mr. Pumblechook, conceitedly. "This is the way to have him! We are beginning to hold our own, I think, mum?"

"I am sure, uncle," returned Mrs. Joe; "I wish you had him always; you know so well how to deal with him."

"Now, boy! What was she a-doing of, when you went in today?" asked Mr. Pumblechook.

"She was sitting," I answered, "in a black velvet coach."

Mr. Pumblechook and Mrs. Joe stared at one another—as they well might—and both repeated, "In a black velvet coach?"

"Yes," said I. "And Miss Estella—that's her niece, I think—handed her in cake and wine at the coach window, on a gold plate. And we all had cake and wine on gold plates. And I got up behind the coach to eat mine, because she told me to."

Mr. Pumblechook and Mrs. Joe stared at one another again, in utter amazement. I was perfectly frantic—a reckless witness under the torture—and would have told them anything.

"Did you ever see her in it, uncle?" asked Mrs. Joe.

"How could I," he returned, forced to the admission, "when I never see her in my life? Never clapped eyes upon her!"

"Goodness, uncle! And yet you have spoken to her?"

"Why, don't you know," said Mr. Pumblechook testily, "that when I have been there, I have been took up to the outside of her door, and the door has stood ajar, and she has spoken to me that way. What did you play at, boy?"

"We played with flags," I said. (I beg to observe that I think of myself with amazement, when I recall the lies I told on this occasion.)

"Flags!" echoed my sister.

"Yes," said I. "Estella waved a blue flag, and I waved a red one, and Miss Havisham waved one sprinkled all over with little gold stars, out at the coach window. And then we all waved our swords and hurrahed."

If they had asked me any more questons, I should undoubtedly have betrayed myself. The subject still held them when Joe came in from his work to have a cup of tea. To whom my sister, more for the relief of her own mind than for the gratification of his, related my pretended experiences.

Now, when I saw Joe open his blue eyes and roll them all round the kitchen in helpless amazement, I was overtaken by penitence. Toward Joe, and Joe only, I considered myself a young monster, while they sat debating what results would come to me from Miss Havisham's acquaintance and favor. They had no doubt that Miss Havisham would "do something" for me. My sister stood out for "property." Mr. Pumblechook was in favor of a handsome premium [1] for binding me apprentice to some genteel trade—say, the corn and seed trade, for instance.

After Mr. Pumblechook had driven off, and when my sister was washing up, I stole into the forge to Joe, and remained by him until he had done for the night. Then I said, "Before the fire goes out, Joe, I should like to tell you something."

"Should you, Pip?" said Joe, drawing his shoeing stool near the forge. "Then tell us. What is it, Pip?"

"Joe," said I, taking hold of his rolled-up shirt sleeve, and twisting it between my finger and thumb, "you remember all that about Miss Havisham's?"

"Remember?" said Joe. "I believe you! Wonderful!"

"It's a terrible thing, Joe; it ain't true."

"What are you telling of, Pip?" cried Joe, falling back in the greatest amaze-

ment. "You don't mean to say it's—"

"Yes, I do; it's lies, Joe."

As I fixed my eyes hopelessly on Joe, Joe contemplated me in dismay. "Pip, old chap! This won't do, old fellow! I say! Where do you expect to go to?"

"It's terrible, Joe; ain't it?"

"Terrible?" cried Joe. "Awful! What possessed you?"

"I don't know what possessed me, Joe," I replied, letting his shirt sleeve go, and sitting down in the ashes at his feet, hanging my head; "but I wish you hadn't taught me to call knaves at cards jacks, and I wish my boots weren't so thick nor my hands so coarse."

And then I told Joe that I felt very miserable, and that I hadn't been able to explain myself to Mrs. Joe and Pumblechook, who were so rude to me, and that there had been a beautiful young lady at Miss Havisham's who was dreadfully proud, and that she had said I was common, and that I knew I was common, and that I wished I was not common, and that the lies had come of it somehow, though I didn't know how.

"There's one thing you may be sure of, Pip," said Joe, "namely, that lies is lies. Howsever they come, they didn't ought to come, and they come from the father of lies, and work round to the same. Don't you tell me no more of 'em, Pip. *That* ain't the way to get out of being common, old chap. And as to being common, I don't make it out at all clear. You are oncommon in some things. You're oncommon small. Likewise you're a oncommon scholar."

"No, I am ignorant and backward, Joe."

"Why, see what a letter you wrote last night! Wrote in print even! I've seen letters—ah! and from gentlefolks!— that I'll swear weren't wrote in print," said Joe.

---

[1] **premium** (prē′mē·əm): an initial fee paid to a master artisan by a prospective apprentice. In former times, apprenticeship was the most common way to learn a trade. A boy (with his parents or guardian) signed a contract, called "indentures," by which he was bound to serve a master artisan without pay for five to seven years. In return for this service, he was taught the master's trade.

"I have learned next to nothing, Joe. You think much of me. It's only that."

"Well, Pip," said Joe, "you must be a common scholar afore you can be a on-common one, I should hope!"

"You are not angry with me, Joe?"

"No, old chap. That's all, old chap, and don't never do it no more."

When I got up to my little room and said my prayers, my young mind was in that disturbed and unthankful state that I thought long after I laid me down, how common Estella would consider Joe, a mere blacksmith, how thick his boots, and how coarse his hands. I thought how Joe and my sister were then sitting in the kitchen, and how I had come up to bed from the kitchen, and how Miss Havisham and Estella never sat in a kitchen, but were far above the level of such common doings. I fell asleep recalling what I "used to do" when I was at Miss Havisham's; as though I had been there weeks or months, instead of hours.

That was a memorable day to me, for it made great changes in me. But it is the same with any life. Imagine one selected day struck out of it, and think how different its course would have been. Pause, you who read this, and think for a moment of the long chain of iron or gold, of thorns or flowers, that would never have bound you, but for the formation of the first link on one memorable day.

CHAPTER 9

A mysterious stranger appears with a surprise for Pip.

THE FELICITOUS idea occurred to me a morning or two later when I woke, that the best step I could take toward making myself uncommon was to get out of Biddy everything she knew. I mentioned to Biddy when I went to Mr. Wopsle's great-aunt's at night, that I had a particular reason for wishing to get on in life, and that I should feel very much obliged to her if she would impart all her learning to me. Biddy, who was the most obliging of girls, immediately said she would, and indeed began to carry out her promise within five minutes.

The educational scheme or course established by Mr. Wopsle's great-aunt may be resolved into the following synopsis. The pupils ate apples and put straws down one another's backs until Mr. Wopsle's great-aunt collected her energies and made an indiscriminate totter at them with a birch rod. After receiving the charge with every mark of derision, the pupils formed in line and buzzingly passed a ragged book from hand to hand. The book had an alphabet in it, some figures and tables, and a little spelling. Biddy gave out the number of the page, and then we all read aloud in a frightful chorus, Biddy leading with a high, shrill, monotonous voice, and none of us having the least notion of, or reverence for, what we were reading about.

It appeared to me that it would take time to become uncommon under these circumstances; nevertheless, I resolved to try it, and that very evening Biddy entered on our special agreement by lending me, to copy at home, a large Old English *D* which she had imitated from the heading of some newspaper, and which I supposed, until she told me what it was, to be a design for a buckle.

Of course there was a public house in the village, and of course Joe liked sometimes to smoke his pipe there. I had received strict orders from my sister to call for him at the Three Jolly Bargemen that evening, on my way from school, and bring him home at my peril. To the Three

Jolly Bargemen, therefore, I directed my steps.

Joe was smoking his pipe in company with Mr. Wopsle and a stranger. Joe greeted me as usual with "Halloa, Pip, old chap!" and the moment he said that, the stranger turned his head and looked at me.

He was a secret-looking man whom I had never seen before. His head was all on one side, and one of his eyes was half shut up, as if he were taking aim at something with an invisible gun. He had a pipe in his mouth, and he took it out, and, after slowly blowing all his smoke away and looking hard at me all the time, nodded. So I nodded, and then he nodded again, and made room on the settle beside him that I might sit down there.

But, as I was used to sit beside Joe whenever I entered that place of resort, I said, "No, thank you, sir," and fell into the space Joe made for me on the opposite settle. The strange man, after glancing at Joe, and seeing that his attention was otherwise engaged, nodded to me again when I had taken my seat, and then rubbed his leg—in a very odd way, as it struck me.

"You were saying," said the strange man, turning to Joe, "that you was a blacksmith. What'll you drink, Mr. Gargery? At my expense? To top up with?"

"Well," said Joe, "to tell you the truth, I ain't much in the habit of drinking at anybody's expense but my own."

"Habit? No," returned the stranger, "but once and away, and on a Saturday night, too. Come! Put a name to it, Mr. Gargery."

"I wouldn't wish to be stiff company," said Joe. "Rum."

"Rum," repeated the stranger. "And will the other gentleman originate a sentiment?"

"Rum," said Mr. Wopsle.

"Three rums!" cried the stranger, calling to the landlord. "Glasses round!"

The stranger put his legs up on the settle that he had to himself. He wore a flapping broad-brimmed traveler's hat and under it a handkerchief tied over his head in the manner of a cap, so that he showed no hair.

"I am not acquainted with this country, gentlemen, but it seems a solitary country toward the river."

"Most marshes is solitary," said Joe.

"No doubt, no doubt. Do you find any gypsies, now, or tramps, or vagrants of any sort, out there?"

"No," said Joe; "none but a runaway convict now and then. And we don't find *them* easy."

"Seems you have been out after such?" asked the stranger.

"Once," returned Joe. "Not that we wanted to take them, you understand; we went out as lookers-on, me and Mr. Wopsle and Pip. Didn't us, Pip?"

"Yes, Joe."

The stranger looked at me again and said, "He's a likely young parcel of bones, that. What is it you call him?"

"Pip," said Joe.

"Christened Pip?"

"No, not christened Pip."

"Surname Pip?"

"No," said Joe; "it's a kind of a family name what he gave himself when a infant, and is called by."

"Son of yours?"

"Well—" said Joe meditatively, "well—no. No, he ain't,"

"Nevvy?" [1] said the strange man.

"Well," said Joe, "he is not—no, not to deceive you, he is *not*—my nevvy."

"What the blue blazes is he?" asked the stranger.

Mr. Wopsle expounded the ties between me and Joe. All this while the strange man looked at nobody but me, and looked at me as if he were determined to have a shot at me at last, and bring me down. But he said nothing until the glasses were brought: and then he made his shot, and a most extraordinary shot it was.

He stirred his rum-and-water pointedly at me, and he tasted his rum-and-water pointedly at me—not with a spoon that was brought to him, but *with a file*.

He did this so that nobody but I saw the file; and when he had done it, he wiped the file and put it in a breast pocket. I knew it to be Joe's file, and I knew that he knew my convict, the moment I saw the instrument. I sat gazing at him, spellbound. Joe got up to go, and took me by the hand.

"Stop half a moment, Mr. Gargery," said the strange man. "I think I've got a bright new shilling somewhere in my pocket, and if I have, the boy shall have it."

He looked it out from a handful of small change, folded it in some crumpled paper, and gave it to me. "Yours!" said he. "Mind! Your own."

I thanked him, staring at him far beyond the bounds of good manners, and holding tight to Joe. On the way home I was in a manner stupefied by this turning up of my old misdeed and old acquaintance, and could think of nothing else.

My sister was not in a very bad temper when we presented ourselves in the kitchen, and Joe was encouraged by that unusual circumstance to tell her about the bright shilling. "A bad un, I'll be bound," said Mrs. Joe triumphantly, "or he wouldn't have given it to the boy. Let's look at it."

I took it out of the paper, and it proved to be a good one. "But what's this?" said Mrs. Joe, throwing down the shilling and catching up the paper. "Two one-pound notes?" [2]

Joe caught up his hat again, and ran with them to the Jolly Bargemen to restore them to their owner. While he was gone I sat down on my usual stool and looked vacantly at my sister, feeling pretty sure that the man would not be there.

Presently Joe came back, saying that the man was gone, but that he, Joe, had left word at the Three Jolly Bargemen concerning the notes. Then my sister sealed them up in a piece of paper, and put them under some dried rose leaves in an ornamental teapot on the top of a press in the parlor. There they remained a nightmare to me many and many a night and day.

I had sadly broken sleep when I got to bed, through thinking of the strange man and of the guiltily coarse and common thing it was to be on secret terms of conspiracy with convicts—a feature in my low career that I had previously forgotten. I was haunted by the file too. A dread possessed me that when I least expected it, the file would reappear. I coaxed myself to sleep by thinking of Miss Havisham's next Wednesday; and in my sleep I saw the file coming at me out of a door, without seeing who held it, and I screamed myself awake.

[1] **Nevvy:** nephew.

[2] **Two one-pound notes:** forty shillings, or almost ten dollars in American money in Dickens' time, a considerable sum of money at that time.

CHAPTER 10

*We meet Camilla and her husband,
Miss Sarah Pocket, Georgiana,
and a pale young gentleman.*

At the appointed time I returned to Miss Havisham's, and my hesitating ring at the gate brought out Estella. She locked it after admitting me, as she had done before, and took me to quite another part of the house, a small paved courtyard, the opposite side of which was formed by a detached dwelling house. There was a clock in the outer wall of this house. Like the clock in Miss Havisham's room, and like Miss Havisham's watch, it had stopped at twenty minutes to nine.

We went in at the door, which stood open, and into a gloomy room with a low ceiling, on the ground floor at the back. There was some company in the room, and Estella said, "You are to go and stand there, boy, till you are wanted." "There" being the window, I crossed to it and stood "there," in a very uncomfortable state of mind, looking out.

I divined that my coming had stopped conversation in the room, and that its other occupants were looking at me. There were three ladies in the room and one gentleman. Before I had been standing at the window five minutes, they somehow conveyed to me that they were all toadies and humbugs.

They all had a listless and dreary air of waiting somebody's pleasure. The most talkative of the ladies, whose name was Camilla, very much reminded me of my sister, with the difference that she was older and of a biunter cast of features. "Poor dear soul!" said this lady. "Nobody's enemy but his own!"

"It would be much more commendable to be somebody else's enemy," said the gentleman; "far more natural."

"Cousin Raymond," observed another lady, "we are to love our neighbor."

"Sarah Pocket," returned Cousin Raymond, "if a man is not his own neighbor, who is?"

"Poor soul!" Camilla presently went on (I knew they had all been looking at me in the meantime), "he is so very strange! Would anyone believe that when Tom's wife died, he actually could not be induced to see the importance of the children's having the deepest of trimmings to their mourning? 'Good Lord!' says he, 'Camilla, what can it signify so long as the poor bereaved little things are in black?' So like Matthew! The idea!"

"Good points in him, good points in him," said Cousin Raymond, "but he never had and he never will have any sense of the proprieties."

The ringing of a distant bell, combined with the echoing of some cry or call along the passage by which I had come, interrupted the conversation and caused Estella to say to me, "Now, boy!"

As we were going with our candle along the dark passage, Estella stopped all of a sudden and, facing round, said in her taunting manner, with her face quite close to mine:

"Well?"

"Well, miss," I answered, almost falling over her and checking myself.

She stood looking at me, and of course I stood looking at her.

"Am I pretty?"

"Yes; I think you are very pretty."

"Am I insulting?"

"Not so much as you were last time," said I.

"Not so much so?"

"No."

She slapped my face with such force as she had.

"Now?" said she. "You little coarse monster, what do you think of me now?"

"I shall not tell you."

"Because you are going to tell upstairs. Is that it?"

"No," said I, "that's not it."

"Why don't you cry again, you little wretch?"

"Because I'll never cry for you again," said I. Which was, I suppose, as false a declaration as ever was made; for I was inwardly crying for her then, and I know what I know of the pain she cost me afterward.

We went on our way upstairs after this episode; and, as we were going up, we met a gentleman groping his way down.

"Whom have we here?" asked the gentleman, stopping and looking at me.

"A boy," said Estella.

He was a burly man of an exceedingly dark complexion, with an exceedingly large head. He took my chin in his large hand and turned up my face to have a look at me by the light of the candle. He was prematurely bald on the top of his head, and had bushy black eyebrows that wouldn't lie down, but stood up bristling. His eyes were set very deep in his head, and were disagreeably sharp and suspicious. He had a large watch chain, and strong black dots where his beard and whiskers would have been if he had let them. He was nothing to me, and I could have had no foresight then that he ever would be anything to me, but it happened that I had this opportunity of observing him well.

"Boy of the neighborhood? Hey?" said he.

"Yes, sir," said I.

"How do *you* come here?"

"Miss Havisham sent for me, sir," I explained.

"Well! Behave yourself. I have a pretty large experience of boys, and you're a bad set of fellows. Now mind!" said he, biting the side of his great forefinger, as he frowned at me, "you behave yourself!"

With these words he released me—which I was glad of, for his hand smelt of scented soap—and went his way downstairs. We were soon in Miss Havisham's room. Estella left me standing near the door, and I stood there until Miss Havisham cast her eyes upon me from the dressing table.

"So!" she said. "The days have worn away, have they?"

"Yes, ma'am. Today is—"

"There, there, there!" with the impatient movement of her fingers. "I don't want to know. Are you ready to play?"

I was obliged to answer in some confusion, "I don't think I am, ma'am."

"Not at cards again?" she demanded with a searching look.

"Yes, ma'am; I could do that, if I was wanted."

"Since this house strikes you old and grave, boy," said Miss Havisham impatiently, "and you are unwilling to play, are you willing to work?"

I could answer this inquiry with a better heart than I had been able to find for the other question, and I said I was quite willing.

"Then go into that opposite room," said she, pointing at the door behind me with her withered hand, "and wait there till I come."

I crossed the staircase landing and entered the room she indicated. From that room, too, the daylight was completely excluded, and it had an airless smell that was oppressive. Every discernible thing in it was covered with dust and mold, and dropping to pieces. The most prominent object was a long table with a tablecloth spread on it, as if a feast had been in preparation when the house and the clocks all stopped together. A centerpiece of some kind was in the middle of this cloth; it was so heavily overhung with cobwebs that its form was quite undistinguishable. I saw speckled-legged spiders with blotchy bodies running home to it, and running out from it.

I heard the mice, too, rattling behind the panels.

These crawling things had fascinated my attention, and I was watching them from a distance when Miss Havisham laid a hand upon my shoulder. In her other hand she had a crutch-headed stick on which she leaned, and she looked like the witch of the place.

"This," said she, pointing to the long table with her stick, "is where I will be laid when I am dead. They shall come and look at me here."

"What do you think that is," she asked me, again pointing with her stick; "that, where those cobwebs are?"

"I can't guess, ma'am."

"It's a great cake. A bride cake. Mine!"

She looked all round the room in a glaring manner, and then said, leaning me while her hand twitched my shoulder, "Come, come, come! Walk me, walk me!"

I made out from this that the work I had to do was to walk Miss Havisham round and round the room. Accordingly, she leaned on my shoulder and we went away at a pace.

After a while she said, "Call Estella," so I went out on the landing and roared that name as I had done on the previous occasion. When her light appeared, I returned to Miss Havisham, and we started away again round and round the room.

If only Estella had come to be a spectator of our proceedings, I should have felt sufficiently discontented; but, as she brought with her the three ladies and the gentleman whom I had seen below, I didn't know what to do. I would have stopped; but Miss Havisham twitched my shoulder and we posted on.

"Dear Miss Havisham," said Miss Sarah Pocket. "How well you look!"

"I do not," returned Miss Havisham.

"I am yellow skin and bone."

Camilla brightened when Miss Pocket met with this rebuff; and she murmured, as she plaintively contemplated Miss Havisham, "Poor dear soul! Certainly not to be expected to look well, poor thing. The idea!"

"And how are *you?*" said Miss Havisham to Camilla. As we were close to Camilla then, I would have stopped as a matter of course, only Miss Havisham wouldn't stop. We swept on, and I felt that I was highly obnoxious to Camilla.

"Thank you, Miss Havisham," she returned. "I am as well as can be expected."

"Why, what's the matter with you?" asked Miss Havisham, with exceeding sharpness.

"Nothing worth mentioning," replied Camilla. "I don't wish to make a display of my feelings, but I have habitually thought of you more in the night than I am quite equal to."

"Then don't think of me," retorted Miss Havisham.

"Oh!" cried Camilla. "It's a weakness to be so affectionate, but I can't help it."

Miss Havisham and I kept going round and round the room; now brushing against the skirts of the visitors; now giving them the whole length of the dismal chamber.

"There's Matthew!" said Camilla. "Never mixing with any natural ties, never coming here to see how Miss Havisham is!"

When this same Matthew was mentioned, Miss Havisham stopped me and herself, and stood looking at the speaker. This change had a great influence in bringing Camilla's chemistry to a sudden end.

"Matthew will come and see me at last," said Miss Havisham sternly, "when I am laid on that table. That will be his place— there," striking the table with her stick, "at my head! And yours will be there! And your husband's there! And Sarah

Pocket's there! And Georgiana's there! Now you all know where to take your stations when you come to feast upon me.[1] And now go!"

At the mention of each name, she had struck the table with her stick in a new place. She now said, "Walk me, walk me!" and we went on again.

While Estella was away lighting them down, Miss Havisham still walked with her hand on my shoulder, but more and more slowly. At last she stopped before the fire and said, after muttering and looking at it some seconds:

"This is my birthday, Pip."

I was going to wish her many happy returns, when she lifted her stick.

"I don't suffer it to be spoken of. I don't suffer those who were here just now, or anyone, to speak of it. They come here on the day, but they dare not refer to it."

Of course *I* made no further effort to refer to it.

"On this day of the year, long before you were born, this heap of decay," stabbing with her crutched stick at the pile of cobwebs on the table, but not touching it, "was brought here. It and I have worn away together. The mice have gnawed at it, and sharper teeth than teeth of mice have gnawed at me."

She held the head of her stick against her heart as she stood looking at the table; she in her once white dress, all yellow and withered; the once white cloth all yellow and withered; everything around in a state to crumble under a touch.

"When the ruin is complete," said she, with a ghastly look, "and when they lay me dead, in my bride's dress on the bride's table—which shall be done, and which will be the finished curse upon him—so much the better if it is done on this day!"

[1] **Now . . . me:** that is, to collect their shares of her will after her death.

I remained quiet. Estella returned, and she too remained quiet. At length, Miss Havisham said, "Let me see you two play at cards; why have you not begun?" With that, we returned to her room, and sat down as before; I was beggared as before, and again, as before, Miss Havisham watched us all the time, directed my attention to Estella's beauty, and made me notice it the more by trying her jewels on Estella's breast and hair.

Estella, for her part, likewise treated me as before, except that she did not condescend to speak. When we had played some half dozen games, a day was appointed for my return, and I was taken down into the yard to be fed in the former doglike manner. There, too, I was again left to wander about as I liked.

I strolled into the garden and found myself in the dismal corner upon which I had looked out of window. Never questioning for a moment that the house was now empty, I looked in at another window, and found myself, to my great surprise, exchanging a broad stare with a pale young gentleman with red eyelids and light hair.

This pale young gentleman quickly disappeared and reappeared beside me. He had been at his books when I had found myself staring at him, and I now saw that he was inky.

"Who let *you* in?" said he.

"Miss Estella."

"Who gave you leave to prowl about?"

"Miss Estella."

"Come and fight," said the pale young gentleman.

What could I do but follow him? I have often asked myself the question since; but, what else could I do? His manner was so final and I was so astonished that I followed where he led, as if I had been under a spell.

"Stop a minute, though," he said, wheeling round before we had gone many paces. "I ought to give you a reason for fighting, too. There it is!" In a most irritating manner he instantly slapped his hands against one another, daintily flung one of his legs up behind him, pulled my hair, slapped his hands again, dipped his head, and butted it into my stomach.

I hit out at him, and was going to hit out again, when he said, "Aha! Would you?" and began dancing backward and forward in a manner quite unparalleled within my limited experience.

"Laws of the game!" said he. Here, he skipped from his left leg on to his right. "Regular rules!" Here, he skipped from his right leg on to his left. "Come to the ground, and go through the preliminaries!" Here, he dodged backward and forward, and did all sorts of things while I looked helplessly at him.

I was secretly afraid of him when I saw him so dexterous; but I followed him without a word to a retired nook of the garden. On his asking me if I was satisfied with the ground, and on my replying "Yes," he begged my leave to absent himself for a moment, and quickly returned with a bottle of water and a sponge dipped in vinegar. "Available for both," he said, and fell to pulling off, not only his jacket and waistcoat, but his shirt, too, in a manner at once lighthearted, businesslike, and bloodthirsty. Although he did not look very healthy, these dreadful preparations quite appalled me. I judged him to be about my own age, but he was much taller.

My heart failed me when I saw him squaring at me with every demonstration of mechanical nicety, and eyeing my anatomy as if he were minutely choosing his bone. I never have been so surprised in my life as I was when I let out the first blow and saw him lying on his back, looking up at me with a bloody nose.

But he was on his feet directly, and after sponging himself began squaring again. The second greatest surprise I have ever had in my life was seeing him on his back again, looking up at me out of a black eye.

His spirit inspired me with great respect. He seemed to have no strength, and he never once hit me hard, and he was always knocked down. He got heavily bruised, but he came up again and again until at last he got a bad fall with the back of his head against the wall. Even after that, he got up and turned round confusedly a few times; but finally went on his knees to his sponge and threw it up, panting out, "That means you have won."

He seemed so brave and innocent that although I had not proposed the contest, I felt but a gloomy satisfaction in my victory. However, I got dressed and said, "Can I help you?" and he said, "No, thankee," and I said, "Good afternoon," and *he* said, "Same to you."

When I got into the courtyard, I found Estella waiting with the keys. But she neither asked me where I had been, nor why I had kept her waiting; and there was a bright flush upon her face, as though something had happened to delight her. Instead of going straight to the gate, too, she stepped back into the passage and beckoned me.

"Come here! You may kiss me if you like."

I kissed her cheek as she turned it to me. I think I would have gone through a great deal to kiss her cheek. But I felt that the kiss was given to the coarse common boy as a piece of money might have been, and that it was worth nothing.

What with the birthday visitors, and what with the cards, and what with the fight, my stay had lasted so long that when I neared home, the light off the point on the marshes was gleaming against a black night sky, and Joe's furnace was flinging a path of fire across the road.

Social Realism in Art

During the year 1848 the French people rose in a revolution that overthrew an oppressive monarchy. In London, Charles Dickens was at work on his novel *David Copperfield,* in which he recalled the miseries of his own poverty-stricken childhood. The cry of the day was for social reforms to better the lot of poor and ordinary people who had thronged to the cities as a result of the Industrial Revolution. Artists and writers alike began to devote their talents to depicting the life and condition of these masses of people.

At the height of this new interest, an English artist named William Maw Egley painted *Omnibus Life in London* (PLATE 1). Who are these people with packages and umbrellas who are crowded into a public transport car? No one of any importance. Yet down to the last button and lace flounce, the painter has depicted them with loving care. He has avoided making any of them ugly, however. Probably he believed in the old theory that if a painting is to be beautiful, everything represented in it must be beautiful too.

More daring painters had other ideas. With eyes open to the everyday world, they found meaning in much that was not beautiful. They sacrificed beauty to reality and started a tradition known today as *social realism.* One of these painters was Honoré Daumier, a political and satirical cartoonist for Parisian newspapers. For his own pleasure, Daumier painted pictures like *The Drama* (PLATE 2). Ordinary people, it seemed to him, were generally 'not beautiful, but he was fascinated by their emotional reactions to public spectacles. With a few sketchy lines Daumier not only characterized individuals in a crowd but at the same time expressed the feelings they shared as a group in response to the melodrama on the stage. Humor and sympathy are combined in the artist's view of both audience and actors. Many people consider the art of this Frenchman closer in spirit to the writing of Dickens than any English art of the time.

A generation later, social realism is seen again in *The Court* by Jean Louis Forain (PLATE 3). Now the characters have become really grubby, though rendered with brilliant brushwork in a sort of painter's shorthand. We see a ragged defendant pleading before a self-righteous magistrate, while a raffish young mother ignores the proceedings and gossips with a friend. The painter seems to take pleasure in observing that for downtrodden people life goes on and has its amusing moments in spite of hard times and unsympathetic officials.

The nineteenth-century European tradition of social realism also found a responsive home in twentieth-century America. The artist Edward Hopper, however, seems more concerned with the loneliness of people in cities than with the plight of the poor. In *Nighthawks* (PLATE 4) garish light shines on deserted streets from an all-night cafeteria. It illuminates the bleak image of unnamed people who are up late for unknown reasons and who perhaps find a little warmth in coffee and doubtful human contact. Over this unglamorous scene Hopper has cast the glamour of art.

Aaron Bohrod painted *Landscape Near Chicago* (PLATE 5) at a low point in the great American economic depression of the 1930's. Here the theme is the intrusion of industrial society, with all its problems, into the fields and trees of a once rural landscape. A service station seems to be under construction and at the same time falling into disrepair. The ungainly cinderblock house with its shingles falling off stands in a work area recently cleared of grass. Here we see old cars, junked signs, a half-new garage, and a new gas pump not yet installed. A fire hydrant and distant high tension wires foretell the future development of this place near a big city, though for the moment it is attended only by a small mechanic putting gas in an old phaeton.

In *Miners' Wives* (PLATE 6) Ben Shahn has adapted some of the elements of modern nonrealist style to treat the theme of poor people and their personal worries in the face of a large, impersonal industrial plant. Here Shahn has used his art to express his sympathy for the American labor movement, which in the 1940's often focused its attention on disasters faced by coal miners and their families. In this painting, the death of a miner is suggested by the anxiety on the faces of the two women, presumably survivors of the tragedy. Through the door in the wall two "company men" stand with backs turned toward the bereaved family. Hot reds and orange, cold blues and violet, and chalky whites combine to suggest the shock felt over their loss.

Social realist painters have invited us to sympathize with poor and ordinary people, people to whom life often presents more misery than happiness, more ugliness than beauty. They have wanted to show us what life *is* rather than what it *should be*—sometimes with the hope that we will be inspired to do something about it.

PLATE 1. WILLIAM MAW EGLEY (English, 1826–1916): *Omnibus Life in London*, 1859. Oil on wood, $17\frac{1}{2}$ x $16\frac{1}{2}$ inches. (Reproduced by courtesy of the Trustees, The Tate Gallery, London)

PLATE 2. HONORE DAUMIER (French, 1808–1879): *The Drama*. 1864. Oil on canvas, 38⅛ x 35 inches. (Neue Pinakothek, Munich)

PLATE 3. JEAN LOUIS FORAIN (French, 1852–1931): *The Court*. 1908. Oil on canvas, $25\frac{5}{8}$ x 32 inches. (Reproduced by courtesy of the Trustees, The Tate Gallery, London)

PLATE 4. EDWARD HOPPER (American, 1882–1967): *Nighthawks.* 1942. Oil on canvas. 33¾₆ x 60⅛ inches. (Courtesy of The Art Institute of Chicago)

PLATE 5. AARON BOHROD (American, 1907–): *Landscape Near Chicago*. 1934. Oil on composition board, 24 x 32 inches. (Collection of the Whitney Museum of American Art, New York)

PLATE 6. BEN SHAHN (American, 1898–   ): *Miners' Wives*. 1948. Tempera on board, 48 x 36 inches. (Philadelphia Museum of Art)

600

CHAPTER 11

Pip becomes Joe's apprentice.

MY MIND grew very uneasy on the subject of the pale young gentleman. The more I thought of the fight, and recalled the pale young gentleman on his back, the more certain it appeared that something would be done to me. When the day came round for my return to the scene of the deed of violence, my terrors reached their height. However, go to Miss Havisham's I must, and go I did. And behold! nothing came of the late struggle. It was not alluded to in any way, and no pale young gentleman was to be discovered on the premises.

On the broad landing between Miss Havisham's own room and that other room in which the long table was laid out, I saw a garden-chair—a light chair on wheels, that you pushed from behind. I entered, that same day, on a regular occupation of pushing Miss Havisham in this chair (when she was tired of walking with her hand upon my shoulder) round her own room, and across the landing, and round the other room. Over and over and over again, we would make these journeys, and sometimes they would last as long as three hours at a stretch. I fall into a general mention of these journeys as numerous, because it was at once settled that I should return every alternate day at noon, and because I am now going to sum up a period of at least eight or ten months.

As we began to be more used to one another, Miss Havisham talked more to me, and asked me such questions as what had I learned and what was I going to be? I told her I was going to be apprenticed to Joe, I believed; and I enlarged upon my knowing nothing and wanting to know everything, in the hope that she might offer some help toward that desirable end. But she did not; on the contrary, she seemed to prefer my being ignorant. Neither did she ever give me any money or anything but my daily dinner—nor even stipulate that I should be paid for my services.

Estella was always about, and always let me in and out, but never told me I might kiss her again. Sometimes, she would be quite familiar with me; sometimes, she would tell me energetically that she hated me. Miss Havisham would often ask me in a whisper, or when we were alone, "Does she grow prettier and prettier, Pip?" And when I said "Yes" (for indeed she did), would seem to enjoy it greedily. Also, when we played at cards, Miss Havisham would look on, with a miserly relish of Estella's moods, whatever they were. And sometimes, when her moods were so many and so contradictory that I was puzzled what to say or do, Miss Havisham would embrace her with lavish fondness, murmuring something in her ear that sounded like "Break their hearts, my pride and hope, break their hearts and have no mercy!"

Perhaps I might have told Joe about the pale young gentleman if I had not previously been betrayed into those enormous inventions to which I had confessed. I reposed complete confidence in no one but Biddy; but I told poor Biddy everything. Why it came natural for me to do so, and why Biddy had a deep concern in everything I told her, I did not know then, though I think I know now.

Meanwhile, councils went on in the kitchen at home. Pumblechook and my sister would pair off in nonsensical speculations about Miss Havisham, and about what she would do with me and for me. In these discussions, Joe bore no part. But he was often talked at, while they were in progress, by reason of Mrs. Joe's perceiving that he was not favorable to my being taken from the forge.

We went on in this way for a long time, when, one day, Miss Havisham stopped short as she and I were walking and said with some displeasure:

"You are growing tall, Pip!"

She said no more at the time, but she presently stopped and looked at me again; and after that looked frowning and moody. On the next day of my attendance, she stayed me with a movement of her impatient fingers:

"Tell me the name again of that blacksmith of yours."

"Joe Gargery, ma'am."

"Meaning the master you were to be apprenticed to?"

"Yes, Miss Havisham."

"You had better be apprenticed at once. Would Gargery come here with you, and bring your indentures,[1] do you think?"

"At any particular time, Miss Havisham?"

"There, there! I know nothing about times. Let him come soon, and come along with you."

When I delivered this message at home, my sister "went on the Ram-page," threw a candlestick at Joe, got out the dustpan —which was always a very bad sign—and cleaned us out of house and home so that we stood shivering in the backyard. It was ten o'clock at night before we ventured to creep in again.

It was a trial to my feelings, on the next day but one, to see Joe arraying himself in his Sunday clothes to accompany me to Miss Havisham's. At breakfast time, my sister declared her intention of going to town with us, and being left at Uncle Pumblechook's and called for "when we had done with our fine ladies."

The forge was shut up for the day, and

Joe inscribed in chalk upon the door (as it was his custom to do on the very rare occasions when he was not at work) the monosyllable HOUT,[2] accompanied by a sketch of an arrow supposed to be flying in the direction he had taken. When we came to Pumblechook's, my sister bounced in and left us. As it was almost noon, Joe and I held straight on to Miss Havisham's house. Estella opened the gate as usual, and led us the way that I knew so well.

Estella told me we were both to go in, so I took Joe by the coat cuff and conducted him into Miss Havisham's presence. She was seated at her dressing table, and looked round at us immediately.

"Oh!" said she to Joe. "You are the husband of the sister of this boy?"

I could hardly have imagined dear old Joe looking so unlike himself or so like some extraordinary bird, standing, as he did, speechless, with his tuft of feathers ruffled, and his mouth open as if he wanted a worm.

"You are the husband," repeated Miss Havisham, "of the sister of this boy?"

It was very aggravating; but, throughout the interview, Joe persisted in addressing me instead of Miss Havisham. It was quite in vain for me to make him sensible that he ought to speak to Miss Havisham. The more I made faces and gestures to him to do it, the more confidential, argumentative, and polite he persisted in being to me.

"Have you brought his indentures with you?" asked Miss Havisham.

"Well, Pip, you know," replied Joe, as if that were a little unreasonable, "you yourself see me put 'em in my 'at, and therefore you know as they are here." With which he took them out, and gave them, not to Miss Havisham, but to me. I am afraid I was ashamed of the dear

---

[1] **indentures** (in·den'chərz): contract binding an apprentice to a master.

[2] **hout:** out.

good fellow—I *know* I was ashamed of him—when I saw that Estella stood at the back of Miss Havisham's chair, and that her eyes laughed mischievously. I took the indentures out of his hand and gave them to Miss Havisham.

"You expected," said Miss Havisham, as she looked them over, "no premium with the boy?"

"Joe!" I remonstrated; for he made no reply at all. "Why don't you answer—"

"Pip," returned Joe, cutting me short as if he were hurt, "which I meantersay that were not a question requiring a answer betwixt yourself and me, and which you know the answer to be full well 'No.' You know it to be 'No,' Pip, and wherefore should I say it?"

Miss Havisham glanced at him as if she understood what he really was, better than I had thought possible; and took up a little bag from the table beside her.

"Pip has earned a premium here," she said, "and here it is. There are five-and-twenty guineas [1] in this bag. Give it to your master, Pip."

Joe, even at this pass, persisted in addressing me. "This is very liberal on your part, Pip," said Joe, "and it is as such received and grateful welcome, though never looked for. And now, old chap," said Joe, "may you and me do our duty, both on us by one and another."

"Good-by, Pip!" said Miss Havisham. "Let them out, Estella."

"Am I to come again, Miss Havisham?" I asked.

"No. Gargery is your master now. Gargery! One word!"

Thus calling him back as I went out of the door, I heard her say to Joe, in a distinct emphatic voice, "The boy has been a good boy here, and that is his reward.

Of course, as an honest man, you will expect no other and no more."

In another minute we were outside the gate, and it was locked, and Estella was gone. When we stood in the daylight alone again, Joe backed up against a wall and said to me, "Astonishing!" And there he remained so long, saying "Astonishing" at intervals so often that I began to think his senses were never coming back. At length he prolonged his remark into, "Pip, I do assure *you* this is as-TON-ish-ing!" and so, by degrees, became conversational and able to walk away.

"Well!" cried my sister, addressing us both at once, when we arrived at Pumblechook's. "I wonder you condescend to come back to such poor society as this, I am sure I do! And, what did she give young Rantipole here?"

"She giv' him," said Joe, handing the bag to my sister, "five-and-twenty pound."

"It's five-and-twenty pound, mum," echoed that basest of swindlers, Pumblechook, rising to shake hands with her; "and it's no more than your merits (as I said when my opinion was asked), and I wish you joy of the money!"

"Goodness knows, Uncle Pumblechook," said my sister (grasping the money), "we're deeply beholden to you."

"Never mind me, mum," returned that diabolical corn chandler. "A pleasure's a pleasure all the world over. But this boy, you know; we must have him bound. I said I'd see to it—to tell you the truth."

The justices were sitting in the town hall near at hand, and we at once went over to have me bound apprentice to Joe. I say we went over, but I was pushed over by Pumblechook, exactly as if I had that moment picked a pocket or fired a rick. [2] Indeed, it was the general impression in

---

[1] **guinea** (gin′ē): a gold coin worth twenty-one shillings, a little over five dollars in American money then.

[2] **fired a rick:** set fire to a haystack.

court that I had been taken red-handed; for, as Pumblechook shoved me before him through the crowd, I heard some people say, "What's he done?" and others, "He's a young 'un, too, but looks bad, don't he?" One person of mild and benevolent aspect even gave me a tract entitled, TO BE READ IN MY CELL.

When we had come out again, we went back to Pumblechook's. And there my sister became so excited by the twenty-five guineas that nothing would serve her but we must have a dinner at the Blue Boar, and that Mr. Pumblechook must go over in his chaise-cart and bring the Hubbles and Mr. Wopsle.

My only remembrances of the great festival are that they wouldn't let me go to sleep, but whenever they saw me dropping off, woke me up and told me to enjoy myself and that when I got into my little bedroom, I was truly wretched, and had a strong conviction on me that I should never like Joe's trade. I had liked it once, but once was not now.

It is a most miserable thing to feel ashamed of home. Home had never been a very pleasant place to me, because of my sister's temper. But Joe had sanctified it, and I believed in it. I had believed in the best parlor as a most elegant saloon; I had believed in the kitchen as a chaste though not magnificent apartment; I had believed in the forge as the glowing road to manhood and independence. Within a single year all this was changed. Now, it was all coarse and common, and I would not have had Miss Havisham and Estella see it on any account.

How much of my ungracious condition of mind may have been my own fault, how much Miss Havisham's, how much my sister's, is now of no moment to me or anyone. The change was made in me; the thing was done. Well or ill done, it was done.

Once it had seemed to me that when I should at last roll up my shirt sleeves and go into the forge, Joe's 'prentice, I should be distinguished and happy. Now I only felt that I was dusty with the dust of the small coal, and that I had a weight upon my daily remembrance to which the anvil was a feather. There have been occasions in my later life when I have felt for a time as if a thick curtain had fallen on all its interest and romance, to shut me out from anything save dull endurance any more. Never has that curtain dropped so heavy and blank, as when my way in life lay stretched out straight before me through the newly entered road of apprenticeship to Joe.

But I am glad to know that I never breathed a murmur to Joe while my indentures lasted. It is about the only thing I *am* glad to know of myself in that connection. It was not because I was faithful, but because Joe was faithful, that I never ran away and went for a soldier or a sailor. It was not because I had a strong sense of the virtue of industry, but because Joe had a strong sense of the virtue of industry, that I worked with tolerable zeal against the grain. It is not possible to know how far the influence of any amiable, honest-hearted, duty-doing man flies out into the world, but I know right well that any good that intermixed itself with my apprentice-ship came of plain, contented Joe, and not of restless, aspiring, discontented me.

What I dreaded was that in some un-lucky hour I, being at my grimiest and commonest, should lift up my eyes and see Estella looking in at one of the wooden windows of the forge. I was haunted by the fear that she would, sooner or later, find me out, with a black face and hands, doing the coarsest part of my work, and would exult over me and despise me. Often after dark, when I was pulling the bellows for Joe, I would fancy that I saw her just drawing her face away, and would believe that she had come at last.

After that, when we went in to supper, the place would have a more homely look than ever, and I would feel more ashamed of home than ever, in my own ungracious breast.

CHAPTER 12

Introducing Orlick.

As I was getting too big for Mr. Wop-sle's great-aunt's room, my education under that preposterous female termi-nated; not, however, until Biddy had im-parted to me everything she knew, from the little catalogue of prices to a comic song she had once bought for a halfpenny. Although the only coherent part of the latter piece of literature was the opening lines,

> When I went to Lunnon town, sirs,
> > Too rul loo rul!
> > Too rul loo rul!
> Wasn't I done very brown, sirs?
> > Too rul loo rul!
> > Too rul loo rul!

—still, in my desire to be wiser, I got this composition by heart with the utmost gravity. In my hunger for information, I made proposals to Mr. Wopsle to bestow some intellectual crumbs upon me; with which he kindly complied. As it turned out, however, that he only wanted me for a dramatic lay-figure, to be contradicted and embraced and wept over and bullied and clutched and stabbed and knocked about in a variety of ways, I soon declined that course of instruction, though not until Mr. Wopsle in his poetic fury had severely mauled me.

Whatever I acquired, I tried to impart to Joe. This statement sounds so well that I cannot in my conscience let it pass unexplained. I wanted to make Joe less ignorant and common, that he might be worthier of my society and less open to Estella's reproach.

The old Battery out on the marshes was our place of study, and a broken slate and a short piece of slate pencil were our edu-cational implements, to which Joe always added a pipe of tobacco. I never knew Joe to remember anything from one Sunday to another, or to acquire, under my tuition, any piece of information whatever. Yet he would smoke his pipe at the Battery with a far more sagacious air than anywhere else—even with a learned air—as if he considered himself to be advancing im-mensely. Dear fellow, I hope he did.

It was pleasant and quiet, out there with the sails on the river. Whenever I watched the vessels standing out to sea with their white sails spread, I somehow thought of Miss Havisham and Estella. One Sunday I resolved to mention a thought concerning them that had been much in my head.

"Joe," said I, "don't you think I ought to pay Miss Havisham a visit?"

"Well, Pip," returned Joe, slowly considering. "What for?"

"What for, Joe? What is any visit made for?"

"There is some wisits p'r'aps," said Joe, "as forever remains open to the question, Pip. But in regard of wisiting Miss Havisham. She might think you wanted something—expected something of her."

I had thought of that too, and it was very far from comforting to me to find that he had thought of it; for it seemed to render it more probable.

"But, Joe."

"Yes, old chap."

"Here am I, getting on in the first year of my time, and since the day of my being bound I have never thanked Miss Havisham, or asked after her, or shown that I remember her."

"Well," said Joe, "if I was yourself, Pip, I wouldn't. No, I would *not.*"

"But, Joe; what I wanted to say was, that as we are rather slack just now, if you would give me a half holiday tomorrow, I think I would go uptown and make a call on Miss Est—Havisham."

"Which her name," said Joe gravely, "ain't Estavisham, Pip, unless she has been rechris'ened."

"I know, Joe. It was a slip. What do you think of it, Joe?"

In brief, Joe thought that if I thought well of it, he thought well of it. But he was particular in stipulating that if I were not received with cordiality, or if I were not encouraged to repeat my visit, as a visit which had no ulterior object, but was simply one of gratitude for a favor received, then this experimental trip should

have no successor. By these conditions I promised to abide.

Now, Joe kept a journeyman [1] at weekly wages whose name was Orlick. He was a broad-shouldered, loose-limbed, swarthy fellow of great strength, never in a hurry, and always slouching. He never even seemed to come to his work on purpose, but would slouch in as if by mere accident. He lodged at a sluice keeper's [2] out on the marshes, and on working days would come slouching from his hermitage, with his hands in his pockets and his dinner loosely tied in a bundle round his neck and dangling on his back.

This morose journeyman had no liking for me. When I was very small and timid, he gave me to understand that the Devil lived in a black corner of the forge, and that he knew the fiend very well; also that it was necessary to make up the fire, once in seven years, with a live boy, and that I might consider myself fuel. When I became Joe's 'prentice, Orlick was perhaps confirmed in some suspicion that I should displace him; howbeit he liked me still less.

Orlick was at work and present, next day, when I reminded Joe of my half holiday. He said nothing at the moment, for he and Joe had just got a piece of hot iron between them, and I was at the bellows; but by and by he said, leaning on his hammer:

"Now, master! Sure you're not a-going to favor only one of us. If Young Pip has a half holiday, do as much for Old Orlick." I suppose he was about five-and-twenty, but he usually spoke of himself as an ancient person.

"Why, what'll you do with a half holi-

---

[1] **journeyman** (jûr′nē·mən): one who has learned a craft and is no longer an apprentice, but who still works for a master artisan.

[2] **sluice** (slo͞os) **keeper:** person in charge of a gate which regulates the flow of water in a sluice, an artificial stream used for drainage or irrigation.

day if you get it?" said Joe.

"What'll *I* do with it? What'll *he* do with it? I'll do as much with it as *him*," said Orlick.

"As to Pip, he's going uptown," said Joe.

"Well then, as to Old Orlick, *he's* a-going uptown," retorted that worthy. "Two can go uptown. 'Tain't only one wot can go uptown."

"Don't lose your temper," said Joe.

"Shall if I like," growled Orlick. "Now, master! Come. No favoring in this shop. Be a man!"

"Then, as in general you stick to your work as well as most men," said Joe, "let it be a half holiday for all."

My sister had been standing silent in the yard, within hearing—she was a most unscrupulous spy and listener—and she instantly looked in at one of the windows.

"Like you, you fool!" said she to Joe, "giving holidays to great idle hulkers like that. You are a rich man, upon my life, to waste wages in that way. I wish *I* was his master!"

"You'd be everybody's master if you durst," retorted Orlick, with an ill-favored grin.

"Let her alone," said Joe.

"I'd be a match for all noodles and all rogues," returned my sister, beginning to work herself into a mighty rage. "And I couldn't be a match for the noodles without being a match for your master, who's the dunderheaded king of the noodles. And I couldn't be a match for the rogues without being a match for you, who are the blackest-looking and the worst rogue between this and France. Now!"

"You're a foul shrew, Mother Gargery," growled the journeyman. "If that makes a judge of rogues, you ought to be a good 'un."

"Let her alone, will you?" said Joe.

"What did you say?" cried my sister, beginning to scream. "What did you say? What did that fellow Orlick say to me, Pip? What did he call me, with my husband standing by? Oh! Oh! Oh!" Each of these exclamations was a shriek. "Oh! Hold me! Oh!"

"Ah-h-h!" growled the journeyman, between his teeth. "I'd hold you, if you was my wife. I'd hold you under the pump and choke it out of you."

"I tell you, let her alone," said Joe.

"Oh! To hear him!" cried my sister, with a clap of her hands and a scream together. "To hear the names he's giving me! That Orlick! In my own house! Me, a married woman! With my husband standing by! Oh! Oh!"

What could the wretched Joe do now but stand up to his journeyman? They went at one another like two giants. But if any man in that neighborhood could stand up long against Joe, I never saw the man. Orlick was very soon among the coal dust, and in no hurry to come out of it. Then Joe picked up my sister, who had dropped insensible at the window, and carried her into the house. Afterward came that calm and silence which succeed all uproars—and I went upstairs to dress.

When I came down again, I found Joe and Orlick sweeping up, without any other traces of discomposure than a slit in one of Orlick's nostrils. A pot of beer had appeared from the Jolly Bargemen, and they were sharing it by turns in a peaceable manner. Joe followed me out into the road to say, as a parting observation that might do me good, "On the Ram-page, Pip, and off the Ram-page, Pip—such is life!"

With what absurd emotions (for, we think the feelings that are very serious in a man quite comical in a boy) I found myself again going to Miss Havisham's, matters little here. Nor, how I passed and repassed the gate many times before I could make up my mind to ring.

Miss Sarah Pocket came to the gate. No Estella.

"How, then? You here again?" said Miss Pocket. "What do you want?"

When I said that I only came to see how Miss Havisham was, Sarah let me in, and presently brought the sharp message that I was to "come up."

Everything was unchanged, and Miss Havisham was alone.

"Well!" said she, fixing her eyes upon me. "I hope you want nothing? You'll get nothing."

"No indeed, Miss Havisham. I only wanted you to know that I am doing very well in my apprenticeship, and am always much obliged to you."

"There, there!" with the old restless fingers. "Come now and then; come on your birthday.—Aye!" she cried suddenly, turning herself and her chair toward me. "You are looking round for Estella? Hey?"

I had been looking round—in fact, for Estella—and I stammered that I hoped she was well.

"Abroad," said Miss Havisham; "educating for a lady; far out of reach; prettier than ever; admired by all who see her. Do you feel that you have lost her?"

There was such a malignant enjoyment in her utterance of the last words, and she broke into such a disagreeable laugh, that I was at a loss what to say. She spared me the trouble of considering, by dismissing me. When the gate was closed upon me, I felt more than ever dissatisfied with my home and with my trade and with everything.

As I was loitering along the High Street, looking at the shop windows and thinking what I would buy if I were a gentleman, who should come out of the bookshop but Mr. Wopsle. He insisted on my accompanying him to the Pumblechookian parlor. I made no great resistance; conse-quently, we turned into Pumblechook's just as the street and shops were lighting up.

It was a very dark night when I set out with Mr. Wopsle on the walk home. Beyond town we found a heavy mist out, and it fell wet and thick. The turnpike lamp was a blur, and its rays looked solid substance on the fog. We were noticing this when we came upon a man, slouching under the lee of the turnpike house.

"Halloa!" we said, stopping. "Orlick there?"

"Ah!" he answered, slouching out. "I was standing by a minute on the chance of company."

"You are late," I remarked.

Orlick not unnaturally answered, "Well? And *you're* late."

"We have been," said Mr. Wopsle, "indulging, Mr. Orlick, in an intellectual evening."

Old Orlick growled, as if he had nothing to say about that, and we all went on together. I asked him presently whether he had been spending his half holiday up and down town?

"Yes," said he, "all of it. I come in behind yourself. I didn't see you, but I must have been pretty close behind you. By the bye, the guns is going again."

"At the Hulks?" said I.

"Aye! There's some of the birds flown from the cages. The guns have been going since dark, about. You'll hear one presently."

In effect, we had not walked many yards further when the well-remembered boom came toward us, deadened by the mist.

"A good night for cutting off in," said Orlick. "We'd be puzzled how to bring down a jailbird on the wing tonight." Orlick, with his hands in his pockets, slouched heavily at my side. I thought he had been drinking, but he was not drunk.

Thus we came to the village. The way

by which we approached it took us past the Three Jolly Bargemen, which we were surprised to find—it being eleven o'clock—in a state of commotion, with the door wide open, and lights scattered about. Mr. Wopsle dropped in to ask what was the matter (surmising that a convict had been taken), but came running out in a great hurry.

"There's something wrong," said he, without stopping, "up at your place, Pip. Run all!"

"What is it?" I asked, keeping up with him. So did Orlick, at my side.

"I can't quite understand. The house seems to have been violently entered when Joe Gargery was out. Supposed by convicts. Somebody has been attacked and hurt."

We were running too fast to admit of more being said, and we made no stop until we got into our kitchen. It was full of people; the whole village was there or in the yard, and there was a surgeon, and there was Joe, and there was a group of women, all on the floor in the midst of the kitchen. The unemployed bystanders drew back when they saw me, and so I became aware of my sister—lying without sense or movement on the bare boards where she had been knocked down by a tremendous blow on the back of the head, dealt by some unknown hand when her face was turned toward the fire—destined never to be on the Ram-page again, while she was the wife of Joe.

Joe had been at the Three Jolly Bargemen, smoking his pipe, from a quarter after eight o'clock to a quarter before ten. While he was there, my sister had been seen standing at the kitchen door and had exchanged good night with a farm laborer going home. When Joe went home at five minutes before ten, he found her struck down on the floor, and promptly called in assistance.

Nothing had been taken away from any part of the house. But there was one remarkable piece of evidence on the spot. She had been struck with something blunt and heavy, on the head and spine; after the blows were dealt, something heavy had been thrown down at her with considerable violence, as she lay on her face. And on the ground beside her, when Joe picked her up, was a convict's leg iron which had been filed asunder.

Now, Joe, examining this iron with a smith's eye, declared it to have been filed asunder some time ago. The hue and cry going off to the Hulks, and people coming thence to examine the iron, Joe's opinion was corroborated. They claimed to know for certain that that particular manacle had not been worn by either of two convicts who had escaped last night. Further, one of those two was already retaken, and had not freed himself of his iron.

Knowing what I knew, I believed the iron to be my convict's iron—the iron I had seen and heard him filing at, on the marshes—but my mind did not accuse him of having put it to its latest use. For I believed one of two other persons to have become possessed of it, and to have turned it to this cruel account. Either Orlick, or the strange man who had shown me the file.

Now, as to Orlick; he had gone to town exactly as he told us when we picked him up at the turnpike, he had been seen about town all the evening, he had been in several public houses, and he had come back with myself and Mr. Wopsle. There was nothing against him, save the quarrel; and my sister had quarreled with him, and with everybody else about her, ten thousand times. As to the strange man: if he had come back for his two bank notes, there could have been no dispute about them, because my sister was fully prepared to restore them. Besides, there had been no altercation; the assailant had come in so silently and suddenly that she had been felled before she could look round.

The constables were about the house for a week or two. They took up several obviously wrong people, and they ran their heads very hard against wrong ideas, and persisted in trying to fit the circumstances to the ideas, instead of trying to extract ideas from the circumstances.

Long after these constitutional powers had dispersed, my sister lay ill in bed. Her sight was disturbed, so that she saw objects multiplied; her hearing was greatly impaired; her memory also; and her speech was unintelligible. It was necessary to keep my slate always by her, that she might indicate in writing what she could not indicate in speech.

However, her temper was greatly improved, and she was patient. We were at a loss to find a suitable attendant for her, until a circumstance happened conveniently to relieve us. Mr. Wopsle's great-aunt conquered a confirmed habit of living into which she had fallen,[1] and Biddy became part of our establishment. Biddy came to us with a small speckled box containing the whole of her worldly effects and became a blessing to the household. Above all she was a blessing to Joe, for the dear old fellow was sadly cut up by the constant contemplation of the wreck of his wife. Biddy instantly taking the cleverest charge of her, Joe became able in some sort to appreciate the greater quiet of his life, and to get down to the Jolly Bargemen now and then for a change that did him good.

Biddy's first triumph in her new office was to solve a difficulty that had completely vanquished me. Again and again and again, my sister had traced upon the slate a character that looked like a curious

T, and then with the utmost eagerness had called our attention to it as something she particularly wanted. I had in vain tried everything producible that began with a *T,* from tar to toast and tub. At length it had come into my head that the sign looked like a hammer, and on my lustily calling that word in my sister's ear, she had begun to hammer on the table and had expressed a qualified assent. Thereupon, I had brought in all our hammers, one after another, but without avail.

When my sister found that Biddy was very quick to understand her, this mysterious sign reappeared on the slate. Biddy looked thoughtfully at it, heard my explanation, looked thoughtfully at my sister, looked thoughtfully at Joe (who was always represented on the slate by his initial letter), and ran into the forge, followed by Joe and me.

"Why, of course!" cried Biddy with an exultant face. "Don't you see? It's *him!*"

Orlick, without a doubt! She had lost his name, and could only signify him by his hammer. We told him why we wanted him to come into the kitchen, and he slowly laid down his hammer, wiped his brow with his arm, took another wipe at it with his apron, and came slouching out.

[1] **Mr. Wopsle's . . . fallen:** she died.

I confess that I expected to see my sister denounce him, and that I was disappointed by the different result. She manifested the greatest anxiety to be on good terms with him, was evidently much pleased by his being at length produced, and motioned that she would have him given something to drink. She watched his countenance as if she were particularly wishful to be assured that he took kindly to his reception. After that, a day rarely passed without her drawing the hammer on her slate, and without Orlick's slouching in and standing doggedly before her, as if he knew no more than I did what to make of it.

CHAPTER 13

Pip opens his heart to Biddy.

I NOW fell into a regular routine of apprenticeship life, which was varied, beyond the limits of the village and the marshes, by no more remarkable circumstance than the arrival of my birthday and my paying another visit to Miss Havisham. The interview lasted but a few minutes, and she gave me a guinea when I was going, and told me to come again on my next birthday. I may mention at once that this became an annual custom. I tried to decline taking the guinea on the first occasion, causing her to ask me angrily if I expected more. Then, and after that, I took it. So unchanging was the dull old house, it bewildered me, and under its influence I continued at heart to hate my trade and to be ashamed of home.

Imperceptibly I became conscious of a change in Biddy, however. Her shoes came up at the heel, her hair grew bright and neat, her hands were always clean. She was not beautiful—she was common, and could not be like Estella—but she was pleasant and wholesome and sweet-tempered. I observed to myself one evening that she had curiously thoughtful and attentive eyes; eyes that were very pretty and very good. I laid down my pen, and Biddy stopped in her needlework without laying it down.

"Biddy," said I, "how do you manage it? Either I am very stupid, or you are very clever."

"What is it that I manage? I don't know," returned Biddy, smiling.

She managed her whole domestic life, and wonderfully too; but I did not mean that, though that made what I did mean more surprising.

"How do you manage, Biddy," said I, "to learn everything that I learn, and always to keep up with me?" I was beginning to be rather vain of my knowledge, for I spent my birthday guineas on it and the greater part of my pocket money.

"I suppose I must catch it—like a cough," said Biddy quietly, and went on with her sewing.

"You are one of those, Biddy," said I, "who make the most of every chance. You never had a chance before you came here, and see how improved you are!"

Biddy looked at me for an instant and went on with her sewing. "I was your first teacher, though, wasn't I?" said she, as she sewed.

"Yes, Biddy," I observed, "you were my first teacher, and that at a time when we little thought of ever being together like this in this kitchen. I must consult you a little more, as I used to do. Let us have a quiet walk on the marshes next Sunday, Biddy, and a long chat."

My sister was never left alone now; and Joe more than readily undertook the care of her on that Sunday afternoon, and Biddy and I went out together. It was summertime and lovely weather. When we came to the riverside and sat down on the bank, I resolved that it was a good time and place for the admission of Biddy into my inner confidence.

"Biddy," said I, after binding her to secrecy, "I want to be a gentleman."

"Oh, I wouldn't, if I was you!" she returned. "I don't think it would be right."

"Biddy," said I, with some severity, "I have particular reasons for wanting to be a gentleman."

"You know best, Pip; but don't you think you are happier as you are?"

"Biddy," I exclaimed impatiently, "I am not at all happy as I am. I am disgusted with my calling and with my life. Don't be absurd."

"Was I absurd?" said Biddy, quietly raising her eyebrows. "I am sorry for that; I didn't mean to be. I only want you to do well and be comfortable."

"Well, then, understand once for all that I never shall or can be comfortable—or anything but miserable—there, Biddy!—unless I can lead a very different sort of life from the life I lead now."

"That's a pity!" said Biddy, shaking her head with a sorrowful air.

"If I could have settled down," I said to Biddy, "I know it would have been much better for me. You and I and Joe would have wanted nothing then, and Joe and I would perhaps have gone partners when I was out of my time, and I might even have grown up to keep company with you. I should have been good enough for *you;* shouldn't I, Biddy?"

Biddy sighed and returned for answer, "Yes; I am not over-particular." It scarcely sounded flattering, but I knew she meant well.

"Instead of that, see how I am going on. Dissatisfied and uncomfortable, and—what would it signify to me, being coarse and common, if nobody had told me so!"

Biddy turned her face suddenly toward mine and looked attentively at me.

"It was neither a very true nor a very polite thing to say," she remarked. "Who said it?"

"The beautiful young lady at Miss Havisham's, and she's more beautiful than anybody ever was, and I admire her dreadfully, and I want to be a gentleman on her account."

"Do you want to be a gentleman to spite her or to gain her over?" Biddy quietly asked me, after a pause.

"I don't know," I moodily answered.

"Because, if it is to spite her," Biddy pursued, "I should think—but you know best—that might be better and more independently done by caring nothing for her words. And if it is to gain her over, I should think—but you know best—she was not worth gaining over."

"It may be all quite true," said I to Biddy, "but I admire her dreadfully."

I turned over on my face when I came to that, and got a good grasp on the hair on each side of my head, and wrenched it well. Biddy was the wisest of girls, and she tried to reason no more with me. She put her hand, which was a comfortable hand though roughened by work, upon my hands and gently took them out of my hair. Then she softly patted my shoulder in a soothing way, while with my face upon my sleeve I cried a little—exactly as I had done in the brewery yard—and felt vaguely convinced that I was very much ill-used by somebody, or by everybody; I can't say which.

"I am glad of one thing," said Biddy, "and that is, that you have felt you could give me your confidence, Pip." So, with a quiet sigh for me, Biddy rose from the bank and said, with a fresh and pleasant change of voice, "Shall we walk a little farther or go home?"

"Biddy," I cried, getting up, putting

my arm around her neck, and giving her a kiss, "I shall always tell you everything."

"Till you're a gentleman," said Biddy.

"You know I never shall be, so that's always. Not that I have any occasion to tell you anything, for you know everything I know—as I told you at home the other night."

"Ah!" said Biddy, quite in a whisper, and then repeated, with her former pleasant change, "shall we walk a little farther or go home?"

We talked a good deal as we walked, and all that Biddy said seemed right. Biddy was never insulting, or capricious, or Biddy today and somebody else tomorrow; she would have derived only pain, and no pleasure, from giving me pain.

I began to consider whether I was not more naturally and wholesomely situated, after all, in these circumstances, than playing beggar my neighbor by candlelight in the room with the stopped clocks, and being despised by Estella. How could it be, then, that I did not like her much the better of the two?

"Biddy," said I, when we were walking homeward, "I wish you could put me right."

"I wish I could!" said Biddy.

"If I could only get myself to fall in love with you—you don't mind my speaking so openly to such an old acquaintance?"

"Oh, dear, not at all!" said Biddy. "Don't mind me."

"If I could only get myself to do it, *that* would be the thing for me."

"But you never will, you see," said Biddy.

When we came near the churchyard, we had to cross an embankment and get over a stile near a sluice gate. There started up, from the rushes, Old Orlick.

"Halloa!" he growled. "Where are you two going?"

"Where should we be going, but home?"

"Well, then," said he, "I'm jiggered if I don't see you home!"

Biddy said to me in a whisper, "Don't let him come; I don't like him." As I did not like him either, I took the liberty of saying that we thanked him, but we didn't want seeing home. He dropped back, but came slouching after us at a little distance.

Curious to know whether Biddy suspected him of having had a hand in that murderous attack of which my sister had never been able to give any account, I asked her why she did not like him.

"Oh," she replied, glancing over her shoulder as he slouched after us, "because I—I am afraid he likes me!"

"Did he ever tell you he liked you?" I asked indignantly.

"No," said Biddy, glancing over her shoulder again, "he never told me so;

but he dances at me whenever he can catch my eye."

I kept an eye on Orlick after that night. He had struck root in Joe's establishment, by reason of my sister's sudden fancy for him, or I should have tried to get him dismissed. He quite understood and reciprocated my good intentions, as I had reason to know thereafter.

And now my mind was confused. At times, I would decide that my disaffection to dear old Joe and the forge was gone, and that I was growing up in a fair way to be partners with Joe and to keep company with Biddy—when all in a moment some remembrance of the Havisham days would fall upon me and scatter my wits again. Scattered wits take a long time picking up; and often they would be dispersed in all directions by one stray thought, that perhaps after all Miss Havisham was going to make my fortune when my time was out.

If my time had run out, it would have left me still at the height of my perplexities, I dare say. It never did run out, however, but was brought to a premature end, as I proceed to relate.

CHAPTER 14

Mr. Jaggers, a lawyer,
brings astonishing news.

I T WAS in the fourth year of my apprenticeship to Joe, and it was a Saturday night. There was a group assembled round the fire at the Three Jolly Bargemen, attentive to Mr. Wopsle as he read the newspaper aloud. Of that group I was one.

I became aware of a strange gentleman leaning over the back of the settle opposite me, looking on. There was an expression of contempt on his face, and he bit the side of a great forefinger as he watched the group of faces.

"Well!" said the stranger to Mr. Wopsle, when the reading was done. "You have settled it all to your own satisfaction, I have no doubt?"

The strange gentleman, with an air of authority not to be disputed, and a manner expressive of knowing something secret about every one of us came into the space between the two settles, in front of the fire.

"From information I have received," said he, looking round at us as we all quailed before him, "I have reason to believe there is a blacksmith among you, by name Joseph—or Joe—Gargery. Which is the man?"

"Here is the man," said Joe.

The strange gentleman beckoned him out of his place, and Joe went.

"You have an apprentice," pursued the stranger, "commonly known as Pip? Is he here?"

"I am here!" I cried.

The stranger did not recognize me, but I recognized him as the gentleman I had met on the stairs on the occasion of my second visit to Miss Havisham. I had known him the moment I saw him looking over the settle. I checked off again in detail his large head, his dark complexion, his deep-set eyes, his bushy black eyebrows, his large watch chain, his strong black dots of beard and whisker, and even the smell of scented soap on his great hand.

"I wish to have a private conference with you two," said he, when he had surveyed me at his leisure. "It will take a little time. Perhaps we had better go to your place of residence."

Amidst a wondering silence, we three walked out of the Jolly Bargemen and in a wondering silence walked home. Joe went on ahead to open the front door. Our conference was held in the parlor, which was feebly lighted by one candle.

It began with the strange gentleman's sitting down at the table, drawing the candle to him, and looking over some entries in his pocketbook.

"My name," he said, "is Jaggers, and I am a lawyer in London. I am pretty well known. I have unusual business to transact with you, and I commence by explaining that it is not of my originating. If my advice had been asked, I should not have been here. It was not asked, and you see me here. What I have to do as the confidential agent of another, I do. No less, no more.

"Now, Joseph Gargery, I am the bearer of an offer to relieve you of this young fellow, your apprentice. You would not object to cancel his indentures at his request and for his good? You would want nothing for so doing?"

"Lord forbid that I should want anything for not standing in Pip's way," said Joe, staring.

"Lord forbidding is pious, but not to the purpose," returned Mr. Jaggers. "The question is, would you want anything? Do you want anything?"

"The answer is," returned Joe sternly, "no."

I thought Mr. Jaggers glanced at Joe, as if he considered him a fool for his disinterestedness. But I was too much bewildered between breathless curiosity and surprise to be sure of it.

"Very well," said Mr. Jaggers. "Now, I return to this young fellow. And the communication I have got to make is that he has Great Expectations."

Joe and I gasped and looked at one another.

"I am instructed to communicate to him," said Mr. Jaggers, throwing his finger at me sideways, "that he will come into a handsome property. Further, that it is the desire of the present possessor of that property that he be immediately removed from his present sphere of life and from this place and be brought up as a gentleman—in a word, as a young fellow of great expectations."

My dream was out; my wild fancy was surpassed by sober reality; Miss Havisham was going to make my fortune on a grand scale.

"Now, Mr. Pip," pursued the lawyer, "I address the rest of what I have to say to you. You are to understand, first, that it is the request of the person from whom I take my instructions that you always bear the name of Pip. You will have no objection, I dare say, but if you have any objection, this is the time to mention it."

My heart was beating so fast, and there was such a singing in my ears, that I could scarcely stammer I had no objection.

"I should think not! Now you are to understand, secondly, Mr. Pip, that the name of the person who is your liberal benefactor remains a profound secret until the person chooses to reveal it at first hand by word of mouth to yourself. When or where that intention may be carried out, no one can say. It may be years hence. It is not the least to the purpose what the reasons of this prohibition are; they may be the strongest and gravest reasons, or they may be a mere whim. This is not for you to inquire into. The condition is laid down. Your acceptance of it, and your observance of it as binding, is the only remaining condition that I am charged with by the person from whom I take my instructions. That person is the person from whom you derive your expectations, and the secret is solely held by that person and by me. If you have any objection to it, this is the time to mention it. Speak out."

Once more, I stammered that I had no objection.

"I should think not! Now, Mr. Pip, I have done with stipulations. We come next to mere details of arrangement. You must know that although I use the term 'expectations' more than once, you are not endowed with expectations only. There is already lodged in my hands a sum of money amply sufficient for your suitable education and maintenance. You will please consider me your guardian.

"Oh!" for I was going to thank him. "I tell you at once, I am paid for my services, or I shouldn't render them. It is considered that you must be better-educated, in accordance with your altered position."

I said I had always longed for it.

"Never mind what you have always longed for, Mr. Pip," he retorted. "Keep to the record. If you long for it now, that's enough. Am I answered that you are ready to be placed at once under some proper tutor? Is that it?"

I stammered yes, that was it.

"There is a certain tutor who I think might suit the purpose," said Mr. Jaggers. "The gentleman I speak of is one Mr. Matthew Pocket."

Ah! I caught at the name directly. Miss Havisham's relation. The Matthew whom Mr. and Mrs. Camilla had spoken of. The Matthew whose place was to be at Miss Havisham's head when she lay dead in her bride's dress on the bride's table.

"You know the name?" said Mr. Jaggers, looking shrewdly at me. "What do you say of it?"

I said that I was much obliged to him for his mention of Mr. Matthew Pocket, and that I would gladly try that gentleman.

"Good. You had better try him in his own house. The way shall be prepared for you, and you can see his son first, who is in London. When will you come to London?"

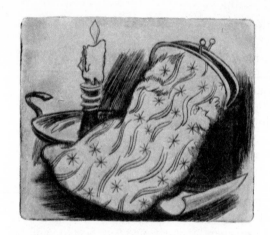

I said (glancing at Joe, who stood looking on, motionless) that I supposed I could come directly.

"First," said Mr. Jaggers, "you should have some new clothes to come in, and they should not be working clothes. Say this day week.[1] You'll want some money. Shall I leave you twenty guineas?"

He produced a long purse, with the greatest coolness, and counted them out on the table and pushed them over to me, and sat swinging his purse and eyeing Joe.

"Well, Joseph Gargery? You look dumfoundered?"

"I *am!*" said Joe, in a very decided manner.

"It was understood that you wanted nothing for yourself, remember?"

"It were understood," said Joe. "And it are understood. And it ever will be similar according."

"But what," said Mr. Jaggers, swinging his purse, "what if it was in my instructions to make you a present, as compensation?"

"As compensation what for?" Joe demanded.

"For the loss of his services."

Joe laid his hand upon my shoulder with

[1] **this day week:** a week from today.

the touch of a woman. "Pip is that hearty welcome," said Joe, "to go free with his services, to honor and fortun', as no words can tell him. But if you think as money can make compensation to me for the loss of the little child—what come to the forge—and ever the best of friends!—"

Oh, dear good Joe, whom I was so ready to leave and so unthankful to, I see you again, with your muscular blacksmith's arm before your eyes, and your broad chest heaving, and your voice dying away.

But I encouraged Joe at the time. I begged Joe to be comforted, for (as he said) we had ever been the best of friends, and (as I said) we ever would be so. Joe scooped his eyes with his wrist, but said not another word.

Mr. Jaggers, had looked on at this, as one who recognized in Joe the village idiot, and in me his keeper. When it was over, he said, "Now, Joseph Gargery, I warn you this is your last chance. If you mean to take a present that I have in charge to make you, speak out, and you shall have it. If on the contrary you mean to say—" Here, to his great amazement, he was stopped by Joe's suddenly working round him with every demonstration of a pugilistic purpose.[1]

"Which I meantersay," cried Joe, "that if you come into my place bull-baiting and badgering me, come out! Which I meantersay as sech if you're a man, come on!"

I drew Joe away, and he immediately became placable. Mr. Jaggers backed near the door and there delivered his valedictory remarks:

"Well, Mr. Pip, I think the sooner you leave here, the better. Let it stand for this day week, and you shall receive my printed address in the meantime. You can

take a hackney-coach at the stagecoach office in London, and come straight to me."

Something came into my head which induced me to run after him.

"I beg your pardon, Mr. Jaggers."

"Halloa!" said he. "What's the matter?"

"I wish to be quite right, Mr. Jaggers. Would there be any objection to my taking leave of anyone I know about here, before I go away?"

"No," said he, looking as if he hardly understood me.

"I don't mean the village only, but uptown?"

"No," said he. "No objection."

I thanked him and ran home again, and there I found that Joe had already locked the front door and was seated by the kitchen fire with a hand on each knee, gazing intently at the burning coals. I too sat down before the fire and gazed at the coals, and nothing was said for a long time.

My sister was in her cushioned chair in her corner, and Biddy sat at her needlework before the fire, and Joe sat next Biddy.

At length I got out, "Joe, have you told Biddy?"

"No, Pip," returned Joe, "I left it to yourself, Pip."

"I would rather you told, Joe."

"Pip's a gentleman of fortun', then," said Joe, "and God bless him in it!"

Biddy dropped her work and looked at me. Joe held his knees and looked at me. I looked at both of them. After a pause they both heartily congratulated me; but there was a certain touch of sadness in their congratulations that I rather resented.

I took it upon myself to impress Biddy (and through Biddy, Joe) with the grave obligation I considered my friends under, to know nothing and say nothing about

[1] **working . . . purpose:** Joe assumed a fighting position.

the maker of my fortune. Biddy nodded her head thoughtfully at the fire and said she would be very particular; and Joe said, "Ay, ay, I'll be ekervally partickler, Pip," and then they congratulated me again, and went on to express so much wonder at the notion of my being a gentleman that I didn't half like it.

"Saturday night," said I, when we sat at our supper of bread-and-cheese and beer. "Five more days, and then the day before *the* day! They'll soon go."

"Yes, Pip," observed Joe, whose voice sounded hollow in his beer mug. "They'll soon go."

"I have been thinking, Joe, that when I go downtown on Monday and order my new clothes, I shall tell the tailor that I'll come and put them on there, or that I'll have them sent to Mr. Pumblechook's. It would be very disagreeable to be stared at by all the people here."

"Mr. and Mrs. Hubble might like to see you in your new genteel figure, too, Pip," said Joe. "So might Wopsle. And the Jolly Bargemen might take it as a compliment."

"That's just what I don't want, Joe. They would make such a business of it— such a coarse and common business— that I couldn't bear myself."

Biddy asked me here, "Have you thought about when you'll show yourself to Mr. Gargery, and your sister, and me? You will show yourself to us, won't you?"

"Biddy," I returned with some resentment, "you are so exceedingly quick that it's difficult to keep up with you. I shall bring my clothes here in a bundle one evening—most likely on the evening before I go away."

Biddy said no more. Handsomely forgiving her, I soon exchanged an affectionate good night with her and Joe, and went up to bed. When I got into my little room, I sat down and took a long look at

it, as a mean little room that I should soon be parted from and raised above forever.

As I put the window open and stood looking out, I saw Joe come slowly forth at the dark door below and take a turn or two in the air; and then I saw Biddy come and bring him a pipe and light it for him. He never smoked so late, and it seemed to hint to me that he wanted comforting, for some reason or other. I drew away from the window and sat down in my one chair by the bedside, feeling it very sorrowful and strange that this first night of my bright fortunes should be the loneliest I had ever known.

I put my light out and crept into bed; and it was an uneasy bed now, and I never slept the old sound sleep in it any more.

CHAPTER 15

Pip visits Trabb, the tailor, and has a brief encounter with Trabb's boy.

MORNING MADE a considerable difference in my general prospect of life. After breakfast, Joe brought out my indentures from the press in the best parlor, and we put them in the fire, and I felt that I was free.

After our early dinner, I strolled out alone. As I passed the church, I thought— with something akin to shame—of my companionship with the fugitive whom I had once seen limping among those graves. My comfort was that he had doubtless been transported a long way off, and that he was dead to me, and might be veritably dead into the bargain. I made my way to the old Battery, and, lying down there to consider the question whether Miss Havisham intended me for Estella, fell asleep.

When I awoke, I was much surprised to find Joe sitting beside me, smoking his pipe. He greeted me with a cheerful smile on my opening my eyes, and said:

"As being the last time, Pip, I thought I'd foller."

"And, Joe, I am very glad you did so."

"Thankee, Pip."

"You may be sure, dear Joe," I went on, after we had shaken hands, "that I shall never forget you."

"No, no, Pip!" said Joe, in a comfortable tone. "*I'm* sure of that. Aye, aye, old chap!"

"It's a pity now, Joe," said I, "that you did not get on a little more when we had our lessons here, isn't it?"

"Well, I don't know," returned Joe. "I'm so awful dull. I'm only master of my own trade. It were always a pity as I was so awful dull; but it's no more of a pity now than it was—this day twelve-month [1]—don't you see!"

What I had meant was that when I came into my property and was able to do something for Joe, it would have been much more agreeable if he had been better qualified for a rise in station. He was so perfectly innocent of my meaning, however, that I thought I would mention it to Biddy in preference.

So, when we had walked home and had had tea, I took Biddy into our little garden and said I had a favor to ask of her.

"And it is, Biddy," said I, "that you will not omit any opportunity of helping Joe on a little."

"How helping him on?" asked Biddy, with a steady sort of glance.

"Well! Joe is a dear good fellow—in fact, I think he is the dearest fellow that ever lived—but he is rather backward in some things. For instance, Biddy, in his learning and his manners."

"Oh, his manners! Won't his manners do, then?" asked Biddy, plucking a black-currant leaf.

"My dear Biddy, they do very well here—"

"Oh! they *do* very well here?" interrupted Biddy, looking closely at the leaf in her hand.

"Hear me out—but if I were to remove Joe into a higher sphere, as I shall hope to remove him when I fully come into my property, they would hardly do him justice."

"And don't you think he knows that?" asked Biddy.

It was such a provoking question (for it had never in the most distant manner occurred to me) that I said, snappishly, "Biddy, what do you mean?"

"Have you never considered that he may be proud?"

"Proud?" I repeated, with disdainful emphasis.

"Oh! there are many kinds of pride," said Biddy, looking full at me and shaking her head; "pride is not all of one kind—"

"Well? What are you stopping for?" said I.

"Not all of one kind," resumed Biddy. "He may be too proud to let anyone take him out of a place that he is competent to fill, and fills well and with respect."

"Now, Biddy," said I, "I am very sorry to see this in you. You are envious, Biddy, and grudging. You are dissatisfied on account of my rise in fortune, and you can't help showing it."

"If you have the heart to think so," returned Biddy, "say so. Say so over and over again, if you have the heart to think so."

"If you have the heart to be so, you mean, Biddy," said I, in a virtuous and

[1] **this day twelvemonth:** a year ago today.

superior tone. "Don't put it off upon me. I am extremely sorry to see this in you, Biddy. It's a—it's a bad side of human nature."

I walked away from Biddy, and Biddy went into the house, and I went out at the garden gate and took a dejected stroll until suppertime, again feeling it very sorrowful and strange that this, the second night of my bright fortunes, should be as lonely and unsatisfactory as the first.

But morning once more brightened my view, and I extended my clemency to Biddy, and we dropped the subject. Putting on the best clothes I had, I went into town as early as I could hope to find the shops open, and presented myself before Mr. Trabb, the tailor, who was having his breakfast in the parlor behind his shop, and who did not think it worth his while to come out to me, but called me in to him.

"Well!" said Mr. Trabb, in a hail-fellow-well-met kind of way. "How are you, and what can I do for you?"

"Mr. Trabb," said I, "it's an unpleasant thing to have to mention, because it looks like boasting, but I have come into a handsome property."

A change passed over Mr. Trabb. He got up from the bedside and wiped his fingers on the tablecloth, exclaiming, "Lord bless my soul!"

"I am going up to my guardian in London," said I, casually drawing some guineas out of my pocket and looking at them, "and I want a fashionable suit of clothes to go in. I wish to pay for them," I added, "with ready money."

"My dear sir," said Mr. Trabb, "may I venture to congratulate you? Would you do me the favor of stepping into the shop?"

Mr. Trabb's boy was the most audacious boy in all that countryside. When I had entered, he was sweeping the shop, and he had sweetened his labors by sweeping over me. He was still sweeping when I came out into the shop with Mr. Trabb, and he knocked the broom against all possible corners and obstacles, to express equality with any blacksmith, alive or dead.

"Hold that noise," said Mr. Trabb with

the greatest sternness, "or I'll knock your head off! Do me the favor to be seated, sir. Now," said Mr. Trabb, taking down a roll of cloth.

I selected the materials for a suit, and re-entered the parlor to be measured. When he had at last done and had appointed to send the articles to Mr. Pumblechook's, he said, "I know, sir, that London gentlemen cannot be expected to patronize local work, as a rule; but if you would give me a turn now and then, I should greatly esteem it. Good morning, sir, much obliged.—Door!"

The last word was flung at the boy, who had not the least notion what it meant. But I saw him collapse as his master rubbed me out with his hands, and my first decided experience of the stupendous power of money was that it had morally laid upon his back Trabb's boy.

After this memorable event I went to the hatter's, and the bootmaker's, and the hosier's, and felt rather like Mother Hubbard's dog whose outfit required the services of so many trades. I also went to the coach office and took my place for seven o'clock on Saturday morning. When I had ordered everything I wanted, I directed my steps toward Pumblechook's, and, as I approached that gentleman's place of business, I saw him standing at his door.

He was waiting for me with great impatience. He had been out early with the chaise-cart, and had called at the forge and heard the news. He had prepared a collation [1] for me in the parlor, and he too ordered his shopman to "come out of the gangway" as my sacred person passed.

"To think," said Mr. Pumblechook, after snorting admiration at me for some moments, "that I should have been the humble instrument of leading up to this, is a proud reward."

---

[1] **collation** (kə·lā′shən): light meal, usually cold.

I begged Mr. Pumblechook to remember that nothing was to be ever said or hinted on that point. I mentioned that I wished to have my new clothes sent to his house, and he was ecstatic on my so distinguishing him. I mentioned my reason for desiring to avoid observation in the village, and he lauded it to the skies. There was nobody but himself, he intimated, worthy of my confidence. Then he asked me tenderly if I remembered our boyish games at sums, and how we had gone together to have me bound apprentice, and, in effect, how he had ever been my favorite fancy and my chosen friend. If I had taken ten times as many glasses of wine, I should have known that he never stood in that relation to me, and should in my heart of hearts have repudiated the idea. Yet for all that, I remember feeling convinced that I had been much mistaken in him, and that he was a sensible, practical, good-hearted, prime fellow.

Tuesday, Wednesday, and Thursday passed, and on Friday morning I went to Mr. Pumblechook's to put on my new clothes and pay my visit to Miss Havisham. My clothes were rather a disappointment, of course. Probably every new and eagerly expected garment ever put on fell a trifle short of the wearer's expectation. But after I had had my new suit on some half an hour, it seemed to fit me better.

I went to Miss Havisham's by all the back ways, and rang at the bell. Sarah Pocket came to the gate and positively reeled back when she saw me so changed.

"You?" said she. "You? Good gracious! What do you want?"

"I am going to London, Miss Pocket," said I, "and want to say goodby to Miss Havisham."

I was not expected, for she left me locked in the yard while she went to ask if I were to be admitted. After a very short delay, she returned and took me up, staring at me all the way.

Miss Havisham was taking exercise in the room with the long spread table, leaning on her crutch stick. The room was lighted as of yore, and at the sound of our entrance, she stopped and turned. She was then just abreast of the rotted bride cake.

"Don't go, Sarah," she said. "Well, Pip?"

"I start for London, Miss Havisham, tomorrow." I was exceedingly careful what I said. "And I thought you would kindly not mind my taking leave of you."

"This is a gay figure, Pip," said she, making her crutch stick play round me, as if she, the fairy godmother who had changed me, were bestowing the finishing gift.

"I have come into such good fortune since I saw you last, Miss Havisham," I murmured. "And I am so grateful for it, Miss Havisham!"

"Aye, aye!" said she, looking at the envious Sarah with delight. "I have seen Mr. Jaggers. *I* have heard about it, Pip. So you go tomorrow?"

"Yes, Miss Havisham."

"And you are adopted by a rich person?"

"Yes, Miss Havisham."

"Not named?"

"No, Miss Havisham."

"And Mr. Jaggers is made your guardian?"

"Yes, Miss Havisham."

She quite gloated on these questions and answers, so keen was her enjoyment of Sarah Pocket's jealous dismay. "Well!" she went on. "You have a promising career before you. Be good—deserve it—and abide by Mr. Jaggers' instructions." She looked at me, and looked at Sarah, and Sarah's countenance wrung out of her watchful face a cruel smile. "Good-by,

Pip!—you will always keep the name of Pip, you know."

"Yes, Miss Havisham."

"Good-by, Pip!"

She stretched out her hand, and I went down on my knee and put it to my lips. I had not considered how I should take leave of her; it came naturally to me at the moment to do this. She looked at Sarah Pocket with triumph in her weird eyes, and so I left my fairy godmother, with both her hands on her crutch stick, standing in the midst of the dimly lighted room beside the rotten bride cake that was hidden in cobwebs.

And now, those six days which were to have run out so slowly had run out fast and were gone, and tomorrow looked me in the face more steadily than I could look at it. As the six evenings had dwindled away, I had become more and more appreciative of the society of Joe and Biddy. On this last evening, I dressed myself out in my new clothes for their delight and sat in my splendor until bedtime. We had a

hot supper on the occasion, graced by the inevitable roast fowl. We were all very low, and none the higher for pretending to be in spirits.

I was to leave our village at five in the morning, and I had told Joe that I wished to walk away all alone. I am afraid that this purpose originated in my sense of the contrast there would be between me and Joe if we went to the coach together. I had pretended with myself that there was nothing of this taint in the arrangement; but when I went up to my little room on this last night, I felt compelled to admit that it might be so, and had an impulse upon me to go down again and entreat Joe to walk with me in the morning. I did not.

It was a hurried breakfast with no taste in it. I got up from the meal, saying with a sort of briskness, as if it had only just occurred to me, "Well! I suppose I must be off!" and then I kissed my sister, who was nodding and shaking in her usual chair, and kissed Biddy, and threw my arms around Joe's neck. The last I saw of them was when dear old Joe waved his strong right arm above his head, crying huskily, "Hoo-roar!" and Biddy put her apron to her face.

I walked away at a good pace, thinking it was easier to go than I had supposed it would be. The village was very peaceful and quiet, and all beyond was so unknown and great that in a moment with a strong heave and sob I broke into tears. I was better after I had cried than before—more sorry, more aware of my own ingratitude, more gentle. If I had cried before, I should have had Joe with me then.

When I was on the coach, and it was clear of the town, I deliberated with an aching heart whether I would not get down when we changed horses and walk back, and have another evening at home, and a better parting.

We changed, and I had not made up my mind, and still reflected for my comfort that it would be quite practicable to get down and walk back, when we changed again. We changed again, and yet again, and it was now too late, and too far to go back, and I went on. And the mists had all solemnly risen now, and the world lay spread before me.

This Is the End of the First Stage of Pip's Expectations.

FOR STUDY AND DISCUSSION

1. In the first stage of his expectations, Pip is involved in events in three very different "worlds": the forge, the marsh, and the strange mansion of Miss Havisham. Which characters does he encounter in each of these? Make a list of the main characters under these three headings. In which "world" is Pip happiest and most content? Why? In which "world" does he have the greatest expectations?

2. Pip, the main character of *Great Expectations,* undergoes many changes in his character, just as people do in real life. What do we learn about Pip from his encounters with the convict on the marsh? Is he generous? Is he honest? Does he feel sympathy for those less fortunate than himself? Which character has had the most influence on Pip in making him this kind of person?

3. What kind of person is "Mrs. Joe"? In what ways is she the opposite of Joe? How does she act toward Pip? Of what does she keep reminding him? Why do you think she does this?

4. How does Pip's opinion of himself, Joe, the forge, and many other things change after his first visit to Miss Havisham's mansion? What causes this change? Do you think it is a change for the better? Why or why not? What does Pip think?

5. Miss Havisham is one of the most fascinating characters in all fiction. From the objects in her rooms and the things she says

about them, what can we suppose about Miss Havisham's past? Why do you think she sends for Pip? How does she treat him? What kind of feelings does she seem to enjoy arousing in other people? Why do you think she takes pleasure in doing this?

6. When Pip first encounters each of the two convicts, the first one frightens him, and the second is frightened by him. Despite this, Pip likes the first convict better. Why? What are some of the differences between the two? Why does the first convict tell the sergeant he stole the food Pip brought him? What does this show about his feelings toward Pip?

7. What kind of person is Joe? What are his feelings toward Pip? Do you think Pip fully appreciates Joe's good qualities, or does he tend to look down on him because of his lack of "learning"? What makes you think so? When Mr. Jaggers offers Joe some money for releasing Pip from his apprenticeship, what is Joe's reaction? What does it show about his attitude toward life?

8 In what ways is Biddy the opposite of Estella? How does each girl influence Pip? Why does he choose Estella over Biddy? Do you think this is a wise choice? Why or why not? Do you like Estella? Do you think it is believable that Pip should love her?

9. In Chapter 6, Mrs. Joe comes home knowing something that Pip and Joe do not. How does she act in this situation? If you were Pip, would her way of breaking the news make you angry? Why or why not? In Chapter 8, Pip comes home knowing something that Mrs. Joe does not. How does Mrs. Joe act in this situation? How does Pip get his revenge? Can you imagine a scene in which Mrs. Joe was trying to find out something from someone just like herself? Why would such a scene be likely to end in blows?

10. What do Mrs. Joe and Mr. Pumblechook expect that Miss Havisham will do for Pip? From what you know of Miss Havisham and her attitude toward people, do you think these expectations are realistic and reasonable or foolish and unfounded? Why?

11. The plot of the novel is built around Pip's "great expectations." What is the meaning of this phrase? Who first uses it in the novel? What facts and circumstances lead Pip to believe that the source of his "great expectations" is Miss Havisham? Do you think he is right? If not, what makes you think otherwise? Who else in the story so far might possibly take such an interest in Pip?

12. Compare the Pip of the first few chapters with the Pip who leaves for London. How has he changed? What has caused this change in him? Which Pip would you rather have for a friend? Why?

THE CRAFT OF THE NOVELIST

1. The action of the story begins very dramatically with Pip's encounter with the convict in the graveyard. How does the setting in the graveyard add to the excitement and suspense of this scene? Which details of the setting and of the convict's appearance are especially effective in creating an atmosphere of mystery and terror? Where do you think Dickens is most successful in describing the place and the man as a child would see them?

2. Throughout the novel, the atmosphere of the marshes suggests loneliness and gloom. What might Dickens have intended the atmosphere of the marshes to symbolize? What other places in Pip's life are associated with a specific mood? What influence on Pip do you think is symbolized by each?

3. Because *Great Expectations* is told from the point of view of the person telling the story —that is, from the first-person point of view— we are able to share Pip's reactions to the other characters and everything they do. Does Pip always react as you would? If not, in which situation would you have acted differently? Why? Would you do as Pip does in the following situations? Why or why not?

Steal food for the convict on the marshes
Continue going to "play" at Miss Havisham's
Leap at the chance to become wealthy

4. What makes the Christmas dinner with Uncle Pumblechook such a funny scene? Reread the scene and point out the comic touches used by Dickens to make each thing that happens funnier than the last.

5. *Great Expectations* was first published

in weekly installments in a magazine, which was edited by Dickens, called *All the Year Round*. To keep people interested in the story—and eager to buy the next issue of the magazine—Dickens made skillful use of mystery and suspense. Look back at the chapter endings in the First Stage and note how often many of them arouse your curiosity about what will happen next. At the end of the First Stage, several questions have been left unanswered, such as, "Who was the pale young gentleman?" and "Who attacked Mrs. Joe?" What are some other unanswered questions?

LANGUAGE AND VOCABULARY

1. As a blacksmith, Joe has two helpers, Pip and Orlick. They are his *apprentice* and his *journeyman,* respectively, and Joe is their *master*. The apprenticeship system is very old, going back as far as ancient Babylonia and Egypt.

In the England of Pip's day, a boy's apprenticeship had to be paid for. A legal contract called his *indentures* provided that his master be paid a certain sum, in return for which the boy received his room and board and training in the master's craft or trade.

Then, as now, a journeyman was an artisan who had completed an apprenticeship and was qualified to earn wages in a trade. A master was an experienced artisan who was capable of doing work of the highest quality.

Our trade unions today still use these old terms and titles. A *master* plumber is the person you would want to fix a leaky sink; you would probably prefer not to have an *apprentice* carpenter build your new garage. We also use such expressions as "He is a journeyman playwright" and "She is a master architect." What do these expressions mean? What other examples can you think of of old terms that are still used in our language today?

2. In making Pip ashamed of his way of speaking, Estella was guilty of *pretension*. Look up the exact meaning of *pretension, pretense,* and *pretend*. What are the Latin roots of *pretend?* What picture do they give of someone who is being *pretentious?* How would a peacock fit this picture?

FOR COMPOSITION

1. Which of the characters that you have met so far do you find most interesting? Reread Dickens's description of this character where he (or she) first appears in the novel. How does Dickens describe the character to make you understand what he is like? Using the most essential of Dickens's details and adding some of your own, write a description of the character that will describe to the rest of the class just what you think.

2. At breakfast, Mr. Pumblechook gives Pip "as much crumb as possible in combination with as little butter." What does this show about Mr. Pumblechook? Which other characters in the novel would do the same? Which would not? Give your opinions in a short composition, being sure to consider the following characters: Joe, Mrs. Joe, Miss Havisham, Estella, Biddy, Pip's convict, Sarah Pocket, Orlick, Pip. For each person, tell what incidents in the novel reveal the real character of each.

LOOKING AHEAD TO STAGE II

In many ways, the problems that Pip faces are much like those a young person might face today. In Stage I he has already begun to change under the pressures of the world around him. Do you think Pip is satisfied with the change in his life and his new expectations? Will he become a "gentleman" and win Estella as his love? Will he show proper gratitude toward Joe and Biddy? What do you think lies ahead for Pip in London?

The Second Stage
of Pip's Expectations

CHAPTER 16

*Pip meets Wemmick, Mr. Jaggers'
clerk, and Herbert Pocket.*

THE JOURNEY from our town to the
metropolis was a journey of about five
hours. It was a little past midday when the
four-horse stagecoach by which I was a
passenger got into the ravel of traffic
frayed out about the Cross Keys, Wood
Street, Cheapside, London. We Britons
had at that time particularly settled that
it was treasonable to doubt our having
and our being the best of everything;
otherwise, while I was scared by the im-
mensity of London, I think I might have
had some faint doubts whether it was not
rather ugly, crooked, narrow, and dirty.

Mr. Jaggers had duly sent me his address: it was Little Britain. A hackney-
coachman packed me up in his coach and
hemmed me in with a folding and jingling
barrier of steps, as if he were going to
take me fifty miles. I had scarcely had
time to enjoy the coach when I observed
the coachman beginning to get down, as if
we were going to stop presently. And stop
we presently did, in a gloomy street, at
certain offices with an open door, whereon
was painted MR. JAGGERS.

I went into the front office and asked
was Mr. Jaggers at home?

"He is not," returned the clerk. "He is
in court at present. Am I addressing Mr.
Pip?"

I signified that he was addressing Mr.
Pip.

"Mr. Jaggers left word would you wait
in his room. He couldn't say how long he
might be, having a case on. But it stands to
reason, his time being valuable, that he
won't be longer than he can help."

With those words, the clerk opened a
door and ushered me into an inner chamber at the back. Mr. Jaggers' room was
lighted by a skylight only, and was a most
dismal place. I sat wondering and waiting
in Mr. Jaggers' close room, until I really
could not bear it and got up and went out.

I told the clerk that I would take a turn
in the air while I waited, and turned into
a street where I saw the great black dome
of Saint Paul's bulging at me from behind a grim stone building which a bystander said was Newgate Prison. Following the wall of the jail, I found the
roadway covered with straw to deaden the
noise of passing vehicles; and from this
and from the quantity of people standing
about smelling strongly of spirits and beer,
I inferred that the trials were on.

I dropped into the office to ask if Mr.
Jaggers had come in yet, and I found he
had not, and I strolled out again. I became
aware that other people were waiting
about for Mr. Jaggers, as well as I. There
were two men of secret appearance lounging in Bartholemew Close, one of whom
said to the other when they first passed
me that "Jaggers would do it if it was to
be done." There was a knot of three men
and two women standing at a corner, and
one of the women was crying on her dirty
shawl, and the other comforted her by
saying as she pulled her own shawl over
her shoulders, "Jaggers is for him, 'Melia,
and what more *could* you have?" These
testimonies to the popularity of my guardian made a deep impression on me, and I
admired and wondered more than ever.

At length I saw Mr. Jaggers coming
across the road toward me. All the others
who were waiting saw him at the same
time, and there was quite a rush at him.

Mr. Jaggers addressed himself to his followers.

First, he took the two secret men.

"Now, I have nothing to say to *you*," said Mr. Jaggers. "I told you from the first it was a tossup. Have you paid Wemmick?"

"Yes, sir," said both the men together.

"Very well; then you may go. If you say a word to me, I'll throw up the case."

"We thought, Mr. Jaggers—" one of the men began, pulling off his hat.

"That's what I told you not to do," said Mr. Jaggers. *"You* thought! I think for you; that's enough for you."

"And now *you!"* said Mr. Jaggers, suddenly stopping and turning on the two women with the shawls. "Once for all; if you come here, bothering about your Bill, I'll make an example of both your Bill and you, and let him slip through my fingers. Have you paid Wemmick?"

"Oh, yes, sir! Every farthing."

"Very well. Say another word—one single word—and Wemmick shall give you your money back." This terrible threat caused the two women to fall off immediately.

Without further interruption we reached the front office. My guardian then took me into his own room, and while he lunched, informed me what arrangements he had made for me. I was to go to Barnard's Inn, to young Mr. Pocket's rooms, where a bed had been sent in for my accommodation; I was to remain with young Mr. Pocket until Monday; on Monday I was to go with him to his father's house on a visit. Also, I was told what my allowance was to be—it was a very liberal one—and had handed to me the cards of certain tradesmen with whom I was to deal for all kinds of clothes and such other things as I could in reason want. "You will find your credit good, Mr. Pip," said my guardian, "but I shall by this means be able to check your bills, and to pull you up if I find you outrunning the constable. Of course you'll go wrong somehow, but that's no fault of mine."

After I had pondered a little over this encouraging sentiment, I asked Mr. Jaggers if I could send for a coach. He said it was not worth while, I was so near my destination; Wemmick should walk round with me, if I pleased.

I then found that Wemmick was the clerk in the next room. I accompanied him into the street, after shaking hands with my guardian. We found a new set of people lingering outside, but Wemmick made a way among them by saying coolly yet decisively, "I tell you it's no use; he won't have a word to say to one of you"; and we soon got clear of them and went on side by side.

Casting my eyes on Mr. Wemmick as we went along, to see what he was like in the light of day, I found him to be a dry man, rather short in stature, with a square wooden face. He wore his hat on the back of his head, and looked straight before him, walking in a self-contained way as if there were nothing in the streets to claim his attention. His mouth was such a post-office of a mouth that he had a mechanical appearance of smiling.

"Do you know where Mr. Matthew Pocket lives?" I asked Mr. Wemmick.

"Yes," said he, nodding in the direction. "At Hammersmith, west of London."

"Is that far?"

"Well! Say five miles."

"Do you know him?"

"Why, you are a regular cross-examiner!" said Mr. Wemmick, looking at me with an approving air. "Yes, I know him. *I* know him!"

There was an air of toleration about these words that rather depressed me; and I was still looking sideways at his block of a face in search of any encouraging note when he said here we were at Barnard's Inn. I had supposed that establishment to be a hotel kept by Mr. Barnard, to which the Blue Boar in our town was a mere public house. Whereas I now found Barnard to be a fiction and his inn the dingiest collection of shabby buildings ever squeezed together in a rank corner as a club for tomcats. We entered a melancholy little square that looked to me like a flat burying ground. I thought it had the most dismal trees in it, and the most dismal sparrows, and the most dismal cats, and the most dismal houses that I had ever seen. The windows of the houses were in every stage of dilapidated blind and curtain, crippled flowerpot, cracked glass, dusty decay, and miserable makeshift.

So imperfect was this realization of the first of my great expectations that I looked in dismay at Mr. Wemmick. He led me up a flight of stairs, which appeared to be slowly collapsing into sawdust, to a set of chambers on the top floor. MR. POCKET, JUN., was painted on the door, and there was a label on the letter box, "Return shortly."

"He hardly thought you'd come so soon," Mr. Wemmick explained. "You don't want me any more?"

"No, thank you," said I.

"As I keep the cash," Mr. Wemmick observed, "we shall most likely meet pretty often. Good day."

When he was gone, I opened the staircase window and had nearly beheaded myself, for the lines had rotted away, and it came down like the guillotine. After this escape, I was content to stand dolefully looking out, saying to myself that London was decidedly overrated.

Mr. Pocket, Junior's, idea of "shortly" was not mine, for I had nearly maddened myself with looking out for half an hour,

and had written my name with my finger several times in the dirt of every pane in the window, before I heard footsteps on the stairs. Gradually there arose before me the hat, head, waistcoat, trousers, boots, of a member of society of about my own standing. He had a paper bag under each arm and a pottle [1] of strawberries in one hand, and was out of breath.

"Mr. Pip?" said he.

"Mr. Pocket?" said I.

"Dear me!" he exclaimed, "I am extremely sorry; but I knew there was a coach from your part of the country at midday, and I thought you would come by that one. The fact is, I have been out on

[1] **pottle** (pot'l): small basket for holding fruit (*British*).

your account—not that that is any excuse—for I thought, coming from the
country, you might like a little fruit after
dinner, and I went to Covent Garden
Market to get it."

For a reason that I had, I felt as if my
eyes would start out of my head. I began
to think this was a dream.

"Pray come in," said Mr. Pocket, Junior. "Allow me to lead the way. I am
rather bare here, but I hope you'll be able
to make out tolerably well till Monday.
My father thought you would get on more
agreeably through tomorrow with me than
with him, and might like to take a walk
about London. I am sure I shall be very
happy to show London to you. As to our
table, it will be supplied from our coffeehouse here, and (it is only right I should
add) at your expense, such being Mr.
Jaggers' directions. As to our lodging, it's
not by any means splendid, because I
have my own bread to earn, and my father
hasn't anything to give me, and I shouldn't
be willing to take it if he had. This is our
sitting room—just such chairs and tables
and carpet and so forth, you see, as they
could spare from home. This is my little
bedroom; rather musty, but Barnard's *is*
musty. This is your bedroom; the furniture's hired for the occasion, but I trust
it will answer the purpose; if you should
want anything, I'll go and fetch it. The
chambers are retired,[1] and we shall be
alone together, but we shan't fight, I dare
say."

As I stood opposite to Mr. Pocket, Junior, I saw the starting appearance come
into his own eyes that I knew to be in
mine, and he said, falling back:

"Lord bless me, you're the prowling
boy!"

"And you," said I, "are the pale young
gentleman!"

---

[1] **retired:** secluded; having few neighbors.

CHAPTER 17

Pip gets a new name.

THE PALE young gentleman and I stood
contemplating one another in Barnard's Inn, until we both burst out laughing.

"The idea of its being you!" said he.
"The idea of its being *you!*" said I. And
then we contemplated one another afresh,
and laughed again. "Well!" said the pale
young gentleman, reaching out his hand
good-humoredly, "it's all over now, I
hope, and it will be magnanimous in you if
you'll forgive me for having knocked you
about so."

I derived from this speech that Mr. Herbert Pocket (for Herbert was the pale
young gentleman's name) still rather confounded his intention with his execution.
But I made a modest reply, and we shook
hands warmly.

"You hadn't come into your good fortune at that time?" said Herbert Pocket.

"No," said I.

"No," he acquiesced. "I heard it had
happened very lately. *I* was rather on the
lookout for good fortune then."

"Indeed?"

"Yes. Miss Havisham had sent for me,
to see if she could take a fancy to me. But
she couldn't—at all events, she didn't."

I thought it polite to remark that I was
surprised to hear that.

"Bad taste," said Herbert, laughing,
"but a fact. Yes, she had sent for me on a
trial visit, and if I had come out of it successfully, I suppose I should have been
provided for; perhaps I should have been
what-you-may-called-it to Estella."

"What's that?" I asked, with sudden
anxiety.

He was arranging his fruit in plates
while we talked, which divided his attention, and was the cause of his having made

this lapse of a word. "Affianced," he explained, still busy with the fruit. "Engaged. Betrothed."

"How did you bear your disappointment?" I asked.

"Pooh!" said he. "I didn't care much for it. *She's* a Tartar." [1]

"Miss Havisham?"

"I don't say no to that, but I meant Estella. That girl's hard and haughty and capricious to the last degree, and has been brought up by Miss Havisham to wreak revenge on all the male sex."

"What relation is she to Miss Havisham?"

"None," said he. "Only adopted."

"Why should she wreak revenge on all the male sex? What revenge?"

"Lord, Mr. Pip!" said he. "Don't you know?"

"No," said I.

"Dear me! It's quite a story, and shall be saved till dinnertime. Mr. Jaggers is your guardian, I understand?" he went on.

"Yes."

"You know he is Miss Havisham's man of business and solicitor, [2] and has her confidence when nobody else has?"

This was bringing me (I felt) toward dangerous ground. I answered with a constraint I made no attempt to disguise that I had seen Mr. Jaggers in Miss Havisham's house on the very day of our combat, but never at any other time, and that I believed he had no recollection of having ever seen me there.

"He was so obliging as to suggest my father for your tutor, and he called on my father to propose it. Of course he knew about my father from his connection with Miss Havisham. My father is Miss Havisham's cousin; not that that implies familiar intercourse between them, for he is a bad courtier and will not propitiate [3] her."

Herbert Pocket had a frank and easy way with him that was very taking. I have never seen anyone who more strongly expressed to me, in every look and tone, a natural incapacity to do anything secret and mean. There was something wonderfully hopeful about his general air, and something that at the same time whispered to me he would never be very successful or rich. He was still a pale young gentleman, without much strength. He had not a handsome face, but it was better than handsome, being extremely amiable and cheerful.

As he was so communicative, I told him my small story, and laid stress on my being forbidden to inquire who my benefactor was. I further mentioned that as I had been brought up a blacksmith in a country place, and knew very little of the ways of politeness, I would take it as a great kindness in him if he would give me a hint whenever he saw me at a loss or going wrong.

"With pleasure," said he, "though I venture to prophesy that you'll want very few hints. Will you begin at once to call me by my Christian name, Herbert?"

I thanked him and said I would. I informed him in exchange that my Christian name was Philip.

"I don't take to Philip," said he, smiling, "for it sounds like a moral boy out of the spelling book. Would you mind Handel for a familiar name? There's a charming piece of music by Handel called the Harmonious Blacksmith."

"I should like it very much."

"Then, my dear Handel," said he, turning round as the door opened, "here is the dinner."

[1] **Tartar** (tär′tər): a person of cruel and unrelenting nature, impossible to deal with.

[2] **solicitor** (sə·lis′ə·ter): in England, a lawyer who handles a client's legal affairs, as distinguished from a barrister (bar′is·tər), who pleads cases in court.

[3] **propitiate:** court the favor of.

We had made some progress in the dinner, when I reminded Herbert of his promise to tell me about Miss Havisham.

"True," he replied. "Let me introduce the topic, Handel, by mentioning that in London it is not the custom to put the knife in the mouth—for fear of accidents —and that while the fork is reserved for that use, it is not put farther in than necessary. It is scarcely worth mentioning, only it's as well to do as other people do. Also, the spoon is not generally used overhand, but under. This has two advantages. You get at your mouth better (which after all is the object), and you save a good deal of the attitude of opening oysters on the part of the right elbow."

He offered these friendly suggestions in such a lively way that we both laughed.

"Now," he pursued, "Miss Havisham was a spoiled child. Her mother died when she was a baby, and her father denied her nothing. He was very rich and very proud. So was his daughter."

"Miss Havisham was an only child?" I hazarded.

"Stop a moment, I am coming to that. No, she was not an only child; she had a half brother. Her father privately married again—his cook, I rather think."

"I thought he was proud," said I.

"My good Handel, so he was. He married his second wife privately, because he *was* proud, and in the course of time *she* died. When she was dead, I apprehend he first told his daughter what he had done, and then the son became a part of the family, residing in the house you are acquainted with. As the son became a young man, he turned out riotous, extravagant, undutiful—altogether bad. At last his father disinherited him; but he softened when he was dying and left him well off, though not nearly so well off as Miss Havisham.

"Miss Havisham was now an heiress, and was looked after as a great match. Her half brother had now ample means again, but wasted them most fearfully. There were strong differences between him and her, and it is suspected that he cherished a deep and mortal grudge against her. Now, I come to the cruel part of the story.

"There appeared upon the scene a certain man, who made love to Miss Havisham. I have heard my father mention that he was a showy man, and the kind of man for the purpose. But he was not to be mistaken for a gentleman. Well! This man pursued Miss Havisham closely and professed to be devoted to her. There is no doubt that she perfectly idolized him. He got great sums of money from her, and he induced her to buy her brother out of a share in the brewery (which had been weakly left him by his father) at an immense price, on the plea that when he was her husband he must hold and manage it all. Your guardian was not at that time in Miss Havisham's councils, and she was too haughty and too much in love to be advised by anyone. Her relations were poor and scheming, with the exception of my father; he was poor enough, but not timeserving or jealous. The only independent one among them, he warned her that she was doing too much for this man, and was placing herself too unreservedly in his power. She took the first opportunity of angrily ordering my father out of the house, in his presence, and my father has never seen her since."

I thought of her having said, "Matthew will come and see me at last when I am laid dead upon that table."

"To return to the man and make an end of him. The marriage day was fixed, the wedding dresses were bought, the wedding guests were invited. The day came, but not the bridegroom. He wrote a letter—"

"Which she received," I struck in,

"when she was dressing for her marriage? At twenty minutes to nine?"

"At the hour and minute," said Herbert, nodding, "at which she afterward stopped all the clocks. What was in it, further than that it most heartlessly broke the marriage off, I can't tell you, because I don't know. When she recovered from a bad illness, she laid the whole place waste, as you have seen it, and she has never since looked upon the light of day."

"Is that all the story?" I asked, after considering it.

"All I know of it. But I have forgotten one thing. It has been supposed that the man to whom she gave her misplaced confidence acted throughout in concert with her half brother; that it was a conspiracy between them; and that they shared the profits."

"What became of the two men? Are they alive now?"

"I don't know."

"You said just now that Estella was not related to Miss Havisham, but adopted. When adopted?"

Herbert shrugged his shoulders. "There has always been an Estella, since I have heard of a Miss Havisham. I know no more."

"And all I know," I replied, "you know."

"I fully believe it. And as to the condition on which you hold your advancement in life—namely, that you are not to inquire or discuss to whom you owe it— you may be very sure that it will never be even approached by me."

He said this with so much delicacy that I felt he as perfectly understood Miss Havisham to be my benefactress as I understood the fact myself.

We were very gay and sociable, and I asked him in the course of conversation what he was. He replied, "An insurer of ships. I shall not rest satisfied with merely insuring ships. I think I shall trade," said he, leaning back in his chair, "to the East Indies for shawls, spices, dyes, drugs, and precious woods. It's an interesting trade."

Quite overpowered by the magnificence of these transactions, I asked him where the ships he insured mostly traded to at present.

"I haven't begun insuring yet," he replied. "I am looking about me."

Somehow, that pursuit seemed more in keeping with Barnard's Inn. I said (in a tone of conviction), "Ah-h!"

"Yes. I am in a countinghouse,[1] and looking about me."

"Is a countinghouse profitable?" I asked.

"Why, n-no; not to me. Not directly profitable. That is, it doesn't pay me anything, and I have to—keep myself. But the thing is, that you look about you. *That's* the grand thing. You are in a countinghouse, you know, and you look about you."

This was very like his way of conducting that encounter in the garden; very like. His manner of bearing his poverty, too, exactly corresponded to his manner of bearing that defeat. It seemed to me that he took all blows and buffets now, with just the same air as he had taken mine then. It was evident that he had nothing around him but the simplest necessaries, for everything that I remarked upon turned out to have been sent in on my account from the coffeehouse or somewhere else. Yet, having already made his fortune in his own mind, he was so unassuming that I felt quite grateful to him for not being puffed up. It was a pleasant addition to his naturally pleasant ways, and we got on famously.

---

[1] **countinghouse:** an office or building where business is transacted.

CHAPTER 18

Pip meets Mr. Matthew Pocket.

On Monday morning at a quarter before nine, Herbert went to the countinghouse to report himself—to look around him, too, I suppose—and I bore him company. He was to come away in an hour or two to attend me to Hammersmith, and I was to wait about for him. When Herbert came, we went and had lunch and then took coach for Hammersmith. We arrived at two or three o'clock in the afternoon. Lifting the latch of a gate, we passed into a garden overlooking the river, where Mr. Pocket's children were playing about.

Mr. Pocket came out to make my acquaintance. He was a gentleman with a rather perplexed expression of face, and with his very gray hair disordered on his head, as if he didn't quite see his way to putting anything straight. Mr. Pocket said he was glad to see me, and he hoped I was not sorry to see him. "For I am really not," he added, with his son's smile, "an alarming personage." He was a young-looking man, in spite of his perplexities and his very gray hair, and his manner seemed quite natural.

Mr. Pocket took me into the house and showed me my room, which was a pleasant one. He then knocked at the doors of two other similar rooms, and introduced me to their occupants, by name Drummle and Startop. Drummle, an old-looking young man of a heavy order of architecture, was whistling. Startop, younger in years and appearance, was reading and holding his head, as if he thought himself in danger of exploding it with too strong a charge of knowledge.

By degrees I learned, chiefly from Herbert, that Mr. Pocket had been educated at Harrow and Cambridge,[1] where he had distinguished himself. He had come to London and here, after gradually failing in loftier hopes, he had turned his acquirements to the account of literary compilation and correction.

In the evening there was rowing on the river. As Drummle and Startop had each a boat, I resolved to set up mine, and to cut them both out. I was pretty good at most exercises in which country boys are adepts, but as I was conscious of wanting elegance of style for the Thames,[2] I at once engaged to place myself under the tuition of the winner of a prize wherry[3] who plied at our stairs, and to whom I was introduced by my new allies.

After two or three days, when I had established myself in my room and had gone backward and forward to London several times, Mr. Pocket and I had a long talk together. He knew more of my intended career than I knew myself, for his having been told by Mr. Jaggers that I was not designed for any profession, and that I should be well enough educated for my destiny if I could "hold my own" with the average of young men in prosperous circumstances.

When I had begun to work in earnest, it occurred to me that if I could retain my bedroom in Barnard's Inn, my life would be agreeably varied, while my manners would be none the worse for Herbert's society; so I went off to Little Britain and imparted my wish to Mr. Jaggers.

"If I could buy the furniture now hired for me," said I, "and one or two other little things, I should be quite at home there."

"Go it!" said Mr. Jaggers, with a short

---

[1] **Harrow and Cambridge:** Harrow is a preparatory school, and Cambridge a famous university in England.

[2] **Thames** (temz): a river passing through London.

[3] **wherry** (hwer'ē): A light, fast rowboat; sometimes used for racing.

laugh. "I told you you'd get on. Well! How much do you want?"

I said I didn't know how much.

"Come!" retorted Mr. Jaggers. "How much? Fifty pounds?"

"Oh, not nearly so much."

"Five pounds?" said Mr. Jagger.

This was such a great fall, that I said in discomfiture, "Oh! more than that."

"More than that, eh!" retorted Mr. Jaggers. "How much more?"

"It is so difficult to fix a sum," said I, hesitating.

"Wemmick!" said Mr. Jaggers, opening his office door. "Take Mr. Pip's written order, and pay him twenty pounds."

This strongly marked way of doing business made a strongly marked impression on me, and that not of an agreeable kind. As he happened to go out now, and as Wemmick was brisk and talkative, I said to Wemmick that I hardly knew what to make of Mr. Jaggers' manner.

"Tell him that, and he'll take it as a compliment," answered Wemmick. "He don't mean that you *should* know what to make of it.—Oh!" for I looked surprised, "it's not personal; it's professional, only professional."

He went on to say in a friendly manner:

"If at any odd time when you have nothing better to do, you wouldn't mind coming over to see me at Walworth, I could offer you a bed, and I should consider it an honor. I have not much to show you but such two or three curiosities as I have and a bit of garden and a summer-house."

I said I should be delighted to accept his hospitality.

"Thankee," said he. "Then we'll consider that it's to come off, when convenient to you. Have you dined with Mr. Jaggers yet?"

"Not yet."

"Well," said Wemmick, "he'll give you wine, and good wine. I'll give you punch, and not bad punch. And now I'll tell you something. When you go to dine with Mr. Jaggers, look at his housekeeper."

"Shall I see something very uncommon?"

"Well," said Wemmick, "you'll see a wild beast tamed. It won't lower your opinion of Mr. Jaggers' powers. Keep your eye on it."

I told him I would do so, with all the interest and curiosity that his preparation awakened.

CHAPTER 19

Pip's friendships increase.

Bᴇɴᴛʟᴇʏ Dʀᴜᴍᴍʟᴇ, who was so sulky a fellow that he even took up a book as if its writer had done him an injury, did not take up an acquaintance in a more agreeable spirit. Heavy in figure, movement, and comprehension, he was idle, proud, niggardly, reserved, and suspicious. He came of rich people who had nursed this combination of qualities until they made the discovery that it was just of age and a blockhead. Thus, Bentley Drummle had come to Mr. Pocket when he was a head taller than that gentleman, and half a dozen heads thicker than most gentlemen.

Startop had been spoiled by a weak mother and kept at home when he ought to have been at school, but he was devotedly attached to her and admired her beyond measure. He had a woman's delicacy of feature. It was but natural that I should take to him much more kindly than to Drummle, and that even in the earliest evenings of our boating, he and I should pull homeward abreast of one another, conversing from boat to boat, while

Bentley Drummle came up in our wake alone.

Herbert was my intimate companion and friend. I presented him with a half share in my boat, which was the occasion of his often coming down to Hammersmith; and my possession of a half share in his chambers often took me up to London. We used to walk between the two places at all hours.

These were the surroundings among which I settled down and applied myself to my education. I soon contracted expensive habits and began to spend an amount of money that within a few short months I should have thought almost fabulous. But through good and evil I stuck to my books. Between Mr. Pocket and Herbert I got on fast.

I had not seen Mr. Wemmick for some weeks when I thought I would write him a note and propose to go home with him on a certain evening. He replied that it would give him much pleasure, and that he would expect me at the office at six o'clock. Thither I went, and found him, putting the key of his safe down his back as the clock struck.

"Did you think of walking down to Walworth?" said he.

"Certainly," said I, "if you approve."

"Very much," was Wemmick's reply, "for I have had my legs under the desk all day, and shall be glad to stretch them. Now I'll tell you what I've got for supper —a cold roast fowl. You don't object to an aged parent, I hope?"

I really thought he was still speaking of the fowl, until he added, "Because I have got an aged parent at my place." I then said what politeness required.

"So you haven't dined with Mr. Jaggers yet?" he pursued, as we walked along.

"Not yet."

"He told me so this afternoon. I expect you'll have an invitation tomorrow. He's going to ask your pals, too. Three of 'em, ain't there? Well, he's going to ask the whole gang."

Mr. Wemmick and I beguiled the time talking, until he gave me to understand that we had arrived in the district of Walworth. It appeared to be a collection of black lanes, ditches, and little gardens. Wemmick's house was a little wooden cottage in the midst of plots of garden, and the top of it was cut out and painted like a battery mounted with guns.

"My own doing," said Wemmick. "Looks pretty, don't it?"

I highly commended it. I think it was the smallest house I ever saw.

"That's a real flagstaff, you see," said Wemmick, "and on Sundays I run up a real flag. Then look here. After I have crossed this bridge, I hoist it up—so— and cut off the communication."

The bridge was a plank, and it crossed a chasm about four feet wide and two deep. But it was very pleasant to see the pride with which he hoisted it up and made it fast, smiling as he did so, with a relish and not merely mechanically.

"At nine o'clock every night, Greenwich time," said Wemmick, "the gun fires. There he is, you see! And when you hear him go, I think you'll say he's a Stinger."

The piece of ordnance referred to was mounted in a separate fortress, constructed of latticework. It was protected from the weather by an ingenious little tarpaulin umbrella.

"Then, at the back," said Wemmick, "there's a pig, and there are fowls and rabbits; and I grow cucumbers. So, sir," said Wemmick, smiling again, but seriously, too, as he shook his head, "if you can suppose the little place besieged, it would hold out a devil of a time in point of provisions."

Then he conducted me to a bower about

a dozen yards off, and in this retreat our glasses were already set forth.

"I am my own engineer, and my own carpenter, and my own plumber, and my own gardener, and my own Jack-of-all-trades," said Wemmick, in acknowledging my compliments. "Well, it's a good thing, you know. It brushes the Newgate [1] cobwebs away, and pleases the Aged. You wouldn't mind being at once introduced to the Aged, would you? It wouldn't put you out?"

I expressed the readiness I felt, and we went into the castle. There we found, sitting by a fire, a very old man in a flannel coat; clean, cheerful, comfortable, and well cared for, but intensely deaf.

"Well, Aged Parent," said Wemmick, shaking hands with him in a cordial way, "how am you?"

"All right, John; all right!" replied the old man.

"Here's Mr. Pip, Aged Parent," said Wemmick, "and I wish you could hear his name. Nod away at him, Mr. Pip; that's what he likes. Nod away at him, if you please."

---

[1] **Newgate:** Newgate Prison. Wemmick's dealings as Mr. Jaggers' clerk were largely with persons who sought either to get out or keep out of Newgate.

"This is a fine place of my son's, sir," cried the old man, while I nodded as hard as I possibly could.

"You're as proud of it as Punch; ain't you, Aged?" said Wemmick, contemplating the old man, with his hard face really softened; "*there's* a nod for you," giving him a tremendous one; "*there's* another for you," giving him a still more tremendous one; "you like that, don't you? If you're not tired, Mr. Pip—though I know it's tiring to strangers—will you tip him one more? You can't think how it pleases him."

I tipped him several more, and he was in great spirits. We left him bestirring himself to feed the fowls, and we sat down to our punch in the arbor, where Wemmick told me, as he smoked a pipe, that it had taken him a good many years to bring the property up to its present pitch of perfection.

"I hope Mr. Jaggers admires it," I said.

"Never seen it," said Wemmick. "Never heard of it. Never seen the Aged. Never heard of him. No; the office is one thing, and private life is another. When I go into the office, I leave the Castle behind me, and when I come into the Castle, I leave the office behind me. If it's not in any way disagreeable to you, you'll oblige me by doing the same. I don't wish it professionally spoken about."

Of course I felt my good faith involved in the observance of his request. The punch being very nice, we sat there drinking it and talking until it was almost nine o'clock. "Getting near gunfire," said Wemmick then, as he laid down his pipe. "It's the Aged's treat."

Proceeding into the Castle again, we found the Aged heating the poker, with expectant eyes, as a preliminary to the performance of this great nightly ceremony. Wemmick stood with his watch in his hand until the moment was come for him to take the red-hot poker from the Aged, and repair [1] to the Battery. He took it, and went out, and presently the Stinger went off with a bang that shook the crazy little box of a cottage as if it must fall to pieces, and made every glass and teacup in it ring. Upon this the Aged—who I believe would have been blown out of his armchair but for holding on by the elbows —cried out exultingly, "He's fired! I heared him!" and I nodded at the old gentleman until I absolutely could not see him.

The supper was excellent. I was heartily pleased with my whole entertainment. Nor was there any drawback to my little turret bedroom.

Our breakfast was as good as the supper, and at half-past eight we started for Little Britain. By degrees, Wemmick seemed to get drier and harder as we went along. At last when we got to his place of business and he pulled out his key, he looked as unconscious of his Walworth property as if the Castle and the drawbridge and the arbor and the Aged had all been blown into space together by the last discharge of the Stinger.

[1] repair: go.

CHAPTER 20

Pip has dinner at Mr. Jaggers'
and observes his housekeeper.

It FELL OUT, as Wemmick had told me it would, that my guardian gave me the invitation for myself and friends. "No ceremony," he stipulated, "and no dinner dress, and say tomorrow."

When I and my friends repaired to him at six o'clock next day, he conducted us to Gerrard Street, Soho, to a house on the south side of that street, rather a stately house of its kind, but dolefully in want of painting, and with dirty windows. We went up a dark brown staircase into a series of three dark brown rooms on the first floor.

Dinner was laid in the best of these rooms. The table was comfortably laid and at the side of his chair was a dumbwaiter, with a variety of bottles and decanters on it and four dishes of fruit for dessert. I noticed throughout that he kept everything under his own hand, and distributed everything himself.

As he had scarcely seen my three companions until now—for he and I had walked together—he stood on the hearthrug, after ringing the bell, and took a searching look at them. To my surprise, he seemed at once to be principally, if not solely, interested in Drummle.

"Pip," said he, putting his large hand on my shoulder and moving me to the window, "I don't know one from the other. Who's the Spider?"

"The Spider?" said I.

"The blotchy, sprawly, sulky fellow."

"That's Bentley Drummle," I replied. "The one with the delicate face is Startop."

Not taking the least account of "the one with the delicate face," he returned,

"Bentley Drummle is his name, is it? I like the look of that fellow."

He immediately began to talk to Drummle. I was looking at the two when there came between me and them the housekeeper, with the first dish for the table.

She was a woman of about forty, tall, of a lithe, nimble figure, extremely pale, with large faded eyes and a quantity of streaming hair. She set the dish on, touched my guardian quietly on the arm with a finger to notify that dinner was ready, and vanished. No other attendant appeared.

Induced to take particular notice of the housekeeper, both by her own striking appearance and by Wemmick's preparation, I observed that whenever she was in the room, she kept her eyes attentively on my guardian. I fancied that I could detect in his manner a purpose of always holding her in suspense.

Dinner went off gaily, and although my guardian seemed to follow rather than originate subjects, I knew that he wrenched the weakest part of our dispositions out of us. I found that I was expressing my tendency to lavish expenditure, and to patronize Herbert, and to boast of my great prospects. It was so with all of us, but with no one more than Drummle. He informed our host that he much preferred our room to our company, and that as to skill he was more than our master, and that as to strength he could scatter us like chaff. He fell to baring and spanning his arm to show how muscular it was, and we all fell to baring and spanning our arms in a ridiculous manner.

Now the housekeeper was at that time clearing the table, my guardian taking no heed of her. Suddenly, he clapped his large hand on the housekeeper's like a trap, as she stretched it across the table. "If you talk of strength," said Mr. Jaggers, "*I*'ll show you a wrist. Molly, let me see your wrist."

Her entrapped hand was on the table, but she had already put her other hand behind her waist. "Master," she said, in a low voice, with her eyes attentively and entreatingly fixed upon him. "Don't."

"*I*'ll show you a wrist," repeated Mr. Jaggers, with an immovable determination to show it. "Molly, let them see your wrist."

"Master," she again murmured. "Please!"

"Molly," said Mr. Jaggers, not looking at her, "let them see *both* your wrists. Show them. Come!"

He took his hand from hers, and turned that wrist up on the table. She brought her other hand from behind her, and held the two out side by side. The last wrist was much disfigured—deeply scarred and scarred across and across. When she held her hands out, she took her eyes from Mr. Jaggers, and turned them watchfully on every one of the rest of us in succession.

"There's power here," said Mr. Jaggers, coolly tracing out the sinews with his forefinger. "Very few men have the power of wrist that this woman has. It's remarkable what mere force of grip there is in these hands. I have had occasion to notice many hands; but I never saw stronger in that respect, man's or woman's, than these. That'll do, Molly. You have been admired, and can go." She withdrew her hands and went out of the room, and Mr. Jaggers filled his glass and passed round the wine.

"At half-past nine, gentlemen," said he, "we must break up. Pray make the best use of your time. I am glad to see you all. Mr. Drummle, I drink to you."

If his object in singling out Drummle were to bring him out still more, it perfectly succeeded. In a sulky triumph Drummle showed his morose depreciation of the rest of us in a more and more offensive degree, until he became downright intolerable. Through all his stages, Mr. Jaggers followed him with the same strange interest.

In our boyish want of discretion I dare say we took too much to drink, and I know we talked too much. We became particularly hot upon some boorish sneer of Drummle's to the effect that we were too free with our money. Startop tried to turn the discussion aside with some small pleasantry that made us all laugh. Resenting this little success more than anything, Drummle, without any threat or warning, pulled his hands out of his pockets, dropped his round shoulders, swore, took up a large glass, and would have flung it at his adversary's head, but for our entertainer's dexterously seizing it at the instant it was raised.

"Gentlemen," said Mr. Jaggers, deliberately putting down the glass, "I am exceedingly sorry to announce that it's half-past nine."

On this hint we all rose to depart. Before we got to the street door, Startop was cheerily calling Drummle "old boy," as if nothing had happened. But the old boy would not even walk to Hammersmith on the same side of the way; so Herbert and I, who remained in town, saw them going down the street on opposite

sides, Startop leading, and Drummle lagging behind in the shadow of the houses.

In about a month after that, the Spider's time with Mr. Pocket was up for good, and, to the great relief of all the house, he went home to the family hole.

CHAPTER 21

Pip has a visitor.

MY DEAR MR. PIP:

I write this by request of Mr. Gargery, for to let you know that he is going to London in company with Mr. Wopsle and would be glad if agreeable to be allowed to see you. He would call at Barnard's Hotel Tuesday morning at nine o'clock, when if not agreeable please leave word. Your poor sister is much the same as when you left. We talk of you in the kitchen every night, and wonder what you are saying and doing. If now considered in the light of a liberty, excuse it for the love of poor old days. No more, dear Mr. Pip, from

> Your ever obliged,
> and affectionate servant,
> *Biddy.*

P.S. He wishes me most particular to write *what larks*. He says you will understand. I hope and do not doubt it will be agreeable to see him even though a gentleman, for you had ever a good heart, and he is a worthy man. I have read him all excepting only the last little sentence, and he wishes me most particular to write again *what larks*.

I received this letter by post on Monday morning, and therefore its appointment was for next day. Let me confess exactly with what feelings I looked forward to Joe's coming.

Not with pleasure, though I was bound to him by so many ties; no, with considerable disturbance and some mortification. If I could have kept him away by paying money, I certainly would have paid money. My greatest reassurance was that he was coming to Barnard's Inn, not to Hammersmith. I had little objection to his being seen by Herbert or his father, for both of whom I had respect; but I had the sharpest sensitiveness as to his being seen by Drummle, whom I held in contempt. So throughout life, our worst weaknesses and meannesses are usually committed for the sake of the people whom we most despise.

I had got on so fast of late that I had even started a boy in boots [1]—top boots—and had clothed him with a blue coat, canary waistcoat, white cravat, creamy breeches, and the boots already mentioned. I had to find him a little to do and a great deal to eat; and with both of these horrible requirements he haunted my existence.

I came into town on Monday night to be ready for Joe, and I got up early in the morning, and caused the sitting room and breakfast table to assume their most splendid appearance.

Presently I heard Joe on the staircase. I knew it was Joe by his clumsy manner of coming upstairs. When at last he stopped outside our door, I could hear his finger tracing over the painted letters of my name. Finally he gave a faint single rap, and Pepper [2] announced, "Mr. Gargery!"

"Joe, how are you, Joe?"

"Pip, how AIR you, Pip?"

With his good honest face all glowing and shining, and his hat put down on the floor between us, he caught both my hands

[1] **started . . . boots:** hired a serving boy.
[2] **Pepper:** the serving boy.

and worked them straight up and down.

"I am glad to see you, Joe. Give me your hat."

But Joe, taking it up carefully with both hands, like a bird's nest with eggs in it, wouldn't hear of parting with that piece of property.

"Which you have that growed," said Joe, "and that gentlefolked," Joe considered a little before he discovered this word; "as to be a honor to your king and country."

"And you, Joe, look wonderfully well."

"Thank God," said Joe, "I'm ekerval to most. And your sister, she's no worse than she were. And Biddy, she's ever right and ready."

Herbert had entered the room, so I presented Joe to Herbert. Joe, being invited to sit down to table, looked all round the room for a suitable spot on which to deposit his hat and ultimately stood it on an extreme corner of the chimney piece, from which it ever afterward fell off at intervals.

"Do you take tea or coffee, Mr. Gargery?" asked Herbert, who always presided of a morning.

"Thankee, sir," said Joe, stiff from head to foot, "I'll take whichever is most agreeable to yourself."

"What do you say to coffee?"

"Thankee, sir," returned Joe, evidently dispirited by the proposal, "since you *are* so kind as to make chice of coffee, I will not run contrairy to your own opinions. But don't you never find it a little 'eating?"

"Say tea, then," said Herbert, pouring it out.

Here Joe's hat tumbled off the mantelpiece, and he started out of his chair and picked it up, and fitted it to the same exact spot.

"When did you come to town, Mr. Gargery?"

"Were it yesterday afternoon?" said Joe, after coughing behind his hand. "No it were not. Yes it were. Yes. It were yesterday afternoon" (with an appearance of mingled wisdom, relief, and strict impartiality).

"Have you seen anything of London, yet?"

"Why, yes, sir," said Joe, but his attention was attracted by his hat, which was toppling. Indeed, it demanded from him a constant attention. He made extraordinary play with it, and showed the greatest skill, now rushing at it and catching it neatly as it dropped; now merely stopping it midway, beating it up, finally splashing it into the slop basin, where I took the liberty of laying hands upon it.

Then he fell into such unaccountable fits of meditation, with his fork midway between his plate and his mouth; had his eyes attracted in such strange directions; was afflicted with such remarkable coughs; sat so far from the table; and dropped so much more than he ate, and pretended that he hadn't dropped it; that I was heartily glad when Herbert left us for the city.

I had neither the good sense nor the

good feeling to know that this was all my fault, and that if I had been easier with Joe, Joe would have been easier with me. I felt impatient of him and out of temper with him.

"Us two being now alone, sir—" began Joe.

"Joe," I interrupted pettishly, "how can you call me sir?"

Joe looked at me for a single instant with something faintly like reproach. I was conscious of a sort of dignity in the look.

"Us two being now alone," resumed Joe, "and me having the intentions and abilities to stay not many minutes more, I will now conclude—leastways begin—to mention what have led to my having had the present honor.

"Well, sir, this is how it were. I were at the Bargemen t'other night, Pip" (whenever he subsided into affection, he called me Pip, and whenever he relapsed into politeness he called me sir), "when there come up in his shay-cart Pumblechook. Well, Pip; this same identical come to me at the Bargemen and his word were, 'Joseph, Miss Havisham she wish to speak to you.'"

"Miss Havisham, Joe?"

"'She wished,' were Pumblechook's word, 'to speak to you.'" Joe sat and rolled his eyes at the ceiling.

"Yes, Joe? Go on, please."

"Next day, sir," said Joe, looking at me as if I were a long way off, "having cleaned myself, I go and I see Miss A."

"Miss A., Joe? Miss Havisham?

"Which I say, sir," replied Joe, with an air of legal formality, as if he were making his will, "Miss A., or otherways Havisham.[1] Her expression air then as follering: 'Mr. Gargery. You air in corre-

---

[1] **Miss A. . . . Havisham:** Joe pronounced Havisham " 'avisham."

spondence with Mr. Pip?' Having had a letter from you, I were able to say 'I am.' 'Would you tell thim, then,' said she, 'that which Estella has come home, and would be glad to see him.' "

I felt my face fire up as I looked at Joe.

"Biddy," pursued Joe, "when I got home and asked her fur to write the message to you, a little hung back. Biddy says, 'I know he will be very glad to have it by word of mouth; it is holiday time, you want to see him, go!' I have now concluded, sir," said Joe, rising from his chair, "and, Pip, I wish you ever well and ever prospering to a greater and greater height."

"But you are not going now, Joe?"

"Yes I am," said Joe.

"But you are coming back to dinner, Joe?"

"No I am not," said Joe.

Our eyes met, and all the "sir" melted out of that manly heart as he gave me his hand.

"Pip, dear old chap, life is made of ever so many partings welded together, as I may say, and one man's a blacksmith, and one's a whitesmith, and one's a goldsmith, and one's a coppersmith. Diwisions among such must come, and must be met as they come. If there's been any fault at all today, it's mine. You and me is not two figures to be together in London; nor yet anywheres else but what is private, and beknown, and understood among friends. It ain't that I am proud, but that I want to be right, as you shall never see me no more in these clothes. I'm wrong in these clothes. I'm wrong out of the forge, the kitchen, or off th' meshes. You won't find half so much fault in me if you think of me in my forge dress, with my hammer in my hand, or even my pipe. You won't find half so much fault in me if, supposing as you should ever wish to see me, you come and put your head in at the forge window and see Joe the blacksmith, there at the old anvil, in the old burned apron, sticking to the old work. I'm awful dull, but I hope I've beat out something nigh the rights of this at last. And so God bless you, dear old Pip, old chap, God bless you!"

I had not been mistaken in my fancy that there was a simple dignity in him. The fashion of his dress could no more come in its way when he spoke these words than it could come in its way in Heaven. He touched me gently on the forehead, and went out. As soon as I could recover myself sufficiently, I hurried out after him and looked for him in the neighboring streets; but he was gone.

CHAPTER 22

The mysterious stranger returns, and so does Orlick.

IT WAS clear that I must repair to our town next day, and in the first flow of my repentance it was equally clear that I must stay at Joe's. But when I secured my box-place by tomorrow's coach, I began to invent reasons for putting up at the Blue Boar. All other swindlers upon earth are nothing to the self-swindlers, and with such pretenses did I cheat myself. I settled that I must go to the Blue Boar.

At that time it was customary to carry convicts down to the dockyards by stage-coach. As I had often seen them on the highroad dangling their ironed legs over the coach roof, I had no cause to be surprised when Herbert came up and told me there were two convicts going down with me. But I had a reason that was an old reason now for faltering whenever I heard the word convict.

"You don't mind them, Handel?" said Herbert.

"Oh, no!"

"I thought you seemed as if you didn't like them?"

"I can't pretend that I do like them, and I suppose you don't particularly. But I don't mind them."

"See! There they are," said Herbert, "and what a degraded and vile sight it is!"

The two convicts were handcuffed together, and had irons on their legs—irons of a pattern that I knew well. They wore the dress that I likewise knew well. One was a taller and stouter man than the other, and his attire disguised him, but I knew his half-closed eye at one glance. There stood the man whom I had seen on the settle at the Three Jolly Bargemen on a Saturday night!

But this was not the worst of it. It came out that the whole of the back of the coach had been taken by a family, and that there were no places for the two prisoners but on the seat in front, behind the coachman. The convict I had recognized sat behind me with his breath on the hair of my head.

"Good-by, Handel!" Herbert called out as we started. I thought what a blessed fortune it was that he had found another name for me than Pip.

The weather was miserably raw. I dozed off myself in considering the question whether I ought to restore a couple of pounds sterling to this creature before losing sight of him, and how it could best be done. In the act of dipping forward, I woke in a fright and took the question up again. Cowering forward for warmth and to make me a screen against the wind, the convicts were closer to me than before. The very first words I heard them interchange, as I became conscious, were the words of my own thought, "Two one-pound notes."

"How did he get 'em?" said the convict I had never seen.

"How should I know?" returned the other. "He had 'em stowed away somehows. Give him by friends, I expect."

"I wish," said the other, with a bitter curse upon the cold, "that I had 'em here."

"Two one-pound notes, or friends?"

"Two one-pound notes. I'd sell all the friends I ever had, for one, and think it a blessed good bargain. Well? So he says—?"

"So he says," resumed the convict I had recognized "—it was all said and done in half a minute, behind a pile of timber in the dockyards—'You're a-going to be discharged!' Yes, I was. Would I find out that boy that had fed him and kep' his secret, and give him them two one-pound notes? Yes, I would. And I did."

"More fool you," growled the other. "I'd have spent 'em on wittles and drink. He must have been a green one. Mean to say he knowed nothing of you?"

"Not a ha'porth. Different gangs and different ships. He was tried again for prison breaking, and got made a lifer."

"And was that the only time you worked out, in this part of the country?"

"The only time."

"What might have been your opinion of the place?"

"A most beastly place. Mudbank, mist, swamp, and work; work, swamp, mist, and mudbank."

They both execrated the place in very strong language, and gradually growled themselves out, and had nothing left to say.

After overhearing this dialogue, I resolved to alight as soon as we touched the town and put myself out of his hearing. This device I executed successfully. As to the convicts, they went their way with the coach, and I knew at what point they would be spirited off to the river. In my fancy, I saw the boat with its convict crew waiting for them at the slime-washed stairs—again heard the gruff "Give way, you!" like an order to dogs—again saw the wicked Noah's Ark [1] lying out on the black water. I could not have said what I was afraid of, but there was great fear upon me.

Betimes in the morning I was up and out. It was too early yet to go to Miss Havisham's, so I loitered into the country on Miss Havisham's side of town—which was not Joe's side; I could go there tomorrow—thinking about my patroness, and painting brilliant pictures of her plans for me.

She had adopted Estella, she had as good as adopted me, and it could not fail to be her intention to bring us together. I loved Estella with the love of a man; I loved her simply because I found her irresistible. I knew to my sorrow, often and often, if not always, that I loved her against reason, against promise, against peace, against hope, against happiness, against all discouragement that could be. I loved her none the less because I knew it, and it had no more influence in restraining me than if I had devoutly believed her to be human perfection.

I so shaped out my walk as to arrive at the gate at my old time. I heard the side door open, and steps come across the courtyard, and started to find myself confronted by a man in a sober gray dress —the last man I should have expected to see in that place of porter at Miss Havisham's door.

"Orlick!"

"Ah, young master, there's more changes than yours. But come in, come in. It's opposed to my orders to hold the gate open."

I entered and he swung it, and locked it,

and took the key out. "Yes!" said he, facing round. "Here I am!"

"How did you come here?"

"I come here," he retorted, "on my legs."

"Are you here for good?"

"I ain't here for harm, young master, I suppose."

I was not so sure of that. "Then you have left the forge?" I said.

"Do this look like a forge?" replied Orlick.

I had gone up the staircase in the dark, many a time. I ascended it now and tapped in my old way at the door of Miss Havisham's room. "Pip's rap," I heard her say, immediately; "come in, Pip."

She was in her chair near the old table, in the old dress, with her two hands crossed on her stick, her chin resting on them. Sitting near her was an elegant lady whom I had never seen.

"Come in, Pip," Miss Havisham continued. "Come in, Pip. How do you do, Pip? So you kiss my hand as if I were a queen, eh?—Well?"

"I heard, Miss Havisham," said I, rather at a loss, "that you were so kind as to wish me to come and see you, and I came directly."

"Well?"

The lady whom I had never seen before lifted up her eyes and looked archly at me, and then I saw that the eyes were Estella's eyes. But she was so much changed, was so much more beautiful, so much more womanly, that I slipped hopelessly back into the coarse and common boy again. Oh, the sense of distance and disparity that came upon me, and the inaccessibility that came about her!

"Do you find her much changed, Pip?" asked Miss Havisham, with her greedy look, and striking her stick upon a chair that stood between them as a sign for me to sit down there.

---

[1] **Noah's Ark:** the Hulks, the prison boat.

"When I came in, Miss Havisham, I thought there was nothing of Estella in the face or figure; but now it all settles down so curiously into the old—"

"What? You are not going to say into the old Estella?" Miss Havisham interrupted. "She was proud and insulting, and you wanted to go away from her. Don't you remember?"

I said confusedly that that was long ago, and that I knew no better then. Estella smiled with perfect composure and said she had no doubt of my having been quite right, and of her having been very disagreeable.

"Is *he* changed?" Miss Havisham asked her.

"Very much," said Estella, looking at me.

"Less coarse and common?" said Miss Havisham, playing with Estella's hair.

Estella laughed. She treated me as a boy still, but she lured me on.

It was settled that I should stay there all the rest of the day, and return to the hotel at night, and to London tomorrow. When we had conversed for a while, Miss Havisham sent us two out to walk. Estella and I went into the garden, I trembling in spirit and worshiping the very hem of her dress; she, quite composed and decidedly not worshiping the hem of mine.

As the garden was too overgrown and rank for walking, we came out again into the brewery yard. I showed her where I had seen her walking that first old day, and she said with a cold and careless look in that direction, "Did I?" I reminded her where she had come out of the house and given me my meat and drink, and she said, "I don't remember." "Not remember that you made me cry?" said I. "No," said she, and shook her head and looked about her. I verily believe that her not remembering and not minding in the least made me cry again, inwardly—and that is the sharpest crying of all.

"You must know," said Estella, condescending to me as a brilliant and beautiful woman might, "that I have no heart—if that has anything to do with my memory. I have no softness there, no—sympathy—sentiment—nonsense. If we are to be thrown much together, you had better believe it at once."

Her handsome dress had trailed upon the ground. She held it in one hand now, and with the other lightly touched my shoulder as we walked. We walked round the ruined garden twice or thrice more. At last we went back into the house, and there I heard with surprise that my guardian had come down to see Miss Havisham on business, and would come back to dinner. Estella left us to prepare herself, and Miss Havisham turned to me and said in a whisper:

"Is she beautiful, graceful, well grown? Do you admire her?"

"Everybody must who sees her, Miss Havisham."

She put an arm around my neck and drew my head close down to hers as she sat in the chair. "Love her, love her, love her! How does she use you?"

Before I could answer (if I could have answered so difficult a question at all), she repeated, "Love her, love her, love her! If she favors you, love her. If she wounds you, love her. If she tears your heart to pieces—and as it gets older and stronger it will tear deeper—love her, love her! Hear me, Pip! I adopted her to be loved. I bred her and educated her to be loved. I developed her into what she is, that she might be loved. Love her!"

"I'll tell you," said she in the same hurried passionate whisper, "what real love is. It is blind devotion, unquestioning self-humiliation, utter submission, trust and belief against yourself and against the whole world, giving up your whole heart and soul to the smiter—as I did!"

She rose up in the chair, in her shroud of a dress, and struck at the air as if she would as soon have struck herself against the wall and fallen dead. All this passed in a few seconds. As I drew her down into her chair, I turned and saw my guardian in the room.

Miss Havisham had seen him as soon as I, and was (like everybody else) afraid of him. She made a strong attempt to compose herself, and stammered that he was as punctual as ever.

"As punctual as ever," he repeated. "And so you are here, Pip?"

I told him when I had arrived, and how Miss Havisham wished me to come and see Estella.

"Well, Pip! How often have you seen Miss Estella before?" said he.

"How often?"

"Jaggers," interposed Miss Havisham, much to my relief; "leave my Pip alone, and go with him to your dinner."

He complied, and we groped our way down the dark stairs together.

"Pray, sir," said I, "may I ask you a question?"

"You may," said he, "and I may decline to answer it. Put your question."

"Estella's name, is it Havisham or—?" I had nothing to add.

"Or what?" said he.

"Is it Havisham?"

"It is Havisham."

This brought us to the dinner table, where she and Sarah Pocket awaited us. Mr. Jaggers scarcely directed his eyes to Estella's face once during dinner. When she spoke to him, he listened, and in due course answered, but never looked at her that I could see. On the other hand, she often looked at him, with interest and curiosity, if not distrust, but his face never showed the least conciousness.

Afterward we went up to Miss Havisham's room, and we four played at whist.[1] We played until nine o'clock, and then it was arranged that when Estella came to London I should be forewarned

[1] **whist:** a card game, the forerunner of modern contract bridge.

of her coming and should meet her at the coach; and then I took leave of her, and touched her and left her.

My guardian slept at the Boar in the next room to mine. Far into the night, Miss Havisham's words, "Love her, love her, love her!" sounded in my ears. I said to my pillow, "I love her, I love her, I love her!" hundreds of times.

Ah me! I thought those were high and great emotions. But I never thought there was anything low and small in my keeping away from Joe, because I knew she would be contemptuous of him. It was but a day gone, and Joe had brought the tears into my eyes; they had soon dried, God forgive me! soon dried.

CHAPTER 23

Trabb's boy has some fun with Pip.

AFTER WELL considering the matter while I was dressing at the Blue Boar in the morning, I resolved to tell my guardian that I doubted Orlick's being the right sort of man to fill a post of trust at Miss Havisham's. He listened in a satisfied manner while I told him what knowledge I had of Orlick. "Very good, Pip," he observed, when I had concluded. "I'll go round presently and pay our friend off." Rather alarmed by this summary action, I was for a little delay, and even hinted that our friend himself might be difficult to deal with. "Oh, no, he won't," said my guardian. "I should like to see him argue the question with *me*."

As we were going back together to London by the midday coach, and as I breakfasted under such terrors of Pumblechook that I could scarcely hold my cup, this gave me an opportunity of saying that I wanted a walk, and that I would go on along the London road while Mr. Jaggers was occupied, if he would let the coachman know that I would get into my place when overtaken. I was thus enabled to fly from the Blue Boar immediately after breakfast. By then making a loop of about a couple of miles into the open country at the back of Pumblechook's premises, I got round into the High Street again, a little beyond that pitfall, and felt myself in comparative security.

It was interesting to be in the quiet old town once more, and it was not disagreeable to be here and there suddenly recognized and stared after. My position was a distinguished one, and I was not at all dissatisfied with it, until Fate threw me in the way of that unlimited miscreant, Trabb's boy.

Casting my eyes along the street at a certain point of my progress, I beheld Trabb's boy approaching. Suddenly the knees of Trabb's boy smote together, his hair uprose, his cap fell off, he staggered out into the road, and crying to the populace, "Hold me! I'm so frightened!" feigned to be in a paroxysm of terror occasioned by the dignity of my appearance. As I passed him, his teeth loudly chattered in his head, and with every mark of extreme humiliation, he prostrated himself in the dust.

This was a hard thing to bear, but this was nothing. I had not advanced another two hundred yards, when, to my inexpressible amazement and indignation, I again beheld Trabb's boy approaching. He was coming round a narrow corner. He staggered round and round me with knees more afflicted, and with uplifted hands as if beseeching for mercy. His sufferings were hailed with the greatest joy by a knot of spectators, and I felt utterly confounded.

I had not got as much farther down the street as the post office when I again beheld Trabb's boy shooting round by a back way attended by a company of delighted young friends to whom he exclaimed, with a wave of his hand, "Don't know yah!" The disgrace attendant on his immediately afterwards taking to crowing and pursuing me across the bridge, culminated the disgrace with which I left town.

The coach, with Mr. Jaggers inside, came up in due time, and I took my box-seat again, and arrived in London safe—but not sound, for my heart was gone. As soon as I arrived, I sent a penitential codfish and a barrel of oysters to Joe (as reparation for not having gone myself), and then went on to Barnard's Inn.

I found Herbert dining on cold meat, and delighted to welcome me back, and I felt that I must open my breast that very evening to my friend and chum. Dinner done and we sitting with our feet upon the fender, I said to Herbert, "My dear Herbert, I have something very particular to tell you."

"My dear Handel," he returned, "I

shall respect your confidence."

"It concerns myself, Herbert," said I, "and one other person."

Herbert looked at the fire with his head on one side, and looked at me because I didn't go on.

"Herbert," said I, laying my hand upon his knee. "I love—I adore—Estella. I have never left off adoring her. And she has come back, a most beautiful and most elegant creature. And I saw her yesterday. And if I adored her before, I now doubly adore her."

"Lucky for you then, Handel," said Herbert, "that you are picked out for her and allotted to her. Have you any idea yet of Estella's views on the adoration question?"

I shook my head gloomily. "Oh! She is thousands of miles away from me," said I.

"Patience, my dear Handel; time enough, time enough. But you have something more to say?"

"I am ashamed to say it," I returned, "and yet it's no worse to say it than to think it. You call me a lucky fellow. Of course, I am. I was a blacksmith's boy but yesterday; I am—what shall I say I am—today?"

"Say a good fellow, if you want a phrase," returned Herbert, smiling, "a good fellow, with impetuosity and hesitation, boldness and diffidence, action and dreaming, curiously mixed in him."

"Herbert," I went on, "you say I am lucky, and yet, when I think of Estella, I cannot tell you how dependent and uncertain I feel. I may say that on the constancy of one person (naming no person) all my expectations depend. And at the best, how indefinite and unsatisfactory, only to know so vaguely what they are!"

"Now, Handel," Herbert replied, in his gay, hopeful way, "it seems to me that we are looking into our gift horse's mouth with a magnifying glass. Didn't you tell me that your guardian, Mr. Jaggers, told you in the beginning that you were not endowed with expectations only? And even if he had not told you so, could you believe that of all men in London, Mr. Jaggers is the man to hold his present relations toward you unless he was sure of his ground?"

"What a hopeful disposition you have!" said I, gratefully admiring his cheery ways.

"I ought to have," said Herbert, "for I have not much else. And now, I want to make myself seriously disagreeable to you for a moment—positively repulsive."

"You won't succeed," said I.

"Oh, yes, I shall!" said he. "I have been thinking that Estella cannot surely be a condition of your inheritance, if she was never referred to by your guardian. Am I right in so understanding what you have told me, as that he never referred to her, directly or indirectly, in any way? Never even hinted, for instance, that your patron might have views as to your marriage ultimately?"

"Never."

"Now, Handel, I am quite free from the flavor of sour grapes, upon my soul and honor! Not being bound to her, can you not detach yourself from her?—I told you I should be disagreeable."

I turned my head aside, for, with a rush and a sweep, a feeling like that which had subdued me on the morning when I left the forge, smote upon my heart again. There was silence between us for a little while.

"My dear Handel," Herbert went on, "think of her bringing-up, and think of Miss Havisham. Think of what she is herself. This may lead to miserable things."

"I know it, Herbert," said I, with my head still turned away, "but I can't help it."

"Well!" said Herbert, getting up with a lively shake as if he had been asleep, and stirring the fire. "Now I'll endeavor to make myself agreeable again! I was going to say a word or two, Handel, concerning my father and my father's son. May I ask you if you have ever had an opportunity of remarking that the children of not exactly suitable marriages are always most particularly anxious to be married? Indeed, I think we are all engaged, except the baby."

"Then you are?" said I.

"I am," said Herbert; "but it's a secret."

"May I ask the name?" I said.

"Name of Clara," said Herbert.

"Live in London?"

"Yes. Her father had to do with the victualing [1] of passenger ships. I think he was a species of purser."

"What is he now?" said I.

"He's an invalid now," replied Herbert. "I have never seen him, for he has always kept his room overhead since I have known Clara. But I have heard him constantly. He makes tremendous rows—roars, and pegs at the floor with some frightful instrument." In looking at me and then laughing heartily, Herbert for the time recovered his usual hearty manner.

"Don't you expect to see him?" said I.

"Oh, yes, I constantly expect to see him," returned Herbert, "because I never hear him, without expecting him to come tumbling through the ceiling. But I don't know how long the rafters may hold."

When he had once more laughed heartily, he became meek and told me that the moment he began to realize Capital, it was his intention to marry this young lady. He added, "But you *can't* marry, you know, while you're looking about you."

---

[1] **victualing**: supplying of victuals (vit'lz), food.

CHAPTER 24

Estella arrives in London.

ONE DAY when I was busy with my books and Mr. Pocket, I received a note by the post. It has no set beginning, as Dear Mr. Pip, or Dear Pip, or Dear Sir, or Dear Anything, but ran thus:

I am to come to London the day after tomorrow by the midday coach. I believe it was settled you should meet me? At all events Miss Havisham has that impression, and I write in obedience to it. She sends you her regard.

—Yours, ESTELLA.

My appetite vanished instantly, and I knew no peace or rest until the day arrived. Then I was worse than ever, and began haunting the coach office in Wood Street, Cheapside, before the coach had left the Blue Boar in our town. I felt as if it were not safe to let the coach office be out of my sight longer than five minutes at a time, and in this condition of unreason I performed the first half-hour of a watch of four or five hours.

In her furred traveling dress, Estella seemed more delicately beautiful than she had ever seemed yet, even in my eyes. Her manner was more winning than before, and I thought I saw Miss Havisham's influence in the change.

"I am going to Richmond," she told me. "The distance is ten miles. I am to have a carriage, and you are to take me. This is my purse, and you are to pay my charges out of it. Oh, you must take the purse! We have no choice, you and I, but to obey our instructions. We are not free to follow our own devices, you and I."

As she looked at me in giving me the purse, I hoped there was an inner meaning in her words. She said them slightingly, but not with displeasure.

"A carriage will have to be sent for, Estella. Will you rest here a little?"

"Yes, I am to rest here a little, and I am to drink some tea, and you are to take care of me the while."

She drew her arm through mine, as if it must be done, and I requested a waiter to show us a private sitting room. Upon that, he pulled out a napkin, as if it were a magic clue without which he couldn't find the way upstairs, and led us to the black hole of the establishment. On my objecting to this retreat, he took us into another room with a dinner table for thirty. I was sensible that the air of this chamber, in its strong combination of stable with soup stock, might have led one to infer that the coaching department was not doing well, and that the enterprising proprietor was boiling down the horses for the refreshment department. Yet the room was all in all to me, Estella being in it. I thought that with her I could have been happy there for life. (I was not at all happy there at the time, observe, and I knew it well.)

"Where are you going to, at Richmond?" I asked Estella.

"I am going to live," said she, "at a great expense, with a lady there, who has the power—or says she has—of taking me about and introducing me and showing people to me and showing me to people. How do you thrive with Mr. Pocket?"

"I live quite pleasantly there; at least—" It appeared to me that I was losing a chance.

"At least?" repeated Estella.

"As pleasantly as I could anywhere, away from you."

"You silly boy," said Estella, quite composedly, "how can you talk such nonsense? Your friend Mr. Matthew, I believe, is superior to the rest of his family?"

"Very superior indeed."

"He really is disinterested, and above

small jealousy and spite I have heard?"

"I am sure I have every reason to say so."

"You have not every reason to say so of the rest of his people," said Estella, "for they beset Miss Havisham with reports to your disadvantage. They watch you, misrepresent you, write letters about you (anonymous sometimes), and you are the torment and occupation of their lives. You can scarcely realize the hatred those people feel for you."

"They do me no harm, I hope?"

"No, no, you may be sure of that," said Estella. "Oh, what satisfaction it gives me to see those people thwarted! Two things I can tell you. First, these people never will impair your ground with Miss Havisham, in any particular, great or small. Second, I am beholden to you as the cause of their being so busy and so mean in vain, and there is my hand upon it."

As she gave it me playfully, I held it and put it to my lips. "You ridiculous boy," said Estella, "will you never take warning? Or do you kiss my hand in the same spirit in which I once let you kiss my cheek?"

"If I say yes, may I kiss the cheek again?"

"You should have asked before you touched the hand. But, yes, if you like."

I leaned down, and her calm face was like a statue's. "Now," said Estella, gliding away the instant I touched her cheek, "you are to take care that I have some tea, and you are to take me to Richmond."

Her reverting to this tone as if our association were forced upon us and we were mere puppets, gave me pain; but everything in our intercourse did give me pain. Whatever her tone with me happened to be, I could put no trust in it, and build no hope on it; and yet I went on against trust and against hope. Why re-peat it a thousand times? So it always was.

I rang for the tea, and the waiter brought in by degrees some fifty adjuncts to that refreshment, but of tea not a glimpse. A teaboard, cups and saucers, plates, knives and forks, spoons, saltcellars, a meek little muffin confined with the utmost precaution under a strong iron cover, a fat family urn. After a prolonged absence he came in with a casket of precious appearance containing twigs. These I steeped in hot water and extracted one cup of I don't know what, for Estella.

The bill paid, and the waiter remembered, and the chambermaid taken into consideration—in a word, the whole house bribed into a state of contempt and animosity, and Estella's purse much lightened—we got into our post coach and drove away. Turning into Cheapside and rattling up Newgate Street, we were soon under the walls of which I was so ashamed.[1]

"Mr. Jaggers," said I, "has the reputation of being more in the secrets of that dismal place than any man in London."

"He is more in the secrets of every place, I think," said Estella, in a low voice.

"You have been accustomed to see him often, I suppose?"

"I have been accustomed to see him at uncertain intervals ever since I can remember. But I know him no better now than I did before I could speak plainly. What is your own experience of him?"

"Once habituated to his distrustful manner," said I, "I have done very well."

"Are you intimate?"

"I have dined with him at his private house."

"I fancy," said Estella, shrinking, "that must be a curious place."

"It is a curious place."

[1] the walls . . . ashamed: Newgate prison.

I should have been chary of discussing my guardian too freely even with her; but I should have gone on with the subject so far as to describe the dinner in Gerrard Street, if we had not then come into a sudden glare of gas.[1] When we were out of it, we fell into other talk, principally about the way by which we were traveling and about London.

It was impossible for me to avoid seeing that she cared to attract me; that she made herself winning; and would have won me even if the task had needed pains. Yet this made me none the happier, for I felt that she held my heart in her hand because she willfully chose to do it, and not because it would have wrung any tenderness in her to crush it and throw it away.

When we passed through Hammersmith, I showed her where Mr. Matthew Pocket lived, and said it was no great way from Richmond, and that I hoped I should see her sometimes.

"Oh, yes, you are to see me; you are to come when you think proper; you are to be mentioned to the family; indeed you are already mentioned."

I inquired was it a large household she was going to be a member of?

"No, there are only two, mother and daughter. The mother is a lady of some station, though not averse to increasing her income."

"I wonder Miss Havisham could part with you again so soon."

"It is a part of Miss Havisham's plans for me, Pip," said Estella, with a sigh, as if she were tired. "I am to write to her constantly and see her regularly, and report how I go on—I and the jewels—for they are nearly all mine now."

It was the first time she had ever called me by name. Of course she did so purposely, and knew that I should treasure it up.

[1] **gas:** gaslight.

We came to Richmond all too soon, and at our destination two cherry-colored maids came fluttering out to receive Estella. The doorway soon absorbed her boxes, and she gave me her hand and a smile, and said good night, and was absorbed likewise. And still I stood looking at the house, thinking how happy I should be if I lived there with her, and knowing that I never was happy with her, but always miserable.

CHAPTER 25

Pip and Herbert
examine their affairs.

As I HAD grown accustomed to my expectations, I had insensibly begun to notice their effect upon myself and those around me. Their influence on my own character I disguised from my recognition as much as possible, but I knew very well that it was not all good. I lived in a state of chronic uneasiness respecting my behavior to Joe. My conscience was not by any means comfortable about Biddy. When I woke up in the night I used to think, with a weariness in my spirits, that I should have been happier and better if I had never seen Miss Havisham's face, and had risen to manhood content to be partners with Joe in the honest old forge. Many a time of an evening, when I sat alone looking at the fire, I thought, after all, there was no fire like the forge fire and the kitchen fire at home.

Now, concerning the influence of my position on others, I perceived it was not beneficial to anybody, and above all, that it was not beneficial to Herbert. My lavish habits led his easy nature into expenses that he could not afford, corrupted the simplicity of his life, and disturbed his peace with anxieties and regrets. I began to contract a quantity of debt. I could hardly begin but Herbert must begin too, so he soon followed.

In my confidence in my own resources, I would willingly have taken Herbert's expenses on myself; but Herbert was proud, and I could make no such proposal to him. So he got into difficulties in every direction, and continued to look about him. When we gradually fell into keeping late hours and late company, I noticed that he looked about him with a desponding eye at breakfast time; that he began to look about him more hopefully about midday; that he drooped when he came in to dinner; that he seemed to descry Capital in the distance rather clearly after dinner; that he all but realized Capital toward midnight; and that about two o'clock in the morning he became so deeply despondent again as to talk of buying a rifle and going to America, with a general purpose of compelling buffaloes to make his fortune.

We spent as much money as we could, and got as little for it as people could make up their minds to give us. We were always more or less miserable, and most of our acquaintance were in the same condition. There was a gay fiction among us that we were constantly enjoying ourselves, and a skeleton truth that we never did. To the best of my belief, our case was in the last aspect a rather common one.

At certain times I would say to Herbert, as if it were a remarkable discovery:

"My dear Herbert, we are getting on badly."

"My dear Handel," Herbert would say to me, in all sincerity, "if you will believe me, those very words were on my lips, by a strange coincidence."

"Then, Herbert," I would respond, "let us look into our affairs."

We always derived profound satisfac-

tion from making an appointment for this purpose. Dinner over, we produced a bundle of pens, a copious supply of ink, and a goodly show of writing and blotting paper. For there was something very comfortable in having plenty of stationery.

I would then take a sheet of paper, and write across the top of it, in a neat hand, the heading, "Memorandum of Pip's debts." Herbert would also take a sheet of paper, and write across it, "Memorandum of Herbert's debts."

Each of us would then refer to a confused heap of papers at his side. The sound of our pens going refreshed us exceedingly, insomuch that I sometimes found it difficult to distinguish between this edifying business proceeding and actually paying the money.

When we had written a little while, I would ask Herbert how he got on.

"They are mounting up, Handel," Herbert would say; "upon my life they are mounting up."

"Be firm, Herbert," I would retort. "Look the thing in the face. Look into your affairs. Stare them out of countenance."

"So I would, Handel, only they are staring *me* out of countenance."

However, my determined manner would have its effect, and Herbert would fall to work again. After a time he would give up once more, on the plea that he had not got Cobbs's bill, or Lobbs's, or Nobbs's, as the case might be.

"Then, Herbert, estimate; estimate it in round numbers, and put it down."

"What a fellow of resource you are!" my friend would reply, with admiration. "Really, your business powers are very remarkable."

I thought so too. I established with myself, on these occasions, the reputation of a first-rate man of business—prompt, decisive, energetic, clear, cool-headed. When I had got all my responsibilities down upon my list, I compared each with the bill, and ticked it off. My self-approval when I ticked an entry was quite a luxurious sensation. When I had no more ticks to make, I folded all my bills up uniformly, docketed each on the back, and tied the whole into a symmetrical bundle. Then I did the same for Herbert (who modestly said he had not my administrative genius), and felt that I had brought his affairs into focus for him.

But there was a calm, a rest, a virtuous hush, consequent on these examinations of our affairs, that gave me, for the time, an admirable opinion of myself. Soothed by my exertions, my method, and Herbert's compliments, I would sit with his symmetrical bundle and my own on the table before me among the stationery, and feel like a bank of some sort, rather than a private individual.

We shut our outer door on these solemn occasions in order that we might not be interrupted. I had fallen into my serene state one evening, when we heard a letter drop through the slit in the said door and fall on the ground. "It's for you, Handel," said Herbert, going out and coming back with it, "and I hope there is nothing the matter." This was in allusion to its heavy black seal and border.

The letter was signed TRABB & CO., and its contents were to inform me that Mrs. J. Gargery had departed this life on Monday last at twenty minutes past six in the evening, and that my attendance was requested at the interment on Monday next at three o'clock in the afternoon.

CHAPTER 26

Pip returns to the forge.

IT WAS the first time that a grave had opened in my road of life, and the figure of my sister in her chair by the kitchen fire haunted me night and day. Whatever my fortunes might have been, I could scarcely have recalled my sister with much tenderness. But I suppose there is a shock of regret which may exist without much tenderness. I went down early in the morning and alighted at the Blue Boar, in good time to walk over to the forge. At last I came within sight of the house, and saw that Trabb and Co. had taken possession. Poor dear Joe, entangled in a little black cloak tied in a large bow under his chin, was seated apart at the upper end of the room, where, as chief mourner, he had evidently been stationed by Trabb. When I bent down and said to him, "Dear Joe, how are you?" he said, "Pip, old chap, you know'd her when she were a

fine figure of a—" and clasped my hand and said no more.

Biddy, looking very neat and modest in her black dress, went quietly here and there, and was very helpful. When I had spoken to Biddy, as I thought it not a time for talking, I went and sat down near Joe.

"Pocket handkerchiefs out, all!" cried Mr. Trabb at this point, in a depressed businesslike voice—"Pocket handkerchiefs out! We are ready!"

So, we all put our pocket handkerchiefs to our faces and filed out two and two: Joe and I, Biddy and Pumblechook, Mr. and Mrs. Hubble, the remains of my poor sister being carried by six bearers.

We went through the village, and now the range of marshes lay clear before us, and we went into the churchyard, close to the graves of my unknown parents, Philip Pirrip, late of this parish, and Also Georgiana, Wife of the Above. And there my sister was laid quietly in the earth while the larks sang high above it, and the light wind strewed it with beautiful shadows of clouds and trees.

When we got back and when they were all gone, Biddy, Joe, and I had a cold dinner together; but we dined in the best parlor, not in the old kitchen, and Joe was so exceedingly particular what he did with his knife and fork and the saltcellar and what not, that there was great restraint upon us. But after dinner, when I made him take his pipe, and when I had loitered with him about the forge, and when we sat down together on the great block of stone outside it, we got on better.

He was very much pleased by my asking if I might sleep in my own little room, and I was pleased too; for I felt that I had done rather a great thing in making the request.

When the shadows of evening were closing in, I took an opportunity of getting into the garden with Biddy for a little talk.

"Biddy," said I, "I think you might have written to me about these sad matters."

"Do you, Mr. Pip?" said Biddy. "I should have written if I had thought that."

She was so quiet, and had such an orderly, good, and pretty way with her that I did not like the thought of making her cry again. After looking a little at her downcast eyes as she walked beside me, I gave up that point.

"I suppose it will be difficult for you to remain here now, Biddy, dear?"

"Oh! I can't do so, Mr. Pip," said Biddy, in a tone of regret, but still of quiet conviction. "I have been speaking to Mrs. Hubble, and I am going to her tomorrow.

I hope we shall be able to take some care of Mr. Gargery together until he settles down."

"How are you going to live, Biddy? If you want any mo—"

"How am I going to live?" repeated Biddy, striking in, with a momentary flush upon her face. "I'll tell you, Mr. Pip. I am going to try to get the place of mistress in the new school nearly finished here. I can be well recommended by all the neighbors, and I hope I can be industrious and patient, and teach myself while I teach others. The new schools are not like the old, but I learned a good deal from you after that time, and have had time since then to improve."

"I think you would always improve, Biddy, under any circumstances." I walked a little farther with Biddy, looking silently at her downcast eyes. "I have not heard the particulars of my sister's death, Biddy."

"They are very slight, poor thing. She had been in one of her bad states for four days, when she came out of it in the evening, just at teatime, and said quite plainly, 'Joe.' As she had never said any word for a long while, I ran and fetched in Mr. Gargery from the forge. She made signs to me that she wanted him to sit down close to her, and wanted me to put her arms round his neck. So I put them round his neck, and she laid her head down on his shoulder quite content and satisfied. And so she presently said 'Joe' again, and once 'Pardon,' and once 'Pip.' And so she never lifted her head up any more, and it was just an hour later when we laid it down on her own bed, because we found she was gone."

Biddy cried; the darkening garden, and the lane, and the stars that were coming out, were blurred in my own sight.

"Nothing was ever discovered, Biddy?"

"Nothing."

"Do you know what is become of Orlick?"

"I should think from the color of his clothes that he is working in the quarries."

"Of course you have seen him then? Why are you looking at that dark tree in the lane?"

"I saw him there on the night she died."

"That was not the last time either, Biddy?"

"No; I have seen him there since we have been walking here. It is of no use," said Biddy, laying her hand upon my arm, as I was for running out. "You know I would not deceive you; he was not there a minute, and he is gone."

It revived my utmost indignation to find that she was still pursued by this fellow, and I told her that I would spend any money or take any pains to drive him out of that country. By degrees she led me into more temperate talk, and she told me how Joe loved me, and how Joe never complained of anything—she didn't say, of me; she had no need; I knew what she meant—but ever did his duty in his way of life, and with a strong hand, a quiet tongue, and a gentle heart.

"Indeed, it would be hard to say too

much for him," said I, "and of course I shall be often down here now. I am not going to leave poor Joe alone."

"Are you quite sure, then, that you *will* come to see him often?" asked Biddy, stopping in the narrow garden walk, and looking at me with a clear and honest eye.

"Oh, dear me!" said I as I found myself compelled to give up Biddy in despair. "This really is a very bad side of human nature! Don't say any more, if you please, Biddy. This shocks me very much."

For which cogent reason I kept Biddy at a distance during supper, and when I went up to my own little room, took as stately a leave of her as I could. As often as I was restless in the night, and that was every quarter of an hour, I reflected what an unkindness, what an injury, what an injustice, Biddy had done me.

Early in the morning I was to go. Early in the morning I was out, and looking in, unseen, at one of the wooden windows of the forge. There I stood, for minutes, looking at Joe, already at work with a glow of health and strength upon his face that made it show as if the bright sun of the life in store for him were shining on it.

"Good-by, dear Joe! No, don't wipe it off—give me your blackened hand! I shall be down soon and often."

"Never too soon, sir," said Joe, "and never too often, Pip!"

Biddy was waiting for me at the kitchen door, with a mug of new milk and a crust of bread. "Biddy," said I, when I gave her my hand at parting, "I am not angry, but I am hurt."

"No, don't be hurt," she pleaded quite pathetically, "let only me be hurt, if I have been ungenerous."

Once more, the mists were rising as I walked away. If they disclosed to me, as I suspect they did, that I should *not* come back, and that Biddy was quite right, all I can say is—they were quite right too.

CHAPTER 27

Miss Skiffins helps serve tea.

HERBERT and I went on from bad to worse, in the way of increasing our debts; and time went on; and I came of age. Herbert himself had come of age, eight months before me. As he had nothing else than his majority to come into, the event did not make a profound sensation in Barnard's Inn. But we had looked forward to my one-and-twentieth birthday with a crowd of speculations and anticipations, for we had both considered that my guardian could hardly help saying something definite on that occasion.

I had taken care to have it well understood in Little Britain when my birthday was. On the day before it, I received an official note from Wemmick, informing me that Mr. Jaggers would be glad if I would call upon him at five in the afternoon of the auspicious day. This convinced us that something great was to happen, and threw me into an unusual flutter when I repaired to my guardian's office, a model of punctuality.

Wemmick offered me his congratulations, and incidentally rubbed the side of his nose with a folded piece of tissue paper that I liked the look of. It was November, and my guardian was standing before his fire with his hands under his coattails.,

"Well, Pip," said he, "I must call you Mr. Pip today. Congratulations, Mr. Pip."

We shook hands and I thanked him.

"Take a chair, Mr. Pip," said my guardian.

As I sat down, I felt at a disadvantage which reminded me of that old time when I had been put upon a tombstone.

"Now, my young friend," my guardian began, as if I were a witness in the box, "I am going to have a word or two with you."

"If you please, sir."

"What do you suppose," said Mr. Jaggers, "you are living at the rate of?"

"At the rate of, sir?"

"At," repeated Mr. Jaggers, "the—rate—of?"

Reluctantly, I confessed myself quite unable to answer the question. This reply seemed agreeable to Mr. Jaggers, who said, "I thought so! Now, I have asked *you* a question, my friend. Have you anything to ask *me?*"

"Of course it would be a great relief to me to ask you several questions, sir."

"Ask one," said Mr. Jaggers.

"Is my benefactor to be made known to me today?"

"No. Ask another."

"Is that confidence to be imparted to me soon?"

"Waive that a moment," said Mr. Jaggers, "and ask another."

"Have—I—anything to receive, sir?" On that, Mr. Jaggers said, triumphantly, "I thought we should come to it!" and called to Wemmick to give him that piece of paper. Wemmick appeared, handed it in, and disappeared.

"Now, Mr. Pip," said Mr. Jaggers, "attend if you please. You have been drawing pretty freely here; your name occurs pretty often in Wemmick's cash-book; but you are in debt, of course?"

"I am afraid I must say yes, sir."

"You know you must say yes, don't you?" said Mr. Jaggers.

"Yes, sir."

"I don't ask you what you owe, because you don't know; and if you did know, you wouldn't tell me; you would say less. Yes, yes, my friend," cried Mr. Jaggers, waving his forefinger to stop me, as I made a show of protesting; "it's likely enough that you think you wouldn't, but you would. Now, take this piece of paper in your hand. Now, unfold it and tell me what it is."

"This is a bank note," said I, "for five hundred pounds."

"You consider it, undoubtedly, a handsome sum of money. Now, that handsome sum of money, Pip, is your own. It is a present to you on this day, in earnest of your expectations. And at the rate of that handsome sum of money per annum, and at no higher rate, you are to live until the donor of the whole appears. That is to say, you will now take your money affairs entirely into your own hands, and you will draw from Wemmick one hundred and twenty-five pounds per quarter until you are in communication with the fountain-head and no longer with the mere agent. As I have told you before, I am the mere agent. I execute my instructions, and I am paid for doing so. I think them injudicious, but I am not paid for giving any opinion on their merits."

After a pause, I hinted:

"There was a question just now, Mr. Jaggers, which you desired me to waive for a moment. I hope I am doing nothing wrong in asking it again?"

"What is it?" said he.

"Is it likely," I said, after hesitating, "that my patron, Mr. Jaggers, will soon come to London," said I, "or summon me anywhere else?"

"Now here," replied Mr. Jaggers, fixing me for the first time with his dark deep-set eyes, "we must revert to the evening when we first encountered one another in your village. What did I tell you then, Pip?"

"You told me, Mr. Jaggers, that it might be years hence when that person appeared.

"Just so," said Mr. Jaggers. "That's my answer."

"Do you suppose it will still be some years hence, Mr. Jaggers?"

"Come!" said Mr. Jaggers. "I'll be plain with you, my friend Pip. That's a question I must not be asked. When that person discloses, you and that person will settle your own affairs. My part in this business will cease. And that's all I have got to say."

"If that is all you have to say, sir," I remarked, "there can be nothing left for me to say."

He nodded assent and asked me where I was going to dine. I replied at my own chambers, with Herbert. As a necessary sequence, I asked him if he would favor us with his company, and he promptly accepted the invitation. But first he had a letter or two to write, and I said I would go into the outer office and talk to Wemmick.

The fact was that when the five hundred pounds had come into my pocket, a thought had come into my head which had been often there before; and it appeared to me that Wemmick was a good person to advise with.

"Mr. Wemmick," said I, "I want to ask your opinion. I am very desirous to serve a friend. This friend is trying to get on in commercial life, but has no money and finds it difficult and disheartening to make a beginning. Now, I want somehow to help him to a beginning."

"With money down?" said Wemmick, in a tone drier than any sawdust.

"With *some* money down," I replied, for an uneasy remembrance shot across me of that symmetrical bundle of papers at home; "with *some* money down, and perhaps some anticipation of my expectations."

"Mr. Pip," said Wemmick, "pitch your money into the Thames and you know the end of it. Serve a friend with it, and you may know the end of it too—but it's a less pleasant and profitable end."

"And that," said I, "is your deliberate opinion, Mr. Wemmick?"

"That," he returned, "is my deliberate opinion in this office."

"Ah!" said I, pressing him, for I thought I saw him near a loophole here; "but would that be your opinion at Walworth?"

"Mr. Pip," he replied with gravity, "Walworth is one place, and this office is another. Much as the Aged is one person, and Mr. Jaggers is another. They must not be confounded together. My Walworth sentiments must be taken at Walworth; none but my official sentiments can be taken in this office."

"Very well," said I, much relieved, "then I shall look you up at Walworth, you may depend upon it."

"Mr. Pip," he returned, "you will be welcome there, in a private and personal capacity."

We had held this conversation in a low voice, well knowing my guardian's ears to be the sharpest of the sharp. As he now appeared in his doorway, we all three went into the street together, and from the doorstep Wemmick turned his way, and Mr. Jaggers and I turned ours.

I devoted the next Sunday afternoon to a pilgrimage to the Castle. On arriving before the battlements, I found the Union Jack flying and the drawbridge up, but undeterred by this show of defiance and resistance, I rang at the gate, and was admitted by the Aged.

"My son, sir," said the old man, after securing the drawbridge, "left word that he would soon be home from his afternoon's walk. He is very regular in his walks, is my son. Very regular in everything, is my son."

I nodded at the old gentleman, and we went in and sat down by the fireside.

"You made acquaintance with my son, sir," said the old man, in his chirping way, while he warmed his hands at the blaze, "at his office, I expect?" I nodded. "Hah! I have heered that my son is a wonderful hand at his business."

I was startled by a sudden click in the

wall on one side of the chimney, and the ghostly tumbling open of a little wooded flap with "JOHN" upon it. The old man, following my eyes, cried with great triumph, "My son's come home!" and we both went out to the drawbridge. The Aged was so delighted to work the drawbridge that I made no offer to assist him, but stood quiet until Wemmick had come across, and had presented me to Miss Skiffins, a lady by whom he was accompanied.

Miss Skiffins was of a wooden appearance, like her escort. The cut of her dress from the waist upward, both before and behind, made her figure very like a boy's kite, and I might have pronounced her gown a little too decidedly orange and her gloves a little too intensely green; but she seemed to be a good sort of fellow, and showed a high regard for the Aged. I was not long in discovering that she was a frequent visitor at the Castle.

While Miss Skiffins was taking off her bonnet (she retained her green gloves during the evening as an outward and visible sign that there was company), Wemmick invited me to take a walk with him round the property and see how the island looked in wintertime. Thinking that he did this to give me an opportunity of taking his Walworth sentiments, I seized the opportunity as soon as we were out of the Castle.

I informed Wemmick that I was anxious in behalf of Herbert Pocket, and I told him how we had first met, and how we had fought. I alluded to the advantages I had derived in my first ignorance from his society, and I confessed that I feared I had but ill repaid them, and that he might have done better without me and my expectations. For all these reasons (I told Wemmick), and because he was my young companion and friend, I sought advice how I could best help Herbert to some present income—say of a hundred a year,

to keep him in good hope and heart— and gradually to buy him onto some small partnership. I begged Wemmick to understand that my help must always be rendered without Herbert's knowledge or suspicion, and that there was no one else in the world with whom I could advise. I wound up by laying my hand upon his shoulder and saying, "I can't help confiding in you, though I know it must be troublesome to you; but that is your fault in having ever brought me here."

Wemmick was silent for a little while, and then said, "Mr. Pip, I'll put on my considering cap, and I think all you want to do may be done by degrees. Skiffins (that's her brother) is an accountant and agent. I'll look him up and go to work for you."

After a little further conversation to the same effect, we returned into the Castle, where we found Miss Skiffins preparing tea. The responsible duty of making the toast was delegated to the Aged, and that excellent old gentleman prepared such a haystack of buttered toast that I could scarcely see him over it. We ate the whole of the toast and drank tea in proportion, and it was delightful to see how warm and greasy we all got after it. The Aged especially might have passed for some clean old chief of a savage tribe, just oiled. Then we drew round the fire, and Wemmick said, "Now, Aged Parent, read us the paper."

Wemmick explained to me while the Aged got his spectacles out that this was according to custom, and that it gave the old gentleman infinite satisfaction to read the news aloud. "I won't offer an apology," said Wemmick, "for he isn't capable of many pleasures—are you, Aged P.?"

"All right, John, all right," returned the old man, seeing himself spoken to.

"Only tip him a nod every now and then when he looks off his paper," said Wem-

mick, "and he'll be as happy as a king. We are all attention, Aged One."

As Wemmick and Miss Skiffins sat side by side, I observed him slowly and gradually stealing his arm round Miss Skiffins' waist. In course of time I saw his hand appear on the other side of Miss Skiffins; but at that moment Miss Skiffins neatly stopped him with the green glove, unwound his arm again as if it were an article of dress, and with the greatest deliberation laid it on the table before her. Miss Skiffins' composure while she did this was one of the most remarkable sights I have ever seen.

At last the Aged read himself into a light slumber. Of course I knew better than to offer to see Miss Skiffins home, and under the circumstances I thought I had best go first; which I did, taking a cordial leave of the Aged, and having passed a pleasant evening.

Before a week was out, I received a note from Wemmick, dated Walworth, stating that he hoped he had made some advance in that matter appertaining to our private and personal capacities. The upshot was that we found a worthy young merchant, not long established in business, who wanted intelligent help, and who wanted capital, and who in due course of time would want a partner. Between him and me secret articles were signed of which Herbert was the subject, and I paid him half of my five hundred pounds down, and engaged for other payments; some to fall due at certain dates out of my income; some contingent on my coming into my property. Miss Skiffins' brother conducted the negotiation.

The whole business was so cleverly managed that Herbert had not the least suspicion of my hand being in it. I never shall forget the radiant face with which he came home one afternoon, and told me, as a mighty piece of news, of his having fallen in with one Clarriker (the young merchant's name), and of his belief that the opening had come at last. Day by day as his hopes grew stronger and his face brighter, he must have thought me a more and more affectionate friend, for I had the greatest difficulty in restraining my tears of triumph when I saw him so happy.

At length, the thing being done, and he having that day entered Clarriker's House, and he having talked to me for a whole evening in a flush of pleasure and success, I did really cry in good earnest when I went to bed, to think that my expectations had done some good to somebody.

A great event in my life, the turning point of my life, now opens on my view. But, before I proceed to narrate it, and before I pass on to all the changes it involved, I must give one chapter to Estella. It is not much to give to the theme that so long filled my heart.

CHAPTER 28

Estella warns Pip.

THE LADY with whom Estella was placed, Mrs. Brandley by name, was a widow, with one daughter several years older than Estella. They were in what is called a good position, and they visited, and were visited by, numbers of people.

In Mrs. Brandley's house and out of Mrs. Brandley's house, I suffered every kind and degree of torture that Estella could cause me. She made use of me to tease other admirers; and she turned the very familiarity between herself and me to the account of putting a constant slight on my devotion to her. And while I think it likely that it almost maddened her other lovers, I knew too certainly that it almost maddened me. She had admirers without end. No doubt my jealousy made an admirer of everyone who went near her; but there were more than enough of them without that.

I saw her often at Richmond, I heard of her often in town, and I used often to take her and the Brandleys on all sorts of pleasures—and they were all miseries to me. I never had one hour's happiness in her society, and yet my mind all round the four-and-twenty hours was harping on the happiness of having her with me unto death. She habitually reverted to that tone which expressed that our association was forced upon us. There were other times when she would come to a sudden check in this tone and in all her many tones and would seem to pity me.

"Pip, Pip," she said one evening, when we sat apart at a darkening window of the house in Richmond; "will you never take warning?"

"Of what?"

"Of me."

"Warning not to be attracted by you, do you mean, Estella?"

"Do I mean! If you don't know what I mean, you are blind."

"At any rate," said I, "I have no warning given me just now, for you wrote to me to come to you this time."

"That's true," said Estella, with a cold careless smile that always chilled me. "The time has come round when Miss Havisham wishes to have me for a day at Satis. You are to take me there, and bring me back, if you will. She would rather I did not travel alone, and objects to receiving my maid, for she has a sensitive horror of being talked of by such people. Can you take me?"

"Can I take you, Estella!"

"You can then? The day after tomorrow, if you please. You are to pay all charges out of my purse. You hear the condition of your going?"

"And must obey," said I.

We went down on the next day but one, and we found Miss Havisham in the room where I had first beheld her. She hung upon Estella's beauty, hung upon her words, hung upon her gestures, and looked at her, as though she were devouring the beautiful creature she had reared.

From Estella she looked at me, with a searching glance that seemed to pry into my heart and probe its wounds. "How does she use you, Pip, how does she use you?" she asked me again, with her witchlike eagerness, even in Estella's hearing. But when we sat by the flickering fire at night, she was most weird, for then, keeping Estella's hand drawn through her arm and clutched in her own hand, she extorted from her by dint of referring back to what Estella had told her in her regular letters the names and conditions of the men she had fascinated. I saw in this that Estella was set to wreak

Miss Havisham's revenge on men. I, too, was tormented even while the prize was reserved for me. I saw in this the reason for my being staved off so long, and the reason for my late guardian's declining to commit himself to the formal knowledge of such a scheme.

The candles that lighted that room were placed in sconces on the wall.

They were high from the ground, and they burned with the steady dullness of artificial light in air that is seldom renewed. As I looked round at them, and at the pale gloom they made, and at the stopped clock, and at the withered articles of bridal dress upon the table and the ground, and at her own awful figure with its ghostly reflection thrown large by the fire upon the ceiling and the wall, I saw in everything the construction that my mind had come to, repeated and thrown back to me.

It happened on the occasion of this visit that some sharp words arose between Estella and Miss Havisham. It was the first time I had ever seen them opposed.

Miss Havisham still clutched Estella's hand in hers, when Estella gradually began to detach herself. She had shown a proud impatience more than once before, and had rather endured that fierce affection than accepted or returned it.

"What!" said Miss Havisham, flashing her eyes upon her. "Are you tired of me?"

"Only a little tired of myself," replied Estella, disengaging her arm.

"Speak the truth, you ingrate!" cried Miss Havisham, passionately striking her stick upon the floor. "You are tired of me."

Estella looked at her with perfect composure, and again looked down at the fire. Her graceful figure and her beautiful face expressed a self-possessed indifference to the wild heat of the other that was almost cruel.

"You stock and stone!" exclaimed Miss Havisham. "You cold, cold heart!"

"What!" said Estella. "Do you reproach me for being cold? You?"

"Are you not?" was the fierce retort.

"You should know," said Estella. "I am what you have made me."

"So proud, so proud!" moaned Miss Havisham, pushing away her gray hair with both her hands.

"Who taught me to be proud?" returned Estella. "Who praised me when I learned my lesson?"

"So hard, so hard!" moaned Miss Havisham, with her former action.

"Who taught me to be hard?" returned Estella. "Who praised me when I learned my lesson?"

"But to be proud and hard to *me!*" Miss Havisham quite shrieked, as she stretched out her arms. "Estella, Estella, Estella, to be proud and hard to *me!*"

"So," said Estella, "I must be taken as I have been made. The success is not mine, the failure is not mine, but the two together make me."

Miss Havisham had settled down, upon the floor, among the faded bridal relics with which it was strewn. I took advantage of the moment—I had sought one from the first—to leave the room, after beseeching Estella's attention to her with a movement of my hand. When I left, Estella was yet standing by the great chimney piece, just as she had stood throughout. Miss Havisham's gray hair was all adrift upon the ground, among the other bridal wrecks, and was a miserable sight to see.

It was with a depressed heart that I walked in the starlight for an hour and more, about the courtyard, and about the brewery, and about the ruined garden. When I at last took courage to return to the room, I found Estella sitting at Miss Havisham's knee. Afterward Estella and I played cards, as of yore—only we were skillful now, and played French games—and so the evening wore away, and I went to bed.

I lay in that separate building across the courtyard. It was the first time I had ever lain down to rest in Satis House, and sleep refused to come near me. At last I felt that I absolutely must get up. I put on my clothes and went out across the yard into the long stone passage. But I was no sooner in the passage than I extinguished my candle, for I saw Miss Havisham going along it in a ghostly manner, making a low cry. I followed her at a distance and saw her go up the staircase. She carried a bare candle in her hand and was a most unearthly object by its light. Standing at the bottom of the staircase, I heard her walking across into her own room, never ceasing the low cry. After a time, I tried in the dark both to get out and to go back, but I could do neither until some streaks of day strayed in and showed me where to lay my hands. During the whole interval, I heard her footstep, saw her candle pass

above, and heard her ceaseless low cry.

Before we left next day, there was no revival of the difference between her and Estella, nor was it ever revived on any similar occasions; and there were four similar occasions, to the best of my remembrance.

It is impossible to turn this leaf of my life without putting Bentley Drummle's name upon it, or I would, very gladly.

On a certain occasion when the Finches [1] were assembled, the presiding Finch called the Grove to order, forasmuch as Mr. Drummle had not yet toasted a lady, it was the brute's turn to do so that day. What was my indignant surprise when he called upon the company to pledge him to "Estella!"

I tell this lightly, but it was no light thing to me. For I cannot express what pain it gave me to think that Estella should show any favor to a contemptible, clumsy, sulky booby, so very far below the average.

It was easy for me to find out, and I did soon find out, that Drummle had begun to follow her closely, and that she allowed him to do it. A little while, and he was always in pursuit of her, and Estella held him on; now with encouragement, now with discouragement, now almost flattering him, now openly despising him. The Spider, as Mr. Jaggers had called him, was used to lying in wait, however, and had the patience of his tribe.

At a certain Assembly Ball at Richmond, I resolved to speak to her concerning him. I took the opportunity when she was waiting for Mrs. Brandley to take her home.

"Are you tired, Estella?"

"Rather, Pip."

"You should be."

"Say, rather, I should not be; for I have

[1] **Finches:** a social club to which Pip, Herbert, and Bentley Drummle belonged.

my letter to Satis House to write before I go to sleep."

"Recounting tonight's triumph?" said I. "Surely a very poor one, Estella."

"What do you mean?"

"Estella," said I, "do look at that fellow in the corner yonder who is looking over here at us."

"Why should I look at him?" returned Estella. "What is there in that fellow in the corner that I need look at?"

"Indeed, that is the very question I want to ask you," said I. "For he has been hovering about you all night."

"Moths and all sorts of ugly creatures," replied Estella, with a glance toward him, "hover about a lighted candle. Can the candle help it?"

"But, Estella, do hear me speak. It makes me wretched that you should encourage a man so generally despised as Drummle. You know he is despised."

"Well?" said she.

"You know he is an ill-tempered, lowering, stupid fellow."

"Well?" said she.

"You know he has nothing to recommend him but money, don't you?"

"Pip," said Estella, casting her glance over the room, "don't be foolish about its effect on you. It may have its effect on others, and may be meant to have. It's not worth discussing."

"Yes, it is," said I, "because I cannot bear that people should say, 'she throws away her graces and attractions on a mere boor, the lowest in the crowd.'"

"I can bear it," said Estella.

"Oh! don't be so proud, Estella, and so inflexible."

"Calls me proud and inflexible in this breath!" said Estella, opening her hands. "And in his last breath reproached me for stooping to a boor!"

"There is no doubt you do," said I, "for I have seen you give him looks and smiles this very night, such as you never give to—me."

"Do you want me then," said Estella, turning suddenly with a fixed and serious look, "to deceive and entrap you?"

"Do you deceive and entrap him, Estella?"

"Yes, and many others—all of them but you. Here is Mrs. Brandley. I'll say no more."

And now that I have given the one chapter to the theme that so filled my heart, and so often made it ache and ache again, I pass on unhindered to the event that had impended over me longer yet; the event that had begun to be prepared for before I knew that the world held Estella.

All the work, near and afar, that tended to the end, had been accomplished; and in an instant the blow was struck, and the roof of my stronghold dropped upon me.

CHAPTER 29

Pip has a midnight caller.

I WAS three-and-twenty years of age. Not another word had I heard to enlighten me on the subject of my expectations. We had left Barnard's Inn a year before, and lived in the Temple.[1] Our chambers were in Garden Court, down by the river. Mr. Pocket and I had for some time parted company as to our original relations, though we continued on the best terms.

Business had taken Herbert on a journey to Marseilles. I was alone, and had a dull sense of being alone. I sadly missed

[1] **Temple:** several groups of famous buildings, built on courtyards near the Thames River, which were occupied by lawyers and court officials and clerks.

the cheerful face and ready response of my friend. It was wretched weather; stormy and wet, stormy and wet; mud, mud, mud, deep in all the streets. We lived at the top of the last house, and the wind rushing up the river shook the house that night, like discharges of cannon or breakings of a sea. I saw that the lamps in the court were blown out, and that the lamps on the bridges and the shore were shuddering, and that the coal fires in barges on the river were being carried away before the wind like red-hot splashes in the rain.

I read with my watch upon the table, purposing to close my book at eleven o'clock. As I shut it, all the church clocks in the city struck that hour. The sound was curiously flawed by the wind; and I was listening, when I heard a footstep on the stair.

What nervous folly made me start, and awfully connect it with the footstep of my dead sister, matters not. It was past in a moment, and I listened again, and heard the footstep stumble in coming on. Remembering then that the staircase lights were blown out, I took up my reading lamp and went out to the stairhead. Whoever was below had stopped on seeing my lamp, for all was quiet.

"There is someone down there, is there not?" I called out, looking down.

"Yes," said a voice from the darkness beneath.

"What floor do you want?"

"The top. Mr. Pip."

"That is my name. There is nothing the matter?"

"Nothing the matter," returned the voice. And the man came on.

I stood with my lamp held out over the stair rail, and he came slowly within its light. I saw a face that was strange to me, looking up with an incomprehensible air of being touched and pleased by the sight of me.

Moving the lamp as the man moved, I made out that he was substantially dressed, but roughly, like a voyager by sea. That he had long iron-gray hair. That his age was about sixty. That he was a muscular man, strong on his legs, and that he was browned and hardened by exposure to weather. As he ascended the last stair or two, I saw, with a stupid kind of amazement, that he was holding out both his hands to me.

"Pray what is your business?" I asked him.

"My business?" he repeated, pausing. "Ah! Yes. I will explain my business, by your leave."

"Do you wish to come in?"

"Yes," he replied. "I wish to come in, master."

I took him into the room I had just left and, having set the lamp on the table, asked him as civilly as I could to explain himself.

He looked about him with the strangest air—an air of wondering pleasure, as if he had some part in the things he admired—and he pulled off a rough outer coat, and his hat. Then I saw that his head was furrowed and bald, and that the long iron-gray hair grew only on its sides. But I saw nothing that in the least explained him. On the contrary, I saw him next moment once more holding out both his hands to me.

"What do you mean?" said I, half suspecting him to be mad.

He stopped in his looking at me and slowly rubbed his right hand over his head. "It's disappointing to a man," he said, in a coarse broken voice, "arter having looked for'ard so distant, and come so fur; but you're not to blame for that—neither on us is to blame for that. I'll speak in half a minute. Give me half a minute, please."

He sat down on a chair that stood before the fire, and covered his forehead with his large brown hands. I looked at him attentively then, and recoiled a little from him; but I did not know him.

"There's no one nigh," said he, looking over his shoulder, "is there?"

"Why do you, a stranger coming into my rooms at this time of the night, ask that question?" said I.

"You're a game one," he returned. "I'm glad you've grow'd up a game one! But don't catch hold of me. You'd be sorry arterwards to have done it."

I relinquished the intention he had detected, for I knew him! Even yet I could not recall a single feature, but I knew him! If the wind and the rain had driven away the intervening years, had swept us to the churchyard where we first stood face to face on such different levels, I could not have known my convict more distinctly than I knew him now, as he sat in the chair before the fire. No need to take a file from his pocket and show it to me; no need to take the handkerchief from his neck and twist it round his head; no need to hug himself with both his arms, and take a shivering turn across the room, looking back at me for recognition. I knew him before he gave me one of those aids, though a moment before I had not been conscious of remotely suspecting his identity.

He came back to where I stood and again held out both his hands. Not knowing what to do—for in my astonishment I had lost my self-possession—I reluctantly gave him my hands. He grasped them heartily, raised them to his lips, kissed them, and still held them.

"You acted nobly, my boy," said he. "Noble Pip! And I have never forgot it!"

At a change in his manner as if he were even going to embrace me, I laid a hand upon his breast and put him away.

"Stay!" said I. "Keep off! If you are grateful to me for what I did when I was a little child, I hope you have shown your gratitude by mending your way of life. If you have come here to thank me, it was not necessary. There must be something good in the feeling that has brought you here, and I will not repulse you; but surely you must understand—I—"

My attention was so attracted by the singularity of his fixed look at me that the words died away on my tongue.

"You was a-saying," he observed, when we had confronted one another in silence, "that surely I must understand. What surely must I understand?"

"That I cannot wish to renew that chance intercourse with you of long ago, under these different circumstances. I am glad to believe you have repented and recovered yourself. I am glad to tell you so. I am glad that, thinking I deserve to be thanked, you have come to thank me. But our ways are different ways, none the less. You are wet, and you look weary. Will you drink something before you go?"

He had replaced his neckerchief loosely, and had stood, keenly observant of me, biting a long end of it. "I think," he answered, still observant of me, "that I *will* drink (I thank you) afore I go."

I made him some hot rum-and-water. I tried to keep my hand steady while I did so. When at last I put the glass to him, I saw with amazement that his eyes were full of tears. I was softened by the softened aspect of the man, and felt a touch of reproach. "I hope," said I, "that you will not think I spoke harshly to you just now. I had no intention of doing it, and I am sorry for it if I did. I wish you well and happy!"

As I put my glass to my lips, he stretched out his hand. I gave him mine, and then he drank, and drew his sleeve across his eyes and forehead.

"How are you living?" I asked him.

"I've been a sheep farmer, stock-breeder, other trades besides, away in the new world," said he; "many a thousand mile of stormy water off from this."

"I hope you have done well?"

"I've done wonderful well. No man has done nigh as well as me. I'm famous for it."

"I'm glad to hear it."

"I hope to hear you say so, my dear boy."

Without stopping to try to understand those words or the tone in which they were spoken, I turned off to a point that had just come into my mind.

"Have you ever seen a messenger you once sent to me," I inquired, "since he undertook that trust?"

"Never set eyes upon him. I warn't likely to."

"He came faithfully, and he brought me the two one-pound notes. I was a poor boy then, as you know, and to a poor boy they were a little fortune. But, like you, I have done well since, and you must let me pay them back. You can put them to some other poor boy's use." I took out my purse.

He watched me as I laid my purse upon the table and opened it, and he watched me as I separated two one-pound notes from its contents. They were clean and new, and I spread them out and handed them over to him. Still watching me, he laid them one upon the other, folded them longwise, gave them a twist, set fire to them at the lamp, and dropped the ashes into the tray.

"May I make so bold," he said then, with a smile that was like a frown, and with a frown that was like a smile, "as to ask you *how* you have done well, since you and me was out on them lone shivering marshes?"

He emptied his glass, got up, and stood at the side of the fire, with his heavy brown hand on the mantelshelf. He put a foot up to the bars to dry and warm it, and the wet boot began to steam; but he neither looked at it nor at the fire, but

steadily looked at me. It was only now that I began to tremble.

When my lips had parted, I forced myself to tell him that I had been chosen to succeed to some property.

"Might a mere warmint ask what property?" said he.

I faltered, "I don't know."

"Might a mere warmint ask whose property?" said he.

I faltered again, "I don't know."

"Could I make a guess, I wonder," said the convict, "at your income since you come of age? As to the first figure, now. Five?"

With my heart beating like a heavy hammer of disordered action, I rose out of my chair, and stood with my hand upon the back of it, looking wildly at him.

"Concerning a guardian," he went on. "There ought to have been some guardian or such-like, whiles you was a minor. Some lawyer, maybe. As to the first letter of that lawyer's name, now. Would it be J?"

All the truth of my position came flashing on me; and its disappointments, dangers, disgraces, consequences of all kinds, rushed in in such a multitude that I was borne down by them and had to struggle for every breath I drew. "Put it," he resumed, "as the employer of that lawyer whose name begun with a J, and might be Jaggers—put it as he had come over sea to Portsmouth, and had landed there, and had wanted to come on to you. Well! however did I find you out? Why, I wrote from Portsmouth to a person in London for particulars of your address. That person's name? Why, Wemmick."

I could not have spoken one word, though it had been to save my life. I stood, with a hand on the chair back and a hand on my breast, where I seemed to be suffocating—I stood so, looking wildly at him, until I grasped at the chair, when the room began to surge and turn. He caught me, drew me to the sofa, put me up against the cushions, and bent on one knee before me: bringing the face that I now well remembered, and that I shuddered at, very near to mine.

"Yes, Pip, dear boy, I've made a gentleman on you! It's me wot has done it! I swore that time, sure as ever I earned a guinea, that guinea should go to you. I swore arterwards, sure as ever I spec'-lated and got rich, you should get rich. I lived rough, that you should live smooth; I worked hard that you should be above work. What odds, dear boy? Do I tell it fur you to feel a obligation? Not a bit. I tell it fur you to know as that there hunted dog wot you kept life in got his head so high that he could make a gentleman—and, Pip, you're him!"

The abhorrence in which I held the man, the dread I had of him, the repugnance with which I shrank from him, could not have been exceeded if he had been some terrible beast.

"Look'ee here, Pip. I'm your second father. You're my son—more to me nor any son. I've put away money, only for you to spend. When I was a hired-out shepherd in a solitary hut, not seeing no faces but faces of sheep till I half forgot wot men's and women's faces wos like, I see yourn. I drops my knife many a time in that hut when I was a-eating my dinner or my supper, and I says, 'Here's the boy again, a-looking at me whiles I eats and drinks!' I see you there a many times as plain as ever I see you on them misty marshes. I says each time, 'If I gets liberty and money, I'll make that boy a gentleman!' And I done it. Why, look at you, dear boy! Look at these here lodgings of yourn, fit for a lord! A lord? Ah! You shall show money with lords for wagers, and beat 'em!"

In his heat and triumph, and in his

knowledge that I had been nearly fainting, he did not remark on my reception of all this. It was the one grain of relief I had. Again he took both my hands and put them to his lips, while my blood ran cold within me.

"Don't you mind talking, Pip," said he. "You ain't looked slowly forward to this as I have; you wosn't prepared for this, as I wos. But didn't you never think it might be me?"

"Oh no, no, no," I returned. "Never, never!"

"Well, you see it *wos* me, and single-handed. Never a soul in it but my own self and Mr. Jaggers."

"Was there no one else?" I asked.

"No," said he, with a glance of surprise. "Who else should there be? And, dear boy, how good-looking you have growed! There's bright eyes somewheres—eh? Isn't there bright eyes somewheres, wot you love the thoughts on?"

O Estella, Estella!

"They shall be yourn, dear boy, if money can buy 'em. Let me finish wot I was a-telling you, dear boy. From that there hut and that there hiring-out, I got money left me by my master (which died, and had been the same as me), and got my liberty and went for myself. It all prospered wonderful. As I giv' you to understand just now, I'm famous for it. It was the money left me and gains of the first few years wot I sent home to Mr. Jaggers —all for you—when he first come arter you, agreeable to my letter."

Oh, that he had never come! That he had left me at the forge—far from contented, yet, by comparison, happy!

"And, then, dear boy, I held steady afore my mind that I would for certain come one day and see my boy, and make myself known to him, on his own ground."

He laid his hand on my shoulder. I shuddered at the thought that for anything I knew his hand might be stained with blood.

"Where will you put me?" he asked presently. "I must be put somewheres, dear boy."

"To sleep?" said I.

"Yes. And to sleep long and sound," he answered, "for I've been sea-tossed and sea-washed, months and months."

"My friend and companion," said I, rising from the sofa, "is absent; you must have his room."

"He won't come back tomorrow, will he?"

"No," said I, answering almost mechanically, "not tomorrow."

"Because, look'ee here, dear boy," he said, dropping his voice, and laying a long finger on my breast in an impressive manner, "caution is necessary."

"How do you mean? Caution?"

"It's death!"

"What's death?"

"I was sent for life. It's death to come back. There's been overmuch coming back of late years, and I should of a certainty be hanged if took."

Nothing was needed but this; the wretched man, after loading me with his wretched gold and silver chains for years, had risked his life to come to me, and I held it there in my keeping!

My first care was to close the shutters so that no light might be seen from without, and then to close and make fast the doors. He asked me for some of my "gentleman's linen" to put on in the morning. I brought it out, and laid it ready for him, and my blood again ran cold when he again took me by both hands to give me good night.

I got away from him, without knowing how I did it, and for an hour or more I remained too stunned to think. It was not until I began to think that I began fully to know how wrecked I was, and how the ship in which I had sailed was gone to pieces.

Miss Havisham's intentions toward me, all a mere dream; Estella not designed for me; I only suffered in Satis House as a convenience, a sting for the greedy relations, a model with a mechanical heart to practice on when no other practice was at hand. But sharpest and deepest pain of all —it was for the convict, guilty of I knew not what crimes, that I had deserted Joe.

In every rage of wind and rush of rain, I heard pursuers. Twice I could have sworn there was a knocking and whispering at the outer door. With these fears upon me, I began to either imagine or recall that I had had mysterious warnings of this man's approach. Crowding up with these reflections came the reflection that I had seen him with my childish eyes to be a desperately violent man; that I had heard that other convict reiterate that he had tried to murder him; that I had seen him down in the ditch, tearing and fighting like a wild beast. Out of such remembrances, I brought into the light of the fire a half-formed terror that it might not be safe to be shut up there with him in the dead of the wild, solitary night. This impelled me to take a candle and go in and look at my dreadful burden.

He had rolled a handkerchief round his head, his face was set and lowering in his sleep. But he was asleep, and quietly, too, though he had a pistol lying on the pillow. I softly removed the key to the outside of his door, and turned it on him before I again sat down by the fire. Gradually I slipped from the chair and lay on the floor. When I awoke, the clocks were striking five, the candles were wasted out, the fire was dead, and the wind and rain intensified the thick black darkness.

This Is the End of the Second Stage of Pip's Expectations.

1. As a result of his life in London, further changes occur in the character of Pip. How is Pip's life in London different from his life at the forge? What new habits has he acquired in London? Do you think anyone in his position would have done the same? Why or why not?

2. The change in Pip's attitude toward other people since he came to live in London is illustrated in the last chapter of Stage II by his reaction to the old convict. On learning that it was the convict who has been his benefactor, does Pip feel grateful for what the convict has done for him? What is his strongest feeling? Is his reaction understandable? Would you, in his place, have felt the same? Why or why not?

3. In London, many people and many influences have a hand in wrenching Pip away from the simple trust, affection, and loyalty of Joe. Which of his new acquaintances influence Pip most strongly? Which ones might remind him, if he would let himself be reminded, of his old life at the forge? How does Pip act when he is with these people? Does he seem to feel superior to them, or does he admire their genuine affection? What makes you think so?

4. Do you think Pip is happy in London? Why or why not? Is he able to pursue the goal he wishes—becoming a gentleman? Has he made any real friends?

5. When they meet in London, Estella says to Pip: "We have no choice, you and I, but to obey our instructions. We are not free to follow our own devices, you and I." Is this true? Has Pip blindly followed his benefactor's instructions, or has he a definite goal in mind? Is he becoming a gentleman because he enjoys being one or because his benefactor expects him to become one? Why might this add to his shock when he discovers that his benefactor is not Miss Havisham, but a convict?

6. Pip wants to become a gentleman so that he will be worthy of Estella. How are the hopes he has of being happy with her different from the way he actually feels when he is with her? Why do you think he continues to hope? If you were he, would you be hopeful?

7. How has Pip become a snob toward Joe and Biddy? Does he feel superior to Joe?

Why? Why is he ashamed of Joe in front of his new friends? Do you think he should be? If Pip had taken Herbert Pocket to visit Joe at the forge, might Herbert have seemed equally uncomfortable and out of place? Why doesn't this occur to Pip?

8. Which arouses greater emotion in Pip: his meeting with Joe or the note from Miss Havisham? Which do you think he should care about more? Why? After visiting Miss Havisham, why does Pip decide to return immediately to London? What is the real reason he wants to stay at the Blue Boar instead of at the forge?

9. On his trip to Satis House, Pip meets several characters from an earlier part of the story. Who are they? What is Pip's attitude toward them, now that he is a gentleman? Which of his old acquaintances gains revenge by embarrassing him? Why do you think Pip is so easily embarrassed?

10. From the tone of Biddy's note in Chapter 21, what can you tell about her attitude toward the new Pip? Does she approve of him? Why or why not? When he returns to the forge, what does she remind him about regarding Joe? What is Pip's reaction to her simple question? Why do you think he has such a strong reaction?

11. What is your opinion of Herbert Pocket? Where had Pip previously encountered him in Stage I of the novel? What characteristics shown by Herbert in that encounter are still evident in him? Which of his qualities are a good influence on Pip? Which of his weaknesses does Pip pick up all too easily?

12. What changes have taken place in Estella since she lived at Miss Havisham's? Do you like her more now or less? Do you think that, despite what she says, she has a genuine liking for Pip? What might make you think so?

13. How does Miss Havisham's relationship to Estella change in Stage II of the novel? During Pip's last visit to Satis House, what does Miss Havisham realize about Estella? Later the same night, how does she react to this realization? Does this incident make her a more or a less sympathetic character? Why?

14. Where in the novel does Pip for the first time make up his own mind to do something

for someone else? Is the person who will benefit from his action deserving of it? What does this decision show about Pip's inner feelings, whatever "gentlemanly" habits he may have fallen into?

THE CRAFT OF THE NOVELIST

1. What new characters does Dickens introduce in Stage II of the novel? Which are most important in the action? One of the most interesting is Bentley Drummle. How does Dickens's description of Drummle make you, like Pip, immediately dislike him? What character from Pip's past does Drummle remind you of in physical appearance and personality?

2. Another character prominent in Stage II is Mr. Jaggers. How does Dickens make him seem mysterious and interesting? What is intriguing about his behavior when Pip first sees him in London? What new facts does Pip later learn that make Jaggers seem even more mysterious? Would you like to know more than Dickens tells you about Jaggers's past and what goes on inside his mind? Do you think, if you knew more about him, Jaggers would seem more or less interesting?

3. Herbert Pocket tells Pip Miss Havisham's story soon after Pip arrives in London. How does knowing what has made Miss Havisham the way she is affect your attitude toward her? How do you think it affects Pip's attitude? Why do you suppose Dickens waited until this point in the novel to reveal the causes of her strange behavior?

4. Wemmick, his Aged Parent, and Miss Skiffins provide much of the humor in *Great Expectations*. What is amusing about the Aged? about Miss Skiffins? about Wemmick's "Castle" and its customs? How does Dickens achieve his comic effects in the scenes at the Castle?

5. Compare Dickens's description of the weather on the night Pip's convict arrives at his London lodgings with the weather in the marshes on the day of their first meeting. How are the two descriptions similar? What words are used in both descriptions? Do you think this is intentional? Why might Dickens want to foreshadow the convict's return with such a similar description?

LANGUAGE AND VOCABULARY

1. Herbert Pocket says about his father's relationship to Miss Havisham, "He is a bad courtier and will not propitiate her." What is the meaning of *propitiate?* Some other words that Dickens might have used instead are *appease, conciliate, mollify, pacify,* or *placate.* In your dictionary check on the exact meaning of each of these. Why, of all these words, does *propitiate* best suggest the exact relationship between Matthew Pocket and Miss Havisham? Which of the other words comes closest to suggesting this relationship? If you had to replace *propitiate* in this sentence with a synonym, which of the other five would you choose?

The English language has many synonyms, but few words have exactly the same meaning as another. Nearly all words have a unique shade of meaning that makes them more suitable in a given context than any other. In your speaking and writing, always try to use the word that most exactly fits your meaning.

2. At one point Pip speaks of "the *hypocritical* Pumblechook." Earlier in the novel he referred to Miss Havisham's greedy relatives as "toadies and humbugs." The word *hypocritical* is from the Greek word *hypokritēs,* and refers to people who try to give the impression that they are better (kinder or perhaps more honest) than they are.

A *toady* plays up to people who are influential or rich. (Some dictionaries define a toady as a "toadeater.") A *humbug* is someone whose actions are deliberately deceptive and misleading.

Today we would be more likely to use the word *snob* than either *toady* or *humbug* to describe the Havisham relatives. Essentially, snobs are people who seek to associate with those whom they regard as their superiors; they are quite cool toward people they consider inferior to themselves.

Which of these four words do you think most exactly describes Mr. Pumblechook?

FOR COMPOSITION

1. In many respects, Pip's going away to London is like anyone's going off alone for the first time. What does Pip do right? What mistakes does he make? What influences keep him from making even more mistakes? Judging from Pip's example, what qualities do you think are necessary in someone who wants to live away from home and disprove Mr. Jaggers's gloomy prediction: "Of course you'll go wrong somehow, but that's no fault of mine"? Think out your ideas and organize your answers to these questions, and then express your opinion on the subject in a short and convincing composition.

2. In Chapter 21, when Pip is ashamed to have Bentley Drummle see him with Joe, he says, "So throughout life, our worst weaknesses and meannesses are usually committed for the sake of the people whom we most despise." What exactly does he mean? In a short composition, explain what you think he means and why you agree or disagree. To support your argument, use at least one example involving someone you have known. Be sure to organize your ideas in a logical manner.

3. Understanding the reasons why people act the way they do can often make us feel more sympathetic toward them and more tolerant of actions that would otherwise seem evil or annoying. Such a person is Miss Havisham. When we realize the cause of her misery, we can at least partly excuse what she has done. Have you ever changed your attitude toward someone after getting better acquainted? Write a short account of such an experience.

LOOKING AHEAD TO STAGE III

At the end of Stage II, what is the dilemma confronting Pip? In his place, what would you do: refuse shelter to your benefactor, a condemned criminal, who has risked his life to return to see you, or run the risk of hiding a wanted man? Which would you expect Pip to choose? Besides his main problem, Pip has had two shattering realizations: he has deserted Joe and the life at the forge for "expectations" that are not more respectable, but less; and Miss Havisham has never had the least intention that he shall someday marry Estella. What do you think Pip will do as a result of these realizations?

The Third Stage
of Pip's Expectations

CHAPTER 30

Pip confronts Jaggers.

IT WAS fortunate for me that I had to take precautions to insure (so far as I could) the safety of my dreaded visitor; for, this thought pressing on me when I awoke held other thoughts at a distance. The impossibility of keeping him concealed in the chambers was self-evident. I was looked after by an inflammatory old female, assisted by an animated rag-bag whom she called her niece; and to keep a room secret from them would be to invite curiosity. I resolved to announce in the morning that my uncle had unexpectedly come from the country.

This course I decided on while I was yet groping about in the darkness for the means of getting a light. Not stumbling on the means after all, I was fain to go out to get the watchman to come with his lantern. Now, in groping my way down the black staircase, I fell over something, and that something was a man crouching in a corner. As the man made no answer when I asked him what he did there, I ran to the lodge and urged the watchman to come quickly. We examined the staircase from the bottom to the top and found no one there.

It troubled me that there should have been a lurker on the stairs on that night of all nights in the year, and I asked the watchman whether he had admitted at his gate any gentleman who had been dining out.

"The night being so bad, sir," said the watchman, "uncommon few have come in at my gate. Besides them three gentlemen that I know, I don't call to mind another since about eleven o'clock, when a stranger asked for you."

"My uncle," I muttered. "Yes."

"You saw him, sir?"

"Yes. Oh, yes."

"Likewise the person with him?"

"Person with him!" I repeated. "What sort of person?"

The watchman had not particularly noticed; he should say a working person; to the best of his belief, he had a dust-colored kind of clothes on, under a dark coat.

My mind was much troubled by these two circumstances taken together. I lighted my fire, which burned with a raw pale flare at that time of the morning, and fell into a doze before it. I was not able to consider my own situation, nor could I do so yet. At last the old woman and the niece came in. I imparted how my uncle had come in the night and was then asleep, and how the breakfast preparations were to be modified accordingly.

By-and-by, his door opened and he came out. I could not bring myself to bear the sight of him, and I thought he had a worse look by daylight.

"I do not even know," said I, speaking low as he took his seat at the table, "by what name to call you. I have given out that you are my uncle."

"That's it, dear boy! Call me uncle."

"You assumed some name, I suppose, on board ship?"

"Yes, dear boy. I took the name of Provis."

"Do you mean to keep that name?"

"Why, yes, dear boy, it's as good as another—unless you'd like another."

"What is your real name?" I asked him in a whisper.

"Magwitch," he answered in the same tone; "chrisen'd Abel."

"When you came into the Temple last night," said I, "and asked the watchman the way here, had you anyone with you?"

"With me? No, dear boy."

"But there was someone there?"

"I didn't take particular notice," he said dubiously, "not knowing the ways of the place. But I think there *was* a person, too, come in alonger me."

"Are you known in London?"

"I hope not," said he, giving his neck a jerk with his forefinger that made me turn hot and sick.

"Were you known in London once?"

"Not over and above, dear boy. I was in the provinces mostly."

"Were you—tried—in London?"

"Which time?" said he, with a sharp look.

"The last time."

He nodded. "First knowed Mr. Jaggers that way. Jaggers was for me. And what I done is worked out and paid for!"

He ate in a ravenous way that was very disagreeable, and all his actions were uncouth, noisy, and greedy. Some of his teeth had failed him since I saw him eat on the marshes, and as he turned his food in his mouth, and turned his head sideways to bring his strongest fangs to bear upon it, he looked terribly like a hungry old dog. "I'm a heavy grubber, dear boy," he said, as a polite kind of apology when he had made an end of his meal. "Sim-ilarly, I must have my smoke." He got up and brought out a short black pipe and a handful of loose tobacco. Having filled his pipe, he took a live coal from the fire with the tongs and lighted his pipe at it, and turned round on the hearthrug with his back to the fire. He took out of his pocket a great thick pocketbook, bursting with papers, and tossed it on the table.

"There's something worth spending in that there book, dear boy. It's yourn. All I've got ain't mine; it's yourn. Don't you be afeerd on it. There's more where that come from. I've come to the old country fur to see my gentleman spend his money *like* a gentleman. That'll be *my* pleasure. *My* pleasure 'ull be fur to see him do it. And blast you all!" he wound up. "Blast you every one, from the judge in his wig to the colonist a-stirring up the dust, I'll show a better gentleman than the whole kit on you put together!"

"Stop!" said I, almost in a frenzy of fear and dislike. "I want to speak to you. I want to know what is to be done. I want to know how you are to be kept out of danger, how long you are going to stay, what projects you have."

"Look'ee here, Pip," said he, laying his hand on my arm in a suddenly altered and subdued manner. "I forgot myself half a minute ago. What I said was low; that's what it was; low. Look'ee here, Pip. Look over it. I ain't a-going to be low."

"First," I resumed, half groaning, "what precautions can be taken against your being recognized and seized?"

"Well, dear boy, the danger ain't so great. Without I was informed agen, the danger ain't so much to signify. There's Jaggers, and there's Wemmick, and there's you. Who else is there to inform?"

"Is there no chance person who might identify you in the street?" said I.

"Well," he returned, "there ain't many. Still, look'ee here, Pip. If the danger had been fifty times as great, I should ha' come to see you, mind you, just the same."

"And how long do you remain?"

"How long?" said he, taking his black pipe from his mouth and dropping his jaw as he stared at me. "I'm not a-going back. I've come for good."

"Where are you to live?" said I. "What is to be done with you? Where will you be safe?"

"Dear boy," he returned, "there's disguising wigs can be bought for money, and there's hair powder, and spectacles, and black clothes—and what not. As to the where and how of living, dear boy, give me your own opinions on it."

It appeared to me that I could do no better than secure him some quiet lodging hard by. That the secret must be confided to Herbert was plain to me. But it was by no means so plain to Mr. Provis (I resolved to call him by that name), who reserved his consent to Herbert's participation until he should have seen him. "And even then, dear boy," said he, pulling a greasy little clasped black Testament out of his pocket, "we'll have him on his oath." The book had the appearance of having been stolen from some court of justice.

There being a respectable lodging house in Essex Street, almost within hail of my windows, I repaired to that house and was so fortunate as to secure the second floor for my uncle, Mr. Provis. I then went from shop to shop, making such purchases as were necessary to change his appearance. This business transacted, I turned my face, on my own account, to Little Britain. Mr. Jaggers was at his desk, but seeing me enter, got up immediately and stood before his fire.

"Now, Pip," said he, "be careful."

"I will, sir," I returned.

"Don't commit yourself," said Mr. Jaggers, "and don't commit anyone. You understand—anyone."

Of course I saw that he knew the man was come.

"I merely want, Mr. Jaggers," said I, "to assure myself what I have been told is true. I have been informed by a person named Abel Magwitch that he is the benefactor so long unknown to me."

"That is the man," said Mr. Jaggers, "—in New South Wales." [1]

"And only he?" said I.

"And only he," said Mr. Jaggers.

"I am not so unreasonable, sir, as to think you at all responsible for my wrong conclusions; but I always supposed it was Miss Havisham."

"As you say, Pip," returned Mr. Jaggers, "I am not at all responsible for that."

"And yet it looked so like it, sir," I pleaded with a downcast heart.

"Not a particle of evidence, Pip," said Mr. Jaggers. "Take nothing on its looks; take everything on evidence. There's no better rule."

"I have no more to say," said I, with a sigh, after standing silent for a little while. "I have verified my information, and there's an end."

"I communicated to Magwitch—in

[1] **New South Wales:** now a state in Australia; formerly a territory to which many convicts were transported, or exiled. Magwitch had been sentenced there for life.

New South Wales—when he first wrote to me—from New South Wales—the caution that he was not at all likely to obtain a pardon, that he was expatriated for the term of his natural life, and that his presenting himself in this country would be an act of felony, rendering him liable to the extreme penalty of the law. I gave Magwitch that caution," said Mr. Jaggers, looking hard at me. "I wrote it to New South Wales. He guided himself by it, no doubt."

"No doubt," said I.

"I have been informed by Wemmick," pursued Mr. Jaggers, still looking hard at me, "that he has received a letter, from a colonist of the name of Purvis, or—"

"Or Provis," I suggested.

"Or Provis—thank you, Pip. Perhaps it *is* Provis? Perhaps you know it's Provis?"

"Yes," said I.

"You know it's Provis. A letter from a colonist of the name of Provis, asking for the particulars of your address, on behalf of Magwitch. Wemmick sent him the particulars, I understand, by return of post. Probably it is through Provis that you have received the explanation of Magwitch—in New South Wales?"

"It came through Provis," I replied.

"Good day, Pip," said Mr. Jaggers, offering his hand. "Glad to have seen you. In writing by post to Magwitch—in New South Wales—or in communicating with him through Provis, have the goodness to mention that the particulars and vouchers of our long account shall be sent to you, together with the balance; for there is still a balance remaining. Good day, Pip!"

Next day the clothes I had ordered all came home, and he put them on. To my thinking there was something in him that made it hopeless to attempt to disguise him. The more I dressed him, and the better I dressed him, the more he looked like the slouching fugitive on the marshes. He dragged one of his legs as if there were still a weight of iron on it, and from head to foot there was convict in the very grain of the man.

For five days, expecting Herbert all the time, I dared not go out except when I took Provis for an airing after dark. At length, one evening when dinner was over and I had dropped into a slumber quite worn out, I was roused by the welcome footstep on the staircase. Provis, who had been asleep too, staggered up at the noise I made, and in an instant I saw his jackknife shining in his hand.

"Quiet! It's Herbert!" I said.

"Handel, my dear fellow, how are you, and again how are you, and again how are you? I seem to have been gone a twelvemonth! Why, so I must have been, for you have grown quite thin and pale! Handel, my—Halloa! I beg your pardon."

He was stopped in his running on and in his shaking hands with me, by seeing Provis. Provis, regarding him with a fixed attention, was slowly putting up his jackknife and groping in another pocket for something else.

"Herbert, my dear friend," said I, shutting the double doors, while Herbert stood staring and wondering, "something very strange has happened. This is—a visitor of mine."

"It's all right, dear boy!" said Provis, coming forward, with his little clasped black book, and then addressing himself to Herbert. "Take it in your right hand. Lord strike you dead on the spot if ever you split in any way sumever. Kiss it!"

"Do so, as he wishes it," I said to Herbert. So Herbert, looking at me with a friendly uneasiness and amazement, complied, and Provis immediately shaking hands with him, said, "Now you're on your oath, you know. And never believe me on mine, if Pip shan't make a gentleman on you!"

CHAPTER 31

*Two men, named Compeyson
and Arthur, step out
of the past.*

In VAIN should I attempt to describe the astonishment and disquiet of Herbert, when he and I and Provis sat down before the fire, and I recounted the whole of the secret. Enough that I saw my own feelings reflected in Herbert's face, and, not least among them, my repugnance toward the man who had done so much for me.

"Look'ee here, Pip's comrade," he said to Herbert, after having discoursed for some time, "I know very well that once since I come back I've been low. But don't you fret yourself on that score. I ain't made Pip a gentleman, and Pip ain't a-goin' to make you a gentleman, not fur me not to know what's due to ye both."

Herbert said, "Certainly," but remained perplexed and dismayed. We were anxious for the time when he would go to his lodging and leave us together, but it was midnight before I saw him safely in at his own dark door. When it closed upon him, I experienced the first moment of relief I had known since the night of his arrival.

Herbert received me with open arms, and I had never felt before so blessedly what it is to have a friend. When he had spoken some sound words of sympathy and encouragement, we sat down to consider the question, What was to be done?

"What," said I to Herbert, "what is to be done? He is intent upon various new expenses—horses, and carriages, and lavish appearances of all kinds. He must be stopped somehow."

"You mean that you can't accept—"

"How can I?" I interposed, as Herbert paused. "Think of him! Look at him!"

An involuntary shudder passed over both of us.

"Then," said I, "after all, stopping short here, never taking another penny from him, think what I owe him already! Then again, I am heavily in debt—very heavily for me, who have now no expectations—and I have been bred to no calling, and I am fit for nothing."

"Well, well, well!" Herbert remonstrated, "Don't say fit for nothing."

"What am I fit for? I know only one thing that I am fit for, and that is to go for a soldier."

"You would be infinitely better in Clarriker's house, small as it is. I am working up toward a partnership, you know."

Poor fellow! He little suspected with whose money.

"But there is another question," said Herbert. "This is an ignorant determined man, who has long had one fixed idea. More than that, he seems to me (I may misjudge him) to be a man of a desperate and fierce character. Think of this! He comes here at the peril of his life, for the realization of his fixed idea. After all his toil and waiting, you destroy his idea, and make his gains worthless to him. Do you see nothing that he might do under the disappointment?"

"I have seen it, Herbert. Nothing has been in my thoughts so distinctly as his putting himself in the way of being taken."

"Then you may rely upon it," said Herbert. "That would be his reckless course if you forsook him. The first and the main thing to be done is to get him out of England. You will have to go with him, and then he may be induced to go. That done, extricate yourself, in Heaven's name, and we'll see it out together, dear old boy."

Provis came round at the appointed

time, took out his jackknife, and sat down to his meal. He was full of plans "for his gentleman's coming out strong and like a gentleman" and urged me to begin speedily upon the pocketbook, which he had left in my possession. When he had made an end of his breakfast, and was wiping his knife on his leg, I said to him, without a word of preface:

"After you were gone last night, I told my friend of the struggle that the soldiers found you engaged in on the marshes. You remember?"

"Remember!" said he. "I think so!"

"We want to know something about that man—and about you. It is strange to know no more about either, and particularly you, than I was able to tell last night. Is not this as good a time as another for our knowing more?"

"Well," he said, after consideration. "You're on your oath, you know, Pip's comrade?"

"Assuredly," replied Herbert.

"And look'ee here! Wotever I done, is worked out and paid for," he insisted again.

He stuck his pipe in a buttonhole of his coat, spread a hand on each knee, and, after turning an angry eye on the fire for a few silent moments, looked around at us and said what follows:

"Dear boy and Pip's comrade, I am not a-going fur to tell you my life, like a song or a storybook. But to give it you short and handy, I'll put it at once into a mouthful of English. In jail and out of jail, in jail and out of jail, in jail and out of jail. There, you've got it. That's *my* life pretty much, down to such times as I got shipped off, arter Pip stood my friend.

"I've been done everything to, pretty well—except hanged. I've been locked up, and stuck in the stocks, and whipped and worried and drove. I've no more notion where I was born than you have. I first became aware of myself down in Essex, a-thieving turnips for my living. Summun had run away from me—a man— a tinker—and he'd took the fire with him, and left me wery cold. I knowed my name to be Magwitch, christened Abel. So fur as I could find, there warn't a soul that see young Abel Magwitch, with as little on him as in him, but wot caught fright at him, and either drove him off or took him up.[1] When I was a ragged little creetur as much to be pitied as ever I see, I got the name of being hardened. 'This is a terrible hardened one,' they says to prison wisitors, picking out me. 'May be said to live in jails, this boy.' They always went on agen me about the Devil. But what the devil was I to do? I must put something into my stomach, mustn't I?

"Tramping, begging, thieving, working sometimes when I could—though that warn't as often as you may think, till you put the question whether you would ha' been overready to give me work yourselves—a bit of a poacher, a bit of a laborer, a bit of a wagoner, a bit of a haymaker, a bit of a hawker, a bit of most things that don't pay and lead to trouble, I got to be a man.

"At Epsom races, a matter of over twenty years ago, I got acquainted wi' a man whose skull I'd crack wi' this poker, like the claw of a lobster, if I'd got it on this hob. His right name was Compeyson; and that's the man, dear boy, what you see me a-pounding in the ditch. He set up fur a gentleman, this Compeyson, and had learning. He was a smooth one to talk and was a dab at the ways of gentlefolks. He was good-looking too.

"Compeyson took me on to be his man and pardner. And what was Compeyson's business in which we was to go pardners? Compeyson's business was the swindling,

---

[1] **took him up:** put him under arrest.

handwriting forging, stolen bank note passing, and suchlike. All sorts of traps as Compeyson could set with his head, and let another man in for, was Compeyson's business. He'd no more heart than a iron file, he was as cold as death, and he had the head of the Devil.

"There was another in with Compeyson, as was called Arthur. Him and Compeyson had been in a bad thing with a rich lady some years afore, and they made a pot of money by it; but Compeyson betted and gamed, and he'd have run through the king's taxes. So, Arthur was a-dying and a-dying poor and with the horrors on him, and Compeyson's wife was a-having pity on him when she could and Compeyson was a-having pity on nothing and nobody.

"I might a-took warning by Arthur, but I didn't. I begun wi' Compeyson, and a poor tool I was in his hands. Arthur lived at the top of Compeyson's house. The second or third time as ever I see him, he came a-tearing down into Compeyson's parlor late at night, in only a flannel gown, with his hair all in a sweat, and he says to Compeyson's wife, 'Sally, she really is upstairs alonger me, now, and I can't get rid of her. She's all in white,' he says, 'wi' white flowers in her hair, and she's awful mad, and she's got a shroud hanging over her arm, and she says she'll put it on me at five in the morning.'

"Says Compeyson: 'Why, you fool, don't you know she's got a living body? And how should she be up there, without coming through the door, or in at the window, and up the stairs?'

"'I don't know how she's there,' says Arthur, shivering dreadful with the horrors, 'but she's standing in the corner at the foot of the bed. And over where her heart's broke—*you* broke it!—there's drops of blood.'

"Compeyson's wife and me took him up to bed agen, and he raved most dreadful. 'Why, look at her!' he cries out. 'She's a-shaking the shroud at me! She'll put it on me, and then I'm done for! Take it away from her, take it away!' And then he kep on a-talking to her, and answering of her, till I half believed I see her myself.

"He rested pretty quiet till it might want a few minutes of five, and then he screams out, 'Here she is! She's got the shroud again. She's unfolding it. She's coming out of the corner. She's coming to the bed. Hold me, both of you—one on each side—don't let her touch me with it.' Then he lifted himself up hard, and was dead.

"Compeyson took it easy as a good riddance for both sides. Him and me was soon busy, and I'll simply say to you, dear boy, and Pip's comrade, that that man got me into such nets as made me his slave. I was always in debt to him, always under his thumb, always a-working, always a-getting into danger. My missis as I had the hard time wi'—Stop though! I ain't brought *her* in—"

He looked about him in a confused way, turned his face to the fire, and spread his hands broader on his knees. "There ain't no need to go into it," he said, looking round once more. "At last, me and Compeyson was both committed for felony—on a charge of putting stolen notes in circulation. Compeyson says to me, 'Separate defenses, no communication,'[1] and that was all. And I was so miserable poor that I sold all the clothes I had, except what hung on my back, afore I could get Jaggers.

"When he was put in the dock, I noticed first of all what a gentleman Compeyson looked, wi' his curly hair and his black clothes and his white pocket hand-

[1] **Separate . . . communication:** each man would handle his own case and there would be no communication between them while defending themselves.

kercher, and what a common sort of a wretch I looked. When the prosecution opened, I noticed how heavy it all bore on me, and how light on him. When the evidence was giv in the box, I noticed how it was always me that had come for'ard, and could be swore to, how it was always me that the money had been paid to, how it was always me that had seemed to work the thing and get the profit. But when the defense come on, then I see the plan plainer; for, says the counselor for Compeyson, 'My lord and gentlemen, here you have afore you, side by side, two persons as your eyes can separate wide; one well brought up, one ill brought up.'

"And when the verdict come, warn't it Compeyson as was recommended to mercy on account of good character and bad company, and giving up all the information he could agen me, and warn't it me as got never a word but guilty? And when I says to Compeyson, 'Once out of this court, I'll smash that face of yourn!' ain't it Compeyson as prays the judge to be protected, and gets two turnkeys stood betwixt us? And when we're sentenced, ain't it him as gets seven year, and me fourteen, and ain't it him as the judge is sorry for, because he might a-done so well, and ain't it me as the judge perceives to be a old offender of wiolent passion, likely to come to worse?"

He had worked himself into a state of great excitement, but he checked it, and stretching out his hand toward me, said, "I ain't a-going to be low, dear boy!

"We was in the same prison ship, but I couldn't get at him for long, though I tried. At last I come behind him and hit him on the cheek to turn him round and get a smashing one at him, when I was seen and seized. The black hole of that ship warn't a strong one. I escaped to the shore, and I was a-hiding among the

graves there, envying them as was in 'em and all over, when I first see my boy!"

He regarded me with a look of affection that made him almost abhorrent to me again, though I had felt great pity for him.

"By my boy, I was giv to understand as Compeyson was out on them marshes too. Upon my soul, I half believed he escaped in his terror to get quit of me, not knowing it was me as had got ashore. I hunted him down. I smashed his face. 'And now,' says I, 'as the worst thing I can do, caring nothing for myself, I'll drag you back.' And I'd have swum off, towing him by the hair, if it had come to that, and I'd a got him aboard without the soldiers.

"Of course he'd much the best of it to the last and his punishment was light. I was put in irons, brought to trial again, and sent for life. I didn't stop for life, dear boy and Pip's comrade, being here."

He slowly took his tangle of tobacco from his pocket, plucked his pipe from his buttonhole, slowly filled it, and began to smoke.

"Is he dead?" I asked after a silence.

"Is who dead, dear boy?"

"Compeyson."

"He hopes *I* am, if he's alive, you may be sure," with a fierce look. "I never heard no more of him."

Herbert had been writing with his pencil in the cover of a book. He softly pushed the book over to me, as Provis stood smoking with his eyes on the fire, and I read in it:

"Young Havisham's name was Arthur. Compeyson is the man who professed to be Miss Havisham's lover."

I shut the book and nodded slightly to Herbert, and put the book by; but we neither of us said anything, and both looked at Provis as he stood smoking by the fire.

CHAPTER 32

Pip and Drummle
exchange sharp words.

A NEW fear had entered in my mind by his narrative. If Compeyson were alive and should discover his return, I could hardly doubt the consequence. That Compeyson would hesitate to release himself for good from a dreaded enemy by the safe means of becoming an informer, was scarcely to be imagined.

Never had I breathed, and never would I breathe—or so I resolved—a word of Estella to Provis. But I said to Herbert that before I could go abroad, I must see both Estella and Miss Havisham. On my presenting myself at Mrs. Brandley's, Estella's maid was called to tell me that Estella had gone into the country. Where? To Satis House. She had never gone there before without me, and I went home again in complete discomfiture.

Next day, I had the meanness to feign that I was under a binding promise to go down to Joe. Provis was to be strictly careful while I was gone, and Herbert was to take the charge of him that I had taken.

Having thus cleared the way for my expedition to Miss Havisham's, I set off by the early morning coach. When we drove up to the Blue Boar, whom should I see come out under the gateway, toothpick in hand, to look at the coach, but Bentley Drummle!

As he pretended not to see me, I pretended not to see him. It was a very lame pretense on both sides; the lamer because we both went into the coffee room. I sat at my table while he stood before the fire. By degrees it became an enormous injury to me that he stood before the fire, and I got up, determined to have my share of it. I had to put my hands behind his legs for the poker when I went up to the fireplace to stir the fire, but still pretended not to know him.

"Is this a cut?"[1] said Mr. Drummle.

"Oh?" said I, poker in hand. "It's you, is it? How do you do? I was wondering who it was who kept the fire off."

With that I poked tremendously, and having done so, planted myself side by side with Mr. Drummle, my shoulders squared, and my back to the fire.

"Large tract of marshes about here, I believe?" said Drummle.

"Yes. What of that?" said I.

Mr. Drummle looked at me and laughed.

"Are you amused, Mr. Drummle?"

"No," said he, "not particularly. I am going out for a ride in the saddle. I mean to explore those marshes for amusement. Out-of-the-way villages there, they tell me. Curious little public houses—and smithies—and that. Waiter!"

[1] **cut:** a refusal to recognize a person.

"Yes, sir."

"Is that horse of mine ready?"

"Brought round to the door, sir."

"I say. Look here. The lady won't ride today; the weather won't do."

"Very good, sir."

"And I don't dine, because I am going to dine at the lady's."

"Very good, sir."

Then Drummle glanced at me with an insolent triumph. One thing was manifest to both of us, and that was that until relief came, neither of us could relinquish the fire. There we stood, well squared up before it, shoulder to shoulder and foot to foot, with our hands behind us, not budging an inch.

After glancing at him once or twice, in an increased state of smoldering ferocity, I said:

"Mr. Drummle, I did not seek this conversation, and I don't think it's an agreeable one."

"I am sure it's not," said he superciliously, over his shoulder.

"And therefore," I went on, "with your leave, I will suggest that we hold no kind of communication in future."

"Quite my opinion," said Drummle. "But don't lose your temper. Haven't you lost enough without that?"

"What do you mean, sir?"

"Waiter," said Drummle, by way of answering me.

The waiter reappeared.

"Look here, you sir. You quite understand that the young lady don't ride today, and that I dine at the young lady's?"

"Quite so, sir!"

How long we might have remained in this ridiculous position it is impossible to say, but for the incursion of three thriving farmers, who came into the coffee room unbuttoning their greatcoats and rubbing their hands, and before whom, as they charged at the fire, we were obliged to give way. I saw him through the window, seizing his horse's mane, and mounting in his blundering brutal manner, and calling for a light for the cigar in his mouth. A man in a dust-colored dress appeared, and as Drummle leaned down from the saddle and lighted his cigar and laughed, with a jerk of his head toward the coffee-room windows, the slouching shoulders and ragged hair of this man, whose back was toward me, reminded me of Orlick.

Too heavily out of sorts to care, I washed the weather and the journey from my face and hands and went out to the memorable old house that it would have been so much the better for me never to have entered, never to have seen.

In the room where the dressing table stood, and where the wax candles burned on the wall, I found Miss Havisham and Estella; Miss Havisham seated on a settee near the fire, and Estella on a cushion at her feet. Estella was knitting and Miss Havisham was looking on. They both raised their eyes as I went in, and both saw an alteration in me. I derived that from the look they interchanged.

"And what wind," said Miss Havisham, "blows you here, Pip?"

Though she looked steadily at me, I saw that she was rather confused. Estella paused a moment in her knitting with her eyes upon me.

"Miss Havisham," said I, "I went to Richmond yesterday to speak to Estella; and finding that some wind had blown *her* here, I followed. What I had to say to Estella, Miss Havisham, I will say before you presently—in a few moments. It will not surprise you; it will not displease you. I am as unhappy as you can ever have meant me to be."

Miss Havisham continued to look steadily at me. I could see in the action of Estella's fingers as they worked that she attended to what I said, but she did not look up.

"I have found out who my patron is. It is not a fortunate discovery, and is not likely ever to enrich me in reputation, station, fortune, anything. There are reasons why I must say no more of that. It is not my secret, but another's. When you first caused me to be brought here, Miss Havisham; when I belonged to the village over yonder, that I wish I had never left; I suppose I did really come here, as any other chance boy might have come—as a kind of servant, to gratify a want or a whim, and to be paid for it?"

"Aye, Pip," replied Miss Havisham, steadily nodding her head, "you did."

"And that Mr. Jaggers—"

"Mr. Jaggers," said Miss Havisham, taking me up in a firm tone, "had nothing to do with it, and knew nothing of it. His being my lawyer, and his being the lawyer of your patron is a coincidence."

"But when I fell into the mistake I have so long remained in, at least you led me on?" said I.

"Yes," she returned, again nodding steadily, "I let you go on."

"Was that kind?"

"Who am I," cried Miss Havisham, striking her stick upon the floor and flashing into wrath so suddenly that Estella glanced up at her in surprise, "who am I that I should be kind?"

"I was liberally paid for my old attendance here," I said, to soothe her, "in being apprenticed, and I have asked these questions only for my own information. What follows has another purpose. In humoring my mistake, Miss Havisham, you punished your self-seeking relations?"

"I did. Why, they would have it so! So would you. You made your own snares. *I* never made them."

Waiting until she was quiet again—for this, too, flashed out of her in a wild and sudden way—I went on.

"I have been thrown among one family of your relations, Miss Havisham, since I went to London. And I should be false and base if I did not tell you that you deeply wrong both Mr. Matthew Pocket and his son Herbert, if you suppose them to be otherwise than generous, upright, open, and incapable of anything designing or mean."

"They are your friends," said Miss Havisham.

"They made themselves my friends," said I, "when Sarah Pocket, Miss Georgiana, and Mistress Camilla were not my friends, I think."

This contrasting of them with the rest seemed, I was glad to see, to do them good with her. She looked at me keenly for a little while, and then said quietly:

"What do you want for them?"

"I do want something, Miss Havisham. If you could spare the money to do my friend Herbert a lasting service in life, but which from the nature of the case must be done without his knowledge, I could show you how."

"Why must it be done without his knowledge?" she asked, settling her hands upon her stick that she might regard me the more attentively.

"Because," said I, "I began the service myself, more than two years ago, without his knowledge, and I don't want to be betrayed. Why I fail in my ability to finish it, I cannot explain. It is a part of the secret which is another person's and not mine."

"What else?"

"Estella," said I, turning to her now, and trying to command my trembling voice, "you know I love you. You know that I have loved you long and dearly."

She raised her eyes to my face on being thus addressed, and her fingers plied their work, and she looked at me with an unmoved countenance. I saw that Miss Havisham glanced from me to her, and from her to me.

"I should have said this sooner, but for my long mistake. It induced me to hope that Miss Havisham meant us for one another. But I must say it now."

Preserving her unmoved countenance, and with her fingers still going, Estella shook her head.

"I know," said I, in answer to that action; "I know. I have no hope that I shall ever call you mine, Estella. I am ignorant what may become of me very soon, how poor I may be, or where I may go. Still, I love you. I have loved you ever since I first saw you in this house."

Looking at me perfectly unmoved and with her fingers busy, she shook her head again.

"It would have been cruel in Miss Havisham to torture me through all these years with a vain hope and an idle pursuit, if she had reflected on the gravity of what she did. But I think she did not. I think that in the endurance of her own trial, she forgot mine, Estella."

I saw Miss Havisham put her hand to her heart and hold it there, as she sat looking by turns at Estella and at me.

"It seems," said Estella very calmly, "that there are sentiments, fancies—I don't know how to call them—which I am not able to comprehend. When you say you love me, I know what you mean, as a form of words, but nothing more. You address nothing in my breast, you touch nothing there."

"Is it not true," said I, "that Bentley Drummle is in town here, and pursuing you?"

"It is quite true," she replied, referring to him with the indifference of utter contempt.

"That you encourage him, and ride out with him, and that he dines with you this very day?"

She seemed a little surprised that I should know it, but again replied, "Quite true."

"You cannot love him, Estella?"

Her fingers stopped for the first time, as she retorted rather angrily, "What have I told you? Do you still think, in spite of it, that I do not mean what I say?"

"You would never marry him, Estella?"

She looked toward Miss Havisham. Then she said, "Why not tell you the truth? I am going to be married to him."

I dropped my face into my hands, but was able to control myself better than I could have expected, considering what agony it gave me to hear her say those words.

"Estella, dearest, dearest Estella, do not let Miss Havisham lead you into this fatal step. Put me aside forever—you have done so, I well know—but bestow yourself on some worthier person than Drummle. Miss Havisham gives you to him, as the greatest slight and injury that could be done to the many far better men who admire you, and to the few who truly love you. Among those few, there may be one who loves you even as dearly, though he has not loved you as long, as I. Take him, and I can bear it better for your sake!"

My earnestness awoke a wonder in her.

"I am going," she said again, in a gentler voice, "to be married to him. The preparations for my marriage are making, and I shall be married soon. Why do you injuriously introduce the name of my mother by adoption? It is my own act."

"Your own act, Estella, to fling yourself away upon a brute?"

"On whom should I fling myself away?" she retorted, with a smile. "Should I fling myself away upon the man who would the soonest feel that I took nothing to him? I shall do well enough, and so will my husband. As to leading me into what you call this fatal step, Miss Havisham would have had me wait, and not marry yet; but I am tired of the life I have led, which has very few charms for me, and I am willing enough to change it. Say no more. We shall never understand each other."

"Such a mean brute, such a stupid brute!" I urged in despair.

"Don't be afraid of my being a blessing to him," said Estella. "I shall not be that. Come! Here is my hand."

"Oh, Estella!" I answered, as my bitter tears fell fast on her hand, do what I would to restrain them. "Even if I remained in England and could hold my head up with the rest, how could I see you Drummle's wife?"

"Nonsense," she returned, "nonsense. This will pass in no time."

"Never, Estella!"

"You will get me out of your thoughts in a week."

"Out of my thoughts! You are part of my existence, part of myself. You have been in every line I have ever read, since I first came here, the rough common boy whose poor heart you wounded even then. Estella, to the last hour of my life, you cannot choose but remain part of my character, part of the little good in me, part of the evil. But I associate you only with the good, for you must have done me far more good than harm. Oh, God bless you, God forgive you!"

I held her hand to my lips some lingering moments, and so I left her. But ever afterward, I remembered that the spectral figure of Miss Havisham, her hand still covering her heart, seemed all resolved into a ghastly stare of pity and remorse.

It was past midnight when I crossed London Bridge. I was not expected till tomorrow, but I had my keys, and, if Herbert were gone to bed, could get to bed myself without disturbing him.

The night porter examined me with much attention as he held the gate a little way open for me to pass in. To help his memory I mentioned my name.

"I was not quite sure, sir, but I thought so. Here's a note, sir. The messenger that brought it said would you be so good as to read it by my lantern?"

Much surprised by the request, I took the note. It was directed to Philip Pip, Esquire, and on the top of the superscription were the words, "PLEASE READ THIS HERE." I opened it, the watchman holding up his light, and read inside, in Wemmick's writing:

"DON'T GO HOME."

CHAPTER 33

*Pip meets Clara,
Herbert's fiancée*

TURNING from the Temple gate as soon as I had read the warning, I made the best of the way to Fleet Street, and there got a late hackney chariot and drove to the Hummums in Covent Garden. In those times a bed was always to be got there at any hour of the night, and the chamberlain, letting me in at his ready wicket, lighted the candle next in order on his shelf, and showed me straight into the bedroom next on his list.

What a doleful night! How anxious, how dismal, how long! The closet whispered, the fireplace sighed, the little washing-stand ticked, and one guitar string played occasionally in the chest of drawers. Why I was not to go home, and what had happened at home, and when I should go home, and whether Provis was safe at home, were questions occupying my mind so busily that one night have supposed there could be no more room in it for any other theme. Even when I thought of Estella, and how we had parted that day forever, I was pursuing here and there and everywhere the caution DON'T GO HOME. At last I dozed, in sheer exhaustion of mind and body.

I had left directions that I was to be called at seven; for it was plain that I must see Wemmick before seeing anyone else, and equally plain that this was a case in which his Walworth sentiments only could be taken.

The Castle battlements arose upon my view at eight o'clock. The little servant happening to be entering the fortress with two hot rolls, I crossed the drawbridge in her company and so came without announcement into the presence of Wemmick as he was making tea for himself and the Aged.

"Halloa, Mr. Pip!" said Wemmick. "You did come home, then?"

"Yes," I returned, "but I didn't go home."

"That's all right," said he, rubbing his hands. "I left a note for you at each of the Temple gates, on the chance. Which gate did you come to?"

I told him.

"I'll go round to the others in the course of the day and destroy the notes," said Wemmick. "It's a good rule never to leave documentary evidence if you can help it. Now, Mr. Pip, you and I understand one another. I accidentally heard, yesterday morning, that a certain person not altogether of uncolonial pursuits, and not unpossessed of portable property—we won't name this person—"

"Not necessary," said I.

"—had made some little stir in a certain part of the world where a good many people go, not always in gratification of their own inclination, by disappearing from such place and being no more heard of thereabouts. I also have heard that you at your chambers in Garden Court, Temple had been watched, and might be watched again."

"By whom?" said I.

"I wouldn't go into that," said Wemmick evasively. "It might clash with official responsibilities. I heard it."

As I saw that he was restrained by fealty to Little Britain from saying as much as he could, I could not press him. But I told him, after a little meditation over the fire, that I would like to ask him a question, subject to his answering or not answering, as he deemed right.

"You have heard of a man of bad character, whose true name is Compeyson?"

He answered with one nod.

"Is he living?"

One other nod.

"Is he in London?"

He gave me one last nod and went on with his breakfast.

"Now," said Wemmick, "questioning being over," which he emphasized and repeated for my guidance; "I come to what I did, after hearing what I heard. I went to Garden Court to find you; not finding you, I went to Clarriker's to find Mr. Herbert."

"And him you found?" said I, with great anxiety.

"And I found him. Without mentioning any names or going into any details, I gave him to understand that if he was aware of anybody—Tom, Jack, or Richard—being about the chambers, or about the immediate neighborhood, he had better get Tom, Jack, or Richard out of the way while you were out of the way."

"He would be greatly puzzled what to do?"

"He *was* puzzled what to do; not the less because I gave him my opinion that it was not safe to try to get Tom, Jack, or Richard too far out of the way at present. Mr. Pip, I'll tell you something. Under existing circumstances there is no place like a great city when you are once in it. Don't break cover too soon. Lie close. Wait till things slacken before you try the open, even for foreign air."

I thanked him for his valuable advice, and asked him what Herbert had done.

"Mr. Herbert," said Wemmick, "after being all of a heap for half an hour, struck out a plan. He mentioned to me as a secret that he is courting a young lady who has, as no doubt you are aware, a bedridden pa. Which pa, having been in the purser line of life, lies a-bed in a bow window where he can see the ships sail up and down the river. You are acquainted with the young lady, most probably?"

"Not personally," said I.

"The house with the bow window," said Wemmick, "being kept, it seems, by a very respectable widow, who has a furnished upper floor to let, Mr. Herbert put it to me, what did I think of that as a temporary tenement for Tom, Jack, or Richard? Now, I thought very well of it, for three reasons. Firstly. It is well away from the usual heap of streets. Secondly. Without going near it yourself, you could always hear of the safety of Tom, Jack, or Richard, through Mr. Herbert. Thirdly. After a while, and when it might be pru-

dent, if you should want to slip Tom, Jack, or Richard on board a foreign packet boat,[1] there he is—ready."

Much comforted by these considerations, I thanked Wemmick again and again, and begged him to proceed.

"Well, sir! Mr. Herbert threw himself into the business with a will, and by nine o'clock last night he housed Tom, Jack, or Richard—whichever it may be—you and I don't want to know—quite successfully. At the old lodgings it was understood that he was summoned to Dover. Now, another advantage of all this is that it was done without you. This diverts suspicion and confuses it, and you want confusion."

Wemmick, having finished his breakfast, here looked at his watch, and began to get his coat on.

"And now, Mr. Pip," said he, with his hands still in the sleeves, "I have probably done the most I can do. Here's the address. There can be no harm in your going here tonight and seeing for yourself that all is well with Tom, Jack, or Richard, before you go home. I must be off. If you had nothing more pressing to do than to keep here till dark that's what I should advise."

I soon fell asleep before Wemmick's fire, and the Aged and I enjoyed one another's society by falling asleep before it more or less all day. Eight o'clock had struck before I got into the air that was scented, not disagreeably, by the chips and shavings of the longshore boatbuilders, and mast, oar, and blockmakers. All that waterside region of the upper and lower Pool below London Bridge was unknown ground to me, and when I struck down by the river, I found that the spot I wanted was anything but easy to find. It

---

[1] **packet boat:** a steamship which carried mail and passengers along a regular route, in this instance, from England to the Continent.

was called Mill Pond Bank, Chinks's Basin; and I had no other guide to Chinks's Basin than the Old Green Copper Rope-Walk.

Selecting from the few queer houses upon Mill Pond Bank a house with a wooden front and three stories of bow window, I looked at the plate upon the door, and read there Mrs. Whimple. That being the name I wanted, I knocked, and an elderly woman of a pleasant and thriving appearance responded. She was immediately deposed, however, by Herbert, who silently led me into the parlor and shut the door.

"All is well, Handel," said Herbert, "and he is quite satisfied, though eager to see you. My dear girl is with her father, and if you'll wait till she comes down, I'll make you known to her, and then we'll go upstairs.—*That's* her father."

I had become aware of an alarming growling overhead, and had probably expressed the fact in my countenance.

"I am afraid he is a sad old rascal," said Herbert, smiling, "but I have never seen him. Don't you smell rum? He is always at it." While he thus spoke, the growling noise became a prolonged roar, and died away.

"To have Provis for an upper lodger is quite a godsend to Mrs. Whimple," said Herbert, "for of course people in general won't stand that noise."

As we were thus conversing, a very pretty, slight, dark-eyed girl of twenty or so came in with a basket in her hand: whom Herbert tenderly relieved of the basket, and presented, blushing, as "Clara." There was something confiding, loving, and innocent in her modest manner of yielding herself to Herbert's embracing arm. I was looking at her with pleasure and admiration when suddenly the growl swelled into a roar again, and a frightful bumping noise was heard above,

as if a giant with a wooden leg were trying to bore it through the ceiling to come at us. Upon this, Clara said to Herbert, "Papa wants me, darling!" and ran away.

Clara returned soon afterward, and Herbert accompanied me upstairs to see our charge. I found Provis comfortably settled. He expressed no alarm, and seemed to feel none that was worth mentioning; but it struck me that he was softened—indefinably, for I could not have said how.

The opportunity that the day's rest had given me for reflection had resulted in my fully determining to say nothing to him respecting Compeyson. For anything I knew, his animosity toward the man might otherwise lead to his seeking him out and rushing on his own destruction. Therefore, when Herbert and I sat down with him by his fire, I asked him first of all whether he relied on Wemmick's judgment and sources of information.

"Aye, aye, dear boy!" he answered with a grave nod. "Jaggers knows."

"Then I have talked with Wemmick," said I, "and have come to tell you what caution he gave me and what advice."

I told him how Wemmick had heard in Newgate Prison that he was under some suspicion, and that my chambers had been watched; how Wemmick had recommended his keeping close for a time, and my keeping away from him; and what Wemmick had said about getting him abroad. I added that of course I should go with him. What was to follow that, I did not touch upon; neither indeed was I at all clear or comfortable about it in my own mind, now that I saw him in that softer condition, and in declared peril for my sake.

He was very reasonable throughout. His coming back was a venture, he said, and he had always known it to be a venture, and he had very little fear of his safety with such good help.

Herbert, who had been looking at the fire and pondering, here said, "We are both good watermen, Handel, and could take him down the river ourselves when the right time comes. No boat would then be hired for the purpose, and no boatmen; that would save at least a chance of suspicion, and any chance is worth saving. Don't you think it might be a good thing if you began at once to keep a boat at the Temple stairs, and were in the habit of rowing up and down the river? You fall into that habit, and then who notices or minds? Do it twenty or fifty times, and there is nothing special in your doing it the twenty-first or fifty-first."

I liked this scheme, and Provis was quite elated by it. We agreed that it should be carried into execution, and that Provis should never recognize us if we came below Bridge and rowed past Mill Pond Bank. But we further agreed that he should pull down the blind in that part of his window which faced upon the east whenever he saw us and all was right.

Our conference being now ended, and everything arranged, I rose to go, remarking to Herbert that he and I had better not go home together, and that I would take half an hour's start of him. "I don't like to leave you here," I said to Provis, "though I cannot doubt your being safer here than near me. Good-by!"

"Dear boy," he answered, clasping my hands, "I don't know when we may meet again, and I don't like good-by. Say good night!"

"Good night! Herbert will go regularly between us, and when the time comes, you may be certain I shall be ready. Good night, good night!" Looking back at him, I thought of the first night of his return, when our positions were reversed, and when I little supposed my heart could ever be as heavy and anxious at parting from him as it was now.

Next day, I set myself to get the boat. It was soon done, and the boat was brought round to the Temple stairs, and lay where I could reach her within a minute or two. Then I began to go out as for training and practice, sometimes alone, sometimes with

Herbert. I was often out in cold, rain, and sleet, but nobody took much note of me after I had been out a few times. At first, I kept above Blackfriars Bridge; but as the hours of the tide changed, I took toward London Bridge. The first time I passed Mill Pond Bank, Herbert and I were pulling a pair of oars; and, both in going and returning, we saw the blind toward the east come down. Herbert was rarely there less frequently than three times in a week, and he never brought me a single word of intelligence that was at all alarming.

Still, I was always full of fears for the rash man who was in hiding. Herbert had sometimes said to me that he found it pleasant to stand at one of our windows after dark, when the tide was running down, and to think that it was flowing, with everything it bore, toward Clara. But I thought with dread that it was flowing toward Magwitch, and that any black mark on its surface might be his pursuers, going swiftly, silently, and surely to take him.

CHAPTER 34

*Wemmick tells Pip
the story of Molly.*

Some weeks passed without bringing any change. We waited for Wemmick, and he made no sign. My worldly affairs began to wear a gloomy appearance, and I was pressed for money by more than one creditor. Even I myself began to know the want of ready money in my own pocket, and to relieve it by converting some easily spared articles of jewelry into cash. But I had quite determined that it would be a heartless fraud to take more money from my patron in the existing state of my uncertain thoughts and plans. Therefore, I had sent him the unopened pocketbook by Herbert, to hold in his own keeping, and I felt a kind of satisfaction in not having profited by his generosity since his revelation of himself.

It was an unhappy life that I lived. Condemned to inaction and a state of constant restlessness and suspense, I rowed about in my boat, and waited, waited, waited, as I best could.

One afternoon, late in February, I came ashore at the wharf at dusk. I had pulled down as far as Greenwich with the ebb tide and had turned with the tide. It had been a fine bright day, but had become foggy as the sun dropped, and I had had to feel my way back among the shipping pretty carefully. Both in going and returning, I had seen the signal in his window, all well.

I had strolled up into Cheapside when a large hand was laid upon my shoulder, by someone overtaking me. It was Mr. Jaggers' hand, and he passed it through my arm.

"As we are going in the same direction, Pip, we may walk together. Come and dine with me."

I was going to excuse myself, when he added, "Wemmick's coming." So I changed my excuse into an acceptance.

We went to Gerrard Street, all three together, and as soon as we got there, dinner was served.

"Did you send that note of Miss Havisham's to Mr. Pip, Wemmick?" Mr. Jaggers asked, soon after we began dinner.

"No, sir," returned Wemmick; "it was going by post, when you brought Mr. Pip into the office. Here it is." He handed it to his principal, instead of to me.

"It's a note of two lines, Pip," said Mr. Jaggers, handing it on, "sent up to me by Miss Havisham, on account of her not being sure of your address. She tells me that she wants to see you on a little matter of business you mentioned to her. You'll go down?"

"Yes," said I, casting my eyes over the note, which was exactly in those terms.

"When do you think of going down?"

"I have an impending engagement," said I, glancing at Wemmick, "that renders me rather uncertain of my time. At once, I think."

"If Mr. Pip has the intention of going at once," said Wemmick to Mr. Jaggers, "he needn't write an answer, you know."

Receiving this as an intimation that it was best not to delay, I settled that I would go tomorrow, and said so. Wemmick drank a glass of wine and looked with a grimly satisfied air at Mr. Jaggers, but not at me.

"So, Pip! Our friend the Spider," said Mr. Jaggers, "has played his cards. He has won the pool."

It was as much as I could do to assent.

"So, here's to Mrs. Bentley Drummle," said Mr. Jaggers, taking a decanter of choicer wine from his dumbwaiter, and filling for each of us and for himself. "Now, Molly, Molly, Molly, Molly, how slow you are today!"

She was at his elbow when he addressed her, putting a dish upon the table. As she withdrew her hands from it, she fell back a step or two, nervously muttering some excuse. And a certain action of her fingers as she spoke arrested my attention.

"What's the matter?" said Mr. Jaggers.

"Nothing. Only the subject we were speaking of," said I, "was rather painful to me."

The action of her fingers was like the action of knitting. She stood looking at her master, not understanding whether she was free to go, or whether he had more to say to her and would call her back if she did go. Her look was very intent. Surely, I had seen exactly such eyes and such hands on a memorable occasion very lately!

He dismissed her, and she glided out of the room. But she remained before me, as plainly as if she were still there. I looked at those hands, I looked at those eyes, I looked at that flowing hair; and I compared them with other hands, other eyes, other hair, that I knew of, and with what those might be after twenty years of a brutal husband and a stormy life. I looked again at those hands and eyes of the housekeeper. And I felt absolutely certain that this woman was Estella's mother. Only twice more did the housekeeper reappear, and then her stay in the room was very short, and Mr. Jaggers was sharp with her. But her hands were Estella's hands, and her eyes were Estella's eyes, and if she had reappeared a hundred times I could have been neither more sure nor less sure that my conviction was the truth.

Wemmick and I took our leave early, and left together. I asked him if he had ever seen Miss Havisham's adopted daughter, Mrs. Bentley Drummle? He said no. To avoid being too abrupt, I then spoke of the Aged, and of Miss Skiffins. He looked rather sly when I mentioned Miss Skiffins.

"Wemmick," said I, "do you remember telling me, before I first went to Mr. Jaggers' private house, to notice that housekeeper?"

"Did I?" he replied. "Ah, I dare say I did."

"I wish you would tell me her story. I feel a particular interest in being acquainted with it. You know that what is said between you and me goes no further."

"Well!" Wemmick replied. "I don't know her story—that is, I don't know all of it. But what I do know, I'll tell you. We are in our private and personal capacities, of course."

"Of course."

"A score or so of years ago that woman was tried at the Old Bailey for murder and was acquitted. She was a very handsome young woman, and I believe had some gypsy blood in her. Anyhow, it was hot enough when it was up, as you may suppose."

"But she was acquitted."

"Mr. Jaggers was for her," pursued Wemmick, with a look full of meaning, "and worked the case in a way quite astonishing. It was a desperate case. The murdered person was a woman, a good ten years older, very much larger, and very much stronger. It was a case of jealousy. They both led tramping lives, and this woman in Gerrard Street here had been married very young to a tramping man, and was a perfect fury in point of jealousy. The murdered woman—more a match for the man, certainly, in point of years—was found dead in a barn. There had been a violent struggle, perhaps a fight. She was bruised and scratched and torn, and had been held by the throat at last and choked. Now, there was no reasonable evidence to implicate any person but this woman, and on the physical improbabilities of her having been able to do it, Mr. Jaggers principally rested his case. You may be sure," said Wemmick, touching me on the sleeve, "that he never dwelt upon the strength of her hands then, though he sometimes does now."

I had told Wemmick of his showing us her wrists that day of the dinner party.

"Well, sir!" Wemmick went on. "This woman was so artfully dressed from the time of her apprehension that she looked much slighter than she really was; her sleeves are always remembered to have been so skillfully contrived that her arms had a delicate look. But the backs of her hands were lacerated, and the question was, was it with fingernails? Now, Mr. Jaggers showed that she had struggled through a great lot of brambles which she could not have got through and kept her hands out of; and bits of those brambles were actually found in her skin and put in evidence. But the boldest point he made was this. It was attempted to be set up in proof of her jealousy that she was under strong suspicion of having, at about the time of the murder, frantically destroyed her child by this man—some three years old—to revenge herself upon him. Mr. Jaggers worked that in this way. 'We say these are not marks of fingernails, but marks of brambles, and we show you the brambles. You say they are marks of fingernails, and you set up the hypothesis that she destroyed her child. You must accept all consequences of that hypothesis. For anything we know, she may have destroyed her child, and the child in clinging to her may have scratched her hands. What then? You are not trying her for the murder of her child; why don't you? As to this case, if you *will* have scratches, we say that, for anything we know, you may have accounted for them, assuming for the sake of argument that you have not invented them.' To sum up, sir," added Wemmick, "Mr. Jaggers was altogether too many for the jury, and they gave in."

"Has she been in his service ever since?"

"Yes," said Wemmick, "she went into his service immediately after her acquittal, tamed as she is now."

"Do you remember the sex of the child?"

"Said to have been a girl."

"You have nothing more to say to me tonight?"

"Nothing."

We exchanged a cordial good night, and went home, with new matter for my thoughts, though with no relief from the old.

CHAPTER 35

*Pip visits Miss Havisham
for the last time.*

PUTTING Miss Havisham's note in my
pocket, I went down by coach next day.
The best light of the day had gone
when I passed the High Street. The cathedral chimes had at once a sadder and more
remote sound to me; they seemed to call
to me that the place was changed, and that
Estella was gone out of it forever.

Miss Havisham was not in her own
room, but was in the larger room across
the landing. Looking in at the door, after
knocking in vain, I saw her sitting on the
hearth in a ragged chair, close before the
ashy fire. I went in and stood where she
could see me when she raised her eyes.
There was an air of utter loneliness upon
her. As I stood compassionating her, and
thinking how in the progress of time I too
had come to be a part of the wrecked fortunes of that house, her eyes rested on me.
She stared and said in a low voice, "Is it
real?"

"It is I, Pip. Mr. Jaggers gave me your
note yesterday, and I have lost no time."

"Thank you. Thank you."

"I want," she said, "to pursue that subject you mentioned to me when you were
last here, and to show you that I am not
all stone. You said, speaking for your
friend, that you could tell me how to do
something useful and good. Something
that you would like done, is it not?"

"Something that I would like done very,
very much."

"What is it?"

I began explaining to her that secret
history of the partnership. I told her how
I had hoped to complete the transaction
out of my means, but how in this I was
disappointed.

"So!" said she, assenting with her head,
but not looking at me. "And how much
money is wanting to complete the purchase?"

I was rather afraid of stating it, for it
sounded a large sum. "Nine hundred
pounds."

"If I give you the money for this purpose, will you keep my secret as you have
kept your own?"

"Quite as faithfully."

"And your mind will be more at rest?"

"Much more at rest."

"Are you very unhappy now?"

"I am far from happy, Miss Havisham;
but I have other causes of disquiet than
any you know of. They are the secrets I
have mentioned."

After a little while, she raised her head
and looked at the fire again.

"Can I only serve you, Pip, by serving
your friend? Regarding that as done, is
there nothing I can do for you yourself?"

"Nothing. I thank you for the question.
I thank you even more for the tone of the
question. But, there is nothing."

She presently rose from her seat and
looked about for the means of writing.
There were none there, and she took from
her pocket a yellow set of ivory tablets,
mounted in tarnished gold, and wrote
upon them with a pencil in a case of tarnished gold that hung from her neck.

"You are still on friendly terms with
Mr. Jaggers?"

"Quite. I dined with him yesterday."

"This is an authority to him to pay you
that money, to lay out at your discretion
for your friend. I keep no money here; but
if you would rather Mr. Jaggers knew
nothing of the matter, I will send it to
you."

"Thank you, Miss Havisham; I have
not the least objection to receiving it from
him."

She read me what she had written, and

it was direct and clear, and evidently intended to absolve me from any suspicion of profiting by the receipt of the money. I took the tablets from her hand and it trembled as she took off the chain to which the pencil was attached, and put it in mine.

"My name is on the first leaf. If you can ever write under my name, 'I forgive her,' though ever so long after my broken heart is dust—pray do it!"

"Oh, Miss Havisham," said I, "I can do it now. I want forgiveness and direction far too much to be bitter with you."

She turned her face to me for the first time since she had averted it, and to my amazement, I may even add to my terror, dropped on her knees at my feet with her folded hands raised. To see her with her white hair and her worn face, kneeling at my feet, gave me a shock through all my frame.

"Oh!" she cried despairingly. "What have I done! What have I done!"

"If you mean, Miss Havisham, what have you done to injure me, let me answer. Very little. I should have loved her under any circumstances. Is she married?"

"Yes!"

It was a needless question, for a new desolation in the desolate house had told me so.

"What have I done! What have I done!" She wrung her hands, and crushed her white hair, and returned to this cry over and over again. "What have I done! Until you spoke to her the other day, and until I saw in you a looking glass that showed me what I once felt myself, I did not know what I had done. What have I done! What have I done!"

"Miss Havisham," I said, when her cry had died away, "you may dismiss me from your mind and conscience. But Estella is a different case, and if you can ever undo any scrap of what you have done amiss in keeping a part of her right nature away from her, it will be better to do that than to bemoan the past through a hundred years."

"Yes, yes, I know it. But, Pip—my dear!" There was an earnest womanly compassion for me in her new affection. "My dear! Believe this: when she first came to me, I meant to save her from misery like my own. At first I meant no more. But as she grew, and promised to be very beautiful, I gradually did worse, and with my praises, and with my jewels, and with my teachings, I stole her heart away and put ice in its place."

"Better," I could not help saying, "to have left her a natural heart, even to be bruised or broken."

"If you knew all my story," she pleaded, "you would have some compassion for me and a better understanding of me."

"Miss Havisham," I answered, as delicately as I could, "I believe I may say that I do know your story, and have known it ever since I first left this neighborhood. Does what has passed between us give me any excuse for asking you a question relative to Estella?"

She was seated on the ground, with her arms on the ragged chair, and her head leaning on them. She looked full at me and replied, "Go on."

"Whose child was Estella?"

She shook her head.

"You don't know?"

She shook her head again.

"But Mr. Jaggers brought her here, or sent her here?"

"Brought her here."

"Will you tell me how that came about?"

She answered in a low whisper and with caution, "I had been shut up in these rooms a long time when I told him that I wanted a little girl to rear and love, and save from my fate. He told me that he would look about him for such an orphan child. One night he brought her here asleep, and I called her Estella."

"Might I ask her age then?"

"Two or three. She herself knows nothing, but that she was left an orphan and I adopted her."

So convinced I was of that woman's being her mother that I wanted no evidence to establish the fact in my mind. But, to any mind, the connection here was clear and straight.

What more could I hope to do by prolonging the interview? I had succeeded on behalf of Herbert, Miss Havisham had told me all she knew of Estella, I had said and done what I could to ease her mind.

Twilight was closing in when I went downstairs into the natural air. I called to the woman who had opened the gate when I entered that I would not trouble her just yet, but would walk round the place before leaving. For I had a presentiment that I should never be there again, and I felt that the dying light was suited to my last view of it.

I made my way to the ruined garden. I went all round it; round by the corner where Herbert and I had fought our battle; round by the paths where Estella and I had walked. So cold, so lonely, so dreary all!

Passing on into the front courtyard, I hesitated whether to call the woman to let me out at the locked gate, of which she had the key, or first to go upstairs and assure myself that Miss Havisham was as safe and well as I had left her. I took the latter course and went up.

I looked into the room where I had left her, and I saw her seated in the ragged chair upon the hearth close to the fire, with her back toward me. In the moment when I was withdrawing my head to go quietly away, I saw a great flaming light spring up. In the same moment I saw her

running at me, shrieking, with a whirl of fire blazing all about her, and soaring at least as many feet above her head as she was high.

I had a double-caped greatcoat on, and over my arm another thick coat. I got them off, closed with her, threw her down, and got them over her; I dragged the great cloth from the table for the same purpose, and with it dragged down the heap of rottenness in the midst and all the ugly things that sheltered there. The closer I covered her, the more wildly she shrieked and tried to free herself. I knew that we were on the floor by the great table, and

that patches of tinder yet alight were floating in the smoky air, which a moment ago
had been her faded bridal dress.

Then I looked round and saw the disturbed beetles and spiders running away
over the floor, and the servants coming in
with breathless cries at the door. She was
insensible, and I was afraid to have her
moved, or even touched. Assistance was
sent for, and I held her until it came, as if
I unreasonably fancied that if I let her
go, the fire would break out again and
consume her. When I got up, on the surgeon's coming to her with other aid, I was
astonished to see that both my hands
were burned; for I had no knowledge of
it through the sense of feeling.

On examination it was pronounced that
she had received serious hurts, but that
the danger lay mainly in the nervous
shock. By the surgeon's directions, her
bed was carried into that room and laid
upon the great table, which happened to
be well suited to the dressing of her injuries. When I saw her again, an hour
afterward, she lay indeed where I had
seen her strike her stick, and had heard
her say she would lie one day.

Toward midnight she began to wander
in her speech and said innumerable times,
in a low solemn voice, "What have I
done!" And then, "When she first came,
I meant to save her from misery like
mine." And then, "Take the pencil and
write under my name, 'I forgive her'!"
She never changed the order of these
three sentences.

As I could do no service there, and as
I had, nearer home, that pressing reason
for anxiety and fear, I decided that I
would return by the early morning coach.
At about six o'clock of the morning, therefore, I leaned over her and touched her
lips with mine, just as they said, "Take
the pencil and write under my name, 'I
forgive her.'"

CHAPTER 36

Pip hears more about Provis.

My HANDS had been dressed twice or
thrice in the night, and again in the morning. My left arm was a good deal burned to
the elbow, and less severely as high as the
shoulder; it was very painful, but I felt
thankful it was no worse. My right hand
was not so badly burned but that I could
move the fingers. My left hand and arm I
carried in a sling; and I could only wear
my coat like a cloak, loose over my shoulders and fastened at the neck.

Herbert devoted the day to attending
on me. He was the kindest of nurses, and
at stated times took off the bandages and
steeped them in the cooling liquid that
was kept ready, and put them on again,
with a patient tenderness that I was
deeply grateful for.

Neither of us spoke of the boat, but we
thought of it. That was made apparent by
our avoidance of the subject and by our
agreeing—without agreement—to make
my recovery of the use of my hands a
question of so many hours, not of so many
weeks.

My first question when I saw Herbert
had been, of course, whether all was well
down the river.

"I sat with Provis last night, Handel,
two good hours. Do you know, Handel,
he improves?"

"I said to you I thought he was softened
when I last saw him."

"So you did. And so he is. He was
very communicative last night, and told
me more of his life. You remember his
breaking off here about some woman that
he had had great trouble with? He went
into that part of his life, and a dark wild
part it is. Shall I tell you?"

"Tell me by all means!"

"It seems, that the woman was a young woman, and a jealous woman, and a revengeful woman; revengeful, Handel, to the last degree."

"To what last degree?"

"Murder! She was tried for it, and Mr. Jaggers defended her, and the reputation of that defense first made his name known to Provis. It was another and a stronger woman who was the victim, and there had been a struggle—in a barn."

"Was the woman brought in guilty?"

"No; she was acquitted. This acquitted young woman and Provis had a little child, a little child of whom Provis was exceedingly fond. On the evening of the very night when the object of her jealousy was strangled, the young woman presented herself before Provis for one moment, and swore that she would destroy the child (which was in her possession), and he should never see it again; then she vanished. You don't think your breathing is affected, my dear boy? You seem to breathe quickly."

"Perhaps I do, Herbert. Did the woman keep her oath?"

"There comes the darkest part of Provis' life. She did."

"That is, he says she did."

Why, of course, my dear boy," returned Herbert, in a tone of surprise, and again bending forward to get a nearer look at me. "He says it all. I have no other information."

"No, to be sure."

"Now, whether," pursued Herbert, "he had used the child's mother ill or well, Provis doesn't say; but she had shared some four or five years of the wretched life he described to us at this fireside, and he seems to have felt pity for her. Therefore, fearing he should be called upon to depose [1] about this destroyed child, and

so be the cause of her death, he hid himself (much as he grieved for the child), kept himself dark, as he says, out of the way and out of the trial, and was only vaguely talked of as a certain man called Abel, out of whom the jealousy arose. After the acquittal she disappeared, and thus he lost the child and the child's mother."

"I want to ask—"

"A moment, my dear boy, and I have done. That evil genius, Compeyson, the worst of scoundrels, knowing of his keeping out of the way at that time, of course afterward held the knowledge over his head as a means of keeping him poorer and working him harder."

"I want to know," said I, "and particularly, Herbert, whether he told you when this happened?"

"Particularly? Let me remember, then, what he said as to that. His expression was, 'a round score o' year ago, and a'most directly after I took up wi' Compeyson.' How old were you when you came upon him in the little churchyard?"

"I think in my seventh year."

"Aye. It had happened some three or four years then, he said, and you brought into his mind the little girl so tragically lost, who would have been about your age."

"Herbert," said I, after a short silence, "the man we have hiding down the river is Estella's father."

CHAPTER 37

Pip receives a mysterious letter.

EARLY next morning I took my way to Little Britain. Although I had sent Mr. Jaggers a brief account of the accident as soon as I had arrived in town, yet I had

---

[1] **depose** (di·pōz′): testify under oath.

to give him all the details now. My narrative finished, I then produced Miss Havisham's authority to receive the nine hundred pounds for Herbert. Mr. Jaggers' eyes retired a little deeper into his head when I handed him the tablets, but he presently handed them over to Wemmick with instructions to draw the check for his signature. From Little Britain I went, with my check in my pocket, to Miss Skiffins' brother, the accountant; and he going straight to Clarriker's and bringing Clarriker to me, I had the great satisfaction of concluding that arrangement. It was the only good thing I had done, and the only completed thing I had done, since I was first apprised of my great expectations.

Clarriker informed me that he would now be able to establish a small branch house in the East and that Herbert in his new partnership capacity would go out and take charge of it. And now indeed I felt as if my last anchor were loosening its hold, and I should soon be driving with the winds and waves.

We had now got into the month of March. My left arm took in the natural course so long to heal that I was still unable to get a coat on. My right arm was tolerably restored—disfigured, but fairly serviceable.

On a Monday morning, when Herbert and I were at breakfast, I received the following letter from Wemmick by the post.

Walworth. Burn this as soon as read. Early in the week, or say Wednesday, you might do what you know of, if you felt disposed to try it. Now burn.

When I had shown this to Herbert and had put it in the fire—but not before we had both got it by heart—we considered what to do. For, of course, my being disabled could now be no longer kept out of view.

"I have thought it over again and again," said Herbert, "and I think I know a better course than taking a Thames waterman. Take Startop. A good fellow, a skilled hand, fond of us, and enthusiastic and honorable."

I had thought of him more than once.

"But how much would you tell him, Herbert?"

"It is necessary to tell him very little. Let him suppose it a mere freak, but a secret one, until the morning comes; then let him know that there is urgent reason for your getting Provis aboard and away. You go with him?"

"No doubt."

"Where?"

It seemed to me almost indifferent what port we made for—Hamburg, Rotterdam, Antwerp—the place signified little, so that he was out of England. Any foreign steamer that fell in our way and would take us up would do. I had always proposed to myself to get him well down the river in the boat; certainly well beyond Gravesend, which was a critical place for search or inquiry if suspicion were afoot. As foreign steamers would leave London at about the time of high water, our plan would be to get down the river by a previous ebb tide, and lie by in some quiet spot until we could pull off to one. The time when one would be due where we lay, wherever that might be, could be calculated pretty nearly, if we made inquiries beforehand.

Herbert assented to all this, and we went out immediately after breakfast to pursue our investigations. We found that a steamer for Hamburg was likely to suit our purpose best, and we directed our thoughts chiefly to that vessel. But we noted down what other foreign steamers would leave London with the same tide, and we satisfied ourselves that we knew the build and color of each. We then separated for a few hours; I to get at once such passports as were necessary; Herbert, to see Startop at his lodgings. When we met again at one o'clock I, for my part, was prepared with passports; Herbert had seen Startop, and he was more than ready to join.

Those two would pull a pair of oars, we settled, and I would steer; our charge would be sitter, and keep quiet. We arranged that Herbert should prepare Provis to come down to some stairs hard by the house, on Wednesday, when he saw us approach, and not sooner; that all arrangements with him should be concluded that Monday night. These precautions well understood by both of us, I went home.

On opening the outer door of our chambers with my key, I found a letter in the box, directed to me—a very dirty letter, though not ill written. It had been delivered by hand and its contents were these:

If you are not afraid to come to the old marshes tonight or tomorrow night at nine, and to come to the little sluice house by the limekiln, you had better come. If you want information regarding *your uncle Provis,* you had better come and tell no one and lose no time. *You must come alone.* Bring this with you.

What to do now, I could not tell. And the worst was that I must decide quickly, or I should miss the afternoon coach, which would take me down in time for tonight. Tomorrow night I could not think of going, for it would be too close upon the time of the flight. For anything I knew, the information might have some important bearing on the flight itself. I resolved to go.

I had to read this mysterious epistle again, twice, before its injunction to me to be secret got into my mind. Yielding to it, I left a note in pencil to Herbert,

telling him that I had decided to hurry down and back to ascertain for myself how Miss Havisham was faring. I caught the coach just as it came out of the yard. I was the only inside passenger, jolting away knee-deep in straw. And now I began to wonder at myself for being in the coach, and to doubt whether I had sufficient reason for being there, and to consider whether I should get out presently and go back, and to argue against ever heeding an anonymous communication, and, in short, to pass through all those phases of contradiction and indecision to which I suppose very few hurried people are strangers. Still, the reference to Provis by name mastered everything. I reasoned that in case any harm should befall him through my not going, how could I ever forgive myself!

It was dark before we got down. Avoiding the Blue Boar, I put up at an inn of minor reputation down the town and ordered some dinner. While it was preparing, I went to Satis House and inquired for Miss Havisham; she was still very ill, though considered something better.

As I was not able to cut my dinner, the old landlord with a shining bald head did it for me. This bringing us into conversation, he was so good as to entertain me with my own story—of course with the popular feature that Pumblechook was my earliest benefactor and the founder of my fortunes.

"Do you know the young man?" said I.

"Know him?" repeated the landlord. "Ever since he was—no height at all."

"Does he ever come back to this neighborhood?"

"Aye, he comes back," said the landlord, "to his great friends, now and again, and gives the cold shoulder to the man that made him."

"What man is that?"

"Him that I speak of," said the land-

lord. "Mr. Pumblechook."

"Is he ungrateful to no one else?"

"No doubt he would be, if he could," returned the landlord, "but he can't. And why? Because Pumblechook done everything for him."

"Does Pumblechook say so?"

"Say so!" replied the landlord. "He han't no call to say so."

"But does he say so?"

"It would turn a man's blood to white wine winegar to hear him tell of it, sir," said the landlord.

I thought, "Yet Joe, dear Joe, *you* never tell of it. Long-suffering and loving Joe, *you* never complain. Nor you, sweet-tempered Biddy!"

I had never been struck at so keenly for my thanklessness to Joe, as through the brazen impostor Pumblechook. The falser he, the truer Joe; the meaner he, the nobler Joe.

My heart was deeply and most deservedly humbled as I mused over the fire for an hour or more. The striking of the clock aroused me, and I got up and had my coat fastened round my neck, and went out. I had previously sought in my pockets for the letter, that I might refer to it again, but I could not find it, and was uneasy to think that it must have been dropped in the straw of the coach. I knew very well, however, that the appointed place was the little sluice house by the limekiln on the marshes, and the hour nine. Toward the marshes I now went straight, having no time to spare.

CHAPTER 38

Trabb's boy leads a rescue party.

It was a dark night, there was a melancholy wind, and the marshes were very dismal. A stranger would have found them insupportable, and even to me they were so oppressive that I hesitated, half inclined to go back. It was a half hour before I drew near to the kiln. The lime was burning with a sluggish, stifling smell, but the fires were made up and left, and no workmen were visible. Hard by was a small stone quarry.

Coming up to the marsh level out of this excavation, I saw a light in the old sluice house. I quickened my pace and knocked at the door. There was no answer, and I knocked again. No answer still, and I tried the latch.

The door yielded. Looking in, I saw a lighted candle on a table, a bench, and a mattress on a truckle bedstead.[1] As there was a loft above, I called, "Is there anyone here?" but no voice answered. Then I looked at my watch, and finding that it was past nine, called again, "Is there anyone here?" There being still no answer, I went out at the door, irresolute what to do.

It was beginning to rain fast. Seeing nothing, I turned back into the house. While I was considering that someone must have been there lately and must soon be coming back, or the candle would not be burning, it came into my head to look if the wick were long. I had taken up the candle in my hand, when it was extinguished by some violent shock, and the next thing I comprehended was that I had been caught in a strong running noose, thrown over my head from behind.

"Now," said a suppressed voice with an oath, "I've got you!"

"What is this?" I cried, struggling. "Who is it? Help, help, help!"

Not only were my arms pulled close to my sides, but the pressure on my bad arm caused me exquisite pain. A strong man's hand was set against my mouth to deaden my cries, and with a hot breath always close to me, I struggled ineffectually in the dark until I was fastened tight to the wall. "And now," said the suppressed voice with another oath, "call out again, and I'll make short work of you!"

Faint and sick with pain, I tried to ease my arm, but I was bound too tight. After groping about for a little, he began to strike a light. Presently I saw his lips breathing on the tinder, and then a flare of light flashed up and showed me Orlick.

Whom I had looked for, I don't know. I had not looked for him. Seeing him, I felt that I was in a dangerous strait indeed, and I kept my eyes upon him.

He lighted the candle from the flaring match with great deliberation, and dropped the match, and trod it out. Then he put the candle away from him on the table, so that he could see me, and sat with his arms folded on the table, and looked at me. I made out that I was fastened to a stout perpendicular ladder a few inches from the wall—a fixture there—the means of ascent to the loft above.

"Now," said he, when we had surveyed one another for some time, "I've got you."

"Why have you lured me here?"

"Don't you know?" said he, with a deadly look.

"Why have you set upon me in the dark?"

"Because I mean to do it all myself. One keeps a secret better than two. Oh, you enemy, you enemy!"

His enjoyment of the spectacle I furnished, as he sat with his arms folded on the table, shaking his head at me, made me tremble. As I watched him in silence, he put his hand into the corner at his side, and took up a gun with a brass-bound stock.

"Do you know this?" said he, making as if he would take aim at me. "Do you know where you saw it afore? Speak, wolf!"

"Yes," I answered.

"You cost me that place.[2] You did. Speak!"

"What else could I do?"

"You did that, and that would be enough, without more. How dared you come betwixt me and a young woman I liked?"

[1] **truckle bedstead:** low bed on wheels, usually rolled underneath another bed.

[2] **that place:** Orlick's position at Satis House.

"When did I?"

"When didn't you? It was you as always give Old Orlick a bad name to her."

"You gave it to yourself; you gained it for yourself. I could have done you no harm, if you had done yourself none."

"You're a liar. And you'll take any pains, and spend any money, to drive me out of this country, will you?" said he, repeating my words to Biddy in the last interview I had with her. "Now, I'll tell you a piece of information. It was never so worth your while to get me out of this country as it is tonight." As he shook his heavy hand at me, with his mouth snarling like a tiger's, I felt that it was true.

"What are you going to do to me?"

"I'm a-going," said he, bringing his fist down upon the table with a heavy blow, and rising as the blow fell, to give it greater force, "I'm a-going to have your life!"

He leaned forward staring at me, slowly unclenched his hand and drew it across his mouth as if his mouth watered for me, and sat down again.

"You was always in Old Orlick's way since ever you was a child. You goes out of his way this present night. He'll have no more on you. You're dead."

I felt that I had come to the brink of my grave. For a moment I looked wildly round my trap for any chance of escape; but there was none.

"More than that," said he, "I won't have a rag of you, I won't have a bone of you, left on earth. I'll put your body in the kiln—I'd carry two such to it, on my shoulders—and, let people suppose what they may of you, they shall never know nothing."

My mind with inconceivable rapidity followed out all the consequences of such a death. Estella's father would believe I had deserted him, would be taken, would die accusing me; even Herbert would doubt me when he compared the letter I had left for him with the fact that I had called at Miss Havisham's gate for only a moment; Joe and Biddy would never know how sorry I had been that night.

Orlick had been drinking, and his eyes were red and bloodshot. Around his neck was slung a tin bottle. He brought the bottle to his lips and took a fiery drink from it.

"Wolf!" said he, folding his arms again. "Old Orlick's a-going to tell you something. It was you as did for your shrew sister."

"It was you, villain," said I.

"I tell you it was your doing—I tell you it was done through you," he retorted, catching up the gun, and making a blow with the stock at the vacant air between us. "I come upon her from behind, as I come upon you tonight. I giv' it her! I left her for dead, and if there had been a lime-kiln as nigh her as there is now nigh you, she shouldn't have come to life again. But it warn't Old Orlick as did it; it was you. You was favored, and he was bullied and beat. Old Orlick bullied and beat, eh? Now you pays for it. You done it; now you pays for it."

He drank again, and became more ferocious. He took up the candle, and shading it with his murderous hand so as to throw its light on me, stood before me, looking at me and enjoying the sight.

"Wolf, I'll tell you something more. It was Old Orlick as you tumbled over on your stairs that night. And why was Old Orlick there? I'll tell you something more, wolf. You and her *have* pretty well hunted me out of this country, so far as gettin a easy living in it goes, and I've took up with new companions and new masters. Some of 'em writes my letters when I wants 'em wrote. They writes fifty hands; they're not like sneaking you as writes but one. I've had a firm mind and a firm will to have your life, since you was down here at your sister's burying. I han't seen a way to get you safe, and I've looked arter you to know your ins and outs. For, says Old Orlick to himself, 'Somehow or another I'll have him!' What! When I looks for you, I finds your Uncle Provis, eh?

"*You* with a uncle, too! But when Old Orlick come for to hear that your Uncle Provis had mostlike wore the leg iron wot Old Orlick had picked up on these meshes ever so many year ago, and wot he kept by him till he dropped your sister with it —when he come to hear that—hey?—"

In his savage taunting, he flared the candle so close at me that I turned my face aside to save it from the flame.

"Ah!" he cried, laughing, after doing it again. "The burned child dreads the fire! Old Orlick knowed you was burned, Old Orlick knowed you was a-smuggling your Uncle Provis away, Old Orlick's a match for you and knowed you'd come tonight! Now I'll tell you something more, wolf, and this ends it. There's them that's as good a match for your Uncle Provis as Old Orlick has been for you. There's them that can't and that won't have Magwitch —yes, *I* know the name!—alive in the same land with them, and that's had sure information of him when he was alive in another land, as that he shouldn't leave it unbeknown and put them in danger. P'raps it's them that writes fifty hands, and that's not like sneaking you as writes but one. 'Ware Compeyson, Magwitch, and the gallows!"

There was a clear space of a few feet between the table and the opposite wall. Within this space he now slouched backward and forward with his hands hanging loose and heavy at his sides, and with his eyes scowling at me. I had no grain of hope left.

Of a sudden he stopped, took the cork out of his bottle, and tossed it away. Light as it was, I heard it fall like a plummet.[1] He swallowed slowly, tilting up the bottle by little and little, and now he looked at me no more. The last few drops of liquor he poured into the palm of his hand and licked up. Then with a sudden hurry of violence and swearing horribly, he threw the bottle from him, and stooped; and I saw in his hand a stone hammer with a long heavy handle.

I shouted out with all my might, and struggled with all my might. It was only my head and my legs that I could move, but to that extent I struggled with all the force that was within me. In the same instant I heard responsive shouts, saw figures and a gleam of light dash in at the door, heard voices and tumult, and saw Orlick emerge from a struggle of men, clear the table at a leap, and fly out into the night!

After a blank, I found that I was lying unbound on the floor, in the same place, with my head on someone's knee. My eyes were fixed on the ladder against the wall when there came between me and it, a face. The face of Trabb's boy!

"I think he's all right!" said Trabb's boy, in a sober voice. "But ain't he just pale, though!"

At these words, the face of him who supported me looked over into mine, and I saw my supporter to be—

"Herbert! Great Heaven!"

"Softly," said Herbert. "Gently, Handel. Don't be too eager."

"And our old comrade, Startop!" I cried, as he too bent over me.

"Remember what he is going to assist us in," said Herbert, "and be calm."

The allusion made me spring up, though I dropped again from the pain in my arm.

[1] **plummet** (plum′it): a lead weight attached to a string, used by carpenters to test the straightness of a wall. When the weight is dropped, the string becomes straight.

"The time has not gone by, Herbert, has it? What night is tonight? How long have I been here?"

"The time has not gone by. It is still Monday night."

"Thank God!"

"And you have all tomorrow, Tuesday, to rest in," said Herbert. "Can you stand?"

"Yes, yes," said I, "I can walk, I have no hurt but in this throbbing arm."

They did what they could until we could get to the town and obtain some cooling lotion to put upon it. Trabb's boy—Trabb's overgrown young man now—went before us with a lantern. But the moon was a good two hours higher than when I had last seen the sky, and the night though rainy was much lighter.

Entreating Herbert to tell me how he had come to my rescue, I learned that I had in my hurry dropped the letter, open, in our chambers, where he, coming home to bring with him Startop, found it very soon after I was gone. Its tone made him uneasy, and he set off for the coach office with Startop. Finding that the afternoon coach was gone, he resolved to follow in a post-chaise. So he and Startop arrived at the Blue Boar, fully expecting there to find me, or tidings of me; but, finding neither, went on to Miss Havisham's, where they lost me. Hereupon they went back to the hotel to refresh themselves and to get someone to guide them upon the marshes. Among the loungers under the Boar's archway happened to be Trabb's boy. Thus Trabb's boy became their guide, and with him they went out to the sluice house. Herbert left his guide and Startop on the edge of the quarry, and went on by himself, and stole round the house two or three times. As he could hear nothing but indistinct sounds of one deep rough voice, he began to doubt whether I was there, when suddenly I cried out loudly, and he answered the cries, and rushed in, closely followed by the other two.

We relinquished all thoughts of pursuing Orlick at that time. For the present, under the circumstances, we deemed it prudent to make rather light of the matter to Trabb's boy. When we parted, I presented him with two guineas (which seemed to meet his views), and told him that I was sorry ever to have had an ill opinion of him (which made no impression on him at all).

It was daylight when we reached the Temple, and I went at once to bed, and lay in bed all day.

My terror, as I lay there, of falling ill and being unfitted for tomorrow, was so besetting that I wonder it did not disable me of itself. I started at every footstep and every sound, believing that he was discovered and taken, and this was the messenger to tell me so. I persuaded myself that I knew he was taken. It happened sometimes that in the mere escape of a fatigued mind, I dozed for some moments or forgot; then I would say to myself with a start, "Now it has come, and I am turning delirious!"

They kept me very quiet all day, and kept my arm constantly dressed, and gave me cooling drinks. Whenever I fell asleep, I awoke with the notion I had had in the sluice house, that a long time had elapsed, and the opportunity to save him was gone. About midnight I got out of bed and went to Herbert with the conviction that I had been asleep for four-and-twenty hours, and that Wednesday was past. It was the last self-exhausting effort of my fretfulness, for after that, I slept soundly.

Wednesday morning was dawning when I looked out of the window. Herbert lay asleep in his bed, and our old fellow student lay asleep on the sofa. I could not dress myself without help, but I made up the fire, which was still burning, and got some coffee ready for them. In good time they too started up strong and well, and we admitted the sharp morning air at the windows, and looked at the tide that was still flowing toward us.

"When it turns at nine o'clock," said Herbert cheerfully, "look out for us, and stand ready, you over there at Mill Pond Bank!"

CHAPTER 39

An informer goes to his death.

IT WAS one of those March days when the sun shines hot and the wind blows cold: when it is summer in the light, and winter in the shade. We had our peacoats [1] with us, and I took a bag. Of all my worldly possessions I took no more than the few necessaries that filled the bag. Where I might go, what I might do, or when I might return, were questions utterly unknown to me; nor did I vex my mind with them, for it was wholly set on Provis' safety. We loitered down to the Temple stairs, and stood loitering there, as if we were not quite decided to go upon the water at all. Of course I had taken care that the boat should be ready, and everything in order. After a little show of indecision, we went on board and cast off; Herbert in the bow, I steering. It was then about high water—half-past eight.

Our plan was this. The tide, beginning to run down at nine, and being with us until three, we intended still to creep on after it had turned, and row against it until dark. We should then be well in those long reaches below Gravesend, between Kent and Essex, where the river is broad

and solitary, where the waterside inhabitants are very few, and where lone public houses are scattered here and there, of which we could choose one for a resting place. There, we meant to lie by all night. The steamer for Hamburg and the steamer for Rotterdam would start from London at about nine on Thursday morning. We should know at what time to expect them and would hail the first; so that if by any accident we were not taken aboard, we should have another chance. We knew the distinguishing marks of each vessel.

Old London Bridge was soon passed, and old Billingsgate market with its oyster boats and Dutchmen, and we were in among the tiers of shipping. Here were steamers, loading and unloading goods, and here, at her moorings, was tomorrow's steamer for Rotterdam, of which we took good notice; and here tomorrow's for Hamburg, under whose bowsprit [2] we crossed. And now I, sitting in the stern, could see, with a faster beating heart, Mill Pond Bank and Mill Pond stairs.

"Is he there?" said Herbert.

"Not yet."

"Right! He was not to come down till he saw us. Can you see his signal!"

"Not well from here; but I think I see it. Now I see him! Pull both. Easy, Herbert. Oars!"

We touched the stairs lightly for a single moment, and he was on board and we were off again. He had a boat cloak with him, and a black canvas bag, and he looked as like a river pilot as my heart could have wished.

"Dear boy!" he said, putting his arm on my shoulder, as he took his seat. "Faithful dear boy, well done. Thank'ee, thank'ee!"

Again among the tiers of shipping, in

[1] **peacoats:** thick, woolen jackets, often worn by sailors.

[2] **bowsprit** (bou'sprit): a pole or spar projecting from the bow (front) of a ship.

and out, avoiding rusty chain cables, frayed hempen hawsers,[1] and bobbing buoys, sinking for the moment floating broken baskets, scattering floating chips of wood and shaving, cleaving floating scum of coal in and out—upon the clearer river, where the ships' boys might take their fenders [2] in, no longer fishing in troubled waters with them over the side, and where the festooned sails might fly out to the wind.

At the stairs where we had taken him aboard, and ever since, I had looked warily for any token of our being suspected. I had seen none. He had his boat cloak on him, and looked, as I have said, a natural part of the scene. It was remarkable that he was the least anxious of any of us.

"If you knowed, dear boy," he said to me, "what it is to sit here alonger my dear boy and have my smoke, arter having been day by day betwixt four walls,

you'd envy me. But you don't know what it is."

"I think I know the delights of freedom," I answered.

"Ah," said he, shaking his head gravely. "But you don't know it equal to me. You must have been under lock and key, dear boy, to know it equal to me—but I ain't a-going to be low."

"If all goes well," said I, "you will be perfectly free and safe again, within a few hours."

"Well," he returned, drawing a long breath, "I hope so."

We made what way we could until the sun went down. At length we descried a light and a roof, and presently afterward ran alongside a little causeway made of stones. I stepped ashore, and found the light to be in the window of a public house. It was a dirty place enough, and I dare say not unknown to smuggling adventurers; but there was a good fire in the kitchen, and there were eggs and bacon to eat. Also, there were two double-bedded rooms—"such as they were," the landlord said. No other company was in the

[1] **hawsers** (hô′zərz): ropes.
[2] **fenders:** anything used as padding against the sides of ships, to protect them from damage in bumping against wharves or other ships.

house than the landlord, his wife, and a grizzled male creature, the "Jack"[1] of the little causeway.

With this assistant, I went down to the boat again, and we all came ashore, and brought out the oars, and rudder, and boat hook, and all else, and hauled her up for the night. We made a very good meal by the kitchen fire, and then apportioned the bedrooms: Herbert and Startop were to occupy one; I and our charge the other. We considered ourselves well off, for a more solitary place we could not have found.

While we were comforting ourselves by the fire after our meal, the Jack asked me if we had seen a four-oared galley going up with the tide. When I told him no, he said she must have gone down then, and yet she "took up too," when she left there.

"They must ha' thought better on't for some reason or another," said the Jack, "and gone down."

"A four-oared galley did you say?" said I.

"A four," said the Jack, "and two sitters."

"Did they come ashore here?"

"They put in with a stone two-gallon jar for some beer."

This dialogue made us all uneasy, and me very uneasy. The dismal wind was muttering round the house, the tide was flapping at the shore, and I had a feeling that we were caged and threatened. A four-oared galley hovering about in so unusual a way as to attract this notice was an ugly circumstance that I could not get rid of. When I had induced Provis to go up to bed, I went outside with my two companions (Startop by this time knew the state of the case) and held council. On the whole we deemed it the better

[1] **Jack:** a sailor.

course to lie where we were, until within an hour or so of the steamer's time, and then to get out in her track, and drift easily with the tide. Having settled to do this, we returned into the house and went to bed.

I lay down with the greater part of my clothes on, and slept well for a few hours. When I awoke, the wind had risen. I looked out of the window. It commanded the causeway where we had hauled up our boat, and I saw two men looking into her. They passed by under the window, looking at nothing else, and they did not go down to the landing place but struck across the marshes. In that light, however, I soon lost them, and feeling very cold, lay down to think of the matter and fell asleep again.

We were up early. As we walked to and fro, all four together, I deemed it right to recount what I had seen. Again our charge was the least anxious of the party. However, I proposed that he and I should walk away together to a distant point, and that the boat should take us aboard there. This being considered a good precaution, soon after breakfast he and I set forth, without saying anything at the tavern.

He smoked his pipe as we went along, and sometimes stopped to clap me on the shoulder. One would have supposed that it was I who was in danger, not he, and that he was reassuring me. We spoke very little.

We waited until we saw our boat coming round. We got aboard easily and rowed out into the track of the steamer. By that time it wanted but ten minutes of one o'clock, and we began to look out for her smoke.

But it was half-past one before we saw her smoke, and soon after we saw behind it the smoke of another steamer. As they were coming on at full speed, we got the two bags ready, and took that opportunity of saying good-by to Herbert and Startop. We had all shaken hands cordially, and neither Herbert's eyes nor mine were quite dry, when I saw a four-oared galley shoot out from under the bank but a little way ahead of us, and row out into the same track.

I called to Herbert and Startop to keep before the tide, that the steamer might see us lying by for her, and adjured Provis to sit quite still, wrapped in his cloak. He answered cheerily, "Trust to me, dear boy," and sat like a statue. Meanwhile the galley, which was skillfully handled, had crossed us, let us come up with her, and fallen alongside. Leaving just room enough for the play of the oars, she kept alongside, drifting when we drifted, and pulling a stroke or two when we pulled. Of the two sitters, one held the rudder lines, and looked at us attentively—as did all the rowers; the other sitter was wrapped up, much as Provis was, and seemed to shrink and whisper some instruction to the steerer as he looked at us. Not a word was spoken in either boat.

Startop could make out, after a few minutes, which steamer was first, and gave me the word "Hamburg," in a low voice as we sat face to face. She was nearing us very fast, and the beating of her paddles grew louder and louder. I felt as if her shadow were absolutely upon us, when the galley hailed us. I answered.

"You have a returned transport there," said the man who held the lines. "That's the man, wrapped in the cloak. His name is Abel Magwitch, otherwise Provis. I apprehend that man, and call upon him to surrender, and you to assist."

At the same moment, without giving any audible direction to his crew, he ran the galley aboard of us. They had pulled one sudden stroke ahead, had got their oars in, had run athwart us, and were holding on to our gunwale before we knew what they were doing. This caused great confusion on board of the steamer, and I heard them calling to us, and heard the order given to stop the paddles, and heard them stop, but felt her driving down upon us irresistibly. In the same moment, I saw the steersman of the galley lay his hand on his prisoner's shoulder, and saw that both boats were swinging round with the force of the tide, and saw that all hands on board the steamer were running forward frantically. Still in the same moment, I saw the prisoner start up, lean across his captor, and pull the cloak from the neck of the shrinking sitter in the galley. Still in the same moment, I saw that the face disclosed was the face of the other convict of long ago. Still in the same moment, I saw the face tilt backward with a white terror on it that I shall never forget, and heard a great cry on board the steamer and a loud splash in the water, and felt the boat sink from under me.

It was but for an instant that I seemed to struggle; that instant past I was taken on board the galley. Herbert was there, and Startop was there; but our boat was gone, and the two convicts were gone.

What with the cries aboard the steamer, and the furious blowing off of her steam, and her driving on, and our driving on, I could not at first distinguish sky from water or shore from shore; but the crew of the galley righted her with great speed, and, pulling certain swift strong strokes ahead, lay upon their oars, every man looking silently and eagerly at the water astern. Presently a dark object was seen in it, bearing toward us on the tide. No man spoke, but the steersman kept the boat straight and true before it. As it came nearer, I saw it to be Magwitch, swimming, but not freely. He was taken on board, and instantly manacled at the wrists and ankles.

The galley was kept steady, and the silent eager lookout at the water was resumed. But the Rotterdam steamer now came up, and apparently not understanding what had happened, came on at speed. By the time she had been hailed and stopped, both steamers were drifting away from us, and we were rising and falling in a troubled wake of water. The lookout was kept long after all was still again and the two steamers were gone; but everybody knew that it was hopeless now.

At length we gave it up, and pulled under the shore toward the tavern we had lately left. Here, I was able to get some comforts for Magwitch—Provis no longer —who had received some very severe injury in the chest and a deep cut in the head.

He told me that he believed himself to have gone under the keel of the steamer, and to have been struck on the head in rising. The injury to his chest (which rendered his breathing extremely painful) he thought he had received against the side of the galley. He added that he did not pretend to say what he might have done to Compeyson, but that in the moment of his laying his hand on his cloak to identify him, that villain had staggered up and back, and they had both gone overboard together; when the sudden wrenching of Magwitch out of our boat had capsized us. He told me in a whisper that they had gone down, fiercely locked in each other's arms, and that there had been a struggle underwater, and that he had disengaged himself, struck out, and swum away.

I never had any reason to doubt the exact truth of what he had told me. The officer who steered the galley gave the same account of their going overboard.

When I asked this officer's permission to change the prisoner's wet clothes by purchasing any spare garments I could get at the public house, he gave it readily, merely observing that he must take charge of everything his prisoner had about him. So the pocketbook which had once been in my hands passed into the officer's. He further gave me leave to accompany the prisoner to London, but declined to accord that grace to my two friends.

We remained at the public house until the tide turned, and then Magwitch was carried down to the galley and put on board. Herbert and Startop were to get to London by land, as soon as they could. We had a doleful parting, and when I took my place by Magwitch's side, I felt that that was my place henceforth while he lived.

For now my repugnance to him had

all melted away, and in the hunted, wounded, shackled creature who held my hand in his, I only saw a man who had meant to be my benefactor, and who had felt affectionately, gratefully, and generously toward me with great constancy through a series of years. I only saw in him a much better man than I had been to Joe.

His breathing became more difficult and painful as the night drew on, and often he could not repress a groan. I tried to rest him on the arm I could use, in any easy position; but it was dreadful to think that I could not be sorry at heart for his being badly hurt, since it was unquestionably best that he should die. That there were, still living, people enough who were able and willing to identify him, I could not doubt. That he would be leniently treated, I could not hope—he who had been presented in the worst light at his trial, who had since broken prison and been tried again, who had returned from transportation under a life sentence, and who had occasioned the death of the man who was the cause of his arrest.

As we returned toward the setting sun we had yesterday left behind us, and as the stream of our hopes seemed all running back, I told him how grieved I was to think he had come home for my sake.

"Dear boy," he answered, "I'm quite content to take my chance. I've seen my boy, and he can be a gentleman without me."

No. I had thought about that while we had been there side by side. I foresaw that, being convicted, his possessions would be forfeited to the Crown.[1]

"Look'ee here, dear boy," said he. "It's best as a gentleman should not be knowed

---

[1] **forfeited** (fôr'fit·id) **to the Crown:** confiscated by the government, which had the legal right to the possessions of a prisoner in Magwitch's position.

to belong to me now. Only come to see me as if you come by chance alonger Wemmick. Sit where I can see you when I am swore to, for the last o' many times, and I don't ask no more."

"I will never stir from your side," said I, "when I am suffered to be near you. Please God, I will be as true to you as you have been to me!"

I felt his hand tremble as it held mine, and he turned his face away as he lay in the bottom of the boat, and I heard that old sound in his throat—softened now, like all the rest of him. It was a good thing that he had touched this point, for it put into my mind what I might not otherwise have thought of until too late: that he need never know how his hopes of enriching me had perished.

CHAPTER 40

Mr. Wemmick takes a walk.

HE WAS taken to the Police Court next day, and would have been immediately committed for trial, but that it was necessary to send down for an old officer of the prison ship from which he had once escaped, to speak to his identity. Nobody doubted it; but Compeyson, who had meant to depose to it, was dead. I had gone direct to Mr. Jaggers at his private house, on my arrival overnight, to retain his assistance, but he told me that no power on earth could prevent its going against us.

I imparted to Mr. Jaggers my design of keeping him in ignorance of the fate of his wealth. Mr. Jaggers was angry with me for having "let it slip through my fingers," and said we must try at all events for some of it. But he did not conceal from me that although there might be many cases in which forfeiture would not be exacted, there were no circumstances in this case to make it one of them. I understood that very well. I was not related to the outlaw, or connected with him by any recognizable tie. I had no claim, and I resolved that my heart should never be sickened with the hopeless task of attempting to establish one.

There appeared to be reason for supposing that the drowned informer had hoped for a reward, and had obtained some accurate knowledge of Magwitch's affairs. When his body was found, many miles from the scene of his death, notes were still legible, folded in a case he carried. Among these were the name of a banking house in New South Wales where a sum of money was, and the designation of certain lands of considerable value. Both those heads of information were in a list that Magwitch, while in prison, gave to Mr. Jaggers, of the possessions he supposed I should inherit. His ignorance, poor fellow, at last served him; he never mistrusted but that my inheritance was quite safe, with Mr. Jaggers' aid.

After three days' delay, he was committed to take his trial at the next session, which would come on in a month.

It was at this dark time of my life that Herbert returned home one evening, a good deal cast down, and said:

"My dear Handel, I fear I shall soon have to leave you."

His partner having prepared me for that, I was less surprised than he thought.

"We shall lose a fine opportunity if I put off going to Cairo, and I am very much afraid I must go, Handel, when you most need me."

"Herbert, I shall always need you, because I shall always love you; but my need is no greater now than at another time."

"You will be so lonely."

"I have not leisure to think of that," said I. "You know that I am always with him to the full extent of the time allowed, and that I should be with him all day long, if I could. And when I come away from him, you know that my thoughts are with him."

"My dear fellow," said Herbert, "let the near prospect of our separation be my justification for troubling you about yourself. Have you thought of your future? In this branch house of ours, Handel, we must have a—"

I saw that his delicacy was avoiding the right word, so I said, "A clerk."

"A clerk. And I hope it is not at all unlikely that he may expand into a partner. Now, Handel—in short, my dear boy, will you come to me? Clara and I have talked about it again and again," Herbert pursued, "and the dear little thing begged me only this evening to say that if you will live with us when we come together, she will do her best to make you happy."

I thanked her heartily, and I thanked him heartily, but said I could not yet make sure of joining him.

"But if you thought, Herbert, that you could, without doing any injury to your business, leave the question open for a little while—"

"For any while," cried Herbert. "Six months, a year!"

"Not so long as that," said I. "Two or three months at most."

Herbert was highly delighted when we shook hands on this arrangement, and said he could now take courage to tell me that he believed he must go away at the end of the week.

On the Saturday in that same week, I took my leave of Herbert as he sat on one of the seaport mail coaches. I then went to my lonely home—if it deserved the name, for it was now no home to me, and I had no home anywhere.

On the stairs I encountered Wemmick. I had not seen him alone since the disastrous issue of the attempted flight; and he had come, in his private and personal capacity, to say a few words in reference to that failure.

"The late Compeyson," said Wemmick, "had by little and little got at the bottom of half of the regular business now transacted, and it was from the talk of some of his people in trouble that I heard what I did. I kept my ears open until I heard that he was absent, and I thought that would be the best time for making the attempt. I can only suppose now that it was a part of his policy, as a very clever man, habitually to deceive his own instruments. You don't blame me, I hope, Mr. Pip? I'm sure I tried to serve you, with all my heart."

"I am as sure of that, Wemmick, as you can be, and I thank you most earnestly for all your interest and friendship."

I invited Wemmick to come upstairs and refresh himself with a glass of grog before walking to Walworth. He accepted but appeared rather fidgety.

"What do you think of my meaning to take a holiday on Monday, Mr. Pip?"

"Why, I suppose you have not done such a thing these twelve months."

"These twelve years, more likely," said Wemmick. "Yes. I'm going to take a holiday. More than that; I'm going to take a walk. More than that; I'm going to ask you to take a walk with me. It ain't a long walk, and it's an early one. Say it might occupy you (including breakfast on the walk), from eight to twelve. Couldn't you stretch a point and manage it?"

He had done so much for me that this was very little to do for him. I said I could manage it—would manage it—and he was so very much pleased that I was pleased too.

Punctual to my appointment, I rang at the Castle gate on the Monday morning, and was received by Wemmick himself, who struck me as looking tighter [1] than usual, and having a sleeker hat on.

When we had fortified ourselves with biscuits and were going out for the walk, I was considerably surprised to see Wemmick take up a fishing rod and put it over his shoulder. "Why, we are not going fishing!" said I. "No," returned Wemmick, "but I like to walk with one."

I thought this odd; however, I said nothing, and we set off. We went toward Camberwell Green, and when we were thereabouts, Wemmick said suddenly:

"Halloa! Here's a church!"

There was nothing very surprising in that; but again, I was rather surprised when he said, as if he were animated by a brilliant idea:

"Let's go in!"

We went in, Wemmick leaving his fishing rod in the porch, and looked all round. In the meantime, Wemmick was diving into his coat pockets and getting something out of paper there.

"Halloa!" said he. "Here's a couple of pair of gloves! Let's put 'em on!"

As the gloves were white kid gloves, I now began to have my strong suspicions. They were strengthened into certainty when I beheld the Aged enter at a side door, escorting a lady.

"Halloa!" said Wemmick. "Here' Miss Skiffins! Let's have a wedding."

The clerk and clergyman then appeared, and true to his notion of seeming to do it all without preparation, I heard Wemmick say to himself as he took something out of his waistcoat pocket before the service began, "Halloa! Here's a ring!"

I acted in the capacity of best man to the bridegroom, while the responsibility of giving the lady away devolved upon the Aged.

---

[1] **tighter:** neater.

"*Now*, Mr. Pip," said Wemmick, triumphantly shouldering the fishing rod as we came out, "let me ask you whether anybody would suppose this to be a wedding party!"

Breakfast had been ordered at a pleasant little tavern a mile or so away. We had an excellent breakfast, and when anyone declined anything on the table, Wemmick said, "Provided by contract, you know; don't be afraid of it!" I drank to the new couple, drank to the Aged, drank to the Castle, saluted the bride at parting, and made myself as agreeable as I could.

CHAPTER 41

Pip takes final leave of Magwitch.

HE LAY in prison very ill during the whole interval between his committal for trial and the coming round of the sessions. He had broken two ribs, they had wounded one of his lungs, and he breathed with great pain and difficulty, which increased daily. Being far too ill to remain in the common prison, he was removed, after the first day or so, into the infirmary. This gave me opportunities of being with him that I could not otherwise have had. And but for his illness he would have been put into irons, for he was regarded as a determined prison breaker, and I know not what else.

Although I saw him every day, it was for only a short time. I do not recollect that I once saw any change in him for the better; he wasted and became slowly weaker and worse day by day from the day when the prison door closed upon him.

When the sessions came round, Mr.

Jaggers caused an application to be made for the postponement of his trial and was refused. The trial came on at once, and when he was put to the bar, he was seated in a chair. No objection was made to my getting close to the dock and holding the hand that he stretched out to me.

The trial was very short and very clear. Such things as could be said for him were said—how he had taken to industrious habits, and had thriven [1] lawfully and reputably. But nothing could unsay the fact that he had returned, and was there in presence of the judge and jury. It was impossible not to try him for that, and do otherwise than find him guilty.

At that time it was the custom (as I learned from my terrible experience of that sessions) to devote a concluding day to the passing of sentences, and to make a finishing effect with the sentence of death. I saw two-and-thirty men and women put before the judge to receive that sentence together. Foremost among the two-and-thirty was he; seated, that he might get breath enough to keep life in him.

Penned in the dock, as I again stood outside it at the corner with his hand in mine, were the two-and-thirty men and women; some defiant, some stricken with terror, some sobbing and weeping, some covering their faces, some staring gloomily about. There had been shrieks from among the women convicts, but they had been stilled, and a hush had succeeded.

Then, the judge addressed them. Among the wretched creatures before him whom he must single out for special address, was one who almost from his infancy had been an offender against the laws; who, after repeated imprisonments and punishments, had been at length sentenced to exile for a term of years; and

[1] **thriven** (thriv'ən): thrived; succeeded; prospered.

who, under circumstances of great violence and daring, had made his escape and been resentenced to exile for life. That miserable man would seem for a time to have become convinced of his errors, when far removed from the scenes of his old offenses, and to have lived a peaceable and honest life. But in a fatal moment, he had quitted his haven of rest and repentance, and had come back to the country where he was proscribed. Being here presently denounced, he had for a time succeeded in evading the officers of justice, but being at length seized while in the act of flight, he had resisted them, and had—he best knew whether by express design, or in the blindness of his hardihood—caused the death of his denouncer, to whom his whole career was known. The appointed punishment for his return to the land that had cast him out being death, he must prepare himself to die.

The sun was striking in at the great windows of the court, through the glittering drops of rain upon the glass, and it made a broad shaft of light between the two-and-thirty and the judge. Rising for a moment, a distinct speck of face in this way of light, the prisoner said, "My Lord, I have received my sentence of death from the Almighty, but I bow to yours," and sat down again.

I began that night to write out a petition to the Home Secretary of State, setting forth my knowledge of him and how it was that he had come back for my sake. I wrote as fervently and pathetically as I could, and when I had finished it and sent it in, I wrote out other petitions to such men in authority as I hoped were the most merciful, and drew up one to the Crown itself. For several days and nights after he was sentenced I took no rest, except when I fell asleep in my chair. but was wholly absorbed in these appeals. The

daily visits I could make him were shortened now, and he was more strictly kept. Nobody was hard with him or with me. There was duty to be done, and it was done, but not harshly. Sometimes he was almost unable to speak; then, he would answer me with slight pressures on my hand, and I grew to understand his meaning very well.

The number of the days had risen to ten, when I saw a greater change in him than I had seen yet. His eyes were turned toward the door, and lighted up as I entered.

"Dear boy," he said, as I sat down by his bed, "I thought you was late. But I knowed you couldn't be that."

"It is just the time," said I. "I waited for it at the gate."

"You always waits at the gate; don't you, dear boy?"

"Yes. Not to lose a moment of the time."

"Thank'ee, dear boy, thank'ee. God bless you! You've never deserted me, dear boy."

I pressed his hand in silence, for I could not forget that I had once meant to desert him.

"And what's the best of all," he said, "you've been more comfortable alonger me since I was under a dark cloud, than when the sun shone. That's best of all."

He lay on his back, breathing with great difficulty. Do what he would, and love me though he did, the light left his face ever and again, and a film came over the placid look at the white ceiling.

"Are you in much pain today?"

"I don't complain of none, dear boy."

"You never do complain."

He had spoken his last words. He smiled, and I understood his touch to mean that he wished to lift my hand, and lay it on his breast. I laid it there, and he smiled again, and put both his hands upon it.

The allotted time ran out while we were thus; but, looking round, I found the governor of the prison standing near me, and he whispered, "You needn't go yet." I thanked him gratefully, and asked, "Might I speak to him, if he can hear me?"

The governor stepped aside and beckoned the officer away. The change, though it was made without noise, drew back the film from the placid look at the white ceiling, and he looked most affectionately at me.

"Dear Magwitch, I must tell you, now, at last. You understand what I say?"

A gentle pressure on my hand.

"You had a child once, whom you loved and lost."

A stronger pressure on my hand.

"She lived and found powerful friends. She is living now. She is a lady and very beautiful. And I love her!"

With a last faint effort, which would have been powerless but for my yielding to it, and assisting it, he raised my hand to his lips. Then he gently let it sink

upon his breast again, with his own hands lying on it. The placid look at the white ceiling came back, and passed away, and his head dropped quietly on his breast.

I thought of the two men who went up into the Temple to pray, and I knew there were no better words that I could say beside his bed than, "O Lord, be merciful to him, a sinner!"

CHAPTER 42

An old friend comes to Pip's rescue.

Now THAT I was left wholly to myself, I gave notice of my intention to quit the chambers in the Temple as soon as my tenancy could legally determine, and in the meanwhile to underlet them.[1] I was in debt, and had scarcely any money, and I began to be seriously alarmed by the state of my affairs. Moreover, I was falling very ill. The late stress upon me had enabled me to put off illness, but not to put it away; I knew that it was coming on me now.

For a day or two I lay on the sofa, or on the floor—anywhere, according as I happened to sink down—with a heavy head and aching limbs, and no purpose, and no power. Then there came one night which appeared of great duration, and which teemed with anxiety and horror; and when in the morning I tried to sit up in my bed and think of it, I found I could not do so. Then I saw two men looking at me.

"What do you want?" I asked, starting. "I don't know you."

"Well, sir," returned one of them, bend-

---

[1] **I gave ... them:** Pip gave notice that he would leave his apartment as soon as his lease could be terminated and in the meantime would sublet the rooms.

ing down and touching me on the shoulder, "you're arrested."

"What is the debt?"

"Hundred and twenty-three pound, fifteen, six. Jeweler's account, I think."

I made some attempt to get up and dress myself. When I next attended to them, they were standing a little off from the bed, looking at me. I still lay there.

"You see my state," said I. "I would come with you if I could; but indeed I am quite unable. If you take me from here, I think I shall die by the way."

As they hang in my memory by only this one slender thread, I don't know what they did, except that they forbore to remove me.

That I had a fever and was avoided, that I suffered greatly, I know of my own remembrance, and did in some sort know at the time. I was delirious and sometimes struggled with real people, in the belief that they were murderers, but above all, I knew that there was a constant tendency in all these people to settle down into the likeness of Joe.

After I had turned the worst point of my illness, I opened my eyes in the night, and I saw in the great chair at the bedside, Joe. I opened my eyes in the day, and, sitting on the window seat, smoking his pipe in the shaded open window, still I saw Joe. I asked for cooling drink, and the dear hand that gave it me was Joe's. I sank back on my pillow after drinking, and the face that looked so hopefully and tenderly upon me was the face of Joe.

At last one day I took courage, and said, *"Is* it Joe?"

And the dear old home voice answered, "Which it air, old chap."

"Oh, Joe, you break my heart! Look angry at me, Joe. Strike me, Joe. Tell me of my ingratitude. Don't be so good to me!"

For Joe had actually laid his head down on the pillow at my side and put his arm round my neck, in his joy that I knew him.

"Which dear old Pip, old chap," said Joe, "you and me was ever friends. And when you're well enough to go out for a ride—what larks!"

After which, Joe withdrew to the window and stood with his back toward me, wiping his eyes. And as my extreme weakness prevented me from getting up and going to him, I lay there, penitently whispering, "O God, bless him! O God, bless this gentle Christian man!"

Joe's eyes were red when I next found him beside me, but I was holding his hand and we both felt happy.

"Have you been here all the time, dear Joe?"

"Pretty nigh, old chap. For, as I says to Biddy when the news of your being ill were brought by letter, you might be amongst strangers, and you and me having been ever friends, a wisit at such a moment might not prove unaccepta-bobble. And Biddy, her word were, 'Go to him, without loss of time.'" There Joe cut himself off short, and informed me I was to be talked to in great moderation. So I lay quiet while he proceeded to indite a note to Biddy, with my love in it.

Evidently Biddy had taught Joe to write. As I lay in bed looking at him, it made me, in my weak state, cry with pleasure to see the pride with which he set about his letter. He got on very well indeed, and when he had signed his name, he got up and hovered about the table, trying the effect of his performance from various points of view, with unbounded satisfaction.

Not to make Joe uneasy by talking too much, even if I had been able to talk much, I deferred asking him about Miss Havisham until next day. He shook his head when I then asked him if she had recovered.

"Is she dead, Joe?"

"Why, you see, old chap," said Joe, by way of getting at it by degrees, "I wouldn't go so far as to say that, for that's a deal to say; but she ain't living."

"Did she linger long, Joe?"

"Arter you was took ill, pretty much about what you might call a week," said Joe, still determined, on my account, to come at everything by degrees.

"Dear Joe, have you heard what becomes of her property?"

"Well, old chap," said Joe, "it do appear that she had settled the most of it on Miss Estella. But she had wrote out a little coddleshell [1] in her own hand a day or two afore the accident, leaving a cool four thousand to Mr. Matthew Pocket. And why do you suppose, above all things, Pip, she left that cool four thousand unto him? 'Because of Pip's account of him, the said Matthew.' I am told by Biddy, that air the writing," said Joe.

This account gave me great joy, as it perfected the only good thing I had done. I asked Joe whether any of the other relations had any legacies.

"Miss Sarah," said Joe, "she has twenty-five pound per annium fur to buy pills. Miss Georgiana, she has twenty, Mrs.—— what's the name of them wild beasts with humps?"

"Camels?" said I, wondering why he could want to know.

Joe nodded. "Mrs. Camels," by which I understood he meant Camilla, "she have five pounds fur to buy rushlights to put her in spirits when she wake up in the night. And now," said Joe, "you can take in one more shovelful today. Old Orlick he's been a-bustin' open a dwelling 'ouse."

"Whose?" said I.

"Not, I grant you, but what his manners

---

[1] **coddleshell:** Joe means *codicil* (kod'ə·səl), an item of instruction added to a will.

---

is given to blusterous. Still, an Englishman's 'ouse is his castle, and castles must not be busted 'cept when done in wartime. And wotsume'er the failings on his part, he were a corn and seedsman in his heart."

"Is it Pumblechook's house that has been broken into, then?"

"That's it, Pip," said Joe, "and they took his till, and they took his cashbox, and they drinked his wine, and they partook of his wittles, and they slapped his face, and they pulled his nose, and they tied him up to his bedpust, and they stuffed his mouth full of flowering annuals to perwent his crying out. But he knowed Orlick, and Orlick's in the county jail."

By these approaches we arrived at unrestricted conversation. I was slow to gain strength, but I did slowly and surely become less weak, and Joe stayed with me, and I fancied I was little Pip again.

For the tenderness of Joe was so beautifully proportioned to my need that I was like a child in his hands. He would sit and talk to me in the old confidence, and with the old simplicity, and in the old unassertive protecting way, so that I would half believe that all my life since the days of the old kitchen was one of the mental troubles of the fever that was gone.

We looked forward to the day when I should go out for a ride. And when the day came and an open carriage was got into the lane, Joe wrapped me up, took me in his arms, and carried me down to it, as if I were still the small helpless creature to whom he had so abundantly given of the wealth of his great nature. When we got back again and he carried me across the court and up the stairs, I thought of that eventful Christmas Day when he had carried me over the marshes. We had not yet made any allusion to my change of fortune, nor did I know how much of my late history he was acquainted with.

"Have you heard, Joe," I asked him that evening, as he smoked his pipe at the window, "who my patron was?"

"I heered," returned Joe, "as it were not Miss Havisham, old chap."

"Did you hear who it was, Joe?"

"Well! I heered as it were a person what sent the person what give you the bank notes at the Jolly Bargemen, Pip."

"So it was."

"Astonishing!" said Joe, in the placidest way.

"Did you hear that he was dead, Joe?"

"Which? Him as sent the bank notes, Pip?"

"Yes."

"I think," said Joe, after meditating a long time, and looking rather evasively at the window seat, "as I *did* hear tell that how he were something or another in a general way in that direction."

"Did you hear anything of his circumstances, Joe?"

"Not partickler, Pip."

"If you would like to hear, Joe—" I was beginning, when Joe got up and came to my sofa.

"Look'ee here, old chap," said Joe, bending over me. "Ever the best of friends; ain't us, Pip?"

I was ashamed to answer him.

"Wery good, then," said Joe, as if I *had* answered, "that's all right; that's agreed upon. Then why go into subjects, old chap, which as betwixt two sech must be forever onnecessary?"

The delicacy with which Joe dismissed this theme made a deep impression on my mind. But whether Joe knew how poor I was, and how my great expectations had all dissolved, like our own marsh mists before the sun, I could not understand.

Another thing in Joe that I could not understand when it first began to develop itself, was this. As I became stronger and better, Joe became a little less easy with me. In my weakness and entire dependence on him, the dear fellow had fallen into the old tone, and called me by the old names, the dear "old Pip, old chap," that now were music in my ears. I too had fallen into the old ways, only happy and thankful that he let me. But imperceptibly, though I held by them fast, Joe's hold upon them began to slacken; and I soon began to understand that the fault of it was all mine.

It was on the third or fourth occasion of my going out walking that I saw this change in him very plainly. We had been sitting in the bright warm sunlight, looking at the river, and I chanced to say as we got up:

"See, Joe! I can walk quite strongly. Now, you shall see me walk back by myself."

"Do not overdo it, Pip," said Joe; "but I shall be happy fur to see you able, sir."

The last word grated on me; but how could I remonstrate! I walked no farther than the gate of the gardens, and then pretended to be weaker than I was, and asked Joe for his arm. Joe gave it me, but was thoughtful.

I, for my part, was thoughtful too. I was ashamed to tell him exactly how I was placed. He would want to help me out of his little savings, I knew, and I knew that he ought not to help me, and that I must not suffer him to do it.

It was a thoughtful evening with both of us. Before we went to bed, I had resolved that I would wait over tomorrow, tomorrow being Sunday, and would begin my new course with the new week. On Monday morning I would speak to Joe and tell him what I had in my thoughts.

We had a quiet day on the Sunday, and we rode out into the country, and then walked in the fields. At night, when I had gone to bed, Joe came into my room, as he had done all through my recovery. He asked me if I felt sure that I was as well as in the morning.

"Yes, dear Joe, quite."

"And are always a-getting stronger, old chap?"

"Yes, dear Joe, steadily."

Joe patted the coverlet on my shoulder with his great good hand and said, in what I thought a husky voice, "Good night!"

When I got up in the morning, refreshed and stronger yet, I was full of my resolution to tell Joe all, without delay. I went to his room, and he was not there. Not only was he not there, but his box was gone.

I hurried then to the breakfast table and on it found a letter. These were its brief contents.

Not wishful to intrude I have departured fur you are well again dear Pip and will do better without

Jo.

P.S. Ever the best of friends.

Enclosed in the letter was a receipt for the debt and costs on which I had been arrested. Down to that moment I had vainly supposed that my creditor had withdrawn until I should be quite recovered. I had never dreamed of Joe's having paid the money; but Joe had paid it, and the receipt was in his name.

What remained for me now, but to follow him to the dear old forge and there to have out my disclosure to him, and my penitent remonstrance with him, and there to relieve my mind and heart of another idea, which had begun as a vague something lingering in my thoughts and had formed into a settled purpose.

The purpose was that I would go to Biddy, that I would show her how humbled and repentant I came back, that I would tell her how I had lost all I once hoped for. Then I would say to her, "Biddy, I think you once liked me very

well, when my errant heart, even while it strayed away from you, was quieter and better with you than it ever has been since. If you can like me only half as well once more, if you can take me with all my faults and disappointments on my head, if you can receive me like a forgiven child, I hope I am a little worthier of you than I was—not much, but a little. And, Biddy, it shall rest with you to say whether I shall work at the forge with Joe, or whether I shall try for any different occupation down in this country, or whether we shall go away to a distant place where an opportunity awaits me which I set aside when it was offered, until I knew your answer. And now, dear Biddy, if you can tell me that you will go through the world with me, you will surely make it a better world for me, and me a better man for it, and I will try hard to make it a better world for you."

Such was my purpose. After three days more of recovery, I went down to the old place, to put it in execution. And how I sped in it is all I have left to tell.

CHAPTER 43

Biddy and Joe have news for Pip.

THE TIDINGS of my high fortunes having had a heavy fall had got down to my native place and its neighborhood before I got there. I found the Blue Boar in possession of the intelligence, and I found that it made a great change in the Boar's demeanor.

It was evening when I arrived, much fatigued by the journey. The Boar could not put me into my usual bedroom, which was engaged (probably by someone who had expectations), and could only assign me a very indifferent chamber among the pigeons. But I had as sound a sleep and the quality of my dreams was about the same as in the best bedroom.

Early in the morning I strolled round by Satis House. There were printed bills on the gate announcing a sale by auction of the household furniture and effects next week. The house itself was to be sold as old building materials, and pulled down. The ivy had been torn down, and much of it trailed low in the dust and was withered already. Stepping in for a moment at the open gate and looking around me with the uncomfortable air of a stranger who had no business there, I saw the auctioneer's clerk walking on the casks and telling them off for the information of a catalogue compiler, pen in hand, who made a temporary desk of the wheeled chair I had so often pushed along.

It was the pleasanter to turn to Biddy and to Joe. I went toward them slowly, for my limbs were weak, but with a sense

of increasing relief as I drew nearer to them, and a sense of leaving arrogance and untruthfulness farther and farther behind.

The June weather was delicious. The sky was blue, the larks were soaring high over the green corn. I thought all that countryside more beautiful and peaceful by far than I had ever known it to be yet. Many pleasant pictures of the life that I would lead there, and of the change for the better that would come over my character when I had a guiding spirit at my side whose simple faith and clear home wisdom I had proved, beguiled my way. They awakened a tender emotion in me, for my heart was softened by my return, and such a change had come to pass that I felt like one who was toiling home barefoot from distant travel, and whose wanderings had lasted many years.

The schoolhouse where Biddy was mistress, I had never seen, but the little roundabout lane by which I entered the village for quietness' sake took me past it. I was disappointed to find that the day was a holiday; no children were there, and Biddy's house was closed. Some hopeful notion of seeing her, busily engaged in her daily duties, before she saw me, had been in my mind and was defeated.

But the forge was a very short distance off, and I went toward it under the sweet green limes, listening for the clink of Joe's hammer. But the clink of Joe's hammer was not in the midsummer wind.

Almost fearing without knowing why to come in view of the forge, I saw it at last, and saw that it was closed. No gleam of fire, no glittering shower of sparks, no roar of bellows; all shut up, and still.

But the house was not deserted, and the best parlor seemed to be in use, for there were white curtains fluttering in its window, and the window was open and gay with flowers. I went softly toward it, meaning to peep over the flowers, when Joe and Biddy stood before me, arm in arm.

At first Biddy gave a cry, as if she thought it was my apparition, but in another moment she was in my embrace. I wept to see her, and she wept to see me; I, because she looked so fresh and pleasant; she, because I looked so worn and white.

"But, dear Biddy, how smart you look!"

"Yes, dear Pip."

"And, Joe, how smart *you* look!"

"Yes, dear old Pip, old chap."

I looked at both of them, from one to the other, and then—

"It's my wedding day," cried Biddy, in a burst of happiness, "and I am married to Joe!"

They had taken me into the kitchen, and I had laid my head down on the old deal table. Biddy held one of my hands to her lips, and Joe's restoring touch was on my shoulder. "Which he warn't strong enough, my dear, to be surprised," said Joe. And Biddy said, "I ought to have thought of it, dear Joe, but I was too happy." They were both so overjoyed to see me, so proud to see me, so touched by my coming to them, so delighted that I should have come by accident to make their day complete!

My first thought was one of great thankfulness that I had never breathed this last baffled hope to Joe. How often, while he was with me in my illness, had it risen to my lips.

"Dear Biddy," said I, "you have the best husband in the whole world, and if you could have seen him by my bed you would have—But no, you couldn't love him better than you do."

"No, I couldn't indeed," said Biddy.

"And, dear Joe, you have the best wife in the whole world, and she will make you as happy as even you deserve to be, you dear, good, noble Joe!"

Joe looked at me with a quivering lip, and fairly put his sleeve before his eyes.

"And Joe and Biddy both, receive my humble thanks for all you have done for me, and all I have so ill repaid! And when I say that I am going away within the hour, for I am soon going abroad, and I shall never rest until I have worked for the money with which you have kept me out of prison, and have sent it to you, don't think, dear Joe and Biddy, that if I could repay it a thousand times over, I suppose I could cancel a farthing of the debt I owe you, or that I would do so if I could!"

They were both melted by these words, and both entreated me to say no more.

"But I must say more. Dear Joe, I hope you will have children to love, and that some little fellow will sit in this chimney corner of a winter night who may remind you of another little fellow gone out of it forever. Don't tell him, Joe, that I was thankless; don't tell him, Biddy, that I was ungenerous and unjust; only tell him that I honored you both, because you were both so good and true, and that, as your child, I said it would be natural to him to grow up a much better man than I did."

"I ain't a-going," said Joe, from behind his sleeve, "to tell him nothink o' that natur, Pip. Nor Biddy ain't."

"And now, though I know you have already done it in your own kind hearts, pray tell me, both, that you forgive me! Pray let me hear you say the words, that I may carry the sound of them away with me, and then I shall be able to believe that you can trust me, and think better of me, in the time to come!"

"Oh, dear old Pip, old chap," said Joe. "God knows as I forgive you, if I have anythink to forgive!"

"Amen! And God knows I do!" echoed Biddy.

"Now let me go up and look at my old

little room and rest there a few minutes by myself. And then when I have eaten and drunk with you, go with me as far as the fingerpost, dear Joe and Biddy, before we say good-by!"

I sold all I had, and put aside as much as I could for my creditors—who gave me ample time to pay them in full—and I went out and joined Herbert. Within a month, I had quitted England, and within two months I was clerk to Clarriker and Co., and within four months I assumed my first undivided responsibility. For the beam across the parlor ceiling at Mill Pond Bank had then ceased to tremble under the old purser's growls and was at peace, and Herbert had gone away to marry Clara, and I was left in sole charge of the Eastern Branch until he brought her back.

Many a year went round before I was a partner in the house; but I lived happily with Herbert and his wife, and lived frugally, and paid my debts, and maintained a constant correspondence with Biddy and Joe. It was not until I became third in the firm that Clarriker betrayed me to Herbert; but he then declared that the secret of Herbert's partnership had been long enough upon his conscience, and he must tell it. So he told it, and Herbert was as much moved as amazed, and the dear fellow and I were not the worse friends for the long concealment. I must not leave it to be supposed that we were ever a great house, or that we made mints of money. We were not in a grand way of business, but we had a good name, and worked for our profits, and did very well. We owed so much to Herbert's ever cheerful industry and readiness that I often wondered how I had conceived that old idea of his inaptitude, until I was one day enlightened by the reflection that perhaps the inaptitude had never been in him at all, but had been in me.

CHAPTER 44

Pip and Estella meet again.

FOR ELEVEN YEARS I had not seen Joe nor Biddy when, upon an evening in December, an hour or two after dark, I laid my hand softly on the latch of the old kitchen door. I touched it so softly that I was not heard, and I looked in unseen. There, smoking his pipe in the old place by the kitchen firelight, as hale and as strong as ever, though a little gray, sat Joe; and there, fenced into the corner with Joe's leg, and sitting on my own little stool looking at the fire, was—I again!

"We giv' him the name of Pip for your sake, dear old chap," said Joe, delighted when I took another stool by the child's side, "and we hoped he might grow a little bit like you, and we think he do."

I thought so too, and I took him out for a walk next morning, and we talked immensely, understanding one another to perfection. And I took him down to the churchyard, and set him on a certain tombstone there, and he showed me from that elevation which stone was sacred to the memory of Philip Pirrip, late of this parish, and Also Georgiana, Wife of the Above.

"Biddy," said I, when I talked with her after dinner, as her little girl lay sleeping in her lap, "you must give Pip to me, one of these days; or lend him, at all events."

"No, no," said Biddy gently. "You must marry."

"So Herbert and Clara say, but I don't think I shall, Biddy. I have so settled down in their home that it's not at all likely. I am already quite an old bachelor."

Biddy looked down at her child, and put its little hand to her lips, and then put the good matronly hand with which she had touched it into mine. There was something in the action and in the light pressure of Biddy's wedding ring that had a very pretty eloquence in it.

"Dear Pip," said Biddy, "you are sure you don't fret for her?"

"Oh, no—I think not, Biddy."

"Tell me as an old friend. Have you quite forgotten her?"

"My dear Biddy, I have forgotten nothing in my life that ever had a foremost place there, and little that ever had any place there. But that poor dream, as I once used to call it, has all gone by, Biddy, all gone by!"

[Dickens originally wrote only two more paragraphs to end the story, but because so many of his friends were dissatisfied with the conclusion, he rewrote the final paragraphs of the novel to read as follows. You will find the original ending on page 726.]

Nevertheless, I knew while I said those words that I secretly intended to revisit the site of the old house that evening, alone, for her sake. Yes, even so. For Estella's sake.

I had heard of her as leading a most un-happy life, and as being separated from her husband, who had used her with great cruelty, and who had become quite renowned as a compound of pride, avarice, brutality, and meanness. And I had heard of the death of her husband, from an accident consequent on his ill treatment of a horse. This release had befallen her some two years before; for anything I knew she was married again.

The early dinner hour at Joe's left me time to walk over to the old spot before dark. There was no house now, no brewery, no building whatever left, but the wall of the old garden. The cleared space had been enclosed with a rough fence, and looking over it, I saw that some of the old ivy had struck root anew and was growing green on low quiet mounds of ruin. A gate in the fence standing ajar, I pushed it open and went in.

A cold silvery mist had veiled the afternoon, and the moon was not yet up to scatter it. But the stars were shining beyond the mist, and the moon was coming,

and the evening was not dark. I could trace out where every part of the old house had been and was looking along the desolate garden walk, when I beheld a solitary figure in it.

The figure showed itself aware of me as I advanced. It had been moving toward me, but it stood still. As I drew nearer, I saw it to be the figure of a woman. Then, it faltered as if much surprised, and uttered my name, and I cried out:

"Estella!"

"I am greatly changed. I wonder you know me."

The freshness of her beauty was indeed gone, but its majesty and its charm remained. Those attractions in it, I had seen before; what I had never seen before was the saddened softened light of the once proud eyes; what I had never felt before was the friendly touch of the once insensible hand.

We sat down on a bench that was near, and I said, "After so many years, it is strange that we should thus meet again, Estella, here where our first meeting was! Do you often come back?"

"I have never been here since."

"Nor I."

The moon began to rise, and I thought of the placid look at the white ceiling, which had passed away. The moon began to rise, and I thought of the pressure on my hand when I had spoken the last words he had heard on earth.

Estella was the next to break the silence.

"I have very often hoped and intended to come back, but have been prevented by many circumstances. Poor, poor old place!"

The silvery mist was touched with the first rays of the moonlight, and the same rays touched the tears that dropped from her eyes. Not knowing that I saw them, and setting herself to get the better of them, she said quietly:

"Were you wondering, as you walked along, how it came to be left in this condition?"

"Yes, Estella."

"The ground belongs to me. It is the only possession I have not relinquished. Everything else has gone from me, little by little, but I have kept this. It was the subject of the only determined resistance I made in all the wretched years."

"Is it to be built on?"

"At last it is. I came here to take leave of it before its change. And you," she said, in a voice of touching interest to a wanderer, "you live abroad still."

"Still."

"And do well, I am sure?"

"I work pretty hard for a sufficient living, and therefore—yes, I do well!"

"I have often thought of you," said Estella.

"Have you?"

"Of late, very often."

"You have always held your place in *my* heart," I answered.

And we were silent again until she spoke.

"I little thought," said Estella, "that I should take leave of you in taking leave of this spot. I am very glad to do so."

"Glad to part again, Estella? To me, parting is a painful thing. To me, the remembrance of our last parting has been ever mournful and painful."

"But you said to me," returned Estella, very earnestly, "'God bless you, God forgive you!' And if you could say that to me then, you will not hesitate to say that to me now—now, when suffering has been stronger than all other teaching, and has taught me to understand what your heart used to be. I have been bent and broken, but—I hope—into a better shape. Be as considerate and good to me as you were, and tell me we are friends."

"We are friends," said I, rising and bending over her, as she rose from the bench.

"And will continue friends apart," said Estella.

I took her hand in mine, and we went out of the ruined place; and as the morning mists had risen long ago when I first left the forge, so the evening mists were rising now, and in all the broad expanse of tranquil light they showed to me, I saw no shadow of another parting from her.

[*Great Expectations* originally ended with the following two paragraphs. In the original version, the final chapter was the same as the present one, up to the point where Pip tells Biddy, "That poor dream, as I once used to call it, has all gone by, Biddy, all gone by!" (See page 724.) From that point on, the original ending was as follows:]

It was two years more before I saw Estella. I had heard of her as leading a most unhappy life, and as being separated from her husband, who had used her with great cruelty, and who had become quite renowned as a compound of pride, brutality, and meanness. I had heard of the death of her husband from an accident consequent on ill treating a horse, and of her being married again to a Shropshire doctor who, against his interest, had once very manfully interposed on an occasion when he was in professional attendance on Mr. Drummle, and had witnessed some outrageous treatment of her. I had heard that the Shropshire doctor was not rich, and that they lived on her own personal fortune. I was in England again—in London, and walking along Piccadilly with little Pip—when a servant came running after me to ask would I step back to a lady in a carriage who wished to speak to me. It was a little pony carriage which the lady was driving, and the lady and I looked sadly enough on one another.

"I am greatly changed, I know; but I thought you would like to shake hands with Estella too, Pip. Lift up that pretty child and let me kiss it!" (She supposed the child, I think, to be my child.) I was very glad afterward to have had the interview; for in her face and in her voice, and in her touch, she gave me the assurance that suffering had been stronger than Miss Havisham's teaching, and had given her a heart to understand what my heart used to be.

FOR STUDY AND DISCUSSION

1. In the first two stages of *Great Expectations,* Pip did what other people told him to. What is different about his actions in Stage III? Which of his actions toward the end of the novel show a new independence of spirit?

2. In the third stage of *Great Expectations,* Pip finds himself. How has he changed from the snob who felt superior to everyone in his past? What is his new attitude toward those who have been kind to him in the past? How is this change in Pip shown in his actions toward Magwitch during and after his trial?

3. In this last stage of the novel, the threads of the plot come together, for Pip as well as for us, into a logical design. In this final stage, what discoveries does Pip make about other people that help to remove the last of his illusions? Who does Magwitch turn out to be related to? How did the other convict, Compeyson, swindle Miss Havisham? Who is Estella's mother? What effect do these discoveries have on Pip's attitude toward Magwitch, Estella, and Miss Havisham?

4. Throughout the novel, the events of the plot profoundly influence Pip's character. In the third stage, which of Pip's experiences teach him the value of real friendship and affection? In particular, what does he learn from each of the following: meeting Clara, Herbert's fiancée; hearing the story Pumblechook has told about him; being held prisoner by Orlick; being cared for by Joe.

5. Just as plot has its effect on character, so character to some extent determines plot.

Which of Dickens's two endings do you prefer? Why? Which do you think is most faithful to the nature of the characters involved? Does Pip, by the end of the novel, still want to marry Estella? Does he deserve to? Does Estella, because of what she has experienced, deserve to be forgiven by Pip? Is it believable that she could have come to love him? Do you think that, after all that Estella has done to Pip and Miss Havisham has done to Estella, these two can still care for each other? Why or why not? Is Pip the sort of person who could, even after all his disappointments, still have such expectations?

6. Both Magwitch and Miss Havisham try to make someone into a certain kind of person. How well does each succeed? At what point in the story might they have felt that their plans backfired and worked to their own disadvantage?

7. How has Estella changed since she was a child? Why does she marry Bentley Drummle? What does Miss Havisham finally realize about the consequences of what she has done to Estella?

8. What does Miss Havisham offer to do for Pip? What does he ask her help in doing? What do you think is her final opinion of Pip? Does she like him? respect him? admire him? What makes you think so?

9. Do you think Biddy would have made a better wife for Pip than Estella, when Estella was older and more gentle? Why or why not?

10. What is your final opinion of Herbert Pocket? How does he help Pip when he needs help? Would you want him for a friend? Why or why not?

11. While holding Pip prisoner, Orlick tells him why he hates him. Why is he envious of Pip? Do you think anyone in his situation might feel the same, or is his envy due mainly to his evil nature? What makes you think so?

12. Was Magwitch's life of crime something that could happen to anyone? How did he become a criminal? How was he treated in the courts and prisons? How do you think you would have reacted to such treatment? Why? What was the great injustice in Magwitch's trial with Compeyson?

13. What is the difference between Wemmick's behavior in Mr. Jaggers's office and his behavior in his "private, personal capacity"? What change comes over Wemmick when he leaves his "Castle" and goes to his office? Do you think many people, like Wemmick, adopt a special manner in certain situations to live up to what they think other people expect of them?

14. While ill with fever, Pip realizes, "My great expectations had all dissolved, like our own marsh mists before the sun." How is this statement, in a way, a summing-up of all that Pip has learned? In your own words, state what you think is the theme of *Great Expectations*.

THE CRAFT OF THE NOVELIST

1. Which would you say were the most exciting or dramatic incidents in Stage III? How does Dickens make them so exciting? Choose one especially exciting incident and show how Dickens builds up suspense and tension.

2. Dickens's masterful handling of plot and suspense is especially evident in his treatment of Molly. What clues does he provide to Molly's real identity? How does Molly's behavior, as observed by Pip, help to make Wemmick's story of her past convincing?

3. By telling the life stories of Magwitch and Miss Havisham, Dickens makes us, as well as Pip, more sympathetic toward them. Do you think you would feel more sympathetic toward Orlick, Compeyson, or Bentley Drummle if Dickens had also told their life stories? Why or why not? Why do you think Dickens left their background unexplained?

4. In the last two stages of the novel, most of the action alternates between Pip's old home on the marshes and his new home in London. As the characters journey back and forth between these two locations, Dickens prepares us for their arrivals or departures by means of the letters Pip receives. These letters either call Pip back to the marshes or prepare him for a visitor. How does each of these letters make the comings and goings of the characters more realistic and convincing?

5. What are the most amusing moments in the chapter "Mr. Wemmick Takes a Walk"? What devices does Dickens use in this chapter to achieve humorous effects?

LANGUAGE AND VOCABULARY

1. Pip's first feeling toward Magwitch is one of *repugnance*—a strong dislike. The word comes from the Latin prefix *re-* (back) and *pugnare* (to fight). What do these roots suggest about the conditions that first gave rise to *repugnance?* Also from the same root come the words *pugnacious* and *impugn*. What is the meaning of each of these? Another strong word, *pungent*, comes from the Latin *pungere* (to prick or sting), but it is also related to both *pugnare* and *pugnus* (fist). What is the meaning of *pungent?* How does the word's sound fit its meaning?

2. Many English words use the Latin root *-pos-* or *-pon-* (to place or put). In *Great Expectations*, Compeyson had meant to *depose* to the real identity of Magwitch. *Depose,* which means "to testify under oath," comes from the Latin *deponere* (to put down). Other words in this family are *postpone, interpose, propose,* and *composure*. From the root *-pon-* or *-pos-* in each, what would you guess to be each word's meaning? After guessing, check each word's exact meaning in a dictionary.

THE NOVEL AS A WHOLE

1. Reading *Great Expectations* should have given you a good idea of the characteristics of the novel as a literary type—especially in the way it differs from the short story. For one thing, the novel, because of its greater length, usually has more characters and examines their lives in greater detail than is possible in a short story. What are some other differences? Make a list of the most important differences, keeping in mind such elements as plot, central characters, setting, and time.

2. Mr. Jaggers is the one character in the novel who seems able to get along without love. How does he treat those who are waiting to see him when Pip first comes to London? Why, of the three young men he has to dinner, do you think he is most interested in Bentley Drummle? Does he expect the worst or the best from people? What in the story makes you sure?

3. Mr. Jaggers's final advice to Pip is: "Take nothing on its looks; take everything on evidence. There's no better rule." Do you agree? Why or why not? Would this have been good advice for Pip when he first came to London? If he had followed it, what do you think he would have done differently? Do you think it would be good advice in any situation? Why or why not?

4. In a way, Satis House is a symbol of Miss Havisham. How has she made it reflect her own state of mind? What is suggested by the stopped clocks? the dark passageways? the yellowed bridal gown? When Pip pulls the tablecloth off the table, spiders and beetles run out of the wedding cake. What does this suggest about Miss Havisham's lost love?

5. From what you know about the life of Charles Dickens (see pages 313–16 and page 559), which scenes in *Great Expectations* do you think might have been drawn from his own experience? What makes you think so?

6. The novels of Charles Dickens helped to bring about reforms in many of the institutions of his time, such as the prisons and schools. Which scenes in *Great Expectations* might have aroused Dickens's readers to demand such reforms?

FOR COMPOSITION

1. Did you notice that, as different as Dickens's two endings were, he used several incidents from the original ending in his rewritten one? Reread both endings and make a list of the incidents used in both of them. Could these same incidents be used in still another ending? What other way might the story end? Write your own ending for *Great Expectations,* being sure to include all the incidents that Dickens included in rewriting.

2. Of all the characters in *Great Expectations,* which one seems to you the most admirable? the most villainous? the most humorous? the most memorable? Write a short paragraph about each one of these, telling why he (or she) seems so to you.

3. In growing up, Pip learns many things about life and people. In a short composition tell what you think are the most important things he learns and why you think they are important.

Reading and Writing about a Novel

You will find that reading critical comments and opinions will often enlarge your own understanding of a given poem, story, essay, play, or novel. Consider, for example, one critic's opinion of what Dickens had in mind in writing *Great Expectations:*

Dickens' idea of Pip was . . . a young man who could be interpreted in detail as his character deteriorates under the stimulus of "great" or "undeserved" expectations of wealth and position. Dickens invented a series of events which would let Pip come close to ruin as a person because of his expectations, reach a climax of disappointment when they turn out to be "false" (false in the sense of caste and prestige), achieve maturity in the experience, then find gradual regeneration by learning to work for proper rewards in life. *Great Expectations* is planned on this concept of character, and all the action revolves around it. (Earle Davis, *The Flint and the Flame: The Artistry of Charles Dickens.*)

How does Pip's character deteriorate in the course of the novel? At what point does he experience a "climax of disappointment"? How does this help him to "achieve maturity"?

WRITING ABOUT A NOVEL

The following quotations about *Great Expectations* all bear upon one of Dickens' major themes: the power and the value of money in our lives. After reading these opinions, write a short essay supporting or refuting one of them on the basis of your own knowledge of *Great Expectations.*

For Pip, the money from the convict, fat and sweltering from the cattle markets, is a very different thing from that of Miss Havisham, "clean and new." But he is wrong in his benefactor, and he is wrong in thinking that some money is mysteriously cleaner than other money. When Magwitch burns the clean money, Dickens means more by it than Magwitch does. Magwitch means to shock and waken Pip, but he also burns Pip's dreams of a clean gentlemanly fortune. (Christopher Ricks, *Dickens and the Twentieth Century.*)

The attitude of Pip toward Magwitch in *Great Expectations* is extremely interesting. Pip is conscious all along of his ingratitude toward Joe, but far less so of his ingratitude toward Magwitch. When he discovers that the person who had loaded him with benefits for years is actually a transported convict, he falls into frenzies of disgust. (George Orwell, "Charles Dickens.")

Great Expectations is the perfect expression of a phase of English society: it is a statement, to be taken as it stands, of what money can do, good and bad; of how it can change and make distinctions of class; how it can pervert virtue, sweeten manners, open up new fields of enjoyment and suspicion. (Humphrey House, *The Dickens World.*)

ART AND LITERATURE

One definition of *realism* is that it portrays everyday life convincingly. To be realistic and convincing, paintings as well as novels must include the little details of ordinary life. Look again at the paintings on pages 595–600 and reread some of Dickens' descriptions in *Great Expectations.* Then write an essay comparing the paintings and the novel and telling which you find most realistic and convincing. In your argument, cite specific details from the novel and the paintings.

THE COMPOSITION AND LANGUAGE PROGRAM

Unless otherwise indicated, all composition assignments appear in the anthology under the heading "For Composition." Number references in parentheses are to the numbered items in the text under the heading "For Composition." Variant headings are listed as appropriate.

Assignments Based on Selections

DESCRIPTION

Description of a possession. (number 2) 48
"The Pacing Goose," Jessamyn West
Description of a person, contrasting outer appearance with inner reality. (number 1) 61
"All the Years of Her Life,"
Morley Callaghan
Description of an event from a particular point of view 93
"A Gray Sleeve," Stephen Crane
Description of a place, contrasting its present with its past appearance. (number 1) '103
"The House with the Grapevine,"
H. E. Bates
Description of a painting. *Art and Literature* 105
Description conveying a main impression 105, 120, 292, 347, 511
Writing a Description. 105
"The Ambitious Guest,"
Nathaniel Hawthorne 120
Art and Literature 292
Your Own Writing. (number 2) 347
Romeo and Juliet, William Shakespeare. (number 4) 511
Description of a place 173, 191, 203, 278, 345
"London Town," John Masefield. (number 1) 173
"The Summit Temple," Li Po. 191

NARRATION

Writing the conclusion to a story 9
"The Lady or the Tiger?"
Frank R. Stockton
Retelling and expanding an incident from a story 13, 98, 553
"Charles," Shirley Jackson 13
"The Secret Life of Walter Mitty,"
James Thurber 98
The Odyssey, Homer. (number 1) 553
Writing a narrative that conveys a strong impression of a character's feelings. (number 1) 36
"The Silver Mine," Selma Lagerlöf
Narration in support of a proverb or moral point. (number 2) 36
"The Silver Mine," Selma Lagerlöf
A personal narrative about the recognition of a person's character 61, 673
"All the Years of Her Life,"
Morley Callaghan. (number 2) 61
Great Expectations, Charles Dickens. (number 3) 673
First-person narrative to prove a point 65, 226
"Luck," Mark Twain. (number -1) 65
"See the Trees," Carl Sandburg. (number 4) 226
Narrative developing a theme 81
"The Gift of the Magi," O. Henry

EXPOSITION

Developing a topic 18, 226, 289, 333, 553
"The Interlopers," H. H. Munro. (number 2) 18
"Boxes and Bags," Carl Sandburg. (number 3) 226
"Of Studies," Francis Bacon 289
"The Day the Dam Broke,"
James Thurber. (number 2) 333
The Odyssey, Homer. (number 2) 553
Expressing and supporting an opinion of a character 25, 65, 728
"The Necklace," Guy de Maupassant. (number 1) 25
"Luck," Mark Twain. (number 2) 65
Great Expectations, Charles Dickens. (number 2) 728
Explaining a procedure. (number 1) 148
"The Gift," John Steinbeck
Comparison of city life and country life. (number 3) 148
"The Gift," John Steinbeck
Essay of opinion 173, 250, 252, 286, 347, 422, 673, 728
"London Town," John Masefield. (number 2) 173
Five Poets: A Closer Look (number 2) 250
Art and Literature (number 2) 252
"The Decline of Sport," E. B. White. 286

Literary Terms and Techniques

Glossary of Literary Terms

ALLITERATION The repetition of initial consonant sounds. Although alliteration sometimes appears in prose, it is mainly a poetic device. Like other forms of sound repetition, alliteration in poetry serves important purposes: it is pleasing to the ear, and it emphasizes the words in which it occurs. (See page 157.) William Shakespeare uses alliteration in this line from a song (page 427) from his play *The Tempest:*

Full fathom five thy father lies

Alliteration has a wide and persistent appeal, which is shown by its frequent use in CLICHÉS, such as "a dime a dozen," "bigger and better," and "jump for joy."

ALLUSION A reference to a person, a place, an event, or a literary work which a writer expects the reader to recognize and respond to. An allusion may be drawn from history, geography, literature, or religion. (See page 179.) An allusion to history is found in these lines from Rudyard Kipling's "Recessional" (page 233):

Lo, all our pomp of yesterday
Is one with Nineveh and Tyre!

In these lines Kipling alludes to two ancient cities that no longer exist. According to the Bible, both Nineveh and Tyre caused God to be angry, for they did not recognize God or obey God's commands.

ANALOGY A comparison made between two things to show the similarities between them. Analogies are often used for illustration (to explain something unfamiliar by comparing it to something familiar) or for argument (to persuade that what holds true for one thing holds true for the thing to which it is compared). Washington Irving uses an analogy in *Diedrich Knickerbocker's History of New York* (page 273) when he says his readers will compare the citizens (burghers) to beavers:

Their own imaginations will doubtless present to them the good burghers, like so many painstaking and persevering beavers, slowly and surely pursuing their labors . . . .

ANAPEST A poetic FOOT consisting of two unstressed syllables followed by a stressed syllable ($\smile\smile\,'$). Generally, a poem with *anapestic* meter has a light, tripping sound. The following lines from Lewis Carroll's playfully satiric poem "Father William" (page 213) use anapestic feet:

"You are old, Father William," the young
    man said,
    "And your hair has become very white;
And yet you incessantly stand on your
    head—
    Do you think, at your age, it is right?"

ANECDOTE A very short story that is told to make a point. Anecdotes are often humorous; at times, they are jokes. Anecdotes are used in all forms of literature. John Steinbeck uses an anecdote in "Travels with Charley" (page 335) when he interrupts his narrative with a very short amusing story to illustrate what happened when people noticed his New York license plates. The point of his little anecdote is that everyone he met said what this local man said about New York City: "Anyway, I hated it. Wouldn't live there if you paid me."

ANTAGONIST A person or force opposing the PROTAGONIST in a narrative; a rival of the hero or heroine. *Antagonist* comes from a Greek word meaning "to struggle against." Famous antagonists in literature include Professor Moriarty, Sherlock Holmes' antagonist in Arthur Conan Doyle's detective stories, and the great white whale Moby Dick, Captain Ahab's antagonist in Herman Melville's novel *Moby Dick*.

APOSTROPHE A FIGURE OF SPEECH in which an absent or a dead person, an abstract quality, or something inanimate or intangible is addressed directly. Robert Burns uses apostrophe when he addresses the Afton river in "Sweet Afton" (page 237):

Flow gently, sweet Afton! among thy green braes

ASSONANCE The repetition of vowel sounds, especially in poetry, as in "high flier." Assonance is used to please the ear and to emphasize certain sounds. (See pages 160 and 204.) Here is an example of assonance in a line from "The Bells" by Edgar Allan Poe:

From the molten-golden notes

ATMOSPHERE The prevailing mood or feeling of a literary work. Atmosphere is often developed, at least in part, through descriptions of SETTING. Such descriptions help to create an emotional climate for the work, which serves to establish the reader's expectations and attitudes. For example, Edgar Allan Poe develops a gloomy and ominous atmosphere for his story "The Fall of the House of Usher" with this description of setting in the first paragraph:

During the whole of a dull, dark, and soundless day in the autumn of the year, when the clouds hung oppressively low in the heavens, I had been passing alone, on horseback, through a singularly dreary tract of country, and at length found my-

self, as the shades of the evening drew on, within view of the melancholy House of Usher. I know not how it was—but, with the first glimpse of the building, a sense of insufferable gloom pervaded my spirit.

AUTOBIOGRAPHY A person's account of his or her own life. An autobiography is generally written in narrative form and includes some introspection. Autobiographies are distinct from diaries, journals, and letters, which are not unified life stories written for publication. Autobiographies are also different from memoirs, which often deal, at least in part, with public events and important persons other than the author. "The Genuine Mexican Plug" (page 260) is from Mark Twain's autobiographical account of his adventures in the Far West.

BALLAD A story told in verse and usually meant to be sung. *Folk ballads* are composed anonymously and transmitted orally. In many countries the folk ballad was one of the earliest forms of literature. The subject matter of the folk ballads stems from the everyday life of the common people. The most popular themes, often tragic ones, are disappointed love, jealously, revenge, sudden disaster, and deeds of adventure and daring. "The Wife of Usher's Well" (page 154) is a folk ballad. In America, a folk ballad tradition has flourished in the Appalachian mountains, among cowpokes, and within labor movements. *Literary ballads* are written by known writers who are imitating folk ballads. "The Ballad of William Sycamore" by Stephen Vincent Benét (page 165) is a literary ballad. (See pages 155 and 156.)

BALLAD STANZA A type of stanza of four lines. The first and third lines have four stressed words or syllables; the second and fourth lines have three stresses. The number of unstressed syllables in each line may vary. The second and fourth lines rhyme. (See page 155.) Here is a ballad stanza from an American folk ballad, "The Lover's Lament":

My déarest déar, the tíme draws néar
When yoú and Í must párt;

But little do you know the grief or woe
Of my poor troubled heart.

BIOGRAPHY A detailed account of a person's life written by another person. Biographies in English have taken many different forms since they were first written in medieval times to praise the virtues of saints and to celebrate the feats of heroes. The modern biographer aims at accuracy and usually makes an attempt to interpret the personality of the subject. Details of the social and historical circumstances in which the subject lived are often included. "The Young Shakespeare" by Marchette Chute (page 294) is an excerpt from a biography. (See page 293.)

BLANK VERSE Verse written in unrhymed IAMBIC PENTAMETER. Blank verse is the verse form used in some of the greatest English poetry, including that of William Shakespeare. Here is an example from *Romeo and Juliet* (page 434):

But soft! What light through yonder window breaks?
It is the east, and Juliet is the sun!
Arise, fair sun, and kill the envious moon,
Who is already sick and pale with grief
That thou her maid art far more fair than she.

CAESURA A light break or pause in a line of poetry, which contributes to the RHYTHM of the poem. There are several caesuras in these lines from Alfred, Lord Tennyson's "Bugle Song" (page 167), which are indicated by double lines (‖):

Blow, ‖ bugle; ‖ answer, ‖ echoes, ‖ dying, ‖ dying, ‖ dying.

CHARACTER A person—or an animal, a thing, or a natural force presented as a person—appearing in a short story, novel, play, or narrative poem. Characters in this book range from the noble Odysseus in Homer's *Odyssey* (page 517), to the goose Samantha in Jessamyn West's story "The Pacing Goose" (page 36), to Time in Ralph Hodgson's poem "Time, You Old Gypsy Man" (page 206). (See pages 3, 35, 433, and 557.)

CHARACTERIZATION The personality a character displays; also, the means by which an author reveals that personality. Generally, a writer develops a character in one or more of the following ways: (1) by showing the character acting and speaking; (2) by giving a physical description of the character; (3) by revealing the character's thoughts; (4) by revealing what other characters think about the character; (5) by commenting directly on the character. (See pages 3, 35, and 557.) Frank R. Stockton uses the last three methods in characterizing the princess in "The Lady or the Tiger?" (page 4):

This semibarbaric king had a daughter as blooming as his most rosy fancies, and with a soul as fervent and imperious as his own. As is usual in such cases, she was the apple of his eye, and was loved by him above all humanity. Among his courtiers was a young man of that fineness of blood and lowness of station common to the heroes of romance who love royal maidens. This royal maiden was well satisfied with her lover, for he was handsome and brave to a degree unsurpassed in all this kingdom, and she loved him with an ardor that had enough of barbarism in it to make it exceedingly warm and strong.

CLASSICISM A movement or tendency in art, literature, or music which reflects the principles manifested in the art of ancient Greece and Rome. Classicism emphasizes the traditional and the universal, and places value on reason, clarity, balance, and order. Francis Bacon's essays (page 287) are considered models of classical prose. Classicism, with its concern for reason and universal themes, is traditionally opposed to ROMANTICISM, which is concerned with emotions and personal themes.

CLICHÉ Any expression that has lost its forcefulness because it has been used too often. Here are some examples of clichés: "tried and true," "easy come, easy go," "last but not least," and "a barrel of laughs."

CLIMAX That point of greatest emotional intensity, interest, or suspense in a narrative. The climax usually marks a story's turning point. (See page 557.) The climax in *Romeo and Juliet* (page 434) takes place in Act III, when Romeo slays Tybalt and reopens the feud between the Montagues and the Capulets. At this point, Romeo's and Juliet's fates are sealed.

COMEDY In general, a literary work which ends happily with a healthy, amicable armistice between the PROTAGONIST and society. Comedy is distinct from TRAGEDY, which is generally concerned with a protagonist who meets an unhappy or disastrous end. The comic protagonist may be a person of ordinary character and ability, who does not usually achieve the heroic stature of the tragic hero or heroine. Comedies are often concerned, at least in part, with exposing human folly, and frequently depict the overthrow of rigid social fashions and customs. Wit, humor, and a sense of festivity are found in many comedies. Anton Chekhov's play *The Boor* (page 351), subtitled *A Jest in One Act,* is a comedy. It makes us laugh at the foolishness of people and at their poses. Like many comedies, it ends with a kiss between the two fighting lovers, and a marriage is anticipated by the audience.

CONFLICT A struggle between two opposing forces or CHARACTERS in a short story, novel, play, or narrative poem. Conflict can be external or internal, and it can take one of these forms: (1) a person against another person; (2) a person against society; (3) a person against nature; (4) two elements or ideas within a person struggling for mastery. Many works of fiction contain more than one of these forms of conflict. (See page 2.) In Jesse Stuart's story "The Split Cherry Tree" (page 66), there is conflict between the students and the farmer and their teacher, between Dave and his father, and between the father and the teacher. There is also a larger conflict in that story between two ways of life.

CONNOTATION All the emotions and associations that a word or phrase may arouse. Connotation is distinct from DENOTATION, which is the literal or "dictionary" meaning of a word or phrase. For example, the word *springtime* literally means that season of the year between the vernal equinox and the summer solstice, but the word usually makes most people think of such things as youth, rebirth, and romance. The word *shroud* literally means a cloth used for burial purposes, or anything that covers or protects. However, most people associate the word *shroud* with death, gloom, darkness, and other unpleasant things. Advertisers are especially sensitive to the connotations of words. For example, you'd probably never find a section of a department store called "Cheap Clothes"; it would more likely be called "Bargain Basement." (See pages 9 and 175.)

CONSONANCE The repetition of consonant sounds within words or at the ends of words, a device often used in poetry. (See pages 177 and 205.) Here are examples of consonance in several lines from Edgar Allan Poe's "The Bells":

> Hear the sledges with the bells,
>   Silver bells!
> What a world of merriment their melody
>   foretells!

CONTEXT The words and phrases closely surrounding another word or phrase, or, the general meaning conveyed by those words or phrases. (See page 25.) Context often determines a particular word's meaning, as in the following examples:

> That book has a fascinating *plot.*
> I'd like to build a house on that *plot.*
> Morgan will *plot* the fleet's position on on the map.

Context is also the situation and circumstances that surround an event; we discuss a character's action in the *context* of the entire story.

CONTRAST A striking difference between two things. In expository writing, two ideas may be contrasted for clarification and emphasis. In imaginative writing, contrasting settings, characters, and events are often presented for dramatic effect. In "The Secret Life of Walter Mitty" (page 94), James

Thurber humorously contrasts Walter Mitty's daydreams, in which he is a romantic, virile hero, with reality, in which he is a meek little man who is dominated by his wife.

COUPLET Two consecutive lines of poetry that rhyme. (See page 169.) Here is a couplet from Robert Louis Stevenson's "Travel" (page 178):

> There I'll come when I'm a *man*
> With a camel cara*van*

DACTYL A poetic FOOT consisting of a stressed syllable followed by two unstressed syllables (′ ◡◡). Dactyls are often found in nonsense poetry, in children's rhymes, and in advertising jingles. Notice the dactyls in these lines of nursery rhyme:

> Hickory dickory dock,
> The mouse ran up the clock

DENOTATION The literal or "dictionary" meaning of a word, which is distinct from its CONNOTATION. For example, the denotation, or dictionary definition, of the word *star* (as in "movie *star*") is "a prominent actor or actress," but the connotation of the word *star* is an actor or actress who is adored by fans and who leads a fascinating and glamorous life.

DÉNOUEMENT (dā·noo·män′) From the French word for "untying" or "solution." The dénouement is that part of a play or other narrative in which CONFLICTS are resolved, or untied, and mysteries and secrets connected with the PLOT are explained. (See page 557.)

DESCRIPTION That type of writing that is concerned with re-creating pictures or other sensory impressions: sounds, smells, textures, and tastes. Description is one of the major forms of discourse. (See also NARRATION, EXPOSITION, and PERSUASION). Although descriptions are often written to stand on their own, they are more frequently written to enhance other forms of writing.

(See page 104.) Here is part of the famous description of Miss Havisham in her bridal dress from Charles Dickens' novel *Great Expectations* (page 560):

> But I saw that everything within my view which ought to be white had lost its luster, and was faded and yellow. I saw that the bride within the bridal dress had withered like the dress, and like the flowers, and had no brightness left but the brightness of her sunken eyes. I saw that the dress had been put upon the rounded figure of a young woman, and that the figure upon which it now hung loose had shrunk to skin and bone.

DIALECT The characteristic speech of a particular regional or social group. Dialect differs from standard English in sentence pattern, vocabulary, and pronunciation. Writers use dialect to aid in characterization and to give their stories a realistic historical or regional quality. (See page 76.) Jesse Stuart uses a Kentucky mountain dialect in "The Split Cherry Tree" (page 66):

> . . . I'll take keer o' 'im. He ain't from this country nohow. . . ."

DIALOGUE A conversation between two or more characters in a literary work. Dialogue can be used to make characters come alive, to advance the action, and to establish ATMOSPHERE. Dialogue appears in every form of literature: short stories, novels, biographies, essays, poetry, and plays. Plays are made up almost entirely of dialogue. In other forms of literature, dialogue can be used extensively (see "The Pacing Goose," page 36), or sparingly or not at all (see "The Lady or the Tiger?," page 4).

DICTION A writer's choice of words, particularly for clarity, effectiveness, and correctness. A writer's diction can be formal or informal, abstract or concrete. In choosing "the right word," writers must think of their subject and their audience. Words that are appropriate in informal dialogue would not always be appropriate in a formal essay. A writer might have a character use "tubby" in an insulting remark, but the word would be inappropriate in a medical article. (See pages 48 and 61.) The impact that diction can have on a piece of writing is illustrated by the following versions of a nursery rhyme. The story is the same; the diction is different.

> Three blind mice,
> See how they run.
> They all ran after the farmer's wife,
> Who cut off their tails with a carving knife.
> Have you ever seen such a sight in your life
> As three blind mice?

> Three rodents with defective vision,
> Observe their rate of motion.
> They all pursued an agriculturalist's spouse,
> Who severed their spinal extremites with a common kitchen utensil.
> Have you ever observed such a phenomenon in the span of your existence
> As three rodents with defective vision?

(See also CONNOTATION and STYLE.)

DRAMATIC POETRY Poetry in which one or more characters speak. Each speaker always addresses a specific listener. This listener may be silent but identifiable, as in a DRAMATIC MONOLOGUE. Or the listener may be another character who carries on a dialogue with the speaker, as in "Uphill" by Christina Rossetti (page 189).

ELEGY A poem of mourning, usually over the death of an individual. It may also be a lament over the passing of life and beauty or a meditation on the nature of death. An elegy is a type of LYRIC poetry, usually formal in language and structure, and solemn or even melancholy in tone. An elegy called "Dirge" by Percy Bysshe Shelly is on page 189.

EPIC A long narrative poem telling about the deeds of a great hero and reflecting the values of the society from which it originated. Many epics were drawn from an oral tradition and were transmitted by song and recitation before they were written down. Two of the most famous epics of Western civilization are Homer's *Iliad*

and *Odyssey*. (See page 513.) Rome's national epic, the *Aeneid*, was modeled on the epics of ancient Greece and was written by the poet Virgil to give the ancient Romans a sense of their own destiny. One of the earliest literary works in history is the *Epic of Gilgamesh* from ancient Mesopotamia. The great epic of the Middle Ages is the *Divine Comedy*, written by the Italian poet Dante. The seventeenth-century English poet John Milton wrote two great Christian epics called *Paradise Lost* and *Paradise Regained*. One of the longest epics in the world is the national epic of India (*c.* 300 B.C.), the *Mahabharata*, which contains 100,000 COUPLETS.

EPIGRAM A short, witty poem or a terse, witty statement. Here is an example from William Shakespeare's *Romeo and Juliet* (page 434):

> What's in a name? That which we call a rose
> By any other name would smell as sweet.

EPITAPH An inscription on a gravestone, or a short poem written in memory of someone who has died. (See page 218.) Many epitaphs are actually EPIGRAMS, or short witty sayings, and are not intended for serious use as monument inscriptions. John Wilmont wrote this epitaph for Charles II:

> Here lies our sovereign lord the King,
> Whose promise none relies on;
> He never said a foolish thing,
> Nor ever did a wise one.

EPITHET A descriptive name or phrase used to characterize someone or something, such as "yellow-bellied coward" or "Catherine the Great." Homer's *Odyssey* is filled with epithets, such as "wine-dark sea" and "keen-edged sword." (See page 553.)

ESSAY A piece of prose writing, usually short, that deals with a subject in a limited way and expresses a particular point of view. An essay is never a comprehensive treatment of a subject (the word comes from a French word for "attempt" or "try"). An essay may be serious or humorous, tightly organized or rambling, restrained or emotional. The two general classifications of essay are the INFORMAL ESSAY (also called the *familiar* or *personal essay*) and the FORMAL ESSAY. However, many essays cannot be so easily pigeonholed. (See page 253.)

EXAGGERATION Overstatement for emphasis, for added interest, or for humorous effect. We use exaggeration in many everyday expressions:

> The batter hit the ball a mile.
> I'll never get to sleep.
> I'm so hungry I could eat a horse.

Folk tales and tall tales use exaggeration to make heroes and events seem more extraordinary. Exaggeration is also a basic ingredient of humor. "The Genuine Mexican Plug" by Mark Twain (page 260), for example, is filled with humorous exaggeration, as is E. B. White's essay "The Decline of Sport" (page 282). (See also HYPERBOLE.)

EXPOSITION The kind of writing that is intended primarily to present information. Exposition is one of the major FORMS OF DISCOURSE. (See also NARRATION, DESCRIPTION, and PERSUASION.) The commentaries in this book which introduce the major sections are exposition. (See page 290.)

Also, exposition is that part of a short story, a novel, a narrative poem, and especially of a play which helps the reader understand essential background information. For example, in *Romeo and Juliet*, Shakespeare provides essential background information, or exposition, in the first three scenes. Before the plot begins to unfold, the audience is informed of the feud between the Capulets and the Montagues and is introduced to the major characters. (See page 361.)

FABLE A brief story that is told to present a MORAL, or practical lesson. The characters of fables are often animals who speak and act like human beings. Some of the most familiar fables, such as the following example, are attributed to Aesop:

> The tortoise and the hare argued about who was swifter, and they agreed to run

a race. The hare sprinted out well ahead of the tortoise. Seeing how slow his adversary was, the hare became so confident that he relaxed and even lay down for a nap by the roadside. Meanwhile, the tortoise plodded on without stopping, passed the hare asleep on the road, and got to the finish line first. MORAL: *Slow and steady wins the race.*

"Fable" by Ralph Waldo Emerson (page 210) is an example of a fable told in verse.

FARCE A type of COMEDY based on a far-fetched humorous situation, often with ridiculous or STEREOTYPED characters. The humor in a farce is largely slapstick — that is, the clowning involves crude physical action. The characters in a farce are often the butts of practical jokes: pies land in their faces or beds cave in on them. The films of Laurel and Hardy, Abbott and Costello, and the Three Stooges are farces. (See page 423.)

FIGURATIVE LANGUAGE Language that is not intended to be interpreted in a literal sense. (See page 48.) Shakespeare uses figurative language in the following lines from his play *As You Like It* (page 429):

> All the world's a stage,
> And all the men and women merely
>   players.
> They have their exits and their entrances,
> And one man in his time plays many parts

Shakespeare is not saying that the world is actually a large, constructed platform; nor is he saying that all the people in the world are actually employed as actors and actresses. Rather, he is drawing a comparison between life and a play, pointing out special and surprising similarities between the two.

By appealing to the imagination, figurative language provides new ways of looking at the world. Figurative language consists of FIGURES OF SPEECH. (See also HYPERBOLE, METAPHOR, PERSONIFICATION, and SIMILE.)

FIGURE OF SPEECH A word or an expression that is not meant to be interpreted in a literal sense. Everyday language abounds with many different kinds of figures of speech, in which we say one thing but mean something else. More than two hundred different kinds of figures of speech have been classified, but the ones found most frequently in literature are HYPERBOLE, METAPHOR, PERSONIFICATION and SIMILE. (See pages 48, 162, and 164.)

FLASHBACK A scene in a short story, novel, play, or narrative poem that interrupts the action to show an event that happened at an earlier time. Many narratives present events as they occur in time—that is, in chronological order. Sometimes, however, a writer interrupts this natural sequence of events and "flashes back" to a past event, to tell the reader or audience what happened earlier in the story or in a character's life. Often a flashback takes the form of a reminiscence by one of the characters, as in "Luck" by Mark Twain (page 62).

FOOT A unit used to measure the METER, or rhythmic pattern of a line of poetry. A foot is made up of one stressed syllable, and, usually, of one or more unstressed syllables. A line of poetry has as many "feet" as it has stressed syllables. For example, the following lines from "Travel" by Robert Louis Stevenson (page 178) has four feet— that is, each line has four stressed syllables (marked here by ′):

I should like to rise and go
Where the golden apples grow

There are several patterns of feet (or stressed and unstressed syllables) in poetry. Stevenson's lines use TROCHEES — that is, feet made up of one stressed syllable followed by one unstressed syllable. (See IAMB, TROCHEE, ANAPEST, and DACTYL.)

FORESHADOWING The use of hints, or clues, to suggest what will happen later in a story, novel, or play. Writers use foreshadowing to create interest and to build suspense. Foreshadowing also prepares the reader for the end of the story. For example, in the first paragraph of the story "The Ambitious Guest" (page 114), Hawthorne mentions that the family lives in a dangerous spot, with a mountain towering over their heads. In paragraph two, he says that the wind howls at their door with a sound of "wailing and lamentation," which "saddened" them for a moment. In the third paragraph, he says of a stranger who knocks at their door: his "fate was linked to theirs." All of these details hint that something terrible might happen, a suspicion that is confirmed by the story's end. (See page 13.)

FORM The structure and organization of a work of literature or art. The *form* of a literary work is different from its *content*, which is what a work is about. (See page 151.) Some of the different literary forms are drama, the novel, the short story, the essay, biography, and poetry.

FORMAL ESSAY An essay that is tightly organized, dignified in style, and serious in tone. The purpose of a formal essay is usually to communicate information rather than to share personal thoughts. Francis Bacon's "Of Studies" is an example of a formal essay. (See page 287, and INFORMAL ESSAY.)

FORMS OF DISCOURSE A classification of writing into types, according to the writer's main purpose. Four forms of discourse are DESCRIPTION, NARRATION, EXPOSITION, and PERSUASION.
Description is the kind of writing that aims to create pictures or impressions perceived by the senses. (See page 104.)
Narration is the kind of writing that relates a series of events. (See page 149.)
Exposition is the kind of writing that explains a subject. (See page 290.)
Persuasion is the kind of writing that is intended to convince the reader to accept a particular point of view.

FREE VERSE Poetry that does not have a fixed RHYTHM or RHYME scheme. (See page 181.) The following lines are from a free-verse poem by Walt Whitman, who was the first poet to use free verse extensively.

The Dismantled Ship
In some unused lagoon, some nameless bay,
On sluggish, lonesome waters, anchor'd near the shore,

An old, dismasted, gray and batter'd ship,
    disabled, done,
After free voyages to all the seas of earth,
    haul'd up at last and hawser'd tight,
Lies rusting, mouldering.

"Night Clouds" by Amy Lowell (page 176) and "Poem" by William Carlos Williams (page 181) are written in free verse.

HYPERBOLE A FIGURE OF SPEECH using EXAGGERATION, or overstatement, for special effect. In these lines from *Romeo and Juliet* (page 434), William Shakespeare uses hyperbole to emphasize a sense of danger:

There lies more peril in thine eyes
Than twenty of their swords.

IAMB A poetic FOOT consisting of an unstressed syllable followed by a stressed syllable (⏑ ′). The iamb is the most common metrical unit in English poetry, perhaps because the natural rhythm of the English language tends to be *iambic*. The following example is from Alfred, Lord Tennyson's "The Eagle" (page 247).

The wrinkled sea beneath him crawls;
He watches from his mountain walls,
And like a thunderbolt he falls.

IAMBIC PENTAMETER The most common verse line in English poetry. It consists of five verse FEET (*penta* is from a Greek word meaning "five"), with each foot an IAMB, that is, an unstressed syllable followed by a stressed syllable. The following line from William Shakespeare's *Romeo and Juliet* (page 434) uses iambic pentameter:

But soft! What light through yonder window breaks?

Shakespeare's plays are written almost entirely in iambic pentameter. Unrhymed iambic pentameter is called BLANK VERSE.

IMAGERY Words or phrases that create pictures, or images, in the reader's mind. (See

pages 176 and 182.) Images are primarily visual, that is, they usually appeal to the reader's sense of sight, as in these lines from Alfred, Lord Tennyson's poem "The Lotus-Eaters" (page 248):

They saw the gleaming river seaward flow
From the inner land; far off, three mountaintops,
Three silent pinnacles of aged snow,
Stood sunset-flushed

Images can also appeal to senses other than sight: touch, taste, smell, and hearing. The images in the following passage from Stephen Crane's story "A Gray Sleeve" (page 82) describe sounds:

Over the noise of the scudding hoofs could be heard the creaking of leather trappings, the jingle and clank of steel, and the tense, low-toned commands or appeals of the men to their horses.

IMAGISTS A group of poets organized in the early 1900's, whose principles for writing poetry were radical at the time but are widely accepted today. The Imagists felt that poetry should be based on precise, concrete images; that it should use the language of common speech, rather than lofty or ornamental diction; and that it should not be limited to the traditional "poetic" subjects, but rather should have absolute freedom of content. One of the leaders of the Imagist school of poetry was Amy Lowell, whose poem "Night Clouds" is on page 176.

INCREMENTAL REPETITION A device commonly used in ballads, in which a stanza repeats a line or lines from another stanza, but adds a few new details (*increments*) to advance the story. For example, in these three opening stanzas of the ballad "The Wife of Usher's Well" (page 154), stanzas two and three use incremental repetition:

There lived a wife at Usher's Well,
    And a wealthy wife was she;
She had three stout and stalwart sons,
    And sent them o'er the sea.

They hadna been a week from her,
    A week but barely one,

When word came to the carline wife
That her three sons were gone.

They hadna been a week from her,
A week but barely three,
When word came to the carline wife
That her sons she'd never see.

INFERENCE The act of deriving a reasonable conclusion based on certain clues or facts. For example, the reader can tell, by inference, what season John Keats is describing in these stanzas from his poem "La Belle Dame sans Merci":

"O what can ail thee, knight-at-arms,
  Alone and palely loitering?
The sedge has withered from the lake,
  And no birds sing.

"O what can ail thee, knight-at-arms!
  So haggard and so woebegone?
The squirrel's granary is full,
  And the harvest's done."

The reader is told that the sedge, or grass, has withered from the lake, that no birds sing, that the squirrel has stored food for the winter, and that the harvest is over. From these clues, the reader can *infer* that the action of the poem is set in late autumn or early winter.

INFORMAL ESSAY A prose work, usually brief, written as if the writer is informally talking with the reader about some topic, using a conversational style and a personal or humorous tone. In an informal essay (which is sometimes called a *familiar* or *personal essay*), a writer might digress from the topic at hand, or express some amusing, startling, or absurd opinions. In general, an informal essay reveals as much about the personality of its author as it does about its subject. J. B. Priestley's essays from *Delight* (page 254) are informal essays. (See pages 253 and 278, and FORMAL ESSAY.)

IN MEDIAS RES A Latin phrase meaning "in the middle of things." The term refers to a technique of plunging into the middle of a story and only later using a FLASHBACK to tell what has happened previously. The

most famous examples of this technique are found in epics. Book I of Homer's *Odyssey,* for example, opens ten years after the Trojan War has ended. The goddess Athena is telling Odysseus's son to go to Sparta to inquire about his father, who should have returned home from the war ten years before. Only later, in Book IX (page 517), do we hear Odysseus tell about all the adventures that happened to him in the previous ten years.

IRONY A contrast or an incongruity between what is stated and what is really meant, or between what is expected to happen and what actually does happen. Three kinds of irony are: (1) *verbal irony,* in which a writer or speaker says one thing and means something entirely different (see page 9); (2) *dramatic irony,* in which a reader or an audience perceives something that a character in the story or play does not know; (3) *irony of situation,* in which the writer shows a discrepancy between the expected result of some action or situation and its actual result (see pages 25 and 214).

An example of *dramatic irony* is found in William Shakespeare's *Romeo and Juliet* (page 434). The audience of the play knows that Juliet is not dead but is merely drugged and appears lifeless. Romeo, however, does not know this. Presuming that his young wife is dead, Romeo kills himself.

LIGHT VERSE Verse that is intended to be humorous or entertaining, rather than serious or profound. Light verse is often characterized by catchy rhythms and strong, often humorous, rhymes. Limericks are examples of light verse, as are these lines by an anonymous poet:

Get up, get up, you lazyhead,
Get up, you lazy sinner,
We need these sheets for tablecloths,
It's nearly time for dinner.

LOCAL COLOR The use of specific details to describe the dialect, dress, customs, and settings associated with a particular region or section of the country. The purpose of "local color" is to suggest the unique flavor of a specific locale. In the years following the War Between the States, stories of "local color" flourished in the United States. Mark Twain re-created the "local color" of the West in his frontier sketches (pages 260).

LYRIC A poem, usually a short one, that expresses a speaker's personal thoughts or feelings. The ELEGY, ODE, and SONNET are all forms of the lyric. As its Greek name indicates, a lyric was originally a poem sung to the accompaniment of a lyre, and lyrics to this day have retained a melodic quality. (See pages 184 and 185.) Lyrics may express a range of emotions and reflections: Wordsworth's lyric "My Heart Leaps Up" (page 184) expresses the joy and confidence he receives from nature, while Frost's lyric "Desert Places" (page 183) expresses the loneliness and fright he feels when looking on a natural scene.

MELODRAMA Originally, melodramas were so-called because melodies accompanied certain actions (*melo* means "song" in Greek). Also, each character in a melodrama had a theme melody, which was played each time he or she made an appearance on stage. Today we use the term *melodrama* to mean a drama that has STEREOTYPED CHARACTERS and a CONFLICT that pits an all-good hero or heroine against an all-evil villain. The good characters always win and the evil ones are always punished. Melodramas are often meant to be tear-jerkers: many soap operas on television are melodramas.

METAPHOR A FIGURE OF SPEECH that makes a comparison between two things which are basically dissimilar. "Life is a dream," "Life is a vale of tears," "Life is a bowl of cherries" are all examples of metaphor. Unlike a SIMILE, a metaphor does not use a connective word such as *like, as, than,* or *resembles* in making the comparison. (See pages 48 and 164.) In *Romeo and Juliet* (page 434), Romeo uses a metaphor when he calls Juliet the sun:

> But, soft! What light through yonder window breaks?
> It is the east, and Juliet is the sun!

Many metaphors are implied, or suggested. An *implied metaphor* does not directly state that one thing *is* another, different thing. Homer uses an implied metaphor in the *Odyssey* (page 517) when he describes the dawn as "rose-fingered." This implies that dawn is a woman with rose-tipped fingers that stretch across the morning sky.

An *extended metaphor* is a metaphor that is extended throughout a poem. William Shakespeare uses an extended metaphor which compares the world to a stage, in "The Seven Ages of Man" (page 429).

A *dead metaphor* is a metaphor which has become so commonplace that it seems literal rather than figurative. Some examples are the *foot* of a hill, the *head* of the class, a *point* in time, and the *leg* of a chair.

A *mixed metaphor* is the use of two or more inconsistent metaphors in one expression. When they are examined, mixed metaphors make no sense. Mixed metaphors are often unintentionally humorous: "The storm of protest was nipped in the bud" or "To hold the fort, he'd have to shake a leg."

METER A generally regular pattern of stressed and unstressed syllables in poetry. In these lines from Edgar Allan Poe's "Eldorado" (page 159), the stressed syllables are marked (´) and the unstressed (˘):

> Gáilў bedíght,
> Ă gállant kníght,
> Ĭn súnshĭne ánd ĭn shádŏw

For the common metrical patterns, see ANAPEST, DACTYL, IAMB, and TROCHEE.

MORAL A shrewd, practical lesson about human conduct or ethics that is pointed out in didactic literary works such as FABLES. The moral of a fable may be stated directly, or it may be implied. Some well-known morals are "Slow and steady wins the race" (from "The Hare and the Tortoise"), "It is easy to propose impossible remedies" (from "The Belling of the Cat"), and "Liars are not believed, even when they tell the truth" (from "The Boy Who Cried Wolf").

MOTIF A recurring feature (such as a name, an image, or a phrase) in a work of literature. A motif generally contributes in some way to the THEME of a short story, novel, poem, or play. For example, a motif used by Poe in his story "The Tell-Tale Heart" (page 108) is the quick staccato phrasing, which continually suggests the extreme nervousness of the narrator. The story opens with one of these staccato sentences: "True!—nervous—very, very dreadfully nervous . . ."

At times, *motif* is used to refer to some commonly used plot or character type in literature. The "ugly duckling motif" refers to a plot that involves the transformation of a plain-looking person into a beauty. Two other commonly used motifs are the "Romeo and Juliet motif" (about doomed lovers), and the "Horatio Alger motif" (about the clerk who becomes the corporation president).

MOTIVATION   The reasons, either stated or implied, for a character's behavior. To make a story believable, a writer must provide characters with motivation sufficient to explain what they do. Characters may be motivated by outside events, or they may be motivated by inner needs or fears.

MYTH   A story, often about immortals and sometimes connected with religious rituals, that attempts to give meaning to the mysteries of the world. An example of a myth is the Greek story of Demeter, the goddess associated with the harvest, and Persephone, her daughter. Persephone was kidnaped from earth by the god of the underworld, Hades. Hades finally agreed to let Persephone return to her mother for only part of each year. Demeter decreed that the earth would be fertile only during the part of the year that Persephone was with her. This myth, which was intended to account for the growing season of crops, was also connected with religious rituals that were held periodically in honor of Demeter.

In myths, the gods and goddesses are identified with the immense powers of the universe: in the Greek myths, Zeus is associated with the sky, Hades with the underworld, Poseidon with the seas, Apollo with the sun, Athena with wisdom, Ares with war. But the gods are also given the forms and feelings of human beings. Thus, myths make it possible for people to understand and deal with things that they cannot control and often cannot see.

Eventually, myths are gathered together to form a *mythology*, which is a body of related stories that at some time are accepted by a particular society as true. A mythology tells a society what it is most concerned about: who its gods are, where it came from, what its most sacred rituals are, and what its destiny is.

NARRATION   The kind of writing or speaking that tells a story (a *narrative*). Narration is one of the four major forms of discourse. (See also DESCRIPTION, EXPOSITION, and PERSUASION.) Narration may take the form of prose or poetry. A narrative may be book-length, such as a NOVEL or an EPIC, or it may be paragraph-length, such as a FABLE or an ANECDOTE. The short stories, the ballads and other narrative poems, the epic, and the novel in this book are all examples of narration. (See page 149.)

NARRATIVE POEM   A poem that tells a story. (See page 153.) One kind of narrative poem is the EPIC, a long poem which sets forth the heroic ideals of a particular society. Homer's the *Odyssey* (page 513) is an epic. The BALLAD is another kind of narrative poem. "The Wife of Usher's Well" (page 154) is an example of a ballad.

NARRATOR   One who narrates, or tells, a story. A writer might choose to have a story told by a *first-person* narrator, someone who is either a major or minor character in the story. Or, a writer might choose to use a *third-person* narrator, someone who is not in the story at all. Third-person narrators are often omniscient, or "all-knowing"—that is, they are able to enter into the minds of all the characters in the story.

Frank R. Stockton's short story "The Lady or the Tiger?" (page 4) is told by a third-person narrator.

Jesse Stuart's short story "The Split Cherry Tree" (page 66) is told by an "I" who is one of the characters in the story. This narrator can reveal his own thoughts, of course, but he can report only what he thinks goes on in the minds of the other characters. Thus, we know only what the narrator can tell us. (See POINT OF VIEW.)

The word *narrator* can also refer to a character in a drama who guides the audience through the play, often commenting on the action and sometimes participating in it. Thornton Wilder uses such a narrator in his play *Our Town*.

NOVEL A book-length fictional prose narrative, having many characters and, often, a complex plot. (See page 555.) Charles Dickens' *Great Expectations* (page 560) is a novel.

ODE A complex and often lengthy LYRIC poem, written in a dignified, formal style on some lofty or serious subject. Odes are often written for a special occasion, to honor a person or a season, or to commemorate an event. Some examples of famous odes are Percy Bysshe Shelley's "Ode to the West Wind," John Keats's "Ode on a Grecian Urn," and William Wordsworth's "Ode: Intimations of Immortality."

ONOMATOPOEIA The use of a word whose sound in some degree imitates or suggests its meaning. The names of some birds are onomatopoetic, imitating the cry of the bird named: *cuckoo, whippoorwill, owl, crow, towhee, bobwhite.* Some onomatopoetic words are *hiss, clang, rustle,* and *snap.* (See page 239.) In these lines from Percy Bysshe Shelley's poem "Dirge" (page 189), the word *moanest* is onomatopoetic:

> Rough wind, that *moanest* loud
> Grief too sad for song

PARABLE A very short, simple tale, usually about an ordinary, familiar event, from which a MORAL or a religious lesson is drawn. The Zen masters in Japan frequently use parables for religious or moral instructions. Some of the most famous parables are those used by Jesus in the New Testament. E. B. White's essay "The Decline of Sport" (page 282) is subtitled "A Preposterous *Parable*." (See page 286.)

PARADOX A statement that reveals an element of truth, although it seems at first to be self-contradictory and untrue. (See pages 184 and 202.) Juliet, in William Shakespeare's *Romeo and Juliet* (page 434), uses a paradox when she says:

> Good night, good night! Parting is such
> sweet sorrow

PARALLELISM The use of phrases, clauses, or sentences that are similar or complementary in structure or in meaning. (See pages 187 and 289.) Francis Bacon, in his essay "Of Studies" (page 287), uses sentences with parallel structure:

> Crafty men contemn studies, simple men admire them, and wise men use them . . . .

The technique of parallelism is used extensively in the psalms in the Bible, where the idea of one line is repeated in the next:

> I will sing unto the Lord as long as I live:
> I will sing praise to my God while I have my being. (Psalm 104)

PARODY The humorous imitation of a work of literature, art, or music. A parody often achieves its humorous effect through the use of EXAGGERATION or mockery. In literature, parody can be made of a plot, a character, a writing style, or a sentiment or theme. For example, Lewis Carroll's poem "Father William" (page 213) is a humorous parody of a serious poem by Robert Southey, called "The Old Man's Comforts: And How He gained Them." Here is Southey's poem:

> "You are old, Father William," the young
> man cried,
> "The few locks which are left you are
> gray;
> You are hale, Father William, a hearty old
> man,
> Now tell me the reason, I pray."

> "In the days of my youth," Father William
> replied,
> "I remembered that youth would fly
> fast,
> And abused not my health, and my vigor
> at first,
> That I never might need them at last."

> "You are old, Father William," the young
> man cried,
> "And pleasures with youth pass away;
> And yet you lament not the days that are
> gone,
> Now tell me the reason, I pray."

"In the days of my youth," Father William replied,
  "I remembered that youth could not last;
I thought of the future, whatever I did,
  That I never might grieve for the past."

"You are old, Father William," the young man cried,
  "And life must be hastening away;
You are cheerful, and love to converse upon death,
  Now tell me the reason, I pray."

"I am cheerful, young man," Father William replied,
  "Let the cause thy attention engage;
In the days of my youth I remembered my God!
  And He hath not forgotten my age."

PENTAMETER A poetic line that consists of five verse FEET. The following lines (page 428) from William Shakespeare's play *The Merchant of Venice* are written in pentameter—that is, there are five stressed syllables in each line. The stressed syllables are marked (′), the unstressed (˘):

How sweet the moonlight sleeps upon this bank!
Here will we sit and let the sounds of music
Creep in our ears. Soft stillness and the night
Become the touches of sweet harmony.

(See also IAMBIC PENTAMETER.)

PERSONIFICATION A FIGURE OF SPEECH in which an animal, an object, a natural force, or an idea is given personality, or described as if it were human. (See page 177.) In the following lines from "Dirge" (page 189), Percy Bysshe Shelley personifies the storm. He addresses it as if it were a person who could feel sadness and shed tears:

Sad storm, whose tears are vain

PERSUASION The type of speaking or writing that is intended to make its audience adopt a certain opinion or perform an action or both. Persuasion is one of the major FORMS OF DISCOURSE. (See also NARRATION, DESCRIPTION, and EXPOSITION.) Modern examples of persuasion include political speeches, television commercials, and newspaper editorials.

PLOT The sequence of events or actions in a short story, novel, play, or narrative poem. Plots may be simple or complex, loosely constructed or close-knit. But every plot is made up of a series of incidents that are related to one another. The most important element of plot is CONFLICT. (See pages 2, 433, and 557.)

POINT OF VIEW The vantage point from which a narrative is told. (See pages 103 and 558.) There are two basic points of view. (1) In the *first-person point of view*, the story is told by one of the characters in his or her own words. First-person point of view is a limited point of view, since the reader is told only what this character knows and observes. Here is an example of first-person point of view from Charles Dickens' novel *Great Expectations* (page 560):

My father's family name being Pirrip, and my Christian name Philip, my infant tongue could make of both names nothing more explicit than Pip. So I called myself Pip, and came to be called Pip.

(2) In the *third-person point of view*, the narrator is not a character in the story. The third-person narrator might tell a story from the point of view of only one character in the story, as Guy de Maupassant does in "The Necklace" (page 19). All the action in that story is told by a third-person narrator, from the *limited* point of view of Mme. Loisel. A third-person narrator, on the other hand, might be an *omniscient*, or "all-knowing," observer who can describe and comment on *all* the characters and actions in the story. Saki's story "The Interlopers" (page 14) is written from an omniscient third-person point of view:

The two enemies stood glaring at one another for a long silent moment. Each had a rifle in his hand, each had hate in his heart and murder uppermost in his mind. The chance had come to give full play to the passions of a lifetime.

PROTAGONIST The central character of a drama, novel, short story, or narrative poem. The protagonist is the character on whom the action centers and usually the one with whom the reader sympathizes most. Usually the protagonist strives against an opponent, or ANTAGONIST. The protagonist can be either heroic or ordinary, good or bad. For example, Odysseus (page 517) is a brave and wise king. Walter Mitty (page 94) is a very ordinary man. The protagonist of "The Tell-Tale Heart" (page 108) is a murderer.

PUN The humorous use of a word or phrase to suggest two or more meanings at the same time. A famous pun on the word *grave* occurs in William Shakespeare's *Romeo and Juliet* (page 434). Mercutio, who is always joking, is fatally wounded and knows that he does not have long to live. He says, "Ask for me tomorrow, and you shall find me a grave man."

QUATRAIN Usually a stanza or poem of four lines. However, a quatrain may also be any group of four lines unified by a rhyme scheme. Quatrains usually follow an *abab, abba,* or *abcb* rhyme scheme. Here is a quatrain from Henry Wadsworth Longfellow's "Curfew" (page 204):

Song sinks into silence,	*a*
The story is *told,*	*b*
The windows are darkened,	*c*
The hearthstone is *cold.*	*b*

REALISM The attempt in literature and art to represent life as it really is, without sentimentalizing or idealizing it. Realistic writing often depicts the everyday life and speech of ordinary people. This has led, sometimes, to an emphasis on sordid details. (See page 93.) The following passage, from Guy de Maupassant's "The Necklace" (page 19), is an example of realistic description:

Mme. Loisel appeared an old woman now. She became heavy, rough, harsh, like one of the poor. Her hair untended, her skirts askew, her hands red, her voice shrill, she even slopped water on her floors and scrubbed them herself.

REFRAIN A word, phrase, line, or group of lines repeated regularly in a poem, usually at the end of each stanza. Refrains are often used in ballads and other narrative poems to create a songlike rhythm and to help build suspense. Refrains can also serve to emphasize a particular idea. (See page 159.) A modern example of the use of refrain is in Rudyard Kipling's "Recessional" (page 233). William Shakespeare uses this refrain in "When Icicles Hang by the Wall" (page 426):

Then nightly sings the staring owl—
    "Tu-whit,
Tu-who!"—a merry note,
While greasy Joan doth keel the pot.

RHYME The repetition of sounds in two or more words or phrases that appear close to each other in a poem. For example: *river-shiver, song-long, leap-deep.* (See pages 168 and 169.) If the rhyme occurs at the ends of lines, it is called *end rhyme.* Here is an example of end rhyme from Ralph Waldo Emerson's "Music" (page 185):

It is not only in the *rose,*
It is not only in the *bird,*
Not only where the rainbow *glows,*
Nor in the song of woman *heard,*
But in the darkest, meanest *things*
There always, always something *sings.*

If the rhyme occurs within a line, it is called *internal rhyme.* Here is an example of internal rhyme from Alfred, Lord Tennyson's "Bugle Song" (page 167):

The spendor *falls* on castle *walls*

Approximate rhyme is rhyme in which the final sounds of the words are similar, but not identical (as opposed to *exact rhyme*). *Cook-look* is an exact rhyme; *cook-lack* is an approximate rhyme. Rudyard Kipling uses approximate rhyme in these lines from "Recessional" (page 233):

For frantic boast and foolish *word*—
Thy Mercy on Thy People, *Lord!*

A *rhyme scheme* is the pattern of rhymes in a poem.

RHYTHM The arrangement of stressed and unstressed syllables into a pattern. Rhythm is most apparent in poetry, though it is part of all good writing. (See pages 169 and 170.) Rhythm often gives a poem a distinct musical quality, as in these lines from Sir Walter Scott's "Hunting Song" (page 168):

Wăkĕn, lórds ănd ládiĕs gáy,

On thĕ móuntaĭn dáwns thĕ dáy,

All thĕ jóllў cháse ĭs hére,

With hăwk, ănd hórse, ănd húnting-spéar!

Poets also use rhythm to echo meaning. In these lines from Alfred, Lord Tennyson's "Bugle Song" (page 167), the rhythmic repetition of *dying* suggests the actual sound of a fading echo:

Blów, búglĕ; ánswĕr, échoĕs, dýĭng,

dýĭng, dýĭng.

ROMANCE Originally, a term used to describe a medieval tale dealing with the loves and adventures of kings, queens, knights, and ladies, and including unlikely or supernatural happenings. (See page 555.) One of the most famous examples of a romance is the legend of King Arthur and the Knights of the Round Table. In a more general sense, a romance is any form of imaginative literature that is set in an idealized world and that deals with heroic adventures and battles between good characters and villains or monsters. For example, the modern trilogy of novels called *The Lord of the Rings,* by J. R. R. Tolkien, is a romance.

ROMANTICISM A movement that flourished in literature, philosophy, music, and art in Western culture during most of the nineteenth century, beginning as a revolt against CLASSICISM. There have been many varieties of Romanticism in many different times and places. Many of the ideas of English Romanticism were first expressed by the poets William Wordsworth (pages 184, 205, and 219) and Samuel Taylor Coleridge. Romanticism, essentially, idealizes life. Whereas REALISM attempts to show life as it really is, Romanticism attempts to show life as it should be, or as the writer, reader, or audience would like it to be. Romanticism tends to soften life, favoring the picturesque, the emotional, the exotic, and the mysterious. Romanticism tends to uphold the notion that people are basically good and perfectible. Romanticism also tends to glorify nature, showing that those who live closest to nature and imitate it are the noblest kind of people. (See pages 92 and 120.) Percy Bysshe Shelley (page 189) was a famous Romantic poet.

SATIRE A kind of writing that holds up to ridicule or contempt the weaknesses and wrongdoings of individuals, groups, institutions, or humanity in general. The aim of satirists is to set a moral standard for society, and they often attempt to persuade the reader to see their point of view through the force of laughter. (See page 282.) E. B. White satirizes Americans' compulsion for competitive sports in his essay "The Decline of Sport" (page 282). James Thurber satirizes a man who daydreams of being a romantic hero while being bossed by his wife, in "The Secret Life of Walter Mitty" (page 94).

SETTING The time and place in which the events in a short story, novel, play, or narrative poem occur. A setting may serve simply as the physical background of a story, or a skillful writer may use setting to establish a particular ATMOSPHERE, which, in turn, contributes to the PLOT and THEME of the story. (See page 558.) For example, in *Great Expectations* (page 560), Charles Dickens uses the setting to create a mood of bleakness:

Ours was the marsh country, down by the river, within twenty miles of the sea. My first vivid impression of things seems to me to have been gained on a memorable raw afternoon toward evening. At such a time I found out for certain that this bleak place was the churchyard; and that Philip Pirrip, late of this parish, and Georgiana, wife of the above, were dead and buried. I knew that the dark flat wilderness beyond was the marshes; and that the low leaden line beyond was the river; and that the distant savage lair from which the wind was rushing was the sea; and that the small bundle of shivers growing afraid of it all and beginning to cry was Pip.

SIMILE A comparison made between two dissimilar things through the use of a specific word of comparison, such as *like, as, than,* or *resembles.* The comparison must be between two essentially unlike things. To say "Dorothy is like her grandmother" is not to use a simile. But to say "Dorothy is like a golden flower" is to use a simile. (See pages 48 and 162.) Like all FIGURES OF SPEECH similes help us to see things in vivid new ways. In "A Narrow Fellow in the Grass" (page 182), Emily Dickinson uses a simile to describe how a snake moves through grass:

The grass divides as with a comb

In "The Eagle" (page 247), Alfred, Lord Tennyson uses a simile to describe the flight of an eagle:

And like a thunderbolt he falls.

SONNET A fourteen-line LYRIC poem, usually written in rhymed IAMBIC PENTAMETER. Sonnets vary in structure and rhyme scheme, but are generally of two types: the *Petrarchan,* or *Italian sonnet,* and the *Elizabethan,* or *Shakespearean sonnet.* Sonnets usually express a single THEME or idea. (See page 192.)

The *Italian sonnet* is a form that originated in Italy in the thirteenth century. The Italian sonnet has two parts, an octave (eight lines) and a sestet (six lines). It is usually rhymed *abbaabba, cdecde.* The two parts of the Italian sonnet play off each other in a variety of ways. Sometimes the octave raises a question which the sestet answers. Sometimes the sestet opposes what the octave says, or extends it. The following sonnet by American poet Henry Wadsworth Longfellow is written in the Italian form, though the rhyme scheme varies from the traditional one:

Oft have I seen at some cathedral door	a
A laborer, pausing in the dust and heat,	b
Lay down his burden, and with reverent feet	b
Enter, and cross himself, and on the floor	a
Kneel to repeat his paternoster o'er;	a
Far off the noises of the world retreat;	b
The loud vociferations of the street	b
Become an undistinguishable roar.	a
So, as I enter here from day to day,	c
And leave my burden at this minster gate,	d
Kneeling in prayer, and not ashamed to pray,	c
The tumult of the time disconsolate	d
To inarticulate murmurs dies away,	c
While the eternal ages watch and wait.	d

The Italian sonnet is often called the Petrarchan sonnet, because the Italian poet Francesco Petrarch used it so extensively. Petrarch dedicated more than 300 sonnets to a woman named Laura.

The *Shakespearean sonnet,* a form made famous by William Shakespeare, consists of three QUATRAINS and a concluding COUPLET, with the rhyme scheme *abab cdcd efef gg.* Here is Shakespeare's Sonnet 18:

Shall I compare thee to a summer's day?	a
Thou art more lovely and more temperate:	b
Rough winds do shake the darling buds of May,	a
And summer's lease hath all too short a date;	b
Sometimes too hot the eye of heaven shines,	c
And often is his gold complexion dimmed;	d
And every fair from fair sometimes declines,	c
By chance, or nature's changing course, untrimmed.	d
But thy eternal summer shall not fade	e
Nor lose possession of that fair thou owest;	f
Nor shall Death brag thou wanderest in his shade,	e
When in eternal lines to time thou growest—	f
So long as men can breathe, or eyes can see,	g
So long lives this, and this gives life to thee.	g

STEREOTYPE A type of character that appears so often in literature that his or her nature is immediately familiar to the reader. Stereotypes, also called *stock characters,* always look and act the same way and reveal the same personality traits. Examples of stereotypes are the temperamental movie star, the talkative cab driver, the mad scientist, the villain with a waxed mustache, and the wise-cracking, hard-boiled detective.

STYLE A writer's characteristic way of writing, determined by the choice of words, the arrangement of words in sentences, and the relationship of the sentences to one another. Thus one writer, such as Francis Bacon (page 287), may write long, complex sentences, while another, such as Jesse Stuart (page 66), may write shorter ones. One writer may use few adjectives, while another uses many. Style also refers to the particular way in which a writer uses IMAGERY, FIGURATIVE LANGUAGE, and RHYTHM. Style is the sum total of qualities and characteristics that distinguish the writings of one person from those of another. (See pages 13, 253, 283, and 558.)

SUSPENSE That quality of a short story, novel, drama, or narrative poem that makes the reader or audience uncertain or tense about the outcome of events. Suspense makes readers ask, "What will happen next?" or "How will this work out?" and impels them to read on. Suspense is greatest when it focuses attention on a sympathetic character. Thus the most familiar kind of suspense involves a character hanging from the ledge of a tall building, or tied to railroad tracks as a train approaches, or ascending a staircase to open a suspicious door. But suspense may also simply arise from curiosity, as when a character must make an important decision, or seek an explanation for something. One of the reasons for the popularity of "The Lady or the Tiger?" (page 4) is that the author does *not* relieve our suspense. When that story is over, we are still wondering, "What happened?"

SYMBOL Any object, person, place, or action that has a meaning in itself and that also stands for something larger than itself, such as a quality, an attitude, a belief, or a

value. A rose is often a symbol of love and beauty; a skull is often a symbol of death; spring and winter often symbolize youth and old age; a dove usually symbolizes peace. (See pages 148 and 183.) In "Uphill" (page 189), Christina Rossetti uses the climb up a hill to symbolize life's journey.

TETRAMETER A line of poetry made up of four verse FEET. Thus a tetrameter line has four groupings of stressed and unstressed syllables. The first and third lines of this verse from Robert Herrick's "To Daffodils" (page 207) are written in tetrameter:

> Fair daffodils, we weep to see
> You haste away so soon;
> As yet the early rising sun
> Has not attained his noon.

THEME The general idea or insight about life that a writer wishes to make in a literary work. All the elements of the literary work — PLOT, SETTING, CHARACTERIZATION, and FIGURATIVE LANGUAGE — contribute toward the development of its theme. A simple theme can often be stated in a single sentence. But sometimes a literary work is rich and complex, and a paragraph or even an essay is needed to state the theme. Not all literary works have a controlling theme. For example, the purpose of some simple ghost stories is to frighten the reader, and some detective stories seek only to thrill and intrigue. (See pages 3, 65, and 76.)

TONE The attitude a writer takes toward his or her subject, characters, and readers. In writing about his experiences in the West, Mark Twain (page 260) takes a humorous, self-mocking tone. In his essay called "Of Studies" (page 287), Francis Bacon takes a serious, formal tone. Through tone, a writer can amuse, anger, or shock the reader. Tone is created through the choice of words and details. (See pages 81 and 190.)

TOTAL EFFECT The final, overall impression that a short story, novel, essay, poem, or play leaves on the reader or spectator. (See pages 3, 93, 98, and 103.)

TRAGEDY In general, a literary work in which the PROTAGONIST meets an unhappy or disastrous end. Unlike COMEDY, tragedy often depicts the problems of a central character of dignified or heroic stature. Through a related series of events, this main character, or tragic hero (or heroine), is brought to a final downfall. The causes of a tragic hero's downfall vary. In traditional dramas, the cause is often an error in judgment or a combination of inexplicable outside forces that overwhelm the hero. In modern dramas, the causes range from moral or psychological weakness to the evils of society. The tragic hero, though defeated, usually gains a measure of wisdom or self-awareness. William Shakespeare's *Romeo and Juliet* (page 434) is a tragedy.

TROCHEE A poetic FOOT, consisting of a stressed syllable followed by an unstressed syllable (ˊ ˘). Here is an example of *trochaic* verse from Robert Louis Stevenson's "Travel" (page 178):

ˊ ˘ ˊ ˘ ˊ ˘ ˊ
I should like to rise and go
ˊ ˘ ˊ ˘ ˊ ˘ ˊ
Where the golden apples grow;
ˊ ˘ ˊ ˘ˊ ˘ ˊ
Where below another sky
ˊ ˘ ˊ ˘ ˊ ˘ ˊ
Parrot islands anchored lie.

UNDERSTATEMENT A restrained statement in which less is said than is meant. If it is ten degrees below zero and someone says, "It's a bit cool out today," that person is making an understatement. The understatement points out how cold it really is. Mark Twain uses understatement in "The Genuine Mexican Plug" (page 260) when he describes a camel as "uncomely." What he really means is that the camel was very ugly and funny looking.

VERSE PLAY A drama written mostly or entirely in verse. Verse plays are often written in BLANK VERSE. William Shakespeare's *Romeo and Juliet* (page 434) is a verse play.

Exercises in the Text

This index indicates the exercises presented in the text under a separate heading (e.g., "Alliteration," "Allusion," etc.). Further exercises on many of the topics will be found in the "For Study and Discussion" sections.

Index of Fine Art

Glossary

Listed below are words from selections in this book that you will find useful to add to your vocabulary. Proper names and words that are specialized, archaic, or not generally useful are not included in this glossary but have been footnoted, as appropriate, in the text. The pronunciation key is that of the Funk and Wagnalls *Standard College Dictionary* and the definitions are based on the *Standard College Dictionary*.

A

abhorrence (ab·hôr'əns) *n.* A feeling of loathing; disgust.

abide (ə·bīd') *v.* To continue in a place.

ablution (ab·lōo'shən) *n.* A washing or cleaning, especially of the body; a bath.

abode (ə·bōd') *n.* Home; dwelling place.

abstraction (ab·strak'shən) *n.* 1. The process of generalizing qualities from the individual objects to which they belong. 2. A product of this process; a concept; a generalization.

accentuate (ak·sen'chōō·āt) *v.t.* 1. To strengthen or heighten the effect of; emphasize. 2. To mark or pronounce with an accent.

accomplice (ə·kom'plis) *n.* A partner in crime; an associate in wrongdoing.

acquiesce (ak'wē·es') *v.i.* To consent or concur; agree.

acquit (ə·kwit') *v.t.* To free or clear, as from blame; declare innocent.

acute (ə·kyōōt') *adj.* Keenly sensitive.

adept (ə·dept') *adj.* Skillful. — *n.* One skilled in any art; an expert.

adjourn (ə·jûrn') *v.t.* To put off to another day or place, as a meeting or session. — *v.i.* To move or go to another place.

adjure (ə·jōor') *v.t.* 1. To charge or entreat solemnly, as under oath or penalty. 2. To appeal to earnestly.

adroitness (ə·droit'nis) *n.* Skillfulness.

adulation (aj'ōō·lā'shən) *n.* Exaggerated or hypocritical praise; flattery.

adversity (ad·vûr'sə·tē) *n.* A condition of hardship; severe trial.

affably (af'ə·blē) *adv.* In a very pleasant, polite, and friendly way.

affectation (af'ek·tā'shən) *n.* A studied pretense; showy display.

affliction (ə·flik'shən) *n.* 1. Distress of body or mind. 2. A cause of suffering; misfortune; calamity.

affray (ə·frā') *n.* A public brawl or fight; a disturbance of the peace.

affright (ə·frīt') *n.* Sudden fear.

aggravate (ag'rə·vāt) *v.t.* 1. To make worse; intensify, as an illness. 2. *Informal* To provoke or exasperate; arouse to anger. — **ag'gra·vat'ing** *adj.*

agile (aj'əl) *adj.* Able to move or do something quickly and easily.

agitation (aj'ə·tā'shən) *n.* 1. Commotion. 2. Extreme nervousness. 3. The exciting of public interest and feeling.

ague (ā'gyōō) *n.* 1. A chill accompanied by shivering. 2. A fever marked by chills, fever, and sweating in sequence.

air (âr) *n.* 1. Peculiar or characteristic appearance; manner: a haughty *air;* an *air* of elegance. 2. *Music* A melody or tune, especially one for a solo instrument or voice.

alien (āl'yen, ā'lē·ən) *adj.* 1. Owing allegiance to another country; foreign. 2. Strange. — *n.* 1. An unnaturalized foreign resident. 2. A foreigner.

alight (ə·līt') *v.* To get out of a vehicle such as a car, coach, or carriage, or off a horse.

allude (ə·lōod') *v.i.* To refer without express mention; make indirect or casual reference.

allusion (ə·lōō'zhən) *n.* Indirect reference; suggestion.

altercation (ôl'tər·kā'shən, al'-) *n.* A heated dispute; angry controversy; argument.

amble (am'bəl) *v.i.* To move with an easy, swaying motion; proceed leisurely.

amiable (ā'mē·ə·bəl) *adj.* 1. Pleasing in disposition; kindly. 2. Friendly.

amorous (am'ər·əs) *adj.* 1. Tending to fall in love; affectionate; loving. 2. Of or related to love.

amphibious (am·fib'ē·əs) *adj.* Living or adapted to life on land and in water.

PRONUNCIATION: add, āce, câre, pälm; end, ēven; it, īce; odd, ōpen, ôrder; tŏŏk, pōōl; up, bûrn; ə = a in *above*, e in *sicken*, i in *flexible*, o in *melon*, u in *focus*; yōō = u in *fuse*; oil; pout; check; go; ring; thin; this; zh, vision.

754

anguish (ang′gwish) *n.* Extreme mental or bodily pain; agony; torture.

animation (an′ə·mā′shən) *n.* **1.** The act of imparting life, or the state of possessing life. **2.** The quality of being lively or quick.

animosity (an′ə·mos′ə·tē) *n.* Active and vehement enmity; hatred.

annexation (an′ek·sā′shən) *n.* **1.** The act of adding or attaching. **2.** That which is added or attached.

annihilate (ə·nī′ə·lāt) *v.t.* To destroy; abolish.

anoint (ə·noint′) *v.t.* **1.** To smear with oil or any soft substance; apply oil or ointment to. **2.** To put oil on as a sign of consecration, as in a religious ceremony.

antiquity (an·tik′wə·tē) *n.* **1.** Times long past. **2.** The quality of being very old.

apothecary (ə·poth′ə·ker′ē) *n.* One who keeps drugs for sale and puts up prescriptions; a druggist.

appall (ə·pôl′) *v.t.* To fill with dismay or horror; terrify; shock.

apparition (ap′ə·rish′ən) *n.* **1.** A phantom or ghost. **2.** A startling or remarkable sight.

appertain (ap′ər·tān′) *v.i.* To have reference to, to be appropriate.

apprehend (ap′prə·hend) *v.t.* **1.** To grasp mentally; understand; perceive. **2.** To dread. **3.** To arrest; take into custody.

apprehension (ap′rə·hen′shən) *n.* **1.** Fear concerning the future. **2.** Understanding.

apprehensive (ap′rə·hen′siv) *adj.* Fearful about the future; anxious; uneasy.

apprise (ə·prīz′) *v.t.* To notify, as of an event; inform.

aptitude (ap′tə·tood, -tyood) *n.* **1.** Natural ability. **2.** Quickness of understanding; intelligence.

arbitrary (är′bə·trer′ē) *adj.* **1.** Based on or subject to one's opinion, judgment, prejudice, etc. **2.** Absolute; tyrannical.

archaic (är·kā′ik) *adj.* Ancient; no longer in use.

archly (ärch′lē) *adv.* In a playful manner.

ardor (är′dər) *n.* **1.** Warmth or affection; eagerness; zeal. **2.** Great heat, as of fire.

arrogant (ar′ə·gənt) *adj.* Excessively proud; overbearing.

artful (ärt′fəl) *adj.* **1.** Crafty; skillful. **2.** Artificial. — **art′ful·ly** *adv.*

artifact (är′tə·fakt) *n.* Anything made by human work or art.

artless (ärt′lis) *adj.* **1.** Lacking craft or deceit. **2.** Natural; simple. **3.** Clumsy.

ascertain (as′ər·tān′) *v.t.* To learn with certainty; discover; determine.

aspiration (as′pə·rā′shən) *n.* **1.** Lofty ambition. **2.** A breath.

aspire (ə·spīr′) *v.i.* To have an earnest desire or ambition, as for something high and good.

assent (ə·sent′) *v.i.* To express agreement; consent; concur. — *n.* **1.** Agreement. **2.** Consent.

assets (as′ets) *n. pl.* All the property of a person or partnership.

assuage (ə·swāj′) *v.t.* **1.** To make less harsh or severe. **2.** To calm.

assumption (ə·sump′shən) *n.* The act of supposing that something is a fact, or that which is supposed to be true; a general idea; belief.

astern (ə·stûrn′) *adv. & adj. Naut.* In the rear; at any point behind a vessel.

asunder (ə·sun′dər) *adv.* Apart; into pieces. — *adj.* Separated; apart.

attain (ə·tān′) *v.t.* To achieve.

attest (ə·test′) *v.t.* **1.** To confirm as accurate, true, or genuine. **2.** To certify.

attire (ə·tīr′) *n.* Dress or clothing.

audacious (ô·dā′shəs) *adj.* **1.** Showing no fear; daring; bold. **2.** Presumptuous; shameless.

audacity (ô·das′ə·tē) *n.* Boldness; daring.

auspicious (ôs·pish′əs) *adj.* **1.** Of good omen. **2.** Fortunate; lucky; prosperous.

auxiliary (ôg·zil′yər·ē, -zil′ər-) *adj.* **1.** Giving or furnishing aid. **2.** Supplementary; reserve. — *n.* A person or thing which aids or helps.

averse (ə·vûrs′) *adj.* Opposed; unfavorable.

aversion (ə·vûr′zhən, -shən) *n.* Extreme dislike; opposition; antipathy.

B

baffle (baf′əl) *v.* To confuse mentally; perplex.

barbarism (bär′bə·riz′əm) *n.* **1.** The use of words or forms not approved or standard in a language. **2.** A primitive stage of civilization.

barricade (bar′ə·kād′, bar′ə·kād) *v.t.* To enclose with a barrier for the purpose of defense.

base (bās) *adj.* **1.** Mean; vile; contemptible. **2.** Befitting an inferior person or thing. **3.** Low in value.

bazaar (bə·zär′) *n.* **1.** An Oriental market or street of shops. **2.** A shop or store for the sale of miscellaneous wares.

beggar (beg′ər) *v.t.* **1.** To exhaust the resources of. **2.** To reduce to want; impoverish.

beguile (bi·gīl′) *v.t.* **1.** To deceive. **2.** To cheat. **3.** To while away pleasantly.

belligerent (bə·lij′ər·ənt) *adj.* **1.** Warlike. **2.** Engaged in or pertaining to warfare.

benefactor (ben′ə·fak′tər, ben′ə·fak′-) *n.* One who gives help; a patron.

benign (bi·nīn′) *adj.* **1.** Of a kind disposition; kindly. **2.** Gentle. **3.** Favorable. — **be·nign′ly** *adv.*

bereave (bi·rēv′) *v.t.* **1.** To deprive, as of hope or happiness. **2.** To leave desolate or saddened through loss.

PRONUNCIATION: add, āce, câre, pälm; end, ēven; it, īce; odd, ōpen, ôrder; took, pool; up, bûrn; ə = a in *above*, e in *sicken*, i in *flexible*, o in *melon*, u in *focus*; yoo = u in *fuse*; oil; pout; check; go; ring; thin; this; zh, vision.

755

beseech (bi·sēch′) *v.t.* To beg for earnestly. — past tense **besought.**

besiege (bi·sēj′) *v.t.* **1.** To attack on all sides; surround. **2.** To overwhelm.

bestir (bi·stûr′) *v.t.* To rouse to activity.

bias (bī′əs) *n.* A preference or prejudice.

bid (bid) *v.t.* **1.** To offer as a price for something. **2.** To order; command. — past tense **bade.**

bland (bland) *adj.* Gentle and soothing in manner; mild.

bondage (bon′dij) *n.* Slavery; serfdom.

bower (bou′ər) *n.* **1.** A shaded recess; arbor. **2.** *Poetic* A private room.

brandish (bran′dish) *v.* To wave threateningly or triumphantly.

brooch (brōch, brōōch) *n.* An ornamental pin.

brusque (brusk) *adj.* Rude or curt; blunt. Also **brusk. — brusque′ly** *adv.*

buccaneer (buk′ə·nir′) *n.* A pirate.

burgeon (bûr′jən) *v.i.* **1.** To flourish; grow. **2.** To bud; sprout.

burlesque (bər·lesk′) *n.* A literary or dramatic composition that provokes laughter by fanciful satire or humorous imitation.

burnish (bûr′nish) *v.t. & v.i.* To polish; make or become shiny.

C

callow (kal′ō) *adj.* Inexperienced; not mature.

candid (kan′did) *adj.* **1.** Honest and open; sincere. **2.** Impartial; fair.

candor (kan′dər) *n.* Frankness; openness; honesty.

canter (kan′tər) *v.* To ride or go at a slow, gentle gallop.

capricious (kə·prish′əs) *adj.* Fickle; changeable; whimsical.

carnal (kär′nəl) *adj.* **1.** Of the body or flesh, as opposed to spiritual. **2.** Worldly.

cascade (kas·kād′) *n.* **1.** A fall of water over steep rocks or one of a series of such falls. **2.** Anything resembling a waterfall, as the zigzag fall of lace trimming on a dress.

casement (kās′mənt) *n.* A type of window that hinges at the side.

cassock (kas′ək) *n.* A close-fitting robe, usually black, reaching to the feet, and worn by clergy, choir singers, etc.

cataract (kat′ə·rakt) *n.* **1.** A waterfall of great size. **2.** A heavy downpour of water.

catastrophe (kə·tas′trə·fē) *n.* A great and sudden disaster.

charitable (char′ə·tə·bəl) *adj.* **1.** Generous. **2.** Kindly; tolerant. — **char′i·ta·bly** *adv.*

chary (châr′ē) *adj.* Cautious; careful; wary.

chloroform (klôr′ə·fôrm, klō′rə-) *n. Chem.* A colorless, rapidly evaporating, sweetish liquid compound, used as an anesthetic and solvent. — *v.t.* **1.** To administer chloroform to. **2.** To anesthetize or kill with chloroform.

chorister (kôr′is·tər, kor′-) *n.* A choir member; a singer.

chronicle (kron′i·kəl) *v.t.* To record events in the order of their occurrence.

cipher (sī′fər) *v.t.* To calculate arithmetically.

circumscribe (sûr′kəm·skrīb′) *v.t.* To mark out the limits of; define; especially, to confine within bounds.

circumvent (sûr′kəm·vent′) *v.t.* **1.** To surround or trap, as an enemy. **2.** To outwit. **3.** To avoid.

clemency (klem′ən·sē) *n.* Leniency; mercy.

cloister (klois′tər) *v.t.* **1.** To seclude or confine. **2.** To withdraw from the world, as in a place of religious seclusion.

cogent (kō′jənt) *adj.* Compelling, in the sense of appealing to the mind; convincing.

coherent (kō·hir′ənt) *adj.* **1.** Sticking together, as particles of the same substance. **2.** Observing logical order and connection. **3.** Capable of being understood: *coherent* speech.

commiserate (kə·miz′ə·rāt) *v.t.* To feel or express sympathy for; pity.

communion (kə·myōōn′yən) *n.* A mutual sharing of thoughts and feelings; fellowship.

compassionate (kəm·pash′ən·it) *adj.* Sympathetic; charitable; pitying.

compilation (kom′pə·lā′shən) *n.* **1.** The act of compiling or collecting. **2.** A collection.

compile (kəm·pīl′) *v.t.* **1.** To put together from materials collected from other sources. **2.** To gather into a volume. **3.** To collect.

composure (kəm·pō′zhər) *n.* Calmness of mind; peacefulness.

comprehend (kom′pri·hend′) *v.t.* **1.** To understand fully. **2.** To take in or embrace; include.

conceive (kən·sēv′) *v.* **1.** To form in the mind; develop mentally. **2.** To form a notion of; imagine. **3.** To believe; think.

conciliatory (kən·sil′ē·ə·tôr′ē, -tō′rē) *adj.* Tending to win over or gain the good will of.

condescend (kon′di·send′) *v.i.* **1.** To come down voluntarily to equal terms with inferiors; be affable. **2.** To lower oneself (to do something). **3.** To behave in a patronizing manner.

condolence (kən·dō′ləns) *n.* **1.** Expression of sympathy with a person in pain or sorrow. **2.** *pl.* A declaration of sympathy.

conflagration (kon′flə·grā′shən) *n.* A great· or extensive fire.

confound (kon·found′, kən-) *v.t.* **1.** To confuse, amaze, or bewilder. **2.** To confuse with something else.

PRONUNCIATION: add, āce, câre, pälm; end, ēven; it, īce; odd, ōpen, ôrder; tŏŏk, pōōl; up, bûrn; ə = a in *above*, e in *sicken*, i in *flexible*, o in *melon*, u in *focus*; yōō = u in *fuse*; oil; pout; check; go; ring; thin; this; zh, vision.

756

confute (kən·fyo͞ot′) *v.t.* **1.** To prove to be wrong, false, or invalid. **2.** To overwhelm with proofs.

congestion (kən·jes′chən) *n.* An overcrowded condition.

conjecture (kən·jek′chər) *v.* To guess; suppose.

conservative (kən·sûr′və·tiv) *adj.* **1.** Inclined to preserve the existing order of things; opposed to change. **2.** Moderate; cautious.

conspiracy (kən·spir′ə·sē) *n.* An agreement or plan by two or more people to do an evil act.

consternation (kon′stər·nā′shən) *n.* Sudden fear or amazement; panic.

construe (kən·stro͞o′) *v.t.* **1.** To analyze the grammatical structure of a clause or sentence. **2.** To interpret; explain.

contemplate (kon′təm·plāt) *v.t.* **1.** To look at attentively; gaze at. **2.** To consider thoughtfully; meditate upon. **3.** To intend or plan.

contemplation (kon′təm·plā′shən) *n.* The act of meditating or musing.

contemporary (kən·tem′pə·rer′ē) *n.* A person living at the same time as another.

contemptuous (kən·temp′cho͞o·əs) *adj.* Showing disdain, scorn. — **con·temp′tu·ous·ly** *adv.*

contingent (kən·tin′jənt) *adj.* **1.** Liable to happen; possible. **2.** Occurring by chance; accidental. **3.** Dependent upon an uncertain event or condition.

contradictory (kon′trə·dik′tər·ē) *adj.* Opposite; contrary.

contrite (kən·trīt′, kon′trīt) *adj.* Deeply and humbly sorry for one's sins.

contrive (kən·trīv′) *v.t.* **1.** To plan cleverly. **2.** To plot or scheme. **3.** To invent. — *v.i.* To plan, scheme, or plot.

contumacious (kon′to͞o·mā′shəs) *adj.* Stubbornly disobedient; rebellious. —**con′tu·ma′·cious·ly** *adv.*

convent (kon′vent, -vənt) *n.* **1.** A religious community, especially of nuns. **2.** The building or buildings of such a community.

converse (kon′vûrs) *adj.* Turned about so that two parts are interchanged; reversed; contrary. — **con·verse′ly** (kən·vûrs′lē, kon′vûrs·lē) *adv.*

convulsive (kən·vul′siv) *adj.* **1.** Involving violent muscular contractions. **2.** Having the quality of a violent disturbance, as an earthquake.

coquet (kō·ket′) *v.i.* To treat a person with pretended affection.

cordiality (kôr·jal′ə·tē, -jē·al′) *n.* Sincerity of feeling; warmth.

corroborate (kə·rob′ə·rāt) *v.t.* To strengthen or support; to confirm.

counsel (koun′səl) *v.t.* **1.** To give advice to. **2.** To recommend. — *v.i.* To give or take counsel.

countenance (koun′tə·nəns) *n.* **1.** The face or features. **2.** Facial expression; appearance.

coupé (ko͞o·pā′) *n.* A two-door automobile, seating two to five people.

courtier (kôr′tē·ər, tyər, kōr′) *n.* **1.** A member of a sovereign's court. **2.** One who seeks favor by flattery.

covet (kuv′it) *v.t.* To desire eagerly; long for; especially to desire something belonging to another. — *v.i.* To feel desire or longing.

craven (krā′vən) *adj.* Lacking in courage; cowardly. — *n.* A base coward. — *v.t.* To make cowardly.

credit (kred′it) *n.* **1.** Trust; faith. **2.** The quality of being trustworthy. **3.** Reputation. **4.** Approval for some action or quality.

cress (kres) *n.* One of various plants of the mustard family, such as watercress, pungent in taste and used in salads.

crusade (kro͞o·sād′) *n.* Any strong, enthusiastic movement, especially a reform movement.

culprit (kul′prit) *n.* One guilty of some offense or crime.

cumulative (kyo͞om′yə·lā′tiv, -lə·tiv) *adj.* **1.** Gained or acquired by additions. **2.** Steadily increasing.

curate (kyo͞or′it) *n.* A member of the clergy assisting a parish priest, rector, or vicar.

currency (kûr′ən·sē) *n.* Money.

curtail (kər·tāl′) *v.t.* To cut off or cut short; lessen; reduce.

cynical (sin′i·kəl, -ə-) *adj.* Distrusting or disbelieving of virtue in others; sneering; sarcastic. — **cyn′i·cal·ly** *adv.*

D

damsel (dam′zəl) *n.* A young single woman.

dapple (dap′əl) *v.t.* To make spotted — *adj.* Spotted: also *dappled.*

decadent (di·kād′nt, dek′ə·dənt) *adj.* Falling into, or characteristic of, decay and decline.

declamation (dek′lə·mā′shən) *n.* **1.** The act of giving a formal speech. **2.** A prepared speech.

decorum (di·kôr′əm, -kō′rəm) *n.* Conforming to the requirements of good taste; correctness in behavior, dress, etc.

deem (dēm) *v.t. & v.i.* To judge; think; believe.

defer (di·fûr′) *v.* To put off until later; postpone.

degradation (deg′rə·dā′shən) *n.* **1.** The act of lowering in character, morals, etc. **2.** The state of being reduced in rank, honor, quality, etc.

dejection (di·jek′shən) *n.* Lowness of spirits; depression; melancholy.

deliberation (di·lib′ə·rā′shən) *n.* Careful and prolonged consideration.

PRONUNCIATION: add, āce, câre, pälm; end, ēven; it, īce; odd, ōpen, ôrder; to͝ok, po͞ol; up, bûrn; ə = a in *above*, e in *sicken*, i in *flexible*, o in *melon*, u in *focus*; yo͞o = u in *fuse*; oil; pout; check; go; ring; thin; this; zh, vision.

delirium (di·lir′ē·əm) *n.* **1.** A temporary mental disturbance characterized by confusion, mixed-up speech, and wild imaginings. **2.** Frenzy.

delusion (di·lōō′zhən) *n.* **1.** The act of deluding; deceiving. **2.** The state of being deluded or led astray.

demagoguery (dem′ə·gôg′ər·ē, -gog′ər·ē) *n.* Leading the public by appealing to prejudices and passions; the practices of an unprincipled politician.

demonstration (dem′ən·strā′shən) *n.* **1.** The act of making known; a pointing out or proving. **2.** A system of reasoning showing how, from given facts, a certain conclusion must follow.

demoralize (di·môr′əl·īz, -mor′-) *v.t.* **1.** To corrupt. **2.** To undermine or destroy the courage, confidence, etc. of; dishearten.

demure (di·myōor′) *adj.* **1.** Having a serious manner; reserved. **2.** Prim; coy. — **de·mure′ly** *adv.*

denomination (di·nom′ə·nā′shən) *n.* **1.** The act of naming. **2.** A name, designation, or title. **3.** A religious group. **4.** A specific class of units in a system of measures, weights, money, etc.

dependent (di·pen′dənt) *adj.* **1.** Conditioned by something else. **2.** Subject to outside control; subordinate. **3.** Relying on someone or something for support or aid. **4.** Hanging down.

depict (di·pikt′) *v.t.* **1.** To portray by drawing, sculpturing, painting, etc. **2.** To describe in words.

deplete (di·plēt′) *v.t.* **1.** To reduce or lessen, as by use or waste. **2.** To empty completely or partially: to *deplete* the supply.

depose (di·pōz′) *v.* To remove or oust from office or, usually, from a position of importance.

depreciate (di·prē′shē·āt) *v.* **1.** To lessen the value of; lower the price or rate of. **2.** To belittle.

depreciation (di·prē′shē·ā′shən) *n.* A loss of value or efficiency resulting from deterioration, usage, age, etc. **2.** A decline in the purchasing value of money. **3.** A disparagement or belittling.

depute (di·pyōōt′) *v.t.* **1.** To appoint as an agent. **2.** To transfer authority to another.

deputy (dep′yə·tē) *n.* One appointed to act for another.

deranged (di·rānjd′) *adj.* **1.** Insane. **2.** Disordered.

derision (di·rizh′ən) *n.* Ridicule; the act of treating with scornful mirth.

derisive (di·rī′siv) *adj.* Mocking.

descry (di·skrī′) *v.t.* To see in the distance or obscurity; discern; detect.

desiccation (des′ə·kā′shən) *n.* **1.** Drying out.

2. The removal of moisture, as from foods in order to preserve them.

designate (dez′ig·nāt) *v.t.* To indicate by some mark, sign, or name.

desolate (des′ə·lit) *adj.* **1.** Deserted; abandoned. **2.** Gloomy; dreary.

desolation (des′ə·lā′shən) *n.* **1.** The condition of being ruined or deserted. **2.** Loneliness; dreariness; sadness.

despicable (des′pi·kə·bəl, di·spik′ə·bəl) *adj.* contemptible; mean; vile.

despondency (di·spon′dən·sē) *n.* Lowness of spirits from loss of hope or courage.

despondent (di·spon′dənt) *adj.* Dejected in spirit; disheartened. — **de·spon′dent·ly** *adv.*

destitute (des′tə·tōot, -tyōot) *adj.* **1.** Not having or possessing. **2.** Extremely poor.

devastate (dev′ə·stāt) *v.t.* To lay waste; destroy.

devastation (dev′ə·stā′shən) *n.* The act of devastating, or the condition of having been devastated; destruction.

devoid (di·void′) *adj.* Not possessing; empty: with *of.*

devolve (di·volv′) *v.t.* To cause to pass to a successor or substitute.

devour (di·vour′) *v.t.* **1.** To eat up greedily. **2.** To absorb.

dexterous (dek′strəs, stər·əs) *adj.* Skillful or adroit; artful.

diabolic (dī′ə·bol′ik) *adj.* **1.** Of, belonging to, or proceeding from the devil. **2.** Very wicked or inhuman; fiendish. Also **di′a·bol′i·cal.**

diagnosis (dī′əg·nō′sis) *n.* **1.** *Med.* The process of recognizing diseases by their characteristic symptoms. **2.** A summary of symptoms and the conclusion reached.

diagnostic (dī′əg·nos′tik) *adj.* **1.** Pertaining to a diagnosis. **2.** Aiding in diagnosis.

differentiate (dif′ə·ren′shē·āt) *v.* **1.** To be the substance of the difference between; serve to contrast between. **2.** To see and indicate the differences in or between.

diffidence (dif′ə·dəns) *n.* Want of confidence in oneself; self-distrust; timidity; shyness.

dilapidated (di·lap′ə·dā′tid) *adj.* Fallen into decay or partial ruin.

diligence (dil′ə·jəns) *n.* **1.** Persistent application to one's work or duty. **2.** Care.

diligent (dil′ə·jənt) *adj.* Showing persistence and application in whatever is undertaken; industrious.

disaffection (dis′ə·fek′shən) *n.* A loss of fond feelings; estrangement.

disapprobation (dis′ap·rə·bā′shən) *n.* Disapproval.

discernible (di·zûr′nə·bəl, -sûr′-) *adj.* Perceptible; capable of being seen and recognized.

PRONUNCIATION: add, āce, câre, pälm; end, ēven; it, īce; odd, ōpen, ôrder; tōōk, pōōl; up, bûrn; ə = a in *above,* e in *sicken,* i in *flexible,* o in *melon,* u in *focus;* yōō = u in *fuse;* oil; pout; check; go; ring; thin; this; zh, vision.

discomfit (dis·kum′fit) *v.t.* **1.** To defeat the plans or purposes of; frustrate. **2.** To throw into confusion. **3.** To rout in battle; vanquish.

discomfiture (dis·kum′fi·chər) *n.* Defeat; frustration.

discommode (dis′kə·mōd′) *v.t.* To cause inconvenience to; trouble; disturb.

discomposure (dis′kəm·pō′zhər) *n.* Uneasiness; agitation.

disconsolate (dis·kon′sə·lit) *adj.* **1.** Unable to be consoled; dejected. **2.** Producing or marked by gloominess; cheerless; saddening. — **dis·con′so·late·ly** *adv.*

discordant (dis·kôr′dənt) *adj.* Characterized by lack of agreement; differing; clashing.

discourse (dis′kôrs, -kōrs, dis·kôrs′, -kōrs′) *n.* Conversation; talk.

discreet (dis·krēt′) *adj.* Tactful, especially in dealing with others; careful not to say or do the wrong thing.

disdainful (dis·dān′fəl) *adj.* Scornful; arrogant.

dismal (diz′məl) *adj.* **1.** Dark and gloomy. **2.** Joyless; bleak. — **dis′mal·ly** *adv.*

dismember (dis·mem′bər) *v.t.* **1.** To cut off or pull off the limbs. **2.** Divide forcibly into pieces.

disparagement (dis·par′ij·mənt) *n.* **1.** The act of treating or speaking with disrespect; belittling. **2.** Discrediting. **3.** Something that belittles or discredits.

disparity (dis·par′ə·tē) *n.* **1.** Lack of equality as in age or rank. **2.** Unlikeness; dissimilarity.

disperse (dis·pûrs′) *v.* **1.** To cause to scatter in various directions. **2.** To drive away; dispel.

dispirited (dis·pir′it·id) *adj.* Downcast in spirit; sad; dejected.

dissemble (di·sem′bəl) *v.* **1.** To conceal or disguise the actual nature of intentions or feelings. **2.** To make a false show of.

dissever (di·sev′ər) *v.t.* **1.** To divide; separate. **2.** To separate into parts.

dissimulation (di·sim′yə·lā′shən) *n.* False pretense.

distend (dis·tend′) *v.t. & v.i.* **1.** To expand by pressure from within. **2.** To stretch out; swell.

distill (dis·til′) *v.* To extract the fundamental nature of something.

distraught (dis·trôt′) *adj.* Deeply worried or tense; emotionally disturbed.

diversion (di·vûr′zhən, -shən, dī-) *n.* **1.** The act of turning aside as from a course. **2.** Something that distracts from worry or work.

divine (di·vīn′) *v.t.* To find out; discover; guess.

divulge (di·vulj′) *v.t.* To tell as a secret; disclose; reveal.

docile (dos′əl) *adj.* **1.** Easy to manage. **2.** Easily worked or handled. — **doc′ile·ly** *adv.*

doleful (dōl′fəl) *adj.* Mournful.

domestic (də·mes′tik) *adj.* Of or pertaining to the home or family.

dote (dōt) *v.i.* **1.** To lavish extreme fondness: with *on* or *upon*. **2.** To be feeble-minded as a result of old age.

draught (draft, dräft) *n.* A quantity of liquid for drinking; a drink; a dose.

dreary (drir′ē) *adj.* **1.** Causing or showing sadness or gloom. **2.** Dull or monotonous.

droll (drōl) *adj.* Humorously odd; comical; funny.

drollery (drō′lər·ē) *n.* **1.** The quality of being droll; humor. **2.** An amusing way of acting or talking.

dubious (dōō′bē·əs, dyōō′-) *adj.* **1.** Doubtful. **2.** Causing doubt. **3.** Uncertain. **4.** Questionable.

E

ecology (i·kol′ə·jē, ē-) *n.* The division of biology that treats of the relations between organisms and their environment. — **ec·o·log·ic** (ek′ə·loj′ik) or **·i·cal** *adj.*

economy (i·kon′ə·mē) *n.* Thrift; careful management of money, materials, resources, and the like.

ecstasy (ek′stə·sē) *n.* **1.** The state of being beside oneself through some overpowering emotion. **2.** Intense delight. **3.** A trance or frenzy thought to attend prophetic, mystic, or poetic inspiration.

eddy (ed′ē) *n.* A backward-circling current of water or air; whirlpool.

edifice (ed′ə·fis) *n.* A building or other structure, especially one that is large and imposing.

edify (ed′ə·fī) *v.t.* To enlighten and benefit, especially morally or spiritually.

egoistic (ē′gō·is′tik, eg′ō-) *adj.* **1.** Selfish. **2.** Conceited. Also **e′go·is′ti·cal.**

emancipation (i·man′sə·pā′shən) *n.* The act of setting free, or the state of being set free; liberation.

embark (im·bärk′) *v.t.* **1.** To put or take aboard a ship. *v.i.* **2.** To go aboard a ship for a voyage.

embellish (im·bel′ish) *v.t.* **1.** To beautify by adding ornamental features. **2.** To heighten the interest of a story by adding imaginative details.

eminent (em′ə·nənt) *adj.* **1.** Distiguished; prominent. **2.** Noteworthy; conspicuous. **3.** High; lofty.

endurance (in·dōōr′əns, -dyōōr′) *n.* **1.** The act or capacity of bearing up, as under hardship or prolonged stress. **2.** The state or power of lasting.

PRONUNCIATION: add, āce, câre, pälm; end, ēven; it, īce; odd, ōpen, ôrder; tŏŏk, pōōl; up, bûrn; ə = a in *above*, e in *sicken*, i in *flexible*, o in *melon*, u in *focus*; yōō = u in *fuse*; oil; pout; check; go; ring; thin; ᵺis; zh, vision.

engorge (en·gôrj′) *v.t.* **1.** To fill with blood, as an artery. **2.** To swallow greedily.

engross (in·grōs′) *v.t.* To occupy completely.

ennoble (i·nō′bəl, en-) *v.t.* To make honorable or noble in nature, quality, etc.; dignify.

enshroud (in·shroud′) *v.t.* To conceal.

ensign (en′sīn) *n.* A flag or banner; especially a national standard or naval flag.

ensue (en·sōō′) *v.i.* **1.** To occur afterward. **2.** To follow as a consequence.

entrails (en′trālz, -trəlz) *n. pl.* The internal parts of a person or animal.

entreat (in·trēt′) *v.t.* To ask earnestly; beg; implore.

entrench (in·trench′) *v.* To dig trenches for defense. — **entrenched** *adj.* Dug in; protected in trenches.

epistle (i·pis′əl) *n.* A letter, especially when long or formal.

errant (er′rənt) *adj.* **1.** Roving or wandering, especially in search of adventure. **2.** Straying from the proper course.

erudition (er′yōō·dish′ən, er′ōō-) *n.* Great learning; scholarship.

ethnic (eth′nik) *adj.* Belonging to or distinctive of a particular racial, cultural, or language division of humanity.

eulogy (yōō′lə·jē) *n.* A spoken or written piece of high praise, especially when formal and delivered publicly.

evince (i·vins′) *v.t.* To indicate clearly; prove.

excavation (eks′kə·vā′shən) *n.* A hole or hollow made by digging.

execrate (ek′sə·krāt) *v.t.* **1.** To call down evil upon; curse. **2.** To denounce violently.

exhilaration (ig·zil′ə·rā′shən) *n.* The state of being in high spirits; glowing with happiness.

exhort (ig·zôrt′) *v.* To urge or advise earnestly.

expatriate (eks·pā′trē·āt) *v.t.* **1.** To drive (people) from their native land; exile; banish. **2.** To withdraw (oneself) from one's native land.

expedient (ik·spē′dē·ənt) *n.* **1.** A means to an end. **2.** Device.

expound (ik·spound′) *v.t.* **1.** To set forth in detail. **2.** To explain the meaning of; interpret.

exquisite (eks′kwi·zit, ik·skwiz′it) *adj.* **1.** Marked by rare beauty. **2.** Being of a high degree of excellence; admirable. **3.** Discriminating. **4.** Extremely refined.

extract (eks′trakt) *n.* **1.** Something drawn out. **2.** A passage selected from a book and used for some purpose; quotation; excerpt.

extricate (eks′trə·kāt) *v.* To free from something that tangles, holds back, embarrasses, or endangers.

exuberant (ig·zōō′bər·ənt) *adj.* **1.** Abounding in high spirits and vitality; full of joy and vigor. **2.** Overflowing; lavish.

exultant (ig·zul′tənt) *adj.* Triumphant; elated. — **ex·ul′tant·ly; ex·ult′ing·ly** *adv.*

F

fabulous (fab′yə·ləs) *adj.* Incredible; passing the limits of belief.

falter (fôl′tər) *v.* To say in an unsteady or stumbling way.

fancy (fan′sē) *v.t.* To believe without proof; suppose. — *n.* An idea or notion not based on fact.

fealty (fē′əl·tē) *n.* Faithfulness; loyalty.

feign (fān) *v.t.* To pretend; sham; fabricate.

felicitous (fə·lis′ə·təs) *adj.* Particularly well chosen; most appropriate; apt.

felicity (fə·lis′ə·tē) *n.* **1.** Happiness, especially when very great. **2.** An agreeably affective manner.

fervor (fûr′vər) *n.* **1.** Great warmth or intensity, as of emotion.

festoon (fes·tōōn′) *v.t.* To decorate with flowers or leaves linked together.

fetter (fet′ər) *n.* A chain around the ankles to prevent movement or escape. — *v.t.* To hold in check; confine.

fodder (fod′ər) *n.* Coarse feed for horses, cattle, etc.; for example, the stalks and leaves of field corn.

foliage (fō′lē·ij) *n.* The growth of leaves on a tree or other plant; also leaves collectively.

forbear (fôr·bâr′) *v.t.* **1.** To restrain oneself from performing some action: to *forbear* speaking. **2.** To stop. — *v.i.* To be patient.

foresight (fôr′sīt, fōr′-) *n.* **1.** The act or capacity of foreknowledge. **2.** Anticipation of what the future may hold.

forge (fôrj) *n.* A blacksmith's shop.

forlorn (fôr·lôrn′, fər-) *adj.* **1.** Deserted. **2.** Wretched. **3.** Hopeless; despairing. —**forlorn′ly** *adv.*

fountainhead (foun′tən·hed′) *n.* **1.** A spring of water from which a stream takes its source. **2.** The source or origin of anything.

fraternal (frə·tûr′nəl) *adj.* Pertaining to or befitting a brother; brotherly.

G

galley (gal′ē) *n.* **1.** A long, low vessel used in ancient and medieval times. **2.** A large rowboat. **3.** The kitchen of a ship.

gallows (gal′ōz) *n.* A framework, usually consisting of two or more upright beams supporting a crossbeam, used for executing a condemned person by hanging.

PRONUNCIATION: add, āce, câre, pälm; end, ēven; it, īce; odd, ōpen, ôrder; tōŏk, pōōl; up, bûrn; ə = a in *above*, e in *sicken*, i in *flexible*, o in *melon*, u in *focus*; yōō = u in *fuse*; oil; pout; check; go; ring; thin; this; zh, vision.

760

gaunt (gônt) *adj.* **1.** Thin and hollow-eyed as from illness or age. **2.** Gloomy in appearance.

genial (jēn'yəl, jē'nē·əl) *adj.* Kindly and pleasant in manner.

gesticulation (jes·tik'yə·lā'shən) *n.* The act of making emphatic or expressive gestures.

gild (gild) *v.t.* **1.** To coat with a thin layer of gold. **2.** To brighten.

gingerly (jin'jər·lē) *adv.* In a cautious, careful, but rather unwilling way.

gird (gûrd) *v.t.* **1.** To surround or fasten with a belt. **2.** To prepare oneself for action. **3.** To clothe or equip.

girt (gûrt) Past participle of GIRD.

graft (graft, gräft) *v.t.* **1.** To insert a shoot into a tree or plant. **2.** To obtain a tree or plant as a result of this procedure.

grievous (grē'vəs) *adj.* **1.** Causing grief, sorrow, or misfortune; distressing. **2.** Meriting severe punishment or censure. **3.** Expressing grief or sorrow; mournful. **4.** Causing pain or physical suffering.

grisly (griz'lē) *adj.* **1.** Inspiring fear or horror; gruesome. **2.** Forbidding; grim.

grovel (gruv'əl, grov'-) *v.i.* **1.** To lie or crawl face downward, as in fear. **2.** To humble oneself.

guileless (gīl'lis) *adj.* Free from guile or cunning; innocent.

guillotine (gil'ə·tēn, gē'ə·tēn) *n.* A machine for beheading a person by means of a weighted blade that slides between two vertical guides.

gut (gut) *n.* **1.** The alimentary canal or any part of it. **2.** The specially prepared intestines of certain animals, used as strings for musical instruments, surgical sutures, etc.

H

haft (haft, häft) *n.* A handle; especially of a sword or knife.

haggard (hag'ərd) *adj.* Having a worn, gaunt, or wild look, as from worry, hunger, or tiredness.

harrow (har'ō) *n.* A farm tool set with spikes or disks for leveling plowed ground or breaking clods of earth. — *v.t.* **1.** To draw a harrow over. **2.** To disturb someone's mind or feelings.

haven (hā'vən) *n.* **1.** A harbor; port. **2.** A refuge or safe place.

heathen (hē'thən) *n.* **1.** A member of a tribe or people that has not adopted Christianity, Judaism, or Islam, especially a person worshipping many gods; idolater. **2.** Any irreligious or uncultivated person.

heed (hēd) *v.t.* To pay attention to; listen to.

herald (her'əld) *n.* **1.** Any bearer of important news; messenger. **2.** One who (or that which) announces what is to follow. — *v.t.* To announce publicly.

hew (hyoō) *v.t.* To cut or strike with an ax, sword, or some other cutting tool. — *v.i.* **1.** To make cutting and repeated blows. **2.** To conform, as to a principle or rule of conduct.

hieroglyph (hī'ər·ə·glif') *n.* **1.** A picture or symbol representing an object, idea, or sound, as in the writing system of the ancient Egyptians. **2.** Any symbol or character having an obscure or hidden meaning.

hilarious (hi·lâr'ē·əs, hī-) *adj.* Noisily gay or cheerful.

homespun (hōm'spun') *adj.* **1.** Spun or woven at home. **2.** Plain and simple in character: *homespun* humor. **3.** Made of homespun fabric, as a garment.

homestead (hōm'sted) *n.* A house and its land, etc., occupied as a home.

homily (hom'ə·lē) *n.* **1.** A sermon, especially one based on a Biblical text. **2.** A solemn speech, especially on morals or conduct.

humility (hyoō·mil'ə·tē) *n.* The state or quality of being modest, free from pride, unassuming.

hurtle (hûr'təl) *v.i.* To rush headlong or impulsively. — *v.t.* To hurl, throw, or drive violently.

hypochondriac (hī'pə·kon'drē·ak, hip'ə-) *adj.* Related to or affected with worry about one's health. — *n.* A person subject to excessive worry about his or her health.

hypocrite (hip'ə·krit) *n.* **1.** One who falsely gives an impression of virtue or sincerity. **2.** One who is insincere in what one says or does.

hypothesis (hī·poth'ə·sis, hi-) *n.* **1.** An unproved scientific conclusion drawn from known facts and used as a basis for further investigation. **2.** An assumption provisionally accepted as a basis for reasoning or argument.

I

ignominious (ig'nə·min'ē·əs) *adj.* **1.** Shameful; involving disgrace or dishonor. **2.** Despicable. **3.** Humiliating; tending to diminish one's self-respect. — **ig'no·min'i·ous·ly** *adv.*

illimitable (i·lim'it·ə·bəl) *adj.* Not measurable; boundless; infinite.

illuminate (il·oō'mə·nāt) *v.t.* **1.** To light up. **2.** To clarify. **3.** To glorify.

illustrious (i·lus'trē·əs) *adj.* Greatly distinguished; famous.

immaculate (i·mak'yə·lit) *adj.* **1.** Completely clean. **2.** Pure. **3.** Without error. — **im·mac'u·late·ly** *adv.*

PRONUNCIATION: add, āce, câre, pälm; end, ēven; it, īce; odd, ōpen, ôrder; toōk, poōl; up, bûrn; ə = a in *above*, e in *sicken*, i in *flexible*, o in *melon*, u in *focus*; yoō = u in *fuse*; oil; pout; check; go; ring; thin; this; zh, vision.

761

impeccable (im·pek′ə·bəl) *adj.* **1.** Free from error or fault. **2.** Incapable of doing wrong.

impediment (im·ped′ə·mənt) *n.* An obstacle; that which hinders.

impel (im·pel′) *v.* To force or drive to an action; urge on.

impend (im·pend′) *v.i.* **1.** To be about to occur. **2.** To be suspended; hang: with *over.*

imperceptible (im′pər·sep′tə·bəl) *adj.* **1.** That can barely be perceived. **2.** Not discernible by the mind or senses. — **im′per·cep′ti·bly** *adv.*

imperious (im·pir′ē·əs) *adj.* **1.** Commanding; domineering. **2.** Urgent. — **im·per′a·tive·ly** *adv.*

imperturbable (im′pər·tûr′bə·bəl) *adj.* Not able to be disturbed or upset; unruffled; calm.

implore (im·plôr′, -plōr′) *v.t.* **1.** To make a humble or urgent request; beseech. **2.** To beg for urgently.

impostor (im·pos′tər) *n.* One who pretends to be someone else.

imprecation (im′prə·kā′shən) *n.* A curse.

impressionable (im·presh′ən·ə·bəl) *adj.* Easily influenced; sensitive.

improvise (im′prə·vīz) *v.t.* To produce without previous thought or preparation; especially to perform or invent without notes or prepared material.

impunity (im·pyōō′nə·tē) *n.* Freedom or exemption from punishment or harm.

imputation (im′pyōō·tā′shən) *n.* The act of charging a fault to someone; accusation.

inalienable (in·āl′yən·ə·bəl) *adj.* Not able to be transferred or taken away.

incendiary (in·sen′dē·er′ē) *adj.* **1.** Of or related to the burning of property. **2.** Tending to inflame mob passion.

incessant (in·ses′ənt) *adj.* Continuing without interruption; never stopping; continual. — **in·ces′sant·ly** *adv.*

incident (in′sə·dənt) *adj.* Naturally or usually found with: with *to.*

incipient (in·sip′ē·ənt) *adj.* Not fully developed, but beginning, or beginning to be.

inclemency (in·klem′ən·sē) *n.* Harshness; severity.

incomprehensible (in′kom·pri·hen′sə·bəl, in·kom′-) *adj.* Incapable of being understood; unintelligible.

inconsequential (in′kon·sə·kwen′shəl, in·kon′-) *adj.* Having little or no importance.

incredulity (in′krə·dōō′lə·tē, -dyōō′-) *n.* Disbelief; doubt.

inculcate (in·kul′kāt, in′kul·kāt) *v.* To teach, or impress upon the mind, by frequent, forceful repetition.

incursion (in·kûr′zhən) *n.* An invasion or raid,

especially a brief and sudden one.

indignation (in′dig·nā′shən) *n.* Righteous anger.

indiscriminate (in′dis·krim′ə·nit) *adj.* **1.** Showing no preference; not recognizing differences. **2.** Lacking in judgment.

induce (in·dōōs′, -dyōōs′) *v.t.* **1.** To persuade. **2.** To bring on; produce; cause.

inevitable (in·ev′ə·tə·bəl) *adj.* Unavoidable; certain; cannot be prevented from happening; fateful.

infatuation (in·fach′ōō·ā·shən) *n.* A silly or foolish love or passion.

infectious (in·fek′shəs) *adj.* **1.** Liable to produce infection. **2.** Tending to excite similar reactions in others: *infectious* laughter.

infer (in·fûr′) *v.t.* **1.** To derive by reasoning; conclude or accept from evidence; deduce. **2.** To imply, hint.

infernal (in·fûr′nəl) *adj.* Inhuman; fiendish. **2.** Hateful.

infidel (in′fi·dəl) *n.* One who rejects all religious belief; an unbeliever.

inflammatory (in·flam′ə·tôr′ē, -tō′rē) *adj.* Tending to arouse excitement, violence, or anger.

inflection (in·flek′shən) *n.* Meaningful change or changes in a word such as those which show case, number, gender, etc.

ingenious (in·jēn′yəs) *adj.* Cleverly conceived; skillful.

ingot (ing′gət) *n.* A mass of metal cast into a convenient shape for storage or transportation.

injunction (in·jungk′shən) *n.* An order, direction, or command.

innumerable (i·nōō′mər·ə·bəl, i·nyōō′-) *adj.* Too numerous to be counted; very many.

inquisition (in′kwə·zish′ən) *n.* **1.** An official investigation of the beliefs and activities of individuals or groups for the purpose of enforcing conformity to social and political rules. **2.** The act of inquiring or searching out.

inscrutable (in·skrōō′tə·bəl) *adj.* Mysterious; cannot be looked into or understood; unable to be pierced.

insensible (in·sen′sə·bəl) *adj.* **1.** Unconscious; not aware. **2.** Not capable of feeling or recognizing. — **in·sen′sib·ly** *adv.*

insight (in′sīt′) *n.* Keen perception or understanding; intuition.

insolent (in′sə·lənt) *adj.* Insulting; disrespectful; overbearing in conduct or speech. — **in′so·lent·ly** *adv.*

instigate (in′stə·gāt) *v.t.* **1.** To spur on or goad to some drastic course or deed; to incite. **2.** To provoke.

institute (in′stə·tōōt, -tyōōt) *v.t.* **1.** To set up or establish; found. **2.** To set in operation; initiate; start.

PRONUNCIATION: add, āce, câre, pälm; end, ēven; it, īce; odd, ōpen, ôrder; tŏŏk, pōōl; up, bûrn; ə = a in *above*, e in *sicken*, i in *flexible*, o in *melon*, u in *focus*; yōō = u in *fuse*; oil; pout; check; go; ring; thin; this; zh, vision.

762

institution (in'stə·tōō'shən, ·tyōō'-) *n.* **1.** A principle, custom, system, etc. that forms part of a society or civilization. **2.** A corporate body organized to perform a particular function: an *institution* of learning; a financial *institution*. **3.** *Informal* A familiar and characteristic object, custom, or person. **4.** The act of instituting, establishing, or setting in operation.

insupportable (in'sə·pôr'tə·bəl, -pōr'-) *adj.* **1.** Not bearable. **2.** Unjustifiable.

interlope (in'tər·lōp') *v.i.* To intrude in the affairs of others. — **in'ter·lo'per** *n.* One who meddles.

interment (in·tûr'mənt) *n.* Burial.

interminable (in·tûr'mə·nə·bəl) *adj.* Seeming never to end; apparently endless.

interpose (in'tər·pōz') *v.t.* To put between other things; cause to come between, especially as a separation or barrier. — *v.i.* **1.** To come between. **2.** To interrupt.

interposition (in'tər·pə·zish'ən) *n.* **1.** The act of coming between, or the state of being separated. **2.** Intervention.

interrogatory (in'tə·rog'ə·tôr'ē, -tō'rē) *adj.* Pertaining to, expressing, or implying a question.

intervene (in'tər·vēn') *v.i.* **1.** To interfere or take a definite stand, especially with a view to correction, solution, or settlement. **2.** To occur in a way that changes an action, expectation, etc. **3.** To be located between.

intimate[1] (in'tə·mit) *adj.* Familiar; deeply personal; private. — **in'ti·mate·ly** *adv.*

intimate[2] (in'tə·māt) *v.t.* To make known without direct statement; hint; imply.

intimation (in'tə·mā'shən) *n.* **1.** Information given indirectly; a hint. **2.** A declaration or notification.

inundation (in'un·dā'shən) *n.* A flood; overflow; deluge.

inveigle (in·vē'gəl, -vā-) *v.t.* **1.** To lead astray by blinding or deceiving. **2.** To win over by cunning or craftiness.

inventory (in'vən·tôr'ē, -tō'rē) *n.* A list of articles with the description and quantity of each.

inviolable (in·vī'ə·lə·bəl) *adj.* **1.** Sacred; not to be defiled. **2.** Not to be violated or broken: an *inviolable* law. — **in·vi'o·la·bly** *adv.*

irresolute (i·rez'ə·lōōt) *adj.* Not resolved; lacking firmness of purpose; wavering; hesitating.

irretrievable (ir'i·trē'və·bəl) *adj.* Not able to be recovered; not capable of being repaired.

J

jubilation (jōō'bə·lā'shən) *n.* Rejoicing; joy.

K

keel (kēl) *n.* A timber running lengthwise along the center of the bottom of a ship.

ken (ken) *v.t.* *Scot.* To know. — *n.* Range or extent of sight or knowledge.

knead (nēd) *v.t.* **1.** To mix (dough, clay, etc) into a uniform mass by pressing, turning, and pulling with the hands. **2.** To massage.

L

labyrinth (lab'ə·rinth) *n.* An arrangement of winding paths or passages.

lacerate (las'ər·āt) *v.t.* **1.** Tear raggedly; to split. **2.** To injure.

lament (lə·ment') *v.i.* To feel or express sorrow.

lamentable (lam'ən·tə·bəl, lə·ment'ə-) *adj.* Causing grief; sorrowful; pitiable.

lamentation (lam'ən·tā'shən) *n.* **1.** The act of feeling sad. **2.** A lament; wail; moan.

lank (langk) *adj.* Lean; slender and thin.

languid (lang'gwid) *adj.* **1.** Affected by weakness or fatigue. **2.** Feeling little inclination toward anything.

languor (lang'gər) *n.* **1.** Weariness of body; weakness. **2.** A lack of energy or enthusiasm. **3.** A mood of tenderness. **4.** The absence of activity.

lapse (laps) *n.* **1.** A gradual passing away. **2.** A slip or mistake, usually minor.

larceny (lär'sə·nē) *n.* Theft.

laud (lôd) *v.t.* To praise highly.

laudable (lô'də·bəl) *adj.* Praiseworthy.

laxness (laks'nes) *n.* A lack of strictness or discipline; neglect.

leaven (lev'ən) *n.* An agent of fermentation, as yeast, added to dough to produce a light texture.

liberal (lib'ər·l, lib'rəl) *adj.* **1.** Broadminded; not intolerant or prejudiced. **2.** Inclining toward opinions or policies favoring progress or reform, as in politics or religion. **3.** Generous.

limpid (lim'pid) *adj.* Clear.

lithe (līth) *adj.* Bending easily or gracefully.

loath (lōth) *adj.* Strongly reluctant; unwilling.

loiter (loi'ter) *v.i.* **1.** To stand around idly or aimlessly. **2.** To proceed in an aimless manner.

loll (lol) *v.i.* **1.** To lounge in a relaxed manner. **2.** To droop or hang loosely.

longitudinal (lon'jə·tōō'də·nəl, -tyōō'-, long'gə-) *adj.* Of or pertaining to length.

ludicrous (lōō'də·krəs) *adj.* Exciting laughter or ridicule; ridiculous.

luster (lus'tər) *n.* **1.** Soft, reflected light playing over a surface; sheen; gloss. **2.** Brightness or brilliance of light; radiance. **3.** Splendor, glory.

PRONUNCIATION: add, āce, câre, pälm; end, ēven; it, īce; odd, ōpen, ôrder; tōōk, pōōl; up, bûrn; ə = a in *above*, e in *sicken*, i in *flexible*, o in *melon*, u in *focus*; yōō = u in *fuse*; oil; pout; check; go; ring; thin; this; zh, vision.

763

lyre (līr) *n.* An ancient harplike stringed instrument, used by the Greeks to accompany poetry and song.

M

mace (mās) *n.* **1.** A heavy war club, usually with a spiked metal head for use against armor. **2.** A club-shaped staff of office or authority.

macrocosm (mak'rə·koz'əm) *n.* The whole universe or great world, in contrast to individual people.

magnanimous (mag·nan'ə·məs) *adj.* Showing generosity in forgiving insults or injuries; not given to resentment or envy; honorable.

magnitude (mag'nə·tōōd, -tyōōd) *n.* **1.** Size or extent. **2.** Greatness or importance.

malignant (mə·lig'nənt) *adj.* **1.** Tending to do great harm. **2.** Having an evil disposition toward others; evil.

manacle (man'ə·kəl) *n.* A handcuff or other device for restraining the hands. — *v.t.* To hold back or hamper.

mangy (mān'jē) *adj.* Shabby; poverty-stricken; wretched.

mania (mā'nē·ə, mān'yə) *n.* **1.** An extreme interest, enthusiasm, or craving. **2.** Frenzy.

maniac (mā'nē·ak) *n.* An insane person; one who is mad.

manifest (man'ə·fest) *v.t.* To reveal; show; display.

matrimonial (mat'rə·mō·nē·əl) *adj.* Of or pertaining to marriage.

maul (môl) *v.t.* **1.** To abuse; handle roughly. **2.** To beat and bruise.

mean (mēn) *adj.* Poor or inferior in grade or quality. — **mean'ly** *adv.*

meditate (med'ə·tāt) *v.* **1.** To engage in continuous and deliberate thought. **2.** To think about doing; plan.

mendicant (men'də·kənt) *adj.* **1.** Begging; depending on alms for a living. **2.** Characteristic of a beggar.

meretricious (mer'ə·trish'əs) *adj.* Showy and meant to attract, but actually false or cheap.

metropolis (mə·trop'ə·lis) *n.* **1.** A principal city in a particular country, state, or area. **2.** An urban center of activity, culture, trade, etc.

microcosm (mī'krə·koz'əm) *n.* **1.** A little world; the universe in miniature. **2.** A being thought of as representing the universe.

mien (mēn) *n.* Manner, bearing, expression, or outward appearance.

minaret (min'ə·ret') *n.* A high slender tower attached to a Moslem temple.

mince (mins) *v.t.* To cut or chop into small bits. — *v.i.* To walk with short steps or affected daintiness or primness.

mineralogist (min'ə·ral'ə·jist, -rol') *n.* One who specializes in the science of minerals.

minion (min'yən) *n.* A follower (a term of contempt).

mirth (mûrth) *n.* Spirited gaiety, especially when accompanied by laughter.

miscreant (mis'krē·ənt) *n.* An evildoer; a person without principles.

misrepresentation (mis'rep·ri·zen·tā'shən) *n.* A false picture or statement.

mode (mōd) *n.* **1.** Way; method. **2.** Current style or fashion, as in dress.

monolithic (mon'ə·lith'ik) *adj.* **1.** Pertaining to or resembling a monolith, a single, usually huge, block of stone. **2.** Having a massive, uniform structure that does not permit individual variations.

monosyllable (mon'ə·sil'ə·bəl) *n.* A word of one syllable.

moorings (mōōr'ingz) *n. pl.* A place where a ship or boat is tied up.

morose (mə·rōs') *adj.* Ill-humored; sullen; gloomy, as a person, mood, etc.

mosque (mosk) *n.* A Moslem temple of worship.

muddle (mud'l) *v.t.* **1.** To mix in a confused way. **2.** To confuse or bewilder. — *v.i.* To act or think in a confused manner.

N

naturalize (nach'ər·əl·īz') *v.t.* **1.** To confer rights of citizenship upon an alien. **2.** To adapt to the environment of a particular area. — *v.i.* To become like a native; adapt.

naught (nôt) *n.* **1.** Nothing. **2.** A zero.

negotiate (ni·gō'shē·āt) *v.i.* To bargain or confer with the aim of reaching an agreement. — *v.t.* To arrange by means of a conference or by means of a discussion.

negotiation (ni·gō'shē·ā'shən) *n.* A conference or discussion designed to produce an agreement.

nicety (nī'sə·tē) *n.* **1.** A fine point; a small or subtle detail or distinction. **2.** A delicacy or refinement.

niggardly (nig'ərd·lē) *adj.* **1.** Meanly stingy. **2.** Meanly insufficient.

nimble (nim'bəl) *adj.* Light and quick in movement; lively.

notoriety (nō'tə·rī'ə·tē) *n.* The state of being generally disapproved of.

nourish (nûr'ish) *v.t.* To supply food or other material to sustain life and promote growth; to feed. — **nour'ish·er** *n.*

nuptial (nup'shəl) *adj.* Suitable for a wedding.

PRONUNCIATION: add, āce, câre, pälm; end, ēven; it, īce; odd, ōpen, ôrder; tōōk, pōōl; up, bûrn; ə = a in *above*, e in *sicken*, i in *flexible*, o in *melon*, u in *focus*; yōō = u in *fuse*; oil; pout; check; go; ring; thin; this; zh, vision.

764

nurture (nûr′chər) *v.t.* **1.** To feed or support; nourish. **2.** To bring up or train.

O

oblige (ə·blīj′) *v.t.* **1.** To give someone cause for gratitude: with *to:* I am *obliged* to you. **2.** To compel or constrain, as by command, promise, etc. **3.** To do a favor or service for.

obliterate (ə·blit′ə·rāt) *v.t.* **1.** To destroy totally. **2.** To blot or wipe out; abolish.

obnoxious (əb·nok′shəs) *adj.* Highly disagreeable; objectionable; offensive.

obscure (əb·skyoor′) *adj.* **1.** Not clear or plain to the mind; hard to understand. **2.** Hidden, remote.

obstinate (ob′stə·nit) *adj.* Stubborn; unyielding; unreasonably fixed in one's purpose or opinion.

obviate (ob′vē·āt) *v.t.* To prevent or counter (an objection, difficulty, etc.) by effective measures; dispose of; provide for.

odium (ō′dē·əm) *n.* **1.** Extreme dislike; hatred. **2.** Disgrace associated with something hateful.

omnipotent (om·nip′ə·tənt) *adj.* All-powerful; having complete authority.

opportune (op′ər·toon′, -tyoon′) *adj.* **1.** Meeting some need; especially right or fit. **2.** Occurring at the right moment; timely.

oppressive (ə·pres′iv) *adj.* **1.** Burdensome; tyrannical; harsh; cruel. **2.** Producing a feeling of weight or constriction.

oracle (ôr′ə·kəl, or′-) *n.* **1.** A prophecy given by a priest or divinity in ancient times; also the place where these prophecies were made. **2.** A person of great wisdom or knowledge. **3.** A wise saying.

ordnance (ôrd′nəns) *n.* **1.** Military weapons, ammunition. **2.** Cannon or artillery.

P

painstaking (pānz′tā′king, pān′stā-) *adj.* Careful; attentive to details.

paling (pā′ling) *n.* One of a series of upright pickets forming a fence.

palpable (pal′pə·bəl) *adj.* **1.** Capable of being touched or felt. **2.** Readily perceived; obvious.

pandemonium (pan′də·mō′nē·əm) *n.* **1.** The abode of demons; hell. **2.** A place or gathering marked by disorder and uproar.

parapet (par′ə·pit, -pet) *n.* A low wall around the edge of a roof, terrace, bridge, etc.

parasitic (par′ə·sit′ik) *adj.* Living at another's expense without making proper return; destructive.

parley (pär′lē) *n.* A conference, as with an en-emy; a discussion of terms; a conversation.

parochial (pə·rō′kē·əl) *adj.* **1.** Pertaining to, supported by, or confined to a parish. **2.** Narrow; restricted in scope.

paroxysm (par′ək·siz′əm) *n.* A sudden and violent outburst of emotion or action.

parsimony (pär′sə·mō′nē) *n.* Undue sparingness in the expenditure of money; stinginess.

patent (pāt′nt) *adj.* Apparent to everybody; obvious.

pathos (pā′thos) *n.* The quality of human experience which arouses feelings of pity, sympathy, and sorrow.

patronize (pā′trən·īz, pat′rən-) *v.t.* **1.** Give support to. **2.** To trade with as a regular customer.

pecuniary (pi·kyoo′nē·er′ē) *adj.* Consisting of or relating to money.

pedagogue (ped′ə·gog, -gôg) *n.* A schoolmaster; educator.

penitence (pen′ə·təns) *n.* The state of feeling regret for sins or offenses; repentance; remorse.

pensively (pen′siv·lē) *adv.* In a quiet, thoughtful way, often also with a touch of sadness.

perceive (pər·sēv′) *v.t. & v.i.* **1.** To become aware of something through the senses; to see, hear, feel, taste, or smell. **2.** To come to understand.

perception (pər·sep′shən) *n.* **1.** The act or process of becoming aware of something through the senses. **2.** The result or effect of awareness.

peril (per′əl) *n.* Danger; risk.

peripatetic (per′i·pə·tet′ik) *adj.* Wandering about from place to place.

pernicious (pər·nish′əs) *adj.* **1.** Having the power of destroying or injuring; tending to kill or hurt. **2.** wicked.

perpetual (pər·pech′oo·əl) *adj.* Lasting forever or for an unlimited time.

perpetuate (pər·pech′oo·āt) *v.t.* **1.** To make lasting or enduring. **2.** To cause to remain known.

perplex (pər·pleks′) *v.t.* To cause to hesitate or become confused by doubt or difficulties; to puzzle.

perplexity (pər·plek′sə·tē) *n.* The state, quality, or condition of being confused; doubt; bewilderment.

persevere (pûr′sə·vir′) *v.i.* To continue striving in spite of difficulties .

pertinacious (pûr′tə·nā′shəs) *adj.* Holding strongly to an opinion or purpose.

phantom (fan′təm) *n.* Ghost.

phenomenal (fi·nom′ə·nəl) *adj.* Extraordinary; remarkable.

phlegmatic (fleg·mat′ik) *adj.* Not easily moved or excited; sluggish; indifferent.

PRONUNCIATION: add, āce, câre, pälm; end, ēven; it, īce; odd, ōpen, ôrder; took, pool; up, bûrn; ə = a in *above*, e in *sicken*, i in *flexible*, o in *melon*, u in *focus*; yoo = u in *fuse*; oil; pout; check; go; ring; thin; this; zh, vision.

765

phraseology (frā′zē·ol′ə·jē) *n.* The choice and arrangement of words and phrases in expressing ideas.

picturesque (pik′chə·resk′) *adj.* Having a striking, irregular beauty, quaintness, or charm.

pigeonhole (pij′ən·hōl) *n.* A small compartment, as in a desk, for filing papers. — *v.t.* To place in a pigeonhole; to file.

pillage (pil′ij) *n.* The act of taking money or property by violence. — *v.t.* **1.** To rob openly. **2.** To take as loot.

pine (pīn) *v.* To grow thin or weak with longing, grief, or the like.

pinion (pin′yən) *v.t.* **1.** To cut or bind the wings of a bird. **2.** To bind or hold the arms of a person so as to make that person helpless.

pious (pī′əs) *adj.* **1.** Marked by a spirit of reverence. **2.** Practiced in the name of religion.

pique (pēk) *n.* A feeling of irritation or resentment.

pitiless (pit′i·lis) *adj.* Having no pity or mercy; ruthless.

placable (plā′kə·bəl, plak′ə-) *adj.* Appeasable; yielding; forgiving.

placid (plas′id) *adj.* Having a smooth, unruffled surface or nature; calm.

plaintive (plān′tiv) *adj.* Expressing a subdued sadness; mournful. — **plain′tive·ly.** *adv.*

plight (plīt) *n.* A condition or circumstance of a dangerous or complicated nature; a predicament.

poach (pōch) *v.i. & v.t.* **1.** To trespass on another's property, especially for the purpose of taking game or fish. **2.** To take game or fish unlawfully.

poise (poiz) *v.t. & v.i.* **1.** To bring into or hold in balance. **2.** To hold; to support, as in readiness. — *n.* **1.** The state or quality of being balanced. **2.** Dignity of manner; self-possession.

pomp (pomp) *n.* Stately display; splendor.

pompous (pom′pəs) *adj.* Marked by exaggerated dignity or self-importance.

ponder (pon′dər) *v.t.* To weigh in the mind; consider carefully. — *v.i.* To meditate; reflect.

ponderous (pon′dər·əs) *adj.* Having great weight; huge; bulky.

portal (pôr′təl, pōr′-) *n.* An entrance door or gate, especially one that is grand and imposing.

portentous (pôr·ten′təs) *adj.* Warning of things to come; ominous.

portray (pôr·trā′, pōr-) *v.t.* To describe or depict in words.

posterity (pos·ter′ə·tē) *n.* **1.** Future generations. **2.** All one's descendants.

precinct (prē′singkt) *n.* **1.** An election district. **2.** An area in a town under the jurisdiction of a police unit. **3.** A place or area marked off by fixed limits.

precipitous (pri·sip′ə·təs) *adj.* **1.** Very steep. **2.** Hasty.

precise (pri·sīs′) *adj.* **1.** Sharply and clearly defined. **2.** Exact in amount.

preliminary (pri·lim′ə·ner′ē) *adj.* Introductory; preceding the main event. — *n.* A preparatory step or act.

premature (prē′mə·choor′, toor′, tyoor′) *adj.* Existing, happening, or developed before the natural or proper period; unusually early. — **pre′·ma·ture′ly.** *adv.*

pre-nuptial (prē·nup′shel) *adj.* Concerning a time before the marriage ceremony.

preposterous (pri·pos′tər·əs) *adj.* Absurd; contrary to nature, reason, or common sense.

presentiment (pri·zen′tə·mənt) *n.* A prophetic sense of something to come; a foreboding.

presumable (pri·zoo′mə·bəl) *adj.* That may be assumed or taken for granted; reasonable. — **pre·sum′a·bly** *adv.*

pretentious (pri·ten′shəs) *adj.* **1.** Making an ambitious outward show. **2.** Making claims, especially when false.

preternatural (prē′tər·nach′ər·əl) *adj.* **1.** Exceeding the common order of nature, but not outside the natural order. **2.** Outside the natural order; supernatural.

prevail (pri·vāl′) *v.i.* **1.** To gain mastery; be victorious. **2.** To use persuasion or influence successfully.

primeval (prī·mē′vəl) *adj.* Primitive; belonging to the first ages.

procure (prō·kyoor′) *v.t.* **1.** To obtain by some effort or means; acquire. **2.** To bring about.

prodigious (prə·dij′əs) *adj.* **1.** Enormous or extraordinary in size, quantity, or degree; vast. **2.** Marvelous; amazing. — **pro·dig′ious·ly** *adv.*

profound (prə·found′, prō-) *adj.* **1.** Wise; deep. **2.** Thorough; complete. — *adv.* **pro·found′ly.**

proliferate (prō·lif′ə·rāt) *v.t. & v.i.* To produce, reproduce, or grow rapidly.

prominent (prom′ə·nənt) *adj.* **1.** Jutting out. **2.** Outstanding in position, character, or importance.

propitiate (prō·pish′ē·āt) *v.t.* To cause to be favorably disposed; appease; conciliate.

proponent (prə·pō′nənt) *n.* **1.** One who makes a proposal or puts forward a proposition. **2.** One who advocates or supports a cause or doctrine.

propriety (prə·prī′ə·tē) *n.* Proper; the character or quality of being proper.

prowess (prou′is) *n.* Strength and courage, especially in battle.

prudence (prood′ns) *n.* The quality or state of being cautious; judgment; shrewdness.

pugilistic (pyoo′jə·list·ik) *adj.* Pertaining to fighting with the fists.

PRONUNCIATION: add, āce, câre, pälm; end, ēven; it, īce; odd, ōpen, ôrder; tŏŏk, pōōl; up, bûrn; ə = a in *above*, e in *sicken*, i in *flexible*, o in *melon*, u in *focus*; yōō = u in *fuse*; oil; pout; check; go; ring; thin; this; zh, vision.

766

Q

qualm (kwäm, kwôm) *n.* **1.** A feeling of sickness. **2.** A sensation of fear or misgiving.

quarry (kwôr′ē, kwor′ē) *n.* **1.** A beast or bird hunted, seized, or killed. **2.** Anything hunted, slaughtered, or eagerly pursued.

quench (kwench) *v.t.* **1.** To put out, as a fire. **2.** To put an end to. **3.** To satisfy thirst.

R

raiment (rā′mənt) *n.* Clothing.

ramble (ram′bəl) *n.* Aimless or leisurely stroll.

rapturous (rap′chər·əs) *adj.* Experiencing, expressing, or characterized by joy or ecstasy.

rasp (rasp, räsp) *n.* **1.** A file. **2.** The sound of filing. — *v.t.* **1.** To scrape or rub roughly. **2.** To utter in a rough voice.

raucous (rô′kəs) *adj.* **1.** Rough in sound; hoarse; harsh. **2.** Boisterous; unruly.

ravage (rav′ij) *v.t.* To lay waste as by burning. — *v.i.* To be destructive. — *n.* ruin, devastation.

rebuff (ri·buf′) *n.* **1.** A sudden repulse; curt denial. **2.** A sudden check; defeat.

rebuttal (ri·but′l) *n.* The act of disproving by offering contrary evidence or proof.

reciprocate (ri·sip′rə·kāt) *v.* **1.** To cause to move backward and forward alternately. **2.** To give, feel, do, etc., in return for something.

recollect (rek′ə·lekt′) *v.t.* To call back to memory; remember.

recollection (rek′ə·lek′shən) *n.* **1.** The act or power of remembering. **2.** Something remembered; memory.

refrain (ri·frān′) *v.t.* To keep oneself back.

remonstrance (ri·mon′strəns) *n.* The act of protesting; objection.

remonstrate (ri·mon′strāt) *v.t.* To say or plead in protest or opposition. — *v.i.* To urge strong reasons against any course or action; protest; object.

remorse (ri·môrs′) *n.* The pain caused by a sense of guilt; repentance.

replenish (ri·plen′ish) *v.t.* To fill again something that has been emptied.

repose (ri·pōz′) *n.* **1.** The act of taking rest or the state of being at rest. **2.** Freedom from excitement or anxiety. **3.** Graceful and dignified calmness. **4.** That which leads to rest or calm. — *v.t.* To lay or place in a position of rest. — *v.i.* To lie at rest.

reproach (ri·prōch′) *v.t.* **1.** To criticize or blame for something wrong. **2.** To bring discredit and disgrace upon.

repudiate (ri·pyōō′dē·āt) *v.t.* **1.** To refuse to accept as valid or binding; reject. **2.** To cast off; disown.

repugnance (ri·pug′nəns) *n.* A strong dislike, distaste, or aversion.

resin (rez′in) *n.* An organic substance discharged from plants and fir and pine trees.

retort[1] (ri·tôrt′) *n.* A direct answer or reply, often sharp and biting.

retort[2] (ri·tôrt′) *n.* **1.** *Chem.* A vessel with a bent tube for the heating of substances. **2.** *Metall.* A vessel in which ore may be heated for the removal of its metal content.

reverie (rev′ər·ē) *n.* Dreaming; absent-minded musing. Also **rev′er·y.**

revert (ri·vûrt′) *v.* To go or turn back to a former condition, attitude, or place.

revolution (rev′ə·lōō′shən) *n.* **1.** The act or state of revolving. **2.** A round or cycle of successive events or changes.

rift (rift) *n.* **1.** An opening made by splitting; a cleft. **2.** Any disagreement or lack of harmony, as between friends, nations, etc.

rigorous (rig′ər·əs) *adj.* Severe; unbending; harsh.

rimy (rī′mē) *adj.* **1.** White with frost. **2.** Cold.

rive (rīv) *v.t.* To tear apart; split.

rivulet (riv′yə·lit) *n.* A small stream or brook.

rogue (rōg) *n.* **1.** A dishonest and unprincipled person; trickster; rascal. **2.** One who is innocently mischievous or playful.

romancer (rō·mans′ər) *n.* Writer of romantic tales.

rumination (rōō′mə·nā′shən) *n.* **1.** The act or process of chewing the cud. **2.** The act of meditating; thoughtfulness.

russet (rus′it) *n.* A reddish or yellowish brown.

S

sagacious (sə·gā′shəs) *adj.* **1.** Characterized by shrewdness and wisdom. **2.** Able to comprehend and decide on a course of action.

sagacity (sə·gas′ə·tē) *n.* Shrewdness; wisdom.

salve (sav, säv) *n.* **1.** A thick ointment for local injuries. **2.** Anything that heals or soothes.

satire (sat′īr) *n.* The use of sarcasm, irony or wit in exposing abuses or follies; ridicule. — **sa·tir′ic** or **sa·tir′i·cal** *adj.*

saturate (sach′ə·rāt) *v.t.* **1.** To soak thoroughly. **2.** To fill completely.

scourge (skûrj) *v.t.* **1.** To whip severely. **2.** To punish severely; afflict.

scrutiny (skrōō′tə·nē) *n.* Close examination or investigation.

secession (si·sesh′ən) *n.* The act of withdrawing, especially from political or religious association.

PRONUNCIATION: add, āce, câre, pälm; end, ēven; it, īce; odd, ōpen, ôrder; tŏŏk, pōōl; up, bûrn; ə = a in *above*, e in *sicken*, i in *flexible*, o in *melon*, u in *focus*; yōō = u in *fuse*; oil; pout; check; go; ring; thin; this; zh, vision.

767

sectionalism (sek'shən·əl·iz'əm) *n.* Regard for a particular section of the country rather than the whole.

semblance (sem'bləns) *n.* **1.** Pretense. **2.** A likeness or resemblance.

sensibility (sen'sə·bil'ə·tē) *n.* Power to perceive or feel.

sentiment (sen'tə·mənt) *n.* **1.** Noble, tender, or artistic feeling. **2.** An idea.

serene (si·rēn') *adj.* Calm; peaceful; unruffled.

servile (sûr'vīl, -vil) *adj.* **1.** Having the spirit of a slave. **2.** Appropriate for slaves or servants.

severity (si·ver'ə·tē) *n.* **1.** Harshness. **2.** Extreme strictness; exactness.

shrew (shrōō) *n.* **1.** Any of numerous small, chiefly insect-eating animals with long pointed snouts and soft fur. **2.** A woman of scolding or nagging disposition.

shrivel (shriv'əl) *v.t. & v.i.* **1.** To shrink and wrinkle. **2.** To wither.

shroud (shroud) *n.* A dress or garment for a dead person.

signify (sig'nə·fī) *v.t.* **1.** To make known by signs or words; announce. **2.** To amount to; to mean.

simultaneous (sī'məl·tā'nē·əs, sim'əl-) *adj.* Occurring, done or existing at the same time.

sinecure (sī'nə·kyōōr, sin'ə-) *n.* Any office or position which involves little responsibility or active service.

sinew (sin'yōō) *n.* A tendon or similar fibrous cord.

singe (sinj) *v.t.* To burn slightly; discolor by burning; scorch.

singular (sing'gyə·lər) *adj.* **1.** remarkable; uncommon. **2.** Odd; unusual.

singularity (sing'gyə·lar'ə·tē) *n.* The state or quality of being uncommon; remarkable; extraordinary.

skirling (skûrl'ing, skirl'-) *n.* The making of shrill or shrieking sounds, like a bagpipe.

slouch (slouch) *v.i.* **1.** To have a downcast or drooping gait, look or posture. **2.** To hang or droop in a careless manner, as a hat.

solemnize (sol'əm·nīz) *v.t.* To perform as a ceremony or solemn rite.

solicitous (sə·lis'ə·təs) *adj.* Full of concern.

solitary (sol'ə·ter'ē) *adj.* **1.** Living, being, or going alone. **2.** Secluded; lonely.

spasmodic (spaz·mod'ik) *adj.* **1.** Of the nature of a muscular spasm. **2.** Fitful; lacking continuity.

spawn (spôn) *v.t.* **1.** To produce. **2.** To give rise to; originate.

speculation (spek'yə·lā'shən) *n.* **1.** The act of forming theories about anything without experiment or investigation. **2.** A theory.

spinney (spin'ē) *n.* *chiefly Brit.* A small wood or thicket.

spurn (spûrn) *v.t.* **1.** To reject with disdain; scorn. **2.** To strike with the foot; kick.

stagnant (stag'nənt) *adj.* **1.** Standing still; not flowing: said of water or air. **2.** Foul from long standing, as water. **3.** Dull; sluggish.

staid (stād) *adj.* Steady and sober; sedate; modest.

starveling (stärv'ling) *n.* A person or animal that is starving. — *adj.* **1.** Starving. **2.** Inadequate.

station (stā'shun) *n.* **1.** The headquarters of some official person or group: a police *station*. **2.** A building serving as a starting and stopping place. **3.** An assigned location. **4.** Social rank or standing: one's *station* in life.

steadfast (sted'fast' -fäst', -fəst) *adj.* Firm in faith or devotion to duty; constant; unchanging.

stimulate (stim'yə·lāt) *v.t.* To rouse to activity.

stipulate (stip'yə·lāt) *v.t.* **1.** To specify, as the terms of an agreement or contract. **2.** To promise; guarantee.

stipulation (stip'yə·lā·shən) *n.* **1.** The act of specifying, as the terms of an agreement. **2.** A condition.

stolid (stol'id) *adj.* Having or showing little feeling or perception; dull. — **stol'id·ly** *adv.*

stupendous (stōō·pen'dəs, styōō-) *adj.* Highly impressive; remarkable.

suave (swäv, swāv) *adj.* Smoothly pleasant in manner; urbane.

suavity (swä'və·tē, swav'ə-) *n.* The state or quality of being suave; smoothness; urbanity.

subaltern (sub·ôl'tərn) *n.* A person of subordinate rank or position.

subjugate (sub'jōō·gāt) *v.t.* To conquer; subdue.

sublime (sə·blīm') *adj.* **1.** Characterized by elevation, nobility, etc.; grand; solemn. **2.** Inspiring awe; moving. **3.** Being of the highest degree; supreme; utmost. — **sublime, sublimity** (sə·blim'ə·tē), **sublimeness** *n.*

subsequent (sub'sə·kwənt) *adj.* Following in time, place of order, or as a result. — **sub'se·quent·ly** *adv.*

subside (səb·sīd') *v.t.* **1.** To become less violent or disturbed; become calm or quiet; decrease. **2.** To sink to a lower level.

subtle (sut'l) *adj.* **1.** Characterized by cunning or craft. **2.** Keen; discriminating. **3.** Executed with nice art; clever. **4.** Of delicate texture.

succor (suk'ər) *n.* **1.** Help or relief from danger, difficulty, or distress. **2.** The person or thing which gives relief. — *v.t.* To go to the aid of; help; rescue.

summary (sum'ər·ē) *adj.* **1.** Greatly condensed; concise. **2.** Instant; hasty; offhand.

PRONUNCIATION: add, āce, câre, pälm; end, ēven; it, īce; odd, ōpen, ôrder; tōōk, pōōl; up, bûrn; ə = a in *above*, e in *sicken*, i in *flexible*, o in *melon*, u in *focus*; yōō = u in *fuse*; oil; pout; check; go; ring; thin; this; zh, vision.

768

sundry (sun'drē) *adj.* Several; various.

supercilious (soo'pər·sil'ē·əs) *adj.* Exhibiting contempt or indifference; haughty; arrogant. — **su'per·cil'i·ous·ly** *adv.*

supersonic (soo'pər·son'ik) *adj.* Characterized by a speed greater than sound.

suppliant (sup'lē·ənt) *n.* One who begs or prays earnestly and humbly.

supposition (sup'ə·zish'ən) · *n.* 1. The act of supposing, thinking, or imagining that something is true. 2. An assumption; theory.

surmise (sər·mīz') *v.t.* To infer on slight evidence; guess.

T

taint (tānt) *v.t.* 1. To imbue with an offensive quality. 2. To render morally corrupt; pollute.

tankard (tangk'ərd) *n.* A large, one-handled drinking cup, usually made of pewter or silver, often with a cover.

tapestry (tap'is·trē) *n.* A woven, ornamental fabric, often hung as a decoration.

tarpaulin (tär·pô'lin, tär'pə-) *n.* A waterproof canvas.

tattoo (ta·too') *n.* A continuous beating or drumming.

taunt (tônt) *n.* A sarcastic, biting remark. — *v.t.* To tease; to provoke with biting remarks.

teamster (tēm'stər) *n.* One who drives or owns a team of animals.

temper (tem'pər) *v.t.* 1. To bring to a state of moderation or suitability: to *temper* justice with mercy. 2. To bring metal to a required hardness and elasticity by heating and suddenly cooling.

tempestuous (tem·pes'choo·əs) *adj.* Stormy; violent.

tendency (ten'dən·sē) *n.* The state of being directed toward some purpose, end, or result; inclination; aptitude.

terrestrial (tə·res'trē·əl) *adj.* Related to, or consisting of, earth or land.

testily (tes'tə·lē) *adv.* In an irritable, touchy way.

throttle (throt'əl) *v.* To choke or strangle, by squeezing the neck of.

timorous (tim'ər·əs) *adj.* 1. Fearful of danger. 2. Indicating or produced by fear.

toil (toil) *n.* Tiring work; labor. — *v.i.* To work hard; labor painfully and tiringly.

token (tō'kən) *n.* A visible sign; evidence.

torrent (tôr'ənt, tor'-) *n.* 1. A stream of water flowing with great speed or in a greatly disturbed state. 2. Any abundant flow: a *torrent* of words.

tortuous (tôr'choo·əs) *adj.* Consisting of or abounding in irregular bends or turns; twisting.

tousle (tou'zəl) *v.t.* To put in a state of disorder, as with the hair or dress.

tract (trakt) *n.* An extended area of land or water.

tranquil (trang'kwil) *adj.* 1. Free from mental disturbance. 2. Quiet and motionless.

tranquility (trang·kwil'ə·tē) *n.* The state of being calm and quiet.

transfix (trans·fiks') *v.t.* 1. To pierce through. 2. To make motionless or fix in place, as with horror, awe, etc.

transient (tran'shənt) *adj.* 1. Passing away quickly; of short duration; brief. 2. Not permanent; temporary.

transpire (tran·spīr') *v.i. Informal.* To happen; occur.

treacherous (trech'ər·əs) *adj.* 1. Traitorous; disloyal. 2. Having a deceptive appearance; unreliable.

tread (tred) *v.t.* 1. To step or walk on. 2. To trample.

treasonable (trē'zən·ə·bəl) *adj.* Pertaining to betrayal, especially of one's government or a particular authority. — **trea'son·a·bly** *adv.*

tremor (trem'ər, trē'mər) *n.* 1. Any involuntary and continued quivering or trembling of the body or limbs; a shiver. 2. Any trembling, quivering effect.

tress (tres) *n.* 1. A lock or ringlet of human hair. 2. *pl.* The hair of a woman or girl, especially when worn loose.

trodden (trod'n) Past participle of **tread.**

truculence (truk'yə·ləns) *n.* Aggressiveness; ferocity.

tuition (too·ish'ən, tyoo-) *n.* 1. The charge or payment for instruction. 2. The act of teaching.

tumult (too'mult, tyoo'-) *n.* The commotion or disturbance of a crowd.

tunic (too'nik, tyoo'-) *n.* 1. In ancient Greece and Rome, a knee-length garment usually worn without a belt. 2. In modern times, a hip-length blouse or coat usually gathered at the waist.

U

ulterior (ul·tir'ē·ər) *adj.* 1. Intentionally unrevealed; hidden. 2. More remote; not so pertinent as something else to the matter spoken of.

unassuming (un'ə·soo'ming) *adj.* Modest, not making ambitious outward show.

uncontaminated (un·kən·tam'ə·nāt·ed) *adj.* Pure; clean.

undeterred (un·di·tûrd') *adj.* Not frightened or turned aside.

undeviating (un·dē'vē·āt·ing) *adj.* Continuing on a straight or appointed course; unswerving.

PRONUNCIATION: add, āce, câre, pälm; end, ēven; it, īce; odd, ōpen, ôrder; took, pool; up, bûrn; ə = a in *above*, e in *sicken*, i in *flexible*, o in *melon*, u in *focus*; yoo = u in *fuse*; oil; pout; check; go; ring; thin; this; zh, vision.

769

unduly (un·dōō′lē, -dyōō′-) *adv.* **1.** Excessively. **2.** Unjustly.

unequivocal (un′i·kwiv′ə·kəl) *adj.* Understandable in only one way. — **un′e·quiv′o·cal·ly** *adv.*

unhampered (un·ham′pərd) *adj.* Unrestrained.

unparalleled (un·par′ə·leld) *adj.* Unmatched; unprecedented; unequaled.

unscrupulous (un·skrōō′pyə·ləs) *adj.* Unprincipled; having no scruples or morals.

untraversed (un·trav′ərst, un′trə·vûrst′) *adj.* Uncrossed; untraveled.

upheaval (up·hē′vəl) *n.* **1.** The act of raising or lifting, or the state of being raised. **2.** A violent disturbance or change.

urbane (ûr·bān′) *adj.* Possessing the quality of refinement or elegance, especially in manner; polite.

usurpation (yōō′zər·pā′shən, -sər-) *n.* The act of seizing and holding without right or legal authority; taking possession by force.

V

vagabond (vag′ə·bond) *n.* A wandering tramp; wanderer.

valedictory (val′ə·dik′tər·ē) *adj.* Pertaining to a leave-taking or departure.

vanquish (vang′kwish, van′-) *v.t.* To defeat in battle; overcome; conquer.

vaunt (vônt, vänt) *v.i.* To speak boastfully. — *v.t.* To boast of.

vehement (vē′ə·mənt) *adj.* **1.** Arising from or marked by impulsive feeling. **2.** Acting with great force or energy.

venerable (ven′ər·ə·bəl) *adj.* **1.** Meriting or commanding respect; worthy of reverence: now usually implying age. **2.** Exciting feelings of reverence because of sacred or historic associations.

veracity (və·ras′ə·tē) *n.* **1.** Truthfulness; honesty. **2.** Agreement with truth; accuracy. **3.** That which is true; truth.

verify (ver′ə·fī) *v.t.* **1.** To prove to be true; confirm. **2.** To test the truth of.

veritable (ver′ə·tə·bəl) *adj.* Unquestionable; doubtlessly true.

vermilion (vər·mil′yən) *adj.* Of a bright red color.

vermin (vûr′min) *n. pl.* Harmful small animals or insects.

versatile (vûr′sə·til) *adj.* **1.** Having an ability to perform various tasks. **2.** Subject to change; variable.

versify (vûr′sə·fī) *v.t.* **1.** To change from prose into verse. **2.** To tell or write in verse — *v.i.* To write poetry. — **ver′si·fi′er** *n.* A poet.

vestibule (ves′tə·byōōl) *n.* An entrance lobby, hall.

vestry (ves′trē) *n.* **1.** A room, as in a church, where robes are put on or kept.. **2.** A room in a church used for Sunday school, for meetings, or as a chapel, etc.

vex (veks) *v.t.* **1.** To irritate or annoy. **2.** To trouble or afflict.

vexation (vek·sā′shən) *n.* **1.** The act of irritating or annoying. **2.** The state of being irritated or annoyed. **3.** A cause of trouble or distress.

vicariously (vī·kâr′ē·əs·lē) *adv.* In a vicarious manner; by or through one or more other persons.

video (vid′ē·ō) *adj.* Of or related to television, especially to the picture portion of a program. — *n.* Television.

vie (vī) *v.i.* To strive for superiority; contend; compete, as in a race; with *for* or *with*.

virile (vir′əl) *adj.* **1.** Having the characteristics of adult manhood; masculine. **2.** Having the vigor or strength of manhood; sturdy.

void (void) *n.* An empty space; a vacuum.

W

waive (wāv) *v.t.* **1.** To give up or relinquish a claim to. **2.** To forgo. **3.** To put off; postpone; delay.

wane (wān) *v.i.* **1.** To diminish in size. **2.** To decline or decrease gradually.

wanton (won′tən) *adj.* **1.** Unjust; malicious. **2.** Of abundant growth; luxuriant. **3.** Playful; unrestrained.

wary (wâr′ē) *adj.* **1.** Carefully watchful and alert. **2.** Shrewd; wily.

wend (wend) *v.* To direct or proceed on (one's course or way).

whet (hwet) *v.* To sharpen, as a knife, by rubbing on a whetstone.

without (with·out′, with-) *prep.* Outside of or beyond the limits of.

wrought (rôt) *adj.* **1.** Beaten or hammered into shape by tools. **2.** Worked; molded.

Z

zeal (zēl) *n.* Strong enthusiasm, especially for a cause.

zenith (zē′nith) *n.* **1.** The point of the celestial sphere that is exactly overhead. **2.** The highest point; peak: the *zenith* of a man's career.

PRONUNCIATION: add, āce, câre, pälm; end, ēven; it, īce; odd, ōpen, ôrder; tŏŏk, pōōl; up, bûrn; ə = a in *above*, e in *sicken*, i in *flexible*, o in *melon*, u in *focus*; yōō = u in *fuse*; oil; pout; check; go; ring; thin; this; zh, vision.

Index of Authors and Titles

Numbers in italics designate pages on which biographical data appear.

PICTURE ACKNOWLEDGMENTS

p. 107, Brown Brothers; p. 113, Essex Institute, Salem, Mass.; p. 128, H. J. Fischer; p. 129, William Ward Beecher, courtesy Viking Press; p. 197, Steinkopf; p. 198, Scala from Shostal; p. 199, Weinberger from Shostal; p. 209, Marion H. Levy, Photo Researchers; p. 221, Edward Steichen; p. 222, Ewing Galloway; p. 227, Brown Brothers; p. 228, The Library of Congress; p. 235, T. and R. Annan & Sons Ltd.; p. 236, New York Public Library, Picture Collection; p. 241, Brown Brothers; p. 269, Musées Nationaux; p. 271, Harbrace; p. 272, John R. Freeman (Photographers) Ltd., London; p. 288, New York Public Library, Rare Books Collection; p. 289, Henry E. Huntington Library, San Marino, Calif.; p. 297, top, Kurt Severin, Black Star; lower left, British Travel Association; lower right, Jean and Tom Hollyman, Photo Researchers; p. 300, top, from *Shakespeare's England,* courtesy American Heritage Publishing Co., Inc.; bottom, Folger Shakespeare Library; p. 323, Lucius Beebe, Territorial Enterprise, from Bettmann Archive; p. 327, New York Public Library, Rare Books Collection; p. 337, Hans Namuth; p. 338, U.S. Forest Service; p. 339, Helen Faye; p. 343, Joe Van Wormer, National Audubon Society; p. 383, Carl and Hannelore Milch; p. 408, The Library of Congress; p. 413, Lloyd Ostendorf; p. 417, New York Public Library; p. 419, Chicago Historical Society; p. 431, New York Public Library, Print Room; p. 432, top, Folger Shakespeare Library; bottom left, United Artists; bottom right, Friedman Abeles, Inc.; p. 433, Folger Shakespeare Library; p. 453, Walter Drayer; p. 455, Musées Nationaux; p. 523, Meyer Erwin; p. 525, Robert Emmet Bright from Rapho-Guillumette; p. 526, Scala from Shostal; p. 595, John Webb F.R.P.S., Brompton Studios; p. 596, Joachim Blauel; p. 597, John Webb F.R.P.S., Brompton Studios; painting © S.P.A.D.E.M. 1966 by French Reproduction Rights, Inc.

ART CREDITS

DONN ALBRIGHT. 116, 118, 119.
BILL BANKS. 206, 207, 237, 247 bottom, 249.
HUNTLEY BROWN. 225, 257, 314, 316, 364, 365, 368, 373, 388, 393, 396, 398, 402.
JOSEPH CELLINI. 261, 263.
NAYED EINSEL. 274, 275, 276, 277, 351, 355, 358.
PAUL GRANGER. 215, 331.
MANNY HALLER. 21, 67, 68, 71, 73, 74, 95, 96, 97, 161, 172, 284 and 285, 565, 573, 579, 586, 604, 610, 613, 616, 620, 622, 628, 636, 639, 641, 645, 648, 653, 655, 656, 661, 664, 666, 668, 675, 681, 686, 690, 696, 701, 707, 710, 715, 721, 724.
AL LEINER. 27, 32, 34, 158, 170, 188, 426, 427 top and bottom, 428, 429, 430, 438, 440, 445, 461, 464, 468, 473, 477, 483, 491, 495, 500, 503.
KEN LONGTEMPS. 5, 8, 16, 111.
JAMES AND RUTH MCCREA. 166, 169, 185, 190, 191, 205, 238, 247 top.
FREDERIC MARVIN. 174, 518, 519, 531, 533, 538, 544, 546, 548, 552.
MARIE NONAST. 37, 39, 41, 46, 78, 80, 101, 225, 281.
SHANNON STIRNWEIS. 83, 85, 88, 91, 134, 135, 137, 141, 144, 163, 167, 231, 232, 233.
HANS ZANDER. 58, 60.